SOURCEBOOK ON PORNOGRAPHY

Franklin Mark Osanka
Sara Lee Johann

LEXINGTON BOOKS

D.C. Heath and Company/Lexington, Massachusetts/Toronto

Library of Congress Cataloging-in-Publication Data

Osanka, Franklin Mark, and Johann, Sara Lee.
  Sourcebook on pornography.

  Bibliography: p.
  Includes index.
  1. Pornography—Social aspects—United States.   2. Obscenity (Law)—United States.
I. Johann, Sara Lee. II. Title.
HQ471.J64 1989   86–46379   86–46379
ISBN 0–669–15858–5 (alk. paper)

Published simultaneously in Canada
Printed in the United States of America
International Standard Book Number: 0–669–15858–5
Library of Congress Catalog Card Number 86–46379

The paper used in this publication meets the minimum requirements of American National
Standard for Information Sciences—Permanence of Paper for Printed Library Materials, ANSI
Z39.48–1984.⊗™

92 8 7 6 5 4 3 2

CONTENTS

The purpose of *Sourcebook on Pornography* is to provide a directory of all the contemporary issues concerning pornography. This is a reference work for lay and professional people who want to familiarize themselves with the different positions and philosophies concerning pornography.

We recognize that there are more nonscholarly than scholarly people interested in pornography, for there is a growing concern among the general public. We would like to help these people obtain information about this issue of public concern. We stress, however, that this is a book for scholars as well. The authors call upon the scholars who have the training and funds to do research to begin taking this issue seriously.

Chapter 1 deals with the difficulties of defining pornography. Here we are reminded of the classic quote from U.S. Supreme Court Justice Potter Stewart, who said that although he could not define hard-core pornography, "I know it when I see it." In the legal realm, concepts such as pornography must be defined. Chapter 1 provides definitions of obscenity along with civil rights definitions of pornography, erotica, and child pornography. The concepts of what pornography is range from any sexually explicit material to only those materials that are sexually explicit and humiliate and subordinate women, including those portraying sexually sadistic or masochistic acts such as torture, rape, mutilation, and bondage. Child pornography becomes a category by itself because legal authorities are given much broader power to include any sexually oriented depictions of children in such regulations.

Chapter 2 deals with the images of pornography. This chapter describes the types of pornographic material available and where pornography is available. It also provides a content analysis of pornography.

Types of pornography include: magazines, books, and films. The Canadian film *Not a Love Story* states that there are more adult bookstores in northern America than there are McDonald's restaurants. There are between fifteen thousand and twenty thousand adult bookstores in the United States. With the widespread use of videotape players, pornographic videotapes have become widely available in many video stores. Some of these include material that used to be found only in adult bookstores, and even hard-core sadomasochistic pornography is now available in some video stores. Newer types of pornography are shows carried on cable television and pornographic phone messages.

In the content of pornography, we see distortions of what would be considered normal or traditional sexual intercourse and sexual interaction. These distortions tend to belittle and subjugate women rather than men. Some pornography belittles, degrades, and uses children or men. One example of such a distortion is the fact that most pornographic films seem to have mandatory ejaculation shots—scenes in which the ejaculation process does not take place inside a person's body but on the body, usually on the woman's face, back, or stomach. It is sadistic to portray ejaculation on the body, for it denies the woman the pleasure of that step in the sexual act and gives the clear message that she is only worth ejaculating on. Group sex, often involving two women and a man, also is common. This illustrates another prevailing theme—that pornography appeals to the prurient interest of males rather than females and is designed to support men's fantasies. Much pornography also portrays abuse of women by groups of men and aggression and violence toward women. Another frequent prevailing theme in pornography is incest.

Among a certain number of people, pornography has legitimized sadomasochistic practices, including discipline and bondage. What used to be considered weird is now considered chic—an area of sexual freedom among consenting adults. Swinger magazines and other forms of pornography teach that a little sadomasochism and bondage and discipline is not so bad if you really want to do it. What is missing from these materials is any warning about the danger of such activities. All extreme forms of torture and violence are contained in pornography, including mutilation, rape, bondage, sex with animals, and murder during sexual acts.

Pornography is not erotica, which can be defined as a description of possible sexual positions and standard sexual ethics, including loving and affectionate sexual activities between consenting persons of equal power. Pornography is, instead, a directory of mayhem in a sense that it is saying that any possible activity can be done in the name of finding sexual satisfaction. The danger of this kind of thinking is that it can distort sexual responsibility. The danger includes the breakup of marriages, sexual abuse, and violence and aggression against persons.

Chapter 3 addresses the nature of the pornography industry. Using materials from the Attorney General's Commission on Pornography and Canadian researcher David Alexander Scott, the authors detail the control of the pornography industry by organized crime.

Chapter 4 deals with pornography victims and perpetrators and clearly shows that in some cases people are victimized. One of the principal themes of pornography is that someone is subservient and someone is dominant. This chapter gives examples of child and adult victims, primarily women, although some men are included. It includes a very chilling segment on the making of a rapist: the case study of Thomas R. Schiro, who began to be exposed to pornography at the age of 7 or 8 and then went on to rape twenty-four women and murder one prior to his 19th birthday.

Chapter 5 discusses scientific research studies of aggressive behavior, women's responses to pornography, the correlation between reading pornography and rape, the influence of pornography on neighborhoods. One of the points we make is that the research design is limited because of the inability to access victims of pornography, particularly through police files and other legal files where confidentiality is maintained.

Chapter 6, the morality perspective, suggests that pornography is wrong and harmful because it goes against traditional values of morality, decency, and religion. Among the wrongs some groups see in pornography are portrayals of sex between unmarried persons, homosexuality, and the mistreatment of persons. Chapter 7, the feminist perspective, emphasizes that pornography should be regulated because it distorts women's sexuality, discriminates against women, and causes men to believe that women want to be sexually abused and degraded. Feminists see this not as a moral issue, but as an issue of harm. Thus, in their view, erotica (loving sexual relations between married persons or single heterosexual or homosexual persons) can be a good thing, while pornography is harmful. In chapter 8, those interested

in private enterprise and civil libertarian maintain that the First Amendment to the U.S. Constitution guarantees freedom of speech and press and that pornography should not be regulated in any way.

Chapter 9 details how to use obscenity laws to prosecute pornographers, as well as how to defend such cases utilizing extensive case histories. Chapter 10 describes the civil rights/sex discrimination approach to fighting pornography and the legal debate surrounding this approach. Chapter 11 discusses other legal methods of regulating pornography, including zoning laws, display to minors laws, nuisance laws, broadcast and cable regulations concerning indecency, and civil remedies for victims such as lawsuits for libel, group libel, privacy violations, and the intentional infliction of emotional distress. Chapter 12 introduces a model law drafted by the authors and intended to regulate pornography.

Chapter 13, summarizes the contents of numerous national studies concerning pornography, including the Attorney General's Commission on Pornography, the Commission on Obscenity and Pornography, and Canadian and British studies.

Chapter 14, traces the history of the anti–child pornography movement, which arose in the mid-1970s. It describes child pornography laws passed as a result of the movement, summarizes the major Supreme Court ruling on child pornography, describes harms to victims of child pornography, and raises current issues about child pornography.

The book's bibliography is intended to be the world's leading bibliography on issues concerning pornography. It is arranged by topic and chapter and is limited to those types of material that reasonable people and researchers would consider valuable to explore.

The appendixes include numerous model laws, standard pornography definitions, and data on where to contact various groups and experts in this field.

Many concerned people are currently addressing the issues of pornography in a haphazard manner with little cooperative effort. This book is offered as a service to them. We would like all these people to consider turning to this book to find out what the contemporary issues in pornography are.

ACKNOWLEDGMENTS

Both authors are unendingly grateful to their families.

Sylvera Johann, Sara Lee Johann's mother and a writer herself, tirelessly provided editorial and clerical assistance to the authors. Eldon Johann and Herold Hillger, Dr. Johann's father and uncle, also provided support throughout the more than three years it took to complete this book. Thanks also to Robert Scott Johann.

Franklin Mark Osanka expresses a special thank you to his wife, Linda, and children, Wendy, Andrew, and Lisa, for being so silently tolerant of the quality time taken from them to complete this major writing project. A special appreciation goes to Jeffrey Osanka, Dr. Osanka's oldest son, who unselfishly took time from his doctoral research to locate and copy isolated resources in the library and on computer.

Both authors wish to thank the following people: Mary "Annie" Steinman of Omaha, Nebraska, whose childhood tragedy with pornography-related sexual abuse served as an inspiration, and who helped the authors research the sourcebook. A summary of her testimony before the Attorney General's Commission on Pornography appears at the beginning of chapter 4.

Jennifer Olson, an EMT from Jackson, Wisconsin, whose library and research skills were invaluable. Wendi Rick of West Bend, Wisconsin, and Robin Schulta of Jackson, Wisconsin, for their invaluable office skills and help with editing the manuscript.

Netta Gilboa, for sharing her considerable research file, which was gathered for the purpose of a doctoral dissertation in sociology at Northwestern University.

Margaret Zusky, Susan Geraghty, Dorothy Lohmann, Lyri Merrill, and Barbara Jatkola, editors at Lexington Books, for their unending faith, patience, and encouragement in the project.

PART I

WHAT IS PORNOGRAPHY?

1 DEFINING PORNOGRAPHY

Pornography is an $8 billion a year business that legitimizes and encourages rape, torture, and degradation of women.[1] It is created by filming real or simulated sexually explicit acts of sexual torture, abuse, degradation or terrorism against real people. Written or verbal descriptions and drawings of these same types of sex acts are also pornography.

Pornographic scenarios are fantasy and fiction. Real women, children, and men do not enjoy being raped, tortured, bound, gang raped, mutilated, penetrated by dogs, horses or snakes, or being murdered. Yet these types of bizarre images are frequent pornographic fare. Consider, for example, this film:

> The first reel shows five eight-year-old girls receiving their first communion, perfect innocents in the perfect ceremony of innocence. Suddenly, a motorcycle gang breaks into the church. Right then, you know what is going to happen, but you can't stop from dropping in the second quarter. And here there is a surprise. For, instead of immediately commencing to rape the girls, the gang pauses to beat up the priest with chains.

Then they crucify him to the cross above the altar. Finally, by reel four, the sex begins. You can actually see the little girls bleeding. All of them are screaming. Except the movie is silent, and you can't hear their cries.[2]

Pornography, in the sense of its effects on human behavior, sometimes is a catalyst for abuse of persons. Police, psychiatric, district attorney, social worker and other professional case notes sometimes contain data about people who were assaulted, molested, or otherwise physically abused by persons acting out pornographic fantasies inspired by the pornography they used. Pornographic influences are elusive and difficult to establish scientifically; we contend, however, that pornography teaches that women and children want to be sexually used and hurt. Persons exposed to pornography often are unaware that it represents bizarre fantasy content which lacks healthy affection and reasonable responsibility for one's actions.

The harm inflicted by pornography is the basis of arguments in favor of regulating it. Before we can deal with this material effectively, however, it must be defined.

DEFINITIONS

Throughout history, endless attempts have been made to define pornography, obscenity, and erotica. Defining these terms, which is so vital to any attempt to regulate such material, remains a major source of conflict and controversy among the many individuals and groups working to control these materials.

As the antipornography forces battle among themselves over definitions, approaches, and strategies, the pornographers continue to make enormous profits with minimal investments. The lack of clear-cut definitions often leaves a legal loophole through which pornographers are able to get the criminal charges against them dismissed. Two frequently advanced arguments sometimes succeed: first, that the definition of pornography or obscenity is so vague and indefinite that the defendant did not know what specific conduct was prohibited by the particular law

at issue; and second, that the range of sexual depictions prohibited by law is so overbroad that it includes types of speech or activities that are protected by the First Amendment to the U.S. Constitution.

Perhaps the classic statement concerning pornography was made by Justice Potter Stewart when he said that although he could not define hard-core pornography, "I know it when I see it."[3] There surely is a range of sexually explicit material in the marketplace that most persons would agree is pornographic, whether or not they believe such depictions should be regulated. It is the task of drawing the boundaries around these elusive terms and concepts that causes debate.

In its *Final Report* of July 1986, the Attorney General's Commission on Pornography found it "tempting to note that 'pornography' seems to mean in practice any discussion or depiction of sex to which the person using the word objects."[4] The commission said that such a definition would not do, nor would any attempt to define the term based on "regulatory goals or condemnation" be appropriate. It expressed concern that defining pornography in purely descriptive language would result in condemning "a wide range of material that may not deserve condemnation." The commission concluded that the best course to follow may be that of the Fraser committee in Canada, "which decided that definition was simply futile."[5] The commission stated:

> We partially follow this course, and pursuant to that have tried to minimize the use of the word "pornography" in this Report. Where we do use the term, we do not mean for it to be, for us, a statement of a conclusion, and thus in this Report a reference to material as "pornographic" means only that the material is predominantly sexually explicit and intended primarily for the purpose of sexual arousal.[6]

Hard-core pornography was described by the commission as "material that is sexually explicit to the extreme, intended virtually exclusively to arouse, and devoid of any other apparent content or purpose."[7] It is worth noting that one of the widest schisms dividing the conservative, morality-oriented antipornography groups and the liberal, feminist-oriented antipornography groups is the issue of whether all sexually explicit material intended to sexually arouse is to be condemned. Some conservatives believe that all material intended to sexually arouse the viewer, reader, or listener is necessarily immoral or bad. Some liberals, however, believe that the type of sexually explicit, arousing material known as erotica is not harmful or to be condemned and is,

in actuality, an excellent form of healthy sex education. According to that viewpoint, *erotica* is defined as "[t]he presentation of mutually pleasurable sexual expression between consenting individuals which involves positive and affectionate human sexual interaction and desires. . . . "[8]

The commission found obscenity easier to define. They used this term to refer to "material that has been or would be likely to be found to be obscene in the context of a judicial proceeding employing applicable legal and constitutional standards."[9] In other words, obscenity is whatever the most recent U.S. Supreme Court and other court decisions say it is.

Concluding that erotica is as hard to define as pornography, the commission again chose not to do so and to avoid the use of the term. It said erotica is generally seen as the opposite of pornography and is used to describe sexually explicit materials "of which the user of the term approves."

> For some the word "erotica" describes any sexually explicit material that contains neither violence nor subordination of women, for others the term refers to almost all sexually explicit material, and for still others only material containing generally accepted artistic values qualifies as erotica.[10]

Unfortunately, those who seek to regulate or control certain types of sexually explicit material do not have the luxury of artfully dodging these issues by declining to define pornography, obscenity, erotica, and related terms. To avoid the legal pitfalls that accompany vague or overbroad antipornography enactments, the object of regulation—that is, pornography—must be clearly defined. In the remainder of this chapter, various approaches to defining pornography used in the United States and Canada are described.

OBSCENITY

Most states that regulate pornography do so by making it a crime to traffic in obscene materials. In *Miller v. California,* the U.S. Supreme Court established the definition of obscenity that is used in the majority of states. The court said:

> [W]e now confine the permissible scope of such regulation [of obscene materials] to works which depict or describe sexual conduct. That conduct must be specifically defined by the applicable state law, as written or authoritatively construed. A state offense must also be limited to works

which, taken as a whole, appeal to the prurient interest in sex, which portray sexual conduct in a patently offensive way, and which, taken as a whole, do not have serious literary, artistic, political, or scientific value.[11]

Citizens for Decency Through Law, Inc., developed a model obscenity statute based on the *Miller* decision and cases interpreting it. That model law, included in appendix A, defines obscene as

> any material or performance, whether through pictures, photographs, drawings, writing, car-

toons, recordings, films, video tapes, telephonic transmissions, or other medium is "obscene" if the following apply:

    (1) The average person, applying contemporary adult community standards, would find that the material or performance taken, as a whole, appeals to the prurient interest.

    (2) The material or performance depicts or describes, in a patently offensive way, sexual conduct, sadomasochistic sexual abuse or lewd exhibition of the genitals.

    (3) The material or performance, taken as a whole, lacks serious literary, artistic, political or scientific value.

Terms such as "contemporary community standards," "prurient interest," and "patently offensive" are examined in chapter 9 of this book.

The model law defines important terms contained in the above obscenity definition:

"Sexual conduct" means ultimate sex acts, normal or perverted, actual or simulated, involving a person or persons, or a person or persons and an animal, including acts of masturbation, sexual intercourse, fellatio, cunnilingus, analingus or physical contact with a person's nude or partially denuded genitals, pubic area, perineum, anal region, or, if such person be female, a breast.

"Sadomasochistic sexual abuse" means actual or simulated flagellation, rape, torture or other physical or sexual abuse, by or upon a person who is nude or partially denuded, or the condition of being fettered, bound or otherwise physically restrained, for the actual or simulated purpose of sexual gratification or abuse or represented in the context of a sexual relationship.

Other definitions can be taken from the comprehensive North Carolina law viewed by supporters and critics as one of the strongest obscenity laws in the nation.

"Sexual conduct" means:
    (1) Vaginal, anal or oral intercourse, whether actual or simulated, normal or perverted; or
    (2) Masturbation, excretory functions, or lewd exhibitions of uncovered genitals; or
    (3) An act or condition that depicts torture, physical restraint by being fettered or bound, or flagellation of or by a nude person or a person clad in undergarments or in revealing or bizarre costume.[12]

As pornography has become more violent and bizarre, concern has grown to make certain material portraying sadistic sexual abuse and masochistic sexual abuse is covered by obscenity laws. In *Ward v. Illinois* and *Mishkin v. New York*,[13] the U.S. Supreme Court found that states can include sadomasochistic materials as part of obscenity definitions, despite the appeal of such pornography primarily to deviant groups. Importantly, in a more recent case, *Brockett v. Spokane Arcades, Inc.*, the court in effect upheld a statute that included in its definitions of obscenity "patently offensive representations or descriptions of . . . violent or destructive sexual acts, including but not limited to human or animal mutilation, dismemberment, rape or torture."[14] In *Brockett*, the court made it clear that material that "provoked only normal, healthy sexual desires"[15] (erotica?) is not obscene. It did not define those terms.

It is also apparent that states choosing to regulate sadomasochistic materials must do so with care. A Louisiana obscenity law that prohibited advertisement, exhibition, or display of sexually violent material was held to be unconstitutional by the supreme court of Louisiana on the ground that it purported to regulate purely violent materials.[16]

A brief history of obscenity law is included here. For more details on this subject, see *The Law of Obscenity, Handbook on the Prosecution of Obscenity Cases, Obscenity Law Reporter,* and *Obscenity and Pornography: The Law under the First Amendment.*[17] See also the chapter 9 bibliography.

The first English case to punish indecency is believed to be *King v. Sedley* in 1663.[18] A definition of obscene was developed in *Regina v. Hicklin,* an English case in 1868: "The test of obscenity is this, whether the tendency of the matter charged as obscenity is to deprave and corrupt those whose minds are open to such immoral influences and into whose hands a publication of this sort may fall."[19]

The *Hicklin* test was applied in most American obscenity cases until 1957, when it was rejected by the U.S. Supreme Court in *Roth v. United States.*[20] Under the *Hicklin* test, obscenity was judged according to its effect on particularly susceptible individuals and was applied to isolated objectionable parts of a work. The focus became the effect of the material instead of the purpose of its creation.[21]

When the Supreme Court rejected the *Hicklin* test, it did so on the basis that that definition of obscenity unduly restricted freedom of speech and press and might cover material legitimately dealing with sex.[22] A new definition of obscenity was created in *Roth:* "[W]hether to the average person, applying contemporary community standards, the dominant theme of the material taken as a whole appeals to the prurient interest."[23]

Importantly, the Court also suggested that

obscenity is utterly without redeeming social importance. Movement toward adding that language and an element known as the patent offensiveness standard occurred in a series of court decisions following *Roth*.[24] Finally, in *Memoirs v. Massachusetts*, the court set forth a new definition of obscenity encompassing all those elements established in the prior cases:

> [I]t must be established that (a) the dominant theme of the material taken as a whole appeals to a prurient interest in sex; (b) the material is patently offensive because it affronts contemporary community standards relating to the description or representation of sexual matters; and (c) the material is utterly without redeeming social value.[25]

It was nearly impossible for criminal prosecutors to establish that any work was "utterly without redeeming social value." Thus, little obscenity regulation took place in the years between *Memoirs* (1966) and *Miller* (1973). Although the Supreme Court threw out the "utterly without redeeming social value" test in *Miller*, some states retain laws that include the test or variations of it.[26]

Attorney Bruce A. Taylor, vice president and general counsel of Citizens for Decency Through Law, Inc., believes that, due to the lack of uniform obscenity laws nationwide and the ineffectiveness of the *Miller* test to "stop the spread and abuses of hard-core pornography which is obviously obscene," an outright prohibition on all hard-core pornography that is "commercially distributed for other than *bona fide* medical, psychological, educational, or other proper non-exploitive uses" might be established.[27] (The Attorney General's Commission on Pornography found that lack of enforcement of obscenity laws already on the books nationally is a major problem.) Taylor's beliefs are shared by the Reverend Dr. Jerry R. Kirk of the National Coalition Against Pornography. Kirk, author of a book titled *The Mind Polluters*, believes that all visual portrayals of ultimate

sex acts for purposes of commercial entertainment should be prohibited.[28]

Taylor's proposal would prohibit the knowing exhibition or distribution of hard-core pornography for commercial purposes or to the public. He would define hard-core pornography as "any material or performance that explicitly depicts ultimate sexual acts, including vaginal or anal intercourse, fellatio, cunnilingus, analingus, and masturbation, where penetration, manipulation, or ejaculation of the genitals is clearly visible." His law would include "an affirmative defense for bona fide scientific, educational, or research purposes, and/or provide an exception for serious literary, artistic, political, or scientific uses." Taylor emphasized that the proposed law would supplement, not replace, obscenity laws.[29]

We believe creation of a new pornography law which eliminates the ineffective and difficult to enforce prurient interest, patent offensiveness and contemporary community standards elements of the *Miller* obscenity test is a move in the right direction. Unlike Taylor, we would propose that such a law replace existing obscenity laws. Under such a plan, the proposed law would need to be both broader and less broad than the Taylor proposal. For example, some people believe that not all portrayals of ultimate sex acts are harmful, immoral or bad. Many believe that erotica is a healthy form of sex education. It seems that the Taylor proposal would cover erotica (unless that were part of the bona fide educational purpose defense he proposes). In addition, under the Taylor proposal many of the worst types of pornography (sadomasochistic acts such as torture, bondage, or flagellation which did not also involve simultaneous sexual acts as described in his proposed law) would escape regulation except by obscenity law. This could bring objections of underinclusiveness from persons who believe that pornography combining sex and violence is the most harmful form and that obscenity law is objectionable or ineffective. The Taylor proposal is a step in the right direction. We propose a new pornography law in Chapter 12.

CIVIL RIGHTS APPROACH

Law Professor Catharine A. MacKinnon and author Andrea Dworkin pioneered the concept of pornography as a civil rights violation when they designed a local human rights ordinance for the City of Minneapolis in 1983. MacKinnon and Dworkin refer to pornography as "a practice of sex discrimination, a violation of women's civil rights, the opposite of sexual equality."[30] Although the Minneapolis ordi-

nance was passed by the city council, it failed to override the veto of the mayor. A similar ordinance was passed by the City of Indianapolis. This law was challenged in *American Booksellers Assn., Inc., v. Hudnut*.[31] The U.S. Supreme Court and lower federal courts found the ordinance to be unconstitutional. This approach and the court decisions are examined in chapters 7 and 10.

Versions of the civil rights law have been considered in other parts of the nation. In some places, opponents of the proposed law took extreme measures to prevent serious consideration of the proposals (see appendix B).

Model Antipornography Law

Dworkin and MacKinnon's model antipornography law is unique in the field of regulating pornography not only because it proposes a distinct definition of pornography, but also because it is aimed at permitting the victims of pornography to sue in civil court to recover damages for the injury done them. Section 1 of the model law provides a statement of policy. Note that while the obscenity law approach to regulating pornography condemns the material as being immoral and indecent, the civil rights approach attacks it because of the harm it does to real people. The model law should be looked at in its entirety by researchers.[32] Section 1 begins:

> Section 1. Statement of Policy. Pornography is sex discrimination. It exists in [PLACE], posing a substantial threat to the health, safety, peace, welfare, and equality of citizens in the community. Existing [state and] federal laws are inadequate to solve these problems in [PLACE].
>
> Pornography is a systematic practice of exploitation and subordination based on sex that differentially harms women. The harm of pornography includes dehumanization, sexual exploitation, forced sex, forced prostitution, physical injury, and social and sexual terrorism and inferiority presented as entertainment. . . .

Section 2 defines pornography:

> 1. *Pornography* is the graphic sexually explicit subordination of women through pictures and/or words that also includes one or more of the following: (i) women are presented dehumanized as sexual objects, things, or commodities; or (ii) women are presented as sexual objects who enjoy pain or humiliation; or (iii) women are presented as sexual objects who experience sexual pleasure in being raped; or (iv) women are presented as sexual objects tied up or cut up or mutilated or bruised or physically hurt; or (v) women are presented in postures or positions of sexual submission, servility, or display; or (vi) women's body parts—including but not limited to vaginas, breasts, or buttocks—are exhibited such that women are reduced to those parts; or (vii) women are presented as whores by nature; or (viii) women are presented being penetrated by objects or animals; or (ix) women are presented in scenarios of degradation, injury, torture, shown as filthy or inferior, bleeding, bruised, or hurt in a context that makes these conditions sexual.
>
> 2. The use of men, children, or transsexuals in the place of women in (1) above is pornography for purposes of this law.[33]

Within the definition of pornography advocated by MacKinnon and Dworkin are numerous other concepts that need further explanation. Dworkin views the term *social subordination*, which is so central to her proposed law, as having four main parts: hierarchy, objectification, submission, and violence. Dworkin states that women experience hierarchy—a group on top and a group on the bottom—in all aspects of their lives. Her concept of objectification is that of depersonalizing human beings, turning them into things or commodities. (In *Take Back the Night*, Diana E.H. Russell and Laura Lederer argue that seeing women as things rather than humans is essential to promoting violence, including rape, toward them. Pornography, they say, feeds that viewpoint. Even nonviolent pornography objectifies female bodies.[34] Kathleen Barry believes that objectification of women is a major cause of their sexual slavery, for this allows them to be treated in cruel and inhuman ways and to be seen as existing only to gratify men.)[35] Persons who are on the bottom of a hierarchy and are dehumanized are expected to be submissive (obedient and compliant), Dworkin explains. Lastly, she states, violence (with submission, hierarchy, and objectification as preconditions), plays a role in subordinating women. Sex, according to Dworkin, is the means through which women are subordinated, and "pornography is the institution of male dominance that sexualizes hierarchy, objectification, submission and violence."[36]

Catharine MacKinnon deals with the issue of what is meant by the term *sex object* in the model law:

> A sex object is defined on the basis of its looks, in terms of its usability for sexual pleasure, such that both the looking—the quality of the gaze, including its point of view—and the definition according to use become eroticized as part of the sex itself.[37]

MacKinnon states that the object world is "constructed according to how it looks with respect to its possible uses."[38]

The definition of pornography written by MacKinnon and Dworkin raises questions of vagueness and overbreadth—the universal attack by pornographers. Wisconsin officials, while employing the civil rights concept, proposed certain changes aimed at eliminating successful legal challenges to the approach.

Dane County, Wisconsin

In one version of County Supervisor Kathleen Nichols's proposed ordinance, the Dworkin–Mac-Kinnon concept of what pornography is would have been narrowed considerably. Nichols removed from the definition of pornography the following: "women are presented in postures or positions of sexual submission, servility, or display"; "women's body parts—including but not limited to vaginas, breasts, or buttocks—are exhibited such that women are reduced to those parts"; "women are presented as whores by nature." The debate over whether to include those three sets of terms in a definition of pornography centers on the view that the inclusion of those concepts could make almost all descriptions or depictions of women in our society pornography, making the definition overbroad. It cannot be disputed, however, that, considering humans learn from and imitate what they view, hear, and read, the pervasive presentation in American society of women as whores by nature and their objectification and presentation in postures of sexual submission, servility, or display have a great deal to do with the persistently unequal treatment of and discrimination against women. As long as women are depicted in that manner (even in what are supposed to be glamour and beauty magazines aimed at women readers), it is difficult to convince people that women are intelligent, caring, worthwhile human beings rather than stupid, unfeeling, worthless sexual objects—playthings to be used, abused, and discarded.

The Nichols ordinance changed the part of the model law that describes women as being "presented dehumanized as sexual objects, things, or commodities" by adding the words "to be used in a sexual manner." She added the term *abasement* to those items listed in part ix of the model law. Interestingly, Nichols proposed to broaden part iii of the model law, which reads: "Women are presented as sexual objects who experience sexual pleasure in being raped." The Nichols version would have read: "Women are presented as sexual objects who experience pleasure *or respond passively to sexual harassment* or sexual assault." (Emphasis added.) She also added the following concept:

> The depiction of children in the following manner, or in any way already covered in the above mentioned depictions, is pornography:

> (vii) presenting children as sexually accessible to or as appropriate sexual partners for adults; or
> (viii) depicting adults in a manner and a context so as to convey that the persons depicted are sexually accessible children.[39]

Wisconsin Legislature

Between April 1985 and February 1986, the civil rights legislation drafted on the legislative level in Wisconsin went through numerous revisions. The final product, which was not introduced due to the break-in described in appendix B, failed to receive the support of Catharine MacKinnon and Andrea Dworkin because they felt it departed too substantially from their original law. In drafting the Wisconsin proposal, Sara Lee Johann attempted to narrow the MacKinnon–Dworkin language and provide more clear-cut definitions of pornography and related terms that would be upheld by the courts. Chapter 12 includes a newly revised draft of a civil law approach to pornography created after the U.S. Supreme Court ruled the civil rights approach to be unconstitutional. Definitions related to pornography in Johann's Wisconsin legislation included:

> Pornography means the graphic sexually explicit subordination of women through pictures and/or words that also includes one or more of the following:
>
> 1. Women are presented involved in violent or destructive sexual acts, including human or animal mutilation, dismemberment, sexual assault or torture; or
> 2. Women are presented as experiencing sexual pleasure from or enjoying being sexually assaulted, pain, humiliation or violence; or
> 3. Women are presented as tied or bound or otherwise physically restrained; or
> 4. Women are presented as cut up, bleeding, mutilated, bruised, physically hurt or injured; or
> 5. Women are presented as dismembered, truncated, fragmented or severed into body parts; or
> 6. Women are presented as being penetrated by objects or animals; or
> 7. Women are presented being tortured, beaten or flagellated; or
> 8. Women are presented as experiencing or being subjected to sexual sadism or sexual masochistic abuse; or
> 9. Fecal matter or urine or the inducement of fecal matter or urine as part of sexual arousal; or

10. Sexual intercourse, other than between husband and wife, between blood relations who are nearer of kin than 2nd cousins where there is a power imbalance or differential or an age difference of more than three years; or

11. Sexual acts or expressions between live persons and dead persons or dead animals; or

12. Bestiality; or

13. Sexual intercourse or masturbation involving a person who has not attained the age of 18 years; or

14. Sexual intercourse which depicts dominance and lacks affectionate or mutually pleasurable sexual interaction.

(i)"Pornography" includes the use of men, children or transsexuals in the place of women in (h) above for purposes of this section.

"Pain" means the sensation due to bodily injury or disorder or acute mental or emotional distress.

"Sexual intercourse" includes actual or simulated genital-genital, oral-genital, anal-genital or oral-anal intercourse, whether between persons of the same or opposite sex.

"Subordination" means any one or more of the following:

1. To be dominated by another person, animal or thing.

2. To be placed in a position of inferiority, inequality, or loss of power.

3. To be demeaned or denigrated.

"Torture" or "tortured" means any severe or intense physical or mental pain inflicted upon a person.

"Violence" or "destructive" means the intentional use of physical force by a person to inflict pain or injury upon another person.[40]

Please note that while Johann chose not to define *sexually explicit* in the civil rights proposal, she did define it in another section that would have made coercing anyone into sexually explicit performances a crime:

"Sexually explicit" means any of the following:

1. Nude

2. Clad in undergarments or in a revealing costume

3. A representation which emphasizes the vagina, breasts, buttocks or genitals

4. A sexually sadistic or sexually masochistic representation.[41]

Under much of the civil rights law, isolated passages or isolated parts of material are not actionable. This language was included to ensure that persons who describe pornography for the purpose of educating people as to how bad it is would not be in violation of this law. The purpose is to require that the entire work or material be examined to determine whether it is pornography.

Under this proposal, erotica would not be pornography. Johann's goal was to narrow the concept of pornography to include primarily those depictions in which sexual explicitness and violence or abuse are combined and those in which someone is portrayed in a sexually explicit, subordinate manner.

Several other interesting definitions of pornography were included in the Canadian *Report of the Special Committee on Pornography and Prostitution* (1985). Helen Longino told the committee:

> What makes a work of pornography, then, is not simply its representation of degrading and abusive sexual encounters, but its implicit, if not explicit, approval and recommendation of sexual behavior that is immoral, i.e., that physically or psychologically violates the personhood of one of the participants. Pornography, then, is verbal or pictorial material which represents or describes sexual behaviour that is degrading or abusive to one or more of the participants *in such a way as to endorse the degradation*.[42]

Longino "writes that behaviour that is degrading or abusive includes physical harm or abuse, and physical or psychological coercion. She would also classify as degrading 'behaviour which ignores or devalues the real interests, desires, and experiences of one or more participants in any way.' "[43]

Longino's definition of pornography emphasizes representations of human females and their status as degraded and demeaned, as sexual objects to be exploited. Her definition is detailed in depth in *Take Back the Night*.[44]

Jillian Riddington dealt with the same aspect of this issue when she defined pornography as follows for the Canadian committee:

> [A] presentation whether live, simulated, verbal, pictorial, filmed or videotaped, or otherwise represented, of sexual behaviour in which one or more participants are coerced overtly or implicitly, into participation; or are injured or abused physically or psychologically; or in which an imbalance of power is obvious, or implied by virtue of the immature age of the participant or contextual aspects of the representation, and in which such behaviour can be taken to be advocated or endorsed.[45]

EROTICA VERSUS PORNOGRAPHY

Erotica, unlike pornography, depicts loving and affectionate human sexual interaction. Erotica is not pornographic, no matter how sexually explicit. Opinions of whether erotica should be regulated vary greatly.

The Canadian Fraser committee concluded that erotic portrayals of sex should be permitted because they will counteract the image of women propagated by pornography. The committee considered the following definitions of erotica:

> Erotica, as defined by Margaret Laurence, is the portrayal of sexual expression between two people who desire each other and who have entered this relationship with mutual agreement.
>
> Gloria Steinem defines the erotic as a mutually pleasurable, sexual expression between people who have enough power to be there by positive choice.[46]

The committee noted that in a recent court case, *R. v. Wagner*, Justice Shannon of the Court of Queen's Bench of Alberta refused to convict the accused of an obscenity violation where the videotape involved was erotic. "In the judge's words, the definition of 'sexually explicit erotica' is material which 'portrays positive and affectionate human sexual interaction, between consenting individuals participating on a basis of equality.' There is no aggression, force, rape, torture, verbal abuse or portrayal of humans as animals."[47]

In *Take Back the Night*, Gloria Steinem contrasts the difference between erotica and pornography: Erotica, rooted in *eros*, involves passionate love and an idea of free will choice, whereas pornography is rooted in *porno*, meaning "female captives" or "prostitution," namely, violence against, and domination of, women. Steinem views erotica as "a mutually pleasurable, sexual expression between people who have enough power to be there by positive choice."[48]

PORNOGRAPHY AND OBSCENITY UNDER THE LAWS OF CANADA

Canada does what some in the United States have urged. It regulates the combination of sex and violence. Under the 1985 Canadian Criminal Code, subsection 159 (8), any publication "a dominant characteristic of which is the undue exploitation of sex, or of sex and any one or more of the following subjects, namely crime, horror, cruelty and violence," is deemed to be obscene.[49] A community standards test, similar to that contained in U.S. obscenity law, is applied to these publications. The issue becomes whether a publication exceeds the contemporary Canadian community standards of tolerance.[50] Like U.S. obscenity law, the application of the test by juries and judges makes the interpretation of the obscenity law quite unpredictable. In Canada, offenses relating to obscene and indecent materials are in the section of the criminal code titled "Offences Tending to Corrupt Morals."

Unlike the United States, Canada has a law prohibiting genocide and hate propaganda, but this law does not prohibit genocide and hate propaganda against women, which most pornography would be. When the Fraser committee completed its report, it recommended the extension of the hate propaganda law to women.[51]

The Canadian Criminal Code provides:

> 281.1 (1) Every one who advocates or promotes genocide is guilty of an indictable offence and is liable to imprisonment for five years.
>
> (2) In this section "genocide" means any of the following acts committed with intent to destroy in whole or in part any identifiable group, namely:
>
> (a) killing members of the group, or
>
> (b) deliberately inflicting on the group conditions of life calculated to bring about its physical destruction.
>
> 281.2 (1) Every one who, by communicating statements in any public place, incites hatred against any identifiable group where such incitement is likely to lead to a breach of the peace is guilty of . . . .
>
> (2) Every one who, by communicating statements, other than in private conversation, wilfully promotes hatred against any identifiable group is guilty of . . . .[52]

Persons violating 281.2 (2) cannot be convicted if they can establish that the statements communicated were true, that they attempted to establish by argument an opinion upon a religious subject, that they reasonably believed the statements to be true and they were made relevant to a subject of public interest the discussion of which was for the public benefit, or that they, in good faith, "intended to point out, for the purpose of removal, matters producing or tending to produce feelings of hatred toward an identifiable group in Canada."[53] Again, women are not considered to be an identifiable group. The law defines *identifiable group* as "any section of the public distinguished by colour, race, religion or ethnic origin."[54]

Schedule C of the Customs Tariff as of 1985 prohibited the importation into Canada of representations of an "immoral or indecent character."[55] The community standards of tolerance test is applied to this. Customs officials issued guidelines to assist in applying this test:

> In these guidelines, "hard-core pornographic pictures" are described as ones which lewdly and explicitly display the male and female sexual organs, sexual intercourse, sexual perversions and acts like bestiality. Prohibited reading material contains "explicit hard-core fictional text dedicated entirely to sexual exploitation and containing no redeeming features."[56]

Canada has gone to great lengths to describe what it considers obscene or pornographic. Definitions describing these items are contained in the Canadian Interpretive Policy, Administration of Tariff Item 99201-1. Those guidelines state that the following materials, insofar as they are considered to be obscene or hate propaganda within the meaning of these terms, are to be prohibited entry:

a) Materials which depict or describe sexual acts that appear to degrade or dehumanize any of the participants, including:

(i) Materials which depict or describe sex with violence, submission, coercion, ridicule, degradation, exploitation or humiliation of any human being, whether sexually explicit or not, and which appear to condone or otherwise endorse such behaviour for the purposes of sexual stimulation or pleasure.

(ii) Portrayals or descriptions of rape. Any materials that depict or describe sexual intercourse between male/female, male/male, or female/female which appear to be without her/his consent and which appear to be achieved chiefly by force or deception.

(iii) Depictions and descriptions of bondage, involuntary servitude and the state of human beings subjected to external control, in a sexual context.

(iv) Portrayals or descriptions which appear to be associating pain and suffering with sexual pleasure or gratification by the use of artificial phalluses or restraints of any type and the mutilation of or letting of blood from any part of the human body, involving violence, coercion, and lack of basic dignity and respect for a human being.

(v) Materials which appear to depict or describe sexual gratification gained through causing physical pain or humiliation or the getting of sexual pleasure from dominating, mistreating, or hurting a human being. This includes depictions and descriptions of physical force which appear to be used so as to injure, damage or destroy; of extreme roughness of action; of unjust or callous use of force or power; of spanking, beating, or violent shoving in a sexual context.

(vi) Depictions or descriptions of mutilation or removal of any part of the human anatomy or the taking of human life, real or implied, for the purposes of sexual arousal.

(vii) The display or description of fecal matter, urine or the inducement of feces through enemas as part of sexual arousal.

(viii) Portrayals or descriptions of the act of buggery (sodomy), including depictions or descriptions involving implements of all kinds.

b) Materials depicting or describing sexual acts between children and/or juveniles, or between children and/or juveniles and adults; and portrayals or descriptions of children or juveniles in total or partial undress, alone or in the presence of other persons, and in which the context is even slightly sexually suggestive.

Children and juveniles are persons actually or apparently under the age of eighteen.

c) Materials depicting or describing sexual acts between members of the same family, other than between husband and wife.

This includes portrayals and descriptions of any sexual activity among members of a family, whether or not they are genetically related (incest), except wife and husband, which generally appear to condone or otherwise endorse this behaviour for the purposes of sexual stimulation or pleasure.

d) Materials depicting or describing sexual acts between human beings and animals. (Bestiality)

This includes depictions and descriptions of bestiality, whether there is actual copulation with an animal or the animal is merely present and copulation is implied.

e) Materials depicting or describing sexual acts between live persons and dead persons or dead animals. (Necrophilia)

f) Materials which advocate or promote genocide or hatred against an identifiable group distinguished by colour, race, religion or ethnic origin.[57]

The Fraser committee proposed changes in the Canadian criminal laws regulating pornography. Essentially, the committee recommended creation of a three-tier system of regulation. Its recommendations included some fascinating and useful definitions of pornography:

Controls on pornographic material should be organized on the basis of a three-tier system. The most serious criminal sanctions would apply to material in the first tier, including a visual representation of a person under 18 years of age, participating in explicit sexual conduct, which is defined as any conduct in which vaginal, oral or anal intercourse, masturbation, sexually violent behaviour, bestiality, incest, necrophilia, lewd touching of the breasts or the genital parts of the body, or the lewd exhibition of the genitals is depicted. Also included in tier one is material which advocates, encourages, condones, or presents as normal the sexual abuse of children, and material which was made or produced in such a way that actual physical harm was caused to the person or persons depicted.

Less onerous criminal sanctions would apply to material in the second tier. Defences of artistic merit and educational or scientific purpose would be available. The second tier consists of any matter or performance which depicts or describes sexually violent behaviour, bestiality, incest or necrophilia. Sexually violent behaviour includes

sexual assault, and physical harm depicted for the apparent purpose of causing sexual gratification or stimulation to the viewer, including murder, assault or bondage of another person or persons, or self-infliction of physical harm.

Material or productions in the third tier would attract criminal sanctions only when displayed to or performed before the public without a warning as to their nature or sold or made accessible to people under 18. Unsolicited mail incorporating such material is also included. In tier three is visual pornographic material or performances in which are depicted vaginal, oral, or anal intercourse, masturbation, lewd touching of the breasts or the genital parts of the body or the lewd exhibition of the genitals, but no portrayal of a person under 18 or sexually violent pornography is included.[58]

Canada is headed in the right direction in trying to create a definition of pornography that gets rid of vague, subjective terminology. The lists of prohibited behavior the Fraser committee proposed are clear-cut and workable. The major category of pornography that does not appear to be included in the Fraser committee proposal is sexual intercourse that depicts dominance and lacks affectionate or mutually pleasurable sexual interaction. This is a major gap likely to be attacked by those who believe much harm is caused by material that depicts women as submissive sexual objects and dehumanizes and degrades them.

Importantly, the committee supported the legislative enactment of a civil cause of action focusing on the violation of civil rights inherent in pornography, including class action suits. It also proposed creating a civil cause of action relating to "promotion of hatred by way of pornography."[59]

CHILD PORNOGRAPHY

A major breakthrough in the arena of regulating child pornography came when the U.S. Supreme Court decided the case of *New York v. Ferber* in 1982.[60] Most importantly, the court found that state laws prohibiting the dissemination of material depicting children engaged in sexual conduct are constitutional, regardless of whether the material is legally obscene. The impact of this was to permit states to establish clear-cut definitions of sexually explicit conduct in much broader terms than those defined under the *Miller* standard. The court justified its ruling by stating that the use of children as subjects of pornographic materials is "harmful to the physiological, emotional, and mental health of the

child." It also found that "prevention of sexual exploitation and abuse of children constitutes a government objective of surpassing importance."[61] Because it is equally true that the use of adult women or men as subjects of pornographic materials is harmful and that the prevention of sexual exploitation and abuse of adult women and men is an important government objective, perhaps someday the court will uphold laws prohibiting specific sexually explicit portrayals involving adults without requiring obscenity standards to be met.

The model law proposed by Citizens for Decency Through Law, Inc. (appendix A in this book), contains a provision prohibiting sexual exploitation of children. It prohibits dissemination of material in which children participate in "sexually explicit nudity, sexual conduct, or sadomasochistic sexual abuse." The definitions of sexual conduct and sadomasochistic sexual abuse are the same ones contained under the obscenity section of this chapter. Sexually explicit nudity is defined as

> the sexually oriented and explicit showing, by any means, including but not limited to, close-up views, poses or depictions in such position or manner as to present or expose such areas to prominent, focal or obvious viewing attention, of

any of the following: post-pubertal, fully or partially developed, human female breast with less than a fully opaque covering of any portion thereof below the top of the areola; the depiction of covered human male genitals in a discernible turgid state; or lewd exhibition of the human genitals, pubic area, perineum, buttocks or anal region, with less than a fully opaque covering.

A complete citation of where the child pornography laws of each state can be located is included in appendix H. Other legal aspects of such laws are dealt with later in the book.

NOTES

1. Pornography Resource Center, *Organizing Against Pornography* (Minneapolis: Pornography Resource Center, 1984).
2. Robert Sam Anson, "The Last Porno Show," *New Times*, 24 June 1977, 46, reprinted in *Protection of Children Against Sexual Exploitation: Hearings Before the Subcommittee to Investigate Juvenile Delinquency of the Senate Committee on the Judiciary*, 95th Congress, 1st Session (1977), 151.
3. *Jacobellis v. Ohio*, 378 U.S. 184, 197 (1964), Stewart, concurring.
4. Attorney General's Commission on Pornography, *Final Report* (Washington, D.C.: United States Department of Justice, 1986), 227 (hereafter cited as AGCOP).
5. Ibid., 227–28.
6. Ibid., 228–29.
7. Ibid., 229.
8. Freedom from sexual violence, *Violent Pornography: What It Is and Who It Hurts* (Milwaukee: Freedom from Sexual Violence, 1985), 3.
9. AGCOP, 229–30.
10. Ibid., 230–31.
11. *Miller v. California*, 413 U.S. 15, 34 (1973).
12. G.S. s. 14-190.1 North Carolina Stats.
13. *Ward v. Illinois*, 431 U.S. 767, 97 S.Ct. 2085, 52 L.Ed.2d 138 (1977); *Mishkin v. New York*, 383 U.S. 502, 86 S.Ct. 950, 16, 1.Ed.2d 56 (1966).
14. *Brockett v. Spokane Arcades, Inc.*, 472 U.S. 491, 493–94.
15. Ibid., 399–400.
16. See Louisiana L.R.S. 14: 106 A (6); 14: 106 A (2) (b) (iii); *State v. Johnson*, 343 So.2d 705 (La. 1977).
17. Fredrick Schauer, *The Law of Obscenity* (Washington, D.C.: BNA Books, 1976); George A. Weaver, *Handbook on the Prosecution of Obscenity Cases* (New York: National Obscenity Law Center, Division of Morality in Media, Inc., 1985); Daniel S. Moretti, *Obscenity and Pornography: The Law under the First Amendment* (New York: Oceana Publications, 1984); *Obscenity Law Reporter*. (New York: National Obscenity Law Center, 1986).
18. Weaver, *Handbook on Obscenity*, 2.
19. *Regina v. Hicklin*, L.R. 3 Q.B. 360 (1868).
20. *Roth v. United States*, 354 U.S. 976 (1957).
21. Weaver, *Handbook on Obscenity*, 2–3.
22. Ibid., 3.
23. *Roth v. United States*, 354 U.S. 976, 489 (1957).
24. *Manual Enterprises Inc. v. Day*, 370 U.S. 478 (1962); *Jacobellis v. Ohio*, 378 U.S. 184 (1964).
25. *Memoirs v. Massachusetts*, 383 U.S. 413 (1966), 418.
26. Bruce A. Taylor, "Pornography and the First Amendment," in *Criminal Justice Reform*, Ed. Patrick B. McGuigan and Randall R. Radder (Chicago: Regnery Gatewood, Inc., 1983), 156–57.
27. Ibid., 165.
28. Jerry R. Kirk, *The Mind Polluters* (Nashville: Thomas Nelson, Inc., 1985), 113.
29. Bruce A. Taylor, "Hard-Core Pornography: A Proposal for a Per Se Rule," *University of Michigan Journal of Law Reform* 21 (Fall 1987 and Winter 1988): 272.
30. Catharine A. MacKinnon, "Pornography, Civil Rights, and Speech," *Harvard Civil Rights–Civil Liberties Law Review* 20 (Winter 1985), 22.
31. *American Booksellers Assn., Inc., v. Hudnut*, 598 F.Supp. 1316 (1984).
32. Andrea Dworkin. "Against the Male Flood: Censorship, Pornography, and Equality." *Harvard Women's Law Journal*. 1985. 8: 1–29.
33. Ibid., 25.
34. Diana E.H. Russell with Laura Lederer, "Questions We Get Asked Most Often," in *Take Back the Night: Women on Pornography*, ed. Laura Lederer (New York: Wm. Morrow & Co., 1980), 24.
35. Kathleen Barry, *Female Sexual Slavery* (Englewood Cliffs, N.J.: Prentice-Hall, 1979), 10. chapter 10.
36. Dworkin, *Against the Male Flood*, 16.
37. MacKinnon, "Pornography, Civil Rights, and Speech," 19.
38. Ibid., 19.
39. Copy of proposed Dane County, Wisconsin, ordinance obtained from County Supervisor Kathleen Nichols.

40. Authors' files. Draft of civil rights antipornography legislation in Wisconsin drafted by Attorney Sara Lee Johann.

41. Ibid.

42. Canada, Minister of Supply and Services, *Pornography and Prostitution in Canada: Report of the Special Committee on Pornography and Prostitution* (Ottawa, 1985), 54–55 (hereafter cited as Fraser committee).

43. Ibid., 55, quoting Helen E. Longino, "Pornography, Oppression, and Freedom: A Closer Look," in *Take Back the Night: Women on Pornography*, ed. Laura Lederer (New York: Wm. Morrow & Co., 1980), 29.

44. Longino, "Pornography, Oppression, and Freedom," 40–54.

45. Fraser committee, 55, from Jillian Ridington, "Freedom from Harm or Freedom of Speech?" (Paper prepared for the National Association of Women and the Law, Ottawa, Ontario, Canada, 1983).

46. Fraser committee, 57, from Margaret Laurence, "On Censorship" (Speech to the Ontario Provincial Judges and Their Spouses, Peterborough, Ontario, Canada, 2 June 1983).

47. Fraser committee, 57–58.

48. Gloria Steinem, "Erotica and Pornography: A Clear and Present Difference," in *Take Back the Night: Women on Pornography*, ed. Laura Lederer (New York: Wm. Morrow & Co., 1980), 37–38.

49. Canadian Criminal Code, s. 159 (8).

50. Fraser committee, 45–46.

51. Fraser committee, 67.

52. Canadian Criminal Code, s. 281.

53. Ibid.

54. Ibid.

55. Canadian Customs Tariff, Schedule C.

56. Ibid.

57. Canadian Customs Tariff, Canadian Interpretive Policy, Administration of Tariff Item 99201-1.

58. Fraser committee, 271–72.

59. Ibid., 313–15.

60. *New York v. Ferber*, 458 U.S. 747 (1982).

61. Ibid., 757, 758.

2 IMAGES OF PORNOGRAPHY

We have chosen to take a very realistic approach in describing the types and amount of pornography available and the contents of that pornography. In some cases, graphic details are given. We found this necessary in order to refute the commonly held belief that pornography is merely pinup-style photographs of naked women and to paint a true-to-life picture of what pornography really is and how pervasive it has become in American society. While much of this material is offensive, much of pornography is offensive and harmful. This chapter takes the reader into the real pornographic world.

TYPES OF PORNOGRAPHIC MATERIAL

In the United States, pornography is estimated to be a four to six billion dollar a year industry.[1] The outlets for this diversified product include pornographic bookstores, telephones, video stores, general interest stores, the mail, computers, newsstands, vending machines, military bases, prisons, swinger and singles clubs, and private homes. Some large cities offer live sex shows.[2]

It has been estimated that at least one million children, ages 1 to 16, have been sexually molested and filmed for profit or pleasure in the United States.[3]

There are four times as many sex emporiums (pornographic bookstores, peep shows, live sex shows) in the United States as there are McDonald's restaurants.[4] Adult book stores number more than fifteen thousand.[5] In the 1970s, distribution locations for sexually explicit materials in Los Angeles alone increased from eighteen to more than four hundred.[6]

The pornography industry in the United States is said to be larger than the commercial movie and record industries combined.[7] And "[t]he circulation of *Playboy* and *Penthouse* is twice that of *Newsweek* and *Time* combined."[8]

Peep Show Loops

Peep show loops account for more than $2 billion a year in profits for the pornography industry. The 3-by 5-foot booths cost about $25,000 each, including equipment. It costs customers 25 cents to view two minutes of a ten- to ninety-minute 8mm film loop. Pornographic stores frequently generate more than $1,500 per day from loops.[9] (Loops are now videos.)

The walls of a peep show booth are usually covered with sex-oriented graffiti, from prostitutes' phone numbers to pornographic drawings. Holes in the side walls of the booths permit customers to engage in anonymous sex with each other. The sex is mostly oral or anal and between males. Some patrons leave the doors to their booths open, allowing other customers to enter and offer to engage in sex. The floors and walls of the booths are usually wet with semen, urine, feces, used prophylactics, saliva, gels, and alcohol. Add disinfectants, and the booths give off a nauseating smell. The unsafe sex that takes place in pornography store peep shows is considered a major health risk as a possible breeding ground for AIDS.[10]

Videocassettes

In 1985, more than 75 million adult videos were rented (20 percent of the total video market), up from 54 million in 1984.[11] In 1985, there were about nineteen thousand video specialty stores in the United States; such stores were expected to increase to twenty-seven thousand in 1987.[12] Women Against Pornography estimates that 75 percent of the video stores sell pornographic cassettes, with such videos making up 50 to 60 percent of all prerecorded cassette sales. While adult videos were said to constitute 13 percent of the market in 1984, this figure excluded most sexually violent material (found in the action/adventure, science fiction, and horror categories) and music videos.[13] In 1986, 28 percent of American homes had videocassette recorders.[14]

Adult Video News estimated that seventeen hundred new sexually explicit videos were released in 1985. A sixty-minute video can be produced at a cost of between $4,000 and $8,000, while a ninety-minute pornographic video costs between $10,000 and $20,000. Such videos sell for between $60 and $80 each. A video producer often sells to a distributor at 100 percent profit. A distributor's profit margin is between 100 and 400 percent. The sexually explicit video industry's profits are into the hundreds of millions of dollars a year.[15] Profits for each video range from $200,000 to several million dollars.[16]

At least 80 percent of the sexually explicit videotapes, 8mm films, and sexual devices and paraphernalia produced in the United States are produced and distributed in Los Angeles County.[17]

Motion Pictures

Approximately one hundred full-length sexually explicit films were distributed to close to seven hundred adults-only pornographic theaters in the United States in 1985. These theaters sold an estimated two million tickets weekly. Annual box office receipts for such films were estimated at $500 million.[18] In 1978, the Adult Filmmakers Association claimed an average weekly audience of 2.5 million and annual receipts of $455 million.[19]

The average cost of producing a feature length 35mm or 16mm sexually explicit movie is around $75,000. One well-known pornographic film, *Deep Throat*, cost $25,000 to produce and has earned more than $50 million. It is believed that there are twelve to twenty-four production companies involved in making theatrical release sexually explicit films.[20]

Dial-a-Porn

There are two types of dial-a-porn. The first is obtained by calling a number to receive a recorded sexually explicit message. The message typically describes sexual acts as if they were happening during the call and as if the performer were a participant in the act. The sex acts described may include rape, lesbian sex, sodomy, excretory functions, sadomasochistic abuse, incest, bestiality, and sex acts with children. The second type of dial-a-porn is when someone phones and obtains sexually explicit conversation from a performer who may encourage him or her to perform sexual acts during the communication.[21]

It is widely known that many calls to dial-a-porn numbers come from children, including boys and girls in elementary school. More than 800,000 calls are made daily to dial-a-porn companies in New York alone.[22] *High Society*'s Hotline Service gets an estimated 500,000 calls daily.[23] New York Telephone

Co. facilitated 96 million calls in 1985, generating $56 million in income for the utility.[24]

It costs only $25,000 to set up twenty-five dial-a-porn lines, including advertising.[25] A dial-a-porn recording can give its fifty-seven-second message to 50,000 callers per hour without any customer getting a busy signal. One such service got 800,000 calls in one day in May 1983. In the year ending February 28, 1984, 180 million calls were made to that same phone number.[26]

Pornographic Magazines

More than twenty million pornographic magazines are sold in the United States each month.[27] The combined readership of *Penthouse* and *Playboy* is twenty-four million.[28] (Table 2–1 details the average monthly circulation of the thirteen best-selling pornographic magazines for 1975, 1980, and 1984.) Newsstand pornographic publications increased from zero in 1953 (the year *Playboy* arrived) to more than forty in 1981.[29]

As of July 1986, it was estimated that there were between fifty thousand and sixty thousand different sexually explicit magazine titles available in the United States, and hundreds of new titles appear each month. When the Attorney General's Commission on Pornography surveyed sixteen pornographic stores in six major eastern cities, it discovered more than twenty-three hundred different magazine titles in those stores alone.[30]

At least one-half of the retail sales of sexually explicit magazines are by pornographic outlets, and

Table 2–1
Average Circulation per Month of Sexually Explicit Magazines

	1975	1980	1984
Cheri	N/A	395,805	360,993
Chic	N/A	268,340	N/A
Club International	318,728	241,761	185,532
Club Magazine	255,146	528,192	463,605
Forum	318,728	721,233	438,132
Gallery Magazine	647,173	583,123	475,321
Genesis	342,589	361,481	284,897
High Society	N/A	443,142	360,723
Hustler	554,559	1,531,855	N/A
Oui	1,276,498	780,420	N/A
Penthouse	3,966,109	4,542,910	3,275,677
Playboy	5,663,149	5,308,553	4,209,824
Playgirl	1,061,010	772,406	562,778
Total	14,084,961	16,479,221	10,617,482

Source: Attorney General's Commission on Pornography Final Report, July 1986, pp. 1409–11, based on audits by the Audit Bureau of Circulation.

the rest are by mail order. Many pornographic magazines are sold in neighborhood convenience stores and general interest bookstores. Pornographic magazines are marked up by as much as 400 to 500 percent from wholesale to retail and by up to 100 percent at the retail level.[31]

Sexual Enhancers

The Institute for the Advanced Study of Human Sexuality has estimated that at least five thousand different sexual enhancers have been marketed in the United States.[32] These items are available at pornographic outlets and through the mail.

The following list of devices may strike readers as something out of a horror story. Remember, however, that these sexual aids are used on real people. The sexual enhancers include dildos, penis rings, stimulators, French ticklers, aphrodisiacs, inhalants, inflatable dolls with orifices, and police and detective equipment. For those with sadomasochistic leanings, devices include rubber clothing, masks, chains, manacles, clamps, whips, paddles, orifice spreaders, body or testicle harnesses, penis stretchers, branding irons, enema bags, crosses, hoists, horse penises, rubber hands for anal insertion, lock restraints, handcuffs, leather straitjackets, pins, rectal catheters, racks, stocks, restraining tables, nipple clamps, and breast chains.

Paperback Books

Sexually explicit paperback books contain very detailed descriptions of sexual acts and are available, among other places, in pornographic bookstores and through the mail. They appear to be very popular. The 1970 Presidential Commission on Obscenity and Pornography estimated that five thousand new titles were published yearly. The Attorney General's Commission on Pornography reported that there were probably not that many in 1986 but that the number of such books published is very large.[33]

Cable and Satellite Television

In 1983, two million Americans subscribed to cable television services featuring pornographic programs.[34] Cable television was present in forty million American homes in 1986. The largest pornographic service, the Playboy Channel, went to 700,000 homes, and satellite networks distributed pornography to 50,000 subscribers.[35] Even regular television features sexual violence of the type found harmful by the Attorney General's Commission on Pornography.

Computer Pornography

A computer system now offers a shop-at-home service for selling and swapping sexually explicit merchandise.[36] Subscribers to a computer porn service can type out sexually explicit messages and get answers from pornographic performers. Pornographic movies and magazines are reviewed on these networks, which also feature dating services.[37] Children have access to such computer pornography, and pedophiles use computers to exchange information about child victims.[38]

Other Types of Pornography

Although there are a few national sexually explicit tabloids, most are regional. Some are issued by swinger or sex clubs, and most are filled with advertisements for sexually explicit products.[39]

Audiotapes of sexually explicit activities also are available, and in some large cities, live sex acts can be observed by customers. The acts range from nude dancers to actual sex activities.

Another type of pornographic material is custom-made photo sets. One company made $600,000 in one year selling such items. Some of these sets feature extreme acts of sexual abuse, including piercing (piercing skin and genitals with pins, needles, and other sharp objects), scat (ingestion or use of feces), extreme sadomasochism, bestiality (sex with animals), extreme mutilation, and child pornography.[40]

WHAT THE PUBLIC THINKS ABOUT PORNOGRAPHY

Twenty-one percent of more than six thousand readers in a *Woman's Day* survey said that they had been assaulted as a direct result of pornography, and 88 percent of those surveyed said that pornography encourages violence against women.[41] In a random survey of raped wives, 24 percent said they were forced to enact pornography.[42]

In 1985, three out of every ten adult Americans

watched an X-rated film, according to an ABC News–*Washington Post* poll.[43] That same poll, taken in early 1986, found that 57 percent of the people favored stricter antipornography laws. Interestingly, that poll revealed what some feminists have called a gender gap on pornography. The poll asked whether respondents thought that laws against pornography in the United States were too strict, not strict enough, or just about right. Ten percent of the men said the laws were too strict, 41 percent said they were not strict enough, and 47 percent said they were just about right. Two percent of the women said the laws were too strict, 72 percent said they were not strict enough, and 23 percent said they were just about right. More than two-thirds of the men said that they do not believe pornography does any damage to adults who see it. In a marked contrast, a decisive majority of women said pornography is harmful to adults.[44]

On March 6 and 7, 1985, *Newsweek* interviewed 1,020 adults by telephone about pornography.[45] The respondents were almost equally split over whether obscenity should be based on a national or community standard. Only 5 percent felt there should be no standard. While 48 percent of those surveyed said standards for the sale of sexually explicit material should be kept as they are, 43 percent felt standards should be stricter.

Nearly three-quarters of the people surveyed said that magazines showing sexual violence should be banned, while 68 percent felt that such movies should be banned. Most of the other respondents felt that there should be no public display of such violence, while only a small percentage felt that there should be no restriction. Sixty-three percent favored banning the rental or sale of videocassettes featuring sexual violence, while only 32 percent wanted to ban X-rated cassettes and another 39 percent favored no public display of such cassettes. Nearly half of all the adults surveyed wanted to ban magazines that show adults having sexual relations, while another 40 percent said there should be no public display of such magazines. Nine percent of the respondents said that they had rented or purchased an X-rated movie or cassette in the previous year; 37 percent said that they sometimes read or bought magazines like *Playboy*, while 13 percent said that they read or bought magazines like *Hustler*.

Importantly, 73 percent of those surveyed by *Newsweek* said that explicit sexual movies, magazines, and books lead some people to commit rape or sexual

violence, and 76 percent said they lead some people to lose respect for women. While 67 percent saw them as leading to a breakdown of public morals, only 35 percent thought they provided a safe outlet for people with sexual problems.

A 1985 National Population Survey in Canada found that two-thirds of Canadian adults use adult entertainment media, while one-third uses none.[46] Consumers of adult entertainment magazines were found to have certain characteristics that differentiated them from nonconsumers:

1. Men outnumbered women by 3 to 1.
2. Those with less than eight years of education bought fewer magazines than those with more education.
3. The unemployed were overrepresented among the magazine buyers.
4. Younger buyers outnumbered older buyers.
5. Single buyers outnumbered married buyers.[47]

In the survey, 31 percent said all sexually explicit material for adult entertainment is obscene, while 42 percent disagreed. Forty-five percent found sex magazines to be unacceptable in "our society," while 35 percent disagreed. However, 66 percent said everyone has the right to view sexually explicit material in private, while only 16 percent disagreed. Thirty-two percent found use of sexually explicit material by adults to be unacceptable, while 43 percent disagreed. Thirty-eight percent said violent sexual scenes shown in magazines should be banned, while 14 percent said offensive parts should be removed and another 4 percent called for fining or jailing the producer. Thirteen percent said children should not be permitted access to such magazines, 13 percent said the magazines should carry a disclaimer saying that they may be offensive to some people, 9 percent said nothing should be done or it should be left to personal discretion, and 9 percent gave no response.[48]

Two-thirds of Americans surveyed by *Time* magazine were very or fairly concerned about the pervasiveness of pornography in the United States, and 72 percent said they would like the government to crack down harder on pornography. In the *Time* poll, 54 percent said pornography leads to acts of sexual violence, 56 percent said it causes rape, 57 percent said it causes a breakdown in social morals, and 65 percent said they believe it leads to sexual promiscuity.[49]

CHILDREN WHO HAVE SEEN PORNOGRAPHY

A Canadian study found that youths between the ages of 12 and 17 were pornography's prime purchasers and had the highest interest in such material.[50]

Another study surveyed one hundred females and one hundred males in each of these age groups: adults (19–39), high school, and junior high school. Of the total surveyed, 91 percent of the males and 82 percent of the females had seen a magazine showing groups or couples engaged in sexually explicit acts. The average age for first viewing pornographic magazines was 13½. More high school students had seen X-rated films than any other age group surveyed. The average age for first viewing a pornographic film was just over 14½. Forty-six percent of junior high school students had seen one or more X-rated movies.[51]

Another survey studied 450 sixth-graders who watch cable television. Sixty-six percent of them said that they view at least one program monthly containing heavy sexual content, and 70 percent said that their parents do not monitor what they watch.[52]

CONTENT ANALYSIS OF PORNOGRAPHY

Introduction

Commissioner Park Elliott Dietz of the Attorney General's Commission on Pornography wrote this in the commission's *Final Report:*

> Pornography is a medical and public health problem because so much of it teaches false, misleading, and even dangerous information about human sexuality. A person who learned about human sexuality in the "adults only" pornography outlets of America would be a person who had never conceived of a man and woman marrying or even falling in love before having intercourse, who had never conceived of two people making love in privacy without guilt or fear of discovery, who had never conceived of tender foreplay, who had never conceived of vaginal intercourse with ejaculation during intromission, and who had never conceived of procreation as a purpose of sexual union. Instead, such a person would be one who had learned that sex at home meant sex with one's children, stepchildren, parents, step-parents, siblings, cousins, nephews, nieces, aunts, uncles, and pets, and with neighbors, milkmen, plumbers, salesmen, burglars, and peepers, who had learned that people take off their clothes and have sex within the first five minutes of meeting one another, who had learned to misjudge the percentage of women who prepare for sex by shaving their pubic hair, having their breasts, buttocks, or legs tattooed, having the nipples or labia pierced, or donning leather, latex, rubber, or child-like costumes, who had learned to misjudge the proportion of men who prepare for sex by having their genitals or nipples pierced, wearing women's clothing, or growing breasts, who had learned that about one out of every five sexual encounters involves spanking, whipping, fighting, wrestling, tying, chaining, gagging, or torture, who had learned that more than one in ten sexual acts involves a party of more than two, who had learned that the purpose of ejaculation is that of soiling the mouths, faces, breasts, abdomens, backs, and food at which it is always aimed, who had learned that body cavities were designed for the insertion of foreign objects, who had learned that the anus was a genital to be licked and penetrated, who had learned that urine and excrement are erotic materials, who had learned that the instruments of sex are chemicals, handcuffs, gags, hoods, restraints, harnesses, police badges, knives, guns, whips, paddles, toilets, diapers, enema bags, inflatable rubber women, and disembodied vaginas, breasts and penises, and who had learned that except with children, where secrecy was required, photographers and cameras were supposed to be present to capture the action so that it could be spread abroad.[53]

David Alexander Scott reports that one hundred content analyses of pornography done between 1970 and 1985 (with seventy of them between 1980 and 1985) showed that pornographic themes and imagery increased in prevalence and virulence over the previous three decades.[54] According to Scott, sex and violence have proliferated as a prominent theme in entertainment media. He believes that the pornography industry has marketed the following four messages over the past two decades and that these have been cloned by motion picture producers, advertising executives, and television programmers: "1) that sexual repression is unhealthy; 2) that regressive fantasy and promiscuity is healthy; 3) that sexual deviance, including homosexuality, is not deviant, and 4) that mature love is not sophisticated."[55]

Scott suggests that pornography promotes promiscuity, homosexuality, drug-enhanced sadomasochism, and sex with children as more fulfilling and enlightened than heterosexual marital relationships.

As early as 1959, a study by the Kronhausens characterized pornography as acts profaning the sacred, defloration, incest, seduction, and the use of the permissive–seductive parent figure.[56]

According to Kathleen Barry, pornography is the media of misogyny (woman hatred).[57] Barry says that pornographic themes often involve seduction or abduction of female victims who are willing collaborators. They are taken by surprise, initially resist, and are deflowered (whether virgins or not) by men in groups performing sadistic acts. Rape is not unusual. No matter how much pain is inflicted on the victim, she is not concerned about it, Barry states. Males are portrayed as supersexed and females as nymphomaniacs. Frequent pornography themes include bondage, discipline, and slavery. Although sex is forced, the women crave it. Sadism is prominent, and it is presented as a source of sexual pleasure for women. Bruises and blood usually are not shown, Barry says.

A study of 428 pornographic paperback books published between 1968 and 1974 uncovered 4,588 sex episodes, of which one-fifth involved an act of rape.[58] This study found that 91 percent of these acts involved rape of a female by a male, 86 percent of the rapists were known to their victims, and 21 percent involved raping a virgin. The rape of married housewives also was common. The average number of rape acts in books involving rape increased from two in 1968 to four in 1974 with an increase in explicit sexual content from one-third to two-thirds.

Smith found that the books described the females' terror at what was about to happen to them in great detail. They also described the women's physical resistance. Yet before the rapes were over, the victims were cooperating and begging for sex. One prominent theme noted by Smith was "that the victim really wants to be subjugated—wants to be forced to submit."[59] According to Smith, the victim rarely reports the rape in pornography, and few of the rapists experience negative consequences from the acts. Attackers are often rewarded with the victim's sexual devotion, and victims go on to richer sex lives.

Dietz and Sears analyzed 5,132 book, magazine and film covers in four major American cities. Approximately one-quarter of all images analyzed are designed to correspond with paraphilic interests. Fifteen percent of all images are designed to appeal to male homosexuals. Eleven percent depicted group

sexual activity. Items depicting particular sexual acts included fellatio (22%), anal insertion of the penis (12%), vaginal intercourse (7%), (of this 7%, the imagery included group sex activity or various deviant sexual activities) etc. Less than 5% of all materials depicted sexual intercourse between only one man and one woman.

The authors classified members of the public as sexually traditional, moderate or liberal. From the viewpoint of the sexually traditional, approximately 13% of the materials surveyed would be regarded as violent, 87% as nonviolent, but degrading and none or almost none as free of violence, degradation or humiliation. The sexually moderate viewed the material as 13% being violent, 35% as nonviolent and nondegrading or humiliating and 52% as degrading or humiliating. The sexually liberal viewed the material as 13% being violent, 23% degrading or humiliating and 64% nonviolent, nondegrading and nonhumiliating.[60]

In "The Propaganda of Misogyny," Beverly LaBelle applies eight techniques used in propaganda campaigns to pornography.[61]

First, *stereotypes* are used to create a fixed, unfavorable image of the scapegoat group. Women and men are portrayed as having opposite characteristics in pornography. Women are shown as submissive, whore-victims, carnal, and "repeatedly subdued and conquered by the eternally worshipped phallus."[62]

Second, *name substitution* creates a negative and biased reaction to the scapegoat group with terms such as cunt, twat, tramp, and so on.

The third technique, *selection*, is a process of presenting only facts that are favorable to the propagandist and unfavorable to his opponent. In pornography, this means presenting an image of women as sexually subservient to men, liking rape, and so on. Another example is the theme that pornography is good and has no adverse effects.

The fourth technique is *downright lying*. Pornography is a downright lie about women. For example, *Chic* magazine ran a feature titled "Columbine Cuts Up." A young woman is shown thrusting a large kitchen knife into her vagina. While blood spurts from the wounds, the woman's face shows sexual ecstasy. A real women who had hurt herself in that manner would be in severe pain.

The fifth technique is *repetition*. As concepts are repeated, they become more persuasive and influential. In pornography, the main theme is that women are inferior and males should do whatever they please with them. Another theme is that all women secretly want to be raped.

Assertion, the sixth technique, is used to promote an idea. Pornography is assertive in two main ways:

first, in its pervasive presence in society, and second, in the pornographers' campaign to silence their opponents by invoking the First Amendment and securing the right to promote antiwoman ideas in the name of free speech.

Seventh, the enemy is *pinpointed*. In pornography, the enemy is women, who are to be subdued and vanquished.

Finally, *authority is appealed to*. This is vital to proving that the ideas are intelligent and respectable. Thus, there are "expert" quotations, testimonials from famous people, and historical references. With pornography, there is an underlying assumption that it is portraying sex in a natural way. Famous people often are featured in articles in soft-core magazines. Psychological and sociological studies are used to describe the benefits of pornography and are quoted as proof that pornography is not harmful.

Thus, according to LaBelle, pornography propagates the "philosophy of male supremacy." It establishes that women exist only to sexually gratify men. Because such "dehumanized" ideas of women are so widely accepted, pornography is not recognized as propaganda designed to "misrepresent the sexual differences between men and women."[63]

In their study, Ashley and Ashley found that women in pornography are treated as meat.[64] They beg for or crave bizarre sex—anal ecstasy, big cocks, double fucking, painful climaxes, and gang bangs. They concluded that pornography is cruel without being truly sadistic, for its hatred and cruelty goes unnoticed. Most people who appear in pornography are anonymous, so consumers can identify with them as everyman and everywoman. Ashley and Ashley found that it is thirty or forty times more common to see men subjugating women in pornography than vice versa. For example, domination is shown in most contemporary pornographic movies when men ejaculate on women's faces. In fact, dominance and submission are the defining characteristics of pornography, according to the authors. Another common pornographic theme is thrusting an erect penis down another person's bulging and often unwilling throat. Ashley and Ashley give the following examples of specific material:

A sexualized "Dracula" movie in which a female vampire bites the man on his genitals and sex is had in a coffin.

A hard-core film in which one male sodomizes another. The second man is clearly not aroused, for his penis is flacid and expression pained. The first male rams his fecal-stained penis down the other's unwilling throat.

In a bondage magazine, women are tied up and scissors, torches, knives, hot irons are held to their vaginas and breasts.

A dagger is plunged into a pregnant woman's stomach.

A man cuts open a woman's abdomen and holds her insides above his head in a scream of orgasmic conquest.

Three men kidnap a 12-year-old girl and a grandmother, beat and kick them senseless and rape them.

Father Bruce Ritter, who works with child victims of pornography and prostitution, and a member of the Attorney General's Commission on Pornography, says that the message of pornography is that "sex bears no relationship to love and commitment, to fidelity in marriage, that sex has nothing to do with privacy and modesty and any necessary and essential ordering toward procreation. . . . [P]leasure—not love and commitment—is what sex is all about."[66]

Susan Brownmiller calls pornography antifemale propaganda. She notes that females in pornography are portrayed as "virgins" who are caught and "banged" or "nymphomaniacs" who are never sated. The most popular pornographic fantasy combines the two. An innocent, sexually untutored female is raped, subjected to unnatural sex practices, and turned into a "raving, slobbering nymphomaniac," a sexual slave who can never get enough. The female is the property of the male. The male's penis is the patriarchal instrument of his power by which he rules by force over her. Brownmiller disputes those who claim that pornography frees sensuality from moralistic inhibition. Instead, she states, it is a male invention designed to dehumanize women and reduce females to objects of sexual access.[67] Another feminist, Andrea Dworkin, states that pornography promotes the idea that real love is the erection, not the orgasm.[68]

A 1984 article by Joseph W. Slade contains a history of pornography that indicates even in the early 1900s, such films were used in brothels and clubs.[69] Slade looked at 1,333 examples of pornography from 1915 to 1972 and found that rape was portrayed in only 5 percent of the total. (Some researchers have found that depictions of rape have increased since the early 1970s.[70]) According to Slade, the concept of women in pornography is false and unfair. Having raised their desire to "nymphomaniac peaks," the stag denies them pleasure for their efforts when he ejaculates into space.[71] Slade found fetish films to be a minority. Although urination showed up frequently in hard-core films since 1915, filmed copulation with animals—dogs, horses, snakes, eels, ducks, and pigs—appeared in less than 1 percent of the films Slade surveyed. These could be considered inherently violent, he suggests, although they rarely employ force. According to Slade, a random sampling of pornography from 1980 to 1983 suggested that violence occurred in about 16 percent of the films, but mild aggression outweighed brutality. Slade perceives a theme in pornography requiring that women recognize the fact that world stability depends on their respect for the penis. There is a danger that in their insatiability that recognition of that fact will be occluded as their lust leads them to mate with anything from animals, other women (hence, near-obligatory lesbian scenes), and phallic substitutes such as dildos or vegetables. Ultimately, however, women confirm their preference for the penis.

As Slade points out, females in pornography always acquiesce. They must be willing to have sex and be as randy as the males want themselves to be. Pornography aimed at males thus invests the female with male sexual traits. Because "male psyches are so often inflamed by voyeurism," Slade notes, pornography often contains the doubtless erroneous idea that erotic photos can trigger female sexual appetites.[72]

In 1982, Dietz and Evans classified 1,760 heterosexual pornographic magazines based on cover imagery.[73] For the study, Dietz and Evans selected four shops in the notorious pornography district on 42nd Street in New York City. They found that 37.3 percent of the covers showed a couple in sexual activity, 16.7 percent showed domination and bondage, 10.7 percent showed a woman posed alone, and 9.8 percent involved group sex. Other images were less common—for example, anal intercourse (1.5 percent) and enema administration (1 percent). Pseudochild images occupied 3.4 percent of the covers.

According to Dietz and Evans, the relative presence of certain fantasy images in pornography corresponds to the preexisting fantasy imagery of the consumer (the various sexual perversions). They describe the sorts of images found in some of the categories listed above. Most of the magazines depicted women wearing high heels and lingerie. Fellatio was shown about as frequently as vaginal intercourse and much more often than cunnilingus. In the bondage and discipline materials, however, if there was direct sex, it tended to be cunnilingus. Material showing a woman posed alone was the mainstay of the 1970 pornography market but constituted only a small percentage of the 1982 sample. Much of the material in the Dietz and Evans survey was unavailable or sold only under the counter

in 1970. The authors state that the fact that 17.2 percent of the material reviewed was devoted to bondage and domination is the most important finding of their research. They also found many paperback novels about pedophilia and incest and a few films of bestiality in the shops.

Another survey by Smith involved sampling pornographic paperback books obtained in places where the general public would shop (not pornographic bookstores).[74] In 1968 through 1974 (excluding 1971), every fifth pornographic paperback was taken from the shelves of eight newsstands and regular bookstores in five states. A total of 468 paperbacks were analyzed. These books revolved around a series of sex episodes tied together by transition pages of nonsexual activity. The sexual scenes rarely contributed to the story line. Smith measured the proportion of pages devoted to sex episodes to determine the frequency of sex episodes in the books. He found a trend indicating the inclusion of more material depicting sexual activity with time. Index scores were .29 in 1967, .36 in 1968, .47 in 1969, .64 in 1970, .61 in 1972, .60 in 1973, and .63 in 1974. The index of sexual content in these books ranged from .15 to .79, while mass market "sex novels" such as *Fear of Flying, Valley of the Dolls, Couples, The Seven Minutes,* and *Portnoy's Complaint* seldom had an index value of more than .05.

Smith also examined the attributes of the principal characters in the books. The typical character was single, young, white, physically attractive, and heterosexual. The males tended to have professional or business occupations, while the females were primarily housewives or clerical workers. Twenty-three percent of the females were students, compared to 20 percent of the males. The physical characteristics of the females were detailed "down to the last dimple,"[75] while the males' physical attributes were given little attention. In the books, 17 percent of the females were bisexual, and another 7 percent were homosexual. Smith notes, however, that female homosexuality and bisexuality was male dominated, with these types of sexual acts frequently forced, instigated, or watched by males.

Few of the sexual episodes studied by Smith needed inducement. In the 17 percent that did use a catalyst, one-third of the time it was alcohol, another third of the time it was some form of drug, and the rest of the time it consisted mainly of pornography and live models. The inducements were usually used to encourage the female, rarely the male.

Importantly, although the Smith study involved the earlier and supposedly milder pornography of the late 1960s and early 1970s, many of the features of today's pornography were apparently present in that material. In only 9 percent of the sex acts was there overt or even implicit expression of love toward the other partner. Of these, approximately 3 percent involved mutual expressions of love, and almost 6 percent involved expressions of love by the female that were not returned by the male. Less than 1 percent involved expressions of love by the male that were not returned by the female.

Sixty percent of the sex episodes involved physical gratification devoid of any feeling toward the partner as a human being. Importantly, Smith discovered that almost one-third of the episodes contained the use of force (physical, mental, or blackmail), usually by the male, to encourage the female into an initially unwanted sex act. Despite the force used, however, in most cases the female became aroused by the male. Despite her verbal protests, she responded physically, much to her shame. The male did not have any particular skill or finesse. The female seemed to respond to his sheer sexuality and the size of his sex organ.

Smith found that machismo themes dominated the pornography. Males dominated the sexual activity and rarely experienced sexual inadequacies. Males even dominated acts of female self-masturbation, frequently forcing such acts on them. Such acts were portrayed as males would like them to be rather than as they really are. In these books, females performed fellatio or anal intercourse as their ultimate submission to the male or the male inflicted these ultimate degradations or humiliations on the female. When cunnilingus was presented, it was not as a form of homage to the female, but rather a way to turn a poised, unobtainable beauty into a lustful nympho-maniac. Bestiality, although uncommon, was forced on the female by the male in 70 percent of its cases. In short, the most common theme was to turn a woman who was young, beautiful, and sexually unstirred into a lustful nymphomaniac. Smith notes that the plots in the books remained consistent through the years of the study and concluded that it remains a male's world.

The fact that pornography is consumed primarily by males was confirmed by a study conducted in 1973.[76] Nawy observed 2,791 adult movie theater patrons, 96.7 percent of whom were males. Sixty-three percent of these said they sometimes used a book or magazine to help achieve orgasm. In addition, 950 adult bookstore patrons were observed, 96.5 percent of whom were males. The 367 arcade patrons observed were all males, for females were prohibited from entering the viewing machine area.

According to Drakeford and Hamm, the "indictment" against pornography involves seven counts.[77]

First, pornography has created a mythical woman. This woman is the fulfillment of masculine wishes: a female who spends her time pursuing males who will satisfy her sexual desires.

Second, pornography undermines family life. It emphasizes sex without relationship, attacks the concept of a well-rounded love, and downgrades commitment to a mate that will provide a setting for raising children. This attack is aimed at a family unit that consists of a husband and wife committed to each other and a warm, loving climate for developing the children's personalities around models of masculine and feminine roles. (Please note that a concept of masculine and feminine roles is sexist and would not be followed by those who seek equality of the sexes).

Third, pornographic presentations divorce sex from love.

Fourth, pornography presents the wrong role models in its portrayals of sexuality. Much learning is by imitation, Drakeford and Hamm state. They express the concern that children will identify with portrayals of men using brutality, force, sex without love, and callous exploitation of women instead of affection.

Fifth, the world of pornography is completely fictional and unreal. It presents sex out of context by severing it from its human context.

Sixth, according to Drakeford and Hamm, the "pornographers are guilty of a monstrous hypocrisy."[78] For example, pornographic movies are called "adult" and "mature." Other examples of hypocrisy by pornographers include pretending that books that describe sexual activities from a male viewpoint are written by women, promoting pornography as educational, and hiding behind the First Amendment and patriotism.

Seventh, the true nature of human sexuality is misrepresented by pornography.

Finally, "Pornography Destroys the Individual's Right to Privacy." When sex becomes public, the viewer does not see the sentiments and the ideals, only the "animal coupling," thus debasing a human relationship "into mere animal connection."[79]

Drakeford and Hamm also make other comments about the content of pornography. They state that pornography is not concerned about reality, it concentrates on building up sexual tension by moving from milder sexual scenes to more variety and increasingly unorthodox acts, and it utilizes certain themes, including the following:

Defloration. For the pornographer, the surrender of virginity is like an army conquering an enemy.

Incest. Pornography upsets normally held taboos concerning human sexuality. Thus, it portrays fathers seducing or being seduced by daughters and seductive stepmothers with their stepsons. In this material, a mother might be shown applauding a husband as he has a sex orgy with his daughter and niece.

Debasement of religion. For example, pornographers try to show that most religious persons are really sensualists. Thus, a priest might be portrayed as having sex with a girl who attends his church.

Use of gutter language.

Violence. The pornographer has to explore all forms of human sexuality in the search for something new. Sadomasochism is one example of this. Thus, a typical theme is a seductive girl leading a man into sex, then being surprised by a gang of four men who quickly knock out her lover and sexually assault her simultaneously. After her initial struggle, she overcomes her inhibitions and thinks (according to the pornographer), "Rip me to pieces . . . isn't this what every girl dreams of secretly to herself?"[80] This perpetuates the myth of women loving rape. Other examples include whippings, bondage, and use of hot enemas. In the real world, women prefer men who are kind and considerate, not brutal.

Super-sexed males. Men in pornography are portrayed with enormous sex organs and unlimited powers of sexual endurance.

Seductive females. While women in real life are often modest, restrained, and anxious about sex, the females in pornography are passionate and seductive and spend their time resisting a consuming lust that can be satisfied only by bedding a partner—animal or human. Pornographic women are lustful nymphomaniacs. Real women, however, often enjoy cuddling as much or more than intercourse.

Bestiality.

Detailed description. Sexual acts are the focus of pornography, and these are described in minute detail. Females are portrayed as having sexual responses similar to those of males. Orgasms are shown as explosive experiences.

Drakeford and Hamm note that pornography is "committed to techniques of sexual arousal." Some realities of sexual activities are conveniently overlooked by the pornographer. There are "no pregnancy—no venereal disease—no pimps—no police raids—no sadistic patrons."[81]

According to Ronald M. Holmes, by age 18, 80 percent of males and 70 percent of females will have seen some form of pornography.[82] Holmes mentions another common pornographic theme: two females engaged in kissing and oral-genital sex. This scene is directed not at lesbians but at heterosexual males who are aroused by viewing women having sex with other women. Rarely do films depict males involved in homosexual acts. Holmes also notes that pornographic novels ignore any problems that could result from the various sexual acts they portray, including divorce, venereal disease, and mental or emotional problems.

In *Take Back the Night,* Judith Bat-Ada (interviewed by Laura Lederer) describes the *Playboy* genre pornography.[83] She says that *Playboy* portrays men as boys who are "forever playing" and women as their toys. Everyday adult responsibilities such as fatherhood, loving, and family duties are "invisible." Wives and family members are ridiculed, and sexual exploitation is portrayed as a winning image. Females are portrayed as "nonhuman, as whores, as animals," which, Bat-Ada says, eliminates any requirement for men to treat women as equals.[84]

According to Bat-Ada, one common technique of the *Playboy* genre pornography is to use fairy tales in cartoons. Thus, a wolf molests Little Red Riding Hood, the Seven Dwarfs rape Snow White, or Goldilocks sleeps with Baby Bear. This type of pornography is based on the belief that readers will understand that the imagery is fantasy and is just a joke or all in good fun. Bat-Ada, however, refers to pornography as "sexual fascism." According to Bat-Ada, fascism is a belief in one's superiority and that one can take control and secure power without regard to how it will affect others. She states: "For women, sexual fascism means that men, and in particular a few powerful men, control our behavior, attitudes, fantasies, concepts of love and caring, integrity, that in which we believe and hope, as well as the ways in which we love and to whom and how we make our genitalia available."[85]

Sarah McCarthy also has dealt with the macho images of pornography. She cites a case in which one character in a popular pornographic magazine declares that there's "still something to be said for bashing a woman over the head, dragging her off behind a rock, and having her."[86] She notes that another popular magazine displayed a nude woman on a plate covered with ketchup and looking like a chicken, while another was posed on a hamburger bun.

Child pornography includes boys and girls with rectums enlarged to accommodate adult men and vaginas penetrated with pencils, toothbrushes, and guns. One Times Square shop in New York City had forty-six films for sale with women having intercourse or performing oral sex with animals such as pigs, dogs, donkeys, and horses. In some pornography, men give enemas or whippings to each other. Some feature 3-foot rubber penises, while in others women are shown penetrated by broom handles, smeared with feces, urinated on, covered in blood, kneeling submissively in the act of fellatio, with genitals shaved, with metal bars holding their legs apart, or sipping ejaculate from champagne glasses.[87]

According to Teresa Hommel, women are portrayed in pornography as either passive, weak victims or aggressive bitch/witch sexual torturess types who cannot be trusted.[88] She notes that pornography is often devoid of the caring, tenderness, and foreplay that sex researchers have found to be important parts of women's sexuality. She believes fellatio is popular in pornography partly because it shuts women up. And, she says, some porn is nothing but violence with no explicit sex. Hommel concludes that the constant portrayal of women as lustful whores provides men with a rationale for rape and other types of sexual aggression.

According to Davis and Braucht, who summarized the content analysis of pornography done by Kronhausen and Kronhausen in 1959 and 1967,

> pornography is characterized by an absence of the reality constraints that mark erotically realistic works of fiction. . . . A prominent theme is that of the seduction of someone who is in fact a willing collaborator. Another theme is that of rape and defloration in which the victim shows little concern for the pain involved and no resentment for having been used. Also prominent among the themes are portrayals of incest or parental encouragement and participation in sexual behavior. One might say that the primary aim is to create a state of increasing sexual arousal in the reader by portraying sexual relations in which all standards are violated and in which the only psychological feelings involved are lust and a mindless sexual joy. In such work, there is an absence of any serious development of the other human emotions and feeling typical of such intimate relationships.
>
> In contrast, erotically realistic work may be just as graphic in its description of sexual intercourse and deviance, but there is also some emphasis on the complexities of feelings involved (such as fear, guilt, ambivalence, disgust) and a concern with the characters as human beings rather than merely as sexual animals.[89]

Susan Griffin's *Pornography and Silence* deals, in large part, with the images of pornography from a feminist perspective.[90] Griffin writes of a pornographic mind obsessed with humiliation of the soul (destroying a virgin's spirit). Thus, in pornography, a virgin becomes a whore after she is raped. The virgin, who has the soul of a whore beneath her innocence, thus loves being raped. In the pornographic mind, the bestiality of "a man's nature is expressed in a woman's body." This, Griffin believes, explains the common association in pornography "between women and animals" (that is, having sex with animals or becoming animals to be trained with whips).[91] Such images do not portray women realizing a unity with nature. Instead, they contain ridicule, revulsion, and degradation. Another common pornographic image is the idea that a man's body soils a woman's body. One point of high drama in pornography is the moment at which a woman begins to remove her clothing to reveal her body. Yet this mystery of the female body is revealed "to be nothing more than flesh, and flesh under culture's control."[92]

According to Griffin, at the very core of pornography is the concept of woman as object (showing her goods). The pornographic mind believes it is the body of the woman and not the woman it loves. The function of the pornographic woman (object) is to please a man. Thus, Griffin notes, a popular porn image is a penis in a woman's mouth. Pornographic women have no rights. They are reduced to objects so they can be mastered and controlled. Thus, sex in pornography is an act of dominance (kidnaping, rape, bondage, orders, imprisonment). Yet, Griffin points out, a real object does not require mastery. Pornography promotes an idea that physical pleasure can be sought and found from physical pain. In pornography, a woman (usually), a man (sometimes), a child (often) "is abducted by force, verbally abused, beaten, bound hand and foot and gagged, often tortured, often hung, his or her body suspended, wounded, and then murdered."[93]

Griffin notes that Wilhelm Stekel described the essence of the sadomasochistic act to be humiliation.[94] She believes that objectification of another is a sadistic act. The mere revealing of a woman's body (as done in porn) is a degradation, for an anonymous viewer considers the pornographic nude his object, which he owns and masters. The classic sadomasochistic relationship requires the invulnerability of the sadist and the vulnerability of the masochist, so this fits. When a woman submits to the threat, another sadistic act has occurred, for there is a loss of will and soul.

Griffin believes that pornography promotes an idea that women are inferior beings. Also, in pornography female silence is a virtue and outbursts result in more punishment. In short, the pornographic world is one of male gestures, ethos, and language. Common themes of pornography show power relationships such as parent-child, teacher-student, doctor-nurse, and master-slave. Those with feelings suffer in pornography, and unfeeling people get ahead. One genre of pornography portrays men abusing men or boys. Not surprisingly, these enslaved males are made to resemble females in every way. They are treated like females and react like females. The pornographer tries to convince us that women want to be punished. Thus, we see abuse of the breasts of women in pornography by fingernails, pinching, and slashing. Women also are urinated or defecated upon. According to Griffin, one of the functions of pornography is to "offend sensibility," for ugliness numbs us into not feeling.[95] The pornographer's desire is to suppress and silence sexual knowledge. She says, "This is the message of the brutality of pornography: the pornographer is a censor."[96] Pornography's heroes seek liberty, release from slavery, the power to do what one likes. Yet in the pornographic mind, woman is nature and he must take away her liberty and silence her. Even the sex in pornography appears to be aimed more at overpowering and silencing women than at pleasure. In pornography, women's expressions of freedom and will are met with violence. Griffin cites examples of gags, bondage, and hoods. In pornography (and real-life rape trials), women victims become the criminals, and heroes who feel trapped by their own desire use violence to free themselves. The pornographer, as part of his delusion, projects what is natural in him onto the body of a young woman, thus denying his own desire by describing her as a nympho.[97]

Ironically, in some pornography, the pornographer is shown fantasizing that his images become events (heroes look at pornography then imitate it). According to Griffin, the women in pornography represent all women, with each image a sadistic act accomplishing the humiliation of all women. In the real world, pornography actresses must appear to enjoy their work in order to keep the actors hard. And Griffin believes real women need emotions for sexual experience. Griffin believes the porn producer loves the power it gives him over his audience, that of "sadistic humiliation of other men." Yet beneath every pornographic image of female glamour "is the conviction that a woman does not really exist."[98]

In the *Story of O*, a pornographic novel, the character, will, and spirit of a woman are undone through a systematic torture of her body. O gradually unlearns natural bodily responses such as defending herself. Griffin describes how O's control over her own body is taken away and she is subjected to extreme temperature changes, beatings, and sexual abuse. Tubes are used to gradually enlarge her anus.

Corsets make her waist smaller. Her master brands his initials on her buttocks. A hole is made in her vagina so that a chain can be attached. O, in short, is a complete sexual slave.[99]

Paraphilias in Pornography

The American Psychiatric Association's *Diagnostic and Statistical Manual of Mental Disorders, III* (DSM III)[100] is the commonly used reference work referred to in court when cases may involve persons with mental disorders. In the chapter on psychosexual disorders, there is a subgroup called "paraphilias," which are important to researchers of pornography because much pornographic material concerns these paraphilias and caters to them.

In DSM III, paraphilias are described as existing when "unusual or bizarre imagery or acts are necessary for sexual excitement." These images or acts tend to be repetitive and generally involve either: "(1) preference for use of a nonhuman object for sexual arousal, (2) repetitive sexual activity with humans involving real or simulated suffering or humiliation, or (3) repetitive sexual activity with nonconsenting partners."[101] Paraphiliac imagery is necessary for erotic arousal.

DSM III describes the following paraphilias:

1. Fetishism
2. Transvestism (sometimes evolving into transsexualism)
3. Zoophilia
4. Pedophilia
5. Exhibitionism
6. Voyeurism
7. Sexual masochism
8. Sexual sadism
9. Coprophilia (feces)
10. Frotteurism (rubbing)
11. Klismaphilia (enema)
12. Mysophilia (filth)
13. Necrophilia (corpse)
14. Telephone scatologia (obscene phone calls)
15. Urophilia (urine)

It is interesting to add that DSM III includes among its psychosexual disorders nymphomania and Don Juanism.

Lebegue studied the titles of 2,173 publications reviewed by the Victorian State Classification of Publications Board in Australia between February 1, 1979, and October 15, 1983, to find out how many had DSM III paraphilias (aberrant sexual behavior) inherent in the titles.[102] Lebegue found the following:

Fetishism comprised 2.3 percent of all titles and 8.9 percent of paraphilia titles.

Transvestism made up 7.2 percent of all titles and 27.9 percent of paraphilia titles.

Zoophilia (bestiality) was not present at all.

Pedophilia/incest comprised 3.5 percent of all titles and 13.5 percent of paraphilia titles.

Exhibitionism was not present in any of the titles.

Voyeurism made up 0.4 percent of all titles and 1.2 percent of paraphilia titles.

Sado-masochism (combined in a group by Lebegue) comprised 12.4 percent of all titles and 47.8 percent of paraphilia titles.

Atypical paraphilias made up 0.1 percent of all titles and 0.5 percent of paraphilia titles.

Lebegue also noted that another 3.4 percent of all titles involved teen or young sex that would not be considered pedophilia under the strict DSM III criteria but were certainly concerns of the law.

The Marquis de Sade

History's best-known pornographer is the Marquis de Sade (Donatien Alphonse Francois de Sade), for whom sadism is named. De Sade used his aristocratic background to act on his violent sexual desires. He was imprisoned numerous times for sexually abusing women. One victim, Rose Keller, is said to have been tied to a bed, whipped, cut with a knife, and had hot wax poured in the wounds. De Sade kidnapped and abused girls, poisoned and sodomized prostitutes, and in short was a rapist, torturer, batterer, kidnapper, and child abuser.[103]

Andrea Dworkin dubbed de Sade the "consummate literary snuff artist," who teaches that orgasm eventually requires murder.[104] According to Dworkin, the ethic of de Sade is the absolute right of men to brutalize and sexually abuse any object of desire at will. She believes that de Sade's work celebrated brutality as the essence of eroticism; fused fucking, torture, and killing; and made violence and sex synonymous.[105]

As Dworkin points out, the themes in the Marquis de Sade's pornography are the same themes that appear in contemporary pornography:

Those in control are mostly aristocratic older men.

As time passes, arousal and orgasm require more cruelty.

Female victims outnumber male victims.

When men are whipped or sodomized, they remain in control and are never maimed.

Bonding occurs between the men on top as they share victims.

Excrement is ingested.

De Sade's two best-known victims, Justine and Juliette, are both raped, tortured, and violated. They are the two prototypical female figures in all pornography: (1) the woman victim who hates it but is provocative in her suffering, and (2) the woman victim who loves it and revels in all that men do to her.

The female libertines are always subordinate to their male counterparts.

Women are evil and must be punished.

Intense hatred of female genitalia is conveyed.

Pregnancy demands murder.

The arrogance of women claiming rights over their own bodies is offensive.

Adult men are especially gratified by the celebration of sexual violence against children.

Incest is encouraged.

The father is the source of life. Contempt is shown for mothers who are repressed. They are portrayed as ignorant prudes who would be better off as whores (or as the whores they truly are). A person owes nothing to one's mother. Daughters turn on their mothers and force them to submit to sexual abuse and torture.

Intercourse and cruelty are fundamentally linked.

Women were born to be fucked and meant to be prostitutes.

Men have the right to compel women's submission, and violence is one of the effects of those rights.

De Sade pioneered the concept of collective ownership of women by men with no woman ever justified in refusing to have sex with any man. (He invented state brothels.)[106]

Videofilms

From here on, we will use the term *videofilms* to refer to super 8, 16mm, and 32mm films (used in movie theaters) as well as all other projections of motion. We believe that of all the pornography images and of all the ways in which pornography is projected, the videofilm is probably the most influential in terms of molding permanent ideas in the mind of the viewer. This is because it combines images in motion with sound, making these images more lifelike and credible than other materials. The influence of videofilms is enhanced by the ease of acquisition. These films are available in most family video stores, and there is no stigma attached to going there, as there is when going to a pornographic bookstore. Because of the low cost of renting videofilms (usually between $1 and $5), it is likely an individual will be able to see more films per month than when the only source of such films was the adult theater. Now films or selected portions of them can be easily copied at little cost. Therefore, a person with a particular sexual deviance can locate that deviance being acted out on film and reproduce those portions of the film for permanent retention, allowing the person to view them over and over. Unlike nonpornographic motion pictures, there is a tendency for the viewer to masturbate to the videofilms, thereby allowing the person to develop a fantasy relationship and a desire relating to the act being depicted.

Thousands of videofilms are available. Some are newly produced materials made for the video format, while others are transfers from 16mm and other motion picture formats. The depictions are extraordinarily graphic, involving close-up detail camera work and behaviors heretofore considered deviant from the norm. These abnormal sexual behaviors are depicted as common, desirable, and even progressive or advanced. The implication is that those who do not have these experiences or do not have a mate who performs in this way are limited.

Certain characteristics of videofilms can be more readily seen through a content analysis. Videofilms are replete with distortions of reality, and they have misrepresentations of normal sexual standards. For example, ejaculation almost always occurs outside the body regardless of the sexual interaction that is being depicted. The surface of the body is usually the receptacle of the semen—the woman's mouth, face, chest, stomach, or back. Another distortion is the presentation of sex without pain—that is, a particular oral or anal copulation represented as nonpainful. In reality, among many partners, oral sex requires conditioning over a period of time, whereas the films show a ramming of the penis into the mouth of the woman in ways that would normally be choking and assaultive, not comfortable. While some couples do derive satisfaction from anal intercourse, these acts require pacing with special consideration for reduction of the pain that is part of the experience. Presumably, the average man who views these films does not realize that. Therefore, trying to repeat these images is harmfully aggressive for the woman or women in his life. We believe, and have seen in victim studies of child sexual abuse and battered women, that the woman's failure to conform to the standards exhibited in the films results in dissension because of the man's unrealistic expectations, as well as a feeling of failure on the part of the woman.

Another unreasonable expectation on the part of the man is the emphasis on two women servicing one man. In these videofilms, two women are often shown performing analingus, fellatio, and different forms of intercourse with the man. The man is the object of all their attention and affection, and the women's role is to please the man. The women, who are usually physically attractive, are projected as being enthusiastically involved in the role being depicted. Such activity is portrayed as normative as opposed to a-normative. If a man who is having sexual intimacies with his mate keeps fantasizing that he is with two women who are servicing him sexually, it is likely that he will not be satisfied with one woman. He will probably relate this feeling of dissatisfaction without confiding that he was fantasizing about an image that would be impossible for his mate to fulfill. Or perhaps the man might begin to insist that the woman find another female to join them in bed. Because the films persuasively suggest that such an act is normal and pervasive, the habitual viewer might get the feeling that everybody is doing it that way, pressure the woman to find a third party for the bed, and place all the responsibility on her. These unreasonable demands—giving the woman the impression that she is not adequate to fulfill the sexual needs of the man and demanding that the woman find another partner to join them—are interpreted by many women as a claim that they have failed to fulfill their responsibility as a sexual partner.

Many videofilms also contain lesbian scenes. These scenes involve two women or more having sex together. In most of these cases, a man is a voyeur (watching) or eventually enters the scene and participates, leading to the conclusion that these events meet the fantasy, sexual, and emotional needs of males rather than females. One of the authors feels that these sex scenes between females might be included as an attraction for women who have bisexual tendencies, are actively bisexual, or might even be lesbian. Videofilms of a pornographic nature are rarely strictly lesbian, and this may be almost the only way in which lesbians can get access to such images. Since it is so easy to fast-forward through the film, the viewer can select only those portions that interest her or him. The other author feels that these pornographic images of women involved in sex are aimed at a male heterosexual market that gets turned on by psuedolesbian images. The images would not appeal to genuine lesbians because they lack erotic and loving relationships and are clearly portrayed as taking place for the viewing pleasure of the male(s) who become involved with the pseudo-lesbians later in the film. This viewpoint is substantiated by the fact that organizations representing lesbians have protested pornographic films and noted the absence of genuine lesbian erotica on the market.

Another theory is that the pornographers have discovered an underlying sexual image appreciated by males—that is, the fascination with viewing two women in love sexually. Still another theory is that the male would not encourage his female sexual partner to become sexually practiced with males because of jealousy, but by allowing her to be sexually practiced with females, he stands to profit by the thought and sometimes the reality of that other female eventually joining him and his mate in sexual activity. (This, of course, is something that a real lesbian would not do.) In addition, many males would not view another woman as competition, primarily because of her anatomy. Another male would be direct competition. Thus, when more than one male is involved with a single female in pornography, it is usually a rape or gang rape situation.

More recent films have begun to feature cunnilingus. It is not clear whether this is an attempt to make pornographic videofilms more acceptable and interesting to female viewers. Past pornography was so blatantly ribald and bizarre and male pleasure dominated it so much that it was truly of little interest to most women, in terms of meeting a romantic sexual image that is more likely to be part of a female's erotic fantasy.

We see the harmful effects of videofilms as many. Among these is the emphasis on male domination and control of women and the subjugation of women to men's needs as opposed to a caring, sharing, mutually consenting interaction. Also dangerous is the misrepresentation of sexual standards between men and women—that is, the impression that women like to be forced, expect to be forced, or will finally agree once they are forced into sexual involvement. In our view, both blatant descriptions and subtle portrayals of rape are too frequent to be healthy for our society. Videofilms have become the principal sex education vehicle. They are particularly handy for people who do not like to read or do not read well. They are packaged in dramatic, exciting ways, often with the accompaniment of music that is arousing. In the absence of anything else, they become the primary transmitter of sexual education, norms and ethics. In addition to rape themes, there is an emphasis on hurting one's mate. While some films have males being put into bondage and being spanked and whipped, the majority have females in these roles. Bondage and discipline can be a dangerous activity for the women. Other sadomasochistic pornography usually involves torturing women. Some male homosexual films also involve sadomasochistic and bondage and discipline treatment of males, and we have the same concern that these materials misrepresent appropriate, healthy, and safe sexual behavior.

Something should be said about what the videofilms mean to women. We bring with us our experiences in a male and female culture, along with other experiences the world has presented to us. It is possible that some women may rent these films out of curiosity, just as most men start out renting them out of curiosity. Women may be curious about the endowments of the male and female performers. For the most part, however, we believe that women would vote for an elimination of pornograhic videofilms as they exist today.

Many of the videofilms are fairly short (seventy minutes or less), do not develop a plot or dialogue, and contain little, if any, romantic content. There is very little romantic seduction. The sexual encounters shown are either outright rape or a category called "no preliminaries, let's do it." While this content meets men's impatient needs, it certainly does not appeal to what women have traditionally perceived to be respectful romantic behavior. The following are examples of types of pornographic videofilms we are concerned about.

A Little Bit of Hanky Panky has a series of sexual situations. In one, a woman in a jogging outfit jogs in an isolated area. She is accosted by a male motorcycle rider. The motorcyclist pursues the woman, accompanied by arousing music and flashes to him revving up his motorcycle and to the boot knife strapped to his leg. The man yells obscenities and tells the woman he is going to use her body. She goes off and sits by herself, masturbating while the man watches in the bushes. Then he comes upon her. She struggles. He says, "I'm not going to have sex with you unless you beg for it." He goes away. She goes back to playing with herself. Eventually, he and she enthusiastically have intercourse and fellatio. At one point in the film, we learn that this woman paid money to go to a sex farm to have the experience of being raped. The message is that there are not enough rapists to go around and that women who like rape have to pay for it.

In another movie, Joy (the title character) is a high school student. Her boyfriend tries to talk her into having sex. She says that she is saving herself for marriage because her mother wants her to. He threatens to break up with her. When she is home alone, two men of Hispanic origin who are pretending to be delivery men rape her. In the process of the rape, she becomes turned on and begs for more rape, more sex. They become fearful of her, thinking she is crazy and leave. She goes to her boyfriend's house, where she seduces and rapes him. Then she stalks a man on the street and rapes him in an alley. She goes home and seduces her mother. The male "rape" victims go to the police station and behave as though they have been brutalized, yet they are mesmerized. A rape epidemic in which women are raping men takes over the city. The film ends with the police officer giving Joy the option of going to jail or getting out of town. She flies away and rapes a couple of sailors, a civilian, and an airline pilot in the men's bathroom at the airport.

Obviously these ideas are ludicrous, but the message is that true rape is not a serious problem. The films also reinforce a male myth that all one has to do to make nymphomaniacs out of females is to have sexual intercourse with them. Once they have had sex, they cannot live without it. It is suggested that women cannot resist, intellectually or physically, so it is better for them in the long run to succumb. Put more succinctly, the message is that a man is doing a woman a favor by raping her.

Another dangerous portrayal involves piercing of nipples, clitorides, or labias. The films show this followed by the insertion of chain hooks with snap locks to which doggy chains are attached. The women are then led around by the chains.

Especially dangerous are films that depict sexual assault of women as nonpainful or at least not permanently painful. The actresses eventually behave as if they do not mind being assaulted. This is a misrepresentation of physical abuse and ignores the long-term emotional trauma victims experience in reality when men act out these behaviors based on ideas obtained from the videofilms. It is our view that the average man or woman would never think of the kinds of abnormal behavior projected in videofilms, nor would they think of the methodology incorporated in these films to achieve the interactions.

Examples of Pornographic Videofilms: Dr. Neil Malamuth has listed the following common characteristics of X-rated films[107]:

1. Focus on exposing the female body and showing the female being "screwed." Much of the material portrays the woman engaged in sexual acts in a demeaning context.
2. The emphasis is on exploitive sexuality. The woman uses her body as a means of reaching some other goal. The man uses the woman's body as an orifice, an object for his physical pleasure.
3. The female is often portrayed as an insatiable, animalistic creature who loses total control.
4. Social taboos are broken. Examples include rape, incest, and sex with children (that is, adults are made to look like kids).

Only a small percentage of the films portray sex within a caring relationship.[108]

The movie *Taboo* is about incest with a notion that the woman precipitated it. *Debbie Does Dallas* involves high school girls who use their bodies to make money. *Deep Throat* glamorizes rape of the throat, teaching that women should be able to take men's penises deep into their throats without choking or gagging. (Linda Lovelace, the actress in that film, was forced to perform for it and other pornographic films.) *The Devil and Miss Jones* involves the sexual initiation of a virgin schoolteacher who becomes a sex-enslaved creature.

One film features a woman and man covered with gray clay or paint having sex. Another shows a naked woman on a kitchen table getting decorated with whipped cream, chocolate syrup, and cherries. She takes a man's chocolate-covered penis into her mouth and sucks until he ejaculates on her neck and chest.

Rape films are common in pornography. In one film, a woman is abused by her sadomasochistic male master. She gets raped anally by two thugs hired by her master. But she and another woman get revenge by drugging the master, tying him to a bed, placing a leather hood over his face, strapping on a huge dildo, and violently having anal intercourse with him. Another film features a boyfriend who is angry at his girlfriend for spending his money. He forces her to service him sexually in every possible way. The video magazine description of the film states that "by the time he's through she's a whimpering obedient little girl!"[109] In a third film, a man threatens to make a woman "fuck" an alligator, but has her gang-raped instead. She turns into a nymphomaniac who "out-fucks" everyone. Her final line is: "If you ever find that alligator, why don't you give me a call?"

In one of the school-genre porn films, a Bible-beating pervert ravages his teenage daughter. An idealistic teacher is committed to bringing about morality in "this suburban Sodom." A student in her class, his father, and several "horny" buddies "give Miss Martin an old-fashioned gang bang that leaves the sexually repressed teacher begging for more."[110] They threaten to send photographs of the rape to the local paper and blackmail her into leaving town. Other films portray women participating in each other's rape in an attempt to justify or legitimize the abuse. In another, a runaway orphan hitchhiker is held down over a bike by a motorcycle gang and "not one of her orifices remains unplugged." Then the gang's "moll" "fist-fucks" her.[111]

A videofilm about one of the Marquis de Sade's works features sexual torture, mutilation, degradation, and killing. One film is about four kinky ladies who decide to end their lives by getting "literally fucked to death." One blows up masturbating with a lit stick of dynamite. Another drowns in a "sea of cum." The third "is fucked to death by a non-stop satyr with a perpetual hard-on."[112] The fourth carries the message that terminal sex ends all grief and pain to the world. She manages to populate an entire cemetery. In another movie, a young woman has passionate dreams of being repeatedly raped in broad daylight by a gang of "crude and powerful" construction workers.[113] Young housewives are captured and forced to become sexual slaves in another film. Even in a film about a sadistic female operator of a sex parlor who kills men, a man whom she plans to kill gets a confession out of her by having intercourse with her.

A mid-seventies movie features a couple who pick up a woman in a bar and degrade and torture her in every possible way. Eventually, they apply clamps to her nipples and make her tear off her own nipples. The movie review in *Hustler* said, "It has been a night of absolute bliss."[114] One movie features a bride who is shackled, beaten, and raped from all angles by a gang of male and female sadists. Another videofilm shows a woman with legs tied apart having her vagina pierced and a ring put through it. She later gets whipped. In another, a woman gets bound and beaten by a man for not cleaning the house.

The story line in a film that features women whipping, binding, and otherwise abusing other women is that the women were being trained in obedience for their master, a man. One film contains abuse of both women and men. Two women are raped in front of an audience (including women who enjoy watching other women being abused). One of the female victims' brother is tied down with his legs apart. She is forced to put her whole fist into his anus, which she resists at first, then later loves. This is shown in graphic close-up color. She then puts a giant dildo into his anus. Another man is chained spread-eagled by a dominatrix. Clothespins are attached to his penis and nipples. She urinates on him and lets him ejaculate.

In another videofilm, a man's wife brings him to be trained to be submissive to her and take orders from her. He gets hooded, ball-gagged and blindfolded, bound in a chair, and made up like a woman (including clothing and a wig). A bondage and discipline video shows a woman suspended in air on a broomstick-like pole protruding from her vagina. This same film shows women bound in painful positions, with sink stopper gags, hanging by their feet from the ceiling, wearing stiletto heels, hanging from their knees from a steel bar, and with latex hoods. The abuse of the women is carried out by another woman.

Among the most bizarre videofilms are those featuring women having sex with animals. These commonly involve women having intercourse with or fellating dogs. Some show women being penetrated by larger animals such as donkeys. The women, in typical pornographic fashion, are made to look like they are sexually aroused by such sex.

Slasher and Snuff Videofilms: An advertisement for *Filmgore*, a collection of clips from R-rated slasher films, read: "See blood thirsty, butcher killer drillers, crazed cannibals, zonked zombies, mutilating maniacs, hemoglobin horrors, plasmatic perverts and sadistic slayers slash, strangle, mangle and mutilate bare breasted beauties in bondage."[115]

Slasher and snuff films promote a belief that the most thrilling, orgasmic sexual experience results from sadistic and sexually violent acts toward women and sometimes men. Because of the ratings system, images of a partially nude woman in a bathtub who gets mutilated are considered less of a concern than an erotic scene of a nude woman in a tub who is not surrounded by bubbles. This value system teaches that loving sex is not all right, but violence is. Media violence may so desensitize people that real violence becomes meaningless. Sexually violent films capitalize on the sexist stereotypes by punishing women's libbers more often and making women into victims. The films add to real women's fear, and, as one guest on "Donahue" (October 3, 1984) stated, a woman who is scared at a movie clings to and rubs against her male companion.

According to the Attorney General's Commission on Pornography, some profits from the pornographic film *Deep Throat* were allegedly used by reported members of an organized crime family to develop Bryanston Films of Hollywood, which distributed the slasher film *The Texas Chainsaw Massacre*.[116]

A film titled *Snuff* depicted a male pulling off a female's nipple with pliers. The sexual climax of the film portrayed a man slitting a woman open from neck to abdomen and holding her insides up in a triumphant gesture as he reached orgasm.[117] The film claimed to show the actual murder and dismemberment of a young woman. This type of film teaches that the combination of sex and death is a necessary aphrodisiac.[118] The plot in the movie *Snuff* involves a cult leader named Satan whose followers, all females, beat, rob, and murder at his command and are initiated by torture into the cult. The cult shoots a pregnant woman's wealthy lover. She cowers on a bed under the covers. A dagger is plunged into her stomach, "which explodes with the sounds of gushing blood and gurgling amniotic fluid."[119] A pretty film production assistant tells her director that she was sexually aroused by that scene. The director asks her if she would like to go to bed with him and act out her fantasies. They fumble about in bed until she notices the crew is filming and tries to get up. The director says, "Bitch, now you're going to get what you want." He butchers her slowly. The scene is filled with blood, cut-off legs and fingers, and so on, with the ending described above.[120] *Snuff* did receive an X rating, and attempts were made to have it prosecuted under obscenity laws, with most of the requests for action coming from feminists.[121]

The 1983 film *Pieces* also involved the murder of beautiful young women for sexual pleasure. In the opening scenes, a kid's mother is cut into pieces. A coed's head is cut off with a chain saw by a man who puts the instrument to her neck. The headless body is shown shaking. A creepy scene in a dark and deserted pool area shows a girl in a bikini with bare breasts. The slasher nets her, causing blood damage to her neck, then drags her from the pool and attacks her with a chain saw. The pieces of the woman are shown in graphic, bloody detail. A dancer gets her arms cut off, and her bloody body is shown on the floor. The film is filled with scenes where women are stalked by the killer, and the man keeps pieces from each body.

In *Pieces*, the "good guys" are portrayed unrealistically. The murders (mainly at a school) are hidden from the public. Only a lovely policewoman is assigned to the case in an undercover role. A male student plays a major investigative part, being shown as brilliant compared to the older, more experienced policewoman. The lad's girlfriend, whom he leaves in bed to go to the policewoman and help investigate, snoops around and gets herself killed. She hears breathing, then she is stabbed repeatedly with a knife on a pool table. She is shown screaming and with blood all over her white dress. The knife sticks out of her mouth. A girl is shown hanging from a door, while the killer fits more pieces of his human body puzzle together. Another girl who is bathing nude gets cut in half at the waist while still alive.

The policewoman goes to see the campus bigwig, a suspect. He drugs her coffee. She cannot move but can hear and sense everything. He puts on gloves and gets out a huge butcher knife. Naturally, the helpless policewoman gets rescued by the kid and cops, who kill the slasher. The ending shows a woman's body—made up of pieces from many different bodies—falling out of the closet. This body reaches up, grabs the male student in the groin area, and tears him apart. His groin is a mass of blood as he screams.

The 1977 film *I Spit on Your Grave* is filled with graphic sexual violence. An independent woman (a novelist who rents a cabin to do her work) is captured by four young men while sunbathing in her boat. Her suit is torn off. One man rapes her while the other three hold her down. She thinks she has escaped them in the woods, but they recapture her. They force her, breasts down, over a rock, and one man anally rapes her while she screams in pain. A lot of complete nudity of the victimized woman is shown throughout the movie. She finally reaches her cabin, crawling. When she tries to dial the phone, it is kicked from her hand by the men, who are now in her house. She is severely beaten. Blood and bruises are shown. They read her fiction love story and make fun of it (that is, the woman's career is not taken seriously). Three of the men finally convince the third, a wimpy guy (a grocery clerk who fell in love with the woman earlier in the movie) who has never had sex to rape her. He fails to orgasm. Another man slaps her, sits on her face, and tries to make her suck his penis. Outside, the men plot to kill the woman so she cannot tell on them. The sissy guy is sent back inside with a gleaming knife to kill her. The woman is nude and unconscious, with blood all over her chin. The man holds the knife above her chest, but does not kill her. He lets the other men believe he murdered her.

The woman washes herself off, cries, and goes through the usual emotional problems experienced by rape victims. But she does not report the crime. Two weeks later, the men discuss the "murder" in a cafe. They cannot figure out why her body was not discovered, for it would have smelled. When they boat past the cabin, they see her sitting outside. They turn on the wimpy guy who failed to kill her. The woman goes to a church and prays for God to forgive her. She has a gun. She orders some groceries, and the wimpy guy is sent to deliver them.

She waits outside for him in a white gown—ghostlike. He follows her with a knife when she runs into the woods. She seduces him, and he says he will kill her this time. The woman undresses and kisses the man who raped her. She pulls his pants off. He makes love to her. She acts as if she loves it. She puts a rope around his head and chokes him, then hangs him from a tree and leaves him in the river.

Next she shows up at the gas station where the most sadistic rapist works. He gets in her car and says, "I knew you'd like it here." She pulls a gun on him in the woods and makes him undress. He begs, telling her he has a family. He says she asked for the rape by the way she dressed and that any man would have done it. She lets him take the gun and seduces him. They wind up together in her bathtub. He explains how he loves his kids, but one gets used to a wife after a while. She tells him she killed the sissy guy and that he finally "came." Then she cuts his penis off with a knife. He bleeds profusely. She locks him in the bathroom and ignores his screams for help. She burns his clothes and is shown cleaning the bloody tub. The dead man is shown curled up, bloody, in a fetal position. His wife, a real tough lady, is shown cussing at his two friends.

The woman who was raped chases the other two rapists with a motorboat. One gets hit in the back of the head with a hatchet. The other gets his penis cut off with the boat's motor (after the woman acts as if she likes him).

I Spit on Your Grave was the best example we found of sadistic, sexually explicit violence in a film that was not considered pornographic or obscene or X-rated. We believe that films like this should be legally considered pornographic because all the pornographic themes are present and the danger of causing or desensitizing people toward sexual violence exists. Although there is sexual violence against the men in the film, it is brought about in a way that portrays the female victim behaving in ways that a real rape victim would not: She gives her body to these rapists again before she murders them, thus feeding the myth that women want to be raped. In real life it is unlikely that such men would have allowed themselves to be seduced by her and then killed. It is more likely that they would have returned and murdered her.

An older film, *Last House on the Left,* deals with the gang rape of two young girls. The rapists wind up spending the night at the home of one of the girls' parents. The parents figure out that the men murdered their daughter and sadistically murder them. In one scene, for example, the mother bites off the sex organ of one of the men. Here we have the theme of normal people turning into crazed, psychotic killers and taking the law into their own hands in a type of vigilante justice.

The movie *Beyond Erotica* opens with a woman clad in a skimpy bunny costume (complete with ears) running through the woods pursued by a man on a horse and dogs. Her foot gets caught in an animal trap (shown in graphic detail). While she lies on the ground screaming in pain, a dog bites her in the neck (graphically shown) while the man watches her get killed by the animal. Then the aristocratic man gets his mother (who knows he abuses women and condones it) to acquire a new female servant for him. The film details his pursuit of this woman. He locks her in an animal pen without food or water until she agrees to have sex with him. The mother knows she

is locked in there and does not help her. The young woman finally agrees to have sex. She welcomes the rape, begging him to give it to her. Despite the title, there is nothing erotic about this film.

Dressed to Kill begins with a woman enjoying rape fantasies. She pursues and is pursued by a strange man in an art museum, gets into a cab with him and has sex, then goes to his hotel for more sex. When she tries to go back to his room (having forgotten her wedding ring), she gets sliced up by a maniac killer in the elevator. This is shown in graphic, bloody detail. The man is dressed as a woman and has a cleaver. Another woman witnesses some of the elevator torture and reaches for the dying woman's hand. But the door closes, and the murderer completes his deed. The witness turns out to be a prostitute, so the cops mistreat her and instead of believing her, accuse her of the murder. While this adult woman is humiliated and treated like an idiot, the murdered woman's teenage son turns into a clever detective.

The murderer, a transsexual, stalks the prostitute. A gang of black men plan to rape this white woman, but they run when they see the attacker corner her. The teenage boy turned detective rescues her from the attacker, who is wearing a blond wig. The cops do not believe the woman was attacked. The boy and prostitute believe that the murdered woman's psychiatrist knows who the murderer is. One cop suggests that the prostitute break into the doctor's office to get the name of the suspect—or he will book *her* for murder the next day. The prostitute goes to the doctor (to get his appointment book) and tells him she has dreamed of a man with a razor making her strip. She tries to seduce the doctor, stripping to her black sexy underwear while the boy watches from outside. The boy gets grabbed by the transsexual, who turns out to be the doctor. The police rescue them. The cop tells the prostitute the doctor is going to the hospital and might get turned into a woman. The prostitute goes home with the young boy hero for a vacation.

The prostitute dreams: At the hospital, the doctor chokes a female nurse and strips her to her expensive underwear while the crazy people watch and cheer. He escapes. He shows up in the boy's home and slashes the prostitute's throat while she is in the shower. One concludes that the boy will probably have to sleep with the prostitute to prevent further nightmares.

The 1984 film *Silent Night, Deadly Night* is about a Santa Claus killer. A 3-year-old boy's crazy grandfather tells him that Santa Claus will punish him. A man dressed as Santa stops the family car, shoots the father, drags the mother out, rips her shirt, bares her breasts, slaps her, and slits her throat.

The boy, who witnesses this, is raised by nuns in an orphanage. He sees a nun use a belt to beat a boy and girl who are making love and hears her call them filthy devils. Nipples and buttocks are shown. The sadistic nun (Mother Superior) tells him punishment is good and beats him for witnessing the sex. In one scene, the boy gets tied to a bed.

Then the boy is an older teen. He dreams of sleeping with a girl whose body is knifed starting at her breasts by a Santa Claus. The young man plays Santa Claus at the store where he works. At the Christmas Eve party, he sees a male co-worker start to rape a female co-worker whom he likes. He chokes the man and hangs him with a cord of lights. The woman, rather than being grateful for the rescue, calls him a bastard and crazy and tells him to get away from her. He slits her abdomen open. He kills the manager with a hatchet, then shoots another female co-worker with a bow and arrow. All these murders are shown in graphic, bloody detail. When women are involved, sexual violence is suggested because of the baring of breasts.

A young couple make love on a pool table. The woman leaves to let the cat in and is shown looking out the door wearing only shorts. Santa Claus grabs her and carries her, struggling, to a moose head on the wall. He impales her on the antlers, which are shown pushing through her breasts. The young man gets killed by being thrown through a second-story window. A little girl in the house thinks he is Santa, and he gives her a knife as a present.

Santa beheads a boy on a sled. At the orphanage, the police shoot the wrong Santa, and the other one hatchets a cop in the stomach. Police shoot him just as he is about to hatchet the nun who was so sadistic to him as a child. A little boy who witnesses this says "naughty" and looks like he, too, will grow up to be a psychotic killer.

In 1979, the movie *Cruising* provoked protests from homosexual groups. The movie is about a detective who trails a psychopathic killer into gay leather bars in New York. It involves the mutilation murders of gays by a homophobic psychopath. The killer, when engaged in anal intercourse, plunges a knife into each of his victims' backs at the moment of orgasm. He chops off their penises and stuffs them into their mouths. Graphic fist intercourse, fellatio, and whipping are shown. The killer is never caught.

Another movie that caused much concern about possible violence against homosexuals and lesbians was *Windows*. In that movie, a lesbian falls in love with a straight woman. She hires a man to rape the woman so she will turn against men. The lesbian records the rape and often plays the tape to sexually arouse herself. The lesbian kills men who were involved with the straight woman. She reenacts the rape with the same knife. In the end, she has a breakdown.

Films like *Pieces, I Spit on Your Grave, The Texas Chainsaw Massacre,* and *Last House on the Left* are not X-rated and are not considered obscene under the *Miller* guidelines (see chapter 1). The Attorney General's Commission and some of the sexual aggression and pornography research dealt with in chapter 5 found these types of films harmful. Under the authors' proposed new law, such films would be considered pornographic and subject to criminal prosecution and/or civil lawsuits. (See chapter 12.)

Many of the slasher/snuff genre movies have resulted in protests at the time of their release. The protests stem from a belief that such movies encourage sexual violence against women (and in some cases lesbians or gays). These movies are highly influential, for they typically take up about 10 percent (or more) of the shelf space in video stores. The movies summarized in this chapter are only a small sampling of the titles available. We obtained the movies mentioned here at video stores in small cities in the generally conservative Midwest.

Magazines

In its Final Report, the Attorney General's Commission on Pornography described a content analysis done of the April 1986 issues of *Cheri, Chic, Club International, Gallery, Genesis, High Society, Hustler, Oui, Penthouse, Playboy,* and *Swank,* eleven of the most widely circulated magazines.[122] The amount of sex-related advertising ranged from 100 percent in *Club International* and *High Society* to 20 percent in *Penthouse* and 10 percent in *Playboy.* Forty-nine percent of all of the ads in the magazines were for phone sex, 16 percent for sexually explicit videos, and 10 percent for sex-oriented magazines. The sex-related editorial content ranged from 100 percent in *Club International* and in the 90 percent range for *Cheri, Club,* and *High Society* to 40 percent in *Penthouse* and 33 percent in *Playboy.* Of the total pictorial content, 20 percent of the acts portrayed were female "split-beaver" shots, 19 percent showed fondling or touching, 12 percent featured oral-genital activities, and 9 percent involved sex between two women.

The commission cited a 1983 Canadian study of *Playboy, Penthouse, Hustler, Gallery, Cheri, Playgirl,*

Forum, Oui, Club, Swank, and *Genesis.*[123] That study found the following:

1. A large percentage of the photos were of partially dressed females.
2. The largest category of photographic depictions was for female body parts (breasts/nipples, 17 percent; genitals, 14 percent.
3. The most common sex acts featured were masturbation (24 percent) and oral–genital contact (14 percent).
4. Ten percent of the sex acts in the textual depictions were of the use of force (anal sex, bondage equipment, weapons, rape, or murder).
5. "Sexually oriented products featuring children were most heavily advertised in Hustler magazine."

According to David Scott,[124] the Canadian study found that while most of the photographs showing sexual acts were vividly graphic, they were simulations. However, the text of the magazines was filled with explicit sexual activities that were not simulated. The study found twenty-four situations in the magazines in which children were portrayed in sexually explicit activities.

In 1982 Dietz and Evans classified 1,760 heterosexual pornographic magazines based on cover photograph images.[125] While pictures of a woman posed alone predominated in 1970, in 1980 such pictures were only 11 percent of the total. In 1980, bondage and domination was the most common image (17 percent), followed by group sex (10 percent).

The Attorney General's Commission on Pornography report included long lists of titles of pornographic magazines. A few examples are *Ass Masters, Boobs and Beavers, Cock Stuffed Sluts, Double-Fucked Gal, Fat Fucks, Fucking Virgin Ass, Lick My Balls, Over 289 Pregnant and Milk Mamas, Painful Pleasures, Sluts in Uniform, Swedish Erotica, Taboo, These Gals Need Deep Penetration, Trainers and Gags, TV Queens, Up Her Ass, Water Works, 3 on 1, Blonde Bitches,* and *Mistress of Pain.*

Playboy, like other pornographic magazines, features women not as human beings, but as sexual objects—vaginas, breasts, and buttocks—that exist only to satisfy male sexual desires. Women are portrayed as sexual playthings—bunnies, playmates, pets, bitches in heat—no matter what their educational or professional background. A cartoon of a male executive having intercourse with his secretary while she takes dictation encourages sexual harassment of women workers by treating it as a joke or turn-on. *Playboy* also is racist: A black woman shown with a snake coming out of her mouth is accompanied by the caption "They say women are all vipers." According to Women Against Pornography (WAP),[126] the magazine thinks women of color should be animals, slaves, and prostitutes and trivializes their liberation goals. WAP also notes that *Playboy* makes adult women look infantile and eroticizes little girls, finding "child molestation humorous and titillating."[127] One *Playboy* cartoon shows a little girl leaving the room of an older man saying, "You call *that* being molested!" The magazine ridicules older women, depicting them as laughable and grotesque. WAP also believes that lesbianism is distorted by *Playboy.*[128] The magazine always implies the presence of a male viewing portrayals of lesbian scenes, thus perpetuating the myth that women cannot be sexually independent of men. According to WAP, *Playboy* finds the rape and murder of women erotic."[129] Beneath its image is a message that women want to be raped, abused, and humiliated.

A *Playboy* cartoon shows cops saying "Beating his wife? The radio call said some guy was eating his wife in the middle of Third Street." Another feature shows a woman wrapped in plastic wrap and plastic tubelike valves and other women participating in sadomasochistic activities involving whips, chains, hoods, boots, gloves, masks, and bondage. A cartoon shows a partially nude woman who has been bound to a chair by a burglar. Caption: "Before you go, would you mind tightening my ankles a little?" A woman is shown against a backdrop in a skimpy costume. She has had knives thrown at her (as in a magician's trick). The caption lists the size, brand, and price of each knife. A doctor in another cartoon tells a mother not to be concerned because her little girl has developed bunny ears and a tail. One woman featured in a cartoon says she keeps her door double-locked "because I'm scared of being raped by someone unattractive." A woman is shown with a snake-head mask. *Playboy* also made fun of a now well-known feminist sexuality expert by showing old pornographic photographs of her having simulated sex with a dog. In a cartoon, a minister orders a young boy who has just had sex with a young girl to go home—implying that the minister intends to have sex with the girl after the boy leaves.

According to Lederer in the introduction to *Take Back the Night, Penthouse* magazine ran a feature titled "The Joy of Pain" showing a woman's painted fingernail and finger pierced by a large needle.[130] The magazine also featured a severely bound Oriental woman with one photo showing her hanging from a tree (apparently dead). One cartoon in this magazine shows a dazed, smiling woman who was just raped calling out to her attacker, "Encore!" *Penthouse* also included a "humor" article about "female rapists."

A pseudolesbian sadomasochistic photo feature shows women clothed in tight black latex gloves, boots, corsets, and hoods. The women are doing what their male master commands. "We are groomed and collared, like prized domestic pets, our leashes serving to further unleash his desires, to stir frenzied dreams of pain and pleasure in each other. . . ." In one photo, a woman has another on a leash held in her mouth and on all fours as though she is being ridden. The sharp heel of one woman's boot gets licked, and the pointed heel is held to another woman's anus. Leather collars also are worn. A *Penthouse* subscription form features part of a woman's nude body with the form covering her vagina. Caption: "Have You Got What It Takes to Fill the Space Below?" In a 1978 *Penthouse* photo feature, a woman answers a "liberated woman" who asks if she wants to be autonomous in this way: "I want to be free—free to find a man who'll make me his slave!" A cartoon in *Penthouse* shows a woman obediently trying out numerous bizarre sex acts suggested in a *Penthouse* magazine. The man says that for the second letter "we need a rubber sheet, a baby snake and a jar of apple butter!"

Penthouse publishes several other magazines that are booklike and word-oriented and contain a few pictures: *Penthouse Variations, Penthouse Hot Talk,* and *Penthouse Forum.* In 1981, *Penthouse Variations* presented "The World of S & M." One story features a woman who was strong and independent on the job but vulnerable, submissive, and craving dominance with her lover. Another is titled: "How Bondage Liberated Me: it was only when tied down that she first felt free." A visit by a gay male to a place featuring leather, whips, chains, hoods, and other torture devices is portrayed as exciting. The man gets shackled, has a ring put around his penis, and is whipped on his buttocks, gagged, and led around on a collar and leash. The issue is filled with letters from readers who are into sadomasochistic activities. Some of the items involve submissive males and dominant women. One woman's favorite fantasy is of being gang-raped by every man in a theater featuring "erotic" films. Another dreams of being anally fucked by a crew of pirates. A female fantasizes about her husband tying her to a bed and bringing four young men to sexually abuse her. Each of the men gives her an anal fist-fucking that has her "screaming with pleasure and coming repeatedly." They stick tiny pins in her breasts. There are also letters from "gay" slaves. One accepts urine in his mouth. Some of the letter writers said they crave spankings. Some "expanded their horizons" by cross-dressing. One man got branded on his buttocks with a hot iron.

Penthouse Variations is advertised as being for "liberated lovers." In this magazine, one finds standard pornographic themes. The women portrayed are beautiful. They love to masturbate with dildos and other objects. A married couple needs a woman to join them to make their sex exciting. A man works as an escort "stud" for lonely women. Group sex is primarily two women servicing one man and enjoying each other. Bondage and other sadomasochistic activities and equipment are portrayed and encouraged. Women love to be raped and "fucked" by several men at once. Anal and oral sex are described. Swinging and group sex is popular. Extramarital sex, lesbianism, and homosexuality are encouraged.

Penthouse also publishes a magazine called *Penthouse Hot Talk.* The content is similar to that of *Penthouse Variations.* One article is about a woman being pierced through her nipple. Antipornography movements are ridiculed. One story contains the "confessions of a cock worshiper." Another makes fun of a hunchbacked man. A series of letters promote cunnilingus. One item states that "every man should take a sex vacation at least once" and teaches that Thai women are wonderful lovers. Techniques for oral sex and masturbation are discussed by letter writers.

Penthouse Forum, also published by *Penthouse,* is similar in content to the other magazines.

Hustler images have included "humorous" photographs of women with rats crawling from their vaginas (a common torture in South America); a cover featuring a woman's body being stuffed into a meat grinder and coming out as ground meat; a "Dream Lover" series in which the man slugs a woman in her face, drags her by her hair, shoves her head into the toilet, and rapes her from behind; and a parody glorifying the Hillside Strangler.[131] "Chester the Molester"—a cartoon showing child molesting techniques—was a regular feature of *Hustler* at one time. One *Hustler* item shows a man sticking a gun into a woman's mouth and forcing her to suck it. (This is a common pornographic theme.) In its racism, this magazine shows a heavily endowed nude black man offering $5,000 to anyone who can surpass the size of his penis. Another item shows a dominatrix wearing a black leather hood with her vagina on a bound man's face. In a parody titled "The Bible by Satan," Noah flashes his kids, Susannah is raped by the elders, there is sodomy in Gomorrah, men wash each other's feet, and Oral Roberts has "never seen so much sex in one book!" A *Hustler* "porn from the past" feature has a woman in pain as her breast is caught in a wringer washing machine.

The same company publishes another magazine, *Hustler Fantasies.* The content of this is similar to that of *Penthouse Variations* and *Penthouse Forum*. A caveman cartoon shows a woman being dragged by the hair. Caption: "What happened . . . did she say no?" One woman says she has never refused her "big milk jugs" to a man who needs or craves them. Another gets obedience trained by her husband to sexually service other men. The article teaches that "a wife should be humble and obedient if a couple expects real sexual happiness!" At one point in the story, the husband makes his wife say that she is a whore and a "degenerate nymphomaniac" and "nothing but a piece of meat to be fucked by all men." He humiliates her further by making her dance with a candle in her anus and by making her lick feces off his penis. Still another item is about anal enemas. A pseudolesbian article pictures a woman blowing a hot dryer on another's vagina.

There are numerous other magazines similar to those described above. *Couples Today* ran an article in which a man is aroused by performing cunnilingus on his girlfriend while she has her period. When her period ends he falls into a deep depression. Another *Couples Today* edition is billed as an "Anal Sex Special!" *Letters Magazine: Fantasies* ran an item about a man who loves having sex with midgets. Bondage, rape, and other violence are featured in this magazine. So are advertisements for *Family Letters* and *Adult Baby World*. One article is about a man who likes to wear diapers. Another edition of *Letters Magazine* tells the story of a woman who has been having sex with both of her husband's parents. One article begins with the statement that the writer and her sister would, by today's standards, be considered the victims of incest by the "do-gooders." She states that in reality they were included in their parents' love life and shown that "sex is not a dirty work or action, but something given out of love to be enjoyed, cherished, and shared." *Juggs Letters* features women with large breasts. In *Velvet's Love Letters!* a man loves the feel of women's silky panties on him. Another article teaches that cheating on one's mate can have some "very sexy" results. Still another promotes exhibitionism in public parks.

An entire series of monthly magazines promotes incest themes. These magazines have names such as *Family Affairs*, *Family Touch*, *Family Secrets*, and *Family Letters*. They feature articles such as "Family Reunion," "The Night Mom Taught Me How to Make Love! She was hot for my young hard-on," "I Left My Husband—For Dad! Only his cock could make me cum," "My Sister Made Me Her Sex Slave," "Pimping Popa," "My Son, My Lover," "Hot Nights With My Niece," "I Made My Son My Pussy Slave!" "The Night I Made Aunt Marge! A

horror flick made her hot for my dick," "My Brother & I Share a Wife!" and "I Got It On with Grandma!"

We conclude that many of the same concerns detailed in the videofilms section of this chapter are equally applicable to pornographic magazines and books, for they promote the same behavior and attitudes.

Paperback Books

We believe that pornographic paperback books are influences on behavior because they require the reader to do something—use his or her intelligence to actively read the content, rather than just sit back and absorb the message of the film or picture. Words, written or oral, are what give meaning. In pornographic books, magazines, or films, it is often the words that accompany the pictures that tell the reader what is really going on. Thus, it makes a big difference whether the words accompanying a photograph of a woman and man engaged in sexual intercourse say "Darling, I love you so much!" or "I know all you bitches love being raped!" Unfortunately, in pornography, it is virtually guaranteed that the words will be of an abusive, nonloving nature.

Pornographic books commonly contain themes of incest, rape, torture, gang rape, group sex, lesbianism, sexual abuse of children, nymphomania, and sadomasochism. These activities are portrayed in a manner in which the victims (usually females) wind up loving and craving the sexual abuse. Because these books are replete with graphic sexual violence and abuse and obviously promote such violence and abuse toward real persons, we cannot agree with the conclusions of the Attorney General's Commission on Pornography[132] or the Williams committee in Great Britain[133] that such books should be the lowest priority for prosecution or not be prosecuted as obscenity at all. These books are detailed road maps for sexual terrorism. We believe that the words contained in such books influence behavior and attitudes, just as the words in school textbooks do.

The following titles of pornographic books suggest their content (incest): *All the Way In Mom*, *A Mother's Loving Son*, *Aunt Brenda Sex Tutor*, *Making Mother Suck*, *Daddy Tastes So Sweet*, *His Daughter's Big Tits*, *Nights with Daddy*, *Punishing His Wife and Daughter*, *Spanked Son*, *Loving Her Brother*, *Raped Stepdaughter*, *Hot Black Brother*, and *Abused by Her Uncle*.

Another line of books promotes physical and sexual abuse of another type: *Battered Bride*, *Bizarre Sisters in Submission*, *Campus Gang Bang*, *Chained*

Slave Secretary, Greta's Dungeon Ordeal, I Want All Night Abuse, Humiliate Me, Leather Licking Slut, Lesbian Dildo Slave, Mom's Doggy Days, My Wife the Nymph, Pound That Pussy, San Quentin Slaveboy, She-Male in Bondage, Spread for Her Pet, Tongue Fucked Asshole, The Schoolgirl's Rape Night, Sally's Anal Punishment, Take Me Hard, Virgin Slave's Torment, Bound Bitch in Heat, Devil Woman's Whip, Madame Made Him Crawl, and *Lesbian Lieutenant.*

Some books promote transsexualism: *High Heeled Husband, A Bra for Bobby, Boys Will Be Girls, Daddy in Drag, Jock in Jewels,* and *Barbara with Balls.*

Many porn paperbacks promote sex with children: *Bound, Whipped and Raped Schoolgirls, A Girl and Her Dog, Chained Up Babysitter, Gang Bang Teens, Sluts of Tuckerville High, Teen Rape Orgy, Teen Whip Mistress, Trained Teen Slave, Young Girls Who Like It Kinky,* and *Young Legs Wide Open.*

A book titled *Turned-On Tourists* features a man who has committed adultery because his wife is frigid and who is sexually attracted to his 15-year-old daughter. When they get kidnaped in Mexico by two young Hispanic men with guns, the wife is excited at the thought of being forced to have sex with the men. One of the men rapes her in front of the daughter, a virgin. The daughter reacts by wanting to be raped, too. She helps the man get undressed and begs him to fuck her. She has both vaginal and oral intercourse at once. Later, the girl watches her teenage brother get seduced by an older woman, who also performs cunnilingus on the girl. Group sex finally involves the girl having sex with her brother, father, and several other men. Meanwhile, the mother experiences vaginal and anal intercourse with two other men at the same time and enjoys it, despite the pain. She feels like a "captive of perversion." The husband blames the wife for being raped (i.e., not saying no). The daughter turns into a nymphomaniac and begs a man to have anal sex with her. "Since she had no chance of resistance against any of these men—even her own father—she did not have to feel guilty about what she was doing." The wife gets raped in front of the husband and begs for it. At the end of the book, the wife suddenly loves having sex with her husband, and the daughter engages in intercourse with her brother and another man. The book closes with incestuous thoughts by the son toward his mother and sister.

Beaten Prisoner Wife is about a wife who is imprisoned for a crime her husband committed (stealing *her* money). The guards in charge of delivering her to the prison chain her to a tree in the woods spread-eagled, beat her with a tree branch, and orally and anally rape her. She is aroused by the rapes. The prison officials are clothed in Nazi-like sadomasochist garb. Female prisoner guards make Lena perform cunnilingus on them and whip her breasts. She gets strapped into a chair to observe the sexual torture of other women, which horrifies and excites her. Her body reacts with lust. Women are whipped and made to suck men's penises. One woman is strapped spread-eagled to a massive frame and whipped on her clitoris and breasts while she is subjected to anal intercourse. Lena's body burns with desire. She gets whipped later for masturbating without orders. Abuse of women by women is prominent in this book.

Lena is repeatedly gang-raped by four huge men, including while she is bound to cell bars. Her female guards amuse themselves by having sex with the men of their choice. The guards call Lena a slut. She is whipped and repeatedly triple-fucked in her vagina, mouth, and anus. Yet she gets angry because she is not allowed to perform oral sex on the men to the point where they ejaculate in her mouth. Lena is allowed to rest and heal for days, then gets paraded before fifty men who are all being sexually serviced by women at their feet. She is called the new bride. When tied down, Lena performs oral sex on the prison master, is whipped, and begs for more "cum." She is "utterly beside herself with lust." After she is repeatedly assaulted in her vagina by men's fingers, her husband, who previously called her frigid, has anal sex with her while she is suspended from a ceiling hook.

The husband says, "I might take you back, you little whore." But he will do this only if she promises to be a "good little slave" and agrees to fuck everyone he says. She promises to do whatever he wants if he will give her more oral sex. Then she watches her husband have sex with other women while she is gang-raped. She wants to prove she will be a good little girl for him and is in a "sea of lust she never wanted to climb out of."

Tying Up Rebecca concerns a male gym coach's fantasy of having sex with a 13-year-old female student, Becky, at a Catholic school. Becky masturbates, masturbates her friend Patty's boyfriend to ejaculation, kisses her father's penis while he sleeps, and has a stick inserted in her vagina by her friend. The coach's wife understands his failure to stay erect near her and his desire for Becky, so she masturbates. And she has sex with Becky's father. He makes her put on a leather hood, calls her a slut and a bitch, ties her ankles and wrists to the bed, stuffs her panties in her mouth, and slaps her. He makes her perform analingus, including eating bits of feces from his hairs. At a gymnastics competition, the coach has sex with numerous teenage girls, and they love it. The female Soviet coach observes this and makes him go down on his knees, inserts a butt plug, and whips his buttocks. She has an aide bite out some of his anal hair. But then the male coach gains control, ties her to a toilet, makes the aide perform analingus on a boy, and urinates in her mouth. Becky's father's ex-wife shows up, says it was wrong of her to leave, and tells him how a black man had sex with her. He assures her he can do better. When Becky shows up, the mother performs cunnilingus on her. The coach finally corners Becky in the gym. He strips her and ties her wrists to parallel bars, then performs cunnilingus on her. After she kicks him in the groin when he attempts intercourse, he straps her spread-eagled across the uneven bars. When he forces her to fellate him, she chokes and spits half of the ejaculation out. He demands that she swallow it. He puts a wooden scoring peg into her anus, then has anal intercourse and ejaculates in her. After Becky faints, he unties her and removes her from the bars.

Once Upon an Orgy begins with a 15-year-old girl begging a male psychiatrist to have sex with her. He willingly obliges, with the full details given in the book. She tells him his penis is bigger and longer than her father's. The doctor is assigned to counsel the members of a teenage sex club that was exposed. The therapist has sex with many of the girls. He initiates some into anal sex. They cry out in pain at first, then love the anal rape. The doctor tells one girl to relax and "let Daddy do the work." He says, "I began my campaign of total assault on the tiny child." She screams that she loves it and orgasms. He makes her lick the feces off his penis. The doctor found it easy to psychologically overwhelm the "young cunts." A frigid woman is cured by having sex with a teenage boy. Virgins also are initiated (willingly) into sex. Group sex involving several teenage girls, the doctor, the sheriff, and the father of one of the girls takes place. Eventually, even the judge gets involved.

Another book is about a young woman who practices incest with her brother. She is caught and is repeatedly raped and humiliated by her two stepbrothers while the brother is held captive. In the end, she and her brother run away.

Another concerns a female schoolteacher who turns into a nymphomaniac after being repeatedly sexually assaulted by different groups of male and female students, teachers, and administrators. She is thrilled by the rapes and begs to be raped in her anus. She also turns on to lesbian activities. She learns to enjoy being taken orally, anally, and vaginally at once. The teacher is the sex sacrifice at a party where she gets repeatedly raped (and repeatedly orgasms) by groups of boys, girls, and school officials. She gets raped until she's uncon-

scious. Although she transfers to another school, she finds out that that school is even more "progressive," starting the students in sex in the freshman year.

While Hubby Watches portrays a frigid wife being initiated, through drugs, into lesbian and group sex—and she loves it. "She didn't want the ravishment to ever end . . . She loved it . . . LOVED IT!"

One book concerns a sex therapist who gets his therapy groups involved in sex and joins in the orgies. Another is about a young girl who is sexually aroused by being whipped and marries a man who abuses her in that way. In *Rita's Ravished Behind*, the woman is constantly subjected to anal sex by her employers and dates, and she indicates she loves it. And in *Degrading Ann*, a woman is kidnapped by a rapist, is repeatedly abused in scenes made to look like seduction, and winds up staying with the rapist and falling in love with him.

Many pseudolesbian paperbacks also are on the market. These portray men as being in control and highly valued by so-called lesbians. In one book, for example, a group of lesbians is controlled by a male pimp. In another, a young woman becomes a lesbian after having been raped by a male schoolteacher. Most of the book is taken up with graphic descriptions of the rape and how she indicates she loves it.

In general, pornographic books portray the sexual abuse of persons much more graphically and in much more detail than other media.

Swingers

The cover of one 1984 swinger magazine shows a woman portrayed in typically pornographic style: on her back on a platform with legs straight up in the air and long blond hair hanging off the end of the platform. This seductively beautiful woman is braless (but her arm hides her breasts) and wears skimpy black panties, a garter belt with black fishnet stockings, elbow-length black gloves, and black shoes with five-inch heels.

Swinger magazines promote the "alternative" lifestyle known as swinging (mate swapping, social sex, group sex, and so on). They contain photographs of couples and singles, nude or in sexy lingerie. Most are of a pinup style, but some show persons engaged in genital or oral sex. Most of the photographs emphasize sex organs such as vaginas, penises, breasts, and buttocks. Some show the faces of the persons who wish to participate in swinging, but others show only their bodies. In a typically sexist style, some of the couples advertisements in these magazines picture only the female of the couple. Unlike the stars in pornographic films and magazines, the swingers who place their photographs in advertisements in pursuit of other swingers are frequently unattractive (fat, bad posture, poor facial features, small penises, and so on).

The magazine described above features interviews with swingers and shows photographs from a swinging weekend. People at the party dance with bare bottoms and breasts. One man has a paper bag over his head and is putting a 2-foot-long imitation penis with giant testicles into a woman's mouth. The magazine also urges a boycott of a hotel chain that canceled a sex convention.

Swinger magazines contain a typical supply of advertisements for sex-oriented products: lingerie, adult bookstore videos, leather goods, sex aids, massage books, pornograhic films, phone sex, soiled panties, escort services, and so on. There are also listings of swinger clubs and swinger events.

A large portion of the typical swinger magazine is devoted to advertisements by couples and singles who wish to have sex with other couples, singles, or groups. The ads usually are accompanied by a photograph and ask the respondent to write to a box number at the magazine. Many seek "sexplicit" photos and letters. The ads give some details about the advertiser, such as size, age, and physical features. They detail the type of sex sought (threesomes, groups, genital–genital, oral, anal, sadomasochistic, bondage and discipline, masturbation, fondling, and so on). They specify the type of partners wanted (white, black, women, men, bisexual, and so on). Comments of the following type are typical: "She's tasty, he's lasting"; "Very oral"; "No pain"; "No drugs"; He can "cum all night"; "No weirdos"; "We're hot and submissive"; "Woman wants 1–3 men"; "She's multi-orgasmic"; "Husband has weakness for heavy women"; and "Husband enjoys hairy beavers." Some advertise for a specified penis length. Others state that they have and enjoy pornographic movies. (Such movies are typically shown at swinger events.) Some ads specify that the female can be bisexual but the male cannot.

In sharp contrast to the swinger magazines are the more mainstream lonely hearts clubs and magazines for singles who seek to meet other singles. These magazines contain no ads for sex-oriented products. They spotlight successful single persons and contain helpful financial and beauty advice. Features typically focus on restaurants, travel, and fashion. Singles events are advertised. The closest thing to pornography is lingerie ads that have erotic, equality-based images. These magazines attempt to appeal to both females and males. Friendship and love, not sex, is emphasized. The personal ads con-

tained in such magazines are tasteful and not pornographic and are a convenient way for single persons to meet each other. They are similar to profiles used by computer dating services, only cheaper and less detailed.

In 1984, Paul Miller, an authority on alternative lifestyles, conducted a survey of 733 male and female swingers and interviewed 286 leaders of swing clubs.[134] Ninety percent of the survey population were couples, with 78 percent married and 12 percent living together. Of the sample, 44 percent most frequently attended social clubs (a place for meeting, mingling, and planning private parties), 35 percent preferred on-premises swing clubs, and the rest relied on friends for contacts or placed and answered ads in swinger magazines.

Miller concluded that swinging has become a thriving social scene in which there is greater openness between lovers than in the 1960s. This openness permits enjoyment of both sexual and emotional intimacy. He cites Dr. William Stayton, who wrote an article published by the Sex Information and Education Council of the United States in 1984 stating that there are an estimated ten million swinging couples today.[135]

While 24 percent of the survey sample said they swing for pleasure only, 61 percent said they "seek lasting friendships and emotional satisfaction through mate sharing in addition to sexual pleasure, and another 14 percent seek these rewards *over* sex."[136] This, Miller feels, runs contrary to the mythical image of swingers as impersonal thrill seekers. Thirty-two percent of those surveyed preferred closed swinging (sex in private areas with usually no more than two couples), 44 percent preferred open swinging (groups of various sizes intermingling throughout the club), and 17 percent preferred group sex (any number of men and women interlocked on a large bed).

However, swinging is not without its problems, Miller notes. The number one reason for persons to drop out of swinging is jealousy. Although only 36 percent of the survey group said they were sometimes jealous, persons who dropped out for that reason were not surveyed. In addition, swing club directors reported large turnovers in their memberships every year. About one-third of the couples operating the major swing clubs broke up during the previous five years, Miller found. Although swinging subscribes to a blend of freedom and fidelity (purging this adultery of disloyalty and deceit), another study found that 15 percent of swingers have sex without their spouse's knowledge or consent.[137] While 70 percent of the swingers Miller surveyed felt swinging improved their marriage or primary relationship, 30 percent felt that it did not. Eighty percent of the participants felt swinging made their mate a more skillful lover.

Miller believes that women have replaced men as the privileged sex at the clubs. He states that 40 percent of the clubs will accept single women without partners, while only 24 percent will accept single men. If dues are charged, the single women pay nothing or a nominal fee, while the single men are often charged more than couples. He attributes this to supply and demand—thousands of single males weekly seek admission to orgies, while females typically do not. Miller notes that men carefully avoid touching in group sex, while females are encouraged to make love "for their own enjoyment and for the voyeuristic pleasure of all."[138] He sees this as another area in which women have greater license. Thus, 80 percent of the females surveyed had practiced bisexuality, while less than 50 percent of the males had.

Miller feels that, demographically, swingers are part of mainstream society, although they have not come out of the closet. In a letter to one of the authors dated January 6, 1987, Miller stated that the organized swinger club scene has declined of late due to fears over sexually transmitted disease, especially AIDS. He said club leaders believe this influence is temporary. Miller said he believes the swingers have "severely underestimated the potential impact of AIDS" and that they should be giving this risk serious attention. Miller is so concerned about this risk that he is heading an alliance of swing clubs formed to promote an awareness of sexually transmitted disease risks and safeguards. The alliance is named ABATE—A Barrier Against the Epidemic. The goal is to carry out risk-reduction counseling and put swingers in touch with local disease-reduction services. He states: "It has been found that swingers apprised of their risks will often choose to quit the lifestyle. If they desire full protection from AIDS risks, this of course is what we recommend."

Sex Services

Newspapers and magazines openly advertise escort services (sometimes a front for prostitution), nude dancers, fantasy phone operators, massage parlors, and swinger and sex clubs. Many of the advertisements include photographs or drawings of nude or scantily clad women in seductive poses. The advertisements for sex and swinger clubs make it clear that sexually

explicit services are being offered: "Strangers at First Sight, Lovers by Midnight"; "Cupid's Retreat"; "The Zoo—On Premises Sex Club"; "Swingers, call [a specified number] for names of swingers in your area."

In December 1978, *High Society* ran an ad for a national hookers guide, said to contain ways to reach five thousand hookers from coast to coast. Another magazine ran an ad that read: "Beginner? Meet Hot Women who want to teach you the pleasures of oral and anal sex, light B/D and much more!" Or how about this ad for filming pornography: "You Make the Love. We Make the Tape."

Phone sex, or dial-a-porn, is a popular service. Few, if any, of the advertisements offer phone sex with men. Perhaps most women would not be interested in phoning a man they do not know for sexual arousal over the phone. One ad from a "sentimental deviant" said, "I Reflect Your Fantasies!" Pandora's Box phone fantasies suggested, "Let's get it on together." Even *Playgirl* advertised a "Provocative New Hotline." One woman specializes in phone sex with married men. She says she does what their wives cannot possibly do for them and talks about sexual subjects they would not dare talk to their wives about. How about trying the "Naughty Lady's Telephone Fantasies"? Or you can "Meet Hot Oriental Dolls Who Want Only to Please You!"

A woman (face not shown) is seductively depicted with her jeans down to her thighs and a nude ass exposed to the reader. Caption: "Want to Get into My Pants? Just Phone Me!" Another ad says, "I'm Getting Myself Moist for You!" Others include those for a phone nympho, a promise of intense orgasm over the phone, and a promise to show "you" all the forbidden ways. Captions read: "I've started without you—Please help me finish"; "Wet and wild phone sex"; "Full Climax Phone Sex"; "I need it—bad."

Phone sex also is available for those interested in sadomasochism. The Fetish Hot Line promises live dominant and submissive women and men. One woman who does fetishes by phone states, "There's nothing too 'kinky' for me." Another ad promises, "Painful Pleasures Await As I Bring You to Your Knees! Call Me If You Dare!! SLAVE." One ad pictures a woman with a whip and states that "Your mistress is waiting" and will fulfill all fetishes and fantasies. And there is "Baroness Frieda. Goddess of Pain and Pleasure." A leather-clad woman—a "bitch goddess"—promises dominance over the phone. Kinky sex with two horny nymphos is offered in another ad. "Call me if you can take the punishment," one ad challenges.

In a leaflet titled *Dial-a-Porn and Children*,

Citizens for Decency Through Law provided one example of a phone message.[139] The recorded message, by a female, tells the caller to imagine that he is in bed with a woman and a dog—"Just you and me and our dog Duke." The woman then describes the bizarre sexual activities between woman, man, and dog in detail, ensuring that the caller will develop a graphic image.

Perhaps the following ad sums up the intent of the dial-a-porn messages: "Cum with Me."

Sex Games, Toys, and Enhancers

There is a lot of sexual innuendo in American society. T-shirts declare: "Teachers Do It with Class," "Golfers Do It on the Green," "Waitresses Do It for Tips," "Telephone Operators Do It Person-to-Person," and "Bookkeepers Do It in Numbers." "Sexual Trivia" and other sex-oriented games are available, playing cards feature sexually explicit photographs of women and men, and drinking glasses picture females and males who undress when ice is added.

Some games are not amusing. A California video firm produced an X-rated game called "Custer's Revenge." The nude man is supposed to be General George Armstrong Custer. An Indian woman is nude and bound with ropes. The player can score points based on the number of times Custer can couple with (rape) the Indian woman without being hit by an arrow.[140] Another sex video game titled "Bachelor Party" involves rape. Another game is called "Beat 'Em, and Eat 'Em".[141]

Life-size female and male dolls are available for men and women to have sex with. These are commonly advertised in pornographic media. An ad in the November 1976 issue of *Sir* states, "Fulfill Your Wildest Dreams with male and female electronic everything dolls." The dolls feature humanlike sex organs—vaginas, breasts, mouths (for deep-throating), and penises. Some even vibrate, and some include ways of lubricating their phony organs to make them more realistic.

Skimpy lingerie and underclothing is promoted in the pornographic media. Some are see-through, others barely cover penises, breasts, vaginas, and buttocks, and still others may have parts cut out specifically for the purpose of exposing those body parts. A full line of leather and rubber clothing is on the market for sadomasochists. One catalog even advertised cutesy clothing for penises, such as a Superman outfit and a coat and tails.

Many pornographic outlets carry inhalant products intended to enhance sexual orgasms. One such product, butyl nitrite, is known to cause health problems in some persons.

A wide variety of so-called aphrodisiacs are marketed: "We Can Help You Turn On Any Girl You Want!" "Brute Vitality in Seconds! The Truckdriver's Magic Capsule!" "Nipple Lick 'Ems." Products include body glitter, anal lube, erection lotion, and jac-off lube.

Other sexual enhancement devices also are common. Among these are love pillows, pleasure swings, a wind-up penis toy to let "her" know when "you're" ready for sex, ceiling mirrors, and a "Flick-My-Dick-Lighter" that looks like a man's penis. Men can try "cock enlargement techniques." One ad states that a "10 INCH PENIS IS NOW POSSIBLE . . . AND IT'S GUARANTEED." Penis pumps, male masturbators, and penis extensions also are available. You can buy a penislike gun and fill it with milk or the Squirting Banana, a plastic penis covered by a banana disguise that can be filled with liquid.

The pleasure enhancers are endless. As noted earlier in this book, it is believed that about five thousand different devices have been marketed in the United States. There are plastic "Ben Wa Eggs" that can be inserted by women to allegedly provide constant intense feelings of pleasure. Vibrating eggs also are available, and dildos and vibrators come in all shapes and sizes. One catalog advertises a 14-inch-long, 3-inch-thick vibrator. Another sells a "two-headed dildo." Seashell-shaped and butterfly vibrators can be purchased to stimulate the clitoris. A G-spot penis extension "brings her to exquisite ecstasy and shuddering orgasms." Other so-called sex enhancers include vibrating "cock rings," "pocket pussies," vibrating anal probes, liplike devices for oral sex, and an "anal intruder kit." French ticklers are another common item.

A whole subgroup of items are available for persons involved in sadomasochistic sexual activities, including a "Love Torture Pole: The Newest S/M Play Toy, Enslave Your Lover." An advertisement for a leather goods catalog in the February 1986 issue of *Penthouse Variations* pictures women involved with or wearing the following: a latex bra with a nipple free, a latex mask with nose holes, a leather hood with a mouth zipper, latex pants with a vibrating dildo, a pecker gag, a horsey bit, a ball gag, a blindfold, a leather dildo, D-ring shackles for wrist or ankle "domination," a waist to wrist restraint, a neck to wrist restraint, leather paddles, a penis whip, and a "Deluxe Playswing—Leather, wood and metal durability will give you years of sensual use and abuse. . . ."

Detective Magazines

Some who have studied the content of detective magazines, including Park Elliott Dietz, a member of the Attorney General's Commission on Pornography, postulate that such magazines are pornography for sexual sadists.[142] These magazines, which contain factual accounts of real crimes and rarely contain nude photographs, pair violent and sadistic images with erotic images. The detective magazines are displayed with general interest magazines and thus are easily available to children.

In the 1960s, H.A. Otto studied eleven detective magazines and concluded that they explicitly described the kind of violence, how the crime was committed, and the result.[143] In the mid-1980s, Dietz, Harry, and Hazelwood studied the content of nineteen different detective magazines with the following results.[144]

Illustrations: Most of the magazines had front cover images of a woman in an inferior or submissive position, with 38 percent of the covers showing a woman in bondage. Other common cover images, in order of decreasing frequency, were "violent struggles, brassieres, guns, accentuated breasts, strangulation, corpses, blood, and knives or other cutting instruments."[145] In contrast, most of the article illustrations were of buildings and conventionally dressed people such as male police officers. When violent or erotic images appeared, however, the most common were of domination and submission.

Advertisements: Ads for weapons and underwear were common. In the nineteen magazines, seventy-three ads promoted "enhancement of sexual control, appeal, or function."[146] Other advertising included sixty-eight ads for detective or law enforcement training; fifty-nine promoting official badges or IDs; thirty-five offering mind control techniques; eighteen for female wrestlers and nineteen for male wrestlers; mail-order brides; lonely hearts clubs; locksmith training, equipment to pick locks, and other crime techniques.

Titles and Text: The following are illustrative of the types of headlines commonly found in detective magazines: "A Trunk Full of Flesh," "Anna Took the Blade 90 Times!" "Satanist Smiled as He Snuffed the Snitch," "Roast a Family of Six," "The Holy Vampire Drank His Victim's Blood," "Ordeal of the Kidnapped Girl in the Pit," and "Weird Fetishes of Washington's Rape-Slayer."[147] Obviously, these are meant to titillate the reader and sensationalize the real-life crimes in a way no modern-day newspaper would.

The researchers found the following themes in article titles of detective magazines, in order of frequency: killing, roles (such as whore, slut, or mistress), mental state, death, law enforcement, sex, strangulation, weapons, mutilation, relentless pursuit, secret location, and life. In the thirty-eight sampled articles, there were forty killings, fifteen involving torture; forty-four sexual violence episodes (with thirteen sex mutilations); fifty shootings; forty stabbings; and ten episodes of binding and gagging. Forty-three of the offenders were male, while only four were female. There were forty-three male victims and fifty-six female victims. Interestingly, seventeen of the females were prostitutes. While almost all of the women were sexually attacked before death, none of the men were sexually molested. The articles contained details of violent acts using descriptive language. The researchers state that the magazines juxtaposed erotic images (such as descriptions of sex acts and scantily clad women) with images of violence and suffering. They note that detective magazines teach techniques for committing crimes and enjoy a wide circulation.

Fantasy Turned into Crime: Dietz, Harry, and Hazelwood detail six real-life cases where criminals used detective magazines as sources of fantasy material and acted out their fantasies. They believe that sexual sadists are particularly drawn to detective magazines and that some of them translate their fantasies into action. They suggest that clinicians should ask their patients about reading habits. While only unethical experiments could prove or disprove causation, the authors believe that the harmful effects of detective magazines outweigh the benefits and they should be considered pornography.[148]

We checked several detective magazines from the early 1980s through 1986 to verify that the content analysis performed by Dietz, Harry, and Hazelwood was accurate. We discovered article titles such as these: "The Psycho Ripped out the Blonde's Heart," "Teen Was Lured into a Fatal Sex Frenzy!" "The Little Girl and the Lusting Brute!" "Pam Was Mutilated with a Roasting Fork," "The Sex Freak's Incredible Reign of Terror," "I had to Kill Her . . . She Asked Me for Sex," "Two Lovely Girls Raped and Strangled," and "Jill Never Reached Home."

We also uncovered the following types of images and words. A cover photo in the May 1981 issue of *Official Police Detective* shows a girl leaning against a tree using an arm to ward off a man who is coming at her with a chain saw. Caption: "The Power Saw Killer: He Dismembered Eight of His Victims—

Keeping the Heads As Gory Souvenirs of His 'Conquests.'" This description appears in the same issue under the title "Sex-Crime That Cleaned Up a City": "They lured the 12-year-old to the room over the sex shop, then took turns raping him. They photographed the boy's ordeal and, when they got bored with it, they killed him. . . ."[149] The child is described as resisting attempts to tranquilize him, having bruises and whip marks all over, and having his anus and surrounding area torn wide open. He was tied to all four corners of the bed and gagged. They drowned him in the sink.

The June 1983 issue of *Official Detective* has a cover portraying a semiclad woman being choked by a man's hand. It contains a story that, like other forms of pornography, tries to blame the female victim for her abuse. The story, titled "Which Lover Slashed the Porno Girl?" describes a woman who, in true nymphomaniac fashion, paid men to have sex with her. Her male murderer killed her after she pulled a switchblade on him and said he could either perform oral sex on her or die. The man was found guilty of unintentional homicide and sentenced to only one year in prison.

In *Best True Fact Detective* (September 1980), one article is titled "Let's Rape the Girl Next Door!" The accompanying photo shows two men holding down a woman who is clad only in underwear. She dies by having her throat slashed twice. The same magazine contains a story about men who force a 14-year-old boy to watch while they take turns raping his female companion. Then they toss both teenagers, still alive, from a 165-foot bridge.

An article in *Front Page Detective* (June 1980) titled "Too Many Rapes to Count" tells how women were dragged from their cars and subjected to "unspeakable defilements."[150] One woman was assaulted by up to ten men. In the same magazine, we find a feature headlined "An Old Woman Lay Dead Obscenely Violated." The story tells how her face was battered beyond recognition, her hands were bound behind her back with twine, sixteen ribs were broken, both ears were sliced open, one eye was almost pulled from its socket, and her right breast was almost severed. A 13-inch stick thrust up her vagina was discovered only in the autopsy. Four men were arrested for the crime.

Inside Detective (January 1980) contains several accounts of sexual abuse. A 16-year-old virgin dies because a man she trusted "was insatiable in his sex drives."[151] Another woman was raped, tied alive to railroad tracks, run over by a train, and slashed into three pieces. Little girls were raped, had their heads chopped off, or were beaten to death. Another female victim had her abdomen repeatedly slashed, a deep cut on her forehead, and both breasts cut to shreds. What remained of her vaginal area was "just a mass of stab wounds,"[152] as she had been raped with a large knife. Even the subscription ad for the magazine shows covers of partially clad women with men holding knives to their throats or strangling them.

The advertising content of some of the detective magazines also is sex-oriented. *Inside Detective* (September 1986) combines ads for a striptease pen, a missing child, the *Illustrated Encyclopedia of Sex,* sexy scripts, Asian women who desire correspondence, lovely Mexican girls who want friendship, love, and marriage, and a claim to "Get Any Girl within Five Minutes and PAY NOTHING!" *Official Detective* (June 1983) has advertisements for the encyclopedia of sex, a truck driver's magic capsule, Filipino women who seek friendship, love, and marriage, sexy girls who want men for dates, and an "enchanting bust." *Best True Fact Detective* (September 1980) has a variety of ads ranging from sex devices, girls, witchcraft, tarot fortune-telling cards, a friendship club, and a device to protect against rape and robbery. This magazine also has ads for teen sex dolls and a doll pictured with its ass in the air. One advertisement read: "Guaranteed to spread her legs: We GUARANTEE that she will spread her legs for you again and again or your MONEY BACK! . . . Positive results in less than 10 minutes." There are also ads for pornographic films with pictorial illustrations and a book titled *How to Eat Away Your Impotence! Inside Detective* (January 1980) contained an ad stating: "Make Any Girl Do Anything You Mentally Command—With Your Mind Alone!" (she'll act as your "submissive slave").

Official Police Detective (May 1981) seems to have it all: ads for leather goods, sexual aphrodisiacs, a pinup calendar, all kinds of foreign girls, pictures of girls wrestling, time-release capsules to make sex last for hours, sex comics, swinger phone books, adult magazines, hard-on drops, penis extensions, a "Screw Her Good—Flexible Rubber Penis," penis exercisers, sexy 5-inch-heel shoes, fetish fashions, bizarre books, solid life-size love dolls, a pump to make a penis grow, and an erection ring. Other ads include "Fetish Phone Club"; "Get It Up! Thick and Big"; "Spanish Fly Supplant—Make Any Girl Hot for Sex with This Powerful New Formula"; and "Now you can turn any party into an orgy with Zingers." There are even ads for gay pornography. The subscription ad for this magazine features a nearly nude woman who is bound and gagged.

After studying the content of detective magazines, we must conclude that many of these do indeed contain pornography.

Rock Porn

The violent lyrics and images in some rock music and rock videos are pornographic. The recording business is a $4.5 billion a year industry. It has been revitalized by music videos. MTV (Music TV) is now in twenty-six million homes. It provides music twenty-four hours a day and is estimated to show three hundred rock videos a day.[153] In the fall of 1983, MTV was monitored for one month.[154] More than half the music videos featured or strongly suggested violence, and 35 percent of that violence was of a sexual nature. Many videos added violent imagery not contained in the song lyrics. Sadism and sexually sadistic violence were common.

The Canadian-sponsored Symposium on Media Violence and Pornography included examples of such music videos.[155] A Billy Idol video shows an apparently naked woman behind a translucent sheet with a rope around her neck. Her wrists are in chains. A man in the foreground is shown sharpening something on a leather strop. In another video, two Doberman pinschers on leashes dissolve into two women on leashes. A third example shows a man in a torture rack being given repeated electric shocks by a woman. There is also an image of a woman with no eyes playing a harp.

Many rock stars, who are idolized by teens and preteens, use pornographic rock images and lyrics. Tipper Gore, co-founder of the Parents Music Resource Center headquartered in Washington, D.C., gave a presentation on this topic at the National Conference on Pornography in June 1986.[156] This organization urges people to become aware of rock groups and their messages. Gore believes that commercialized sex and violence are not benign images. She stated that a minority of powerful artists are promoting songs that deal with incest, suicide, sadism, masochism, thrill-killings, and explicit sex. Gore noted that even people in the recording industry have been speaking out, including one performer who called this music "auditory pornography."[157] Gore pointed out that six thousand teenagers commit suicide each year, with some doing so while listening to pro-suicide music. She also cited another startling statistic: In the United States, ninety-six out of every one thousand teenage girls get pregnant each year, with more than thirty thousand teens under age 15 becoming pregnant each year. Gore noted that a 1986 issue of *Time* magazine stated that social workers are almost unanimous in believing that the media encourage the trend toward precocious sexuality. According to Gore, these materials reach very young children as well as teenagers. She also noted that the average teenager listens to between three and six hours of music each day.

Gore gave the following examples of what we have nicknamed "rock porn." (For more details about artists and titles, contact her. See note 156).

Motley Crüe's *Shout at the Devil* album has sold more than two million copies. Its songs emphasize violence against women. One song, for example, is about "not a woman, but a whore." It talks about killing her and watching her face turn blue. Another song glorifies rape, including talk of breaking her face, taping down her legs, and going in for the kill. Still another is about knifing a "bastard" to death.

Prince sings a song, "Darling Nikki," about meeting a girl in a hotel lobby who is masturbating with a magazine.

A 1985 hit record by Sheena Easton has her asking men to come spend the night inside her sugar walls.

Twisted Sister has a fan club called "The Sick Mother-Fucking Friends of Twisted Sister."

Gore notes that rock porn glorifies violence and sexual violence, usually against women and sometimes against children. Here are some more examples of rock porn:

One song talks about loving a woman to death and killing her if the singer cannot have her.

Another is about a homicidal maniac who butchers women with a 12-inch blade.

One cover of a rock album features a disemboweled woman being eaten by a mutant. The back cover portrays a blood-covered woman. This same rock group uses stage acts in which scantily clad or naked women are brutalized (in simulation).

The group WASP (We Are Sexual Perverts) appears on a major record company label with songs such as "Fuck Like a Beast" and "Ball Crusher." Two typical concert features of this group were (1) tying a naked woman onto a torture rack and pretending to slit her throat, and (2) beating a naked woman who had a black hood over her head until blood came down her breasts, then simulating a rape with a chain saw blade.

Lyrics to a Nasty Savage song tell about a "bitch" who is bound and helpless and screaming for more. That "sweet and innocent girl is really hard core." She is obsessed with pain. She eagerly indulges as he gives her the whip.

Savage Grace features a naked woman chained to a motorcycle.

One Rolling Stones album has a picture of a woman

who is bound and bruised from beating. "I'm Black and Blue from the Rolling Stones—and I Love It!"

One group sings about loving "you" to pieces and a flesh eater. The song "Easy Prey" is accompanied by an image of a woman walking down a beach stalked by a man with a knife.

Devil worship and satanism are common themes of some of rock music.

Thrasher has a song that talks about tying a woman down—she knows what's waiting for her. Nothing is too cruel. "Beat her 'til she's red and raw. Crack the whip—it hardly stings the bitch."

These, Gore said, are the images American children are facing day after day.

Another speaker at the conference was Bobby Dee, director of Teen Vision, Inc., of Pittsburgh.[158] This organization emphasizes helping teenagers choose music and puts out a magazine periodically. Dee is a former deejay. He attributes the following four attitudes, which he hears teenagers express over and over, to desensitization:

1. Denial of any problem
2. Denial of awareness ("I don't listen to the words.") (Yet, Dee says, if listening to something over and over does not influence people's behavior, the people in the advertising business are wasting a lot of money.)
3. Denial of any influence
4. Anticensorship feelings ("I have the right to do or sing what I want.")

Dee mentioned numerous examples of rock porn:

"Stick It Out" by Frank Zappa says, "Fuck me, you ugly son-of-a-bitch . . . stick out your hot curley weenies. . . . make it go in and out, . . . fast 'til it squirts, squirts, squirts."

Other Zappa songs include "Titties and Beer" and "Why Does It Hurt When I Pee," in which he sings of something from the toilet seat jumping up and grabbing his "meat."

An album called *Virgin Killer* was made by RCA in Germany. Although it was not supposed to be imported into the United States, it managed to appear in some stores. The album features a sexually abused 8- or 10-year-old girl.

Dee remarked that magazines for young girls emphasize how you look, not who you are, and that advertisements in such magazines encourage all types of sexual behavior. He notes that even *Mad* magazine,

a favorite of young boys, has nude comics. His examples continue:

One song talks about making love on an elevator.

Another song talks about bringing a girlfriend or two to make pornographic movies and making a "star" out of "you."

The Purple Rain movie features a woman's body being grabbed all over.

Madonna's live version of "Like a Virgin" on MTV showed her simulating the act of sexual intercourse on stage.

Duran Duran's "Girls on Film" video includes lesbian acts.

Some rock stars, through their music, videos, and comments in magazines, glorify sexual behavior between unmarried kids, promote sexual violence, encourage drug and alcohol abuse, promote suicide, and glorify the occult. For example, according to Dee, Madonna starred in a porn movie in 1979 and got fan mail from boys wanting to make love to her and girls wanting to be like her. One rock star said: "I tried to hang myself just to see what it was like." Another suggested crucifixes are sexy because there is a naked man on them. Others have extolled their adventures of sharing women and going through women "the way most people go through socks." One man was portrayed with a stocking around his neck (in a manner related to autoerotic asphyxiation). And one star was found guilty of indecent exposure after he exposed his private parts on stage and simulated masturbation and oral copulation.

At the conference, both Dee and Gore emphasized the need for parents to become involved in what their children are seeing and hearing in this new genre we call rock porn.

Fashion Chic and Sexism in Advertising

Jean Kilbourne, an expert on sexism in advertising, has stated that "the advertiser is America's real pornographer." She finds a consistent message that men reign supreme, that they are the intelligent ones and the complex decision makers.[159] Women, according to Kilbourne, are generally presented in only two roles: (1) a frantic housewife who is obsessed with cleanliness and (2) a sex object. Only 7 percent of the advertisements she analyzed for her 1980 doctoral dissertation portrayed women outside those two roles. She also found that only 2 percent of the ads pictured men as anything other than the traditional strong, macho type.[160]

A 1971 study of the roles of women in magazine advertisements found that the ads reflected these stereotypes:

1. A woman's place is in the home.
2. Women do not do important things and do not make important decisions.
3. Women need men's protection and are dependent on men.
4. Men are not interested in women as people; they regard women primarily as sex objects.[161]

Some researchers argue that advertisements use pornographic themes. These include women being bought and sold like commodities, bondage, the baby doll or teasing temptress image, and violence.[162] Aggressive images of women being mugged and beaten create concern because they not only reflect values but also create them.[163]

Feminists claim that in both pornography and advertising, women are regarded as objects. They argue that objects, stripped of human dignity and personality, are more likely to be treated in violent and degrading ways.[164] In addition, they say, pornographic myths turn up in advertising.[165] Examples of this follow:

The theme of "woman as evil temptress" appears in a perfume ad showing a black woman wearing a serpent necklace and makeup giving her eyes a feline look.

The theme of "woman as perpetual virgin" is reflected in a perfume ad that implies one should be "Sensual . . . but not too far from innocence."

The theme of "woman to be dominated" appears in an advertisement for footwear that says, "Some men treat their boots better than their women. Hardly admirable but certainly understandable."

Feminist author Andrea Dworkin attributes the new style of advertisements to pornography.[166] She gives examples of punk-type video commercials with imminent violence and sexy scenes, female body parts (such as breasts, legs, and buttocks) shown by themselves, and preteens in provocative poses. Dworkin believes that such ads convey the message that women are sexually available, they are all the same, men have the right to an endless number of women, and all women want sex. Catharine MacKinnon concludes that the overall effect of pornographic images is to feed the myth that women want to be raped and that sexual violation is normal.[167]

Jean Kilbourne believes that ads such as those for Maidenform underwear (in which women in professions are shown wearing only underwear and coats) send out a message that women in professional positions should not be taken seriously.[168] As long as women are made to feel inferior through objectification, Kilbourne claims, they will doubt their abilities and settle for lower pay and poor jobs. She points out that men in advertising are shown in positions of dominance and control.

We examined some of the more popular women's magazines to verify the claim that many portrayals are indeed sexist. We found women in contorted, ridiculous poses wearing skimpy clothes that emphasized body parts. In many depictions, only body parts (such as legs, buttocks, hands, or breasts) were shown. Many of today's fashion models are posed with vacant, nonhuman faces. It is, apparently, considered chic to wear uncomfortable clothes in flashy shades and images that do not look right together—that, in fact, make women look ridiculous. Hair that is standing straight up or streaked with fluorescent colors is promoted. Shoes have heels so high that it would be almost unbearable to walk in them. Some women are pictured with mean facial features, while others are smiling seductively, promoting the image of either the bitch/whore or virgin. This strange mixture of beauty combined with ugliness reminds us of the images of pornography. The overall impact is to treat women as sex objects— inhuman things that lack intelligence and exist only to be used by males for their sexual pleasure. In contrast, the men in magazines are portrayed as macho and strong.

Following are descriptions of some of what we considered the most sexist advertisements in fashion magazines.

We found sadomasochistic themes in some advertisements. A jeans ad pictures four men, two wearing only jeans, surrounding a female who is seated on the ground with two of the men. The men look mean, and one man has his hands on the girl's shoulders, holding her down. Could this convey a rape theme? A hair spray ad shows three Oriental women with blue lips and the upper halves of their bodies pressed together. Their bodies are nude, except for the bondage-type twine wrapped around their breasts, necks, and arms. A statue of a male god is in the corner of the ad. Could this convey bondage and lesbian themes? An ad for jeans captioned "seamless CHEEKS" shows a man with his hand raised about to paddle the buttocks of a woman who is bent at her waist. Another woman is shown lying on the floor lovingly looking at a man's shoe. Caption: "Keep her where she belongs . . ."

A perfume ad, surrounded by dark colors, shows a naked woman being sexually aroused by one man, while a second man also appears in the photograph.

This has appeared on a billboard as well as in magazines. A cocktail ad for "The Club" shows a smiling woman and carries the caption "Hit me with a club." An ad for men's perfume shows a woman lying at a macho man's feet. Her skirt and blouse are open, and she is wearing a "just-fucked" look. The caption reads, "All the Power a Man Needs." Three women wearing only lingerie are shown on a stage in front of a group of men. Caption: "Once you've worn it you can never plead innocent." In a punk-style clothing ad, the woman holds a knife to a man's hip. A men's slacks advertisement pictures the lower half of a man who is stepping on a tiger rug. The rug has the head of a woman, however, and his foot is on her head. Caption: "It's nice to have a girl around the house."

Even in an ad for skates, a woman is nude from the waist up and is wearing tight leatherlike pants. A clothing ad features a nude woman hitchhiker. A jewelry ad proclaims "Put her in chains." Another jewelry ad shows a woman with part of a chain necklace in her mouth. A cigarette ad shows a man blowing smoke in a woman's face and claims that if he blows in her face, she will follow him anywhere. Two other ads by the same advertiser show a crazy-looking woman perched on a spiked iron fence wearing only a flimsy gown and another woman pushing at a wall as though she might jump from the building. A series of fashion displays show women being beaten and roughed up. A clothing ad shows a scared-looking teenage girl hiding in a corner of an animal pen wearing a skirt and halter top. Her bra straps are showing. Two buttons on her halter top are open and her belly button is showing. There are cows in the pen. The next frame show her struggling with a man (their hands against each other's) and her bra creeping above the halter. The third photo shows her only from the bust up. She is subdued. The man's hand is on her shoulder. Her bust is partially unclothed, with part of her bra showing. Again, does this suggest a rape scene? Is this fashion chic or something close to pornography?

Jeans ads show men and women nude from the waist up. A beer mug ad shows a faceless woman with a nude breast holding the mug. Even a *Time* magazine ad shows the back of a nude, seated woman forming the shape of the I. The woman in a cigarette ad proclaims that she was never so insulted as when her boyfriend said he loved her for her mind. Nude women are shown pulling on jeans. An underwear ad has a paper doll woman with panties that can be interchanged. An ad for men's underwear shows several women's hands frisking his undershirt. A man's hand squeezes a woman's nude breasts in a jewelry ad. A men's cologne ad features drawings of a woman attacking a man and claims to include self-defense instructions in every package for the men. One leading women's magazine even ran an article encouraging readers to use dial-a-porn and frequently runs features encouraging sex between persons who are not married.

One photo shows women wearing skimpy body-suits where nipple buds and buttocks cracks are clearly visible. A perfume ad shows a woman in a skimpy dance outfit surrounded by ten men who seem to be fighting over her. Another fragrance ad showing a costume ball carries the caption "Unleash Your Fantasies." A masked man and woman are shown. He is clothed in shirt and pants. She has a gown with flimsy straps. He is kissing her neck and has pulled the side zipper of her dress down to reveal her bare hips. In an underwear ad, a woman's buttocks are uncovered except for the crack. An ad for stockings features the lower half of a woman's body with her legs spread, while a huge hat hides her body from her waist to her upper thigh. An ad for a moisturizer shows a woman with bare shoulders wrapped in fur with a man's hand on her shoulder.

One presidential candidate ran an ad against the marriage tax, but the caption read: "Wife Beating . . . Government Style!" An automatic bank teller ad says, "What you do with Mary Ann after hours is your business." And lastly, there are ads where little girls are made up to look like women. "Because innocence is sexier than you think," one proclaims. Another ad shows pictures of a girl from baby to teen. In the teen pictures, she is in a shapely dress with earrings and makeup. One pose shows her crouched down and her legs emphasized. Caption: "Show me the child and I'll give you the woman!"

Romance Novels and Confession Magazines

One topic of debate is whether romance novels for women are pornography. According to Joseph Slade, romances depict males as powerful yet vulnerable, both rough and gentle, worldly and domestic, impatient yet skilled at kissing, fondling, and caressing.[169] The men in romances are objects of desire shaped in the images women wish for. This, according to Slade, is pornography for women.

Feminists, while not going so far as to label romance novels pornography, object strongly to the themes those mass market books perpetuate.[170] Romances, the feminists claim, depict men as superior and support old stereotypes of female and male roles. Heroines are ineffectual, helpless, and weak. The men they fall in love with are macho and masterful. While the heroine is a chaste beauty, he is a lustful beast. These portraits suggest images of child/parent and victim/rescuer. Romances perpetuate the myth that women should depend on men. And, of course, every one ends with a declaration of eternal love, and the heroine and her hero live happily ever after.

Since 1980 romance novels have become a $250 million industry, suggesting they have a pervasive influence on women's thinking.[171] In 1982, 264 million Harlequin romances were sold, according to the publisher. And four out of every ten paperbacks sold in the United States in 1980 were romances.[172]

Teen romances, which are quite popular, are as unrealistic as the adult romances. Personal appearance is emphasized, while intelligence is something to hide. According to *Media Report to Women,* the same old "deadly" sexist messages are espoused by these books.[173] In short, girls are taught to be dependent on males. Scholastic, Inc., sells 2.25 million teen romances annually, and other publishers are said to have similar success.

For an excellent description of contemporary romance novels, see Snitow, who describes Harlequin genre romances as being filled with "phallic worship" of the hero by the heroine.[174] Women, she notes, are stereotyped in helping roles and are portrayed as passive. Snitow speculates that romances command a large audience because they offer sexual release. She also believes that the women in romances are portrayed just as they are in pornography—as being helplessly at the mercy of men with the heroine surrendering to the force of her hero's masculinity.

We found that the romance genre often stereotypes males as captors, females as captured, males as sexually aggressive and domineering, and females as submissive. Women are occupied with capturing a man or getting married and may give up their careers, if necessary, to reach that all-important goal. Men's roles focus primarily on their careers, while sex and family are secondary. The women in romances fall in love with the men before they have sex with them or during sex, while the men hold out on declarations of love. The women have a goal of making the men love them.

We believe, however, that there are differences between pornography and female-oriented romance novels. Although sex is portrayed more explicitly in romances today, it is not as explicit as sex in pornography and does not take up the major portion of the novel. The sex portrayed in romances is often more equal, loving, and affectionate (despite perpetuating the old stereotype of women liking macho men). The heroines usually do not get raped. They get seduced or seduce the heroes. There is no group sex or sex for the sake of pleasure alone. The heroine and hero are in love and show it in many ways (such as sharing meals and expressing concern for each other's work) besides participating in sexual activities. And the novels end with a marriage commitment. Heroes in these books are allowed to have feelings, and most see the heroines as persons, not sex objects. Gentle, passionate, and loving feelings toward each other are often shown by heroine and hero. Books of this type, therefore, often come closer to the mutuality, equality, and love characteristic of erotica rather than pornography. Many, however, are not even sexually explicit enough to be considered erotic. Some do contain sexually explicit passages. When rape or other sexually abusive acts are involved, such books could be considered pornographic.

Confession magazines likewise lack the explicitness of pornography. Some do promote an immoral lifestyle (extramarital sex, premarital sex, and so on), but many of the articles deal with everyday images of women (cooking, child care, and so on) and everyday problems of women (battering, alcohol, breakups, jealousy, and health). These items primarily concern finding love and making choices in love. The confession magazines seem to cater primarily to young women (at least the women in the stories are mostly young). A few sexual aid and lingerie advertisements appear in these type of magazines.

We conclude that romance novels and confession magazines for the most part are not pornographic. There is no doubt, however, that these influential and widely read works do perpetuate sexist stereotypes about females.

Pornography and Racism

Pornography, Nazis, and Other Fascists

In November 1984, Betty Wein presented a Jewish perspective on pornography to the Seventh World Media Conference in Japan.[175] In her paper, Wein relates today's United States to the pre-Nazi Weimer Republic in Germany, and pornography is part of that comparison. She sees the moral crisis in the United States as paralleling the decadence of prewar Germany and surpassing that of Sodom. She notes that many Americans see the struggle against these decadent forces as futile, and, like many Germans, they go inside, bolt the door, and attempt to shut it all out. According to Wein, many Nazi symbols of sadism are present in mainstream America today—on television, in rock music, in the fashion world, and on our streets during gay pride parades. Pamela Hansford Johnson notes:

> We are in danger of creating an affectless society in which no one cares for anyone but himself or for anything but instant self gratification. We demand sex without love, violence for kicks. We are encouraging the blunting of sensitivity. And this, let us remember, was not the way to an earthly paradise, but the way to Auschwitz.[176]

Wein claims that great civilizations have fallen when their masses became so busy pursuing lust that they stopped thinking. She also notes that during Machado's dictatorship in Cuba, when the police saw an uprising, protest, or cry of independent will, "they announced programs of indecent films in Havana theaters to turn men's minds to other things."[177]

Wein also comments on certain features in 1984's *The Best of Hustler*.[178] In that issue, a satirical magazine titled *Gestupo* is advertised as "sex mag entertainment for horny Nazis" with articles such as "Sex in the Shower Can Be a Gas." One page has a photo of "Klaus Barbie Doll," which has a swastika, gestapo outfit, and "working guillotine." This doll is described as the "Butcher of Lyons," who is entitled to "play with your kids." *Gestupo*, it says, is "bound to cause a fuehrer." Wein notes that adult pornography bookstores in New York City feature paperback books with titles such as *Black Bitch, Nazi Train, Teen Slaves, Gestapo Training School, Japanese Sadist Dungeon, Mother's Black Lovers,* and *Abused Vietnamese Virgins.*[179] She views these types of books as launching an invitation to rape:

Women do indeed suffer most at the hands of pornographers. They are depicted performing oral sex on a goat, being mounted by a dog, being penetrated by an eel or cockroach. Feminists Fighting Pornography have compiled unbelievable depictions of women with their nipples being cut off by pliers or pierced with a sharp weapon, women hanging upside down or right side up, women bound and gagged, etc. *Hustler* feeds a woman into a meat grinder. *High Society,* published by a woman, features, in its December 1983 issue, a woman wearing a dog collar and chain while torching her own genital area with raging flames. Concentration camp chic.[180]

Wein believes that the United States today is at the same stage Nazi Germany was at when people "suspended their humanity in the face of dehumanization."[181] She views the American Civil Liberties Union as functioning in an intellectual vacuum, continuing to defend the free flow of pornography by arguing that a book never harmed anyone but saying, in the next breath, that the best weapon against bad ideas is good ideas. Wein calls this a delusionary pattern of reversing the truth. According to Wein, we must "[a]dd to these delusions, 'you cannot legislate morality' even as law after law is passed endorsing immorality."[182]

On the link between pornography and Nazism, Wein points out that the Nazis flooded Poland with pornography after invading that nation "in a deliberate attempt at social castration."[183]

> And let us never forget that the seeds of fascism, leading not only to book burning, but also to the crematoria for six million Jews, were planted in the 1920's in the democratic, sexually permissive Weimar Republic where dehumanizing, sadomasochistic pornography flowed unabated . . . The moral relativism of the Weimar Republic was translated into "anything goes" and what went was the ability of the German people to differentiate right from wrong.[184]

Wein cites David Holbrook's *The Pseudo-Revolution* on the issue of why there was so little protest when the first concentration camps were set up, when Jews disappeared, and when mentally deficient children were carted off for experiments, along with the equally compelling question of why there is so little protest today over dehumanizing pornography.[185] Holbrook answered those questions with one word: dissociation. He explained that people, preferring not to experience the anguish created by breaking away from herd trends, pretend the manifestation has not happened or they have not seen it or that what happened is normal and can be reconciled with normal life, behavior, and values.

Wein worries that one of the most serious problems facing this nation today—the insidious desensitization of the masses to dehumanizing pornography—goes largely unrecognized. This treacherous desensitization, she warns, is fostered by the relative silence of Americans in the face of a porn industry that preys on the weak and weakens the resolve of the strong.

With one of the last bastions of safety from decadence—the home—invaded by dial-a-porn, cable porn, video porn, computer porn, mail porn, and, increasingly, radio and television porn, Wein asks, "When will Americans, who are quick to rail against bodily assaults, ever wake up to the stark reality that pornographic assaults on the spiritual dimensions of man can be even more devastating?"[186]

On that note, she paraphrases Edmund Burke's widely quoted admonition to relate to contemporary America: "The only thing necessary for the triumph of evil is for good men not to even recognize it as such."[187] Isn't that what happened, she asks, not only to the Nazis who turned off the lights and turned on the gas in the gas chambers, but also to the railroad engineers who transported masses of Jewish children, women, and men in cattle cars, to the German finance division that paid the fare, to countries that stood by idly as Jews were being rounded up for slaughter?

The Germans in World War II and the prewar years were experts at using photographs, slogans, and other propaganda to influence human behavior. The Nazis understood the advantages of combining pornography with political propaganda advocating violence.[188] Hitler realized that associating the "inferior races" with pornography was a powerful means of demoralizing them. Nazi victims were "rapidly broken by enforced participation in public sex—by being, for instance, photographed during masturbation and totally deprived of privacy for sustained periods."[189]

Great Britain's Longford report addressed the Nazi use of pornography this way:

> We cannot ignore the lesson to be learned here from what is perhaps the only historical instance where pornography was deliberately and consciously used for political ends—the activities of Julius Streicher (hanged as a Nazi war criminal in 1946), in violent stimulation of anti-Semitism by means of his magazine Der Stürmer. . . .

The magazine, which contained stories about how "the Jew" was ordered by the Talmud and the Elders of Zion to "despoil aryan maidenhood," to slaughter "aryan children" for ritual and use their blood in passover baking, depended chiefly on lurid anatomical cartoon-style drawings. The cover, with sickening monotony, would depict a revoltingly ugly old Jew lecherously leering at the breasts of a blonde girl whose last shreds of clothing he was about to tear away; the Jew's unshaven face was emphasized to imply that his fiendish sexuality was intent only on rape. Der Stürmer, which began in Nuremberg in 1923, rapidly grew to a circulation of hundreds of thousands—and even this is no indication of its readership, since after Hitler's accession to power, it was publicly displayed all over the country in glass-covered boxes on the walls—Stürmer-Kasten—for those who preferred not to buy it. At the same time as Streicher—a self-confessed sadist who boasted he frequently used the whip he always carried—rose in the Nazi hierarchy, his magazine became a means of denouncing any Jew alleged to have had sexual relations with an "aryan" girl; to be mentioned—and no pornographic detail of "evidence" was left out of the description—in Der Stürmer was tantamount, for any Jew, to a concentration camp sentence.

Streicher himself, although loathed by stern puritans in Hitler's entourage such as Himmler and Goering, had a huge library of pornography. Very little is known about Hitler's own interest in pornographic materials, although he was a keen and regular reader of Der Stürmer; it is generally accepted that he suffered from sexual inadequacy, probably from impotence, which may have led to his violent denunciations of sexual decadence and emphasis on procreation—of "aryan offspring for the Fatherland"—as the only justification for intercourse. There are in existence collections of pornographic photographs taken, probably by each other, of his mistress Eva Braun and her sister, who may, it is thought, have had a lesbian relationship. And despite the national insistence during the thirties on "purity"—the banning of nudist camps and nightclubs, for instance—much of the approved art proudly proclaimed by the Nazis as "healthy" and "aryan" would to most of us today appear obscenely preoccupied with detail of anatomy, down to the meticulous painting of each pubic hair on giantesque Germanic women. The two-edged weapon of pornography—to provide prurient excitement and sadistic titillation—has never been so effectively or cynically put to use in order to influence the mass of society.[190]

The Nazi Germany bearing children became the most important part of a woman's life. "If she was fertile, pregnant by order of the Fuhrer, everything was due her. If she was intellectual, independent, childless, she was exposed to the violent onslaughts of the breeding experts."[191] In June, 1936 women were banned from being judges. The Nazis took the position that "women were only able to make decisions emotionally and were thus unqualified to hand down justice, among other things."[192] Some 800,000 women were removed from the labor market from 1933 to 1935 as a result of these types of governmental decrees. Women were also kept out of party positions and political power in Nazi Germany. It was, in short, a patriarchal society in which males held all the power and women were forced into the role of forced motherhood and treated as childbearing sexual objects.[192]

According to Dorchen Leidholdt, the collective mind of the Nazis and the pornographers have such ideological similarities and operate in such similar ways that one must conclude that they are the same. In support of her belief, Leidholdt gives these examples: (1) A Jewish couple is pictured. A Jewish girl chases a dollar bill attached to a string. The string is pulled by a man hiding behind a building. He wears a swastika on his arm and raises a baseball bat. (2) A naked woman leans against a draped counter with her pelvis thrust forward and her arms behind her back as if tied. With legs slightly spread, her posture suggests submission, sexual desire, and helplessness. Her face is devoid of intelligence or emotion. A gleaming, gigantic python circles her leg, penetrates her thighs, and coils behind her. The first is a *Hustler* cartoon. The second is a painting by Franz von Stuck, the favorite artist of Adolf Hitler.

Leidholdt believes that both fascism and pornography are based on biological determinism—that there is a genetic, natural hierarchy of groups of human beings expressed in a political hierarchy. Both claim that the dominant and subordinate groups in the hierarchy have overwhelming genetic differences. the attributes possessed by the dominant group are designated as important, superior, and human. The traits it assigns to the subordinate group are inferior and subhuman. In Nazism, these groups were the Aryan and the Jew. In pornography, it is the biological fact of being born with a penis rather than a vulva that determines superiority. Within pornography, Leidholdt says, a racial hierarchy in which women are rated according to their skin color also exists. The Nazis, like the pornographers, divested women of civil and reproductive rights.

Leidholdt cites Theodore Adorno's book *The Authoritarian Personality* as documenting the convergence of the pornographic and fascistic mind.[194] She notes that Adorno found certain attitudes that distinguish potential fascists. They include the following:

1. Masculine and rough, independent, and successful
2. Lacking softness and passivity
3. Belief in the superiority of men and inferiority of women (dominant/submissive)
4. See sex as a way to achieve masculine status through conquests
5. Tend to regard women as objects and cannot become personally or emotionally involved with women
6. While outwardly pretending to admire women, secretly disrespect and resent them
7. Stereotype all women as virgins or whores and have contempt for the latter, with the highest scorers in this category expressing contempt for all women
8. Have an exploitive and manipulative attitude toward women
9. Associate sex with aggression and display a sadomasochistic orientation.

These, of course, are the same attitudes possessed by pornographers and certain consumers of pornography. And, as Leidholdt points out, sadomasochism is the type of sexuality that pornography celebrates and documents. Even so-called soft-core pornography is sadomasochistic, she says, with females exhibiting masochism by pretending pleasure in the humiliation of being displayed as "cunt", "tits", and "ass" and male viewers exhibiting sadism in the pleasure they derive from witnessing the women's humiliation.[195]

Leidholdt notes that Hitler adopted the whip as his personal symbol and was delighted to watch scantily clad women risk their lives. She says that sadomasochism (dominance) characterized Hitler's interaction with his immediate subordinates and the German people. Both pornographers and fascists direct their sadism against people considered weaker, lesser, and feminine. Both reject responsibility for their sadistic acts, instead projecting responsibility onto the victims. Leidholdt believes that the seeds of mass violence lie within this ideology.

In addition, when the Nazis gained control of the government of Poland, they flooded Poland with pornography on the theory that by making the individuals conscious of the need for personal sensation, the social combination of forces would be difficult.[196]

In *Pornography and Silence,* Susan Griffin has a chapter titled "The Sacrificial Lamb" that deals with the relationship between racism, the anti-Semitism of the Nazis, and pornography.[197] She speaks of two kinds of delusion: (1) a private delusion where the person is often perceived as insane, and (2) a mass delusion, "a shared set of beliefs which are untrue and which distort reality."[198] According to Griffin, pornography, racism, and the Nazi Germany belief that Jews were evil are all forms of mass delusion, despite the fact that in some time periods whole segments of society have accepted these beliefs, just as some people in the United States perceive the pornographic ideology as reasonable today.

Griffin considers the pornographic and racist minds to be identical both in their symbolic content and in the psychological purposes of the delusions they express. She describes a classic mental pattern in which images must accelerate in their violence until they become human events that devastate countless lives.

Thus, she states, the image of a dark man raping a white woman embodies all that the racist fears. This image is prevalent in pornography. Griffin cites the following examples of pornographers being obsessed with racism:

1. In a *Hustler* magazine cartoon titled "Chester the Molester," a man wearing a swastika on his arm tries to entice a little girl away from her parents. The child and parents are wearing yellow Stars of David (Jewish symbols).
2. Nazi memorabilia such as uniforms and photographs of the atrocities of concentration camps are sold as pornography along with pornographic books and films.
3. Pornographic films sometimes bear titles such as *Golden Boys of the SS, Leibencamp,* and *Ilse, the Shewolf of the SS.*

Lucy Davidowicz, cited in Griffin, has mentioned a rock group called the dictators who declare "we are the members of the master race."[199] Davidowicz also has knowledge of articles found in the apartment of a Hell's Angels motorcycle gang member that included torture devices, Nazi propaganda, and pornography. She believes that "pornography and propaganda have reinforced each other over the decades."[200] Indeed, it is true that two anti-Semitic ideologues, Gobineau and Houston Chamberlain, who greatly influenced the philosophy of Adolf Hitler and the Third Reich, were deeply influenced by the pornographic writing of the Marquis de Sade.

As Griffin correctly points out, the fantasized portraits drawn by pornographers and racists (including Nazis) resemble one another. She claims that these are all creations of one mind—a "chauvinist mind"—which projects all its fears within itself onto others and which defines itself by what it hates.[201] Among the examples cited by Griffin are portrayals of black men and women as stupid and unthinking; Jews as a dark race; women as whores, virgins, and slaves; Jews as effeminate; Africans as unclean; black women as lustful; Jewish and black men with enormous sexual endowment; the materialism of Jews, blacks, and women; and women or Jews who take away white men's jobs.

According to Griffin, where one finds the racist idea of another person as evil or inferior, one also finds a racial ideal—a portrait of the self as superior, good, and righteous. She cites as examples the southern white male slave owner and the anti-Semite.

The racist's idea of black intelligence, the anti-Semite's idea of Jewish intelligence, and the pornographer's idea of female intelligence resemble each other, Griffin says, as all three are described as possessing an animal cunning. The intelligence of all three classes of people is made to appear evil. The chauvinist mind Griffin describes has, at times, imagined that the Jew or the witch (that is, a woman) gained power by desecrating the religious symbols of the dominant culture.

Griffin notes that Nazi propaganda, like pornography, became translated into events. Similarly, the Marquis de Sade justified his philosophy of cruelty by describing nature as cruel. Hitler described his vision of violence against Jews as natural. Griffin sees chauvinists conferring upon themselves the right to manipulate nature. Thus, in the pornographer's world, the natural act of sexual intercourse becomes an act of aggression, rape, and violence.

Under the Nazi campaign against emancipated women, women were forced out of public life and back into the home with the principle of "Küche, Kinder, Kirche ('kitchen, children, church')."[202]

Hitler grew up in an atmosphere where anti-Semitic politics and ideas flourished. Anti-Semitic writing and propaganda were available in a steady stream. Hitler followed the work and the magazines of a writer named George Lanz von Liebenfels and surely was familiar with the notion that inspired this writer—namely, that Jews, Slavs, and blacks were closer to the apes than Aryans and were a dark force against the Aryan race. Liebenfels also had a theory that in a happy marriage, men should be physically and psychologially brutal to their wives. If Hitler read *Ostara,* Liebenfels's magazine, he saw anti-Semitic propaganda freely mixed with pornography, Griffin points out. One example is the magazine's lurid illustrations depicting Aryan women succumbing to the powers of hairy and apelike men of dark races. Similarly, the popular magazine *Der Stürmer* was both racist and pornographic. One scene played out by racists, and especially anti-Semites, during that period was a pornographic drama in which an Aryan woman was raped or seduced by a Jewish man.

According to Griffin, Hitler's personality suggests that he was a sadomasochist. Some sources, she says, claim that he practiced sadomasochistic rituals and regularly visited prostitutes, whom he paid to tie him up and beat him. Another claims that he demanded that his lovers humiliate him by urinating on his body. Clearly, if these allegations are true, Hitler had a taste for pornography.

As Griffin notes, pornography resembles nothing in modern times so much as it resembles the scheme of lies, images, and rituals that we know as Nazi propaganda. Both lie by reversing the order of truth. After Nazi rallies that spewed forth anti-Semitic propaganda, anti-Jewish riots took place in which Jewish people were attacked in the streets and their shop windows broken. Thus, as with the connection between consuming pornography and committing acts of sexual violence against women and children, Nazi hate propaganda provoked violence against the Jews. Griffin states:

> In every detail, the concentration camp resembled an enacted pornographic fantasy. Even the hardware of sadomasochism was present. Men and women were chained and shackled, and the SS officer, who wore high leather boots, carried a whip. And just as in a pornographic fantasy, the Jew was beaten. He was "disciplined." A man who attempted to escape, for example, was "beaten to a pulp." And then he was made to stand for hours in his beaten state under a hot sun, in rain before being lashed again, thrown into a dungeon or hanged before the assembled camp.[203]

Jewish prisoners were disciplined for trifling offenses. The scientific experiments that the Nazis carried out on the Jewish inmates in the concentration camps attained what Griffin calls a most obvious pornographic symbolism: "In one experiment men were immersed in ice water and then put between the bodies of naked women. Gypsy children were sterilized without anesthetic. Chemical irritants which would burn through tissue were introduced into women's wombs. Men were castrated surgically and with radiation."[204]

Jewish survivors of the concentration camps have said that the purpose of the camps was to humiliate and degrade the Jews, Griffin says. Similarly, in pornography, men murder women, but first humiliate and degrade them. In one novel, the pornographer recalls the scientific experiments of the concentration camps as he forces an enema on his victim. In

another, as a man cuts apart a woman's breast, he systematically tortures her sexual body in an atmosphere of humiliation.

The Nazis painstakingly documented every act of torture, humiliation, and murder. Hitler watched, in his private rooms, photographs of men and women being tortured. Griffin believes that by creating these images, the Nazis made a pornographic fantasy out of real Jews. From these images, she says, we can recognize that the pornographic and Nazi mind are identical both in form and content.

She explains that Hitler's idea of the feminine was a pornographic idea, for he saw women as weak, in need of control, and crying out for fatherly authority and commands. Thus, he decided females did not want freedom, she says. Both the Nazi and pornographic ideologies show the dominant aesthetic as nothing sensual but as ugliness verging on brutality. Toughness and strength are seen as physical ideals. Indeed, Hitler's favorite painter, von Stuck, painted pictures of bestiality—women having sex with animals.

Nazi Images in Pornography

The German *Playboy* pictures a Jewish-type woman in bondage with destructive, burning laser beams binding her and penetrating her vagina.[205] Pornograhic books bear titles such as *Hot Cock Nazi Master, Nazi Abuse, Nazi Dungeon Slave, Nazi Lust, Nazi Masters, Nazi Sex Slave, Nazi Slave Used by the Gestapo*[206], *Concentration Camp Tortures*, and *Dachau Desire*.[207] Books are sold in which Nazi victims supposedly describe Nazi sex horrors.

The September 1980 issue of *Penthouse* ran a multipage cartoon spread making fun of the Nazis. Women were shown abusing other women, and Hitler was depicted being dominated by Eva Braun. He was on all fours with Braun riding his back, holding whip, and gripping the harness in his mouth. Indeed, Nazi-style boots, whips, and black leather clothing abound much of pornography.

Nazi women are portrayed in pornography as mean and hateful, yet they are shown as sex objects, partially clothed in Nazi uniforms with breasts and vaginas exposed. Nazi men are often fully uniformed.

A magazine titled *Fascist Femmes* contains numerous Nazi-type pornographic images.[208] A partially uniformed female in high boots whips a nude man. A uniformed man then hits him with a rifle while the man is forced to suck the woman's vagina. The caption suggests that the man is not sure whether he will die from the rifle blows or from the woman's powerful stench, conveying the idea that the woman is dirty or bad. A nymphomaniac loves to satisfy the desires of the cruel male Nazis. She is shown in a hat, a uniform jacket on one arm and shoulder with the other arm and breast bare, and her pants unzipped to reveal pubic hair. Another woman seduces an RAF (Royal Air Force) officer by her aggressiveness and cruelty, getting him to submit totally to her and tell her military secrets while having a painful enema up his ass. Yet another Nazi woman rams a quirt up a man's ass and shoves it in his mouth, making him her sex slave. The caption says he died with smile on his face. One Nazi uniformed woman finger-fucks herself while saluting Hitler.

The same magazine features several woman in Nazi uniforms with guns pointed at their vaginas and mouths. One exclaims that a fantasy of hot lead and the final blast filling her head is the "ultimate blow job." Another woman is turned on by pain and violence. Her idea of a real blow job is firing the hard, cold metal barrel of her luger up her vagina. The magazine also contains scenes of women whipping each other.

The cover of a book titled *War Horrors* depicts two "Nazi Experimental Victims." One is lashed nude to a chair. The other has her hands tied behind her back attached to the ceiling and her feet in 5-inch heels tied to the floor. She wears a skimpy costume, but her breasts and vagina are bare. A doctor is present in the scene, as is a needle.

Ilsa, Queen of the S.S.: Nazi File No. 76 shows a woman in a Nazi uniform wearing boots with stiletto heels and riding a nude man who is on all fours, animal-like. He has a muzzle in his mouth, and she has a whip.

Slaves for the Master Race: Nazi File No. 77 is sadomasochism at its worst. The cover shows a teenage girl, nude from the waist down, lying on her stomach on a hard table. Her arms are held apart by ropes, and two men hold her legs spread-eagled. A third man is dropping his pants, and his bulging erection is revealed in his underpants. The back cover tells how the teenager was so lovely that German Youth leaders chose her to become a sexual plaything for the government's highest ranking members. She underwent sex training, learning to perform the "most lewd and perverse acts" for women and men. Within six months, she knew as much about giving sexual pleasure as the most famous courtesans of history.

As you can see, all the standard images of pornography are present in the Nazi genre of pornography. Women are shown as sex objects, as nymphomaniacs who crave continual sex—no matter how cruel, painful, or humiliating—and as bad, cruel, domineering bitches.

Pornography in Israel

In 1983, Judith Bat-Ada noted that the sharp increase in the incidence of rape in Israel paralleled the upsurge in pornography, which, she believes, contributes to violence against women in that nation.[209] In the early 1980s, topless teenage girls were used to advertise children's clothing, a rape scene ran as part of an ad for a woman's perfume, and another advertisement (in a leading family magazine) portrayed a terrified woman in panties and bra with Holocaust imagery such as trains, a furnace, and a shower-head type fixture.[210]

Bat-Ada states that "pornography can be seen as the anti-Semitism of women."[211] According to Bat-Ada, themes of child pornography, sadism, and pseudohomosexuality are woven into family, women's and general interest media in Israel. Child pornography is openly displayed. Semi-erect penises are shown, as are images of naked 15-year-old girls and couples engaged in foreplay. One billboard advertising a film depicted a naked teenage girl astride an adult male with an adult female watching. While a graduate school screens pornographic films at all major student events and porn videos sell successfully, laws that regulate pornography are not enforced.[212]

A family magazine in Israel has run photos of nude battered women, women tortured and bound, and rape-murder scenes. Women portrayed on the cover have vacant or hate-filled eyes, Bat-Ada notes. The magazine also has featured sexually sadistic photo displays.[213] Throughout the media of Israel, children are displayed in provocative poses, clothing and shoe ads feature females stripping in front of males, and women are portrayed in life-threatening situations. A boot ad depicts two naked children, around age 3, in boots and hats standing on a shag rug in front of a full-length mirror. The boy is embracing and about to kiss the girl. A popular song has lyrics claiming that men do not want virgin girls anymore but would rather have the ones from the magazines. And pseudolesbian clothing and shampoo ads picture models nuzzling each other and gazing into the eyes of the beloved. These images promote the *Playboy* lifestyle, Bat-Ada believes.[214]

Racist Pornography

According to Tracey A. Gardner, it is the way pornography uses underlying myths and the history of the oppression of blacks, not the physical appearance of a person of color, that makes pornography racist.[215] Those myths, she says, include the following:[216]

1. White is pure and moral. Black is carnal, satanic, and diabolical.
2. African males were beastlike, with huge genitals. They were phallic symbols and feared by white men as sexual rivals.
3. Black men are portrayed as pathological rapists of white women (when, in reality, most of the interracial rapes in the United States were of black woman by white men).
4. Black women are portrayed as bad, mean, and wicked.
5. A black man having a relationship with a white woman degrades her.
6. A white man having a relationship with a black woman elevates her.
7. The image of the black woman is that of a slut who can take anything sexually.

These images certainly are promoted by racist pornography.

Gardner makes an interesting comparison between the inhuman treatment of black men by white men—based in part on the economic threat they posed—and the current inhuman treatment of women (especially white women) by white men in pornography and real life. She states that white women, who are striving for their own independence in the sexual and economic spheres, now threaten the power and masculinity of white men as black men and women used to.[217]

She also notes that while white men like pornographic images of black women in leather with whips looking bad, black men like pornographic portraits of black women helpless and submissive and in bondage.[218] Both Gardner and Luisah Teish believe that white women in pornography tend to be portrayed as soft, pure, beautiful, and innocent, whereas black women are shown as sadistic, ugly, animalistic, and "undeserving of human affection."[219] We also have seen much pornography portraying white women as sadists and feel strongly that most pornography dehumanizes the women featured in it, whether they are white or black. There is no doubt, however, that pornography containing images of women of color reinforces cultural values of racism, male dominance, and white supremacy. Van F. White, a black man who, as a member of the Minneapolis City Council, co-sponsored the civil rights pornography ordinance, states that users of pornography, "by looking at other human beings as a lower form of life, . . . are perpetrating the same kind of hatred that brings racism to society."[220]

Alice Walker describes a real concern felt by women of color when their men masturbate to pornographic photographs of white women: Will he think of them when he makes "love to me?"[221] This same man may masturbate to pornographic images of women of color, she notes. The woman looks in a mirror and decides that she is not beautiful or hip. She later realizes that she must fight the pornographic messages and make the man realize that he "can never have her again sexually the way he has had her since their second year of marriage, as though her body belonged to someone else. He sees, down the road, the dissolution of the marriage, a constant search for more perfect bodies, or dumber wives."[222] Walker considers it to be a problem that pornography has escaped the eye of black activists. As an example, she cites an advertisement for a pornographic movie titled *Slaves of Love*. The ad shows two black women in chains, naked, with a white man standing over them with a whip. Walker suggests that the black man considers his wife to be "still" black, "whereas he feels himself to have moved to some other plane."[223] This image of the woman in chains excites rather than horrifies him. Thus, Walker explains, the lynching of the black woman's body has never stopped. She states that black women in pornography are depicted as "shit," while white women are depicted as "objects." Black men are portrayed as "being capable of fucking anything . . . even a piece of shit," and are defined solely by the size of their penis and its readiness and unselectivity.[224]

We selected the following examples of titles of racist pornographic books and magazines from the report of the Attorney General's Commission on Pornography[225]: *Jewels of the Orient; Long Black Super Cock; Lusty Latin, Vanessa Del Rio; Mulatto Splits & Tits; Oriental Cock; Oriental Fetishes; Sexy Senoritas; Slut from Shanghai; Tan Tigress, A Cocksucking Slave; Black Nurse, White Cock; Black Tit & Body Torture; Black Whore; Brown Juicy Bitch; Dark & Dirty; Dominant Black Bitch; Geisha Girls; Guys Who Fuck Tight Black Pussy; Asian Suck Mistress; Asian Anal Girls; Black & Kinky; Black & White Fetish Exchange; Black Beaver Fever; Black Hot Honey; Japanese Sadist Dungeon; Jap Sadist's Virgin Captives; Raped by Arab Terrorists; Slant-Eyed Savages; Soviet Sadist's Slave; Virgin's Black Stud;* and *White Masters: Black Slave Girls.*

In pornography, scenes of black women slaves seducing white slave owners are shown, while in real life, the slave owners exploited the slaves. Andrea Dworkin cites the following examples of racist pornography.[226] One film called *Foxy Brown* features a woman chopping off a man's penis with a knife and presenting it to his girlfriend in a jar. When Foxy is bound and gang-raped, she rakes the rapists' eyes out with a coat hanger and ignites both white men with gasoline. She also slices a man up with an airplane propeller and blows a man's head off with a pistol. Another film is about an Indian "maiden" who runs into prejudice from both races when she has a love affair with a white man and about a white girl who is raped by Indian men. "Her initial fear turns into lust as she gets banged in the teepee."[227] Yet another is about parents who sell their Oriental daughters into sex slavery to be disciplined and abused by pimps and others. A film magazine contains an ad for "Japanese Girls" who are described as having been trained from childhood in the "art of pleasing men." According to the ad, they are exactly what men want for friendship, love, and marriage. In one pornographic story, a Mexican jail scene shows a "hot-blooded senorita" offering herself to a Mexican cop in order to have intercourse with her lover who is jailed. The Mexican male is portrayed as a brute, while the white male is shown as sensitive. Finally, a book features a black fashion model who is in love with a white man who molests little girls. Kelly, the model, is kidnaped, raped, and photographed for pornography. The abuse she suffers includes bondage, double-intercourse, and lesbian scenes—and she loves it all. A newspaper prints the pornographic photos, and her career is ruined. She returns to anonymity with her white man.

There is no doubt in our minds that these types of images attempt to foster racial hatred and violence toward persons of color in the United States and that they play a role in continuing racial and sexual inequality in our nation.

CONCLUSION

Believe it or not, we have not even touched on some special forms of pornography. A magazine account of a Halloween party describes a "dog and cat" having sex in "doggy fashion" while the "cat" performs oral sex on a man, a huge "hairy gorilla fucking a delicate, pale angel" with a penis that gives the appearance of being too big for her vagina, and a guy in a rat costume with his "whiskery snout" buried in a maid's vagina. A lovely naked woman gives Santa a "blowjob" in a poem titled "Santa's Christmas Present." There is a pregnancy genre of pornography that displays pregnant women being sexually exploited. Handicap porn features the following kinds of images:

A white deaf-mute girl with a 9-inch tongue services a group of "horny blacks."
A *Hustler* image shows a man's scrotum pushed against the ear of a retarded girl with semen squirting out the other ear. The text reads: "Good Sex with Retarded Girls—you can do anything you want cause who would believe a scrunched face retarded girl?"
A film involves a "sex-driven, mentally disturbed" girl with masturbation problems that a psychiatrist attempts to solve. She seduces the doctor.

In the "art" world, a sculpture of three boys in peering at a centerfold insults women. Drawings of women in bondage and mutilated are part of a college art exhibit. And a university special collections room features a photo display of nude women lying in pools of blood—apparently dead, often bound and gagged, some with knife wounds—accompanied by a stack of whole wheat pancakes. These photos are part of a boxed package called "The Incredible Case of the Stack O' Wheats Murders."

The images of pornography are many and varied, but the message is clear: Women are inhuman, lack intelligence, do not deserve equal treatment, live only for the sexual pleasure of men, and love to be abused, degraded, and humiliated sexually. In this process, men, to some extent, become dehumanized also and are portrayed as sadistic, unloving, and sexist. The images that exist in our society (whether pictures or words) influence and shape our thinking and culture. We suggest that the pornographic image has nothing of value to offer society and does, in fact, pose a variety of harms.

NOTES

1. Women Against Pornography, *Did You Know That . . .* (New York: Women Against Pornography, undated).
2. Citizens For Decency Through Law, *Legal Aspects* (Phoenix: Citizens for Decency Through Law, undated), 7.
3. Ibid.
4. Ibid., 9.
5. U.S. Department of Justice, Attorney General's

Commission on Pornography, *Final Report* (Washington, D.C.: U.S. Department of Justice, 1986), 1363 (hereafter cited as AGCOP).

6. Ibid.

7. Task Force on Prostitution and Pornography (Ed.), "Prostitution and Pornography: Major Industries in the U.S." *The Sex for Sale Industries*. (Madison, WI." Task Force on Prostitution and Pornography, 1985), 6. (Hereafter TOPP).

8. Ibid.

9. AGCOP, 1471–76.

10. Dan Allegretti, "AIDS Forcing Porn Shop Regulation," *Capital Times* (Madison, Wis.), 9 December 1986, 1.

11. "Current Statistics on the Pornography Industry, 1986," in TOPP 8, reprinted from *The National Anti-Pornography Civil Rights Organization Reporter* (Hereafter NAPCRO), September 1986.

12. AGCOP, 1394.

13. Ibid., 1388–89.

14. Ibid., 1387.

15. Ibid., 1368–69, 1481, 1391–93.

16. NAPCRO, 8.

17. AGCOP, 1366.

18. David T. Friendly, "This Isn't Shakespeare," *Newsweek* 18 March 1985, 62.

19. Kathleen Barry, *Female Sexual Slavery* (Englewood Cliffs, N.J.: Prentice-Hall, 1979), 84.

20. AGCOP, 1365–84.

21. Ibid., 1429–30.

22. Ibid., 78.

23. Women Against Pornography, *Did You Know That . . . .*

24. NAPCRO, 8.

25. Ibid., 8.

26. Women Against Pornography, *Did You Know That . . . .*

27. NAPCRO, 8.

28. Women Against Pornography, *Did You Know That . . . .*

29. Laura Lederer, "*Playboy* Isn't Playing: An Interview with Judith Bat-Ada," in *Take Back The Night: Women on Pornography*, ed. Laura Lederer (New York: Wm. Morrow & Co., 1980), 121.

30. Ibid., 1413–14.

31. Ibid., 1414.

32. Ibid., 1446.

33. Ibid., 1451–53.

34. Women Against Pornography, *Did You Know That . . . .*

35. NAPCRO, 8.

36. Women Against Pornography, *Did You Know That . . . .*

37. Morality in Media, Inc., *Report on the Billion Dollar Traffic in Pornography* (New York: Morality in Media, Inc., 1986), 5–6.

38. AGCOP, 1443–45.

39. Ibid., 1463–66.

40. Evelyn Radison, "Feminists Speak Out to the Pornography Commission," *Women Against Pornography Newsreport* 7 (Spring/Summer 1986): 4.

41. Ibid., 4.

42. "Why Porn Thrives," *Cedar Rapids Gazette*, 18 June 1986.

43. Harrison Donnelly, "Pornography: Setting New Limits," *Congressional Quarterly Editorial Research Report*, 16 May 1986, 349–68, 351.

44. "Post Poll Shows 'Gender Gap' on Pornography," *Women Against Pornography Newsreport* 7 (Spring/Summer 1986): 2.

45. "A Newsweek Poll: Mixed Feelings On Pornography," *Newsweek*, 18 March 1985, 7.

46. Canada, Minister of Supply & Services, *Pornography and Prostitution in Canada: Report of the Special Committee on Pornography and Prostitution*, vol. 1 (Ottawa, 1985), 90–92 (hereafter cited as Fraser committee).

47. Ibid.

48. Ibid., 104–06.

49. "Americans Want Obscenity Laws Enforced," *NFD Journal* 10 (August 1986): 15.

50. "Study Finds Children Consuming Pornography," *NFD Journal* 11(2) (February 1987): 13–14.

51. Ibid., 12.

52. "Did You Know? Some Facts about Pornography and the Victories Being Won Against It," *Bible Advocate*, January 1985, 8.

53. AGCOP, 42–44.

54. David Alexander Scott, *Pornography: Its Effects on the Family, Community and Culture* (Washington, D.C.: The Free Congress Foundation, 1985), 10–12.

55. Ibid.

56. Barry, *Female Sexual Slavery*, 175.

57. Ibid., 174–178.

58. Don Smith, "Sexual Aggression in American Pornography: The Stereotype of Rape." Paper presented at the annual meeting of the American Sociological Association, New York City, 1976; cited in Lederer, *Take Back the Night*, 213–214.

59. Ibid., 214.

60. Park Elliott Dietz and Alan E. Sears, "Pornography and Obscenity Sold in 'Adult Bookstores': A Survey of 5,132 Books, Magazines, and Films in Four American Cities," *University of Michigan Journal of Law Reform*, 21 (Fall 1987 and Winter 1988): 46.

61. Beverly LaBelle, "The Propaganda of Misogyny," in *Take Back the Night: Women on Pornography*, ed. Laura Lederer (New York: Wm. Morrow & Co., 1980), 174–78.

62. Ibid., 175.

63. Ibid., 176–78.

64. Barbara Renchkowsky Ashley and David Ashley, "Sex as Violence: The Body Against Intimacy," *International Journal of Women's Studies* September-October, 1984, 7, no. 4 ( ):, 352–71.

65. Ibid., 359.

66. AGCOP, 95–96.

67. Susan Brownmiller, *Against Our Will: Men, Women, and Rape* (New York: Simon & Schuster, 1975), 394.

68. Andrea Dworkin, *Pornography: Men Possessing Women* (New York: G.P. Putnam's Sons, 1981), 128.
69. Joseph W. Slade, and Judith Yaross Lee "Violence in the Hard-Core Pornographic Film: A Historical Survey," *Journal of Communication* 34 (Summer 1984) 34:148–163.
70. Ibid., 8.
71. Ibid., 9.
72. Ibid., 6.
73. Park Elliott Dietz and Barbara Evans, "Pornographic Imagery and Prevalence of Paraphilia," *American Journal of Psychiatry* 139 (November 1982): 1493–95.
74. Don D. Smith, "The Social Content of Pornography," *Journal of Communication* 26 (Winter 1976), 16–24.
75. Ibid., 21.
76. Harold Nawy, "In Pursuit of Happiness?" Consumers of Erotica in San Francisco," *Journal of Social Issues* 24, no. 3 (1973): 147–61.
77. John W. Drakeford and Jack Hamm, *Pornography: The Sexual Mirage* (Nashville: Thomas Nelson, Inc., 1973), 28–48, 135–52.
78. Ibid., 149.
79. Ibid., 150, 152.
80. Ibid., 38.
81. Ibid., 47, 48.
82. Ronald M. Holmes, *The Sex Offender and the Criminal Justice System* (Springfield, Ill., Charles C. Thomas, 1983), 105–20.
83. Lederer, "*Playboy Isn't Playing*," 124–25.
84. Ibid.
85. Ibid., 127.
86. Sarah J. McCarthy, "Pornography, Rape, and the Cult of Macho," *The Humanist*, September/October 1980, 15–16.
87. AGCOP, 74–76.
88. Teresa Hommel, "Images of Women in Pornography and Media," *New York University Review of Law and Social Change* 8, no. 2 (1978—79): 207–15.
89. Keith E. Davis and George N. Braucht, "Exposure to Pornography, Character, and Sexual Deviance: A Retrospective Survey," in *Technical Report of the Commission on Obscenity and Pornography* vol. 7, (Washington, D.C.: U.S. GPO, 1971), 175–76.
90. Susan Griffin, *"Pornography and Silence: Culture's Revenge Against Nature* (New York: Harper & Row, 1981).
91. Ibid., 24.
92. Ibid., 26, 28, 33.
93. Ibid., 36, 38, 39, 47–49.
94. Ibid., 47.
95. Ibid., 84.
96. Ibid., 88.
97. Ibid., 88–101.
98. Ibid., 118–214.
99. Ibid., 218–231.
100. American Psychiatric Association, *Diagnostic and Statistical Manual of Mental Disorders III* (Washington, D.C.: American Psychiatric Association, 1980), 261–85.
101. Ibid., 266.
102. Breck J. Lebegue, "Paraphilias in Pornography: A Study of Perversions Inherent in Title," *Australian Journal of Sex, Marriage & Family* 6, no. 1: 33–36.
103. Dworkin, *Pornography: Men Possessing Women*, 72, 74, 76–78.
104. Ibid., 92.
105. Ibid., 70–71.
106. Ibid., 92–100.
107. Quoted in David Scott, ed., *Symposium on Media Violence and Pornography: Proceedings and Resource Book* (Toronto: Media Action Group, Inc., 1984), 64–65.
108. Ibid.
109. "Sweet Captive," *Cinema X* 2, no. 3.
110. "Vista Vally P.T.A.," *Video X*, December/January 1981.
111. "Little Orphan Dusty," *Hustler*, February 1979.
112. "The Kinky Ladies of Bourban Street," *High Society*, June 1977.
113. "Sweet Dreams, Susan," *Hooker*, November 1980.
114. "Slaves of Pleasure," *Hustler*, May 1986; 1, no. 6(1980).
115. Scott, *Symposium on Media Violence and Pornography*, 82.
116. AGCOP, 467.
117. Scott, *Symposium on Media Violence and Pornography*, 137.
118. Beverly Labelle, "Snuff—The Ultimate in Woman-Hating," in *Take Back the Night: Women on Pornography*, ed. Laura Lederer (New York: Wm. Morrow & Co., 1980), 272–73.
119. Ibid., 273.
120. Ibid., 274.
121. Ibid., 275–78.
122. AGCOP, 1400–04.
123. Ibid., 1402.
124. David Alexander Scott, *Pornography: Its Effect on the Family, Community and Culture*, 11.
125. Dietz and Evans, "Pornographic Imagery."
126. Women Against Pornography, *Why Women Against Pornography Is Demonstrating Against Playboy* (New York: Women Against Pornography,).
127. Ibid.
128. Ibid.
129. Ibid.
130. Laura Lederer, "Introduction," in *Take Back the Night: Women on Pornography*, ed. Laura Lederer (New York: Wm. Morrow & Co., 1980), 17.
131. The Preying Mantis Women's Brigade, "A Celebration of First Amendment Rights." (Oshkosh, Wisc.: The Preying Mantis Women's Brigade, March 8, 1981), 1.
132. AGCOP, 381–85.
133. Ibid.
134. Paul Miller. "The Miller Report: A Survey of Swingers in America Today," *Gallery* 12 (November 1984): 59–75.
135. Ibid., 2.
136. Ibid.
137. Ibid., 2–3.

138. Ibid., 3.
139. Citizens for Decency through Law, *Dial-a-Porn and Children* (Phoenix: Citizens for Decency Through Law, 1986).
140. Jacquelyn Mitchard, " 'Custer' Game Isn't Funny; It's Sadistic," *Capital Times* (Madison, Wisc.), 30 October 1982.
141. "The Sex Video Games Are Everywhere, Nationwide-A Report From The West Coast." *Media Report to Women* 11 (January/February 1982): 8.
142. Park Elliott Dietz, Bruce Harry, and Robert R. Hazelwood, "Detective Magazines: Pornography for the Sexual Sadist?" *Journal of Forensic Sciences* (January 1968): 197–211.
143. Herbert A. Otto, "Sex and Violence on the American Newsstand," *Journalism Quarterly* 40 (Winter 1963): 19–26.
144. Dietz, Harry, and Hazelwood, "Detective Magazines," 199.
145. Ibid.
146. Ibid., 200.
147. Ibid., 201.
148. Ibid., 202–09.
149. Arthur Kaplan, "Sex-Crime That Cleaned Up a City," *Official Police Detective*, May 1981, 7.
150. C. Cleveland, "Too Many Rapes to Count," *Front Page Detective*, June 1980, 30.
151. Stafford Mann, "Even Two Wives Couldn't Satisfy His Lust," *Inside Detective*, 58 (January 1980): 21.
152. Terry Ecker, "Who Butchered Erlene and Left Her in the Lonely Field?" *Inside Detective*, 58 (January 1980): 58.
153. *Symposium on Media Violence and Pornography: Proceedings and Resource Book,* ed. David Scott (Toronto: Media Action Group, Inc., 1984), 56.
154. Ibid.
155. Ibid., 57, 58.
156. Tipper Gore, speech at the Morality in Media, Inc., National Conference on Pornography, St. Louis, June 1986; audiotape. See also Tipper Gore, *Raising PG Kids in an X-Rated Society* (New York: Bantam Books, 1988). For more information on rock artists and lyrics, contact Gore at the Parents Music Resource Center, 1500 Arlington Blvd., Arlington, Virginia 20009; (703) 527-9466.
157. Gore, audiotape.
158. Bobby Dee, speech at the Morality in Media, Inc, National Conference on Pornography, St. Louis, June 1986; audiotape. For more information on rock artists and lyrics, contact Dee at Teen Vision, P.O. Box 4505, Pittsburgh, Pennsylvania 15205.
159. Mary Maynard, "The Naked Truth," *Equal Times*, May 13, 1979, 10.
160. Ann Baker, "Hard-sell or Hard-core?: Critics Say Ads Use Pornographic Themes," *St. Paul Pioneer Dispatch*, 16 October 1983.
161. Alice E. Courtney and Sarah Wernick Lockeretz, "A Woman's Place: An Analysis of the Roles Portrayed by Women in Magazine Advertisements, *Journal of Marketing Research* 3 (February 1971): 92–95.
162. Baker, "Hard-sell or Hard-core?"
163. Ibid.
164. Ibid.
165. Ibid.
166. Ibid.
167. Ibid.
168. Ibid.
169. Slade and Lee, "Violence in the Hard-Core Pornographic Films," 153.
170. "A Few Publishers Distribute Hundreds of Millions of Books Showing Men Superior," *Media Report to Women* 11 (March/April 1983): 12.
171. Ibid.
172. Ibid.
173. "Scholastic Publisher Used Its School Channels to Create Demand for Teen Romances, and Sold 1,800,000 in 1 Year." *Media Report to Women* 11 (September-October 1983): 9: Teaching Girls to Be Dependent on Men," *Media Report to Women* 11 (March-April 1983): 12.
174. Ann Barr Snitow, "Mass Market Romance: Pornography for Women Is Different," in *Powers of Desire*, ed. Ann Barr Snitow, (New York: Monthly Review Press, 1983), 248.
175. Betty Wein, "The Chilling Effects of Pornography" (Paper presented at the Seventh World Media Conference, Tokyo, November 1984), 1–39.
176. Ibid., 2.
177. Ibid., 25.
178. Ibid., 27.
179. Ibid., 28.
180. Ibid., 28–29.
181. Ibid., 29.
182. Ibid., 30.
183. Ibid., 25.
184. Ibid., 26.
185. Ibid.
186. Wein, Letter to Authors, 6 May, 1987.
187. Ibid.
188. *Pornography: The Longford Report* (London: Coronet Books, Hodder Paperback, Ltd., 1972), 157.
189. Ibid., 89–90.
190. Ibid., 46–48.
191. Marc Hillel and Clarissa Henry, *Of Pure Blood*, trans. Eric Mossbacher (New York: McGraw-Hill Book Co., 1976), 34.
192. Ibid.
193. Dorchen Leidholdt, "Where Pornography Meets Fascism," *WIN*, 15 March 1983, 18–22.
194. Ibid., 18.
195. Ibid., 21.
196. Irene Diamond, "Pornography and Regression: A Reconsideration of 'Who' and 'What'," in *Take Back the Night*, ed. Laura Lederer, 202.
197. Griffin, *Pornography and Silence*, 157–199.
198. Ibid., 156.

199. Ibid., 159.
200. Ibid.
201. Ibid., 160.
202. Hillel and Henry, *Of Pure Blood*, 34.
203. Ibid., 189.
204. Ibid., 190.
205. Dworkin, *Pornography: Men Possessing Women*, 138–43.
206. AGCOP, 1555, 1561.
207. Liedholdt, "Where Pornography Meets Fascism," 3.
208. *Fascist Femmes* 4, no. 4 (1979).
209. Judith Bat-Ada, "Porn in the Promised Land, *Lilith*, Fall 1983, 9–14.
210. David M. Szonyi, "Lilith Magazine Charges: Pornography Contributes to Violence Against Women in Israel," *Long Island Jewish World*, 2–8 March 1984, cover, 8, 9.
211. Bat-Ada, "Porn in the Promised Land", 11.
212. Ibid.
213. Ibid., 12.
214. Ibid., 13.
215. Tracey A. Gardner, "Racism in Pornography and the Women's Movement," in *Take Back the Night: Women on Pornography*, ed. Laura Lederer (New York: Wm. Morrow & Co., 1980), 105–14.
216. Ibid., 105–14.
217. Ibid., 111.
218. Ibid., 113.
219. Luisah Teish, "A Quiet Subversion," in *Take Back the Night: Women on Pornography*, ed. Laura Lederer (New York: Wm. Morrow & Co., 1980), 117.
220. Van F. White, "Pornography and Pride," *Essence*, September 1984, 186.
221. Alice Walker, "When Women Confront Porn at Home," *Ms.*, February 1980, 7.
222. Ibid., 69.
223. Ibid., 70.
224. Ibid., 75.
225. AGCOP, 1506, 1508, 1509, 1513, 1517, 1522, 1525, 1526, 1534, 1538, 1543.
226. Dworkin, *Pornography: Men Possessing Women*, 210–17.
227. *Adam Film World*, February, 1976, 9–10; *Velvet*, November 1979.

3 THE NATURE OF THE PORNOGRAPHY INDUSTRY

Distribution of pornography in the United States is controlled by organized crime. This fact is detailed in the two lengthy excerpts that make up most of this chapter.

A definition of what we mean by organized crime is appropriate here. We have adopted the definitions given by H. Robert Showers, then assistant U.S. attorney for the Eastern District of North Carolina, in his statement to the Attorney General's Commission on Pornography on January 22, 1986:

> Organized crime is a self-perpetuating, continuing criminal conspiracy for power and profit using fear and corruption seeking immunity from the law. The term is divided into Class I traditional organized crime and racketeering groups as the La Cosa Nostra, Mafia Syndicate and closely controlled and large allied organizations like Reuben Sturman's Sovereign News Empire in pornography. Class II Organized Crime is also a criminal syndicate consisting of groups operating in criminal cartels across the nation, banded together which corresponds to a corporation with a board of directors at the top to settle problems such as territorial disputes and to enforce discipline. However, Class II involves non-traditional LCN organizations sometimes more on a regional basis controlling narcotics smuggling, large scale white collar frauds, pornography distribution like the DIXIE Mafia in drugs and gambling and the

Thevis or Atkinson organization controlling pornography.[1]

Thus, as David Alexander Scott points out in the second excerpt,

> professional pornographers are not, as some civil libertarians often argue, the D.H. Lawrences, Henry Millers and Allen Ginsbergs of the world. They are for the most part highly organized, professional criminals who derive their power and perpetuity from two principal sources: fear generated through violence and threat of violence, and control over corrupted public officials and political leaders.

Those seeking further details about specific individuals and organizations involved in the pornography industry in the United States should refer to pages 1072–1238 of the Attorney General's Commission on Pornography's *Final Report*. It is worth noting, as was pointed out in the report, that the same criminal elements involved in the pornography industry are involved in other criminal activities such as murder, arson, extortion, physical violence, damage to property, prostitution, narcotics distribution, money laundering and tax evasion, copyright violations, fraud, child pornography, illegal gambling, and possession, transfer, and sale of machine guns and silencers.

EXCERPT FROM THE FINAL REPORT OF THE ATTORNEY GENERAL'S COMMISSION ON PORNOGRAPHY*

[Please note that spellings appear as in the original. Footnotes, however, have been renumbered for the convenience of the reader.]

I. PREFACE

The Commission has relied heavily on information and intelligence provided by experienced federal, state, and local law enforcement authorities regarding

---

*U.S. Department of Justice, Attorney General's Commission on Pornography, *Final Report* (Washington, D.C.: U.S. Department of Justice, 1986), 1039–71.

the involvement of organized crime in the pornography industry. This first hand knowledge is based upon years of investigative experience in the highly complex and covert area of organized crime. Many of these law enforcement authorities testified before the Commission on January 21–22, 1986, in New York City, at a hearing devoted primarily to matters relating to organized crime. The Commission has also used investigative reports prepared by the United States Department of Justice, the office of the Attorney General of California, the Middle Atlantic–Great Lakes Organized Crime Law Enforcement Network (MAGLOCLEN), the Pennsylvania Crime Commission, the Washington, D.C., Metropolitan Police Department and others. Reliance on the investigative reports and the experience of these law enforcement authorities was necessary because the Commission operated without the authority to subpoena witnesses or compel their testimony regarding this sensitive area of inquiry.

II. INTRODUCTION

Organized crime involvement in the pornography industry has been described by law enforcement officers and by organized crime operatives themselves. A retired veteran Federal Bureau of Investigation agent said of traditional[1] organized crime members, "you cannot be in the field and distribute pornography without their consent. . . ."[2] He added that the pornography trade is attractive to organized crime because "[i]t's a fast way of making a buck."[3] Aladena Fratianno whose involvement in La Cosa Nostra [LCN] dates back to the late 1940's has reached the same conclusion.[4] In an interview with a Commission investigator, Fratianno described the connection as he knew it to be in the 1970's as follows:

> Interviewer: Is it possible for any person to become a major distributor of pornography in the United States without becoming involved in organized crime?
> Fratianno: I doubt it. I doubt it.
> Interviewer: Okay, why do you doubt it?
> Fratianno: Well, because there's so much involved and I don't think they would let them.
> Interviewer: Okay, so if someone tried to operate without an involvement
> Fratianno: Well, somebody would report 'em, they'd say look it, he's taking my business.

> Interviewer: . . . what would they do? Shut them down, or take them over?
> Fratianno: Well, they would do something. I really couldn't answer that. You know, they would do something. They might go so far as killing them, who knows.[5]

Another individual who was the owner and operator of an "adult" bookstore and spent many years in the pornography business described his experience in dealing with organized crime:

> Interviewer: . . . If the mob says, "I do not want this, boy."
> Subject: You don't sell it. Even if they don't even talk to you. You're not going to sell it nowhere. If you go to the store on 14th street and put it in there, they're gonna bust his ass. Or they're gonna break your legs when you start going through them. There was a man who went from New York City . . . went into Atlanta. Had films to sell . . . They found him at the airport, with a $5,000 Rolex watch on and about eight grand in his pocket, and four rolls of film in his hands, with his head blown up in the trunk of his car. Nobody robbed him, nobody took a dime off him. They didn't even take the film. But he was at the airport with a New York ticket shoved in his coat pocket. Don't come down from New York selling unless you've been sent down.[6]

III. ORGANIZED CRIME INVOLVEMENT IN PORNOGRAPHY

The 1970 President's Commission on Obscenity and Pornography was unable to draw conclusions regarding the role of organized crime in the distribution of obscene and pornographic materials. The 1970 Commission on Obscenity and Pornography found:

Although many persons have alleged that organized crime works hand-in-glove with the distributors of adult materials, there is at present no concrete evidence to support these statements.

The hypothesis that organized criminal elements either control or are "moving in" on the distribution of sexually oriented materials will doubtless continue to be speculated upon. The panel finds that there is insufficient evidence at present to warrant any conclusion in this regard.[7]

There is some question about how the earlier Commission reached this conclusion.[8] It is clear that the role of traditional organized crime in the pornography trade has increased substantially since the 1970 report was issued. Until 1970, only one LCN family, the Columbo organization, was known to have been involved significantly in the pornography business.[9]

The Attorney General's Commission on Pornography has received reports from law enforcement officials, prosecutors, and legislators describing the substantial role which organized crime, both in traditional (LCN) and non-traditional forms, plays in the pornography business in the United States today.[10]

In addition to attorneys, many other professional persons assist organized crime families and their associates in the pornography business. Realtors handle land transactions knowing the ultimate purpose of the transaction is to facilitate the sale of obscene material.[11] Landlords rent property to organized crime families knowing they will be used to warehouse obscene material or to sell, produce, distribute, or display obscene merchandise.[12] Bankers process accounts and provide all manner of banking services (including the failure to report currency transactions as required by Title 31 United States Code.) Printers and film processors develop the visual images taken by pornographers and turn them into finished products for sale or reproduction. Transportation companies and interstate carriers show no discretion in shipping obscene materials to increase organized crime family profits. Academics are paid to act as experts on behalf of organized crime members and associates who are brought to trial and challenged in public debates. Public figures including prosecutors, judges, city, county and state officials, zoning board members, and health department officials may be subjected to monetary and political influence. These people sometimes may ignore the organized criminal activity or impose minimal sanctions when punishment is unavoidable.

Following are highlights of reports provided to this Commission relating to traditional organized crime involvement in and control of the pornography industry.

One report came from a group of law enforcement officers, coordinated through the Investigative Serv-ices Division of the Washington, D.C., Metropolitan Police Department, which undertook a study in 1978 to determine the extent of organized crime involvement in the pornography industry.[13] One reason for the study was, "(knowledge) that organized crime generally involves itself in situations where the gain far outreaches the risk. The pornography industry fits this description."[14] "An initial probe determined that law enforcement could document Organized Crime control in certain geographic areas. However, it did not appear in 1977 that *any* single law enforcement body *was in possession of documentation* reflecting the situation on a national level".[15] (emphasis added)

The project participants determined that traditional organized crime was substantially involved in and did essentially control much of the major pornography distribution in the United States during the years 1977 and 1978. The group further concluded that the combination of the large amounts of money involved, the incredibly low priority obscenity enforcement had within police departments and prosecutors' offices in an area where manpower intensive investigations were essential for success, and the imposition of minimal fines and no jail time upon random convictions resulted in a low risk and high profit endeavor for organized crime figures who became involved in pornography.[16] During its seventy-eight year history, the Federal Bureau of Investigation (FBI) has been engaged periodically in investigation of persons and organizations who violate the federal obscenity laws. Though the FBI has not recently been involved in many large scale obscenity related investigations,[17] Federal Bureau of Investigation director, William H. Webster, along with present and former special agents of the FBI have provided current information about the pornography industry.[18] In the late 1970s' the FBI prepared a report detailing the extent of organized crime involvement in pornography. In preparing that report, the Bureau conducted a survey of the fifty-nine FBI field offices.[19] Based on the survey and other sources, FBI intelligence analysts concluded:

> Information obtained (during the course of the enclosed survey) points out the vast control of the multi-million dollar pornography business in the United States by a few individuals with direct connections with what is commonly known as the organized crime establishment in the United States, specifically, La Cosa Nostra. . . . Information received from sources of this Bureau indicates that pornography is (a major) income maker for La Cosa Nostra in the United States

behind gambling and narcotics. Although La Cosa Nostra does not physically oversee the day-to-day workings of the majority of pornography business in the United States, it is apparent they have "agreements" with those involved in the pornography business in allowing these people to operate independently by paying off members of organized crime for the privilege of being allowed to operate in certain geographical areas.[20]

In 1985, at the request of the Attorney General's Commission on Pornography, Director Webster conducted a brief survey of the fifty-nine FBI field offices concerning their knowledge of involvement of traditional organized crime in pornography. Director Webster advised this Commission, "About three quarters of those offices indicated that they have no verifiable information that organized crime was involved either directly or through extortion in the manufactures or distribution of pornography. Several offices did, however, report some involvement by members and associates of organized crime."[21]

The FBI reported that on April 30, 1981, Joseph Palladino, a known dealer in pornography in Boston and Worcester, Massachusetts, met with Gennaro J. Angiulo in Boston.[22] Angiulo is the underboss of the New England Organized Crime Family.[23] Palladino complained that one Carlo Mastrototaro was opening an adult bookstore in the Worcester area to compete with the one jointly owned by Pallidino and Mastrototaro. Palladino could not understand why the New York family had authorized Mastrototaro to operate a competing pornography business. Prior to this, Palladino said he had considered Robert DiBernardo of the New York family to be his "compare". In response, Angiulo became angry because Palladino had first sought an explanation from DeBernardo. Angiulo said this prevented him from contacting DeBernardo's boss in New York and he would now have to deal with Sam Cufari, capo of the Genovese family in Massachusetts.[24]

One former FBI agent told the Commission:

In my opinion, based upon twenty-three years of experience in pornography and obscenity investigations and study, it is practically impossible to be in the retail end of the pornography industry (today) without dealing in some fashion with organized crime either the mafia or some other facet of non-mafia never-the-less highly organized crime.[25]

The Chicago Police Department has been involved in the investigation of organized crime families who are engaged in the distribution of pornography in the *Midwest*.[26] Thomas Bohling of the Chicago Police Department Organized Crime Division, Vice Control Section reported, ". . . it is the belief of state, federal, and local law enforcement that the pornography industry is controlled by organized crime families. If they do not own the business outright, they most certainly extract street tax from independent smut *peddlers*."[27]

An overwhelming majority of obscene and pornographic materials are produced in the Los Angeles, California, area.[28] Organized crime families from Chicago, New York, New Jersey, and Florida are openly controlling and directing the major pornography operations in Los Angeles.[29] According to Chief Daryl F. Gates of the Los Angeles Police Department, "Organized crime infiltrated the pornography industry in Los Angeles in 1969 due to its lucrative financial benefits. By 1975, organized crime controlled eighty percent of the industry and it is estimated that this figure is between eighty-five to ninety percent today."[30]

An investigative report submitted to the California Legislature by the Attorney General of California discussed organized crime infiltration into the pornography industry:

In the early 1970's . . . four organized crime groups moved in on pornography operations in California. They met relatively little resistance because the weak-structured organized crime group of Southern California lacked the necessary strength to deter the infiltration of organized crime from the East.

Organized crime figures first focused on production and retail operations in California. In this effort, they used the influence of their established national distribution network and effectively resorted to illegal and unfair business tactics. The newly arrived organized crime groups formed film duplication companies which illegally duplicated the films of independent producers and displayed them at nationwide organized crime controlled theaters. Faced with continued piracy and lost of profits, many legitimate producers were forced to deal with organized crime controlled distribution companies and film processing labs.

After gaining control or ownership of many California wholesale and retail companies, organized crime forced other independent retailers out of business through price manipulation. Wholesale prices to independent retailers were raised while prices to organized crime controlled outlets were lowered. Independents were undersold by organized crime controlled outlets until lost profits forced them out of business. Many competitors were bought out which allowed the subsequent raising of prices in other parts of the market. Some dealers that openly opposed this takeover were silenced by means of extortion and arson.[31]

In 1984, California Attorney General John Van De Kamp reported that the arrival of home video cassette recorders on the market in 1979 was accompanied by a growing demand for adult video tapes.[32] California pornographers, linked to the Gambino, DeCavalcante, Luchese and Columbo organized crime families entered this market through companies that produce, duplicate, distribute and sell adult video tapes.[33]

Law enforcement agents have described the control of organized crime families in the pornography industry. Organized crime figures and associates are involved in the commerce essential to the pornography business through ownership of the distribution sources of the material. The 1970 Commission on Obscenity and Pornography reported ". . . crime syndicate members reported in interviews that it was not worthwhile for the syndicate to enter the business, primarily because there was no real economic inducement."[34] In 1986, there are tremendous profits in the pornography industry. These profits are of the type that can be easily hidden from the Internal Revenue Service, because of the cash transactions and the policy of no cash receipts for merchandise.[35]

Law enforcement officials have described large profit margins in the pornography business today.[36] Magazines which cost fifty cents to produce wholesale for five dollars and the retail price is ten dollars or more.[37] A fifty minute eight millimeter film wholesales for three dollars and retails for twenty dollars.[38] Video cassette tapes which wholesale for fifteen dollars often retail for eighty to ninety-five dollars.[39]

The well-known pornographic film "Deep Throat" was produced by the Periano brothers of the Columbo organized crime family for $25,000 and is reliably estimated to have grossed fifty million dollars as of 1982.[40] The film was " . . . the biggest money maker of any film to that time and possibly since, in the state of Florida."[41]

Joseph, Anthony, and Louis Periano all became millionaires as a result of "Deep Throat."[42] They used profits from the film to build a vast financial empire in the 1970s that included ownership of garment companies in New York and Miami, investment companies, a sixty-five-foot yacht in the Bahamas, "adults only" pornographic theaters in Los Angeles, and record and music publishing companies on both the east and west coasts.[43] From 1973 to 1976, their corporate empire included Bryanston Distributors, Inc., a motion picture company that earned twenty million dollars in its first year of operation.[44] The Perianos also used profits from "Deep Throat" to finance drug smuggling operations in the Caribbean.[45]

Aladena Fratianno, a.k.a., Jimmy Fratianno, a made member of a La Cosa Nostra organized crime family and a former Capo and later acting boss of the Los Angeles crime family, told this Commission that large profits have kept organized crime heavily involved in the obscenity industry.[46] Fratianno described this involvement to a Commission investigator as follows:

> Interviewer: Could you describe the nature and type of involvement organized crime would have in the pornography industry when you were active in organized crime?
>
> Fratianno: Well, it's very, very big. . . . I'd say, 95 percent of the families are involved in one way or another in pornography. . . . It's too big. They just won't let it go.
>
> Interviewer: Okay, does organized crime reap a lot of money from their involvement in pornographic industry?
>
> Fratianno: Absolutely. Absolutely.[47]

The Attorney General's Commission on Pornography concludes that organized crime in its traditional LCN forms and in other forms exerts substantial influence and control over the obscenity industry. Though a number of significant producers and distributors are not members of LCN families, all major producers and distributors of obscene material are highly organized and carry out illegal activities with a great deal of sophistication.[48]

This influence and control has increased since the report of the 1970 Commission on Obscenity and Pornography and is particularly evident in the distribution of pornographic materials.[49] Organized crime elements have found that the large financial gains to be reaped from pornography far outweigh the risks associated with the trade.

IV. RELATED CRIMES AND ACTIVITIES

In addition to the myriad of other harms and antisocial effects brought about by obscenity[50] there is a link between traditional organized crime group involvement in the obscenity business and many other types of criminal activity. Physical violence, injury, prostitution and other forms of sexual abuse are so interlinked in many cases as to be almost inseparable except according to statutory definitions. Among the crimes known to be interlinked with the pornography industry are:

(1) *Murder*—One of the largest pornographers in the United States during the 1970's was Michael George Thevis who headed Peachtree News in Atlanta, Georgia, and 106 other corporations.[51] In October, 1979 Thevis was convicted in the United States District Court for the Northern District of Georgia for Racketeer Influenced and Corrupt Organizations Act (RICO) violations including murder, arson, and extortion.[52]

A leading figure in the national distribution of the film "Deep Throat", Robert DeSalvo, has been missing since January, 1976 and is presumed to have been murdered.[53] DeSalvo provided evidence on behalf of the United States in the Periano trial arising from the "Deep Throat" film distribution.[54]

During the late 1970s a number of persons involved in the pornography business were murdered in what were believed by law enforcement agents to be pornography turf wars.[55] The son of Joseph Periano, one of the producers of "Deep Throat" along with an innocent woman, was murdered "gangland style".[56]

Immediately prior to this Commission's hearing in Chicago, Illinois, in July, 1985, Patsy Ricciardi owner of the Admiral Theater there, was found murdered. Chicago Police believe his murder was related to his dealings in the pornography business.[57]

(2) *Physical violence damage to property*—The damage and injuries range from those sustained by performers[58] forced to engage in physically harmful acts which can often result in permanent injury,[59] to damage to property,[60] "knee-breaking"[61] and arson.[62]

A veteran FBI agent told the Commission "Over the years there has been heavy violence associated with the pornography industry. Some of the current well-known names in the industry have reported threats against them or physical brutality."[63]

A bookstore operator, associated with members of organized crime families, described the "discipline" within the pornography industry for those who choose to disobey rules regarding pricing, territory and other matters.[64] He said, " . . . Bonjay a year and half ago, took one of the guys held him by his arms up against the wall in the alley, and it's common knowledge, the car ran into him, with the front bumper up against the wall and shattered his knees. That's a pretty good discipline."[65] This same witness also reported bombs being thrown into stores that

were not complying with general price agreements or failed to pay a street tax to organized crime families.[66]

(3) *Prostitution and other sexual abuse*—"'Prostitution is the foundation upon which pornography is built. . . . Pornography cannot exist without prostitution. . . . It is impossible to separate pornography from prostitution. The acts are identical except in pornography there is a permanent record of the woman's abuse."[67]

It is estimated that there are between 400,000 and 500,000 adult women who have been used in prostitution in America.[68] A recent study found that the average age of the working prostitute was twenty-two; the average age a woman started working as a prostitute was seventeen; sixty-three percent of the prostitutes had run away from home; eighty percent were victims of sexual abuse; eighty percent had pimps; and eighty-three percent had no savings or other financial resources.[69] These women, who have been subject to every form of rape, sexual assault, and battery, and whose lives are totally controlled by their pimps, are used and abused by pornographers for the creation of their wares.[70] It is impossible for most sexually explicit books, magazines, or films to be produced without acts of prostitution.[71]

Michael Joseph Glitta one of the two major pornography distributors in Chicago, and a lieutenant in the Accardo organized crime family, controlled a "strip joint" where numerous persons have been arrested for prostitution related offenses.[72] Pornographer Martin Hodas was identified by his former bodyguard as the one-time owner of a massage parlor and prostitution empire in the northeast.

(4) *Narcotics distribution* Narcotics are often distributed to performers who appear in pornographic materials to lower their inhibitions and to create a dependency.[73] Profits earned by organized crime from pornography sales have been used to finance drug smuggling.[74]

Joseph Periano, a soldier in the Columbo organized crime family, invested proceeds from the movie "Deep Throat" in drug smuggling. New York State Senator Christopher Mega, Chairman of the New York Organized Crime Commission, said, "Few have imagined that the profits of "Deep Throat" may have been part of the capital invested in the development of Norman's Cay into the major drug smuggling base north of the Panama Canal."[75]

Local police also report that "narcotic transactions are present in these deteriorating neighborhoods (where "adult bookstores" locate) and go hand-in-hand with the rampant criminal activity in those areas."[76]

(5) *Money laundering and tax violations*—The na-

ture of the pornography business provides inviting opportunities for skimming on[77] every level. There is often dishonesty among producers, wholesalers, distributors, retailers and others who attempt to cheat each other.[78] The often "cash only" business creates immense opportunities to launder money received from other organized crime activity.

Bookstores which primarily sell sexually explicit material have a consistent sales format throughout the United States.[79] Generally there are two separate operations for accounting purposes, loosely identified as "frontroom" and "backroom" operations.[80] The frontroom operation generally consists of a sales area for paperback books, magazines, rubber goods, lotions, stimulants and other materials.[81] The front room operations profits are generally used to pay for rent, utilities, materials, and employee wages.[82] The back room operations consist of peep machines which are coin operated and produce substantial income that is usually not reported as taxable income.[83] A local police officer noted, "The backroom operation usually takes in twice the amount as the frontroom operation."[84] A bookstore operator and associate of known organized crime family members, reported to this Commission that such "skimming" commonly occurs with video cassette rentals and magazines as well as the peep machine coin boxes.[85]

Organized crime associate Martin Hodas, who was convicted in federal court, Buffalo, New York, in 1985 for obscenity violations has been heavily involved in peep machines.[86]

Michael Thevis, once a major distributor of pornography in the South, told a meeting of organized crime family members and associates that he owned ninety percent of the movie viewmatic machines in the United States. Thevis was interrupted by Robert DiBernardo, a person alleged to be a member of the Gambino (and/or DeCalvalcante)[87] organized crime family, who reminded him that though he might have "proprietary rights" the machines were owned by "the family."[88]

The idea of converting run down theatres in the Midwest into pornographic adult movie houses to launder cash from other illegal rackets was the brain child of Chicago organized crime figure Patsy Riccardi who was murdered in July, 1985.[89]

Myron and Michael Wisotsky were convicted in the United States District Court for the Southern District of Florida in late 1985, for tax evasion which arose from skimming activities at their sexually oriented book-stores.[90]

A bookstore operator told the Commission:

Subject: 80 percent of the skimming goes on in coin boxes.

Interviewer: Right, how does that happen?

Subject: Because who can tell how many customers come in today, and drop how many quarters, in how many machines. Alright?

Subject: I had a machine. I'm running a hundred stores. I'm doing $1,200 to $1,600 a day in quarters (per store). I'm doing maybe three hundred to five hundred dollars a day in cassette rentals, club memberships . . . if you pay $69.95 per year membership then you also charge $3.95 a day for the rental of each film, right, okay, I'm doing maybe $350 a day in magazines and pocketbook sales. And at the time maybe five or ten rolls or film a day comes to maybe one hundred or five hundred dollars. So we're talking three thousands dollars a day roughly. Okay. Your magazines and your films and pocketbooks and your straightline pocketbooks. . . . It pays your rent, electric, gas, pays your overhead. If I don't something's happening wrong. Plus, now with the videos coming in, the video rentals go in your pocket too. It's another thing that gets bringing up. It's coming up all the time.

Subject: Alright, the guy who collects the machine is either a manager, or owner, or owner/manager or just somebody like I was in (city) in total control. They know I wouldn't steal they knew I didn't steal.

Subject: The only way you can catch me stealing, is if I got partners, and I'm going to keep those records till the 30th of the month, to the last day of each month. Because the last day of each month I have been figuring on the coin boxes and the end figure on the coin boxes.[91]

(6) *Copyright Violations*—Organized crime elements involved in the production of videocassettes and movies have been known to infringe copyrights by the "pirating" of films produced by legitimate studios and the use of music or other parts of a legitimate enterprise without royalty agreements.[92]

(7) *Fraud*—Layers of corporations and hidden transactions of all descriptions are used by organized crime families involved in pornography to conceal true ownership and activities.[93]

Other crimes associated with organized crime involvement in obscenity include child pornography,[94] possession, transfer and sale of machine guns and silencers,[95] and illegal gambling.[96]

V. REUBEN STURMAN

Reuben Sturman, also known as Robert Stern, Roy C. English, Robert Butler, Paul Shuster, and Paul Bekker, of Cleveland, Ohio, Los Angeles, California, and elsewhere, is widely believed to be the largest distributor of pornography in the world.[97] Law enforcement authorities believe that the Sturman empire has financial control of nearly two hundred businesses in nineteen states, one Canadian province and six foreign countries.[98] Sturman is closely associated with known organized crime family members.

James Fratianno described Sturman's connection with Robert DiBernardo, a member of the LCN Gambino (and/or de Cavlacante) Family: ". . . if he has a problem he goes to Debe.[99] Sturman and DiBernardo have had a long term business relationship, ". . . they were partners, plus . . . if Debe wanted [Sturman] to do something, he [Sturman] would do it."[100]

More than twenty years ago Sturman was a small time candy, tobacco and comic book distributor who moved slowly into pornographic magazines.[101] Avoiding any serious legal problems, he built the business into a mammoth operation encompassing all phases from production to retail sales with a myriad of corporate identities.

One account describes his organization as follows:

> "[Sturman] structured his many companies from retail stores to video production firms, in a honeycomb of nominees, false names and dead associates to avoid local obscenity prosecutions. [A 1985 tax case] reveals that the corporate structure has grown hydra-headed over the years, apparently with the more serious intent of avoiding taxes.[102]

Sturman's influence on the pornography industry is so great because his enterprise produces a very wide range of items and distributes them to retailers through countless disguised channels.[103] According to Los Angeles police, 580 of the 765 adult video arcade machines there are owned by companies controlled by Sturman.[104] Police report that Sturman typically installs equipment worth $22,000 to $60,000 at no cost to the store owner.[105] In exchange, he reaps fifty percent of the income from the peep-shows.[106] A store owner in San Diego, California, described Sturman's hold on the industry there by saying, "People are afraid of him because of his power. He could just cut people off. You could just die out there. Paranoia sets in and I'm sure he uses it to his advantage."[107]

Over the past few years, a number of Sturman associates and corporations have been convicted on obscenity charges and other violations of law.[108] Sturman, himself, however, has evaded any serious consequences for his acts.[109]

An indictment returned by a federal grand jury in Cleveland in 1985 alleged Sturman conspired to evade millions of dollars in taxes by laundering seven million dollars through foreign bank accounts and also charges that he destroyed records subpoenaed by the grand jury.[110] One of his co-defendants, Scott Dormen, plead guilty in late 1985 to his part in the conspiracy, admitting that he skimmed money from Sturman's income and delivered at least $450,000 in cash, to Sturman that went unreported.[111] When Sturman is the subject of prosecution,

> [he] professes indignity when legally attacked— as he always is—and fights back savagely. He also covers legal fees and fines of associates and gives them bonuses when they face the consequences of arrest.[112]

Reuben Sturman controls General Video of America (GVA), one of the largest distributors of sexually explicit video tape cassettes in the United States.[113] GVA recently released and distributed a "White Paper" to video cassette retailers giving them notice of government action to prosecute obscenity violations. The "White Paper" also announced the creation of a legal defense fund for GVA and others involved in the distribution of such video cassettes. In addition, they offer a toll-free number for retailers to call an attorney provided by GVA to advise them on legal matters.[114]

VI. CONCLUSION

A local law enforcement officer told this Commission, "The industry is very difficult to investigate as a local police officer, as a business in one jurisdiction, in general, is incorporated in another jurisdiction, receives materials from another jurisdiction and is controlled by individuals in another jurisdiction. Federal law enforcement involvement is an absolute necessity to attack the real problem of organized crime influence."[115] While no known additional organized crime families may live in a particular state, the effect of their production, distribution and sale of obscene material can be readily apparent. Another local law enforcement officer concluded, "Left unchecked, organized crime, in a traditional sense, can suck the lifeblood out of a community. Many times, their enterprises have been viewed as "service" oriented or victimless crimes. However, it tears at the moral fiber of society and through unbridled corruption, it can weaken the government."[116]

The findings of the 1978 Federal Bureau of Investigation analysis remain essentially correct:

In conclusion, organized crime involvement in pornography . . . is indeed significant, and there is an obvious national control directly, and indirectly by organized crime figures of that industry in the United States. Few pornographers can operate in the United States independently without some involvement with organized crime. Only through a *well coordinated all out national effort*, from the investigative and prosecutive forces can we ever hope to stem the tide of pornography. More importantly, the huge profits gathered by organized crime in this area and redirected to other lucrative forms of crime, such as narcotics and investment in legitimate business enterprises, are certainly cause for national concern, even if there is community apathy toward pornography.[117]

NOTE

1. H. Robert Showers, "Statement of H. Robert Showers, Assistant United States Attorney, Eastern District of North Carolina Before the Attorney General's Commission on Pornography," New York City, 22 January 1986, 6–7.

NOTES

1. For a more complete explanation of traditional organized crime structures and influence see the textual discussion of organized crime, *supra*.
2. New York Hearing, Vol. I, Homer Young, p. 40.
3. *Id*. at 41.
4. New York Hearing, Vol. I, Fratianno interview, Interview by Senior Investigator Edward H. Chapman, Attorney General's Commission on Pornography, p. 112.
5. *Id*. at 112–15.
6. New York Hearing, Vol. I, "Bookstore Operator" interview, p. 141–44; *See also*, New York Hearing, Vol. II, William Johnson, p. 82A-1 on "16 November 1970, Kenneth Herbert (Jap) Hann's bullet riddled body was found in the trunk of a car at Atlanta International Airport."
7. *The Report of the Commission on Obscenity and Pornography*, 141–43 (1970).
8. New York Hearing, Vol. I, Homer Young, p. 10; Former Federal Bureau of Investigation Obscenity Specialist Young reported that a staff member of the 1970 Commission interviewed him for approximately four hours about the role of organized crime in pornography in the 1968/1969 era. Young advised that he furnished the individual with documentation of organized crime involvement which for some unknown reason was not included in the earlier Commission's final report.
9. New York Hearing, Vol. I, William Kelly, p. 69.
10. *See*, Appendix One, *infra*.
11. New York Hearing, Vol. I, James D. Harmon, p. 14A-5.
12. "The building in which Star [Distributors, Inc.] rent space is managed and partly owned by John Zaccario . . . a fact first revealed in a New York City Tribune Copy story . . ." Selle, *Pornography Warehouse Target of Irate Protesters*, N.Y. City Trib., Oct. 29, 1984.
13. *Organized Crime's Involvement in the Pornography Industry*, Investigative Services Division, Metropolitan Police Dept., Washington, D.C. (1978).
14. New York Hearing, Vol. I, Carl Shoffler, p. 214.
15. *Id*. at 215.
16. *Id*.
17. *See*, Washington, D.C., Hearing, Vol II, William H. Webster, p. 77–81.
18. *Id*. at 75; New York Hearing, Vol I, Homer E. Young, p. 16.
19. Washington, D.C., Hearing, Vol. II, William H. Webster, p. 81.
20. *Federal Bureau of Investigation Report Regarding the*

Extent of Organized Crime Development in Pornography, 6 (1978).

21. Letter, William H. Webster, Director, Federal Bureau of Investigation to Henry E. Hudson, chairman, Attorney General's Commission on Pornography, Nov. 15, 1985.

22. Letter to the Attorney General's Commission on Pornography from the Federal Bureau of Investigation, March 24, 1986.

23. *Id.*

24. *Id.*

25. New York Hearing, Vol. I, William P. Kelly, p. 86.

26. New York Hearing, Vol. I, Thomas Bohling, p. 178.

27. *Id.* at 189.

28. *See,* Los Angeles Hearing, Vol. I, James Docherty, p. 6.

29. Los Angeles Hearing, Vol. I, Robert Peters, p. 32.

    Detective Peters estimates that eighty to ninety percent of the pornography in the United States is produced in the Los Angeles area. *See also,* The discussion of production and distribution of sexually explicit materials.

30. Los Angeles Hearing, Vol. I, Robert Peters, p. 32.

31. *Investigative Report on Organized Crime and Pornography Submitted to the Attorney General of California,* 2–3.

32. State of California, Department of Justice, *Organized Crime in California,* (1984) 6.

33. *Id.* at 5.

34. *Investigative Report on Organized Crime and Pornography Submitted to the Attorney General of California* 5.

35. New York Hearing, Vol. II, William Johnson, p. 82A; *See,* the discussion of the production and distribution of sexually explicit materials for a detailed explanation of the profitability of the industry.

36. *See,* Los Angeles Hearing, Vol. I, James Docherty, p. 6.

37. New York Hearing, Vol. II, William Johnson, p. 73.

38. *Id.* at 82A-5.

39. *Id.*

40. New York Hearing, Vol. I, William Kelly, p. 108A-3.

41. *Id.*

42. *Id.* at 108A-4.

43. Cong. Rec., S433 (daily ed. Jan. 30, 1984). (statement of Senator Jesse Helms).

44. *Id.*

45. New York Hearing, Vol. II, Christopher J. Mega, p. 160.

46. New York Hearing, Vol. I, Interview with James Fratianno by Senior Investigator Edward Chapman, Attorney General's Commission on Pornography, p. 112.

47. New York Hearing, Vol. I, Interview with Jimmy Fratianno, by Senior Investigator Edward H. Chapman, Attorney General's Commission on Pornography, p. 115–16.

48. *See, Investigative Report on Organized Crime and Pornography Submitted to the Attorney General of California;* State of California, Department of Justice, *Organized Crime in California* (1984).

49. *See,* The discussion of the production and distribution of sexually explicit materials for further information.

50. *See,* The sections discussing social and behavioral science research, harms and victimization for a more complete explanation.

51. New York Hearing, Vol. I, William Kelly, p. 76.

52. *See, United States v. Thevis,* 665 F.2d 616(5th Cir. 1982).

53. New York Hearing, Vol. I, William Kelly, p. 75.

54. *Id.;* Cong. Rec. S433 (daily ed. Jan. 30, 1984) (Statement of Sen. Jesse Helms).

55. New York Hearing, Vol. I, Thomas Bohling, p. 180–87. New York Hearing, William Johnson, Vol. II.

56. New York Hearing, Vol. I, Christopher J. Mega, p. 162.; Cong. Rec. S433 (daily ed. Jan. 30, 1984) (statement of Sen. Jesse Helms).

57. New York Hearing, Vol. II, Thomas Bohling, p. 182–83

58. *See,* Chapter 2 in this Part for a more complete discussion about performers.

59. Los Angeles Hearing, Caryl and Brian Cid, p. 127–53; New York Hearing, Vol. I, Linda Marchiano, p. 51; Washington, D.C., Hearing, Vol. I, Valerie Heller, p. 217–41; Washington, D.C., Hearing, Vol. II, Charles Sullivan, p. 65–77; *See also,* The discussion of performers and harms attributable to their work.

60. New York Hearing, Vol. I, Bookstore Operator, p. 152.

61. *Id.* at 141.

62. New York Hearing, Vol. I, Thomas Bohling, p. 179.

63. New York Hearing, Vol. I, William P. Kelly, p. 83.

64. New York Hearing, Vol. I, Bookstore Operator, p. 131; The FBI reported such a territorial dispute in 1981 involving pornography stores in New England. The dispute arose between Joseph Palladino, an operative of New England LCN Boss Gennaro Angiulo, and Carlo Mastrototaro, who had been authorized by the New York LCN family to open a competing business in Worcester, Massachusetts. Letter to Attorney General's Commission on Pornography from Federal Bureau of Investigation, March 24, 1986.

65. New York Hearing, Vol. I, Bookstore Operator, p. 131.

66. *Id.*

67. New York Hearing, Vol. IV, W.H.I.S.P.E.R. Statement, p. 398.

68. *Id.*

69. *Id.*

70. Washington, D.C., Hearing, Vol. I, Sarah Wynter, p. 175–84.

71. *See,* Chapter 2 of this Part for a discussion of performers.

72. New York Hearing, Vol. I, Thomas Bohling, p. 185.

73. An investigator reported to the Commission that child pornographers use cocaine to lure children, create an addiction and thus a lasting relationship of molestation

and pornography production. Miami Hearing, Vol. II, Dennis Shaw, p. 107. Los Angeles Hearing, Vol. I, Chris, p. 94–95; "I had been taking drugs throughout the time I was in prostitution and pornography. They had been supplied and doled out to me by my pimp." Washington, D.C., Hearing, Vol. I, Sharah Wynter, p. 185.

74. New York Hearing, Vol. I, Christopher J. Mega, p. 167.

75. *Id.*

76. Los Angeles Hearing, Vol. I, James Docherty, p. 8.

77. Skimming is the practice of fraudulently reporting income so as to avoid tax liability.

78. New York Hearing, Vol. I, Bookstore Operator, p. 146–51.

79. *See,* The discussion of production and distribution of sexually explicit materials for a further explanation.

80. New York Hearing, Vol. I, Bookstore Operator, p. 146–51; New York Hearing, Vol. II, William Johnson, p. 73–74.

81. New York Hearing, Vol. II, William Johnson, p. 73–74.

82. *Id.*

83. *Id.*

84. *Id.* at 73. *See also,* The discussion of the production and distribution of sexually explicit materials for more detailed description of bookstores.

85. New York Hearing, Vol. I, Bookstore Operator, p. 124–25.

86. New York Hearing, Vol. I, Christopher J. Mega, p. 167.

87. Several law enforcement agencies for years have identified Mr. Di Bernardo as an associate of the de Cavalcante family of New Jersey. However, during the trial of Di Bernardo and Rothstein in the Miporn case in June of 1981, a New York City FBI agent identified Di Bernardo as a "soldier" of the Gambino family of the Mafia, based upon information provided to the FBI office in New York.

Now, is it possible to be involved with both families? I don't know, but that's what the information is, that he is involved with both. It could be right and it might not be right. I don't know. New York Hearing, Vol. I, William P. Kelly, p. 77–78.

88. New York Hearing, Vol. I, Homer Young, p. 34.

89. New York Hearing, Vol. I, Thomas Bohling, p. 182.

90. New York Hearing, Vol. II, Marcella Cohen, p. 32; *United States v. Wisotsky,* 83-741-Cr EBD (S.D.Fla.).

91. New York Hearing, Vol. I, Bookstore Operator, p. 144–45.

92. "Arno said he had been previously somewhat reluctant to inform the agents that he was involved in the reproduction of pirated motion pictures as this was a violation of federal copyright statutes. Arno said that there were several problems connected with the production of these video tape cassettes, because there was a lot of pressure from the FBI recently in this area and that several producers of pirated films had been busted in the recent past and were now working for the FBI." New York Hearing, Vol. II, Marcella Cohen, p. 17, 38.

93. *See,* The discussion in the Recommendations for Law Enforcement Agencies. "To effectively conceal the full extent of its involvement in the nation's pornography industry, organized crime has developed a maze of organization structures through complex legal maneuvering. Pornography businesses are often represented on corporate papers by persons with no apparent ties to the company's true owner. Business transactions are commonly conducted with hidden corporate affiliates which creates an appearance of legitimate competitive business practices. Foreign corporations and banks have been used to circumvent normal business accounting methods.

For protection purposes, pornographers frequently form several corporations for one operation. They know that law enforcement authorities, when serving search warrants as a result of possible obscenity violation, are restricted to search only the corporation named. The other corporations remain protected from police inspections." *Investigative Report on Organized Crime and Pornography Submitted to the Attorney General of California,* 5, 6(1978).

94. New York Hearing, Vol. II, Marcella Cohen, p. 38.

95. *Id.*

96. Pornographer Michael Joseph Glita, member of Accardo family was reported to the United States Senate Rackets Committee as the number two man in a North Side Chicago numbers racket. New York Hearing, Vol. I, Thomas Bohling, p. 182.

97. New York Hearing, Vol. I, Marilyn Sommers, p. 199; E. Whelan, *Prince of Porn,* Cleveland Magazine 143(Aug. 1985).

98. New York Hearing, Vol. I, Marilyn Sommers, p. 200.

99. New York Hearing, Vol. I, Interview with Jimmy Fratianno, Edward Chapman, p. 115.

100. *Id.*

101. E. Whalen, *Prince of Porn,* Cleveland Magazine, 82(Aug. 1985).

102. *Id.*

103. *The Porn Peddlers,* San Diego Reader, Vol. 15, No. 10, Mar. 13, 1986, p. 17.

104. *Id.*

105. *Id.*

106. *Id.*

107. *Id.*

108. *See, e.g., United States v. Sovereign News Co.,* et al, United States District Court, Western District of Kentucky.

109. In 1980 Sturman was charges in the MIPORN investigation. The charges were ultimately dismissed. Sturman was also charged with a prior obscenity violation in Cleveland in 1976. He was acquitted.

110. New York Testimony, Vol. I, Marilyn B. Sommers, p. 1–15;

111. *Id.*

112. E. Whalen, *Prince of Porn*, Cleveland 82(Aug. 1985).
113. New York Hearing, Vol. I, Marilyn Sommers, p. 209.
114. The "White Paper" fails to disclose that some of the video cassettes sold by GVA have been found to be obscene by state and federal courts and that individuals and corporations have been convicted of felonies for their distribution. *See*, New York Hearing, Vol. II, William Johnson, p. 79.

115. New York Hearing, Vol. 1, Carl Shoffler, p. 217–18.
116. New York Hearing, Vol. II, William Johnson, p. 82A-10.
117. *Federal Bureau of Investigation Report Regarding the Extent of Organized Crime Involvement in Pornography* (1978).

EXCERPT FROM *PORNOGRAPHY: ITS EFFECTS ON THE FAMILY, COMMUNITY AND CULTURE**

CHAPTER VII. THE ROLE OF ORGANIZED CRIME

Marketing Addiction, Regression and Vice

The average citizen rarely, if ever, becomes aware of the impact or influence of organized crime on their daily lives. Each year, in its many manifestations, organized criminal activity siphons hundreds of billions of dollars out of our economy. The pornography industry accounts for only a small fraction of organized criminal activity in this country.[1]

The apparent prevalence and public acceptance of pornography, however, help to create and foster a psychological climate conducive to criminal activity: acceptance of violence, acceptance of deviance and tolerance of political corruption.[2]

Marketing a View of Man in Which Deviance Is Not Deviant

The pornography industry markets a view of man in which deviance is not deviant and in which abnormal behavior is redefined to be normal. It markets a line of products which supports that view: drugs, prostitution, pornographic materials and products and services that support sexually deviant lifestyles,

lifestyles which are aggressively marketed in the media, and even taught in our classrooms.[3]

Many law-enforcement officials and media observers believe that national organized crime groups effectively control the domestic and international distribution of adult and child pornography materials, and also exercise substantial control over their production.[4]

A National Consortium that Controls Adult and Child Pornography

Numerous federal, state and local law-enforcement commissions and investigations over the past 15 years in New York, New Jersey, Pennsylvania, Ohio, Indiana, Illinois, Florida, California and in the District of Columbia have generated public testimony that describe and detail *a national pornography consortium* dominated by five traditional New York, La Cosa Nostra (LCN) families: the Bonanno family, the Colombo family, the Luchese family, the Gambino family and the Genovese family.[5]

Undercover surveillance by the FBI and local law-enforcement agencies, detailed in public testimony and described by investigative journalists, attributes the day-to-day oversight of consortium interests to Robert DiBernardo, a "caporegime" in the LCN DeCavalcante family in New Jersey and the vice-president of Star Distributing, Ltd., one of

---

*David Alexander Scott, *Pornography: Its Effects on the Family, Community and Culture* (Washington, D.C.: Free Congress Foundation, 1985), 25–26, 51–52.

the principal U.S. distributors of pornographic materials, headquartered in New York City.[6]

"Labyrinthine Business Dealings"

The labyrinthine business dealings among Star, DiBernardo and other major pornography distributors such as Reuban Sturman, the president of Sovereign News Company in Cleveland, Ohio, have been extensively described in confidential law enforcement reports recently tabled before the New York Crime Commission. Although a number of obscenity trafficking (many in the 1980 FBI "MIPORN" sting operation in Miami), they are often not LCN "criminal associates" or "made" LCN members.[7]

In association with approximately 50 sub-distributors, according to law-enforcement observers, the consortium effectively controls the distribution of the lion's share of the pornographic books, magazines, films, videotapes, sexual "aids" and paraphernalia produced both in this country and abroad. These materials are then distributed through a network of more than 15,000 adult bookstores and over 500 adult theaters throughout the United States, Canada and Western Europe.[8]

"These Decisions Are Not Made by the Hugh Hefners of the World"

With their accumulated "know-how" and encyclopedic knowledge of the industry and its operation, DiBernardo and Sturman are believed in effect to control much of the decision-making process in this country and abroad relating to *who* makes pornography, *what* pornography is made, *when* it is made and *where* it is made. Exceptions, such as the material produced in the Far East by the *Yakuza* in Japan and the Chinese *Triad's*, observers argue, only prove the rule.[9]

From time to time, the consortium is reported to exert influence on decisions about feature Hollywood films, the production of movies for television, the production of feature "X"-rated films and videotapes, and the distribution patterns of pornographic films over scrambled-signal, pay-cable and direct-broadcast satellite.[10]

Despite what many people think, these decisions are not always made by the Hugh or Christie Hefners, Bob Gucciones and Larry Flynts of the world.[11]

Pornography Is Not Just Another Mob Business

There is a consensus among law-enforcement officers who track the consortium that gross revenues from the sale of pornography approach $4 billion a year. Up to $2 billion comes from adult pornography bookstore revenues (most of it from "peep-show" income) with the balance generated from the sale of hard-core books, magazines, films and videotapes, under-the-counter child pornography, "sex aids" and paraphernalia. The remaining $2 billion is generated from the sales and advertising revenues of soft-core magazines, adult-theater proceeds and a variety of mail-order activities.[12]

It is important to remember, observers note, that pornography is not just another LCN business. There are important economic and political reasons for LCN involvement in pornography that are an integral part of the LCN's political economy and its longer-range political and social agenda.[13]

"An Almost Perfect Vehicle for Laundering Money"

For example, many law-enforcement officials believe that the loose but near-monopolistic structure of the industry is an almost perfect vehicle for laundering revenues from drug distribution, gambling and other criminal activities, as well as for concealing monies skimmed from other LCN-controlled "legitimate" businesses. Some law-enforcement officials estimate that as much as $10 billion could be laundered or otherwise disguised in this way. Remember that pornography is essentially an all cash business.[14]

More important, they argue, is that the pornography industry has become an almost ideal marketing device for the economic interests of the larger vice industry, helping to create a greater demand for products such as drugs, gambling and prostitution. In producing films and television programs that glorify drug dealers, gamblers, prostitutes, pimps and pornographers, the industry is facilitated in *marketing the message that deviance is not deviant*. The media "happy face" also blurs the public perception about what is believed to be LCN involvement in and control of the pornography industry.[15]

The Industry Helps Create a Demand for Drugs and Prostitution

The consortium, according to these officials, is willing to spend large sums of money to market the message that deviance is not deviant, and to nurture the public perception created by widespread exposure to pornographic imagery that the recreational use of sex and drugs is much more prevalent than it actually is.[16]

These tactics, they argue, help to create a psychological climate that, in turn, encourages and promotes a dependence on pornographic imagery and on drugs for sexual arousal and gratification. This *climate of deception* also primes the pump for further consumption of pornography.[17]

Organized Crime then Supplies the Demand It Helped To Create

The addiction model demonstrates how repeated exposure to pornography inhibits normal sexual arousal, leading in some cases to a growing dependence on viewing increasingly aberrant pornographic images in order to restore prior levels of sexual arousal, and how a desire to inflict or experience pain can often shadow this dependency.[18]

Ultimately, in addition to a need for the pornographic imagery and artificial sex aids, some researchers have noted that at this point drugs often become necessary to achieve sexual arousal and release. At this juncture, law-enforcement sources note, organized crime re-surfaces as the major domestic supplier not only of the imagery and the sex aids, but the drugs.[19]

Main Points in the Historical Development of the Pornography Industry

The pornography industry went through its infancy in the late 1950s and early 1960s. Early entrepreneurs included Reuban Sturman at Sovereign News in Cleveland: Teddy Rothstein at Star Distributors in New York City and Mickey Zaffarano, then a Colombo family "capo," at All State Films in New York; Milton Luros, and subsequently Teddy Gaswirth at Erotic Words and Pictures in Los Angeles; Mike Thevis at Peachtree Distribution in Atlanta; and later on Harry Mohney in Michigan.

Together they developed a nationwide distribution network for pornographic magazines, books and short-subject films: Zaffarano producing eight-millimeter "peep-show" films at All State, Sturman manufacturing equipment to show them at Automatic Vending in Reno, and both Sturman at Sovereign and Rothstein at Star producing books and magazines.

Ultimately, they were able to pyramid a series of corporate takeovers into effective control over a loose confederation of over 500 adult theaters and 15,000 adult bookstores, operating more often then not with a battery of Sturman's machines showing Zaffarano's films and selling either Sturman's or Rothstein's books and magazines. Even at that time, the confederation generated several hundred million dollars a year in revenues.

Following John Kennedy's murder in 1963, the pornography business boomed. Bob Guccione started *Penthouse* magazine in 1965, and the Supreme Court's *Redrup v. New York* decision in 1967 reversed many obscenity convictions, serving as a green light to many of the LCN families in New York, who rushed into all aspects of the pornography business. By 1970, Appalachian-style pornography industry meetings were taking place bi-annually, convening the 40 to 50 key industry players of any given era. However, Sturman, Thevis and Luros had already come under FBI scrutiny. Their meetings had attracted J. Edgar Hoover's personal interest.

As 1970 unfolded, territorial disputes over pornography began to erupt between individual LCN families in New York and elsewhere. Joe Bonanno struck a deal with Joe Colombo to bring Mickey Zaffarano in as overboss to bring order to the industry and peace to the warring factions. This also set the stage for the consortium. Thevis was already under indictment in Atlanta, Luros under investigation in Los Angeles, and the New York Crime Commission had begun to investigate Star, All State and many of their associates.

But business was never better. The turmoil of 1970 laid the groundwork for 1971, which ushered in the industry's golden era. In July of 1971, Louis Peraino, a Colombo family "soldier," and co-owner of All State with Mickey Zaffarano, founded "twin" companies: Bryanston Distributors, Inc., and Damiano Film Productions. Bryanston was to lay dormant for two years, but Damiano went on to make quick, low-budget films starring Damiano friend Linda Traynor, a.k.a. Linda Lovelace: *Sex USA* and *Deep Throat*. Almost overnight, *Deep Throat* became legendary and also revolutionary.

It not only became one of the higher grossing films of all times, earning as much as $100 million, its success propelled Peraino, his father and brother, and the consortium to Hollywood. Two years later, however, *Deep Throat* would collide with the Supreme Court's *Miller v. California* decision and lead to an obscenity trial in Memphis that would sow the seeds of the Perainos' downfall. That same collision, however, would also create a mechanism for laundering money that was to be an education in itself for organized crime.

For the pornography industry, 1971 was a red-banner year. The success of *Deep Throat* was consecrated by the highly contentious findings of the Johnson Administration's Commission on Obscenity and Pornography (i.e., that pornography had "no effect" on human behavior. The Commission report became what the Commission Minority Report's author Father Morton Hill characterized as a "Magna Carta" for the pornography industry. History proved him right.

As 1971 unfolded, Al Ruddy, the producer of *The Godfather*, went to New York to get Joe Colombo's blessing to make the film, set in Colombo's Brooklyn. Colombo's fascination with the film, however, on top of his high-profile activity with the Italian American Civil Rights League, was the last straw for his more conservative fellow bosses. Within weeks, he was seriously wounded in a failed assassination attempt.

Legitimate distribution of *Deep Throat* continued on into the summer of 1973, generating tens of millions of dollars a year for the Perainos, Zaffarano, and the Colombo family. In 1973 the consortium went to Hollywood. Bryanston opened with a bang, acquiring and distributing three straight box-office hits: Andy Warhol's *Frankenstein, Return of the Dragon* (starring the late Bruce Lee, allegedly murdered by *Triad* interests) and *The Texas Chainsaw Massacre*. Until its demise three years later, Bryanston was directly involved in at least two dozen other films, launching the careers of such people as John Travolta, Jodie Foster and Chuck Norris, as well as director John Carpenter of *Halloween* fame, and involving producers such as Al Ruddy (*The Godfather*) and Sandy Howard, who later produced *Vice Squad*. June of 1973 brought the Supreme Court's *Miller* decision. *Deep Throat*, now legally obscene, went underground.

The Perianos (Louis and his father Anthony and brother Joe) formed a company called AMMA with Florida porn movie distributor, theater owner, and convicted counterfeiter Bob DeSalvo. *Deep Throat* was no longer shipped openly. It was transported across state lines by "checkers." They delivered the prints to theaters, stayed on to count the customers and to collect the distributor's share of the box-office receipts, usually half, normally all cash. "Sweepers" then went from checker to checker collecting the money daily, then either mailing it or hand-carrying it on plane flights back to company offices in New Jersey and Florida. As the money flowed into Florida, partners Anthony Periano and DeSalvo funneled the funds through a succession of companies. The funds finally ended up in the Bahamian and Cayman Island bank accounts or in Periano family companies in Florida and New Jersey. At the same time, the Assistant US Attorney in Memphis, Larry Parrish, began gathering information to prosecute the Perianos. Bryanston and *Deep Throat* actor Harry Reems on obscenity charges.

The year 1974 found Thevis in jail, Luros and the Perianos under indictment and *Frankenstein, Dragon,* and *Chainsaw* runaway box-office successes. Zaffarano and Bob DiBernardo were commuting between New York and Los Angeles overseeing consortium interests. It was time for Sturman to make his move. After consolidating a number of Thevis interests, he moved in to take over the Luros interests, buying out Erotic Words and Pictures (EWAP). At the same time, he was expanding into England and Europe under the Lasse Braun label with his associate Alberto Ferro in Amsterdam. His final gesture that year was to front the money to fellow-Clevelander Larry Flynt to produce the first issues of *Hustler* magazine. This same year, the Supreme Court further tightened the noose on obscenity with the *Paris Adult Theater I v. Slaton* decision.

The year 1975 was quiet. The handwriting was on the wall for the Perianos in Memphis. On October 12, the *New York Times* published a major article linking Bryanston with organized crime interests. The Perainos hedged their bet. In November, looking astutely into the future, they began a company in Florida to turn out pornography on videotape just a few weeks after Sony put the first home videocassette recorder on the market. Today, videocassette pornography generates almost $500 million a year for the consortium.

On March 1, 1976, the *Deep Throat* trial began in Memphis. By April 30 it was over. All three Perianos were convicted. A month later Bryanston folded, almost overnight. DeSalvo became a fugitive, fleeing first to the Bahamas, then dropping out of sight. He is believed to be dead.

In August, the FBI in Los Angeles began the first of a series of LCN pornography-related undercover operations. The first, code-named "PORNEX," lasted three months. Though it led to indictments, FBI informer Frank Bonpensiero was killed in a gangland slaying that sufficiently unnerved LCN Los Angeles family boss "Jimmy the Weasel" Fratianno that he became an FBI informant.

Nonetheless, the consortium had left its mark on Hollywood and achieved its goals. It had firmly established new levels of tolerance of sex and violence on the screen, standards soon to be accepted by the TV networks. It gave the consortium practical "hands on" working knowledge of the motion picture industry and its financial structure, and a foot in the door in the video business. In practical terms, it consolidated the consortium's grip on the distribution of pornography both in the United States and abroad. The Perianos were expendable. It was time to fade back to New York and leave things to Zaffarano and DiBarnardo.

In the waning days of the Ford administration, senior FBI agents taking early retirement left one last operation on the drawing board, a "sting" operation that became known as "MIPORN." The formal operation ran from August of 1977 until the net fell on Valentine's day in 1980. "MIPORN" ensnared 54 of the top members of the consortium including Sturman, DiBernardo, Zaffarano and Rothstein in a 13-city sweep by a synchronized force of 400 FBI agents and local police.

The impact of the sweep was so powerful for Zaffarano that he died of a heart attack minutes before FBI agents arrived with a warrant for his arrest. His death left a serious power vacuum for the consortium to resolve. DiBernardo, even though briefly jailed following his "MIPORN" conviction, filled part of the vacuum. Sturman took up some of the slack on an interum basis.

The moral of the story (if there is one) is that professional pornographers are not, as some civil libertarians often argue, the D. H. Lawrences, Henry Millers and Allen Ginzbergs of the world. They are for the most part highly organized, professional criminals who derive their power and perpetuity from two principal sources: fear generated through violence and threat of violence, and control over corrupted public officials and political leaders.

Joe Periano was gunned down in January of 1982. His father and brother went to jail a month later on "MIPORN" convictions. The Periano family still collects *Deep Throat* royalties, and Bob DiBernardo is now out of jail and back in charge at Star. Since the Carter inauguration eight years ago, the Department of Justice has failed to carry out any significant *new* pornography prosecutions. The last of the "MIPORN" trials are now taking place in Miami. The absence of prosecution has given the pornography industry a green light and strong signals about future potential activity. Some feel the "MIPORN" convictions to have been a Pyrrhic victory. Consequently, many people are anticipating the work of the new Attorney General's Commission on Pornography that is now underway.

NOTES

1. (1981) Abadsky, J. *Organized crime.* New York: Allyn & Bacon.

(1971) Albini, J. *The American mafia: Genesis of a legend.* New York: Appleton.

(1965) Barzini, L. *The Italians.* New York: Antheum.

(1973) Hess, H. *Mafia & Mafiosi: The structure of power* (trans. E. Osers). Lexington, MA: Lexington Books.

(1972) Ianni, F., & Reuss-Ianni, E. A *family business, kinship and social control in organized crime.* New York: Russell Sage.

(1964) Lewis, N. *The honored society.* New York: G.P. Putnam's Sons.

(1971) Messick, H. *Lansky.* New York: G.P. Putnam's Sons.

(1933) Mori, C. *The last struggle with the mafia* (trans. O. Williams). New York: Putnam.

(1976) Nelli, H. *The business of crime: Italians and syndicate crime in the United States.* New York: Oxford University Press.

(1975) Pace, D., & Styles, J. *Organized crime: Concepts & control.* Englewood Cliffs, N.J.: Prentice Hall. (pp. 16–25).

(1966) Pantaleone, M. *The mafia and politics.* New York: Coward-McCann.

(1983) Peterson, V. *The mob: 200 years of organized crime in New York.* Ottawa, IL: Green Hill Publishers.

(1962) Schiavo, G. *The truth about the mafia and organized crime in America.* New York: Vigo Press.

(1976) Servaido, G. *Mafioso: A history of the mafia from its origins to the present day.* New York: Stein and Day.

Also Supra, note 1, and Infra, note 5.

2–3. (1979) Fahringer. If the trumpet sounds an uncertain note. . . . *New York University Review of Law and Social Change,* 8 (251), 251.

(1970) Gardiner, J. *The politics of corruption: Organized crime in a American city.* New York: Sage.

Also Supra, note 5, Ciccotelli, E., Smith, W., & Webster, W.

4. (1980) Bergsman, S. (1980, July 22). Local porno businesses tied to organized crime: Phoenix's largest porno operation part of Rubin Sturman's Cleveland syndicate. *Phoenix Weekly Gazette.* pp. 1–3.

(1078) Brockett, D., Frank, A., & Diernan, M. (1978, February 13). Mystery man quietly gives up holdings in the world of smut. *The Washington Star.*

(1978) Brockett, D., Frank, A., & Diernan, M. (1978, February 13). Pornography cash is an invitation to corruption. *The Washington Star,* p. 1.

(1980) Dorschmer, J. (1980, June 8). The case of the naive porn lawyer: Inside Miami's FBI scam. *The Miami Herald/Tropic Magazine,* p. 17–44.

(1982) Farley, E., & Knoedelseder, W. (1982, June 13). Family business, episode 1, "The pornbrokers." *Los*

Angeles Times/Calender, pp. 3–13.

(1982) Farley, E., & Knoedelseder, W. (1982, June 20). Family business, episode 2, "The hollywood years." *Los Angeles Times/Calander*, pp. 3–9.

(1982) Farley, E., & Knoedelseder, W. (1982, June 27). Family business, episode 3, "The fall." Los Angeles Times/Calander, pp. 3–8.

(1985) Hanlon, M. (1985, March 2). The caper that caught a porn king. *The Toronto Star/Saturday Magazine*, pp. M1, M5, M6.

(1985) Hanlon, M. (1985, March 9). Can Rayne beat the test? *The Toronto Star/Saturday Magazine*, p. M1.

(1980) Langelan, M. The political economy of pornography. *Oasis*. Washington, D.C.

(1980) Lovelace, L. *Ordeal*. Seacaucus, NJ: Citadel Press.

(1981) May, D., & Hosenball, M. (1981, September 6). Worldwide tentacles of Mr. Porn. *The London Times*, London, England.

(1976) Payne, D. (1975, May 3). Shy pornographers. *Macleans Magazine*, pp. 34–41.

(1979) Satchell, M. (1979, August 19). The big business of selling smut: Five little known men dominate sleazy network of pornography that may gross $4 billion a year. *Parade Magazine*, pp. 4–5.

Also Infra, note 5–6.

5–6. (1977) California Assembly Committee on Criminal Justice (1977, October 31). Hearing on Obscenity and the Use of Minors in Pornographic Material, San Diego, CA.

(1983) California Department of Justice, Office of the Attorney General, Bureau of Organized Crime and Criminal Intelligence. *Organized crime in California 1982–1983: Annual report to the California Legislature*. Sacramento, CA.

(1984) Ciccotelli, E. (1983, July 11). Report on organized crime in New York City. (Testimony on behalf of the Organized Crime Control Bureau, New York City Police Department, before the Committee on the Judiciary, Sen. Thurmond (Ch.), U.S. Senate). In *Organized crime in America* (Part 2, pp. 111–167, 189–277)., (S. Hrg. 98-184, Pt. 2). Washington, DC: USGPO.

(1983) Dintino, J. (1983, February 16). The structure of organized crime in New Jersey. (Testimony on behalf of the New Jersey State Police before the Committee On The Judiciary, Sen. Thurmond (Ch.), U.S. Senate). In *Organized crime in America* (Part 1, pp. 152–299)., (S. Hrg. 98-184, Pt. 1). Washington, DC: USGPO.

(1984) Dworin, W. (1984, May 16). *State and local enforcement efforts related to obscenity*. (Paper presented at the Obscenity Prosecution Seminar, L. Lippe (Ch.), conducted by the Department of Legal Education, U.S. Department of Justice)., Washington, DC.

(1978) Federal Bureau of Investigation. *The extent of organized crime involvement in pornography*. Washington, D.C.

(1983) Higgins, S. (1983, March 2). Characteristics of America's "war" with organized crime. (Testimony on behalf of the Bureau of Alcohol, Tobacco and Firearms before the Committee on the Judiciary, Sen. Thurmond (Ch.), U.S. Senate). In *Organized crime in America* (Part 1, pp. 311–326)., (S. Hrg. 98-184, Pt. 1). Washington, DC: USGPO.

(1951) Kefauver Committee Hearings. Committee to Investigate Organized Crime, U.S. Senate. In *Investigation of organized crime in interstate commerce: Hearing on S. 202*. (81st Cong. 2nd sess., and 82nd Cong. 1st sess.)., Washington, DC: USGPO.

(1963) Kennedy, R. (Cross-examination of Joe Valachi before the Subcommittee on Investigations of the Committee on Government Operations, U.S. Senate). In *Organized crime and illicit traffic in narcotics: Hearings on S. 17* (Pt. 1, 88th Congress)., Washington, DC: USGPO.

(1976) National Advisory Committee on Criminal Justice Standards and Goals. *Organized Crime: Report of the task force on organized crime* (pp. 226–228). Washington, DC: USGPO.

(1982) New York Select Committee on Crime (1982, July 26). *An investigation of racketeer infiltration into the sex-oriented materials industry in New York City* (pp. 195–244). Report to the State of New York Commission of Investigation, New York, N.Y.

(1982) Ohio Law Enforcement Consulting Committee. *Report to the Governor of Ohio: Organized crime*, Colombus, OH.

(1984) Pennsylvania Crime Commission. La Cosa Nostra. In *1984 report: Pennsylvania law enforcement* (pp. 38–43). St. Davids, PA.

(1967) Presidential Commission on Law Enforcement and Administration of Justice. *Organized crime: Task force report* (pp. 6, 61–79, 114–126). Washington, DC.

(1984) Shoffler, C. Pornography—The victims and perpetrators. In D. Scott (Ed.), *Symposium on media violence & pornography: Proceedings, resource book & research guide* (pp. 210–211). Toronto: Media Action Group.

(1982) Smith, W. (1982, October 4). *Memorandum: Enforcement of anti-pornography laws*. (Available from U.S. Department of Justice, Washington, D.C.).

(1983) Smith, W. (1983, January 27). (Testimony on behalf of the United States Department of Justice before the Committee on the Judiciary, Sen. Thurmond (Ch.), U.S. Senate). In *Organized crime in America* (Part 1, pp. 10–18)., (S. Hrg. 98-184, Pt. 1). Washington, DC: USGPO.

(1983) Trott, S. (1983, August 24). *Memorandum: Enforcement of anti-pornography laws*. (Available from U.S. Department of Justice, Washington, D.C.).

(1977) United States Department of Justice. (1977, June 8). *Organized crime involvement in pornography*. Washington, DC.

(1984) Von Raab, W. (1983, May 20). (Testimony on behalf of the United States Customs Service before the Committee on the Judiciary, Sen. Thurmond (Ch.), U.S. Senate). In *Organized crime in America* (Part 2, pp. 2–22, 40–93)., (S.Hrg. 98-184, Pt. 2). Washington, DC: USGPO.

(1984) Von Raab, W. (1983, May 20). Remarks at the White House Meeting on Obscenity, March 28, 1983. (Entered on the record during testimony on behalf of the United States Customs Service before the Committee on the Judiciary, Sen. Thurmond (Ch.), U.S. Senate). In *Organized crime in America* (Part 2, pp. 24–29)., (S.Hrg. 98-184, Pt. 2). Washington, DC: USGPO.

(1978) Washington, D.C. Metropolitan Police Department, Investigative Services Division, Organized Crime Criminal Intelligence Unit (1978, November). *Organized crime's involvement in the pornography industry*. Washington, DC.

(1983) Webster, W. (1983, January 27). (Statement on behalf of the Federal Bureau of Investigation before the Committee on the Judiciary, Sen. Thurmond (Ch.), U.S. Senate). In *Organized crime in America* (Part 1, pp. 50–62, 76–85)., (S. Hrg. 98-184, Pt. 1). Washington, DC: USGPO.

(1983) White House Working Group on Pornography. (1983, December 6). *Summary report: Federal Bureau of Investigation*. Washington, D.C.

(1984) Confidential Law Enforcement Source Material: Los Angeles, Phoenix, Toronto, Indianapolis, Cleveland, Miami, New York & Washington, DC Police Departments; Michigan State Police, Ontario Provincial Police, F.B.I., R.C.M.P. Department of Justice, Ministry of Justice, & Eastern States Vice Investigators Association (E.S.V.I.A.).

7. (1977) *Sovereign News Co. vs. Falke*, 448 F.Supp. 306 (N.D. Ohio 1977).

(1982) *Sovereign News Co. vs. Falke*, 674 F.2d 484 (6th Circuit 1982).

Supra, notes 4 & 266, C.L.E.S.M.

8–14. Supra, notes 1, 4, 5 & 21 C.L.E.S.M.

15–16. (1982) Andrews, P., Longfellow, C., & Martens, F. Zero-sum enforcement: Some reflections on drug control *Federal Probation*, March, 14–20.

(1984) Baker, J. (1984, July 27). An approach to pornography as a copyright problem. (Memo to the White House Working Group on Pornography)., Washington, D.C.

(1980) Daniels, A. The Supreme Court and obscenity: An exercise in empirical Constitutional policy-making, *San Diego Law Review*, 17 (757), 795–798.

(1983) Edelhertz, H., Cole, R., & Berk, B. *The containment of organized crime*. Lexington, MA: Lexington Books.

(1976) Ehrlich, I. Participation in illegitimate activities: A theoretical and empirical investigation. In L. McPheters, & W. Strong (Eds.), *The economics of crime and law enforcement* (pp. 141–196). Springfield, IL: Charles C. Thomas.

(1983) McGuigan, P., & Rader, R. (Eds.), *Criminal justice reform: A blueprint*. Washington, DC: Regnery/Gateway & Free Congress Research and Education Foundation.

(1983) Moore, M. Controlling criminogenic commodities: Drugs, guns, and alcohol. In J. Wilson (Ed.), *Crime and public policy*. San Francisco: Institute for Contemporary Studies.

(1984) Morality in Media, Inc. (1984, October 16) 'Obscenity now covered by 'RICO' statute (18 U.S.C. 1961) as a result of Congressional passage on October 11, 1984 of the "Helm's Ammendment" to the "Comprehensive Crime Control Act of 1984." News Release: Author. (Available from Author: 475 Riverside Drive, New York, NY 10115).

(1982) Nossen, R. *The detection, investigation and prosecution of financial crimes: White collar, political corruption and racketeering*. Richmond, VA: Nossen, Richard A., & Associates.

(1984) Nossen, R. *Overview of civil and criminal forfeiture statutes and procedure*. Richmond, VA: Nossen, Richard A., & Associates.

(1984) Parrish, L. (1984, May 16). *The development of obscenity cases: Targeting of obscenity investigations*. (Paper presented at the Obscenity Prosecution Seminar, L. Lippe (Ch.), conducted by the Department of Legal Education, U.S. Department of Justice)., Washington, DC.

(1984) Parrish, L. (personal communication, May 16, 1984).

(1983) Taylor, B. Pornography and the First Ammendment. In P. McGuigan, & R. Rader (Eds.), *Criminal justice reform: A blueprint* (pp. 155–170). Washington, DC: Regnery/ Gateway & Free Congress Research and Education Foundation.

(1984) Taylor, B. (1984, May 16). *The trial of obscenity cases*. (Paper presented at the Obscenity Prosecution Seminar, L. Lippe (Ch.), conducted by the Department of Legal Education, U.S. Department of Justice)., Washington, DC.

(1984) Taylor, B. (personal communication, November, 1984).

Also Supra, 21, C.L.E.S.M., 6, 15, 16, 17 & 19.

17. Supra, notes 141–146, 237–238, Gerbner, G., & 2–3.

18. Supra, note 65.

19. Supra, notes 41, Zillmann, D., 54, & 2–3.

4 PORNOGRAPHY'S VICTIMS AND PERPETRATORS

My name is Mary "Annie" Steinman. I'm from Omaha, Nebraska. I was sexually molested as a child in my own home. My abuse started at the age of 3. My father kept suitcases full of pornographic pictures and magazines. From the earliest years he would have me perform oral sex on him. He would hang me upside down in a closet and push objects like screwdrivers or table knives inside me. Sometimes he would heat them first; all the while he would have me perform oral sex on him. He would look at his porno pictures almost everyday using them to get ideas of what to do to me or my siblings. I've had my hands tied, my feet tied, my mouth taped to teach me big girls don't cry. He would tell me I was very fortunate to have a father who would teach me the facts of life. Many of the pictures he had were of women in bondage, with their hands tied, feet tied and their mouth taped. There was one picture I remember with a woman with a chain around her neck and her hands and feet were chained to the head and foot of a bed. Some of the magazines he had showed adults having sex with children and children having sex with children. He had a lot of pictures depicting group sex. My father had an easel that he put by the bed. He'd pin a picture on the easel and like a teacher he would tell me this is what you're going to learn today. He would then act out the picture on me. As early as the age of four my father would rent me out to other people for the purpose of sex. Along with me went part of his pornographic collection which was included in the price and had to be returned. This abuse continued until I was 14.

I had no childhood. The relationship with my father was sexual from the age of 3. I was nothing but a pornographic tool for his use. I cannot distinguish the difference between sex and pornography. Because of my sexual abuse as a child I am extremely against pornography, and because of pornography I cannot enjoy sex. The word love is very painful to me. My father said he loved me and his love hurt me. The mere mention of the word sometimes gives me flashbacks to the abuse I endured as a child.

I have appeared on numerous radio and television shows, both national and local, in an effort to help other victims of child sexual abuse and to inform the listening audiences of the dangers of the use of pornography. I have testified at numerous legislative hearings concerning anti-pornography and obscenity laws. I have helped Dr. Osanka in his workshops and seminars concerning the prevention of child sexual abuse as a guest speaker and resource person.

In my travels around this country, I have met many other victims of child sexual abuse and in practically all of their situations, as well as mine, the use of pornography was a common denominator. I have very strong feelings about both child and adult pornography. I think it should be abolished.

—Condensation of testimony before the Attorney General's Commission on Pornography, 1985

The case histories of pornography victims and perpetrators that follow present overwhelming documentation that pornography serves as a catalyst for sexual abuse and violence and other physical abuse of women and children and sometimes men. While evidence of pornography-related abuses abounds, little, if any, evidence exists to demonstrate any value of or justification for pornography. We found close to five hundred different offenders in our limited files whose acts of sexual abuse, violence, or physical abuse were pornography related. Unfortunately, many of these offenders victimized multiple victims. Few professionals who are in positions to document pornography-related abuse ask the right questions of abuse victims and offenders; therefore, most pornography-related offenses go undocumented. We suggest that the questionnaire for victims and perpetrators we include at the end of this chapter be used to document the relationship between pornography and abuse.

STATISTICAL INFORMATION

U.S. police departments routinely find sizable pornography collections in the possession of serial murderers and pedophiles. In fact, a study of thirty-six serial killers by the Federal Bureau of Investigation (FBI) revealed that twenty-nine were attracted to pornography and incorporated it into their sexual activity, which included serial rape-murder.[1] In attempting to profile the sex killers, the FBI found that 81 percent of the thirty-six reported that "their biggest sexual interest was in reading pornography and in 'compulsive' masturbation."[2] Donald Wildmon cites a Paul Harvey column that mentions a National Institute of Mental Health study of serial killers. One of the suspected common denominators among these killers, Harvey said, is that "most feed on pornography."[3] Scott states that a small group of the most violent individuals collectively and compulsively murder more than one thousand young victims a year in the United States—often stimulated and fueled by the fantasies of violent pornography.[4]

Almost half the rapists interviewed in a study by William Marshall used soft-core consenting sex pornography to arouse themselves in preparation for seeking a victim.[5] Nineteen percent of the sex offenders used sadistic-bondage, forced-sex pornography to incite them to rape, while 38 percent used consenting-sex pornography immediately before committing an offense. Of the homosexual child molesters Marshall studied, 55 percent used child pornography to instigate their crimes.

The State of Michigan keeps standardized reports of all sex crimes in its computer. As of May 1979, there were between thirty-five thousand and thirty-eight thousand such cases in the computer. According to a report by Detective Lieutenant Darrell Pope, head of the Michigan State Police Investigative Resources Unit on May 1, 1979, " . . . in 41 percent of all sexual assault cases, pornography was involved just prior to the act or during the act."[6]

A 1973 study found that 57 percent of rapist subjects had tried the sexual behavior depicted during peak adolescent exposure to pornography.[7] Seventy-seven percent of the child molesters with male targets and 87 percent with female targets reported trying or imitating the sexual behavior modeled by the pornography. Interestingly, 85 percent of the control group subjects also indicated that they had imitated behavior modeled by the pornography.

Diana Scully, a sociologist at Virginia Commonwealth University, interviewed 114 convicted rapists and concluded that "the scenes depicted in violent porn are repeated in rapists' accounts of their crimes."[8] Dr. Scully conducted more than five hundred hours of structured interviews with the rapists. She found that 65.3% of the rapists (compared to 56.7% of the nonrapist incarcerated control subjects) said they had used pornography. The rapists believed in the rape myths espoused by pornography, she concluded.[9] Similarly, rapists who participate in the Lino Lakes, Minnesota, program for sex offenders must "swear off hard-core pornography, which one psychologist describes as being 'like a shot of whiskey to an alcoholic.' "[10]

In July 1985, a representative of Washington County (Minnesota) Human Services, Inc., completed a survey designed by Sara Lee Johann (one of the authors) as part of the background material compiled to support antipornography legislation in Wisconsin. The survey concerned the relationship between pornography and abuse, battering, sexual assault, and exploitation of persons. The results, based on six years of experience with the program and 2,380 sexual assault victim and offender clients, were interesting. The representative estimated the following:

1. Abusers often used pornographic material portraying women, children, and men involved in all sorts of sexual activity from intercourse to bestiality, child molestation, rape, and group sex. This material included depictions of violence such as torture, pain, humiliation, mutilation, bleeding, bruises, beatings, physical injury, whips, chains, and ropes.
2. In 68 percent of the 2,380 cases, the abuser beat or sexually abused the victim or someone else after looking at pornographic material.
3. Fifty-eight percent of the abusers pointed out pornographic pictures or articles to their victims.
4. Forty-seven percent of the victims were upset by someone, often the abuser, trying to get them to do what he or she had seen in pornographic materials. (Such materials were used as a preconditioning to abuse.)
5. In 23 percent of the cases, the abuser was influenced to act in a violent manner from viewing pornography.
6. In 14 percent of the cases, the abuser took pornographic photos of the victim or someone else.

According to one director of a battered women's shelter in Illinois,

[i]n shelters we see women who have been burned, bitten (with chunks of flesh actually bitten from her body), beaten, sexually mutilated, kicked, tortured, and psychologically degraded. Battered women tell us of their husbands' or lovers' preoccupation with pornography in some form.[11]

Dr. Kathleen Barry, professor of sociology and author of *Female Sexual Slavery*, reports that prior to "turning out" women to prostitution, many pimps break down their victims through sessions of sexual abuse, including rape.[12] Some of the sessions are filmed or photographed, and the pimps use the pictures to blackmail the victims by threatening to send them to their families or sell them to pornographers for mass market production. Barry says this use of pornography is a form of torture and terms the marketing of actual torture sessions a pleasure commodity.

According to the December 1983 issue of the *Arizona Republic*, an estimated fifty thousand children "disappear nationwide annually," and "many are forced into a life of sexual exploitation."[13]

Douglas Besharove, former director of the National Center on Child Abuse and Neglect, estimated that close family friends or family members sexually abuse between 60,000 to 100,000 children annually in the United States.[14] Lloyd, writing in 1976, reported that more than sixty thousand children in the United States die each year from child abuse.[15] The *Capital Times* in Madison, Wisconsin, reported in September 1984 that an American Psychiatric Association study of sixty-six children involved in sex rings "showed that 54.8 percent of them had been used in pornography."[16]

The interest in sexual use of children appears to be sizable. For instance, the motto of the Rene Guyon Society in California, which has a membership of five thousand, is "Sex before eight or it's too late."[17] In 1972 officers of the Los Angeles Police Department arrested a child pornographer who had produced a travel guide for child molesters that listed 378 places in fifty-nine cities and 34 states where a child could be found. Records found by investigators revealed that the publication, titled *Where the Young Ones Are*, sold more than seventy thousand copies.[18] Catherine Wilson, who controlled mail-order child pornography in the United States, had a mailing list of thirty thousand customers. An investigation by the Los Angeles Police Department revealed that 30 to 40 percent of her customers were registered sex offenders.[19]

The sexual violence statistics in the United States are cause for great concern. One woman is raped every three minutes. One wife is battered every eighteen seconds. One woman in four will be sexually assaulted in her lifetime. Approximately twenty-five million women in the United States will experience sex with a male adult before age 13. An estimated 50 percent of all women will be battering victims at some point in their lives.[20]

Statistics from the U.S. General Accounting Office (1982) said that around 2.4 million American teenagers are involved in prostitution.[21] Similarly, the Reverend Bruce Ritter, who operates Covenant House, a home for runaway teens near Times Square in New York City and was a member of the Attorney General's Commission on Pornography, told a U.S. Senate committee that more than 60 percent of the fifty thousand young people who have come to his shelter since it opened in 1977 have had some contact with prostitution and pornography.[22]

In a 1984 study, two hundred juvenile and adult, former and current street female prostitutes in the San Francisco Bay Area were interviewed.[23] Out of 193 cases of rape mentioned by the women, 24 percent included allusions to pornographic material by the rapist. The rapists referred to pornography and insisted victims enjoy rape and extreme violence. Of 178 cases of juvenile sexual exploitation brought up by this group of females, 22 percent of the cases mentioned the use of pornographic materials by the adult prior to the act. These findings are especially important because the researchers did not ask the subjects whether pornography was involved in their abuse; the subjects brought up the pornographic connection themselves. The researchers also found that 38 percent of the prostitutes had had sexually explicit photographs taken of them when they were children. They said that their results lend support to the imitation model of pornography.

Of the twenty-eight boy prostitutes interviewed by Ann Burgess, all had been asked to participate in pornography, and 75 percent participated.[24] According to the boys, most of the pornography was for the private use of the pornographer. The boys were concerned about the loss of control over the use of the pictures and experienced loss of esteem for themselves or others.[25] Burgess also found that of those police agencies that investigated at least one child prostitution case, "a mean percentage of 26.2 percent investigated prostitution cases that also involved child pornography."[26] And of those police departments that had at least one arrest for a sexual assault against children, the percentage responding that the assault involved the use of a camera for movies, videotapes, or photographs ranged from 8.9 percent in Illinois to 20.3 percent in the Northeast, with a mean over the five regions of 15.1 percent.

(We believe that the figures may be much lower than they would be if more police departments asked pornography-related questions of their child sexual assault victims.)

Russell and Trocki conducted a random survey of 930 women in San Francisco.[27] Their findings suggest that the connection between pornography and abuse of women is strong and that many women have been harmed by pornography. We suggest that many other studies similar to Russell and Trocki's research be done to further document this connection. Russell and Trocki found that

[o]f those women who said they had seen pornography, 44% said they were upset by it. This is clearly a large minority.

Fourteen percent (14%) of the 930 women— or almost one in every seven women—reported that they had been asked to pose for pornographic pictures.

And 10% of the women interviewed said they had been upset by someone trying to get them to enact what had been seen in pornographic pictures, movies or books.[28]

As Russell and Trocki note, the figures may be underestimated, for some of the women may have been unaware that the "sexual behavior or requests that upset them were influenced by the viewing of pornography."[29]

Nonetheless, applying the percentages arrived at by their study to the entire population of American women (and, perhaps, adolescents), it seems likely that an enormous number of American females have experienced harms associated with pornography. While documentable harms from pornography have been found, we have yet to discover any redeeming qualities, values, or justifications for pornography's existence.

Other researchers have documented harms from pornography. Hollis Wheeler worked with more than one hundred adult females who were sexually assaulted or abused as children. An incomplete survey of them showed that more than 10 percent were used to make pornography, either for commercial sale or the offender's personal use.[30] Dr. Victor Cline told the Attorney General's Commission on Pornography that he had treated around 225 individuals who had their lives disrupted because of their involvement with pornography.[31] In a letter to the editor of the *Wausau Sunday Herald,* Dom Gordon said that a national study by the University of Chicago's Dr. Morris Lipkin and Dr. Donald Carns found that 254 therapists said they had had patients who were damaged or harmed by exposure to pornography. Another 325 doctors indicated that they had had

patients whose cases showed partial evidence suggesting harms associated with the use of pornography.[32] Charles H. Keating, Jr., founder of Citizens for Decency Through Law, told a U.S. Senate committee that one research study found that 77 percent of child molesters of boys and 87 percent of child molesters of girls admitted imitating the sexual behavior they had seen modeled in pornography.[33]

We, in our work, have found that police officials (who work directly with the victims and offenders) frequently note a direct connection between pornography and crimes of sexual abuse or violence against women and children. The pornography is read or viewed and imitated abusively. According to J. Edgar Hoover, who testified at the Granahan hearings in 1961, "We know that an overwhelmingly large number of sex crimes are associated with pornography. We know that sex criminals read it, are clearly influenced by it."[34] Hoover, at one time director of the FBI, believed that pornography was a major source of sexual violence and that if distribution of pornography were eliminated, the United States' crime rate would be greatly reduced.[35]

The Los Angeles Police Department's Sexually Exploited Child Unit has found that there is "a strong correlation between child pornography and the sexual exploitation of children."[36] Chief of police Daryl Gates and Captain J.J. Docherty said that children must be victimized in order for child pornography to be produced and that it is common for child pornography to be used to lower the inhibitions of child sexual abuse victims. Los Angeles Police Department Detective William Dworin has estimated that of the seven-hundred child molesters in whose arrest he has participated more than half had child pornography in their possession. In addition, he states that about eighty percent own either child or adult pornography.[37]

Detective Terry Hall of the Indianapolis Police Department said that he has worked on numerous child molesting cases where pornography was used to indoctrinate the children into molestation.[38] Similarly, William Fortune of the New York Police Department said that there are many cases in the department's files in which pedophiles used pornography to entice children into sex acts.[39] Similar findings were noted by Lee P. Brown, Houston's chief of police.[40] Milwaukee's chief of police noted that most pedophiles have large collections of pornography,[41] and Dane County, Wisconsin, sheriff Jerome Lacke said that studies have shown that the single most "distinctive" characteristic of a pedophile is "his consummate interest in adult and child pornography."[42] He noted that concrete information is hard to obtain because many abusers refuse to admit an interest in pornography and not all victims are shown it.

Charles Keating quoted a former Detroit police inspector as saying, "There has not been a sex murder in the history of our department in which the killer was not an avid reader of lewd magazines."[43] Inspector Harry Fox of the Philadelphia Police Department told the Granahan committee in 1959 that the department found pornography in the possession of juvenile sex offenders and in some cases adults used it to entice juveniles into sex acts.[44] After questioning hundreds of adults and juveniles involved in sex offenses, the Philadelphia Police Department concluded that "this material acts as an aphrodisiac resulting in rapes, seduction, sodomy, indecent assaults and indecent exposure."[45]

According to Wildmon, U.S. Postal Service inspectors "have found that 80 percent of the child pornography collectors they investigate abuse children sexually." He states that Chicago police say that "almost all collectors they investigate convict themselves with their own evidence—[P]olaroid photos, videotapes and movies."[46]

Justice Tom C. Clark, dissenting, in *Memoirs v. Massachusetts* said: "[S]ex murder cases are invariably tied to some form of obscene literature . . . [T]he files of our law enforcement agencies contain many reports of persons who patterned their criminal conduct after behavior depicted in obscene material."[47]

Andrea Dworkin entered into the December 12, 1983, Minneapolis hearings record on the civil rights ordinance before the Minneapolis City Council Government Operations Committee a letter from a New York City crisis worker concerning the increased

existence of rape of the throat since distribution of the movie *Deep Throat*.[48] Patricia Foscato, a social worker who treats families troubled by sexual abuse, told the Attorney General's Commission on Pornography that around 40 percent of the incest families she evaluated or treated "mentioned pornography as a concern."[49] In Marathon County, Wisconsin, there were four hundred reported cases of child sexual assault in one year. Professionals who worked with the victims said pornography is frequently used to convince and teach children that it is okay to do sex acts with perpetrators.[50]

Carol Plumer, a Michigan therapist who has worked with children who were used in child pornography and sexually abused, wrote that virtually all the children were shown adult and child pornography as part of the preparation for abuse. Victims, as adults, feared that the photographs and negatives could be used. There was no way they could recover them or feel the violation had ended.[51] A Florida child psychologist and a social worker told Brad Curl about the alarming increase in sexually abused children being treated. They mentioned a growing tragedy—3- and 4-year-old girls sexually abused by 7- to 10-year-old boys "who have been stimulated by pornography."[52] Ann Jones, who interviewed many battered women who killed their attackers, became convinced that there was a connection between pornography and violence against women when pornography kept coming up again and again in such cases.[53] And Harry Clor cites statements from a psychiatrist, a psychologist, and the National Council of Juvenile Court Judges from the 1950s that delinquent, antisocial, and criminal behavior can result from stimulation of juveniles by pornography.[54]

PORNOGRAPHY'S ACTRESSES AND ACTORS

The women and men who prostitute themselves in pornography are, in some cases, victims of pornography. Linda Marchiano (known as Linda Lovelace in pornographic movies) was held captive as a sex slave for more than two years and was forced to perform for pornography. To this day, she has found no legal remedy against the persons who abused her and no legal remedy to get the pornography that was the product of her abuse off the streets. Linda told her story in her books, *Ordeal* and *Out of Bondage*.[55] We reprint below part of her testimony at the Minneapolis hearings.

MS. MARCHIANO: I feel I should introduce myself and tell you why I feel I am qualified to

speak out against pornography. My name today is Linda Marchiano. Linda Lovelace was the name I bore during a two and a half year period of imprisonment. For those of you who don't know the name, Linda Lovelace was the victim of this so-called victimless crime.

Used and abused by Mr. Traynor, her captor, she was forced through physical, mental, and sexual abuse and often at gunpoint and threats of her life to be involved in pornography. Linda Lovelace was not a willing participant but became the sex freak of the '70's.

It all began in 1971. I was recuperating from a near fatal car accident at my parents' home in Florida. A girlfriend of mine came to visit me with a person by the name of Mr. Charles Traynor. He came off as a considerate gentleman, asking us what we would like to do and how we would like to spend the afternoon and opening doors and lighting cigarettes and all so-called manners of society.

Needless to say I was impressed, and started to date him. I was not getting along with my own parents. I was 21 and resented being told to be home at 11:00 o'clock and to call and say where I was and to call and give the phone number and address where I would be.

Here comes the biggest mistake of my life. Seeing how upset I was with my home life, Mr. Traynor offered me his assistance. He said I could come and live at his home in Miami. The relationship was platonic, which was fine with me. My plan was to recuperate and then go back to New York and live. I thought then he was being kind and a nice friend. Today I know why the relationship was platonic. He was incapable of a sexual act without inflicting some type of pain or degradation upon a human being.

When I decided to head back north and informed Mr. Traynor of my intention, that was when I met the real Mr. Traynor and my two and a half years of imprisonment began. He began a complete turnaround and beat me up physically and began the mental abuse, from that day forward my hell began.

I literally became a prisoner. I was not allowed out of his sight, not even to use the bathroom. Why, you may ask, because there was a window in the bathroom. When speaking to either of my friends or my parents, he was on the extension with a .45 automatic 8 shot pointed at me. I was beaten physically and suffered mental abuse each and every day thereafter.

In my book *Ordeal*, an autobiography, I go into greater detail of the monstrosity I was put through. From prostitution to porno films to celebrity satisfier. The things that he used to get me involved in pornography went from a .45 automatic 8 shot and M-16 semi-automatic machine gun to threats on the lives of my family. I have seen the kind of people involved in pornography and how they will use anyone to get what they want.

So many people ask me why didn't you escape? Well, I did, I'm here today. I did try during the two and a half years to escape on three separate occasions. The first and second time I was caught and suffered a brutal beating and an awful sexual abuse as punishment. The third time I was at my parents' home and Mr. Traynor threatened to kill my parents. I said, "No, you won't, my father is here in the other room" and he said, "I will kill him and each and every member of your family." Just then my nephew came in through the kitchen door to the living room, he pulled out the .45 and said he would shoot him if I didn't leave immediately. I did.

Some of you might say I was foolish but I'm not the kind of person who could live the rest of my life knowing that another human being had died because of me.

The name, Linda Lovelace, gave me a great deal of courage and notoriety. Had Linda Borman been shot dead in a hotel room, no questions would be asked. If Linda Lovelace was shot dead in Los Angeles, questions would have been asked. After three unsuccessful attempts at escaping, I realized I had to take my time and plan it well. It took six months of preparation to convince Mr. Traynor to allow me out of his sight for 15 minutes. I had to tell him he was right, a woman's body was to be used to make money, that porno was great, that beating people was the right thing to do. Fortunately for me, after I acquired my 15 minutes out of his presence, I also had someone that wanted to help me.

I tried to tell my story several times. Once to a reporter, Vernon Scott, who works for the UPI. He said he couldn't print it. Again on the Regis Philbin Show and when I started to explain what happened to me, that I was beaten and forced into it, he laughed. Also at a grand jury hearing in California after they had watched a porno film, they asked me why I did it. I said, "Because a gun was being pointed at me" and they just said "Oh, but no charges were ever filed."

I also called the Beverly Hills Police Department on my final escape and I told them that Mr. Traynor was walking around looking for me with an M-16. When they first told me that they couldn't become involved in domestic affairs, I accepted that and asked them and told them that he was illegally possessing these weapons and they simply told me to call back when he was in the room.

During the filming of *Deep Throat*, actually after the first day, I suffered a brutal beating in my room for smiling on the set. It was a hotel room and the whole crew was in one room, there was at least 20 people partying, music going, laughing, and having a good time. Mr. Traynor started to bounce me off the walls. I figured out of 20 people, there might be one human being that would do something to help me and I was screaming for help, I was being beaten, I was being kicked around and again bounced off of walls. And all of a sudden the room next door became very quiet. Nobody, not one person came to help me.

The greatest complaint the next day is the fact that there was bruises on my body. So many people say that in *Deep Throat* I have a smile on my face and I look as though I am really enjoying myself. No one ever asked me how those bruises got on my body.

Mr. Traynor stopped searching for me

because he acquired Marilyn Chambers who I believe is also being held against her will.

A reporter from the Philadelphia newspaper did an interview, his name is Larry Fields. During the course of the interview Ms. Chambers asked for permission to go to the bathroom and he refused it. Mr. Fields objected and said, why don't you let the poor girl go to the bathroom, she is about to go on stage and he came back with, I don't tell you how to write your newspaper, don't tell me how to treat my broads.

I have also been in touch with a girl who was with Mr. Traynor two months prior to getting me, who was put through a similar situation but not as strong. And as it stands today, she still fears for her life and the life of her family. Personally, I think it is time that the legal system in this country realize that one, you can't be held prisoner for two and a half years and the next day trust the society which has caused your pain and resume the life you once called yours. It takes time to overcome the total dehumanization which you have been through.

It is time for something to be done about the civil rights of the victims and not criminals. The victims being women. But realize, please, it is not just the women who are victims but also children, men and our society. . . .

Could you describe for us the first time that Mr. Traynor prostituted you?

MS. MARCHIANO: It happened in Florida. I had thought we were going to visit a friend of his and we pulled up to a Holiday Inn. So my second reaction was a buffet, I thought we were going to lunch. And he took me up to a room and there was five men in the room and told me that I was there to satisfy each and every one of them. And I said that I wouldn't do it so what he did is he took me into this little dressing area and he told me that if I didn't do it that he would shoot me. And I said, you won't shoot me, there is five men in this room, you just won't do it, somebody will say something and do something. And he just laughed hysterically. He said that my body would be found and I would be another prostitute who was shot in her hotel room or something like that and that none of the men would do anything, they would just laugh.

During this event, I started to cry and while these five men were doing whatever they wanted to do, and it was really a pitiful scene because here I was, they knew I wasn't into it. One of the men complained and asked for his money back because I was crying and I wasn't the super freak that Mr. Traynor usually brought around. And he was given back his money. And the other four men proceeded to do what they wanted to do through my tears and all. . . .

MS. DWORKIN: One of the situations that is commonly portrayed in pornography is women being—women having sexual intercourse and doing various sex acts with animals. You were forced to make such a film, could you describe for us the situation in which you were forced to make this film?

MR. DAUGHTERY: Would you like to respond?

MS. MARCHIANO: Yes, I think it is important that everyone understands.

Prior to that film being made, about a week, Mr. Traynor suggested the thought that I do films with a D-O-G and I told him that I wouldn't do it. I suffered a brutal beating, he claims he suffered embarrassment because I wouldn't do it.

We then went to another porno studio, one of the sleaziest ones I have ever seen, and then this guy walked in with his animal and I again started crying. I started crying. I said I am not going to do this and they were all very persistent, the two men involved in making the pornographic film and Mr. Traynor himself. And I started to leave and go outside the room where they make these films and when I turned around there was all of a sudden a gun displayed on the desk and having seen the coarseness and the callousness of the people involved in pornography, I knew that I would have been shot and killed.

Needless to say, the film was shot and still is one of the hardest ones for me to deal with today.

MS. DWORKIN: . . . There was one other incident that you described in your book *Ordeal* that involved Mr. Hefner, Hugh Hefner at the Playboy Mansion that was about the same theme. Would you tell us briefly about that?

MS. MARCHIANO: Yes. Well, we first met Mr. Hefner. Mr. Traynor and him sat around discussing what they could do with me, all kinds of different atrocities. And it seemed that Mr. Hefner and Mr. Traynor both enjoyed seeing a woman being used by an animal. And so Mr. Hefner had Mr. Traynor's dog flown in from Florida to the L.A. Mansion. And one evening they decided that it was time and they had one of the security guards bring the animal down to Mr. Hefner's bathhouse and fortunately, during my two and a half years in imprisonment there was a girl that tried to help me in her own sort of way. She told me the tricks to avoid that kind of a situation and I did what I could to avoid it but Mr. Traynor and Mr. Hefer were both very disappointed.

MS. DWORKIN: Thank you. Would you explain to us how it was that Mr. Traynor taught you to do what is now known popularly in this culture because of the movie *Deep Throat* as the sex act of deep throating?

MS. MARCHIANO: Well, he used hypnotism. He told me that it would overcome the natural reflexes in your throat that would prevent you from gagging and it was through hypnotism that I was able, I guess, to accomplish the feat, I guess you could say.

MS. DWORKIN: So that hypnotism was added to the prostitution?

MS. MARCHIANO: Yes, it was.

MS. DWORKIN: My final question is this: Some people may think that you could have gotten away, for instance, when Mr. Traynor was sleeping. Could you explain to us why that was impossible?

MS. MARCHIANO: Well, at night what he would do is put his body over my body so that if I did try to get up he would wake up. And he was a very light sleeper. If I did attempt to move or roll over in my sleep he would awaken.

MS. DWORKIN: Thank you very much.

MS. MacKINNON: How do you feel about the existence of the film *Deep Throat* and its continually being shown?

MS. MARCHIANO: I feel very hurt and very disappointed in my society and my country for allowing the fact that I was raped, I was beaten, I was put through two and a half years of what I was put through. And it's taken me almost 10 years to overcome the damage that he caused.

And the fact that this film is still being shown and that my three children will one day walk down the street and see their mother being abused, it makes me angry, makes me sad. Virtually every time someone watches that film, they are watching me being raped.[56]

Other pornographic stars also have been victims. Colleen Applegate (known as Shana Grant in the films), a small-town girl who appeared in numerous pornographic films, committed suicide, taking her own life with a gun. A PBS "Frontline" documentary titled "Death of a Porn Queen" explored her life and suggested that she took her life because she was emotionally upset by her involvement in pornography.

The Killing of the Unicorn: Dorothy Stratton 1960–1980[57] tells how Dorothy Stratton, not quite 18, met Paul Snider (who later became her husband), a small-time pimp and drug dealer who claimed to be a big-time promoter and tried to convince Stratton to pose nude for *Playboy*. He seduced her, and she fell in love with him. He eventually tricked her into posing nude, saying the pictures were only for him. When her mother refused to sign a release on the photos, he forged the signature. Stratton became *Playboy's* Playmate of the Month and Playmate of the Year. In August 1980, Paul Snider raped, sexually tortured, and sodomized Dorothy Stratton in a manner directly patterned after a film, *Autumn Born*, in which she had starred, then murdered her and committed suicide. All this took place in a room papered with pornographic pictures of her.

In 1987, an agent and two film producers were indicted in Los Angeles for using X-rated film star Norma Kuzma (known as Traci Lords in the films) in a sexually explicit movie when she was 16.[58] Kuzma used a phony identification—Christie Elizabeth Nussman. She turned 18 in May 1986. During her two and a half years in the adult movie business, Kuzma made at least 105 sexually explicit films. (Note: Filmmakers can defend against such charges if they make good-faith efforts to make certain that porn actresses and actors are adults.)

A male, George, acted in pornographic films and testified before the Attorney General's Commission on Pornography.[59] At age 19 he started dancing and nude modeling in New York. Magazine representatives approached him. At 21 he got into X-rated movies. According to George, getting paid to have sex with all those beautiful women was an ego trip. It was easy work, easy money.

George got paid per sex scene, which could be $200 to $250 for one scene a day or $300 to $400 for two scenes. He earned more for having anal sex. Girls made more when they were working with two guys. Porn stars just say they are getting paid to act to keep their jobs and make it sound legitimate, George said, but they are paid per sex act and not for acting. Producers and directors do not care about their models developing acting skills. They care only about getting a product out, he said. George told the commission that the producers and directors "are nothing but pimps" and that they don't "give a hoot about the girls or the guys" and don't help people who have been hurt.[60]

One of the best-known male pornography stars, John Holmes, died in 1988 from AIDS. The disease problem is one reason George left the pornography business. He contracted sexually transmitted diseases a couple of times and says that diseases are rampant in the industry. According to George, one person with AIDS could infect the whole industry.

George also left because he said the industry dehumanized him and the women he worked with. He said he hates what it does to the women, who are almost forced to do things they would rather not do—for example, perform in anal sex scenes with large guys. He saw them crying in pain. "It just destroys their personalities when they are forced to do things like that," he said. The filmmakers will threaten to call the woman's agent and ask for someone who will do the scene. Or they will offer the woman an extra $50. But when she gives in, she always regrets it afterward, George said. He said he has seen sweet 18-year-old girls go through "total changes in personality and lifestyle." Once in, a woman finds it hard to get out, for many have an alcohol or drug habit to support, he said. He estimated that 80 to 90 percent of the models delve into cocaine and "definitely use pot and alcohol." George has seen cocaine handed out on the set "to relax the girls" and to entice them into scenes they do not want to do. Many bring drugs for relaxation between scenes, he said.[61]

Actors and actresses also get into pornography for the money, George said. It is the only way to get $1,000 to $2,000 a week without being street prostitutes. These people could not make that kind of money in the jobs they would find. Many of the women have boyfriends sponging off them and pushing them to stay in the business, he noted.

Once involved in pornographic acting, one cannot leave it behind, George said. He almost lost his current job because his boss found out about his past. It destroyed his family life. His parents will not talk to him. His wife divorced him. It will hurt him for the rest of his life.

George said his dad always had pornography around the house. When George was a junior in high school, his dad would throw pornographic magazines on his bed for him to look at and took him to X-rated films. George believes that if he had not been exposed to so much pornography, he would not have had much interest in becoming a porn actor.

The harms resulting from acting in pornography are discussed at length in the Attorney General's Commission on Pornography's report.[62]

Laura Lederer interviewed a former female pornography model in *Take Back the Night*.[63] The woman's parents were sexually abusive, so she ran away from home and lived with a boyfriend. She signed up to model for pornography because she needed money. She said most women who model for pornography are "hurt or crazy—women under stress."[64] They are usually desperate economically. Many female high school graduates are not skilled at anything but marketing their bodies and making themselves pretty, the woman commented. A big part of the pornography business consists of runaways, she said.

The model said women are socialized "to passively accept tremendous amounts of pain, indignity and humiliation." Her boyfriend lived off her. She said pornographic acting was "all a form of rape because women who are involved in it don't know how to get out."[65] While porn models can fool themselves, street prostitutes are more honest about what they are doing, she said. Women resist pressure to do hard-core pornography because you cannot ever go back to the more legitimate modeling. Yet some hook onto the money.

The woman told Lederer of physical abuse on the job (being worked to death, exposed to diseases and forced to assume physically dangerous positions) and emotional abuse (being subject to suggestive sexual comments, treated like a piece of meat, and referred to in the third person). She said that she was once drugged and raped. Her sex life has not been normal, for she cannot equate sex with affection. She still fears that her picture will show up somewhere, noting that as soon as you sign a model's release form, you sign away those pictures for life. She modeled in the late 1960s when hard-core meant just sex, not violence and brutality as it does today. The model believes that by allowing the widespread proliferation of pornography, children are being trained to think that sadomasochistic behavior is normal. This, she said, victimizes women, because pornography is made for male purchasers.

Sylvester Stallone made a pornographic movie when he was a young man because he was literally starving and saw his only other option as robbing someone.[66] Suzanne Somers once let a boyfriend take nude pictures of her. They were published in *Playboy* ten years later. A company considered canceling her lucrative commercial because of the photographs.[67] Vanessa Williams lost her Miss America crown when *Penthouse* published sexually explicit pictures of her that she said were made for private use, and at most, for silhouettes. She said she did not consent to their publication.[68] And, more recently, *Wheel of Fortune* star Vanna White sued *Playboy* for $5.2 million for publishing revealing photos of her that were meant for private use. White posed for a photographer in sheer lingerie at a time when she was poverty-stricken, "when I couldn't eat or pay the rent." White's attorney alleged that after she achieved stardom, the photographer sold the photographs to *Playboy* for $100,000.[69]

Like pornographic acting, writing pornography is not a glamorous job. Ron Sproat, author of several pornographic novels, wrote a piece for *New York Magazine* in 1974 that was reprinted in *Sexual Deviance and Sexual Deviants*.[70] Sproat was expected to produce a two-hundred page novel in one week (forty pages a day) for $120. Writers were assigned subjects such as straight sex, gay-male, and gay-female. He was told there was quite a turnover of staff writers. Sproat learned that quantity of production, not quality of the writing, was important to his employers. The books were printed elsewhere, and he never saw his finished work.

Sproat had to sign a paper saying he would produce forty pages a day that were acceptable to the company or he could be fired or forfeit salary for the missing pages. There were no benefits or guaranteed right to work until he had been there three months, and he could be arbitrarily fired. The books were published under pseudonyms, and the authors did not know under what titles or pseudonyms the books they wrote would be published.

Sproat finally began talking to other writers during coffee breaks. They hated the "forbidding assembly-line atmosphere,"[71] the unending sex scenes, and the boredom of writing the same scene again and again. Although Sproat worked for this company for almost a month and wrote two and a half novels, he never averaged more than thirty-five pages a day.

One of Sproat's assignments was a novel about pedophilia. The guidelines said to emphasize the children's innocence and the adults' lechery. Child features such as lack of pubic hair or breasts and tiny privates were to be emphasized. The children written about were to be from 6 to 15 years old. Sproat also was given a guide to writing about bestiality. He could not carry out his assignment because his 8-year-old nephew had come close to being molested and he did not know how to write such a thing. Sproat asked to be invited if "ever anyone wants to have a book-burning party to destroy all of these things."[72]

THE PLAYBOY EXAMPLE

Miki Garcia, Ms. January 1973 for *Playboy* and later director of Playmate Promotions, told the Attorney General's Commission on Pornography that playmates had lots of problems for which she counseled them. For instance, "at Playboy's Mansion West, Playboy's corporate house, Hefner and his staff encouraged playmates to use illegal drugs and coerced them into bisexual activities and orgies to satisfy Hefner's interests."[73]

Garcia said, "Hugh Hefner suppresses the truth about his organization through extensive connections in the media and political world." She resigned in May 1982 when she confirmed that some Playmates "were involved in an international call girl ring which had ties to the Playboy Mansion. Because of Playboy security's influence with the LAPD [Los Angeles Police Department] a major investigation of the Playmates was thwarted."[74]

Models for *Playboy* sign releases, she explained. They do not know at the time what types of photos they will be required to pose for. While they cannot be forced to pose, they are manipulated, she said. The playmates eventually get dumped after they lose attractiveness, begin to abuse drugs, and so on. They often end up in prostitution or hard-core films, she said. Garcia said she was raped by a celebrity while traveling for Playboy.

A former Playboy bunny testified that she was suicidal and had sought psychiatric help to deal with the eight years she had lived in a sexually promiscuous fashion. In Los Angeles, her roommate, also a bunny, slashed her wrists.[75] Another former bunny said the group sex held in Hefner's mansion was accompanied by the pornographic movie *The Devil in Miss Jones*.[76] We suggest that you consult Russell Miller's book about the Playboy operation for further details.[77]

PORNOGRAPHY'S PERPETRATORS

The authors have chosen three pornography crime-linked perpetrators to present in depth. All three case histories are presented as reprints of Dr. Frank Osanka's testimony before the Attorney General's Commission on Pornography on July 23, 1985, in Chicago.

By age 19, Thomas Schiro had sadistically raped and murdered one woman and raped more than twenty others. Arthur Gary Bishop murdered several young boys. John Wayne Gacy murdered thirty-three boys and young men. Their stories are excellent examples of the negative influence pornography can have on human behavior.

Text of Dr. Frank Osanka's Remarks[78]

Thank you, ladies and gentlemen, for this opportunity to share with you some of my findings regarding the association between exposure to pornography and crimes against persons. Because of limited time, I will restrict my comments to one specific case study (see Attachments I & II for two additional examples) which involved the painful death of an innocent female victim. In this case, the male victimizer was prematurely exposed to explicit pornography films at the tender age of seven. He developed an addiction to pornography and by the age of nineteen he had raped over twenty women; the last victim he raped, murdered and sexually used her body after she was dead.

The victimizer is Thomas N. Schiro and he was convicted September 12, 1981 of brutally raping and strangling to death a young woman in Evansville, Indiana that same year. He was sentenced to die in the electric chair on January 21, 1982, and he is today still awaiting his fate in the Indiana State Prison in Michigan City.

My data about Mr. Schiro was gathered and tape recorded in two Indiana jails where I evaluated him in preparation for testimony during his trial. I spent over fifty clinical hours with Mr. Schiro and subsequently testified as to my findings about his state of mind at the time of the murder.

During my evaluation of the question of Schiro's sanity I was surprised by discovering how pervasive pornography was in the development of his personality and his warped beliefs about human sexuality. Schiro's development from an innocent seven-year-old to a vicious nineteen-year-old rapist and murderer should give us cause to seriously examine the potentially dangerous effects of premature exposure to pornography.

My methodology today is designed to be brief. I will provide a summary of Schiro's premature and gradual exposure to pornography and his subsequent addiction to pornography; the integration of the deviant sexual values of pornography into his personality resulting in subsequent behavior of sexual crimes against others; and finally, I will let you hear Schiro himself describing some of the above developments. I have not provided for public record his descriptions of the brutal rape and murder but I am available to consult with the Commission on these matters in closed session. The portions that I will share with you are from a tape recording that I made of some of the fifty hours of clinical interviews of Schiro. . . .

Premature Exposure and Subsequent Addiction to Pornography—The Schiro Case: Thomas Schiro's first exposure to pornography happened before he was eight years old. He discovered two of his father's WW II–vintage pornography films. Viewing the films motivated him to masturbate and develop a need for additional exposure to additional pornography. One of the films was entitled, "Bedtime" and illustrated a man and a woman engaged in a variety of sexual interactions. The significant aspect of the film was the depiction of the woman's body as being sexually enthusiastic, while at the same time the camera frequently drew attention to her anguished facial features. The message to young Schiro was that

women enjoyed sexually-related pain to them. Later he learned that most women did not enjoy such pain and humiliation, but by that time he did not care because he had developed sadistic needs to hurt women either in thoughts or actions.

Within a few years, Schiro was stealing or buying "skin magazines" from drug stores or finding such materials in trash dumps. In his early teen years he would sneak into x-rated drive-in movies. Schiro paired masturbation with all of the above exposures. By the time he raped and murdered his last victim, he had been exposed to "skin magazines," pornographic picture books, and pornographic films. Many of these materials included violent sadistic acts against women.

Schiro's psychosexual development regressed to the point where he could not achieve an erection in any sexual act unless he coupled this desired behavior with viewing pornography. He would often place "centerfolds" next to the head of his victim and demand that she lay perfectly still. Schiro's live-in girlfriend testified at his trial that she finally concluded that she was nothing more than his "jack-off machine."

Schiro's psychosexual responses were conditioned to achieve primary sexual satisfaction, either alone or with another person, by pairing masturbation with viewing pornography.

Schiro's Sexually Deviant Behavior and Crimes Against Persons: What follows is a list of sexual dysfunctions that Schiro learned and reinforced through viewing pornography paired with masturbation.

Voyeurism. Schiro began "peeping" into other persons' windows when he was twelve. He continued this behavior until he was arrested for murder. When he found unsuspecting victims he would often knock on their window moments before he ejaculated. In later years he used his night prowling as a form of reconnaissance to his later breaking and entering for the purpose of sexual assault.

It should be noted that viewing pornography is a form of voyeurism.

Exhibitionism. Schiro began "flashing" in his late teens. He walked busy streets of Vincennes, Indiana, wearing brief cut-off jeans which left the head of his penis slightly exposed. He also sat in his car masturbating to pornography with the practice of calling a woman over to the car just prior to achieving ejaculation.

Telephone Scatology. Schiro began making obscene telephone calls when he was ten years old. He would watch the film, "Bedtime," then call a victim.

Urolagnia. Schiro urinated on some of his victims as a means of imitating the images in much of the pornography that he viewed.

Rape. Schiro committed nineteen to twenty-four sexual assaults of women before the final rape and murder episode. In these cases, he would need to view pornography in order to achieve an erection to accomplish the sexual assault. He defined accomplishment as ejaculating on or in his victim, or both. He would break and enter with a flashlight and "skin magazine," lay on the kitchen floor looking at the pornography until he achieved an erection, and then proceeded to carry out the sexual assault. He developed a desire for rape and the methodology of rape from pornography.

Cross-Dressing (Pseudotransvestism). Schiro experimented with wearing women's underwear while masturbating to pornography.

Sexual Sadism. Schiro received maximum sexual pleasure from fantasizing about inflicting pain on women or actually inflicting pain on women. This need was introduced by the film, "Bedtime," and reinforced by countless pornography magazines, books, and films.

Pygmalionism. Schiro developed a sexual and personal fixation on a manikin in a shop window in downtown Evansville, Indiana. The connection between this sexual interest, his requiring many of his victims to lay perfectly still, and his sexual abuse of his last victim after she was dead, is obvious.

Lust Murder. Schiro raped and murdered his last victim after incorporating all of the above-outlined sexual deviances, including the next one—necrophilia.

Necrophilia. Schiro used sexually the body of his last victim after he took her life. All of the above sexually-deviant behavior was modeled in the pornography that he was exposed to.

Attachments. For comparative purposes, I have attached pertinent previously unpublished documentation about two other convicted sex murderers who were addicted to pornography and used such materials tactically to compromise their victims. They are John Wayne Gacy, convicted in 1980 of the sexual assault

deaths of thirty-three boys and young men in Illinois and Arthur Gary Bishop who was convicted of sexual assault deaths of five boys in Utah. Both of these murderers are incarcerated today.

Attachment I is a hand-written letter by Arthur Gary Bishop which was provided to me by Mr. Wendell J. Ashton, Publisher, *Deseret News*, Salt Lake City, Utah. Mr. Ashton made a significant reference to this letter in his address before the Denver National Conference on Pornography on June 1, 1985.

Attachment II is a reprint of my evaluation of John Wayne Gacy prepared on March 6, 1980 while under contract as a paid consultant to the three-attorney prosecution team of the Cook County State's Attorney's Office in Chicago.

Attachment I[79]

Dear Bishop Guertz:

Since our brief discussion about pornography on April 30, I have done considerable thinking about it and its effects. Pornography is a widespread social problem, so prevalent that many people accept it as normal. I wish I could present a solution to effectively combat this disease, but I can't. Perhaps, though, you could derive some insight from my experiences with it.

During my trial Dr. Victor Cline testified about the adverse effects of pornography. As I listened to his explanations, I could discern how my own life corresponded to these consequences. He stated that as people become addicted to it, their desires escalate, their normal feelings become desensitized and they tend to act out what they have seen.

So it was with me. I am a homosexual pedophile convicted of murder, and pornography was a determining factor in my downfall. Somehow I became sexually attracted to young boys, and I would fantasize them naked. Certain bookstores offered sex education, photographic, or art books which occasionally contained pictures of nude boys; I purchased such books and used them to enhance my masturbatory fantasies. But it wasn't enough. I desired more sexually-arousing pictures, so I enticed boys into letting me take pictures of them naked. From adult magazines I also located addresses of foreign companies specializing in "kiddie porn," and spent hundreds of dollars on their magazines and films. Such materials would temporarily satisfy my cravings, but soon I would need pictures that were more explicit and revealing. Some of the material I received was shocking and disgusting, at first, but it shortly became commonplace and acceptable—and provided ideas on how to make my own pictures more sensual.

As I continued to digress further into my perverted behavior, more stimulation was necessary to maintain the same level of excitement. Finding and procuring sexually arousing materials became an obsession. For me, seeing pornography was like lighting a fuse on a stick of dynamite; I became stimulated and had to gratify my urges or explode. I persisted in taking photographs of boys, encouraging suggestive and perverted stances; shortly this became a starting point for me to physically fondle and involve them in mutual masturbation. I knew that what I was doing was wrong, but I perceived my money and gifts as compensation for any emotional harm sustained by them. I guess I was seeking the love and companionship generated between a man and his wife, but such tender feelings were incapable of being produced under these conditions. All boys became mere sexual objects, their only purpose being to heighten and intensify my sensual feelings. My conscience was desensitized, and my sexual appetite entirely controlled my actions. The day came when I invited a small neighborhood boy into my apartment, molested him, and then killed him in fear of being caught. Over the next few years I kidnapped, sexually abused, and murdered four other boys.

Pornography wasn't the only negative influence in my life, but its effect on me was devastating. I lost all sense of decency and respect for humanity and life, and I would do anything or take any risk to fulfill my deviant desires. If pornographic material would have been unavailable to me in my early stages, it is most probable that my sexual activities would not have escalated to the degree they did.

Sincerely,
Arthur Bishop

Attachment II[80]

The text of Dr. Frank Osanka's evaluation of convicted multiple-murderer, John Wayne Gacy.

March 6, 1980 letter to Mr. William J. Kunkle, Jr., Chief Deputy State's Attorney, Cook County, Illinois.

Dear Mr. Kunkle:

This report concerns your requested evaluation of the Defendant, Mr. John W. Gacy (born: March 17, 1942), currently on trial in Cook County. Specifically, this report will reflect my opinion concerning the following:

On the occasion of the crimes with which the Defendant is charged, did he:

a. Have the capacity to appreciate the criminality of his conduct?

b. Have the capacity to conform his conduct to the requirement of the law?

In order to objectively conclude an answer to these questions I have thoroughly reviewed and evaluated the following:

1. Since December, 1978, at least ninety percent of the printed news accounts of the case and twelve hours of television news spots and special reports. All of these materials are in my personal possession and I continually referred to them. I took a professional interest in this case from the first indications that a heinous crime has been committed as the issues involved (runaways/missing persons, rape, deviant crimes, the insanity defense, sexual abuse, etc.) are serious social justice issues that are thoroughly examined in the Lewis University Social Justice Graduate Program in which I teach.

2. The research files of Mr. Clifford L. Linedecker, author of *The Man Who Killed Boys: A True Story of a Mass Murderer in a Chicago Suburb*. New York: St. Martin's Press, 1980. Mr. Linedecker turned over to me clippings, interview notes, and his tape-recorded interviews of respondents on which he based his book. Mr. Linedecker gave me these items plus a typed draft of the book in 1979.

3. I have also reviewed extensive files of evidence, opinion and data held by the State's Attorney, among which are:

   a. Mr. Gacy's medical and social history, including material records from childhood to adulthood.

   b. Police reports, including the defendant's statements to the police, and the investigator's reports.

   c. The extensive "Defense Psychological/Psychiatric Evaluations" and the "Prosecution Psychological/Psychiatric Evaluations," much of which has been testified to in the trial to date.

   d. Interviews of family members of Mr. Gacy.

   e. Interviews of acquaintances of Mr. Gacy.

   f. Interviews of persons who allege to have been sexually intimate with Mr. Gacy.

   g. The legal, medical, correctional reports from Mr. Gacy's trial, conviction and incarceration in Iowa.

   h. Consultation with various investigators assigned to this case.

4. I have also studied pertinent psychiatric, psychological, social psychological, sociological, criminological books and journals relative to many of

the issues in this case. In addition, I have consulted law literature relative to the elements of this case.

5. For the sake of insuring complete objectivity, I prefer to make this evaluation without interviewing the Defendant. The Defendant's ability to ingratiate and persuade is frequently documented. Therefore, I prefer to be free of such possible influences.

After a thorough analytical review and examination of the foregoing data and evidence, it is my opinion that at the time of the crimes with which the Defendant is charged, Mr. John W. Gacy did have the capacity to appreciate the criminality of his conduct and did have the capacity to conform his conduct to the requirements of the law.

Because the crimes that Mr. Gacy is accused of are heinous crimes, crimes that are beyond the imagination of most people, there is a natural tendency to look for complex psychiatric explanations for the acts and to assume that the acts were carried out by a person who must not be aware of what he was doing. While this may be true in some cases, it is my opinion that there is no convincing evidence, data, or other indicators that would suggest that Mr. Gacy lacks control of his faculties. The only exception might be when he is under the influence of alcohol and/or drugs. However, it is clear that Mr. Gacy was not continually in such a drug or alcohol-induced state of mind between the years 1972 and 1979, so therefore drugs and alcohol cannot be used as an indicator that Mr. Gacy did not have the capacity to appreciate the criminality of his conduct or did not have the capacity to conform his conduct to the requirements of the law at the times of the thirty-three (33) murders.

In my opinion, a more reasonable conclusion would be that we are reviewing an individual who knows the difference between right and wrong, but he knows that there is a great deal of latitude in society's definitions of right and wrong in any given place at any given time with any given social group. Basically, Mr. Gacy is aware of the differences between right and wrong and uses blatant exhibitions of "right" to build an aura of not being capable of doing any "wrong," especially something as wrong as murder.

In other words, Mr. Gacy has absorbed the values and norms of the social world around him and has noted people's strengths and weaknesses in terms of the prevailing prejudices and behavioral labelling. Specifically, he recognizes people's moral and social strengthened weaknesses. His motivation for absorbing the culture around him is not altruistic but rather to satisfy his own selfish, mostly sexual needs. He is acutely conscious of these sexual needs as evidenced by his incessant insistence and defense that he is not a homosexual but rather a bisexual. This preoccupation with labelling of his sexual predisposition is the only consistent non-logical indicator of his behavior. It is commonly recognized that homosexuality is included in the meaning of bisexuality. Mr. Gacy is aware of his need for erotic homosexual experimentation, including sadistic forms. Pornography, sexual paraphernalia such as the dildo, leg-spreader, handcuffs, chains, and the board found in the house clearly indicate his conscious awareness of and self-pandering to his desire for erotic homosexual experimentation. Witnesses have testified and statements have been taken supporting his practice of using these items in his sexual ritual.

Mr. Gacy planned his adult life in ways which would provide him opportunities to seduce boys and young men. With the possible exception of some employment as a shoe salesman and as a cook, most of Mr. Gacy's employment have been situations where he would be in a position to meet and influence a variety of boys and young men. For example, his position in Iowa as a manager of several Fried Chicken franchises gave him the chance to influence through hiring. The nature of that business, with a constant turnover of customers, gave him opportunities to size-up the potential sexual possibilities of some of his customers. These kinds of impersonal and transitory establishments lend themselves to "opportunistic sex," especially for male homosexuals. This type of location is similar to the impersonal nature of highway oases, establishments that are known by many homosexuals as opportunities for "spot sex."

Mr. Gacy established his general contracting firm in a particular occupational design that would serve his need for erotic homosexual experimentation. The new firm provided lucrative self-employment (no supervisor), high status in the community, a reasonable explanation for keeping odd hours, and endless opportunities to use high wages as the means to attract and influence boys and young men.

Mr. Gacy was known to be an excellent chef and an untalented construction worker. Mr. Gacy managed the food franchises in Iowa, was a cook while in prison in Iowa, worked as a cook when he returned to Illinois from Iowa and often catered his own massive parties at his home on Summerdale Street. It is my interpretation that employment as a cook in a restaurant in Chicago did not provide the same opportunities to gratify his need for erotic homosexual experimentation with boys and young men. The job of cook requires almost constant attention to the product at a static location for a set period of time each working day. The job of a general contractor, however, allows for flexibility of time and distance (inconsistent hours at many different places) and the opportunity to attract boys and young men who could, because of the transitional nature of the job, appear and disappear with little notice. Mr. Gacy became so secure in his personal safety and financial comfort that he began to do what he wanted to do for a long time—intensify his pleasure for erotic homosexual experimentation. On some occasions in the data he is attributed with an unusually large number of successful homosexual encounters.

Mr. Gacy has been gifted with a quality of charisma to an unusual extent. It is a quality that has served to allow him to assimilate and, ingratiate himself into many different social strata. He is keenly aware of role playing and certain stereotypical roles in society. He understands that often people respond to the aura of a person rather than take the time to precisely evaluate what a person is saying or what the person's real intent may be. So, he is able to assume the behavioral characteristics prescribed to certain role models. Indeed, in the same day he can actively convince people that he is a good husband, considerate neighbor, cooperative co-worker, authoritative policeman, happy-go-lucky clown, political activist, and sadistic homosexual opportunist. The evidence of his agility at role transformations at will is the ample testimony of entirely different descriptions of him as seen at given points in space and time. Mr. Gacy consciously adapts his role behavior to his view of the prevailing values, norms and standards that he finds operational in the social situation he places himself in. He doesn't talk about the drug culture with those neighbors and friends that he recognizes would disapprove but he uses the opportunity for drugs as a means of influencing boys and young men. He displays a picture of himself standing next to the wife of the President of the United States for viewing by all but only shows his considerable collection of pornography, especially depicting homosexual acts, to boys and young men that he has solicited into his home for the purposes of gratifying his need for erotic homosexual experimentation. His ability at role adaption is so perfected that neighbors, family, friends, sexual partners, and jailers are widely inconsistent in their descriptions of the Mr. Gacy that they have experienced.

Briefly, role adaption requires the capacity to appreciate the reality of the social situation and Mr. Gacy continually conforms his behavior to the requirements of the situation that serves his advantage.

In summary, it would be comfortable to say that the repeated acts of murder of thirty-three boys and young men in such a heinous manner was the work of the mentally ill. And so we begin to look for classifications of behavior and mental states that must account for the derangement and thus will explain the behavior. Various professionals with different kinds of psychology and psychiatry backgrounds have been conditioned towards the same explanatory goals—convenient classification of the behavior of this case into or on the edge of existing theories of mental illness. In my opinion, to classify Mr. Gacy's behavior in principally psychiatric and psychological terms of mental illness is an exercise in deception and a clear injustice to those who truly suffer from mental diseases and who deserves society's sympathy and society's interactions toward lessening their pain and confusion and totally rehabilitating them. To attempt to apply psychotherapeutic analysis to explain Mr. Gacy's alleged behavior as a mental illness requires becoming a participant in his design of social theater. Mr. Gacy has stage managed what has to be his greatest manipulation in a lifetime of manipulative behavior. Indeed, if successful, it may be the greatest manipulation ever.

It would be comfortable to explain the heinous behavior under question as an uncontrollable mental illness. However, the explanation of episodic psychotic states simply cannot explain multiple murders, committed essentially at the same location, in essentially the same methodical manner, hiding the remains in essentially the same methodical manner, over a period of eight years by a man labelled acceptable and successful by his neighbors and in his business. Considering all of the available data in this case I can only conclude that while we stretch and pull and expand and clothe Mr. Gacy's behavior into neat niches that might be accounted for in psychological and psychiatric theory a layman can see the behavior described and can understand the behavioral dynamics in lay terms. That behavior is demonstrably premeditated murder. The murders were calculated in terms of planning, execution of the murders, eliminating traces of the murders, disposing of the remains, and preparation for the deposit of the remains of future victims. All clearly cognitive behavior.

In conclusion, it is my opinion, as a behavioral and social scientist, that the Defendant at the time of the crimes with which he is charged suffered neither with a mental illness nor mental defect which prevented him from appreciating the criminality of his behavior or from conforming his conduct to the requirements of the law.

Respectfully submitted,
Frank Osanka, Ph.D.
cc: Mr. Samuel Amirante
Counsel for Defense

Conclusions and Recommendations[81]

This Commission should take into consideration that in the absence of reasonable sex education for children at home, through the Church, or at school, pornography may be the primary source of sex education for youngsters, especially males. Pornography is much more accessible to young persons today than when Schiro was developing his sexual values. Pornography is easily available openly through neighborhood convenience stores and video rental stores. Usually these materials are purchased or rented by the parents but the parents are often careless about the need to secure the materials in order to guard against premature one-sided exposure to impressionable minds. As children generally are not exposed to a reasonable explanation of healthy sexual attitudes and behavior they have no way to recognize that pornography represents bizarre fantasy content and there is an absence of healthy affection and reasonable responsibility for one's actions. In addition, much pornography projects negative attitudes and messages about females.

I am serious when I recommend to this Commission that they consider the idea of recommending that all materials labeled pornography carry a warning sign similar to that found on cigarettes. For example:

Warning: Absorbing of this material may be dangerous to your health and/or the health of others.

Ladies and gentlemen, thank you for this opportunity to share some of my work with you.

DEATH FROM PORNOGRAPHY

People have died as a result of pornography-related crimes. (See, for example, the accounts of the murder activities of John Wayne Gacy, Thomas Schiro, and Arthur Gary Bishop in the previous section.)

In early June of 1985, five large bags of human bones, some charred, were collected from shallow graves at a remote cabin site in Calaveras County, California, about 140 miles northeast of San Francisco.

It was alleged that Leonard Lake, 39, and Charles Chatt Ng, 24, "acted out and videotaped sexual torture fantasies." According to Calaveras County Sheriff Claud Ballard, "The best evidence we have are movies of a woman pleading with Lake and Ng to give her back her baby, and being abused and forced at gunpoint to engage in sex acts with them."[82] It was believed that up to twenty-five men, women, and children may have been victims.

Lake killed himself while in custody on other charges. A woman who knew him told authorities that he once claimed membership in a San Francisco cult that practiced murder. Ng became the subject of an international search and was later arrested.

The remains of a child, woman, and man were previously found on the three-acre site used by Lake. Police also found jewelry, clothes, handcuffs, and "pornographic photographs and videotapes showing scenes of sexual torture involving Lake, Ng and women victims."[83] Also confiscated were Lake's diaries. These detailed his daily activities since 1983, giving an account of his practice of "keeping women in captivity as sexual slaves." The torture apparently took place in a cinder-block bunker with a secret chamber, mattress, and two-way mirror.

According to Calaveras County Sheriff Claud Ballard, one of Lake's diaries had fifty pages of his philosophy "that God meant women for cooking, cleaning house and sex and when they are not in use, they should be locked up."[84] The *San Francisco Chronicle* reported the diary had detailed scripts of up to one dozen videotapes showing the torture of victims.

The killings were thought to be linked to "fantasies of sadistic sexual domination, war games and survival."[85] There were videotapes of women being threatened with death. Ng appears in one allegedly slashing a woman's clothing with a knife. Police also found a videotape machine belonging to a San Francisco couple who disappeared last summer with their 16-month-old son.

In August 1973 the nation was shocked by the news disclosure that a sadistic trio led by former candy maker Dean Corll had raped and murdered at least twenty-seven male youths in Houston, Texas. Corll's teenage accomplices, Elmer Wayne Henley and David Owen Brooks, procured young victims for Corll. The long list of homicides stopped when Elmer Wayne Henley fatally shot Dean Corll in an argument over the intended rape and possible murder of other youths whom Henley brought to Corll's home, where the youths had earlier passed out as a result of intoxication due to sniffing paint, drinking hard liquor, and smoking marijuana. Police investigations subsequent to the Corll killing uncovered the twenty-seven victims under the floor of a utility shed, a dry riverbed, and an isolated wooded area.[86]

In another raid, Houston police found a warehouse full of homosexual literature, obscene photographs, and movies, slides, and magazines picturing boys ranging from age 8 or 9 to their late teens. There were strong indications that eleven of the boys in the photographs were among the twenty-seven Houston mass murder victims, but this connection was not pursued. The pornography leader, Roy Ames, had a prior record of child abuse. His distribution of pornography was worldwide.[87]

The Nueces County (Corpus Christi, Texas) medical examiner, Dr. Joseph Rupp, lectures extensively on child abuse and sex crimes and believes that pornography causes sexual abuse.[88] He has about thirty thousand slides of various forensic subjects, five hundred concerning sexual abuse deaths.

In 1978, Dr. Rupp said that since his office was created seven years earlier, there had been fifteen murders with sexual overtones.

> Two deaths in the past two years created considerable community concern about the problem of sexual abuse and pornography. One was the death of a young boy, sodomized and strangled to death after being abducted on the way home from school. Another was the death of an 18 year old girl with a vibrator in her rectum, laceration marks on her wrist, and stuffed in a refrigerator. Gags and strips of cloth were present in the room along with pornographic magazines. Some of them were depicting bondage and sadomasochism similar to the murdered girl's situation.[89]

In Great Britain, a man and woman tortured two children to death and made tape recordings of their screams. Ian Brady and Myra Hindley forced the 10-year-old girl and 12-year-old boy to pose for obscene pictures before killing them.[90]

In Iowa, a man was convicted of kidnapping and murdering an 8-year-old girl. He said she reminded him of a young girl he had seen in a pornographic magazine and was incited to the sexual attack and the murder.[91] And in New Jersey, a young boy who was exposed to pornography by a man, became so aroused that he "brutally raped and murdered a 10-year-old girl."[92]

In St. Petersburg, Florida, two brothers, ages 7 and 9, killed a baby. The boys assaulted the infant with a coat hanger and a pencil, imitating acts they had seen in pornographic magazines.[93]

Psychologist Edward Donnerstein, in testimony in the trial of convicted rapist-murder Thomas Schiro said that Schiro believed "sadism, masochism and rape are just part of sex and . . . Schiro enjoys modeling what he has seen in movies and on television."

In December 1984, *Penthouse* featured pictures of Asian women, bound from ankles to neck with ropes, hanging from trees. Two months later, a Chinese girl was found hanging from a tree in North Carolina. Her body's position and the location where it was found resembled the *Penthouse* layout. The girl had been kidnapped and murdered. Rape had been attempted.[95]

In the mid-1970s, a Hamilton, Ontario, resident killed his children and wife by "tieing them up in sleeping bags and dropping them in the Welland Canal. He used intricate knots, in binding his victims that he got from his collection of bondage magazines."[96] Also in Ontario, this time in Mississauga, a 19-year-old man raped and murdered a 16-year-old girl, "then burnt her breasts and pubic hair with a lighter before urinating on her body. He told police he got the idea from *Penthouse Forum*."[97]

In June 1983 in Thunder Bay, Ontario, a young man shot a 16-year-old girl through the heart, then cut off her breasts and removed her reproductive organs, which he left on her stomach. He had pornographic material at home showing the development of the female breast and reproductive organs.[98] And

> [i]n 1975 in Ottawa a 17 year old, Robert Poulin, overpowered a teenage girl, raped and killed her. Her body was found tied to a bed and had been set on fire. There was evidence of anal and vaginal intercourse. Poulin then shot up a classroom at his high school killing another student before taking his own life. A search of his bedroom revealed he was a collector of violent obscene photography and also possessed a blow-up sex doll.[99]

Use of pornography has been linked to other major crimes, including those of mass murderer Ted Bundy, who was interviewed by Dr. James C. Dobson, psychologist, hours before Bundy's execution in Florida in 1989. Among other things, Bundy said:

> My experience with pornography that deals on a violent level with sexuality is that once you become addicted to it—and I look at this as a kind of addiction—I would keep looking for more potent, more explicit, more graphic kinds of materials. Until you reach the point where the pornography only goes so far. You reach that jumping-off point where you begin to wonder if maybe actually doing it will give you that which is beyond just reading about it or looking at it.[100]

In New York, "Son of Sam" killer David Berkowitz had pornographic magazines at his bedside. Pornographic pictures also papered the walls of the shack where Melvin Rees tortured Mildred Jackson and her five-year-old daughter, Susan.[102] A rapist in Cambridge, Great Britain, had a vast stock of pornography,[103] while large quantities of pornography were found at Charles Manson's commune in California.[104] And a man who gunned down fourteen people in an Oklahoma post office had pornographic and paramilitary magazines, guns, and ammunition in his home.[105]

Linda Lee Daniels, 22, was kidnapped from in front of her fiancé's home on January 12, 1986, in Albuquerque, New Mexico. The four male kidnappers took her to a motel room, where they drugged and raped her. This was done for the production of a pornographic film. When her disappearance was publicized, the men murdered Linda.[106]

Roger Lange, 28, was charged with enticing a child for immoral purposes, kidnapping, first degree sexual assault, and first degree murder in connection with the March 1, 1982, death of 10-year-old Paula McCormick of Madison, Wisconsin. A police detective cried on the witness stand as he described how Paula's body was found bound and gagged in a television box after Lange led police to a rented warehouse area. Pathologist Dr. Billy Bauman said Paula died of strangulation and was sexually assaulted after she died. Dozens of pornographic books and sexual devices were confiscated from Lange.[107]

Charise Kamps, 19, also was murdered in Madison on June 24, 1984. Charise was disemboweled with a knife in a manner similar to that shown in the movie *Caligula*. She and the accused had seen the movie together.[108]

In Milwaukee, Lucille Ann Nelson, 20, was stabbed six times, struck on the head twelve times with a tire iron, and left naked in a snowbank with her hands tied behind her back with her underwear. Harold Koput was convicted of her murder in May 1984. He told a psychiatrist that he had viewed a television movie in which "an actress was maimed with a knife, slashed to death and raped." Koput told the doctor, "I wanted to do what they did." The prosecutor said the pornography Koput viewed stimulated his perversions and "gave him ideas on how to act out his . . . hatred of women."[109]

In a paper presented to the 1984 Seventh World Media Conference in Tokyo, Betty Wein mentions two West German cases from 1983 where killers were found to have large collections of violent videos. In one case, a woman and her husband killed her lover, cut his body into small pieces, and canned it. In the other, a mother and her two small children were murdered, and their bodies were slashed to bits.[110]

In Georgetown, Texas, a man beat his wife to death because she refused to have sex with him on his birthday. The man had watched a pornographic videotape immediately before the killing.[111] In *Presnell v. State*, 243 S.E.2d 496 (1978), a man was convicted of kidnapping and murdering an 8-year-old child and kidnapping and raping a 10-year-old child. He said one of the girls " 'reminded me of a girl in a pornographic book.' "[112] And in Cleveland, Ohio, a man who was charged with the rape, kidnapping, and murder of an 8-year-old girl reportedly told police he had been in an adult bookstore earlier that day and had magazines portraying nude children in his possession.[113]

In the state of Washington a man who was charged with murdering two women had rented two pornographic videotapes. He returned the tapes without winding them back. One of the tapes was stopped just after a scene depicting a woman in a position similar to that in which one of the murder victims' body was found.[114]

A Boston police captain told the Granahan committee in 1961 that pornography is frequently linked to crime and vice such as rape, child molestation, suicide or murder of children, wife swapping, and homosexuality. He noted that one child was found crucified with a mound of pornography at the foot of a cross.[115]

In Fullerton, California, Edmund Kemper III was convicted of murdering his grandparents at age 15, his mother at age 24, and six other women in between. He said he frequented snuff movies and read magazines to find depictions of corpses.[116] Another California man who pled not guilty by reason of insanity in the stabbing deaths of an elderly couple said he saw flashbacks from the slasher movie *Halloween II* before the stabbing.[117] And in India, two men saw a movie about a sex maniac who kills and rapes young girls. The men then killed two girls, ages 5 and 7, after deciding to imitate the man in the movie.[118]

In 1966, a 14-year-old boy slayed a 9-year-old girl. Her body was found in a shed along with pornographic magazines. Also in 1966, two male youths watched pornographic pictures and drank alcohol. Later that day, one of them killed a young woman after trying to rape her.[119]

Elise Taliaferro of Madison, Wisconsin, died in sexual bondage after her husband subjected her to torture using the pornographic magazine *Housewives in Bondage* as a manual.[120] And in East Austin, Texas, a 21-year-old man said he shot and killed a 32-year-old man who forced him to perform oral sex on him. Numerous sex devices and sex magazines, some depicting homosexuals, were found in the murdered man's apartment.[121]

Snuff pornography, "produced for men who

derive sexual pleasure from viewing it, requires the dismemberment, torture, mutilation and death of the women and children used to make it." According to experts such as Paul Gerber of the Minnesota Bureau of Criminal Apprehension, "some pornography depicts the actual murders of children."[122]

In Orange County, California, Fred Berre Douglas and Richard Felix Hernandez (also known as Richard Manuel Hernandez) were each charged on August 3, 1983, with two counts of murder, one count of conspiracy to commit murder, and one count of conspiracy to engage in and solicit prostitution. Beth M. Jones, 19, and Margaret Krueger, 16, had agreed to perform in a pornographic film for the men because they had no jobs and needed the money. "The girls disappeared on August 13, 1982, and their skeletal remains were found on March 30, 1983, 80 miles southeast of Anaheim, California." Douglas and Hernandez allegedly lured the girls to the California desert to make snuff-type films. They were later charged with murdering them.

Douglas had been tried five years before for allegedly plotting to torture women to death while making a pornographic film. His first trial ended in a hung jury. He then pled guilty to a lesser charge of conspiracy to commit assault with a deadly weapon. He received a six-month jail sentence and was placed on three years' probation.[123]

In Sacramento, California, the 10-year-old daughter of a man accused of child molestation said she saw her father and other men "film the ritual killings of three small children." According to the girl, her father said he would "cut her in half" if she told.

The father, Arthur Dill, and four persons who worked for him were charged with a combined total of 169 counts of felony child molestation.

The alleged victims included three of Dill's four children, ages 4 to 10, and five other children. The allegations included sexual incidents with the father and his friends and Dill's charging the men between $55 and $85 each to molest the children while he took photographs.[124]

The film *Snuff*, a pornographic film made in South America, shows a woman dismembered and disemboweled while alive, then murdered. There is much debate about whether the film shows an actual or simulated murder. When *Snuff* was shown in Monticello, New York, the district attorney refused to bring an obscenity prosecution. A group named Women Against Violence Against Women began its own court action. The City of Minneapolis also brought obscenity charges against the movie.[125]

After *Snuff* opened in New York City, the mutilation killing of two women was reported.[126] And in Buenos Aires, Argentina, at least three prostitutes were found dead. All were mutilated, and one had her arms cut off. The women were believed to have participated in snuff films.[127]

In the cases cited in this section, the harms from pornography were fatal to innocent victims. We believe that these and other deaths show that the risks of harm from pornography are greater than its value (which, we believe, is none).

AUTOEROTIC DEATHS

According to Jane E. Brody, teenage boys and others in the United States are following an extremely dangerous sexual practice "in which self-induced erotic pleasure is enhanced by near asphyxiation, usually induced by a noose around the neck."[128] The technique is used to heighten orgasm in masturbation. In the Brody article, two doctors describe the death scene when an accidental sexual asphyxiation has occurred: Victims of such deaths leave no suicide note and are found partly or totally undressed or in female underclothing. A cloth is around the person's neck (to prevent marks or burns). Pornography is nearby. Ropes or chains may bind the victim. Devices that can asphyxiate a person are positioned so that the victim could have applied or released them. It appears that masturbation took place. Victims are found suspended by their necks. The activities usually seem to have taken place alone.

The best source of information on autoerotic deaths is *Autoerotic Fatalities* by Robert R. Hazelwood, Park Elliott Dietz, and Ann Wolbert Burgess.[129] That work includes an excellent bibliography of articles about autoerotic deaths. According to these authors, the four common ways for such deaths to occur are compression of the neck through hanging or strangulation, exclusion of oxygen with a plastic bag or other device on the head, airway obstruction, and chest compression. (p. 49)

Hazelwood, Dietz, and Burgess studied 157 suspected autoerotic fatalities. They speculate that between five hundred and one thousand such deaths occur annually in the United States and Canada.

These authors note that bondage pornography is found in the possession of a sizable proportion of autoerotic asphyxia decedents (p. 56). (We have noted that autoerotic asphyxia typically involves being bound in pornographic-type bondage poses and the use of devices common to pornographic fantasies, including ropes, chains, handcuffs, leather hoods, gags, and vibrators.) Of the 157 cases Hazelwood, Dietz, and Burgess studied, commercial "erotica" (pornography) was found at the death scene or at the victim's home in forty-four cases. Several of those cases are described below.

Bondage magazines depicting the use of complex bindings such as the 21-year-old man had used were found at the man's attic death scene (p. 67).

A man was found dead with a belt around his neck and a rope tied to the belt. An open bondage magazine was on the coffee table near the man. In a desk drawer, police found rope, more bondage books, and photographs of the man engaged in bondage activity. The wife showed authorities a box of photos of her and her husband in bondage acts. She said the magazine on the table was his favorite, open to his favorite picture. She told them, "Whenever possible, he wanted to be tied exactly like the person in the photo, duplicating every twist, knot, and wrapping of the rope to the most minute detail" (p. 83).

Another autoerotic fatality victim had drawn sketches of sadistic sexual fantasies (scantily clad women with knives plunged into their chests) (pp. 87–89).

A 25-year-old man found hanging by a belt wore a sweater and skirt and had photos of women in sweaters on the bed nearby. *"Many of his sketches depicted a man embracing and kissing a woman wearing a sweater, while he stabbed her in the abdomen. Splashes of blood in the sketch were surrounded by the printed word* orgasm" (pp. 87, 89).

A woman was found suspended by a rope wrapped around her breasts and crotch. At her death, the woman wore a harem girl costume. A story about a harem in which women were hung around the walls had been read so often that its pages were loosened from the binding (p. 102).

Both of a dead victim's hands grasped magazines depicting women in stages of undress, and newspaper ads with similar photos were scattered about his body (p. 106).

One man was found with a bag of pornography nearby. He had pasted photographs of his family and friends over the faces of the porn models. He died from exposure after practicing autoerotic asphyxia (p. 113).

A man was found with his head in a black leather discipline mask (p. 114).

In a case of a 17-year-old male, police found photographic negatives that, when developed, showed the victim in sexual poses, including a prior asphyxial scene. One photo documented another hanging episode and had been altered by piercing through the nipples. Sketches of females in positions approximating the man's position at death and in his previously photographed episodes, as well as those showing nipple piercing, also were found (p. 129).

Diana Herceg sued *Hustler* magazine, claiming that a how-to article on autoerotic asphyxia had incited her 14-year-old son to replicate the act and caused his death in 1981. A copy of the article was found at her dead son's feet. *Hustler's* attorney said that the article had warned the reader at least twenty-two times that the practice of autoerotic asphyxia can result in death. Herceg received damages of $182,000 to compensate her for the death of her son.[130] The appellate court, however, reversed on First Amendment grounds.

In Dane County, Wisconsin, an attorney died in a sexual bondage episode. Pornographic magazines and homosexual films were at the death scene. A rag soaked with butyl nitrite was stuffed in his mouth. The man was tied and suspended from the ceiling.[133]

Pope cites two cases in which two males, ages 17 and 19, were found dead from autoerotic practices. Both had pictures depicting exactly what had happened to them next to them.[132] Morton A. Hill reports on six boys, ages 12 to 19, who died from autoerotic asphyxiation and had bondage magazines in their possession.[133] And Keating mentions an autoerotic death of a man. Just above him on the bed were five or six magazines open to nude female forms.[134]

The relationship between pornography exposure and the learning of autoerotic asphyxiation practices is clear. Considering that a number of persons die from this practice, the relationship should cause concern.

SEX RINGS

Countless children have been harmed by use in pornography and prostitution sex rings. Burgess describes three types of sex rings. In *solo sex rings,* several children are involved in sex with an adult who uses his or her legitimate role in their lives to recruit them. Children are conditioned by the adult to provide sex in exchange for rewards. Initiation into sex usually begins with indirect approaches such as showing them pictures of naked people in magazines. In *transition sex rings,* multiple adults are sexually involved with the children. The victims are usually pubescent, and they may be propelled quickly into prostitution. *Syndicated sex rings* are well-structured organizations that recruit children, produce pornography, deliver sexual services, and establish an extensive network of customers.[135]

The Indianapolis Police Department has identified a number of pedophile characteristics.[136] (Pedophiles are adults who have a sexual interest in children.) Importantly, pornography was mentioned in the profile of pedophiles. The pedophiles maintain inventories of all the child pornography they own. In fact, Kenneth V. Lanning of the FBI writes that pedophiles "are usually avid collectors of child pornography and child erotica."[137] This includes children describing sex acts in audio form. Children, he said, recognize the permanency of photographs. (This is significant because the children can never escape the possibility that the photographs will reappear and embarrass them. The children may be recognized in the photographs by significant others. Maturity makes them realize that men might be masturbating to the pictures forever, thereby making the children involuntary victims of others and continuing the sexual abuse.)

Lanning addresses the issue of why pedophiles collect child pornography. He says it may help them reinforce or satisfy persistent sexual fantasies about children and may help fulfill a need for validation of behavior and camaraderie (sharing with other pedophiles). In the photo, the child stays young forever; in real life, there cannot be a long-term sexual relationship. Lanning details pedophile uses of child pornography and erotica (pp. 83–85):

1. Sexual arousal and gratification (In most cases, the fantasy and arousal fueled by the porn is only a prelude to actual sex with children.)
2. To lower children's inhibitions (Adult pornography also is used.)
3. For blackmail of children (to silence them)
4. To exchange with other pedophiles
5. For profit

According to Burgess, collectors of child pornography believe that they are not harming the child.[138] We believe that collectors create a demand for child pornography, which means more children must be exploited and abused to meet this demand.

Burgess and others studied fifty-five sex rings.[139] Fifty-three of the ring leaders were male, mostly middle and upper class, with 90 percent between the ages of thirty and fifty-nine. Children were accessed by occupation (38.2 percent), by means of their living situations (27.3 percent), and by means of other children (14.5 percent). Many of the offenders had no previous offenses, but 34.6 percent had prior sex offenses. In at least 40 percent of the cases, mental health services were suggested for the children. Only boys were involved in 49.1 percent of the rings, only girls in 23.6 percent, and both boys and girls in 27.3 percent.

The following types of sex were involved in the rings: fondling, 89.1 percent; oral sex, 80 percent; vaginal sex (those with only females), 60.7 percent; anal sex (those with only boys), 63 percent. Of the syndicated rings, almost half had sadomasochistic activity; 9.7 percent of the solo rings had such acts, and no such acts were found in the transitional rings. Importantly, 52.9 percent of the syndicated rings videotaped sexual activities, while 12.9 percent of the solo rings and none of the transitional rings did so.

The study found that 61.8 percent of the rings showed adult pornography to the children, 18.2 percent did not, and no data were available for 20 percent of the rings. Of the syndicated rings, 84.4 percent showed adult pornography to the children, and 76.5 percent were involved in the commercial use of pornography.

In 1982, Cathy Stubblefield Wilson, a divorced mother of five, was arrested and accused of being the nation's largest dealer in child pornography. Operating with European connections, Wilson allegedly netted about $500,000 a year from her porn business. Los Angeles Police Department sources believed that Wilson controlled 80 percent of the distribution of child pornography in the United States. Police confiscated a mailing list of thirty thousand names from Wilson. A Los Angeles Police Department Investigation found that 30 to 40 percent of her clients were registered sex offenders.[140] Wilson pled guilty to one count of distributing child pornography and was sentenced to four years in prison.[141]

John Norman, who ran a boy-by-mail child pornography operation with more than thirty thousand customers, was imprisoned in 19xx for child molestation. After he was released, he was again arrested, and a list of fifty thousand names was confiscated.[142]

In another case, approximately three hundred girls were enticed into posing for nude photographs on the promise that the photographer would help them become movie stars. At first the mothers would accompany the girls to the sessions, which were perfectly innocent, and then later they stopped attending, trusting the photographer. In these later sessions, the younger girls were given Quaaludes and marijuana, then encouraged to pose nude. Seven men were involved in the operation, and the diary of one offender detailed sex acts with girls. Boxes of photographs of children in "compromising positions" also were found. The man was sentenced to life in prison, but a judge later suspended his sentence, credited him with the seven months he had served, and put him on probation for five years.[143]

In February 1987, a grammar-school teacher on the Hopi Indian Reservation was accused of "engaging in sexual activities and nude photography with 142 victims, apparently Indian boys."[144]

In Bulgaria, Joseph Groto, the reputed kingpin of a child pornography racket, was beaten by angry mothers while he was out on bond for child molesting. Groto, who could not swim, drowned when he ran into a lake. An Interpol agent said Groto and his sex ring had used at least three thousand children.[145]

In Tennessee, the Reverend Claudius I. "Bud" Vermilye founded Boys' Farm, Inc., a home for troubled youths, in 1971. (In 1966, Vermilye had been accused of trying to seduce one of the boys in a home he had started in Georgia. He had resigned as pastor to avoid an investigation.) In a November 4, 1976, raid on the Tennessee farm, more than one thousand photos of nude boys and adults in homosexual acts were uncovered. Vermilye and adult patrons of Boys' Farm were in some of the photos. The operation was eventually traced to a dozen states. Vermilye was sentenced to twenty-five to forty years in prison.[146]

In San Jose, California, a 15-year-old girl and her parents filed a $7 million lawsuit against two men who allegedly used her as part of an international pornography business. The two men, Earl Magoun, 60, and Walter Holbrook, 58, allegedly ran a pornography ring involving San Jose schoolgirls out of a house for ten years. Officials said the men allegedly lured girls into the business by ads for housekeepers on local bulletin boards. The two men were charged with sexually molesting children and procuring children for prostitution.[147]

In the late 1970s, a band of pederasts became involved as leaders of a Boy Scout Troop in New Orleans, Louisiana. The men seduced and used young boys in a child prostitution and pornography ring, which was uncovered when a photo processing studio reported child pornography snapshots to police. Child pornography confiscated in this investigation included bestiality, rings piercing nipples and penises, and a set of pictures with a man jamming his fist into another man's rectum almost up to the elbow. The investigation led to a private school in Coral Gables, Florida, where boys had been raped. The probe went into thirty-four states. Twenty-two men were eventually convicted and sentenced for sex offenses involving children.[148]

Seventeen New England men were accused of participating in a prostitution ring involving seventy boys, ages 8 to 13, who were Massachusetts state wards placed in foster homes. Heterosexual stag films, drugs, beer, and cash were used to induce the boys into sex. One ring member was convicted of raping young boys. More than one hundred photos of naked boys were confiscated from him.[149]

A Los Angeles Police Department detective told the Attorney General's Commission on Pornography that a man befriended a woman and her two young girls, set child pornography around for the children to see, and molested, photographed, and distributed photos of another young girl. He corresponded with some three hundred people, sending photographs to them. Police identified sixteen children, ages infant to sixteen, who were involved in the operation.[150]

In Orlando, Florida, Donald Eugene Masken, 44, was arrested for distribution of child pornography. Officials confiscated ten thousand different slides.[151]

In Los Angeles, more than twenty-two hundred slides of nude children, ages 2 to 4, were found in the home of the owners of a private nursery school. The slides portrayed nineteen different children from the school nude and in sexually explicit poses. On May 7, 1982, Edwin James Meacham was convicted on eleven counts of child molestation and sentenced to twenty-six years in prison.[152]

In Chicago, two men were arrested and accused of operating a sex ring involving more than twenty-five boys. The boys were offered $20 for each new boy they recruited. Drugs and dozens of pornographic photos of young boys were seized. The men allegedly drugged the boys, showed them nude photos of other young boys in sex acts, and paid them with money or drugs for performing similar acts.[153]

Burgess describes a sex ring in which police

found nude photos and pornographic films in the apartment of a child molester. Sixty-three of the youths depicted in the pornography were eventually found.[154] Burgess also writes about Ernie, a pedophile, who took instant photos of his 7-year-old niece with his finger inserted in her genitals. Ernie also took photographs of male and female children's genitals while they slept. He processed, through a photo lab, fifteen hundred photos a week believed to be sold for $2 each, grossing an estimated $3,000 weekly.[155]

Eugene Abrams of Nassau County, New York, was a child pornographer who ran a child sex ring that earned an estimated $250,000 annually. More than four thousand nude and obscene photos of girls, some showing Abrams in sex with prepubescent girls, were found in his possession. His own daughter appeared in some of the pornography. Nearly a dozen adults were arrested in this investigation. Parents and other adults brought the children to Abrams to be photographed in response to magazine ads.[156]

Gerald S. Richards of Port Huron, Michigan, recruited approximately thirty boy models for pornography and kept a blackmail photo of each. He worked at a pornographic bookstore and resold prints from the store. He eventually left the store and went into the mail-order pornography business. With a chicken hawk (man who uses boy prostitutes) named Dyer Grossman, he formed a children's mission and a nature camp. A newspaper reporter later linked that camp to an international network of camps. At the camp, runaways and troubled boys were introduced to oral and anal sex with boys and adult males. They were seduced by affection and phony friendship. Police said alcohol and stag films were sometimes used to stimulate the boys before they took part in the orgies. At least ten photos believed to have been taken at the camp appeared in hard-core pornographic magazines. Richards had about six hundred customers.[157]

In Indiana, police confiscated more than twenty-five thousand pictures of nude girls from the home of Bill Smith. They also found a file of names from two dozen states and nations.[158] In Nevada, a day-care teacher was charged with molesting and was believed to have had fifty to sixty victims, according to police.[159] A truckload of child pornography was found in his home.

A Los Angeles grand jury inducted nine men on forty-four counts involving an international child pornography and prostitution ring. Children were shown pornography before being photographed in sex acts with their peers and adults. A photograph of one of the victims appeared in a child pornography magazine.[160]

A Pennsylvania man was charged with twenty-one complaints of sexual abuse of thirteen young boys. He told police he was a pedophile. Police confiscated "half a roomful" of pornographic videotapes, photos, magazines, and books, some of which portrayed the man's victims.[161]

ABUSE OF CHILDREN BY CHILDREN

The effectiveness of pornography as a learning tool for abuse of persons is perhaps most clearly demonstrated in victim cases where children, imitating pornographic scenarios, sexually or otherwise physically abuse other children.

A gang of youths savagely attacked and raped a 14-year-old girl for several hours. The leader had a large stock of pornography at home detailing each practice the boys carried out on the victim.[162]

A 10-year-old girl was sexually assaulted on a pool table in Providence, Rhode Island, by a 12-year-old boy who may have taken the idea from watching a gang rape trial on television. The boy was accused of making the girl perform oral sex, then further assaulting her while other children watched.[163]

Six adolescent boys gang-raped a juvenile girl. They used a porn magazine's pictorial and editorial lay-out to re-create a rape in the woods in their housing development.[164]

Seven Oklahoma youths gang-raped a 15-year-old girl from Texas and forced her to commit "unnatural acts" with them. Four of the boys admitted to being incited to commit the assaults by reading obscene magazines and looking at lewd photos.[165]

A woman who testified at the Minneapolis antipornography hearings in 1983 said her daughter was gang-raped by four tenth-grade boys who used pornographic magazines to threaten and terrify her. They made the victim pose in the positions shown in the pornography magazines.[166]

Two Dallas boys, ages 8 and 9, were held for questioning for an alleged serious and brutal sexual assault of a 6-year-old girl. Rape crisis officials said this was one of a growing number of sexual assaults on children by other children. According to the victim's mother, the 8-year-old boy began abusing boys and girls in the neighborhood after he saw pornographic movies.[167]

A 10-year-old boy in London, England, was

charged with raping a 12-year-old girl. Dozens of pornographic magazines and nude photos were found in his room. The boy said he wanted to be like the men he saw in the magazines and on television and that he got his ideas from the pornography.[168]

In San Antonio, Texas, police found a 16-year-old boy who had raped a 10-year-old girl in possession of three homosexual playing cards. Other neighborhood boys also had such cards.[169]

In Milliard, Ohio, police charged a local juvenile with two counts of rape and another youth with two counts of complicity in connection with the rape of a 10-year-old retarded youth. All were males ages 9 to 11. Police found pornographic literature where the incident took place. The boy who raped the retarded child had been reading the pornography.[170]

A 15-year-old boy sodomized a 5-year-old boy. The youth admitted committing these acts on several small boys and said he had seen a number of homosexual playing cards and "heard men and older boys talk about such acts."[171]

A 17-year-old boy picked up a 5-year-old boy and a 7-year-old boy in his car. He showed them a cutout from a nude magazine. At knifepoint, "he copulated the 5-year-old boy" and forced the child "to copulate him." He had a prior record for similar offenses.[172]

In *Seduction of the Innocent*, Dr. Fredric Wertham details his ten-year study of crime comic books (those that emphasize and exploit violence and sex) and their effects.[173] Wertham concludes that such materials often are a significant contributing factor in causing delinquency, sexual maladjustment, and acts of violence by children and adolescents. Constant exposure to such books can, he says, result in imitation or promote a buildup of emotional tension that may or may not find release by action. This, he says, could result in harmful behavior, psychological harm, or masturbatory or deliquent acts. Wertham cites these examples: A 7-year-old boy was hanged nude from a tree with his hands tied behind him, then burned with matches. The offenders, ages 3, 6, and 8, were reenacting a comic book plot. A 14-year-old Chicago boy strangled an 8-year-old girl. He left fifty comic books in the room with the victim. The

books showed different ways of killing people and abusing girls, including strangling.

In West Covina, California, police discovered two youths engaged in sodomy. A *Playboy* spread was being used as a means of excitement.[174]

A 6-year-old LaCrosse, Wisconsin, boy forced other children to remove their clothes and touch each other. He was charged with sexual assault and taken from his mother's custody. Police said the boy reportedly met children in a wooded area, showed them pictures of nude women, and told them "to remove their clothes and touch each other." When some refused, he forcibly removed their pants.[175]

Pornography was shown to a woman's two daughters by an 11-year-old neighbor boy. He tried to imitate the sex acts portrayed in the photographs with the woman's 11-year-old daughter. The other daughter witnessed this.[176]

When she was a child, a woman was pushed into a shed by a boy who sexually assaulted her with his fingers and made her masturbate him. She had previously seen him with pornography.[177]

In Duluth, Minnesota, police reported the increase in juvenile sex crimes in which pornography served as a model. For example, a 12-year-old boy was caught experimenting sexually with two 6-year-old girls. Pages of pornographic magazines (belonging to the girls' father) were opened to color photographs showing sexual activities among adults.[178]

A 13-year-old male admitted attacking a girl in a downtown office in 1965. He said he was "stimulated by sexual arousal from a stag magazine article he had previously read in a public drugstore."[179]

In San Antonio, Texas, a 15-year-old boy dragged a 9-year-old girl into the brush and tried to rip off her clothes. He fled when she screamed. He admitted to police that he had done similar things in other communities. He read his father's pornographic picture books, which, he said, resulted in the urge to attack victims.[180]

Wildmon cites a letter from a 15-year-old boy to columnist Ann Landers. His 12-year-old girlfriend said she was pregnant, although they had had sex only once. He said they were just seeing what it was like after watching a cable television movie.[181]

PORNOGRAPHY AND WIFE ABUSE

We have uncovered dozens of cases in which pornography played a known role in the abuse of wives by husbands. We believe that if battered women shelters, police, doctors, social workers, attorneys, psychologists, and other professionals who

work with domestic abuse victims were to ask victims whether their abuser used pornography and whether pornography played any role in their abuse, the response would be overwhelmingly affirmative. We encourage professionals to begin investigating, in an organized fashion, the relationship between pornography and the abuse of women and children.

Ms. P. testified at the 1983 Minneapolis hearings.[182] She said her husband read pornography like a textbook. Most of the scenes they enacted were the exact scenes he read in the magazines. Finally, they divorced. Ms. P. said:

> I could see how I was being seasoned to the use of pornography and I could see what was coming next. I could see more violence and I could see more humiliation and I knew at that point I was either going to die from it, I was going to kill myself or I was going to leave. And I was feeling strong enough that I left.[183]

Ms. P. emphasized that pornography was not a fantasy but a reality that involved the abuse of her body. Her husband tried to get her to go up on stage and let him take photographs of her having sex with other men. She refused. He raped her several times while she slept. Ms. P. saw Oriental pornography portraying bestiality, women in cages, gang rapes, sexual slavery, women led around by collars, anal penetration, and sadomasochism. She was repulsed when her husband read her excerpts from pornography about group sex, wife swapping, anal intercourse, and bondage. They and his friends also went to pornographic theaters and live sex shows.

When people came over for dinner, her husband had them strip and act out scenes he had read in the magazines. She refused to participate. Once she woke up, and a male friend was in bed with them. To prevent more group sex scenes, she agreed to act out, in private, a lot of the scenes he read to her.

Ms. P. said she felt worthless as a person, was suicidal, and saw her dreams of a career as a doctor washed away. She realized her life was just like that of the prostitutes she and her husband had seen on stage when he was transferred overseas. It was at this point that she found the strength to leave the relationship. "I spent the next few years of my life, through the help of therapy, education and friends, healing myself," she said.[184]

On December 13, 1983, Ms. W. told of a home in which she had stayed where the ex-husband used pornographic materials to terrorize and rape her and his wife:

> Over a period of 18 years the woman was regularly raped by this man. He would bring pornographic magazines, books, and paraphernalia into the bedroom with him and tell her that if she did not perform the sexual acts that were being done in the "dirty" books and magazines he would beat and kill her. I know about this because my

bedroom was right next to hers. I could hear everything they said. I could hear her screams and cries. In addition, since I did most of the cleaning in the house, I would often come across the books, magazines, and paraphernalia that were in the bedroom and other rooms of the house. . . . Eventually the woman admitted to me that her ex-husband did in fact use pornographic materials to terrorize and rape her.

> Not only did I suffer through the torture of listening to the rapes and tortures of a woman, but I could see what grotesque acts this man was performing on her from the pictures in the pornographic materials. I was also able to see the systematic destruction of a human being taking place before my eyes.[185]

The man threatened Ms. W. He said that if she told anyone or tried to run away, he would beat her, break and cut off her legs and arms, cut up her face, and kill her. He whipped Ms. W. with belts and electrical cords, beat her with pieces of wood, and touched her and grabbed her where she did not want to be touched or grabbed. She also was locked in closets and in the basement. He did the same types of things to his wife and children but abused them even worse. Ms. W. said:

> I knew that if he wanted to, he could do more of the things that were being done in those magazines to me. When he looked at the magazines, he could make hateful obscene, violent remarks about women in general and about me. I was told that because I am female I am here to be used and abused by him and that because he is male he is the master and I am his slave. I was terrorized into keeping silent and it wasn't until three years after escaping from him that I was psychologically and emotionally strong enough to tell anyone what had happened to me.[186]

Ms. W. said she was not saying that pornography caused the man to do those things to her and others, only that pornography is an extension of the hatred and violence against women that already exists in American society.

Ann, a victim who testified before the Attorney General's Commission of Pornography, said that her husband, Tom, introduced her to pornography and treated it as normal for people to read.[187] Tom began tying her up for sex (after discussing techniques shown), which frightened her. Ann thought something was wrong with her because she was not receptive. Tom admitted to fantasizing with magazines. Ann wondered what was wrong that he could have sex with magazines but not with her.

Tom tried to get Ann to have sex with one of

her friends, who was also his lover. "I was so dead inside that all I could do was watch the two of them and feel disgust and contempt for myself because I had allowed my marriage to get to this point," Ann said.[188]

Tom spent much of their joint income on pornography, resulting in the loss of their home. Ann said that pornography cripples the mind and body and warps a person's perception of himself or herself and others. Ann divorced Tom, but she is afraid of relationships with other men, even though she wants to believe she will find someone to love and trust who will feel the same about her.

Another woman's husband sometimes suggested that she try to imitate Linda Lovelace's performances. He tied her with clothesline to the four corners of the bed frame while their 9-month-old son watched. He held a butcher knife on her and fed her three strong tranquilizers. When she cried, he beat her face and body (causing welts and bruises) and tried to smother her with a pillow. He had vaginal sex with her and forced her to perform oral sex on him.[189]

Bonnie testified that her husband, Leon, had a substantial collection of pornography.[190] He could not perform sexually without the pornography, and he forced her to perform violent sexual acts while he leafed through the pictures. He tied both her daughters to their beds and put his fingers in their rectums. He had done the same to her. She left him to divorce.

After Bonnie divorced Leon, she married Paul, who had a large collection of sadomasochistic pornography and bondage material that he kept in the nightstand in their bedroom. Once he tied her to the bed and sodomized her after she refused to be bound as some of the pornography depicted. Her daughters were molested while she was out of the house. Some of the acts could be linked to poses shown in the pornography. Paul sometimes tied the girls' feet with rope and periodically showed them child pornography. Bonnie said that she felt Paul was obsessed with pornography and violence, even though he was a prominent person in the community. As a result of the abuse, her daughters are afraid of men.

Sharon told the Attorney General's Commission on Pornography that her husband, a dentist, kept pornography around the house and had asked her to do several sexual acts with him and other persons.[191] She refused. Sharon said her husband was fascinated with lesbian and masturbation poses. All his relationships were superficial, she said. When watching television with Sharon and their small child in the room, he would read pornography, open his fly, and masturbate. He would call his daughter's attention to his penis, calling it a snake. He insisted he wanted interracial and group sex.

In November 1979, Sharon found her husband with his hands on their small baby daughter's pubic area in an improper manner. He belittled her for thinking he was doing anything improper. They divorced, and Sharon learned that he was obsessed with all forms of pornography. Sharon said he had molested ten of his patients by giving them nitrous oxide and then touching them.

A woman wrote to Wildmon that she had been involved in pornography from ages 15 to 25.[192] She said that her mind became filled with all types of sexual action. She performed oral sex with her boyfriend's dog and tried to force her neighbor's 3-year-old child to perform oral sex on her when she was 15, but he refused. During her marriage, she was controlled by her "insane" thoughts, such as imagining rape during the sex act with her husband.

Wanda Richardson of the Harriet Tubman Women's Shelter in Minnesota told the Minneapolis hearing about a man who imprisoned his wife in their house.[193] He brought pornographic videos home, tied her to a chair and made her act out what they saw on the screen. The woman was severely injured and came to the shelter.

Donna Dunn of Women's Shelter, Inc., in Minnesota, related three cases:[194]

One woman's spouse collected *Penthouse, Hustler,* and other pornography. Bondage was his favorite form of abuse. He liked to play a "game" of slavery and whipping. The woman knew what he did to her was directly related to articles about sex and bondage. He wanted to involve her female friend in the scenes, and when the wife refused to comply, he anally assaulted her.

A second woman's husband had rape and bondage magazines all over the house and was obsessed with tying up women. She found two suitcases of Barbie dolls with ropes tied around their legs and arms and tape across their mouths. He would tie her up and try those things on her.

A third woman's spouse always had pornography around the house. He acted out one scene from a magazine that ended their marriage. In it, he forcibly stripped, bound, and gagged her. Then, with the husband's help, she was raped by a German shepherd. The man's second wife sought support from the shelter because of magazines and bondage equipment she found in the house.

On June 4, 1984, a woman told the Minneapolis City Council that she was hit and punched because she refused to allow her partner to put his fist in her vagina in the same way this was portrayed in one of his pornographic magazines.[195]

Tanya Vonnegut Beck of a battered women's shelter testified that for ten years one husband would wake up his wife, beat her, then demand that she perform acts depicted in pornography.[196] He cut her with a razor; slapped, hit, and kicked her; tied her to a bed; and required her to do demeaning sex acts with him and other people.

Russell and Trocki reported that one woman said her "old man" and she went to a show featuring lots of anal intercourse and tying up.[197] When they made love at home, he got two belts, tied her feet together with one, and "kinda beat me" with the other. "But when he tried to penetrate me anally," she said "I couldn't take it, it was too painful. I managed to convey to him verbally to quit it. He did stop, but not soon enough to suit me."[198] The same woman still has a scar on her buttocks from a time when the man put a wax initial on a hot plate and branded her behind.

Diann said that she developed low self-esteem and felt powerless as a result of her husband's coercing her into acting out sex fantasies he had from reading or viewing pornography.[199] This happened at least three times a week during the first several years of their marriage. He showed her pornography to convince her that spankings and other acts portrayed in pornography were okay. If there was any sex, it had to be preceded by looking at the magazines, Diann said.

Wildmon cites one man who said he became addicted to pornography and it robbed him of a great deal of joy and love he might have shared with his wife.[200] Another man told Wildmon that pornography totally perverted his imagination and ruined his marriage (pp. 131–32). A third man told how his pornography addiction drove him to drugs, affairs, adultery, and divorce. Even though he later became a Christian, he said that he has to guard his thoughts, for his minds replays images of the pornography he used to read (p. 140).

A woman wrote to Wildmon saying that her husband frequented a pornography store and practiced what he read and learned on her, forcing degradation on her. She said he believed the pornographic myth that women need and enjoy being dominated and humiliated (p. 139).

Effects on women whose husbands are addicted to pornography are many. One woman became suicidal and attempted suicide several times.[201] Another woman threw up after viewing a film, which involved sex with children, with her stepfather-in-law, mother-in-law, husband, neighbors, and children.[202] A woman became depressed, confused, and ashamed after her boyfriend took her to a party to watch pornography, sexually used her on a living room couch, then went back to the party.[203]

One woman told the Attorney General's Commission on Pornography that she had a good marriage for thirty years.[204] Then, in 1983, her husband began watching pornography on cable television. He thought he was shortchanged because what he saw in the pornography was not what happened in their marriage. He tried to get her to act out the pornography, but she found the acts portrayed nauseating. Her husband chased other women and finally moved in with one. He demanded a divorce, and she got one. The woman later learned that two of her friends had similar problems. She said that one friend's husband changed his sexual interest to men as a result of exposure to pornography and another's husband felt the need to be with other women.

Other common effects of pornographic addiction include an emphasis on male masturbation and demands for sex orgies and spouse swapping. Some addicts prefer masturbating and looking at pornography to having sex with their wives.[205] According to one woman who wrote to the Minneapolis City Council, as a result of Linda Lovelace's convincing performance in *Deep Throat*, "our husbands began to think that they were cheated in life . . ." Younger women, she said, were brainwashed to believe this and wanted to show "our husbands that they could be a better Linda Lovelace [performer of oral sex] than the wife they had at home." She saw heartbreaks, nervous breakdowns, and use of tranquilizers by women who were coerced into sex acts they did not enjoy. She admonished women not to let men force them to be receptacles rather than cherished wives.[206]

PORNOGRAPHY AND PROSTITUTION

A former prostitute, Terese, referred to as Ms. Q. in the hearings report, described the connection between pornography and prostitution when she spoke on behalf of a group of women who were all former Minneapolis prostitutes at the Minneapolis hearings.[207] Terese also testified before the Attorney General's Commission on Pornography.[208]

We were all introduced to prostitution through pornography, there were no exceptions in our group, and we were all under 18. Pornography was our textbook. We learned the tricks of the trade by men exposing us to pornography and us trying to mimic what we saw. I could not stress enough what a huge influence we feel this was. Somehow it was okay. These pictures were real men and woman who appeared to be happy and consenting adults, engaged in human sexuality.[209]

Terese had spoken to older prostitutes who got involved when they were adults and found they experienced the same sense of powerlessness and victimization. She told how one prostitute was paid by a client to go to a house. She found a group of physically disabled men and able-bodied men watching pornographic films of intercourse, oral sex, and women being penetrated by animals. The films were played continuously. There were two weapons in the room. The disabled men were undressed, and the prostitute was held down by the able-bodied men and forced to engage in sex with the disabled men. Then the able-bodied men said they would show the others how "real men" do it. They forced the woman to act simultaneously with the movie, including having sex. They also urinated on her.

In another case described by Terese, a prostitute met a man in a hotel room. She was tied up and gagged while sitting nude on a chair. After an hour, the man returned with two other men. They attached nipple clips to her breasts and burned her with cigarettes. The men had many sadomasochistic magazines with them and showed her photos of women appearing to consent to, enjoy, and encourage this abuse. They held her for twelve hours, continually raping and beating her.

One woman was in a room with two clients. After one man told the other that he had seen some pictures of women who shaved their pubic hair and it had turned him on, they removed the woman's pubic hairs with a jackknife, burning and plucking what the knife missed. The men told her that her hairless vagina reminded them of their young daughters' genitals and then engaged in intercourse. Another man paid a woman $35 to recruit another woman so he could direct them in a lesbian scene he had seen in a movie.

After the release of *Deep Throat*, the prostitutes experienced men demanding oral sex and joking about it. Terese said, "Women were forced to constantly enact specific scenes that men had witnessed in pornography. They would direct women to copy postures and poses of things they had seen in magazines and then they would take their own pictures of the women."[210]

Terese said that the men the prostitutes had serviced were very powerful in the community, including men in the media—"the same men that perpetuate the myth that Minneapolis is a clean city with exceptional morals and a high quality of life."[211]

Terese stated that there is a clear relationship between pornography and the systematic abuse of women. She stressed that everything seen in pornography is happening to real women right now.

Terese reported that another woman was forced by her pimp to go to a house where the women who ran it kept a room with a projector, porn films, and stacks of pornography. The tricks would look at the pornography to get psyched up, then the girl would be sent in. Her trick stripped her, tied her spread-eagled on the bed, and squeezed her nipples hard. He showed her a pornographic magazine with a photo of a beaten woman. He told her he wanted her to look like that and to hurt. He then beat her, and "when I didn't cry fast enough, he lit a cigarette and held it right above my breast for a long time before he burned me."[212] She told him he had better kill her or untie her or she would tell the police and his wife. He let her go. The house continued to provide that service.

The same woman worked at massage studios where the owners expected the girls to look at magazines with the waiting men to get them titillated. According to Terese, the men used soft porn to help them work up the courage to try the acts described in the magazines. The woman also was involved in an apartment where a larger group of men would drink and watch pornographic movies, then act out what they had seen in the films, with other men watching.

Another woman was the main prostitute for a pimp who filmed sexual acts almost every night in the pimp's home. Women, whom she assumes were forced to be there, were filmed having sex with dogs. The pimp used this pornography to blackmail people.

Terese said:

[Y]oung women would be picked up on the street, off the street, and everyone's first experience was always the same which was that the man would show either magazines or take you to a movie and then afterwards instruct her to act in the way that the magazines or the films had depicted. Usually after, I call it a training period, what would happen then is that these men or different men would set up scenarios of usually more than one woman to very, very specifically copy and reproduce scenes that were portrayed in magazines and books that they had witnessed. And then they would make their own movies using home video equipment and also Polaroid cameras and they would all collect their own library of pornography involving these women.[213]

In endorsing the proposed Minneapolis ordinance, the Prostitutes Union of Massachusetts said, "There are many women we know personally who have been held captive since their youth, often sold and transferred from one porno group to another."[214]

Sara, a victim of pornography, told her story to the Attorney General's Commission on Pornography.[215] Sara ran away at age 13 in the 1960s. She was raped the first night and gang-raped the second night. A man befriended her. He was kind, then kept her drugged and took nude photos of her. A few weeks later, he sold her to a pimp named Bob. The pimp raped her and stole her I.D. She was repeatedly beaten and raped. He kept her in line by threatening her life and the lives of her family. He also threatened to turn her over to police and to tell her mother she was a prostitute. She believed him. Sara often tried to escape, but he caught her. He dragged her out of restaurants, beating her, but no one would help. Many of her tricks were prominent, and they knew she was a child and was not acting of her own free will.

They showed Sara pornography to teach her about sex. They told her to act like the women in the pictures. One regular customer had a vast collection and made videos of the sex he had with her. She was sent to stag parties with twenty men who viewed pornography. Then she and another woman were forced to have sex with some of the men. This took place in public places. She was forced to work conventions. Pornographic films were followed by sex with her and other women. The films set the tone for the types of acts they were expected to perform. At an apartment where Sara was sent, several men had sex with her. They took pictures of her in pornographic poses. It turned out to be a porn production firm. She was taken to New Jersey to meet men whom she was told were gangsters. There was a large set. She and another woman were told to act out a lesbian scene. Later she realized she had been used for the illegal production of pornography.

Police were paid off by having sex with Sara. The authorities would not help her, she said, because they were also her exploiters. At age 16, she was put in a juvenile facility and sexually abused by the male employees. When she was transferred to a facility upstate, she escaped, but the only place to go was back to prostitution.

Sara's last pimp was a pornographer. He got aroused by pornography, forced his women to have sex with him, and filmed them. He taped their screams when he beat them and threatened to kill them. He humiliated them by playing the pornography for his friends and used it to terrorize them. He raped and beat Sara, taped it, and delighted in repeatedly playing it for them.

In her early 20s, Sara married an alcoholic who beat her and forced sex on her. He always read *Playboy* and other soft-core pornography and once insisted they see an X-rated movie together, then demanded sex at home. After he died in a car accident before age 25, Sara discovered that he had participated in pornography as an adolescent. She saw a picture of him as a child performing in pornography.

Sara said it took her close to twenty years to undo what had been done to her by pornography and prostitution. At the time of her testimony, she was an undergraduate college student planning to counsel women who experienced the same things she had. She had the support of a loving husband, but her thighs were permanently scarred from repeated beatings, and the porn she was forced to make still exists and could be used to humiliate and blackmail her and to ruin her career.

Sara asked, what good is the First Amendment to victims of pornography? She asked why people defend rapists, pimps, and pornographers but not women like her.

Other victims of pornography who also were prostitutes tell their stories in the final report of the Attorney General's Commission on Pornography.[216] Linedecker describes a case in which prostitute mothers sold their 3-year-old and 5-year-old girls into pornography.[217]

PORNOGRAPHY AND INCEST

In our research, we found that pornography is sometimes involved in incestuous abuse. Mary "Annie" Steinman, whose story is told in the introduction to this chapter was abused as a child by a father who was addicted to pornography. He acted out pornographic scenes with her and her siblings.

According to Dr. Judianne Densen-Gerber, in 1977 all twenty-seven cases of incest reported in Rockingham County, New Hampshire, included child pornography preceding and accompanying the assaults on the children.[218]

One woman, Mary Wells, had sex with her father

more than five hundred times between ages 12 and 17. She said he set up a camera to photograph sex acts with her. She once contemplated suicide, said she finds the thought of hugging a man repellent, and said she has had no relationships with men other than her father.[219]

Oklahoma parents forced their four daughters, ages 10 to 17, to engage in family sex while pornographic pictures were being filmed. The mother also drove the girls to dates with men and watched while they had sex for money.[220]

A father and stepmother convicted of incest and second degree sexual assault received ten-year sentences in 1987. The girl said her father began to have sex with her age 11 and had her fitted for a birth control device. The stepmother also regularly had sex with her. She endured nine years of abuse. The father also had the girl engage in sex with another man while he took photographs.[221]

John took sexually explicit photographs of his daughter from shortly after birth to age 6. He was a collector of child pornography and owned three detective magazines, each of which had at least one story of a pedophile who killed at least one child. John wrote a manuscript on how to train a child between birth and the age of 15 months to be capable of sexually handling one or two customers per night. He wrote sexual abuse stories in which children could endure abuse and survive. He was convicted of molesting his 6-year-old daughter since birth.[222]

Al, a 48-year-old grandfather, sexually molested his two granddaughters and grandson. He exploited them in photos and let a friend molest them. He created what Burgess calls fake sadomasochistic pornography. Photos show that he hung them naked by their feet, put them in bondage, and held a candle near the girl's genitals. There were pictures of the 6-year-old granddaughter with a fake substance that appeared to be a great amount of blood covering her genitals. He also sketched the 6-year-old with her bound and gagged while rats chewed on her genitals.[223]

Danny, at age 11, was forced to have sex with his father, who then turned him over to his friend, child pornographer Roy Ames, who made him a "star." He appeared in more than fifty porn movies, usually involving sex with other boys. Ames was sentenced to ten years in federal prison for sending obscene material through the mail.[224]

An Alabama woman reported that on three occasions, from ages 9 to 16, her father forced her to be a pornography model.[225] A 17-year-old male who raped his 5-year-old sister said he got the idea from an adult pornography magazine that he had purchased that day.[226] And Katherine Brady, author

of *Father's Days*, an autobiography of incest abuse, told the U.S. Senate Subcommittee on Juvenile Justice, "Pornography trained me to respond to my father's sexual demands."[227]

A Red Bank, Tennessee, father of three runaway sisters, ages 10, 12, and 14, was arrested for sexually molesting them (short of intercourse). A search uncovered some four hundred pornographic books and magazines and nude photographs of the girls.[228] In Los Angeles, a father had incestuous relations with his son beginning at age 6. By the time the boy was 11, he had been in pornographic magazines and movies, had been twice sold as a sex slave, and had been involved in swap clubs.[229] In a Chicago case, parents posed for pornography with their minor son and daughter. More than four hundred photos were found of the family sexually involved and involved with other adults.[230]

Valerie Heller told the story of her own incestuous abuse by male members of her family, including a stepfather and stepbrothers. One of the men took soft-core pornographic photos of her when she was 14 and expressed an intent to use her for prostitution. She was repeatedly raped by family members. One threatened to publish the pornography if she kept telling her story.[231]

One teenage boy reported sexual abuse by an uncle. He was shown pornography and used in the production of pornographic films. The boy attempted suicide several times.[232]

The Attorney General's Commission on Pornography received several reports of diseases transmitted as a result of actions inspired by pornography. For example, a citizens group from Oklahoma wrote to the commission about a 3½-year-old girl with gonorrhea of the throat and a painful vagina stretched many times its normal size. The group said her father, who used her sexually, was a pornography addict.[233] Dr. Simon Miranda, a clinical psychologist, told the commission that he had found several cases where pornography (such as requests for group sex) had caused marital problems and had seen several children who had been sexually abused by parents who were avid pornography users. Miranda said he had seen cases with a "clear relationship, almost cause/effect—certainly a dispositive cause—in the abuse of the child, resulting from the use or the involvement of pornography by the adults." Miranda cited a case in which a 10-year-old boy and his sister had been sexually abused since age 2 by a father who showed the boy pornography.[234]

Los Angeles Police Department detective William Dworin told the commission that one pedophile had sexually molested his daughter (by licking her vagina) since she was an infant. Police found photos of sex involving the infant.[235] Another father used pornographic pictures to help his daughter learn more about sex and to convince her that incest was okay and that all fathers do it with their daughters.[236] In a similar case, an 8-year-old girl was shown pictures of family members having sexual intercourse.[237]

When one girl was 12, her 16-year-old brother got hooked on *Playboy* and listened to filthy tape recordings. He sexually molested her.[238] Another woman reported that when she was a child, her father wrote her name across a *Playboy* centerfold and put it under the covers so she would find it. He then joined her in bed and sexually molested her.[239] A 5-year-old girl told her foster mother that her father showed porn movies with naked people when her mother was gone and that she and Daddy did the same thing the people in the movies did.[240] A woman who was incestuously abused by an older brother felt that pornography contributed to the types of abuse she suffered. For example, oral sex did not occur until after pornographic magazines arrived in the home.[241]

Dane County's Committee on Sexual Assault (Madison, Wisconsin), reported that a male, age 20, used pornography to get ideas of what to do to an 11-year-old female cousin. In another case in which pornography was found, a male cousin, age 14, fondled two girls, ages 8 and 3.[242] A teen-age boy told a minister that his girlfriend wanted him to run away with her because her father kept her up late to watch Playboy movies with him.[243] A Milwaukee man was accused of sexually assaulting his daughter when she was 7, 8, and 9, as well as his daughter's 7-year-old friend. He showed the girls pornographic magazines.[244] A 74-year-old widower was convicted of sexually abusing six girls, ages 9 to 11, including his granddaughter. The sex involved oral and vaginal intercourse. The girls were shown sexually explicit magazines.[245] Milwaukee police reported a case where a suspect advertised his daughter in a national magazine and sent pictures of her in pornographic poses to various people.[246]

Ingrid Horton told the Attorney General's Commission on Pornography that she was involved in a lot of child sexual abuse cases where the children were shown pornography (adult or mixed) to lower their inhibitions and guide their behavior and poses. Her own father had abused her and shown her pornography. Another witness told the commission that she was forced to view pornography during the course of an incestuous relationship with her father. She said that viewing pornography brings back memories of painful incidents with her father.[247]

PORNOGRAPHY AND ABUSE OF ADULTS

We found numerous case histories of adults who were victimized by adult pornography users. For example, a 19-year-old female was offered a ride home by a 19-year-old man she knew. He took her to the country and demanded a sex act. She refused. He had piercing or stabbing magazines in his car. She was sexually assaulted by every possible means and stabbed fifty-seven times.[248]

Mr. O. was exposed to heterosexual pornography at a young age and learned that sex was violence. Mr. O. is gay. When his gay lover was violent, Mr. O. believed that the violence was normal. His ex-lover used pornography, and Mr. O. believes it influenced his behavior. The lover threatened Mr. O. with a knife, battered him on different occasions, and forced sex on him. Pornography helped convince Mr. O. to accept sexual violence and to continue in a destructive relationship.[249]

Twelve women, some of whom had worked as Playboy bunnies, were promised by a ring of five men that they would have a chance to be taped for a television promotion. When the women arrived at the address where they were told to report for an audition, they were drugged, tortured, forced into pornographic poses and scenes, and photographed. Then the women were blackmailed. The blackmail ring was busted when one of the women reported the operation to police. Police raided the building and found Polaroid pictures and videotapes of the women. The bedrooms were equipped with video cameras and recording equipment.[250]

A man kidnapped a married woman and made nine hours of color videotapes of the repeated sexual rapes committed on her.[251] Tanya Vonnegut Beck testified that a rapist put a woman through demeaning sexually violent acts, twisted her body into unbelievable shapes, and tied her hands and legs together. He made her have sex with an animal, shaved her, marked Xs on her back, showed her pornography while performing sex acts on himself, and raped her. The man pointed to pictures and said, "This is how it ought to be with women."[252] Another rapist made a woman imitate bondage pornography and took pictures of her doing the imitations.[253]

A woman told an emergency room nurse that the men who raped her said, as she was becoming unconscious, "Let's Deep Throat her before she passes out."[254] In Madison, Wisconsin, an adult male broke into and burglarized the home of a female victim, age 24. He raped her and took a photograph.[255] A ticket clerk at a triple-X theater in Des Moines, Iowa, was raped at the theater. The man was convicted of a felony assault.[256] One woman's boyfriend, who used pornography, had her pose nude in murderlike scenes and pose in a plaster cast.[257] A 16-year-old boy who raped a woman told police he had watched a movie about rape and thought it was a good idea.[258]

A California man was sentenced to prison for eleven years for kidnapping two young women and sexually assaulting one. In his car, police found a gun, rope, knives, a syringe and needle, pornography magazines, and a catalog of bondage devices.[259] A man suspected in twenty-five or more Austin, Texas, rapes took pictures of his victims during the attacks. Officers found a pornography magazine, a Polaroid camera, and a nude photo of one of his victims in his car.[260] In 1967, a woman was raped on the way to church in Cleveland, Ohio. The rapist had been reading obscenity in his truck just prior to the attack.[261]

A video game called "Custer's Last Stand" involves trying to get a white man, Custer, to rape an Indian woman who is bound. A real Indian woman was attacked by two white men who made it clear they hated Indians. They raped her at knifepoint, and as they threw her to the ground, they screamed in her face, "This is more fun that Custer's Last Stand."[262]

One court found a rapist's pornography collection to be relevant evidence in showing his "bent of mind."[263] Philip Hughes, a rapist/mutilator of women, made his wife bring him violent pornography, from which he learned ways to kill.[264] And a rapist in England blamed pornographic films for his crimes. He received life imprisonment for seven rapes and an act of sodomy.[265]

In Madison, Wisconsin, a male in his 20s had anal intercourse with another male, age 20. The victim had pornography in his room, and, according to the victim, the offender said he wanted the victim just like the woman in the picture.[266] In Milwaukee, a man was accused of rape, false imprisonment, and armed robbery involving a 22-year-old woman. The woman was allegedly forced at gunpoint into an adult bookstore and then forced into two sexual acts in a booth. The man then took the woman to a motel and raped her twice. At a second adult bookstore,

she tricked him into releasing her, the criminal complaint said.[267]

Helen Gualtieri, a social worker, told the Attorney General's Commission on Pornography of the abuse one of her clients suffered as a result of pornography. The client, a 29-year-old foreign woman, had accepted a mail-order marriage proposal from a man she had corresponded for six years. He showed her pornographic video films and told her to perform the acts she had seen portrayed with the men. She refused to prostitute herself. He beat her for days until she escaped.[268]

Russell and Trocki told the commission of numerous cases in which women had been upset by someone trying to get them to imitate pornography:

1. This guy had seen a movie where a woman was being made love to by dogs. He suggested that some of his friends had a dog and we should have a party and set the dog loose on the women. He wanted to put a muzzle on the dog and put some sort of stuff on my vagina so that the dog would lick there. (p.11).
2. He forced me to go down on him. He said he'd been going to porno movies. He'd seen this and wanted me to do it. He also wanted to pour champagne in my vagina. I got beat up because I didn't want to do it. He pulled my hair and slapped me around. After that I went ahead and did it, but there was no feeling in it. (p.15).
3. This person showed me a porno magazine with pictures of two women. He said he'd like to see two women doing that—me being one of them. That upset me. (p.13).
4. It was urinating in someone's mouth. (p. 14).
5. My boyfriend and I saw a movie in which there was masochism. After that he wanted to gag me and tie me up. He was stoned. I was not. I was really shocked at his behavior. I was nervous and uptight. He literally tried to force me, after gagging me first. He snuck up behind me with a scarf. He was hurting me with it and I started getting upset. Then I realized it wasn't a joke. He grabbed me and shook me by my shoulders and brought out some ropes, and told me to relax, and that I would enjoy it. Then he started putting me down about my feelings about sex, and my inhibitedness. I started crying and struggling with him, got loose, and kicked him in the testicles, which forced him down on the couch. I ran out of the house. Next day he called and apologized, but that was the end of him.[269] (pp. 15–16).

Russell and Trocki also detailed other cases. One woman was asked if she would participate in being beaten up after a man viewed sadomasochistic pornography. A couple who had just read a porn book tried to get a woman's boyfriend to persuade her to participate in group sex. They were running around naked, making her uncomfortable. When she said she had to leave on a plane, they left. One man, after seeing oral sex in movies, unsuccessfully tried to persuade a woman to have oral sex with him. He said it would be fun to mentally and physically torture a woman. Another man saw pornography involving anal sex and forced a woman to submit to it.[270]

A survey of women at battered women's shelters received results similar to those of Russell and Trocki. Photographs of rape and violence were shown to a victim, and then she was raped and beaten. Another victim was shown photographs or pornography, including penetration of people with instruments, sex with animals, and violence against persons. Her abuser tried to get her to do what was shown in the pornography.[271]

Wanda Richardson of the Harriet Tubman Women's Shelter reported that a woman was repeatedly taken to a theater and made to watch X-rated movies by her boyfriend. At home, he made her act out the movies with him. She ended up in the hospital after one such episode.[272]

Women also have been sexually harassed on the job because of pornography. A Montana woman who held a nontraditional job (brakewoman for the railroad) saw her name printed below pornographic pictures of a woman with spread thighs being raped by a huge disembodied penis.[273] In May 1984, a woman reported that her employer had pushed her down on the floor of his office and stuffed a gun into her vagina. A picture on the lunchroom wall showed a woman sucking a gun.[274] And a convenience store manager was fired for refusing to sell pornography.[275]

Ms. R. was in the construction trade. When she went into the shack on the job site for lunch, she found it completely decorated with pictures out of magazines such as *Hustler, Playboy, Penthouse,* and *Oui*. Some of the photos were very explicit, including sex and women in bondage. Ms. R. said, "It was very uncomfortable for me to go down there and have dinner and lunch with about 20 men and here is me facing all these pictures and hearing all these men talking about all the wonderful things they did on the weekend with all of these women."[276]

One day Ms. R. ripped all the pictures off the wall. When she came back at lunch, half the photos were back up, and her co-workers called her names. The men were very hostile. She took the photos down again, and some went back up. Then she began to eat elsewhere, and the men would not talk to her at work. The Minneapolis Affirmative Rights Office investigated the case, and she later found her car door bashed in. She was then transferred to another job.

A Minnesota woman wrote that pornographers and the values they represent ruined her life. She said men are unwilling to end the exploitation and degradation of women. She felt that she could no longer live in a society that considered her a piece of meat, so she chose to take her life. The 23-year-old woman set herself on fire in an adult bookstore.[277]

The State of Wisconsin paid $60,000 to a former Waupun prison inmate who said he was raped and beaten by a cellmate after an X-rated movie was shown in their cell. Authorities at Waupun halted the showing of X-rated films thereafter.[278] It is interesting to note that Michigan prison officials withheld the November 1985 *Hustler* from their inmates because "they feared it would incite violence against women guards." California and New Jersey officials also withheld the issue, which had a photo layout of a woman guard being raped by prisoners.[279]

People who have been used in pornography sometimes fear the future dissemination of the pornography. As one victim told the Attorney General's Commission, "I know the men who made it. I know where they are, and there is nothing I can do about it. I live knowing that any time it could surface and could be used to humiliate me and my family [and] ruin my professional life in the future. . . ."[280] Many other witnesses told the commission that they had to seek medical and mental assistance because of injuries they attribute to pornographic materials.[281]

PORNOGRAPHY AND ABUSE OF CHILDREN

An excellent description of how pornography is involved in the abuse of children is in "Hell Is for Children: And Madison's Child Pornographers Want to Keep It That Way" by Margaret Camlin, reprinted in Appendix I of this book. We found hundreds of cases where pornography and sexual abuse of children were connected. Some are described below. The sex rings section of this chapter contains similar cases.

David Eugene Pyles, 29, abducted a Joyce, Washington, girl, 17, at knifepoint, raped her, stabbed her, and cut her throat. He threw her in a ravine, returned, and struck her head with a rock. Her hands were severely cut from fending him off. Pyles had watched many sex and horror movies. When arrested, he possessed pornographic pictures from magazines in a scrapbook, a notebook describing brutal sex acts and torture, and parts of sexually explicit novels describing brutal sex acts torn out and stapled together.[282]

In England, Peter Samuel Cook received seven concurrent life sentences after he admitted raping six girls and committing sodomy on a seventh. The hooded "rapist of Cambridge" said pornographic films drove him to commit the crimes.[283]

A 14-year-old Minnesota girl was stopped on her bike at knifepoint and forced into a car. Her hands were tied with a belt. The abductor cut off her clothes and fingers with the knife, then inserted fingers and a knife into her vagina. He ordered the girl to stick a safety pin into the nipple of her breast and forced her to ask him to hit her. Then he made her perform fellatio, submit to anal penetration, and burn her breasts and near pubic area with a cigarette. The man defecated and urinated on the girl's face and forced her to ingest some of the excrement and urine. He made her urinate in a cup and drink it. The man choked the girl to the point of unconsciousness with a string from her blouse, leaving burn marks on her neck, and cut her in a couple of places. Then he drove her back to where he had abducted her and let her go. The man had books depicting sadomasochistic and bizarre sex crimes and others depicting enemas and "golden showers" (urination). The Minnesota Supreme Court said, "It appears, in committing these acts the defendant was giving life to some stories he had read in various pornographic books."[284]

In Michigan, two males watched a drive-in movie about two males who picked up two teenage girls who were hitchhiking. The movie detailed obscene acts against the girls. The two males left the movie and picked up two teenage hitchhikers. In his report, Pope reported that "when the officers found those two girls, the 16 year old girl was lying in the middle of a road with her back broken, fighting off these two men and their attack. The 13 year old sister to that girl was sexually assaulted in every conceivable way that you can think of, as was the 16 year old. She escaped totally nude into the bushes and was found incoherent that morning, babbling."[285]

At age 13, Ms. L. went camping with the Girl Scouts in northern Wisconsin. While walking through the forest, Rita came upon three deer hunters reading magazines, talking, and joking around. As she started to walk away, one man yelled, "There is a live one."

She thought they meant a deer, ducked, and tried to run. The men came after her and caught her when she tripped. They forced her up, said she wasn't going anywhere, and called her little Godiva. Although it was November, they made her take off her clothes. They threatened to blow her head off if she made a sound. Two held guns at her head and another hit her breast with his rifle. They laughed.

The first man raped her. They joked about her being a virgin, joked about how they could have used something like this when in the military. The second man raped her. They just wanted intercourse, not kissing or touching. When the third man could not get an erection, he forced his penis into her mouth. She did not know what to do, so he swore at her and called her a bitch. When one man pulled the trigger of his gun, she tried hard to perform fellatio. The third man then had an erection and raped her. The men kicked leaves and needles on her and said if she wanted more she should come back the next day. Ms. L. put her clothes back on. She then looked down and saw that they had been reading pornographic magazines with nude women on the covers. She did not tell anyone she had been raped until she was 20 years old. She had seen pornography before. Her father and older brothers kept it under their mattresses and beds. As a child, she had assumed that was how it would be when she grew up. When she was being raped, she thought the men would kill her.[286]

A convicted child molester, age 50, told a Senate panel that he had victimized a total of twenty-two girls, ages 6 to 14, from 1949 to 1978. He said he had used pornographic films and photos of children to diminish the girls' resistance to sexual activities. The man, Joseph Henry, said, "If a pedophile wants a little girl to do a certain act and she doesn't want to do it, he can say, 'Look, this little girl is doing it.' "[287] Convicted sex offender Bill Smith (not his real name) told a Senate subcommittee, "I see pornography itself as a catalyst to the fantasies of a sex offender."[288] And John Ferguson (not his real name), another sex offender who victimized young girls, said pornography was a contributing factor to his problems. "It gives you ideas . . . gets your body going. . . . Pornography Ok's the act."[289]

Dan, a professional man, was a pornography addict for more than forty years. He was introduced to it as a child. At age 9, he met a young man in his early 20s at the pool. The young man won his confidence. He showed him cartoon pornography with explicit sex. The man masturbated to the pornography and fellated Dan. They did it three times a week that summer. Thus, Dan began to associate pornography with masturbation. He did not masturbate in the next two years because pornography was absent from his life. Then he got cartoon pornography from friends at school. At age 15, he threw it away because he was starting to notice real girls. During a military tour in Europe, he purchased actual photographs, books, and magazines of explicit sex. He resumed his habit of masturbating to pornography for two years.

Then Dan met and married his wife and stopped buying pornography. But he was still conditioned to relate pornography to his sexual experiences. He avoided close friendships with males. There were times when all he could concentrate on were mental images of sexually explicit material. He blamed this on pornography. Dan saw the first edition of *Playboy*, and it was like a magnet. He bought it and every issue that followed. The whole process began again. Dan collected more than two hundred books, magazines, and films in three years. It was hard to conceal this from his family. Hard-core pornography became more plentiful. During the 1960s and 1970s, Dan purchased thousands of sexually explicit materials. He saw hundreds of films at adult theaters. Dan tried many times to stop the habit (by burning thousands of dollars worth of material), but it would start again. Each time his appetite became more bizarre, although he never bought material involving sadomasochism, bondage, children, animals, or homosexuality, all of which he felt were subhuman and revolting. But he knew in time they, too, could become a stimulus.

Dan got counseling. He realized then that sexually explicit material is like substance abuse—it exercises tremendous control over the mind. He recognized his problem and had the desire to overcome it. He was not cured, but he was in control of his habit. At one point he had not purchased pornography for four years but said, "The demon is still there." He has to avoid pornography. Dan said he believes that there are thousands of people like him and knows many users personally. Sooner or later, he said, many will be hooked just as he was.[290]

A 38-year-old man managed a girls' softball team comprising girls ages 9 to 11. He talked to girls whose parents did not show up to determine which ones did not feel wanted or loved at home, then he selected his next lover. He had 835 slides, 32 rolls of 8mm film, and 2 large boxes of child pornography when arrested. There were photos of him having sex with a 10-year-old girl with blood running down her legs. That same scene was pictured on the headboard of the bed.[291]

A 35-year-old man on trial for kidnapping said on the witness stand that he had developed a compulsion to act out the bizarre photos in pornographic magazines he purchased at adult bookstores. He used a knife to force a girl into his car. When arrested, two boxes containing 177 porn books were found in his car.[292]

Police in Duluth, Minnesota, reported a case where a baby-sitter was sexually assaulted by a man who had just seen an X-rated movie with a rape scene. They also reported a case involving the attempted rape of three female hitchhikers by a man who said he was goaded by pornography he viewed in an adult bookstore.[293]

An eighth-grade boy was raped by a 19-year-old neighbor who tied him up in a game to see if he could get loose, then showed him pictures of sadomasochism.[294] *Easy Prey*, a television movie about a serial killer/rapist, may have prompted the abduction, bondage, beating, cutting, and repeated rape of a 16-year-old girl by a 35-year-old Michigan man. The case bore a striking resemblance to the movie.[295]

A 33-year-old man was arrested in Milwaukee for allegedly assaulting an 8-year-old boy. Police found child pornography and a letter seeking to purchase six boys, ages 5 to 12, for sex slaves. The letter stated that the boys would be used in sex films in which one or all would be killed.[296]

A baby abducted from a shopping center was forced to perform sex acts, including those with an 11-year-old Vietnamese refugee, also abducted. Many of the assaults were recorded with a camera.[297]

Linedecker states that when the Reverend Richard Ginder, once a leading crusader against obscenity, was arrested in Pittsburgh, pornographic magazines were in his apartment. Also found were two thousand color photographs of teenage boys and girls with Father Ginder, "all naked and engaging in a variety of sex acts."[298]

In St. Louis in December 1979, Mark Molasky made a thirty-minute videotape of his then fiancée, Karen Yates, engaged in sex with a 3-year-old boy. He received a 32-year sentence for rape, sodomy, and child abuse.[299]

Garrett Gilbert, 16, told the Attorney General's Commission on Pornography that a longtime family friend, an attorney, exposed her to pornography at age 10. This happened numerous times in his car. He masturbated and had her masturbate him. He also showed her bestiality. He kissed and fondled her while she looked at the magazines. The he got her to perform oral sex and have sex with a vibrator. When she was 11½, he had her act out pornographic pictures and took pictures of her doing so. At age 13½, she tried to commit suicide.[300]

Two children, ages 6 and 7, were allegedly traumatized when they saw triple-X-rated sex scenes spliced onto the end of a rented cartoon videotape. A psychiatric report said that the children suffered behavioral changes and emotional trauma after seeing the sexually explicit video.[301]

Linedecker reports that in Michigan City, Indiana, in 1979 a stage musician was accused of sexually molesting two 7- and 10-year-old boys and taking nude photos of them. Ten years earlier, the man had been arrested and sentenced to two to fourteen years in prison when he pled guilty in a sodomy case involving about seventy-five boys ages 9 to 14.[302] Linedecker also writes about Guy Strait, who, in his twenty-year career as a child pornographer, made between $5 million and $7 million (p. 227). Another case noted by Linedecker concerns a man who produced child pornography (police confiscated thirty cartons of pictures, negatives, and film, mostly of 7 to 10-year-old girls) and then died from hanging in jail. He was reportedly beaten by other inmates (p. 223).

Linedecker tells the story of Frank Collin, age 35, the former chief of the National Socialist Party of America (Nazis). Collin was accused of picking up boys for sex. Some boys told officials he took nude photos of them posed with rifles. Collin attracted national attention two years earlier when he went to court over the right of the Nazis to march in Skokie, Illinois, which has a large Jewish population, including concentration camp survivors. Collin was purged from the party a few weeks before his arrest when former comrades learned of his pederastic activities and told police (p. 173).

According to Linedecker, a 14-year-old runaway girl from Georgia met a boyfriend who got her into posing for heterosexual and lesbian pornography (pp. 131–32). Linedecker also reports on Luz Valentin, who was raped by her brothers starting at age 6 and became a prostitute. At age 15, she made pornographic movies, posed for pornographic magazine pictures in South Florida, and appeared in live sex shows (pp. 124–26). In Denver, Linedecker says, a nurse and her male companion were accused of luring 11- to 17-year-old girls to a makeshift photo studio in a former ambulance parked in a shopping center. The girls were enticed with offers of $20 to $50 to model for catalogs, then forced to pose for pornography (p. 100).

In 1979, Illinois officials looked into reports that teenage boys placed in a foster home in Chicago were involved in sex with their foster father. Officials had seen a photo album of nude photos of the teens and the foster father.[303]

Linedecker writes about a case in New York in which two men were arrested for drugging fifteen high school and junior high school girls and photographing them during group sex.[304] Linedecker also describes a case in Nassau County, New York, in which a man was accused of luring at least twenty-five teenage girls to his apartment with promises of drugs, then photographing them in sex acts with him. He was accused of drugging the girls prior to the sessions. More than five hundred pornographic photos were confiscated in the apartment (p. 30). And in Elgin, Illinois, Linebecker tells of a construction worker who enticed almost forty teenage girls to pose naked for him in exchange for marijuana. Five hundred color photos of naked children were found in his possession. (p. 30).

A man and his wife were accused of molesting and taking nude photos of the children at the nursery school they owned. Thousands of photographs and pornographic slides of victims between ages 2 and 5 were found. The defense disputed that there was a sexual intent behind the photographs. Burgess describes the impact the experience had on the children.[305]

Joey, a gay prostitute, claimed to earn $200 to $300 a night. He was molested by a man in a sex ring and was involved in all types of sex with males, including beatings, bondage, and group sex. He started taking drugs when participating in sex and photo sessions.[306]

In St. Louis, a Catholic priest and lay teacher were charged with deviant sexual assault concerning a 16-year-old boy. Pornographic photos of boys were found in the priest's rectory room. A large amount of child pornography was seized from both suspects' homes.[307]

A 55-year-old man was arrested on suspicion of molesting four girls, ages 8 to 10. He was accused of sometimes holding them at gunpoint and forcing them to pose for sexually explicit pictures. Many pornographic films and magazines were found in his home.[308]

In Alabama, 6-, 12-, and 13-year-old girls were assaulted by a man who produced obscene pictures. Police found photos showing him sexually involved with one of the girls. His wife took pictures of the acts between him and the 6-year-old girl. Photos of the wife and girl in explicit scenes also were found.[309]

In Marlin, Texas, a man believed to have molested up to fifty-four poor minority boys was shot to death by a 16-year-old boy who lived with him. Police found a footlocker with snapshots of young males, about twenty pornographic magazines, and fifteen porn videos.[310]

A Chicago pornographer took pictures of children posing for sadomasochistic shots. The children were brought to the pornographer by victimized women, primarily divorced or unwed mothers who had themselves posed for this man. Almost a half a million pornographic pictures were seized by police, along with sadomasochistic paraphernalia. Half of the pictures seized were of nude children on torture devices.[311]

In Batavia, Illinois, police arrested a couple who allegedly used their own three young children and at least fifty other children to pose for their pornographic photo business. More than fifteen hundred explicit photos were confiscated from the couple.[312]

An Illinois teacher was charged with child pornography and aggravated criminal sexual assault after a 9-year-old girl alleged he had fondled her at school. Police found his home wallpapered with nude photographs of children, mostly 7- to 14-year-old girls, and found suitcases of children's underwear tagged with names and dates. More than ten thousand photos of nude children were confiscated at his home, and it was discovered that he had been fired from a previous teaching job because of allegations that he had improperly touched a female pupil.[313]

Dr. Simon Miranda told the Attorney General's Commission on Pornography that a 4-year-old boy's mother found him trying to insert his erect penis into the mouth of the centerfold in a pornographic magazine. He had seen oral sex on television at his uncle's house. Miranda also told of a 10-year-old boy who was the victim of repeated anal intercourse by his mother's live-in boyfriend. The man showed him pornography. And, Miranda said, a 16-year-old girl who had the mentality of a 6-year-old was shown pornography by a 34-year-old man, then sexually assaulted.[314]

An 11-year-old boy was shown child pornography to coerce his participation in sexual abuse. He, in turn, sexually assaulted a 7-year-old youth.[315] A 19-year-old woman was charged with having sexual intercourse with a 15-year-old boy, serving alcohol to minors, and showing obscene videos to minors.[316] An Ohio man showed porn movies to four girls, ages

10 to 12, and sexually molested them. He was sentenced to four months in jail and received a $500 fine.[371] And in *Ross v. State*, a man used pornography in connection with the seduction and assault of a 15-year-old boy.[318]

Keating cites numerous cases in which pornography was linked to sexual abuse of children. For example, a 20-year-old male who raped a 12-year-old girl left a pornographic magazine at the attack scene. The girl said that the magazine was in the man's possession at the time of the attack.[319]

Peggy Davis of St. Paul, Minnesota, was sexually abused as a child by a neighbor who had a workshop full of pornography. Her live-in lover sexually abused her own two children and used pornography as a teaching tool. And four teens forced her junior high school daughter to pose like the women they saw in pornographic magazines.[320]

In Dothan, Alabama, a man was arrested for raping and sodomizing a 7-year-old girl. Thousands of pornographic pictures involving children were found in the man's home. These included pornographic storybooks about Mother Goose, Snow White, and Cinderella.[321]

A man made his girlfriend's 10-year-old daughter strip and do housework nude. He would then strap her bare bottom. Later he suspended her by her ankles from the rafters in the garage and performed cunnilingus on her. He was found to have catalogs about bondage.[322]

In Miami, a former Big Brother volunteer was indicted for photographing his two Little Brothers and a third child in homosexual acts for child pornography magazines.[323] And in Syracuse, New York, a photo lab owner was convicted of dealing in child pornography. The lab processed photos of persons under age 16 involved in bestiality and extreme sadomasochistic abuse.[324]

In the abuse of children alone, we found more than 150 other cases of pornography related abuse.

CONCLUSION

These case histories of victims and perpetrators of pornography demonstrate that pornography serves as a catalyst for sexual and other physical abuse of human beings. We firmly believe that if the perpe-

trators had not been exposed to or involved in creating pornography, many of the victims whose stories were detailed in this chapter would not have been killed, raped, or otherwise abused.

QUESTIONNAIRE: PORNOGRAPHY'S RELATIONSHIP TO ABUSE

The following questionnaire, taken primarily from the Final Report of the Attorney General's Commission on Pornography[325] (except for the pornography definitions) is intended to be used by police, district attorneys, social workers, psychologists, psychiatrists, attorneys, battered women's center employees, counselors, and other professionals who come in contact with persons who have been sexually abused or assaulted, battered, molested, involved in prostitution or pornography, or otherwise physically or emotionally abused. The purpose of the questionnaire is to begin to compile detailed documentation of the relationship between pornography and abuse of persons in the hope of aiding efforts to prevent future abuse of this nature.

Whenever pornography is mentioned in the following questions, it refers to material, in pictures or words, communicating any of the following activities, whether or not such depictions are considered legally obscene. Under each category, indicate the approximate number of women, men, girls, and boys depicted in the manner described.

Women Men Girls Boys

Activity Depicted (Underline those that apply.)

(Whether Actual or Simulated)

Nude
In lingerie or underwear
In leather, latex, or rubber clothing or equipment
Wearing leather boots (high heels?) or shoes with extremely high heels
Male dressed in female clothing or underwear
Bound with ropes, chains, or _____
Physically restrained (How? _____)
Specific body parts bound or physically restrained _____
Gagged with _____
Being beaten by whip, belt, chain, or _____ .
Heterosexual activities
Homosexual activities
Lesbian activities
Transvestite(s)
Sexual activities showing
    Love
    Affection
    Mutually pleasurable interaction
    Equal power among the participants
Being fondled or touched by _____ on
    Vagina
    Breasts
    Buttocks
    Penis
Actual or simulated sexual intercourse
    Genital-genital
    Oral-genital
    Anal-genital
    Oral-anal
Bestiality (Animals or creatures involved _____)
Necrophilia (with dead persons or dead animals)
Fecal matter (Where? _____)
Urine (Where? _____)
Enemas
Incest (Describe _____)
Sexual sadism (Describe _____)
Sexual masochism (Describe _____)
Ejaculation on a _____'s body
Penetration of vagina, ass, or mouth, by [name object(s)] _____
Sexual violence (What kind? _____)
Being sexually assaulted or raped
Infliction of pain on _____
Murder
Mutilation, dismemberment, or severed into body parts

Physical coercion or abuse
Psychological coercion or abuse
Discipline or punishment
Bleeding
Bruises
Injured or hurt (How? _____)
_____ having power over _____
Sexual abuse (Describe _____)
_____ sexually degrading _____
_____ sexually humiliating _____
_____ sexually subordinating _____
(or making them submit)
_____ being debased by _____
(How? _____)
Pimps (Glorified? How? _____)
Prostitutes (Glorified? How? _____)
Inflicting harm on self
Receiving sexual pleasure from
    Violence
    Pain
    Sexual assault or rape
    Humiliation
Masturbating

Considering all the pornographic material at issue in this case, approximately _____% depicted females being abused and approximately _____% depicted males being abused.

Considering all the pornographic material in this case, approximately _____% depicted adults and approximately ____% depicted children.

Considering all the pornographic material in this case, approximately _____% depicted lesbian activities and approximately _____% depicted male homosexual activities.

Considering all the pornographic material in this case, what percentage depicted the following: (Note: Percentages need not equal 100%, as some will overlap.)

Sexually violent or
sadomasochistic activity   _____

Activities that were degrading,
humiliating, or debasing to one
or more participants   _____

Activities in which the
participants engaged in mutually
pleasurable, loving, affectionate
sexual relationships of equal
power   _____

Were weapons depicted? (Describe _____)
Describe the settings of the pornographic scenes _____
What percentage of the participants in the pornography were *not* Caucasian (white)? _____%
What percentage of the participants in the pornography were in each of the following categories:

    Ages 0 to 12   _____
    Ages 13 to 18   _____
    Ages 19 to 30   _____
    Ages 31 to 45   _____
    Ages 46 to 60   _____
    Over 60   _____

What types of pornographic material were used or possessed? Include percentages and indicate the approximate number of each type of material used.

    Books   _____% (_____)
    Videocassettes   _____% (_____)
    Audiocassettes   _____% (_____)
    Motion pictures   _____% (_____)
    Peep shows   _____% (_____)
    Dial-a-porn   _____% (_____)
    Computer porn   _____% (_____)
    Cable television   _____% (_____)
    Photographs (snapshots)   _____% (_____)
    Magazines   _____% (_____)

What percentage of the pornography contained words without pictures? _____%

In sexual assault or molestation cases, and perhaps in other assault cases, a report similar to the Illinois Division of Criminal Investigation Sex Motivated Crime Analysis Report (Appendix 4A) should be filled in.

If the Assailant Lived with or Was Known to the Victim

1. The victim is a female/male.
2. The assailant is a female/male.
3. Did/do you live with the person who assaulted you?
4. If so, what was/is your relationship? How do you know him/her?
5. Did/does your assailant use or collect pornography?
6. If so, what kind? (Have the pornography questionnaire above filled in at this point.)
7. Did/does he/she use pornography for masturbation?
8. Did/does he/she use it to get aroused before sexual relations?
9. Did he/she ever ask you to view, read, or hear pornography with him/her?
10. Did he/she ever pressure you to view, read, or hear pornography with him/her?
11. Did he/she ever force you to view, read, or hear pornography with him/her?
12. Do you know the specific names or titles of the pornography? If so, what are they?
13. Was pornography used as part of your normal sexual encounters with him/her?
14. If so, how was it used?
15. Did he/she ever ask you to act out scenes from pornography?
16. Did he/she ever pressure you to act out scenes from pornography?
17. Did he/she ever force you to act out scenes from pornography?
18. Did he/she ever mention pornography in your sexual encounters?
19. Did he/she ever ask you to pose for nude or pornographic material?
20. Did he/she ever pressure you to pose for nude or pornographic material?
21. Did he/she ever force you to pose for nude or pornographic material?
22. Did he/she ever send nude or pornographic photographs of you to a magazine or wife-swapping club newsletter?
23. Did he/she ever show nude or pornographic photographs of you to his/her friends?
24. Did he/she ever sell nude or pornographic photographs of you?
25. Did he/she refer to pornography when he/she assaulted you? For example, did he/she say anything like "This is what women ask for in the magazines I read" or "This is what the woman did in the movie, and she loved it"?
26. Did he/she, or anyone involved in the assault, take nude or pornographic pictures of you before, during, or after the assault?
27. Did he/she show you pornography prior to or after the assault?
28. Did/does he/she use pornography to learn or teach you sexual techniques? To teach you how to dress in a way that turns him/her on? To learn how to tie you up? To learn how to sexually abuse you? Other?
29. Did he/she ever act out scenes from pornography on you?
30. Does/did he/she use pornography to justify, pressure or force you to perform sex acts that you don't want to participate in? For example, does he show you pictures and say, "A lot of couples do this" or "Look how much she likes doing it."
31. Did/does he/she use dial-a-porn services?
32. Did/does he/she frequent X-rated establishments that have live sex shows?
33. Did/does he/she attend peep shows or visit pornographic bookstores?
34. Did/does he/she attend topless and/or bottomless bars and clubs?
35. Did/does he/she attend swingers clubs or activities?
36. Did/does he/she attend pornographic movies?
37. If you answered yes to any of numbers 31 through 36, has he/she ever asked, pressured, or forced you to attend these establishments with him/her?
38. Did/does he/she go to massage parlors, use escort services, or use prostitutes?
39. Did he/she ever batter, assault, sexually assault or molest, or otherwise physically abuse you after consuming pornography?
40. Did he/she ever emotionally abuse you after consuming pornography? For example, did he/she call you names such as slut, whore, bitch, or cunt?
41. Do you know whether his/her use or collection of pornography has ever been involved in his/her physical or emotional abuse of anyone other than you? If yes, explain.

42. Has anyone other than the assailant ever
    a. Sexually assaulted you
    b. Battered you
    c. Physically abused you
43. Was that person a user or collector of pornography?
    (Note: It is extremely important to get as much detail from the victim about the relationship between pornography and the assault as possible. Thus, for example, questions 8, 9, 10, 11, 13, 15, 16, 17, 18, 19, 20, 21, 22, 23, 24, 25, 26, 27, 28, 29, 30, 39, 40, and 41 should contain details of the types of pornography or pornographic acts involved.)

If the Victim Did Not Know Her/His Assailant(s)

Use questions 1, 2, 5, 6, 7, 8, 9, 10, 11, 12, 15, 16, 17, 18, 19, 20, 21, 25, 26, 27, 28, 29, 30, 39, 40, 41, 42, and 43. Add:

44. Did he/she show nude or pornographic depictions of you to other persons?
45. Did he/she ever sell or trade nude or pornographic pictures of you or state that he/she planned to do so?
46. Was there pornography in the place in which you were assaulted?
47. Did your assault take place in an area in which there are a lot of pornographic establishments such as X-rated movie theaters or bookstores?

If the Victim Has Been Used in Pornography

48. Were you a runaway? If so, when did you leave home?
49. Had you been sexually abused before you left home? If so, by whom? How? How old were you when the abuse took place? How old was the person who abused you? Was that person a family member or friend?
50. If you were abused before you left home, was pornography part of the abuse? How was it used?
51. Were you involved in prostitution? Did you have a pimp? Was there an older man/woman who told you what to do, made you have sex for money, and collected the money afterward?
52. How did you first become involved in pornography? What were the circumstances of your life? How old were you?
53. What kind of pornography were you used in?

54. Were forced into the making of pornography by
    a. Threats
    b. Violence
    c. Poverty
    d. Trickery
    e. Pressure by a relative, friend, or lover
    f. Enticement
    g. I was not forced into pornography.
    h. Other

    Please explain.

55. Was pornography shown or communicated to you to convince you to perform for pornography?
56. Was pornography shown or communicated to you to force you to perform for pornography?
57. Do you know other people who have been forced, pressured, or enticed into posing for pornography?
58. Were you ever beaten, whipped, spanked, or physically hurt in the making of pornography? Were you ever tied up? Did you have to act out violent scenes? Was the sex physically painful? Were you ever given drugs, alcohol, or similar substances before or during the pornography making?
59. Do you know people who were physically hurt in the making of pornography?
60. Do you know who produced or profited from the pornography you were used in? Do you know if they were involved in organized crime?
61. Do you know about or have you heard about people being murdered in the making of pornography?
62. Were you in prostitution while you were being used to make pornography? Were other persons you know in pornography also in prostitution?
63. How has your experience in pornography affected how you feel about yourself? How has it affected your relationships with others? How has it affected your schooling and/or job performance?
64. Do you ever have flashbacks or nightmares about your experience in pornography?
65. Do you suffer from phobias?
66. How do you feel now when you see pornography?
67. Have you had upsetting experiences with pornography outside your experiences in the sex industry?
68. What would you like to see done to help persons who have been used/abused in pornography?
69. Would you like to be able to take legal action against the people who abused you? Would you like to be able to sue them? Would you like them to be criminally prosecuted? Would you like to be able to stop the pornography used against you and/or which you performed in from being shown?

70. When (If) you were in prostitution, were you ever asked, pressured, or forced to imitate scenes from pornography? Explain. By whom?

Sexual Harassment and Pornography

71. Is pornography displayed in public places in your community?
72. If so, where is it, and what kinds of pornography are displayed?
73. How does this material make you feel about yourself? How does it make you feel about your relationships with others?
74. Have you ever been upset by pornographic materials you've seen? Explain.
75. Have any people you know been upset by pornographic materials they've seen?
76. Have you ever been sexually harassed by men/women in pornography districts, in front of pornography theaters or bookstores, in front of the pornography sections of a newsstand, in grocery stores, or in drugstores?
77. If so, how did this make you feel?
78. Does pornography make you frightened to perform your daily activities, such as traveling to and from your job?
79. Have you ever been sexually harassed by men/women who referred to pornography or made comments to you that seemed to come from pornography?
80. Is pornography used or displayed at your place of employment?
81. If so, what kind? Where do you see it? Who uses it?
82. Have you ever been sexually harassed on the job? If so, was pornography involved in harassment—i.e., did your boss, co-worker, or customer show you pornography, display pornography, or make verbal references to pornography?
83. Have your bosses, co-workers, or customers ever compared you to models in pornography?
84. How has the presence or use of pornography in your place of work made you feel about yourself and your ability to perform your job?
85. Have you ever complained to anyone about sexual harassment on the job involving pornography? If so, to whom? If not, why not?

86. Were any steps taken about the harassment?
87. Have you ever been forced to leave your job, or have you ever considered leaving your job because of sexual harassment involving or related to pornography?
88. Do you think that pornography has contributed to the way your bosses, co-workers, or customers view you and relate to you?
89. Is pornography used or displayed in your school?
90. If so, what kind? Where do you see it? Who uses it?
91. Has pornography ever been used in your classroom—i.e., in a course on human sexuality? Have any of your teachers or professors ever used pornographic slides or made reference to pornography?
92. Have you ever complained about the presence or use of pornography at your school? If so, to whom? Was any action taken? If not, why not?
93. Have your teachers of fellow students ever used pornography to sexually harass you? Have they ever made verbal references to pornography that have made you feel uncomfortable?
94. Have you ever had pornography imposed on you in social situations at school, such as in fraternity parties or during fraternity or sorority initiations?
95. Is there pornography in your home?
96. Do any of your relatives or friends use pornography or make verbal references to it?
97. If so, how does it make you feel?
98. Have you ever attempted to remove the pornography from your home? Were you successful?
99. Do your children see or know about pornography that is kept in your home? If so, has it influenced the way they think about women and sexuality?

Questions for Abusers, Molesters, and Batterers

When an abuser, molester, or batterer is willing to answer questions, administer the pornography questionnaire to find out whether he/she used or collected pornography and what kind. Then ask him/her questions 1 through 43, changing the wording to find out whether he/she ever used pornography against his/her victims in the manner described. For example, question 17 should be changed to read: Did you ever force her/him to act out scenes from pornography?

NOTES

1. David Alexander Scott, *Pornography: Its Effects on the Family, Community and Culture* (Washington, D.C.: Free Congress Foundation, 1985), 1.
2. "Sex Killers Can't Tell Fact from Fantasy," *Morality in Media of Wisconsin, Inc. Newsletter*, Summer 1987, 3.
3. Donald E. Wildmon, *The Case Against Pornography* (Wheaton, Ill.: Victor Books, 1986), 15.
4. Scott, *Pornography*, 9.
5. Ibid.
6. Darrell Pope, "Does Pornographic Literature Incite Sexual Assaults?" Memorandum to the Western Michigan Committee for Decency in Media, 1 May 1979, 1–13, 5.
7. Michael J. Goldstein and Harold Sanford Kant with John J. Hartman, *Pornography and Sexual Deviance: A Report of the Legal and Behavioral Institute, Beverly Hills, California* (Berkeley: University of California Press, 1973).
8. Aric Press, Tessa Namuth, Susan Agrest, MacLean Gander, Gerald C. Lubenow, Michael Reese, David T. Friendly, and Ann McDaniel, "Justice: The War Against Pornography, *Newsweek*, 18 March 1985, 65.
9. Phyllis Schlafly, ed., *Pornography's Victims*, (Westchester, Ill.: Crossway Books, 1987), 151–59.
10. "Rape: The Sexual Weapon," *Time*, 5 September 1983, 29.
11. Commission on the Status of Women State of Illinois, *Report and Recommendations to the Governor and the General Assembly*, February 1985, 26–27.
12. Andrea Dworkin citing a letter from Kathleen Barry on Ordinances to Add Pornography as Discrimination Against Women, Minneapolis City Council Government Operations Committee, 12 and 13 December 1983, 17 (hereafter cited as Minneapolis hearings).
13. "Child-Abducting Uncovered by FBI," *Arizona Republic*, 22 December 1983.
14. Clifford L. Linedecker, *Children in Chains* (New York: Everest House, 1981), 90.
15. Robin Lloyd, *For Money or Love: Boy Prostitution in America* (New York: Vanguard Press, 1976), 104–05.
16. Richard T. Pienciak, "Child Smut Law Hurt, Didn't Help Us, Officials Say," *Capital Times* (Madison, Wisc.), 19 September 1984.
17. C. Benes, "The Current Status of Pornography and Its Effects on Society," (Los Angeles, Police Department, Administrative Vice Division, November 1984), 10.
18. Ibid., 14; Lloyd, *For Money or Love*, 100.
19. Benes, 14.
20. Freedom from Sexual Violence, *Violent Pornography: What It Is and Who It Hurts* (Milwaukee: Freedom from Sexual Violence, 1985), 10.
21. Judith A. Reisman, in *"Rape And Sexual Assault,"* ed. Ann Wolbert Burgess (New York: Garland Publishing, 1985), 367.
22. Robert Barnes, "Child Pornography 'Cottage Industry' Continues to Thrive Despite Tougher Laws and Police Efforts," *St. Petersburg Times*, 21 August 1983.
23. Mimi H. Silbert and Ayala M. Pines, "Pornography and Sexual Abuse of Women," *Sex Roles* 10, nos. 11, 12 (1984): 857–68.
24. Mark-David Janus, Barbara Scanlon, and Virginia Price, "Youth Prostitution" Chap. 7 in *Child Pornography and Sex Rings*, ed. Burgess and Clark, 139.
25. Ibid.
26. Albert Belanger et al., "Scope of the Problem: Investigation and Prosecution," Chap. 2 in *Child Pornography and Sex Rings*, ed. Burgess and Clark, 33.
27. Diana E.H. Russell and Karen F. Trocki, "The Impact of Pornography on Women" (Testimony before the Attorney General's Commission on Pornography, Houston, 11 September 1985), 1–19.
28. Ibid., 2.
29. Ibid., 3.
30. Ann Wolbert Burgess, ed., *Rape and Sexual Assault* (New York: Garland Publishing, 1985), (fn. 11).
31. Victor B. Cline, "The Effects Of Pornography on Human Behavior" (Testimony before the Attorney General's Commission on Pornography, Houston, 11 September 1985), 1.
32. Dom Gordon, Letter, *Wausau Sunday Herald* (Wausau, Wisc.), 6 May 1985.
33. Wildmon, *The Case Against Pornography*, 13.
34. Harry M. Clor, *Obscenity and Public Morality: Censorship in a Liberal Society* (Chicago: University of Chicago Press, 1969), 137.
35. Neil Gallagher, *The Porno Plague* (Minneapolis: Bethany House Publishers, 1981), 19.
36. Letter from Los Angeles chief of police Daryl F. Gates and Captain J.J. Docherty to Wisconsin state representative James A. Rutkowski and his aide, Sara Lee Johann, 28 May 1985.
37. *Report of the U.S. Congress Permanent Subcommittee on Investigations on Child Pornography and Pedophilia*, Ninety-Ninth Congress, Second Session, 1986 (Washington, D.C.: U.S. Government Printing Office, 1986), 9.
38. Letter from city of Indianapolis police detective Terry Hall to Sara Lee Johann, 21 October 1985.
39. Letter from William Fortune, New York Police Department, to Wisconsin state representative James A. Rutkowski, 22 July 1985.
40. Letter from Houston chief of police Lee P. Brown to Wisconsin state representative James A. Rutkowski, 13 August 1985.
41. Letter from Milwaukee police chief Robert J. Zianik to Wisconsin state representative James A. Rutkowski, 21 May 1985.
42. Letter from Dane County, Wisconsin, sheriff Jerome

Lacke to Wisconsin state representative James A. Rutkowski, 20 May 1985.

43. Charles H. Keating, Jr., "Memorandum Re Statistical Study of Relationship of Obscenity to Crime and Other Antisocial Behavior," letter to William B. Lockhart, 11 August 1969; Exhibit C of the "Report of Commissioner Charles H. Keating, Jr.," in *The Report of the Commission on Obscenity and Pornography* (New York: Bantam Books, 1970), 637.

44. Clor, *Obscenity and Public Morality*, 140.

45. *Ibid.*

46. Wildmon, *The Case Against Pornography*, 13.

47. *Memoirs v. Massachusetts*, 383 U.S. 413, 452–53 (1966), Justice Tom C. Clark, dissenting.

48. Dworkin, Minneapolis hearings, 17.

49. *Pornography's Victims*, ed. Phyllis Schlafly (Westchester, Ill.: Crossway Books, 1987), 33.

50. "Let the Victims Be Heard!" *Morality in Media of Wisconsin, Inc. Newsletter*, Summer 1987, 3.

51. Letter from Carol Plumer to Sara Lee Johann, 23 October 1985.

52. Letter from Brad Curl to friends of Morality in Media, Inc., December 1986.

53. Ann Jones, "A Little Knowledge," in *Take Back the Night: Women on Pornography*, ed. Laura Lederer (New York: Wm. Morrow & Co., 1980), 179–86.

54. Clor, *Obscenity and Public Morality*, 139–42.

55. Linda Lovelace, *Ordeal* (Secaucus, N.J.: Citadel Press, 1980).

56. Linda Marchiano, Minneapolis hearings, 13–16.

57. Peter Bogdanovich, *The Killing of the Unicorn: Dorothy Stratton 1960–1980* (New York: Wm. Morrow & Co., 1984). Dorothy Stratton's story also was told in the following films: *Death of a Centerfold*, MGM/UA Home Video Presentation, 1981; *Dorothy Stratton: Untold Story*, Playboy Video Programs, 1985; *Star 80*, Warner Bros. Home Video, 1983.

58. Karen E. Klein, "3 Indicted in Porn Case Involving 16-year-old," *Los Angeles Daily News*, 6 March 1987.

59. Tom Minnery, ed., *Pornography: A Human Tragedy* (Wheaton, Ill. Christianity Today, Inc. 1986), 179–83.

60. Ibid., 180.

61. Ibid., 181–82.

62. U.S. Department of Justice, Attorney General's Commission on Pornography, *Final Report* (Washington, D.C.: U.S. Department of Justice, 1986), 837–900, 1371–74 (hereafter cited as AGCOP).

63. Laura Lederer, "Then and Now: An Interview with a Former Pornography Model," in *Take Back the Night: Women on Pornography*, ed. Laura Lederer (New York: Wm Morrow & Co., 1980, 57–70.

64. Ibid., 58.

65. Ibid., 62.

66. AGCOP, 627.

67. Fred Robbins, "Suzanne's Agony: Telling Her Son about Those Nude Pix," *The Globe*, 11 March 1980.

68. Catherine A. MacKinnon, "Pornography, Civil Rights, and Speech," *Harvard Civil Rights–Civil Liberties Law Review* 20 (Winter 1985): 36.

69. Leon Freilich, "Vanna Wages War over Sexy Photos," *Star*, 3 March 1987.

70. Ron Sproat, "The Working Day in a Porno Factory," in *Sexual Deviance and Sexual Deviants*, eds. Erich Goode and Richard R. Troiden (New York: Wm. Morrow & Co., 1974), 83–92.

71. Ibid., 91.

72. Ibid., 92.

73. Miki Garcia, "Transcript of Proceedings," presented at Attorney General's Commission on Pornography Hearings, Houston, 12 September 1985, 116.

74. Ibid., 117.

75. Phyllis Schlafly, ed., *Pornography's Victims* (Westchester, Ill.: Crossway Books, 1987), 91–92.

76. AGCOP, 779.

77. Russell Miller, *Bunny: The Real Story of Playboy* (London: Michael Joseph Ltd., 1984).

78. Dr. Frank Osanka, Testimony before the Attorney General's Commission on Pornography, Chicago, 23 July 1985.

79. Letter from Arthur Gary Bishop to Heber J. Guertz, 3 May 1985.

80. Letter from Dr. Frank Osanka to William J. Kunkle, Jr., 6 March 1980.

81. Osanka, Testimony before the Attorney General's Commission on Pornography.

82. *The Milwaukee Journal*, 10 June 1985.

83. "Many Bones Found at Site in California," *Milwaukee Sentinel*, 11 June 1985.

84. "Family of 5 Missing in California Case," *Milwaukee Journal*, 11 June 1985.

85. "Sex-Torture Killing Suspect May Surrender," *Milwaukee Sentinel*, 13 June 1985.

86. Linedecker, *Children in Chains*, 186–87.

87. Lloyd, *For Money or Love*, 85–86.

88. Beverly Heinrich, "Extent Report," (Texas) House Select Committee on Child Pornography: It's Related Causes and Control, 14 September 1978, 28.

89. Ibid.

90. Clifford L. Linedecker, *Children in Chains* (New York: Everest House, 1981), 184.

91. National Federation for Decency, *Real Life Tragedies* (Tupelo, Miss.: National Federation for Decency, 1984).

92. Ibid.

93. "Pornography Provides Boy with How-To in Baby Girl's Death," *Women Against Pornography Newsreport* 6 (Spring/Summer 1984): 4.

94. Patrick W. Wathen. "Schiro's Behavior Linked to Pornography," *The Evansville Courier*, 12 September 1981, 11.

95. Evelyn Radison, "Child Murderer Convicted," *Women Against Pornography Newsreport* 7 (Spring/Summer 1986): 7.

96. Joint Forces of the Ontario Provincial Police and the Metropolitan Toronto Police Pornography and Hate Literature Section, *Obscenity Investigator's Manual* (Toronto: Ontario Provincial Police, 1986), 107.

97. Ibid., 108.

98. Ibid.

99. Ibid., 109.

100. Rolf Zettersten, "Ted Bundy: A Fatal Attraction," *Focus on the Family* 13 (March 1989): 23.

101. Jones, "A Little Knowledge," in *Take Back the Night*, ed. Laura Lederer, 181.

102. *Ibid.*

103. Dusty Rhodes and Sandra McNeill, eds., *Women Against Violence Against Women* (London: Onlywoman Press, Ltd., 1985), 16.

104. Robin Morgan, "How to Run the Pornographers out of Town and Preserve the First Amendment," *Ms.*, November 1978, 55.

105. "Mass Killer Fed Mind with Violent, Porn Magazines," *NFD Journal* 10 (October 1986): 6.

106. "College Student Kidnapped and Killed by Porn King," *Women Against Pornography Newsreport* 7 (Spring/Summer 1986): 5.

107. "The Chairman's Corner," *Citizens Concerned for Our Community Bulletin* (Madison, Wisc.), 1 September 1980.

108. *Ibid.*

109. "TV 'Smut' Gets Blame, Murderer Gets Life," *Green Bay Press Gazette*, 18 May 1984.

110. Betty Wein, "The Chilling Effects of Pornography: A Jewish Perspective" (Paper presented at the Seventh World Media Conference, Tokyo, November 1984), 34.

111. Carlos Sanchez, "Williamson Killing Linked to Sexual Rage," *Citizens Against Pornography Newsletter* (Austin, Texas), March 1987.

112. William A. Stanmeyer, *The Seduction of Society: Pornography and Its Impact on American Life* (Wheaton, Ill.: Victor Books, 1986), 81.

113. Gallagher, *The Porno Plague*, 23–24.

114. Wildmon, *The Case Against Pornography*, 88.

115. Clor, *Obscenity and Public Morality*, 140–41.

116. Valerie J. Hamm, "The Civil Rights Pornography Ordinances—An Examination under the First Amendment," *Kentucky Law Journal*. 73 (1984–85): 1081, (citing Mark Starr et al., "The Random Killers," *Newsweek*, 26 November 1984, 104–105).

117. "Jurors See Movie," *Milwaukee Journal*, 25 May 1984.

118. "Crime Cruel Imitators," *India Today*, 16–30 November 1979, 16.

119. Keating, "Memorandum," 640–41.

120. Task Force on Prostitution and Pornography, *A Partial List of Victims of Sexploitation* (Madison, Wisc.: Task Force on Prostitution and Pornography, undated), 1.

121. Patrice Gravino, "Forced Sex Claimed in Slaying Trial," *Citizens Against Pornography Newsletter*, September 1987.

122. Pornography Resource Center, Minneapolis, undated press release.

123. "Two Accused of Murder in 'Snuff' Films," *Oakland Tribune*, 6 August 1983; "Slain Teens Needed Jobs, Tried Porn," newspaper article from unknown source; Felony Complaint—Criminal No. NF 800382 in *California v. Fred Berre Douglas and Richard Felix Hernandez and Richard Manuel Hernandez*, [John Does I through III] dated 5 August 1983, in the Municipal Court, North Orange County Judicial District, County of Orange, State of California.

124. "Girl Says Father Filmed Murder of 3 Children," *Daily Herald* (Wausau–Merrill, Wisc.), 15 January 1985; "Girl Says She Watched Father Film Killings of Three Children," *Oakland Tribune*, 15 January 1985.

125. Women Against Violence Against Women, *We Say That Film "Snuff" Should Not Be Shown* (Monticello, N.Y.: Women Against Violence Against Women, undated); Charlie Crist, "DA Won't Prosecute in 'Snuff' Obscenity Case," *Times Herald Record*, (New York, NY) 24 March 1976; "Anti-'Snuff' Organization Hires Lawyers for Obscenity Battle," *Times Herald Record*, 31 March 1976; "Snuff Stirs Woe for Other Porno," *Variety*, 3 March 1976.

126. Women Against Violence Against Women, *We Say That Film "Snuff" Should Not Be Shown.*

127. Ibid.

128. Jane E. Brody, "Autoerotic Death of Youth Causes Widening Concern," *New York Times*, 27 March 1984.

129. Robert R. Hazelwood, Park Elliott Dietz, and Ann Wolbert Burgess, *Autoerotic Fatalities* (Lexington, Mass: Lexington Books, 1983).

130. "Auto-Erotic Asphyxiation," *Pornwatch* (Milwaukee chapter of the National Federation for Decency), July/August 1987, 6; AGCOP, 797; *Herceg v. Hustler*, 814 F.2d 1017 (5th Cir. 1988).

131. Wildmon, *The Case Against Pornography*, 86.

132. Pope, "Does Pornographic Literature Incite Sexual Assaults?" 6–8.

133. Letter from Morton A. Hill, S.J., to friends of Morality in Media, Inc., Fall 1982.

134. Keating, "Memorandum," 647–48.

135. Albert J. Belanger et al. "Typology of Sex Rings Exploiting Children," chap. 3 in *Child Pornography and Sex Rings*, ed. Burgess and Clark 52, 53, 61–63.

136. Belanger et al., "Scope of the Problem," chap. 2 in *Child Pornography and Sex Rings*, ed. Burgess and Clark, 29–30.

137. Kenneth V. Lanning, "Collectors," ch. 4 in *Child Pornography and Sex Rings*, ed. Burgess and Clark 83.

138. Carol R. Hartman, Ann W. Burgess, and Kenneth V. Lanning, "Typology of Collectors," chap. 5 in *Child Pornography and Sex Rings*, ed. Burgess and Clark 96.

139. Ibid, 73.

140. Benes, "The Current Status of Pornography," 14.

141. " 'Kiddie Porn Queen' Gets 4 Years in Jail," *Chicago Tribune*, 6 May 1984.

142. Linedecker, *Children in Chains*, 212–18; Lloyd, *For Money or Love*, 80–82.

143. Belanger et al., "Typology of Sex Rings Exploiting Children," chap. 3 in *Child Pornography and Sex Rings*, ed. Burgess and Clark 67–68.

144. "FBI Affidavit Accuses Teacher of Molesting Hopi

Indian Boys," *Dallas Morning News*, 25 September 1984.

145. "Angry Moms Drown Child Molester," *Weekly World News*, 25 September 1984.

146. Linedecker, *Children in Chains*, 51–72.

147. John Flinn, "Girls, Parents Sue over Porno Pics," *San Francisco Examiner*, 5 May 1984.

148. Linedecker, *Children in Chains*, 73–89.

149. Ibid., 110–111.

150. Phyllis Schlafly, ed., *Pornography's Victims* (Westchester, Ill.: Crossway Books, 1987), 184–87.

151. "Fugitive Caught in Orlando Charged in Child Porn Sales," *Miami Herald*, 19 August 1984.

152. Letter from Daryl F. Gates, chief of police, and J.J. Docherty, captain, commanding officer, Administrative Vice Division, Los Angeles Police Department, to Wisconsin state representative James A. Rutkowski, 28 May 1985.

153. Phillip J. O'Connor, "2 Arrested in N. Side Boys' Sex Ring," *Chicago Sun-Times*, 17 April 1978.

154. Burgess, *Child Pornography and Sex Rings*, 62–63.

155. Belanger et al., "Typology of Sex Rings Exploiting Children," chap. 3 in *Child Pornography and Sex Rings*, ed. Burgess and Clark, 62–63.

156. Belanger et al., "Scope of the Problem: Investigation and Prosecution," chap. 2 in *Child Pornography and Sex Rings*, ed. Burgess and Clark, 26–27.

156. Linedecker, *Children in Chains*, 13–17.

157. Ibid., 37–50.

158. Ibid., 221.

159. "Suspect Has 'Truck Load' of Child Pornography," *NFD Journal* 10 (March 1986): 17.

160. Linedecker, *Children in Chains*, 179–80.

161. "User of Pornography Abuses 13 Young Boys," *NFD Journal* 10 (August 1986): 18.

162. Rhodes and McNeill, *Women Against Violence*, 17.

163. "Boy, 12, May Have Taken Rape Idea from TV Trial, Officials Say," *Minneapolis Star Tribune*, 18 April 1984.

164. AGCOP, 777.

165. Keating, "Memorandum," 640.

166. *Brief Amici Curiae of Women Against Pornography et al. in American Booksellers Association, Inc. v. Hudnut, et al.*, Case No. 84-3147, U.S. Court of Appeals for the Seventh Circuit, date unknown, 13 (hereafter cited as Brief of Women Against Pornography).

167. Wildmon, *The Case Against Pornography*, 58.

168. Ibid., 60.

169. Keating, "Memorandum," 641.

170. Wildmon, *The Case Against Pornography*, 57.

171. Keating, "Memorandum," 643.

172. Gallagher, *The Porno Plague*, 22.

173. Cited in Clor, *Obscenity and Public Morality*, 143–44.

174. Keating, "Memorandum," 642.

175. "Child Exposed to Pornography, Forces Others to Participate," *NFD Journal* 10 (November/December 1986): 11.

176. AGCOP, 785.

177. Ibid., 777.

178. Gallagher, *The Porno Plague*, 24.

179. Keating, "Memorandum," 640.

180. Ibid., 641.

181. Wildmon, *The Case Against Pornography*, 86.

182. Ms. P., Minneapolis hearings, 43–46.

183. Ibid., 44.

184. Ibid.

185. Ms. W., Minneapolis hearings, 65.

186. Ibid., 66.

187. Minnery, *Pornography*, 163.

188. Ibid., 164.

189. AGCOP, 774–75.

190. Minnery, *Pornography*, 171–75; [Phyllis Schlafley (Ed.) *Pornography's Victims* (Westchester, Illinois: Crossway Books, A Division of Good News Publishers, 1987), 34–38.]

191. *Pornography's Victims*, ed. Phyllis Schlafly (Westchester, Ill.: Crossway Books, 1987), 25–31.

192. Wildmon, *The Case Against Pornography*, 133–34.

193. Wanda Richardson, Minneapolis hearings, 68.

194. Donna Dunn, Minneapolis hearings, 69–71.

195. Brief of Women Against Pornography, 14.

196. Tanya Vonnegut Beck, "Women in Pornography" (Submitted to the Administration Committee, Indianapolis/Marion County City Council, 16 April 1984).

197. Russell and Trocki, "The Impact of Pornography," 15.

198. Ibid.

199. Diann, "Destroyed Marriage," in *Pornography's Victims*, ed. Phyllis Schlafly (Westchester, Ill.: Crossway Books, 1987), 83–85.

200. Wildmon, *The Case Against Pornography*, 134–35.

201. AGCOP, 801.

202. Ibid., 803–04.

203. Ms. N., Minneapolis hearings, 41.

204. Anonymous, "Destroyed Marriage," *Pornography's Victims*, ed. Phyllis Schlafly (Westchester, Ill.: Crossway Books, 1987), 221–28.

205. A frequent response of addicts evaluated by Dr. Osanka, for example, Thomas R. Schiro, 1981 (convicted multiple rapist and murderer) and Randy Wedding, 1989 (convicted multiple rapist). See also the works of psychologist Victor Cline listed in the Bibliography.

206. MacKinnon, "Pornography, Civil Rights, and Speech," 35.

207. Ms. O., Minneapolis hearings, 46–49.

208. Terese, Testimony before the Attorney General's Commission on Pornography, Chicago, July 1985.

209. Ms. Q., Minneapolis hearings, 46.

210. Ibid., 47.

211. Ibid.

212. Ibid., 48.

213. Ibid., 49.

214. Susan Batkin, "42% of Cambridge Voters Support Anti-Porn Ordinance," *Women Against Pornography Newsreport* 7 (Spring/Summer 1986): 7.

215. Minnery, *Pornography*, 166–71; Schlafly, *Pornography's Victims*, 39–49.

216. AGCOP, 780–81, 792–93, 809–10, 823–25.

217. Linedecker, *Children in Chains*, 70–71.

218. J. Densen-Gerber. "Child Prostitution . . . Exploitation of Children," in *Sexual Abuse of Children: Selected Readings* (National Center on Child Abuse and Neglect, 1980), 78.

219. Steve Payne, "Night Smokes Panic Woman," *Toronto Sun*, 7 September 1986.

220. AGCOP, 780.

221. "Pornography Is Not a 'Victimless' Crime," *Pornwatch* (Milwaukee Chapter of the National Federation for Decency. July/August 1987, 3.

222. Kenneth V. Lanning, "Collectors," chap. 4 in *Child Pornography and Sex Rings*, ed. Burgess and Clark, 90–92.

223. Belanger et al., "Scope of the Problem," chap. 2 in *Child Pornography and Sex Rings*, ed. Burgess and Clark, 27–28.

224. James Neff, "I'll Never Forget," *Cleveland Plain Dealer*, 16 March 1980.

225. Brief of Women Against Pornography, 14.

226. Gordon, Letter.

227. Joan Radovich, "Pornography Called Trigger for Child Molesting," *Los Angeles Times*, 9 August 1984.

228. Linedecker, *Children in Chains*, 95–96.

229. Ibid., 33.

230. Ibid., 26.

231. Valerie Heller, "Commentary: Pornography and My Life," *Women Against Pornography Newsreport* 7 (1985): 2, 19.

232. AGCOP, 800.

233. Ibid., 795–96.

234. Dr. Simon Miranda, "Psychologist," *Pornography's Victims*, ed. Phyllis Schlafly (Westchester, Ill.: Crossway Books, 1987), 216–20.

235. William Dworin, "Child Porn," in *Pornography's Victims*, ed. Phyllis Schlafly (Westchester, Ill.: Crossway Books, 1987) 191.

236. AGCOP, 785–786.

237. AGCOP, 786.

238. "Victim of Abuse Tells of Playboy's Role," *NFD Journal* 10 (March 1986): 17.

239. AGCOP, 775.

240. Ibid.

241. Ibid., 778.

242. Judy Witt of Dane County (Wisconsin) Committee on Sexual Assault 1985 correspondence with Sara Lee Johann, undated, case number 704416 and CSD 167473-4 (hereafter cited as Witt, Correspondence with Johann, with specific case numbers).

243. Minnery, *Pornography*, 190.

244. "Daughter and Friend Assaulted," *Pornwatch* (Milwaukee chapter of the National Federation for Decency), September 1987, 6.

245. Belanger et al., "Typology of Sex Rings Exploiting Children," chap. 3 in *Child Pornography and Sex Rings*, ed. Burgess and Clark 25.

246. Letter from Milwaukee police captain Thomas A. Perlewitz to Attorney General's Commission on Pornography, 23 July 1985.

247. AGCOP, 801–02.

248. Pope, "Does Pornographic Literature Incite Sexual Assaults?" 11–12.

249. Mr. O., Minneapolis hearings, 41–42.

250. Kathleen Barry, *Female Sexual Slavery* (Englewood Cliffs, N.J.: Prentice-Hall, 1979), 91.

251. *United States v. Ming Sen Shiue*, 504 F.Supp. 360 (1980).

252. Beck, "Women in Pornography."

253. Jim Phillips, " 'He Said I Was Very Lucky': 5-Hour Rape Ordeal Is Described in Punishment Hearing," *American Statesman*, date unknown.

254. MacKinnon, "Pornography, Civil Rights, and Speech," 35.

255. Witt, Correspondence with Johann, case number 794325 (Madison Police Department, 1984).

256. "Pornography Effects Evident Again," *NFD Journal* 10 (March 1986): 15.

257. AGCOP, 782.

258. "Movie Rape Emulated," *Morality in Media Newsletter*, December 1986, 4.

259. "Criminal Possessed Bondage Devices," *NFD Journal* 11 (January 1987): 17.

260. Wildmon, *The Case Against Pornography*, 86.

261. Keating, "Memorandum," 641.

262. Ms. X., Minneapolis hearings, 66–67.

263. *Watson v. State*, 147 Ga. 847, 250 S.E.2d 540 (1978).

264. Gary E. McCuen, *Pornography and Sexual Violence* (Hudson, Wisc.: Gary McCuen Publications, Inc., 1985), 13.

265. Ibid.

266. Witt, Correspondence with Johann, case number 865653 (Madison Police Department, 1985).

267. "Man Accused of Rape in Adult Bookstore," *Milwaukee Journal*, 21 February 1985.

268. Helen Gualtieri, "Alien Victim," *Pornography's Victims*, ed. Phyllis Schlafly (Westchester, Ill.: Crossway Books, 1987), 128–30.

269. Russell and Trocki, "The Impact of Pornography," 11, 13–16.

270. Ibid., 11, 13–15.

271. These pornography victim cases were obtained in a response to a survey sent by Sara Lee Johann to battered women centers in Wisconsin in 1985.

272. Wanda Richardson, Minneapolis hearings, 68.

273. AGCOP, 827.

274. Brief of Women Against Pornography, 13.

275. "Another Manager Loses Job for Refusal to Sell Porn Magazines," *NFD Journal* 11 (April 1987): 11.

276. Ms. R., Minneapolis hearings, 50–52.

277. "Blaming Pornographers, Woman Sets Self on Fire," *Capital Times* (Madison, Wisc.), 12 July 1984.

278. Roger McBain, "Inmate Gets $60,000 in Rape Suit," *Milwaukee Journal*, 21 September 1984.

279. Evelina Kane, "Prison Officials Fear Effect of Porn," *Women Against Pornography Newsreport* 7 (Spring/Summer 1986): 6.

280. AGCOP, 808.

281. Ibid., 827–28.

282. Thomas Guillen, "Assault Linked to Sex Movies?"

Seattle Times, 10 December 1984; see also Wildmon, *The Case Against Pornography,* 89–91.

283. Gallagher, *The Porno Plague,* 24–25.

284. MacKinnon, "Pornography, Civil Rights, and Speech," 46–50.

285. Pope, "Does Pornographic Literature Incite Sexual Assaults?" 8.

286. Ms. L., Minneapolis hearings, 38–39.

287. Marlene Cimons, "Used Films, Photos to 'Diminish Resistance' of Young Girls: Child Molester Tells Panel of Porno Ties," part 1, *Los Angeles Times,* 22 February 1985.

288. Wildmon, *The Case Against Pornography,* 85.

289. Wildmon, *The Case Against Pornography,* 85–86.

290. Minnery, *Pornography,* 175–79.

291. Pope, "Does Pornographic Literature Incite Sexual Assaults?" 10–11.

292. Stanmeyer, *The Seduction of Society,* 29.

293. Gallagher, *The Porno Plague,* 24.

294. Wildmon, *The Case Against Pornography,* 143.

295. "Rapes Reflect ABC Movie," *NFD Journal* 11 (January 1987): 16.

296. "The Chilling Effects of Pornography," *Morality in Media of Wisconsin, Inc. Newsletter,* Summer 1987, 3.

297. Annie Laurie Gaylor, "Pornography through the Eyes of Women: Minneapolis Ordinance to Spawn Madison Version?" *The Feminist Connection,* January/February 1984.

298. Linedecker, *Children in Chains,* 244.

299. Nancy Nau Sullivan, "Molasky Shows Remorse for 'Bizarre' Sex Crime," *St. Louis Globe-Democrat,* 30 May 1986.

300. Garrett Gilbert, "Child Victim," in *Pornography's Victims,* ed. Phyllis Schlafly (Westchester, Ill.: Crossway Books, 1987), 206–09.

301. "Risque Disney Tape," *Pornwatch* (Milwaukee chapter of the National Federation for Decency), 16 December 1986, 1.

302. Linedecker, *Children in Chains,* 244.

303. Mitchell Locin, "State Probes Foster Home Sex Reports," *Chicago Tribune,* 13 September 1979.

304. Linedecker, *Children in Chains,* 30.

305. Ann W. Burgess et al., "Impact of Child Pornography and Sex Rings on Child Victims and Their Families," chap. 6 in *Child Pornography and Sex Rings,* ed. Burgess and Clark, 119.

306. Ibid., 119.

307. "Porn Involved in Another Crime," *NFD Journal* 11 (April 1987): 13.

308. "Accused Child Molester Collected Porn," *NFD Journal* 11 (April 1987): 11.

309. "Pornography Is Not a 'Victimless' Crime," 3.

310. "Pornography Was a Part of Life for Pedophile Who Molested 54 Boys," *NFD Journal* 11 (September 1987): 1, 17.

311. Lloyd, *For Money or Love,* 89–90.

312. "Charges Filed Against Parents," *Milwaukee Sentinel,* 28 October 1981.

313. "Substitute Teacher Charged in Sex Case," *Milwaukee Sentinel,* 19 April 1985; Mike Christopulos, David Doege, and John Higgins, "Racine Pastor Fired Teacher in Child Pornography Case," *Milwaukee Sentinel,* 20 April 1985.

314. Dr. Simon Miranda, "Psychologist," *Pornography's Victims,* ed. Phyllis Schlafly (Westchester, Ill.: Crossway Books, 1987), 216–20.

315. Letter from Farley B. Miles, sergeant, commanding officer, Youth Division, Special Investigating Unit, and Joe P. Mayo, commander, Youth Division, Chicago Department of Police, to Sara Lee Johann, 4 July 1985.

316. "Child Molesting Charges Filed Against Inwood Woman," *Plymouth Pilot News* (Plymouth, Ind.), 25 August 1987.

317. "Judge Gives Molester Light Sentence," *NFD Journal* 11 (April 1987): 11.

318. *Ross v. State,* 475 A.2d 481 (Md. App. 1984).

319. Keating, "Memorandum," 640.

320. Press et al., "Justice: The War Against Pornography," 65.

321. Wildmon, *The Case Against Pornography,* 59.

322. Keating, "Memorandum," 653.

323. "Big Brother Volunteer Sought on Child Pornography Charges," *Chicago Tribune,* 10 December 1977.

324. "Child Porn Conviction," *Morality in Media Newsletter,* October 1983, 4.

325. AGCOP, 739–45.

APPENDIX 4A

DEPARTMENT OF LAW ENFORCEMENT
ILLINOIS DIVISION OF CRIMINAL INVESTIGATION
SEX MOTIVATED CRIME ANALYSIS REPORT

DLE 4-46

THE INFORMATION CONTAINED HEREON IS IN ACCORDANCE WITH CHAPTER 127, IRS, WHICH EMPOWERS THE DIVISION OF CRIMINAL INVESTIGATION TO INVESTIGATE THE ORIGINS, ACTIVITIES, PERSONNEL AND INCIDENTS OF CRIME. THIS REPORT SHOULD BE SUBMITTED WHETHER OR NOT THE PERPETRATOR HAS BEEN IDENTIFIED OR AFTER THE APPREHENSION OF THE ACCUSED. THIS INFORMATION SHALL BE KEPT CONFIDENTIAL AND SHALL BE AVAILABLE FOR EXAMINATION BY ANY AUTHORIZED LAW ENFORCEMENT AGENCY.

Dept. Submitting Report:	Your Case # :	Date of Offense:	Officer Making Report:
County of Occurrence	Office Use Only District:	File # Entry Type:	Date of Report

VICTIM INFORMATION

Name: Last, First, Middle	Sex	Ethnic Origin	D.O.B.	Blood Type	Marital Status

Address:	Telephone Number:

Height	Weight :	Hair Color:	Eye Color:	Complexion:	Location Where Offense Occurred

VEHICLE INFORMATION

License #:	State:	Year:	Make:	Model:	Year:	Color:	Style:	Drivers License #:

Employer:	Address:	Occupation:

NUMBER OF ASSAILANTS: [ ]

(This crime - one form per assailant)

P. VICTIM RESIDES WITH:
[ ] 1. Parents
[ ] 2. Spouse
[ ] 3. Family other than above
[ ] 4. Alone
[ ] 5. Roommate-male
[ ] 6. Roommate-female
[ ] 7. Children and other family
[ ] 8. Children only
[ ] 9. Phone number published
[ ] 10. Phone number unpublished

Q. RELATIONSHIP OF ASSAILANT TO VICTIM:
[ ] 1. Date
[ ] 2. Pick up
[ ] 3. Hitchhiker
[ ] 4. Friend/Social Acquaintance
[ ] 5. Babysitter
[ ] 6. Relative (Immediate family) (Father, brother, etc.)
[ ] 7. Relative (Uncle, cousin, etc.)
[ ] 8. Boyfriend/Girlfriend
[ ] 9. Business relationship
[ ] 10. Same school
[ ] 11. Neighbor
[ ] 12. Has been seen in neighborhood
[ ] 13. Nickname known
[ ] 14. Full name known
[ ] 15. Name and address known
[ ] 16. Co-worker
[ ] 17. Landlord
[ ] 18. Total stranger
[ ] 19. Unknown-No information

OO. PRIOR TO CRIME
[ ] 1. Peeping Toms
[ ] 2. Obscene Telephone calls
[ ] 3. Prior burglaries
[ ] 4. Prior home repairs
[ ] 5. Name/Picture in newspaper
[ ] 6. Visited tavern/bar
[ ] 7. Other
[ ] 8. Nothing unusal

R. CLOTHING
[ ] 1. Neat
[ ] 2. Flashy clothing
[ ] 3. Rough
[ ] 4. Uniform
[ ] 5. Ear rings
[ ] 6. Sun glasses
[ ] 7. Rings
[ ] 8. Gloves
[ ] 9. Cap (baseball, etc.)
[ ] 10. Hat
[ ] 11. Bathing attire
[ ] 12. Pants suit
[ ] 13. Shirts
[ ] 14. Shorts
[ ] 15. Skirt/Blouse
[ ] 16. Slacks/Jeans
[ ] 17. Suit
[ ] 18. Work clothes
[ ] 19. Other_____
[ ] 20. None

S. BUILD
[ ] 1. Slender
[ ] 2. Medium
[ ] 3. Heavy, stocky
[ ] 4. Muscular

T. HAIR TYPE
[ ] 1. Long (Entire ear covered)
[ ] 2. Medium (Part of ear showing)
[ ] 3. Short (Entire ear showing)
[ ] 4. Afro
[ ] 5. Bald
[ ] 6. Corn Row
[ ] 7. Partially bald
[ ] 8. Bushy
[ ] 9. Crew cut
[ ] 10. Curly
[ ] 11. Fad
[ ] 12. Greasy
[ ] 13. Kinky
[ ] 14. Processed
[ ] 15. Straight
[ ] 16. Thin or receding
[ ] 17. Wavy
[ ] 18. Sideburns (Over 1")
[ ] 19. Sideburns (1" or less)
[ ] 20. Other_____

W. FACE
[ ] 1. Broad- full
[ ] 2. Long- rectangle
[ ] 3. Round- oval
[ ] 4. Square
[ ] 5. Thin- narrow
[ ] 6. Other_____

QQ. VICTIM INCAPACITATION
[ ] 1. Drugs
[ ] 2. Emotionally disturbed
[ ] 3. Handicapped
[ ] 4. Ill health
[ ] 5. Liquor/Alcohol
[ ] 6. Old age
[ ] 7. Retarded
[ ] 8. Young age
[ ] 9. Other_____
[ ] 10. Not incapacitated

A. TYPE OF CRIME
[ ] 1. Arson
[ ] 2. Auto theft
[ ] 3. Burglary
[ ] 4. Forgery
[ ] 5. Fraud
[ ] 6. Home invasion
[ ] 7. Murder
[ ] 8. Robbery
[ ] 9. Theft
[ ] 10. Other_____
[ ] 11. Child molestation
[ ] 12. Deviate sexual assault
[ ] 13. Indecent exposure
[ ] 14. Peeping Tom
[ ] 15. Rape

B. TIME OF DAY
[ ] 1. Daytime (6 a.m. - 6 p.m.)
[ ] 2. Evening (6 p.m. - 12 M)
[ ] 3. Morning (12M - 6 a.m.)
[ ] 4. Unknown
ACTUAL TIME [   ]

C. DAY OF WEEK
[ ] 1. Monday
[ ] 2. Tuesday
[ ] 3. Wednesday
[ ] 4. Thursday
[ ] 5. Friday
[ ] 6. Saturday
[ ] 7. Sunday
[ ] 8. Unknown

RH. WEATHER CONDITIONS
[ ] 1. Seasonal (No precipitation)
[ ] 2. Rain
[ ] 3. Snow
[ ] 4. Exceptionally hot
[ ] 5. Exceptionally cold
[ ] 6. Foggy

II. AREA OF CONTACT
[ ] 1. Commercial
[ ] 2. Industrial
[ ] 3. Residential
[ ] 4. Rural
[ ] 5. Inside private building
[ ] 6. Inside public building
[ ] 7. Outside_____

[ ] 8. School
[ ] 9. Park/Recreational area
[ ] 10. Other_____
[ ] 11. Unknown

PP. PENILE PENETRATION
[ ] 1. Once
[ ] 2. Twice
[ ] 3. Three times
[ ] 4. More than three times
[ ] 5. None
[ ] 6. Unknown

Additional crime information: (Including assailants comments, if any, and any pertinent information not covered elsewhere on this form.

Fold Here

_____

_____

Please include all known information requested on this form and check at least one response for each catagory.)

When completed, attach offender's photo (if known and available) and mail to:

Offender's photograph if available

Attention: Analytical Section

SUSPECT INFORMATION

Name: Last, First, Middle	Sex	Ethnic Origin	D.O.B.	Blood Type	Marital Status

Address:		Telephone Number:

Height	Weight :	Hair Color:	Eye Color:	Complexion:	Scars, marks, amputations, etc.

VEHICLE INFORMATION

License #:	State:	Year:	Make:	Model:	Year:	Color:	Style:	Drivers License #:

Employer:	Address:	Occupation:

ISB NUMBER	FBI NUMBER	SOCIAL SECURITY NUMBER	LOCAL AGENCY OR OTHER NUMBER

R. CLOTHING:
- [ ] 1. Neat
- [ ] 2. Flashy Clothing
- [ ] 3. Rough
- [ ] 4. Uniform
- [ ] 5. Ear Rings
- [ ] 6. Sun Glasses
- [ ] 7. Rings
- [ ] 8. Gloves
- [ ] 9. Cap (Baseball, etc.)
- [ ] 10. Hat
- [ ] 11. Bathing Attire
- [ ] 12. Pants Suit
- [ ] 13. Shirt
- [ ] 14. Shorts
- [ ] 15. Skirt/Blouse/Dress
- [ ] 16. Slacks/Jeans
- [ ] 17. Suit
- [ ] 18. Work Clothes
- [ ] 19. Other
- [ ] 20. None

S. BUILD
- [ ] 1. Slender
- [ ] 2. Medium
- [ ] 3. Heavy, Stocky
- [ ] 4. Muscular

T. HAIR TYPE
- [ ] 1. Long (Ear covered)
- [ ] 2. Med. (Part of " ")
- [ ] 3. Short (None of " ")
- [ ] 4. Afro
- [ ] 5. Bald
- [ ] 6. Corn Row

- [ ] 7. Partially bald
- [ ] 8. Bushy
- [ ] 9. Crew cut
- [ ] 10. Curly
- [ ] 11. Fad
- [ ] 12. Greasy
- [ ] 13. Kinky
- [ ] 14. Processed
- [ ] 15. Straight
- [ ] 16. Thin or receding
- [ ] 17. Wavy
- [ ] 18. Sideburns (Over 1")
- [ ] 19. Sideburns (1" or less)
- [ ] 20. Other

U. EYE PECULIARITIES
- [ ] 1. Bulging
- [ ] 2. Cataracts
- [ ] 3. Crossed
- [ ] 4. Different colors
- [ ] 5. Missing or glass eye
- [ ] 6. Squints or blinks
- [ ] 7. Slanted
- [ ] 8. Glasses
- [ ] 9. Other
- [ ] 10. None

V. EYEBROWS
- [ ] 1. Arch
- [ ] 2. Bushy
- [ ] 3. Meeting
- [ ] 4. Straight
- [ ] 5. Thin
- [ ] 6. Other

W. FACIAL CHARACTERISTICS
- [ ] 1. Broad - full
- [ ] 2. Long - rectangle
- [ ] 3. Round - oval
- [ ] 4. Square
- [ ] 5. Thin - narrow
- [ ] 6. Other

W. FACIAL ODDITIES
- [ ] 7. Birthmark(s)
- [ ] 8. Freckles
- [ ] 9. Pockmarks
- [ ] 10. Pimples
- [ ] 11. Thin lips
- [ ] 12. Thick lips
- [ ] 13. Hollow cheeked
- [ ] 14. Moles
- [ ] 15. Other
- [ ] 16. None

X. FACIAL SCARS
- [ ] 1. Left cheek
- [ ] 2. Right cheek
- [ ] 3. Chin
- [ ] 4. Left ear
- [ ] 5. Right ear
- [ ] 6. Left eyebrow
- [ ] 7. Right eyebrow
- [ ] 8. Forehead
- [ ] 9. Hare-lip
- [ ] 10. Lower lip
- [ ] 11. Upper lip
- [ ] 12. Nose
- [ ] 13. Pierced earlobes

- [ ] 14. Other
- [ ] 15. None

Y. CHIN
- [ ] 1. Round
- [ ] 2. Square
- [ ] 3. Pointed
- [ ] 4. Jutting
- [ ] 5. Receding
- [ ] 6. Cleft
- [ ] 7. Double
- [ ] 8. Other

Z. EARS
- [ ] 1. Large
- [ ] 2. Small
- [ ] 3. Close to head
- [ ] 4. Protruding
- [ ] 5. Cauliflower
- [ ] 6. Normal

AA. TEETH
- [ ] 1. Chipped
- [ ] 2. False
- [ ] 3. Gaps
- [ ] 4. Gold
- [ ] 5. Good
- [ ] 6. Irregular
- [ ] 7. Missing
- [ ] 8. Protruding
- [ ] 9. Special dental work
- [ ] 10. Stained/decayed
- [ ] 11. Normal

BB. NOSE
- [ ] 1. Large
- [ ] 2. Small

- [ ] 3. Broken, crooked
- [ ] 4. Broad
- [ ] 5. Flat
- [ ] 6. Hooked bulged
- [ ] 7. Long
- [ ] 8. Short
- [ ] 9. Thin
- [ ] 10. Pointed
- [ ] 11. Straight
- [ ] 12. Upturned, pug
- [ ] 13. Other
- [ ] 14. Normal

CC. FACIAL HAIR
- [ ] 1. Beard
- [ ] 2. Goatee
- [ ] 3. Mustache, heavy
- [ ] 4. Mustache, medium
- [ ] 5. Mustache, thin-light
- [ ] 6. Fu Manchu
- [ ] 7. None

DD. DEFORMITIES
- [ ] 1. Bow-legged
- [ ] 2. Pigeon-toed
- [ ] 3. Hunchback
- [ ] 4. Crippled left arm
- [ ] 5. Crippled right arm
- [ ] 6. Crippled fingers
- [ ] 7. Crippled hand
- [ ] 8. Crippled leg (limp)
- [ ] 9. Other
- [ ] 10. None

EE. TYPE OF TATTOO
- [ ] 1. Initials
- [ ] 2. Names
- [ ] 3. Words/Pharses

- [ ] 4. Pictures
- [ ] 5. Designs
- [ ] 6. Pachuco
- [ ] 7. Numbers
- [ ] 8. Other
- [ ] 9. None

FF. SPEECH/VOICE
- [ ] 1. Soft
- [ ] 2. Loud
- [ ] 3. High voice
- [ ] 4. Low voice
- [ ] 5. Lisping
- [ ] 6. Raspy/gruff
- [ ] 7. Stutters
- [ ] 8. Mute
- [ ] 9. Rapid speech
- [ ] 10. Refined
- [ ] 11. Vulgar
- [ ] 12. Mexican/Spanish
- [ ] 13. Southern accent
- [ ] 14. Other foreign accent
- [ ] 15. Mumbles
- [ ] 16. Other
- [ ] 17. Unknown

GG. DISGUISES USED
- [ ] 1. Cloth or hankie
- [ ] 2. Hood
- [ ] 3. Mask
- [ ] 4. Hand held over face
- [ ] 5. Head cloth or bag
- [ ] 6. Silk stocking mask
- [ ] 7. Wig
- [ ] 8. Any other disguise
- [ ] 9. None

HH. PHYSICAL CHARACTERISTICS
- [ ] 1. Abnormal genitals
- [ ] 2. Fingernails long
- [ ] 3. Fingernails bitten close
- [ ] 4. Hands stained, greasy, dirty
- [ ] 5. Handsome
- [ ] 6. Left handed
- [ ] 7. Narcotic user
- [ ] 8. Smells (Body order, greasy, etc.)
- [ ] 9. Other

HH. MENTAL CHARACTERISTICS
- [ ] 10. Cries during/after offense
- [ ] 11. Grins, stares, leers
- [ ] 12. Had been drinking
- [ ] 13. Jostles women
- [ ] 14. Laughs at victim
- [ ] 15. Mentally disturbed
- [ ] 16. Offers victim liquor, beer, etc.
- [ ] 17. Ransacks house
- [ ] 18. Rips/cuts telephone

JJ. APPROACH TO VICTIM
- [ ] 1. Answers ad
- [ ] 2. Babysitter
- [ ] 3. Claims to be sent by parents
- [ ] 4. Exposes him/herself
- [ ] 5. Friendly approach/then grabs
- [ ] 6. Follows victim to elevator, etc.
- [ ] 7. Follows and sneaks up from behind
- [ ] 8. From concealment, bushes, alley, etc.
- [ ] 9. Knocks/rings at door
- [ ] 10. Knocks at windows
- [ ] 11. Loiters in area
- [ ] 12. Meets victim at party, bar, etc.

- [ ] 13. Offers job
- [ ] 14. Offers gift and/or money
- [ ] 15. Offers assistance
- [ ] 16. Pretext of medical treatment
- [ ] 17. Poses as public/police official
- [ ] 18. Poses as repairman
- [ ] 19. Poses as salesman/surveyor, etc.
- [ ] 20. Requests assistance
- [ ] 21. Shows pornography (Commercial)
- [ ] 22. Shows pornography (Homemade)
- [ ] 23. Shows child pornography
- [ ] 24. Sits near bus, theatre, home, etc.
- [ ] 25. Writes notes
- [ ] 26. Other

LL. CONVERSATION OF ASSAILANT
- [ ] 1. Abusive language to victim
- [ ] 2. Apologizes
- [ ] 3. Asks victim about sex experiences
- [ ] 4. Asks victim to meet again
- [ ] 5. Demands money
- [ ] 6. Demands jewely
- [ ] 7. Indicates he knows victim
- [ ] 8. Obscene language during crime
- [ ] 9. Orders victim to be quiet
- [ ] 10. Polite
- [ ] 11. Reveals racial hostility
- [ ] 12. Says he has been in jail or prison
- [ ] 13. Says he has raped or murdered
- [ ] 14. Say he will return/returns
- [ ] 15. Silent makes no comment
- [ ] 16. Talkative
- [ ] 17. Threatens to harm victim's children, family, etc.
- [ ] 18. Other

KK. HOW VEHICLE INVOLVED
- [ ] 1. Assaults victim in car
- [ ] 2. Carries victim to car
- [ ] 3. Demands transportation after crime
- [ ] 4. Exposes from car
- [ ] 5. Follows victim's car
- [ ] 6. Forces victim into assailant's car
- [ ] 7. Forces victim into own car
- [ ] 8. Forces victim to lie (sit) on floor or seat
- [ ] 9. Happens after victim parks car
- [ ] 10. Hides in victim's car
- [ ] 11. Hitchhiker (assailant or victim)
- [ ] 12. Jumps into victim's car
- [ ] 13. Lures victim to or into his car
- [ ] 14. Parks car and follows on foot
- [ ] 15. Stops victim's car on highway
- [ ] 16. Tells victim car is sparking
- [ ] 17. Other
- [ ] 18. No vehicle involved
- [ ] 19. Unknown

MM. TREATMENT OF VICTIM
- [ ] 1. Attempts to kill victim
- [ ] 2. Battery to breast
- [ ] 3. Battery to buttocks
- [ ] 4. Other battery (sexual implication)
- [ ] 5. Covers victim's head (blanket, etc.)
- [ ] 6. Cuts victim's clothing
- [ ] 7. Forces victim into concealment
- [ ] 8. Grabs with hand over mouth
- [ ] 9. Rips/tears victim's clothing
- [ ] 10. Removes victim's clothing
- [ ] 11. Sadist (beats victim)
- [ ] 12. Torture (any form)
- [ ] 13. Victim attacked with hands/feet
- [ ] 14. Victim beaten with weapons
- [ ] 15. Victim blindfolded
- [ ] 16. Victim gagged
- [ ] 17. Victim grabbed around neck-choked
- [ ] 18. Victim handcuffed
- [ ] 19. Victim kidnapped

- [ ] 20. Victim killed
- [ ] 21. Victim stabbed
- [ ] 22. Victim suffocated
- [ ] 23. Victim tied, bound
- [ ] 24. Victim thrown to ground
- [ ] 25. Other

I. WEAPONS
- [ ] 3. Club
- [ ] 4. Electronic device
- [ ] 5. Explosives
- [ ] 6. Garrotte
- [ ] 9. Knife
- [ ] 11. None
- [ ] 14. Pistol
- [ ] 15. Rifle
- [ ] 16. Shotgun
- [ ] 19. Other

NN. SEX ACTS (COMMITTED BY ASSAILANT)
- [ ] 1. Disrobes him/herself
- [ ] 2. Forces victim to disrobe assailant
- [ ] 3. Lifts or raises victims clothing
- [ ] 4. Intercourse canine position
- [ ] 5. Lies on top of victim
- [ ] 6. Places victim on lap
- [ ] 7. Shows/uses contraceptives
- [ ] 8. Uses lubricant on victim
- [ ] 9. Unable to achieve erection
- [ ] 10. Requests help in accomplishing sex act
- [ ] 11. Masturbates
- [ ] 12. Forces victim to masturbate him/herself
- [ ] 13. Forces victim to masturbate offender

- [ ] 14. Bites
- [ ] 15. Licks
- [ ] 16. Fondles or sucks breast
- [ ] 17. Sexual penetration cunnilingus to victim
- [ ] 18. Sexual penetration fellatio to victim
- [ ] 19. Sexual penetration cunnilingus to assailant
- [ ] 20. Sexual penetration fellatio to assailant
- [ ] 21. Other oral perversion to victim
- [ ] 22. Other oral perversion to offender
- [ ] 23. Inserts finger into vagina or rectum
- [ ] 24. Inserts foreign object into rectum
- [ ] 25. Inserts foreign object into vagina
- [ ] 26. Plays with victim's genitals

- [ ] 27. Places genitals between victim's legs
- [ ] 28. Rubs genitals against victim
- [ ] 29. Other non-penile penetration
- [ ] 30. Engages in sodomy/animals
- [ ] 31. Forces victim to engage in sodomy/animals
- [ ] 32. Urinates on victim
- [ ] 33. Has victim urinate on offender
- [ ] 34. Defecates on victim
- [ ] 35. Has victim defecate on assailant
- [ ] 36. Cleans him/herself (or attempt)
- [ ] 37. Cleans victim (or attempts)
- [ ] 38. Photographs victim during/after offense
- [ ] 39. Takes souvenir
- [ ] 40. Other

5 SCIENTIFIC RESEARCH STUDIES

This chapter summarizes scientific research studies that attempt to assess the social impact of pornography. The studies are massive and extensive and defy easy comparison or even brief description. Our objective here is to provide an identification and summation of the extent, nature, and results of scientific research studies about pornography, all of which implicitly or explicitly address the question of the effects of pornography. Readers can then refer to the original studies for details and clarifications.

PROBLEMS WITH PORNOGRAPHY RESEARCH

Various factors affect the credibility, accuracy, and usefulness of pornography effects research. These include the following:

Devices and methods to measure sexual arousal
Differences in how pornography is defined and in the types of pornography used
Subjective versus objective arousal measures
Volunteer bias
Males' ability to control erection responses
Laboratory settings (as opposed to real-world settings)
Researcher bias
Characteristics of the people used as experimental subjects (sex, age, education, and so on)
Length of exposure to stimuli
Questionnaire styles and contents

Lab found flaws in the Attorney General's Commission on Pornography's conclusion that there is a causal link between substantial exposure to sexually violent materials and acts of sexual violence and between degrading, dominating, and humiliating pornography and "sexual violence/coercion." He says the commission accepted much of the research "at face value and without question" and ignored identified problems with the research such as methodological shortcomings.[1] (Lab, however, considers only studies since the 1970 commission, concentrates on studies dealing with aggression, and does not include all relevant research or report in detail on those studies he includes. Useful charts reporting on major aspects of some studies are used.)

The aggression studies, according to Lab, have "highly equivocal" results—some of which support and some of which negate a pornography–aggression relationship. He notes that only one study (Jaffee et al.) did *not* involve prior provocation. Because the general public is not "aggressively provoked" before consuming pornography, he argues, these results are not valid. In addition, he says, some of the results seem to show that the provocation, not the "erotic" stimuli, enhances aggression.

Lab presents an excellent methodological critique, emphasizing that one cannot generalize results. It includes the following points:[2]

1. Studies set in the laboratory may not reflect "behavior of subjects in the real world."
2. There is no control over "unknown factors" brought to the lab by the subjects, researcher, or assistants.
3. People are concerned about pornography's effect "in day to day living," not in restricted settings.
4. The experimental subjects used are usually university undergraduate students from introductory psychology courses who are coerced to participate as part of the course or for extra credit. These students are not representative of college students or the general population.
5. The studies usually couple erotic stimulus with anger/provocation. These are not coupled in the real world.
6. The form of aggression the aggressor uses in the experiments is usually an obnoxious noise, electric shock, or overinflated blood pressure cuff. Attempts to equate these with rape or sexual assault raise serious questions. Although in the real-world females are usually raped by males, many of the studies use only male targets. And, in the studies, subjects are often provoked in the same manner and by the same person against whom they aggress. Yet "few rapists or sexual assaulters are subject to sexual offenses by their victims prior to an erotic stimulus."

7. The artificial lab setting might facilitate the aggression. Lab suggests that the subjects probably know that the researcher cannot allow actual harm to subjects. And the experimenter, by providing subjects the opportunity to aggress, suggests that aggression or retaliation is viable and acceptable in that setting. Some studies, he says, present aggression as a tool to enhance the learning of the target, and subjects might see themselves as being benevolent.

8. The use of selected excerpts from films, books, and other media might "enhance the effect of the aggressive or erotic scene beyond the level that an individual would experience in common everyday exposure."

9. Most studies use a *short* length of exposure. Concerning those that include exposure every day for weeks, Lab says that it is questionable how many people really consume pornography every day.

10. The lag time between lab exposure to pornography and aggression is usually only a few minutes. Studies that look at extended consequences get varied results.

11. Other studies measure attitudes and aggression, but it is not evident what effect this has on real behavior. The attitude studies suffer from the same defects as the aggression tests.

Lab also attacks studies that compare pornography readership rates and rape rates by noting that any relationship could be due to other factors. He argues that interviews with victims cannot determine whether pornography causes an offense, for an offender may have acted without pornography. Likewise, studies of offender arousal to rape cannot show causation, for offenders might have acted anyway, and the rapists used in the studies may not be representative of rape offenders. He notes that field studies such as these are mainly "correlational," with a large range of qualifications and a lack of adequate controls for extraneous factors. He attacks rapist studies and prostitute studies as not representative of the general population.

Lab concludes that inferring a causal relationship between pornography and aggression is "ill-advised." He suggests that exposure to pornography in the lab should be with conditions similar to life. (Lab does not point out that health authorities have prohibited such testing due to the health risk to the public— that is, the prospect that massive, real-life–like exposure to pornography would result in sexual violence and aggression against real victims.) He admits that if one accepts alternative definitions of harm (that is, changes in morality, attitudes, and

callousness toward women) as viable, many of the Attorney General's Commission's recommendations and comments are justifiable with the available scientific and other types of evidence, for these are not measurable.

Linz, Donnerstein, and Penrod conclude that the social science data relied on by the 1986 Pornography Commission do not justify the commission's conclusions about harm or the call for more stringent law enforcement. These authors are advocates of educational programs aimed at mitigating the effects of media sexual violence rather than stricter legal controls. One of their main points is that the themes of sexual violence against women are also found in nonpornographic material and it is inappropriate to single out pornography for regulation.[3]

In an article dealing with public policy and psychological research, researchers Donn Byrne and Kathryn Kelley argue that reasons for changes in public policy should be well established. They say they are "disturbed" by the 1986 Pornography Commission's conclusion that exposure to pornography has a causal relationship to sexual aggression, coercion, and violence. They also are disturbed by the policy recommendations involving changes in pornography laws. They believe that the Attorney General's Commission's recommendations do not have a firm data base, saying that the recommendations were based on "extremely weak data such as vivid case histories." They refer to publications such as *Penthouse* and *Playboy* as being "erotically dull."[4]

One dispute among the behavioral scientists is whether to emphasize the affective versus the rational aspect of human behavior. Byrne and Kelley emphasize the affective. They note that pornography has different impacts on different people, with some feeling excited, joyous, and interested, and others becoming angry, nauseated, or anxious. They suggest that a simple solution would be for those who respond negatively to avoid such material and those who respond positively not to be deprived of it. Yet they admit that solution would not work in the real world.

They note the difficulty in settling disputes because scientists are influenced by their own emotional responses and the need to justify those responses. In addition, they note that scientific questions can never be settled forever. Thus, they conclude, objectivity is usually an "impossible dream," saying, "We select, believe, remember and conclude in large part on the basis of our existing emotions, attitudes, beliefs and values."[5]

One example of this would be people seeking out that which they already believe and avoiding that which they do not. Even science is guided by such beliefs. The most unethical extreme would be to falsify data.

They note considerable disagreement among people about the effects of exposure to pornography. Although they state that "almost everyone" agrees that sexual coercion is not acceptable, they urge caution in moving from sex research results to making public policy. For example, coercive sex cannot be directly investigated. This is one of the few fields in which the "prime dependent variable" gets excluded from the process of research. Therefore, researchers end up asking people what they have done in the past and what they might do in the future, and they test people's responses to depictions of activities such as torture, rape, or child abuse. They take the attitude that case histories (in other words, victim and police reports indicating that pornography might result in people being victimized) are not valid. In fact they call the case type of evidence clearly ludicrous if it was not for the widespread acceptance of such data.[6] (We find case data to be much more realistic than the scientific studies.)

Byrne and Kelley also emphasize that existing beliefs can guide research and the interpretation of research.

They ask the important question of whether we want to prevent the modeling of all sexual activity. They point out that modeling literature strongly supports the idea that persons who are exposed to sexually explicit materials will show an increased tendency to imitate the sexual activities presented. They note that inhibiting factors such as religious beliefs, legal restrictions, anxiety, and various emotional responses can intervene in their acting upon such feelings. They note that people in general disapprove of coercive sex and generally approve of love and procreational sex in the context of marriage, but point out that there are a vast number of other possibilities that result in disagreements over acceptability. They raise the issue of whether using certain erotic or pornographic depictions with sexually dysfunctional people to initiate sexual intercourse with spouses is acceptable. Similarly, they ask whether sex education that involves prevention of sexually transmitted diseases and use of contraceptives is acceptable. They ask, however, whether reactions to depictions of homosexuality, adultery, and promiscuity are the same. Sexist television commercials, slasher films, and reckless car chases also raise behavior concerns, they note.

Another concern is that correlations do not necessarily indicate a cause and effect relationship. Individual differences must also be taken into account in sex research. Such differences might include things such as hypermasculinity, sex guilt, authoritarianism, and erotophobia, as well as different types of personality that respond differently to erotic or pornographic depictions. (Byrne and Kelley showed their bias when they liken general laws restricting pornography to banning the sale of peanut butter because some people are allergic to it.)

Another experimental problem Byrne and Kelley raise is that although response alternatives for subjects must be limited, experimenters' attitudes can influence their selection of the alternatives and thus bias the effects. For example, studies may give persons an opportunity to behave aggressively in response to pornography but not give them a chance to behave in a pro-social way following such exposure.

There is also the problem of limited exposure to pornography versus massive exposure. Brief exposures and tests of short-term effects might result in erroneous conclusions that there is little or no effect from the pornography. In fact, as Byrne and Kelley suggest, measurable effects might require years of exposure. They also note that these effects would differ from those resulting from massive exposure in a series of days or weeks. For comparison, they note that the effect of drinking one bottle of soda daily for five years may not be the same as that of drinking seventy-three bottles daily for twenty-five days.

Their overall conclusion is that there is not enough information available about the effects of "erotica" to be able to achieve a consensus on this issue, and, therefore, public policy should not be changed at this time.

In an August 1983 paper, Baron and Straus discuss ethical and conceptual problems in pornography research. They state that one problem is with the conceptualization of pornography—in other words, the "subjective nature" of what pornography is. They establish dimensions along which pornography could be "operationalized." These dimensions include the following: the degree of explicitness; the social context of the stimulation; sexual objectification; the type of sexual act depicted; the distribution of enjoyment; suffering; power; violent/nonviolent; the extent of injury; the gender of participants; and age and kinship relation.[7]

According to Baron and Straus, the second concern in pornography research is the ethical considerations that constrain the research. For example, there are federal regulations aimed at protecting human subjects from certain types of experiments, as well as institutional review boards charged with safeguarding the rights of such subjects. The federal code does not require that the research involve no risk, for that would end all research. Rather the code considers people to be "at risk" if the risks involved in the experiment are greater than those to which the people would encounter in the normal course of their activities. There is, however, a tendency not to approve projects because of fears that universities might be sued if something goes wrong in the research laboratory, and on topics such as pornography, the review boards are likely to be conservative.

Baron and Straus argue that most pornography research is not subject to regulation by these boards. One category of pornography research that is not exempt from regulation involves studies investigating whether exposure to pornography causes an attitude or behavior change on the part of the subject. In these cases, boards usually emphasize the importance of debriefing.

In *Take Back the Night,* Russell critiques pornography research. She points out that the research rarely distinguishes between pornography, erotica, and explicit sexual materials and that precise descriptions of the stories, films, or pictures used in the experiments are lacking. Many focus on the effects of pornography on sexual behavior but do not distinguish between healthy nonsexist behavior and destructive sexist behavior. She emphasizes that research designs have not used certain types of pornography, such as magazines based on rape myths, and that women and feminists have not been given money to do this type of research. Russell believes that the 1970 commission reached a "false conclusion that pornography is harmless." She notes the insensitivity of some researchers, such as asking females whether they are likely to enjoy being victims of rape. She points out that men do not tend to be asked whether they would enjoy another man sodomizing them.[8]

Russell argues that if pornography or erotica can be used to change behavior in a doctor's office, "its potential to effect change in other circumstances is thereby also proven." She also points out that Marvin Wolfgang, one of the authors of the 1970 Commission report, seems to have changed his view on pornography's effects, having made a more recent statement that the weight of the evidence now suggests that portrayals of violence tend to encourage the use of aggression among those exposed to the violence.[9]

Thelma McCormack critiques research on pornography in *Women Against Censorship.* She emphasizes that the studies do not use the term *effects* consistently or precisely. There is no coherent or cumulative body of knowledge. She feels that in many of the violence and pornography stimulus and response type studies, violence is taken out of context, inhibiting variables that normally influence human behavior are left out, the physiological effects may be of short duration, and responses might be to something other than violence on the screen.

She feels that, depending on the circumstances, tension or anger can either be reduced through vicarious experience (a cathartic effect) or intensified.

McCormack criticizes social learning or modeling studies that teach that aggression is learned behavior. She says it is questionable whether people really imitate what they see (for example, on television) and also wonders why they would imitate some behaviors and not others. Social values could come into play, she suggests.

McCormack also critiques the cultivation hypothesis, which argues that the problem is what violence represents in terms of dominance, submission, and power in other social relationships. She says that people who are made anxious by what they see would not continue to be heavy viewers.

She notes that the desensitization theory, which says that watching a great deal of violence will lower anxiety and cause gradual unlearning and extinction of spontaneous reactions, is difficult, "if not impossible, to prove." She wonders whether desensitization can be reversed and whether it is always undesirable. Instead, she suggests desensitization could be essential in selecting wise policies and engaging in rational discussions.

McCormack critiques the 1970 Pornography Commission studies, concluding that they showed exposure to pornography leads to short-term sexual arousal and stimulates sexual activity and fantasy but does not alter established sexual behaviors. She also finds little systematic evidence to link pornography with rape. McCormack believes that it is only in exceptional circumstances that the media convert someone from one viewpoint to another, and therefore it would be unreasonable to expect pornography to have such an impact. She feels that rather than there being strong evidence that people copy pornography, there is strong evidence that established sex patterns and strong inhibiting factors keep responses within cultural norms.[10]

In a 1970 Pornography Commission study, Amoroso et al. noted the definitional problem with pornography. Another major problem with studies of pornography is how to measure sexual arousal (that is, self-report versus physiological indices) and how to differentiate this from more general arousal. In addition, there are technical, measurement, definitional, and ethical problems in investigating pornography and behavior.

In their first study, Amoroso et al. reinvestigated ratings of pornographic stimuli as they might be affected by whether the subject was attached to devices recording physiological responses, whether the person was alone or with other subjects, and the order of presentation of the stimuli. They used twenty-seven slides, including themes such as dressed and undressed couples, females nude or in underwear, a female on a bed with anus and genitals exposed, a female masturbating, close-ups of female genitals, a nude male, a male masturbating, a couple in bed under a blanket, a couple with genitals exposed and manual genital oral breast contact and manual genital kissing, cunnilingus, and fellatio, a male ejaculating on a female's breasts, and a variety of positions of intercourse. The subjects were sixty males ages 18 to 25 from a university.

The researchers found that the order of presentation and whether it was done alone or in a group did not significantly influence any of the slide ratings. But there were "significant effects due to measures (physiological "hookup" versus not)."[11] The subjects rated the material as more pornographic when they were hooked up to the device. There was also a small increase in autoerotic (masturbation) activities after viewing the slides. Thus, the context—either hooked up or not—in which the slides were viewed resulted in the stimuli being seen as more pornographic and stimulating. The researchers also felt that hooking up increased the subjects' candor in their self-reports.

An interesting result was that even though masturbation was common for the subjects and it was the behavior most affected by viewing the slides, male masturbation in the slides tended to be rated as very unpleasant by the male subjects. [The stimuli were considered pornographic by the subjects to the extent that they were highly arousing and quite unpleasant.] There were only small reported changes in sexual behavior overall.

The second study by Amoroso et al. was a measure of viewing time, which was expected to increase if the stimuli were pleasant. There were fifty-six male subjects ages 18 to 25 from a university. Fifteen of the twenty-seven slides used in the first study also were used here, and the experimenters measured heart rate, finger pulse volume, and gross eye movements. They also asked questions about sex during the week before and after viewing the slides.

The results showed that the viewing time was much shorter when the subjects were grouped together (10.43 seconds) than when they were alone (21.16 seconds). The viewing time for the male masturbation and male nude slides was extremely low. Subjects saw explicitly pornographic materials as dirty, unpleasant, and bad but also stimulating. In general, sexual behavior was reported to be affected little by looking at the slides. There were effects on sexual dreams, masturbation, and spontaneous erections. The slides were seen as more pornographic by those subjects who reported themselves as being highly religious and who had relatively conservative attitudes toward sex. To the researchers' surprise, students from larger hometowns saw the slides as more unpleasant and pornographic than students from smaller towns.

In their study, Beck, Sakheim, and Barlow question the reliability of the vaginal photoplethysmograph, which was devised in 1975 by Sintchak and Geer to measure sexual arousal in women. They also note that other physiological measures do not differentiate sexual arousal from other types of "autonomic arousal."[12]

In 1966, Masters and Johnson reported vasocongestion to be a physiological indicator of sexual arousal in females. Beck et al. explain that the vaginal probe works on the premise that as arousal occurs, "opacity changes due to vasocongestion" take place within the vagina. The two active parts of the probe are a light source aimed at the vaginal wall and a photocell that "detects the backscattered incident light." Photocell output changes to show that the vaginal tissue reflects less light as vasocongestion takes place.

Beck et al. note:

> The probe can be DC coupled, with the resulting record showing "vaginal blood volume" (VBV). This signal is thought to reflect slow changes in pooling of blood within the vaginal wall. When AC coupled, the probe produces a signal that can be analyzed either as vaginal pulse amplitude (VPA) or vaginal pressure pulse (VPP). This signal is thought to indicate the pulse wave in the peripheral vascular vessels within the vagina.[13]

Both types of signals have been used to measure female genital arousal. According to the authors, some studies suggest that the two signals do not produce the same information, and some suggest that the VPA may be more sensitive to measuring responses to pornography.

The researchers mention the problem of what to use as a baseline in such tests. Most studies allow three to five minutes to adapt after the probe is inserted. Yet women do not return to the base level after stimulus onset. There is also a problem with multiple stimulus tests. Some set a new baseline for each stimulus.

Beck et al. say that the vaginal photoplethysmograph has not had reliable results with different subjects and sessions. They emphasize that the reliability (or lack thereof) of the instrument is critical to its use as a main dependent variable in research. While calling for more research, they conclude that this instrument may not reliably measure the strength of vasocongestive response.

Beck, Sakheim, and Barlow also tested several different types of vaginal photoplethysmographs. These were stored in lightproof containers for weeks to prevent light history effects, given an interface cable connection, and allowed a one-hour warm-up to eliminate the chance of drift caused by the heating up of the potentiometer. Then each was wrapped in gauze, tightly enclosed in a dark paper cylinder, and placed in a dark room that was temperature controlled. [connected to the measurement instruments.]

They found that when the instrument was operated on DC, a substantial amount of baseline drift took place over time. This occurred despite the fact that they used the lowest sensitivity setting on the polygraph. It is particularly important that they discovered the greatest instability during the first two hours of operation, as most research tests occur within that time. The researchers report that the most disturbing result is that the drift did not take the same form across sessions or devices.

The devices also were tested for temperature sensitivity. Beck et al. found the original design device to be extremely sensitive to temperature, especially in the 95- to 100-degree range, the very range in which the vaginal temperature exists.

Beck, Sakheim, and Barlow conclude that the temperature responsivity and DC draft of these devices should be considered serious contraindications to using them in experiments. The DC drift could explain problems that have occurred in some experiments, such as females tested as failing to return to baseline levels during intermissions between stimuli. This drift also creates much uncertainty about how much of the result is due to the drift characteristic of the device and how much to actual opacity changes in the vagina. Because the drift across devices and sessions is inconsistent, the problem cannot be statistically adjusted using a correction factor. This, the researchers say, could account for the reported low reliability for measurement across subjects and sessions. Another factor that cannot be statistically controlled is the change in vaginal temperature, which can change the probe signal output and confound the data. The researchers conclude that the data raise serious questions about using vaginal photoplethysmography in experiments.

Laws and Rubin tested whether penile erection is an exclusively involuntary reflex. Seven male employees, ages 25 to 32, of a state hospital were the subjects. Because the pornographic/erotic film did not produce full erections in three of the men, they were not used. The stimuli used was 200 feet of 8mm motion pictures "chosen for their erotic content." (It is not clear what the film depicted.) A mercury strain gauge measured changes in penile circumference. The measurement of full erection was determined based on each man's verbal self-report during a sample film. Each subject was shown the same film three times in succession. They were alternately told to do nothing to inhibit their sexual response to the film and "to avoid getting an erection by any means except not watching the film."[14]

When, during the first film, subjects were told not to inhibit their penile erection, each of the four men produced a full erection. When told to inhibit their erections, the average erection for all four subjects was only 14 percent of the maximum. With the third showing of the film, when told not to inhibit their response, every man again had an almost full erection. Similar results were achieved when the men were tested with a different film. However, it should be noted that there were considerable differences in response among individual men. (For example, in the second test, when told to inhibit their penile response, two of the four men reached peaks of about 75 percent of the maximum while the other two subjects did not exceed 15 percent.)

There was a noticeable lack of arousal when the men were instructed to "develop an erection in the absence of an erotic film." The average erection over time was only 13 percent of the maximum, with three subjects having peaks of 30 percent and one of 90 percent.

The researchers conclude that all four men were able to inhibit their penile erections. This was not due to them looking away from the film, or satiation by the film, or general fatigue. The subjects said they inhibited their erections by concentrating on things such as song lyrics, poetry, and multiplication tables. Erection development without the erotic film was accomplished by thinking about sexually exciting events or things. The fantasy erections had long "latencies, low peak levels (partial erection)," and some variability across time. The film-elicited erections had "short latencies to the maximum level (full erection) and a generally smooth and regular response recording."[15]

According to Laws and Rubin, this study has significant implications for using changes in penile volume in response to pornographic/erotic pictures to "diagnose sexual pathology." It raises the issue of the extent to which persons can influence such a diagnosis by inhibiting erections.[16] They explain that sexual deviation is usually diagnosed based on erection responses to deviant stimuli. Thus, a person could influence a diagnosis by inhibiting an erection to deviant stimuli, with the result that he would not be diagnosed as deviant.

The researchers also state that because penile erection is needed to consummate most male sexual acts, voluntary control of erections could be used to change "the probability of occurrence of a particular sexual act."[17]

Abel et al. studied sexual arousal in male homosexuals. They argue that there are problems associated with the use of penile erection as the means to measure male sexual arousal. The first problem is that different methods of stimulus can elicit different results, and the second problem is that male heterosexuals appear to have a fair degree of voluntary control of their erections. This study checked to see whether male homosexuals had that same sort of control.

Here the subjects were twenty male homosexuals who had sought evaluation or treatment. They ranged in age from 15 to 41. A strain gauge was used to measure penile tumescence. Subjects were allowed an adaptation period to get used to wearing the penile transducer, and watching sexual slides while wearing it, and being able to respond to the visual stimuli. Three types of stimuli were used with two examples of each. The first was a black-and-white videotape showing explicit homosexual behaviors, including anal intercourse and fellatio. The second was two pictures or slides that the subject had selected as erotic. These varied from nude males to explicit homosexual acts. The third was a series of audiotaped descriptions of homosexual behaviors tailored to the individual subjects. These typically included references to preferred sex acts and partners. Each stimuli was presented for two minutes. Three conditions were used: one in which subjects were instructed to imagine themselves involved with the different stimuli situations and let themselves become sexually aroused; a second where they were instructed to imagine themselves involved but to voluntarily suppress erections by any mental means; and a third, which was a repeat of the first set. The same stimuli were used during each setting.

The researchers found that under the initial arousal setting, the videotape generated significantly more arousal than the slides, which in turn generated significantly more arousal than the audiotapes. Under suppression, the videotape was again significantly more arousing than the slides or audiotapes, which did not differ. Abel et al. concluded that videotape is clearly superior to slides or audiotape in generating erections, even under instructions to suppress arousal. Yet they also found that male homosexuals could substantially and voluntarily suppress erections to slides and videotape. However, as a group the subjects were not able to suppress their erections to the audiotapes. They concluded: "One must be careful in using erection as a dependent variable in sex research because of the susceptibility of that response

to instructional influences and the effect of the choice of stimulus modality used to generate that response."[18]

Kolarsky and Madlafousek studied fifty-six subjects, all males. Stimuli included black-and-white silent film scenes of the same young woman lasting ten seconds. For example, she was shown in a two-piece swimming suit without a smile, completely nude from the front, and lying on her back demonstrating a high level of sexual arousal. The penile effects of the stimuli depended to some extent on the impact of the preceding stimulus. The authors also found that focusing the subject's attention on nonsexual matters interfered with penile reaction.[19]

Gibbons studied fifty-two male undergraduate psychology students. They were assigned to self-aware and non-self-aware conditions under which they had to rate the attractiveness and excitability of pictures of nude women. The self-aware condition involved having a large mirror in the cubicle where they were taking this test. (We note the sexist nature of this sort of study, which tries to measure the attractiveness of various women.) The subjects were given attitude pretests involving their feelings toward "erotica." These revolved around whether laws should be passed preventing the sale of pornography, whether they considered X-rated movies to be in bad taste and offensive, and whether they enjoyed reading magazines such as *Playboy* and *Penthouse*. The excitement ratings by the subjects who were self-aware because of the mirror was in line with their expressed attitudes. However, the subjects with no mirror ignored their attitudes and enjoyed themselves with the pornographic pictures.

A second study involved fifty-one female undergraduate psychology students. They were divided into high, medium, and low sex guilt groups. They were exposed to either a sexual or nonsexual anagram and told to write as many new English words they could think of using the letters in the sentence. They also were exposed to a passage from a pornographic novel that had been somewhat changed and asked to rate the passage as sexually arousing, enjoyable, and so on. The anagrams were troublesome for the students. Those subjects in the self-aware condition again had a strong correlation between their pretest scores and their responses to the erotic passage, while those in the no mirror condition did not have this relationship.

A third experiment used forty-eight female undergraduates. The anagrams were given after the passage ratings. Again there was a significant correlation between the pretest score and responses to the erotic passages in the mirror condition but a weak relationship in the no mirror condition. Gibbons concludes that behavior is more likely to be in line with personal standards when self-awareness is enhanced.[20]

Adamson et al. studied responses to sexual stimuli. In the first experiment, they produced their own film stimulus. They did not wish to use stag films because of "possible ethical complications." The five-minute film was in color and showed a bedroom encounter between a woman and man with the second half of the movie "apparently portraying coitus." A sound track from the motion picture *Man and Woman* (1965) was used. Ten married male Caucasian volunteers, mostly hospital employees, were used as subjects. The control medium comprised neutral color slides and fifteen color slides of "girlie pictures" from a men's magazine. All ten subjects found the movie sexually stimulating and more stimulating than the slides. Seven reported some degree of penile erection. Three reported anxiety, and one experienced "mild disgust."[21]

In the second experiment, an unpleasant movie was prepared by editing a film about the concentration camps of World War II, including scenes of dismembered bodies and corpses bulldozed into open graves. The subjects were thirty-nine married males ranging in age from 22 to 56 and recruited from a university class. The researchers also used the same sexual movie as in experiment one. Physiological measures were altered. (The various measures included skin resistance, a thermistor, and an electromiograph, which was used in the first experiment but not in the second.) Subjects were aroused by both films, and Adamson et al. found that both movies resulted in "significant increases in SBP, DBP and GSRs and significant decreases in palm or skin resistance and finger temperature." Heart rates significantly increased only after subjects viewed the sexually explicit movie. They concluded that the differences they hypothesized between dysphoric and sexual arousal were not shown.[22]

Barclay and Little tested their theory that urinary acid phosphates (AP) is a specific indicator of sexual arousal. They note that one previous study had shown that people have a degree of cognitive control over the secretion of AP. They also say that when subjects view a sexually arousing movie, they might say they are aroused even if they are not for fear of being labeled deviant because the movie was called sexually arousing.

The seventy-three undergraduate male subjects in this study were assigned to one of five conditions: laughter, aggressive, sexual, anxiety, or control. The study was said to be a biochemistry experiment that required two urine samples taken half an hour apart. During the half-hour waiting period, the subjects were asked to rate the effectiveness of videotaped vignettes. Depending on which condition they were assigned, subjects viewed videotapes of alleged psychodramas that focused on a physical battle, an interracial argument, a paper airplane assembly line, a shaving cream fight, or sexual behavior. Subjective reports of sexual arousal were then assessed through a questionnaire. Urine samples were collected. In this case, the sexually explicit film consisted of a young engaged couple sitting down together and talking. Then they began kissing and fondling one another and continued to do so for the remainder of the fifteen- to sixteen-minute tape. The results showed that the subjects became significantly aroused in all arousal conditions except for the laughter condition. These subjects actually found the laughter condition less amusing than the sex condition. As the researchers had predicted, the AP increased only among those who were in the sexual arousal condition. A general type of activation was not present, for the urinary AP secretion did not increase in the aggressive and anxiety conditions, yet Barclay and Little felt it was possible that the secretion of the AP might partially be a response to an element of general arousal or a link between sex and anxiety.[23]

Wincze et al. studied the effects of subjective monitoring on physiological measures of genital response to pornography/erotica. They questioned whether having a person monitor their subjective (that is, self-report) sexual arousal continuously causes distraction from the sexual stimuli or nonerotic thoughts that interfere with results and confound the usefulness of monitoring techniques such as the self-report lever.

The researchers tested six men and eight women, ages 19 to 27, recruited from hospital and university communities. All were exclusively heterosexual and experienced in intercourse and petting. Physiological arousal indexes were the vaginal pulse amplitude for women (measured by a photoplethysmographic system) and penile tumescence (measured by an electromechanical strain gauge for men). Cognitive (subjective) arousal was measured by a self-report scale between 0 and 10 using a potentiometer driven by a mechanical lever, which could be operated effortlessly and comfortably with one hand by a sitting or reclining subject.[24]

Four two-minute videotape sequences were used:[25]

1. A control film of two minutes of the word *relax*
2. A two-minute travelogue of an island off the coast of Nova Scotia
3. A low-arousing stimulus of a clothed young woman and man engaged in three minutes of "lip kissing and embracing"

4. A moderate- to high-arousing film of a completely naked young woman and man involved in about two and a half minutes of intercourse

No audio track was used. All subjects were found to be in the normative range for all prescreening measures (which included a pornography experience scale). Each subject saw the two control films and then viewed the two low- and high-arousing films twice. For one set of films, subjects were told to use the self-report lever. For the other, they were instructed only to watch. Same-sex experimenters were used.

The researchers note, "It is impossible to ascertain the exact initial level of vasocongestion in women." However, because most women fall within a narrow basal range in a prearousal phase, arousal can be measured "by subtracting average basal amplitude from evoked amplitude." Return to basal levels was "markedly rapid" during the intervals between stimuli in this test. Insertion of the probe evokes the same neutral, nonarousing response in women as does inserting a tampon. The male device has also been shown to be nonarousing.[26]

Wincze et al. found that the women as a group did not show an overall correlation between subjective and physiological arousal measures, while the men as a group did show a significant correlation. For functional women, the continual self-monitoring (by lever) of their sexual arousal did not appear either to facilitate or to inhibit their physiological sexual arousal while they viewed "erotic" films. However, the use of the monitoring lever did interfere with the men's physiologically measured sexual arousal.

The researchers conclude, "The validity of the lever, i.e., the extent to which it accurately represents an individual's cognitive state, needs further investigation."[27]

Wolchik, Spencer, and Lisi address the issue of volunteer bias in sex research. They argue that because of the intrusiveness of the vaginal photoplethysmograph, the number of women willing to participate in such experiments "may be extremely low." Thus, generalization of results from such studies is limited.

The researchers note that Farkas did a similar study of male volunteers for an experiment with the penile plethysmograph. The volunteers reported "less guilt, less sex fear, more sexual experience, and a higher incidence of erectile difficulties than nonvolunteers." Farkas concluded that limits on generalization were needed. In his study of male volunteers, Farkas found no differences between volunteers and nonvolunteers in experience with commercialized "erotica" or in objection to viewing sexually explicit films.[28]

In the Wolchik, Spencer, and Lisi study, 296 introductory psychology female students were required to participate in several studies to fulfill course requirements but were given their choice of studies. These subjects had been recruited for a questionnaire about personality and sexuality. A female experimenter was used. The last pages of the questionnaire described an additional study for which they could volunteer to be considered, in exchange for one hour of experimental credit. The new study was said to involve individual subjects who would watch "erotic movies depicting explicit sexual scenes." Their sexual arousal level would be measured by the vaginal plethysmograph, a tamponlike device that they would insert in their vaginas. They would not be observed.[29]

Only 15 percent of the 296 students volunteered to participate in the experiment involving the sexually explicit movies and the vaginal plethysmograph. A significantly greater percentage of the volunteers reported having experienced sexual trauma (such as rape or incest) than nonvolunteers. A significantly larger percentage of the nonvolunteers objected to viewing sexually explicit films. The two groups did not differ on sexual experience. The female volunteers "masturbated more frequently, were initially exposed to commercialized erotica at an earlier age, viewed more erotic pictures and slides, and read more erotic literature than nonvolunteers. In addition, volunteers scored significantly lower on all subscales of the sex fear inventory."[30]

The researchers caution that the group of 296 females was selective in that these women had volunteered to participate in a study of personality and sexuality. They note that different factors may influence the decisions of men and women to participate in studies involving genital measures. Older women and women with different educational backgrounds might respond differently, they said. They also note that they tested only the response to the prospect of using the vaginal plethysmograph, not other measures of genital arousal.

Barker and Perlman contend that volunteer bias can create problems in sex research. For example, Kinsey's critics claimed such volunteers were a "small, atypically permissive group." There was, they said an inflation of those who experienced "disapproved" or "unconventional" sexual behavior. Studies suggest volunteers are as or more liberal than nonvolunteers.[31]

The researchers tested 126 males and 128 females in an introductory psychology course at a large Canadian university. All, as part of the course, took a personality test. Two to five months later, in a seemingly unrelated study, 149 received the sexual standards questionnaire, and 105 received the parent–child questionnaire. No credit was given for completing the questionnaires, which were supposedly anonymous but were coded with invisible ink.

Barker and Perlman found that none of the ways in which the "sex research volunteers were unique was significantly related to greater permissiveness." They also note that the way people are solicited can affect the "magnitude of bias introduced."[32]

Wolchik, Braver, and Jensen studied volunteer bias in sex research. They conducted a test to determine which of the following components are responsible for the low volunteer rate in sex research:

1. "[E]xposure to a sexually explicit film"
2. The knowledge that the subject's "sexual responsiveness" was being monitored
3. "[A]ssessment procedures that require attachment to a physiological recording instrument"
4. "[A]ssessment of genital response to sexual material"
5. The requirement of becoming partially undressed
6. "[A]ttachment of a physiological device to the genitals."[33]

The researchers also expressed concern about gender differences. Reports that women are as or more responsive to "erotica" than men may be due to "cultural changes in the acceptability of sexual arousal of women" or "to the fact that the women in these studies represent a much more select sample than do the men."[34]

The subjects were 424 female and 324 male introductory psychology college students who were, as part of a course requirement, given a choice of studies for which they could volunteer. These students volunteered for a questionnaire study concerning "sexuality and personality." A female experimenter was used.

At the end of the questionnaire, participants were solicited for another research project involving "watching 'erotic movies depicting explicit sexual scenes.' "[35] They were told they would be alone and not observed and that the data would be confidential. Six groups were created:

1. The "*film* group," which was given no further information
2. The "*subjective arousal* group," which was told members would subjectively rate their sexual arousal several times on a scale of 1 to 7
3. The "*nongenital* group," where sexual arousal would be measured by an electrode "measuring

'changes in forehead temperature which are correlated with sexual arousal' "
4. The "*clothed* group," whose sexual arousal would be rated by a "thermogram" (an instrument that resembles a heating pad and, through heat sensors, assesses "changes in genital blood flow and volume")
5. The "*unclothed* group," which was told members would be tested as described to all participants but would be partially undressed from the waist down
6. The "*intrusive* group," in which the vaginal photoplethysmograph for females and the penile strain gauge for males were described (Subjects were told that the devices would be attached or inserted after the experimenter left the room and that they were "harmless and unnoticed once applied.")[36]

The researchers found that female volunteers were more sexually experienced, worried less about their arousal, reported more sexual trauma, valued sex research more, had more sexual curiosity, had more experience with commercialized "erotica," and were about twice as likely to agree to participate in an experiment involving aversive noise than female nonvolunteers.

Male volunteers were more sexually experienced, reported greater difficulties with erection or ejaculation, were more sexually curious, had less sexual anxiety, valued sex research more, had been exposed to more "erotica" and objected less to it, and had significantly higher masculinity scores than male nonvolunteers. While 45 percent of all female subjects objected to commercialized "erotica," only 20 percent of male subjects objected.

The male subjects were more likely to volunteer for sexual arousal-related laboratory experiments than were the female subjects. Volunteer rates for conditions requiring partial undressing were significantly lower for both male and female subjects than for less intrusive conditions. The volunteers across the conditions differed little in sexual attitudes and behaviors. (In most laboratory studies, women are more likely to volunteer than men; sex research is an exception. This could be due to lower exposure of women to pornography and a less positive response to it, the researchers suggest.)

Fifty percent of the men and 49 percent of the women volunteered for the film experiment, which involved exposure to a sexually explicit film. The percentages volunteering for the other conditions were as follows:

Subjective: males, 57%; females, 44%
Nongenital: females, 41%; males, 66%
Clothed: males, 67%; females, 38%
Unclothed: females, 13%; males, 30%
Intrusive: males, 26%; females, 13%

Both female and male volunteers were more likely to agree to participate in the noise experiment than nonvolunteers. The researchers note that those who volunteer for sex research possibly are more committed to participating in any kind of research and are more likely to seek new and unusual experiences.

Wolchik, Braver, and Jensen conclude that the generalizability of results from studies that measure sexual arousal with devices such as the penile strain gauge or vaginal photoplethysmograph is limited. They also urge caution in conducting experiments that are less intrusive, noting that persons who volunteer to watch sexually explicit films in labs are more liberal on sexual dimensions than nonvolunteers. Such persons may not be a representative sample, they warn, cautioning against generalizing the results of such studies. In this particular study, some narrowing had already occurred because subjects had volunteered for a questionnaire study of sexuality and personality.

Kant, Goldstein, and Lepper in a 1970 Pornography Commission study, compared results to two different questionnaires that measured exposure to pornography. The same ten male Caucasians answered both questionnaires. The researchers compared answers to similar questions in the studies. Both studies asked about books as a source of sex information, but only 30 percent of the subjects said they received information from books on one questionnaire, while 90 percent of these same subjects claimed they received such information on the other questionnaire. Among the more bizarre results were from one subject who on one questionnaire reported twenty-five exposures to sadomasochistic pictorial material and on the other questionnaire reported no such exposure. There was also a lack of consistent reporting of exposure to homosexual and oral genital pornography on the two questionnaires.

The authors say that the in-depth probing nature of one of the questionnaires rather than the sex of the interviewer resulted in evoking more extensive and earlier memories than the other questionnaire. They also note that distortions appeared to be limited to a few individuals and to certain types of questions.

The discrepancies did not concern attitudes toward pornography and its control but rather estimates of personal experience with pornography. The authors believe that differences were due to variations in question wording and to questions requiring the respondent to define what is pornographic. For example, some respondents had seen films depicting sexual intercourse but did not regard them as pornographic.[37] (We suggest that this study points out that the type of questions in studies concerning the effects of pornography can make a big difference and can even inject bias into such studies.)

Ashley and Ashley found that a major problem with the social science research concerning pornography is that subjects in different experiments are exposed to different kinds of sexually explicit material. They believe that the failure to consider the type of material subjects were exposed to was a major flaw in the 1970 Pornography Commission data, rendering its results useless. They also note that the research does not consider the way different people interpret and render pornographic or erotic scenes meaningful.[38]

Some of the issues raised by McNamara and St. George about phony experts and fraudulent research used in court testimony regarding the community standards aspect of obscenity cases might be applicable in some situations involving scientific pornography related research. They note that the basic rule of scientific research is that it must be objectively done and honestly reported. That rule is protected by self-regulation (that is, teaching researchers a code of ethics), ethics codes, licensing, colleague evaluations, and similar procedures. However, as McNamara and St. George point out, this emphasis on autonomy may open the door to unscrutinized practices. In an opinion survey, for example, one cannot be certain that the questions, pictures, and other reasons said to have been presented to participants were truly presented in the manner claimed or that those said to have been interviewed really were.[39]

High, Rubin, and Henson studied color as a variable in making "erotic" films more arousing. They used eight adult males as subjects and measured arousal with a mercury and rubber strain gauge transducer. Subjects saw black-and-white and color erotic films. They found that each person had the highest arousal level during the first erotic film regardless of whether it was color or black-and-white. (Apparently, the same films were shown in color and in black-and-white.) They concluded that researchers need not be concerned about whether the erotic films they use are in color or in black-and-white.[40]

SEXUAL AROUSAL MEASUREMENT TECHNIQUES

To accurately assess the results of the pornography research studies, we must understand the techniques used to measure sexual arousal. Kelley and Byrne did an excellent summary piece on this topic. They argue that behavior changes in response to "erotic fantasy." Some of the behavioral changes can bring potential sexual partners closer together and increase the likelihood of sexual behavior. Positive reactions to fantasy can result in "activation, pursuance of further stimulation, and approach responses," while negative reactions can result in avoidance of added excitement, except in some cases where negative "affective" responses to erotica cause temporary increases in sexual behavior, including masturbation.

It is typical for people to engage in increased sexual behavior in the few hours after exposure to "erotic stimuli," Kelley and Byrne state. They describe sexual arousal as a "drive state that is based on the need for sexual release," which "[p]resumably" leads a person "to engage in consummatory behavior such as sexual intercourse or masturbation." They say that learning greatly influences the sex drive.[41]

According to Kelley and Byrne, sex researchers rely on three major types of response measures in measuring sexual arousal:[42]

1. Self-rating scales, which range from "not at all aroused" to "highly aroused." These are not standardized.
2. Nonstandardized self-report scales that ask people to estimate their physiological responses "along dimensions such as 'no erection' to 'full erection' or 'no breast sensations' to 'strong breast sensations.' "
3. Direct physiological measurements based on knowledge that sexual arousal results in "vaso-congestion, especially in the genitalia," which, in turn, results in bodily changes that can be measured. These changes include genital temperature increases, penile erection changes, and increased vaginal wall opacity.

Most reliability concepts such as "the coefficient of internal consistency" cannot be applied to the devices used to measure sexual arousal, Kelley and Byrne state. Different arousal levels to different erotic stimuli are assumed to show different responses rather than errors in measurement. Only the "coefficient of equivalence" seems to apply, for different self-reporting scales or measures of "penile tumescence" should highly correlate.[43]

These researchers believe that current sexual arousal measures have "face validity" because what is usually meant by arousal is a subjective excitement feeling and genital changes that involve erotic sensations, tissue swelling, and temperature increases. "Construct validity" has been shown for most of the sexual arousal measuring devices because they show arousal in response to erotic stimuli and nonarousal in response to nonerotic stimuli and because they "are appropriately related to subsequent behavior with appropriate sex objects." Kelley and Byrne report that "predictive validity"—the most important validity concept for arousal measures—has not received much attention. They say that persons most aroused in a situation are more likely to engage in a sex act in subsequent situations than persons who are initially unaroused. They note that the specific stimuli that arouse a person (for example, forced sex or mutually consenting sex) reflect the specific type of sexual behavior in which the person engages.[44]

Male arousal is measured in a variety of ways. Two ways are to determine the amounts of urinary acid phosphatase and plasma testosterone in the urine and blood. Yet, Kelley and Byrne state, studies have found testosterone level to be an inadequate measure of sexual activity. There are also questions about whether urinary acid phosphatase levels reflect sexual arousal and/or general arousal.

A third way to measure male sexual arousal is to use devices to determine circumferential or volumetric changes (that is, measurement of penile tumescence). Circumference measures detect changes in volume brought about by blood engorgement (plethysmograph). A thermistor has been used to record changes in penile skin temperature. An anal probe has been used to detect pelvic contractions during orgasm.

The authors also note that early measurements of female sexual arousal such as vaginal secretions, the kolpograph, and indices of general arousal have drawbacks.

In 1975, Geer invented a photoplethysmograph system that "reliably measures vaginal vasocongestion during the cycle of sexual arousal." A vaginal probe "indirectly measures blood volume by detecting changes in the optical density of the tissue surrounding it." Kelley and Byrne also found that measurement of "pressure pulse amplitude"—which they call an important measure of female sexual arousal—reliably records changes in arousal during exposure to nonerotic versus erotic films and during masturbation that leads to orgasm.[45]

Another measure of female sexual arousal is the thermistor which attaches to a woman's labia via a temperature clip, and is sensitive to arousal during erotic films. It is hard to keep the clip attached to the genitals, however, as it is blood engorgement of the tissue that results in a temperature increase at the site.

Questions have been raised about the "reactivity" and "nonvalidity" of some of these sexual arousal measures. Kelley and Byrne note that experimenters in few other areas need be concerned about venereal disease being transmitted through the use of contaminated devices, unsuspected pregnancy being interfered with, or embarrassment to subjects caused by strangers mistakenly opening lab room doors. Literal and psychological intrusiveness of such devices also can be a problem.

Subjective sexual arousal levels usually "correlate in the .40 to .80 range with objective physiological measurement of sexual arousal," Kelley and Byrne state, although there is higher correspondence for males than females and coefficients drop "as low as zero in some dysfunctional groups." The *timing* of subjective measurement (that is, during or after erotic stimulation) could make a difference. Different cultural teachings—with females taught to be less attentive or neutral to their physical responses—could account for such differences, they suggest. (We note that other writers suggest the differences in female subjective and objective arousal could be due to invalidity of devices.) They also note that anatomical differences make it easier for males to perceive their genital reactions. In addition, they say that males can inhibit erection occurrence. They point out that little information is available about how emotional states influence measures of sexual arousal.[46]

CATHARSIS THEORY

Some researchers ask the questions "Does viewing sexual aggression and violence reduce aggressive tendencies in the viewer?" and "Is viewing of sexual aggression therapeutic in that it may release pent-up emotions heretofore repressed?"

Scott, states that there is "virtually no support" for the "catharsis hypothesis"—the idea that viewing sexual aggression and violence reduces aggression, is therapeutic, or releases pent-up emotion. According to Scott, psychologist Seymour Feshbach, who developed the catharsis hypothesis decades ago, changed his views about catharsis. Yet, as Scott states, the belief in the catharsis theory is "deeply ingrained in popular culture."[47]

In a newspaper article dealing with catharsis, Edward Donnerstein responded to a contention by supporters of survival games (in which people pay to act out simulated guerrilla warfare in the woods) that such games are a good way to relieve anger and an outlet for built-up hostility. Donnerstein said, "There is no basis in research to support that view. What it does is to desensitize them to violence and (sometime) in a state of anger they are going to make a response."[48]

Clor argues that the "safety-valve theory" conflicts with the "man-in-the-street understanding of human motivation and conduct, according to which one does not weaken or gain control of harmful impulses by stimulating them." While the safety-valve idea may work in a few cases under controlled conditions, more harm than good usually results from "systematic indulgences in vicious thoughts, imaginations, and desires." He believes that public policy should not be based on such a tenuous theory. At the same time, he says, there is "no significant body of tested opinion against the view that the influence of obscenity is harmful."[49]

Dr. Gordon Russell says that the general public believes in the notion of a safety valve of release of hostility, but field studies and social experimental lab results contradict that belief. Researchers studied large numbers of people at professional wrestling matches, hockey games, and other sports events and found nothing resembling catharsis. In fact, they found an increase in the hostility of both male and female fans at those events. Yet he suggests that even desensitized people can recognize the limits of entertainment and that there are limits involving "how attractive violence will become."[50]

Feshbach writes about the catharsis hypothesis. He is one of the major authors of the catharsis theory. As noted previously, the basis of this theory is that providing outlets for aggressive behavior, whether in film or contact sports such as football, wrestling, or hockey, channels aggressive impulses, which are biologically rooted, into other areas. Feshbach admits that the contrary has been shown in numerous instances, namely "stimulus situations that were soon to be carthartic have resulted in an increment in aggressive behavior. Most of these situations entail exposure to aggression depicted in the media." This has raised a serious question about whether there is any validity to the catharsis concept.

Feshbach describes several types of psychological processes that have used the term *catharsis,* and the reader is urged to consult his article for that data. He concludes that "the question of whether exposure to violence in drama has a cathartic effect depends upon audience and dramatic vehicle characteristics that relate to the expression of inhibited anger." He admits that the evidence for the catharsis theory has been sparse but argues that it is too early to discard the hypothesis. He says we should not rely on catharsis "as a potent mechanism for reducing war or criminal violence" but feels there might be opportunities for the catharsis of aggression to be used to maintain sound mental health and harmonious social relationships.[51]

Geer, Stonner, and Shope studied the catharsis hypothesis by conducting an experiment with ninety introductory psychology students. They found that "the opposite of catharsis" occurred "when an experimental situation was arranged to [minimize restraints against] aggression. . . ."[52]

EARLY PORNOGRAPHY RESEARCH

Cairns, Paul, and Wishner reviewed pre-1970 Pornography Commission studies of pornography for the commission. They examined research from 1961 to 1968 involving sex censorship and arrived at the following conclusions:[53]

1. Words and pictures depicting human sexuality produce sexual arousal in "a large proportion of the adult population."
2. Females are aroused by romantic stories, expressions of affection, and subtle depictions that would not be considered obscene. Men are highly aroused by pictures or words of sexual relations and female nudity and are less likely to be aroused by "romantic" stimuli.
3. "There are sharp individual differences in personal preferences for and responses to sexual stimuli." (For example, homosexuals are more aroused by homosexual stimuli.)
4. The setting in which pornography is viewed is "a significant determinant" of the amount of arousal the subject will experience. (An inhibiting setting will result in anxiety rather than arousal.)

Readers should consult this study for summaries of the specific early pornography studies. A few of those studies are described below.

Jakobovitz (1965) used twenty 700-word short stories (half of which were erotically realistic and the other half of which were defined as hard-core pornography). Volunteers from among Jakobovitz's acquaintances passed out research booklets among friends, then returned them. Although the women and men studied did not respond differently to the realistic stories, in contrast to other researchers' findings, women found the hard-core material more sexually arousing than did the men. (Note that we do not know the content of the stories.) Both sexes found the materials increasingly more stimulating, which contradicts the satiation theory.

In a related vein, Cairns, Paul, and Wishner note that attempts to link pornography with sex crimes had thus far gotten negative results and emphasize that data based on self-reports of sex criminals might be unreliable. However, they find it premature to reject the possibility that pornography might trigger or elicit behavior by sex offenders.

Walters, Bowen, and Parke (1964) "found that sexually significant responses can be disinhibited by observing the behavior of another individual."[54] They showed college men pictures of nude or nearly nude women and men. They were told that a spot of moving light on the pictures indicated where the previous test subject had focused his or her attention. In some cases, the experimenter focused the light on the nude bodies, emphasizing genital and breast areas. In other cases, the experimenter directed the light toward the background of the pictures, suggesting that the previous viewer had avoided looking at the pictures. After being exposed to one of those two conditions, subjects viewed a set of similar pictures. An eye-marker camera traced their eye movements.

The main outcome of this study was that persons who followed "uninhibited" viewers spent significantly more time looking at the nude pictures than did those who followed "inhibited" viewers. Apparently, the authors concluded, following an uninhibited viewer relaxed subjects' inhibitions about viewing the nude photos. They said that " 'observers who are emotionally aroused and uncertain how to respond in a social situation are readily influenced by the behavior of a model.' "[55] Subjects imitated the prior subject's behavior only when "emotionally arousing stimuli" (nudes) were used. They did not imitate the behavior of prior subject when the pictures were unrelated to sex or nonthreatening. They suggested that persons, who are the "least stable in their sexual patterns," such as children, are likely to be influenced by the sexual behavior of models.[56]

Martin (1964) found that persons given permissive instructions spent significantly more time looking at nude photos than did persons given inhibitory instructions.

Byrne and Sheffield (1965) showed that college students reported anxiety feelings after reading "erotic" stories. In relation to this, Cairns, Paul, and Wishner state: "It seems that exposure to hard-core obscenity is a stressful experience, even for 'sophisticated' normal young adults."[57]

Cairns, Paul, and Wishner also cite studies that found that the pupils of male subjects' eyes dilated in response to nude photographs of women but showed little change in response to nude photos of men, while females responded similarly (dilation) to photos of nude men. They emphasize that there is no single measure that should be looked at as "the index of sexual arousal." They encourage researchers to use multiple measures of arousal and to use a variety of groups of people for experimental studies (that is, not just "normal" college students). They conclude that the data between 1962 and 1968 did not provide any definitive answers about the effects of pornography.[58]

PORNOGRAPHY'S AROUSAL ABILITY

Some studies confirm something instinctively recognized by many: Pornography and erotica sexually arouse men and women. Studies have found the following to be true:

Movies and videotapes are more arousing than pictures, slides, audiotapes, or words of similar content.

Female and male responses to pornography differ.

Individual differences such as gender, age, sexual experience, political attitudes, marital status, sex guilt, and authoritarianism can make a difference in arousal.

Differences were found between subjective self-reports of arousal and objective (device-measured) arousal, especially for females. Some of these differences could be due to the use of unreliable devices.

People tend to be most aroused by material that fits their own sexual preferences—for example, heterosexual, homosexual, rape, and child molesting. Some themes seem more arousing to the average male than others—for example, heterosexual themes such as intercourse and oral sex are more arousing than rape, bestiality, and other extreme practices.

Gender Differences

Jakobovits studied reactions to erotically realistic and unrealistic literature, the content of which was not clear. There were twenty different stories. While there were no significant differences between the females and males regarding how they found the realistic stories stimulating, the females found the unrealistic stories more stimulating than the males. Both sexes showed ambivalence toward the stories, with both pleasant and unpleasant reactions.[59]

Weaver studied the effects on women's perceptions of portrayals of violence against women and female sexuality. He found that brief exposure to such media induced substantial changes in attitudes toward women and men and toward punishment of a rapist who had been convicted. Weaver said his most important finding was that when female and male undergraduates were exposed to sexually explicit materials of a nonviolent nature perceptions of the sexual receptiveness of peer-group females who were sexually nonpermissive were adversely affected (while other personality assessments were not). Rape, as a result, was trivialized as a criminal offense. In Weaver's study, sexually violent materials resulted in weaker effects. Weaver concluded that such media can have an adverse influence on people's judgments of others in everyday life.[60]

Byrne et al. studied similarities in responses to pornography of husbands and wives. They noted the general feeling that similarity of personalities, attitudes, and ideals is positively related to marital satisfaction and that one area in which such agreement is needed is that of sexual behavior. The subjects in this study were forty-two married couples at a university who volunteered to participate in a study dealing with opinions about pornography. (Again, there is bias built into the sample here.) Three different conditions were used. One had subjects view photographic slides, another had them read the script of passages, and the third had them picture in their minds a series of themes including heterosexual, homosexual, and autosexual acts. Subjects were exposed to nineteen themes used in research by Levitt and Brady and were asked to indicate whether they thought each was pornographic. The definition of pornography provided was "obscene or licentious; foul, disgusting or offensive; tending to produce lewd emotions."[61]

The various stimuli used in this experiment produced no relevant differences, so the researchers combined all three groups for analysis purposes. They found highly correlated total arousal for husbands and wives, with the most similarity arising in forms of heterosexual activity and the least involved in autosexual, homosexual, or group sex activities. They did not find a pattern of similarity in these spouses' judgments of pornography regarding specific themes. The wives and husbands were similar in their overall restrictiveness attitudes. In addition, the authoritarianism and equalitarianism scores for the husbands and wives correlated highly, with those involved in authoritarian relationships reporting greater arousal yet labeling more themes as pornographic and advocating greater restrictions on sexual stimuli than those involved in equalitarian relationships. While the spouses showed similar judgments about pornography and censorship and similar sexual arousal, the feelings aroused by the stimuli did not yield similar effects.

Schmidt, Sigusch, and Schafer studied differences between men and women in responding to reading "erotic stories." The subjects were 120 female and 120 male students at the University of Hamburg who had volunteered to be involved in an experiment about "psychosexual stimulation." Two stories with sexual themes were used in this experiment. It is important to emphasize that in creating the text, the researchers made certain that the woman and man displayed pleasure, satisfaction, sexual initiative, and activity to the same degree. Both stories involved sexual explicitness. One story showed no affection between the lovers, but the other story did involve affection. The plot and descriptions of specific sexual acts in the stories did not vary. The first story had 3,400 words and the second story had 4,100 words.

Half the subjects read one story, and the other half read the other story. They completed a questionnaire after reading the story on which they rated their sexual arousal and their favorable and unfavorable reactions. While the men reported somewhat higher arousal than did the women and the story with affection was described as more stimulating by both women and men, there was no significant sex difference. The researchers were not able to prove

that the type of story had a different influence on men and women. After reading the story that contained no affection, both sexes were more agitated and emotionally activated, had greater emotional tension and emotional instability, and revealed emotional avoidance reaction involving disgust and repellence. On a variety of items, the women were more strongly disgusted, repelled, and shocked during the story. There was more repellence and disgust at the story without affection than the story with affection. There were, however, no significant [interactions] between sex and the type of story.

Schmidt, Sigusch, and Schafer found that on the day after reading either of the stories, both women and men experienced a general increase in general activity and inner uneasiness. There was also "a significant increase of aggressiveness and autonomic complaints." However, "the extent of emotional change was only slight." The story that lacked affection caused greater inner uneasiness and greater aggressiveness. Self-reports of the subjects showed that the majority of the men and women did experience physiological reactions to the story.[62]

The researchers found that there was no statistically significant difference between the two stories in effects on the subjects' type and degree of sexual behavior within the twenty-four hours after exposure. Females experienced an increase in coital activity in the twenty-four hours after exposure and an increase in the number of orgasms, sexual fantasy activity, talks about sex, tendency to look at pictures, text, or films that are sexual in content, and arousability through external stimuli. The men experienced these increases: increase in sexual fantasy, talks about sex, watching or reading films, books, and pictures with sexual content, and attendance at bars in quest of sexual activity. Overall, however, the changes were only slight when behavior was involved, and changes were observed only among a minority of those tested.

Overall these experimenters conclude that narrative sexually explicit material such as pictorial stimuli generates sexual arousal. They found few sex differences in arousability to narrative versus pictorial stimuli. They did, however, admit that it was possible that their stories did not have sufficient differences involving affection because neither of the stories was a romantic or love story. They felt that their experiment refuted a claim that "female sexuality is basically more dependent on affection than male sexuality."[63]

In 1973, Mosher studied differences in sex guilt, sex experience, and sex differences and reactions to explicit sexual films. (We believe that this study might have a sex bias built into it in and that gender differences in attitudes were perhaps not taken into account. For example, lack of sexual experience or certain attitudes toward sex are considered to reflect guilt rather than wisdom. It is not clear what questions were used in determining sex guilt, and it is not clear whether reactions could reasonably differ between the sexes.)

Mosher studied 194 single male undergraduates and 193 single female undergraduates from an introductory psychology course. The subjects were divided into groups of thirty of the same sex. They filled out questionnaires about sexual attitudes, experience, behavior, and guilt and were then shown pornography. They completed self-reports of physiological and affective judgments and did a twenty-four-hour follow-up report and a two-week follow-up report. There was no control group that did not view these films.

Films from the U.S. President's Commission from the Institute for Sex Research in Hamburg, Germany, were used. These were silent films in color. Both films had the same couple in the same setting and nearly identical act sequences. The length of the films was not mentioned. The researchers suggested that the speeding up the films distracted the subjects. The first film was called *Petting Two*. It showed a couple undressing each other and involved in kissing, manual genital petting, cunnilingus, and fellatio to ejaculation. The second group saw *Coitus One*. This involved the couple undressing each other and involved in kissing, manual genital petting, and face-to-face coitus. The films had no sadomasochism, fetishes, homosexuality, profaning the sacred, or group sex. Fewer genital close-ups and more affection were portrayed than in most commercial pornography films. Mosher had hypothesized that these films would be more appealing to the sexually experienced and uninhibited adults of both sexes than would regular pornography, which is oriented toward a male audience and involves more kinky sex.

Immediately after the film, the subjects filled out a physiological reaction form (self-report) rating their sexual arousal on a scale of 1 to 7. Males also had to state whether they had partial or full erections and for how long and whether they had preejaculatory secretions or ejaculations. The females stated whether they had mild, moderate, or strong vaginal sensations, breast sensations, vaginal lubrication, or orgasms. Feeling or mood changes also were reported on a scale that rated the films as pornographic, containing abnormal behavior, enjoyable, offensive, or disgusting. Again, the scale consisted of subjective terms.

Twenty-four hours later, subjects reported on which of thirteen sexual behaviors they had exhibited in the twenty-four hours before and twenty-four hours after the film and compared eight emotional reactions. A two-week follow-up tested attitudes toward items such as marital intercourse, extramarital intercourse, standards of sexual behavior, their own attitudes compared to the average person's, and any new sexual behavior they had performed since they had seen the films. They also noted detrimental or beneficial changes due to the films. Similar items had been included on the prefilm questionnaire.

The prefilm questionnaire showed that those with high sex guilt had different attitudes than those with less guilt. For example, those with high guilt were less likely to have had coitus, felt more guilty about pornography, and masturbated less. Overall, after the films, the males reported significantly more sexual arousal than the females. There was little sex difference in arousal to the *Coitus One* film, but the males were more aroused and the females less aroused by the *Petting Two* film. Almost all the males and 85 percent of the females reported physiological sensations in their genitals.

Mosher concludes that the hypothesis that sex guilt "precludes sexual arousal to explicit sexual stimuli is untenable," but suggests that more research into non-self-report methods of measuring this is needed. Both the men and the women reported statistically significant changes in their "affective" states after the films, but most were mild decreases or increases. No negative affective states increased to a large extent. Both sexes became somewhat restless. The females were somewhat "disgusted," but the males were not. The men "reported an increase in general activation and in affects associated with approaching a sex object and decreases in negative affects as a function of viewing films of either coital or oral genital activity."[64] (We authors find it very interesting that people are referred to as sex objects in some of these studies.) The females had much higher increases in general activation to the coitus rather than the petting film, which they were more "disgusted" by. Both high and low guilt males were eager for contact after viewing the films, but only the low guilt females showed much increase in this affect. High sex guilt also related to feelings of shame, depression, and disgust.

Mosher found that there were statistically significant sex differences in that the females rated the films as showing "less normal sexual behavior" and as more pornographic, offensive, and disgusting and less enjoyable. There were also big differences between high and low sex guilt subjects. Oral sex was seen as less normal. The females were higher on sex guilt, were less experienced, and had a more conservative attitude toward sex. (We again question how such things are measured. It is not necessarily true that people who have less sex experience or have guilty or shameful feelings toward sex have a wrong attitude.) Even while the men saw the petting film as more offensive, they were as aroused by it as by the coitus film and had no more negative affects from it than from the coitus film. The women were less aroused by the petting film and more disgusted by it.

Most subjects had the same sexual behavior pattern in the twenty-four hours before and after the films, although some talked about sex more. Mosher concludes that there was no evidence that pornography can "trigger sexual behavior at least among single college students." He says that erotic films lead to increased sex immediately after viewing only if there is a well-established sex pattern. He found only mild changes in sexual tension and other measures within 24 hours and little change in attitudes or behavior two weeks later.[65]

Mosher's bias comes out when he states that as a result of the findings, he agrees more with the need for sex education and feels obscenity laws should be repealed. He based this belief on a finding that there was no evidence that "explicit sexual films had untoward consequences on those who viewed them."[66]

Steele and Walker studied male–female differences in response to pornography as related to sexual adjustment. One hundred male and one hundred female undergraduate students viewed twenty slides depicting sexual acts including homosexual, heterosexual, and sadomasochistic themes. Subjects rated the slides along dimensions of "liking," "sexual stimulation," and "extremeness." While both sexes reported only minimal liking for the slides as a whole, the males reported greater liking than the females. The subjects did not find the slides very extreme, except that the males rated the slide of heterosexual coitus with the female on top as significantly more extreme than did the females. The more extreme slides were rated less sexually stimulating and less liked (with the females displaying this response more than the males). They found the males to be more responsive to the visual "erotica" than the females.[67]

Steele and Walker hypothesize that the classroom setting may have caused the subjects to rate the slides as less arousing than they would have otherwise. The fact that the subjects were from a private church-related university may also have had an influence, they say.

In another study, Steele and Walker examined feminine perspectives of "erotic" films. They used twenty unmarried female undergraduate students who were at least 21 years old. The stimuli used were seven color films of five minutes each depicting

behavior such as heterosexual behavior, heterosexual behavior stressing genital activity, group sex with two males and one female, group sex with three males and three females, sadomasochism involving forcing sexual behavior on a female and roughness "but not brutal or cruel behavior toward her" (we see this as a contradiction), sadomasochism with more brutal behaviors including scenes in which the females appear to be physically harmed by the males, and male homosexual behavior. The subjects viewed the films in random order and rated their degree of sexual arousal from each film. Most of the films produced at least moderate sexual arousal. The females found the heterosexual as opposed to brutal sadomasochistic or homosexual activities to be sexually exciting. They found the homosexual, cruel sadomasochistic, oral genital, and lack of affection depictions to be unappealing and/or disgusting most frequently.

One interview question asked these subjects what would they include if they were to construct a movie designed for marital counseling that would be as sexually exciting as they could make it.

> The responses overwhelmingly included a sequence involving a male and female in private starting out dressed, then undressing, kissing, having a significant amount of foreplay, being affectionate and including various positions of coital activity. Additional suggestions for the "ideal" erotic film included gentleness on the part of both participants, depiction of the female as an active partner, the addition of sound tracks to the movies, an emphasis on the satisfaction of participants after the sex act.[68]

These researchers found that the females were more sexually aroused by and preferred the stimuli in which a male related to a female (even if in a brutal and cruel manner such as sadomasochism) over a homosexual film of a male relating to a male.

Griffitt, May, and Veitch studied eighty female and eighty male introductory psychology students. One-half of the subjects were given mimeographed booklets of nineteen short passages, one per page, describing heterosexual, autosexual, and homosexual acts. They were asked to judge whether each was pornographic. The other subjects were put in a nonarousal condition, reading passages that were nonsexual in content. The subjects in the arousal condition were significantly more sexually aroused than those in the nonarousal condition. Subjects also had to evaluate strangers of the same or opposite sex. Males tended to respond more positively to females whether or not they were aroused, whereas sexually aroused females responded more positively to males than females.

A second experiment involved fourteen males and twenty-two females. In the arousal condition, subjects saw nineteen slides with depictions similar to those in the passages mentioned earlier. The subjects then had to choose whether to sit next to a female or male confederate. The aroused females and males looked more at persons of the opposite sex than did the nonaroused people. The researchers concluded that sexual stimulation due to pornography exposure can cause more subtle "heterosexual behaviors such as positive affective responses, visual attention and physical approach responses to heterosexual targets." Persons who had positive affective responses to the "erotica" established closer proximity to the opposite sex targets than did those whose responses were negative. This caused the researchers to conclude that the influence of erotica-produced sexual stimulation largely depends on the nature of the affective and emotional responses caused by that stimulation.[69]

Griffitt studied thirty female and thirty male unmarried introductory psychology students. He found that different types of sexual experience associated positively with the degree of responsiveness to depictions of those same types of experience. The persons with the most sexual experience were the most sexually aroused by explicit depictions of sexual activities. For the females, both their heterosexual and masturbatory experiences were related to their emotional and sexual responsiveness to the stimuli used; for the males, only the frequency of masturbation related consistently to their positive affective and sexual responses to the pornography. The researchers say that this suggests that "masturbation experience is superior to heterosexual experience as an indicant of male sexual responsiveness."[70]

Schmidt studied differences in female and male sexual arousal and behavior based on exposure to sexually explicit material. Five studies were done involving 562 females and 562 males enrolled at the University of Hamburg, Germany. One study used black-and-white slides that portrayed nudes of the opposite sex, seminudes, and necking, petting, and intercourse scenes. The second study used both black-and-white and color films and slides portraying intercourse, petting, and necking. The third study used two stories describing a sexual experience of a young couple. This involved detailed descriptions of petting, necking, and coitus. The fourth study used black-and-white and color films and slides but portrayed masturbation of a man and masturbation of a woman. The fifth study used four films involving aggressive sexual content. One showed flagellant activity between women, a second showed a sadomasochistic ritual, the third showed four men raping a woman in a bar, and the fourth was a controlled stimulus involving nonaggressive sexuality.

In each of the studies, subjects were left alone to view the films or slides or read the stories. A questionnaire was administered immediately after the experiment and twenty-four hours later. The women said they were only slightly less aroused than the men. Most of the subjects noticed some sort of physiological sexual reactions to the stimuli. Both sexes showed a slight general increase in sexual behavior during the twenty-four hours following the exposure to the stimuli compared to the twenty-four hours before exposure, as well as an increase in sexual desire and fantasies. Both sexes showed a moderate inclination to incorporate the stimuli into their masturbatory fantasies and into their fantasies during coitus. There was a "negligible" influence of the sexually explicit material on coital techniques. The stimulation led immediately to emotional agitation and activation for both sexes. It also caused increases in the emotional tension and instability and emotional avoidance reactions, which were stronger in the women than in the men. The increase in emotional instability and emotional activation were still found among both sexes twenty-four hours after the exposure. Overall, Schmidt found similar reactions to the stimuli for the men and women. He cautions that other groups, such as older people and those from different social strata, might differ according to sex.

Schmidt then addresses the issue of whether the content of the stimuli changed the above general effects. For example, his findings are contrary to earlier findings of researchers that women's sexuality in Western society is more dependent on affection than is men's. The studies Schmidt has done with other researchers have found that this was not the case. However, he does admit that they might not have used sufficient differences in affection in the stories. He concludes that affection is not necessary for women to react sexually to such stimuli. Even with the films of aggressive sexual content, he and his co-researchers found similar behavior patterns among the women and men. Here he reports that the strongest arousal of both the females and males came in response to the control stimulus, which involved nonaggressive sex. Both sexes responded to the sadomasochistic film with low arousal, but they had strong emotional avoidance and "emotional labilization, dysphoric mood and moderate aggressiveness." Both sexes responded to the group rape film with high arousal and strong emotional avoidance reactions, "emotional labilization, dysphoric mood and much aggressiveness." This film evoked a strong conflict reaction—in other words, the combination of sexual arousal and strong aversion. The women did show stronger emotional avoidance reaction to the aggressive films. In the women, "the rape film produces sexual arousal and by identification with the female victim, fears of being helplessly overpowered. In men this conflict is more characterized by guilt feelings and dismay that they are stimulated by aggressive sexual activities incompatible with their conscious ideas of sexuality."[71]

Schmidt says that the most important finding is that "films which do not describe sexual aggression as a deviant or strange ritual (as in the sadomasochistic film) can induce strong sexual arousal in both men and women." He found that strong aggression in a sexual content did not inhibit the student's ability to react with sexual arousal and feels that aggression might have added a sexually stimulating effect for both sexes.[72]

Gebhard critiques the 1973 study by Schmidt, Sigusch, and Schafer. He found differences among the Schmidt findings, the Schmidt et al. findings, and the findings reported by Kinsey et al. He says the discrepancy is due largely to "differential cultural conditioning which (1) made the Kinsey question phraseology less applicable to females and (2) caused females to respond more to stimuli presented gradually rather than quickly, a tendency not taken into account in comparing male and female responsiveness." Gebhard believes both sexes have an inherent ability to respond to visual sexually explicit stimuli.[73]

Stauffer and Frost studied male reactions to *Playboy* and female reactions to *Playgirl*. While 70 percent of the males had positive reactions to the pornography, only 26 percent of the females did. The great majority of the men gave the combined centerfold and photo essay features of *Playboy* high ratings, while only 46 percent of the women rated these features in *Playgirl* highly. All of these features were of frontal nudity of members of the opposite sex. The researchers found that the female ambivalence toward the male nudity in *Playgirl* might be due to traditional social pressures and social meanings instead of reactions to sexual content.[74]

Dienstbier suggests that rather than ignoring or faulting the 1970 Pornography Commission research, the use of the social learning model to interpret the data should be questioned.[75]

Hatfield, Sprecher, and Traupmann hypothesized that men and women would be most sexually aroused when seeing a person of the opposite sex masturbating and least aroused when seeing someone of the same sex doing so. Fifty-eight summer school students were exposed to a film of a female masturbating and

a film of a man masturbating. The hypothesis was strongly confirmed.

A second study involved 556 men and women enrolled in an introductory human sexuality class. They were exposed to a variety of films that depicted male and female homosexuality, male and female masturbation, and heterosexuality among adolescents and elderly people. They found that the women and men were most sexually aroused by seeing someone of the opposite sex masturbating, engaged in homosexual activity, or engaged in heterosexual activity. They were least aroused by seeing someone of the same sex engaged in such activities. The men found female homosexuality extremely arousing and male homosexuality extremely unarousing. The women had a much less intense reaction. They found "male homosexuality only slightly more arousing than female homosexuality."[76]

Griffitt and Kaiser studied forty male and forty female introductory psychology students. They measured sex guilt scores. The high and low sex guilt subjects were randomly assigned to an experimental or control group. Experimental group subjects were shown black-and-white slides depicting a variety of explicit sexual acts. The high-sex-guilt subjects had less positive affects and more negative affects than did the low-sex-guilt subjects. Males had more positive affects than did females. Correct choices "in a discrimination task" resulted in the subject being shown "erotic" slides. Males saw the slides as rewarding (desirable). Females and high-sex-guilt subjects considered the slides to be punishing (to be avoided, condemned, and rejected). However, regardless of gender, those individuals with a positive reaction to the slides saw them as rewards while those people with negative reactions considered the slides to be punishment. Females and high-sex-guilt subjects made fewer responses in the test which led to exposure to the "erotic" slides.[77]

Fisher and Byrne studied sex differences in response to pornography. The subjects used were thirty males and thirty-two females, all unmarried, who were students in undergraduate abnormal psychology classes at a university. The subjects were shown the same film, which depicted a heterosexual interaction in which the partners undressed, pet by manual genital contact, engaged in fellatio and cunnilingus, and reached orgasm. Some subjects were told that the people in the film were a young working man and his wife, who had been recently married, were much in love, and had just returned from a dance. Others were told that the people were a young working man and a prostitute; the prostitute had approached the man at a dance, and he had purchased her services. There were no sex differences in reported arousal responses to the love or lust scenes, but the love scene subjects evaluated the characters more positively. However, the females were more likely to rate the stimuli as pornographic and more in favor of restricting pornographic material.

In a second experiment, the subjects were thirty-six married couples who had responded to local newspaper advertisements. The love and lust themes were presented, and a casual sex scene was introduced by giving them different instructions. This theme suggested that a young working man and a girl had met at a dance, were sexually attracted to each other, and had sex. One of the films shown involved petting and partial nudity in which manual genital contact was made but orgasm was not reached. A second film portraying intercourse, cunnilingus, and fellatio also was shown. The casual sex theme was found to be more arousing than the love or lust themes, which were equally arousing. The females more often than the males expressed the belief that sex should be accompanied by a love relationship and were more opposed to extramarital sex. However, because of the greater arousal to a chance sexual encounter, the researchers concluded that affection or romantic emphasis is not a precondition to female arousal to "erotica." Again, the females were more likely to rate the film as pornographic and more likely to favor restrictions on such material. The researchers concluded that the females' expression of a lack of interest in "erotica" contrasted sharply with the fact that they were not less aroused by it than the males. They note that the social prescription of female interest in pornography might account for the differences in expressed interest.[78] (We again note that some researchers have a tendency not to recognize that women are abused in many types of pornography and therefore women would dislike it. Because of this, we do not favor such material.)

Brown studied thirty female and thirty male students from a Canadian university enrolled in an introductory psychology course. Two female experimenters who differed greatly in age, appearance, personality, impressions of warmth and competence, and other characteristics were used. The subjects were shown twenty-one slides representing a variety of themes such as male and female nudes and masturbation, heterosexual intercourse, oral genital acts, heterosexual group sex, lesbianism, homosexuality, and male transvestism. These were hard-core materials. Subjects were told they could view each slide for as long as they wanted. The males rated the slides more pornographic than the females, and they also looked at the slides significantly longer than the females. The males found many themes more arousing. The slides that the females rated signifi-

cantly more negatively were those of vaginal exposure, heterosexual cunnilingus and fellatio, group sex, and lesbians engaged in mutual masturbation. The males avoided the homosexual themes. Brown found a curve linear relationship between the looking time and pornographic value as rated by the males but no such relationship for the females. There were no experimenter effects.[79]

Malamuth, Heim, and Feshbach studied 308 undergraduate psychology students. They were given one-page descriptions of sexual intercourse. There were rape and nonrape versions of the intercourse. In the rape versions, words such as *forced, forcefully, terrified, paralyzed, screaming, panic,* and *frenzy of tears* were used. In the nonrape versions, there was no reference to any force, and the women were described as being excited, feeling sensuous, and experiencing pleasure and a "frenzy of bliss." Some versions included references to the woman experiencing pain, discomfort, and aching. One version of the rape story indicated that the rapist had planned the rape, and another depicted him as not planning it but going out of control. There were aggressive cues in some of the passages using words such as *assault, slammed,* and *stabbed.* The researchers found that the college student subjects were less sexually aroused by themes involving sexual assault than by themes involving mutual consent.

A second experiment used only the rape stories. The victims were described as experiencing either an involuntary orgasm or nausea and disgust. One hundred thirty-nine female and male introductory psychology students were subjects. The stories that showed the victim as experiencing the involuntary orgasm were found to be more stimulating than the stories that showed her as being nauseated. The female subjects were "relatively highly aroused when the victim was described as experiencing an orgasm and no pain whereas [the] males were most aroused when the victim experienced orgasm and pain." The women were more angered, embarrassed, offended, frustrated, and less positive than the men who read the stories. The researchers describe the female arousal as a form of identification with the rape victim. They say the male arousal fits into a power explanation.[80]

Sherif critiques the Malamuth, Heim, and Feshbach study. She also raises a concern about exposing females to rape depictions because "depiction of sexual attack is a powerful means of social control." She argues that there is no support for the conclusions that the female arousal was due to identification with the victim. She wonders why a parallel finding was not made for the men, alleging that they identified with the sadistic rapist.[81]

Malamuth, Feshbach, and Heim responded to Sherif's critique by arguing that her comments show a lack of understanding of the research and a misinterpretation of their explanations.[82]

Abramson, Repczynski, and Merrill studied 133 women recruited from an introductory psychology class and a women's clinic at a university center. Twenty-eight percent of these subjects were using oral contraceptives. The researchers were testing to find a relationship between phases of the menstrual cycle and responses to "erotic literature." It is not clear what literature the subjects were exposed to. The researchers found that women on the pill who were in the menstrual phase of the cycle experienced the greatest sexual arousal and genital sensation in response to the erotic stories. Women on the pill also experienced the least sexual arousal and genital sensation to the stimuli when they were in the premenstrual phase of the cycle.[83]

Kenrick et al. studied sex differences in responses to erotica. These authors noted that other studies had shown that although females are as aroused physiologically by "erotica" as males, they report less "positive affective responses," favor more restrictions on such stimulations, and say they would avoid pornography more in a free choice setting. In one study, the subjects were forty-one female and fifty-two male undergraduates in an introductory psychology course. The analysis included thirty-eight of the females and forty-eight of the males; there was no control group. They were tested in small groups by one female and one male experimenter. Half of the groups were same sex, and the other half were mixed sex. They were told the test involved reactions to X-rated movies from soft-core erotica to hard-core pornography. Subjects were asked to choose between a film of a very much in love, recently married couple (a soft-core film) and a film of a young man who just purchased the services of a prostitute (a hard-core film). No films were actually shown to the subjects. It was expected that females would be more likely than males to prefer the soft-core film and results confirmed this. Based on this finding, the researchers suggest that females who are negative to "erotica" might avoid signing up for such studies, so samples might not be representative.

The second study by Kenrick et al. involved sex-typed subjects versus androgynous subjects. They included forty-three female and forty-one male psychology course undergraduate subjects. Each was contacted by phone before the class term began and told the psychology department wanted to arrange participation in experiments. Subjects were asked to sign up for one of two experiments to be conducted during the upcoming week. The first experiment involved special perception using geometric figures. The second was a filmed sexual interaction between a male and female. Subjects were told that they could sign up to participate in either the geometric figure perception study or the one involving "erotica." Some were told the second experiment involved hard-core erotica with explicit sexual scenes. Others were told it involved soft-core erotica with suggestive but not very explicit sex scenes. There was no actual exposure to pornography.

Thirty-four females and twenty-six males filled out a questionnaire that divided them into two groups—sex-typed (strong male/female characteristics) and androgynous (a blend of male and female characteristics). The females were less likely than the males to volunteer for the erotic film (51 percent versus 73 percent). Subjects of both sexes were less likely to volunteer for the hard-core film than for the soft-core film (51 percent versus 73 percent). Both sexes were more likely to volunteer for the erotic film when the experimenter was of the opposite sex. Only 31 percent of the sex-typed females volunteered for the erotic film, but 91 percent of the sex-typed males did so. Sixty-seven percent of the androgynous females volunteered for the erotic film, while 60 percent of the androgynous males did so.

The researchers suggest that there is a study bias in these sorts of experiments because subjects are informed of the sexual nature of the tests and those who are likely to have an unpleasant reaction to pornography will not volunteer. Yet, they state, it would be unethical to try to get subjects to view materials that they might find objectionable, and when "erotica" is actually shown, subjects must be forewarned. They also state that experimenter characteristics could make a difference. They say that the use of college students is a limitation and suggest that sex differences of the type found in this study might not be found with a different age group. They suggest that continued differences in responses to erotica may cause continued avoidance of erotica by females. Males, however, might avoid homosexual or male masturbatory erotica. These researchers note that the hypothesized link between pornography and sex crimes has been negative thus far. Yet they say that pornography might hurt concepts of sexual attractiveness and that it might be male adaptive because it differs from the real world. They suggest that this needs more research.[84]

Steinman et al. compared female and male sexual arousal patterns. The issue was whether males and females differed in their sexual response to "erotica." Eight heterosexual males and eight heterosexual females between the ages of 19 and 30 were paid $10 each to participate. One male and female were married. The subjects were tested for heterosexuality, absence of sexual dysfunction, emotional disturbance, and an aversion to explicit sexual material. Vaginal photoplethysmograph and penile strain gauges were used. The subjects also were asked immediately after each stimulus to rate on a scale of 0 to 100 how sexually aroused they felt. Sexual arousal was continually estimated using a hand lever as well. They were asked during the debriefing to rate their arousal during each film in retrospect. Attitudinal ratings of pleasantness also were tested for.

There were 6 four-minute conditions. The first was no film, the second was a neutral film of the Nova Scotia coast, the third involved a male and female couple involved in explicit sex acts, the fourth involved two males engaged in explicit sex, the fifth involved two females involved in explicit sex, and the last was a group sex film involving both males and females. (We do not know the content or context of these films—that is, whether they were loving and affectionate or aggressive and violent.) The films were presented in the same order to each person with three-minute intervals between them.

For the males, the baseline, neutral, and homosexual male films "produced significantly less change in penile circumference than did the heterosexual, lesbian and group conditions." The greatest arousal for them was in this order: group sex, lesbian scenes, and heterosexual activity. For the females, the baseline and neutral conditions produced significantly "less change in vaginal vasocongestion than did the heterosexual and group film conditions." There were no significant differences between the neutral, male homosexual, baseline, and lesbian conditions for the females. Their greatest physiological arousal was during the group sex and heterosexual scenes.[85]

On the subjective measures of arousal, the males said their greatest arousal was with the group sex, lesbian, and heterosexual activities, in that order. For the female subjective arousal, they said they were most aroused during the heterosexual, lesbian, and group sex scenes, in that order.

The researchers note that the measures of penile circumference and vaginal vasocongestion are not directly comparable, so structural patterns of arousal, not absolute amounts, must be compared. They note that males had high arousal to lesbian scenes and females had the lowest arousal to male homosexual scenes, yet both males and females had the greatest arousal to the group sex films. The researchers point out that the physiological and subjective measures of arousal are similar for males but variable for females. They suggest that this might be due to social acceptability or unacceptability and that partial taboos can enhance arousal. The researchers say they consider

lesbian activities to be a partial taboo, while male homosexuality would be a complete taboo and thus not enhance arousal. In addition, males get positive social sanctions for expressing sexual arousal, and females do not. The females in this study might have seen the group sex as more socially taboo than the heterosexuality. And the sexes might have different abilities to recognize sexual arousal.

The researchers found no relationship between ratings of subjective arousal and pleasantness for the females and found strong relationships for the males.

Nevid studied the effects of homosexual stimuli on heterosexual viewers. Subjects were 133 undergraduate students from classes in human sexuality at Hofstra University. Sixty-eight were males and sixty-five were females. All reported a heterosexual orientation. Two color films, twenty minutes in length, were presented. One was a male homosexual film produced in 1976 by Multimedia Resource Center Films. This showed a male homosexual couple engaged in sexual activities such as petting, anal intercourse, and oral genital stimulation. The second was a lesbian film produced in 1974 by the National Sex forum. It showed a lesbian couple engaged in activities such as using a vibrator, petting, mutual masturbation, and oral genital stimulation.

The results showed that the males had more antihomosexual attitudes than did the females. The subjects experienced increased, though still moderate, amounts of hostility and anxiety. This increase occurred among both sexes and in reaction to both films.[86]

Wendy Stock studied the effects of violent pornography on women. She took an excerpt from a letter to a *Penthouse Variations*. It was an account of a woman who went into a bar and headed for the ladies' room. On the way, she was grabbed by a man and forced into the men's bathroom. The man locked the door and tied her up, and the couple had mad, passionate sex. Stock says that this is representative of the typical rape myth of pornography—that is, that even though women say no initially, they really want to be raped. Stock wrote other versions in which the woman's behavior remained the same but the amount of force and the element of whether she enjoyed it or not were varied. She created a mutual consent condition in which the woman met the man, liked his looks, and willingly went into the bathroom. She also created a neutral condition in which the woman and man met and had a boring conversation about jazz music.

Stock found that women were no more genitally aroused or turned on to depictions of rape in which the woman did not enjoy it and suffered realistically than they were to the boring jazz music conversation.

However, the women were turned on to the rape myth. This, she says, does not mean that women are turned on by rape. They are turned on, as are men, to eroticized and mystified depictions of rape. Stock suggests that exposure to this type of porn and later sexual victimization might create inner conflict, and guilt, and self-blame in women.

Stock gave a more detailed account of her dissertation in a paper presented at the annual meetings of the American Psychology Association in August 1983.[87] In her research, Stock used audiotaped stimuli. In the first phase of the experiment, seventy-five female subjects, mean age of 20, completed questionnaires including past experiences of forced sexual interaction and rape and past exposure to pornographic materials. The subjects were randomly assigned to one of the five preexposure groups. The first two groups heard a neutral interaction between a female and a male involving no sexual or aggressive behavior. The third group heard a violent rape in which the male rapist overpowers the female victim and both are sexually aroused. The fourth group heard a description of mutually consenting intercourse between a male and female. The fifth group heard a rape description that emphasized the female victim's fear, pain, and negative response. At the end of that exposure, all subjects heard a second "rape criterion" tape. The sexual arousal of these women was measured through self-reports and physiologically by a vaginal photometer that measured the vaginal pulse amplitude. Subjects completed a second questionnaire after audiotape exposure. Preexposure to the rape myth scenario (group three) increased response to the later depiction of rape. The rape empathy group, (group five) however, was higher on dimensions of anxiety, anger, and frustration.

Stock says that the study does not show strong evidence that exposing women to aggressive/erotic pornography affects their attitudes and beliefs toward rape as "dependent" measures. She tentatively concludes that reported arousal to sexually oriented material and experience with it enhances subjective sexual arousal to depictions of rape. She notes that the females in the study were generally reluctant to put responsibility for the rapes on the female rape victims and to underestimate the trauma of the victims. This, she says, contrasts with previous research findings using male subjects and again suggests that there are sex differences in this area of research. She calls for serious consideration of the impact of pornographic material because the indications are that women and men can be influenced to perceive rape as an arousing event. The female subjects all responded with relatively low subjective and genital arousal to the rape criterion exposure.

(Remember that the rape criterion tape was a realistic depiction of the behavior involved in a rape.)

Bart, Freeman, and Kimball reported on the different attitudes of men and women toward pornography and their responses to a film about pornography titled *Not a Love Story*. These researchers started from a perspective of conceptualizing pornography as "prorate propaganda." Initially they handed out stamped, addressed questionnaires to patrons leaving a theater showing the film *Not a Love Story*. They had a return rate of 15 to 20 percent. They also interviewed some people who had seen the film. Based on this response, they constructed a new questionnaire taken directly from answers to the original questionnaire. These questions were approximately equally divided between anti and pro-pornography attitudes. In this study, they used 668 subjects, most of whom viewed the film *Not a Love Story* at an art film house and some at a university. The questionnaire was handed out before the film, and the lights were left on afterward so that the people could complete the questionnaire. Approximately 90 percent of the audience cooperated. The researchers note that this was a "natural audience" rather than one put together for experimental purposes.

Their hypothesis that there would be gender differences in responses, with the women being more opposed to pornography than the men, was supported overwhelmingly by the respondents. For example, while only 5 percent of the females strongly agreed and 24 percent moderately agreed with the statement that "pornography has its place," 23 percent of the males strongly agreed and 38 percent moderately agreed. Another major difference was in response to the statement that "some of the increase in the rate of rape can be attributed to pornography." Although 35 percent of the females strongly agreed and 46 percent moderately agreed, only 16 percent of the males strongly agreed and 35 percent moderately agreed. (It should be noted that 313 people answered the "pornography has its place" question, whereas only 58 answered the rape rate question, which was introduced later in the survey.)[88]

Bart, Freeman, and Kimball also found support for their hypothesis that there would be information acquired and changes in self-reported attitudes as a result of exposure to the film. Reflecting these changes were statements by people that they had not known that pornography was so violent, that the film made them angrier about it, and that it taught them the fear men have of women and their needs. The researchers also found that the males more than females "may favor a pluralist society tolerant of pornography *regardless* of what is happening to women." They emphasize that the pros and cons of pornography and being for or against it are not the same for women and men, that the choices are made "along different dimensions within a different frame of reference."[89]

They found that the women disliked pornography but that some of the women expressed toleration for pornography in order not to feel like enemies of liberty "or perhaps to gain approval from men."[90] Conversely, the men who said that pornography has its place were more likely to approve of the pornography. The men did appear to take family members into consideration when expressing an opinion about pornography, with more fathers of girls and married men being opposed to pornography and more fathers of boys favoring it.

Another factor that had an impact on attitudes toward pornography was the amount of pornography to which the subjects had previously been exposed. For example, they found that the women who had been exposed to more pornography were "significantly less anti-pornography." For the men, the effect of previous exposure was more than twice as great. The researchers call for studying the hypothesis that "repeated exposure to pornography brings about a pro-porn attitude."[91]

These researchers conclude that the test used in obscenity law—that is, that a work must violate community standards—is based on a false belief. There are, they say, no community standards; rather "there are male standards and female standards." Because the women in pornography are made to behave in ways that reflect male fantasies, the researchers found that it was no accident that the men were more propornography than the women.[92]

Bart, Freeman, and Kimball conclude that pornography does not result in catharsis because if it did, there would be less sexual violence against women. They argue that pornography is not a victimless crime. Instead, it reinforces men's inaccurate fantasies about women and makes them insensitive to women's needs. By creating an expectation that real women should behave like the women in pornography, pornographic material sets the stage for abuse of women.

Becker and Byrne used thirty-four female and thirty-six male undergraduates who viewed twenty-one explicit heterosexual slides. They hypothesized that erotophiles would spend more time viewing "erotica" and more accurately remember the material content than would erotophobes. They also believed that coronary prone persons would spend less time viewing erotica than non–coronary prone people. (The reader should remember that erotophiles are people who are considered to have positive orienta-

tions toward sex. We question the advisability of making it seem that it is a positive thing to favor pornography. It could be positive to be exposed to what is more commonly known as erotica, which includes sexual relationships of equality and mutual affectionate consent, as opposed to pornography, which can include extreme sexual activities such as rape, bestiality, and sadomasochism.)

The color slides showed seminude and nude females and males engaged in heterosexual activities such as manual contact with genitals, oral genital contact, and a variety of sexual intercourse positions. The length of time that each subject chose to expose himself or herself to each slide was recorded. Results showed that the erotophiles spent an average of 4.64 seconds viewing the slides compared to 2.70 seconds for the erotophobes. Interestingly, exposure time for males averaged 4.62 seconds compared to 2.72 seconds for females. Erotophiles and erotophobes who were coronary prone had equivalent exposure times, but non–coronary prone erotophiles looked at the slides longer than did non–coronary prone erotophobes. Duration of exposure had the major impact on the accuracy of recalling the slide content, at least among the non–coronary prone individuals. The erotophiles indicated greater arousal, more positive affects, less sense of being rushed, and more engrossment in the slides than erotophobes. The same was true for males compared to females. The researchers emphasize that one of the more important findings is that a "nonsexual dispositional variable" (that is, the coronary proneness variable) could outweigh a "purely sexual dispositional variable (erotophobia)" when a behavior applies to both dimensions.[93]

Kelley studied responses to heterosexual and masturbatory slides, concentrating on individual difference variables of authoritarianism and sex guilt and responses to "erotica." The subjects were 185 female and 185 male introductory psychology students who received course credit for voluntary participation. The sessions consisted of groups of four or five same sex persons who were randomly assigned to the various cells of the design. All of the subjects viewed three sets of sexual stimuli presented in one of six counterbalanced orders by an experimenter of either the same sex or the opposite sex. They responded to measures of authoritarianism and sex guilt either before or after viewing the slides. Each of the twelve slides per set was shown for fifteen seconds. The sets showed explicit sexual themes of either masturbatory activity or heterosexual activity, which included nude petting, intercourse, and oral genital sex. Each color slide showed a white nude male or female or a couple in an indoor setting. Afterward the subjects were asked to rate whether they thought the experimenter fit any or all of the following descriptions: was homosexual, was sexually promiscuous, thought about sexuality more than the subject did, or would have sexual intercourse with just about anybody.

The males felt more positive than the females about each slide set, except in the case of high sex skilled subjects of both sexes, who responded negatively to the same sex masturbation slides. The low guilt males also were more negative toward same sex masturbation. For both sexes, male masturbation evoked the most negative response. Males had the greatest arousal to heterosexual stimuli and the least arousal to same sex masturbation stimuli. Authoritarianism was found to be negatively related to positive feelings about the same sex slides. The females with low positive feelings about the heterosexual and same sex masturbation slides expressed more dislike toward and derogation of the experimenter.[94]

Other Factors That Influence Responses to Pornography

In 1968, Dean, Martin, and Streiner studied the use of sexually arousing slides with twenty-eight male students from an introductory psychology course. They measured the galvanic skin response (GSR) to the slides. They used red and yellow lights to condition the subjects to respond to slides of seminude or nude females from men's magazines. The researchers found that the sexually arousing slides could serve to maintain a GSR in a classical conditioning paradigm.[95]

Consult J. Mann's "Experimental Induction of Human Sexual Arousal, a 1970 Pornography Commission Technical Report, for other early methods of measuring sexual arousal.[96] Marvin Zuckerman's "Physiological Measures of Sexual Arousal in the Human," also a 1970 commission Technical Report, provides summaries of more studies of this nature.[97]

In a 1970 Pornography Commission study, Byrne and Lamberth used forty-two married couples from a university as subjects for research about pornography opinions. Subjects were given various tests of feelings and assigned to one of three conditions. One condition was the photographic stimuli condition with nineteen slides showing a variety of heterosexual, homosexual, and autosexual activities. Each slide was shown for twenty seconds and rated as to how arousing it was. A second condition, the literary stimuli condition, involved nineteen short passages from books that matched the pictures in the first condition. In the third condition, the imaginary

stimuli condition, subjects were told to use their imaginations to consider sexual themes or activities that they would like and that would be in books and movies. They had twenty seconds to think about each theme and then rated the degree to which the activity or scene aroused them. The themes given the individuals matched those in the slides and literary passages.

Subjects were given a dictionary definition of pornography as "obscene or licentious; foul, disgusting or offensive; tending to produce lewd emotions" and were asked to judge whether each of the nineteen themes was pornographic or not pornographic.[98]

Interestingly, the imaginary stimuli turned out to be the most arousing to these subjects. The most arousing themes for both sectors were female masturbation, nude petting, face-to-face intercourse, cunnilingus, group sex, and fellatio. The least arousing themes were male nudity, homosexual anal intercourse, a man in undershorts, a clothed female, and a female torturing a male.

Authoritarianism was related to the number of scenes found to be pornographic, and people who attended church weekly found more of the themes to be pornographic than any other group. Feelings of disgust were related to the number of themes judged pornographic for both sexes. For females the number of themes found pornographic related to feelings of nausea and anger as well. These subjects found homosexual anal intercourse, homosexual fellatio, homosexual cunnilingus, a male torturing a female, and group sex to be the most pornographic themes. Some themes were seen as pornographic but not sexually arousing. These included torture, homosexual anal intercourse, and homosexual fellatio.

Byrne and Lamberth did not find significant sex differences in beliefs that pornography should or should not be restricted. They did find restrictive attitudes to be related to feelings of disgust, authoritarianism, religious preference, and frequency of church attendance. They did not find effects on these people's sexual behavior that could be attributed to the experiment, with some individual exceptions.

The authors emphasize that conclusions drawn from this study should be considered "tentative" and "evaluated cautiously." (In a very sexist finding, these researchers commented that "it may be hypothesized that women's sexual behavior is affected by erotic stimuli for emotional reasons while men are affected by cognitive intellective variables.") They found that specific sexual themes were different in their arousal qualities. They also found that individual judgments about what is pornographic seem to be based on a negative response to the stimuli, which turns into a desire to legally restrict such stimuli.[99]

Schill and Chapin found that males who chose to read "erotic" material while waiting for an experiment to begin had less sex guilt than males who avoided that material and read the nonerotic material instead.[100]

Check reports on Canadian men who viewed and evaluated sexually explicit videotapes. The evaluations of this group of 117 men indicated that they knew the difference between erotica or affectionate prosocial/realistic sex and violent/degrading pornography. Three types of sexually explicit material were used. The first was sexually violent pornography, which included scenes of beatings, rape, and other forms of physical abuse of and forced sex with women. The women were always shown as enjoying the violence. The second type of material did not contain overt physical violence but portrayed sex as highly dehumanizing and degrading to the women. The third type of material was what is more commonly known as erotica. This was sexually explicit material, but there was no degradation, violence, or abuse of either partner. The participants chose to engage in sex and shared pleasure with mutual respect for each other's needs and wishes.

The men studied rated all three types of videos as equally sexually exciting, arousing, and stimulating. This, Check says, is contrary to the belief that men need sexual degradation and violence to become sexually aroused. (It is interesting, however, that these men were aroused by sexually violent portrayals.) The men found the sexually violent and degrading nonviolent pornography to be more obscene than the erotica. They also found the erotica to be of greater educational value and more realistic. They recognized the differences in content, rating the violent pornography as most aggressive and the erotica as nonaggressive. They also found the erotica to be more nondegrading and affectionate and the violent and degrading pornography to be equally lacking in affection and degrading. They liked the men as persons more in the erotic materials than in the degrading or violent materials. And they rated the women in the degrading and violent pornography as less willing and experiencing less pleasure and more pain than the women in the erotica.

While nearly a quarter of the men thought no one should be allowed to see degrading and violent pornography, less than 3 percent thought that no one should be allowed to see erotica. Thirty-one percent of the men felt erotica should be made available to anyone over age fourteen, while only 17 percent thought degrading pornography should be that available and 15 percent thought violent pornography should be that available. These men, Check empha-

sizes, were evaluating material they had actually seen rather than responding to telephone interview polls.

About half of the men in the study were regular (defined as once a month or more) consumers of pornography.

> Finally both the violent and the degrading pornography was found to create feelings of anxiety, hostility and depression in the viewers. In contrast the erotica did not create any negative feelings in the viewers. These aggressive feelings following exposure to violent and degrading pornography have important implications since it is exactly these feelings which are frequently the precursors of violent acts.[101]

Ray and Thompson studied eighty-seven female subjects who were unmarried undergraduate students. Three movies were shown: a neutral film, a female masturbatory movie, and a heterosexual coital stimulus film. Each person saw only one movie. The more explicit stimuli resulted in greater galvanic skin responses.[102]

Colson studied twenty-three male students and interns at a medical center and twenty-eight male university students. The pornography used consisted of passages of thirty typewritten lines taken from books purchased at newsstands in Chicago. Two passages were about heterosexual intercourse preceded by petting and oral genital contact. In one the male was the dominant active party; in the other the female was dominant. Two other passages described sexual activities between a 9-year-old girl and her aunt. In one the aunt orally stimulated the child's sex organs. In the other the aunt persuaded the child to insert much of her forearm into the aunt's vagina to stimulate her. These passages were labeled as pedophilic. The subjects found the pedophilic passages to be much more undesirable and much more obscene than the heterosexual passages.[103]

McConaghy studied twelve male medical students. Six of them were shown a travelogue-type film with ten moving sequences of orange circles followed by nude women, alternated at one-minute intervals with ten sequences of blue triangles followed by nude males. The subjects then saw a similar series of circles, triangles, and nudes as still slide pictures. The other six students were shown the slides first and then the film. The nudes in the film were not sexually provocative. Changes in the men's penile volumes were recorded by a penile plethysmographic technique. The penile volume increases of these heterosexual men to the moving pictures of nude women was greater than that to the still pictures. There was a less marked difference in penile volume for the nude males, and the penile responses to the nude women were significantly greater than to the nude males.[104]

Galbraith studied eighty-four male introductory psychology students. He measured their sex guilt, then showed them a board with twenty-seven photos of seminude and nude "girls" clipped from magazines pasted on it. They were asked to identify which of the "girls" would most likely fit various stereotypes, such as most and least sexually appealing, most likely to be a virgin or a nymphomaniac, and most likely to be a prostitute or a lesbian. They also took a word association test dealing with sexual words. Galbraith found that exposure to sexual stimulation created a "significant increment in the overt sexual responsivity of low sex guilt Ss but had no significant effect upon the overt responsivity of high sex guilt Ss."[105]

Mavissakalian et al. tested six homosexual males who were seeking treatment or evaluation at a medical center for their patterns of sexual arousal and six male heterosexual medical student volunteers for sexual arousal using a penile transducer and subjective reports of arousal. Two 2-minute black-and-white videotapes of each of the following were used as stimuli:

A young, single, nude adult female engaged in sexually provocative behavior such as "sliding from a sofa down to the floor, caressing thighs and breasts, looking invitingly at the camera, etc."[106]

Lesbian activities of two female adults engaging in explicit behavior such as mutual masturbation, cunnilingus and "general body pressure simulating intercourse, etc."[107]

An adult male and female engaged in various coital sexual intercourse positions

Two adult males involved in explicit homosexual behavior such as anal intercourse and fellatio

The same eight clips were shown to the subjects twice, seven days apart. Both the penile erection arousal measure and subjective (self-reported) arousal measures showed that both heterosexual and homosexual males were almost equally aroused by the heterosexual couple stimuli. The researchers conclude that this was probably due to "the presence of both a man and woman in this stimulus condition, allowing the subject to focus on the figure of his preference." And, they say, "This clearly shows that films of heterosexual intercourse have no usefulness in assessing sexual preference."[108]

The homosexual males were most highly aroused by the homosexual (male) couple scenes, while the heterosexual males found these stimuli to be the least

arousing and most unpleasant. Yet the most highly arousing stimuli for the heterosexual men were the lesbian scenes (which were not very arousing to the homosexual men). In a conclusion that defies logic, the researchers state that this "suggests that the lesbian stimuli are processed as genuine heterosexual cues by males."[109]

A close relationship was found between the physiological and subjective measures of sexual arousal. The researchers caution that subjective reports can be "influenced by instructions or expectancy." They speculate that overestimation or underestimation of sexual response in subjective reports might result from a subject's attitude toward the particular stimulus. The results also refute the common belief that homosexual males have an aversion toward female bodies and female genitalia.[110]

Love, Sloan, and Schmidt hypothesized that high sex guilt subjects would spend significantly different amounts of time exposing themselves to "erotic" slides and have significantly different attitudes toward the material than low sex guilt subjects. They used forty-one male introductory psychology students. (The sexist nature of this study is indicated by their comment that because most of the pornography market is aimed at males, "it was not deemed appropriate to include females in the sample.") Eighteen black-and-white slides of material varying from "pretty girls in bikinis" to graphic portrayals of heterosexual activity were used as stimuli. The slides were rated on the basis of attractiveness, disgust, obscenity, and artistic value. While the high sex guilt subjects did not significantly change slide viewing time as a function of obscenity ratings of the slides, the low sex guilt subjects increased viewing time as obscenity of the slides increased. The high and, to a lesser extent, moderate sex guilt subjects tried to avoid arousal of sex guilt by minimizing their exposure to the stimuli. The low sex guilt subjects rated the slides as less disgusting and obscene than the other group.[111]

Barr and Blaszczynski examined the question of whether homosexual and transsexual males differed in their responses to "erotic" films. Forty male transsexuals, forty-four male homosexuals, and sixty heterosexual male university students were tested. Penile volume changes were measured by pressure transducers. Skin resistance and heart rate also were measured. Ten female sequences alternating with ten male sequences were used. These were of partially clothed or nude young adults, each lasting ten seconds. They were set in a travelogue-type film.

The results showed that the three subject groups responded to the nonpreferred sex with penile volume decreases. The authors conclude that there was no strong relationship between penile volume and galvanic skin responses to the preferred sex. The heterosexual and homosexual patients showed significantly greater galvanic skin responses to the preferred sex. Transsexual patients tended to show greater skin responses to females. The authors point out, however, that galvanic skin responses can be due to other than sexual causes.[112]

Brown, Amoroso, and Ware studied the behavioral effects of watching pornography. Subjects were fifty-six male university students who responded to an ad in a campus newspaper. Their sexual attitudes and behavior were tested. A few weeks later, they were shown fifteen color slides of a couple engaged in masturbation and a variety of heterosexual activities. Some subjects saw these alone and others were observed by graduate students, which was called the audience condition. They completed questionnaires concerning their reactions to the slides and indicated their sexual activity during the week preceding the viewing. Later they were asked about sexual behavior on the day of viewing and during the following six days.

While 77 percent described the experience as enjoyable and 52 percent reported being sexually aroused, 21 percent of the subjects said they were disgusted by the slides. More than half (60 percent) said they had used their imagination to add to the slides, and 21 percent said they had tried to control their arousal. Twenty-nine percent reported having seen activities in the slides that were new to them and that they would like to try. Most of these were oral genital activity and heterosexual anal intercourse. The figures for sexual activities were very similar for the weeks before and after viewing the slides, although those who saw them in the alone condition reported more changes (either increases or decreases) in sexual activity. There was an increase in masturbation on the day the slides were viewed relative to the prior day or the average for the prior week. There was some reason to believe that those whose behavior changed most were those who had engaged in the least sexual behavior to start with.[113]

Wincze, Hoon, and Hoon studied six sexually experienced women who all had some experience with pornography and were not having current sexual problems. They measured groin and breast temperatures, cognitive sexual arousal, and vaginal capillary engorgement. Subjects were shown a videotape with the word *relax* for two minutes, a one-minute travelogue, and then seventeen different scenes of sexual content, including mild heterosexual involvement to heterosexual intercourse, group sex, and a single homosexual scene. All the subjects had a high correlation between groin and breast temperature

measures, and all but one had a positive significant correlation between the vaginal and cognitive measures. Using the vaginal measure, all the subjects were most aroused during the group sex and oral sex scenes. These subjects did not report arousal to the group sex scene during the debriefing period. Again, this contrasts with the physiological measure, and the researchers state that this could be based on the cultural taboo placed on group sex.[114]

Fehr and Schulman studied twelve female undergraduate students. It is not clear exactly what the sexual content of the passages used in this study was. The researchers conclude, however, that the pleasurable passage was significantly more sexually stimulating, less anxiety provoking, less disgusting, and less guilt provoking than the unpleasurable passage.[115]

Dermer and Pyszczynski studied fifty-one male undergraduates who reported heterosexual romantic involvement. They read either a description of the courtship and mating behavior of heron gulls or an explicit account of the sexual fantasies and behaviors of a college woman, which included descriptions of masturbation, cunnilingus, fellatio, and mutual fondling. Exposure to the erotic passage increased scores on several components of love, intimacy, caring, and attachment.

In a second study, sixty-four men and seventy-seven women completed surveys in exchange for psychology course credit. The results showed that the men were more likely to express love-type statements to their loved ones when sexually aroused than when not and that the women were more likely to reinforce a suitor for expressing loving statements than for expressing liking statements.[116]

Fisher and Byrne studied thirty-one male and thirty-one female unmarried university students taking an abnormal psychology class. The subjects saw a ten-minute film in which a male and female undressed, had manual genital contact, fellatio, and cunnilingus, and reached orgasm. The erotophobes had more negative affective reactions than the erotophiles. The erotophobes increased their sexual activity after exposure to the film to a greater extent than the erotophiles, whose sexual behavior did not change appreciably. For the erotophobes, heterosexual activities such as petting and necking, dreaming about sex, and talking and thinking about it increased, but masturbation did not. This brought the erotophobes' sexual activity equal to that of the erotophiles. The researchers conclude that the results highlighted the importance of considering individual differences in responses to pornography.[117]

Mosher and O'Grady studied 215 male undergraduates enrolled in introductory psychology courses. They were randomly assigned to three film conditions—a masturbation film involving a male, a film of two men engaged in homosexual relations, and a film of a woman and a man engaged in heterosexual relations. The color films were silent and lasted ten minutes each.

The heterosexual film resulted in more subjective sexual arousal than either of the other films, although significantly more arousal was reported in response to the homosexuality film than to the masturbation film. The homosexuality film also resulted in more negative affects of anger, shame, disgust, and guilt than the male masturbation film.[118]

Abramson and Mosher studied the use of pornography to induce masturbatory fantasies. They used 96 male and 102 female undergraduate introductory psychology students as subjects. The ten-minute films showed either a man or a woman in similar physical settings exhibiting similar behaviors. They were alone on a bed reading a book, arose and undressed, then fondled their bodies and began to masturbate. Masturbation occurred in sitting and lying positions until ejaculation or orgasm took place. Subjects were then asked to construct stories of masturbation using the film as a stimulus. While the women who saw the film of the woman masturbating wrote fantasies that delineated erotic images, the men who saw the film of the man masturbating did not give erotic details. This, the researchers state, shows that the women had a positive projective identification with the same sex person in the film, while the men had a negative projective identification with the same sex person.[119]

In another study, Mosher and Abramson looked at sexual arousal in response to masturbation films. It appears that they may have used the same subjects and the same films in this experiment as in the other one. The only significant effect was that the females reported significantly more anxiety than the males after viewing the masturbation films. The males reported their highest level of depression, guilt, disgust, and shame after viewing the male masturbation film. The females reported slightly but insignificantly more negative responses to the female masturbation film as opposed to the male film. The males had their highest arousal in response to the female masturbation film, while the females were almost equally responsive to both films.[120]

Abramson et al. studied the effects of experimenters on responses to pornography. Eighty-nine single female undergraduates and fifty-three single male undergraduates were used as subjects. There were two male and two female experimenters. Their attire and manner of interacting with the subjects were controlled. While one of each sex represented a formal personality style, the other two represented an informal style. The pornography used was a film of heterosexual intercourse. The results showed that the males who had an informal experimenter of either sex had significantly greater genital sensations to the pornographic stimuli. The women who had an informal male experimenter were made more anxious by the experimenter. The women reported significantly higher affective sexual arousal to the films than did the males. Those who had the informal experimenters rated the film as significantly more attractive than those who had the formal experimenters, except that females who had a formal female experimenter rated the male actor's physique as more attractive.[121]

Mosher and Greenberg studied female responses to pornography. Subjects were seventy-two introductory psychology students. An erotic passage taken from a book described the seduction of a virginal girl by a young man. These researchers describe this as highly erotic and hypothesized that it would provide the females with a heroine to identify with. (Other researchers have described this book as being sexually exploitive of the girl involved.) An academically oriented passage was used as the neutral condition. Those who read the erotic passage reported greater sexual arousal than those who read the academic passage. The erotic passage also increased the subjects' ultimate feelings of sadness.[122]

Pawlowski studied seventy-two college volunteers who were divided into a variety of sex anxiety groups. Females were much more reluctant to volunteer for this study, with male volunteers outnumbering them four to one. Two films were used, both with explicit heterosexual behavior. While one was about a romantic relationship between a man and woman; the other showed two couples engaging in intercourse in a variety of "acrobatic" positions. Each was ten minutes long. Pawlowski did not find any significant differences in ratings by the groups based on high, medium, and low anxiety.[123]

Malamuth and Check used seventy-seven and sixty-six female students as subjects. They constructed eight versions of an "erotic" story of about a thousand words each. The stories varied in content in that some involved consent, and others did not; some involved pain, and others did not; and some involved a woman's arousal, while other involved a woman's disgust. The subjects rated themselves on a sexual arousal scale containing 11 points. Some of the stories used involved rape depictions.

The researchers found that depictions of women experiencing sexual arousal were more arousing than those that showed women's disgust. They conclude that if a woman is perceived as disgusted by the sexual act, viewers' sexual arousal might be inhibited regardless of whether there were other indications that she might give her consent. However, if the woman is shown as sexually aroused, even if there is a lack of consent, pain, or violence, those inhibitors may have no effect.[124]

Schill, Van Tuinen, and Doty studied forty-two male undergraduates in introductory psychology. They divided the subjects into groups of high and low sex guilt. The stimuli used were eight typewritten pages of "erotic" passages taken from paperback novels. Each page had three passages that dealt with themes of oral sex, intercourse, seduction, and group sex in vivid and explicit detail. After reading each page, subjects rated their feelings of sexual arousal, disgust, guilt, anger, anxiety, boredom, and entertainment. The results showed that both groups had initial moderate levels of sexual arousal, which declined as they read additional passages. Thus, the position that sex guilt might have a differential effect was not supported. As the subjects read more of the pornography, they became less entertained, more bored, slightly more angry, less guilty, and less anxious. High guilt subjects had a bit more negative experience.

In a second study, male undergraduates in psychology were used. Again they were divided into high and low sex guilt categories. Both groups reread the same "erotic" passage for eight trials. Subjects experienced moderate initial arousal, which decreased to slight arousal by the fourth trial. After reading the passage eight times, subjects were less entertained and less anxious. In this case, researchers did find a significant interaction of sex guilt with boredom, disgust, and anger.[125]

Stock and Geer studied forty-eight female undergraduates. Physiological measures were taken by a vaginal photoplethysmograph. The first procedure involved having the women create a sexual fantasy in their own minds for five minutes. After a five-minute baseline rest period, they were exposed to a ten-minute pornographic tape that involved a heterosexual encounter including undressing, foreplay, oral genital sex, and intercourse. Both the fantasy and the taped conditions resulted in genital changes that showed sexual arousal in most of the women. The erotic taped condition resulted in larger vaginal responses than did the fantasy.[126]

Eisenman studied eighty college students. One of their tasks was to write as many sexual fantasies as they could during a twenty-minute period. Some were read a brief description from a sex novel, while others were not. The subjects were told that there was nothing wrong with having antisocial elements in their fantasies. The persons who were provided with an example of a sex fantasy and given a brief

discussion of fantasy wrote an average of 4.25 fantasies compared to an average of 2 fantasies by the subjects without this experience. The persons in the fantasy condition wrote more than twice as many words in their fantasies as those who were not in that condition.[127]

Henson, Rubin, and Henson studied vaginal blood volume and labial responses to visual and other stimuli. These researchers point out that only one physiological change, genital vasocongestion, occurs exclusively because of sexual stimulation in women. The visible changes that occur include changes in color and increases in size of the external genitalia and vaginal barrel.

The subjects in this experiment were five women ages 26 to 33 who had prior experience with one or both of the genital measurements used. The measurements used were the surface thermistor, which records changes in the temperature of the labia minora, and the vaginal photoplethysmograph, which measures changes in pulse pressure amplitude in the vaginal wall or in pooled blood volume. Five women who had participated in a prior study involving genital measurements declined to participate in this study.

Each of the five subjects was involved in two experimental sessions separated by at least one month. In the first session, a color videotape lasting around eleven minutes was used as the erotic stimulus. (The content of the tape was not described.) In the second session, the women sexually stimulated themselves by manual manipulation. They determined the duration of that time and reported whether or not they had experienced an orgasm or wanted to stop the stimulation. During each session, the genital devices were attached by the subjects. Each genital measure was recorded at six-second intervals. Both types of physiological measurement showed increases in each of the five women during the "erotic" film. Both also showed increases during the periods of manual self-stimulation. Following orgasm in the manual stimulation, the vaginal blood volume decreased dramatically; the labial measure did not change during the orgasm but decreased rapidly soon after.[128]

Rubin et al. studied the relationship between the level of testosterone in men and their penile responses to "erotic stimuli." Subjects were six adult male heterosexual volunteers, ages 25 to 44, four of whom were married, each of whom reported drinking alcohol daily, and three of whom reported regular use of marijuana. Changes in penile circumference were measured by a mercury in rubber strain gauge transducer. Color videotapes of two "erotic" films showing a variety of heterosexual behaviors were used as the erotic stimuli. (The content was not described.) Subjects were allowed to try out the transducer and sample erotic stimuli to determine whether they wanted to continue to participate. This also allowed baseline information about penile circumference to be determined.

Subjects participated in six experimental sessions at three- to six-day intervals. Plasma was taken from the subjects immediately prior to their entering the experimental rooms. They were then told to relax and enjoy the tape. The same tape was used during each session. Five of the six developed rather high levels of sexual arousal during each of the sessions. The other person developed smaller increments of erectile response. The researchers found a "significant inverse relationship across subjects between testosterone levels and reported frequency of orgasm during the 72-hour period preceding each experimental session." They conclude that sexual arousability and arousal as measured by the penile response are "directly influenced by fluctuations in the levels of indogenous testosterone at least in apparently healthy sexually functional men." Yet they found that for most of the subjects, a certain level of testosterone on a specific day did not predict the magnitude of penile erection. They state that factors other than testosterone concentrations have a major influence on

"normal" men's sexual responsivity. One such factor is prior sexual activity.[129]

Kelley and Musialowski studied twenty-eight female and twenty-eight male undergraduate introductory psychology students. In their first session, the students responded to the Byrne Sexual Opinion Survey, which tests "affective" reactions to topics dealing with sex. After viewing a film, they responded to a scale of affective and arousal responses.

The subjects then viewed an eleven-minute color film of heterosexual genital intercourse with several positions at twenty-four-hour intervals on four consecutive weekdays in groups of three or four members of the same sex. The experimenter also was of the same sex. On the fifth day, the subjects saw a same-length color film of either (1) the same two actors in nude petting and oral genital sexual acts (not clear whether fellatio or cunnilingus) or (2) a different heterosexual couple in various acts of genital intercourse.

By the third day, the subjects in each group expressed more "negative affect" about the film than in the first session. The negative affect significantly dissipated following the film change. There were no significant differences between groups, except that the erotophobes showed more negative affect and less positive affect at the fourth session in both the same and different actor film conditions.[130]

THERAPEUTIC USES OF PORNOGRAPHY (RECONDITIONING)

This research generally postulates and concludes that exposure to socially acceptable but untried sexual practices through pornography (or sex education materials, more likely) increased patients' sex satisfaction abilities. Researchers have found that pornography is a stimulus in fantasy production in patients and have tested for the role of fantasy in treating sexual deviations. To date research suggests that exposure to nondeviant sexual practices through pornography can successfully recondition some sexual deviants to sexually appropriate practices. The opposite also must be true—but would be unethical to test—that nondeviant persons could be conditioned to practice deviant sexual behavior by being exposed to pornography, perhaps even through accidental or self-chosen exposure (as opposed to exposure in therapy).

Check and Malamuth write about the application of social learning theory as it applies to the feminist view to studies of pornography and sexual aggression. The social learning theory partly involves how

behavior is acquired or affected by observing others and modeling what they do.

> Social learning theorists would predict that modeling influences in pornography can (a) teach novel modes of sexual behavior, (b) serve to facilitate already learned socially acceptable forms of sexual behavior and (c) strengthen or weaken inhibitions over previously learned and socially unacceptable forms of sexual behavior.[131]

Under the social learning theory, it would be possible for some types of pornography to have antisocial effects and other types to have prosocial effects. Check and Malamuth summarize some of the available research from that perspective. They conclude that the social learning theory, as applied to feminist analysis, is very useful in looking at the pornography research.

Byrne studied the imagery of sex. He notes that the primary source of information about sex seems to be same age friends and pornography as a supplemental source material. Individual differences and responses to pornography can be based on religious behavior, liberalism versus conservatism, sex guilt, authoritarianism, and sex differences. For example, he notes some documentation showing female uninterest in stimuli that males consider "erotic" and male and female differences in the types of material which is arousing. He suggests that females might have been taught to avoid sexual excitement in order to protect themselves against male advances. They might thus "equate the arousing properties of sexual imagery with danger."

At the time of his study (1977), Byrne believed it was premature to conclude that erotica could have no "ill" behavioral effects. He notes, for example, that many studies dealt with emotionally adjusted, well-educated, middle-class volunteers and that mal-adjusted, uneducated, low socioeconomic people were not tested, which might have produced different results. He also notes that self-reports by sex offenders might not be accurate and that these offenders might in fact have spent their lives saturated with "erotica" but feel motivated to conceal this from researchers in order to present a socially acceptable image.[132]

Byrne supports the safety-valve theory, accepting the idea that masturbation provoked by erotica could be an effective deterrent to acting out sexually antisocial acts. He also suggests that people who cannot attract sexual partners could live partially satisfied lives with the help of pornography and masturbation. Lastly, he suggests that unhappy spouses could attain satisfaction by imagining forbidden acts or more desirable partners. (As we now know from some victim data, this sort of satisfaction simply is not the case. What happens in contemporary times is that some people who are exposed to the beautiful people and bizarre acts of pornography are no longer satisfied with their sex partners and want to try out these acts.)

Byrne creates a scenario in which erotic imagery could have an effect. For example, he says that a female who has not engaged in fellatio, becomes anxious even thinking about it, and has no desire to change her behavioral attitudes might be exposed through books, movies, and other media to the idea that fellatio is pleasurable and acceptable in hetero-sexual relationships. Her attitudes might then change through desensitization and familiarization. He notes that Zajonc suggested that repeated exposure to a stimulus results in more favorable attitudes toward that stimulus. Through this process, each time the fellatio topic came up, the woman would be less anxious. The expected result would be a more favorable evaluation of fellatio. Once such an attitude

shift has occurred, thoughts of it could occur during coitus or masturbation. If the idea of fellatio has become pleasurable and exciting, there might be an inclination to try it out in real life. Therefore, the erotic images seen by the woman could become translated into behavior.

Byrne concludes that

> for the population as a whole . . . the net long range result of sexual explicitness should be (1) more favorable attitudes toward the depicted activities, (2) an increase in tolerance for the activities and in private fantasies about the activities and (3) an increase in the frequency of the activities themselves.[133]

The effects could be positive in having people derive more joy from a variety of sex practices, but they also could be negative if exposure to certain images led to flagellation, pederasty (sexual molestation of male children), or rape, Byrne notes. Thus, some erotic activities should not be encouraged. (Byrne also argues that there is "no evidence linking sex crimes to exposure to erotica except some indications of a negative effect."[134] It should be noted that Byrne was one of the 1970 Pornography Commission researchers.

Abel and Blanchard write about the role of fantasy in treating sexual deviation. They found numerous references to "the high concordance between presence of deviant fantasies and occurrence of deviant behavior." This, they say, suggests that fantasy might be a precursor to deviant behavior. They also found that deviants who use deviant fantasies during their masturbation exhibited a large amount of deviant behavior. (For the purposes of this book, it is important to consider what role pornography plays in creating the deviant fantasies that lead to such behavior.) The therapies using explicit sexual materials are thus used to alter deviant sexual fantasies. This involves getting people to switch their fantasies from deviant activities to more normal activities. Yet these researchers conclude that although the case reports indicated the effectiveness of such methods, no controlled study had "adequately substantiated fantasy alteration as the relevant variable leading to alteration of sexual behavior patterns."[135]

Bjorksten deals with the use of sexually graphic material in treating sexual disorders. He mentions the secretive nature of sexuality and societal thinking that information about sex is dirty. Many professionals have the same attitudes. Professionals, he says, should at least have witnessed various sexual behaviors before they consider "the psychodynamics of people who engage in those behaviors." He believes that sexually explicit materials can be used therapeutically to educate and desensitize patients.[136]

The Division of Family Study of the University of Pennsylvania Department of Psychiatry uses sexually graphic material as an adjunct to sex therapy. Workers there never use it alone for treatment of any "marital unit which suffers from a sexual dysfunction."[137]

Bjorksten comments on problems with studies of the effects of pornography. He notes that the stimulus varies from study to study, the people studied are typically not representative of the population, few longitudinal studies have been done considering the effects of pornography, and no studies have been done to examine the effects of pornography on sexually dysfunctional couples. He also questions whether it is the pornography or the experimental study that causes the effect.

Bjorksten notes that people's responses to pornography depend on many factors, including the stimulus (duration and reality of the materials), the context, and the individual's personality, need state, socialization, and state of consciousness. He suggests, for example, that a person may respond differently to pornography if he views it with his wife, mother, sister or brother, close male friend, or a stranger. He also suggests that those with high sex guilt would tend to rate films as more pornographic than those with lower guilt and would also see them as more disgusting than enjoyable. He noted that persons with low sex guilt tend to be sexually callous toward women, more exploitive, and more likely to use a forceful technique to gain intercourse.

Bjorksten found the following therapeutic uses for sexually graphic material:

1. *Attitude reevaluation.* Such material is useful to keep people focused on an uncomfortable subject such as sex and possibly to make them aware of attitudes they were not aware of before.

2. *Education.* Such materials can provide sex information more quickly than an explanation and often more accurately. They can be used to teach patients about their anatomy and about sexual techniques. (Here again Bjorksten appears to be talking about films produced by educational institutes for educational purposes.) As a result of seeing such "erotica," couples can develop vocabularies about sexual matters and feel they have permission to enjoy sex. It also provides characters after whom viewers can model themselves. (We note that a modeling effect would be bad if sexually violent or dangerous materials were shown.)

3. *Fantasy building.* Many people are prohibited from having sexual fantasies and thoughts and thus lack such fantasies. Bjorksten states that it is "impossible for a person to have fantasies about things to which he has never been exposed."[138]

4. *Group therapy.* Sexually graphic materials can be used to trigger discussions about sex during group sessions. This can help with group cohesiveness.

5. *Behavior therapy.* Sexually explicit materials can be used in behavior therapy such as aversive conditioning and desensitization. The purpose of aversive conditioning is to change a person's sexual patterns if the person uses "undesirable sex objects." These might include fetish objects and children, among others. In aversive conditioning, explicit sexual pictures that represent the person's "sexual object are paired with some noxious stimulus" so that the person begins to associate an unpleasant feeling with the image of that sex object. Unpleasant stimuli used have included things such as electric shocks and obnoxious odors. Desensitization is a behavior therapy technique in which a person is gradually exposed to things he or she fears "while he is in a state of deep muscular relaxation." For example, a homosexual patient might be gradually exposed to pictures of nude females. According to Bjorksten, when desensitization occurs, one would expect it to alter "(1) anxieties about sexual behaviors; (2) the person's disgust with certain sexual fantasies or behaviors; and (3) anxieties about a person's self image." Because of this feeling change, a person's attitudes might change to make him or her more open to a variety of sexual "values."[139]

According to Bjorksten, the method used to expose people to sexually explicit materials must depend on the practitioner's treatment goals. Atmosphere, setting, whether there is musical accompaniment, and seating arrangement, can all have an impact on the degree and manner in which an audience will respond to the stimuli.

One method of presentation is the mass presentation, which involves a great deal of exposure in a short amount of time. This aims at exhausting people and, in turn, wearing down their anxiety responses. After mass presentations of graphic sexual materials, "the participants [often] experience extreme fatigue and are not surprised or anxious at seeing almost any kind of erotica." They become much more able to discuss sexual topics freely, more receptive to accurate information about sexual matters, and less likely to distort facts because of their anxiety. Bjorksten claims that no harmful effects have been reported from such programs. He describes a number of models that have been used around the nation. Bjorksten says that other effects might include dramatically increased communication between married couples, increased knowledge about sex, and decreased beliefs in myths concerning sex. At page 181 he does note that a number of participants in these types of experiments became acutely upset because they failed to live up to the behaviors, performance, and relationships shown in the films. Interestingly, he states that there have been fewer than five "casualties" (to the best of his knowledge) and thus concludes that these workshops are not harmful to couples in marital therapy. Nowhere does he explain what these so-called casualties were or how many couples in all participated in the programs.[140]

In addition to sexually explicit materials, these types of workshops typically include group discussions, sex education, meetings between each couple and the workshop leader(s), and practice sessions (for example, participants might go to their rooms, undress, and discuss experiences with their partners). Obviously, these conditions do not represent those of the typical pornographic film viewer, who is not exposed to the pros and cons of he or she has seen. According to Bjorksten, these types of treatments seem to work best with problems such as situational orgasmic dysfunction and premature ejaculation. He concludes that desensitization can be produced by showing several hours of sexually explicit material in one day. He expresses some concern that, at least with some types of people, mass exposure might cause such intense reactions that the people would try to avoid the situation by leaving, sticking to old attitudes, or not paying attention. In addition, these presentations might not be very interesting to people who have already had a great deal of exposure to such material, and they would require more intense presentations of the material.

A second method of presentation is the spaced presentation. Here sexually explicit materials are used only occasionally or there is an extended period of time between exposures. This type of presentation might be used to educate people about their anatomy and various sexual techniques. Bjorksten says that it is important for the couple's therapist to expose them to these materials. This can, however, create problems with what as known as transference. For example, this reaction, which occurs between a patient and a therapist, could result in a relationship that is more sexualized, and the patient might perceive the therapist as the perfect partner and wish that he or she had the therapist for a partner instead of his or her spouse. This feeling can cause the person's spouse to become jealous, depressed, or angry.

A therapist also must guard against having vicarious sexual relationships with patients by use of the sexually graphic material if he or she is attracted to one of the partners. Similarly, such materials should not be used by a therapist who dislikes one partner of a couple to try to encourage performance anxiety in that person. Bjorksten urges therapists to remember that it is normal for people to get aroused by these materials. They should not be concerned if they experience such arousal.

Bjorksten lists a variety of reactions to "erotic films," ranging from people claiming to have seen it all before, to trying to protect other group members from the things they are seeing, to claiming that what is being portrayed can't be real because it is not what they do.[141] He suggests that use of sexually explicit material might be helpful when patients are anxious about sexual behaviors, fantasies (or a lack of fantasies), or inhibitions about discussing sex; when one's sexual attitudes are overly restrictive; when someone is ignorant about sex; when there is confusion about sexual identity or unrealistic expectations of one's sexual partner or oneself; and when a couple desires sexual enrichment within marriage. (We note that some of these reasons for using sexually explicit material in therapy could actually be problems caused by pornography—for example, confusion about sexual identity and unrealistic sexual performance expectations.)

Bjorksten notes that people who work with sexually explicit materials and the research literature generally conclude that exposure to such material is very safe. However, he also notes three major "contraindications" to using such material. The first is psychosis, usually organic brain syndromes and schizophrenia. Here there is a concern with precipitating an acute episode of schizophrenia or feeding into a delusional system. Second, there is concern about severe depression being accompanied by feelings of inadequate performance. Seeing "beautiful people" in the films having a "beautiful relationship" could make a person feel more inadequate and could be harmful to someone who is already severely depressed. Third, persons who have strong moral opposition to sexually explicit materials should not be included in groups in which they are "almost by definition" considered deviants.[142] (We would again caution that the material that seems to be the subject of articles on the use of sexually explicit material in therapy is of a sexually educational and erotic nature rather than the mass market pornography of today.)

Abel, Blanchard, and Becker detail the use of sexually explicit stimuli in attempts to change patterns of rapists' sexual arousal. One of the components of such treatment is attempting to change rapists' arousal patterns so that they become aroused by adult females and not aroused to rape stimuli. The researchers note that aversion suppression methods such as electrical aversion, odor aversion, chemical aversion, and biofeedback assisted suppression, as well as covert sensitization, are used to treat excessive arousal to rape stimuli. The lack of arousal to nonrape sexual stimuli is treated by generating arousal to nonrape cues through techniques such as masturbatory conditioning, exposure, fading (fading in pictures of another type of stimuli during periods of sexual arousal to the first type of stimuli), and systematic desensitization.

The researchers note the unreliability of rapists' self-reports. For example, one set of rapists reported little sexual arousal to rape scenes. They emphasize the need to measure in the laboratory excessive erections to descriptions of rape. They state that "all rapists, sadists and pedophiles must have excessive deviant arousal."[143]

Abel, Blanchard, and Becker found problems with penile volume measures. For example, expressing results as rank order scores makes the data difficult to interpret, since only the relative arousal of different stimuli is shown. Thus, results from different laboratories cannot be compared unless similar stimuli were used. A second problem with the devices is their cost. Another problem is in interpreting the relevance of the very small erection responses measured by the device. Other important considerations in measuring the sexual arousal of rapists are what instructions to give the patients during the tests and what stimuli to use. There is also the issue of using appropriate control groups. The authors review numerous other studies dealing with various techniques.

As the researchers note, sexual arousal can be caused by having a patient develop internal fantasies, listen to oral presentations of "erotic scenes," read such passages, view pictures or slides of explicit material, watch movies or videotapes of sexual acts, and actually carry out an act, such as having an exhibitionist expose himself to a female technician. The authors note that ethical considerations can preclude obtaining visual stimuli of specific people (such as a specific incest victim), and in those situations audio descriptions can be used.

Importantly, the authors note (page 175) that even when sophisticated mechanical devices are used, the subjects' erections do not simply reflect responded to pornographic stimuli, but could also be strongly influenced by their fantasies and thoughts. They also note (page 176) that patients could significantly inhibit their erections to sexual stimuli. (These problems point out problems with the reliability of some of these data.)

One method used in reducing deviant sexual arousal is aversion therapy, in which arousal to depictions such as rape are associated with a noxious stimulus such as an electrical shock or a nauseous odor. It is typical in these types of treatments to use erotic or pornographic stimuli depicting deviant fantasies such as rape and more normal sexual acts such as heterosexual intercourse. The idea is to shock or punish the person for arousal to the deviant portrayals and to reward the person for arousal to the more normal sexual activities.

In the covert sensitization technique, imagined stimuli (the patient's fantasies of his or her deviant behavior) are paired with scenes that the subject considers aversive, such as pictures of fecal matter, vomit, or bleeding. Abel, Blanchard, and Becker conclude that aversion therapy works with sexual offenders such as rapists to reduce their deviant arousal. They give an example how covert sensitization was used with a rapist in a case study. The therapist described to the rapist various scenes (which could be considered examples of audio pornography).

For example, in one scene the rapist sees a woman and imagines her body parts, her sleeping in bed, and so on; he then goes into the woman's house and rapes her. Some graphic details such as his hitting and raping her and his erections are given. The therapist went on to describe how family members of the victim corner the rapist's wife, hold her down, and rape her as a means of revenge. The rapist is said to be incarcerated at the time. Graphic descriptions of the wife's rape are given because it is known that the rapist considers his relationship with his wife to be very important. The story ends with the wife being committed to a mental institution, and it is said that she will never recover from the rape. (It is interesting to note that some persons who promote use of the covert sensitization technique consider it to be a form of treatment to encourage rapists to fantasize scenes of rape and aggression against women.)

Abel, Blanchard, and Becker go on to describe how in "classical conditioning," elicited sexual arousal, such as seeing slides of deviant stimuli, is paired with heterosexual stimuli aimed at increasing heterosexual arousal. In a fading technique, heterosexual stimuli slides are faded in after the patient has been sexually aroused by homosexual stimuli. These researchers conclude that classical conditioning, at least when it is used with pedophiles and homosexuals, does not seem to be a reliable procedure.

Another theory is that masturbatory conditioning can be used as a treatment. This theory states that a person's arousal pattern can be altered by changing his or her masturbatory fantasies. Again various media depicting erotica or pornography can be used. As an example of masturbatory conditioning, the authors use the case of a man who was having fantasies of injuring women and masturbating to rape or sadistic fantasies frequently by age 12. He would look at sadistic magazines and think about sadistic things. Group treatment was used to try to reduce and eliminate the man's erections to the sadistic stimuli and to develop his arousal to nonsadistic sexual themes.

It should be emphasized that Abel, Blanchard, and Becker appear to be suggesting that sex education films, not commercially available pornography, be used with these various techniques.

Gillan explains that thereaputic uses of obscenity began as part of the treatment for reconditioning sexual deviants. It is also used to treat dysfunctions and is part of assessment of deviation, reconditioning, and aversion therapy.[144]

H.J. Eysenck discusses desensitization as a way of helping someone overcome his or her fears. In the case of pornography, it is a way to help people tolerate more outspoken material. This could apply to sex and violence, he suggests.

Eysenck says, "One of the most satisfactory methods of desensitization is that of modeling." He notes that violence can be induced by film modeling. Yet, he says, pornography may help potential sex criminals "sublimate" or "suppress" "libidinal impulses." He notes that while the evidence is not conclusive, he doubts that many experts would dispute the fact that sex crimes are *not* increased by the sale of "explicit sexual material" and "may well be curtailed." But, at the same time, he says that it cannot be argued that pornography has no effect on behavior. He concludes that pornography threatens society's emphasis on a permanent, secure, and loving union between a man and a woman.[145]

Quinsey, Chaplin, and Carrigan write about penile response measures of sexual arousal patterns that are used to evaluate the clinical treatment of sexual deviance. For example, behavioral treatments aimed at modifying the inappropriate sex/age preferences of child molesters commonly employ measures of penile responses to slides of persons who vary in sex and age. The use of such strategies is supported by findings that the penile responses and sex profiles differentiate child molesters from nonoffenders and relate very closely to the molesters' histories of victim choice. However, their verbal reports do not so relate. (They cite a 1975 study by Quinsey, Steinman, Bergersen, and Holmes.)

The researchers say that external validity data must be used because changes in sexual arousal patterns due to the therapy might not persist over time. Penile responses might be unrelated to the commission of new sex offenses, and sex offenders might simply fake them under treatment conditions.

They cite data that some "normal" subjects can influence their penile responses to slides in accordance with instructions to do so and that in 1978 Laws and Holman found that a child molester could fake penile responses as well. However, they note that a 1977 study by Rosen and Kepel found recidivism in a transvestite after a biofeedback program had altered his penile responses to a transvestite/exhibitionist videotape.

In their first study, Quinsey, Chaplin, and Carrigan studied thirty patients who had molested children age 13 or younger and at least five years younger than themselves. Each had received biofeedback, biofeedback plus signaled punishment, or biofeedback and/or classical conditioning. Many also had received heterosocial skills training and sex education. Five adult slides, ten child slides, and five neutral slides were used with the patients in this experiment. The adult slides used were female, male, or both, depending on the sex of the adult that the molester said he would prefer as a sex partner. The sexes and ages of the child slides were chosen for each patient to include the types of children that elicited sexual arousal in a preliminary psychophysiological assessment and the types of children he had chosen as victims. Each slide was presented for thirty seconds, and there was a sixty-second or longer period between slides to allow the patient's penile response to return to baseline. The patients in this study had been released to a less secure setting or the community for an average of 28.55 months, and during that time six had committed new offenses against children. The researchers found a relationship between the laboratory measure of sexual preference and sexual reoffending.

A second study used eighteen similar patients, all of whom showed inappropriate sex/age preferences in testing. One of the patients was diagnosed as psychotic, four as retarded, and thirteen as having a personality disorder. In each of ten sessions, each patient was shown twenty slides of thirty seconds each, separated by sixty seconds, consisting of ten adult and ten child slides. A total of one hundred slides were drawn from the same sex and age population as the assessment slides. Different slides were used for each of the first five sessions, with different orders of presentation; the slides were "randomly recombined" after each five sessions, then presented in the same order. Blue and red colored lights were used to inform a patient when his penile arousal to an adult or child slide exceeded a preselected criterion. In the biofeedback sessions, the patients were instructed to gain control of their sexual arousal by minimizing red light time and maximizing blue light time. During signal punishment sessions for thirty seconds during and after a child slide, a shock was delivered to the patient. While thirteen of the eighteen patients overall showed significant improvement, the biofeedback plus signal punishment aversion therapy was found to be more effective than the biofeedback procedure alone in altering the inappropriate sex/age preference of these child molesters. They also concluded that the biofeedback plus signal punishment appeared to be more successful than the classical conditioning aversion therapy procedure employed by Quinsey, Bergersen, and Steinman in 1976.[146]

Laws, Meyer, and Holmes used olfactory (smell) aversion with valeric acid to get their client (a 29-year-old male found to be criminally insane after attacking a woman with an ax) to "reduce his deviant sexual arousal to sadistic materials to a near zero level." Before treatment the man had an eighty-three percent erection to slides of simulated rape and bondage with knives and around eighty percent erections to slides of bondage, bondage with whips, and spanking. He had fantasies of sexual violence including bondage, whipping, torture, and forced oral, anal, and vaginal intercourse. He had masturbated to these themes for fourteen years and on occasion had acted them out. The technique used by Laws, Meyer, and Holmes was that of providing the patient with a bad smell if he became aroused by sadistic pornographic slides. They succeeded in changing the patient's arousal and behavior, and he reported after therapy was ended that on the rare occasions when sadistic fantasies entered his consciousness, he often reexperienced the choking and burning sensations that had been caused by the inhalation of the valeric acid gas.[147]

Evans studied the connection between masturbatory fantasy and sexual deviation. Evans notes that therapy based on learning theory has gained acceptance and success in treating deviant behavior. In 1965, McGuire, Carlisle, and Young had suggested that most theorists supported the hypothesis that "one—trial learning from a crucial, but often accidental, sexual experience is sufficient to explain the habit strength of the sexually deviant behavior." They offered an alternative hypothesis that the initial deviant act was important to supply the fantasy used during masturbation; therefore each time the person masturbated with the deviant activity as fantasy, the habit strength of the deviant behavior was increased. Those researchers also noted that a direct test of the hypothesis, namely attempting to change a normal person into a deviant by using appropriate masturbatory fantasy, would be unethical. An indirect test, however, could be a test of the relative ease with which people having normal and deviant masturbatory fantasies could have their sexual fantasies changed through conditioning.

Evans investigated whether exhibitionists who have normal masturbatory fantasies could be deconditioned more rapidly than exhibitionists who had exhibitionistic masturbatory fantasies. Ten subjects were used in the study, five of whom fit into each of those categories.[148]

Although slides were used in the study, the slides consisted of phrases depicting normal or deviant activities. At each session, the subjects were shown sixty slides, twenty of which were related to deviant behavior and forty of which related to normal activities. Each deviant phrase was connected to an apparatus that produced a shock after a short delay. When the subject advanced the projector to the next normal slide, the shock was terminated automatically. The amount of shock used was that which the subject had earlier indicated he could no longer tolerate. Subjects were told to imagine as vividly as possible the situation suggested by the written slides. There was an initial block of ten weekly trials, followed by booster sessions on a decreasing frequency over a two-year period.

The measure of results in this study was the number of weeks following the initiation of treatment at which the person reported no further acting out or urges to do so. For the normal fantasy group of exhibitionists, this state was reached after a median of four weeks with a range of three to five weeks. For the exhibitionist fantasy group, this state was reached after a median of twenty-four weeks with a range of four to twenty-four weeks. Therefore, Evans concludes that the deviant behavior, in terms of acting out and urges to do so, was deconditioned more rapidly in the normal fantasy group. He also notes that the hypothesis of McGuire, Carlisle, and Young—that deviant masturbatory fantasy can affect the habit strength of a person's sexual deviation— was supported.

Rachman and Hodgson studied conditioning of five subjects to give sexual responses to a picture of a pair of knee-length boots. The unconditioned stimuli in the experiment were colored slides of scantily dressed or nude women projected onto a screen. The conditioned stimulus was a pair of knee-length, fur-lined boots. Five other slides of boots or shoes were used for stimulus generalization. In the experimental condition known as forward conditioning, the boot slide was presented for thirty seconds, followed immediately by the unconditioned stimuli of the nude or scantily dressed women for ten seconds. In the control condition, called backward conditioning, the slides of the women were presented for ten seconds, followed by an interval to allow the response to subside; then the conditional slide, the boots, was presented for thirty seconds. During the backward conditioning experiment, after the subjects saw the boot slide, they reported that they had been imagining the previous slides of the women or imagining some sexual scene involving boots.

These researchers conclude it is possible to establish an experimental model of sexual fetishism. They say that their inability to evoke sexual responses to the boots under the backward conditioning supports their conclusion that they were establishing a genuine conditioned reaction in the forward conditioning procedure. They say they showed that this abnormal sexual reaction can be acquired by a process of conditioning.[149]

Feldman and MacCulloch studied application of anticipatory avoidance learning to treating homosexuality. They begin their article by reviewing the literature about treatment of sexual aberrations with behavior therapy and describe the major techniques of avoidance conditioning. The basic purpose is to alter the direction of a homosexual's interest. (We note that this study occurred in 1965 at a time when homosexuality was still considered to be a major problem.) In this study, the researchers attempted to design a technique that would reproduce the technique used by other researchers who had studied dogs. They recommend use of several different variables relevant to the conditioned avoidance.

The treatment used in this study involved electric shocks. Each patient was shown numerous slides of clothed and nude males. The patient then had to assess the degree of attractiveness of each slide. Some slides were selected and presented in a hierarchy of attractiveness. Each set usually contained eight slides and provided a wide range of homosexual behavior and stimuli. The tests started with a slide that was mildly attractive and proceeded to the more attractive slides. A hierarchy of female slides was set up in the reverse order, beginning with the most attractive. The pictures from which the slides were made came from some magazines intended for heterosexuals and some intended for homosexuals. Patients also could use pictures in their possession that they were fond of. While the researchers used pictures from patients suggesting a variety of homosexual activities, they did not use any of heterosexual activities. In some cases, pictures of males and females known to the patient in real life were used.

A level of shock that the patient said was very unpleasant was used. The basic procedure involved showing the patient a male picture and shocking him several seconds later. Patients were told that they could turn off the slide by pressing a switch and that the shock would end when the slide left the screen.

Patients were told to leave the slide on the screen for as long as they found it sexually attractive. The process was repeated with the next slide after the patient reported that his attraction to the slide had been replaced by actual dislike or indifference and after he tried to switch off the slide within one or two seconds of its appearing. While trying to increase the amount of avoidance to male stimuli, the researchers tried to decrease the amount of avoidance to female stimuli. However, they could not attempt to make the females more attractive, only to make them less unattractive to these males. The sample size used in this experiment was nineteen persons. Number of treatment sessions used varied from five to twenty-eight, with the average being fifteen.

Three of the patients failed to complete the course of treatment. There were a variety of different results with the different men. Some changed from a strong interest in homosexuality to an increased interest in heterosexuality. Some stopped practicing homosexuality, yet an equally large number showed no change in their homosexual patterns after this treatment. The researchers felt that the role of the therapist was critical in these situations.[150]

Abel et al. studied erotic cues in sexual deviations. In this study, subjects were seated in a comfortable reclining chair with their penile erection response measured by a circumferential penile transducer. The subjects began by describing an erotic experience they had had or would like to have. The experimenter checked to see which parts of the person's description created the penile responses. These were made into an audiotaped fantasy specific to that deviant's interest. For example, in one case, the researchers learned by changing the stories that the man was aroused by becoming, in his fantasy, a female and wanting intercourse but not by references to having a woman's ass. Another person was tested to find out whether he was aroused by feet, sandals, or elements of both. While he had reported being aroused by sandals, the results showed that the feet were the cause of the arousal.

The researchers found that many subjects could not identify which specific cues were erotic to them. This puts into serious question conclusions based on self-reports of how people are aroused. (Strangely, the researchers found it unethical to create videotapes or pictorial erotic cues of things such as rape, sadistic acts, and sex involving young boys or girls. They felt it was ethical, however, to create audio descriptions of these acts.) A rapist who had raped victims of both sexes and all ages was tested using such audio descriptions. The result was that the act of rape portrayed generated the sexual arousal rather than the characteristics of the victim.

The researchers caution that a major problem is caused by the ability of some subjects to voluntarily suppress erection responses. They feel that data that confirms erections could be more reliable than data showing an absence of erections to certain cues. This is because the ability to generate erections voluntarily is considered to be much lower than the ability to suppress erections. They also claim that audiotapes are less susceptible to voluntary suppression, at least among homosexuals, than visual stimuli.[151]

Reisinger studied the use of "erotic" stimuli in masturbatory training. His clients were three middle-class, middle-aged women who had been married from eight to fifteen years and had indicated a receptive attitude concerning "explicit erotic materials." These women had a common problem of being unable to achieve orgasm during sexual intercourse or by masturbation. The clients themselves selected a series of hard-core pornographic color films. The film content was limited to heterosexual activity including foreplay and explicit intercourse. The clients first viewed erotic films, choosing the ones they perceived as sexually stimulating and not "primarily aversive." Techniques for masturbation also were reviewed with them during this program.

Erotic films selected by each client were presented during masturbatory activity. The subjects were instructed to concentrate on the pleasurable experiences depicted in the films. Orgasms were reported. The clients were given similar home assignments, and they used reading materials or photos as aids to masturbation at home. Husbands also were taught to stimulate their wives to orgasm using masturbation. As a result, all of the women reported that they succeeded in masturbating to orgasm by the conclusion of the training condition. There were also notable increases in heart rate. Reisinger concludes that this study "demonstrated that use of masturbatory training with erotic film can provide an effective intervention procedure for situational orgasmic dysfunction." Follow-ups indicated that the treatment gains were maintained over time by the wives and by inclusion of their husbands. The author felt that the clients' verbal reports were reliable based on the successes of the client under the controlled clinical conditions.[153]

Wilson argues that pornography can contribute to the prevention of sexual problems. (Wilson was director of the 1970 Commission on Obscenity and Pornography.) Importantly, under Wilson's definition, pornography refers to "depictions of genitalia and sexual activity, either verbal or pictorial, that are potentially sexually arousing for substantial segments of the population." He sees the term as being synonymous with "explicit sexual material." The fact that he uses this broad definition of pornography suggests that the material he considers potentially preventive of sexual problems could include sex education and erotic materials and would not necessarily include sexually violent or humiliating materials.[154]

Wilson states that he is aware of only one major study that deals directly with the issue of whether pornography can contribute to the prevention of sexual problems. He mentions the study by Abelson and his "colleagues" in 1971. (We note that Wilson was one of Abelson's colleagues.) In that study, 2,486 adults age 21 and older from forty-eight states were interviewed about their experience with five different depictions of sexual content: a woman and man having sexual intercourse, sexual acts between people of the same sex, nudity with the sex organs exposed, mouth/sex organ contact between a man and a woman, and sexual activities including belts, whips, or spankings. Respondents were asked a series of questions about the effect reading or seeing those types of materials had on them and on others whom they knew. Wilson argues that the data from this survey were valid, that the self-reports were reasonably valid because only 5 percent said they had been less than candid in responding to the questions, and a pilot study involving a longer clinical interview found similar data.

The Wilson and Abelson et al. study found that 12 percent of the men and 8 percent of the women said that the described materials had improved the sex relationships in their marriages. Four percent of the women and 11 percent of the men said that in their own situations, these materials had caused husbands and wives to do "new things" sexually. One percent of the women and 2 percent of the men said that sexual materials had given them personal relief of sexual problems.

Wilson projects these findings to the entire adult population of the United States and estimates that more than ten million Americans have had an experience in which looking at or reading pornography improved their marital sexual relations and that more than a million Americans have personally obtained relief from a sex problem by reading or looking at pornography. (We remind the reader that it is questionable whether such results are representative of the entire population.) It is worth noting that the 1971 Abelson et al. study found that 47 percent of the men and 51 percent of the women believed that sexual materials "lead people to commit rape." Even more importantly, 10 percent of those men and 8 percent of those women based this belief on personal knowledge, which was defined as something that had happened to them personally or to someone they knew personally. Projecting those figures onto the entire U.S. population using the Wilson technique, it is then estimated that millions of Americans have either been raped or committed rape as a result of being exposed to pornography. That harm is surely more serious an effect than any slight potential benefit some people might experience as a result of exposure to pornography.

It is also worth mentioning that 1971 Abelson et al. study found that even using the not-so-extreme pornography of the late sixties as described in this study, 41 percent of the men and 46 percent of the women believed that pornography leads people to lose respect for women, and more than one third of each sex said that it makes people sex crazy. In addition, 55 percent of the men and 57 percent of the women said that pornography leads to a breakdown of morals. Only 35 percent of the men and 32 percent of the women believed that pornography provided an outlet for bottled-up impulses, and only 28 percent of the men and 27 percent of the women said that it gives relief to people who have sex problems.

The 1971 Wilson and Abelson et al. study also showed that the overwhelming majority of American adults had been exposed to pornography. Much of that exposure had occurred primarily in a social context, with friends being the most common source. There was less exposure to sadomasochistic-type pornography than there was to other types. Importantly, that study found than only 7 percent of all adults felt that people should be allowed to see or read anything they want to even if the materials have harmful effects. Another 35 percent felt that people should not be allowed to see or read some things even if those materials have no harmful effects. A full 44 percent said that their opinion about the availability of pornography would depend on whether or not the material is harmful.

The women consistently wanted to restrict pornography more than the men. Forty percent of the men and 50 percent of the women felt that movies depicting sex organs are not acceptable for any age. Fifty-five percent of the women and 44 percent of the men said that movies showing heterosexual intercourse should not be available for any age. Fifty-eight percent of the men and 67 percent of the women said that movies showing heterosexual oral genital contact should not be available for any age. Fifty-eight percent of the men and 65 percent of the women felt that movies showing homosexual activities should not be available, and a full 68 percent of the women and 61 percent of the men stated that movies with sadomasochistic content are not acceptable for any age. The figures for textual (written) materials depicting the same sexual practices were slightly lower than for movies.

Wilson mentions a series of studies, mostly taken from the 1970 Pornography Commission, which Wilson directed, that found no relationship between amount of exposure to pornography and things such as whether or not parents had talked to their children about sex and how much information children received from other sources such as technical sex material presented in high school or available at home. It is interesting that in a 1971 study of 473 adolescents in Chicago, Berger, Gagnon, and Simon found that 45 percent of the boys and 44 percent of the girls said that exposure to sexual materials had taught them things about sexuality that they had not known before, and similar percentages reported that such materials had given them an idea of what people actually do sexually. (We note that the Berger, Gagnon, and Simon study supports the argument made in this book that pornography is a learning device.) Propper (1971) also found a positive correlation between exposure to pornography and accuracy of sex information. Wilson cites other studies in support of his argument that large numbers of people in American society state that information about sex is an important product of viewing pornography.

Based on the fact that pornography provides sex information, Wilson argues that the information gained from pornography helps to prevent sex problems. (We note that negative information about sex contained in much of today's pornography could in fact cause sex problems.) Wilson makes a lot out of several commission studies that found that sex offenders had less exposure to pornography during adolescence than nonoffenders. From this, Wilson concludes, "We are led to the tentative conclusion that pornography, in our society, can—indeed does—contribute to the prevention of sex problems by providing necessary information for the development of appropriate, mature sexual functioning."[155]

He does state that the sex offender studies have some weaknesses, such as being correlational when in fact what is needed is what he calls experimental "longitudinal designs" aimed at establishing that experience with pornography helps prevent the development of "socially disapproved" patterns of sexual conduct. He also states that those studies do not address the possibility that deviant sexual patterns and their relationship to pornography might not be causally related, but rather both could result from an unidentified third variable, and that the studies cannot necessarily be generalized to "more socially acceptable sexual problems, such as marital sexual dysfunction."[156]

Wilson found little research in the areas of the

"anxiety—and inhibition—relieving function" of pornography and its role in contributing to sexual partners' ability to communicate with each other. He does, however, cite such effects found in various studies where pornography exposure appeared to increase openness in discussing sex and created urges to try new sexual techniques. Thus, he concludes that pornography does facilitate communication with others about sex.[157]

Wilson expresses shock at the possibility that some people do not know when they are aroused sexually. He suggests that pornography could aid people in learning to identify the experiences of sexual arousal. He also notes that much modern sex therapy concentrates on providing "appropriate information, reducing anxiety and inhibitions, and facilitating communication between sexual partners in treating sexual dysfunction." Therefore pornography, which he says accomplishes the same ends, can contribute to the prevention of sexual problems. He is careful to note that he does not argue that pornography is potentially the best or most effective way to prevent sexual problems or that the primary function of pornography is the prevention of such problems.[158]

Wishnoff studied the effects of sexual and nonsexual stimuli on women's behavior and anxiety. Quoting Golden and Golden (1976), he suggests that sexual dysfunction is emerging in our society as a norm rather than an exception and that methods of treating such dysfunctions therefore become important. The subjects in this study were forty-five female undergraduates who were chosen because they were anxious "virgin women." Subjects saw one of three 15-minute videos produced by the researcher. The sexually explicit tape involved eye contact, kissing, undressing, fondling, and various positions of sexual intercourse. The nonexplicit tape involved kissing, eye contact, and light petting over clothing. The control group saw a nonsexual videotape.

Wishnoff found that 100 percent of the women in the explicit group (all of whom were virgins) reported that they would engage in some type of coital activity, while more than 85 percent of the subjects in the control and nonexplicit group reported that they would not engage in such behavior. (It is interesting to note that the majority of these women who suddenly developed an interest in coitus showed a specific interest in intercourse with female on top.) The anxiety levels of the women who were exposed to the sexually explicit material were reduced so that they had the lowest sexual anxiety level of the three groups.[159]

Reynolds studied the facilitation of erection in men with dysfunctions. The subjects were thirty men who had come to the program with a complaint of erection difficulties. Their penile tumescence changes were measured by a mercury strain gauge. The "erotic" film stimuli involved in this study were 8mm color motion pictures depicting sexual activities of a heterosexual couple. There were twelve 90-second segments. Ten slides of nude females and twenty pictures taken from popular men's magazines also were used. The men were divided into three groups. One was the continuous feedback and contingent erotic film group in which subjects were told to concentrate on feelings and fantasies that would allow erection. Subjects received visual and auditory feedback for changes in their erectile responses. They were told that the film would come on only when there was a relatively large increase in erection. The second group received segments of "erotic" films contingent on increases in tumescence, but they did not receive any visual or auditory feedback for changes in their erectile responses. The third group was the noncontingent erotic film group. Subjects saw the ninety-second segments of erotic films, but seeing the films was not contingent on changes in their penile diameter. They were matched with people in the other groups so that the timing of the film segments was identical to the people with whom they were paired. They were not exposed to any continuous feedback.

The third group had significantly greater penile amplitude scores than either of the other groups. While seventeen of the twenty-six subjects reported improvement in their erectile functioning as a result of the study, only seven subjects reported that their functioning was considerably or completely impaired. Reynolds suggests that exposure to pornographic film segments that are contingent on increases in erectile response "may enhance the voluntary facilitation of erection in the laboratory for men with erectile dysfunction." Yet the instructions given some of these men in which their seeing the films was contingent upon erectile performance might have created greater performance anxiety and thus this might have disrupted their ability to function. Providing the continuous tumescence feedback did not promote greater changes in erection, and thus its therapeutic value was not demonstrated. Please note that a control group was not used in this study.[160]

Barr and McConaghy tested sixty freshman university student volunteers who were assumed to be heterosexual and forty-four male patients who had sought treatment for homosexual impulses. Penile volume changes were measured by a method described by McConaghy in 1967. Each person was tested with the aversive and appetitive conditioning procedure on the same day, with twenty minutes between tests.

Ten female nude sequences alternating with ten male nude sequences of ten seconds each at one minute intervals were the unconditioned stimuli. Photographs of a red circle preceding the female pictures and a green triangle preceding the male photos were the conditioned stimuli. In the aversive test, penile "responses to ten unpleasant electric shocks were measured." Fifty-six of the sixty students responded negatively to the electric shocks, and forty-three responded negatively to the male film sequences.[161]

The researchers conclude that "measurement of penile volume changes is a valid method of assessing sexual orientation." (Yet the changes in penile volume in response to the female films was rarely large enough to produce an erection or be "obvious to the subject." Many reported finding the film uninteresting but showed consistent penile volume increases to the female pictures.)[162]

Wincze, Hoon, and Hoon studied the exposure of sexually dysfunctional women to an "erotic" stimulus. Their subjects included six sexually adjusted women and six women who had sought treatment for sexual dysfunction. They exposed the clinical women to only the erotic stimulus and the other women to the erotic, neutral, and dysphoric stimuli. The neutral and dysphoric stimuli were not described by the researchers. The erotic stimulus in this case was a seven-minute black-and-white videotape portraying a couple engaged in foreplay that led up to but did not include intercourse. Sexual arousal was measured by a variety of techniques such as diastolic and systolic blood pressure, vaginal blood volume, skin conductance response (SCR), heart rate, and skin conductance (SC) between the soles of the feet.

The researchers found that there were increases in vaginal blood volume and diastolic blood pressure for the sexually adjusted women relative to the clinical women. This they found to be consistent with the theory that sexually adjusted women become fully aroused by erotic stimuli, whereas clinical women become only slightly aroused. The fact that the heart rate, SCR, and SC did not differ between the sexually adjusted and the clinical women during exposure to the sexually explicit stimulus was found to be consistent with the findings of a study by Hoon et al., which states that those measures are unreliable indicators of erotic arousal. While all the women rated themselves as moderately aroused, the sexually adjusted women showed greater "capillary engorgement" than the clinical women.[163]

Morokoff and Heiman studied twenty-two married women, eleven of whom were in a clinical group because they had experienced a lack of or low frequency of arousal in their sexual relations. The stimuli used were an audiotape of a man's voice describing a sexual encounter on a beach using explicit sexual language and a nine-minute silent color film of heterosexual intercourse depicting a young couple. The genital responses of the low arousal women and the women without an arousal deficit were similar, contrary to expectations. However, the women's subjective ratings of sexual arousal showed that the clinical women reported significantly less arousal. The researchers conclude that one could be aware of genital tumescence and yet have no psychological feeling of being aroused.[164]

McConaghy studied twenty-two homosexual subjects who had been referred for aversion therapy and eleven heterosexual medical student subjects. The researcher concludes that penile volume changes to pictures of female and male nudes were a valid measure of the declared sexual orientation of male subjects who were cooperative.[165]

Van Deventer and Laws studied two patients at a state hospital who experienced high sexual arousal in response to children. Each selected three slides that appealed to his pedophilic interests and three slides of adult females who were not unattractive or sexually attractive to them. The subjects viewed forty slides including those of male and female children and male and female adults. They engaged in directed masturbation. One subject showed shifts in sexual responsiveness away from the male children and toward the female adults. The researchers concluded that "properly conducted and frequently evaluated orgasmic reconditioning appears to be an effective procedure for the reduction of deviant sexual arousal." They do admit that the subjects could have faked their erection responses.[166]

Herman, Barlow, and Agras studied three homosexuals and one homosexual pedophile. They measured penile responses to colored slides of nude males (young boys for the one subject) and females by a mechanical strain gauge. The subjects were taken through phases of exposure to the slides. The researchers found that exposure to "heterosexual" stimuli modified the sexual arousal of the homosexuals. They conclude, however, that this might not be sufficient treatment for homosexuality and that techniques such as aversion therapy might still have to be used to decrease homosexual behavior and arousal.[167]

Jackson treated a case of voyeurism with counterconditioning. The voyeur liked to peep in windows at young nude females. He was treated by getting him to masturbate in private to "the most exciting pornographic picture he had in his collection." His orgasm was paired with a *Playboy* nude picture. Thus the man's voyeuristic fantasies and tendencies were overcome by attraction to more acceptable "objects," (adult women). He later experienced two "satisfactory heterosexual relations."[168]

Langevin and Martin studied sixteen heterosexual male volunteers. Penile volume changes were measured as the men were shown neutral slides and slides from men's magazines. Two "intensities" of slides were used. A second similar experiment used movies. The researchers conclude that the results raise doubts whether "penile tumescence can be classically conditioned."[169]

Barlow outlines procedures for treating sexual deviation. Among them are aversion therapy, which pairs descriptions or pictures of deviant behavior with noxious scenes of vomiting and nausea, electric shocks, odors, and so on. He found that this procedure does not always work. Another goal is to desensitize the deviant person to anxiety or avoidance of heterosexuality. This is done by exposing the person to explicit heterosexual themes. Another technique is called masturbatory conditioning, in which masturbation is paired with heterosexual stimuli. The fading technique consists of fading in pictures of heterosexual stimuli during periods of sexual arousal by deviant stimuli. A final technique discussed by Barlow is heterosocial training.[170]

Conrad and Wincze used pictures of nude females

posed alone and homosexual slides of males engaged in or about to engage in activities such as mutual masturbation, anal intercourse, and fellatio to attempt to recondition the sexual arousal of adult male homosexuals. They used shock aversion therapy. While the subjects said that they had become more sexually adjusted, their behavioral and physiological measures of arousal did not change, and therefore the researchers did not consider the experiment to be a success.[171]

Crawford writes about the need for a comprehensive approach to modifying deviant sexual behavior. He reviews a variety of the studies that used pornography or erotica to try to change deviant arousal patterns.[172]

Quinsey and Marshall also detail ways of reducing inappropriate sexual arousal. They evaluate the research, much of which deals with aversion therapy as well as nonaversive techniques.[173]

Kolarsky and Madlafousek studied exhibitionists and their responses to pornography. They found that the men were not aroused by female anger or fear but they were aroused by female genital exposure, especially a scene of a female pointing at her genitals. This same behavior aroused the control group only when erotic prestimulation immediately preceded the scene.[174]

HABITUATION THEORY

Habituation studies attempt to show that subjects exposed to pornography get habituated (bored) with it. Positive habituation results would run counter to pornography addiction theories.

Howard, Reifler, and Liptzin studied a group of twenty-three subjects and nine controls, all of whom were young adult college males. Their hypothesis was "that repeated exposure to pornography causes decreased interest in it, less response to it, and no lasting effect from it." They tested the subjects and controls, then exposed them to a pornographic movie. Subjects were then exposed to pornography for ninety minutes a day for fifteen days. Subjects and controls were retested after seeing a second pornographic movie. (We do not know what the content of the movies and "pornography" were.) The controls saw only the two movies without exposure to pornography on a daily basis. Twenty of the subjects saw a third pornographic movie. This study measured penile erection, acid phosphatase secretion, and heart rate. Self-reports, standardized tests, and psychiatric interviews also were used.[175] "Results confirmed the hypothesis and it was concluded that exposure to

pornography was a relatively innocuous stimulus without lasting or detrimental effect on the individual or his behavior."[176]

The researchers did not accept homosexuals or subjects whose experience with pornography was extensive. The subjects had movies, still pictures, magazines and novels, and nonpornography available to them. They had to record their activities for each ten-minute segment. The researchers found that there was little or no difference between the results from the subjects before exposure to pornography and after exposure. Even the repeated or extensive exposure had no lasting effect. Twenty-five percent of the subjects reported a change in sexual behavior, sexual interest, and feelings about themselves after the exposure to pornography. Some expressed having fewer guilt feelings about having sex, one had a stronger urge to have intercourse, two reported some decrease in sexual activity, and one of those had a vivid preoccupation with sexual thoughts that he thought were related to exposure to pornography.

All of the subjects reported initial stimulation by the pornography and a marked decrease in interest in it as a result of the exposure. One of the subjects stole some of the magazines, and another one stole three reels of film. The subjects almost unanimously said that pornography was one of the least important problems that our society faces, and none of them reported any permanent health, attitude, or behavior changes as a result of participation in the study.

The physiological measure results supported the hypothesis that repeated exposure to pornography would result in decreased responsiveness toward it. The researchers said that decreased response to such stimuli is a measure of satiation. "At the beginning of the experiment, all the subjects were interested in seeing pornography and were even willing to pay for this privilege. . . . [A]bout nine weeks after the end of the daily exposure all experimental subjects reported being bored by the thought of pornography and a number said that they had refused private opportunities to view it."

Attitudes toward the legal control of pornography changed as a result of the project. While the subjects' initial attitudes varied, after the experiment all except two of the most conservative subjects had moved "toward a more permissive attitude." The researchers found that exposure to pornography did not produce any detrimental or even "enduring effects other than liberalization of attitudes toward pornography itself."[177]

A study by Schaefer and Colgan in New Zealand tested four unmarried and six married males between ages 21 and 43 to see whether habituation occurred with repeated exposure to pornography. A penile gauge was used to measure arousal. The subjects read pornographic material that was described as six pages from *Sexus* by Henry Miller, which contained explicit heterosexual scenes. Responses were measured at the end of each page. Subjects read these same six pages at each of six sessions over a period of two weeks. A single page of pornography from the same book and of similar content was given to the subjects at each session constituting novel material. Control subjects read nonpornographic material after each session until their penile tumescence decreased to less than 25 percent. The experimental subjects followed the reading of pornography with ejaculation. The researchers found that "responding increased over trials when pornography was immediately followed by such a gratification." They conclude that the findings support the conditioning theory for sexual deviation.

There was a higher response by both the controls and the experimental subject to the novel pornography. Schaefer and Colgan emphasize that in studies where reexposure to the same pornography is used, the results should be interpreted cautiously, especially if they are used to measure treatment success, because the effects of treatment "become confounded with the effects of habituation." This study demonstrates that "diminution of an unreinforced response is likely regardless of intervening treatment."[178]

O'Donohue and Geer studied the habituation of sexual arousal. They defined habituation as "a systematic decrease in the magnitude of a response with repeated presentation of an eliciting stimulus, when that decrease cannot be accounted for in terms of fatigue or receptor adaptation." It is regarded as a form of learning not to respond. Habituation shows how permanent modification of behavior can occur because of repeated stimulation.[179]

In experiments involving exposure to erotic or pornographic stimuli and treatment by such stimuli, the effects of treatment can be "confounded" due to habituation. These researchers used forty male volunteers ages 17 to 19, some of whom were enrolled in an introductory psychology course at a university. Strain gauges were used to measure penile responses. Subjects also had to complete three questionnaires involving sexual experiences and attitudes, emotional state, and experiences with sexually oriented materials. The stimuli used were ten color slides. They represented the type of material found in sexually explicit magazines. Five of the slides were described as being in the high erotic condition. These showed "attractive heterosexual couples" performing genital or oral sex." The other five slides were referred to as the medium erotic intensity condition. They had attractive nude or seminude female models.

The subjects were divided into four groups. The first saw a constant stimulus of medium intensity, viewing a single slide of medium erotic intensity. The second had a constant stimulus of high intensity, viewing a single slide of high erotic intensity. The third group saw varied stimuli of medium intensity, viewing five slides of medium erotic intensity. And the fourth group saw varied high erotic intensity stimuli, viewing five slides of high erotic intensity. Each slide presentation lasted one minute, with a one-minute interstimulus interval. Presentations were repeated until each subject habituated up to a maximum of twenty-seven stimulus presentations. Habituation was considered to have occurred if the penile tumescence was near the baseline level, if no increase in penile tumescence was detectable for two sets of slide presentations, and if the subject gave two consecutive ratings of either of the two lowest ratings on the scale of subjective sexual arousal.

O'Donohue and Geer found that sexual arousal to erotic stimuli decreased with repeated presentations. The study also confirmed the theory that a constant stimulus would result in a higher rate of decreases of subjective and physiological responses over presentations that varied stimuli. Controls were used to rule out the theory that physiological fatigue rather than habituation occurred. Again, the researchers emphasized that habituation concerning sexual arousal can confound sex research methods. This must be kept in mind by researchers who use repeated exposure to similar or the same pornographic stimuli in their tests.

The researchers' hypothesis that exposure to stimuli of high erotic intensity would result in a lower rate of habituation of physiological sexual arousal than medium erotic intensity stimuli was not supported by the results. And the finding from trials 13 to 27 that the medium erotic stimuli were associated with a higher amount of subjective responses was unexpected and inconsistent with habituation literature. O'Donohue and Geer suggest that perhaps the two levels of erotic intensity were not different enough and that perception of intensity varied considerably across individuals.

Zillmann and Bryant say that Howard (1971) wrongly concluded that if pornography consumption were unrestricted, people would get bored with it and turn to other forms of entertainment but that Howard correctly showed that consuming the same or similar pornography "becomes dull and boring." Zillmann and Bryant found that enjoyment of uncommon erotica (for example, sadomasochism and beastiality) increased and state that the sexual brutalization of women holds "the greatest promise of exciting men."[180]

These researchers note that in studies such as this one, there is a substantial refusal to participate, which "constitutes a selective bias." They took male and female university undergraduates and random adults from a midwestern city of 150,000 population. There were 160 subjects in all. A laboratory was used for one-hour sessions during six consecutive weeks. The controls saw six hours of television situation comedies, one hour per week in six consecutive weeks. The subjects saw six hours of "commonly available pornography" (which included heterosexual acts of vaginal intercourse, anal intercourse, cunnilingus, and fellatio) one hour per week in six consecutive weeks. Each week, after viewing the material, controls and subjects were asked to evaluate the production quality of the materials.

In the eighth week, the subjects were allowed to view their choice of six tapes for fifteen minutes. Video jackets clearly described the tape contents. The choices were as follows:[181]

1. *Unsinkable Molly Brown,* a sexually innocent (G-rated) musical

2. *Exposed,* (R-rated) which features a passionate encounter, vulgar language, and partial nudity
3. *Amoire,* which shows a couple involved in fellatio, cunnilingus, and coitus but contains no violence or coercion (X-rated)
4. An XXX-rated bondage film in which three virgin females are tied, whipped, and otherwise subjected to torture and forced into servitude
5. An XXX-rated sadomasochistic film in which a leather-clad person whips a male and a male paddles, pinches, and bites a female
6. An XXX-rated bestiality film which shows a female involved in sex with a large dog and a male having intercourse with a ewe

Those subjects who had substantial prior exposure to nonviolent common pornography showed little interest in similar pornography and instead chose to view uncommon pornography (bestiality, bondage, and sadomasochism) when given a choice. Male nonstudents with substantial prior exposure to nonviolent, common pornography consumed the uncommon pornography almost exclusively. A similar, but less extreme pattern was shown by the male students. The same preferences were shown by the females, but to a much less pronounced degree, especially by the female students.

The findings strongly support the view

> that continued exposure to generally available, nonviolent pornography that exclusively features heterosexual behavior among consenting adults arouses an interest in and creates a taste for pornography that portrays less commonly practiced sexual activities, including those involving the infliction of pain.

These researchers say that it is unclear whether this was due to decreasing excitement with common pornography, to satisfying curiosity about common sexual practices, or to the interplay of these factors. It is of concern to society if violent and aberrant sexual conduct (in pornography) can shape behavior, especially among young people, they said. The researchers suggest that it does not matter whether it is nonviolent or violent pornography that trivializes rape, for the consumer of milder pornography will advance to more hard-core material.[182]

Ceniti and Malamuth studied the effects of repeated exposure to nonviolent or sexually violent stimuli on sexual arousal in response to depictions of rape and other scenes. The subjects were twenty-six people who responded to a classified advertisement at a university in Canada. Another forty-eight male volunteers were selected from a pool at the university.

The subjects, all males, took the Minnesota Multiphasic Personality Inventory and a sexual background questionnaire to make sure that they were not severely psychologically impaired and that they had no legal difficulties and were not exclusively homosexuals. A mercury in rubber strain gauge measured penile tumescence. This was described as a "fine bore rubber band which is filled with mercury and encircles the penis." As penile diameter changes the length of the rubber band increases, which causes a contraction of the mercury column.

The stimuli used were three written and three pictorial depictions in a preexposure session. Each of the written stimuli took two to three minutes to read. One described a woman masturbating, and the second and third portrayed rape and nonrape as reported in Abel et al. in 1977. The three pictures depicted nonrape, rape, and lesbianism. Subjects were then assigned to one of the following exposure conditions: control (no exposure), sexually violent stimuli, and sexually nonviolent stimuli. Four weeks after the preexposure session, some of the subjects were exposed to six feature-length films of sexually violent

behavior such as rape and sadomasochism; they saw two films a week for three consecutive weeks. After the last film, they were given pictorial and written materials showing sexually violent and nonviolent activities to take home for the fourth week of exposure. The control group was not exposed to any films during the four weeks. The sexually nonviolent exposure group saw sexually explicit nonviolent films. There was a debriefing session.

The data showed that "repeated exposure to sexually violent or nonviolent pornography resulted in satiation and sexual arousal to rape themes for force oriented subjects (i.e., those who prior to any exposure had shown relatively high levels of arousal to rape stimuli)." No effects were obtained for the unclassifiable subjects and non-force-oriented subjects. Neither force orientation or the type of pornography subjects were exposed to (violent or nonviolent) had a "significant effect on arousal to mutually consenting sex stimuli." The authors suggest that it is possible that repeated exposure to variations of a theme such as group sex or rape may lead to habituation to that type of activity.[183]

PORNOGRAPHY'S EFFECT ON ATTITUDES AND BEHAVIOR OF "NORMAL" PEOPLE

The research shows that some pornography leads to temporarily increased sexual activity, sometimes masturbation. It decreases satisfaction with the person's sexual life and sex partners and increases discussion about sex. It sometimes causes desires to try new sexual techniques, including oral sex, group sex, homosexuality, anal intercourse, bondage, adultery, whipping, rape, bestiality, and child molesting, among others. Exposure to pornography results in greater acceptance of such practices and of practices such as promiscuity and extramarital sex.

In surveys, some people report that they perceive pornography as leading people to commit rape, improving or worsening sexual relations of married couples, and breaking down morals.

Weaver, Masland, and Zillmann studied forty-six male undergraduate students. They were exposed to twenty slides and a six-minute video of nature scenes, "beautiful nude females in sexually provocative poses or engaged in precoital or coital behavior," or rather unattractive females involved in those same activities. (We suggest that this sort of research makes women appear to be sex objects and is very sexist. For example, how did these pictures differ in content, and who decided beauty versus unattractiveness?) An

unrelated test on modern art was given to disguise the study's purpose. Subjects answered a questionnaire about their present girlfriends with whom they shared sexual intimacy. In this study, the subjects rated the busts and buttocks of their sexual partners from flat to hypervoluptuous. They circled the shape that best described their mates' bodies. Further body-part appeals were measured, including legs and face, as well as subjects' sexual satisfaction with their mates.[184]

After exposure to the beautiful females, the "perception of one's mate's bodily characteristics was about half-way between flat and hypervoluptuous." After exposure to the unattractive females, the perception of their mate's body features was "significantly . . . closer to hypervoluptuousness." Perception by subjects in the control condition was an intermediate position similar to that of those who were exposed to the beautiful women. The researchers conclude that "exposure to programs featuring beautiful women, compared with programs featuring unattractive women, may produce a temporary unappraisal of a mate's sexual appeal." According to the researchers, an adverse affect on aesthetic perception does not necessarily translate to sexual dissatisfaction with mates.[185] (We find it peculiar that in this study sex appeal was based on body features only.)

Zillmann and Bryant used as subjects undergraduates at a variety of midwestern universities and adults from an area highly representative of the U.S. population at large (according to test marketers). The subjects were paid to watch television programs or films. Of the persons contacted, 37 percent responded positively to participating in this program. After they were told that it might involve hard-core sexually explicit material, participation dropped 23 percent of those persons contacted. (We wonder whether persons who are antipornography dropped out of participation.)

One hundred sixty persons participated. Twenty subjects were assigned to each of the two experimental conditions. Both males and females were involved. While the students' average ages were early twenties, the nonstudents' average ages were mid-thirties. About 58 percent of all subjects reported being presently sexually active, but some thought this included masturbation. Some 50 to 85 percent of the subjects were cohabitants or married.

The subjects in the two experimental conditions met for one-hour sessions for six consecutive weeks in a laboratory. The material was viewed on a television monitor. It was in color. In the control condition, no pornography was shown. These people saw sexually innocuous situation comedies from prime-time television. In the second condition, subjects saw X-rated pornography. These had twelve to twenty-two minutes of other than sexual behaviors. There was a wide range of heterosexual activity including intercourse, fellatio, cunnilingus, and anal intercourse. There were no pictures of bondage or discipline, beastiality, homosexuality, or sexual violence. After each show, the subjects were asked to rate production quality, lighting, and sound. This was done to disguise the true purpose of the experiment. In the seventh week, the subjects were given tests of "values of marriage" and the inventory of personal happiness. Their sexual practices also were tested. They were debriefed and told of related research and cautioned not to adopt the attitudes and perceptions that consumption of pornography is likely to create.

The researchers found that factors such as gender and educational status (student versus nonstudent) were not significant but that effective exposure to pornography was important. Exposure to pornography diminished satisfaction with the physical appearance of the subjects' sexual partners. It also reduced satisfaction with the partners' affection, sexual behavior, sexual inquisitiveness, and intimate relationship altogether. Those who were exposed to the pornography described the importance of faithfulness as having been diminished, the importance of having sex without any emotional involvement as having been enhanced, and the importance of good family relations as having been diminished. The researchers found that these effects were specific to sex-related areas, for assessments of happiness outside the sexual sphere were not influenced by the pornographic exposure.

The researchers conclude that repeated pornography consumption can induce "dissatisfaction with numerous aspects of sexuality." They note that all the effects, including physical appeal, less gratifying sexual performance, and sexual curiosity and affection, were significant. Importantly, this impact was not gender specific. The women who were exposed to pornography became just as dissatisfied as the men. Zillmann and Bryant note, however, that they do not know the behavioral implications of this dissatisfaction. They speculate that people would seek more sexually gratifying experiences. It is unrealistic to search for better partners, however, and this would result in more dissatisfaction. There is, they suggest, a small group of people with "truly superior physique, with ever present zest for sexual exploration." Some percentage of dissatisfaction could be what leads to pornography consumption, they speculate, but, the pornography is likely to make the situation worse by projecting partners and performances that are out of reach for most people.[186]

They believe that nonpornographic material with stunning beauty also could temporarily reduce "aesthetic appraisals" of oneself and one's mate. Sexual explicitness would not be needed for such appraisals. (In what we consider an extremely sexist remark, the researchers state, "Surely, a man whose female partner has slumping breasts need not see coital action to be reminded of his partner's imperfection. Any pinup—whether nude or in bathing suit—will do.") The researchers conclude, however, that pornography seems to be the only genre that specifically affects sexual dissatisfaction.[187]

> Only pornography exhibits the joy of sex with children and only this genre provides specifics such as fellatio in which women make entire male organs vanish or coition in which penises of extreme proportion cause women to scream in apparent painful ecstasy. The sexual experience of normals must pale by comparison. Partners must seem prudish, insensitive, inhibited, frigid, hypolibidinal and deficient in endowment and skill and who, confronted with the bounty of readily attainable sexual joys that are continually

presented in pornography and nowhere else, would consider his or her sexual life fulfilled?[188]

Davis and Braucht studied reactions of people who viewed films of "erotically realist heterosexual behavior." They used films made for the Institute of Sex Research of Hamburg University. (These films also had been used by Schmidt and Sigusch.) The films portrayed an attractive woman and man. One showed light petting involving manual contact with the genitals short of orgasm in which both partners undressed down to the underwear. The second showed heavy petting involving manual contact with the genitals, cunnilingus, and fellatio until orgasm with both partners naked. The third showed various positions of coitus and foreplay, cunnilingus, and fellatio. Both partners were naked. They noted that research of Sigusch and Schmidt had shown that such "erotically realistic films" aroused women and men physiologically and emotionally.[189]

These researchers solicited volunteers from 256 men who were involved in a retrospective questionnaire study. Volunteers could not be solicited from an additional 109 prison inmates who also had participated in the retrospective study due to a prison warden decision; of those 175 volunteered for this experiment, and only 121 actually showed up for the session. The 121 subjects completed a questionnaire about viewing "erotic" films and another one about their actions and thoughts during the twenty-four hours before and after viewing the films. The films were silent color films of ten minutes each, with breaks of three minutes between them.

Davis and Braucht looked at characteristics of the volunteers to determine what sort of person would voluntarily expose himself to pornography. Those who did not volunteer had the least prior experience with pornography. Those who came to the session had the greatest prior exposure. They also found that the people who actually exposed themselves to the pornography in the experiment were of "higher character" than the nonvolunteers. The researchers concluded that the types of people most likely to volunteer were those who had seen considerable amounts of pornography before and wanted to see more and those with high character scores who would tend to be prone to respond to an appeal to scientifically study pornography.

They found that the films had "marked effects" during viewing and in the twenty-four hours afterward. The immediate effect was that subjects became more sexually aroused, more likely to recommend that such film availability be restricted, and less likely to call themselves deviant for watching pornography. In the twenty-four hours after the films,

subjects "became more tense, engaged in more substitute (for sex) behavior, felt more desire for sex, engaged in more pornography simulated or pornography aided sex, masturbated more . . . but engaged in no more petting or coitus than prior to the film." Before seeing the films, only 24 percent judged them to be unacceptable. Afterward, 57 percent of the subjects had that response. (At one point, the researchers redid their "major data analysis" and omitted 24 of the 121 subjects because they were in a Catholic seminary and almost at the stage of taking vows of sexual abstinence.)[190]

This study did not have a control group, so Davis and Braucht could not be certain that the arousal measured was due to the films. They found that the people who were most aroused were those who did not have established heterosexual relations or histories of coitus and petting and that those people also were more likely to engage in masturbation. A small group of people active in homosexual practices also were highly aroused. The researchers note that they did not test for homosexual or highly deviant heterosexual behaviors in their questionnaires. Reasonably mature college-educated persons used in this study are not the type of people the general public is concerned will develop sexual deviance due to exposure to pornography. There was more concern with effects on younger persons from all socioeconomic levels. The researchers emphasize that only carefully designed longitudinal work would be satisfactory for dealing with concerns such as context of exposure and age of exposure.

Mann, Sidman, and Starr studied the effects of pornographic films on the sexual behavior of married couples. Eighty-five married couples were studied.

Nonstandard erotica was used in one category. This involved a twelve-minute film of two female lesbians fondling and engaged in mutual oral genital activity. This was followed by a twelve-minute film of one male and two females engaged in coitus, fondling, oral genital acts, and anal play. That film also showed one female lapping up semen that had been ejaculated by the man onto the other female's breast. A second sequence in the nonstandard erotic area involved a twelve-minute film of three male homosexuals involved in mutual masturbation and oral genital activity, followed by a twelve-minute film of a Japanese female and male engaging in whipping and coitus.

The first sequence of the more standard erotic films was a ten-minute film showing a female masturbating to orgasm, followed by a "highly realistic" twelve-minute film of a couple engaged in fondling, oral genital acts, and coitus in a variety of positions. Another sequence was a twenty-minute film by a female photographer that was intended to present a female's fantasies about sex. This was produced by the National Sex and Drug Forum. Although there were explicit close-ups of penile insertion, oral genital contact, and other sexual acts, the close-ups were presented in a "highly aesthetic manner." The film incorporated landscapes, birds in flight, and other such scenes and had its own music sound track.

The films were in black-and-white except for the female masturbation film. Control subjects saw nonerotic films, and the other subjects were divided into two groups. One viewed the standard films in the first two weeks and the nonstandard during the second two weeks, and the other saw the films in the reverse order.

These researchers note that the persons who saw the nonerotic films appeared to have initiated as many new sexual behaviors as did most of the persons who saw the erotic films. They found that 77 percent of the men who saw the erotic films and 63 percent of their spouses reported greater frequency of sexual activity on film viewing nights as compared to 41 percent of the males in the control group and 35 percent of their spouses. (We caution readers to notice the apparent sexist bias in this study by emphasizing the males and referring to the females as "spouses.")

The researchers found, based on comments made by subjects in the daily questionnaires, that aspects of the procedure other than viewing the films, such as completing daily questionnaires, also influenced subjects' behavior. In fact, in their self-reports, subjects rated the component of viewing the films as "relatively unimportant both in motivating them to volunteer for the study and in changing their sexual patterns." One change frequently reported was increased openness in discussing sex. However, nearly a quarter of the subjects reported having increased urges to try new sexual techniques and lowered inhibitions toward their spouses. Eleven percent of the males and 3.7 percent of the females also expressed an increased desire for extramarital sex after exposure to the films. Two males and eleven females said that participation in the study was harmful; five of these females did not see the erotic films, but in some cases their spouses did. One person who did not see the pornographic films found it harmful that her husband reported arousal to portions of films showing activities she regarded as aversive.[191] (We point out that this type of reaction is in line with actual victim case histories showing that pornography exposure can lead spouses who have been exposed to sexual activities that the other spouse finds aversive to try to act out those activities

with the spouse and sometimes to force such activities on the spouse.)

The subjects rated the film that was more alive and artistic most favorably and the one showing sadomasochistic activity least favorably. Yet in many cases the males rated "various films" more favorably than did the females. Interestingly, the order of presentation of the films seemed to make a difference. The females who saw those showing standard practices first were significantly less likely to view films as "favorable" than were those who saw the films showing the nonstandard practices first. Both sexes found the intercourse and oral genital activities in the films to be most arousing. They found the male homosexuality and sadomasochism films to be the least arousing. Yet for all the activities except intercourse, the males' ratings fell between the slightly aroused and no reaction scale points, and for the females, most of their ratings fell between the no reaction to "mixed arousal and repulsion" ratings. The males rated five of the seven films unfavorably, while the females rated all but the erotic artistic film unfavorably. The males reported higher proportionate genital sensations compared to the females in response to the female homosexuality and masturbation films. The researchers found that the favorite film (the erotic artistic film) was less arousing than those films that were rated as aversive and anxiety provoking.

While the males exposed to the films became significantly more permissive toward most categories of sex activities after seeing the films, the male control subjects showed no significant change on seven variables, except they did become significantly less permissive toward films depicting group sex. The females who saw the erotic films showed no significant change, except they did become significantly more permissive toward film portrayals of oral genital contact. Those females who saw no films or nonerotic films became significantly less permissive toward all eight activities. The activities at issue included oral genital contact, intercourse, male and female homosexual acts, sadomasochistic acts, group sex, bestiality, and female masturbation. The females who saw the standard films first became "significantly more permissive toward depictions of intercourse . . . oral genital contact . . . sadomasochistic acts . . . and female masturbation."[192]

The researchers found that for the most part the subjects seemed to maintain preexisting frequencies and types of sexual behavior. Most of the subjects who reported any changes attributed them to study aspects other than viewing the films—for example, completing the daily questionnaires. Comments made show that some couples were encouraged to experiment with new techniques (including anal intercourse) after seeing references to those techniques on the daily questionnaires. They did find that denying females the right to see the pornographic films with their spouses led to resentment. Most subjects found the study to have had a positive effect on their sexual and general marital relationships. The males found the group sex, female homosexuality and female masturbation films significantly more arousing than did the females. (Comments made later in the study suggest that it is negative to be inhibited toward viewing such films and that favorable reaction toward films are a positive change. We suggest that this shows the bias of these particular researchers quite clearly.)

The subjects, according to these researchers, were *not* a cross section of the general population, and care should be taken to use these results only with people of similar backgrounds. They also found some strong deviations in individual responses compared to group means. They conclude that exposure to these films did not "appear to produce harmful effects on subjects' behavior," yet it was not possible to show that the films had beneficial effects on the subjects because any benefits reported may have been the result of other parts of the procedure.[193]

Heiby and Becker studied the effects of filmed modeling on masturbation frequency. Filmed modeling is based on the social learning theory "concept of observational or vicarious learning." This theory claims that observational learning can have three major effects: the inhibition of already existing behavior, the acquisition of new behavior, or the disinhibition of existing behavior. For example, modeling films portraying female masturbation demonstrate the method of attaining orgasm and also communicate a message that masturbation is acceptable and normal as a way to attain sexual pleasure. However, some modeling films could result in an inhibitory effect. The researchers suggest that this might be the case if the model were viewed as an unattractive woman who was unable to find a partner.[194]

Heiby and Becker used forty-eight female undergraduate students in their test. None of these women were cohabiting with a male or married at the time of the experiment. Twenty-four of the women were asked to view a film on female masturbation after completing the pretest questionnaire. The film ran for eight and a half minutes and showed a slightly overweight, youthful nude woman exploring her body with her hands and then masturbating to orgasm "by means of digital stimulation." There was a music track and there was a sound track with a woman's voice softly stating phrases such as "relax, enjoy it, discover what feels good."

One month after the initial questionnaire, the women filled out the same questionnaire. While the experimental group reported an increase in masturbation frequency that was statistically significant, the control group reported no change in frequency. At the same time, however, the subjects reported that the film did not affect their sexual behavior or attitudes. The researchers explain this inconsistency by theorizing that subjects might have learned how to masturbate by viewing the film, that the film might have given them permission to report a more realistic masturbation frequency, and that the film might have created an expectation to report a higher frequency of masturbation (a demand characteristic). They could not tell whether any of those hypotheses were valid. The fact that the subjects found the model to be unattractive did not have an inhibitory effect on reported masturbation frequency.[195]

Merritt, Gerstl, and LoSciuto reported on a national sample study on the perceived effects of pornography. They interviewed 2,486 adults. While many reported that they did not know the effects of pornography, 49 percent said sexual material leads people to commit rape, while 29 percent said it does not. Nine percent said pornography had had that effect on someone they knew personally. Forty-one percent said sexual materials make men want to do new things with their wives, while 28 percent said it did not. Thirteen percent said pornography had had this effect on someone they knew personally.

While 47 percent said sexual materials improves sexual relations of some married couples, 30 percent said it does not, and 14 percent said pornography had had this effect on someone they knew personally. Thirty-four percent said they believed catharsis theory that such materials provide an outlet for bottled-up impulses. Forty-six percent said they did not believe this theory, and 5 percent said pornography had had that effect on someone they knew personally. While 37 percent said that pornography makes people sex crazy, 45 percent said that it does not, and 9 percent said it had had this effect on someone they new personally.

A full 56 percent said sexual materials lead to a breakdown of morals, 30 percent said they do not, and 13 percent reported this effect on someone they knew personally. While the respondents were divided on whether sexual materials lead people to lose respect for women, 11 percent reported knowing of this effect on someone they knew personally. (Recall that this survey took place in 1975, before the more violent, humiliating, and aggressive types of pornography were available on a large scale.) The survey showed clear differences between older and younger persons, with the older ones saying that "erotica" has the most undesirable effects, and the younger ones noting the more desirable effects of pornography. More educated persons also were more likely to report desirable effects. Women cited more undesirable and less desirable effects than men.[196]

Kutschinsky studied the immediate and short-term effects of one-hour exposure to hard-core pornography in Copenhagen, Denmark. He did not use a control group and had a selective small group of subjects of forty-three men and twenty-nine women. Twenty-two of these were married couples, mostly graduate students. Seventy-one percent of the men and 40 percent of the women said they were strongly or somewhat interested in pornography, and 66 percent of the women and 47 percent of the men had never seen a pornographic film.

Kutschinsky found no significant differences or changes in the attitudes of these people toward sex crimes in general relative to other crimes and no support for the idea that short-term pornography stimulation leads to a relatively more lenient attitude toward sex crimes. He does say that there might be effects on a single sex crime or different effects for different people with different backgrounds. On the whole, however, these people found the pornography to be inartistic and boring and evaluated it rather unfavorable. He says that he was surprised that both the men and the women disliked the men in the films, while both sexes liked the lesbian couple in one of the films. The men had appreciable amounts of zest and pleasure during the session "in striking contrast to the women." Very few women said they felt lust or arousal.

Eighty-six percent of the men had some erection, and 61 percent of the women reported genital sensations as a result of the experiment. Those men and women who had an interest in deviant sexual practices tended to have an excess of positive reactions, evaluations, and pleasant feelings toward the pornography. The more favorably the pornography was experienced and the more arousing it was, the more likely it was that the person would increase his or her sexual activities in the twenty-four hours after the session. Here, heterosexual activity tended to increase more than masturbation. (Perhaps this can be accounted for by the fact that the subjects were married couples.) Overall, however, the majority reacted negatively to the pornography, and increased heterosexuality was rare among these people. Among the men whose spouses were not present, increased sexual activities were mainly masturbation.[197]

Kutschinsky concludes that "there does not seem to be any doubt that the hypothesis 'pornography breeds prurient interest' has been found false in this study." He says that the real question became whether there was enough basis to conclude that the pornography had the opposite effect—in other words, diminishing prurient interest. He does point out some problems, such as not being able to observe feelings and reactions and having to rely on the person's subjective reports of arousal. He also notes that the questionnaire provoked expectations and sometimes sexual arousal in some subjects in ways that interfered with their responses to the pornography sessions.

The hypothesis that the pornography would create strong emotional reactions such as shame, fear, and urge for sex was rejected because strong emotional reactions among these subjects were rare. The most frequent reactions were "relatively vague feelings of mirth and boredom." The hypothesis that viewing the hard-core pornography would create an interest in deviant practices in subjects also had to be rejected. There was a considerable decrease in this type of interest, which Kutschinsky says seems to favor the catharsis theory. However, the study did not allow for conclusions as to the cause of this change.[198]

(We think that the Kutschinsky study is filled with sex biases—for example, the emphasis on whether the men whose spouses were present during the pornography sessions increased coital frequency versus those whose spouses were not. This does not seem to ask whether the females present during the pornography sessions increased *their* sexual activities. In other words, they are just adjuncts to the males and not considered to be initiators of their own sexual activity.)

SEX FANTASIES

We have included several studies of the sexual fantasies of men because they show how common it is for "normal" men to have fantasies of sexually coercing or aggressing against women. One study showed that these "normal" men found magazines such as *Playboy* and a sadomasochistic book "exciting" and that 62.6 percent of them fantasized themselves as the hero in the pornographic movie

Deep Throat. This shows widespread familiarity with pornography. The fantasies these men had were scenarios typically found in pornography. One wonders whether fantasies resulted from pornography exposure. Some researchers argue that fantasy plays a role in shaping sexual behavior.

Crépault and Coutoure studied men's erotic fantasies. They questioned ninety-four Francophone men, ages 20 to 45, from the Province of Quebec, Canada. The men were volunteers recruited from advertisements in a major newspaper and posters in public places. Each man participated in a two-hour interview and a self-administered questionnaire. Sixty-six percent of the men tested had erotic fantasies outside of sexual activity once or more a day. And 76.6 percent of them had, at least occasionally, such fantasies "during heterosexual activity with their regular partner."

Among the more interesting findings were that 45.8 percent of the men fantasized about being raped by a woman, 33 percent fantasized raping a woman, 39.4 percent imagined a scene in which "the woman that you seduce pretends resisting" 39.4 percent envisioned scenes in which they tied up a woman and stimulated her sexually, and 36.2 percent saw a scene in which they were tied up and sexually stimulated by a woman. A full 84 percent fantasized about being with a woman other than their real sex partner, 77.7 percent imagined "part of a female body" (objectification), 77.7 percent saw scenes in which they had sexual activities "with a perverted woman" (whatever *perverted* means), and 77.7 percent fantasized about a scene from an "erotic film that excited you."[199] (We note that this suggests that many men have seen pornographic films and that they do recall what is pictured.)

Some of these men (no small percentage *if* such results could be generalized to the entire population of men) envisioned scenes of humiliating women, being humiliated, and having sex with an animal; 10.7 percent pictured beating a woman up, and 5.3 percent pictured being beaten. Nineteen percent fantasized about being penetrated in the anus (41.6 percent of the men had "had a homosexual experience during childhood, adolescence, or adult life").[200]

Perhaps most shocking is the fact that 61.7 percent of these men imagined a scene in which they sexually initiated a young girl, and 3.2 percent envisioned sexually initiating a young boy. In their fantasies, 74.5 percent of the men felt sexually powerful enough to satisfy more than one woman at a time.

The researchers categorized some of the men's fantasies into affirmation of sexual power, aggressiveness, masochism, the maternal image, confirmation of sexual identity, and affirmation "of a man's sexual dominance." They also compared fantasy average scores to actual sexual behavior and preferred activities of the men. The researchers conclude that imagery is important in a man's sex life.[201]

Women and men share five popular fantasies, they say: a scene from "an erotic film," fellatio, cunnilingus, being with another sex partner, and memories of prior sexual enocunters. Men's heterosexual fantasies center on confirming sexual power, masochistic fantasies, and being aggressive. Women's fantasies involve narcissism, denying responsibility of pleasure, and dialectic-type fantasies "in which personalization and depersonalization of the object are being opposed."[202]

Greendlinger and Byrne studied coercive sexual fantasies of college men. They note that large numbers of college women have reported sexual aggression against them (with one quarter having been forced to have intercourse according to a 1977 study by Kanin and Parcell) and that these women's reports of aggression are corroborated by the self-reports of college men. For example, a 1974 study by Heisler found that 4.9 percent of the men questioned admitted to having committed rape, and a 1982 study by Koss and Oros found that 25 percent of the men studied admitted to having at least one forcible attempt at intercourse since entering college. Greendlinger and Byrne emphasize that it is unknown to what degree any type of forced sex fantasy gets translated into actual coercive behavior, yet it seems reasonable to hypothesize a link between such fantasies and behavior.

These researchers studied 114 men enrolled in junior level courses in human sexuality and personality at a college. The men responded to a questionnaire about coercive sexual fantasies. The results were very interesting. For example, 80 percent of these men said they would be turned on by being tied up and forced by a woman to have sex with her. At the same time, 69.6 percent of them fantasized about having a woman tied spread-eagle to a bed. Almost as many were turned on by thoughts of bondage; 63.5 percent said, "I get excited when a woman struggles over sex." Slightly over half of the men fantasized about forcing a woman to have sex; 35.7 percent of them fantasized about raping a woman. Almost all (96.5 percent) said they find *Playboy* exciting.

More than 91 percent of the men said they like to dominate a woman, and 90.4 percent of them said they believe the myth that women like to hold out so they do not seem easy. Yet in a seemingly contradictory statement, 89.6 percent agreed that they do not understand how a man could "possibly rape a woman." While 88.7 percent said they like to be in charge of the sex they have with a woman, almost as many (87 percent) said that a strong woman turns them on. More than 83 percent of these men said, "Some women look like they're just asking to be raped," and 82.6 percent of the men found *The Story of O* (a book about the sexual abuse of a woman) exciting. Slightly over three-quarters of the men said they would report their roommate if they knew he had raped a woman. Slightly over 80 percent of the men said they believe that women think of them as sex objects. More than 62 percent of these men said they fantasize about being the hero in *Deep Throat* (the pornographic movie in which the star, Linda Lovelace, was forced to act). Yet only a tiny percentage (3.5 percent) said they lose interest when a woman tries to take charge sexually.

Greedlinger and Byrne found that scores on the coercive sexual fantasy scale related positively to likelihood to rape measures. In a very interesting finding, fewer than 20 percent of these college males complied with the researcher's request to write a coercive sexual fantasy. (The fantasies were supposed to involve rape or force.) The researchers found that the willingness to write such fantasies was related to the likelihood to rape item. Only 6.8 percent of those who said they would not be at all likely to commit a rape wrote a coercive fantasy. Of the people indicating some likelihood that they would commit a rape, 32.4 percent wrote a fantasy. However, of those three persons who said "that committing a rape would be very likely, 100 percent wrote the requested fantasy." It should be noted that 64.9 percent of the men said it would be not at all likely that they would commit a rape. The researchers did not find a significant relationship between the self-report of prior coercive behavior and the likelihood to rape measure. Only 1.6 percent of the subjects said they had raped a woman, and 6.7 percent said they had used physical force for petting. Another 41.7 percent of the sample admitted to saying things they did not mean as a coercive method to gain sex against a woman's will. Twenty-three percent claimed they had become so excited that they could not stop themselves.

These researchers conclude that this study provides additional evidence that fantasy content is an important indicator of a variety of aspects of people's actions and motivations. They speculate that events such as exposure to verbal and written "erotica," nonsexual media violence, and real-life experiences become incorporated into the masturbatory fantasies of some individuals. The fantasies become linked with sexual pleasure, excitement, and orgasm. "As a result of this conditioned relationship violent fantasies influence expectancies about the rewards of coercive activities and hence motivate

aggressive sexual behavior; such fantasies also serve as models for specific aggressive acts." They note that exposure to aggressive sexual imagery increases the probability of engaging in such fantasies, and having the fantasies in turn increases the probability of engaging in such coercive behavior.[203]

These researchers conclude that rape myth acceptance and rape likelihood do not seem to be related to real-life coercive sexual behavior. Instead, they found coercive behavior to be a correlate of aggressive tendencies and coercive fantasies and their interaction.

Przybyla, Byrne, and Kelley argue that cognitive processes such as "imaginative fantasizing, supercede (sic) hormonal processes in initiating and directing sexual arousal" in most persons.[204] They say that humans are primarily aroused in response to visual images. They also see dream imagery as being relevant to sexual dysfunctions and reliving parts of past sexual experiences as being important to a person's imagery catalog. They note that human imagination has no boundaries.

These writers cite Barclay (1973) as finding that college male fantasies " 'contained much visual imagery and anatomical detail, whereas female sexual fantasies emphasized emotions, plot, and dialogue.' "[205] They note that Hunt found that males, in their masturbatory fantasies, were more likely than females to imagine having group sex, forcing someone to have sex, and having intercourse with a stranger, while women were more apt to fantasize being forced to have sex and perform acts in which they would never actually engage. The image of women being sexually dominated is a recurrent theme in literature, Przybyla, Byrne, and Kelley note.[206]

They cite a study by Przybyla and Byrne (1981) in which college students were asked to write about their most exciting sexual fantasies. While women more commonly described interpersonal affection, men wrote about explicit sex, gave information about their partner's body proportions and attractiveness, and described oral sex scenes. Forty-five percent of the males wrote of being fellated, while only a handful mentioned cunnilingus. Only 3 percent of the females mentioned oral sex, and *all* of those fantasies involved cunnilingus, not fellatio.[207]

While these researchers say that erotica "mirrors aspects of the society that produces it," they also note that sexual images play a major role in shaping and initiating behavior.[208] They include a brief review of the sex research literature from the late 1970s, but do not go into detail. They note that while Herrell (1975) found that men were more aroused than women by sexual exploitation of a female by a male, Schmidt (1975) found that both males and females were highly aroused by a movie of a group rape of a female victim. The males felt guilty; the females felt helpless.[209]

Citing other (older) studies, these researchers conclude that the fear that seeing hard-core pornography leads to imitation lacks "empirical support," noting that the only evidence of a modeling effect has been reducing anxiety among non-orgasmic females in therapy. They argue that the data consistently refute the belief that pornography causes sex crimes and that there are "repeated indications" that the opposite may be true. They comment that the typical pornographic consumer is a rich businessman, not an "emotionally disturbed deviant" who leaves a pornographic bookstore to lurk and wait for his victim.[210] (We note that this comment contains a misconception that sexual deviants have a certain appearance, when, in fact, they cross all ages, classes, and occupations.) They argue for the catharsis theory and in favor of using positive sex fantasies to treat sex dysfunctions. For example, they say, one female was instructed to imagine being raped as she masturbated. This helped her overcome her inability to achieve orgasm. It made sexual excitement acceptable because she was not responsible.

These researchers suggest that changes in fantasy can lead to changes in behavior and point out that entertainment, propaganda, and advertising all use procedures designed to alter our fantasies.

Kelley and Byrne postulate that "internal imagination is a mechanism that provides self-control of learned behavior."[211]

Kelley later studied the alteration of sexual fantasies through exposure to erotic images in both entertainment and advertising. She used 123 male and 123 female college students as subjects. All the students viewed two out of three sets of sexual slides consisting of twenty color photographs of an explicit heterosexual nature. These depicted acts of intercourse, nude petting, and oral sex by white actors. Two sets of twenty "mildly erotic color slides showed titillating, partially clad, individual white males or females."[212] Each person saw only one set of these single sex stimuli, which were presented in orders that counterbalanced the viewing of the heterosexual set. Each slide was shown for fifteen seconds to small groups of three to four subjects of the same sex. The experimenter's sex was the same as the subjects' sex. After exposure to each slide set, the subjects responded to scales assessing sexual arousal and affective responses.

Then the subjects were asked to create a sexual fantasy of their own, which was described as an individual's "imaginative story about sexual behavior."[213] They were asked to write down one of their sexual fantasies. The stories were rated by pairs of six persons who looked at the positivity of the story outcome, whether the characters were portrayed as emotionally positive or lustful, the degree of commitment and affection described in any relationship in the fantasy, the number of words used and references to heterosexual intercourse, homosexual activity, and oral genital activity. (We question how it was determined what was negative or positive and whether the ratings were really subjective based on the raters' own opinions. We also wonder whether females or males would differ in such judgments and how the style of writing or writing ability figured into these judgments.)

Next, subjects responded to the sexual opinion survey. Lastly, homophobic attitudes were measured. Persons who viewed the heterosexual slides before the single sex set and had negative sexual attitudes showed the least positive affect. The male slides evoked the least positive affect among the male subjects. Individuals with positive instead of negative sexual attitudes reported more sexual arousal. Both male and female subjects expressed the least sexual arousal after exposure to slides of their own sex and were more aroused by the heterosexual rather than the single sex pictures.

The fantasies written by the female subjects contained more positive themes of commitment and affection "partially confirming descriptions of them as more romantic and more concerned with intimacy." The female fantasies described females in more positive terms "effectively" and in more lustful ways sexually. The males indicated their male characters as more lustful and positive only when the heterosexual slides were presented before the single sex slides. The males with positive sexual attitudes made more request references to homosexual acts in their fantasies after viewing the female slides, but these fantasies were primarily of a male character engaging in sexual activity with "groups of sexually interacting females." This, Kelley states, had a more distinctly heterosexual tone and reconfirmed the tendency of males to fantasize more frequently about group sex with females.[214]

SEX CRIMES AND PORNOGRAPHY

While some reports show a correlation between sex crimes and pornography availability, others suggest sex crime rates decrease with greater availability. It is questionable whether the statistics on amount of pornography available in society are accurate because this is a partially underground industry influenced by organized crime. It is equally questionable whether the rape and other sex crime statistics are reliable because reporting of such crimes is low and crime definitions vary from place to place. Other factors besides pornography also can influence sex crimes.

Nonetheless, the following studies represent some pioneering efforts to test the relationships between pornography and sex crimes.

Kutschinsky attempts to explain the decrease in reported sex crimes in Copenhagen, Denmark. He says that the decrease became "manifest" during the first part of the 1960s and was striking from the middle of the decade on. He surveyed four hundred men and women in Copenhagen to find out their attitudes toward pornography, victimization, and sex crimes. Each interview lasted from twenty-five minutes to one hour. Importantly, the age groups surveyed were limited to people from 18 to 49. People over 50, whom Kutchinsky said made up a large percentage of the Copenhagen population, were excluded from the survey "since the focus of this study was on recent or potential victims of sex crimes (or parents of such victims).[215] (This suggests that older people are not victims of such crimes. We note that it is widely known that older people tend to have attitudes that are tougher on crime and more antipornography.)

The persons surveyed were presented with lists of sex acts and asked to state whether they considered them criminal or not. They also were questioned as to whether any of the things mentioned had ever happened to them. Sixty-one percent of the women and 26 percent of the men said they had experienced at least one of those sorts of things. The acts included things such as exhibitionism, verbal indecency, and peeping. Only 6 percent of the incidents mentioned by the men and 19 percent of the incidents mentioned by the women were reported to police.

Kutschinsky admits that the number of respondents in many of the categories was too small to provide reliable victimization data. (For example, only two rape cases and two incest cases were reported.) Yet he proceeds to state that it would be worthwhile to see if his data had some measure of validity in spite of all the deficiencies. He mentions a general concern with distrusting data about cases that were not reported to the police. (We note that this does not take into account the many reasons why, for example, rape victims do not report to police.) Most of the cases mentioned by the people interviewed were "of a trifling nature," Kutschinsky states.[216] Despite findings that there was a decrease in reporting and little reporting taking place, he concludes that the victimization data had little value in answering the question of why there was a decrease in sex crimes registered by the police.

(We find some results of this study to be amazing. For example, when people were asked whether certain things were criminal acts, these sorts of results were obtained: Only 68 percent thought that a man petting his 16-year-old daughter was committing a criminal act. Only 17 percent of the men and 9 percent of the women thought that a man who raped a woman who had just permitted "impertinent petting" was committing a crime. Only 46 percent of the men and 32 percent of the women thought that touching a woman's breast in a streetcar was a criminal act. Only 52 percent of the people surveyed felt it was criminal to expose oneself to a woman in a park. And only 32 percent of those surveyed felt it was criminal to have consensual coitus with a 14-year-old girl. We believe that these results suggest an amazing degree of permissiveness and acceptability of what, in the United States at least, would be recognized as serious sex crimes.)

The Kutschinsky data also showed that people were slightly less willing to report in 1969 than they were in 1959. For some unexplained reason, Kutschinsky then proceeds to ignore the more serious sex crimes such as rape and molestation of children and concentrates on crimes such as peeping, exhibitionism, and indecency toward women and small children. He found the main reason for people not wanting to report these incidents was that these acts were considered trifling or not dangerous, yet he interprets the fact that 40 percent of the women said it would do no good to report such crimes as meaning that the crimes were not considered serious rather than that the women believed they would not be taken seriously within the criminal justice system.

While many of those surveyed reported becoming more tolerant in their attitudes toward sexual offenses, 7.6 percent of the men and 2.5 percent of the women said they had become more tolerant due to pornography. Kutschinsky does not consider this to be an important finding.

Based on his data, Kutschinsky does not exclude the possibility that the decrease in reported cases of indecency toward women and in exhibitionism might be fully or to a large extent explained by changes in people's attitudes toward the crime and toward reporting. Yet he concludes that this reasoning does not apply to the decrease in reported peeping incidents or in the change in indecency toward girls. He does emphasize that the conclusions in this study are tentative.

Kutschinsky's results are based on the safety-valve theory, which, as he describes it, implicitly includes an inaccuracy.

> It is unquestionable that with few exceptions the purpose of a sexual offender when committing a sex crime is to obtain sexual satisfaction usually in the form of orgasm. In many cases of sex crimes the orgasm is obtained through masturbation either while committing the crime or immediately afterwards. Since pornography is well suited (and quite often used) as a source of sexual stimulation for masturbation . . . it seems likely that some earlier offenders may have stopped or at least reduced their criminal activity while potential offenders may never engage in committing sexual offenses because they get sufficient sexual satisfaction through the use of pornography.[217]

(We note that today, however, it is recognized that many sex offenders commit offenses out of aggressive, violent, and dominant controlling attitudes and behaviors rather than for sexual reasons. Pornography alone, of course, cannot satisfy these aggressive and violent impulses.)

In looking at the influence of pornography on sex crimes, Kutschinsky again ignores the more serious sex crimes (such as rape) and concentrates on crimes such as exhibitionism and peeping. He doubts that a person who wants to be looked at and to expose himself would find relief from this in pornography. Yet, he states, this impact of pornography on victims might be great because its ready availability could cause a decrease in reporting due to fewer numbers of children and women being shocked "by the unexpected exposure of a real life penis."[218] He says that it is unlikely that victims will be directly affected by pornography when peeping is the offense. But, Kutschinsky states, pornography availability created a peeper's paradise, and one would expect pornography to serve as a substitute for peeping among some peepers, particularly the more intelligent.

Kutschinsky says that there is no reason to believe that pornography played a direct role in the decrease in crimes involving indecency toward women. (He suggests that that might be why the decrease in that type of crime was relatively slight.) However, in another category, indecency toward girls involving sexual interference short of intercourse, Kutchinsky feels that pornography could have had a major influence in the decrease in these types of acts because, he says, children are often substitutes for preferred normal heterosexual experiences with adults and pornography could serve as a similar substitute. He notes that the theory that pornography could prevent certain types of sex crimes, especially those against children, should be examined further.

Kutschinsky also reports his results in the *Journal of Social Issues*.[219] There he notes that there had been a considerable decrease in all types of sexual offenses except rape (the most serious offense).

(We note that the statistics on molesting and indecency concerning children appear to be based primarily on reports of these activities by adults and therefore do not seem to have a great deal of validity. We also note that Kutschinsky's conclusions concerning the role of pornography in the sex crime rates appear to be based primarily on his own hypotheses, which remain untested.)

Ben-Veniste studied pornography and sex crimes from the Denmark experience for the 1970 Pornography Commission. He cites a Kinsey researcher conclusion that "inferior intelligence and education of the average sex offender precludes his deriving sufficient sexual arousal from pornography to trigger overt antisocial activity."[220] (We note that this kind of finding is inaccurate, first because many sex offenders are not of inferior education or intelligence, and second because most males, educated or not, appear to become aroused to the visual and audio pornography of today, such as video or movies.)

Ben-Veniste looked at what effect the abolition of restrictions on pornography distribution in Copenhagen, Denmark, had on sex crime in that nation. Prior to 1965, pornography was obtained in a clandestine manner. In 1965, pornography became readily available to the general public. Ben-Veniste hypothesized that if pornography were a cause of sex crimes, there would be a rise in Copenhagen's sex crime rate after 1965. Alternatively, a decrease in the sex crime rate would give credibility to the safety-valve or catharsis theory. Using Copenhagen police statistics, he found that the rate of reported sex crimes had declined sharply during the period that hard-core pornography was freely disseminated.

(We point out that according to this study, it was not until June 1967 that pornographic literature was exempted from the criminal obscenity law of Denmark and that graphic pornography such as magazines, pictures, and films remained prohibited until July 1969, when all forms of pornography were legalized. Thus, it is questionable whether these sex crime figures from the mid-sixties to the late sixties are relevant to the issue of increased availability of pornography. At the same time, however, Ben-Veniste claims that books such as a Danish version of *Fanny Hill* appeared in 1964. The book, found not to be obscene, sold an estimated 300,000 copies in 1964. Publishers then glutted the market with pornographic paperback novels, which at first sold well, from ten thousand to fifteen thousand copies each. He states that by the time the 1967 law removed concern over criminal prosecution, the consumer demand had greatly lessened. Books involving topics such as sadomasochism, bondage, and homosexuality first began to appear in mid-1967, yet these had a small market of six thousand to eight thousand copies per title. It is not clear where Ben-Veniste got these figures, considering that during many of the years in question, these materials were considered illegal.)

Ben-Veniste estimates that in 1965, around two million copies of magazines showing models provocatively posed with full rear or frontal views, legs spread, and so on. But in January 1966, police cracked down, and the sales of those magazines dropped to around 750,000 copies in 1966. Sales of this category of magazine dropped to 100,000 in 1967 because people were buying the more hard-core and petting magazines, Ben-Veniste says. And in 1968, he notes, producers of the softer core materials abandoned Denmark. "Petting magazines," which included all activity except penetration, fellatio, and anal intercourse, first appeared in the fall of 1965, selling up to 35,000 copies per issue, with a total of 150,000 copies that year. Yet in 1966, an estimated one million petting magazines were disseminated. In 1967, prosecution of pornography became a low-priority item for the police, and Danes bought around 1.5 million copies of petting magazines. In 1968, those magazines began to suffer from lack of readership as the more hard core pornographic magazines took over their market.

The new category, which Ben-Veniste defines as graphic pornography, usually had two models in sexual activity. Lesbian activities were common, but male homosexual activities were rare. Masturbation by females with inanimate objects was popular in these magazines. While sales of hard-core publications were around 20,000 in 1966, they had increased to 450,000 in 1967 and 1.6 million in 1968. An estimated 1.8 million copies were consumed in 1969. The first year of serious petting and hard-core 8mm films was 1968, with around 7,500 such films sold during that year and 20,000 such films sold during 1969.

Ben-Veniste notes that there was a significant decrease in reported sex crimes from 1967 to 1969, coinciding with the widespread dissemination of pornography in Copenhagen. However, during that same period, total reported crimes showed a significant increase. His figures show that consensual and nonphysical offenses declined yearly beginning in 1964 and that physical offenses decreased sharply from 1967 to 1969. Offenses against children also decreased consistently. (We note that according to his figure 1, the total rape and attempted rape figures decreased little during the relevant years.) Ben-Veniste theorizes that a combination of increased sexual permissiveness and widespread pornography dissemination was responsible for most of the decrease in reported sex crimes. He says that it is indisputable that pornography "of the type disseminated in Denmark" apparently caused no increase in the sex crime rate. "It follows that this type of pornography should not be considered a cause of sex crimes. Not to be ruled out at this stage, however, is the possibility that pornography portraying some forms of deviant sexual behavior especially sadism may adversely influence potential offenders."[221]

Bachy also studied Danish "permissiveness." He notes that it was not until June of 1969 that Denmark's penal code was changed to make pornography in the form of reading material, objects, and pictures available to all persons age 16 and older. Thus, he feels that the Kutschinsky work was based on just a few months of experience under relaxed pornography permissiveness in that country. Like Kutschinsky, Bachy obtained criminal sex crime records from the Copenhagen police. However, there were marked differences in the official police statistics Bachy obtained and the figures used by Kutschinsky. The Kutschinsky figures were consistently much lower than the police statistics. Bachy says that if the police statistics he obtained are not reliable, they support no case, but if they are reliable, they suggest different conclusions than those in Kutschinsky and the 1970 Pornography Commission reports. He states, "Using these police statistics we can advance the hypothesis that the lifting of censorship on pornography led to a rise of rape cases for three years after which these offenses fell back to the level where they were before 1969."[222]

Bachy also found that the frequency of reported intercourse involving minors rose after censorship was lifted and then declined. He says that this might be partly explained by the fact that Danish youths began having sexual relations at a younger age. While complaints about indecent exposure fell off dramatically after censorship was lifted, he notes that in Denmark, nudity is practiced in the parks and on the beaches and that police seldom bother with arrests. "Pornography has altered the conceptions of decency. Statistics are no longer significant."[223]

Bachy suggests that the only possible conclusions are that the crime situation has not changed much since the legalization of pornography or that it has gotten worse. "We certainly cannot conclude that it has improved."[224] He also notes marked changes caused by the liberalization of pornography in neighborhoods. He says that criminality was installed at the highest level and notes a close relationship among pornography, prostitution, violence, and drugs, as well as politics and shady business. This, he says, would make pornography one of the factors corroding "western society."[225]

In *Take Back the Night*, Diana E.H. Russell quotes from the testimony of a young Danish female who argued that legalized pornography in Denmark made it legal to rape and accost women and regard them as sex objects. This woman was among many who had agreed to be photographed for pornography. She saw pornography as making every woman for sale to all men and to the lowest bidder.[226]

Also in *Take Back the Night*, Swedish feminist Britta Stovling notes that all ages can get even the most extreme pornography, such as child pornography, freely in Sweden. She also says that persons who were researching pornography, rape, wife battering and prostitution in Sweden were threatened and that "you might not allow yourself to feel raped in Sweden because it is a very liberal country."[227] She notes that the women's movement in Sweden does not have a clear-cut definition of rape, and this makes it difficult to gather accurate figures.

Brannigan and Kaparids critique research into pornography and sex crimes. They come out on the side of Kutschinsky's early 70s Denmark study, argue that most of the literature on rape makes no reference to the role of pornography, and attack work by feminists that points out such a role. These researchers do not even recognize that rape is a type of physical assault.[228]

Kupperstein and Wilson mention cases from law enforcement and increases in the rape rate as relating to a causal relationship on the pornographic issue. In their study, they looked at the alleged correlation between availability of "erotica" and reports of sex crimes and illegitimacy. For example, they reported how *Playboy* circulation increased by 311 percent between 1961 and 1968. The number of complaints received by the postal service for unsolicited sexually oriented mail increased during those same years by 170 percent. They say that the number of theaters showing "skin flicks" or "sexploitation films" in-

creased from one hundred in the 1960s to more than five hundred a decade later.

These researchers argue that absolute rape increases are misleading because they do not take into account population increases. They criticize the uniform crime reports and suggest that increases in crime rates could be indicative of social progress rather than decay. Those reports showed that the number of forcible rapes known to the police increased by 116 percent between 1960 and 1969, while arrests rose 56.6 percent during the same time. The total number of arrests for sex offenses increased by 15 percent compared to 24 percent for all nonsexual offenses. But, the researchers say, the general population also increased. They conclude that the statistics do not support the belief that increased availability of "sexual materials leads to sex crime among juveniles."[229] At the same time, they do not "disprove a connection between sexual material and sex offenses such as forcible rape."[230]

According to Kupperstein and Wilson, another possible indication of antisocial sexual behavior is illegitimate births. These increased by 51 percent between 1960 and 1969, but, again, so did the population. The researchers also note that abortion and contraceptives may have changed the number of births as well. The question of whether illegitimate births increased due to increased "erotica" could not be answered.

Dr. John Court, a practicing clinical psychologist from Australia who has worked with patients with sexual problems, has critiqued some of the work of the 1970 Pornography Commission. For example, in his September 12, 1985, testimony before the Attorney General's Commission on Pornography, he found a study by Abelson and Wilson to be "seriously deficient." Specifically, Court attacked the claim that pornography had "improved marital sex for ten million Americans and helped one million in overcoming their sexual problems."[231] He noted that this result arose from a survey of close to twenty-five hundred persons, of whom only thirty-five claimed help. He said that this was a seriously unrepresentative sample and was scientifically invalid.

The only valid uses of pornography that Court noted are as an aversion "paradigm for the paraphilias." He also agreed that sexually explicit materials of an educational sort could have a positive clinical value for treating sexual dysfunctions.

Court specifically critiqued the Kutschinsky data from Copenhagen, Denmark, which was included in the original commission studies. Court studied sex crime data from Denmark and other countries, most of which he visited personally. He emphasized that he does not claim that pornography causes a change in sex crime rates (which, he states, Kutschinsky does), but he noted that three kinds of data show significant psychological harm from pornography. These are serious sex crime traits as opposed to all sex crime traits, laboratory data on attitudinal change from experiments, and legal and clinical evidence of an anecdotal type.

For example, a Court found that in South Australia from 1972 to 1977 there was a decrease in the reporting rate of the offense of carnal knowledge, but at the same time rape reports increased, with such reports surpassing carnal knowledge reports by 1977. (These are 1970 to 1977 data.) He said the contrary trends of minor offenses decreasing and serious sex offenses increasing in countries where pornography has proliferated are common. He said, "I maintain that pornography assaults the sexual taboos of a society, bringing about desensitization to sexual abuse together with lowered inhibitions against acting out antisocial sexual behavior."[232] He called pornography a "facilitator" for "psychological aids," which he said means "acquired insensitivity and disinhibition syndrome."[233]

Yet Court more recently discontinued his research into the effects of pornography, claiming that worldwide sex crime rates are so influenced by public awareness of rape, changed legislation, and changed attitudes toward reporting that any trends can be interpreted in many conflicting ways. That only became the case around 1975, he said. He also said that researchers are at as much risk of desensitization as anyone else. He expressed serious reservations about laboratory research, discounting the impact of sexually explicit materials that are nonaggressive. According to Court, "the laboratory is not the right setting for measuring the kinds of arousal which occur in viewing or reading in privacy or in the company of a sexual partner since the laboratory setting typically creates its own inhibiting environment."[234] He also noted that laboratory studies do not deal with other issues of relevance, such as alcohol as a disinhibitor, and do not keep up with the changing media. For example, he said, lab studies use short amounts of exposure to slides, whereas in the real world it is not uncommon for people to view videos (not necessarily all pornographic) six to thirty hours per week. Lab studies also are conducted in a controlled environment and use volunteers, mostly undergraduates, whereas videos have "sexualized the home environment." Court suggested going beyond rape statistics and looking at child sexual abuse and spouse abuse to measure those increases and see whether they are more than increased recording and awareness. He said, "I believe again from clinical experience it will be only a matter of time before a

proportion of those presenting with anorexia nervosa will be shown to be the indirect victims of exposure to pornography."[235]

Court noted that studies on teenagers and children, compared to those done with university students, have not been conducted. This is strange in that children and teenagers are often the highest risk group in terms of their vulnerability to adults and to their own psychosexual development, yet because of ethical reasons they are not tested.[236]

Court argued that desensitization began with soft-core pornography, which generated dehumanization and objectification, in turn providing foundations for acceptance of "porno violence." He urged the commission to take both types of pornography seriously. He said he saw pornography as one of the causal factors in violent criminal activity. Other factors would include acceptance of law and order, the extent of police intervention, and control of sexual offenses, including convictions and penalties. He told the commission he had personally seen instances where people were psychologically predisposed toward certain violent criminal acts, and because they viewed and consumed pornography, it caused them to act out those fantasies. He notes that he cites 30 pages of such examples in his book *Pornography and the Harm Condition*. He said that he had, for example, come across many wives who were distressed by husbands wanting to treat them like the things in the books.

In a 1982 article, Court reported that rape trends in New South Wales had conflicting evidence. One set of statistics showed a sharp increase in those trends, while another showed none. Both accurately represented official figures and thus raised the question about reliability of statistics and interpretations resulting from them. Despite the conflict, Court found the data showing an increase in rape trends to be more satisfactory.[237]

In a 1984 book, Court details the shortcomings of previous pornography studies. For example, he says that the British Williams Committee Report in 1979 and its researcher, Mr. Yaffe, ignored significant research, particularly that done during the past decade by researchers such as Edward Donnerstein, Neil Malamuth, and Dolf Zillmann. Court argues that the newer studies present a strong case for "postulating a positive enhancement of sexually aggressive behavior after exposure to porno violence without adequate evidence for a decline in such behavior."[238]

Court refers to the 1971 Ben-Veniste study of pornography in Denmark. That study used sex crime rates in Copenhagen based on police reports and concluded that pornography of the sort distributed in Denmark had not caused an increase in the rate of sex crimes. Yet even Ben-Veniste said that the possibility "that pornography portraying some form of deviant behavior especially sadism may adversely affect potential offenders" could not be ruled out at this stage. [239] Porno violence was just becoming available in Denmark at that time. Similarly, Kutschinsky, who also studied sex crimes in Denmark, emphasized that his conclusions were tentative and would have to be re-examined upon a more complete analysis of the data.

Court states that the Denmark evidence is incomplete and has serious flaws. He says that it provides no evidence that serious sex crimes decreased or could be expected to decrease as a result of relaxation of pornography laws and availability. Court found that even the trend of decreasing numbers of minor sexual offenses could be due to changes in the law and in changed attitudes toward reporting rather than any real reduction in the incidence of those types of sex acts. He points out that the researchers used a great variety of data, with some relying on police report data and others relying on arrest data. He also notes that the sex crime studies up to 1970 involved settings where porno violence was rather unusual. Thus, it was too soon for evidence from those statistics to be attributed to such violence, and information relating to pornography from the 1970s would be much more pertinent than that from the 1960s. Court also argues that evidence about a rise or fall in sex crimes is "too crude to relate to the availability of porno violence."[240] In other words, those sex crimes that involve violence should be distinguished from sexual offenses that do not. In Court's view, much of the older data is obsolete because sexually explicit material available then is very different from today's pornography.

Court argues that the statement that a decline in the pornography market followed liberalization of pornography laws in Denmark is not supported by the facts. This argument, he says, was advanced by Kutschinsky in 1973 and 1978. Court notes that changes in reported crime levels, especially for crimes where the reporting level is known to be low, could make a difference. He says that under Kutschinsky's 1971 work, people were consistently "less likely to report sex crimes as pornography became increasingly available."[241] He also notes that changes in rape definitions have resulted in slight reporting increases after 1975. Yet many rape victims turn to counseling centers and obtain emotional support rather than reporting their victimization to police.

Court says that when the number of offenses becomes very large, the likelihood of effective action against the offenders is reduced, and it appears

useless to report. For example, Los Angeles data showed that in 1960 there was a 29 percent chance that a report would result in arrest. By 1972, this had dropped to a 13.5 percent chance. Another trend is toward rapists receiving either no sentence or a short sentence after arrest, and this can reduce the willingness of victims to report. Because a greater number of offenders are out free, actual offenses can increase.

Court feels that factors such as a greater percentage of the population falling within the young adult group are insufficient to account for steep increases in rape reports. He makes the following arguments and backs them up with data:

1. "Rape reports have increased where pornography laws have been liberalized."[242] Here he uses statistics from 1964 and 1974 showing rape reports to police per 100,000 population. For example, in the United States, there was a 139 percent increase during that time; in Australia, there was a 160 percent increase; and in Stockholm, there was a 41 percent increase. (Note that this is based on the presumption that the availability of pornography has "undoubtedly increased" in the nations studied.)

2. "Areas where porno violence is not liberalized do not show a steep rise in rape reports."[243] For example, Court shows that in Singapore, where the government took a strong stand against permissiveness and controlled pornography between 1964 and 1974, rape reports increased by 69 percent, from 2.01 to 3.40 per 100,000 population. (This compares to an increase from 11 to 26.30 per 100,000 population in the United States.) Copenhagen, which has liberalized pornography laws, increased from 8.88 percent to 16.32 percent per 100,000 population, a change of 84 percent. Court does note that cultural differences might invalidate a comparison of Singapore with Western nations. He also uses the example of South Africa, considering only the white population, where it was found that the rate of reported rapes, per 100,000 population, increased from 10.80 in 1964 to 13.87 in 1974, a 28 percent increase. In addition to tough pornography laws, both South African and Singapore have tough penalties for rapists, which might account for the absence of a major increase in rapes. Court also looked at two states within Australia—Queensland, which has had a conservative antipornography policy, and South Australia, which has wide availability of pornography. While rape reports increased for Queensland from 1964 to 1965 and 1974 to 1975 by only 23 percent, there was an increase of 284 percent in South Australia.

3. "Where restrictions have been adopted rape reports have decreased."[244] Court found sparse

evidence to support this proposition. However, he mentions that this might be the case in Japan, which has restrictions on pornography (such as not showing pubic hair) but no restrictions on violent content. There was a decline in rape reports to Japanese police from 1965 to 1974 from 11.5 to 6.28 per 100,000 population.

4. "Intermittent policy changes are reflected in rape report data."[245] Court found a significant downturn in rape reports from 1974 to 1976 in Hawaii, where restrictions on pornography were applied. When the laws were relaxed in 1977, rape reports increased.

5. "Changed laws on pornography are temporally related to changed rates of rape."[246] Court argues that in England and Wales, a major law change that allowed greater freedom of circulation of obscenity in 1959 resulted an increase in reported rapes from 1.10 to 2.13 per 100,000 population, or 94 percent, from 1964 to 1974. These rates have continued to rise since then. Over the 1945 to 1958 period, there was no such significant increase. He states that while the fact that other violent crimes also increased over the same time period does not invalidate the relationship shown, this might lead some people to speculate about "a more general disinhibition with porno violence having a contributory role."[247] He also implicates liberalized laws on obscenity in New Zealand as playing a role in the upward trend in rape reports from 1964 to 1974. He calls the 40 percent increase there very steep.

6. "The nature of the rape attack is changing."[248] Court states that this proposition cannot be scientifically investigated. Official records do not adequately show the nature of offenses against women and how these have changed in conjunction with changes and images in pornographic films and books. He does find support for the proposition in newspaper and police accounts that show rapes as becoming more violent and rapists forcing women into more indecent acts.

7. "Discrepant cases should not occur without adequate explanation."[249] Court emphasizes that there have been no claims that rape reports have declined where pornography has been liberalized, and he states that where factors other than porno violence availability play a major role, there are steeply increased rape rates, such as in Alaska and the northern territory in Australia. For example, Alaska also has a disproportionate male:female ratio and unusually high accessibility to alcohol.

8. "The increase in rape reports does not parallel the increase in serious nonsexual offenses."[250] Court says that although sometimes it can be shown that an increase in rape is greater than increases for nonsexual violent crime, often no such differences can be detected. Therefore, he concludes that there is insufficient evidence to support or deny this proposition. He suggests that laboratory studies would be the best way to investigate this.

Overall, Court suggests that while a causal relationship cannot be excluded, "it is safer to assume a multifactorial situation in which pornography is playing a significant part."[251] Court feels that while there is a demand for freedom of expression, this is offset by the loss of freedom suffered by victims of sexual assault and the general damage done to society as a whole. He says that a strong case can be made for restraining "porno violence" when it is seen in conjunction with what is known about modeling and about the responsiveness of pathological and "normal" groups to pornography, as well as what from studies of media violence have shown.

In 1984, Court addressed the question of using pornography to relieve sexual problems. He concludes that the case for using pornography to treat such problems, including marital problems, has not been made. Although many therapists advocate the use of pornographic materials in sex therapy, he said that there is little satisfactory evidence to demonstrate its effectiveness. Things such as encouraging masturbation as a therapy goal might be considered therapeutic, but things such encouraging incest would not. Yet Court found extreme examples of these uses, such as one medical practitioner who said he would prescribe a picture of a female tied up and in chains with a naked man pointing a sword at her genitals in order to produce a masturbatory situation. He also felt that a picture of a naked man with a cat-o'-nine-tails striking a woman on the genitals could stimulate a man and have great therapeutic value. In response, Court asks what the outcome of stimulating a man to sexual arousal with sadomasochism would be.

Court again critiques the Wilson and Abelson study for the 1970 Pornography Commission that claimed that more than a million people had obtained relief from a sex problem by reading or looking at pornography. As mentioned earlier, the researchers admit that the survey found only thirty-five such people out of close to twenty-five hundred and that some of these people might have been talking about benefits from information taken from a marriage guidance manual rather than real pornography. Court notes that the study found much higher percentages of people citing negative effects from pornography, such as knowing of someone being led to commit rape because of pornography.[252]

Court does not reject use of any explicit sexual materials in therapy. He indicates that there is evidence suggesting that erotica can be valuable in therapy in educational ways. It is important to emphasize that such materials have been specifically prepared for therapy and educational purposes, but this differs from pornography, which is available on the commercial market. He cites Feshbach and Malamuth from 1978 as opposing therapists' use of films of rape or encouraging them to indulge in rape fantasies.

In 1973, Court wrote about the place of "censored material" in treating behavior disturbances. In using such material, it is assumed that the subject will be able to respond with a rich fantasy experience in order to reinforce, either positively or negatively, the properties of the situation being portrayed. It is hoped that this will then have an effect on future behavior. Factors such as the setting in which sexually explicit material is used, the type of stimuli used (such as slides and pictures), and the use of shocks can make a difference, Court says. He believes that carefully planned uses of "erotic stimuli as reinforcers" should be continued.[253]

In 1977, Court stressed that sex crime data that do not differentiate between severe crimes such as rape and lesser crimes are thoroughly unreliable.[254] He also wrote of a reevaluation of pornography and sex crimes in light of recent trends. For example, the decline in sex crimes in Denmark has been associated with large reductions in minor offenses such voyeurism and exhibitionism. Court rejects the satiation hypothesis that people will quickly lose interest if pornography is made readily available, and he notes that there could be differences in reactions among people who are sexually well adjusted versus those who are sexually disturbed. What appears to happen is that material becomes progressively more bizarre. He also found it to be a myth that the pornography in Denmark was primarily for the tourists. There was no evidence showing what percentage of the pornography there was bought by foreigners or citizens of Denmark. A third myth, according to Court, is the idea that children can be "adequately protected while adults retain their right to freedom."[255] In Denmark, for example, children of any age could obtain pornography from machines located on the streets.

The last myth Court examined was the theory that the number of sex crimes would decrease with greater availability of pornography. He concludes that one cannot demonstrate a causal relationship between pornography and increases in sex crimes any more than the supposed declining sex crimes can be causally linked. However, he finds that there are 3 significant trends in reported rape figures related to the circulation of pornography: (1) Upward trends in liberalized countries follow after relatively stable periods of reporting, which (2) appear to coincide closely with the availability of pornography in the community; (3) in a country where controls were exercised, the upward trend was not found. He emphasizes that the Danish data were from a time before sadistic pornography became widely available.

Court and O. Raymond Johnston presented a paper on pornography and harm to the International Conference on Psychology and Law in July 1982. These authors reject suggestions that anecdotal evidence be ignored. They note that much of the most "fruitful work" in fields such as psychiatry is based on exhaustively investigated individual case studies. They do, however, suggest rigorous criteria for assessing such data.

They state that it is wrong to look for a one-on-one relationship between cause and effect in trying to prove the pornography/sex crime case, noting that it is unrealistic to require such an approach of social science data. Contemporary behavior studies aimed at "multifactorial" behavior explanations, along with associations taking into account predisposing factors, individual differences, and opportunities for behavior to take place, have to be considered. Court and Johnston argue that it is inappropriate to use a principle that causation of harm must be proven beyond reasonable doubt. (This was suggested by the Williams committee.)[256]

These authors suggest that harm involves certain effects and damages to healthy functioning or the normal state of someone or something. Harm can be both physical and psychological. Moral judgment is involved in harm that is not purely physical. One has to look at who or what is harmed, including performers, consumers, and others who are threatened by someone else's consumption of pornography. There is also the concept of cultural damage, in which institutions in society are harmed.

In 1984, Court stated that there is no research on effects of pornography on children because it would be "monstrously unethical" to expose children to pornography to determine effects. This is because the risks of harm are too great.[257]

Court quotes Gene Able from a 1982 BBC television program in which Abel said he was convinced of the link between pornography and sexual violence. He said that he had no doubt that potential rapists could become actual rapists after exposure to certain types of pornography. This information was based on his personal experience in working with sex offenders.[258]

In 1984, Beverley Brown also emphasized the

main problem with pornography experiments is medical ethics. Researchers are not allowed to do "efficient research on human beings."[259] The studies linking rape and pornography are not reliable in her view because not much evidence is available on the amount or type of pornography in circulation and because crime figures are not reliable. She states that if people are going to be seriously concerned about rape as an issue, then there are many other more important factors that should be looked at as well, such as patrolling the streets, alcohol use, prosecuting the victim in rape trials, lighting conditions on streets, and commission of rape by people known to victims. She's concerned about concentrating on pornography and its connection to rape rather than looking at rape "as a political problem." She is afraid that this will distract people's attention away from the issue of rape and believe that in this context, pornography is not all that important.

(It should be noted that the Williams committee from England attacks much of Court's work and that Court defends his work in a variety of his writings.)

Baron and Straus studied the relationship between pornography and rape in the United States. They used the FBI's uniform crime reports as the database for rape statistics and admit that the underreporting of rape in those statistics is well known. This study included control variables that were believed to be related to the incidence of rape, such as the percentage of people living in standard metropolitan statistical areas, the percentage with incomes below poverty levels, the percentage of persons aged 15 to 24, the gender ratio for 15- to 24-year olds, and the percentage who were black.[260]

While the researchers looked at all the variables, we report here the relationship found between pornography and rape. They looked at sex magazine readership, which was measured by looking at subscription and newsstand sales of eight sexually explicit magazines in 1979. (Those magazines were *Chic*, *Club*, *Forum*, *Gallery*, *Genesis*, *Hustler*, *Oui*, and *Playboy*. The data were from the Audit Bureau of Circulation.) They converted the number of copies sold to a rate per 100,000 population in each state. The rape rate statistics used were the average number of rapes per 100,000 population during 1980–1982 based upon the Uniform Crime Reports (UCR). They found large differences in those states with the highest readership and those with the lowest readership, along with an "unusually high correlation between the sex magazine readership index (SMRX) and the UCR rape rate."[261] However, they emphasize that there are other plausible explanations for the correlation between the sex literature readership and rape.

For example, validity of this is threatened by large differences in willingness to report rape among the states. Baron and Straus emphasize that their findings do not show that sex magazine readership causes rape, only that there is a strong association between the two.

Baron and Straus found that their study supported three of four 'theories of rape': "(1) the theory that gender inequality contributes to rape; (2) the theory that pornography provides ideational support for rape; and (3) the theory that rape is a function of the level of social disorganization in society."[262] They failed to find support for their additional theory that rape "reflects a spillover from aspects of society in which violence is culturally approved."[263] They found that rape rates were higher where women had a lower status compared to men. Their study compared various factors from each of the fifty states.

Despite the fact that they found a direct relationship between the rape rate and the circulation of eight sex magazines studied, Baron and Straus say that they doubt their finding represent a "cause-effect relationship." They based their opinion on other experimental studies showing that exposure to nonviolent pornography diminishes aggression of men against women, the Kutschinsky type of rape rate studies in European nations, and the high correlation they found between the circulation of "the women's magazine *Playgirl*" and the rape rate (commenting that it is unlikely that female readership of such a magazine contributes to the rape rate). Finding these three bodies of evidence inconsistent with the theory that pornography causes rape, they say that they cannot ignore the chance that their finding is "spurious—that it reflects confounding with other unmeasured variables." For example, they suggest, the link between pornography and rape could be due to "their shared association with hypermasculinity."[264] Baron and Straus conclude that violence, social disorganization, and sexism—not pornography—are the fundamental causes of rape and that these underlying causes of violence toward women should be addressed in social policy and research.

(We note that Kutschinsky-type studies have been criticized elsewhere in this chapter, that studies of whether nonviolent pornography causes or diminishes aggression against women have varied results, and that there is reason to believe that *Playgirl* appeals primarily to a male homosexual market. It is also questionable whether the eight magazines considered in this study are representative of pornography. The researchers ignored other, more hard core magazines, pornographic videos, and other types of pornography.)

PORNOGRAPHY AND ABUSE OF PERSONS

Professionals have concluded that pornography use can lead to the abuse of persons. Details of those conclusions appear in this section. Also see chapter 4 for examples of pornography victimization.

Victor B. Cline, a clinical psychologist, testified before the Attorney General's Commission on Pornography on September 11, 1985. Over a period of sixteen years, he treated around 225 males who "had sexual pathology or family disruption because of their involvement with pornography."[265] He found that these males, almost universally, experienced a four factor syndrome:

The first thing that happens was an ADDICTION effect. There seemed to be a clear psychological addiction to this material. Once involved they kept coming back for more and still more. The material provided a very powerful sexual stimulant or aphrodisiac effect followed by some kind of sexual release. The pornography provided very exciting and powerful fantasies which they frequently recalled and elaborated on at moments of reverie.

Secondly there was an ESCALATION effect. With the passage of time they required more explicit, rougher, more deviant kinds of sexual material to get their "highs" and "sexual turn-ons." In one sense it was reminiscent of individuals afflicted with drug addictions. In time there is an increasing need for more of the stimulant to get the same effects as initially. If their spouses or girl friends were involved with them the same thing occurred. They pushed their partners over time into doing increasingly bizarre and deviant sexual activities. In many cases this resulted in a rupture of the relationship when the spouse or girl friend refused to go further leading to conflict, separation or divorce.

The third thing that happened was DESENSITIZATION. With material (in books, films or magazines) that were originally perceived as shocking, taboo breaking, repulsive or immoral (even though still sexually arousing) in time were seen as acceptable and commonplace. They, in a sense, became legitimized. There was also, increasingly, a sense that "everybody does this"— or at least many people do which gave a kind of permission to do likewise.

The fourth thing that occurred was an increasing tendency to ACT OUT the sexual activities witnessed in the pornography viewed. This involved a great variety of sexual acts including sexual seduction of children, sexual aggression against women, as well as an increasing

reper(sic)toir of sexual activities in the bedroom with one's current partner. Group sex and partner switching were other outcomes. Voyeurism, exhibitionism, fetishism, and necrophilia were other examples of acting out behavior.

It was at this point, often, that the individual was seen in therapy occasioned by court sanctions, acute family and marital disruption, getting a venereal disease, or as an act of conscience when one's current behavior became unacceptable to the individual.[266]

Cline cited the work of McGaugh (1983) concerning memory. McGaugh's work concluded that "experiences at times of emotional (or sexual) arousal get locked in the brain by the chemical epinephrine and become virtually impossible to erase," he said.[267] The memories, graphic and vivid, continue to intrude on the mind's memory screen and arouse and stimulate the viewer. This, Cline said, helps explain the addicting effect of pornography. Pornography's "powerfully sexually arousing experiences" become vivid memories that the mind continually replays, he told the commission.[268] He emphasized that most evidence suggests that sexual deviations are learned behavior, not genetically transmitted. Cline noted that McGuire, Young, and their associates suggest that many sexual deviations are learned or occur "through the process of masturbatory conditioning."[269] Cline said, "Vivid sexual memories and fantasies are masturbated to which at the moment of climax further reinforces their linkage in the brain and leads in time to the increased probability of their being acted out in real life behavior."[270]

Research by Russell and Trocki, based on a random survey of 930 women, concluded that a large percentage of American women have suffered from "pornography-related victimization" (such as being upset by it, being asked to imitate it, or being asked to pose for it). For example, 43 percent of the victims of father–daughter incest reported being asked to pose for pornography (four times the percentage reported by nonincest victims).[271]

In her September 11, 1985, testimony before the Attorney General's Commission, Russell presented a "theory about the causative role of pornography in the occurrence of violence and sexual abuse of women and girls."[272] This is true, she argued, because pornography seems to contribute to the four "preconditions for the occurrence of sexual assault" (developed by David Finkelhor in 1984 to explain child sexual abuse):[273]

1. Someone must want to sexually abuse a person. (Research studies have shown that pornography fosters "rape fantasies and desires in a significant number of men who view it.")
2. The person's "internal inhibitions" against acting upon the desire must be "undermined." (Pornography does this by seeming to legitimize certain criminal and abuse acts, such as the myth that women enjoy rape.)
3. The person's "social inhibitions against acting out this desire (e.g., fear of being caught and punished) have to be undermined." (Pornography rarely shows any negative consequences for rapists or sexual abusers.)
4. The perpetrator must undermine or overcome the victim's ability to resist or avoid the sexual abuse. (For example, pornography is shown to children, wives, and lovers to "undermine their resistance to participate in certain sexual acts.")[274]

Russell admitted that the data do not prove that pornography causes the abusive behavior, but that it is reasonable to conclude that pornography does have "some effect." Ten percent of the women interviewed felt they "had been personally victimized by it."[275]

A survey by the *Regeneration News* of Baltimore, Maryland, a local ministry, found that 60 percent of the homosexuals they questioned said pornography "increased the depth of their homosexual problem." Sixty-eight percent said that using pornography "increased the likelihood that they would act out sexually." Only 24 percent said that using pornography was a release that made it less likely that they would do such acting out. Three-quarters of them agreed that pornography made them focus on certain sexual acts and body parts, and 36 percent said that it made their sexual interests more bizarre.[276]

PORNOGRAPHY AND SEXUAL DEVIANCE

Some studies have found a relationship between exposure to pornography and sexual deviance. Self-reports of rapists and other sexual deviants indicate less use of pornography than reported by "normal" men, greater arousal to coercive sexual images, and imitation or acting out of aggressive pornography against real women victims. It is reasonable to bring into question the veracity of rapists, however, as researchers have yet to find a reliable way to test this veracity.

Scott reports that psychologist William Marshall of Kingston Penitentiary and Queens University (Canada) found that of eighteen rapists who used " 'consenting' " pornography "to instigate a sexual offense," seven said "it *provided a cue to elicit fantasies of forced sex*" and ten "used it to elicit rape fantasies."[277]

Scott also says that research by Marshall and Abel "suggests that a substantial number of rapists and child molesters may be using pornography to start the process that triggers the crime."[278] Scott describes the Marshall study of sexual deviants who were his patients at his Kingston (Ontario) Sexual Offenders Clinic. From 1979 to 1985 he studied 89 deviants (23 rapists, 15 incest offenders, 33 heterosexual child molesters, and 18 homosexual child molesters). His control group of 24 men of similar age, socioeconomic class, and intelligence had no

history of sexual offenses. Nineteen of the 23 rapists studied used hard-core pornography occasionally or frequently.

According to Scott, one of the rapists told Marshall he used pornographic pictures of "people enjoying sex with each other" (that is, nonviolent pornography) "to get aroused enough to rape."[279] He said he did not use pornographic rape scene pictures because the women in the scenes were obviously acting and, in his words, " 'Who would want to rape a willing participant?' "[280] Upon questioning, five of the other rapists made similar claims. Marshall found that the rapists uniformly believed that the " 'girl next door' " shown in the nonviolent pornography would resist rape and would not want to be raped.[281] "This, then, triggered their rape fantasies (and for almost 40 percent of Marshall's subjects, it triggered actual rape.)"[282] These findings are important because they suggest that for a substantial number of rapists, images of consensual sex, not images of rape, trigger the crime of rape. This, Scott says, is the type of pornography that the industry and the American Civil Liberties Union (ACLU) claim is harmless.[283]

Scott reports that Marshall found a similar trend among child molesters. Fourteen of the thirty-three used hard-core pornography to instigate sex crimes. Marshall found that while 37 percent of "normal" males used hard-core pornography, 61 percent of incest offenders, 75 percent of child molesters, and 94 percent of rapists used it.[284]

Schultz reports on conversions with seventy sex offenders in the Waupun prison in Wisconsin. About half of the men she spoke to, mostly the better educated, denied that pornography had played any significant role in their attitudes toward sex. Others, however, reported having been influenced by pornography and wanting to practice what they read. A number of the men told her that they believed they would not have committed their sex offenses if they had had a source of sex information besides pornography.[285]

Barry suggests that there is a problem with comparing convicted rapists to males in the "normal" population. She notes that the FBI estimates that only 10 percent of rapes are reported to police, only a few rape cases go to court, and only a few rapists get convicted. "As a result there is in the normal population a significant percentage of unreported, uncaught, unconvicted rapists."[286]

Davis and Braucht found the following:

Relationships among indices of exposure to pornographic materials, age of exposure, moral character and deviant sexual behavior were evaluated within a retrospective cross-sectional design in which subjects were young men between the ages of eighteen and thirty with a wide range of putative character and records of deviance. A modest relationship was found between exposure to pornography and low scores on a moral character indices but this relationship was due almost entirely to those subjects exposed late (after age seventeen) and it seemed most plausible to attribute the relation to those with low character scores voluntarily exposing themselves to pornographic materials. In the case of sexual deviance positive relationships between amount of exposure to pornography and deviance were found for all age of exposure subgroups. While these data may be interpreted as supporting the hypothesis that exposure to pornography plays a role in the development of sexual deviance and in precocious heterosexual behavior limitations of the research design do not permit a definite conclusion in favor of such an interpretation. It should be emphasized that these same data are also interpretable as supporting the hypothesis that persons who come to engage in sexually deviant behavior also tend to make use of pornography and to expose themselves voluntarily to it.[287]

These researchers were concerned with three aspects of character: moral blindness, quality of moral reasoning, and "defective interpersonal character such as that exhibited in exploitive and shallow interpersonal relationships."[288] The study detailed things such as right and wrong, self-interests, standards of having the most fun possible without regard for the long-term effects, and moral reasoning. These characteristics were used to determine three character aspects.

Davis and Braucht note that pornography lacks reality constraints that mark erotically realistic works of fiction, and this explains why pornography could have a detrimental effect on character development if it is a person's primary source of information about sex. They proposed two porn hypotheses. First, because character is largely formed by early adolescence "exposure to porn is a voluntary matter that largely reflects the character one has."[289] Second, character, although partly formed by early adolescence, "is still open to influence by experience in that the content of pornography exercises a detrimental influence on it particularly in the area of the quality of interpersonal relationship and moral reasoning."[290]

Their sample consisted of 365 males ages 18 to 30. Fifty-five percent of the sample had been arrested one or more times, and 25 percent had been arrested several times. The sample group was divided into jail prisoners, Mexican-American students, black students, liberal fraternity members, liberal Protestants, conservative Protestants, and seminary students. The researchers looked at a variety of measures such as exposure to pornography; deviance in the home, peer group, or neighborhood; labeling selves as deviant for reading or watching pornography; and age of earliest exposure to pornography. The subjects' moral and interpersonal characters were assessed by self-reports and by one male and female who knew each person.

Subjects also were tested for general deviance and sexual deviance. The sexual deviance measure included questions of voyeurism, forcing a girl age 12 or younger to touch their sexual organs, forcing a girl age 16 or younger to have intercourse, forcing a girl age 16 or older to have intercourse, forcing a man or boy to have intercourse, dressing as a woman, allowing other men to use them sexually for money, stealing articles of women's clothing to wear, exhibiting their sex organ to women in public places, and whether or not they were ever arrested for a sexual offense. Drug use, including alcohol use, was examined, as were liberal and conservative sexual attitudes and behavior.

The researchers purposefully studied groups with widely differing backgrounds and levels of deviance. The inmates and liberal fraternity group had the greatest exposure, and the conservative Protestants and seminarians had the least exposure to pornography. The three religious groups had the least home deviance, and the inmates had the most. The minority groups and the inmates showed the most deviance from middle-class standards, and the three religious groups showed the least. While the three religious groups labeled themselves deviant for reading or watching pornography, the inmates minority and liberal fraternity group did not. The earliest age of exposure to pornography varied from 16 to 17 for the religious groups to 13 to 14 for others. (This conflicts with other studies that showed prison populations, particularly sex offenders, having less or later exposure to pornography.) The inmates and liberal fraternity had the most liberal attitudes and behavior. In the category of sexual deviance, the inmates and the black subjects were the only two groups above the grand mean. Again, the three religious groups had the lowest scores. Similar results were found for general deviance and on the test of character.

This study found that "exposure to pornography has a significant correlation with sexual deviance" and that "exposure to pornography is the strongest predictor of sexual deviance among the early age of exposure subjects."[291] While this made a plausible case for the contribution of porn to sexually deviant behavior, it also made a plausible case that use of pornography was simply part of routine social practices of some deviant adolescent subgroups or, perhaps both are true. For the early age of exposure subgroup, the researchers found that the amount of exposure correlated significantly with things such as number of different petting partners in high school, group sex, masturbation frequency, frequency of homosexual intercourse, and " 'serious' sexual deviance." Davis and Braucht say that while the data are not conclusive in support of a causal connection between pornography exposure and engaging in early deviant and heterosexual behaviors, they are not inconsistent with such an interpretation. Three hundred six of the 365 subjects had seen enough pornography and remembered enough for a stable age of exposure scale. (Again this shows high exposure to pornography even among young people.) The researchers found that deviance, exposure to pornography, and sexual deviance were strongly interconnected.

> At the very least this argues for a pattern in which exposure to pornography is part of a strongly deviant lifestyle including in some cases strongly homosexual patterns and including in other cases a high level of heterosexual experience with little regard for the quality and duration of the relationship. While one cannot assign a causal role to exposure to pornography there is good

reason to consider it part of these deviant lifestyles.[292]

Davis and Braucht conclude that those first exposed at age 17 or later already had poor characters and this explained the modest relationship between poor character and pornography at that age. Where sexual deviance was involved, they found a positive relationship between deviance and exposure to pornography at all ages of exposure. They also found a positive relationship between peer pressure to have sex and sexual deviance and exposure to pornography. However, because they did not have age of commission information for the more deviant behavior, they could not pin down this causal hypothesis. They pointed out limits on the design and conclusions. First, most of the data came from self-reports. Second, a causal link, or lack thereof, could be better studied in a longitudinal designed study in which behavior and character could be examined before and after exposure to pornography and other variables such as peer pressure could be examined as they develop. Third, they also note that it might not be mere nakedness or sex that has a detrimental effect, but rather people's attitudes toward sex, other people, and the body that are critical. Fourth, they state that many men read or see large amounts of pornography without any detrimental effects, and they suggest that more attention should be given to what "inoculates persons against the potentially detrimental effects of exposure."[293]

Walker contrasts causal versus catharsis views and labels those with the first view as moralists and those with the second view as professionals. (Readers are cautioned to remember that the pornography of the late 1960s, which Walker studied, differs dramatically from that of today.) Walker claims that early studies were not scientific and thus subject to error. For example, in 1955 Bloomer and Hauser found that male inmates in a penal institution and female delinquents in a state training school for girls were more inclined to participate in antisocial sexual behavior and more sexually aroused following the viewing of erotic pictures or movies. However, no comparison group was used.

A 1969 study of psychologists and psychiatrists by Lipken and Carns found that 80 percent had never encountered cases in which pornography was a cause of antiscoial sexual behavior. But 7.4 percent had encountered cases in which they were somewhat convinced of a link, and another 9.4 percent had had cases in which they suspected but were not convinced that there might be a link between the two.

A 1967 study of psychiatrists and psychologists by the New Jersey Committee for the Right to Read asked, "Have you ever had a patient or patients whose behavior is otherwise within a normal range and who was (were) provoked into antisocial behavior primarily as a result of exposure to sexually oriented literature?"[294] The response was 84.3 percent no, 5.4 percent yes, 9.4 percent no answer, and 1 percent a qualified response. (We point out that the question limited responses to persons otherwise within a normal range, which could perhaps eliminate numerous people who were provoked into antisocial behavior as a result of exposure to pornography.)

In 1965, Gebhard, Gagnon, Pomeroy, and Christenson studied 1,356 white males convicted of sex offenses, 488 white males in the general population, and 888 white males in prison who had never been convicted of sex offenses. They found no observable connection between pornography and sex offenses. Sex offenders were less responsive to pornography than nonoffenders, Walker reports.

In 1935, Von Bracken and Schafers found that when murderers, swindlers, thieves, and sex offenders were allowed to choose books they liked to read, the sex offenders tended to prefer the sex books.

Walker states in summary that the data do not clearly establish whether pornography is or is not related to sexual offenses. While some studies and cases suggest there is such a relationship, the best scientific studies (according to Walker) suggest that the sex offender is less responsive to pornography than the average person.

In his research, Walker asked two questions. First, is the sex offender someone who has been exposed to pornography more frequently than the nonsex offender? Second, does the sex offender have different thoughts, fantasies, and ideas as he views pornography than the average person? The test subjects were thirty male sex offenders who were hospitalized in the maximum security ward of a state hospital. All had been convicted of aggressive sex offenses, mainly rape. The control group was thirty male mental patients who were not charged with sex offenses but were in the same ward as the sex offenders. A second test was conducted with thirty male offenders, mostly rapists, and thirty male prisoners who had not been charged with a sex offense. A third test involved thirty male undergraduates at one university who were age 21 or older and thirty male black undergraduates at another college who were age 21 or older.

In the first and second groups, experimental subjects were not found to be exposed to pornography more or less frequently than their controls. However, the offenders saw and read representations of heterosexual intercourse at a significantly younger age, which Walker suggests might be a chance finding.

There were no significant differences between the subjects and controls on effects of pornography on others, but the subjects reported more frequently than the controls that pornography had led them to commit a sexual crime and that pornography had something to do with their being in the prison or hospital. Also, they thought that their sexual activity had been increased by these materials. For example, fourteen of thirty-six offenders said that they had personally experienced the consequence that pornography led to sexual crime. Only four out of forty-six nonoffenders had that same experience. The sex offenders more frequently than the nonoffenders found usual sexual intercourse to be "very enjoyable." The controls were more exposed to pornography than the subjects, except that one group of nonoffenders saw live sex shows more than the controls. The experimental group collected pornography for a significantly longer time than did the controls. The college sample was more inclined to consider pornography favorable, masturbate to it, and feeling like having sex as a result of it. The control groups saw pornography as having more effects, both in leading to sex crimes and providing a safety valve for antisocial impulses (these are contradictory) and in encouraging sexual behavior. The controls had a more negative reaction to the pornography than the sex offenders. However, most of the men in all the groups studied found pornography appealing and sexually arousing.

Walker notes that the subjects did not respond to the pornography with greater sexual arousal, more pathological sexual ideation, or more aggressive sexual fantasies than did the controls. However, he concludes that the results are only minimally reliable. (We suggest that the stimuli used in the study may not have been adequate to elicit differences in response.) Walker discusses how the sex offenders who were less exposed to pornography than the controls may have said pornography affected their behavior as an excuse. He does admit that a small "but significant minority of sex offenders" said that pornography had "led them to commit their offense."[295] They affirm significantly more often than either the college or men's club sample that they were influenced by pornography to commit a sexual crime. Walker concludes that the study overall lacks validity and is only minimally reliable.

Johnson, Kupperstein, and Peters used as a study population forty-seven white males convicted of sex crimes in Philadelphia and as controls people from the data file of a recent national probability study conducted by Abelson et al. The convicted males were placed on probation and involved in group psychotherapy sessions. Eighteen were convicted for rape, twelve for homosexual offenses, ten for exhibitionism, and seven for pedophilia. The data showed that substantial proportions of both groups had experience with "erotic material" during the previous two years. For the offenders, books were a more frequent source of recent experience with pornography; for the nonoffenders magazines were a more frequent source. While 60 percent of the offenders said they obtained visual erotica from friends, only 24 to 27 percent of the nonoffenders group did so. Forty-four percent of the sex offenders and 40 percent of the controls had encountered erotic material by age 14, but 27 percent of the offenders and from 6 to 13 percent of the controls had not seen pornography until age 21.

The researchers report that "proportionately more of the sex offenders (48 percent) than the nonoffenders (28 percent to 38 percent) reported textual depictions of 'sex activities which include whips, belts or spankings.' "[296] (We note that this study clearly disproves the 1970 Pornography Commission's own finding that sadomasochistic materials were not widely available at that time.) Data not included in the report were said to reveal that offender and nonoffender groups did not differ with respect to the number of occasions on which pornographic materials were read or seen.

The sex offenders were much more likely than the controls to report no effect from their last seen pornography, while the controls reported more disgust. But 16 percent of the offenders and many of the other men did not respond to those questions. The researchers found that the sex offenders more often agreed with socially desirable or neutral effects of pornography, such as the theory that it provides an outlet for bottled-up impulses or gives relief to people who have sex problems. Those persons who said pornography had certain effects were then asked whether it had an effect on them personally, on someone they knew personally, or on no one they knew. For example, 62 percent of the sex offenders and only 34 percent of the nonoffenders said that pornography provides an outlet for bottled-up impulses. Of these, 11 percent of the total sex offenders said it had had an effect on them personally, and 19 percent of the total sex offenders said it had had that impact on someone they knew. The corresponding figures for nonoffenders were 8 and 10 percent. Again we find that 2 percent of the sex offenders, in other words one person, said pornography had led him to commit rape, and 6 percent, or three more sex offenders, said it had led someone they knew personally to commit rape. A full 10 percent of the nonoffenders said pornography had led someone they knew to commit rape.

The researchers conclude that there are important limitations on the study, particularly the small sample size, which resulted in no statistical tests being performed. Therefore, the particular findings did not resolve the critical questions. However, their overall finding was that experience with "erotica" is not a factor that differentiates sex offenders and nonoffenders.

Gebhard et al. analyzed sex offenders in 1965. They note that "the impulse to seek pleasurable sexual visual stimuli is statistically, biologically and psychologically normal. There is nothing pathological or antisocial in enjoying and owning pornography. . . . A few sadistic photographs do not prove the owner a sadist any more than a copy of *Lolita* proves its owner a pedophile."[297]

These researchers found that the aggressors against minors had the largest percentage (21 percent), of men who were sexually aroused by stories and pictures of sadomasochism and the largest proportion (13 percent) who were strongly aroused. Only 8 percent of the control and prison groups responded to such material, and only 3 to 4 percent had strong responses. Among aggressors against minors, 74 percent were sexually aroused by pornography, and 44 percent who were strongly aroused. While three fifths of the offenders against adults said they had little or no response to pornography, they ranked third (with 14 percent) among those who were sexually aroused by sadomasochistic stories or pictures.

They report that the men who were sexually aroused by seeing females also were aroused by seeing representations of heterosexual activity, striptease, and nude female art. Some of the sex bias in the study comes through where they make a comment about "erotica, giving most adults a mild pleasurable response."[298] They do not mention whether this includes women. In fact, women and their responses and feelings appear to be ignored throughout.

The researchers found it striking how few of the men studied had failed to see pornography, yet they were surprised when large portions of these men said they had little or no sexual arousal from pornography. (We wonder how the pornography was defined and also note that these sex offenders may well have had reasons for pretending not be aroused to such material.) Interestingly, these authors felt that factors such as age, marriage, and poor education could mitigate against "conscious sexual response to pornography."[299] (We believe this flies in the face of the reality that responses to pornography are not cognitive but emotional, a factor recognized by authorities such as the Supreme Court.) They comment that uneducated males from lower socioeconomic backgrounds might ask why get worked up about a picture, with which you can do nothing, when responding to a real female would make more sense because she represents an attainable goal. They also say that people whose sexual drives have been met do not respond readily to pornography. (This study appears to have been done long before the use of physiological measures of arousal was common. The results are based on self-reports of questionable reliability.)

Gebhard et al. state that a strong response to pornography "is associated with imaginativeness, ability to project and sensitivity, all of which generally increase as education increases and with youthfulness."[300] They argue that because most sex offenders are not youthful or well educated and because their responsiveness to pornography is less than that of others, it "cannot be a consequential factor in their sex offenses" unless one argues that the inability to respond to "erotica" precludes gaining a curious satisfaction and thereby causes the person to behave overtly, which renders him more liable to be arrested and convicted. They use an analogy comparing men attracted to real women versus those attracted to pornography with men who say that a pot of stew is more stimulating to a hungry man than a photo of a beef roast. Showing their bias against the lower classes, they emphasize that a certain amount of know-how is needed to obtain pornography, and they suggest that those who make a living through illegal activities or are in lower socioeconomic brackets have such know-how and that upper-class and middle-class men usually do not. (Again this goes against the results of in other studies that show that men at all socioeconomic levels have found equal access to pornography.) These researchers conclude that sex offenders and non–sex offenders are not differentiated by the possession of pornography.

Cook and Fosen studied 129 inmates, 63 sex offenders, and 66 criminal code offenders in the Wisconsin State Prison. They were shown a series of twenty-six slides depicting sexual behavior and then were interviewed about their prior exposure to pornography. The researchers found no differences between the sex offenders and criminal code offenders on the measure of sexual arousal to the slides. They did find numerous differences between them concerning past exposure to pornography. The sex offenders in general had experienced milder and less frequent exposure to pornography.

The slides shown to the sex offenders and criminal code offenders would not be considered violent, sadomasochistic, or extreme pornography. Most of them included petting, intercourse, cunnilingus, fellatio, and undressing. The subjects rated their own levels of sexual arousal to each of the slides from neutral to extremely exciting, and they were told the study was for the President's Commission on Obscenity and Pornography. The study data did show that there was a large amount of exposure to pornography by all of the subjects and controls. Many of these men said that the information in the pornography to which they had been exposed was not misleading. Only a few of the sex offenders had viewed pornography within the twenty-four hours before their offense. Many had engaged in sex, masturbation, or both after viewing pornography. The sex offenders came from more sexually repressive home environments. There was little difference in the arousal to the slides between the two groups.[301]

Cook, Fosen, and Pacht also reported the findings of this study in *The Journal of Applied Psychology*. In that report, they emphasize the similarity between the sex offender and the non–sex offender. In this report, however, they describe how the severity of pornography and the frequency of exposure to pornography were determined. For example, a rating of 2 was given for exposure to live entertainment such as go-go dancers and burlesque shows, semierotic movies in regular theaters, soft-core magazines, and "erotic" novels. A rating of 3 was given for exposure to hard-core pornographic drawings, films, or photographs depicting explicit sex acts. (We note that these subjective types of judgments could have had a major impact on the findings relative to exposure to pornography.)

In this report, the researchers state that there were significant differences between the sex offenders and criminal code offenders in the types of sexual behavior reported after viewing pornography. The non–sex offenders more frequently masturbated. Four of the sixty-three sex offenders said viewing pornography had encouraged them to commit their offense. Overall, both groups showed relatively low arousal compared to that of college students who had seen similar material. These researchers conclude that childhood variances that encourage repression of sexual feelings and behavior are associated with "antisocial sexual behavior."[302] However, "[i]n short these data indicate a negative relationship between exposure to pornography and the tendency to commit a sex crime."[303]

These researchers did find that independent factors of erotic response showed that there were marked differences in arousal patterns to different forms or depictions of sexual behavior. For example, the rapists were more aroused by slides showing intercourse and heavy petting, and persons convicted of indecent liberties with females were less aroused by slides showing fellatio. The researchers say that with additional work, verbal reports by offenders of arousal in response to particular pornographic stimuli might usefully aid the treatment and diagnosis of persons with sexual maladjustments.

Goldstein studied fifty-two male users of pornography who volunteered in response to flyers in adult bookstores, institutionalized sex offenders (rapists and pedophiles), nonheterosexuals (homosexuals and transsexuals), and a control sample (males from Los Angeles). They found that the sex offenders and homosexuals had less adolescent experience with pornography than the controls. The homosexuals reported greater current exposure to pornography than the controls, and the "sex offender and sex deviate groups" had a higher incidence of masturbating to erotic materials than the controls. The following percentages of users reported wishing to try an act seen in pornography: 30 percent of the adult controls, 48 percent of the teen controls, 35 percent of the adult rapists, 80 percent of the teen rapists, 35 percent of the adult pedophile male object, 65 percent of the teen pedophile male object, 25 percent of the adult pedophile female object, 40 percent of the teen pedophile female object, 33 percent of the homosexual adults, 39 percent of the homosexual teens, 14 percent of the transsexual adults, 29 percent of the transsexual teens, 58 percent of the adult pornography users, and 66 percent of the teen pornography users. From 6 to 15 percent of the adults tried imitating the pornography, and from 14 to 30 percent of the teens tried imitating it. Anywhere from 0 to 50 percent of the men participated in other sex acts shortly after viewing pornography. Goldstein found that the homosexuals and pornography users showed an obsessive interest in erotica in adulthood.[304]

Goldstein et al. designed a detailed survey administered to institutionalized sex offenders, non-institutionalized sexual deviants, users of pornography, and controls. While these researchers present the overall idea that rapists are less exposed to pornography than "normal" persons, the reader should remember that exposure to pornography is still high and a source of learning. One table in this study shows that the adult rapists were much more likely to masturbate to or use sexual material to get excited to masturbate than the controls and slightly more likely to use this material to get excited to participate in sexual relations. The rapists were slightly more likely to wish to try acts seen and to actually try these acts. They also were more likely to have been punished by parents when caught with pornographic material.

Although more of the rapists had had their first heterosexual intercourse earlier than the controls, they had less sex education and knowledge in youth. A much higher percentage of the rapists and

pedophiles had had homosexual intercourse. The data show that subjects attained through a flyer in pornographic outlets had intercourse much more frequently per week than the control subjects. The rapists and male-object pedophiles said they enjoyed intercourse less than the controls, with 92.5 percent of the controls enjoying it, 73.7 percent of the rapists enjoying it, and 45.0 percent of the male-object pedophiles enjoying it.

The institutionalized sex offenders, homosexuals, transsexuals, and pornography users reported less frequent exposure to pornography during adolescence than the controls. The same was true for the period one year prior to the interview, except that the users and homosexuals showed an obsessive interest in "erotica" in that year. The users also had marked increases in sexual activity after adolescence. All the groups of sexual deviants reported less than average exposure to pornography than did the controls.

> This finding suggests that a reasonable exposure to erotica particularly during adolescence reflects a high degree of sexual interest and curiosity. Sexual curiosity is correlated with an adult pattern of acceptable heterosexual practice. . . . If the pattern of sexual development proceeds along a deviant track then deviant sexual behavior in later life may be correlated to either underexposure to erotica or an obsessive interest in it.
> . . . It appears that unresolved sexual conflicts in adolescence relate to adult sexual patterns in which erotica is a necessary stimulant (in the case of users, homosexuals, sex offenders for example) to obtain gratification. In the normally developed male the adolescent use of erotica as an adjunct to sexual actions declines and the sexual partner becomes the primary source of arousal and gratification.[305]

In another study, Goldstein et al. studied sex offenders, including rapists and pedophiles, sexual deviants, heavy users of pornography who were not institutionalized, and a control group. Relying on the self-reports of these people, they found that the rapists reported significantly less exposure to certain types of pornography than the other groups. They found homosexuals and pornography users compared to controls to have an obsessive interest in sexual stimuli while having much less exposure to "erotica" as teenagers. Sex offenders, pornography users and sexual deviant groups, except the transsexuals, reported greater amounts of masturbation in response to sexually explicit material than did the controls.

The researchers conclude that "a reasonable exposure to erotica particularly during adolescence reflects a high degree of sexual interest and curiosity.

This curiosity is correlated with an adult pattern of accepted heterosexual interest and practice."[306] They found that less than average exposure during adolescence correlated with development in an extremely restrictive atmosphere and low amounts of exposure to heterosexual intercourse. They note that for subjects who developed along deviant sexual tracks, deviant sexual behavior later in life correlated with either underexposure or obsessive interest in erotica. According to the researchers, if sexual conflicts in adolescence are unresolved, this may relate to "adult sexual patterns in which erotica is a necessary stimulus to gratification."[307] For other men, using erotica in adolescence as an adjunct to sexual actions declined, and the sexual partner became the main source of gratification and arousal.

Kercher and Walker studied twenty-eight men convicted of attempted rape, rape, or forcible rape and used a control sample of twenty-eight adult felony offenders convicted of nonsexual crimes. All samples were taken within three weeks of admission to the Texas Department of Corrections. Each group had twelve Caucasians, thirteen Negroes, and three Mexican Americans. The physiological measures used in the study were penile volume and galvanic skin response (GSR). Each person was tested individually in an experimental room. Each stimulus was rated on five subjective responses: boring/interesting, sick/healthy, ugly/pretty, awful/nice, and dirty/clean. There were nine slides, two of a pastoral neutral warm-up nature, one of a clothed young couple in a romantic pose, and one each of the following: nude female, male masturbating, heterosexual petting, heterosexual fellatio, heterosexual coitus, and male active sadomasochism. Each slide was shown for twenty seconds with one minute in between.

The GSR resulted in significant differences, with rapists more reactive to all but two slides (the male masturbating and the sadomasochism) and considerably more aroused than nonrapists to the young clothed couple on the grass. There was no significant difference in penile volume between the rapists and nonrapists. The rapists evaluated the erotic stimuli more negatively than the nonrapists, which these authors say was more important to emotional meaning but may be more anxiety provoking than repulsive.[308]

Quinsey et al. studied penile and skin conductants and ranking responses of child molesters compared to nonmolesters. The subjects were twenty child molesters, a "normal" group of ten non-sex-offending patients, and eleven nonpatients. (The nonpatients were recruited from acquaintances of the experimenters.) Each of the molesters had committed a sexual offense when age 16 or older against a child age 13 or under with a five-year age difference minimum

between him and the victim. Many had committed multiple offenses. Twenty percent had had sexual contact with boys, 20 percent with boys and girls, and 60 percent with girls. Beckman biopotential skin electrodes recorded skin conductants. A mercury in rubber strain gauge recorded penile circumference.

A slide sort test involved two arrays of six black-and-white slides shown to subjects one at a time on a sorter tray that was lighted. A seventh color slide in each array showed a sadomasochistic act. In one array, the figures were nude, and in the other the figures were partially clothed. There was one person of each sex on each of three age levels—between 18 and 30, 12 and 15, and 5 and 11. Each subject was asked to choose the slide that he found most sexually attractive.

In what the researchers called the psychophysiological test, the subjects were instructed to relax in their chairs, look carefully at the slides, and think of the slides in a sexual way. There were two slides in each of the following categories: heterosexual activity involving a partially clothed or nude man and woman depicted on a bed petting; nude or partially clothed adult females, pubescent females, and child females in the same age groups previously mentioned; nude or partially clothed males in the same age categories; children under five; " 'sadistic' or SP (a female nurse being choked by a man and a man being whipped by another man)"; and a neutral chandelier or landscape.[309] The age of the persons depicted in the slides was felt to be a socially relevant variable.

The child molesters tended to respond to the children's slides more than the "normal" subjects. For the child molesters, there was a striking disparity in data between the subjective ratings of the subjects and the penile measurements. The molesters ranked the adult females as most arousing but exhibited the largest penile responses to child females. The penile responses of the heterosexual child molesters peaked on child females, whereas those of the homosexual child molesters peaked on child males.

These researchers conclude that a slide series can be used to differentiate child molesters from other persons by using penile circumference measures. However, they note that there were "marked discrepancies between the penile circumference responses (PCR) and ranking data and between the ranking data and both the child molesters' and normals' histories. In addition, the PCRs did not show high within subject correlations with skin conductance responses (SCRs) in either of the groups."[310] Because of this, they believe that skin conductants cannot differentiate sexual from neutral stimuli.

Abel et al. looked at components of the sexual

arousal of rapists. Importantly, these researchers questioned the usability of certain techniques for measuring sexual arousal. They said: "Although other physiological variables such as respiration, galvanic skin response (GSR), and cardiac rate do correlate with increasing sexual arousal, similar increases are also seen in emotional states unrelated to sexual arousal, such as anger, guilt, anxiety, etc."[311] Only penile erection in males occurs exclusively during sexual arousal.

They also critique the Kercher and Walker study by stating that the lack of differences in penile responses of rapists and nonrapists may have occurred because subjects were not given rape cues, because the slides used were a weak sexual stimulus compared to movies, and because the brief twenty-second presentation might not have "allowed sufficient opportunity for erections to occur."[312] They also argue that the GSR changes found were not specific to sexual arousal and might have indicated some other emotional state. Abel et al. found audio descriptions of sex more useful than movies or slides for generating arousal to sexual stimuli such as rape.

In their small sample, they tested thirteen rapists and seven nonrapists, all of whom were mental health patients. The nonrapists included persons who preferred sex with children, homosexuals, voyeurs, and masochists. None of these people was "normal." All of them suffered from deviant sexual arousal and had been referred for treatment. In these tests, erections were measured by a circumferential penile transducer and also by subjective self-reports.

The subjects listened to vivid two-minute audio-taped descriptions similar to those used in other studies. One of these was a description of mutually enjoyable intercourse. This was very male oriented, with the man described as "you." The second portrayed a rape situation involving the same woman who appeared in the first. The woman resists, and a knife is involved in the incident. The victim described for each man was a female of the age he said he preferred. Thus, some of the females were children. The responses showed that the nonrapists and the rapists were aroused by the mutually consenting sex with mean values of erections in the 60- to 65-percent range. The rapists showed similar arousal to the rape scenes, whereas the nonrapists showed very little arousal to those scenes. The researchers suggest that treatment not aimed at arousal to rape cues had not helped some of these people.

A second study by Abel et al. involved nine subjects chosen from the thirteen rapists. One audiotape used involved a description of the patient physically assaulting a female, including slapping and holding her down but making no reference to attempted sexual intercourse. The second tape described the same victim and setting, but the patient is depicted as raping the victim and the victim as struggling to avoid being raped. The results showed a 55 percent erection mean to the rape scene and a 26 percent erection mean to the aggression scene. The researchers note, however, that the entire study seemed to show a lot of individual differences. Those persons who preferred forcing themselves on a woman or injuring her had deficiencies in their arousal to mutually enjoyable intercourse with a woman. Only when force was added to intercourse, or, in one case, where pure aggression occurred, did adequate erections develop. Abel et al. say that if aggression was needed to arouse, the likelihood of aggression against the real life rape victims of these patients was quite high.

A third study tested whether preference for age of sexual object can be determined by showing subjects slides of nudes of various ages and measuring erection. The researchers developed audiotapes of similar depictions of rapes with different age victims. Results showed that the rapists were more aroused by the age groups they had victimized or said they preferred. Thus the researchers conclude that treatment could focus on reducing arousal to such victims.

The overall results showed that using explicit descriptions of rape and nonrape can separate rapists from nonrapists and also separate the more physically dangerous rapists from the less physically dangerous ones. Such descriptions also can determine the preferred age of victims. However, the study was limited by a small sample size and the patients were cooperative. The researchers note, "Since sexual arousal can in part be significantly controlled by the patient, a patient who chooses to conceal his responses may reflect different findings."[313]

Kolarsky, Madlafousek, and Novotná studied twenty-eight subjects, half of whom had been previously examined by the researchers. After interviewing them, Kolarsky diagnosed fourteen of the subjects as sexual "deviants." These were people in which normal (inoffensive) sexual behavior was either insufficient or absent in providing the person with full sexual satisfaction. All of these people had a preferred "sexual object" of an adult woman. Ten were exhibitionists without other known offenses, four had a history of offensive touches including sexual aggression without rape, and eight had experienced normal intercourse. The control sample consisted of fourteen paid hospital employees and soldier volunteers who were said to be "sexually successful and active."[314] Oral questions showed no evidence that these men suffered from any form of sexual deviation. The subjects' penile volume changes were measured by the phalloplethysmograph.

Eighteen black-and-white silent film scenes of ten seconds each were created for this study. Care was taken to see that sexual arousal dissipated before the next stimulus was presented. In fourteen of the scenes, a young woman was shown naked during the entire scene; over the course of the other scenes, she was shown reaching full nudity. All the scenes contained different sorts of "possible seductive behavior such as chastity or provocative display of the body."[315] (We find it peculiar that chastity would be considered seductive.) All of the behavior shown was precoital. The subject was always sitting or standing and not lying down. The front of her body was usually visible. Before the second set of nine scenes, several nonseductive scenes involving the same actress were shown. These included portrayals of her with a motionless face and a motionless torso, standing without emotion in a swimsuit, and from the front. These were included to test the affects of weaker versus stronger stimuli. For example, one picture portrayed her lying naked on her back "simulating high sexual arousal, being prepared for" intercourse.

The researchers found that overall the normal and deviant subjects responded least to the supposedly weak scenes, and most strongly to the precoital scene, and less strongly to the seductive scene than to the precoital scene. There were no significant differences between them. The various "seductive" scenes had a different arousal effect. Five of the scenes got a strikingly stronger response in the deviants. These researchers attribute this to deviants being aroused by those scenes with an absence of "seductive pseudoretreat." They define this seductive pseudoretreat as "avoidance of the frontal body position with respect to the camera and the tendency to squeeze the thighs together."[316] However, people analyzing these scenes could not even agree on which ones showed the thigh squeezing. This cast doubt on using the deviant scenes for comparison purposes. Therefore, only the remaining thirteen seductive scenes were used, and these showed no significant difference between the deviants and normal men. In an earlier study, these researchers had found that while female nonerotic activity inhibits the sexual arousal of normal men, it does not inhibit that of deviants.

Barbaree, Marshall, and Lanthier studied rapists' deviant sexual arousal, which they say is often used to explain deviant sexual behavior. Their subjects were ten men imprisoned in the Canadian Federal System, seven of whom were in prison for the crime of rape and the others who had admitted to committing rape. The control group was ten university graduate students. A mercury in rubber strain gauge measured sexual arousal. Two sets of audiotaped descriptions of seven episodes each, two minutes per episode, were created. Some of these involved mutually consenting sex, others involved rape activities, and yet another involved a male's nonsexual physical assault of a woman. The amount of consent given by the woman and the force and violence used were varied in these descriptions. The subjects were told "that sexual arousal in response to all these descriptions was natural and that sexual arousal evoked by violent episodes would not indicate a propensity to enact such episodes."[317] (We consider it rather peculiar to tell rapists and normal men that it is normal and natural to be aroused by depictions of rape.) The nonrapists showed significantly lower arousal to rape than to mutually consenting episodes. The rapists, however, did not have significantly lower arousal to rape episodes.

Quinsey, Chaplin, and Upfold studied the sexual arousal of rapists and non–sex offenders to sadomasochistic and nonsexual violence themes. They argue that because some rapists have extremely sadistic fantasies, it might be expected that they would be aroused by sadomasochistic themes in pornography. They noted that rapists were found to masturbate to various sadomasochistic themes and to be aroused by descriptions of inappropriate sexual behaviors. However, responsiveness to sadomasochistic themes is not unusual in the general population if the types of pornography available are any guide. Thus, "real life sadomasochistic activities may or may not be a legal or clinical problem depending on whether real damage is done to the victim/partner and whether the victim/partner consents."[318]

In this study, twenty males, most of whom had been charged with rape, attempted rape, or indecent assault of a female and two of which were charged with homicide as part of a sexual assault, were the subjects. The control group consisted of ten males from the same institution with no history of sexual offenses and ten control subjects from the community recruited through local employment agencies or the newspaper. A mercury and rubber strain gauge measured penile responses. The subjects were told that they would listen to a number of audiotaped descriptions that would last about an hour. The researcher told them, "I want you to listen closely to what is said and imagine you are the person saying it."[319]

Forty audiotaped stories narrated by a male in the first person were used. There were ten categories with four stories each. The categories were "neutral situation, consenting sex with a female partner, rape with a female victim, nonsexual violence with a female victim, consenting sex with a male partner, rape with a male victim, nonsexual violence with a male victim, consenting bondage and spanking with a female partner, masochistic consenting bondage and spanking with a female partner (where the male was tied up and spanked), and nonconsenting bondage with a female victim."[320] The duration of the stories varied between forty-five and fifty-five seconds, with a thirty-second period between the end of each scoring interval and the beginning of the next story. The stories consisted of approximately 155 words, with 10 words to set the theme, 20 describing the victim and partner, 15 describing the intention and approach, 25 describing the victim's or partner's response, 45 dealing with sexual contact (if any) and the partner's or victim's response or resistance, and 40 describing continued response and contact. All of the victims and partners were described as attractive.

The results showed that neither psychotic/nonpsychotic status nor institutionalization was important to the results. The rapists responded less to the consenting sex with a female partner than did the control subjects. The rapists responded more to rape stimuli than to consenting sex stimuli, which did not agree with these researchers' prior work. The finding that the rapists showed substantial arousal to nonsexual violence also was not in agreement with their prior work. They suggest this might be due to inclusion by chance of more sadistic individuals using more strictly controlled stimuli that were of shorter duration. The rapists did not respond to nonsexual violence involving male victims. This, the researchers say, suggests that sexual arousal to descriptions of nonsexual violence occurred because the descriptions resembled violence in a sexual context. The rapists did not respond more than the nonoffenders to the masochistic bondage, sadistic, or spanking stories. The researchers note that it was surprising that the rapists did not respond differently than the nonrapists according to whether the partner or victim consented or not. The researchers attempt to explain these findings by stating that non–sex offenders' arousal is inhibited by victim pain, whereas rapists' arousal is not. (This, however, suggests that the bondage, spanking, and sadistic themes did not involve victim pain.) The researchers note that only stories involving victim injury and vicious attacks differentiated the rapists from the nonrapists. The fact that some of the bondage and sadistic descriptions involved nonconsenting victims was not a differentiation.

AGGRESSION AND PORNOGRAPHY

Researchers interested in determining if there is a relationship between pornography and aggression have studied some effects of R-rated motion pictures and X-rated films and videotapes depicting violence against women. There is a pronounced interest in pornography as it relates to rape myths and even the desire to rape. Does pornography desensitize the viewer to the true exploitive nature of rape? The more socially threatening question is "Does pornography cause people to commit rape?"

Dr. Edward Donnerstein, a psychologist who specializes in research involving aggression, testified at the public hearings on the civil rights ordinance before the Minneapolis City Council Government Operations Committee on December 12, 1983. Donnerstein told the committee that his research showed fairly dramatic results after only five or ten minutes of exposure to pornography. And, he cautioned, when he mentions no effects in the short term for "erotica," he refers to material *made by himself or colleagues* "which is sexually explicit and does not show power orientation between males and females."[321]

While it was expected, in earlier research, that rapists would become aroused to scenes of rape, brutality, and mutilation, Donnerstein said, it was not expected that "normals" would be sexually aroused by such material. Yet, he said, Neil Malamuth found in the late 1970s that normal males were aroused by such scenes when the rape victim showed sexual arousal to the abuse. Malamuth and others have used a Rape Myth Acceptance Scale involving myths such as "Any woman who hitchhikes deserves to get raped," "women who wear provocative clothing are putting themselves in a place to get raped," and "women unconsciously set up situations which force rape on them."[322] Donnerstein found that after only ten minutes of exposure to aggressive pornography (in which women are being aggressed against) males were much more willing to accept such rape myths.[323] He also found that males were more accepting on the Acceptance of Interpersonal Violence Scale, which dealt with spouse battering and ideas that women are turned on by force and aggressiveness.

Donnerstein cited a Malamuth study in which normal males were exposed to five minutes of pornography that showed a woman becoming sexually aroused to being raped. The following results were found: The males said that 25 percent of the women they know would enjoy being raped. They said that 30 percent of the women they know would enjoy being "aggressively forced into sexual intercourse."[324] And up to 57 percent of the males indicated some likelihood that they would commit a rape if guaranteed they would not be caught.

Donnerstein said that in the general population, between 25 and 30 percent of "normal, healthy males" indicate "some willingness they would commit a rape."

> We are not saying they would in fact commit a rape except there is high correlation between items which I have talked about and the use of actual physical force admitted by these individuals.
> I am not going to make that leap, that this would predict actual rape. It predicts attitudes about rapes by offenders.[325]

These men believe that other men would rape if they were guaranteed of not being caught. They basically identify with the rapist. Thus, he said, there is a good chance they would never convict a rapist. They also believe that rape victims "derive pleasure" from their assaults and cause their own assaults, he said. That same 25 to 30 percent become aroused to graphic forms of violence against women, rape images in which women enjoy being raped, and sexual violence in which the woman does not show a "positive" reaction.

He pointed out that 25 to 30 percent of the male population is a large percentage. He noted, "[W]hen you think about the amount of people that might see any particular film, even if it is only one percent, we are talking about an incredible amount of potential harm to women."[326]

For this study, Donnerstein and his colleagues constructed neutral films showing erotic action and one in which there was a negative ending to a rape scene (that is, the women did not enjoy the rape). He found that the 25 to 30 percent of the males who said they would rape if they were guaranteed not to be caught were much more aroused sexually by the rape scenes than by the erotic material. He said if one took the males who saw the market-produced rape film in which the victim was turned on, put them in a room an hour later, and asked them to think of something sexually arousing and write it down when they became aroused, their writings would involve rape scenes. While there is nothing wrong with sexual arousal, he said, it is the "juxtaposition with violence" that is the problem.

Those who have worked in the media violence field for years, such as Donnerstein, believe it "is almost impossible to find individuals becoming aggressive when they see violent films unless they have been angered or predisposed."[327] Yet in the pornography research, they began with a group of subjects who were not predisposed or angered. These were normal, healthy males, not hostile people or sex offenders. The result was an increase in aggressive behavior after seeing sexually violent material in which women enjoy being raped and brutalized. In their research, Donnerstein and others use "very normal people"[328] and expose them to sexually violent material.

> We preselect these people on a number of tests to make sure they are not hostile, anxious or psychotic. Let me point out that the National Institute of Mental Health and the National Science Foundation and our own subjects committee will not allow us to take hostile males and expose them to this type of material because of the risk to the community. They obviously know something some of us do not. . . . They are so normal, incredibly normal, that there is no risk. This works against us in what we are doing.[329]

Donnerstein said that the research shows that "if you can measure sexual arousal to sexual images and measure people's attitudes about rape you can predict aggressive behavior with women, weeks and even months later."[330] This material leads to sexual arousal and changes in attitudes, he explained. "Once you have found those you can predict aggressive behavior," he said.[331] He emphasized that the research is not correlational. "We are not talking about correlations where we get into chicken/egg problems of which came first, we are talking about causality."[332] Predictions of potential aggressive behavior after exposure to certain images can be made independent of people's past viewing habits, background, and initial hostility, he said.

In his own research, Donnerstein and his colleagues took "normal" males and exposed them to R-rated films (in which women are killed in sexual ways), X-rated violent films, and X-rated non-violent films. The results showed the following:

> You see over a time less depressed, less annoyed or bothered by forms of graphic violence. If you ask them about particular perceptions of violence, if you look at the same films from day one to day five, if it is one week or two weeks, they see less blood and less blood and gore and less violent scenes. Over time they find the material more humorous, they are less depressed, they enjoy the material more and are less upset. You also find the same things for the X violent films, those are X-rated in which the main scene is women being

raped, women being bound, hung, aggressed against in general. You find that subjects find less violence, as time goes on, against women in these films over repeated exposure. They are just as sexually aroused over this, however, to the material. Sexual arousal does not decrease. They feel much less likely to censor the material, they are less offended by the material, they see this less graphic and less gory, they look away less. What that means on the first day when they saw women being raped and aggressed against, it bothers them. By day five it does not bother them at all, in fact, they enjoy it.

> If we look again how upset, they were less upset and less debased and they found the material makes a great deal of sense and was more meaningful by the end of the week. . . . They find the material less degrading with time.[333]

Donnerstein and his colleagues used a control group on the last day. Persons who saw the violent or X-rated material saw less injury to a rape victim than those who did not. They considered the woman to be more worthless than did those who did not see the material.

Donnerstein explained that current research has different results from older studies because different techniques are used, different questions are asked, and the material has changed. The 1970 Presidential Commission on Pornography "made a concerted effort not to deal with violence images," he said.[334] Then, he noted, short-term effects, rather than long-term ones, were examined. With long-term exposure, he said, "subtle changes in attitudes" and "sexually calloused" attitudes occur.[335] Donnerstein said that the effects from exposure to pornography differ from the effects of exposure to general violence in the media because they occur "much more rapidly" and are "much stronger."[336]

> [I]f you assume that your child can learn from Sesame Street how to count one, two, three, four, five, believe me, they can learn how to pick up a gun and also learn attitudes. I think the concern should be what attitudes are they learning about male/female relations. Unfortunately, their attitudes are influenced with too much degradation and violence.[337]

In 1980, Donnerstein received a $2,500 grant from the Playboy Foundation to study pornography and aggression against women. He was quoted as saying that he had had a feeling that Playboy was interested in his research, so "why don't they support it?"[338] Thus, he had applied for the grant. He said that his research does not support Playboy-type philosophies because it shows the negative effects of images of women as objects or victims of aggression.

Donnerstein was quoted in the *Wisconsin State Journal* as emphasizing that "censorship is not the answer."[339] He said that getting rid of pornography will not get rid of the problem of the subordination of women. Instead, Donnerstein advocates more sex education.

Mosher and Katz studied 120 males involved in a verbal aggression against women study. The men watched either a neutral or pornographic film. Half of them were told that they had to have a high level aggression against women if they wanted to see the second pornographic or neutral film. Half were told they could see the films regardless of their level of aggression. "When aggression was instrumental to seeing a pornographic film it increased."[340] High sex guilt males who had not seen a pornographic film increased their aggression more than low sex guilt males. High sex guilt males who had seen a pornographic film were less instrumentally aggressive than the low sex guilt males, who were more interested in seeing a second pornographic film. Different female assistants elicited different levels of aggression from the males. The researchers drew a parallel with everyday living: "[T]he expectancy that aggression will lead to a sexual goal makes aggressive behavior more likely."[341]

Tannenbaum exposed male college students to one of three film conditions. These were a neutral film titled *Adventures of Marco Polo*, a student-made erotic film, and a selected aggressive film. The erotic film was considered more arousing but significantly less aggressive than the aggressive film. Subjects were angered by a confederate, exposed to the film, and then given the opportunity to shock the confederate. The researcher found a significantly greater level of aggressive behavior after exposure to the erotic film compared to the aggressive film.

In a second experiment under similar conditions, subjects were required to respond in a nonaggressive manner. Here Tannenbaum found that when "the called-for behavior is inconsistent with the initial encounter, the [drive] model no longer holds." The drive model hypothesizes that nonspecific generalized physiological arousal triggers subsequent behavior, whether aggressive or not, rather than the specific content of a message triggering such behavior.

In a third study, humor was used as a stimulant. The humor film subjects used significantly greater electric shock intensity than subjects exposed to the neutral film, yet the humor film produced a significantly lower level of shocks than did the aggressive film.

A fourth study used a film of a young woman going to an apartment and disrobing in a sensuous manner, apparently in preparation for a lover's arrival. In one version, the woman reminisces about prior lovemaking experiences. In another version, she reminisces about a past affair but recalls the man's infidelity and bad treatment of her. She mentions murder possibilities, and in one version inserts of possible weapons are shown. Here the combined erotic and aggressive content produced a significantly higher shock response.

Tannenbaum concludes that while these data support a drive formulation in which a person aroused by any means behaves more intensely, when put into a specific response situation, the data do not reject the influence of "cognitive cue factors."[342]

In another series of studies, Tannenbaum dealt with the consequences of censorship treatments, in some cases concluding that people's fantasies could be more explicit than what is deleted from films.

Zillmann, Hoyt, and Day studied sixty male university undergraduates. Subjects played teacher roles while another subject, actually an experimental confederate, played a learner role. These involved differences of opinion. The learner exposed the subject to noxious noises when he or she disagreed with the learner's opinions. The subject was then exposed to various communications and told of an opportunity to administer noxious stimuli to the learner. The communications used were a neutral film, an aggressive film showing a prize fight, a violent film in which a prisoner was tortured and mutilated in great detail, and an erotic film that showed a young couple engaged in sexual foreplay and face-to-face intercourse in a variety of nonaggressive positions. After exposure to the erotic film, excitation was consistently higher than in any of the other conditions. This film tended to intensify the postexposure aggressiveness to a higher degree than those communications that showed violent and aggressive acts.[343]

Baron studied thirty-six undergraduate males. They were in an unaroused condition with pictures of scenery and furniture, a mild arousal condition with pictures of young women in various stages of undress, and a moderate arousal condition with pictures of young nude women from issues of *Playboy*. Results confirmed the hypothesis that minimal and moderate levels of sexual arousal would reduce aggression.[344]

Zillmann and Sapolsky studied sixty-six male university students. The subjects were either provoked or not provoked by the first experimenter. Then they were exposed to either neutral slides, slides of nude women from the waist up, or sexually explicit slides showing males and females engaged in intercourse, cunnilingus, and fellatio. A second experimenter showed the slides. The first experimen-

ter later returned and told the second examiner that he had forgotten to have the subjects fill out a required form.

The results showed that exposure to the "erotica" did not have an appreciable effect on the unprovoked subjects. However, the provoked subjects showed greater annoyance overall but less annoyance after exposure to the pornography. It should be emphasized that the pictures used here were mild. Interestingly, the provoked subjects were not more aroused by the photographs of the sexual activities compared to the photographs of the nudes.[345]

Jaffe and Berger studied twenty-nine female introductory psychology students from Tel Aviv. Some of the subjects read erotic material for five minutes. Others read neutral material. The sexual arousal group had significantly greater sexual affect than the control group, and these subjects also delivered significantly higher shocks to other persons than the control group. Jaffe and Berger conclude that the relationship between sex and aggression is a cross-cultural phenomenon.[346]

Donnerstein and Hallam used sixty male introductory psychology undergraduates as subjects. Two erotic films and two aggressive films of three and a half minutes each were used. The erotic films were black-and-white and depicted sexual intercourse, including oral and anal, and female homosexuality. The aggressive films were black-and-white clips from a movie called *The Wild Bunch*. Subjects were given the task of writing an essay on the legalization of marijuana. An alleged confederate rated their essays and gave them shocks. They were then exposed to one of the films and were later given the chance to shock the confederate. The results showed that "highly erotic films can act to increase aggressive responses against females under certain conditions."[347] The condition here was the opportunity to aggress immediately after being exposed to the film. The researchers raise the question of why the pornography influenced aggression against women but not men.

Cantor, Zillmann, and Einsiedel involved sixty female undergraduates from a communications course in a study of defensive and offensive strategies in a game situation. There could be negative or positive feedback in the form of either a loud noxious noise or pleasant music. When a person made an incorrect guess, the other player (an experimenter) could choose either type of feedback. After the first game in which the subject received only minor negative feedback, subjects were shown a film and their physiological responses were monitored. The neutral segment was *Marco Polo's Travels*, the aggressive segment was a prize fight, and the erotic segment showed a couple engaged in intercourse. Each lasted six or seven minutes.

When provocation occurred, retaliation by the subjects was "significantly higher after the erotic film than after both the aggressive film and the neutral film."[349] Surprisingly, among the women who had seen the aggressive film, those who were not provoked reacted significantly more aggressively than the provoked women, which the researchers attributed to an apparent disinhibiting effect of the film on the unprovoked women. They found that whatever the film content, the more arousal the film produced, the more aggressively the subjects tended to behave. They found no evidence that provocation or film exposure affected benevolent responses. They emphasize differences between the ways men and women are affected by viewing violence. The women were not aroused by the aggressive film, so it did not enhance their aggressive behavior when they were provoked. They were aroused by the erotic film and retaliated when provoked. The researchers emphasize the need to study both women and men in media violence research.

White studied ninety-five college males. They were told their task was one of impression formation. In the angry condition, the personality rating of the subject by the confederate was very insulting and unfavorable. In the nonangry condition, it was more favorable. Sample shocks were given, and subjects were then told to rate slides. Four sets of slides depicted a variety of sexual and nonsexual activities. Subjects saw only one set. A control group was used. Subjects later were allowed to shock confederates. Aggressive behavior toward the confederate "was reduced by exposure to erotic stimuli that evoked primarily positive responses relative to the effect of exposure to neutral material."[349] White found a slight tendency for aggressive behavior to be increased by exposure to erotic stimuli reported to be unpleasant and disgusting. He says that the excitement and entertainment from certain sexual stimuli might be compatible with performing aggressive acts and feelings of anger.

Baron and Bell studied eighty-six undergraduate introductory psychology males. Anger was aroused in some of the subjects by showing them unfavorable descriptions of them written by confederates. Some were then shown neutral scenery and furniture-type pictures. Others were shown ten "cheesecake" pictures of young women in negligees and bathing suits, shown ten pictures of nude women taken from *Playboy*, or ten pictures of couples engaged in sexual activities such as intercourse and oral sex. Still others were shown a notebook with ten typed sexual activity descriptions. Subjects were allowed to shock confederates after being exposed to the stimuli.

The angry subjects rated the stimuli as more attractive than the nonangry subjects. Pictures of sexual acts were rated as less arousing than pictures of nude women. Aggression for both the nonangry and angry subjects appeared to have been reduced by exposure to the pictures of women in negligees and bathing suits, nude women, and sexual acts but not to the erotic passages. While exposure to the mild stimuli sharply reduced aggression by the male subjects, the more arousing materials resulted in aggression levels that were similar to those in subjects exposed to the nonerotic stimuli. The experimenters suggest that the stimuli may not have been arousing enough to yield the expected aggression increments. It also can make a difference whether subjects rate the materials before or after their opportunity to aggress.[350]

Baron notes that most studies of arousal and aggression use only male subjects. In his study, he used forty-five undergraduate females who were enrolled in an introductory psychology course. He randomly assigned them to four levels of stimuli and to two levels of prior provocation. He used a modified Buss "aggression machine." This has ten push-button switches that can ostensibly be used to give "electric shocks of varying intensity to another individual."[351] A stop clock measured the duration of shocks.

Each set of two subjects met each other in a waiting room and exchanged information in writing concerning the type of impression they had made on each other. This information was really drafted by the experimenter. Personality sketches were constant and neutral. Ratings were varied. Some contained derogatory remarks intended to anger the subject, while others were favorable. In the next phase, both subjects were taken to another room. One subject was exposed to erotic or nonerotic stimuli, then allowed to aggress against the other in the adjoining room. Mild sample shocks were given to a subject who was allowed to aggress to convince her of its reliability. Subjects were told that the stimuli they were to look at was to be used in another experiment.

The four sets of stimuli were nonerotic, which consisted of scenery, pictures of furniture, and abstract art; beefcake, which consisted of ten pictures of handsome men in shorts and bathing suits; nudes, which consisted of ten nude young men from *Playgirl*; and acts, which consisted of ten pictures from "erotic" magazines showing couples engaged in lovemaking including intercourse and oral sex. These examples were matched to similar studies involving male subjects. The subjects were allowed five minutes to examine the pictures and rate each along dimensions of "calm-excited; disgusted-entertained; relaxed-aroused; pleased-annoyed."[352] Each person then had twenty opportunities to administer shocks to the confederate subject.

The subjects were significantly more aroused by the pictures of sexual acts than by the nonerotic pictures, and they were significantly more excited by these. They rated the acts as significantly more disgusting than the nonerotic or beefcake pictures. There were somewhat less negative reactions to the nudes, and the magnitude of the effects was somewhat greater for the angered rather than the nonangered subjects. Aggression was significantly reduced in the angered subjects by exposure to mild erotic stimuli (the beefcake pictures) but was enhanced by exposure to the more explicit materials depicting explicit sex acts. Aggression was not similarly affected in the nonangered subjects.

A postexperiment questionnaire showed that those in the angered group had more anger and dislike toward the victim. Shock intensity correlated positively with self-reported anger and negatively with reported liking for the victim. Sexually experienced people reported more emotional excitement after the pictures.

Baron concludes that the predicted result occurred, even for women. In other words, mild erotic stimuli (men in swimsuits) inhibited aggression by previously angered females. More arousing materials (pictures of explicit sex acts) enhanced aggression by previously angered individuals. Baron found a contrast with males in other studies in that the females found the sex act pictures and the nudes unpleasant. Baron notes that the women might have labeled their arousal as negative and thus enhanced assaults against the confederate.

Mayerson and Taylor wrote about the effects of rape myth pornography on the attitudes of women. Ninety-six female undergraduates were the subjects, divided into four groups and assigned to three story conditions or a control group. The three written story conditions described a woman at a friend's party using the master bedroom's bathroom, then talking to a man (whom she's met before) who has entered the bedroom. He touches her sexually and eventually engages in sex with her. The three stories differ in their descriptions of the consent and arousal of the woman. All stories included use of sexual force.

Mayerson and Taylor found that: "Compared to not reading a story, reading any story generally led to changes in self-esteem and greater acceptance of rape myths and interpersonal violence. Also as predicted, high, compared to low, SRS" (sex role stereotyping) "subjects generally reported lower self-esteem and more tolerance of rape and other violence."[353]

Zillmann et al. selected ninety-six photographs and fifty-six segments that were erotic and nonerotic. The stimuli were presented with twenty male undergraduates who reported their "hedonic" reactions. Stimuli that were misclassified as erotic or nonerotic were discarded. Eight sets of stimuli were created. Photographs or film segments were transferred onto videocassettes. Each of the four low excitatory potential sets included fifteen photographs displayed for twenty-four seconds each. Each of the high excitatory potential sets consisted of six film segments displayed for sixty seconds each. There was also a control condition.

Nonerotic, low excitatory potential negative hedonic valance scenes included diseased faces, disfiguring tumors, victims of starvation, and the like. Nonerotic, high excitatory potential positive hedonic valance pictures included gourmet food, children with pets, baby animals, and spectacular nature scenes. Nonerotic, high excitatory potential negative hedonic valance pictures included a baby seal slaughter and a distraught child overhearing a parental argument. Nonerotic, high excitatory potential positive hedonic valance pictures showed rock concerts and young people dancing, singing, and joyously interacting.

Erotic, low excitatory potential negative hedonic valance pictures were of obviously pregnant women masturbating with mechanical devices; women gagged, bound, and beaten in bonded rituals; an obese female fellating a gaunt male; and close-ups of deformed female genitals with metal clips and pliers. Erotic, low excitatory potential positive hedonic valance pictures included scantily clad or nude females from soft-core magazines. Erotic, high excitatory potential negative hedonic valance pictures involved bestiality and sadomasochism, such as a male whipped while his genitals were abused and tied, a male being beaten by a female during cunnilingus, a woman and a large dog having intercourse, and a woman masturbating and fellating a dog. Erotic, high excitatory potential positive hedonic valance pictures included film segments from hard-core pornographic movies with a variety of heterosexual precoital and coital behaviors without aggression.

Seventy-four male undergraduates were the subjects. They were randomly assigned to one of the nine experimental conditions. Subjects played a game that involved a defensive position, partially variable defenses, and totally variable defenses in which targets could be moved. Subjects were assigned to the defense and their confederates to the offense. After this game playing, subjects were told they would now watch television segments of an unrelated study. They had previously been asked their opinion of the women's liberation movement. After the physiological measurement devices were attached, the confederates' written reactions to the women's lib questions were shared with the subjects. The confederates disagreed with the subjects, saying, for example, that anyone who supports women's lib is really stupid or anyone who does not support it is really stupid, depending on the individual subject's response. Confederates also insulted the subjects orally on this issue. Then the subjects were exposed to one of the nine experimental stimuli.

The experimenters conclude that the findings give strong support to the "excitation and valance model of erotica on motivated aggression."[354] Exposure to the disturbing and arousing erotica had a strong aggression facilitating effect compared to the no exposure control.

> In practical terms this finding can be taken to mean that a great majority of male college students is both aroused and disturbed by exposure to such sexual activities as flagellation and bestiality and that because of this erotic themes of this kind have the capacity to promote antisocial behaviors at least temporarily. These consequences are not necessarily restricted to erotica that feature rather extreme sexual practices however. They accrue to all erotica that elicit for whatever reason a negative reaction.[355]

They found many individual differences in hedonic responses to erotica and therefore conclude that erotica effects depend "to a high degree on personality considerations."[356] Exposure to the pleasant unarousing erotica did not produce motivated aggressive behavior.

Mueller and Donnerstein studied the effects of arousal due to films on prosocial behavior. They used twenty-eight male subjects enrolled in an introductory psychology course. The subjects were told the experiment concerned stress and distraction and that they would both deliver and receive electric shocks. They wrote essays under stress and were rated by confederates, who put a money value on the essay quality. Subjects were then asked to watch a short film clip. Some saw a television talk show; others saw a brief film of a woman and a man engaged in intercourse. The clips lasted three and a half minutes. Subjects were then given a chance, using a memory-type recall task, to shock the confederates.

Subjects who saw the erotic film showed significantly greater increase in diastolic, systolic, and mean blood pressure. Subjects who were positively treated were more rewarding that those neutrally treated. Subjects who saw the pornographic film were more rewarding than those who saw a control film.

A second study involved forty male introductory psychology students. A similar procedure was used. The erotic film was seen as significantly more erotic, arousing, pleasurable, and interesting. Subjects who were positively treated and shown an arousing film had significantly more reward behavior than those who were similarly treated but saw an unarousing film. The researchers also found that neutrally treated subjects who saw the erotic film were significantly more aggressive than those who saw a control film.[357]

Donnerstein and Berkowitz studied eighty male introductory psychology students. Five-minute black-and-white films were used. The neutral film was a talk show interview. The other films showed a young woman who was supposed to study with two men who had been drinking. The woman sat down between the men, was shoved around, and was forced to drink. She was tied up, slapped, stripped, and sexually attacked. The positive outcome aggressive erotic film showed the woman smiling and not resisting the two men. The negative outcome aggressive erotic film showed her taking actions indicating she was suffering and found the experience disgusting and humiliating. Anger of the subjects was manipulated in this study by having them write a short essay on marijuana legalization, having it judged by an alleged confederate in another room, and having the subject mildly shocked nine times for five seconds each. Subjects were shown one of the films and afterward had the chance to administer shocks to the confederate who had shocked them. Subjects had a choice of the level and number of shocks administered for a task that the confederate performed.

Interestingly, the researchers found that where the confederates were males, there were no increases in aggression due to film exposure. However, for the female confederates, the movies did affect the aggressive behavior. Exposure to either of the aggressive erotic films increased the aggression level toward the female, whereas the purely erotic films did not heighten that aggression. The researchers stress the importance of associating the female confederate with the victim in the aggressive movie.

In a second experiment, the researchers hypothesized that nonangered subjects would not be stimulated to increase the attacks on females after seeing the victim's pain and distress in the films. Again the subjects were eighty male undergraduate psychology students. While the angered subjects increased aggression in response to both the negative and positive aggressive erotic films, the nonangered subjects increased aggression only in response to the aggressive erotic film that showed the woman with a positive arousal outcome. The researchers reason that filmed violence scenes can reduce viewers' inhibition against aggression. They note that there is a frequent combination of aggression and arousal in pornography and say that this "could stimulate aggressively disposed men with weak inhibitions to assault available women."[358] Again the focus is on pornography in which women are shown enjoying being sexually victimized.

Zillmann and Bryant studied pornography, sexual callousness, and rape trivialization by studying eighty male and eighty female undergraduate students. The subjects met in six consecutive weekly sessions. Films of eight minutes each were shown. Some subjects were massively exposed, seeing six such films per session. Others saw three erotic films and three nonerotic films per session. All of the films were nonerotic in the no exposure condition. The films showed activities such as fellatio, cunnilingus, coitus, and anal intercourse. None of the activities involved coercion or the deliberate reception or infliction of pain. Lastly, the subjects were introduced to a rape case involving a hitchhiking that resulted in a sexual offense. They were asked to recommend a sentence. Students then saw a new sexually explicit film and were asked to report their reactions. The males also filled in a measurement of sexual callousness toward women.

Those who were massively exposed to pornography perceived the use of certain sexual practices to be more pronounced than did those who saw less pornography. There were no sex differences in these results. Yet comparing these results to survey data, they indicated that viewing pornography actually corrected distorted views of sexuality, bringing beliefs in line with actual practices in society. However, those massively exposed to the pornography greatly overestimated the popularity of unusual sexual practices. Those who had the most exposure considered the pornography less objectionable and offensive, but the women found the pornography significantly more objectionable than did the men. Those massively exposed to pornography recommended significantly shorter terms of imprisonment in the rape situation. This exposure, the researchers note, "made rape appear a trivial offense."[359] Women also trivialized rape, although they treated it as a more serious offense overall.

Those who had massive exposure showed much less support for the women's liberation movement, which the researchers say shows that massive exposure to pornography generalized to a "loss of compassion for women per se, thus undermining support of dispositions for women's causes."[360] The massive exposure significantly increased the men's sexual callousness toward women. While the researchers do not rule out experimenter demand factors in getting these results, they suggest that a lack of censure of pornography in society would make real world results similar to that of the experiment. They also say that the findings suggest further "antisocial consequences," such as those who are massively exposed to pornography might become more distrusting of their partners and might undermine love and massive exposure might create an increasing dissatisfaction with sexual reality.

Jaffe studied the effects of sexual stimulation on prosocial behavior. The subjects were forty-six male undergraduate students (six of whom were removed as participants because they were suspicious about the study). Subjects were told that the experiment involved the effects of reading materials or films on extrasensory perception (ESP). They were told that another subject, the receiver, was already in an adjacent room. (In reality, there was no such subject. The experimenter operated the receiver's panel "in the bogus ESP equipment used."[361]) Subjects took a checklist test to measure "affective states, including sexual arousal." The men were then assigned, at random, to view one of three six-minute films or to read "some highly arousing erotic passages."[362] One film was a thrilling adventure on the Colorado River. Another was a calm travelogue of Norway. The third was "a highly arousing erotic one, featuring a nude Swedish female acting seductively."[363] (We note that one cannot tell the content of the so-called "erotic" film or passages from these descriptions, but it seems likely that they may have been erotic rather than pornographic or violent.)

After the exposure, the mood change checklist was readministered to the subjects. They were then assigned to the transmitter role and told the other subject would be the receiver in the ESP experiment. The subject had to concentrate on colored cards twenty times, then signal the receiver to use a light signal to indicate which color he thought the card was. For the twelve incorrect responses, the subject could either administer an electric shock to the receiver or show him the correct response by pressing the appropriate colored light button. Subjects were told that the purpose of this was to find out which combination of the two responses was most likely to improve ESP results. Each subject was given a shock to give him a notion of its intensity and to reinforce the experiment's credibility. Afterward, the checklist of mood changes was again administered to the subjects.

The erotic film and erotic passages were both highly effective in producing sexual arousal, while the two control films were not.

Analysis of the behavioral data, i.e., the number of times subjects chose to shock their ostensible victim rather than show him the correct response, indicated that aggression was consistently lower and positive social behavior consistently higher among the sexually aroused than among the nonaroused subjects, regardless of the modality through which sexual arousal was elicited.[364]

Overall, subjects "showed a strong preference for the prosocial as opposed to the aggressive response alternative." The average shock use was 2.80 times out of 12 chances. Jaffe concludes that subjects' initial inclinations are toward prosocial responses and when there is nothing about the experiment that alters the predisposition "into an aggressive one," exposure to relatively high levels of erotic source arousal enhances the prosocial disposition and increases prosocial behavior when there are aggressive and prosocial alternatives.[365]

Zillmann, Bryant, and Carveth tested forty male undergraduates individually in a laboratory. Each subject met a confederate subject who was in reality an experimenter. Subjects were told they would have to assist in taking blood pressure. They were separated by a partition and told not to interact. They were told that if they pumped the pressure higher than 150mm/Hg, measurement would be "uncomfortable if not painful."[366] Pumping it over 150 was the measure of retaliatory aggression. The measure of provocation was a self-report of whether anyone mistreated them in the experiment. The confederates made snide remarks to try to provoke the subjects.

Four conditions were used. The first was nonarousing, pleasing, and nonaggressive. It was made up of fifteen photographs of "highly attractive nude or scantily clothed females."[367] The second set was arousing, displeasing, and nonaggressive. It included six film segments of bestiality. For example, an obese female fellated a dog and a boar; an unattractive woman masturbated with a live snake; and "none of the persons or animals involved expressed pain, reluctance to cooperate or displeasure."[368] (We note the sexist nature of these examples.) The third set of stimuli was arousing, displeasing, and aggressive. It was composed of six segments of sadomasochistic behavior, including a male whipping a male engaged in cunnilingus, a female whipping a male whose genitalia were abused and tied, and a female beating a male during intercourse. There was no exposure to pornography in the fourth condition.

The researchers found that 79.3 percent of the subjects said they were "mistreated by the confederate . . . but not the experimenter." Only five of the forty subjects did not apply excessive pressure. The researchers found that exposure to communication significantly affected retaliatory behavior. The pressure time with exposure to displeasing, arousing erotica—with and without aggressive cues—"produced aggressive behavior at a level above that associated with no exposure."[369] However, aggression after exposure to "nonarousing, pleasant erotica" was especially low but unreliable. This, the researchers say, might be explained by annoyance summation. They note, "If exposure to such erotic fare as bestiality or sadomasochism proves disturbing, . . . this exposure further aggravates the provoked individual and thus promotes motivated aggression."[370]

Ramirez, Bryant, and Zillmann cite prior research that shows that individuals who are provoked aggress more strongly after they are exposed to explicit arousing erotica such as films of sexual intercourse than after exposure to nonerotic materials. They summarize the literature in this field. In their own study, they used seventy-two male university students enrolled in an introductory communications course. The subjects were provoked mildly or severely by the first examiner. (They were shown pictures of birds and sea life in slow motion and the "destruction of a dead mouse by blow-fly maggots in time-lapse photography."[371]) The mild provocation involved subjects being accused twice of not cooperating by a slightly irritated experimenter. The severe provocation involved the examiner accusing the person of not listening to instructions and stating, "Any adult can do that!"[372] The examiner yelled at the subject after ripping up a bogus electrocardiogram (ECG). Then the subject is angrily told the ECG will have to be done over.

The nonerotic condition consisted of thirty-six slides of persons in normal snapshot poses with an equal number of females and males. The slides were changed every 16.5 seconds, and total exposure was nine minutes fifty seconds. In the suggestive, mildly erotic condition, a film of thirty-six slide nudes of the *Penthouse* and *Playboy* type were used. In the explicit, strongly erotic condition, a male and female were shown performing fellatio, cunnilingus, and intercourse in various positions; the film also showed ejaculation in the female's face. This ran for nine minutes fifty seconds. The subjects rated the slides using criteria such as extremely boring versus extremely exciting, extremely displeasing versus extremely pleasing, extremely calming versus extremely disturbing, amount of arousal, amount of eroticism, and amount of interest. They also evaluated the experimenters.

The researchers found that the severe provocation treatment resulted in significantly stronger reactions than the mild provocation. They also found that the film was more exciting than the still photos and that the level of annoyance was significantly higher for the severe provocation. Exposure to the explicit "erotica" facilitated expression of annoyance no matter which degree of provocation was involved, yet exposure to the mild erotica failed to calm severely provoked people. However, the researchers state that these results were reliable only for the explicit erotica.[373]

Overall, they conclude that the results were not statistically reliable in showing that exposure to explicit pornography fostered hostile behavior of significantly higher intensity than exposure to mild erotica regardless of provocation. Yet they say that the findings corroborate earlier studies that "exposure to suggestive mild erotica can under certain circumstances reduce hostile behaviors among males."[374] However, the circumstances are "comparatively low levels of provocation."[375] It would be unreasonable, they say, to think that exposure to mild erotica can help subjects control intense anger reactions to strong provocation. But, they note, anger might have to be directed at the provoker in order to be intensified by exposure to erotica.

Kelley et al. studied forty-eight female and forty-eight male introductory psychology students. The subjects received either a positive or negative evaluation of themselves supposedly made by another subject called a confederate. They were then either allowed to deliver bogus electric shocks to the confederate or not given this opportunity. Next they viewed nonerotic or erotic slides.

The subjects in the nonangered condition were evaluated by their so-called confederate as mature, sincere, intelligent, likable, masculine if male or feminine if female, emotionally stable, and open-minded. The subjects in the angered condition were evaluated negatively on those same dimensions. They were then given the opportunity to be aggressive toward the offender by way of various levels of shock. No real shocks were given.

Three groups of slides were presented for fifteen seconds each. One group of "mildly erotic slides" had five scenes of a female and male kissing and undressing. A second group of "strongly erotic slides" had five scenes of the same female and male engaged in sexual intercourse. A third group of "nonerotic slides" consisted of five scenes of inanimate objects such as paintings and furniture.[376] After evaluating the slides as to how sexually arousing they were, the subjects rated how angry they felt after receiving the evaluation from the other subject. The angered subjects selected higher shock intensity than did the nonangered subjects. However, the researchers

found that contrary to predictions and contrary to previous methodology, neither the manipulation of anger nor the opportunity to aggress affected ratings of sexual arousal. (We note that none of the slides presented in this experiment appeared to involve violent or sexually aggressive scenes.)

In a second experiment, the subjects were thirty-one males and twenty-four females enrolled in an introductory psychology course. The study was conducted in same-sex groups of approximately six subjects. Each person was asked to evaluate one of the other subjects in the group on an Interpersonal Judgment Scale. All the subjects evaluated the same person (created by the experimenter) based on that person's responses to the self-rating questionnaires. All the subjects viewed three strongly erotic and three mildly erotic slides presented in random order for fifteen seconds each. The slides were selected from those used in the prior experiment, and they had been rated by other students for female and male dominance and how arousing they were. The researchers again found that the results did not support the hypothesis that anger increases sexual arousal. The addition of the no evaluation control group, the indirect sexual arousal measure, and differential dominance in the stimuli did not make a difference in the finding that anger did not increase sexual arousal.

A third experiment involved seventy-two male and sixty-four female introductory psychology students. The procedures were identical to those of the second experiment, but the subjects were shown the three strongly erotic slides that varied in dominance and three nonerotic slides depicting an egalitarian relationship, male dominance, and female dominance. Again the negatively evaluated subjects were not more sexually aroused than the positively evaluated or nonevaluated subjects.

In none of the three experiments reported here did anger have an effect on self ratings of sexual arousal or any consistent effect on the perceptions of the sexuality of others. The general hypothesis that anger and/or aggressive behavior acts to facilitate sexual arousal is not supported at all by the present research. This suggests, at best, limitations on the generality of Barkley's results. It may be that anger simply increases the sexual content of fantasies but has no effect on other aspects of sexuality.[377]

Kelley et al. also found that dominance cues in the nonerotic and erotic stimuli had few gender-specific effects on the self-reports of arousal. However, there were strong gender-specific effects on perceptions of the sexuality of others. A male or female stranger shown in a dominant role was perceived as a sexual individual. Such effects were heightened for female subjects exposed to the depiction of a dominant male. It should be noted that the Barkley research created anger by means of negative evaluations delivered orally by an experimenter who had power over the subjects and acted in a dominant and arrogant manner. Kelley et al. suggest that it may be the creation of a dominant–submissive interaction that affects sexual responses.

Leonard and Taylor studied forty male introductory psychology undergraduates. Subjects were assigned to one of four conditions—permissive cues, nonpermissive cues, neutral cues, and no specific cues. The subject and a female confederate were seated in adjacent experiment rooms. Eight slides were rated by the subject and confederate. All except the control condition subjects viewed erotic slides showing nude heterosexual couples engaged in intimate behavior. In the permissive cue condition, the subjects overheard the female confederate make positive comments about the slides such as "I'd like to try that" and "That looks like fun."[378] These were meant to convey that the female confederate had a tolerant, positive attitude toward viewing pornography. In the nonpermissive condition, the female confederate made negative statements about pornography such as "This is disgusting" and "Oh, that's awful."[379] In the no cue condition, the female confederate made no comment. The subjects in the neutral condition saw slides of completely clothed females and males and heard no comments about the slides.

Subjects were told they were competing with the confederate on a reaction time test and that he or his opponent would receive a shock depending on the competition outcome. Each received four trials, and all the subjects won 50 percent of the trials. Subjects also rated the slides on dimensions of arousal, excitement, enjoyableness, pleasantness, and eroticism.

The men rated confederates who provided nonpermissive cues as less of a leader, less reasonable, less accepting, and less relaxed than those who provided permissive cues. Leonard and Taylor found that under conditions of high provocation, exposure to erotica may facilitate aggression. The results support the hypothesis that permissive cues by the females would facilitate "erotica induced aggression while nonpermissive cues would inhibit aggression."[380] The men who competed against a female who gave permissive cues and responses to the slides selected higher shocks for that female than did those provided with no cues. Nonpermissive cues reduced aggression only under high provocation conditions. The researchers conclude that the permissive cues

might have informed the subjects that normally inappropriate behaviors would be tolerated and thus they engaged in the inappropriate behavior of attacking the woman. The opposite result occurred with the nonpermissive cues. Leonard and Taylor suggest that it is possible the cues might have influenced the degree of arousal.

Malamuth studied forty-two men, most of whom were university students. A mercury in rubber strain gauge was used to measure penile tumescence. In each of two sessions separated by eight or nine weeks, subjects read written stories depicting sexual and rape acts. During each session, sexual arousal was generated by having the subjects read a story depicting a woman masturbating. The other stories depicted consenting sex and rape. The rape depictions emphasized the abhorrence of the rape victim. An extrasensory perception (ESP) experiment involving the subject and a female confederate posing as another subject took place; punishment was an aversive noise. Anger was induced by negative evaluations of the subjects. Malamuth found that factors involved in real-world aggression against women "successfully predicted men's laboratory aggression against a female."[381] Among factors were attitudes facilitating violence and sexual arousal to rape.

Check and Malamuth studied 289 female and male introductory psychology students to determine sex role stereotyping. Subjects were exposed to one of three written one-thousand-word stories. All the stories involved sexual acts between a man and a woman told from the man's perspective. In the stranger rape story, a stranger followed a woman home from a disco, got into her apartment, and raped her despite her protests and cries. In the acquaintance rape condition, the man and woman had a first date at a local disco, then went to the man's apartment. The woman had told the man she believed in free love, and they had been drinking. She responded to his kiss and objected when he tried to remove her shirt. During a struggle, the man removed all the woman's clothing, slapped her to quiet her screams and subdue her, and raped her. The third condition was similar to the acquaintance rape depiction up to the point when the man removed the woman's shirt. At this point, they proceeded to have mutually consenting intercourse.

The males were more aroused than the females in all three conditions, and subjects who had low sex role stereotyping had inhibited levels of arousal to the rape relative to consenting sex. Subjects with high sex role stereotyping showed arousal patterns that were similar to those of rapists—in other words, approximately equal levels of arousal to the consenting and rape depictions. Thirty percent of the men showed some likelihood of raping, with 44 percent of the high sex role stereotyping men doing so compared to only 12 percent of the low sex role stereotyping men. All the subjects saw the acquaintance rape victim as reacting more favorably than the stranger rape victim. Check and Malamuth suggest that acquaintance rape might be seen by many as "within the realm of normative acts."[382] They did not find sex differences regarding the influence of sex role stereotyping on reactions to rape.

Malamuth and Check studied individual differences in arousal to rape depictions. Of 307 male introductory psychology students who signed up for an orientation session, 146 signed up for the laboratory phase of the experiment. Subjects were exposed to one of eight audiotaped pornographic messages. In the second phase, they listened to a pornographic passage of either a rape or mutually consenting intercourse and filled out a questionnaire. The volunteers were more force oriented and more oriented toward unconventional sexual activities. When a woman was shown as experiencing disgust, both the high and low likelihood of raping subjects were less aroused by nonconsenting compared to consenting depictions. However, when the woman was shown as becoming sexually aroused, the low likelihood of raping subjects were equally aroused by the nonconsenting and consenting pictures, whereas the high likelihood of raping subjects showed greater arousal to the nonconsenting scenes.[383]

For a detailed analysis of pornography studies relating to aggression, consult *Pornography and Sexual Aggression* by Malamuth and Donnerstein. In that book, Malamuth expresses the concern that pairing of sex and aggression in the media "may result in conditioning processes whereby aggressive acts become associated with sexual arousal, a powerful unconditioned stimulus and reinforcer."[384] He notes that a lot of data indicate that exposure to aggressive pornography may alter perceptions of rape victims and that rape data have shown that exposing male subjects to aggressive pornography can increase aggressive behavior toward female but not male targets. Another key point is that when victims in the portrayals react positively, as they commonly do in aggressive pornography, this can act to justify aggression and decrease inhibitions against aggression. Malamuth concludes that the information from the experiments "strongly supports the assertion that mass media can contribute to a cultural climate that is more accepting of aggression against women."[385] He notes, however, that this does not suggest that the media are the most or among the most powerful influences.

Donnerstein, writing about his studies with Berkowitz, says that depictions that show the suffering and pain of the victim affect only those male subjects who are predisposed toward aggression, while pornography that shows a positive and willing victim influences all subjects. He also notes that sexual arousal does not seem to be a necessary component to facilitate aggression against women. The aggressive cue value of the female target seems to be more important. That occurs when the person associates the victim, who could be a female experimenter, for example, with the female portrayed in the film. Donnerstein states, "We have now seen that there is a direct causal relationship between exposure to aggressive pornography and violence against women."[385] Again he emphasizes that it is the aggressive content and not the sexual content that is the main contributor to the violence.

Sapolsky, writing in Malamuth and Donnerstein, proposes a modification to what is called the excitation-transfer paradigm. This paradigm suggests that "individuals would be expected to behave more aggressively when (1) they are angered, (2) they are then exposed to arousing erotica, and (3) residues of arousal are available to 'energize' the motivated aggression when they are again confronted with an annoyer."[387] The Sapolsky modification recognizes that the affective response to an "erotic" communication might interfere with the aggression facilitating effect of the communication.

In the same book, Abramson and Hayashi deal with pornography and sex crimes in Japan. As of 1984, it was illegal to show pubic hair and adult genitals in sexually explicit materials in Japan. There was an exception for written pornography, and themes of rape and bondage were common in films and novels in that country. The rape statistics in Japan were substantially lower than in the United States. In Japan, there were 2.4 rapes per 100,000 population. In the United States, there were 34.5. The laws were similar, and like American women, Japanese women were reluctant to report rapes. Abramson and Hayashi believe that if there was a direct connection between pornography with images of rape and rape behavior, Japan would have an overwhelming amount of rape, but it does not. Yet they attribute some of these differences to other cultural differences between the United States and Japan. They believe that the Japanese "have recognized the necessity of sexual availability" such as prostitution and believe it contributes to the low incidence of rape. Rape in Japan is treated with public humiliation of rapists and the publication of names of convicted rapists. In addition, it is considered a big disgrace for a family member to commit a rape.[388]

Another good source of summaries of a number of pornography studies is *The Connection Between Sex and Aggression* by Zillmann.[389]

Kelley studied the effects of aggressive and sexual film exposure on hostility, willingness to help the experimenter, and attitudes about the sexes. The subjects were 135 male and 129 female undergraduates in an introductory psychology course. Participants responded to a sexual opinion survey that assessed negative and positive reactions to various sexual topics. Different groups of subjects saw four 11-minute films in the absence of the experimenter. A sexual film showed explicit activity by a heterosexual couple; a control film depicted two males engaged in a bowling match; an aggressive film made up of excerpts from a commercial film, showed physical aggression among males; a sexually aggressive film depicted the brutal rape of a woman by two men. Immediately following exposure to one of the films, subjects responded to a scale indicating their affective and sexual arousal responses to the film.

The males offered less help to the experimenter after viewing the aggressive film than after viewing the other three films, which resulted in similar levels of help. Compared to the females, the males who possessed primarily positive sexual attitudes (erotophiles) expressed "comparatively less hostility toward a female experimenter than toward a male experimenter."[390] Attraction toward the experimenter varied with the film content. Subjects had greater attraction to the experimenter after exposure to the erotic or aggressive film than to the control film.

Kelley found sex differences in conjunction with the erotophilic–erotophobic relationships throughout much of the data, with the males indicating more positive reactions to the aggressive and sexually aggressive films in terms of sexual arousal and affect. While the content of the films had no effect on the helping behavior of the female subjects, the males were least responsive to a request for aid after viewing an aggressive film and most responsive after the control and rape films. For the females, erotophobia was not related to affective responses to the films, but it was strongly related to film content. The sexually aggressive film elicited the least positive feelings for females. The control and erotic films elicited the most positive feelings for the women. Erotophilic males were more positive than erotophobic males, in response to both the rape and the aggressive films, yet the sexually aggressive film elicited the least positive affect and the control and erotic films the most positive.

Kelley found that although erotophilia can promote generally positive responses to sexual stimuli, erotophiles' stereotypic sexist attitudes were most positive in the study after a male experimenter presented a rape film. She found that attitudes toward men and women were most positive after the erotophiles viewed sexual aggression, which suggests that "the negative attitudinal effects of this type of film exposure may be greatest among erotophobes."[391]

Malamuth and Check studied individual differences concerning the effects of aggressive pornography on rape myth beliefs. They cite research by Burt showing that beliefs in rape myths play a major role in actually causing rape and other forms of violence against women. Of the 307 male introductory psychology students who signed up for the orientation session of Malamuth and Check experiment, only 146 signed up for the laboratory phase of the experiment after learning of the measures and procedures to be used. Only one of these subjects dropped out.

Various questionnaires were administered to assess sexual motivation and experience, personality, and likelihood of raping. Eight audiotaped stories of approximately a thousand words each were presented at a speed of about two hundred words per minute. The content of these was manipulated along dimensions of consent versus nonconsent, pain versus no pain, and outcome being the woman's arousal or disgust. The consenting versions portrayed the woman and man in "relatively equal 'power' roles without any suggestion of domination of one person over the other."[392] Rape depictions were used. After the experiment, the subjects filled out another questionnaire. This also inquired into how often the subjects read magazines such as *Playboy* or *Penthouse*. A male voice presented the stories used in this experiment.

The volunteers and nonvolunteers did not differ on measures such as sexual experience, motivations, or personality. Yet the volunteers were more oriented toward unconventional sexual activities and also more force oriented. The volunteers were more likely to have thought about male homosexual acts and to have found the idea of such acts attractive. They also indicated a greater likelihood of engaging in such acts and a greater likelihood of engaging in anal intercourse and group sex. They found the idea of watching lesbian acts more attractive than the nonvolunteers, and they thought about such acts more frequently. The "volunteers were *less* likely to have tried conventional intercourse." The volunteers were more likely to have "thought of forcing a woman into sexual acts."[393] They found the idea of forcing a woman more attractive than the nonvolunteers did. The volunteers also indicated a greater likelihood of raping and felt less disgusted about forcing a female than the nonvolunteers did.

The researchers found that subjects who were

exposed to a depiction of a nonconsenting woman's arousal to rape said that a larger percentage of women would enjoy being forced to do something sexual and enjoy being raped than did persons who were exposed to a depiction of a nonconsenting woman's disgust reaction to rape. While 24.7 percent of the subjects with a high likelihood of raping believed that women would enjoy being raped, 6.63 percent of those with a low likelihood of raping believed this. Those high likelihood of raping subjects who were exposed to the nonconsenting woman's arousal believed that more women would enjoy being raped (36.9 percent). Those high likelihood of raping subjects who heard the nonconsenting woman's disgust reaction to being raped said that 20 percent of women would enjoy being raped. Similar results were found for the questions of whether women would enjoy forced sex. Exposure to the women's disgust and women's arousal in the consenting depictions did not significantly affect beliefs in rape myths for the high likelihood of raping subjects. Of these men, 17.7 percent believed that women would enjoy being raped after exposure to the consenting woman's arousal condition.

The researchers' analysis found that the belief in sexual violence myths was associated with the likelihood of raping, frequency of exposure to pornography, and power motivation. They note that "on the whole the findings strongly support the hypothesis that a depiction portraying the myth that a rape victim becomes sexually aroused increases males' belief in such a rape myth."[394] They also found that men who already have greater "inclinations to aggress against women are particularly likely to be affected by exposure to aggressive pornography that portrays rape myths."[395] They did find an association between the belief that women enjoy sexual violence and a higher level of exposure to pornography in the real world and note that this suggests the possibility that in real-world settings, men are influenced by exposure to the rape myths in pornography. Yet they suggest that any conclusions along those lines should await future research.

Malamuth and Check also looked at the possibility that the effects found might be due to a greater willingness to report a belief that might be seen as socially inappropriate rather than to a change in perceptions or beliefs. They say that this was not likely. They also reject a suggestion that new information in the nonconsenting woman's arousal scenario changed subjects' perceptions of how women react to sexual violence. They found it "doubtful that any of the subjects had not previously encountered the type of myth portrayed in the woman's arousal version of the rape depiction."[396] They found it more likely that the results were based on the

processing of information and retrieval of information from memory. They call this the primary theory, which says that memory can have a significant impact on real-world judgments. The primary theory also suggests that a communication will be more likely to affect attitudes when the communication is consistent with the person's existing beliefs.

Krafka studied the effects of pornography on female viewers. Subjects were 126 female students. She rejected any sexually inexperienced women, choosing not to expose such women to the stimuli.

Subjects saw one film daily for four consecutive days. They were divided into three film-type categories. The first involved sexual encounters in R-rated and X-rated films. X-rated films contained close-up shots of various acts of human intercourse. Primarily females were on display, as indicated by the more graphic and longer periods of exposure of female body parts. The women were often shown as having "voracious sexual appetites" and being responsive to a partner's every sexual demand without regard to appropriate times and places.[397] The women in the film often had to submit to unwanted sex or seduce a more powerful male to reach desired goals. The R-rated films were less sexually explicit. The second category was that of sexual violence. At least one scene in each film involved the sexual abuse of a female. For example, some depicted rapes, and one of the films showed a female stripped, bound, and whipped on numerous occasions to make her the "perfect" woman for her male lover. The females who were abused in these films had either negative or ambiguous consequences as the result of the violence. The final category was composed of slasher films in which nude females were mutilated and violence often followed sexually suggestive scenes.

On the fifth night of the study, subjects were told the last film was not available to be screened and were asked instead to take part in a law school study that turned out to be a mock rape trial. They filled in a voir dire questionnaire, then watched an hour-long tape of a simulated rape trial. The case involved the alleged rape at a fraternity party of a woman by a man with whom she was acquainted. Consent was an issue. Pictures showed severe bruising of the woman's face after this incident. Subjects rated victim and defendant responsibility, injury severity, victim credibility and resistance, and whether the case conformed to their definition of rape. Some subjects were debriefed about the film contents before they participated in the rape trail, and others were debriefed afterward.

The results showed that the groups found the material disturbing but that the negative feelings evoked by early exposure to the films were not cumulative or of lasting duration. Those exposed to the sexually violent material were "significantly less reactive to the material on the last day of exposure than they were on the first day of exposure to their films."[398] Those exposed to the slasher films also were less disturbed in comparison to their initial reactions. No significant changes occurred for the viewers of the sexually explicit material. Those exposed to the slasher films became less critical of the ways in which female characters were depicted as the days went by. Those exposed to the sexually violent and sexually explicit films rated themselves to be less likely to be victims of nonsexual violent crimes than did control subjects. Exposure to the slasher films worked against feelings of victimization and vulnerability in the females exposed to them.

Krafka concludes that her study showed that the women exposed to two of three of these types of movies showed an increase in negative effect. At least for those exposed to the sexually violent and slasher images, desensitization occurred over time. Yet the effect on self-perception and attitudes were "mostly null findings."[399] The exposure did not affect attitudes about rape and violence toward women. There was no evidence of psychological trauma, and there was no support for the theory of escalating aggression. Krafka found that "the effects of exposing subjects to graphic portrayals of violence against women are (1) not restricted to an immediate measure time frame, (2) not restricted to measures of aggression, and (3) not restricted to subjects who are disinhibited by treatment received from the experimenter."[400] The evaluation of the rape trial outcome by those who were exposed to the slasher films was significantly affected by that exposure. These subjects were higher than the other groups in tendency to return an acquittal verdict, to excuse the defendant's conduct, to place responsibility on the victim, to have a restrictive sexual assault definition, and to impeach the victim's credibility on resistance attempts.

Krafka states that the null findings resulting from exposing females to pornography were unexpected and inconclusive. She suggests a number of reasons for not generalizing the results. Among these are the fact that the findings might have been influenced by use of subjects who were sexually experienced and self-selected and also the fact that there were a number of dropouts, particularly in the sexually violent category.

Malamuth, Check, and Briere studied thirty-seven male and forty-three female psychology students. One-thousand-word stories were prepared along dimensions of aggression and sexual explicitness. The aggressive sexual story was a sexually explicit rape depiction similar to those typically found in pornography. It showed nonconsent and pain but also some sexual arousal. The aggressive nonsexual story involved a brutal assault on a woman by a man with a knife and his beating her into unconsciousness. The nonaggressive sexual story was of a woman and man having mutually consenting intercourse. The nonaggressive nonsexual story involved a woman and man having a casual conversation. In relation to the nonaggressive depictions, the women in the aggressive depictions were seen as having more pain, deriving less pleasure, and being less willing. However, the woman who was sexually aggressed against was seen as more willing than the woman who was violently aggressed against without a sexual attack. The researchers conclude that "aggression does not necessarily inhibit the sexual arousal of nonrapists."[401]

A second experiment involved 367 male introductory psychology students in an orientation session, 123 of whom signed up for the laboratory phase. The volunteers scored higher on acceptance of masturbation, explicit sexual materials, and sexual permissiveness than the nonvolunteers. The subjects were more aroused by the nonaggressive stories than by the aggressive ones. The researchers conclude that aggression "may be a sexual stimulant for some individuals from the general population."[402] The subjects' self-reports of sexual arousal to stories of forcing a woman were predictive of the sexual arousal assessed by penile tumescence and self-reports in a later session. For the 30 percent of subjects who had a relatively high level of arousal to force, aggression enhanced sexual arousal.

Malamuth studied the "predictors of naturalistic sexual aggression."[403] In this study, sexual aggression was measured in naturalistic settings and rated by a self-report inventory and genital measures of sexual arousal.

The test subjects were 155 males with an average age of 23; 80 percent of them were university students. The first phase of the experiment involved a questionnaire of sexual aggression, experiences, attitudes facilitating violence, hostility, and so on. The second phase assessed sexual response to rape and mutually consenting depictions by using a penile gauge. Self-reported sexual arousal also was measured. In this phase, subjects were given envelopes containing stories. They read the stories, then indicated their sexual arousal. There were three depictions. The first described a woman masturbating, the second depicted rape, and the third depicted mutually consenting sex.

Malamuth found the subjective and physiological measures of sexual arousal to be highly correlated. He concludes that the results support the belief that sexual arousal in response to aggression is a factor that may cause "an inclination to aggress against women."[404] He notes, however, that other factors must also be present before such an arousal pattern will lead to aggressive behavior.

Malamuth and Briere dealt with the indirect effects of sexual violence in the media on aggression against women. They note that figures suggesting that about one-quarter of North American women have been sexually assaulted or raped at some point in their lives indicate that sexual violence is committed by a large number of men rather than by a few deviant individuals.

Media effects models are based on either indirect or direct methods of influence. For example, indirect models do not rule out cause/effect relationships but propose more complex connections between media depictions and people's behavior. Malamuth and Briere propose such a model and suggest that sexual arousal patterns, thought patterns, and other responses can be "modified by exposure to sexually violent depictions in conjunction with many other influences."[405] These responses can interact factors that might contribute to a variety of antisocial behaviors. The authors emphasize that the media depict sexual aggression differently than nonsexual aggression in that the victims of sexual violence are shown as initially resisting, secretly desiring, and ultimately deriving pleasure from the sexual assault, whereas victims of other types of aggression are shown as intent on avoiding it and abhorring the experience. Also, sexual aggression is often shown without negative consequences for the perpetrator or the victim.

Malamuth and Briere present a model of "indirect effects of mass media exposure on antisocial behavior against women."[406] The model includes originating variables such as "Individual experiences" and "Cultural forces" including the mass media; intermediate variables such as "Attitudes," "Dominance," "Motives," "Hostility toward women," "Sexual arousal to aggression," and "Personality characteristics"; and a "Social network of aggression-supportive peers."[407] The model also includes intermediate variables that are "situational." These include forms of acute arousal such as frustration, priming stimuli such as the mass media, opportunity and access, and disinhibiting events such as approval, alcohol, or immediate pressure. They say that these all lead to "Antisocial behavior against women."[408] Under this category would be criminal aggression such as stranger rape, aggression frequently not viewed as criminal such as date rape (we would suggest that such behavior is criminal), aggression in the laboratory, and nonviolent antisocial acts such as supporting aggression or discrimination.

Malamuth and Briere believe that forces such as the media can change a person's responses and that such changes can ultimately result in the person's aggressive behavior in some circumstances. For example, if media exposure or other factors cause a person to become more tolerant of violence against women, that person's reactions to sexual aggression against others might change, even if his or her own aggressive behavior does not. This model is based on the belief that there are a number of mutually influencing factors.

Malamuth and Briere note that ethical considerations have precluded exposing minors to pornography and exposing people to large amounts of sexually violent material over long periods of time. They indicate that minors might be most susceptible to the conditioning effects of such material.

The authors argue that a number of studies have found that measures of attitudes and beliefs, as well as media exposure, can predict aggressive behavior. They caution against drawing conclusions about causes and effects from the data they present. They explain that ethics stop experiments in which people could be exposed to media portrayals over extended periods of time, which might change their thoughts and behavior. They call for additional research on conditions under which the mass media change thought patterns and how important the media are in comparison to other influences. They also suggest the causal links between intermediate and originating contributors to aggression should be explored further.

Linz studied the effects of sexual violence in the media on male viewers. He exposed subjects to R-rated films in which women were "among other things, stabbed, beaten, tortured, raped, decapitated, burned, drilled with electric drills, cut with saws, scalped and shot in the head with nail guns."[409] He looked at the issue of whether "male viewers become desensitized to graphic depictions of violence against women" after continued exposure to such depictions.[410] He also studied whether the desensitization, if it happens, also applied in other contexts. For example, would these people tend to view victims in real-life situations as less injured or be less sympathetic toward them?

Linz also looked at the impact of prolonged exposure to X-rated nonviolent films that portrayed women mainly as sexual objects. These films contained depictions of fellatio, cunnilingus, heterosexual intercourse, and lesbian activities. The women were portrayed as sexually subordinate to men and as eager and willing to accommodate every male advance. He also exposed people to "teenage sex films."[411] These are films that depict teenage girls and older females as basically "proving grounds" for "young male virgins or as the high school class whore."[412] Linz looked at whether males exposed to either of these categories of films for extended times became more accepting of beliefs that women are sex objects incapable of having more complex emotional and intellectual qualities. He also looked at the issue of whether males exposed to such films would start to believe that women enjoy rape or forced sex and would tolerate more violent forms of sexual behavior.

Linz presents a sample case of a psychologist who was preparing a clinical intervention program based on systematic desensitization techniques. If the psychologist wanted to enable people to calmly view the graphic dismemberment and torture of female bodies, he or she would take steps such as having the subjects read about mutilation and torture. Then a stronger manipulation might be used, such as making them view still photographs of mutilated bodies. They might then be asked to watch models involved in mutilating such bodies. As a result, the subjects' tolerance for the material might become quite high. In fact, one might expect that viewing films of actual mutilation or even viewing a mutilated body could become tolerable.

Linz presented several hypotheses. For example, he argues that while it might be possible that continued exposure to media violence would result in less aggressive behavior due to "decreased priming of aggressive thoughts through habituation,"[413] it is more likely that such exposure would result in aggressive behavior increases. Even if habituation were involved, Linz suggests that subjects might first habituate to ideas inhibiting aggressive responses rather than to ideas facilitating aggression. And he says that other processes that would reduce anxiety due to viewing violence and aggression might take place instead of or in addition to habituation. Linz also suggests that certain types of films might result in a state of desensitization to violence with repeated exposure. He predicts that subjects' attitudes toward the material and toward the victims portrayed in the material would change as they became repeatedly exposed to such material. For example, he says anxiety would be reduced.

Linz expected that subjects exposed to large amounts of either R-rated teenage sex films or X-rated nonviolent pornographic films would accept rape myths, view women as sex objects, be more likely to endorse using force in sex, and support more conservative sex roles than people who were not exposed to the films. He also expected them to be more likely to judge rape victims as responsible for their own plight and defendants less worthy of severe punishment and less responsible when evaluating a videotaped rape trial.

In Linz's first study, his subjects were fifty-two males recruited from various university departments. These students were tested for psychoticism and hostility, and anyone believed to be predisposed toward aggression was eliminated. In this case, that amounted to three of the men. Linz was afraid that subjects who were overly aggressive might be inclined to imitate scenes from the films.

Twelve subjects were assigned to view five R-rated violent films, and twelve subjects were recruited as controls. Slasher films (*Texas Chainsaw Massacre, I Spit on Your Grave, Toolbox Murders, Maniac,* and *Vice Squad*) were shown to the men. These films included violence in which the victims were almost always females. Violent scenes were juxtaposed with erotic or sensual scenes. For example, a woman masturbating in a bathtub was suddenly and brutally attacked. The films did not indicate that the victims enjoyed or were sexually aroused by the violence. Most of the scenes ended in the death of the victim.

After each film, one of which was seen each day for five consecutive days, the subjects rated how they felt and how they viewed the attitudes toward sex and violence, degradation, and the like, in the film. On the last day, after they saw the fifth film, they watched a videotape reenactment of a rape trial that they were told was being substituted for another film that had not arrived. The control subjects also watched this film. Everyone was debriefed after the videotape. These debriefings included an emphasis that women do not seek, like, or deserve to be victims of any type of violence.

Linz found that after prolonged exposure to the violence in the films, the subjects had lower "emotional reactions" to them. They were significantly less anxious and depressed on the final day of viewing and were more likely at that point to enjoy the films. By the last day of the viewing, the films were seen to be significantly less violent, although, Linz notes, not significantly less sexually violent. The subjects rated the films as significantly less degrading and offensive by the last day. After watching the reenactment of the rape trial, the men who saw the films judged the victim to be significantly less injured and less worthy than did those in the control group, who did not see the films. The men who saw the films also were much more likely to judge the victim in the rape trial as offering less resistance and as being more responsible and to judge the rapist as being less responsible. The men also expressed less sympathy for the victim.

Linz concludes that these findings indicate that lengthy exposure to filmed violence can lower sensitivity to violence victims in other contexts. However, Linz says he did not find the "expected positive intercorrelations between enjoyment of the films and perceptions of how degrading and violent they were."[414] In addition, emotional arousal such as depression and anxiety was not a "significant predictor of degradation scores or perceptions of violence."[415] Linz concludes that this suggests that reduced depression and anxiety may not influence changes in people's perceptions of violence, contrary to what he had hypothesized.

In a second study, Linz dealt with the concern that his original study had been too concentrated. Therefore, in this study, half of the subjects viewed five movies and half viewed only two movies. The movies were shown every other day to allow a longer rest period between them. To deal with the possibility that the effects from such films are only short-term ones, Linz had the subjects in the second study participate as mock jurors in the rape trial two days after exposure to the last film rather than immediately after it. In addition, he removed a lot of the ambiguity about the rape victim's injury by including a photograph of the injured victim in the mock trial. He also changed the way the rape trial was shown so that the subjects would be less likely to connect the showing of the trial to the initial phase of the experiment.

Linz tested 638 introductory psychology students on the psychoticism and hostility subscales. Again those who scored high on these tests were eliminated out of fear that they might imitate violent scenes from the films. Fifty-nine of the subjects were eliminated on those grounds. A random sample of 396 subjects were contacted. Only 20 subjects declined to participate due to objections to the material they might have to view; 170 declined because of scheduling difficulties or lack of interest in the study.

In this study, the subjects saw either R-rated violent movies, R-rated nonviolent movies (the teenage sex films), or X-rated nonviolent movies. The X-rated films had scenes of masturbation, coitus, cunnilingus, fellatio, and anal intercourse. There were no sexual assaults or scenes of forced sexual intercourse in the films. However, they often portrayed women in a degrading fashion—as sex objects (that is, as receptacles for male penetration) and as sexually insatiable (that is, willing and eager to have sex with any male). Linz notes that these X-rated films included large power differences between the women and men portrayed, with the women often shown as "only able to attain a valued goal by submitting to unwanted sex or seducing the more socially powerful male."[416] The rape trial involved an alleged rape of a woman by a member of a fraternity during a fraternity party. The subjects saw either an acquaintance version or a nonacquaintance version of the rape trial. The control subjects were exposed to the rape trial but did not see any of the other films. There was extensive debriefing.

Linz found that subjects who were continually exposed to graphic film violence against women had initial feelings of depression and anxiety that began to dissipate. As exposure continued, the subjects reported seeing less violence in the films. They also evaluated the material as less degrading with more exposure. While the increase in enjoyment found in the first study was not found in this one, enjoyment did not decrease with increased exposure. Linz found that exposure to two movies was sufficient to obtain a similar desensitization effect as that obtained after exposure to five movies, which he says suggests that desensitization to film violence occurs rapidly. He suggests studying desensitization as it occurs with each violent act rather than with each movie.

Those subjects exposed to the R-rated films were less sympathetic to the rape victim portrayed in the trial and less likely to emphasize with her in comparison to the control subjects and those exposed to the other types of films. Rape myth acceptance and perceptions of victim injury did not interact with the type of film exposure. Linz found these results "somewhat puzzling" in light of the first study's results. Yet he says it is safe to conclude that exposure to R-rated films depicting brutal violence against women does influence viewer responses to victims in a more realistic context. He found the variables affecting these judgments and the reliability of the effects to be "somewhat unclear."

Linz suggests that showing the picture of the rape victim to the subjects possibly left no doubt that she had been harmed and greatly diminished any film effects. Yet he urges caution in reaching this conclusion because this was not experimentally manipulated. He also found that the reactions to actual victims need not be measured immediately after exposure to violence. He suggests that the best predictor of the trial outcome in this study was the subjects' perception of victim resistance. He writes,

> The results failed to support the hypotheses derived from Zillmann and Bryant's previous work that long term exposure to X-rated sexually explicit or R-rated teenage sex films which portray women as sexual objects will affect the development of subsequent attitudes about women. We did not observe a single statistically significant main effect or interaction for the film type, film dosage or acquaintance independent variables on either the pretrial questionnaire scales assessing rape myth acceptance, belief in women as sexual objects, endorsement of force in sexual relations,

conservative sex roles or the post-trial assessments of the victim and the defendant.[417]

Linz suggests that the expected results may not have been found for a variety of reasons. One is that once subjects do not recognize a connection between exposure to the pornography and the questions measuring their attitudes presented to them, the results might disappear. Linz also suggests that there might have been critical differences between the film stimuli he used and those used in prior studies by Zillmann and Bryant. Yet Linz emphasizes that the X-rated films used in both his study and the previous one contained the same kinds of sexual activities. Linz further suggests that it might not be the frequency of images of female promiscuity that leads to the effects but rather concentrated doses of scenes showing women as "sexually insatiable whores" like those used in the Zillmann and Bryant study. He also suggests that longer term exposure to such films might be needed for those effects to occur.[418]

In a third study, Linz tested to find out whether persons who had high ratings of psychoticism and hostility would react differently toward films of graphic sexual aggression and rape against women than would persons who did not have such characteristics. He expected the high hostility subjects to find the films less harmful and degrading to the women and to show greater enjoyment of the violence. He expected persons high in psychoticism to have less empathy for rape victims in general and those low in psychoticism to have more empathy. He also expected those high in psychoticism to have stronger beliefs about the use of force in sexual relations and in rape myths after exposure to the films than would the other subjects. In the first phase, 638 male introductory psychology students were pretested for hostility and psychoticism measures. Forty-five subjects were recruited from among them. Half of them had high levels of hostility and psychoticism, and the other half were below the criteria that had been established.

In one film condition, subjects saw the films *Eyes of Laura Mars* and *Video Drone*. These films had a small degree of sexual violence but no rape behavior. In another film condition, subjects saw the X-rated movies *Babycakes* and *Easy*. They were sexually explicit and had at least one scene of rape "in which the woman is either held at knife point or tied up and forced to submit to sexual intercourse."[419] In the films, the victims reacted ambiguously to the assaults. The third film condition showed the films *I Spit on Your Grave* and *Lipstick*. Both were R-rated and contained extremely brutal rape scenes in which the victims are shown as emotionally traumatized and severely hurt physically as well.

The results failed to support the hypothesis that those subjects with high hostility would find even the brutal rape films more entertaining and less degrading than the low hostility subjects. Nor did Linz find the expected interaction for rape, empathy, or sympathy based on psychoticism scores. He did find that those with higher psychoticism scored higher on the endorsement of force variable but not on the rape myth issue. While people who scored high in psychoticism and were exposed to violent rape films rated the victims as less attractive, less credible, and less worthy than those with low scores, Linz failed to find a similar pattern of interactions for victim injury, responsibility, and resistance. He concludes that people with relatively high psychoticism "may be more likely to endorse the use of force in sexual relations even after exposure to films depicting the most violent of rapes."[420] (The reader should consult this thesis for debriefing scripts to be used in these types of experiments.)

Mosher and Anderson studied the relationship between macho and aggressive personalities and reactions to images of realistic rape. The rape imagery used described "an average young woman with a flat tire on an isolated road who became the nonconsenting victim of forced-intercourse rape."[421] The imagery was in the form of a twelve-minute audiotape during which subjects were told to imagine they were the man (rapist) in the fantasy. The subjects were 175 male undergraduate introductory psychology students who volunteered in order to fulfill a course requirement. Before the experiment, the men were tested for hypermasculinity and aggressive sexual behavior.

Table 1 of the Mosher and Anderson study showed that many of the men had used aggressive sexual behavior against women. For example, 19 percent of the men studied reporting having gotten drunk and forced a woman to have sex, 10 percent had shared a "party girl" with other men, and 5 percent had forced a woman to have sex with them and some of their friends. Large minorities of the men also reported having used verbal manipulation to get women to agree to sex. Sixty-six percent of the men said they had gotten a woman drunk in order to have sex, and 42 percent said they had gotten a woman high on pills or marijuana "so she would be less able to resist my advances."[422] Anger and threats also had been used to gain sex.

The study found that men with a macho personality and who fit the Calloused Sex Attitudes Subscale "correlated with a history of sexual aggression."[423] The men with macho personalities experienced less "negative affect while imagining themselves committing the crime of rape."[424] Those with a history of sexual aggression experienced "more subjective sexual arousal while imagining committing a rape."[425] They were also more excited or interested. However, contrary to what had been hypothesized, the men with a history of sexual aggression "experienced more, rather than less, anger, distress, fear, shame, guilt and disgust" compared to men with low sexual aggression "as they imagined themselves committing the crime of rape."[426]

During the debriefing, the researchers found that the men experienced surprise, interest, and disgust, very different emotions from the enjoyment, interest, and sexual arousal that results from depictions of consensual sex. The researchers note that the study evoked "mild to moderate levels of negative affect and little sexual arousal or enjoyment in these college men."[427] (They say that the men may have been surprised by the emphasis on the violence of the rape in contrast to typical male fantasies of rape as more erotic than violent. This imagery was of a realistic crime of rape.)

While Mosher and Anderson found that, contrary to expectations, the macho men were not more sexually aroused by imagining themselves raping, they speculated that the "absence of erotic cues kept sexual arousal low."[428]

ADULT BUSINESS STUDIES

Several large cities have conducted studies purporting to show that pornography outlets cause crime increases in and deterioration of neighborhoods where they are located. Much of the increased crime reported consists of indecent exposure (often *in* the pornographic outlets) and prostitution offenses. Although larger rape rates have been shown in some pornographic outlet areas compared to other areas, often differences in area population and economic and property characteristics were not considered. It seems reasonable to conclude that some pornographic outlets attract crime and cause neighborhood deterioration.

In *Hudnut* v. *American Booksellers Association, Inc.*, the Seventh Circuit Court of Appeals amici brief of The Neighborhood Pornography Task Force claimed there was a deterioration of south Minneapolis neighborhoods "caused by the presence of increasing numbers of pornographic bookstores and theaters." The brief also alleged that women were harassed and intimidated there. The brief claimed that crime rates, especially for prostitution-related offenses, were higher in neighborhoods bordering East Lake Street (that is, areas where pornographic outlets were) than in other parts of Minneapolis.

A Community Crime Prevention Agency report of certain personal crimes in Minneapolis in 1983 showed that, for example, the Phillips neighborhood (where pornographic outlets are located) had a higher number of personal crimes (including 41 rapes, 53 other sexual offenses, and 254 stranger-to-stranger assaults) than many other neighborhoods. (We found this data to be too incomplete to draw conclusions. It did not contain information such as the number of pornographic outlets in each neighborhood, population data, economic data, property value data, or which neighborhoods would be comparable in demographic characteristics.)[429]

On May 25, 1979 the Planning Department of the City of Phoenix, Arizona, issued a report titled "Adult Business Study." The report stated that in New York City, where there were concentrated adult business districts at one time, police department reports said that in police districts with pornographic outlets, crime complaints were almost 70 percent higher than in those districts without them. There were higher rates of rape, assault, and robbery in the areas with pornographic outlets. And, in a concentrated adult business area around Times Square, because 2.5 times as many retail jobs were lost there as in the rest of the city, sales taxes dropped by 43 percent in a two-year time span.[430] (Again, we caution that these figures do not detail population characteristics, property values, and nature of the crimes, among other things. Those could probably be found in the original New York study.)

Phoenix passed a zoning ordinance that prevented adult businesses from being concentrated in certain areas. This was done because the community government hypothesized that (1) "there are direct impacts which uniquely relate to this class of land use" and (2) "there are indirect, but equally potent, attitudinal concerns which result from proximity to an adult business."[431] Examples of the first would include litter, noise, criminal activity, unusual hours of business, and possible traffic congestion, the report said. According to the report, the latter is shown by "substantial testimony" that many area residents "dislike" living near an area with an adult business and the claim that financial institutions consider pornographic outlets when financing residential properties.

The Phoenix report said it would show that "there is a relationship between arrests for sexual crimes and locations of adult businesses."[432] This, it said, causes fears for the safety of women, children, and neighborhoods and lowers the livability and desirability of such areas. The Phoenix report paired three neighborhoods with pornographic businesses with three neighborhoods without them. The adult business and control areas were paired using similar population characteristics such as number of residents, median family income, median age of the population, percentage of nonwhite population, percentage of residential and nonresidential acreage uses, and percentage of dwelling units built since 1950. (We note that one of the pornographic areas had a median income more than $2,000 lower than its control and only 57 percent of its buildings built between 1950 and 1970 compared to 93 percent for the control area. This pornographic area had four pornographic outlets, compared to one each for the other two study sites and none for the control areas.)

The data used, based on arrests, showed that the first pornographic area had 127 sex offenses compared to only 12 for its control area. However, 107 of these were for indecent exposure. The data showed a 1.13 per thousand rape rate for the pornographic area compared to a 0.38 per thousand rate for the control area. The indecent exposure data was 8.61 per thousand compared to 0.45 per thousand. The results from the other study and control areas were similar. In the first study area, 89 percent of the indecent exposure crimes "were committed on adult business premises."[433] (We point out that the results of studies such as this rely heavily on inclusion of crimes such as indecent exposure and, in other cases, prostitution-related offenses.)

An August 24, 1977, memorandum from Captain Carl I. Delau to Deputy Inspector John Kukula of the Cleveland Police Department on the topic of contribution of "smut shop" outlets to increased crime rates in census tract areas containing such shops was taken from a talk by Captain Delau at the National Conference on the Blight of Obscenity held in Cleveland on July 28–29, 1977. The memo said that Cleveland had 26 "smut" outlets in 15 census tracts out of 204 in the city. While the city experienced an overall 8.1 percent reduction in crime in 1976 compared to 1975, twelve of the census tracts with the pornography outlets rose in crime rankings or remained the same. Delau reported that the two highest crime tracts had eight pornography establishments and the top five crime tracts had twelve of the twenty-six pornography outlets. The fifteen tracts with pornography outlets had double the citywide average of robberies. The rate for rapes in these fifteen tracts was nearly double the citywide average. Four tracts with ten of the pornography outlets had

an average rape rate four times the city average. (Again, the reader is cautioned that these figures do not detail differences in population or economic and property characteristics.)[434]

In June 1977, the Department of City Planning in Los Angeles released a report titled "Study of the Effects of the Concentration of Adult Entertainment Establishments in the City of Los Angeles." This study said the police department had found a link between the concentration of "adult" businesses (including adult motels, massage parlors, bookstores/arcades, and theaters) and increased crime in the Hollywood community. Public hearing testimony showed that the public had a serious concern about the proliferation of such businesses. The planning department staff concluded that the degree of "deleterious effects" of such businesses depends largely on how the business is operated and the particular type of business. They could not conclude that properties with such businesses directly influenced the assessed values of nearby properties. The department of planning felt that any ordinance passed to control adult businesses should disperse rather than concentrate them.

In Los Angeles, the Hollywood area and portions of Studio City and North Hollywood have the greatest concentrations of adult entertainment establishments. These areas were studied, along with three separate control areas in Hollywood. The three study areas (parts of Hollywood) *and* the control areas all experienced considerably less increase in assessed values between 1979 and 1977 than either the Hollywood community as a whole or the entire City. According to the report,

> there would seem to be some basis to conclude that the assessed valuation of property within the study areas containing concentrations of adult entertainment businesses have *generally* tended to increase to lesser degree than similar areas without such concentrations. However, in the staff's opinion there would appear to be insufficient evidence to support the contention that concentrations of sex-oriented businesses have been the *primary cause* of these patterns of change in assessed valuations between 1979 and 1976.[435]

Hundreds of persons attended public meetings on the topic. At the Hollywood meeting, the most common comment was that of fear of walking in areas where such businesses were concentrated. Other remarks stressed physical or economic deterioration of the area, offensive displays, and an increase in street crime. Most of the speakers felt that concentrated adult businesses in their neighborhoods were "detrimental, either physically by creating blight or economically by decreasing patronage of traditional businesses; or socially by attracting crime."[436] The report emphasized that such testimony was "subjective." The planning department staff again emphasized that certain types of adult businesses are more "objectionable" than others and that negative effects could be minimized based on advertisement and operation of a business.

Businesses, property owners, real estate agents, bank representatives, and others were sent questionnaires. The return rate was 17.4 percent. The great majority of respondents felt that neighborhood business sales and profits and home values and appearances were negatively effected by adult establishments. Many respondents agreed that effects included vacant businesses, tenants moving out, customer complaints, lower rents, deteriorated neighborhood appearances, decreased property values, decreased business activity, and more crime. Only a tiny percentage of the respondents said that there was no effect, and a few indicated a positive impact. Yet the survey could not determine whether the stated negative effects actually occurred or were merely perceived to have occurred.

The Los Angeles planners took care to isolate areas within the city with common characteristics (taken from census data) for their study. But entire census tracts rather than more isolated neighborhoods had to be used.

A police department report indicated there were eleven adult entertainment establishments in the Hollywood area in 1969 and eighty-eight in 1975. During that same time period, reported rape offenses decreased by 7 percent in the Hollywood area and 15.2 percent in the entire city; prostitution arrests rose 372.3 percent in the Hollywood area compared to only 24.5 percent citywide; reported aggravated assaults increased 46.5 percent in the Hollywood area compared to 1.3 percent citywide; homicides increased 94.7 percent in the Hollywood area compared to 52.3 percent citywide; and pandering arrests increased 475.0 percent in the Hollywood area compared to 133.3 percent citywide.

The report said,

> The overwhelming increase in prostitution, robberies, assaults, thefts, and the proportionate growth in police personnel deployed throughout Hollywood, are all representative of blighting results that the clustering of Adult Entertainment Establishments has on the entire community. These adverse social effects not only infect the environs immediately adjacent to the parlors but create a malignant atmosphere in which crime spreads to epidemic proportions. . . . [A]ll officers felt the sex-oriented businesses either contributed to or were directly responsible for the crime problems in the Hollywood area.[437]

THE 1970 AND 1986 COMMISSIONS

The 1970 Commission on Pornography concluded that pornography is harmless. The 1986 commission concluded that some pornography has harmful effects on behavior. The details of those conclusions appear in chapter 13.

Numerous people have criticized the 1970 commission's conclusions.

In his 1974 book, Victor B. Cline concludes that commission's results were biased due to the ideological biases of the commission members and staff. The commission had found that there was no evidence that exposure to sexually explicit materials " 'plays a significant role in the causation of delinquent or criminal behavior among youth or adults . . . or causes social or individual harms such as crime, delinquency, sexual or nonsexual deviancy or severe emotional disturbance.' "[438] Cline basically accuses the commission majority of covering up their own studies, which supported theories that pornography does have an adverse impact on behavior. He uses evidence from modeling and imitative learning

literature that sexual deviations can be treated and created in the laboratory by using "erotica," that sexual orientations can be changed by using pornography, and that pornography does play a role in the formation of sexual deviations. He states that five commission studies found evidence of aggressive arousal in people who were exposed to sexually explicit material.

Cline cites a study by Gilbert Bartell (1970) of group sex among 350 Americans. That author found that many men who had pushed their partners into having sex with other women had gotten the idea from pornographic movies or books. Bartell reported that this resulted in disaster for the males because 65 percent of the females admitted to enjoying their homosexual relationships.[438]

Cline also notes that the Davis and Braucht (1971) study found pornography to be the strongest predictor of sexual deviance among people exposed at an early age.[440] He accuses Goldstein, Kant, and Hartman of misinterpreting their own study findings when they concluded that the work supported the view that pornography "does not incite criminal or antisocial acts."[441] According to Cline, these researchers used the term "rarely satisfying desires to imitate sexual activities shown in pornography" to describe "the 57 percent of the rapists who acted out or imitated the pornography modeled for them."[442] The same data showed that 77 percent of the child molesters who had male targets and 87 percent of the molesters who had female targets modeled pornography seen during peak adolescent experience. Interestingly, they also found that 85 percent of the normal controls imitated behavior they had seen in pornography. Cline concludes that all the groups were stimulated and affected by the pornography, if their self-reports can be believed. He says that apparently if people were normal, they tended to choose safer outlets for the stimulation. If they were rapists or child molesters, they engaged in aggressive antisocial acts.

Cline criticizes the commission report for failing to mention findings by Lipkin and Carns (1970) that a fairly substantial number of psychologists and psychiatrists had found a direct causal relationship between pornography and sex crimes.[443]

He says that another problem with the commission findings is that none of their studies actually investigated crime, delinquency, or antisocial behaviors. Thus, they did not study the issue upon which they made findings. Cline also questions their emphasis on pornography and sex crimes in Denmark and points out that the United States is the country most Americans are concerned about. He argues that since pornography availability grew in the United States to about the same degree as in Denmark, the sex crime increases in the United States should be of concern. He presents numbers showing increases in reported rapes, rape arrests, certain sex offenses, venereal diseases, divorces, and illegitimate births, which he calls major increases in almost every type of "social and sexual pathology" in our country at the same time when the volume of "erotica" increased.[444] He emphasizes that the studies showed that violent sex crimes in Denmark did not decrease during the years studied.

Cline also cites the Walker study, which showed a significant minority (39 percent) of sex offenders stating that pornography had something to do with their committing the sex crime for which they were convicted. Cline admits that the sex offenders could be "scapegoating," but at the same time they might be telling the truth. He also points out findings by Howard et al. (1971) showing that men with high amounts of psychopathic tendencies according to the Minnesota Multiphasic Personality Inventory Psycho-pathic Deviate (MMPI Pd) scale tended not to tire or satiate to pornography as quickly or as much as did normal men.[445]

The commission did not undertake longitudinal studies to determine the long-term effects of exposure to pornography on sex offenses, sex activities, and moral value changes. A properly done longitudinal study, Cline says, could have given the most powerful evidence about pornography's effects. In addition, there were no in-depth clinical studies of individuals and their lives to assess the impact of pornography. Importantly, no attention was paid to sadomasochism or porno violence, which, according to Cline, have become increasingly linked in the media. Nor did the commission study imitative learning data.

Importantly, the commission did not do a single study involving youth (despite their acclaimed findings involving young people). Cline also says that there was possible volunteer bias in the studies because only people who were willing to be exposed to pornography were used. This would be especially limiting for female subjects, he notes. In addition, comparisons between the studies are hard to make because varying amounts of erotic material, different definitions, and different types of pornography were used. Often the subjects' own definitions or interpretations of what pornography was were relied upon. And, Cline emphasizes, many of the studies used very limited exposure and no control groups.

Cline emphasizes that correlation alone can never demonstrate a causal relationship and that in the social sciences it is difficult to prove causal relationships among numerous variables.[446] Often many different things contribute to people's maladjustment or adjustment in society. He says, however, that the evidence that sexual deviations can be treated or created in people by using erotica should be seriously considered in determining its effects, for this suggests that accidental or deliberate exposure to pornography could facilitate antisocial sexual behavior as well. He looks at pornography as one of the casual instigators of such behavior.

Cline addresses the issue of whether people become satiated through overexposure to pornography and concludes that people may get temporarily weary of it after massive exposure, but the interest quickly returns. He cites a commission study by Winick (1971) of real-life consumers of sexually explicit material such as adult bookstore and movie patrons. Winick showed that 52 percent were regular customers and heavy or regular users of pornography.[447] The Nawy (1970) study also showed that patrons of a movie theater showing pornography frequented the theater.[448] And a study by Berger et al. (1970) of 473 working-class adolescents concluded that even high levels of exposure to pornography did not bore the young people in this study.[449]

Cline also suggests that a great deal of commission evidence indicated that young college-educated people, especially men, had already been exposed repeatedly to pornography. Thus, if there was to be a corrupting effect from pornography, it would have already started to occur long before the commission exposed these people to additional pornography. Previous exposure to pornography was not controlled for in many of the studies, and the studies did not ask the people whether they engaged in any antisocial sexual behavior after exposure to pornography. Yet the commission made conclusions on these topics. Cline also attacks the commission for not using matched control groups—for example, people with similar sexual, psychosocial, personality, and family backgrounds.

Readers are encouraged to see Cline (1976)[450] and the Hill–Link Minority Reports[451] of the 1970 commission for additional critiques by Cline of the commission research.

Feminists such as Kathleen Barry have criticized parts of the 1970 Commission on Pornography reports.[452] She says that its liberal bias affected the objectivity of the research. The result was a product of "cultural sadism" instead of "pursuit of truth." This bias was worked into the "design, methodology, and interpretation of findings of the Effects Panel research," she says.[453]

Irene Diamond suggests that the commission framed its research in the prevailing liberal ideology of the time—that is, that sex during the "so-called 'sexual revolution'" was good.[454] Biases, she says, influenced the Final Report of the commission, and influenced choice of research designs, interpretation of data, and integration of studies into the Final Report.

Diamond points out that many commission surveys measured people's opinions toward pornography but did not address the effects question. She suggests that the reason why there are conflicting results concerning "sex offenders" is that different studies included different types of people in that category. For example, studies that referred only to rapists had different pornography-related results than those that included pedophiles, homosexuals, exhibitionists, and persons who took "indecent liberties." Diamond also points out that many of the studies

used materials better defined as sex education materials rather than real-world pornography.

Diamond notes a conflict between commission studies that found that people exhibited a decreased interest in pornography after being exposed to large amounts in a short time and those that showed that real-world consumers of pornography are habitual consumers. She concludes that the commission conclusion that pornography is harmless was not justified on the basis of its own data.

Rist describes the behind-the-scenes workings, organization, and biases of the 1970 commission.[455]

McCormack argues that the 1970 commission research showed sexist biases in the way the research was designed and the manner in which the problems were conceptualized. She points out that pornography was not seen as an extreme form of sexual inequality in which women were sex objects and that the studies did not use subjects of both sexes. In addition, most of the research was carried out by men. For example, she points out that in the Abelson et al. study people were asked whether they thought pornography exposure "makes men want to do new things with their wives."[456] A similar question in which women assumed the sexual initiative "lead people to lose respect for women" was not offset with a statement that such materials "lead people to lose respect for men."[457]

Bart and Jozsa critique some of the 1970 studies in *Take Back the Night.* They point out the difficulty of demonstrating the effects of pornography in the real world because the relationships between what people tell researchers they believe and what they actually believe and between what they think they would do and what they actually would do (and under what circumstances) are not known. These authors also note that this research was conducted in a climate influenced by the sexual revolution and liberalized sexual values. They also argue that sex offenders do not differ much from the general male population and therefore would not differ much from the control group in studies. They say that the research on pornography is inadequate and call for an alternative feminist model that would consider the fact that male and female interests are often in conflict. In particular, they note, "pornography is not in the interests of women."[458]

A variety of other people have critiqued the 1970 commission either favorably or unfavorably. See, for example Wills[459] and Packer.[460]

MISCELLANEOUS STUDIES

In this section, we summarize those studies that do not fall into any of the other categories. These include, among others, topics such as positive effects from debriefings in pornography experiments and a general overview of the related field of television violence effects.

Yaffé and Nelson note the tendency of people to criticize scientific evidence with which they disagree and to accept data with which they agree at face value. They also discuss the problem of measuring people and their responses in clinical isolation. These researchers believe that the findings of the 1970 commission were premature. For example, the commission, they say, should not have drawn conclusions about the effects of pornography on young people because young people were not used in the studies due to ethical considerations. Yaffé and Nelson also reject the catharsis theory. In addition, they say that it is a "misconception" that sexually cruel and violent scenes appeal only to a small minority of warped and stunted individuals. Instead, they suggest, such fantasies are prevalent among "normal" individuals.[461]

Yaffé and Nelson also discuss Schmidt's (1975) interpretation of a Money and Erhardt study that found that men react to pinups and other pornography by seeing the women as sexual objects. They take the women out of the pictures and have sex with them. A woman seeing such pictures projects herself into the pictures and becomes the sexual objects to which men respond. However, if the pornography is a picture of a man, men do not project themselves into the pictures and identify with it. Similarly, women do not identify with the male figure and do not respond to it as a sexual object. They cite a 1976 survey in which women were found to be much less interested in male nudes than men were in female nudes.[462]

Yaffé details therapeutic uses of sexually explicit materials.[463] He emphasizes that such materials have been prepared for education and therapy and are not commercially available pornography. The emphasis in using such materials is to modify deviant sexual orientations and to increase people's orientation to what are considered more normal and appropriate sexual activities. (We suggest that you refer to this book for summaries of uses of sexually explicit material in sex therapy.)

In one of the more unusual studies mentioned by Yaffé, Forgione (1976) had two pedophiles indulge in their unacceptable practice using surrogates (in this case, the surrogates were life-size models of children). The therapist treated these pedophiles by photographing their interactions with the life-size models. The photographs were used as deviant arousal stimuli and coupled with aversion therapy. This led to the elimination of the pedophilic behavior in the subjects.

Nelson reports on studies linking pornography and sexual aggression.[464] He points out that one problem in these types of studies is that the term *pornography* does not have a generally accepted or well-defined definition in the scientific literature. Because different authors use it differently, comparisons are difficult to make. He also notes that research has certain limitations. For example, questionnaire and interview data may be affected by faulty recall, especially when the behavior at issue is personal. There also may be problems with subjects who are unwilling to cooperate or comply with the subject. Another problem is that findings cannot always be generalized to other people. In addition, subjects are often volunteers. For example, Zuckerman et al. (1976) found that single male college students would volunteer for an experiment rating their reactions to an "erotic" film three times as often as single female college students would do so.

Nelson envisions a time when lines in the pornography controversy will be drawn along those "nonaggressive erotic depictions being seen as relatively benign and innocent forms of sexual expression and the sexually violent and deviant portrayals being viewed as dangerous."[465] He found the evidence linking sexually explicit material to harmful aggressive and sexual behaviors to be limited but suggestive. However, he concludes that the concern that viewing "erotica induces people to commit sex crimes seems unfounded since the sex crime rate appears unrelated to this factor—it may not significantly lower the rate but it does not seem to put it up either."[466]

Nelson emphasizes that exposure to material portraying violent sexuality has different effects on people with different attitudes and personalities and also notes that there might be certain characteristics or traits that predispose people away from or toward criminal or violent acts.

He concludes that viewing sexual violence should be considered as a reinforcing or contributing factor to assaultive behavior, but he feels that exposure to such depictions alone would be unlikely to instigate such behavior. He does see depictions that portray victims as becoming sexually aroused by violent or aggressive behavior as a justification for such behavior in the minds of men. He states that conditioning sexual arousal to violent stimuli "would require repeated exposure." This can happen through masturbation to fantasies of sexual violence. Another impact would be creation of behaviors and attitudes that cause men to disregard a woman's nonconsent and reinforce their already existing beliefs about the appropriateness of using intimidation or force to make a woman do what they want her to do.

Nelson sees men as acquiring their negative behaviors and attitudes toward women in a non-media-related context but says that media exposure reinforces existing beliefs and also increases the probability that men may engage in actual assaultive behavior. Nelson feels that although observing violent sexual behavior in the media may be only one of the contributors to aggression, "it may be a very powerful one for at least a brief period of time in highly aroused and angered males."[467] His overall conclusion, however, is that there are extremely variable effects of viewing sexually explicit material.

Dallas comments on the lack of pictorial sex education in British schools. As a result, she says, no information or wrong information would be available to young people, resulting in misinformation and experimentation, as well as exposure to porn, which young people might believe is accurate.[468]

Check and Malamuth looked into whether there could be positive effects from participating in pornography experiments. The theory here was that a debriefing in these experiments could counteract any possible antisocial effects of exposure to rape depictions and also educate people and change their attitudes about pornography and sexual violence.

The subjects were sixty-four male and ninety-four female introductory psychology students. They were exposed to one of four depiction and debriefing combinations. These were a stranger rape depiction followed by a rape debriefing, an acquaintance rape depiction followed by a rape debriefing, a consenting intercourse depiction followed by a rape debriefing, and a consenting intercourse description followed by a nonrape or controlled debriefing. "For obvious ethical reasons there were no conditions in which subjects were exposed to rape depictions without an associated rape debriefing."[469] In the second phase of the experiment, the subjects responded to a newspaper account of a real acquaintance rape and were asked to give their perceptions of the causes of rape. Stories, rather than videotapes or pictures, were used. The debriefings used were typed and distributed in sealed envelopes to the subjects. Subjects were

unaware that the newspaper rape account and survey concerning their attitudes toward rape were related to the earlier experiment phase.

The researchers found that persons who had received the rape debriefing viewed pornography as more of a cause of rape than did persons who received the nonrape or controlled debriefing. This effect occurred regardless of whether the person had read the consenting or rape depictions. In addition, persons who were exposed to either rape story followed by the rape debriefing saw less victim responsibility and gave the rapist a more severe sentence than persons who were exposed to a consenting depiction followed by either debriefing.

The researchers conclude that the outcome suggests that a debriefing stating that aggressive pornography may have undesirable effects can have an impact in and of itself even in the absence of exposure to a pornographic rape depiction. Their debriefings cautioned persons "about the possible undesirable effects of pairing sexually pleasing and violent stimuli within pornography."[470] They note that previous research showed that exposure to pornography without the additional type of debriefing information used in this study generally resulted in reduced perceptions of pornography as causing criminal behavior. They suggest that some of the subjects in the other studies may have believed that if aggressive pornography were given to them by experimenters whom they believed to be conscientious scientists, the effects of violent pornography could not be very negative.

Check and Malamuth say the most important finding of their experiment was that "the rape debriefing had a desirable impact on subjects' later judgment of the man and woman involved in the newspaper account of the real rape."[471] The effect was statistically significant only when exposure to a pornographic rape depiction chosen on the basis of its relevance to the myths mentioned in the rape debriefing preceded the debriefing (that is, the acquaintance rape). There was no significant effect on subjects' reactions to the real rape when the rape debriefing was preceded by exposure to a mutually consenting, nonviolent depiction. The researchers believe that it is important to construct rape debriefings that are relevant to the materials used in the research. The researchers conclude that properly constructed rape debriefings can have a significant impact on the attitudes of subjects toward pornography and rape, thus serving as a means to change subjects' attitudes about those topics.

Thomas Radecki told the Symposium on Media Violence and Pornography that between 25 and 50 percent of the violence in our society stems from "the violence that has been taught to society/the culture of violence that has been established in our society and is reinforced every day in violent entertainment."[472] He found the "daily reinforcement" to be "a serious social problem" and said that these daily events begin to "approximate a world war."[473]

Dr. Leonard Eron told the Symposium on Media Violence and Pornography that he and others studied 875 girls and boys in school in 1960. They did a follow-up ten years later in which they reinterviewed 470 of the people who were now 19 years old. They found that "the best single predictor we had as to how aggressive a young person would be at age nineteen was the violence of the television programs that he preferred when he was eight years old. . . . The best possible explanation for our results was that it was the television violence that was causing the aggressive behavior."[474] He said that continued television violence viewing by children "can have a lasting effect on their character and personality, leading to serious criminal behavior and antisocial violence of all types."[475] He called television a powerful teacher.

Dr. Rowell Huesmann said that the Eron data showed "a significant relationship between television viewing at age 8 and the seriousness of criminal convictions by the time you are an adult at age 30."[476] It is not true, he said, that television violence affects only those children predisposed to aggression or those with lower socioeconomic status or lower IQs.

Some people in the television industry recognize that their shows can influence behavior. In response to the AIDS problem, some shows have created episodes in which characters deal with the issues and have moved away from the promotion of casual sex. According to Michael Filerman, an executive producer of "Knots Landing" on CBS, "If our characters engage in indiscriminate sex, viewers will think they can, too."[477]

Abramson studied the ethical requirements of human sexual behavior research from the perspective of subjects. He notes the failure of researchers and students to agree upon what is ethical in such research. He studied forty females and forty male introductory psychology students. Students were exposed to magazine viewing/reading of neutral or sexual magazines and to reading of an erotic story. Upon questioning, the subjects indicated that they had enjoyed the experiment as a learning experience and had suffered no negative effects. They felt the debriefing was important.[478]

David Lester proposed a hypothesis that "males who habitually attend heterosexual pornographic films" may be gratifying "unconscious homosexual desires."[479] These films, for example, show several males sharing one female. This hypothesis has not been tested.

Linz et al. argue that effective debriefings in sexual violence experiments might give adults "the critical viewing skills necessary to counter the effects of exposure to violence against women in the media."[480]

Athanasiou reviews the pornography research and calls it "simplistic sophistry" to claim that one single factor—exposure to pornography—can have a major effect on complex behavioral responses.[481]

Athanasiou cites a study by Diener et al. (1973) that measured honesty and altruism as they related to exposure to "erotica." These researchers compared the return of wallets lost in a pornographic bookstore and those lost in a general bookstore. They found that people returned wallets found while leaving the stores more often than they returned those found while entering the stores. They concluded that " 'these data do indicate that exposure to erotic stimuli did not lead to an increase in the antisocial behavior of stealing.' "[482]

Kelley studied thirty male and thirty female students enrolled in an introductory psychology course. First, she gave them a sexual opinion survey developed by Byrne and Fisher in 1983 to assess sexual attitudes. She also tested them on a personal feelings scale. The students viewed one of two 13-minute films. The first was a heterosexually explicit film titled *Methods and Positions of Coitus*. The second was a nonerotic film on sexually transmitted diseases titled *Look What's Going Around*. After seeing the films, the students responded to a paired-associate learning task used by Spence et al. in 1956. Competitive and noncompetitive word pairs were used. Those students with positive sexual attitudes (called erotophiles) made more errors and required more trials before succeeding at a competitive learning task after viewing the erotic rather than they did after viewing the nonerotic film. The reverse was true for those erotophiles who completed a noncompetitive task. Kelley says that this study showed that following exposure to explicit "erotica," persons with positive sexual attitudes "respond in a facilitated manner to a relatively easy task and the reverse way to a difficult one."[483]

Spengler studied 245 "manifestly sadomasochistic" West German men who completed an anonymous questionnaire. He found that these men reported purchasing pornography and sadomasochistic literature and magazines and that contact ads were sometimes listed in these media. Sixty-four percent of these men said they found sadomasochistic sex partners through contact ads. The percentages of these men who used pornography in the previous twelve months were once, 9 percent; two to five times, 21 percent; six to twenty-five times, 54 percent; and more often, 15 percent. (This study seems to show a huge use of pornography by men involved in sadomasochistic activities in West Germany.)[484]

As recently as 1983, Kutschinsky argued that "official crime statistics have not disproved the hypothesis that pornography helps prevent certain kinds of sex crimes, such as child molesting."[485] [We note that this statement, taken from an encyclopedia, goes against the reality reported by many police departments (see chapter 4) that child molesters commonly use pornography to arouse themselves for their crimes and to entice children to cooperate in their molestation.]

Bell, who takes a pro-pornography stance, cites Ned Polsky as suggesting that both prostitution and pornography are ways of discharging what our culture defines as "antisocial sex." Pornography provides this outlet via masturbation. Bell sees a social value for pornography in situations where heterosexual outlets are limited or unavailable—such as in the military, boys' schools, and prisons. He also mentions Polsky's suggestion that some people use pornography as a "sex instruction manual."[486]

Briddell et al. tested forty-eight undergraduate males, some of whom received an alcoholic beverage or believed they received an alcoholic beverage that was actually a placebo. Three taped narratives were presented to all of the subjects. The narratives involved forcible rape, mutually enjoyable intercourse, and sadistic aggression without sexual involvement. Those who believed they had consumed alcohol had a greater penile tumescence than the other subjects, and those who believed they had consumed alcohol had high levels of arousal to the forcible rape stimulus, equal to the arousal in response to the heterosexual recording. In fact, their sexual arousal patterns were indistinguishable from those of identified rapists.[487]

Lang et al. also studied the relationship between alcohol and reactions to pornography. Subjects were 436 male introductory psychology students. Some received vodka and tonic mixtures, and others received no alcohol. Subjects were exposed to twenty color slides, which were copies of pornographic material. These showed partially clothed individuals and explicit portrayals of nude heterosexual couples in various activities. Subjects who had been told that

their beverages had alcohol reported greater intoxication even though there was no alcohol in the beverage. The researchers found that individual differences in the people's sexual guilt "mediated the effect of alcohol expectancy cognitions on behaviors relating to sexual stimuli."[488] The high sex guilt subjects who believed they had received alcohol treatments showed an increase in the time they spent viewing the slides as they became more pornographic. This contrasted sharply with high sex guilt people who believed they had consumed only nonalcoholic drinks. The subjects who thought they had had alcohol rated the slides as more sexually stimulating and reported significantly more sexual arousal.

Two 1970 commission studies, one by Kupperstein and Wilson[489] and another by Thornberry and Silverman,[490] looked at previous studies that dealt with juvenile delinquency and pornography exposure. These studies were from the 1950s and 1960s. Both studies conclude that there is no link between juvenile delinquency and pornography, based primarily on the fact that the literature on juvenile delinquency did not deal with the pornography topic.

Laws used a biofeedback method to treat a bisexual pedophile for eighty-eight days. The pedophile's erection response to deviant sexually explicit stimuli was monitored on closed-circuit television. The treatment succeeded in suppressing the pedophile's deviant response to sexually explicit images of young boys and girls. At the same time, it helped him to maintain sexual arousal to nondeviant stimuli.[491]

MacCulloch et al. found a strong association between sadistic persons masturbating to behavior such as bondage, rape, torture, flagellation, buggery, kidnapping, anesthesia, and killing and the acting out of such fantasies. Unfortunately, they did not deal with the issue of where those fantasies came from.[492]

Halpern studied 105 female and 83 male psychology students. They were led to believe that part of the study was to look into the ability of people to form accurate first impressions, and they were shown pictures of other students. Those in the experimental condition were then presented with ten pornographic pictures of nude males and females in various poses. Control subjects were not exposed to the pictures. The subjects were then given a list of trait rating scales to describe the individual from the student pictures whom they had selected as least favorable. The experimenter analyzed the results for the trait "lustful." It was found that the higher sex defensive subjects rated their unfavorable others as more lustful than any other group. The higher sexually defensive subjects were those persons who said, in a questionnaire, that "they do not have sexual fantasies and dreams" and were not aroused by the "potentially sexually arousing situations" presented in the questionnaire.[493]

RESEARCH SUMMARIES

A number of experts have raised the pornography studies literature and summarized their findings. Included here are some of the more inclusive examples.

Zillmann reports on the effects of prolonged pornography consumption. He argues that research in which subjects are exposed to pornography just once and in which effects are measured more or less immediately after exposure are not useful for measuring behavioral, attitudinal, and perceptual effects, especially lasting ones. He argues that effects may be transient without affecting later behavior and that many effects may appear only after repeated exposure to pornography.

Zillmann critiques the Mann et al. study of couples who were married at least ten years, arguing that these people had sexual histories and would find little if anything in the pornography that was not "already part of their sexual repertoire."[494] Alternatively, people with little sexual experience "readily accept and are willing to practice particular sexual behaviors that they have witnessed on the screen."[495]

Zillmann argues that pornography is not usually believed to have undesirable effects on sexual behaviors because instigation of sexual desire and expanding of sexual techniques are often considered positive effects. He notes an exception in which pornography is used to entice children into sexual activities. (We would add to that any behavior portrayed in pornography that encourages modeling of acts such as rape and other coercive sexual behaviors.)

Zillmann believes that studies suggesting that people become bored with or satisfied by pornography show only that they get tired of watching the same materials repeatedly.

Zillmann summarizes numerous research studies discussed earlier in this book. In particular, he notes a finding by Donnerstein that people who have seen X-rated violent films, R-rated violent films, or X-rated sexually explicit films perceive less victim injury and also that the desensitization effect was found to be strongest for nonviolent pornography.[496] Zillmann concludes that "nonviolent pornography thus must contain information that promotes callousness in men toward sexually victimized women."[497]

Zillmann also cites a 1986 study by Weaver that looked at what produces such callousness. Weaver exposed females and males to a control condition of nonerotic nonviolent scenes and scenes featuring rape, nymphomaniacal episodes, or women being terrorized without involving clear sexual threats. While exposure to the different films did not affect subjects' views of a damage suit based on the physical abuse of a female cohabitant, it did greatly affect judgments of appropriate punishment in a rape case scenario.

> Compared with the control condition exposure to the film depicting women as sexually insatiable and socially nondiscriminating—which it should be noticed is a most salient theme in nonviolent pornography—reduced recommended incarceration terms most strongly (by 37 percent). Rape and terror had intermediate effects (28 percent reduction). Diverse sex finally had only an insignificant effect (11 percent reduction). These effects were rather uniform across gender of respondent. The only discrepancy occurred in the terror condition. In this condition females were highly punitive toward the rapists but men were not.[498]

Zillmann interprets this study as showing that certain sexual cues that are without violence are "indeed potent mediators of sexual callousness toward women."[499] He says that it also showed that terrorization of women "fosters such callousness in men," and he notes that the findings suggest that not all nonviolent pornography plays an equal role in mediating callousness concerning rape and rape victims.[500]

Zillmann deals with the fact that both the Linz Study and Krafka Study found that exposure to certain types of violent and erotic materials did not influence punitive recommendations in a significant way. He emphasizes in some detail that [Krafka and Linz's] failure to identify such an influence resulted from alternative procedural features of their research. For example, they used highly ambiguous rape cases, did things that may have created awareness on the parts of subjects about what the experimenters considered important media influences and thus may have caused them to guard against such influences, and might have made subjects more sympathetic toward rape victims by having them respond to questions about empathy.

In 1986 studies, Zillmann and Bryant studied the effects of nonviolent pornography consumption across six weeks. They noticed strong attitudinal and perceptual changes, including both sexes deeming promiscuity in both sexes to be more natural, greater acceptance of extramarital and premarital sex for themselves and intimate partners, and greater belief in health risks from sexual repression. They also noticed anti-gender-equality findings that favored male dominance over egalitarianism in intimate relationships. Zillmann notes that females embraced egalitarianism more than males and students embraced it more than nonstudents.

In addition, the pornography exposure reduced the desire to have children and particularly reduced the desire to have female children. The prolonged pornography consumption also reduced "sexual satisfaction and sexual related personal happiness markedly."[501] Zillmann notes that while pornography is often consumed in the hopes of increasing sexual satisfaction, it can in fact decrease satisfaction with intimate partners. The studies by Zillmann and Bryant also showed that people who had prolonged exposure to common pornography lost interest in it but became very interested in pornography depicting less common practices such as sexual violence and sadomasochism. At the same time, the pornography exposure did not affect these people's moral judgments of nonsexual behaviors such as shoplifting and drunken driving.

Zillmann emphasizes that much so-called common pornography is dehumanizing and demeaning to women. He also reports effects from studies in which prolonged exposure to pornography was shown to influence the reported likelihood of forcing women into unwanted sex acts and the likelihood of raping. Zillmann summarizes the effects of prolonged consumption of pornography this way:

(a) Excitatory responses to pornography, both specifically sexual and general ones, diminish with prolonged consumption. Some degree of recovery occurs spontaneously. It remains unclear, however, which conditions might facilitate or hamper such recovery.

(b) Repulsion evoked by common pornography diminishes and is lost with prolonged consumption.

(c) Prolonged consumption of common pornography does not lead to increased enjoyment of the frequently consumed material. Only less common forms of pornography that depict less common forms of sexuality tend to elevate enjoyment.

(d) Prolonged consumption of common pornography fosters a preference for pornography featuring less common forms of sexuality, including forms that entail some degree of pseudoviolence or violence.

(e) Prolonged consumption of common pornography distorts perceptions of sexuality. Specifically, it fosters presumptions of popularity for all less common sexual practices and of health risks from sexual hypoactivity.

(f) Prolonged consumption of common pornography promotes increased acceptance of pre- and extramarital sexuality. Although it increases distrust among intimates, the violation of sexual exclusivity is more readily tolerated. Moral condemnation of sexual improprieties diminishes altogether.

(g) Prolonged consumption of common pornography spawns doubts about the value of marriage as an essential societal institution and about its future viability.

(h) Prolonged consumption of common pornography leads to diminished desire for progeny. The strongest effect of this kind concerns the desire of females for female offspring.

(i) Prolonged consumption of common pornography breeds discontent with the physical appearance and the sexual performance of intimate partners. To a lesser degree, it breeds discontent with these partners' affectionate behavior.

(j) Prolonged exposure to nonviolent and violent pornography promotes insensitivity toward victims of sexual violence.

(k) Prolonged consumption of common pornography trivializes rape as a criminal offense.

(l) Prolonged consumption of nonviolent and violent pornography, especially of the former, promotes men's propensity for forcing particular sexual acts on reluctant female partners.

(m) Prolonged consumption of nonviolent and violent pornography increases men's propensity for committing rape. This effect is pronounced for normal men manifesting some degree of psychoticism; it is negligible for men with minimal psychotic tendencies.

(n) Habitual consumers of common pornography, in contrast to occasional consumers, are at risk of becoming sexually callous and violent.[502]

C. Everett Koop, Surgeon General of the United States, told the Denver National Conference on Pornography on May 31, 1985, that he believes, based on evidence, that pornography is a "serious contributing factor to certain disorders of human health."[503] He implicated pornography in four health areas: copy-cat rapes, sexual dysfunctions, autoerotic deaths of young people (which often look like suicides), and the effects on children caused by child pornography.

Scott provides an excellent short summary of the results of scientific research concerning pornography's effects (from a conservative's view) and an extensive bibliography. He concludes that the research shows the following:

1) Quite apart from any moral assessment of its depiction, exposure to nonviolent, noncoercive, "soft-core," consenting-sex pornography desensitizes, leads to callousness, and can in some circumstances trigger emotionally violent behavior.

2) "Hard-core," deviant depictions, including graphic violence without sexual content, soft-core depictions of consensual sex between heterosexual couples, and even "neutral," sex-education materials all, differentially, desensitize and habituate the viewer.

3) Significant desensitization has been found to occur in "hi-hostile" individuals following exposure to as few as two violent movies, containing less than 25 acts of violence, and lasting only three hours. This desensitization effect can last for several weeks after exposure.

4) Pornography affects the most dangerous sex-offender as well as the normal person, and it interferes with interpersonal relationships and personal moral development in *everyone* who uses it, not only in the disturbed and demented.

5) The negative effects of pornography impact "normal persons" and their marriages, as well as individuals with a wide variety of personality disorders.

6) Normal, as well as disturbed people, not only become "desensitized" to soft-core materials, they also develop a fondness for more deviant materials. Both incorporate them into their sexual practices, and begin to fantasize about, and even endorse, the use of force in their sexual relationships.

7) Dangerous offenders (i.e., child molesters, incest fathers, killers and rapists), develop a fondness for deviant material and incorporate it into their preparatory stimulation before seeking out a victim, whether it is a child to molest, a woman to rape, or an adolescent boy to assault. Rapists, in particular, report a preference for "soft-core," consenting-sex depictions before seeking out a rape victim in order to enable them to fantasize that the female they stalk will, in fact, resist.

8) Both normal and emotionally disturbed individuals become "habituated" to pornographic materials. They require increasingly deviant and bizarre images to re-establish their original, pre-habituation level of sexual arousal.

9) For the increasingly addicted "normal" consumer of pornography, habituation is overcome: a) by engaging in increasingly unusual and bizarre sex acts which often lead to dissatisfaction within marriage; and b) by seeking out a greater variety of sexual partners, including prostitutes, outside of marriage. Both sets of behavior are soon perceived to be "quite normal." This perception evolves into the belief that these materials do not harm others, even children.

10) The bottom line effect of long-term exposure to these materials has been: a) an increasing callousness and insensitivity towards others; and b) a more gradual, malignantly regressive "primitivization" of emotional relationships that cuts across all social strata.

11) Sex-offending, particularly for the dangerous offender, is compulsive and addictive. His mechanisms for reducing anxiety have become sexualized. Repetitive sexual molestation has become compulsive. The sex-offender's anxiety-reducing "fix" is sex with a child or an adolescent rather than drugs, alcohol or nicotine.

12) His need for a child, or for many different children, or for the same child is just as frequent and urgent as the addict's need for chemical substances. The sex-offender must offend repeatedly in order to maintain his psychic stability. Failure to satisfy this need can presage emotional breakdown, suicidal ideation and even suicidal behavior, for not only the offender, but sometimes his adolescent victims as well.

13) An increasingly visible and steadily growing class of more than two million sexually deviant adults—rapists, pedophiles, "hebephiles," incest fathers, sexual sadists, habitual felons and customers of teenage prostitutes seeking "little girls" (and boys) year-in-year-out are sexually victimizing a like number of children and youth.

14) The actual number of assaults is more than two million due to the repeat offending against the same victim by incest fathers, homosexual and heterosexual pedophiles, and the customers of child and adolescent prostitutes. Relatively few of these incidents are reported to the authorities.[504]

Elsewhere, Scott also has summarized the research of Zillmann, Bryant, Weaver, Donnerstein, Malamuth, Check, Linz, Marshall and Abel.[505]

According to law professor William Stanmeyer,

[T]he main evil of pornography is its general influence on attitudes, feelings, inclinations, emotional stability, and moral standards. The flow of causality is *not* (a) Pornography (causes) anti-social or criminal conduct (always) but rather; (b) Pornography (causes) deviant more psychological attitudes (usually) (which in turn cause or predispose to) anti-social or criminal conduct (more often than such conduct would occur had attitudes not been pre-disposed to tolerate and even enjoy such conduct).[506]

Eysenck emphasizes that it is not ethically possible to expose subjects to pornographic material if the hypothesis being tested is that such material would do them some kind of harm. He emphasizes that sex is "aroused, sustained and directed much more by conditioned stimuli which the individual has learned to perceive as arousing, sustaining and directing and by imaginary acts and ideas taking place in his head than by simple physiological mechanisms."[507] Eysenck believes that while pornography does not induce people to commit sex crimes, it is not reasonable to argue that pornography has no effect on the behavior of people who see or read it.

He compares pornography to drug research in which some drugs are controlled by government agencies. Some products of the mass media are "dangerous," and the public should be protected from them. He argues that drug firms are not given "the benefit of the doubt" and that television and motion picture companies should not be treated differently. He notes that the evidence tends to show that even short segments of media have profound effects on viewers.

In a report based on the Surgeon General's June 1986 workshop on pornography and public health, Mulvey and Haugaard emphasize the lack of directly relevant information on the pornography effects issue due to the ethical dilemmas regarding exposure to pornography. Exposure effects, they state, are likely to differ depending on a child's age and susceptibility to particular influences. The setting and social context in which pornography is experienced also are important. But because of ethics, the effects of pornography on children cannot be tested. Clinical studies of youths who have been involved in pornography can be examined, however. These often do not isolate the effects of pornography exposure from other variables that may have had an influence, and many clinical reports have a bias supporting the beliefs of the persons who write them.

Lab studies also are artificial and do not always have results similar to those that might occur in the real world. Yet they do allow for control over the amount and types of materials seen, as well as control over other variables that might affect the results. However, nonrepresentative samples (for example, college students) are often used, and volunteers for such studies may not be representative of all potential subjects. Because such studies are based on hypothesis testing models, only significant results end up getting reported in the literature, and it is not known how many studies do not produce results. Correlational studies have a problem because of their limited ability to control for numerous variables that may contribute

to any correlation, and causal relationships cannot be demonstrated by use of such studies.

Mulvey and Haugaard conclude that no set of findings or one study using only one method "should be taken as definitive."[508]

Participants in the Surgeon General's workshop included a variety of pornography researchers. They came up with several consensus statements that they felt had been "demonstrated with a required degree of social science accuracy."[509]

1. "Children and adolescents who participate in the production of pornography experience adverse enduring effects."[510] This conclusion appeared to be based primarily on clinical work with children who had been involved in pornography and prostitution.
2. "Prolonged use of pornography increases beliefs that less common sexual practices are more common."[511] This conclusion is taken mainly from the work of Zillmann and Bryant.
3. "Pornography that portrays sexual aggression as pleasurable for the victim increases the acceptance of the use of coercion in sexual relations."[512]
4. "Acceptance of coercive sexuality appears to be related to sexual aggression." The workshop participants note that clear evidence that such attitudes cause the behaviors of interest is lacking.[513]
5. "In laboratory studies measuring short term effects, exposure to violent pornography increases punitive behavior toward women."[514]

The workshop participants concluded that while pornography does have effects, it is not known how powerful or widespread the effects are. And they claim that behaviors are just as likely to influence attitudes as vice versa. Research has shown that attitude changes do not lead to behavior changes, Mulvey and Haugaard state.

The workshop set forth a future research agenda that would include examining the effects of violent sexual material in more realistic settings and working to develop a usable "typology of pornographic materials"[515] in order to guide discussion and research. For example, there could be definitional boundaries between rape and mutually consenting sexual activities. Consumption patterns of adults, children, and adolescents also should be looked at. Individual differences in reaction to sexually explicit and aggressive materials should be considered, and the duration of attitude and behavior changes observed in a laboratory should be studied.

Mulvey and Haugaard emphasize the need for longitudinal investigations of the influence of attitudes on sexual behavior. In other words, the same people should be investigated over time. And there should be research continuing into the use of sexually explicit stimuli for "clinical purposes."

Another session of the workshop focused on ways to mitigate the negative effects of pornography. (Here again emphasis was on children and adolescents while ignoring adults.) In this category, parents or children could be provided with the cues to "sensitize them to the materials that should be watched with caution."[516] A second method might be to produce a media literacy framework for viewing pornographic materials that could "limit the harmful effects of exposure."[517] Another area of concern must be preventing children's involvement in pornography production.

Mulvey and Haugaard include a paper prepared by Malamuth for the Surgeon General's workshop on the topic of whether sexually violent media "indirectly contribute to antisocial behavior."[518] Malamuth listed several processes by which sexual violence and the media might "lead to attitudes that are more accepting of violence against women."[519]

1. "Labeling sexual violence more as a sexual rather than a violent act."
2. "Adding to perceptions that sexual aggression is normative and culturally acceptable."
3. "Altering perceptions of the consequences of sexual aggression, in particular minimizing the seriousness of the consequence to the victim and reinforcing the myth that victims derive pleasure from sexual assault."
4. "Changing attributions of responsibility to place more blame on the victim."
5. "Elevating the positive value of sexual aggression by associating it with sexual pleasure and a sense of conquest."
6. "Reducing negative emotional reactions to sexually aggressive acts."[520]

Malamuth compared sexual and nonsexual media violence. Most sexually aggressive depictions involve males acting against females, while most nonsexual violence involves male victims. Victims of nonsexual violence are often outraged by the experience and intent on avoiding victimization. When sexual violence is shown, there is often a suggestion that "despite initial resistance the victim secretly desired the abusive treatment and eventually derived pleasure from it."[521] This, according to Malamuth, provides a justification for aggression that could not otherwise be justified. And such sexual violence is often shown without negative consequences for the perpetrator or the victim. The sexual violence is often associated

with physical pleasure, while the other violence is not. Malamuth described research studies that he said support the hypothesis that there are "indirect causal influences of media sexual violence on antisocial behavior against women."[522] He described media exposure as exerting a small influence on behavior, noting that this is true for all the contributing causes of such violence and thus does not mean that such exposure should not be examined further.

Eysenck and Nias critique pornography research up to 1978 and offer suggestions for dealing with pornography. Their concern was whether pornography and violent material had an influence on people's conduct. They caution people against using summaries of the various pornography studies, suggesting that some of the summaries do not accurately represent the original work or the conclusions from that work. They also criticize the fact that many of the studies were done by sociologists. Eysenck and Nias, however, see the pornography problem and the methods of "empirical inquiry" as psychological.

They raise the issue of whether any effects are due to pornography or to "erotic fantasies stimulated by the material."[523] They note that the studies do not deal with this issue.

They argue that the evidence is not contradictory, except when studies that are executed, analyzed, and planned properly are contradicted by badly planned and executed studies. They say that many reviewers have not looked at the quality of the studies and that the conclusions some study authors draw are not necessarily justified by their studies. These researchers argue that faulty techniques can cause false conclusions.

Another issue raised by Eysenck and Nias is that much of the evidence is circumstantial. For example, they note, researchers cannot randomly expose youths to pornographic films or prevent them from seeing any. Also of concern is that individual personalities and the effectiveness of exposure to certain individuals should be emphasized. The authors also point out that terms such as *pornography* and *erotica* have different meanings to different study authors. Sometimes these are not defined and thus cannot be compared across studies.

While Eysenck and Nias cite examples and state that they have hundreds of other cases in their files that indicate that pornography might have played a "decisive role in causing individual acts of sexual violence," the material does not show that the pornography was responsible for the crime that was committed.[524]

They cite arguments typically used for believing or disbelieving in harmful effects from pornography. First, it is argued that television and magazine advertising persuades people to buy things by showing models enjoying and buying such things. The same should apply to showing sexual or violent acts. Conversely, it could be argued that people want many of the things advertised in the media but that they do not want violence or sexual perversion. Second, it is argued that the media present a view of society and give examples of how to behave in various situations. The media provide models for young people to imitate. These researchers believe that this argument is partly justified. Third, they cite the case studies in which pornography and television violence appear to have an influence on individuals. However, they argue that the value of such cases is "low." Fourth, it is argued that vulnerable or emotionally disturbed persons are affected by pornography and violence in even a few people can do a great amount of harm. Fifth, some argue that pornography's main effect is to increase people's desire for "normal" sex, which is a good thing.

Eysenck and Nias argue that much of the pornography research is "unimaginative, repetitive and grossly oversimplified; conclusions are often framed without regard to possible alternatives and may betray the a priori inclinations of the investigator."[525] Again they emphasize that secondary sources should not be relied on because they often misinterpret original data, sometimes in the opposite direction in order to support the writer's biases. They say that most differences in findings can be explained by differences in socioeconomic status, age, and other population characteristics, as well as different instructions, materials, time periods of exposure, and follow-up.

According to Eysenck and Nias, the U.S. commissions that were set up in the late sixties to study the effects of pornography and television violence were primarily staffed by people who were selected to represent certain interests. They also state that the final reports of these commissions gave unreliable reviews of the actual studies that had taken place.

They argue that just because the research studies are not perfect, it does not follow that a no-effect conclusion can be drawn. They feel that there is enough high-quality work to allow researchers to arrive at a firm conclusion in this area of media effects. While they feel that the media cannot be held responsible for most of the increase in violence, the influence of the media should not be underrated.

The writers note that factors such as individual differences, duration of exposure to material, previous experience with material, and sexual experience in general should be taken into account. Far-reaching conclusions should not be drawn based on studies that used "highly selected populations, one particular type of material, a small number of exposures to that material . . . and a short time of follow-up."[526] Availability is another issue. For example, a person may see a technique performed in pornography and want to practice the new technique but not have access to a suitable partner for some time.

Eysenck and Nias emphasize the need for a proper control group in these experiments, for the absence of such a group can make an experiment meaningless. They also note that it is counter to psychological theory to believe that someone would immediately imitate a film because it has been shown that lengthy learning periods are usually needed before a change in behavior occurs. They say that much of the research in this area is "naive" because it does not pay attention to established psychological theories. Failure to get results can be due to faulty designs and instruments, they point out. For example, theories of conditioning, including desensitization processes, social theories such as imitation and modeling, and cognitive theories should be considered. They point out how sexual behavior has been found to be "strongly susceptible to methods of conditioning."[527]

The authors talk about the importance of desensitization, which is used to cure patients of fears, anxieties, and other inappropriate feelings. They seem to feel that persons could be desensitized to violence and pornography. Desensitization could be used for therapeutic purposes but also for destructive purposes, such as desensitizing children to explicit sex.

They argue that new behavior is partially acquired by imitating others and that imitation probably occurs not only in children but also in adults. They note that disinhibition also comes into play in these pornography issues. The concern here is that a person's aggression could be disinhibited after he or she witnesses acts of violence. Viewing of the violence is thought to weaken inhibitions against aggression and make it more likely that aggression would be expressed. Eysenck and Nias reject the catharsis theory and note that most experiments show a tendency for people to be more aggressive rather than less after viewing or participating in violence.

In chapter 3, they address various methods of investigation. These include the field study, in which naturally occurring behavior is looked at. This type of study has the arguable advantage of seeming more genuine because of its real-world nature and of allowing media effects to be assessed in relation to other factors that influence real-world behavior. Such results are likely to be taken seriously. However, this method lacks the precision of laboratory work and is not suitable for testing complex theories. For example, subjects cannot be assigned to the conditions being compared and differences between the groups might be due to a wide variety of reasons. Experimental field studies may be better because they use controlled manipulations in natural settings, but these manipulations can add elements of artificiality. For example, if subjects know they are in an experiment, their behavior might be affected.

Laboratory methods have the advantage of allowing subjects to be assigned to conditions that can be compared, and the conditions can be arranged to maximize effect detection. These methods are, however, subject to criticism that they are too far removed from real life to provide useful results. Some people feel that subjects do not behave in their normal way during such experiments. The studies also must be limited to relatively short durations of time. On the positive side, lab studies allow researchers to test theories and maintain various consistencies.

Eysenck and Nias argue that single case histories have "no scientific value and can be used only to illustrate never to prove any points about the effects of the media."[528]

In chapter 4, they critique the 1970 commission. In chapter 5, they look at field studies, many of which have been summarized in this book. They seem to support the view that sex offender statements about pornography influences are of limited value because they are based on subjective judgments. They critique the Goldstein et al. study, which claimed that sex offenders rarely act out pornographic desires, even though the results showed that most of those surveyed said that they had tried out activities shown in pornography. Eysenck and Nias suggest that if those activities are of an aggressive nature, this could have serious consequences. They note that the Denmark studies of the 1970 commission were unreliable because only a few cases are normally reported to the police. They say that the commission's conclusions that pornography availability was associated with a sex crime reduction are "misleading."

In chapter 6, Eysenck and Nias look at some experimental field studies and emphasize that none of them showed that exposure to pornography led to a decrease in sexual activity. Studies have primarily emphasized the issue that people get aroused by erotica or pornography. The conditioning theory of development of sexual preferences argues that "erotic scenes imagined immediately before orgasm are reinforced and thus become a more potent source of stimulation."[529]

Often researchers who conducted these studies did not take the trouble to recruit persons who were not familiar with pornography. Persons already exposed to such material would be unlikely to have much additional effect from it.

These researchers disagree with the theory that people will tire of pornography if it is freely available. This does not happen in real life, they argue, for a real-life pornography addict continues to look for new material.

They conclude that because the studies were not designed to show immediate sexual attitude changes or preferences or behavior changes, it is unfair to use them to conclude that pornography has little effect.

Next they look at laboratory experiments. Here they emphasize it is difficult to determine the extent to which the results of such studies are based on observing pornography rather than on fantasies of the subjects. They feel that in order to claim an important impact from pornography, something beyond that which could be produced by fantasy should be shown. They note that while mild forms of "erotica" have been shown to inhibit aggression, more hard-core material has tended to "facilitate it."

Eysenck and Nias express concern that the conditioning theory combined with evidence from the studies suggests that it might be possible to create a sadist or rapist in the laboratory "by presenting scenes of rape or sadism immediately prior to normally rousing scenes."[530]

They emphasize that films used for sex education are usually made specifically for that purpose because commercial pornography films are generally unsuitable since they do not portray positive sexual experiences and they do not involve gradual sexual arousal.

In chapter 10, these researchers emphasize that individual differences and personality can make a major difference in responses to and effects of pornography. They point out how showing a film could make an activity more popular among males and have the effect of forcing many women to take part in the activity only to please their men even though the women disliked the activity. These authors believe that individual differences might explain the inconsistent results.

In chapter 11, Eysenck and Nias give their recommendations and conclusions. They state, "The evidence is fairly unanimous that aggressive acts new to the subject's repertoire of responses as well as acts already well established can be evoked by the viewing of violent scenes portrayed on film, TV or in the theater."[531] They argue that the effects of pornography cannot be disputed but that they can be "quite variable." They believe that it has been established that portraying "violence in the media can incite some viewers to violence."[532] They feel that the makers of films, television programs, and so on, should be more concerned about portraying violence and social responsibility than they have been. Because the media are not concerned, and because economic interests are often involved, these researchers conclude that "some form of censorship may be essential."[533]

Eysenck and Nias argue that the censorship that they suggest for violence also should apply to portrayals of perverted sexual behavior. They are referring to things such as incest, rape, sadism, and other types of harmful behavior. Other examples would be sex with children or animals, sadomasochism, bondage, and torture. They note that the context of the presentation also is important, as is its prevailing tone.

These authors state that because most pornographic films have a context that is hostile to women, they should fall into a category of "incitement to violence toward minority groups," even though women are not a minority group. The films "constitute a clear case of incitement to maltreat women, downgrade them to a lower status, regard them as mere sex objects and elevate male machismo to a superior position in the scale of values." The authors feel that pornographic presentations affect men's attitudes in ways that are detrimental to women and therefore should be proscribed.[534]

Eysenck and Nias emphasize that more research is required. They feel that a team approach is needed, including psychologists and others. They call for research divorced from commerce, money, and politics.

Bowen discusses two models of aggression. One is the psychopathology model, which states that "sexual aggression represents a manifestation of a psychological disorder in the offender."[535] The aggression is considered an abnormal emotional disorder. The second is the social control model, which states that "sexual aggression is facilitated by cultural attitudes and beliefs concerning male/female relationships and sex roles."[536] Bowen found that the research on aggression and pornography could be condensed into four major themes:

1. Stimulus materials including pain and suffering of a victim affected male participants who were predisposed toward aggression through disinhibition of their self reported high level of likelihood to behave aggressively.

2. Materials including a victim who was willing and who reacted positively influenced all participants through the portrayal of positive consequences for sexual aggression.

3. Depictions of nonsexual aggression toward women influenced subsequent sexual aggression by affecting attitudes based on sex stereotypes (Donnerstein and Linz, 1984).

4. Repeated exposure to violent sexually arousing stimuli resulted in participants being less bothered or anxious by the depictions, less perceptive of violence and injury and less willing to judge the victim as having worth (Donnerstein, 1984).[537]

Bowen suggests using educational interventions to reduce people's vulnerability to sex role rigidity and media influences.

Gray critiques pornography research from the perspective of not opposing pornography. She argues that researchers have hesitated in exposing students to extreme forms of pornography and that research has not shown a strong connection between sexual arousal and reported likelihood of committing rape or tolerance of rape. She says research shows that pornography "facilitates the expression of anger if anger toward a particular target already exists."[538] Nonsexual violence can facilitate similar results, she states. There is evidence, she says, that pornography erodes inhibition of aggression toward both women and men, but she concludes that anger is a greater social problem than pornography. She refers to pornography as a "folk art" form.[539]

A good summary of the pornography research and implications for public policy appears in *The Question of Pornography* by Donnerstein, Linz, and Penrod.[540]

CONCLUSION

Consumption of pornography is a personal and private matter that is still often done in secret. Such conditions defy replication in university settings. The persons selected for study are often university students and criminal offenders. We do not believe that university students are representative of the typical pornography consumers, and we suspect the veracity

of criminal offenders. Consequently, the scientific research, while intriguing, is inconclusive and has proved little reliable scientific knowledge about the effects of pornography. Therefore, the public must rely on common sense. Common sense suggests that pornography is produced and sells because it is stimulating. If the public believes that it is wrong to brutalize and rape women and children, the public must conclude that much pornography represents the potential for social harm and therefore must be taken far more seriously than it has been in the past.

We are apprehensive about the possibility that pornography's practice of illustrating the deviant will turn healthy curiosity into antisocial attitudes or practices in some consumers. That apprehension is the reason we wrote this book. While we applaud the research efforts to date, we are distressed that the results lack uniformity and are inconclusive. Perhaps the nature of pornography, with its inherently bold explicitness and need to challenge established social taboos, defies controlled research. Future researchers must be more realistic and take into consideration the large amount of hard-core pornography now readily available at even the most modest of video rental stores. Perhaps future researchers will find a way to evaluate the consumers of pornography from these outlets.

NOTES

1. Steven P. Lab, "Pornography and Aggression: A Response to the U.S. Attorney General's Commission," *Criminal Justice Abstracts* 19 (June 1987): 301–21, 301.
2. Ibid., 309–11.
3. Daniel Linz, Edward Donnerstein, and Steven Penrod, "The Findings and Recommendations of the Attorney General's Commission on Pornography: Do the Psychological 'Facts' Fit the Political Fury?" *American Psychologist* 42 (October 1987): 946–53.
4. Donn Byrne and Kathryn Kelley, "Psychological Research and Public Policy: Taking a Long Hard Look before We Leap," updated paper, (State University of New York at Albany), 1–30, 2.
5. Ibid., 7.
6. Ibid., 13.
7. Larry Baron and Murray A. Straus, "Conceptual and Ethical Problems in Research in Pornography," (paper presented at the 1983 annual meeting of the Society for the Study of Social Problems, 5 August 1983), 1–19.
8. Diana E.H. Russell, "Pornography and Violence: What Does the New Research Say?" in *Take Back the Night: Women on Pornography*, ed. Laura Lederer (New York: Wm. Morrow & Co., 1980), 218–38, 228.
9. Ibid., 236.
10. Thelma McCormack, "Making Sense of Research on Pornography," in *Women Against Censorship*, ed. Varda Burstyn (Vancouver and Toronto: Douglas and McIntyre, 1985), 181–205.
11. Donald Amoroso, Marvin Brown, Manfred Pruesse, Edward F. Ware, and Dennis W. Pilkey, "An Investigation of Behavioral, Psychological and Physiological Reactions to Pornographic Stimuli," in *Technical Reports of the Commission on Obscenity and Pornography*, vol. 8 (Washington, D.C.: U.S. Government Printing Office, 1971), 1–40, 10.
12. J. Gayle Beck, David K. Sakheim, and David H. Barlow, Ph.D. "Operating Characteristics of the Vaginal Photoplethysmograph: Some Implications for Its Use," *Archives of Sexual Behavior,* 12 (1983): 43–44.
13. Ibid., 44.
14. D.R. Laws and H.R. Rubin, "Instructional Control of an Autonomic Sexual Response," *Journal of Applied Behavior Analysis* 2 (1969): 93–99, 94–95.
15. Ibid., 98.
16. Ibid.
17. Ibid., 99.
18. Gene G. Abel, M.D., David H. Barlow, Edward B. Blanchard, Ph.D., Matig Mavissakalian, M.D., "Measurement of Sexual Arousal in Male Homosexuals: Effects of Instructions and Stimulus Modality," *Archives of Sexual Behavior* 4(6) (1975): 623–29, 628.
19. A. Kolarsky and J. Madlafousek, "Variability of Stimulus Effect in the Course of Phallometric Testing," *Archives of Sexual Behavior* 6 (1977): 135–41.
20. F.X. Gibbons, "Sexual Standards and Reactions to Pornography: Enhancing Behavioral Consistency through Self-Focused Attention," *Journal of Personality and Social Psychology* 36 (1978): 976–87.
21. J.D. Adamson, K.R. Romano, J.A. Burdick, C.L. Corman, and F.S. Chebib, "Psychological Responses to Sexual and Unpleasant Film Stimuli," *Journal of Psychosomatic Research* 16 (1972): 153–62, 153.
22. Ibid., 162.
23. A.M. Barclay and D.M. Little, "Urinary Acid Phosphatase Secretion Resulting from Different Arousals," *Psychophysiology* 9 (1972): 69–77.
24. J.P. Wincze, E. Venditti, D. Barlow, M. Mavissakalian, "The Effects of a Subjective Monitoring Task in the Physiological Measure of Genital Response to Erotic Stimulation," *Archives of Sexual Behavior* 9 (1980): 533–45, 536.
25. Ibid., 537.
26. Ibid., 540.
27. Ibid., 543.
28. Sharlene A. Wolchik, S. Lee Spencer, and Iris S. Lisi, "Volunteer Bias in Research Vaginal Measures of Sexual Arousal," *Archives of Sexual Behavior* 12 (1983): 399–408, 401.
29. Ibid., 401–2.
30. Ibid., 405.
31. W.J. Barker and D. Perlman, "Volunteer Bias and Personality Traits in Sexual Standards Research,"

Archives of Sexual Behavior 9 (1975): 161–71, 161–62.

32. Ibid., 170.

33. Sharlene A. Wolchik, Sanford L. Braver, and Karen Jensen, "Volunteer Bias in Erotica Research: Effects of Intrusiveness of Measure and Sexual Background," *Archives of Sexual Behavior* 14(2).

34. Ibid., 95–96.

35. Ibid., 98.

36. Ibid.

37. Harold S. Kant, J. Goldstein, Derek J. Lepper, "A Pilot Comparison of Two Research Instruments Measuring Exposure to Pornography," in *Technical Reports of the Commission on Obscenity and Pornography,* vol. 7 (Washington, D.C.: U.S. Government Printing Office, 1971), 325–40.

38. Barbara Renchkousky and David Ashley, "Sex As Violence: The Body Against Intimacy," *International Journal of Women's Studies* 7 (September–October, 1984) 352–71, 356–57.

39. Patrick H. McNamara and Arthur St. George, " 'Porno' Litigation, Community Standards, and the Phony Expert: A Case Study of Fraudulent Research in the Courtroom," *Sociological Practice* 3 (Spring 1979): 45–60, 45; Edward Diener and Rick Crandall, *Ethics in Social and Behavioral Research* (Chicago: University of Chicago Press, 1978).

40. R.W. High, H.B. Rubin, and D. Henson, "Color as a Variable in Making an Erotic Film More Arousing," *Archives of Sexual Behavior* 8 (1979): 265–67.

41. Kathryn Kelley and Donna Byrne, "Assessment of Sexual Responding: Arousal, Affect, and Behavior," in *Social Psychophysiology*, eds. J. Capioppo and R. Petty (New York: Gilford, 1983), 467–90.

42. Ibid., 11.

43. Ibid., 12.

44. Ibid., 13.

45. Ibid., 19.

46. Ibid., 22.

47. David Alexander Scott, *Pornography: Its Effects on the Family, Community and Culture* (Washington, D.C.: Free Congress Foundation, 1985), 4.

48. Quoted in Walt Trott, "Are Gun-Toting Games Outlet for Emotions of Pure Hostility?" *Capital Times* (Madison, Wisc.), 1983.

49. Harry M. Clor, *Obscenity and Public Morality: Censorship in a Liberal Society* (Chicago: University of Chicago Press, 1969), 156–57, 166.

50. *Symposium on Media Violence and Pornography*, ed. David Scott (Toronto: Media Action Group, 1984), 39–40.

51. Seymour Feshbach, "The Catharsis Hypothesis, Aggressive Drive and Reduction of Aggression," *Aggressive Behavior*, 10: 91–101, 100.

52. R.G. Green, D. Stonner, and G.L. Shope, "The Facilitation of Aggression by Aggression: Evidence Against the Catharsis Hypothesis," *Journal of Personality and Social Psychology* 31 (1975): 721–26, 725.

53. R.B. Cairns, J.C.N. Paul, and J. Wishner, "Psychological Assumptions in Sex Censorship," in *Technical Reports of the Commission on Obscenity and Pornography,* vol. 1 (Washington, D.C.: U.S. Government Printing Office, 1970), 5–21, 5–6.

54. Ibid., 10.

55. Ibid.

56. Ibid., 11.

57. Ibid., 12.

58. Ibid., 13.

59. Leon A. Jakobovits, "Evaluational Reactions to Erotic Literature," *Psychological Reports* 16 (1965): 985–94.

60. James B. Weaver, "Effects of Portrayals of Female Sexuality and Violence Against Women on Perceptions of Women," July, 1987. Doctoral thesis, Indiana University, Bloomington, Indiana, 1–115.

61. Donn Byrne, Fran Cherry, John Lanberth, and Herman E. Mitchell, "Evaluation of Erotica: Facts on Feelings," *Journal of Personality* 41 (1973): 385–94, 387.

62. Gunter Schmidt, Volkmar Sigusch, and Siegrid Schafer, "Responses to Reading Erotic Stories: Male-Female Differences," *Archives of Sexual Behavior* 2 (1973): 181–99, 191.

63. Ibid., 198.

64. Donald L. Mosher, "Sex Differences, Sex Experience, Sex Guilt, and Explicitly Sexual Film," *Journal of Social Issues* 29 (1973): 95–112, 103, 104.

65. Ibid., 109.

66. Ibid., 111.

67. D. Steele and E. Walker, "Male and Female Differences in Reaction to Erotic Stimuli as Related to Sexual Adjustment," *Archives of Sexual Behavior* 10 (1974): 459–70, 459, 462.

68. D. Steele and E. Walker, "Female Responsiveness to Erotic Films and the 'Ideal' Erotic Film from a Feminine Perspective," *Journal of Nervous and Mental Disease* 162 (1976): 266–73, 271.

69. William Griffitt, James May, and Russell Veitch, "Sexual Stimulation and Interpersonal Behavior, Heterosexual Evaluative Responses, Visual Behavior, and Physical Proximity," *Journal of Personality and Social Psychology* 30 (1974): 367–77, 375.

70. William Griffitt, "Sexual Experience and Sexual Responsiveness, Sex Differences," *Archives of Sexual Behavior* 4 (1975): 529–39, 538.

71. Gunter Schmidt, "Male-Female Differences in Sexual Arousal and Behavior During and After Exposure to Sexually Explicit Stimuli," *Archives of Sexual Behavior* 4 (1975): 352–65, 359.

72. Ibid., 359.

73. P.H. Gebhard, "Sex Differences in Sexual Responsiveness," *Archives of Sexual Behavior* 2 (1973): 201–3.

74. J. Stauffer and R. Frost, "Explicit Sex: Liberation of Exploitation? Male and Female Interest in Sexually Oriented Magazines," *Journal of Communications* 26 (1976): 25–30.

75. R.A. Dienstbier, "Sex and Violence: Can Research Have It Both Ways?" *Journal of Communications* 27 (1977): 176–88.

76. E. Hatfield, S. Sprecher, and J. Traupmann, "Men's

and Wives' Reactions to Sexually Explicit Films: A Serendipitous Finding," *Archives of Sexual Behavior* 7 (1978): 583–92, 590.

77. William Griffitt and D.L. Kaiser, "Affect Sex Guilt, Gender, and the Rewarding and Punishing Effects of Erotic Stimuli," *Journal of Personality and Social Psychology* 36 (1978): 850–58.

78. W.A. Fisher and D. Byrne, "Individual Differences in Affective, Evaluative and Behavioral Responses to an Erotic Film," *Journal of Applied Social Psychology* 8 (1978): 355–65.

79. M. Brown, "Viewing Time of Pornography," *Journal of Psychology* 102 (1979): 83–95.

80. Neil Malamuth, Maggie Heim, and Seymour Feshbach, "Sexual Responsiveness of College Students to Rape Depictions: Inhibitory and Disinhibitory Effects," *Journal of Personality and Social Psychology* 38 (1980): 399–408, 404.

81. Carolyn Wood Sherif, "Comment on Ethical Issues in Malamuth, Heim, Feshbach's "Sexual Responsiveness of College Students to Rape Depictions: Inhibitory and Disinhibitory Effects." *Journal of Personality and Social Psychology* 38 (1980): 409–412, 410.

82. Neil M. Malamuth, Seymour Feshbach, and Maggie Heim, "Ethical Issues and Exposure to Rape Stimuli: A Reply to Sherif," *Journal of Personality and Social Psychology* 38 (1980): 413–415, 414.

83. P.R. Abramson, C.A. Repczynski, and L.R. Merrill, "The Menstrual Cycle and Response to Erotic Literature," *Journal of Consulting and Clinical Psychology* 44 (1976): 1018–19.

84. D.T. Kenrick, D.O. Springfield, W.L. Wagenhals, R.H. Dahl, and H.J. Ransclell, "Sex Differences, Androgyny, and Approach Responses to Erotica: A New Variation on the Old Volunteer Problem," *Journal of Personality and Social Psychology* 30 (1980): 517–24.

85. D.L. Steinman, J.P. Wineze, B.A. Sakhein, D.H. Bartow, and M. Mavissakalian, "A Comparison of Male and Female Patterns of Sexual Arousal," *Archives of Sexual Behavior* 10 (1981): 529–44, 536–37.

86. J.S. Nevid, "Exposure to Hemoerotic Stimuli: Effects on Attitudes and Affects of Homosexual Viewers," *Journal of Social Psychology* 119 (1983): 249–55.

87. David Scott ed., *Symposium on Media Violence and Pornography*, 125–41; Wendy E. Stock, "The Effects of Violent Pornography on Women," paper presented at the annual meetings of the American Psychology Association, August 29, 1983.

88. Pauline B. Bart, Linda Freeman, and Peter Kimball, "The Worlds of Women and Men: Attitudes Toward Pornography and Responses to Not a Love Story— A Film About Pornography," *Women's Studies International Forum* 8 (1985): 307–22, 309.

89. Ibid., 313, 314.

90. Ibid., 315.

91. Ibid., 317, 318.

92. Ibid., 319.

93. Michael A. Becker and Donn Byrne, "Self-Regulated Exposure to Erotica, Recall Errors, and Subjective Reactions as a Function of Erotophobia and Type A Coronary-Prone Behavior," *Journal of Personality and Social Psychology* 48 (1985): 760–67, 766.

94. Kathryn Kelley, "Sex, Sex Guilt and Authoritarianism: Differences to Responses to Explicit Heterosexual and Masturbatory Slides," *Journal of Sex Research* 21 (1985): 68–85.

95. Sanford J. Dean, Randall B. Martin, and David L. Streiner, "The Use of Sexually Arousing Slides as Unconditioned Stimuli for the GSR in a Discrimination Paradigm," *Psychonomic Science* 13(2) (1968): 99–100, 100.

96. J. Mann, "Experimental Induction of Human Sexual Arousal," in *Technical Reports of the Commission on Obscenity and Pornography*, vol. 1 (Washington, D.C.: U.S. Government Printing Office, 1971), 23–101.

97. Marvin Zuckerman, "Physiological Measures of Sexual Arousal in the Human," in *Technical Reports of the Commission on Obscenity and Pornography*, vol. 1 (Washington, D.C.: U.S. Government Printing Office, 1971), 61–102.

98. D. Byrne and J. Lamberth, "The Effect of Erotic Stimuli on Sex Arousal, Evaluative Responses, and Subsequent Behavior," in *Technical Reports of the Commission on Obscenity and Pornography*, vol. 8 (Washington, D.C.: U.S. Government Printing Office, 1971), 41–67, 48–49.

99. Ibid., 64.

100. T. Schill and J. Chapin, "Sex Guilt and Males' Preference for Reading Erotic Magazines," *Journal of Consulting and Clinical Psychology* 39 (1972): 516.

101. James V.P. Check, News release, York University, Toronto, 1984.

102. R.E. Ray and W.D. Thompson, "Autonomic Correlates of Female Guilt Responses to Erotic Visual Stimuli," *Psychological Reports* 34 (1974): 1299–1306.

103. Charles E. Colson, "The Evaluation of Pornography: Effects of Attitude and Perceived Physiological Reactions," *Archives of Sexual Behavior* 3 (1974): 307–23.

104. N. McConaghy, "Penile Volume Responses to Moving and Still Pictures of Male and Female Nudes," *Archives of Sexual Behavior* 3 (1974): 565–70.

105. Gary G. Galbraith, "Effects of Sexual Arousal and Guilt upon Free Associative Sexual Responses," *Journal of Consulting and Clinical Psychology* 32 (1968): 707–11, 709.

106. M. Mavissakalian, E. Blanchard, G. Abel, and D. Barlow, "Responses to Complex Erotic Stimuli in Homosexual and Heterosexual Males," *British Journal of Psychiatry* 126 (1975): 252–57, 254.

107. Ibid., 254.

108. Ibid., 255.

109. Ibid.

110. Ibid., 256.

111. R.E. Love, L.R. Sloan, and M.J. Schmidt, "Viewing Pornography and Sex Guilt: The Priggish, the Prudent, and the Profligate," *Journal of Consulting and Clinical Psychology* 44 (1976): 624–29.

112. R. Barr and A. Blaszczynski, "Autonomic Responses

to Transsexual and Homosexual Males to Erotic Film Sequences," *Archives of Sexual Behavior* 5 (1976): 211–22.

113. Marvin Brown, Donald M. Amoroso, and Edward E. Ware, "Behavioral Effects of Viewing Pornography," *Journal of Social Psychology* 98 (1976): 235–45.

114. John P. Wincze, Emily Franck Hoon, and Peter W. Hoon, "Sexual Arousal in Women: A Comparison of Cognitive and Physiological Responses by Continuous Measurement," *Archives of Sexual Behavior* 6 (1977): 121–33.

115. F.S. Fehr and M. Schulman, "Female Self-Report and Autonomic Responses to Sexually Pleasurable and Sexually Aversive Readings," *Archives of Sexual Behavior* 7 (September, 1978): 433–53.

116. M. Dermer and T.A. Pyszczynski, "Effects of Erotica upon Men's Loving and Liking Responses for Women They Love," *Journal of Personality and Social Psychology* 36 (1978): 1302–10.

117. William Fisher and Donn Byrne, "Individual Differences in Affective, Evaluative, and Behavioral Responses to an Erotic Film," *Journal of Applied Social Psychology* 8 (1978): 355–65, 362.

118. D.L. Mosher and K.E. O'Grady, "Homosexual Threat, Negative Attitudes Towards Masturbation, Sex Guilt, and Males' Sexual and Affective Reactions to Explicit Sexual Films," *Journal of Consulting and Clinical Psychology* 47 (1979): 860–73.

119. P.R. Abramson and D.L. Mosher, "An Empirical Investigation of Experimentally Induced Masturbatory Fantasies," *Archives of Sexual Behavior* 8 (1979): 27–29.

120. Donald Mosher and Paul Abramson, "Subjective Sexual Arousal to Films of Masturbation," *Journal of Consulting and Clinical Psychology* 45 (1977): 769–807.

121. P.R. Abramson, P.A. Goldberg, D.L. Mosher, L.M. Abramson, and M. Gottesdiener, "Experimenter Effects on Responses to Erotic Stimuli," *Journal of Research in Personality* 9 (1975): 136–46.

122. D.L. Mosher and I. Greenberg, "Females' Affective Responses to Reading Erotic Literature," *Journal of Consulting and Clinical Psychology* 33 (1969): 472–77.

123. W. Pawlowski, "Response to Sexual Films as a Function of Anxiety Level," *Psychological Reports* 44 (1979): 1067–73.

124. N.M. Malamuth and J.V.P. Check, "Sexual Arousal to Rape and Consenting Depictions: The Importance of the Women's Arousal," *Journal of Abnormal Psychology* 89 (1980): 763–66.

125. T. Schill, M. Van Tuinen, and D. Doty, "Repeated Exposure to Pornography and Arousal Levels of Subjects Varying in Guilt," *Psychological Reports* 46 (1970): 467–71.

126. W. Stock and J. Geer, "A Study of Fantasy-Based Sexual Arousal in Women," *Archives of Sexual Behavior* 11 (1982): 33–47.

127. R. Eisenman, "Sexual Behavior as Related to Sex Fantasies and Experimental Manipulation of Authoritarianism and Creativity," *Journal of Personality and Social Psychology* 43 (1982): 853–60.

128. D.E. Henson, H.B. Rubin, and C. Henson, "Labial and Vaginal Blood Volume Responses to Visual and Tactile Stimuli," *Archives of Sexual Behavior* 11 (1982): 23–31.

129. H.B. Rubin, D.E. Henson, R.E. Falvo, and R.W. High, "The Relationship Between Men's Endogenous Levels of Testosterone and Their Penile Responses to Erotic Stimuli," *Behavior Research and Therapy* 17 (1979): 305–12, 310.

130. Kathryn Kelley and Donna Musialowski, "Repeated Exposure to Sexually Explicit Stimuli: Novelty, Sex and Sexual Attitudes," *Archives of Sexual Behavior*, 15 (1986): 487–98.

131. J.V.P. Check and N.M. Malamuth, "Pornography and Sexual Aggression: A Social Learning Theory Analysis," in *Communication Yearbook* 9 ed. M.L. McLaughlin (Beverly Hills, Calif.: Sage Publications, 1985), 181–213, 184.

132. Donn Byrne, *"The Imagery of Sex,"* in *Handbook of Sexology,* eds. J. Money and H. Musaph (Elsevier, North Holland: Biomedical Press, 1977), 328–48, 341.

133. Ibid., 346.

134. Ibid., 348.

135. G.G. Abel and E.B. Blanchard, "The Role of Fantasy in the Treatment of Sexual Deviation," *Archives of General Psychiatry* 30 (1977): 467–75, 474.

136. O.J.W. Bjorksten, "Sexually Graphic Material in the Treatment of Sexual Disorders," in *Clinical Management of Sexual Disorders,* ed. J.K. Meyer (Baltimore: Williams and Williams, 1976), 161–93, 162.

137. Ibid., 163.

138. Ibid., 174.

139. Ibid., 175.

140. Ibid.

141. Ibid.

142. Ibid., 176.

143. G.G. Abel, E.B. Blanchard, and J. Becker, "An Integrated Treatment Program for Rapists," in *Clinical Aspects of the Rapist,* ed. R. Rada (New York: Grune and Stratton, 1977), 161–207, 168.

144. Patricia Gillan, "Therapeutic Uses of Obscenity," in *Censorship and Obscenity,* eds. Dhavon and E. Davies (London: Martin Robertson, 1978), 127–47.

145. H.J. Eysenck, "Psychology and Obscenity—a Factual Look at Some of the Problems," in *Censorship and Obscenity,* eds. Rajeer Dhavon and Christie Davies (London: Martin and Robertson & Co., 1978), 168, 175–76.

146. V.L. Quinsey, T. Chaplin, and W. Carrigan, "Biofeedback and Signalled Punishment in the Modification of Inappropriate Sexual Age Preferences," *Behavior Therapy* 11 (1980): 567–76.

147. D.R. Laws, J. Meyer, and M.L. Holmes, "Reduction of Sadistic Sexual Arousal by Olfactory Aversion: A Case Study," *Behavior Research and Therapy* 16 (1978): 281–85, 284.

148. D.R. Evans, "Masturbatory Fantasy and Sexual Deviation," *Behavioral Research and Therapy* 16 (1978): 17–19, 17.

149. S. Rachman and R.J. Hodgson, "Experimentally Induced Sexual Fetishism, Replication and Development," *Psychological Record* 18 (1968): 25–27.

150. M.P. Feldman and M.J. MacCulloch, "The Application of Anticipatory Avoidance Learning to the Treatment of Homosexuality," *Behavior Research and Therapy* 2 (1965): 165–84.

151. G.G. Abel, E.B. Blanchard, D.M. Barlow, and M. Mavissakalin, "Identifying Specific Erotic Cues in Sexual Deviations by Audiotaped Descriptions," *Journal of Applied Behavior Analysis* 8 (1975): 247–60.

152. Wardell B. Pomeroy, "The Use of Audiovisual Materials in Therapy."

153. J.J. Reisinger, "Generalization of Treatment Effects Following Masturbatory Training with Erotic Stimuli," *Journal of Behavior Therapy and Experimental Psychiatry* 10 (1979): 247–50.

154. W.C. Wilson, "Can Pornography Contribute to the Prevention of Sexual Problems?" in *The Prevention of Sexual Disorders*, eds. C.A. Qualls, J.P. Wincze, and D.H. Barlow (New York: Plenum, 1978), 159–76, 162. See also W. Cody Wilson and Herbert I. Abelson, "Experience with and Attitudes toward Explicit Sexual Materials," *Journal of Social Issues* 29 (1973): 19–39.

155. Ibid., 171.

156. Ibid., 170.

157. Ibid., 171.

158. Ibid., 176.

159. R. Wishnoff, "Modeling Effects of Explicit and Nonexplicit Sexual Stimuli on the Sexual Anxiety and Behavior of Women," *Archives of Sexual Behavior* 7 (1978): 455–61.

160. Barry S. Reynolds, "Biofeedback and Facilitation of Erection in Men with Erectile Dysfunction," *Archives of Sexual Behavior* 9 (1980): 101–13.

161. R.F. Barr and N. McConaghy, "Penile Volume Responses to Appetitive and Aversive Stimuli in Relation to Sexual Orientation and Conditioning Performance," *British Journal of Psychiatry* 119 (1971): 377–83, 378.

162. Ibid., 383.

163. John P. Wincze, Emily Franck Hoon, and Peter W. Hoon, "Physiological Responsivity of Normal and Sexually Dysfunctional Women During Erotic Stimulus Exposure," *Journal of Psychosomatic Research* 20 (1975): 445–51.

164. P.J. Morokoff and J.R. Heiman, "Effects of Erotic Stimuli on Sexually Functional and Dysfunctional Women: Multiple Measures Before and After Sex Therapy," *Behavior Research and Therapy* 18 (1980): 127–37.

165. N. McConaghy, "Penile Volume Change to Moving Pictures of Male and Female Nudes in Heterosexual and Homosexual Males," *Behavior Research and Therapy* 5 (1967): 43–48.

166. A.D. Van Deventer and D.R. Laws, "Orgasmic Reconditioning to Redirect Sexual Arousal in Pedophiles," *Behavior Therapy* 9 (1978): 748–65, 759.

167. S.H. Herman, D.H. Barlow, and W.S. Agras, "An Experimental Analysis of Exposure to 'Explicit' Heterosexual Stimuli as an Effective Variable in Changing Arousal Patterns in Homosexuals," *Behavior Research and Therapy* 12 (1974): 335–45.

168. B.T. Jackson, "A Case of Voyeurism Treated by Counter-Conditioning," *Behavioral Research and Therapy* 7 (1969): 133–34, 133.

169. R. Langevin and M. Martin, "Can Erotic Responses Be Classically Conditioned?" *Behavior Therapy* 6 (1975): 350–55, 355.

170. David H. Barlow, "The Treatment of Sexual Deviation: Toward a Comprehensive Behavioral Approach," in *Innovative Treatment Methods in Psychology* eds. K.S. Calhoun, E.E. Adams, and K.M. Mitchell (New York: John Wiley, 1974), 121–43.

171. S.R. Conrad and J.P. Wincze, "Orgasmic Reconditioning: A Controlled Study of Its Effects upon the Sexual Arousal and Behavior of Adult Male Homosexuals," *Behavior Therapy* 7 (1976): 155–66.

172. D.A. Crawford, "Modification of Deviant Sexual Behavior: The Need for a Comprehensive Approach," *British Journal of Medical Psychology* 52 (1979): 151–56.

173. V.L. Quinsey and W. Marshall, "Procedures for Reducing Inappropriate Sexual Arousal: An Evaluation Review," in *The Sexual Aggressor: Current Perspectives on Treatment*, eds. J.G. Geer and I. Stuart (New York: Von Nostrand Reinhold Co., 1983), 267–90.

174. A. Kolarsky and J. Madlafousek, "The Inverse Role of Preparatory Erotic Stimulation in Exhibitionists: Phallometric Studies," *Archives of Sexual Behavior* 12 (April, 1983): 123–48.

175. James L. Howard, Clifford B. Reifler, and Myron Liptzin, "Effects of Exposure to Pornography," in *Technical Reports of the Commission on Obscenity and Pornography* vol. 8 (Washington, D.C.: U.S. Government Printing Office, 1971), 97–132, 97.

176. Ibid., 97.

177. Ibid., 125–27.

178. H.H. Schaefer and A.H. Colgan, "The Effect of Pornography on Penile Tumescence as a Function of Reinforcement and Novelty," *Behavior Therapy* 8 (1977): 938–46, 944.

179. William T. O'Donohue, M.A., and James H. Geer, Ph.D., "The Habitation of Sexual Arousal," *Archives of Sexual Behavior* 14 (1985): 233–46, 234.

180. Dolf Zillmann and Jennings Bryant, "Shifting Preferences in Pornography Consumption," *Communication Research* 12 (October 1986): 560–78, 561, 562.

181. Ibid., 562.

182. Ibid., 574.

183. J. Ceniti and N. Malamuth, "Effects of Repeated Exposure to Sexually Violent and Nonviolent Stimuli on Sexual Arousal to Rape and Nonrape Depictions," *Behavior Research and Therapy* 22 (1984): 535–48,, 537, 544.

184. J.B. Weaver, J. Masland, and D. Zillmann, "Effects of Erotica on Young Men's Aesthetic Perception of

Their Female Sexual Partners," *Personality and Motor Skills* 50 (1984): 929–930, 929.

185. Ibid., 930.

186. Dolf Zillmann and Jennings Bryant, "Pornography's Impact on Sexual Satisfaction," *Journal of Applied Social Psychology* 18 (1988): 1–29, 19.

187. Ibid., 21.

188. Ibid., 21–22.

189. Keith E. Davis and George N. Braucht, "Reactions to Viewing Films of Erotically Realistic Heterosexual Behavior," in *Technical Reports of the Commission on Obscenity and Pornography*, vol. 8 (Washington, D.C.: U.S. Government Printing Office, 1971), 68–69, 69.

190. Jay Mann, Jack Sidman, and Sheldon Starr, "Effects of Erotic Films on the Sexual Behavior of Married Couples," *Technical Reports of the Commission on Obscenity and Pornography*, vol. 8 (Washington, D.C.: U.S. Government Printing Office, 1971), 170–254, 190.

191. Ibid., 214.

192. Ibid., 232.

193. Ibid., 253.

194. E. Heiby and J.D. Becker, "Effect of Filmed Modeling on the Self-Reported Frequency of Masturbation," *Archives of Sexual Behavior* 9 (1980): 115–21, 116.

195. Ibid., 116.

196. C. Gary Merritt, Joel E. Gerstl, and Leonard A. LoSciuto, "Age and Perceived Effects of Erotica—Pornography: A National Sample Study," *Archives of Sexual Behavior* 4 (1975): 605–21.

197. Berl Kutschinsky, "The Effect of Pornography: A Pilot Experiment on Perception, Behavior, and Attitudes," in *Technical Reports of the Commission on Obscenity and Pornography*, vol. 8 (Washington, D.C.: U.S. Government Printing Office, 1971), 133–69, 143.

198. Ibid., 143.

199. C. Crépault and M. Couture, "Men's Erotic Fantasies," *Archives of Sexual Behavior* 9 (1980): 565–81, 569, 573, 575.

200. Ibid., 580.

201. Ibid., 575.

202. Ibid., 581.

203. Virginia Greendlinger and Donn Byrne, "Coercive Sexual Fantasies of College Men as Predictors of Self-Reported Likelihood to Rape and Overt Sexual Aggression," *Journal of Sex Research* 23 (February 1987): 1–11.

204. D.P.J. Przybyla, D. Byrne, and K. Kelley, "The Role of Imagery in Sexual Behavior," in *Imagery: Current Theory, Research, and Application*, ed. A.A. Sheikh (New York: John Wiley, 1983), 436–67, 436.

205. Ibid., 438.

206. Ibid., 438–39.

207. Ibid., 439.

208. Ibid., 441.

209. Ibid., 449.

210. Ibid., 450–51.

211. Kathryn Kelley and Donn Byrne, "The Function of

Imaginative Fantasy in Sexual Behavior," *Journal of Mental Imagery* 2 (1978): 139–46, 139.

212. Kathryn Kelley, "Sexual Fantasy and Attitudes as Functions of Sex of Subject and Content of Erotica," *Imagination, Cognitive and Personality* 4 (1984–85): 339–47.

213. Ibid., 341.

214. Ibid., 345.

215. Berl Kutchinsky, "Toward an Explanation of the Decrease in Registered Sex Crimes in Copenhagen," in *Technical Reports of the Commission on Obscenity and Pornography*, vol. 7 (Washington, D.C.: U.S. Government Printing Office, 1971), 263–310, 267.

216. Ibid., 273–74.

217. Ibid., 288.

218. Ibid., 292.

219. Berl Kutchchinsky, "The Effect of Easy Availability of Pornography on the Incidence of Sex Crimes: The Danish Experience," *Journal of Social Issues* 29 (1973): 163–81.

220. Richard Ben-Veniste, "Pornography and Sex Crime: The Danish Experience," in *Technical Reports of the Commission on Obscenity and Pornography*, vol. 7 (Washington, D.C.: U.S. Government Printing Office, 1971), 245–62, 245.

221. Ibid., 252.

222. Victor Bachy, "Danish 'Permissiveness' Revisited," *Journal of Communication* 26 (Winter 1976): 40–43, 42.

223. Ibid., 42.

224. Ibid.

225. Ibid., 43.

226. Diana E.H. Russell, "Pornography and Violence: What Does the New Research Say?" in *Take Back The Night: Women on Pornography*, ed. Laura Lederer (New York: Bantam Books, 1980), 218–38.

227. Laura Lederer, "Pornography in Sweden: A Feminist's Perspective," in *Take Back the Night: Women on Pornography*, ed. Laura Lederer (New York: William Morrow and Co. Inc., 1980), 86–89, 88.

228. Augustine Brannigan and Andros Kapardis, "The Controversy Over Pornography and Sex Crimes: The Criminological Evidence and Beyond," *Journal of Criminology* 19 (December 1986): 259–84.

229. Lenore R. Kupperstein and W. Cody Wilson, "Erotic and Antisocial Behavior: An Analysis of Selected Social Indicator Statistics," in *Technical Reports of the Commission on Obscenity and Pornography*, vol. 7 (Washington, D.C.: U.S. Government Printing Office, 1971), 311–24, 318–19.

230. Ibid., 318–19.

231. John H. Court, Testimony before the Attorney General's Commission on Pornography, Houston, 12 September 1985, 3–29, 6.

232. Ibid., 13.

233. Ibid., 14.

234. Ibid., 16.

235. Ibid., 17.

236. Ibid., 11.

237. John H. Court, "Rape Trends in New South Wales:

A Discussion of Conflicting Evidence," *Australian Journal of Social Issues* 17 (1982): 202–6.

238. John H. Court, "Sex and Violence: A Ripple Effect," in *Pornography and Sexual Aggression*, eds. N. Malamuth and E. Donnerstein (New York: Academic Press, 1984), 143–72, 144.

239. Ibid., 146.

240. Ibid., 149.

241. Ibid., 152.

242. Ibid., 157.

243. Ibid., 159.

244. Ibid., 162.

245. Ibid.

246. Ibid., 163.

247. Ibid., 164.

248. Ibid.

249. Ibid., 165.

250. Ibid., 166.

251. Ibid., 167.

252. John H. Court, "The Relief of Sexual Problems through Pornography," *Australian Journal of Sex, Marriage and Family* 5 (May 1984), 97–106.

253. John H. Court, "The Place of Censored Material in the Treatment of Behavior Disturbances," *Australian Psychologist* 8 (July 1973), 150–61, 159.

254. John H. Court, "Pornography and Sex-Crimes: A Re-evaluation in the Light of Recent Trends around the World," *International Journal of Criminology and Penology* 5 (1977): 129–57, 137.

255. Ibid., 137.

256. John H. Court and O. Raymond Johnston, "Pornography and Harm," *Swansea*, July 1982, 1–23.

257. John Court, "Pornography-Erotica or Violence?" *Counterpoint Forum*, Murdoch University, 11 October 1984, 2.

258. Ibid., 4.

259. Beverly Brown, "Pornography—Erotica or Violence?" *Counterpoint Forum*, Murdoch University, 11 October 1984, 12.

260. Larry Baron and Murray A. Straus, "Sexual Satisfaction, Pornography, and Rape in American States," (Paper, Family Research Laboratory and Department of Sociology, University of New Hampshire, 18 November 1983), 1–21.

261. Ibid., 9.

262. Larry Baron and Murray A. Straus, "Four Theories of Rape: A Macrosociological Analysis," *Social Problems* 34 (December 1987).

263. Ibid.

264. Ibid.

265. Victor B. Cline, "The Effects of Pornography on Human Behavior," (Testimony before the Attorney General's Commission on Obscenity and Pornography, 11 September 1985), 1.

266. Ibid., 1–2.

267. Ibid., 4.

268. Ibid.

269. Ibid., 4–5.

270. Ibid., 5.

271. Diana E.H. Russell and Karen F. Trocki, "The Impact of Pornography on Women" (Testimony before the Attorney General's Commission on Pornography, Houston, 11 September 1985), 1–19, 8.

272. Ibid., 10.

273. Ibid.

274. Ibid.

275. Ibid., 16.

276. "Survey Shows Connection between Porn, Homosexuality," *NFD Journal* 10 (August 1986): 23.

277. Scott, *Pornography*, 7.

278. Quoted in Tom Minnery, ed., *Pornography: A Human Tragedy*, (Wheaton, Ill.: Christianity Today, Inc., Tyndale House Publishers, 1986), 148.

279. Ibid., 149.

280. Ibid.

281. Ibid.

282. Ibid.

283. Ibid.

284. Ibid., 150.

285. Gladys Denny Shultz, "What Sex Offenders Say About Pornography," *Readers Digest*, July 1971, 1–6.

286. Kathleen Barry, *Female Sexual Slavery* (Englewood Cliffs, N.J.: Prentice-Hall, 1979), 199–214, 200.

287. Keith E. Davis and George N. Braucht, "Reactions to Viewing Films of Erotically Realistic Heterosexual Behavior," in *Technical Reports of the Commission on Obscenity and Pornography*, vol. 8 (Washington, D.C.: U.S. Government Printing Office, 1971), 68–96, 173. Note: Page number references in notes 288 through 293 refer to original manuscript.

288. Ibid., 174.

289. Ibid., 175–76.

290. Ibid.

291. Ibid., 205.

292. Ibid., 211.

293. Ibid., 214.

294. Eugene C. Walker, "Erotic Stimuli and the Aggressive Sexual Offender," in *Technical Reports of the Commission on Obscenity and Pornography*, vol. 8 (Washington, D.C.: U.S. Government Printing Office, 1971), 91–148, 93–94.

295. Ibid., 128–29.

296. Weldon T. Johnson, Lenore R. Kupperstein, and Joseph J. Peters, "Sex Offenders' Experience with Erotica," in *Technical Reports of the Commission on Obscenity and Pornography* (Washington, D.C.: U.S. Government Printing Office, 1971), 163–72, 164–65.

297. P.H. Gebhard, J.H. Gagnon, W.B. Pomeroy, and C.V. Christenson, *Sex Offenders: An Analysis of Types* (New York: Harper & Row, 1965), 404.

298. Ibid., 661, 670.

299. Ibid., 671.

300. Ibid., 673.

301. Robert F. Cook and Robert H. Fosen, "Pornography and the Sex Offenders: Patterns of Exposure and Immediate Arousal Effects of Pornographic Stimuli," in *Technical Reports of the Commission on Obscenity and Pornography* vol. 7 (Washington, D.C.: U.S. Government Printing Office, 1971), 149–62.

302. R.F. Cook, R.H. Rosen, and A. Pacht, "Pornography and the Sex Offender: Patterns of Previous Exposure and Arousal Effects of Pornographic Stimuli," *Journal of Applied Psychology*, 55 (1971): 503–11, 509.
303. Ibid., 509.
304. Michael J. Goldstein, "Exposure to Erotic Stimuli and Sexual Deviance," *Journal of Social Issues*, 29 (1973): 197–225.
305. Michael J. Goldstein, Harold S. Kant, Lewis J. Judd, Clinton J. Rice, and Richard Green, "Exposure to Pornography and Sexual Behavior in Deviant and Normal Groups," in *Technical Reports of the Commission on Obscenity and Pornography*, vol. 7 (Washington, D.C.: U.S. Government Printing Office, 1971), 1–90, 58–59.
306. Michael J. Goldstein, Harold S. Kant, Lewis J. Judd, Clinton J. Rice, and Richard Green, "Experience with Pornography: Rapists, Pedophiles, Homosexuals, Transsexuals, and Controls," *Archives of Sexual Behavior* 1 (1971): 1–15, 13.
307. Ibid., 14.
308. G.A. Kercher and C.E. Walker, "Reactions to Convicted Rapists to Sexually Explicit Stimuli," *Journal of Abnormal Psychology* 81 (1973): 46–50.
309. V.L. Quincey, C.M. Steinman, S.G. Bergersen, and T. Holmes, "Penile Circumference, Skin Conductance, and Ranking Responses of Child Molesters and 'Normals' to Sexual and Nonsexual Visual Stimuli," *Behavior Therapy* 6 (1975): 213–19, 215–16.
310. Ibid., 219.
311. G. Abel, D.H. Barlow, E.B. Blanchard, and D. Guild, "The Components of Rapists' Sexual Arousal," *Archives of General Psychiatry* 34 (1977): 895–903, 895.
312. Ibid., 895.
313. Ibid., 903.
314. A. Kolarsky, J. Madlafousek, and V. Novatná "Stimuli Eliciting Sexual Arousal in Males Who Offend Adult Women: An Experimental Study," *Archives of Sexual Behavior* 7 (1978): 79–87, 81.
315. Ibid., 82.
316. Ibid., 84.
317. H.F. Barbaree, W.L. Marshall, and R.D. Lanthier, "Deviant Sexual Arousal in Rapists," *Behavior Research and Therapy* 17 (1979): 215–22, 217.
318. V.L. Quincey, T.C. Chaplin, and D. Upfold, "Sexual Arousal to Nonsexual Violence and Sadomasochistic Themes Among Rapists and Nonsexual Offenders," *Journal of Consulting and Clinical Psychology* 52 (1984): 651–57, 652.
319. Ibid., 653.
320. Ibid.
321. Edward Donnerstein, Testimony before the Minneapolis City Council Government Operations Committee, 12 and 13 December 1983, 5 (hereafter cited as Minneapolis hearings).
322. Ibid., 6.
323. Ibid.
324. Ibid., 6–7.
325. Ibid., 7.
326. Ibid.
327. Ibid., 8.
328. Ibid., 9.
329. Ibid.
330. Ibid., 8.
331. Ibid.
332. Ibid.
333. Ibid., 10.
334. Ibid., 11.
335. Ibid., 12.
336. Ibid.
337. Ibid., 11.
338. "UW Prof Gets Playboy Grant for Study of Pornography," *Milwaukee Journal*, 16 March 1980.
339. Sunny Schubert, "Revealing Pornography Violence Link," *Wisconsin State Journal*, 26 February 1984.
340. Donald L. Mosher and Harvey Katz, "Pornography Films, Male Verbal Aggression against Women, and Guilt," in *Technical Reports of the Commission on Obscenity and Pornography* vol. 8 (Washington, D.C.: U.S. Government Printing Office, 1971), 357–59, 357.
341. Ibid., 359.
342. Percey N. Tannenbaum, "Emotional Arousal as a Mediation of Erotic Communication Effects," in *Technical Reports of the Commission on Obscenity and Pornography* vol. 8 (Washington, D.C.: U.S. Government Printing Office, 1971), 326–56, 342.
343. D. Zillmann, J.L. Hoyt, and K.D. Day, "Strength and Duration of the Effects of Aggressive, Violent and Erotic Communications on Subsequent Aggressive Behavior," *Communication Research* 3 (1974): 286–306.
344. R.A. Baron, "Sexual Arousal and Physical Aggression: The Inhibiting Influence of 'Cheesecake' and Nudes," *Bulletin of the Psychonomic Society* 3 (1974): 337–39.
345. D. Zillmann and B. Sapolsky, "What Mediates the Effect of Mild Erotica on Annoyance and Hostile Behavior in Males?" *Journal of Personal and Social Psychology* 35(8) (1977): 587–96.
346. Y. Jaffe and A. Berger, "A Cultural Generality of the Relationship Between Sex and Aggression," *Psychological Reports* 41 (1977): 335–36.
347. E. Donnerstein and J. Hallam, "The Facilitating Effects of Erotica on Aggression Towards Females," *Journal of Personal and Social Psychology* 36 (1978): 1270–77, 1275.
348. J.R. Cantor, D. Zillmann, and E.F. Einsiedel, "Female Responses to Provocation After Exposure to Aggressive and Erotic Films," *Communications Research* 5 (1978): 395–411, 405.
349. Leonard A. White, "Erotica and Aggression: The Influence of Sexual Arousal, Positive Affect and Negative Affect on Aggressive Behavior," *Journal of Personality and Social Psychology* 37 (1979): 591–601, 597.
350. R.A. Baron and P.A. Bell, "Sexual Arousal and Aggression by Males: Effects of Type of Erotic Stimuli and Prior Provocation," *Journal of Personality and Social Psychology* 35 (1977): 79–87.

351. R.A. Baron, "Heightened Sexual Arousal and Physical Aggression: An Extension to Females," *Journal of Research in Personality* 13 (1979): 91–102, 93, 94.

352. Ibid., 95.

353. Suzin E. Mayerson and Dalmas A. Taylor, "The Effects of Rape Myth Pornography on Women's Attitudes and the Mediating Role of Sex Role Stereotyping," *Sex Roles*. 1987. 17: 321–338, 321.

354. D. Zillmann, J. Bryant, P.W. Comisky, and N.J. Medoff, "Excitation and Hedonic Valance in the Effect of Erotica on Motivated Intermale Aggression," *European Journal of Social Psychology* 2 (1981): 233–52, 248.

355. Ibid., 248.

356. Ibid., 249.

357. C.W. Mueller and E. Donnerstein, "Film-Facilitated Arousal and Prosocial Behavior," *Journal of Experimental Social Psychology* 17 (1981): 31–41.

358. E. Donnerstein and L. Berkowitz, "Victim Reactions in Aggressive Erotic Films as a Factor in Violence Against Women," *Journal of Personality and Social Psychology* 41 (1981): 710–24, 722.

359. Dolf Zillmann and Jennings Bryant, "Pornography, Sexual Callousness, and the Trivialization of Rape," *Journal of Communication* 32 (Autumn 1982): 10–21, 16.

360. Ibid., 17.

361. Yoram Jaffe, "Sexual Stimulation: Effects on Prosocial Behavior," *Psychological Reports* 48 (1981): 75–81, 77.

362. Ibid., 78.

363. Ibid.

364. Ibid., 80.

365. Ibid.

366. D. Zillmann, J. Bryant, and R.A. Carveth, "The Effect of Erotica Featuring Sadomasochism and Bestiality on Motivated Intermale Aggression," *Personality and Social Psychology Bulletin*, March 1981, 153–59, 156.

367. Ibid., 155.

368. Ibid.

369. Ibid., 157–58.

370. Ibid., 158.

371. John Ramirez, Jennings Bryant, and Dolf Zillmann, "Effects of Erotica on Retaliatory Behavior as a Function of Level of Prior Provocation," *Journal of Personality and Social Psychology* 43 (1982): 971–78, 973.

372. Ibid., 974.

373. Ibid., 976.

374. Ibid., 977.

375. Ibid.

376. K. Kelley, C. Miller, D. Byrne, and P. Bell, "Facilitating Sexual Arousal Via Anger, Aggression, or Dominance," *Motivation and Emotion* 7 (1983): 191–202, 194.

377. Ibid., 195, 200.

378. K. Leonard and S. Taylor, "Exposure to Pornography Permissive and Nonpermissive Cue, and Male Aggression Toward Females," *Motivation and Emotion* 7 (1983): 291–99, 293.

379. Ibid., 293.

380. Ibid., 297.

381. N.M. Malamuth, "Factors Associated with Rape as Predictors of Laboratory Aggression Against Women," *Journal of Personality and Social Psychology* 45 (1983): 432–42, 434–40.

382. J.V.P. Check and N.M. Malamuth, "Sex-Role Stereotyping and Reactions to Depictions of Stranger vs. Acquaintance Rape," *Journal of Personality and Social Psychology* 45 (1983): 344–56, 354.

383. N.M. Malamuth and J.V.P. Check, "Sexual Arousal to Rape Depictions: Individual Differences," *Journal of Abnormal Psychology* 92 (1983): 55–67.

384. Neil Malamuth, "Aggression Against Women: Cultural and Individual Causes," in *Pornography and Sexual Aggression*, eds. Neil Malamuth and Edward Donnerstein (Orlando, Fla.: Academic Press, 1984) 31.

385. Ibid., 40.

386. Edward Donnerstein, "Pornography: Its Effect on Violence Against Women," in *Pornography and Sexual Aggression*, eds. Neil Malamuth and Edward Donnerstein (Orlando, Fla.: Academic Press, 1984), 53–84, 78.

387. B.S. Sapolsky, "Arousal Affect and Aggression Moderating Effect of Erotica," in *Pornography and Sexual Aggression*, eds. Neil Malamuth and Edward Donnerstein (Orlando, Fla.: Academic Press, 1984), 87–88.

388. Paul A. Abramson and Haruo Hayashi, "Pornography in Japan: Cross-Cultural and Theoretical Considerations" in *Pornography and Sexual Aggression*, eds. Neil Malamuth and Edward Donnerstein (Orlando, Fla.: Academic Press, 1984), 173–83.

389. Dolf Zillmann, *The Connection between Sex and Aggression* (Hillsdale, N.J.: L. Earlbaum, 1984).

390. K. Kelley, "The Effects of Sexual and/or Aggressive Film Exposure on Helping, Hostility, and Attitudes about the Sexes," *Journal of Research in Personality* 19 (1985): 472–83, 476.

391. Ibid., 481.

392. Neil M. Malamuth and James V. Check, "The Effects of Aggressive Pornography on Beliefs in Rape Myths: Individual Differences," *Journal of Research in Personality*, 19 (1985): 299–320, 304.

393. Ibid., 307.

394. Ibid., 313.

395. Ibid., 314.

396. Ibid., 315.

397. C.L. Krafka, "Sexually Explicit, Sexually Violent, and Violent Media: Effects of Multiple Naturalistic Exposure and Debriefing on Female Viewers," Ph.D. dissertation, University of Michigan—Madison, 1985, 24.

398. Ibid., 32.

399. Ibid., 40.

400. Ibid.

401. N.M. Malamuth, J.V.P. Check, and J. Briere, "Sexual

Arousal in Response to Aggression: Ideological Aggressive and Sexual Correlates," *Journal of Personality and Social Psychology* 50 (1986): 330–40, 333.

402. Ibid., 338.

403. N.M. Malamuth, "Predictors of Naturalistic Sexual Aggression," *Journal of Personality and Social Psychology* 50 (1986): 953–62.

404. Ibid., 960.

405. N.M. Malamuth and J. Briere, "Sexual Violence in the Media: Indirect Effects on Aggression Against Women," *Journal of Social Issues* 42(3) (Fall, 1986): 75–92, 76.

406. Ibid., 77.

407. Ibid., 78.

408. Ibid.

409. Daniel Linz, "Sexual Violence in the Media: Effects on Male Viewers and Implications for Society," Ph.D. dissertation, University of Wisconsin—Madison, 1985, 3.

410. Ibid., 3–4.

411. Ibid., 4.

412. Ibid.

413. Ibid., 18.

414. Ibid., 26, 31.

415. Ibid., 31.

416. Ibid., 41.

417. Ibid., 68.

418. Ibid., 70.

419. Ibid., 78.

420. Ibid., 86.

421. D.L. Mosher and R.D. Anderson, "Macho Personality, Sexual Aggression, and Reactions to Guided Imagery of Realistic Rape," *Journal of Research in Personality* 20 (1986): 77–94, 80.

422. Ibid., 84.

423. Ibid., 77.

424. Ibid., 86.

425. Ibid.

426. Ibid., 87.

427. Ibid., 89.

428. Ibid., 90.

429. Brief of The Neighborhood Pornography Task Force, *Hudnut et al. v. American Booksellers Association, Inc.*, Seventh Circuit Court of Appeals Case No. 84-3147, date unknown, 1–20.

430. City of Phoenix Planning Department, "Adult Business Study," 25 May 1979, 1–9, 1.

431. Ibid., 2.

432. Ibid., 3.

433. Ibid., 9.

434. Captain Carl I. Delau, Cleveland, Ohio, Police Department, "Smut Shop Outlets, Contribution of These Outlets to the Increased Crime Rates in the Census Tract Areas of Smut Shops" Memorandum to Deputy Inspector John Kukula, Cleveland, Ohio, Police Department, 24 August 1977), 1–2.

435. Department of City Planning of the City of Los Angeles, "Study of the Effects of the Concentration of Adult Entertainment Establishments in the City of Los Angeles," June 1977, 1–55, 25–26.

436. Ibid., 31.

437. Ibid., 55.

438. Victor B. Cline, ed., *Where Do You Draw the Line? An Exploration into Media Violence, Pornography, and Censorship* (Provo, Utah: Brigham Young University Press, 1974), 205.

439. Ibid., 214.

440. Ibid., 214–16.

441. Ibid., 216.

442. Ibid., 218.

443. Ibid., 219.

444. Ibid., 226.

445. Ibid., 227.

446. Ibid., 232.

447. Ibid., 234.

448. Ibid., 235.

449. Ibid.

450. Victor B. Cline, "The Scientists vs. Pornography: An Untold Story," *Intellect*, May/June 1976, 7–9.

451. *The Hill–Link Minority Report of the Presidential Commission on Obscenity and Pornography* (Washington, D.C.: U.S. Government Printing Office, 1971).

452. Kathleen Barry, *Female Sexual Slavery* (Englewood Cliffs, N.J.: Prentice-Hall, 1979), 199–214.

453. Ibid., 199–200.

454. Irene Diamond, "Pornography and Repression: A Reconsideration of 'Who' and 'What,' " in *Take Back the Night: Women on Pornography*, ed. Laura Lederer (New York: Wm. Morrow & Co., 1980) 187–203, 193–94.

455. R. Rist, "Policy, Politics, and Social Research: A Study in the Relationship of Federal Commissions and Social Science," *Social Problems* 21 (Summer 1973): 113–28.

456. Thelma McCormack, "Machismo in Media Research: A Critical Review on Violence and Pornography," *Social Problems* 25(1978): 544–55, 549.

457. Ibid., 549.

458. P.B. Bart and M. Jozsa, "Dirty Books, Dirty Films and Dirty Data," in *Take Back the Night: Women on Pornography*, ed. Laura Lederer (New York: Wm. Morrow & Co., 1980), 204–7, 217.

459. Garry Wills, "Measuring the Impact of Erotica," *Psychology Today*, August 1977, 31, 33–34, 74, 76.

460. Herbert L. Packer, "The Pornography Caper," *Commentary*, February 1971, 72–77.

461. Maurice Yaffe and Edward Nelson, eds., *The Influence of Pornography on Behavior* (New York and London: Academic Press, 1982), 20.

462. Christine Pickard, "A Perspective on Female Responses to Sexual Material," in *The Influence of Pornography on Behavior*, eds. Maurice Yaffe and Edward Nelson (New York and London: Academic Press, 1982) 107–8, 110.

463. Maurice Yaffe, "Therapeutic Uses of Sexually Explicit Material," in *The Influence of Pornography on Behavior*, ed. Maurice Yaffe and Edward Nelson (New York and London: Academic Press, 1982).

464. Edward Nelson, "Pornography and Sexual Aggression," in *The Influence of Pornography on Behavior*,

ed. Maurice Yaffe and Edward Nelson (New York and London: Academic Press, 1982).

465. Ibid., 222.

466. Ibid., 223.

467. Ibid., 236.

468. Dorothy M. Dallas, "The Use of Visual Materials in Sex Education," in *The Influence of Pornography on Behavior*, eds. Maurice Yaffe and Edward Nelson (New York and London: Academic Press, 1982), 65–80.

469. James V. Check and Neil M. Malamuth, "Can There Be Positive Effects on Participation in Pornography Experiences?" *Journal of Sex Research* (20 February 1984): 1–31, 18.

470. Ibid., 27.

471. Ibid., 28.

472. David Scott, ed. *Symposium on Media Violence and Pornography* (Toronto: Media Action Group, Inc., 1984), 44.

473. Ibid.

474. Ibid., 23.

475. Ibid., 30.

476. Ibid., 31.

477. Tamar Lewin, "Sexual Revolution: Realities of Today Will Have a Big Impact on TV in the Future," *Milwaukee Journal*, 15 March 1987.

478. P.R. Abramson, "Ethical Requirements for Research on Human Behavior: From the Perspective of Participating Subjects," *Journal of Social Issues* 33 (1977): 184–92.

479. David Lester, "Pornographic Films and Unconscious Homosexual Desires: An Hypothesis," *Psychological Reports* 54 (April 1984): 606.

480. Daniel Linz, Edward Donnerstein, Michael Bross, and Margo Chipin, "Mitigating the Influence of Violence on Television and Sexual Violence in the Media," *Advances in the Study of Aggression*, vol. 2, eds. Robert J. Blanchard and D. Caroline Blanchard (Orlando, Fla.: Academic Press, 1986), 165–94, 189.

481. Robert Anthansiou, "Pornography: A Review of Research," in *Handbook on Human Sexuality*, ed. John Money (Englewood Cliffs, N.J.: Prentice-Hall, 1980), 252–65, 257.

482. Ibid., 226.

483. Kathryn Kelley, "Sexual Attitudes as Determinants of the Motivational Properties of Exposure to Erotica," 6(1985): 391–93, 393.

484. Andreas Spengler, "Manifest Sadomasochism of Males: Results of an Empirical Study," *Archives of Sexual Behavior* 6(1977): 441–44, 442.

485. Berl Kutchinsky, "Obscenity and Pornography: Behavioral Aspects," in *Encyclopedia of Crime and Justice*, vol. 3, ed. Sanford Kadish (New York: Free Press, 1983), 1079–85, 1085.

486. R. Bell, *Social Deviance* (Homewood, Ill.: The Dorsey Press, 1976), 120–51, 127, 132.

487. D.W. Briddell, D.C. Rimm, G.R. Caddy, G. Krawitz, D. Sholis, and R.J. Wunderlin, "Effects of Alcohol and Cognitive Set on Sexual Arousal to Deviant Stimuli," *Journal of Abnormal Psychology* 87(1978): 420–23.

488. A.R. Lang, J. Searles, R. Lauerman, and V. Adesso, "Expectancy, Alcohol and Sex Guilt as Determinants of Interest in the Reaction to Sexual Stimuli," *Journal of Abnormal Psychology* 89(1980):644–53, 645.

489. Lenore R. Kupperstein and W. Cody Wilson, "Erotic and Antisocial Behavior: An Analysis of Selected Social Indicator Statistics," in *Technical Reports of the Commission on Obscenity and Pornography*, vol. 7 (Washington, D.C.: U.S. Government Printing Office, 1971), 311–24.

490. Terrence P. Thornberry and Robert A. Silverman, "Exposure to Pornography and Juvenile Delinquency: The Relationship as indicated by Juvenile Court Records," in *Technical Reports of the Commission on Obscenity and Pornography*, vol. 1 (Washington, D.C.: U.S. Government Printing Office, 1971), 175–80.

491. D.R. Laws, "Treatment of Bisexual Pedophilia by a Biofeedback-Assisted Self-Control Procedure," *Behavior Research and Therapy*, 1980, 18: 207–11, 207.

492. M.J. MacCulloch, P.R. Snowden, P.J.W. Wood, and H.E. Mills, "Sadistic Fantasy, Sadistic Behavior, and Offending," *British Journal of Psychiatry* 143(1983): 20–29.

493. James W. Halpern, "Projection," *Journal of Abnormal Psychology* 86(1977): 536–42.

494. Dolf Zillmann, "Effects of Prolonged Consumption of Pornography," in *Report of the Surgeon General's Workshop on Pornography and Public Health*, eds. E.P. Mulvey and J.L. Haugaard (Washington, D.C.: U.S. Public Health Service and U.S. Department of Health and Human Services, 1986), 1–33, 3.

495. Ibid., 3.

496. Ibid., 12.

497. Ibid., 12.

498. Ibid., 12.

499. Ibid., 13.

500. Ibid.

501. Ibid., 15.

502. Ibid., 26–28.

503. C. Everett Koop, Surgeon General of the United States, "Keynote Address" (Presented to the Denver National Conference on Pornography, 31 May 1985), 6.

504. Scott, *Pornography*, 3–4.

505. Tom Minnery, *Pornography*, 115–61.

506. William Stanmeyer, "Obscure Evils v. Obscene Truths," *Capital University Law Review* 7(1978): 647–64.

507. H.J. Eysenck, "The Uses and Abuses of Pornography," in *Pornography Is about People*, ed. H.J. Eysenck (London: Allen Lane, The Penguin Press, 1972), 236–86, 270.

508. E.P. Mulvey and J.L. Haugaard, eds. *Report of the Surgeon General's Workshop on Pornography and Public Health* (Washington, D.C.: U.S. Public Health Service and U.S. Department of Health and Human Services, 1986), 12.

509. Ibid., 13.

510. Ibid.
511. Ibid., 17.
512. Ibid., 19.
513. Ibid., 23.
514. Ibid., 28.
515. Ibid., 40.
516. Ibid., 48.
517. Ibid.
518. Neil M. Malamuth, "Do Sexually Violent Media Indirectly Contribute to Antisocial Behavior," Paper included as a background paper in Mulvey and Haugaard, 1.
519. Ibid., 10.
520. Ibid., 7.
521. Ibid., 6.
522. Ibid., 24.
523. H.J. Eysenck and D.K.B. Nias, *Sex, Violence and the Media* (London: Maurice Temple Smith, 1978) 10–11.
524. Ibid., 15.
525. Ibid., 25.
526. Ibid., 38.
527. Ibid., 45.
528. Ibid., 77.
529. Ibid., 135–36.
530. Ibid., 190.
531. Ibid., 253.
532. Ibid., 252–53, 255.
533. Ibid., 255.
534. Ibid., 259.
535. Nancy H. Bowen, "Pornography: Research Review and Implications for Counseling," *Journal of Counseling and Development* 65 (March 1987): 345–50, 345.
536. Ibid.
537. Ibid., 347–48.
538. Susan H. Gray, "Exposure to Pornography and Aggression Toward Women: The Case of the Angry Male," *Social Problems* 29 (April 1982): 387–98, 390.
539. Ibid., 394.
540. Edward Donnerstein, Daniel Linz, and Steven Penrod, *The Question of Pornography: Research Findings and Policy Implications* (New York: Free Press, 1987).

PART II

PHILOSOPHIES ABOUT PORNOGRAPHY

6 THE MORALITY PERSPECTIVE

Six major national organizations are in the forefront of the morality/decency movement against pornography. Addresses for these are listed in appendix D.

1. *Morality in Media, Inc.* (MIM) headquartered in New York, describes itself as "a non-profit, national organization working to stop the traffic in pornography constitutionally through vigorous enforcement of obscenity laws."[1] The organization was formed in 1962 by three clergymen who were concerned about the "effects of pornography on children, youth and the family." The president of MIM, the Reverend Morton A. Hill, S.J., was appointed to the Presidential Commission on Obscenity and Pornography in 1968 and co-authored the Hill–Link minority report of that commission.[2]

Morality in Media began and continues with two aims:

1. To educate and alert parents and community leaders to the problem of, the scale of, and the danger in the distribution of obscene material;
2. To encourage communities to express themselves in a unified, continuous, organized way (a) to law enforcement officials urging vigorous enforcement of obscenity law and (b) to legitimate media requesting responsibility.

Morality in Media does not believe in censorship, that is, prior restraint by government.

Morality in Media does believe in free expression—in the free expression of all the people. Freedom of expression is not the exclusive right of producers, publishers, authors or a handful of media executives. Freedom of expression belongs, too, to readers, listeners, viewers—the entire community.[3]

Morality in Media operates the National Obscenity Law Center, a clearinghouse on obscenity law for prosecutors and others. It has published the *Handbook on the Prosecution of Obscenity Cases* and the *Obscenity Law Reporter* and has two regular newsletters—the *Morality in Media Newsletter* and the *Obscenity Law Bulletin.*

2. *Citizens for Decency Through Law, Inc.* (CDL), with offices in Scottsdale, Arizona, "is a national non-profit organization promoting decency and op-posing the dissemination of obscenity within the framework of the law."[4] Thus, its purpose is to enforce the laws against persons who violate the nation's obscenity laws. It maintains a staff of attorneys who assist prosecutors around the country in handling such cases.[5] The organization was founded as Citizens for Decent Literature by attorney and businessman Charles H. Keating, Jr., in 1957. Since its inception, CDL's two main goals have been to inform the public of problems associated with pornography and to demand and assist in enforcement of the law. Its objectives include:

1. Prevention of the *production* of hard-core pornography which is distributed in violation of state and federal law.
2. Prevention of the *distribution* of hard-core pornography on the local and national level in violation of state and federal law.
3. Elimination of obscene and indecent material from cable and subscription television and from telephone services.
4. Elimination of the display of material or indecent material at locations which are accessible to minors.
5. Prevention of the production and distribution of child pornography.
6. Education of the public that hard-core pornography is causing crime, disease, and dangerous societal change, among children as well as adults.[6]

3. The *National Coalition Against Pornography* (N-CAP), based in Cincinnati, Ohio, was formed in 1983. N-CAP states:

As a coalition, we are in unanimous agreement that hard-core and child pornography, which are not protected by the Constitution, must be eliminated.

These materials, to most Americans, are demeaning, degrading and humiliating. They lower the quality of life wherever present, they are a vicious attack on human dignity, and they serve no beneficial purpose in society.

Because of N-CAP's concern for the quality and sanctity of human life, and its awareness that pornography significantly contributes to the alarming increase in child abuse, violent crimes against women, teenage pregnancies and suicide, drug abuse, broken marriages and broken lives . . . N-CAP encourages and supports the enactment and the full, fair enforcement of constitutional laws prohibiting obscenity and child pornography, and effectively regulating indecency and sexually explicit material that is harmful to minors.[7]

The coalition's president, Reverend Jerry R. Kirk, wrote a book titled *The Mind Polluters*,[8] which outlines the harms of pornography and the religious viewpoint and calls citizens to action against this material.

N-CAP's mission statement is "To mobilize the Christian community and all concerned citizens to combat and eliminate the destructive influence of obscenity, pornography and indecency."[9] The organization envisions its role in combating pornography to be one of uniting, mobilizing, and working with antipornography groups and leaders while respecting each one's autonomy. It plans to coordinate its actions with other agencies of "similar purpose," including Morality in Media, Citizens for Decency Through Law, the American Family Association, and the National Christian Association. Another role of N-CAP is to "teach and model a leadership style incorporating mutual love, trust, individual worth and decision by consensus in dependence on the Holy Spirit."[10]

This group also views its role as one of calling on Christian leaders and concerned citizens to become aware of the role of pornography "in the sexual victimization of men, women and children" and to get these people to mobilize their group members. N-CAP calls upon the president, the U.S. Justice Department, the FBI, the commissioner of customs, the postmaster general, and the Federal Communications Commission (FCC) to enforce existing obscenity and other laws and encourages state officials to do the same. It encourages corporate leaders to assume "their moral responsibility" in combating this "serious social problem."[11]

4. The *American Family Association* (AFA) (formerly known as the National Federation of Decency) of Tupelo, Mississippi, "is a Christian organization promoting the Biblical ethic of decency in American society with primary emphasis on TV and other media."[12] AFA's executive director, Reverend Donald E. Wildmon, links the tendencies of Americans to be violent to violence on television and in pornography.[13]

A key tenant of the AFA is that television has an anti-Christian bias. For a detailed description of this viewpoint, refer to *The Home Invaders* by Rev-

erend Wildmon. In that book, Wildmon states that not one television network series in a modern-day setting has "a single person who is identified as a Christian" and that "the values and morals of the networks are diametrically different from those of the vast majority of our homes."[14] According to Wildmon, the Hollywood "elite" and networks are "openly hostile" toward the Christian faith and desire their "religion—humanism" to "replace the Christian view of man as the foundation of our society." He sees the anti-Christian "hostility" being reflected by censoring of any positive portrayal of Christians in a modern-day setting and presenting them, nearly without exception, in a negative manner.[15]

5. The *National Christian Association* (NCA) is dedicated to decency-oriented values and fighting pornography because it is believed to go against those values. Its president, Brad Curl, outlines the NCA's positions in *A Strategy for Decency*, available from the group's headquarters in Washington, D.C. A bumper sticker for NCA states "Pornography Victimizes Women and Children" and portrays a small girl crying with a man in the shadows behind her.

Curl was involved in producing "The Chicago Statement: A Response to the Effect of the PLAYBOY Mentality on Our Society," released in front of Playboy's headquarters on October 22, 1979. Excerpts from it are illustrative of the philosophy of the NCA:

Mr. Hefner,
Have you ever thought that your 37 story office building in the center of our nation could become a kind of monument to the sacrifice of our future?

You, perhaps more than anyone else in the past 20 years have called America to self-indulge as never before and it appears that we are now reaping the results. It's becoming evident that popular hedonism will eventually wreck a society.

Your slickly marketed recreational sex mentality has contributed to the abortion of over a million and one half babies per year. Your anti-family life-style has helped bring about epidemic divorce rates which leave millions of children in fatherless homes and your self-centered approach to living has helped leave our government with social burdens which no amount of money can solve.

The Playboy philosophy reduces the 'whole man to his private parts.' . . . Surely a society will not long hold together that does not challenge men and women to have some control of their bodies with their minds, especially in the most sensitive and personal realm of sexuality.

Does it not seem ironic to you that you parade as a champion of women's rights and then profit by exploiting women as commercial sex objects?

Have you considered that your entire 37 story office building couldn't begin to hold all the agencies that are needed to help the millions of tormented people you have helped to create— the women who aborted their unwanted babies, the lonely divorcees who thought marriage and infidelity could work, the millions of fatherless children who will grow to vent their hostilities on a society of people who gave them a bad deal?

Do you think our country can continue to tolerate this debasing influence? It may be time the people stop calling you a fun-loving editor and start thinking of you as a pimp-like promoter who has been attempting to make a sexual toy out of the American woman and an irresponsible adolescent out of the American man.[16]

6. The *Religious Alliance Against Pornography* (RAAP) was formed at a meeting co-hosted by Cardinals O'Connor and Bernardin in New York on July 25, 1986. Its first national conference was held in November 1986, calling together leaders of every major religious denomination in the United States. This broad group of religious leaders represents approximately 150 million Americans. These leaders respect the First Amendment and oppose censorship of materials protected by it.

"The sole purpose of the Alliance is to mobilize America's religious community against child pornography which involves children sexually with adults and with each other, and pornography which promotes violence and the abuse, rape and degradation of women."[17] These materials (child pornography and hard-core pornography) are not protected by the Constitution, the RAAP states in its policy statement. The initial communiqué of the organization states:

> As religious leaders, we believe in the inherent dignity of each human being. Created in God's image and likeness, the human person is the clearest reflection of God's presence among us. Because human life is sacred we all have a duty to develop the kind of societal environment that protects and fosters its development. This is why we address a broad range of life-threatening and life-diminishing issues. These assaults on human life and dignity are all distinct, each requiring its own moral analysis and solution. But they must be confronted as elements of a larger picture.
>
> The particular purpose of today's meeting is to bring into clear focus a major factor in the assault on human dignity and the consequent dehumanization that it promotes: hardcore and child pornography.[18]

THE CALL TO ACTION

The morality and decency groups, religious leaders, and others who espouse the morality perspective place great emphasis on motivating people to take an active role in opposing pornography. They recognize the potential power and influence of a united group of people actively promoting a cause.

For example, an episode of the D. James Kennedy Show titled "Pornography: An American Tragedy," broadcast in November 1986, showed how two young women went to neighborhood convenience stores that sold pornography and successfully persuaded the owners to remove the material from the stores. The message is clear: One or two people *can* make a difference.

Neil Gallagher, Ph.D., proclaims, "If EVERY Christian EVERY time he enters EVERY store complains about porno on the shelves, porno, nationally, will disappear in a month."[19] Gallagher espouses the philosophy that people cannot successfully fight pornography on their own—they need to rely on God to give them the power to do so. He points out that most people feel nervous and scared to confront store clerks and owners about the issue.

"It's called fear. And Satan is the author of it. I learned long ago to claim the power of 2 Timothy 1:17, 'For God did not give us the spirit of timidity but a spirit of power and love and self-control.' "[20]

Gallagher says, "I told you at the beginning that if you weren't willing to die to uphold God's standards, don't even start. Because if you start and quit, that discourages others. Unless you *will* pay the price in time, money, and reputation, don't even start. Please."[21]

One of the most moving calls to action against pornography was a speech given by Dr. Elizabeth Holland, a pediatrician from Memphis, Tennessee. In a speech to the 1984 National Consultation on Obscenity, Pornography and Decency, Dr. Holland described how she treated families and children who were injured by people influenced by pornography. A boy, 14 at the time of treatment, had repeatedly raped his younger brother and sisters from the time he was 9. He read pornography for sexual stimulation, then raped the children. Another young boy, from ages 2 to 4, was raped many times each weekend by his father. Holland treated a 4-year-old girl who had a "torn, lacerated vagina." Her brothers, uncle, and father shared pornography to arouse themselves, then took turns sexually abusing the girl. Another doctor had closed his eyes to what was being done to the girl. In another case, a man took stacks of sadistic pornography out onto the porch and shared it with his wife and 10- and 12-year-old daughters. He held a gun to his wife's head, raped her repeatedly in front of the girls, then blew her head off. He then held the gun at each of the girls' heads and raped

them. Another man and woman used their 3-year-old girl and 4-year-old boy as child pornography models.[22]

Holland says that people have a duty to speak out against pornography and that "God and every one of us are an invincible army." Importantly, Holland, like many of the other morality advocates, emphasizes that the reason pornography needs to be regulated is because it is harmful to human beings.[23]

THE RELIGIOUS VIEW OF PORNOGRAPHY

According to Cardinal Joseph Bernardin, "the theological foundation on which opposition to pornography, obscenity and indecency rests is the sacredness of all life and the inherent dignity of the human person."[24]

In 1986, the California Catholic Conference concluded that pornography is far from "harmless" or "victimless." The conference found that pornography "arrests personal development and interferes with interpersonal relationships." It also "creates a hunger for more violent, more deviant and more antisocial sexual materials, driving many who use it to engage in increasingly unusual and bizarre sex acts with a greater variety of partners." Indeed, the conference noted, "child molesters, persons who commit incest, killers and rapists often develop a fondness for pornography and use it as preparatory stimulation before seeking out victims." The conference pointed out that the pornography industry photographs hundreds of thousands of children in the United States each year engaging in sexual acts and that it plays a major role in many of the estimated two million cases of American children who are sexually victimized yearly. Finally, the conference said, "Pornography degrades and dehumanizes women, robs them of dignity and portrays them as if their only value consisted in their being of sexual use to males. Furthermore, the physical safety of women may be endangered by the power of pornography to induce in males a proclivity toward rape and molestation."[25] The conference concluded that pornography must be rejected because of the damage it does to individuals and the threatened danger to society.

Morality in Media, Inc., compiled statements from several religious leaders about pornography. The following are excerpts.

Bishop Jerome J. Hastrich, Diocese of Gallup, New Mexico, stated on December 4, 1984:

Purity is defined as that virtue which properly regulates our use of sex according to our state of life. Human sexuality was made by God and is good as long as it is used according to God's design. In Genesis we read of God creating man in His own image and likeness, and "God looked upon everything He had made and saw it to be very good." Then God joined the first man and woman together and blessed them and said: "Increase and multiply and fill the earth." Thus sex was designed by God to be used only within the context of matrimony. It is something sacred and is necessarily related to the origin of human life as well as an expression of conjugal love and unity.

Today we see a mighty effort to separate sex from its God-given goal, and this has led to a flood of pornography and all its evil consequences which have come in its wake: violence, the degradation of women, humiliation, torture, sadism, incest, child molestation, rape and murder. I might also add that there is a new philosophy being foisted upon us by the mass media today: that anything goes between consenting adults. Thus we have the so-called sexual revolution in the matter of pre- and extramarital relationships, and a tendency to disregard any moral implications in homosexuality.

The word pornography in its literal meaning relates to a form of slavery.[26]

Florida's religious leaders said on December 31, 1985:

Proper expressions of human sexuality are extensions of God's love for each of us. This love is not selfish but calls all people to mutual respect and concern. Pornography distorts the goodness and beauty of human love and sexuality and undermines those beliefs and values which are essential to the stability of any society. It threatens the innate dignity of every person and erodes the general moral fiber. As leaders of churches and synagogues in Florida, we recognize and accept our responsibility to speak clearly and forcefully in condemnation of this contemporary moral plague. We reject pornography in any form and urge all people in our state to join with us.

Modern pornography combines sex with violence and focuses on the abnormal and the immoral. Both men and women are demeaned by being portrayed as cheap sexual objects. Even very young children are cruelly exploited and abused. Frequently, violence and abuse are encouraged as suitable means of gratifying sexual desires. In short, pornography perverts God's high purpose for human sexuality. It degrades us as people and as a nation.[27]

In 1986, the Catholic Bishops of Missouri and the Catholic Bishops of New York prepared a pastoral letter on this issue:

Our Church believes and we Bishops teach these truths:
God created each one of us in His own image calling us into existence through love.
God's gift of sexuality is part of God's own plan of love to involve us in His creative act of giving life and love.
Precisely because God has given to each human being the spark of life and the gift of consciousness, those acts which degrade and dehumanize persons violate fundamental human rights and are evil.
Pornography is such an evil act. Pornography "makes a mockery of human sexuality, corrupting young and old alike and giving rise to further crimes such as molestation, rape and other dehumanizing evils." (Joseph Cardinal Bernardin, Report of U.S. Bishops Committee for Pro-Life Activities, November 1984.)[28]

Archbishop John R. Roach of the Archdiocese of St. Paul and Minneapolis delivered a statement on pornography in January 1986:

The effects of pornography are becoming increasingly clear. Years ago the United States Supreme Court stated, "There is at least an arguable correlation between obscene material and crime." A multitude of studies since then has substantiated that claim.
Law enforcement officers routinely find evidence of pornographic material when investigating sex crimes against children. Despite protests by the pornographers, researchers are showing more and more evidence that the use of the sexually violent material contributes to a social climate in which violence against women is more accepted, and is thus more likely to occur. Pornography is really a form of hate literature. It

promotes and justifies hostility and aggression against a target group of people. Women, children and minorities are particular targets.
One of the terrible aspects of pornography to any of us of faith is the debasing way in which sex and our human sexuality are presented. God's design for human sexuality was based on genuine love. Pornography is loveless. In fact, it is violent.[29]

The Catholic Bishops of Connecticut said on March 25, 1985:

Our Catholic teaching is: to propagate pornography is to cause an occasion of sin for other people, and to accept or to use such evil and obscene material is incompatible with moral and religious living.
In addition, the point should also be made that pornography is a shameful degrading of human dignity. Women, the usual objects of pornography, are all degraded when a woman is used or abused in this way. When a child is used for the so-called "kiddy porn," the psychological effects can harm that human being for all the later years of life. Child pornography is actually a form of child abuse.
. . . Pornography must be eliminated—for the building of a good, decent society, for the human dignity of women and children, and for the health and strength of the next generation.[30]

Elder David B. Haight of the Quorum of the Twelve Apostles, Church of Jesus Christ of Latter-day Saints (Mormon), said at the general conference on October 7, 1984:

Pornography is not a victimless crime. Who are its victims? First, those who either intentionally, or sometimes involuntarily, are exposed to it. Pornography is addictive. What may begin as a curious exploration can become a controlling habit. Studies show that those who allow themselves to be drawn to pornography soon begin to crave even coarser content. Continued exposure desensitizes the spirit and can erode the conscience of unwary people. A victim becomes a slave to carnal thoughts and actions. As the thought is father to the deed, exposure can lead to acting out what is nurtured in the mind.
But there are other victims. Crimes of violence have increased in the United States at up to five times the rate of our population growth. A 1983 University of New Hampshire study found that states having the highest readership of pornographic magazines also have the highest number of reported rapes. Pornography degrades and exploits men, and women, and children in a most ugly and corrupt fashion.

Perhaps the greatest tragedy of all is in the lives of children who become its victims. The saddest trend of our day is the alarming large increase in child abuse. . . .

The Savior reserved His harshest condemnation for those who would offend little children. He said: "Take heed that ye despise not one of these little ones; for . . . it is not the will of your Father which is in heaven, that one of these little ones should perish." (Matt. 18:10, 14.)

The Lord further commanded: "Neither commit adultery . . . nor do anything like unto it." (D&C 59:6.)

"The early apostles and prophets [warned against] sins that are reprehensible. . . . — adultery, . . . infidelity, . . . impurity, inordinate affection, . . . sexual relations outside of marriage, . . . sex perversion, . . . preoccupation with sex in one's thoughts . . . [or] sexual [relations] between persons so closely related that they are forbidden by law to marry." (Spencer W. Kimball, *President Kimball Speaks Out*, Salt Lake City: Deseret Book Company, 1981, p. 6.) Incest is an ugly sin, and this sin particularly may irreparably damage its innocent victims.

Yet, what impels these offenders to such terrible deeds? Police report that some 80 percent of those who molest young boys and girls admitted modeling their attacks on pornography they had viewed.[31]

The Jewish Communal Affairs Commission of the American Jewish Committee stated on May 3, 1984:

Pornography may be defined as any material that demeans the innate dignity of men and women by abstracting sexuality from its human context. . . .

As American Jews, we consider pornography to be offensive to Jewish ethics and potentially destructive to American society.

A core belief of Judaism is that man and woman, created in the image of God, deserve to be treated with dignity and respect. Judaism sanctions, indeed hallows, the positive enjoyment of sexuality within the context of an overall relationship between husband and wife. Pornography represents the very antithesis of our tradition. It makes people into objects by reducing sexuality to an impersonal, mechanical activity. It denies the image of God within us.

Since Judaism abhors sexual violence, we are especially disturbed at the increasingly violent nature of pornography. . . .

The question of whether or not exposure to violent pornography may influence behavior is extremely controversial; no conclusive evidence can be marshaled for either side. However, there is a growing body of research suggesting that extended exposure to violent pornography desensitizes the viewer to the seriousness of sex crimes, so that, if he witnesses an attack on a woman, or serves on a jury in a rape case, he is likely to take the crime less seriously. [references omitted]

Quite aside from pornography's impact on the consumer, it has another harmful consequence. Many of the actors and models are children who are enticed or coerced by the pornographers into acts of sexual debasement, sadism and bestiality. . . .

In view of pornography's offensiveness and destructive potential, we must find ways, within the limits of the Constitution, to combat its influence. The AJC expresses its profound opposition to the dissemination of pornography, which it regards as a serious form of social pathology, approaching epidemic proportions.[32]

Bishop Howard J. Hubbard of the Diocese of Albany, New York, said on August 2, 1984:

The rapid growth of this industry, 90 percent of which is allegedly controlled by organized crime to launder money from drug trafficking, is not surprising because pornography is highly addictive. The addiction often escalates as the user/reader needs rougher material which can lead to desensitization and acting-out behavior.

It is no coincidence, then, that as pornography has exploded in America, so, too, have rape, incest, sexual abuse of children, spouse battering, venereal disease, abortion and out-of-wedlock births. . . .

Opposition to pornography must be rooted ultimately in our personal, social and religious understanding of human sexuality as being a precious gift from God shaping one's own identity and giving one the potential to enter into lasting love relationships with others.

The root evil of pornography, then, is that it runs radically counter to the true meaning of human sexuality and human personhood.[33]

The Greek Orthodox 27th Biennial Clergy Laity Congress stated that the lifestyle propagated by pornography is contrary to New Testament teachings; that church, family, and community values are being seriously threatened by the pornography industry; and that the erosion of values has contributed to the increase in teen pregnancies, sexual assaults, and child prostitution.[34]

John Cardinal Krol said at the Denver National Conference on Pornography on May 31, 1985:

Though we appreciate the Supreme Court's criterion for determining obscenity by contemporary community standards, it is a very precarious criterion. It severs morality from any natural law foundation, and reduces morality to a product of a moment, so that what may have been considered obscene at one time could, because of a changed public conscience or judgment, be considered moral today. Morality by popular consensus is not an acceptable standard. The history of God's chosen people provides us with the example of Sodom and Gomorrah and other instances in which morality by popular consensus was punished by God. Against such a fluctuating concept of obscenity, there is the unchangeable natural law which binds all men, irrespective of religious affiliation or social position. The claim of some artists to absolute independence and unrestricted freedom, or their claim that art is outside the range of morality—*ars gratia artis*—is false. Like all other manifestations of life, art is subject to God's law.

However, inasmuch as the Supreme Court allows the applicability of contemporary community standards in determining obscenity, we the people are members of the community. It is within our competence to set community standards. . . . We have the right to choose to have a public morality. . . .

The very word "pornography" means a harlot's words or picture. Pornography is a degradation of God's gift of sex. God created man in His own image and likeness. He created them male and female. He intended them to be a gift to and for each other. By their sexuality and freedom as persons, they are capable of mirroring the creative activity of God. He ordained that sex is sacred; that sex is for marriage and marriage is for Christ and that sex is both love giving and life giving. It not only expresses conjugal love and unity, but also and necessarily is related to the origin of human life. . . .

George Washington said that religion and morality are the indispensable supports of our form of government. Pornography erodes both. Since the founding of our nation pornography was considered a crime and the Constitutional guarantee of the freedom of the press and expression did not extend to obscenity.[35]

In March 1986, the Missouri Catholic Conference issued its "Joint Statement on Pornography":

Pornography is an evil that desensitizes and degrades the adults who use it, insults and victimizes all women, promotes sexual violence, puts children who have easy access at terrible risk and leads its producers and users to consider themselves and others as mere objects to be used and abused at will. There is considerable evidence of the link between pornography and organized crime. Pornography thus corrupts our whole society by violating society's greatest asset: The God given integrity and dignity of every human being.[36]

The Jehovah's Witnesses share the concern of other religious leaders about the harmful effects of pornography on society. In June 1982, they published a series of articles highlighting the harms of pornography, prostitution, incest, and child abuse.[37]

In his book *The Porno Plague*, Neil Gallagher outlines what he calls the "spiritual strategy" for fighting pornography. He says, "If you're going to do anything about pornography, understand clearly that God *hates* sexual abuse; and, admit that you've been brainwashed and seduced by our 'sexually free' culture." He then quotes Bible passages about nakedness, fornication, adultery, incest, homosexuality, bestiality, and prostitution which he labels as forms of sexual abuse.

Keep away from every kind of evil. (1 Thess. 5:22)

Fix your thoughts on what is true and good and right. Think about things that are pure and lovely. (Phil. 4:8)

Remember, too, that knowing what is right to do and then not doing it is sin. (James 4:17)

For we are not fighting against people made of flesh and blood, but against persons without bodies—the evil rulers of the unseen world, those mighty satanic beings and great evil princes of darkness who rule this world; and against huge numbers of wicked spirits in the spirit world. (Eph. 6:12).

. . . Here is immorality:

In our universe, there is a wide, thick, eternal line. Above the line are people, below the line are things.

People are to be loved. Things are to be used.

Immorality is the reversal. It's immoral to love things. It's immoral to use people.

It's immoral to use people for *any* reason. It's immoral to use people for political, racial, financial, or sexual advantage. People who are used are people who hate. Prostitutes confess that they hate men. Less than 1% of prostitutes successfully marry. They've never learned love. They've been used.

God likes sex. He created it. He wants men and women to enjoy it, not abuse it. It's lovely, passionate, and irreplaceable ecstasy. The Bible commends husbands and wives who sexually enjoy each other. (2 Cor. 7:3, 4). God made Adam and Eve pure and nude. Satan made them prurient and naked. Sex, manipulated by Satan, is abuse, leading to death and banishment from God.

God wants His people to love each other, not use each other. He knows they'll be happier that way.

People who produce, sell and buy pornography are not happy. Their lust, greed, and appetite for shock will never be satisfied. They traffic in hate. And hate is emotional cannibalism. Pornography is an extravaganza of sexual abuse, a relentless, vile outpouring of hate. It is the enemy of love, the enemy of God.[38]

John H. Court, a clinical psychologist, professor of psychology at The Finders University, Australia, and author of several books about pornography, summarized the morality view of pornography. He said pornography is:

1. Anti-life.
2. Anti-relationship and anti-family.
3. Anti-human.
4. Anti-woman.

5. Anti-children.
6. Anti-sex.
7. Anti-social.
8. Anti-environment.
9. Anti-community.
10. Anti-culture.
11. Anti-conscience.
12. Anti-God.[39]

Reverend Jerry Kirk believes that God has allowed pornography into the United States "to make us face the seriousness of our own sin, to break our hearts by revealing the desperate need for righteousness in our lives and in the church. Our own needs must drive us to the Lord and to each other at much deeper levels."[40] Kirk also emphasizes that God can heal victims and abusers. He urges morality group activists not to misdirect their anger and drive pornographers and pornography addicts further from God: "Then we have unwittingly become agents of evil, not of God," he says.[41]

THE VIEW OF FEMINISTS OPPOSING PORNOGRAPHY

A number of differences toward the morality view, perhaps unresolvable, divide the morality and feminist leaders who oppose pornography. The morality advocates favor obscenity laws that attack pornography as being immoral. Feminists support civil laws giving pornography victims the right to sue for harms done and to oppose obscenity laws (for reasons detailed in chapter 7). Most feminists would not regulate erotica—even if it depicts explicit sexual acts between homosexuals, lesbians, or unmarried couples. Many moralists want to regulate depictions of those acts, and some want to ban all depictions of ultimate sexual acts. Morality groups base their positions on the Bible and consider pornography to be an attack on a Christian, family-oriented value system. While these groups almost invariably attack women's liberation, unmarried persons sleeping together, homosexuality, lesbianism, abortion, and the Equal Rights Amendment, many feminists are in the forefront of the movement advocating those rights. While the morality groups see pornography as destroying the moral lifestyle they advocate, feminists view pornography as a force that perpetuates a male system of power and prevents true equality for women. Thus, the moralists and feminists, the right and left wing opponents of pornography, respectively, agree on little except the need to regulate

pornography. So far, that goal has not been enough to unite them in their fight against pornography.

The Christian philosophers entwine their antifeminist and antipornography views in a variety of ways.

Neil Gallagher suggests that "homosexuals (a small minority) and extremist wranglers of ERA (a smaller minority) swing legal clout because they scream. They picket, boycott, sit-in, and march."[42] (Gallagher's point is that the antipornography groups should be using the same tactics.)

On the legal front, Betty Wein, giving a Jewish perspective, suggests, "The recent anti-porn 'civil rights' legislation, unsuccessfully being pushed by feminists and widely regarded as unconstitutional, may be only the first of many well-meaning but nonetheless, First-Amendment threatening efforts if the obscenity laws continue to be ignored."[43]

And, while the Christianity groups attack the civil rights approach as being too broad, some people propose outlawing *all* material that depicts ultimate sexual acts—an approach far broader than that suggested in the civil rights law.[44]

Reo Christenson, a professor of political science at Miami University in Oxford, Ohio, states:

In Minneapolis and Indianapolis, feminists have sought to deal with *some* aspects of porn by declaring it violates women's civil rights and jeopardizes their prospects for obtaining genuine equality. They are doomed to fail. They have come too close to saying that speech which is deemed to be socially harmful has no constitutional protection. The implications are too broad, and I regret that I cannot support the language employed by the well-intentioned people who drafted these statutes. There is almost no chance that the courts will accept such law.

They should have used a more direct, straightforward approach. They should have sought a new federal law which banned the movement in interstate commerce of any material or any performance which involves visually explicit sexual behavior, real or simulated, intended for commercial entertainment.[45]

Another leader of the Christianity-oriented anti-pornography forces, Jerry Kirk, calls Indianapolis's adoption of the civil rights ordinance "courageous" and notes that "the message is being heard across the nation: women are not going to tolerate abuse by porn any longer!"[46]

E. Michael Jones says that pornography has split the feminist movement, quoting feminist Sharon Page as saying, " 'Porn/erotica *can* play a progressive role in showing women taking pleasure apart from the married/reproductive context—if we reclaim it to do so.' "[47] Jones states:

Andrea Dworkin, who seems to have become deranged by reading too much pornography, is typical of the feminist writer who sees pornography as the quintessence of maleness. Males, according to Dworkin, are ipso facto a pathological phenomenon. Pornography is simply the most visible symptom of the disease, in the way that the sore is an indication of herpes. Maleness is the universal *radix malorum*. "Terror," Dworkin writes in *Pornography: Men Possessing Women*, "is the outstanding theme and consequence of male history and male culture. . . . Terror issues forth from the male, illuminates his essential nature and his basic purpose." According to Dworkin, there is virtually no difference between rape and marriage. "Marriage is an institution developed from rape as a practice. Rape, originally defined as abduction, became marriage by capture. Marriage meant the taking was to extend in time, to be not only use of, but lifelong possession of, or ownership." As with most feminist analysis, Dworkin's views preclude the need for explanation. Schiro, one could say, was a rapist because he was a male. Pornography just allowed his maleness free expression. Men exploit women sexually because they are men. Exploitation exists because men exist.

Men are to feminists what the fallen angels are to Christians, although that misstates the case somewhat. Feminists are more Manichean in their beliefs; unlike Christians they believe in the existence of an absolute evil principle, perhaps an omnipotent one, since they don't believe in God.

The belief that sexual perversion and exploitation and pornography are all a function of maleness is, however, becoming less tenable in the face of the evidence. First of all, feminists, especially lesbians, are increasingly frequent users of pornography.[48]

Law professor William A. Stanmeyer summarizes the moralist view of feminists who attack pornography:

Feminists are objecting to pornography, but their understanding of the problem is still incomplete. At the NYU Colloquium, Susan Brownmiller, the feminist author, summed up the feminist case this way.

"What we object to is the *sexual humiliation and degradation of women* that *is the essence of pornography*. Pornography's intent is call of violence against the female body. We object to the presentation of rape, torture, mutilation, and murder for erotic stimulation and pleasure."

This is not exactly the point. Indeed, Ms. Brownmiller and the other feminists seem torn between their rightful concern about the anti-female essence of pornography and their "libertarian" inclination to absolutize the First Amendment. Further, their focus on the degradation of women seems to overlook the fact that pornography also degrades children of both sexes and degrades young men as well (homosexual pornography). One suspects that some feminists at least would tolerate other forms of pornography if only *women* could be factored out of pornographic pictures and films. To put it another way, their concern is *specific* and not *generic*. Feminists do not fully discern the common thread that connects all forms of pornography.

This common thread is predatory hedonism. At root, pornography is the glorification of what one might call "psychological cannibalism"—the use of women, children, and boys for all the pleasure they can disgorge in a passing encounter. Though violent pornography against women deserves women's concern, the issue is deeper: pornography of *any* kind deserves *every* civilized citizen's concern. For all pornography does the same thing: it tells the viewer to take pleasure for its own sake, to cast off all moral and cultural restraints, to treat another human as a thing, not a person. As such, it is a threat not only to women in our civilization; it is a threat to our civilization itself.

Feminists should also reflect on the implications of the sexual "liberation" that seems to be part of their program. Few can argue with the principle, "Equal pay for equal work." Yet a by-product of feminism is the notion that women should have the same opportunity as men to be sexually promiscuous. Women as a group see themselves as less valuable than they once did, as less worthy of the strict codes of chaste courtship that most of their mothers and probably all of their grandmothers preferred. Many young women are willing to embrace a barracks-room attitude toward sex. "My place or yours?" is the usual conclusion to a flirtatious singles bar encounter.

The sexually liberated lifestyle may be more the fantasy of Hollywood television writers than the usual practice of women. Yet is there not a connection between the sexual "liberation" of women and the current explosion of pornography and exploitive sexual activity?

There surely is such a connection and, towards the end of the 1970s, many feminists began to see it. They did not like where they were heading. In freeing women from sexual restraints they had reinforced the male pressures for erotic "freedom" as well. And men were not being gentlemen about it. The billboards and record jackets started appearing, showing half-dressed women tied and beaten, bruised, sometimes bloody, yet smiling through it all. Women reported that men were acting out the sadistic fantasies their pornography lessons taught them. Though many feminists do not like to admit it, they had started to do what the two doctors in Dr. Frankenstein's laboratory had done: create a monster.

Feminists who campaign against pornography have not yet embraced a traditional view of public morality and public decency. They should. They should also develop a more comprehensive understanding of the nature of pornography. Pornography exploits women whether the depictions are violent or voluntary, for it makes women no more than a foil, an organ, a function, with nothing personal or unique or lasting in the encounter. The pornographer portrays sex too closely to make it an art and he removes its sacred and personal character. Even non-violent pornography with women depicted exploits women. It should be obvious, especially to feminists who see the point elsewhere, that when you are exploited you are not "liberated."[49]

CONCLUSION

The morality-centered viewpoints about pornography revolve around a theologically based attitude that pornography is immoral, indecent, and offensive. The supporters of this view range from those who advocate regulation of all anti-religious values (including pornography, television violence and sex, the drug culture, rock music, homosexuality, and abortion) to those who favor a stance more likely to generate broad public support—concentrating on the most harmful pornography (child pornography and that which depicts violence or degradation).

While the religious leaders have found support for their opposition to pornography in the Bible and other religious books, not all of their criticisms of pornography are theological. These leaders, as well as the morality/decency groups, emphasize that pornography needs to be regulated because it influences some people to harm other people by acts such as sexual assault, child molestation, torture, mutilation, incest, battering, and even murder.

The morality and religious leaders emphasize that pornography has been found by the U.S. Supreme Court not to be protected speech covered by the First Amendment to the Constitution. Morality in Media, Inc., addresses the free speech/censorship issues, legislating morality, and other frequently raised concerns in "Cliché Arguments: Designed to Create Confusion Around the Problem of Pornography, Obscenity and Cableporn," which is reprinted as appendix C.

Reverend Jerry Kirk summarizes the morality groups' position in this statement: "If we had gotten together sooner for the battle against pornography, thousands of children would still be alive, millions of women would not have been raped, an entire generation of young people would not have been ravaged through drugs and twisted death-dealing sex."[50]

NOTES

1. Morality in Media, Inc., Correspondence.
2. Morality in Media, Inc., *MTM: Morality in Media* (New York: Morality in Media, Inc., 1987),.
3. Ibid.
4. *The National Decency Reporter,* January 1989, 6.
5. Citizens for Decency Through Law, Inc., *Citizens for Decency Through Law, Inc.: Legal Aspects,* (Phoenix: Citizens for Decency Through Law, Inc., 1–6.
6. Ibid.
7. National Coalition Against Pornography, Inc., *Mission and Objectives for the N-CAP, Inc., 1985,* (Cincinnati: National Coalition Against Pornography, Inc., 1985).
8. Jerry R. Kirk, *The Mind Polluters* (Nashville, Tenn.: Thomas Nelson Publishers, 1985).
9. National Coalition Against Pornography, Inc., *Mission and Objectives,*
10. Ibid.
11. Ibid., 1–2.
12. *NFD Journal* 10(7) (July, 1986): 2.
13. Donald E. Wildmon, *The Home Invaders* (Wheaton, Ill.: Victor Books, 1985), 75–91.
14. Ibid., 14, 15.
15. Ibid., 22, 23, 51.
16. Brad Curl, *A Strategy for Decency,* 2d ed. (Washington, D.C.: National Christian Association, 1986), 148.
17. Religious Alliance Against Pornography, *Policy Statement of the Religious Alliance Against Pornography* (Cincinnati: Religious Alliance Against Pornography, 1986).
18. Ibid.
19. Neil Gallagher, *The Porno Plague* (Minneapolis: Bethany House Publishers, 1981), 53.
20. Ibid., 57.
21. Ibid., 62.
22. Elizabeth Holland, "I Don't Have the Right?" *Bible Advocate,* January 1985, 25–26, from a speech to the 1984 National Consultation on Obscenity, Pornography and Indecency.
23. Ibid., 26.
24. Cardinal Joseph Bernardin, "TV Porno," in *Religious Leaders' Statements on Pornography 1984–1986* (New York: *Morality in Media Inc.,* , 1986), (hereafter cited as *Religious Leaders' Statements 1984–1986*).
25. California Catholic Conference, "Human Dignity and the Sacredness of Sexuality," California 26 May 1986,
26. Bishop Jerome J. Hastrich, Diocese of Gallup, New Mexico, "Greetings to the Clergy, Religious and Laity of the Diocese of Gallup," in *Religious Leaders' Statement: 1984–1986,* 25–26.
27. Florida's Religious Leaders, "Statement Against Pornography," in *Religious Leaders' Statements 1984–1986,* 4–5.
28. Catholic Bishops of Missouri, "To the Catholic People

of Missouri," Catholic Bishops of New York, "Text of Bishops' Pornography Statement"; in *Religious Leaders' Statements 1984–1986,* 1, 8.
29. Archbishop John R. Roach, Archdiocese of St. Paul and Minneapolis, "Statement on Pornography," in *Religious Leaders' Statements 1984–1986,* 6–7.
30. Catholic Bishops of Connecticut, "Pornography: Harmful, Dangerous Exploitation," in *Religious Leaders' Statements 1984–1986,* 16–18.
31. Elder David B. Haight, "Personal Morality," in *Religious Leaders' Statements on Pornography 1984–1985* (New York Morality in Media, Inc., 1986), 28–33 (hereafter cited as *Religious Leaders Statements 1984–1985*).
32. Jewish Communal Affairs Commission of the American Jewish Committee, "Statement on Pornography," in *Religious Leaders' Statements 1984–1986,* 50–53.
33. Bishop Howard J. Hubbard, Diocese of Albany, New York, "The Porno Plague, How to Combat Its Spread," in *Religious Leaders' Statements 1984–1986,* 37.
34. Greek Orthodox Archdiocese, North and South America, "Resolution on Pornography and Obscenity," in *Religious Leaders' Statements 1984–1985,* 21–23.
35. John Cardinal Krol, "Religious Perspectives on Pornography," Statement to the Denver National Conference on Pornography, 31 May 1985.
36. Catholic Bishops of Missouri, "To the Catholic People of Missouri"; Catholic Bishops of New York, "Text of Bishops' Pornography Statement"; in *Religious Leaders' Statements 1984–1986,* 1, 8.
37. "The New Morality"; " 'Chickens' and Hawks' "; " 'Baby Pros' and 'Kiddie Porn' "; "Rape at Home"; "To End Child Abuse," *Awake* 22 June 1982, 3–12.
38. Gallagher, *The Porno Plague,* 41, 45, 46.
39. John H. Court, "What Then Shall We Say and Do?" *Bible Advocate,* December 1985, 22–26.
40. Kirk, *The Mind Polluters,* 91, 92.
41. Ibid., 203, 204.
42. Gallagher, *The Porno Plague,* 101.
43. Betty Wein, "The Chilling Effects of Pornography" (Paper presented at the Seventh World Media Conference, Tokyo, November 1984), 16.
44. See chapter 1, Bruce Taylor's and Jerry Kirk's views are presented.
45. Reo Christenson, "The Truth about Pornography," *Bible Advocate,* January 1985, 6, 7, 23, 24.
46. Kirk, *The Mind Polluters,* 198.
47. E. Michael Jones, "Smut, Sex and Death in Evansville," *Fidelity,* November 1985, 36.
48. Ibid., 36–37.
49. William A. Stanmeyer, *The Seduction of Society* (Ann Arbor, Mich.: Servant Books, 1984), 76–78. Stanmeyer is President of the Lincoln Center for Legal Studies in Arlington, Virginia.
50. Kirk, *The Mind Polluters,* 205.

"Pornography is the theory and rape is the practice."[1] Those oft-quoted words by Robin Morgan describe the feminist antipornography movement. Feminist opposition to pornography is rooted in the belief (supported by cases of pornography victims and scientific studies) that there is a correlation between pornography use and the victimization of women and children through rape, molestation, battering, prostitution, marital rape, and other abuse. Feminist theory also points out that even those women who are not physically abused as a result of pornography are deeply harmed by it. Pornography is the ideology that promotes the continuation of sexist attitudes and behavior and of patriarchal power and control in our culture. Feminists target pornography that is violent, humiliating, or degrading toward women or that objectifies women. They do not oppose "erotica," which is as sexually explicit as pornography but promotes loving, affectionate, consensual, and equal sex between partners of equal power.

Unlike the morality advocates, feminists are divided on the issue of pornography. Some feminists oppose any censorship of pornography out of fear that feminist views about abortion, contraception, sexual freedom, control of one's own body, economics, and social control might be censored as well.

In a memo to the U.S. Attorney General's Commission on Pornography, The Feminist Coalition listed a series of demands that provides an overview of the antipornography feminist view:

1. We demand that the Commission acknowledge that the 8-billion-dollar-a-year pornography industry is built on the sexual enslavement and exploitation of *women*.
2. We demand that the Commission acknowledge that pornography targets *all women* for rape, battery, sexual harassment, prostitution, incest, and murder.
3. We demand that the Commission acknowledge that pornography is a practice of sex discrimination that denies women civil rights and civil liberties.
4. We demand that the Commission acknowledge that pornography sexualizes and profits from racism, anti-Semitism, and hatred of Lesbians and gay men.
5. We demand that the Commissioners rid themselves of their prejudice against the women who have testified before them about the abuse they have been subjected to because of pornography. We demand that they acknowledge that these women are speaking the truth.
6. We demand that the Commission devote two full days of hearings to the testimony of all of the women who wanted to speak out about the ways pornography has injured them, but who have been denied access to this forum.
7. We demand that the Commission reject moralistic, ineffective, sexist obscenity laws, which create a climate of censorship.
8. We demand that the Commission endorse the civil rights antipornography laws proposed in Minneapolis, Indianapolis, Los Angeles, and Cambridge, Massachusetts.
9. We demand that the Commission recommend federal funding for housing, legal and medical services, education, and job training for women escaping prostitution and pornography.
10. We demand that the Commission recommend that fines levied against pornographers, and money and property confiscated from them in criminal proceedings, be allocated to programs for their victims.[2]

These demands were endorsed by a wide range of feminist groups and individuals: The Assault Prevention Training Project, Columbus, Ohio; Kathleen Barry; The Battered Women's Service Directory; Phyllis Chesler; Child Assault Prevention Center, Columbus, Ohio; D.C. CASE (Committee Against Sexism and Exploitation); Feminists Against Pornography, Washington, D.C.; Feminists Fighting Pornography, New York City; Shere Hite; Lesbian Task Force, Chapel Hill, North Carolina; Lesbians and Gays Against Pornography, New York City; Los Angeles Women Against Pornography; Men Against Pornography, New York City; Men Against Sexist Violence, Washington, D.C.; Not in Our Name: Men Working Against Pornography, Washington, D.C.; Robin Morgan; National Assault Prevention Center; Not in Our Name: New York NOW, Lesbian Rights Committee; Organizing Against Pornography, Minneapolis; Pornography Awareness, Chapel Hill, North Carolina; Pro Femina, Cambridge, Massachusetts; PUMA (Prostitutes Union of Massachusetts); Diana E.H. Russell; Gloria Steinem; Street Work Project, New York State Victims Services Department; VOICES (Victims of Incest Can Emerge Survivors); Betsy Warrior; WHISPER (Women Hurt in Systems of Prostitution Engaged in Revolt); Women Against Pornography, New York City; Women's Alliance Against Pornography, Cambridge, Massachusetts.

R. George Kirkpatrick and Louis A. Zurcher, Jr., summarize the feminist perspective in "Women Against Pornography: Feminist Anti-Pornography Crusades in American Society," which is included as appendix F. For an overview of the feminist perspective that pornography is harmful, *Not a Love Story*, a film produced by the National Film Board of Canada, is available. The film contains interviews with numerous pornography "stars" and shows their working conditions.

Feminists who oppose fighting pornography take the position that antipornography laws would hurt women more than help them and create a false sense that steps were being taken to end sexism. They believe that such legislation is dangerous and ineffective and promote educating people about the harms of pornography.

ORGANIZATIONS

Feminist perspectives on pornography are represented by numerous groups throughout the nation. Appendix E contains the addresses of the groups described below. Lists of local groups should be available from these organizations.

1. *Women Against Pornography* (WAP) is a national organization in New York that concentrates on educating the public about pornography through slide shows, feminist-guided tours of the Times Square pornography district, speakers, newsletters, protests, boycotts, and advocacy for women hurt by pornography. WAP periodically holds advertising award ceremonies "zapping" companies for producing ads that demean women and girls. Conferences have addressed issues such as pornography and male sexuality (1981), pornography and women's self-image (1982), the sexual liberals and the attack on feminism (1987), and international trafficking in women (1988). WAP has a national membership of ten thousand women and men.[3]

In correspondence with us, WAP states:

> We are working against pornography because it reinforces women's inferiority in society and promotes violence. Our fight against pornography is a fight for the dignity, autonomy, safety and equality of women's lives.
>
> We support civil rights remedies that would empower women injured by pornography to take legal action against their exploiters and abusers. We oppose censorship and any legal approach based on the male-centered notion of banning or regulating "obscenity;" such laws only reinforce sexism and repression, and they never address the real harm of pornography to women's lives and status.[1]

WAP also details some of the harms of pornography:

1. The fundamental message of pornography is that women are sexual objects that exist primarily for men's use. Pornography denigrates and trivializes women by presenting them as bunnies, pets, and playmates. It dehumanizes women by reducing them to truncated body parts. It slanders women by portraying them as masochists who find their fulfillment in sexual subservience, brutality and rape.

2. Pornography is a powerful agent of socialization for men and boys, many of whom learn most of what they believe about women and sex through pornography. They learn that their own sexual desires are inherently aggressive, that girls and women are things to be dominated and used, that sex is an act of conquest, and that sexual violation and humiliation of women does not constitute real harm because women enjoy it, want it, and deserve it.

3. Pornography also socializes women and girls. It teaches females that they exist primarily for the gratification of men, that their value resides in their desirability and availability to men, and that denigration, exploitation and abuse are their fulfillment as women.

4. Pornography is more than images and ideology: it is the practice of dehumanizing and abusing real women to make materials that are then used against other women. Women are often pressured, deceived, and/or forced to pose or perform for pornography; this is devastating in its effect on them. And then the lessons of pornography are acted out against other women and girls, in marital rape, in domestic battery, in incest, in sexual harassment on the job.[5]

WAP periodically publishes a newsletter titled the *Women Against Pornography Newsreport*. Numerous information packets and slide shows also are available from the organization.

2. *Organizing Against Pornography (OAP: A Resource Center for Education and Action* (formerly known as the Pornography Resource Center) is a feminist group that promotes the civil rights approach to regulating pornography. OAP makes available to researchers in the pornography field one of the most extensive collections of data in the nation. Persons involved in OAP have been active in supporting the civil rights antipornography approach in Minneapolis and nationally. Numerous educational materials, including a slide show titled "Pornography: A Practice of Inequality" are available from OAP. OAP also provides speakers and trainers on pornography for a variety of adult and teenage groups.

OAP states that pornography is violence against women and eroticizes inequality:

Pornography is more than images. Rape, battery, sexual harassment, prostitution and child abuse are pornography. These acts become justified and reinforced by two myths—women enjoy being violated and men have the right to violate them. Men learn how to abuse women from pornography and come to believe that abuse is something women want.

Consumers of pornography find portrayals of dominance and submission sexy and appealing. For example, scenarios of bondage, humiliation, child molestation, Nazi death camps and slave plantations are considered real "turn-ons." All pornography, even *Playboy* and *Penthouse*, relies on these foundations.

Pornography is not a passive means of expression. It is about abusive behavior and harm done to women. Pornography shapes the sexual expression of both men and women—making men's arousal dependent on the objectification and abuse of women. There is growing evidence to confirm that pornography is used in crimes against specific women and that it contributes to the oppression of all women. Because women's lives are at stake, it is imperative that we counter this practice with active resistance.

Organizing against pornography is a way to transform our outrage into action and collectively say 'no' to the makers and users of pornography. Organizing against pornography is a way to confront sexual behaviors and attitudes that rely on humiliation, domination and violence. It is one way to pursue equality and justice for women, children and other disempowered groups.[6]

3. *The Feminist Anti-Censorship Task Force* (FACT), based in New York, is a group of feminists who believe it is dangerous and misguided for feminists to seek legislation prohibiting sexually explicit images. FACT believes that antipornography legislation would hurt women more than it would help them, while at the same time creating a false belief that something effective is being done to combat sexism.[7]

FACT was formed in the fall of 1984 to oppose a Minneapolis-type civil rights ordinance introduced on Long Island, New York. Among its primary purposes is presenting feminist opposition to civil rights type antipornography laws and to laws that would regulate sexually explicit speech. Another goal is to educate people about issues that sexually explicit images raise. FACT wants to show that feminists have diverse views about pornography and its regulation.[8]

A recent publication by FACT is filled with pornographic images and makes it clear to us that this group is not to be taken seriously as a representative of genuine feminist thought.[9] Most of FACT's views are discussed in chapter 8 of this book.

Nan Hunter, a representative of FACT and director of the American Civil Liberties Union Lesbian and Gay Rights Project, told the U.S. Attorney General's Commission on Pornography that the civil rights antipornography law would "perpetuate rather than subvert disabling stereotypes concerning women and sexuality." She said:

The problem with pornography, in our view, lies in the extent to which it reflects, validates and glorifies male supremacy. Unfortunately, the indicia of male supremacy are found throughout society, not just in pornography. Pornography is not the cause of the oppression of women nor is it even the primary channel in which that supremacy is reflected, validated and glorified. Other, much more powerful, established and legitimate institutions contribute far more than does the pornography industry to the second-class status of women. Thus we and many other feminists believe that targeting pornography in a civil rights law, as has been attempted by the ordinance in question, is a fundamentally misguided attempt to get at the root causes of an ideology which tells us that women are inferior and incompetent.[10]

4. *Citizens for Media Responsibility Without Law* (Outlaws for Social Responsibility) is headquartered in Oshkosh, Wisconsin. This organization, started by feminists Nikki Craft and Melissa Farley, states that "Sex Is Not Obscene! The *real* obscenity is the marketing of women as products—The dehumani-

zation and glorification of violence." The organization states:

We Are In Favor Of Nudity & Sensuality

We strive toward a more sexually liberated society. We advocate diverse, consenting sexual experience. . . . We believe that explicit sexual materials have a place in literature, art, science and education, and most of all in the public domain.

We defend sex education, abortion, and access to safe and reliable birth control for men and women.

We seek an end to the body hatred and guilt concerning normal functions that this woman-hating society fosters.

There is a difference between genuine love, acceptance and empowerment of the body, and the marketing of women and exploitation of nudity that is the trademark of pornography.

We are Anti-Censorship

We support unlimited freedom of the press.

We contend that no government is capable of deciding what information individuals should have access to.

We do not want pornography hidden. We want it displayed, discussed and rejected as bigotry.

We do not want censorship. We want a citizens' mandate against violent pornography. We call on liberals, civil libertarians, and all people who say they believe in freedom to take public responsibility for pornography and work towards an end to this trafficking in women.

We Are Opposed To Objectification and Violent Pornography.

We are opposed to the display of women's bodies to sell products in advertising.

We object to women being judged in beauty pageants, clothed or unclothed.

We reject the boring, fetishized pornography that perverts sexuality in our society.

We refuse to tolerate the stripping, binding, rape, torture and humiliation of women for entertainment and men's profit.

We demand corporate and individual responsibility for publishing, printing, distribution and selling of violent pornography.

We Practice Civil Disobedience.

When the multibillion-dollar pornography industry disseminates hateful propaganda that results in real harm to real women, we will not collaborate in our own victimization by remaining silent.

We advocate and commit civil disobedience as retaliation against sexually violent images in the media.[11]

This organization is not working for legislation against pornography. Some of the tactics used to highlight its philosophy are reviewed in other parts of this chapter.

Craft and others have found a new organization called Naturalists Opposing Pornographic Exploitation (NOPE). This group advocates portraying positive images of child and family nudity.[12]

5. The *National Organization for Women* (NOW), a well-known feminist group, took the following position on pornography in 1985:

Whereas, the 1984 NOW Conference resolved that pornography is a factor in creating and maintaining sex as a basis for discrimination, and that pornography, as distinct from erotica, is a systematic practice of exploitation and subordination based on sex, which differentially harms women, and children, through dehumanization, sexual exploitation, forced sex, forced prostitution, physical injury, and social and sexual terrorism presented as entertainment, and that pornography violates the civil rights of women and children; and

Whereas, the pornography issue is receiving widespread attention at this time and action at this juncture by a large, national organization of NOW's stature would serve and extend the interest; and

Whereas, NOW, as the largest feminist organization in the United States, should properly take a leadership position on the issue; and

Whereas, the feminist movement is deeply divided on numerous issues related to pornography—ranging from whether pornography is harmful and to what degree, to whether legislation dealing with the content of pornography will effectively reduce violence against women; and

Whereas, the pro-pornography faction is funded by large and in some cases well-financed organizations, putting local chapters at a severe disadvantage as they try to deal with the issue at their local levels; and

Whereas, the lack of adequate sex education in our schools combined with accessibility of pornography, gives pornography a virtual monopoly over sex education in our society; and

Whereas, pornography promotes sexual assault and is used increasingly and commonly in battery, in rape and in forcing women and children into prostitution;

Therefore, be it resolved, that NOW will develop and produce an educational kit including a visual presentation to be used in educating chapters about the pornography issue, and the feminist analysis of it; and

Be it further resolved that NOW will explore feminist approaches to laws including, but not limited to: products liability law; consumer law; libel law (individual and groups); and civil rights law; and

Be it further resolved that NOW will work to encourage rape crisis centers and battered women shelters nationwide to include questions regarding the use of pornography in instances of violence on intake forms; and

Be it further resolved that the national office serve as a collection point to which subunits of NOW may submit evidence of crimes committed against women in which pornography was a factor; and

Be it further resolved that NOW will explore possible legislative remedies, including but not limited to: a civil rights approach; current ordinance proposals; and law requiring that all pornographic materials carry complete identification of the producer/financier, with the following guidelines: that they are urged to join antipornography alliances that do not support explicitly the equality of women and lesbian and gay rights; and

Be it further resolved that NOW encourages subunits of NOW to participate in education and action on pornography. Recommendations to chapters may include: economic boycotts, primary and secondary; "buycotts" (buying where pornography is not sold); sidewalk counseling at pornographic businesses; houseparties and other educational meetings; locating and reporting to national office of possible litigants (people with standing to sue) in their communities; monitoring of purchasers and distributors of pornography; zap actions; media monitoring; letter-writing campaigns; marches and pickets; and improving accessibility to sex education programs; and

Be it further resolved that the Board Issues Committee shall develop a concept paper on pornography; and

Be it finally resolved that NOW allocate an additional $10,000 to the Action Program line item of the national budget.[13]

6. The *Task Force on Prostitution and Pornography* (TOPP) of Madison (Dane County), Wisconsin, is a local organization concerned about women, children, and teenagers who are involved in prostitution and pornography. TOPP states, "Our purpose is to educate our community about prostitution and pornography and how sexual exploitation hurts everyone." The group works in three areas: research and education, direct action, and legislation.[14] In a March 27, 1985, press release, TOPP endorsed the MacKinnon/Dworkin civil rights antipornography law: "We understand that it is one critical way to empower those harmed by pornography."[15]

TOPP was formed in 1983 from two previously existing groups—Women Against Pornography and the Task Force on Prostitution—when persons working with both groups "came to understand the connections between prostitution and pornography and between pornography and the exploitation and abuse of women and children." TOPP believes that prostitution and pornography are not victimless crimes, "nor are they 'inevitable' institutions that some women supposedly 'choose.' "[16]

TOPP, like most other feminist groups, provides public education via slide shows, speeches, and demonstrations. One of its major efforts was the Pornography Free Zone Campaign in which it offered businesses, groups, and individuals a way to make a visible statement about pornography and its effects on women and children. The campaign promoted stickers and posters reading: "This space is safe for Women and Children. It is a Pornography Free Zone." A booklet, *The Sex for Sale Industries*, is available from TOPP.[17]

FEMINIST VIEWS

Attorney Catharine A. MacKinnon, co-author (with Andrea Dworkin) of the civil rights antipornography approach, believes that pornography has flourished despite various laws against it partly because it is so financially and sexually profitable that it sets community standards. However, the main reason pornography has flourished, she says, is because "its real harm was never identified: the violation of women and children that is essential to its making and inevitable through its use." She says this harm could be overlooked because pornographers (whom she calls pimps) take the already powerless (females, the poor, youths, and so on) and "deepen their invisibility and their silence."[18] In her testimony

before the Attorney General's Commission on Pornography, MacKinnon stated:

> Women in pornography are bound, battered, tortured, humiliated, and sometimes killed. Or, merely taken and used. For every act you see in the visual materials . . . a woman had to be tied or cut or burned or gagged or whipped or chained, hung from a meat hook or from trees by ropes, urinated on or defecated on, forced to eat excrement, penetrated by eels and rats and knives and pistols, raped deep in the throat with penises, smeared with blood, mud, feces and ejaculate. Or merely taken through every available orifice, or posed as though she wanted to be. Pornography

sexualizes women's inequality. Every kind of woman is used, each one's particular inequalities exploited as deemed sexually exciting: Asian women bound so they are not recognizably human, so inert they could be dead; Black women playing plantation struggling against their bonds; Jewish women orgasming in re-enactments of Auschwitz; pregnant women and nursing mothers accessible, displayed; white women splayed across hoods of cars trussed like dead prey; amputees and other disabled or ill women, their injuries or wounds or stumps proffered as sexual fetishes; retarded girls presented as gratifyingly compliant; adult women infantilized as children, children presented as adult women, interchangeably fusing vulnerability with the sluttish eagerness said to be natural to women of all ages; so-called lesbians, actually women arranged with women to be watched and claimed, bought and sold.

The point is, because the profit from the mass production of these mass violations counts and women do not, because these materials are valued and women are not, because the pornographers have credibility and rights and women do not, the products of these acts are protected and women are not. So these things are done, so that pornography can be made of them. I call this a direct causal link between pornography and harm.[19]

Another feminist, Caryn Jacobs, states that pornography harms all women. Some sell their bodies as pornographic performers. Others have pornographic fantasies enacted upon them by men who have learned from pornography how to molest children, batter wives, and rape or force sex upon unconsenting partners. All women live in the "poisoned atmosphere of misogyny to which pornography directly contributes,"[20] she says.

Jacobs sees pornography as both a cause and a symptom of our patriarchal society. It makes female subjugation and male dominance "erotic" and portrays the master/slave relationship as sexually satisfying to both. She describes myths that pornography teaches:

1. Women want to be raped, enjoy rape, and are masochistic.
2. Females merit punishment for their "evil nature."
3. Women are to blame for the violence done to them.
4. Women are bestial/subhuman.
5. Female voices should be silenced.[21]

Pornography is present everywhere, Jacobs notes. Its message shames women, making them timid and causing them to lower their aspirations. It undermines the status of women in the workplace by encouraging sexual harassment of them and causing male superiors and peers to regard them as sex objects. Jacobs describes harms suffered by pornography models, critiques antipornography laws, and makes suggestions for change.[22]

Ann Jones believes that pornography teaches and fosters the violent abuse of women. She says that it also provides the ideological basis for "juries to condemn women who fight back." Thus, it promotes violence in the bedrooms and streets and "reaffirms violence in the courtroom," she states.[23]

Feminists are concerned that the consequence of raising females among humiliating and violent images of women will be to make women accept those images as normal and socially acceptable similar to the way in which slaves develop attitudes of inferiority.[24]

According to Debbie Ratterman, pornography increases women's fear that they will become victims of male violence. In response, women change their behavior by working harder to placate men and consent to sex more readily for fear of the reaction if they say no. She says that pornography silences women in relationships with men by inhibiting the honesty, openness, and trust that are necessary to a meaningful relationship, and she believes that pornography paralyzes women.[25]

Sarah J. McCarthy believes that we can expect "a skyrocketing of rape statistics" rather than a "catharsis" effect from the increase in violent pornography.[26] Pornography, which she states is a primary source of sex education for teenage boys, is incitement to rape, violence, and degradation, not sexuality. Feminists are not antisex, she notes, but are antiviolence, especially sexual violence.[27]

Dorchen Leidholdt of Women Against Pornography in New York City discusses the importance of objectification of women as it relates to the pornography issue. She considers objectification to be a process by a group in power carries out against a less powerful group a mechanism to establish and perpetuate dominance of the group in power. The powerful group attributes human characteristics to itself and inanimate object or animal-like characteristics to the group it is subjugating. By portraying the powerless group as different and caricatured, the powerful group creates a reason to fear, ridicule, and hate the other group, she states.

Leidholdt says that objectification is a psychological method that prevents the powerful group from identifying or empathizing with the subjugated group. It relieves the group in power from any responsibility for its oppressive policies.

When objectification becomes institutionalized, Leidholdt notes, it forms the psychological foundation for institutionalized acts of violence. She cites as an example Hitler's campaign to make Germans hate Jews.

Leidholdt notes that the sexual objectification of women reduces them to body parts and to animals such as foxes and fillies. In this way, men can proclaim their superiority to women. Leidholdt concludes that sexual objectification, institutionalized in pornography, paves the way for sexual violence against women.[28]

One well-known feminist antipornography activist is Andrea Dworkin, author of *Pornography: Men Possessing Women*. Dworkin also is a co-author with Catharine MacKinnon of the civil rights antipornography law, which is discussed in detail in other parts of this book.

In her book, Dworkin paints a picture of pornography as part of a male supremacist society. She outlines what she calls the "tenets" of male supremacist ideology:

1. Men have the self that takes and women must lack it.
2. Men are physically stronger than women and for that reason have dominion over them.
3. Men are aggressive (due to biology), hostile, cruel, and pro-conflict and pro-war.
4. Men have the power of naming. They define experience and values, determine what can and cannot be expressed, and control perception. This power is upheld by force.
5. The male's right to own the female, and whatever he does to effect or maintain ownership, is natural.
6. The power of money is a male power. Money in a man's hands signifies worth and accomplishment; in a women's hands, it is something foul or unwomanly, evidencing ambition or greed.
7. Sexual power authentically originates in the penis.

Dworkin relates these tenets to pornography by stating that the major theme of pornography as a genre is male power.[29] She refers to sex, violence, and death as the "male erotic trinity."[30]

According to Dworkin, objectification is a major theme of men's treatment of women: "Men want women to be objects, controllable as objects are controllable." Pornography she states, portrays such treatment of women.[31]

Violence is the prime component of male identity, Dworkin believes. Men are rewarded by money and admiration for practicing violence in every sphere, she claims, citing examples of both policemen and outlaws being treated as heroes.[32]

According to Dworkin, sex crimes against women are seen as a type of male normalcy, while such crimes against men and boys by men are seen as perversions. Thus, society protects men and boys from male sexual aggression because men are valuable, but it does not protect women and girls from such aggression, which is testimony to the "worthlessness of a female life." Dworkin notes that it is hard to make a credible claim that a crime against a woman matters in a "woman-hating culture."[33] She suggests that the Marquis de Sade (a sadistic pornographer) did (in the sex crimes he committed) what all men want to do and that none of his work takes place outside of common male beliefs. Thus, she says, Sade's importance is as "Everyman."[34]

Dworkin notes that throughout most of "patriarchal" history, women have been men's chattel. Women have been raised and forced to conform to male-defined ideals of female beauty, and this has resulted in deforming or mutilating the natural body. The final value of this beautiful object is its cruel destruction, she says.[35] According to Dworkin, objectification has become necessary for male arousal. Thus, women have become men's fetishes, and sexual behavior toward them, although predatory and hostile, is considered normal, whereas such behavior directed toward real objects would be considered abnormal.[36]

Dworkin claims that in order to justify their social and sexual domination of women, the pornographers (and sexual philosophers) need to believe that women are as or more dangerous and sadistic than men.[37] She details what she calls fundamental truths about pornography, noting that pornography's most enduring attitude, which women cannot understand, is that normal females desire, need, and demand sexual violence.[38] Thus, the first principle of sex in pornography is that the woman is a sexual provocateur or harlot.[39] Dworkin discusses several studies of sexuality that assert that the normal male commits sexual acts against the will of females and that force is intrinsic to male sexuality.[40]

Dworkin believes that pornography depicts the way real women are treated. She says that the idea that pornography is dirty comes from the belief that the sexuality of women is dirty, and pornography promotes that idea.[41] She asserts that pornography belongs to men of both the right and the left:

> The right-wing ideology claims that the division of the mother and whore is phenomenologically real. The virgin is the potential mother. The left-wing ideology claims that sexual freedom is in the unrestrained use of women, the use of women as a collective natural resource, not privatized, not owned by one man but instead used by many.

The metaphysics is the same on the Left and on the Right: the sexuality of the woman actualized is the sexuality of the whore; desire on her part is the slut's lust; once sexually available, it does not matter how she is used, why, by whom, by how many, or how often. Her sexual will can exist only as a will to be used. Whatever happens to her, it is all the same. If she loathes it, it is not wrong, she is.[42]

In the *Harvard Women's Law Journal,* Dworkin describes images of pornography, then relates those images and pornography to male power over women to the creation of sexual inequality, to perceptions of women as whores, to rape myths, and to actual physical injury of women through battering, rape, and other abuse. What would be considered atrocious if done to men is considered entertainment, fun, and a civil liberty when done to women, she notes. Dworkin comments on the insidious nature of this attitude: "What do you want to be when you grow up? *Doggie Girl? Gestapo Sex Slave? Black Bitch in Bondage?* Pet, bunny, beaver? In dreams begin responsibilities, whether one is the dreamer or the dreamed."[43]

In Dworkin's view, most pornographers are pimps who sell the real flesh-and-blood women in the pictures. They like the excitement of domination, are sadistic, hate women, and are greedy for profit, she says. She feels that the pornography these men create is the "distillation of that hate" and that part of the challenge of the pornographers' vocation is to find new and terrible things to do to women.[44]

Dworkin testified before the Attorney General's Commission on Pornography, emphasizing the relationship between pornography and real crimes against real women and children. She claimed that real rapes are filmed and sold in the marketplace: "[T]he major motif of pornography as a form of entertainment is that women are raped and violated and humiliated until we discover that we like it and at that point we ask for more."[45]

Dworkin stated that studies have shown that 65 to 70 percent of the women in pornography are victims of incest or child sexual abuse. They are poor women without opportunities, frequently runaways picked up by pimps. "They are frequently raped, the rapes are filmed, they are kept in prostitution by blackmail. The pornography is used on prostitutes by johns who are expected to replicate the sexual acts in the pornography, no matter how damaging it is." Dworkin emphasized how pornography is used to choreograph and engender the excitement to commit rape, to harass women on jobs and in education, and to create terror and compliance in the home.

The impact of pornography, Dworkin believes, is to keep women socially silent. (This violation of women's First Amendment free speech rights is discussed in chapter 8.[46]) Dworkin concludes that women will know they are free only when pornography goes out of existence. Men are betting that women will comply with the pornography and that their sexual abuse of women will turn real women into "the compliant women of sex," she says. But, she adds, "[t]he boys are wrong."[47]

Two other feminists, Diana E.H. Russell and Laura Lederer, express their views about pornography in *Take Back the Night.* They state that one goal of Women Against Violence in Pornography and Media (WAVPM) is to "put an end to all portrayals of women being bound, raped, tortured, killed, or degraded for sexual stimulation or pleasure."[48]

Lederer and Russell believe that the constant linking of sexuality and violence is dangerous. They object to all pornography because "even the most banal porn . . . objectifies women's bodies." An essential ingredient of violence against women, they feel, is to see them as things instead of as humans. Men are reared to view women as such; pornography feeds this viewpoint, and rape is a consequence, they state.[49]

While WAVPM is dedicated to freedom of speech, pornography is an abuse of free speech, Lederer and Russell note. They say that the First Amendment was never intended to protect material that condones and promotes violent crimes against any group.[50]

Barbara Renchkovsky Ashley and David Ashley discuss the feminist critique of pornography and review contemporary hard-core pornography from that viewpoint. The Ashleys conclude that feminists are correct in the view that pornography is about domination. Pornography, they state, endorses the idea that sexual pleasure is attained by dehumanizing others as a means to achieve self-gratification. Thus, in pornography, women are treated as meat; they beg for or crave bizarre sex, anal "ecstasy," big cocks, double fucking, painful climaxes, and gang bangs. Pornography is always against intimacy, the Ashleys claim. And, they say, it is inherently antierotic.[51] They conclude that feminists see pornography as signifying slavery, not liberation, and as a tool used to subjugate others.[52]

Sociologist Netta Gilboa frequently lectures and presents a slide show on violence and pornography in the media titled "When the Whip Comes Down." She emphasizes the clear difference between the way men and women are portrayed in pornography. While women are shown gagged, bound, tortured, whipped, and naked, men are clothed and in charge. She believes that rather than violence ending as people get bored, more violent and extreme images appear. Her examples include the transition from pinup-style pornography to child pornography and snuff images.[53]

Like many feminists, Gilboa believes in exposing pornography to the public to make them aware of the violence against women it portrays. She also believes that pornography legitimizes the abuse of women. While defining pornography as a link between sex and violence, Gilboa differentiates "erotica" as lacking violence and not implying hatred of women.[54] Gilboa has advanced an interesting concept that the more opposition and public outcry generated against a particular item such as a film or record, the more sales go up, thus suggesting that some methods of protest against pornography could backfire.[55] (We gratefully acknowledge the contribution made to this book by Netta Gilboa, who provided invaluable resource materials for our use, particularly in the areas of feminist thought and images of pornography.)

Susan Brownmiller states that "hard core pornography is not a celebration of sexual freedom, it is a cynical exploitation of female sexual activity."[56] She says that pornography represents hatred of women and "its intent is to humiliate, degrade and dehumanize the female body for the purpose of erotic stimulation and pleasure."[27]

Women, Brownmiller states, are disgusted by pornography because it strips, exposes, and contorts their bodies for men who get a kick and sense of power from "viewing females as anonymous, panting playthings, adult toys, dehumanized objects to be used, abused, broken and discarded." This, she notes, is the same philosophy as that underlying rape. According to Brownmiller, pornography is a male invention geared to male consumption and designed to dehumanize women and support males ruling by force over women.

Brownmiller notes that the same liberal men who understood that the purpose of Hitler's propaganda machine was to give an ideological base to the Holocaust and that "nigger" jokes and portrayals of blacks as ignorant servants gave an ideological base to continuing black oppression and myths of black inferiority maintain that the hatred and contempt for women in pornographic propaganda is a valid extension of freedom of speech and a constitutional right. Brownmiller comments that it is not very courageous of the American Civil Liberties Union to defend the propaganda rights of a lone crazed American Nazi while Jews are not threatened by storm troopers and concentration camps. She wonders whether that position would change if 42nd Street in New York were lined not with propaganda devoted to the humiliation, rape, and torture of women but

with propaganda depicting the sadistic pleasures of gassing Jews or lynching blacks. Brownmiller examines the contradiction inherent in a liberal view that supports blacks who oppose demeaning portrayals of their race but attacks women who object to the hate literature against their sex, labeling them as opponents of free speech. Brownmiller concludes that the antifemale propaganda that permeates American culture promotes "a climate in which acts of sexual hostility directed against women are not only tolerated but ideologically encouraged."[58]

Kathleen Barry's book, *Female Sexual Slavery*, contains a chapter titled "Pornography: The Ideology of Cultural Sadism." Barry states that pornography brings sadistic violence and sexual enslavement into everyday life. It depicts what one can do not just with a prostitute but with "one's lover, one's wife, and even one's daughter." Through it, the gap between love and violence and "madonnas and whores" is closing, she believes. She notes that against no other group (except women and girls) could blueprints and handbooks for "sadistic violence, mutilation, and even gynocide abound with such safety, support, and impunity."[59]

In Barry's view, female sexual slavery exists whenever women or girls cannot change the immediate conditions of their lives, cannot get out of those conditions, or are subject to exploitation and sexual violence. Any forced sex (which she defines as sex with a woman or girl held in sexual slavery) is rape. She asserts that rape is a political crime of violence against women, "an act of power and domination." She says that sexual violence is a way of socially controlling women, not a collection of isolated, unrelated incidents. Sexual violence terrifies victims and nonvictims, she notes, making "sexual terrorism" a way of life for women.[60]

Barry views the representation of women as sexual slaves in pornography and other media as part of masculine culture. She states that pornography "is a practice of cultural sadism" and a means of spreading this sadism into mainstream behavior and people's sexual practices. She defines pornography as "the media of misogyny."[61]

Pornography, Barry believes, is intended to produce both sexual feelings and actions in its consumers. Masturbation commonly occurs while reading or viewing pornography, she states. She notes that personal fantasy sometimes enters into one's sexual interaction with others and points out that fantasy is learned.

Barry believes that the practices of cultural sadism greatly interfere with the rights of women to life, liberty, and the pursuit of happiness.[62] She concludes:

To live in a society where blueprints for female enslavement and gynocide abound is intolerable. For women to accept it means, . . . participation in our own demise. But to demand the elimination of all pornography, as women must, is immediately to be accused of trespassing on the rights of men who have fought so hard to protect the rights they have been granted. Make no mistake: in pornography the right of freedom of speech cannot be separated from the right to sexual access, just as pornography cannot be separated from behavior.[63]

Gloria Steinem defines the differences between pornography and erotica in *Take Back the Night*. Her definition typifies the feminist view that pornography is harmful, while erotica is acceptable and to be encouraged.

Sex and violence are dangerously intertwined and confused in today's pornography, Steinem claims. For example, she notes, snuff movies and some other pornography "insist that a slow death from sexual torture is the final orgasm and ultimate pleasure." She considers the idea that male sexuality is normally aggressive and that female sexuality normally needs male aggression to be a central part of our male-dominant culture. Why else, she states, do we say *she* was penetrated by a man rather than *she* enveloped him? Pornography is the propaganda that teaches and legitimizes what Steinem calls forms of antiwomen warfare: rape, male–female beatings, forced prostitution, and female sexual slavery. Porn, she states, is about an imbalance of male–female power, not about sex.

According to Steinem, feminist groups are not arguing for censorship of pornography, for such laws would define pornography in male-dominant terms. Under those terms, the wrong people might be punished. Freely chosen heterosexual expression might be considered more pornographic than snuff movies, or contraceptive courses for teens more obscene than bondage. Also, she believes, this would drive pornography underground and make it more profitable.[64]

Kate Millet also has described the difference between erotica and pornography. Erotica, she says, portrays sex as good, delightful, and operating out of goodwill. Pornography portrays sex as dirty, evil, and secret. Even so, Millet states, the end of censorship—of sexually explicit materials is a step forward.[65]

Women Against Pornography (WAP) has acknowledged that an antipornography movement can threaten lesbian lifestyles, for lesbianism has often been seen as "pornographic" behavior. WAP has made it clear, as have most feminist antipornography

groups, that it opposes any definition of pornography that includes lesbianism.[66] (We point out that if lesbian sexual activities are portrayed as violent or nonerotic, many feminists would oppose such depictions.)

Charlotte Bunch asks, "[W]hat kind of society . . . calls love and affection between two women perverse, while male brutality is not only considered not perverse but made profitable?" Bunch calls the United States a "pornographic patriarchy." Lesbian love has nothing to do with pornography, she says, which is based on woman hatred and not woman love. She calls lesbian scenes in pornography "phony" because they distort lesbianism to make it fit male fantasies. She believes that women can tell the difference between "eroticism" (which celebrates sexuality) and "anti-female pornography."[67]

Feminist Myrna Kostash believes that pornography, far from being an alternative to sexual repression, is in fact contempt for women and traffic in their sexuality. Thus, pornographer Larry Flynt is no dissident, she says, but rather a pimp. She points out that pornography, viewed as harmless fantasy by some men, is seen by women as humiliating and injurious to womanhood. Kostash says that it is not coincidental that the explosion in imagery of violence toward women comes at the same time as the struggle for women's liberation. As women demand their share of power and wealth, she notes, men desperately defend their authority by depicting women in increasingly "grotesque" ways, as if reducing women to despised sexual functions makes them vanish.

Kostash says that pornography is no more sexually liberating than was the so-called sexual revolution of the 1960s. She quotes English art critic John Perger as stating that the sexual revolution was about male liberation—making women shared property instead of private property. Like other feminists, Kostash believes that sexual violence is a matter of power and control, not sex. She makes it clear that opposition to pornography is not a desire to legislate sexuality. Rather, it is the "need to delegitimize images of male supremacy over women."[68]

Shere Hite, in *The Hite Report on Male Sexuality*, concludes that "our entire gender has been raped, physically, emotionally and spiritually by our culture." That culture, through the media, reinforces the idea that men get or take sex from women, conquer or possess them. One common theme is that women who say no really mean yes. According to Hite, sexual intercourse has traditionally symbolized male ownership and dominion of women. Contrary to being biological sex urges, rape and buying women through pornography are extensions of this ideology, Hite claims.[69]

In Hite's view, pornography reflects our patriarchal society, in which women are used for men's pleasure. This propaganda reinforces in men the idea that all women can be bought. Importantly, when men look at pornography together, the idea of male ownership of women is reinforced in a type of male bonding. Hite notes that most women do not like the way women are portrayed in pornography. While people have the right to see and read about intimate relationships in order to sort out their lives and feelings, pornography does not serve that purpose, Hite notes. Instead, pornography shows a woman submitting to "a stronger, threatening, perhaps hostile and violent male." Women are much more likely than men to be tortured, humiliated, and dominated in pornography. As Hite points out, even in soft-core pornography exhibiting a "come and get me" pose, the woman is dominated—by the primarily male viewer. Hite fears that the continued spread of pornography will reinforce the stereotypical attitudes toward women that have already done much harm and will make relationships between men and women slower to change.[70]

The Hite study was based on questionnaires returned by 7,239 men. This research uncovered some interesting male responses concerning their thoughts about pornography. For example, Hite found that most of the men who were in their 20s or 30s had first seen pornography when they were very young and had first learned about sex from it. (This, clearly, could have frightening consequences in the way men treat women and believe women want to be treated. As we saw in chapter 2, pornography depicts an unrealistic, fantasy-oriented view of sex.)

The men in Hite's survey saw pornography as a type of male bonding. They lusted over pornographic pictures together as a form of entertainment. Pornography was an important part of masturbation for some of the men. Only a few of them had never looked at pornography.

The survey produced interesting results when the men were queried about what type of pornography they liked. Hite found that the key to arousal for most men was eye contact in the photos, which conveyed the feeling that "she wants *me*." Most preferred soft-core pornography, which they described as portraying beauty and being in good taste. However, a minority liked more explicit sex. Interestingly, most of the men surveyed complained that hard-core pornography was degrading, but they said that they would use it if nothing "better" was available. Many men were confused by their reactions to such pornography, for they became excited even when they found the material offensive or degrading. Only a few men spoke out strongly against pornography, calling it dehumanizing and "sexploitation." Others said it was violent, sadomasochistic, and lustful.

While some of the men felt pornography was educational, only a few said it represents "certain elemental truths about how men and women really are—both psychologically and sexually." Several men said pornography gives sexual misinformation: the multiple orgasm myth, the myth that many women would like to be raped, and the idea that women are hot, always ready for sex, when in fact it often takes a full evening of togetherness before women desire sex. However, even when men found pornography to be sexist and misleading, they said they were aroused by it.[71]

In *Pornography and Silence,* Susan Griffin argues that pornography, rather than being a love of the life of the body and an expression of human erotic feeling and desire, is "a fear of bodily knowledge, and a desire to silence eros." She views the entire history of civilization as a struggle between the force of eros and our minds' attempts to forget eros. Pornography, she states, would replace nature (eros) with a delusion of "cultural" power. And yet, she notes, culture need not be opposed to eros, for the individual's unity with all things and knowledge of the body are major characteristics of the "very forms of culture: language and image."[72]

Griffin views culture as opposing nature through violence and taking revenge on it. She calls the "pornographic mind" the "mind of our culture."[73] According to Griffin, women, by inspiring sexual desire in men, remind them of their own bodies; men, when they want women, lose control, for their bodies and natural existence begin to take control of their minds. But in pornography, men picture the natural with them still in control. Griffin states, "[T]he sight of a woman's body reminds him of the power of his own body, which is nature, over his mind, which is culture. Thus, for a few moments, his self-image dies and he is humiliated."[74]

Griffin believes that men make bonds with each other through a pornographic culture that excludes real women and creates a false image of women that men share. Like dolls, women's bodies are molded to please men. She states that pornography's revenge against nature is to deprive matter of spirit, to humiliate women's bodies by pitting their physical survival against the needs of their souls, thus destroying those souls. She notes that sadomasochism does not come from biological behavior; rather, the concepts of women as masochists and men as sadists were shaped by culture.[75]

Pornography promotes an idea of nature as aggressive and cruel, with culture finding "human instinct evil," Griffin notes. A huge body of scientific data seeks to disprove this. While the pornographer claims that pornographic fantasies will release minds from obsession with violence, pornographic images and words teach that only violence will release the mind. It is certainly ironic that the fantasy of silencing women promoted by pornography masquerades as a cry for freedom, Griffin notes.[76]

Griffin finds it illogical that social science tells us that images shape behavior while some social scientists argue that pornographic images have no effect. Mass media advertising that uses porn images to sell products confirms that such images sell. Even the pornographer, who claims that his product does not cause certain events, argues that pornography is a necessary stimulus for some to be able to participate in any sexual act. "Pornography is *intended* to affect behavior, it is *expected* to affect behavior and it does affect behavior," Griffin states. In fact, there is a relationship between culture and the event, she concludes, claiming that the pornographic imagination can lead to actual murder and pointing out that pornography is in itself a sadistic act.[77]

Because the pornographic idea is madness, a delusion, it must assault reality and try to change it to fit the illusion, Griffin argues. The pornographer is not sane and has a madman's commitment to the illusion. He sees himself as invulnerable and places himself (culture) above nature (woman). He fears reality (real women) will destroy him. He imagines his fantasy will become an event, and ultimately it does. The final solution for the pornographic mind is to replace nature (reality) with culture, Griffin believes. Falling under the power of nature (woman) is considered a source of evil and tragedy, she states. Culture chooses to repress knowledge of the body, believing that such knowledge can be had only in the destruction of the body.[78]

According to Griffin, we shape ourselves after cultural images. Thus, our ideas of man and woman are cultural choices and have nothing to do with reality. In reality, the "feminine" traits (grace, sensuality, intuition, carnality, vulnerability, softness, beauty, concrete knowledge, and passion) and the "masculine" traits (language; ability to calculate, create, and generate ideas; desire and capacity to understand; desire to know, master, and craft; longing for meaning) are truly "human" qualities, she states.[79]

"The idea that a woman might reject a man seems to exist at the heart of culture's rage against women, in both pornographic fantasy and actual event," Griffin says.[80] Often, she notes, the theme of rejection is behind male acts of violence. When a woman rejects a man, he does not control her. Thus, rejection implies humiliation. Culture expresses power over nature by rejecting women. Yet few people conform precisely to culture's idea of how they should be.[81]

Griffin argues that women have been silenced throughout history by means such as force, not having their writings published, making them invisible in history, making their testimony suspect in court, rape, wife beating, and ensuring that women of genius are spent obscurely. As women start to believe the pornographic lies all around them and mold themselves to society's image of what they should be, they cease to know themselves, their experience is destroyed, and their real self is silenced and denied. Women become adept at impersonating the female stereotype—the pornographic image. Women are not present as "beings." We imitate what we love, Griffin points out, adding that people make themselves into the images others have of them. In both image and fact, she says, the "pornographic culture annihilates the female self." This is an expression of sadomasochism. Silence is at the heart of women's condition—the "inability to reveal."

Griffin believes that pornographic culture defames the female being by portraying women as attracting rape and making the great women of history look frigid or like whores. Not only does the pornographic mind give us a pornographic image of women, it also erases any image of women that might contradict that pornographic image. Women also are erased by being ignored by culture, by being made invisible. Their presence is not recognized, their work not recognized, their role in history not reported. Thus, women begin to believe that their identity is nothingness. They cannot be content, however, because their souls long for expression—to be seen and heard.[82]

CRITIQUES OF THE FEMINIST VIEW

Helen Hazen critiques the feminist viewpoint of pornography in *Endless Rapture: Rape, Romance and the Female Imagination.* Hazen's chapter on pornography contains an interesting commentary about women's attitudes toward pornography. She cites a 1975 study by Lois Gould. Based on interviews with fifty women, Gould found that women were offended by the nude male pinups in magazines such as *Playgirls, Viva,* and *Foxlady* and that most readers of such magazines were male homosexuals.[82] Surprisingly, Gould found that a top "turn-on" for women was the pornographic novel *Story of O* in which a woman is sexually enslaved, degraded, and tortured at the hands of an aristocrat. Another turn-on was Clark Gable's carrying a struggling Vivien Leigh up the stairs in *Gone with the Wind.* Gould attributed the turn-on of women to these and other rape scenes to the theme of masochism in female sexuality. According to Hazen, Gould agreed with Robin Morgan that the trend of women viewing themselves as masochists will continue until women get a more positive and assertive self-image. Gould found that the women she interviewed had a longing for "overpowering tenderness" and, unlike men, did not want scenes of genital close-ups without it.[84]

Hazen attacks Gloria Steinem's description of the differences between pornography and erotica by suggesting that erotica, too, is just selling sex with no real pleasure. "The message of pornography is not inherently one of violence, nor is its purpose to create or reinforce images of inequality," Hazen states. She says that it is wrong for Steinem to imply that by removing violence and domination from sex, it will turn into love or erotica. To show this, she gives an example of a man who began his career writing pornography and was advised by a publisher to stick to the following five plots:

1. An unsuccessful businessman is seduced and trained by a knowledgeable woman, preferably the boss's wife. In turn, he enchants his wife and becomes successful at work.
2. The unsuspecting repairman stumbles into the home of a lovely and lonely lady.
3. The younger man is trained into successively more interesting episodes by an older woman.
4. Next-door neighbors in suburbia discover each other.
5. Two women and one man.[85]

(We note that the plots described are so vague that one cannot tell whether they would involve violence or domination or subordination of women, but conceivably they might not.)

While Steinem is correct that pornography is evil, Hazen states, her account contradicts "both fact and feminism." For, she argues, pornography is "first and foremost the depiction of sexual acts, and I do not believe that Steinem wishes to banish sex peremptorily. Nor does she want to offer love such unabashed approval, much of feminism being a plea for women not to fall in love." She claims that Steinem's main thesis is that pornography is wrong because women do not like it and therefore it must be changed so that they do. Hazen states that mainstream pornography does not peddle sadism, violence, bondage, or child sex.[86] (Remember that she wrote this in 1975.)

Hazen says that pornography's purpose is "to help men masturbate" and to sexually titillate, but not to exclude love or "the erotic." She believes that the wish to be aroused by pornography "is so foreign to females that the feminists cannot recognize its simplicity." Women will not be able to create their own pornography until they recognize this, she notes.[87]

Although feminists have written about sex explicitly, they have not created pornography, Hazen states, for their writings are intended to describe a woman's attitude toward sex, not to arouse women. By calling for erotica, feminists have worked themselves into a corner where equality demands "sameness" with men. Hazen mentions the difficulty in determining whether or not something is erotic.[88]

Hazen believes that what triggers women's lust is the very literature that feminists would eliminate for its shabby treatment of women—romance. She notes that women try to translate their romantic feelings into sexual desire, while men, when they love women, work at turning sexual desire into romance.[89]

Susan Kappeler in *The Pornography of Representation* states that feminists have shifted the focus of the pornography debate from "dirt" and "obscene" to violence against women and the rights of women. She urges them to move from a content orientation to an analysis of "representation." Like other feminists, Kappeler believes that women have not been heard on this issue because their statements have been overridden by the pornographers, their customers, and male decision makers. She calls obscenity law "the preoccupation of the bourgeois community with its self-image." The real pornography issue, she states, is the harm to women—namely, sexism—not indecency.[90]

Kappeler cites Deirdre English as claiming that feminists have moved beyond advocating prohibition of pornography and recognize the dangers of aligning with censorship forces that would censor feminist books along with pornography. As a result, feminist groups lobbying against pornography lack clear political objectives and tend not to state what action other than protest would be appropriate. English says that a major problem with the feminist position is hopelessly blurring the distinction between pornography and erotica. Kappeler feels that English's call to try to understand male difficulties involving pornography is a waste of feminist effort. She questions English's belief that what men see makes little difference in their behavior if they can distinguish between fantasy and real life.

Kappeler notes that feminists have a dangerous conception that changing the genitals of the porn producers will result in positive sexual images of women, pointing out that many women are "gender traitors" who have been culturally apprenticed to male views and produce "virulent anti-woman dis-course, representations and politics." She believes that making men into sex objects will not solve the problems with pornography and could lead to equal exploitation rather than an end to exploitation.[91]

In Kappeler's view, men's continuing to "see" women as objects of their pleasure is enough "behavior" to qualify for change:

> The fundamental problem at the root of men's behavior in the world, including sexual assault, rape, wife battering, sexual harassment, keeping women in the home and in unequal opportunities and conditions, treating them as objects for conquest and protection—the root problem behind the reality of men's relations with women, is the way men see women, is Seeing.[92]

Thus, she argues, men's cultural self-representation is proof of their behavior. The men in the peep shows and movie theaters fantasizing, viewing, and masturbating are real. The only make-believe part is the woman object. Kappeler calls pornography the "cultural archeplot of power," a plot for the subjugation of women, which women need to recognize.[93]

FEMINIST ACTIONS:
HOW THEY FIGHT PORNOGRAPHY

Feminist author Robin Morgan, who was once jailed as a result of a feminist protest against pornography, states that pornography's message is domination rather than reciprocity: "It defines sex as male aggression and the female body as a target for conquest." She notes that today's pornography depicts the "normal" male as a sadist and the "healthy" female as a willing victim. According to Morgan, even so-called female porn (created by the same purveyors as other pornography) has never been widely read by women, who seem to be more aroused by romance—"emotional contact, affection, passion, tenderness, in other words, *relationships* between persons, not mere organs."[94]

"[P]orncrats," Morgan says, conveniently equate all opposition to pornography with opposition to free speech. But, she notes, the Bill of Rights is very precious to feminists, who are aware that witch-hunts are likely to begin, "again," with "us." For example, while *Playboy* and *Penthouse* thrived with a combined circulation of 29 million readers a month (in 1978), *Ms.* magazine was the target of attempts to restrict its distribution or to ban it.[95]

Morgan suggests numerous ways to oppose pornography that are consistent with the First Amendment:

1. Treat pornography as an exception to First Amendment protections under theories of its interfering with the civil rights of others, its presenting a clear and present danger to women's lives and honor, and its inciting violence against women and its violating general public nuisance laws.
2. Examine communities' experiments with zoning and display laws.
3. Ask how many males use pornography to pressure women into sex acts or sexual frequency that they dislike. Ask how some sex therapists can use pornography to change people's sexual orientation yet claim there is no connection between pornography and sex practices. Ask how some therapists can suggest pornography as a way to liberate women when it means making them fit male views of sexual freedom.
4. Boycott publishers and producers who profit from pornography and products that advertise in "misogynistic contexts."

5. Picket. For example, photograph pornography customers and paste their photos on posters. (Some protesters have gone so far as to paste stickers across pornography stating it degrades women or to paint messages on exploitive billboards. These are referred to as "guerrilla tactics.")

6. Urge newspapers to restrict pornographic advertising.

7. Research and expose the pornographers and their backers.

8. Insist that public officials cease collaborating with the "New Pornocracy."

9. If necessary, resort to civil disobedience.[96]

According to Morgan, "Pornography and its offspring, child pornography, are ways of terrorizing women, of telling us to stay in our place, of telling us who's boss. . . . A woman can't go past a newsstand today without feeling a psychic rape. That's why pornography is a feminist issue."[97]

Since the late 1970s, feminists have sponsored "Take Back the Night" marches aimed at demanding for women the same right men have to walk the streets without fear of physical violence. These demonstrations publicize the right of women to fight back against violence to themselves and other women. At issue is the right of women to be free from physical and emotional abuse by men. Among the "Take Back the Night" organizers' concerns are domestic violence such as battering and rape, violence in institutions, sexual harassment on the job and pornography. Large numbers of people have participated in "Take Back the Night" events.[98] The marches call attention to the problems of violence against women and the violence toward women depicted in pornography.[99]

Some feminists have pointed out that the "legitimate" media contribute to the pornography industry by making it look respectable.[100] Canadian feminists have noted that Canada's education system is built on the assumption that people learn from and imitate images from books and other media. Ironically, in the real world, the few dollars thrown at rape and sexual violence prevention are far outnumbered by "pornographic counter-education."[101]

Some feminist works have been published by the division of *Playboy* that publishes books. Women's rights advocates argue that women should be made aware of the publishers of such books so that they can make informed decisions about whether to buy or use them. A group called Feminists in Alternative Business from Chicago wants authors to consider all other ways of publishing before going to *Playboy*. The group also opposes using *Playboy* money to fund feminist publications and organizations.[102]

Feminist Nikki Craft is well known for her acts of civil disobedience that focus on sexism. Her organization, Citizens for Media Responsibility Without Law (Outlaws for Social Responsibility), sells stickers that read: "Penthouse: RAPE MANUAL." She urges a boycott of major companies that advertise in *Penthouse* and, she says, that support violence against women. She also urges a boycott against the printer and major distributor of *Penthouse*. She suggests that people write to Bob Guccione, the publisher of *Penthouse,* and ask why he has never appeared nude in the magazine. Some of her group's leaflets picture nude caricatures of various pornography publishers.[103]

Craft and her followers have torn up pornography and been arrested many times for civil disobedience. She has marched topless to protest discriminatory nudity laws. She wrote "Violence in the media equals violence in the society" over seventeen miles of sidewalks and roads in Santa Cruz, California. Craft also created the "Myth America Pageant" to boycott the Miss America Pageant, which she believes exploits women's bodies, and she threw meat at beauty contests.[104]

Citizens for Media Responsibility Without Law has a poster with a "nude" picture of Larry Flynt (*Hustler* publisher) with chocolate syrup on him. Caption: "I'm Black and Blue by the Women's Movement and I love it! Wanted! Larry Flynt for Inciting the Rape and Murder of Women and Children." A public service parody from the group targets *Penthouse* printer Meredith Corporation as "successful, white businessmen, and we're people too!" The brochure reprints bondage and torture photos from that magazine and states: "With our exceptional printing technology we make Bob Guccione's dismal morality look good. You might say that his pimping of women, glorification of violence and degradation of sexuality comes out looking as American as apple pie. Won't you write us and let us know what you think."[105]

Craft once published a list of sixteen hundred men who were indicted for sex offenses in Dallas County—to get rid of the anonymity that lets them rape over and over. The American Civil Liberties Union claimed that this violated the men's privacy, she said.[106]

Her group boycotted films such as *Texas Chainsaw Massacre* and *Dressed to Kill* by having a woman lie down on the sidewalk; covering her with a sheet, chocolate, and ketchup; and propping a chain saw next to her with a poster reading "Boycott Texas Chainsaw Massacre: Violence is Not Entertaining."

Craft says that she uses civil disobedience against pornography because she wants a citizens' mandate against it and she believes that education is the way to accomplish that.[107]

FEMINIST COMMENTS ON THE MORALITY PERSPECTIVE

Feminist attorney Martha Langelan believes that pornographers and puritans have a lot in common: both believe that women should be powerless, submissive, and totally controlled by men.[108] Conservatives say that pornography is immoral because it exposes the body. Liberals claim that pornography is one more aspect of our expanding sexuality. Feminists state that pornography is the ideology of a culture that promotes and condones abuse of women.[109]

For moralists, the wrongness of pornography lies in its pleasure. According to Irene Diamond, they also believe that battered women, rape victims, and other female victims of abuse are fallen women responsible for their own fate. (We disagree.) On the other hand, Diamond states, feminists are concerned about the relationship between pornography and actual violence against women.[110]

The Task Force on Prostitution and Pornography (TOPP) says that Christian fundamentalists are the longest existing, most vocal opponents of pornography. TOPP notes that the fundamentalists oppose any material that depicts explicit sexual acts outside the traditional monogamous heterosexual marriage: "Because their interest is in protecting traditional morality and preserving the nuclear family, they see pornography as a threat because it depicts and promotes sexual alternatives to this idealized lifestyle."[111]

Nikki Craft states that her organization, Citizens for Media Responsibility Without Law, refuses to align itself with the right wing or to have its work used to support any effort toward sexual repression. Craft says that she opposes the "very concept of decency."[112]

According to Gloria Steinem, right-wing antipornography groups misdefine pornography and, unlike some feminists, want to censor it. These groups, she believes, define pornography as all that is not virginal or motherly.

Steinem says that one problem concerning pornography is the confusion of all nonprocreative sex with pornography: "Any description of sexual behavior, or even nudity, may be called pornographic or obscene (a word whose Latin derivative means *dirty* or *containing filth*) by those who insist that the only moral purpose of sex is procreative, or even that any portrayal of sexuality or nudity is against the will of God."[113] Yet, Steinem notes, sexual desire exists at times when humans cannot procreate and is a form of bonding.

Steinem also speaks of a fear by some right-wing persons that the patriarchal structure will be upset if women have sexual and reproductive freedom. She claims that antiequality groups denounce sexual education and family planning as pornographic and try to use obscenity laws to prevent mailing of contraceptive information. The target of these groups is any sex or nudity outside of the context of patriarchal marriage, and, she notes, they support forced childbirth.[114]

Helen Hazen, in her critique of the feminist view of pornography, states that feminists do not object to pornography on the traditional ground that sex is a private matter that should not be publicly displayed or the belief that it contains no redeeming social value. Rather, she says, they disapprove because the actors are not having a good time and demand a new pornography based on their own standards. She labels these demands "an embarrassment" that opens the door to treating males as mere bodies, too. Hazen concludes that feminists who seek their own pornography have not discovered its true nature, for all pornography lacks desire and love.[115]

In *Pornography and Silence*, Susan Griffin argues that pornography, the church, and Judeo-Christian culture all reduce women to material objects without souls who "can only be 'loved' physically."[116] While there exists in pornography the idea of spirit (man) separate from matter (woman), the same idea of separation of flesh and spirit is a biblical theme. Griffin notes that the Marquis de Sade's acts resembled the inquisitions. She says that the pornographer is obsessed with the idea of transgressing the morality of the church, and both Sade and the church fathers chose the same victim for their rage—the body of a woman. Both "share an ideology which conceives of women as the vessel of evil."

Griffin states that in the thinking of the church fathers, a virgin is pure, and her soul can be loved because her body has not been touched. In contrast, the whore, who has had sexual experience, is defiled, and only her body can be "loved." She notes that pornographers are obsessed with the virgin and the whore. Pornography reprimands the virgin for prudery, rages against her for rejection, and punishes her for carnality. Satisfaction is derived from humiliating the virgin and destroying her spirit. The virgin in pornography becomes a whore after she is raped. But pornography portrays virgins as enjoying rape, and thus they have the souls of whores beneath their innocence.

The ordeal suffered by women (and sometimes by men, often children) in pornography is a sadomasochistic ritual that Griffin compares to Christ's martyrdom.[117] She describes the whipping, torture and crucifixion of Christ as a sadomasochistic ritual, the "origin" of culture's "torture of the body." She says that we are asked to imitate Christ's death. Thus, the obscene mind and the Judeo-Christian vision of the world are two faces of the same sensibility. She believes that Christianity teaches a hatred of knowing flesh, has a profound distrust for the sensual world as dangerous, and teaches that the danger of beauty leads one to hell. Pornography also distrusts the sensual world and spreads the story of women leading men to the devil with their beauty.[118]

Maureen Burnley believes that the sight of feminists politicizing women with right-wing views over the pornography issue (civil rights approach) is shaking people up. She says that it is inaccurate to think that right-wing women want to use this issue only to advance their own cause, that there is no common cause among women, and that the women's movement can grow only by the growth of the left. The male-controlled media, Burnley states, are trying to make this into a left versus right issue, but all women—right-wing, left-wing or apolitical—are pornography victims. She says that the fact that conservative women have joined feminists in the antipornography fight does not make it any less legitimate.[119]

CONCLUSION

Andrea Dworkin summarized the state of the feminist antipornography movement in a speech during a "Take Back the Night" march. She said that women who see pornography in small bits and pieces will develop a "useful rage," but those who study it in depth will turn into mourners. She stated, "And life, which means everything to me, becomes meaningless, because these celebrations of cruelty destroy my very capacity to feel and to care and to hope. I hate the pornographers most of all for depriving me of hope."

Dworkin described how pornography makes some people want to destroy it by bombing and razing theaters, bookstores, and publishing houses. She said that people can be part of a revolutionary movement, or they can mourn. And she concluded, "Perhaps I have found the real source of my grief—we have not yet become a revolutionary movement."[120]

NOTES

1. Robin Morgan, "Theory and Practice: Pornography and Rape," in *Take Back the Night: Women on Pornography*, ed. Laura Lederer. (New York: Bantam Books, 1980), 131.
2. "Demands," *Women Against Pornography Newsreport* 7 (September/October 1984): 352–71.
3. Women Against Pornography, personal correspondence, 25 June 1988.
4. Ibid.
5. Ibid.
6. Pornography Resource Center *Pornography: A Practice of Inequality* (Minneapolis: Pornography Resource Center, 1986.
7. Feminist Anti-Censorship Task Force, *Who We Are* (New York: Feminist Anti-Censorship Task Force, no date).
8. Ibid.
9. Caught Looking, Inc., *Caught Looking: Feminism, Pornography and Censorship* (New York: Caught Looking, Inc., 1986).
10. Nan Hunter, Testimony before the Attorney General's Commission on Pornography, Chicago, 25 July 1985.
11. Citizens for Media Responsibility Without Law, ["Sex is not Obscene! The real obscenity is the marketing of women as products—The dehumanization and glorification of violence,"] (Oshkosh, Wisc.: Citizens for Media Responsibility Without Law [Outlaws for Social Responsibility], no date).
12. Nikki Craft, personal correspondence, 20 April 1988.
13. "Resolution on Pornography," National NOW Times, August/September 1985, 6–7.
14. Task Force on Pornography and Prostitution, *Prosti-*

tution and Pornography Are Forms of Abuse, (Madison, Wisc.: Task Force on Prostitution and Pornography).

15. Ibid.
16. Ibid.
17. Ibid.
18. Catharine A. MacKinnon, "The Civil Rights Approach To Pornography" (Testimony before the Attorney General's Commission on Pornography 24–25 July 1985), 1–2.
19. Ibid., 3–5.
20. Caryn Jacobs, "Patterns of Violence: A Feminist Perspective on the Regulation of Pornography," *Harvard Women's Law Journal* 7 (1984): 5–55, 9.
21. Ibid., 13–17.
22. Ibid., 18–23.
23. Ann Jones, "A Little Knowledge," in *Take Back the Night: Women on Pornography,* ed. Laura Lederer (New York: William Morrow & Co., 1980), 183.
24. Ann Simonton, "Bust," *City on a Hill,* 18 March 1982.
25. "Pornographic Media Showing Violence Induce Certain Behavior by Women," *Media Report to Women,* January/February 1983, 8.
26. Sarah J. McCarthy, "Pornography, Rape, and the Cult of Macho," *The Humanist,* September/October 1980, 11.
27. Ibid., 14, 16.
28. Dorchen Leidholdt, *Some Notes on Objectification: From Objectification to Violence,* (New York: Women Against Pornography, no date).
29. Andrea Dworkin, *Pornography: Men Possessing Women* (New York: G.P. Putnam's Sons, 1981), 13–24.
30. Ibid., 30.
31. Ibid., 65.
32. Ibid., 51–53.
33. Ibid., 56, 57, 80.
34. Ibid., 89, 100.
35. Ibid., 101–18.
36. Ibid., 122, 124, 129.
37. Ibid., 136.
38. Ibid., 166.
39. Ibid., 178.
40. Ibid., 180–98.
41. Ibid., 200, 201.
42. Ibid., 207.
43. Andrea Dworkin, "Against the Male Flood: Censorship, Pornography, and Equality," *Harvard Women's Law Journal* 8 (1985): 9–11.
44. Ibid., 11, 12.
45. Andrea Dworkin, "Pornography Is a Civil Rights Issue for Women" (Testimony before the Attorney General's Commission on Pornography, New York, 22 January 1986), 1.
46. Ibid., 1–2.
47. Dworkin, Pornography: Men Possessing Women, 224.
48. Diana E.H. Russell with Laura Lederer, "Questions We Get Asked Most Often," in *Take Back the Night: Women on Pornography,* ed., Laura Lederer (New York: William Morrow & Co., 1980), 24.
49. Ibid.
50. Ibid., 29.
51. Barbara Renchkovsky Ashley and David Ashley, "Sex as Violence: The Body Against Intimacy," *International Journal of Women's Studies* 7 (September/October 1984): 352–71.
52. Ibid., 365.
53. Nancy Bell, "Violence to Women Filters into Public Thinking: Gilboa," *News Journal* ( ), 15 April 1983; "Slide Show on Exploitation of Women Runs Thursday," *Northeastern Illinois Print,* 25 May 1982.
54. "Sex Researcher Relates Pornography, Violence," *Chicago Sun-Times,* 19 June 1983.
55. Netta Gilboa, "Violent Art and Interest Groups" (Paper).
56. Susan Brownmiller, *Against Our Will: Men, Women and Rape* (New York: Simon & Schuster, 1975), 393.
57. Susan Brownmiller, "Let's Put Pornography Back in the Closet," in *Take Back the Night: Women on Pornography,* ed. Laura Lederer (New York: William Morrow & Co., 1980), 253.
58. Brownmiller, *Against Our Will,* 394–95.
59. Kathleen Barry, *Female Sexual Slavery* (Englewood Cliffs, N.J.: Prentice-Hall, 1979), 174.
60. Ibid., 33–37.
61. Ibid., 174, 175.
62. Ibid., 211.
63. Ibid., 214.
64. Gloria Steinem, "Erotica vs. Pornography," in *Outrageous Acts and Everyday Rebellions,* (New York: Holt, Rinehart & Winston, 1983), 219–30.
65. "What Do *You* Think Is Erotic? 10 Women Explain What Turns Them On . . ." *Ms.,* November 1978, 80.
66. Women Against Pornography, *Lesbian Feminist Concerns in the Feminist Anti-Pornography Movement* (New York: Women Against Pornography, October 1979).
67. Charlotte Bunch, "Lesbianism and Erotica in Pornographic America" in *Take Back the Night: Women on Pornography,* ed. Laura Lederer, (New York: William Morrow & Co., 1980), 91–93.
68. Myrna Kostash, "Power and Control: A Feminist View of Pornography," *This,* July/August 1978, 4–7.
69. Shere Hite, *The Hite Report on Male Sexuality* (New York: Ballantine Books, 1985), 742.
70. Ibid., 741, 792, 793.
71. Ibid., 779–92.
72. Susan Griffin, *Pornography and Silence: Culture's Revenge Against Nature* (New York: Harper & Row, 1981), 1, 261.
73. Ibid., 255–61.
74. Ibid., 3.
75. Ibid., 28–32, 49.
76. Ibid., 46.
77. Ibid., 94, 102.
78. Ibid., 105, 106, 111.
79. Ibid., 121–41.
80. Ibid., 141–142.
81. Ibid., 142–50.
82. Ibid., 201–45.

83. Helen Hazen, *Endless Rapture: Rape, Romance and the Female Imagination* (New York: Charles Scribner's Sons, 1983), 106.
84. Ibid., 106–8.
85. Ibid., 111.
86. Ibid., 112.
87. Ibid., 112–13.
88. Ibid., 114–16.
89. Ibid., 116–17.
90. Susan Kappeler, *The Pornography of Representation* (Cambridge, England: Polity Press, 1986), 1, 2, 15, 16, 22, 23.
91. Ibid., 34–38, 40, 41, 43, 47, 48, 50.
92. Ibid., 60–62.
93. Ibid., 104–5.
94. Robin Morgan, "How to Run the Pornographers out of Town and Preserve the First Amendment," *Ms.*, November 1978, 55.
95. Ibid., 78.
96. Ibid., 79, 80.
97. Carol Kleiman, "Old Struggles, New Issues: Morgan: Not Liberated but Growing," *Chicago Tribune*, 17 July 1977.
98. Diana Wilkinson, "Marching to 'Take Back the Night,' " Barbara Varro, 5 October 1980; "Feminists Aims to X-out Pornography," *Chicago Sun Times*, 26 November 1979; *Isthmus Equal Times* 12 August 1979.
99. "Women March to Take Back the Night," Program by the New Haven, Connecticut, Take Back the Night Alliance, (date unknown).
100. "Media Contribute to Pornography Industry by Making It Appear to Be 'Respectable,' " *Media Report to Women*, November/December 1982, 7.
101. "Pornography's Real Intent: Control of Women," *Media Report to Women*, May/June 1983, 8–9.
102. "On Making Pornographic Violence to Women an Accepted Institution in Society," *Media Report to Women*, February 1984, 4.
103. Citizens for Media Responsibility Without Law, leaflets provided to authors in 1985.
104. Elizabeth Zima, "There She Is . . . 'Myth America' . . ." *Cedar Rapids Gazette*, 29 September 1984.
105. Citizens for Media Responsibility Without Law, *Penthouse Gives Us the Business*, (Oshkosh, Wisc.: Citizens for Media Responsibility Without Law).
106. Tricia Lootens and Alice Henery, "Interview: Nikki Craft, Activist and Outlaw," *Off Our Backs*, July 1985, 1–7.
107. Ibid.
108. " 'Feminists Against Pornography' Ask ACLU to Apply Its 'Klan' Policy to Pornographers," *Media Report to Women*, November/December 1982, 5.
109. Laura Lederer, "Introduction," in *Take Back the Night: Women on Pornography*, ed. Laura Lederer. (New York: William Morrow & Co., 1980), 19.
110. Irene Diamond, "Pornography and Repression: A Reconsideration of 'Who' and 'What,' " in *Take Back the Night: Women on Pornography*, ed. Laura Lederer (New York: William Morrow & Co., 1980), 192.
111. Task Force on Prostitution and Pornography, *The Sex for Sale Industries: Writings by Women on Prostitution and Pornography* (Madison, Wisc.: Task Force on Prostitution and Pornography, 1986), 12.
112. Lootens and Henery, "Interview: Nikki Craft," 7.
113. Gloria Steinem, "Erotica vs. Pornography," 224–25.
114. Ibid.
115. Hazen, *Endless Rapture*, 105.
116. Griffin, *Pornography and Silence*, 3.
117. Ibid., 14–23, 46.
118. Ibid., 69–74.
119. Maureen Burnley, "Shake It Up: Some Views on Pornography," *Womenews*, April 1985.
120. Andrea Dworkin, "Speech Exhorts March" *Off Our Backs*, January 1979, 4–5.

8 PRIVATE ENTERPRISE INTERESTS AND THE CIVIL LIBERTARIAN PERSPECTIVE

This chapter presents the perspective of civil libertarian groups and individuals and pornographers (private enterprise) toward pornography. Several major national organizations in the forefront of this viewpoint are listed in Appendix G. We have found that many of these organizations are interconnected through their individual activists. For example, Attorney Burton Joseph is special counsel to Playboy Enterprises, Inc., and chairman of the Playboy Foundation. He has served as a member of the ACLU National Board and is chairman of the Media Coalition.[1] Attorney Nan Hunter, a founding member of the Feminist Anti-Censorship Task Force (FACT), is director of the ACLU Lesbian and Gay Rights Project.[2] Marcia Pally of FACT is a senior editor of Penthouse's *Forum*.[3]

Proponents of the private enterprise interests and civil libertarian view

1. The *Media Coalition, Inc.*, headquartered in New York, is composed of the American Booksellers Association, Inc., the Association of American Publishers, Inc., the Council for Periodical Distributors Associations, the International Periodical Distributors Association, Inc., and the National Association of College Stores, Inc. It was founded in 1973. A May 24, 1986, statement describes the coalition as a trade association that defends the First Amendment right to sell and publish magazines and books containing sexual explictness that are not obscene according to U.S. Supreme Court decisions.

The coalition files suits challenging laws that it believes are unconstitutional and submits amicus curiae briefs in cases that involve sexually explicit materials. Typically, the laws opposed by the coalition are those aimed at regulating pornography (such as the civil rights proposal, zoning, and display of pornography to minors). (This puts this civil libertarian group in the position of defending hard-core pornography.) The coalition also informs its members about state legislative actions concerning works that have any sexual content and writes to legislators to advise them about legislative proposals.

The coalition typically argues that a law it is challenging is unconstitutional because it would have resulted in the suppression of publications that are protected by the First Amendment.[4]

2. The *American Civil Liberties Union* (ACLU) describes itself as the guardian of the Bill of Rights, which guarantees civil liberties, including the freedom of press and speech. The organization says that it acts to defend people's Constitutional rights because it is its duty, not because it always agrees with their views. The ACLU is not defending the ideas themselves; rather, it is defending the "right to express" the ideas. The ACLU states that it most often acts on behalf of those who are especially powerless, such as women, children, and minorities.[5] (We argue that the ACLU does not represent the best interests of women or children in its defense of pornography.)

Jane M. Whicher, staff counsel of the ACLU of Illinois, testified before the Attorney General's Commission on July 24, 1985. She said that the ACLU position on censorship is to "oppose any restraint on the right to create, publish and distribute material" and support the right to "choose what materials one may read or view." It does not evaluate the merit of the speech or urge its circulation. Thus, Whicher said, it is not concerned about whether the attorney general's claim that the nature of pornography is changing is true.

According to Whicher, the ACLU believes that the *Miller* obscenity standard is "inadvisable" because it requires subjective judgments, Whicher said. For

286 SOURCEBOOK ON PORNOGRAPHY

example, the judge or jury must make value judgments about what is "of value." Unpopular or controversial viewpoints are often the ones that get censored; yet these are the ones that the First Amendment was designed to protect. She said that because obscenity cannot be precisely defined, the subjectivity required causes unpredictable results, which gives rise to a chilling effect—people steer clear of expression that might be close to the line of law violation.

The ACLU, according to Whicher, believes in concentrating on legally punishing the act that is the harm—for example, the rape, murder, or theft—not the content of the speech based on beliefs of how that content will affect the recipient. Their notion of an appropriate solution to the advocacy of "bad" ideas is to advocate the contrary view—more speech.

The ACLU, said Whicher, condemns the sexual exploitation and abuse of children, including making of child pornography. However, the organization believes that child pornography should be dealt with by punishing those who abuse the children in the making of the pornography:

> We believe that sanctions such as censorship of the publications or criminal prosecutions of those unconnected with the abuse are neither constitutionally permissible nor wise as a matter of policy. The government should not engage in censorship or the suppression of expression no matter how offensive that expression is.

Whicher also argued, on behalf of the ACLU, that government should not concern itself with exposure of pornography to children at home. The availability of pornography in the home is "no one else's business," and control of such access belongs with the parents, not the government, she said.[6]

The remainder of the information in this chapter dealing with the ACLU is taken from a 1986 ACLU public policy report by Barry W. Lynn, legislative counsel for the organization.[7]

The ACLU, in a brief filed in the child pornography case, New York v. Ferber, argues that the First Amendment protected distribution of child pornography. Those who commit the sexual conduct that results in the pornography should be punished, not the pornographer. The group argues that child pornography laws have done nothing to stem the rise in the sexual abuse of children. The ACLU opposes making knowing possession of child pornography a felony. Its response to the commission call to prohibit computerized information exchanges concerning child pornography or children to be used in child pornography was to claim that this proposal could "reach teenage computer dating services if the services

ultimately 'facilitate' sexual conduct between the teens." The report also states:

> A sad irony in this approach is that in most reported cases of pedophile computer use, examination of the information contained in computer files apparently facilitated prosecutions for underlying sexual assaults. If the defendants had not been such meticulous record-keepers, their offenses against children might have gone undiscovered and unpunished.[8]

The ACLU also came out against commission recommendations that would have made it a crime to advertise information about where child pornography can be found, claiming that it would be unfair to hold magazine publishers liable for unwittingly publishing such information. (We note that much child pornography/prostitution is advertised in "coded" advertisements. Because the majority of such ads are found in child pornography or adult pornography type publications—and not in mainstream publications—it is not believable that the publishers are unaware of the nature of such ads.)

The report attacks the commission for polluting the debate over censorship and sexually explicit material by (1) trying to revitalize "archaic" obscenity law by following the dangerous reasoning that speech should be suppressed for causing bad attitudes (Affirmative speech is the best solution.), and (2) attempting to extract a theory that sexual violence is caused by certain pornography from limited scientific studies.

The ACLU alleges that the commissioners were biased against pornography and that 77 percent of the witnesses who spoke before the commission supported more regulation of pornography. For example, the ACLU notes that antipornography witnesses were not seriously cross-examined, but pro-pornography witnesses were sharply grilled about "tangential issues." The ACLU also charges that the commission staff searched to find antipornography witnesses but did not seek the views of major writers' groups. "[A]dult entertainment" representatives faced possible criminal prosecution for testimony because the commission had no legal right to offer witnesses immunity. The ACLU also says that the commission seemed to look for the most offensive pornographic images. The ACLU sued the commission to gain access to its internal papers.

The Lynn report says that the commission found the task of defining pornography impossible. The ACLU believes that speech may be penalized only if there is "a close and demonstrable causal relationship between speech and violence"—and that imminent lawlessness must be shown. It would treat sexual speech the same way and believes that the U.S. Supreme Court's *Miller* obscenity standards are unconstitutional. There is no difference, it argues, between sexually explicit speech and other speech. Such speech fulfills traditional speech functions, including idea transmission, self-realization promotion, and safety-valve service. Pornography can, according to the ACLU, have a purpose of promoting a political viewpoint involving distribution of power in social relationships (in this case, the group states, an idea that has controlled cultures since human history began to be recorded—namely, that men are dominant and powerful and women are submissive and unprotected). It does not matter if pornography appeals to the emotions and other speech appeals to rational communication, the report states.[9]

While alleging that censorship is a real threat, the ACLU report fails to demonstrate that there have been many book removal attempts at libraries. (We point out that "censorship" occurs every time a library decides to carry some books and not others.) The report also says that the commission wrongly concluded that pornography is becoming increasingly violent.

The Lynn report accuses the commission of omitting (from their final report) information that some phone companies were using revenues from dial-a-porn to help subsidize services to the elderly and poor.

The ACLU report states that if there were no laws on obscenity, "there would be no criminal activity, and, thus, no 'organized crime' involvement."[10]

The Lynn report attacks the commission for sending letters to pornography distributing convenience stores indicating that the final report would include them among the purveyors of pornography. The exercise of such free speech (exposure of the list to the public) apparently persuaded some of the companies to withdraw the pornography from their shelves. The ACLU calls this an unconstitutional intimidation of merchants by the government.

The ACLU notes that the commission report read more like a religious or moral tract "than a serious legal or scientific work."[11] It also alleges that the commission did not use a tough enough standard of proof in judging credibility of witnesses, evidence accuracy, or the causality link between pornography and behavior. Lynn says that the victims of pornography had life histories of sexual abuse and questioned how big a role pornography played in such abuse.

The report claims that much sadomasochistic activity is nonviolent and consensual. Lynn says that it is "legally irrelevant" whether or not a majority of

Americans in public opinion polls favor bans on sexually explicit materials. (He suggests that, if polled, many Americans would not favor our nation's basic constitutional freedoms.)[12]

According to the ACLU, the fact that rapists or molesters enjoy depictions of those acts does not mean that pornography caused them to become molesters or rapists. It was not surprising, the Lynn report states, that most of the research discussed by the commission concluded that "exposure to particular ideas and images can, temporarily at least, change perceptions and attitudes." Such is the purpose and result of "most speech," the ACLU asserts. The Lynn report argues, however, that the research studies are of limited value for the following reasons:

1. The research subjects' past experiences and how those made them feel about sex are unexamined factors that may help explain the study outcomes.
2. It is not known how long the reported effects of the pornography studies last.
3. Laboratories are highly artificial settings that limit transferring those results to real-world predictions.
4. The measure of aggression in the tests only analogizes actual aggression because the experimenter allows it with a guarantee that there will be no punishment. Showing films depicting violence may lead test subjects to believe that the experimenter approves of violence in the experiment context.
5. The Donnerstein design does not allow students who become sexually aroused to masturbate. Perhaps one reason they push the shock buttons is out of annoyance at arousal without relief.

The ACLU report emphasizes that the research did not show that men were induced to rape by viewing depictions of rape. The report notes that the subjects were debriefed from the rape myths by providing them with factual data about the impact of sexual assault, with the result of significant improvements in understanding rape. (We wonder why debriefing is necessary if there is no danger that persons who have been exposed to pornography depicting rape will imitate that behavior. Unfortunately, in the real world, most persons exposed to such pornography will not be debriefed by anyone and are not likely to come across alternative ideas that expose the rape myths.)

The ACLU report also argues that there is no evidence to link sex discrimination to pornography, for if that were true, women would be much better off in places where pornography is not available widely, and they are not. In addition, it emphasizes that in our system of government, actions, not attitudes or ideas, are regulated. This organization also believes that television, advertising, and popular literature are more intrusive in our society than pornography and may be more persuasive. According to the report, pornographic offenses are less serious than crimes such as murder, rape, and robbery; therefore, law enforcement personnel should not divert scarce resources away from those serious crimes to combat obscenity.

The ACLU takes the position that laws that require shielding covers of pornographic magazines are unconstitutional under the First Amendment. It argues that civil rights ordinances are unconstitutional (see chapter 10). And, it argues, broadcasting obscene material over electronic media such as television is constitutional, despite *Miller*.

While the ACLU defends the right of people to protest against things with which they disagree and to petition the government to change laws that they believe are wrong, "some forms of protest are unwise and deleterious to other values like diversity and privacy." Sometimes, it suggests, the rights of others and tolerance should result in one's silence. (The ACLU obviously includes pornography in this category.) It is unwise, the ACLU states, to picket, march, demonstrate, or boycott on behalf of removing theater films or library books. While it is all right to urge someone not to view a film, it is wrong to censor it so it is not available.[13]

The ACLU objects to industry rating systems, such as the film rating system, out of concern that creativity will be stifled. It objects to many of the commission's recommendations and argues that they are a substantial threat to civil liberties. The recommendations objected to include enacting forfeiture provisions as part of obscenity laws; making it an unfair business and labor practice for employers to hire persons to be involved in commercial sexual performances; regulating private sexual practices between consenting adults; regulating pornography on cable television; regulating dial-a-porn; enacting obscenity laws; calling for increased (felony) punishment for second offenses of obscenity laws; creating a law enforcement data bank for obscenity information; prosecuting pornography stars as prostitutes; using bankruptcy laws to close pornographic bookstores; enforcing public health laws in pornographic facilities as a way of prosecuting consenting sex; requiring mandatory prison sentences for second or subsequent violations of federal obscenity laws (this would be "grossly disproportionate to the offense" and would make the massive overcrowding of prisons worse); requiring those involved in producing or distributing pornography to maintain records of performers' ages and consent forms (this would violate privacy and help potential criminal investigations against the persons' interest); prohibiting those under 21 from performing in pornography (unconstitutional); requiring photo labs to report child pornography; and passing the civil rights legislation.

3. *Family Affairs,* a pornographic magazine published by Letters Magazine, Inc., of Teaneck, New Jersey, and distributed by Kable News Company of New York and Mount Morris, Illinois, describes itself as the only magazine about incest that the reading public can buy. It claims to be internationally distributed. It concerns sexual intimacy among family members. Typical examples of article titles from *Family Affairs* include "Cum Crazy Cousin," "Bound to My Sister," "Uncle Harry's Wet Dream," "Grandmother in Bonds," and "A Mother's Love." The publisher says that the articles are actual accounts of incestuous love affairs between family members sent in by readers.

An editorial in the *Family Affairs* of February 1984 expresses the belief that *reading* about incest relationships will encourage readers to share their own family incest experiences with the magazine. (We suggest that these editors apparently believe, contrary to the stated positions of some civil libertarians, that reading can influence people to take certain actions and behave in a particular manner.) The editors refer to this anonymous sharing of incest stories through the magazine as "sharing happy times" with other people. They describe a basic need in people to tell about something they are doing that "isn't quite legal." This, they feel, can relieve guilt without risking discovery.

In the same issue, the editors thank their readers for writing in about their incest experiences. This, they state, keeps the magazine in "tune" with what is actually occurring in society. They say that it also brings sexual enhancement, comfort, and joy to others who "find sexual and emotional fulfillment within the bounds of their own family group." The editorial concludes by stating, "FAMILY AFFAIRS loves you."

Despite the fact that real-world incest is a serious criminal offense, the tone of *Family Affairs* (and many similar magazines) is to make incest appear to be a joyous, acceptable, and healthy sexual activity by describing, in vivid detail, sexual acts between family members. Incest themes are promoted in modern pornography by using the terms or code words "family" (literature) and "taboo" (films). A frequently repeated phrase in *Family Letters* (a companion publication) is "The family that plays together stays together" (an obvious pun on the religious theme "The family that prays together stays together").

The pornography producers have invested considerable time, money and resources to produce materials with incest themes. Even though in the real world acts of incest are serious criminal offenses, such acts are portrayed and condoned in widely available "adult" films under the code name "Taboo." (For example, "Taboo: American-Style, Tape I, II, III, IV"; "Taboo, I, II, III and IV"; "Black Taboo", and a recently remarketed seventies-vintage incest film called "Mother, Brother and I.") Taboo-theme films employ adult persons as actors, but the films clearly eroticize the sexual abuse of children.

(We believe that the "family" magazines and the "taboo" films are, in effect, substitutes for child pornography, and we are concerned that their widespread availability and absence of public protest approves and encourages the sexual abuse of children.)

4. The *Adult Film Association of America* (AFAA) represents two hundred distributors, exhibitors, and producers of sexually explicit videos and films. The AFAA credo contains four points:

1. Adult films will only be produced for and exhibited to adults and "persons not of legal age will not be admitted."
2. "Adult" is that term defined by the authorities of each community, but never any person under age 18.
3. "That we will produce and exhibit only films that are in conformity with the Free Speech provisions of the Constitution of the United States of America."
4. "That we in no manner will condone, produce, or exhibit child pornography in any form."

An attorney for the AFAA told the Attorney General's Commission on Pornography that the organization would consider materials depicting excrement or bestiality or made with "unconsenting" children or adults off-limits. Yet the association has no enforcement mechanism to ensure that the guidelines outlined above are followed.[14]

5. The *Feminist Anti-Censorship Task Force* (FACT) is described in chapter 7; FACT views on the civil rights ordinances are presented in chapter 10.

The San Francisco Bay Area chapter of FACT argues that censorship of pornography is more likely to stifle calls for change, especially those of feminists and gays, than it is to control the problems it is intended to solve, such as child abuse. The Bay Area group refers to the controversial sexually explicit book of photographs titled *Show Me* as a first-class sex education book for children and says that that book was one of the first "victims" of child

pornography legislation. The group says that children are "empowered" by more information about sex.[15]

The FACT Book Committee produced a book titled *Caught Looking: Feminism, Pornography and Censorship,* which, aside from being an attack on the civil rights approach to pornography, is filled with pornographic black-and-white photos.

Attorney Nan D. Hunter, a founding member of FACT and director of the ACLU Lesbian and Gay Rights Project, testified before the Attorney General's Commission. FACT, according to Hunter, is a "feminist" organization created to oppose the civil rights ordinances that it believes would "perpetuate rather than subvert disabling stereotypes concerning women and sexuality." Hunter cited Kate Ellis, who argues that while much pornography expresses woman hatred and patriarchal values, it also expresses radicalism by rejecting hypocrisy and sexual repression. (These women view sexual repression as harmful to women as a class.) Hunter also claimed that the assumption that pornography has an all-male audience is "incorrect" and that women are starting to produce sexually explicit materials.[16] She said:

Unfortunately, the indicia of male supremacy are found throughout the society, not just in pornography. Pornography is not the cause of the oppression of women nor is it even the primary channel in which that supremacy is reflected, validated and glorified. Other, much more powerful, established and legitimate institutions contribute far more than does the pornography industry to the second-class status of women. Thus we and many other feminists believe that targeting pornography in a civil rights law, as has been attempted by the ordinance in question, is a fundamentally misguided attempt to get at the root causes of an ideology which tells us that women are inferior and incompetent.

Moreover, such an approach holds real dangers for women which we believe far outweigh the possible benefits from this particular piece of legislation.[17]

Hunter said that FACT opposes the civil rights proposal for the following reasons:

1. FACT believes the proposal has a definitional problem.
2. The ordinance allows the judicial system to interpret its "highly subjective language"—not an advantageous forum for women.
3. The ordinance reinforces sex-based stereotypes and classifications.

4. "We believe that sexually explicit speech as a category should receive greater, not less, protection under the First Amendment."

5. The ordinance is not constitutional. It suppresses protected speech and "creates sex based classifications which are not tailored to remedy the conditions of sexual violence and abuse which do exist."[18]

FACT also opposes obscenity laws and believes that prostitution should be decriminalized. Hunter stated that driving pornography and prostitution underground makes conditions worse for those who work in those industries.

FACT believes that there are more important aspects to remedying porn-related problems, including the need for women to have economic independence; the need for better and more sex education for children and teens; and the need for greater funding for programs for victims of battering, rape, and abuse. Hunter stated that the "demeaning portrayal of women in all media" is a far greater problem than pornography.[19]

The FACT branch in Madison, Wisconsin, describes itself as dedicated to ending sexism, violence against women, and the victimization of children. It stands for true sexual equality and the free choice to pursue and enjoy sexual preferences and alternative lifestyles that do no violence to other people. Its leaders are concerned that the civil rights ordinance could be used against the goals of feminism to which they are committed. They are afraid that the politics, art, and literature of feminists, gays, lesbians, liberals, humanists, socialists, and others with unpopular views and lifestyles also will be targets of censorship.

In a democratic society, FACT (Madison) states, we cannot let some people decide what others can see or read, and we cannot allow thought and idea control. This group encourages debate on the pornography issue and supports expanded community education. FACT expresses a fear that the radical right, which it calls the primary opponent of sexual materials, will decide what to censor. FACT asserts that obscenity laws have been used to deny women access to means of and information about sexual expression, such as birth control and abortion.

FACT has called on feminists to reject the Attorney General's Commission's attempts to censor sexual texts and images as "part of the problem, not part of the solution." These "feminists" believe that the commission agenda was based on conservative beliefs about morality that, in the past, oppressed women by making them dependent on men for "protection," maintaining "the double standard," falsely identifying sexuality as the source of abuse

and violence (rather than pinpointing the inequality of women), and making sex-related information unavailable and shameful. As a result of obscenity campaigns, real people—mostly women, feminists, gay and lesbian artists, those with minority sexual preferences, and independent pornography producers—get jailed, harassed, and prosecuted. This ruining of lives and robbing people of peace of mind is "not the equivalent of ending patriarchy," FACT notes.[20]

6. *Playboy Enterprises, Inc.*, is a private enterprise which profits from pornography. Burton Joseph, special counsel to Playboy Enterprises, Inc., testified before the Attorney General's Commission. He said that censorship of obscenity and pornography is unconstitutional and voiced his opposition to such censorship. According to Joseph, elimination of images, ideas, or words does not make societal problems disappear:

> I have been and continue to be dedicated to what I believe is the foundation of a democratic and free society, that is the assumption that people should be free to choose for themselves, free of governmental restrictions based upon content, what books and magazines they read, what pictures or films they see and what ideas and values they choose to have.
>
> The suggestion that you can keep people from having bad ideas or engaging in anti-social conduct by limiting what books, magazines, pictures, films and art is available is both fallacious and dangerous to a free society. It is the ultimate rejection of the democratic ideal that people are capable of and should be free to have access to the widest range of information, words and images so they can, for themselves, decide what is in their interest.[21]

Joseph described the First Amendment as a check on the power of the majority aimed at protecting the rights of individuals. He stated that "the problem with censorship is that it is insidious. . . . The censor's appetite is insatiable."

Joseph called *Playboy* "an American institution" and said that it has never been found to be obscene in a court of law. He said that the magazine has "an editorial policy that abhors violence" and that there is no sadism, masochism or "celebration of violence" in it.[22] (We note that Joseph's claim does not agree with some of the images we found in *Playboy* and described in chapter 2. Also, it could be argued that the display of women's bodies and body parts for male voyeurism is inherently sadomasochistic.)

The *Playboy* attorney told the commission that

he opposes censorship of "explicit sexual material— 'pornography' " for these reasons:

1. Censorship is unconstitutional and in violation of the First Amendment.
2. Censorship is ineffective to achieve the results desired.
3. Censorship gives false value to that which is censored and creates a demand beyond that which would exist if it was freely available.
4. Censorship is a wasteful allocation of scarce law enforcement resources.
5. Censorship increases the risk of distribution, thereby driving the production into criminal hands who are willing to take greater risks for greater profits and thereby increases the threat of corruption.
6. Censorship is used to justify for the protection of society, but there is no demonstrable evidence showing a causal relationship between explicit sexual imagery and aggression or anti-social conduct that could possibly justify the evils of censorship.
7. Censorship is an attempt to impose moral, religious and social values of some people upon the society as a whole.
8. Censorship is premised upon the infallibility of the judgment of those censoring. This infallibility is contradicted by the judgment of history.
9. Censorship falsely raises the expectation for solutions to social problems and diverts attention from real causes and meaningful attempts at amelioration.
10. Censorship avoids responsibility for individual aggression or antisocial behavior by blaming third parties, and avoids individual responsibility for one's actions by permitting blame to be transferred to "pornography" or television or some other extraneous source as the cause of such conduct.
11. Censorship is incapable of enforcement and thereby demeans the law and diminishes respect for law enforcement and legal process.[23]

The viewpoint of *Playboy* is perhaps best expressed by excerpts from statements written by its publisher, Hugh M. Hefner. The December 1987 issue of that magazine includes excerpts from the "Playboy Philosophy." That philosophy is based on Hefner's belief in the importance of individuals and their right in a free society. He does not believe in permitting government to enter the most private part of people's lives—their bedrooms—and decide what acts may take place there. (We wonder whether Mr. Hefner would prevent government from stopping incest, wife battering, and marital rape in the privacy of people's homes.)

He argues that private acts between two consenting adults should not be outlawed. The publisher of *Playboy* believes that people are hypocritical in protesting against depictions of sexual acts they practice in private. He says that it is wrong for a society to stress the negative side of sex before marriage. Although he prefers personal sex to impersonal sex, Hefner says that he does not oppose the latter unless it harms someone. In his view, suppression of sex is harmful. He says that government should prohibit sexual exploitation and "unwelcome" sexually violent or aggressive acts.

Hefner claims that religious, philosophical, political, medical, social, and racial ideas have, at one time or another, been labeled obscene. He does not believe that books or movies are harmful; their "badness" is a matter of opinion or taste. He opposes paternalistic ideas of keeping some ideas from the general public and says that contemporary psychiatrists know that publications that deal honestly and openly with sex have no or little effect on behavior and any impact they have is healthy.

He also argues that in a society that was sexually free, pornography would lose much of its popularity and that the worst types of pornography flourish in suppressive atmospheres, an argument commonly made by civil libertarians. (We note that real-world experiences do not support this argument. As regulation of pornography has decreased in the United States, more extreme pornography has flourished.)

Hefner believes that when ideas are freely exchanged, the best ones ultimately win out. He states: "Blessed is the rebel—without him there would be no progress."[24]

In the March 1985 issue of *Playboy*, a reply to a letter to the editor argues that giving the power to censor to the state does much more harm than good to society.[25] An example of the type of man whom *Playboy* believes reads *Playboy* is an all-star baseball player who is "Mr. Clean" and "Mr. Conservative."[26]

Playboy has attacked the Attorney General's Commission on Pornography. It accuses the commission of blackmailing retailers into banning men's magazines and calls the commission report its "reptile manifesto." *Playboy* calls the link between pornography and criminal behavior found by the commission a "myth" and argues that it is "societies that practice sexual taboos" that suffer from violence and crime.[27]

In January 1986, *Playboy* called the commission "sexual McCarthyism," accused it of using only witnesses who claimed they were harmed by pornography, and said that the witnesses were not credible. It accused the commission of providing misinformation and reaching unfounded conclusions. Hefner said that the commission was trying to interfere with "our" freedom.[28]

In August 1986, *Playboy*, responding to a letter to the editor, said it was "ludicrous" for the commission to say that there was a link between *Playboy* (and similar magazines) and child abuse. It attacked commission members as "zealots." *Playboy* also printed excerpts from letters to the commission written by members of the Association of American Publishers who argued that they would not trust anyone to decide what pornography is and that people should be free to read and write about what they want.

Playboy also explained why it was suing the commission. The suit claimed that the commission's director sent a letter to numerous companies stating that they had been identified as distributors or sellers of pornography. Partly as a result, some corporations stopped distributing *Playboy* "and certain other lawful publications," the suit claimed. *Playboy* sought to prohibit the commission from blacklisting them and others and taking other actions to censor the sale and distribution of *Playboy* and other publications protected by the Constitution. According to *Playboy*, the letter and threatened public disclosure of the list of corporations achieved results normally achieved by criminal prosecutions without affording constitutional safeguards of the type guaranteed criminal defendants. *Playboy* also claimed that the letter was an "administrative prior restraint" that suppressed lawful speech before it had been ruled upon by a judge. It sought to have the commission declare that it did not consider *Playboy* or other "constitutionally protected materials" to be unlawful or obscene and that it did not suggest distributors be prosecuted for such distribution.[29] (We are of the opinion that, despite its spokespersons' statements, *Playboy* presents women as sexual objects. One edition even contained a full-page cartoon of a little girl leaving the room of an older man saying, "You call *that* being molested!"[30]

7. *Penthouse* is another supporter of the civil libertarian view. The Minotaur Press, Ltd., a Penthouse International Company [according to *Webster's New World Dictionary*, 2d college ed., a minotaur was a Greek mythological monster with the body of a man and the head of a bull (or vice versa in some versions) who was "annually fed seven youths and seven maidens"], published a book by Philip Nobile and Eric Nadler titled *United States of America vs. Sex: How the Meese Commission Lied about Pornography*. The book is based on a series of articles titled "Bedtime for Porno" that had appeared in Penthouse's *Forum* magazine. The articles criticized the regional public hearings of the Attorney General's Commission on Pornography. Nobile is employed by *Forum* as editorial director; Nadler is employed by *Forum* as senior editor.

The book attacks the commission, its members, and some of its witnesses by making fun of them as individuals and ridiculing their beliefs and mannerisms. For example, a feminist antiporn leader is referred to as the "Rubenesque zealot." Linda Marchiano (known as Linda Lovelace in pornographic films) is called the "most famous" pornography victim. Dorchen Leidholt is called "the Squeaky Fromme of Women Against Pornography" (the real Fromme being one of Charles Manson's followers). Dr. Judith Reisman, who did a study (funded by the Justice Department) of cartoons in *Penthouse*, *Playboy* and *Hustler*, is ridiculed for having been a former songwriter for "Captain Kangaroo."[31]

The commission testimony of Dr. Frank Osanka concerning the link between pornography and criminal behavior in the cases of sex murderers such as Thomas Schiro, John Wayne Gacy, and Gary Arthur Bishop is not mentioned in the book. Yet the comment is made that witnesses such as Mary Steinman, the author of the introduction to chapter 4 of this book and a pornography and incest victim, were never taken seriously by the "more sophisticated" commissioners. Nobile and Nadler refer to Steinman as "a little old lady with a heavy past."[32]

In the Nobile and Nadler book, Dr. Victor Cline, a critic of the 1970 Commission report and a psychologist who has worked with pornography victims and offenders, is criticized for not having published the results of his findings. Dr. John Court of Australia is described as looking "fit and handsome in a tight white suit." Dr. Dolf Zillman, well known for his research about the effects of pornography, is described as an "ardent advocate of sadomasochism." Dr. Edward Donnerstein is accused of supporting both sides, being "ambitious," and being "the pivotal figure in the school of slasher criticism."[33]

Patrick Fagan is accused of presenting bogus evidence to the commission and called "a thug from the right-wing Free Congress Research and Education Foundation." Dr. Richard Green is said to have "never met a paraphilia he did not like" and called the "George McGovern of sexology." Former *Playboy* bunnies who testified against pornography are ridiculed in a section titled "Herpes Hideway: Bunny Defectors." Decency supporters are referred to as "the dogs of decency."[34]

Pro-pornography attorney Burton Joseph is described as "a smartly dressed veteran of the obscenity wars" who "carried the *Playboy* standard in Chicago." The book states that *Penthouse* hired its columnist and law professor Alan Dershowitz to debate with the commission in New York. "The fiery law professor put the commission on the griddle. He roasted its 'self-selected, self-serving' witnesses and their testimony."[35]

Marcia Pally of FACT wrote a commentary for the book and an article favoring pornography for the November 1987 issue of *Penthouse*. Pally is employed as a senior editor of Penthouse's *Forum* magazine.

While the Nobile and Nadler book is an editorial of Penthouse International Company, it is not described as such, but is made to look like a civil libertarian work of literature. Penthouse publications such as *Forum*, which has administrative offices in Des Moines, Iowa, and *Hot Talk* advertised the book, beginning with the words "If you think you live in a free society . . . Think Again." They describe the book as perhaps the most important book someone who cares about freedom of speech and the First Amendment will ever read. People are urged to buy it if they are concerned about the censorship movement. The book is described as being a "monumental investigative report" that exposes corruption and abuse of power about the pornography issue.[36]

A postcard included in the book is designed to be sent to the Periodical and Book Association of America for that organization to forward to the president of the United States. The card, addressed to the president, expresses fear of the "growing threat" to "my First Amendment rights" caused by "self-appointed censors" who are taking their lead from the Meese commission. Thus, the book by Penthouse International Company is also a form of political advocacy, action, and lobbying. (We think that it is debatable whether people who buy pornographic publications read the serious articles.)

The April 1985 issue of *Penthouse* contains a "message" from the magazine that depicts fascist dictators and is captioned "The Experts Agree That Censorship Works." Censorship, they state, is the best way to cause agreement on ideas, even bad ones. Censorship succeeded in Nazi Germany and currently works in nations such as Cuba, the Soviet Union, and Iran, the message says. *Penthouse* accuses a "few so-called 'decency' groups" of trying to make censorship work in the United States today. It claims that such groups have tried to censor magazines such as *Penthouse* and *Ms.*, books such as *Ulysses* and *Huckleberry Finn*, and television programs such as "The Day After" and "M*A*S*H." The message notes that Americans "have the freedom to say *No* to censorship. Say it today—tomorrow may be too late."[37]

THE CENSORSHIP ISSUE

Throughout the years, philosophers have debated the pros and cons of censorship. Civil libertarians express the anticensorship viewpoint. In his 1974 book, *Where Do You Draw the Line? An Exploration into Media Violence, Pornography, and Censorship*, Victor B. Cline lists thirty-six arguments typically presented by those who oppose censorship:

1. You can't legislate morality. And even if you could, it would be an inappropriate function of government, especially in a pluralistic society such as ours where so many culturally different subgroups espouse many diverse values and points of view.

2. The censoring of erotica or violence (or anything else) in any of the arts would necessarily mean banning many great works of art and literature, and this would be intolerable in a free society. Permitting the occasionally vulgar or that which is in poor taste is not too great a price to pay, for that would allow and encourage the great work of art or genius without fetters and constraints.

Our society would be enriched overall by such a policy.

3. Censorship laws create crimes without victims. If you send a man to jail for selling a forbidden book or picture or for showing an illegal cinema (which consenting adults have chosen to expose themselves to) we have a "crime" without any victim. This is illogical and tyrannical.

4. The First Amendment to the Constitution of the United States unequivocally suggests that any censorship law is unconstitutional. The wording is clear and unambiguous: Congress shall make no law . . . abridging the freedom of speech or of the press. Thus it is inappropriate for the government to tell any citizen what he can say, see, hear, or read. And to permit punishment for ideas that are offensive to some is totally unacceptable. The prime function of the First Amendment is to keep debate open to liberal-minded as well as staid people.

5. The real obscenities in life are not pornographic books or films but rather war, poverty, prejudice, pollution, and the like.

6. Erotica suggests a uniting of the sexes, of love, of pleasuring and giving to someone else. Sexual imagery, no matter how explicit, merely reflects a universal life function. This is not bad, but good. Only those with sexual hangups and neuroses (which many censors appear to have) will be afraid of the human body and human sexuality and oppose its dissemination to those adults who choose to have it. To deny sex is to deny life. To reject art is to impoverish yourself, rejecting pleasure and growth. To accept sex and art together is to advance oneself, to be positive instead of negative.

7. What is pornography? It is a question beyond definition—almost by definition. It cannot be defined. What is pornographic to one man is mildly risqué to another. Obscenity is in the eye (or groin) of the beholder. Because it is a variable concept this means that its definition is mercurial and constantly shifting depending on ever-changing times, tastes, and morals as well as individual differences. And if you can't define it, it's impossible to legislate against it. No law can be so precisely framed as to indicate what this will-o'-the-wisp is so as to provide a clear guilt. And every man should be able to know with certainty when he is committing a crime. No such certainty exists in the obscenity area.

8. Only one short step separates the censorship of literature and the arts from the censorship of political thought. We can't take that chance. When you set a precedent and allow some censorship, it can easily spread to other kinds of material. Censorship is the hallmark of an authoritarian regime. A society can be strong only when it is truly free.

9. There is no really conclusive evidence that erotic or even violent imagery or words ever harmed anybody. No girl was ever seduced by a book or received physical injury from same (unless it was dropped on her head or thrown at her).

10. Seeing erotic or violent images is probably cathartic and therapeutic. It provides a vicarious outlet for our aggressive and sexual impulses. This could help keep a "rapist off the street," drain his impulses so that he won't commit an antisocial act; in other words this type of material may render some people less socially dangerous by providing a fantasy release for aggressive and sexual impulses, thereby proving beneficial to mankind.

11. If you do enact censorship laws, you have nobody who is really qualified to act as censor. This would include Mrs. Grundy, the Citizens' Puritan League, the PTA president, the district judge, or the vice squad officer; for all of these people will necessarily possess special biases, points of view, and possible neurotic hangups. And what if their biases are different from yours or mine? Why should they censor what I read or see? Won't this mean that censorship will necessarily always be capricious, arbitrary, and variable—depending on who is doing the censoring? And is this tolerable in a free society? There are some individuals who become excited by seeing lingerie ads in the Sears-Roebuck catalog. Should they be censors? But if not they, then who?

12. Censorship always and invariably interferes with the creativity of the artist, writer, sculptor, film producer, playwright, and others. It creates a repressive climate that is antithetical to creativity. This is intolerable and should not be permitted. The artist as creator must necessarily challenge common beliefs and cultural values, for the creative process identifies new relationships out of which come new meanings; and this is good.

13. Even though the majority should rule, they shouldn't be allowed to legislate their prejudices in areas and issues dealing with free speech and expression. Even unpopular ideas and material in poor taste, even shoddy things should have the opportunity of being presented and being accepted or rejected in a free marketplace. The Constitution protects coarse expression as well as refined, and vulgarity no less than elegance.

14. The enjoyment and personal use of erotica or violent imagery is a private, not a public art, and as such is not a matter for the state to involve itself in. The Supreme Court's ruling (Stanley v. Georgia) supports this position and suggests the corollary, that one should have the right to purchase this kind of material if he chooses.

15. Materials (in film, art, and books) reflecting moral heresy (even erotica and violence) should enjoy the same freedom of expression as that reflecting political heresy and unorthodoxy. The rights of the best of men are secured only as the rights of the vilest and most abhorrent are protected.

16. The most outrageously immoral, intolerant, and obscene act is that of someone censoring what consenting adults wish to read or view.

17. Pornography and violence (in images or words) help people overcome their fear of sexuality (or violence) through the process of desensitization. Exposure to this material helps one overcome sexual hangups and neuroses. It demythologizes sex and helps one laugh at it, producing a more healthy view of it.

18. When you censor something, you invest it with a special "forbidden fruit" aura; you

make it tempting and prurient. This actually creates a morbid interest in the material—not a healthy one. You artifically create a desire for it.

19. If we abandon censorship, works of art and "trash" can legitimately compete on their true merits, not on contrived prurience. This would be healthy and good for society.

20. Art can be both pornographic and violent and a great work of art at the same time. To censor this material would mean a loss to our society and a rejection of a possible work of great talent or genius.

21. Pornography is a boon to the lonely, the sexually confused, and the hopelessly ugly. In fantasy it gives them some relief from their sexual frustrations.

22. Sex and violence are a part of life. If you censor these in the arts or hide them, you are hypocritically denying extremely important aspects of living and life. You are creating a distorted and untrue vision of man. You are being artistically and aesthetically dishonest about human experience.

23. By abolishing taboos (eliminating censorship), you liberate the human spirit and free the man. You abolish guilt about sex and violence. But by censorship you indirectly make people feel guilty about sex, you create neuroses, and you may make people sick.

24. Censorship never really works. In a democracy, people see and read what they wish despite what the law says. Just as during prohibition, if you pass a law which everybody violates, it creates an attitude or climate of indifference toward the law and a disrespect which could generalize to other legitimate and valid laws.

25. The government should not enforce widely held moral or religious beliefs which inveigh against communication of sexual stimuli merely on the ground that it is evil, bad, or wrong. This is private morality and is not the province of governmental intrusion or interference. It may be a legitimate area of concern of parent, priest, or teacher, but never of the government. To suppress a book in the interest of the prevailing sexual morality strikes as deep into the First Amendment as the dictator's knife can go.

26. Public opinion is a much better force to deal with pornography and violence than oppressive censorship laws. A majority of the citizens by their public disapproval could keep this sort of thing in check and within tolerable bounds in our society.

27. The less power the police and state have over our private lives the better.

28. If we ignore pornography—let it take its course, people will soon tire of it, and its novelty will wear off. They'll satiate. Pornography will tend to go away, or at least its interest to the general public will greatly diminish. It is better that we deal with it this way than through repressive legislation.

29. Censorship stifles social change and progress by impeding ideological change, which tends to preserve or "freeze" the present morality via the powers of the state.

30. Censorship limits the student's education. It leaves him with a distorted and jaundiced view of society. It suggests that we do not trust his judgment. How can we expect to produce a free, reasoning person who can make his own decisions, understand his culture, and live compassionately with his fellow man if we censor vital elements of his culture and human experience?

31. Censors are a far greater danger to society than the works they attack or seek to proscribe. To vest a few fallible men—prosecutors, judges, and jurors with the vast power of literary and artistic censorship—to convert them into moral police—is to make them despots.

32. Censorship laws to protect children will not work because children can always get older persons to buy the forbidden material for them. And there is nothing in the Constitution that gives the Supreme Court the right to water down the First Amendment to protect young people. To censor material because it is supposedly deleterious to youth is to burn the house to roast the pig.

33. If it is argued that whatever excites sexual longing and interest may possibly produce sexual misconduct, then perfumes, hot pants, and brief bathing suits will have to be banned along with obscenity.

34. Paternalistic guardianship by the government (e.g., "papa knows best") of the thoughts of grown-up citizens enervates their spirit, keeps them immature, makes conformists out of them, and creates a crippling dependence on the state or on others to do their thinking for them. This is undesirable in a democracy.

35. One never hears a judge, a prosecutor, a censor, or a moralist declare that *their* moral fiber has been injured by looking at a dirty picture, a movie, or a book. It's always someone else's moral fiber for which anxiety is felt. It's always "they" who get damaged.

36. Control of improper *conduct*, not of expression, is the proper function of government.[38]

The First Amendment to the U.S. Constitution reads: "Congress shall make no law . . . abridging the freedom of speech, or of the press." Taken literally, *no* form of speech (whether libelous, privacy invading, obscene, or otherwise) could ever be regulated on the federal level. This is, in fact, what First Amendment absolutists believe. Yet in the years B.C. (Before Christ), the Greek philosopher Plato suggested in *The Republic* that censors should reject or accept fictional works to prevent children from receiving ideas that they did not wish them to have when grown up. Plato argued that there was a need to control poetry that feeds the passions, for it could cause one to neglect virtue and justice. And in 1651, Thomas Hobbes expressed the view in *Leviathan* that those who govern must have the right to decide what opinions and doctrines are conducive to keeping the peace and to determine what may be spoken in order to " 'prevent discord and war.' "[39]

A debate exists over whether the founders of the United States were First Amendment absolutists and whether they intended for that amendment to protect pornography. John Stuart Mill argued in *On Liberty* (1859) that the government's power of coercion is " 'illegitimate' " and that it has no right to censor persons of contrary opinions. He argued that freedom of opinion is necessary to the " 'mental well-being of mankind' " for the following reasons:

1. A silenced opinion may be true. To deny this means we assume " 'our own infallibility.' "
2. Prevailing views are rarely the whole truth. Even erroneous silenced opinions may contain some truth. It is only by allowing opposing opinions to collide that the rest of the truth has a chance to be exposed.
3. Even if the opinion is the whole truth, if it is not vigorously contested, it will be " 'held in the manner of prejudice, with little comprehension or feeling of its rational grounds.' "
4. The meaning of the doctrine will be in danger of being lost, and the growth of real and heartfelt conviction will be prevented.[40]

Interestingly, Burton Joseph of Playboy Enterprises, Inc., the ACLU, and the Media Coalition, in testimony before the Attorney General's Commission, said that his own opposition to censorship is grounded in the philosophy of John Stuart Mill:

> "The only freedom which deserves the name is that of pursuing our own good in our own way, so long as we do not attempt to deprive others of theirs or impede their efforts to obtain it. Each is the guardian of his own health, whether bodily, or mental or spiritual. Mankind are greater gainers by suffering each other to like as seems good to themselves, than by compelling each to like as good as seems good to the rest."[41]

Those who oppose pornography could argue that the Mill quote cited by Joseph should be interpreted to recognize that pornography does deprive and impede others, usually women, in their efforts to obtain freedom, equality, and free speech.

Harry Clor notes that Mill recognized the need for limits on freedom of people to live as they please—namely, the right to govern that conduct when it violates the explicit rights of nonconsenting people. Clor quotes from *On Liberty:* "The only purpose for which power can be rightly exercised over any member of a civilized community, against his will, is to prevent harm to others. His own good, either physical or moral, is not a sufficient warrant . . . Over himself, over his own mind and body, the individual is sovereign."[42] (Taking Mill's philosophy to its logical conclusion regarding pornography, *if* one's consensual consumption, production, distribution, display, and so on, of pornography causes or is likely to contribute to harm (rape, child molesting, battering, prostitution, and the like) of others, government power could be rightly exercised to censor pornography.)

There is evidence that early political leaders of our nation recognized the need to limit individual freedom to do as one pleases when other individuals or their rights are injured. For example, in 1799, George Hay, who prosecuted Aaron Burr for treason, defined speech as the power " 'uncontrolled by law, of that speaking either truth or falsehood at the discretion of each individual, provided no other individual be injured.' "[43]

James Madison, writing in 1798, denied that Congress had any power to control the press or restrain its " 'licentiousness.' " However, Clor notes, Madison was concerned with restraints on political criticism and defamatory political speech. It is not clear, he states, what Madison would have thought of nonpolitical speech (a class including obscenity/pornography, according to Clor). Clor points out that Madison and Thomas Jefferson would not deny the states the power to restrain licentiousness of the press. Madison said in 1799 that " 'every libelous writing or expression can receive its punishment in the state courts . . . whether it injured public officers or private citizens.' " Thomas Jefferson said, " 'While we deny that Congress have a right to control the freedom of the press, we have ever asserted the right of the States and their exclusive right to do so.' "[44] Jefferson also said, " 'Printing presses shall be subject to no other restraint than liableness to legal prosecution for false facts printed and published.' "[45]

Thus, it seems arguable that for the founding fathers of our nation, the free speech issue was partially one of federal versus state control—with the right to restrain the press being granted to the states and withheld from the federal government through the Constitution. There is certainly evidence that they intended at least one exception to an absolute prohibition against regulations of speech—namely, libel. And there is no doubt that the United States' founders were never faced with the issue of pornography as we know it today.

John Milton argued in *Areopagitica*, addressed to the Parliament of England in 1644, that men should be able to decide what to read for themselves. He said one can learn evil manners without books and that a fool will remain a fool even with the best book.[46]

Philosopher Alexander Meiklejohn told a U.S. Senate subcommittee on November 14, 1955, that the First Amendment protects only political activities by which " 'free men govern themselves.' " It does not, he said, protect incitement to such action or overt action. However, it does protect " 'advocacy' " of action.[47] Meiklejohn also said that it is never legitimate to subordinate free expression to some other public interest.[48]

Meiklejohn said that the Constitution differentiates between speech concerned with public interests and that concerned with private interests. The First Amendment protects all public discussion and speech about public issues or about " 'the general welfare.' " Speech directed at our private interests and needs gets qualified protection from the due process clause. Thus, he said, libel and slander can be punished, but criticism of government cannot.[49]

Meiklejohn asserted in 1961 that even literature and the arts have First Amendment protection, for "[t]hey lead the way toward sensitive and informed application and response to the values out of which the riches of the general welfare are created."[50] Meiklejohn, while condemning censorship of obscenity, would have denied First Amendment protection to the radio. In 1948, he said that radio was not enlarging human communication; it was just making money.

"The radio, as we now have it, is not cultivating those qualities of taste, of reasoned judgment, of integrity, of loyalty, of neutral understanding upon which the enterprise of self-government depends. On the contrary, it is a mighty force for breaking them down. It corrupts both our morals and our intelligence."[51]

Clor says that Meiklejohn's later ideas suggest that he extended the First Amendment absolute protection to all media.[52]

The U.S. Supreme Court has had a variety of insightful comments about obscenity/pornography and the First Amendment. In *Chaplinsky* v. *New Hampshire*, the court said that obscene and lewd speech is "no essential part of any exposition of ideas, and are of such slight social value as a step to truth that any benefit that may be derived from them is clearly outweighed by the social interest in order and morality."[53]

Justice William O. Douglas believed that censoring obscenity would carry the same dangers as any government censorship of literature or art. He felt that literature played an important role in exposing all aspects of life. While pornography may trigger " 'a seriously ill psychopath into some kind of action,' " in another person it might help avoid the development of " 'neurotic tendencies' " and add to the knowledge of life. Douglas expressed concern about being governed by past traditions and conformity when change is needed—if censorship occurs. Douglas also felt that it is dangerous to bar thoughts of sex by obscenity law, for " 'a person without sex thoughts is abnormal.' " He said that the issue was whether the government can " 'espouse one moral code as against another and apply sanctions against those who write or speak against the norm.' " The only basis to punish obscenity publication is if it causes antisocial conduct, " 'not among psychopaths, but among the average of the group to which it is addressed.' " Offensiveness of pornography is not a reason to ban it, Douglas said.[54]

In *Paris Adult Theatre I.* v. *Slaton*, the court found legitimate state interests in stemming obscenity, including "the interest of the public in the quality of life and the total community environment, the tone of commerce in the great city centers, and possibly, the public safety itself."[55] The *Miller* v. *California* court said:

The dissenting Justices sound the alarm for repression. But, in our view, to equate the free and robust exchange of ideas and political debate with the commercial exploitation of obscene materials demeans the grand conception of the First Amendment and its high purpose in the historic struggle for freedom . . . ."The protection given speech and press was fashioned to assure unfettered interchange of *ideas* for the bringing about of political and social changes desired by the people." (Quoting *Roth*, emphasis added.) . . . But the public portrayal of hard-core sexual conduct for its own sake, and for the ensuing commercial gain, is a different matter.[56]

Rajeev Dhavan and Christie Davies advance the theory that censorship of obscenity reflects a social order in which some groups impose or try to impose their set of moral values on others. These authors believe that juries, over time, have been less willing to convict on obscenity charges, thus encouraging authors and producers to cease precensoring themselves. Dealing with both the British and American treatment of pornography, they note a shift in the British Parliament away from moral thinking to causalist thinking on this issue. This way of conceptualizing the pornography issue would permit an activity if decision makers believe more harm is caused by prohibiting it and prohibit the activity if the reverse is true. Thus, in the United States, extensive research into the effects of pornography is taking place, and, Dhavan and Davies state, even the ACLU recognized in 1967 that they could no longer succeed in preventing censorship by merely invoking the First Amendment in an absolute way. The causalist question is "What is the effect of prohibiting or permitting pornography on people's behavior?"[57]

According to Dhavan and Davies, the U.S. Constitution is a moralist, not a causalist, document. Thus, justification for pornography lies not in beneficial consequences, but in itself. They believe that the causalist debate comes out in favor of the pro-pornography position. Obscenity law in the United States also is moralist, they state. Their book details moralist and causalist arguments.

Dhavan discusses the various viewpoints in support of and in opposition to obscenity laws. Those who favor protection claim that obscenity legislation is necessary "for the protection of the people." This philosophy is based on the idea that permissiveness per se produces an attitude of moral laxity that will affect attitudes of responsibility and on the idea that obscenity panders to the sexual instinct, which results in increased sex crimes. While the protectionist arguments assume that a person needs more than individual discretion to protect himself or herself, the libertarians have more faith in individual will, Dhavan states. Even they, however, might decide not to leave children to their own discretion, based on the belief that they are not mature enough to protect themselves. The second protectionist argument is that literary standards need to be protected. There is also an argument that cities are visually blighted by pornography. Lastly, there can be an indirect protection aimed at specific persons or classes of persons.

Dhavan paints the controversy about pornography as a democracy versus elitism issue. One side argues that people should be free to decide what to read, while the other presupposes a generally accepted community standard.

The libertarian view argues that there are no consensus standards that must be protected, for there are many lifestyles in society. Second, libertarians

state that each person is a free individual after reaching maturity and that the development of the personality should be left in the individual's own hands. Third, libertarians advance the viewpoint that there is a right to privacy to read and see what one likes.

Dhavan suggests several methods advanced by libertarians, of how people can know in advance whether or not their items will be considered obscene:

1. Create an unofficial board of classification to give a warning (but not immunity) to the producers of a film.
2. Provide a consistent line of court precedents.
3. Create an unofficial board of censors.
4. Have courts make declaratory judgments that will carry weight in future legal proceedings.[58]

D.N. MacCormick writes about privacy and obscenity. Curiously, privacy arguments can be used for or against controls on pornography. One privacy claim states that there should be freedom in the use and enjoyment of obscene materials. The other claims that privacy requires controls on the use and dissemination of obscenity to protect people's privacy right not to have pornography forced on them. Both these arguments, MacCormick states, can be advanced at once if one claims that controls are needed only beyond a certain point. MacCormick cites Supreme Court cases in support of this theory. *Stanley* v. *Georgia* held that people have the right to possess obscene materials in their own homes, based on the First Amendment right to receive information and the right to be free from unwarranted government intrusions into one's privacy. In *U.S.* v. *12,200 ft. Reels* and *U.S.* v. *Orito*, however, the court refused to extend those privacy theories to an argued right to import obscene materials for private use.

While one's right to privacy is essentially a right to nonintrusion, MacCormick argues, it is a very loose and indirect connection to claim that there is an invasion of privacy when sexual displays cannot be avoided. If that were true, then anything objectionable in one's environment should be considered an invasion of privacy, he says. He distinguishes between "sexual obscenity"—making public display of things the public display of which is objectionable though the private practice or existence of which is unobjectionable—and "sadistic obscenity" and "indecency"—depiction of acts of violence and cruelty that should not be practiced at all. Each person, within his or her sphere of privacy, can decide whom, if anyone, to become intimate with, MacCormick claims. He argues that what is willingly done in public falls outside of the sphere of any person's privacy.[59]

MacCormick says that individual privacy rights in obscenity issues are invaded only in the following types of situations. First, a magazine publishes a photograph of a man and woman having intercourse. It was made without their knowledge or permission. Second, "exploitive obscenity." Economic or other pressures are put on pornographic actresses and actors to secure their participation in the public obscenity. To the extent that their consent was not really free consent, their privacy has been invaded. Third, delivery of unsolicited obscene mail.[60]

John Trevelyan headed the censorship board for films in Great Britain from 1958 to 1971. The board is an independent, nongovernment organization that at one time provided a type of protection for the film industry by warning producers and distributors when a film might be obscene. Now, Trevelyan says, the board provides no certain protection, for courts have found that films can be prosecuted under the obscenity laws despite board decisions. He says that a real problem is the lack of a legal definition of obscenity in England. Trevelyan says that adults should be free to see and read what they want provided it does not harm other people and recommends repeal of obscenity laws (unless a committee of lawyers can produce an exact definition of obscenity, which he believes they cannot). Trevelyan supports continuation of the film censorship board, with jurisdiction limited to protecting children and young people. Even he, however, would prohibit child pornography and pornography featuring bestiality "out of kindness to animals." He believes that the only kind of censorship that is justifiable is "self-censorship."[61]

An informative description of the interests that freedom of expression concerns is found in "Freedom of Expression and Categories of Expression" by T.M. Scanlon, Jr. Perhaps most interesting is the way Scanlon creates, then critiques, what he calls the Millian principle:

> There are certain harms which, although they would not occur but for certain acts of expression, nonetheless cannot be taken as part of a justification for legal restrictions on these acts. These harms are: (a) harms to certain individuals which consist in their coming to have false beliefs as a result of those acts of expression; (b) harmful consequences of acts performed as a result of those acts of expression, where the connection between the acts of expression and the subsequent harmful acts consists merely in the fact that the act of expression led the agents to believe (or increased their tendency to believe) these acts to be worth performing.

However, in deciding that the Millian principle, created to rule out arguments for censorship, is "implausible," Scanlon notes how laws such as those against cigarette ads or deceptive advertising cannot be squared with this theory. Scanlon says that he believes it would be legitimate for government to promote people's safety by restricting information about how to make nerve gas, but it would not be legitimate to stop political "agitation."[62]

Ray C. Rist calls pornography a "pseudo" problem when compared with other problems such as nuclear war, poverty, racism, and the environment. He believes that pornography has no negative effects and no "victim." He states, "When law becomes a vehicle to enforce a particular moral philosophy, there is the continual danger of its abuse, since the law does not reflect a consensus as to the appropriate social policy for the society, but the power of a particular group engaged in status politics."[63]

First Amendment absolutist attorney Alan Dershowitz has said that the First Amendment was meant to protect incitement to violence. In fact, however, the founding fathers of our nation incited to violence.[64]

Alan Berger argues that pornography is a political ideology because it "is propaganda whose purpose is to perpetuate those habits of authority and submission which belong to the idolatry of power." As such, it cannot be censored, for political speech is exactly what the First Amendment was intended to protect. Yet Berger says that people are wrong to deny the connection between violent depictions of the rape, torture, bondage, and mutilation of women and real violence, which "incarnates" those images, just as they would be wrong to deny the connection between violent representations in Nazi Germany and the Holocaust. Berger suggests that if our society does not do anything about the raping, battering, and killing of women, eventually we will have to "try cauterizing one of its causes with censorship."[65]

Herbert Marcuse says that liberalist tolerance is based on the idea that people are individuals who can learn to feel, hear, and see by themselves. However, the democratic argument for absolute tolerance today " 'tends to be invalidated by the invalidation of the democratic process itself.' " Concentrated political and economic power and technology used as an instrument of domination prevent effective dissent—which is, in effect, a type of censorship.

Marcuse suggests that the speeches of Nazi and Fascist leaders " 'were the immediate prologue to the massacre. . . . [I]f democratic tolerance had been withdrawn when the future leaders started their campaign, mankind would have had a chance of avoiding Auschwitz and a world war.' "[66]

Avrum Stroll views censorship as an essential part of ruling that is applied only to those who are ruled. In order for wise public policies to be enacted, one must have access to the full range of relevant discussion and facts, he says. Political involvement is the answer to Marcuse's dilemma, Stroll suggests.[67]

Arthur M. Schlesinger says that in a libertarian democracy, the majority rule rests on the guarantee that minorities may convert themselves into new majorities. He admits that while this philosophy has had useful results, it also has led to unredressed wrongs and unsolved problems. He notes that censorship would be an effective way to halt human progress.[68]

Widmer cites an interesting argument made by Terence J. Murphy at a 1959 congressional hearing. If, he said, " 'ideas have no consequences,' " then they have no " 'social value.' " Therefore, the First Amendment has no justification, for there is no reason to protect ideas and reading material.[69]

Film critic Judith Crist points out that people are under no requirement to view pornographic movies. People are free to exercise self-censorship, the only kind of censorship in which she believes. She also suggests that movie creators exercise such censorship. (We note that in many areas, streets, and stores, people are confronted by pornography and cannot easily avoid it.) Crist emphasizes the need to protect even those thoughts we hate. However, she declined to testify on behalf of pornographic movies.[70]

Carey McWilliams, liberal editor of *The Nation*, opposes all censorship. He does not like the idea of some persons attempting to protect "the minds and morals of other people." He believes that one cause of a major crisis in law enforcement and the courts is using criminal law for purposes it is not intended for—namely, attempts to regulate the "moral behavior" of people. This includes censorship. McWilliams made these anticensorship arguments:

1. There is difficulty defining concepts such as obscenity and pornography.
2. Who will judge what is obscene?
3. Local passions will often win out in antipornography cases, for few cases go to the U.S. Supreme Court.
4. Pornography is an adult market, but young people are not as innocent or susceptible to suggestion as adults believe.
5. There is no hard evidence that exposure to pornography adversely affects society or individuals. According to some, it may have a therapeutic effect as a safety valve "for the erotic fantasies of disturbed adults."

6. Political censorship is based on the fear that those censored will persuade large numbers to share their view.[71]

Charles Rembar, a propornography attorney who handles a lot of obscenity cases and wrote *The End of Obscenity*, emphasizes that the First Amendment exists to protect all expression, not just that which is beneficial. He says that there is no need to guarantee freedom for what the majority wants. There is, in addition to the political idea of making democracy work, a value of free speech of simply making "us feel good."[72]

According to Clor, the civil libertarian position is "(1) that the censorship of obscenity contravenes the First Amendment and the principles which lie behind it, and (2) that obscenity is not harmful, or, at least, that the circulation of obscenity does not injure individuals or society to any significant degree."[73]

Clor argues that there are three rationales on which moral censorship may be justified:

1. Moral education is a primary function of the law.
2. Censorship is the result of the need, in all communities, "for cohesion or unity." (Yet, he points out, some liberals contend that common belief or moral consensus is not desirable or needed in a free society.)
3. Certain "minimal moral requisites" must exist for social and political duties to be properly performed. Excessive concern with gratifying sexual desires will weaken energies and withdraw them from social concerns.[74]

Just because there is a profit motive behind much of the United States' free press does not make it bad, media lawyer Marshall Berger says. He believes that this is irrelevant to First Amendment protection.[75]

Alan Levine, a partner in a civil liberties law firm and formerly staff counsel to the New York Civil Liberties Union, believes that "every great author has been subject to censorship." He says that censors do not distinguish between pornography and erotica but that they censor both.[76]

Susan Brownmiller says that she has been libeled by pornographic magazines but was told by civil libertarian lawyers not to sue unless she could prove that her work had suffered or that she had lost money. She also felt that a lawsuit would have been made into a media circus, which is what she believes the pornographers wanted.

Civil libertarian attorney Herald Price Fahringer believes that anyone defamed by a publication has the right to sue. While he believes that libel laws have a purpose, he opposes prohibiting publications that print libelous statements. He prefers allowing persons harmed to collect damages from the publisher. (We note that damages cannot fully compensate for the harm to one's reputation and emotions and lost opportunities sometimes caused by libel.) Fahringer notes that if a woman is portrayed "very attractively" in pornography such as *Playboy,* he finds it "enjoyable."[77]

Fahringer says that he opposes censorship because he believes people can see and read "anything without being morally corrupted." He calls the 1970 President's Commission majority conclusion that pornography does not contribute to sexual offenses and does not alter sexual desires "inescapable." In a democracy, unconventional and new ideas must be heard no matter how offensive, in order to discover those that may be "truly enlightening," he says. He says that Ku Klux Klan and American Nazi party literature was "much more obscene" than the pornography on the stands in 1978. (Mr. Fahringer apparently did not recognize that some pornography is hate literature against women; those other groups distribute hate literature against blacks and religious groups. Pornography is, however, much more prevalent.) Fahringer argues that the right to read and see must include all publications, or, eventually, it may include none.[78]

Paul Chevigny opposes any controls on writings concerning "emotions about sex" because he believes speech is effective in changing people's minds and sometimes, when powerful, in hurting people. He concedes that pornography has sometimes been bad for women and effectively creates an atmosphere that is degrading to women. However, he says, it is precisely because speech is effective that he opposes controls on it. He argues that censorship laws are always enforced on the side of powerful people and that "if" women are oppressed, censorship of speech about women would not benefit them. Chevigny believes that censorship would lead to suppression of speech favoring equality for women.[79]

Feminists who oppose censoring pornography give their views in *Women Against Censorship,* edited by Varda Burstyn. Burstyn states that "women's freedom lies not in accepting censorship, but in repudiating it." She calls on women to remember what was learned from early feminists:

1. Even when there is goal agreement, alliances by feminists with nonfeminist and antifeminist forces are "dangerous." These other interests are allied with a male-dominated state. Feminists will not be the ones to decide how the reforms enacted are carried out. These could be used against feminists, such as by applying them to nonsexist, lesbian, gay, educational, and literary publications. The right-wing sanctions sexism by perpetuating the second class status of women and their dependence on men. Conservatives see sex as dangerous and corrupting, want to contain it within marriage, reject women's autonomy, and degrade their sexuality, Burstyn says.

2. State institutions (governments) are biased toward protecting the status quo, in this case patriarchal social relations.

3. Controlling, punitive, top-down government cannot be used to mend or change sexual life. While Burstyn approves of using government to help people become sexually responsible and self-determining, she opposes its use to punish or control deviation from "one dictated sexual norm."[80]

Burstyn believes that all censorship of the media should be stopped and that obscenity and pornography laws should be eliminated. Otherwise, she fears, birth control, abortion, lesbian sex, and other issues of importance to feminists could be censored. Burstyn proposes the use of the following alternatives:

1. Negotiating with pornography proprietors about the offensiveness of their media and trying to get them to eliminate it (We argue that this proposal is unrealistic. It is unlikely that pornographers will give up a product that makes a huge profit to satisfy feminists, who lack political power and economic clout.)
2. Bringing assault charges against rapists, child molesters, and batterers
3. Protesting pornography
4. Women shaping their own sexual culture
5. Sex education based on pluralism (that is, all sexual preferences represented)
6. Widen distribution and production of noncommercial (for example, feminist) publications
7. Creation of a television station of women's own (Burstyn is Canadian, so presumably she means a Canadian station)
8. Decriminalization of prostitution
9. Meaningful alternatives to working in the sex industry

Burstyn argues that only economic independence for women and youths can stop their sexual exploitation, and this, not pornography, is the primary issue. She says that there is no effective "substitute for basic change, no alternative to social transformation." She calls for equal pay and comparable worth, affirmative action (nontraditional jobs), full employment, quality social services for women, and education and jobs for youths. Women must control their bodies and lives, she states, by means such as safe, reliable contraception, the right to abortion, an end to compulsory heterosexuality, and the right to choose or refuse sterilization. She also wants to abolish the age of consent.

She concludes that making sexually explicit material inaccessible "only increases its attraction and heightens its authority."[81]

FACT feminists Lisa Duggan, Nan Hunter, and Carol S. Vance advance numerous arguments for opposing the civil rights antipornography ordinance. They believe that it embraces the idea that sex is dangerous and degrading to women and that women are victims who have sex inflicted upon them by men. They say that the ordinance supports American culture's "repressive approach to sexuality" and incorporates myths about sexuality that feminists have tried to displace. The proposed law's coverage is broader than violence, they believe. For example, if someone is consensually tied up (bondage), this is not violent. And, they note, there is much disagreement over what "subordinate" means. Is fellatio, lesbian activity, or sadomasochism subordinate? What is "inferior," "a sex object," or "degrading"? Why single out sexual explicitness as the cause of the oppression of women?[82]

Vance, Hunter, and Duggan give three reasons why feminists should not support a civil rights law:

1. The pornographic images do not cause any more harm than "other aspects of misogynist culture."
2. Even in a patriarchal society, "sexually explicit speech" has "positive social functions for women." For example, pornography flouts "conventional sexual mores," underscores the importance of sexual needs, and ridicules "sexual hypocrisy." It advocates group sex, sex for pleasure, sex outside of marriage, casual sex, and other practices, some of which appeal to women. Thus, pornography is not as victimizing as the ordinance claims.
3. Such laws "are more likely to impede, rather than advance, feminist goals."[83]

These three feminists believe that the idea that pornography plays a big role in the suppression of women contradicts history. They do not want sex and family issues to be made private, as right-wing supporters do. Existing laws have remedies for genuine problems such as physical assault, sexual harassment, and coercion, they note. They fear that the civil rights law may divert attention from drives to enact other laws (for example, comparable worth laws) to "genuinely empower women."[84] (We argue

that laws supporting equal rights for women are unlikely to be enacted as long as our culture suffers from the woman-hating, sexist, and harmful beliefs propagandized into our cultural beliefs by pornography.)

Mariana Valverde and Lorna Weir argue that lesbians have a lot to lose if pornography is censored—even though the images of lesbian acts in pornography are not genuine—for they are produced by and for heterosexual men. This is true despite the fact that the monthly budgets of all lesbian publications combined probably are not equal to the cost of one photo spread in a publication such as *Penthouse*. They point out that freedom of the press belongs to those who own it and that lesbians hardly have power equal to that of pornographers.

Yet Valverde and Weir strongly believe that censoring pornography would only undermine "attempts to give birth to a lesbian culture." They fear that pornography laws would be used against *actual* lesbian representations and that lesbians would be persecuted. While free speech does not currently exist for lesbians, it is a goal. They favor genuine "sexual pluralism" and note that the antipornography ordinance would hinder this effort.[85]

Lynn King argues that law reform (at least in Canada) is not the answer to pornographic images. Censoring pornography is like using an aspirin to cure cancer: It does not end the disease and can have serious side effects. Free expression is such a tentatively secured right it should not be dismissed lightly, "especially for a doubtful result."

King lists some dangers of censorship laws:

1. Canada's film review process censors those who lack the funds, time, or ability to deal with bureaucracies.
2. The review board has broad discretion due to vague laws.
3. The board's concern is to avoid explicit sexuality and uphold traditional values, which are sexist and hardly feminist values.
4. The board favors the interests of established (patriarchal) power.
5. Feminists do not control the state, judiciary, police, attorney general, or other enforcement authorities.
6. It is up to the judge to decide what community standards are, and the entire community must be considered.
7. Even if the hate literature laws were amended to include women, courts would not be likely to find that pornography advocates genocide of women or that it leads to a breach of peace. Instead, such laws could be used to attack

nontraditional female role images. Other laws passed to help women's equality have failed (except for funding of battered women's shelters and similar things).[86]

According to Lisa Steele, only equal representation on women's own terms within all areas of society, including media imagery, will protect women in the long run. What is needed is a whole new system for the creation and distribution of cultural information. Pornography is the wrong object of attack, Steele believes. Protests against certain specific pornographic images—for example, bondage—results in other pornography and other images being seen as less bad. It is a mistake, she says, to treat any image in the mass media as an aberration, for sexist images of women are deeply embedded in our culture. The focus on pornography only delays the feminist critique of the entire media, Steele argues.

Steele says that censorship will not work because it only reforms the mass media by removing the images that are most offensive to women. She believes that reform is not needed; rather, a complete overhaul that allows values to change is needed. Steele suggests devoting energy to building women's culture by becoming acquainted with and pushing feminist works as part of a protest against pornography. For example, she suggests offering films produced by women with a positive image instead of pornography.[87]

Sara Diamond agrees that there is a need to produce positive sexual images that portray love free from degradation. This alone, she believes, will change the economic and social position of women and men and undermine the demand for "sexist sexual imagery." Like some other feminists, Diamond fears patriarchal, antiwoman state enforcement of censorship laws.

Diamond argues that images are not a liberal view of reality and that there is a wide difference between fantasy and reality. She calls the imitative theory of sexual violence "false and frightening" and believes that there is no "direct relationship between what an image shows and what its viewer acts out." It is not true that pornography is addictive, she states. While the greater acceptability and visibility of sexual images reflect a backlash against women, it also shows "real gains by the women's and gay movements in making sexuality an area of more open and explicit discussion and depiction."

While pornography reinforces existing social structures and pressures women to do sexual acts asked of them without complaining, the real problem is with the mass media, justice system, and values, Diamond claims. Censorship would not end general ideas of violence toward women. Pornography would move underground. Violence would continue as long as "other oppressive structures" remained in place. Suppressing images would not bring about fundamental changes in the learning of sexual behaviors and identities, Diamond says. Pornography is not the main cause of continued male dominance. She notes that "social and economic structures that create dependency on the sex market, reproduce the powerlessness of women and perpetuate women's cultural objectification create misogynist culture, and it is against these we must take aim." She believes that pornography will exist until "the roots of sexism are uncovered and broken."[88]

Only the feminist agenda set forth in Burstyn's book, including economic equality, control of our bodies, and the right to free sexual expression, will resolve the pornography problem, Diamond states. She believes that pornography portrays cultural problems with sexuality rather than causing them. She calls upon women to create images "of equal or greater impact" than pornography. She says there is a need to flood the market with feminists products and to obtain women's access to the mass media in positions of real power.[89]

The Burstyn book theme that feminists should not advocate censorship and should not support government actions against pornography and degradation is echoed in Wendy Kaminer's article in *Take Back the Night*. Kaminer urges feminists to organize politically and to protest material that degrades and endangers women.[90]

Caught Looking: Feminism, Pornography and Censorship, by the FACT book committee presents the same basic arguments as Burstyn's book. However, it has hundreds of photographs of pornography, including bondage and heterosexual and homosexual material. The authors of *Caught Looking* say that they chose images that turned them on for the book. One of the *Caught Looking* authors writes that reading pornography and masturbating with a vibrator is as important to her as the sex she has with friends, lovers, and tricks.

The book accuses antipornography feminists of using the worst examples of pornography to upset women. They describe one of the feminist antipornography groups as an organization "with a right wing philosophy masquerading as a radical feminist organization." Such groups are being used for sexual repression by powerful groups such as the church and business, they charge.[91]

The FACT authors emphasize that there is no proof that pornography is a cause rather than a symptom of more pervasive power imbalances. They are concerned that obscenity laws end freedom of sexual speech and are enforced selectively against homosexual publications and persons involved in unpopular political activities. They worry that such laws could close homosexual bars and silence sexual minority leaders.

Caught Looking includes a list of sexual premises (or beliefs) about pornography that society in general seems to believe but that FACT feels are not necessarily well founded. These include the ideas that men identify with the male pornographic actors, that pornography is female submissive and male dominant, and that pornography users are sexual addicts and therefore potential sex offenders.

Ellen Willis calls it "dangerously simplistic" to include pornography in the same category as rape, for while a woman who is raped is a victim, a woman who enjoys pornography (including a rape fantasy) "is in a sense a rebel, insisting on an aspect of her sexuality that has been defined as a male preserve."

Willis fears that calling pornography a woman's enemy would make a lot more women ashamed of and afraid to be honest about their sexual feelings. It would be better, she says, to state that some sexual images are offensive while others are not.

Willis charges that Susan Brownmiller's statement that the First Amendment was written to protect political debate, not depictions of woman-hating violence, defeats the amendment's purpose because it gives the government the right to define *political*. If pornography is sexist propaganda as the antipornography feminists allege, she argues, it must be political.[92]

The FACT book also contains a large segment attacking the civil rights proposals as "false premises." Because much of this same information is included in chapter 10, it is not repeated here.

RESPONSES TO CIVIL LIBERTARIAN ARGUMENTS

When the First Amendment became part of the U.S. Constitution, pornography, fighting words, libel, and slander were considered to be "expressions of 'licentiousness' " not protected by free speech or press guarantees.[93]

Laws in the United States create numerous court permitted restraints on freedom of speech and the press. These include criminal or civil laws prohibiting disorderly conduct, telephone threats, obscenity, obscene phone calls, bomb scares, child pornography, solicitation of prostitutes, forgery, fraudulent writings, libel, slander, false advertising, threats to injure or accuse of crime, disclosure of polygraph results, publications stating that any public place of accommodation will be denied to a person by reason of sex or race, using another person's trademark, contracts or conspiracies in restraint of trade, bribery of public officials or witnesses, sedition, perjury, copyright infringement, invasion of privacy, cigarette advertising on television, making a political speech over a public address system at 3 A.M., involuntary prayer in public schools, political speeches by some government employees, and release of governmentally classified information.

In addition, it is important to note that a form of "censorship," as the civil libertarians would define it, occurs continually: No library buys every book that is published, and no bookstore offers for sale every book ever published. Likewise, television and movie theaters do not present every movie ever made. In the civil libertarian view, this must be a form of censorship. In fact, books containing politically

unpopular views, educational books that deal with sexual minorities, and books that deal with women as equal human beings receive a lot less distribution and display than books that promote the views of the majority in our culture.

Maureen Burnley notes that pornography puts feminists at odds with a traditional ally—"America's male-defined and controlled left." The "boys" on the left claim that any challenge to pornography is censorship and a threat to the First Amendment, she says. The major deception in the defense of pornography by leftist males is the "myth" that there is such a thing as free speech in the United States, Burnley claims. She correctly points out that the "right" to free speech has no meaning unless it is accompanied by access to the means of such speech. In reality, access requires free time and "lots of dollars." No one will hear what you have to say unless you have the money to get your opinion publicized. Thus, Burnley concludes, the economic realities of mass communication "censor free speech more effectively than any anti-pornography legislation ever could."[94]

Judith Bat-Ada (who is also called Judith Reisman) calls the claim that freedom of press and speech exist in the United States a "popular American myth" and "a media illusion." She alleges that the "Fourth Estate" (the press) controls expression and ideas in our society "in the service of the corporate oligarchy" and suggests that the control is so powerful that it constitutes censorship.

Reisman charges that a pornographic environment

is undemocratic and threatens free speech. Images of women and children that are injurious and distorted are often exploited by the private corporate interests that control the mass media, she says.

According to Reisman, the First Amendment implies equal opportunity for all people to be heard, communicate, and persuade in a "free marketplace of ideas." She maintains that in reality, the ruling "commercial oligarchy" limits the effectiveness and reach of its opposition. While freedom of speech and the press has been paralyzed by this oligarchy, it tries to perpetuate the illusion that free speech exists. Concentration of media ownership prevents all viewpoints from being represented. The media control "our attitudes, opinions, and imaginations," Reisman states, and they help shape reality.

Women and children are shut out of the media because they do not have the financial resources to battle with communications giants. Reisman claims that pornography is a big business that is part of the corporate oligarchy. The pornographers use funds to buy a "legal stable with the capability to pontificate about the sacredness of the freedom of speech."

Reisman attacks the theory that in a free marketplace of ideas, the good and bad words do battle and the truth triumphs. There is no such free marketplace, she states. She notes that intellectual print media cannot compete with today's "electronic–visual" media.

Reisman says that the "slippery slope" free speech concept, which claims prohibiting pornography will "cause a serious erosion of creative freedom" is a myth, for it is based on the falsehood that free speech exists. Instead, we should ask what the pornographic environment has done to "erode art and literature." The pornographers should be "attacked as censors" for shaping and warping our perceptions and attitudes with their warped portrayals.

Reisman believes that for democracy to be obtained, equal access to the media must be obtained. She states that pornography is supported because those who oppose it have been denied freedom of speech by the "mass media monopoly." The media and sponsors should have to provide equal space and time for "uncensored" responses when females are shown as sex objects or to stop such portrayals, she suggests.[95]

Andrea Dworkin notes that the Bill of Rights (including the free press/speech amendment) was not intended to, and has not, protected the rights of women except occasionally by accident. She, like Reisman and Burnley, emphasizes that the First Amendment "belongs to those who can buy it." In our culture, men have the economic power and pornographers have "empires," while women lack economic power and media access. Men, she believes, have "counseled" women to be quiet with tactics such as criticizing them for boycotting or picketing pornography and destroying property. If the First Amendment does not work for women, it does not work at all, Dworkin concludes.[96]

Susan Brownmiller notes that sexual intimidation of females is being "buttressed" by absolutist free speech advocates. She questions whether a group that is "evil," "powerful," "sick," and "mentally unstable" has a right, protected under the law, to promote sexual violence against women (an oppressed group) for commercial gain.

Brownmiller stresses that for absolutists, no rights, including public safety or privacy, supersede the First Amendment. She recalls a strike that shut down all the newspapers in New York City. Why did the liberals not oppose the strike on the grounds that it had a "chilling effect" and denied people's right to know? A good liberal would never suggest using the First Amendment to break a strike, Brownmiller states. She says that she awaits the day when liberals will be as sensitive to women's concerns.[97]

Linda Rosenberg asks why, if pornography is so liberating, women seldom look at it and turn away when they do see it. She suggests that it is a form of male power and degrades and demeans women as objects to be abused. Pornography's freedom, far from being that of females over their destiny, means making women more available to men more often.[98]

A position paper of Women Against Sexist Violence in Pornography and Media emphasizes how press freedom belongs to those who own it. Responding to advertisements about murder being the latest fashion (for the movie *Dressed to Kill*), this group attempted to buy an ad on the theater page of the *Pittsburgh Press* stating that "bomb scares are the latest fashion for theaters showing violence against women." The group notes that the paper routinely featured movie advertisements glamorizing the murder of women. The newspaper refused the proposed ad on the ground that it might lead to actual bomb scares.[99] (If that were so, would it not be just as likely that ads advocating the murder of or violence toward women could lead to actual violence?)

According to Lorenne M.G. Clark, freedom of the individual is the central value of liberalism. Liberals like to remove legal restraints and dislike making legal duties for others. However, such duties are necessary in order to give people the means to do what they want. She calls the absence of restraint a "privilege" or "liberty" right and the imposition of a duty to ensure another individual's freedom a "claim" right. In the pornography area, only a claim right, the imposition of controls on pornography, can ensure the freedom of women to use their rights and to receive equal treatment.[100]

Robert F. Fitch writes:

> [N]o sort of liberty is an absolute right. There are limits to liberty that reside in the moral order itself. As both St. Paul and Plato understood, liberty carried to the point of license results in anarchy for the individual and for society; in the first case, it results in becoming a slave to passion; in the second case it eventuates in tyranny. Liberty is limited by other competing values—such as equality; it is limited by the price we are willing to pay for it; it is limited, as both Shakespeare and Edmund Burke knew, by the need for a framework of law and order within which true liberties can flourish.[101]

Walter Berns, in an excellent description of the relationship between pornography and art, says that censorship helps maintain the difference between art and "trash." Therefore, he says, it protects art and enhances "the quality of this democracy."[102]

Berns suggests that anyone who believes that pornography is a serious problem or wants to prevent it from becoming a problem, or anyone who cares for the American quality of life in our democracy, must be for censorship. Yet he sees a difference between repressive censorship and liberal censorship of words. He suggests that much of the genuine cultural market in our country is being preempted by pornographic books, theaters, and movies. For example, pornographic novels have a better chance of being published than nonpornographic ones, and "quite a few pretty good novels" are not published because they are not pornographic and are less likely to sell.[103]

Irving Kristol points out that if one believes no book ever corrupted anyone, one must also believe no book ever improved anyone. Thus, all art would be trivial and all education "morally irrelevant." No one, he states, really believes that. No one, he says, is a "complete civil libertarian." For example, we would not allow anyone to commit suicide on stage during a performance or allow acts of real physical torture on stage.[104]

Reo M. Christenson, a liberal and longtime ACLU member, argues that stronger pornography legislation is needed. He notes that a variety of laws have abridged freedom of the press and of speech throughout the years and that our entire history makes it clear that what the First Amendment means is that Congress may place no *unreasonable* restraints on that freedom. Christenson makes a case for censorship.[105]

In 1955, Abraham Kaplan found a difference between art and pornography. While art is a "challenge to evil and death, forcing enduring human values out of the sadly deficient and evanescent material of experience," and while conventional, Dionysian, and maybe romantic obscenity play a part in performance of the aesthetic function, pornography—obscenity of the perverse or of violence—does not do this. Kaplan says:

> For these are in the service of death, not of life. They belong to that monstrous morality and taste of the burial ground where death is glorified and the sculpture of Michelangelo is given a fig leaf. The god of such obscenity is not Eros, but Thanatos. Not the wages of sin, but sin itself, in death.[106]

CONCLUSION

In legal terms, *censorship* means "prior restraint." Because no one in the antipornography movement is advocating prevention of publication of pornography, claims by civil libertarians that antipornography activists are trying to "censor" pornography are misleading.

The private enterprise profit interests of the pornographers and civil liberties groups concern us, particularly the financial interrelationships between them. We also are concerned about the lack of self-governing standards. For example, "taboo" films and the "family" literature promote, glorify, legitimize, and eroticize incest, which is recognizably child sexual abuse and thinly veiled substitute child pornography. We are concerned that adults who get aroused by the idea of sex within the family may not restrict their interests to adults who can reject such interests but will turn to the less informed and subordinate family members—children.

The strongest leadership in the pro-pornography and civil libertarian perspective consists of persons linked to the pornography industry. Thus, these philosophical opinions are being shaped by businessmen and businesswomen who intellectualize but whose industry involvement gives one cause for concern about their objectivity.

The private industry representatives and civil libertarians have a number of underlying philosophical beliefs. First, they want people to be able to say or write whatever they please about sex and oppose legal regulation of pornography. As a result, they end up defending even the most hard-core, demeaning, and violent pornography. Some of them even oppose "censorship" of child pornography.

Second, they do not recognize harm from pornography and downplay scientific efforts to find causal links between pornography and abuse of persons, while selectively supporting those studies that conclude that pornography is not harmful or has a cathartic effect.

Third, they argue that the answer to "bad" speech is to counter it with "good" speech—without recognizing that many people do not have the money or power needed to communicate their opposing view effectively and persuasively.

Fourth, they fear that "censorship" of pornography will lead to "censorship" of birth control, homosexuality, and abortion.

Fifth, they use legal suits to argue that pornography and obscenity laws are unconstitutional and to prevent such laws from being effectively enforced.

Sixth, they claim that pornography cannot be defined.

Finally, the most important sophisticated political theorists often use examples from historical pornography and erotic literature and lack exposure to modern exploitive, demeaning pornography.

NOTES

1. Burton Joseph, "Presentation to Attorney General's Commission on Pornography" (Testimony before the Attorney General's Commission on Pornography, Chicago, 24–25 July 1985), 1–18, 1–2 (résumé); 1, 2 of résumé.
2. FACT Book Committee, *Caught Looking: Feminism, Pornography and Censorship* (New York: Caught Looking, Inc., 1986), 94.
3. *United States of America vs. Sex: How the Meese Commission Lied About Pornography*, eds. Philip Nobile and Eric Nadler (New York, N.Y.: Minotaur Press, Ltd. A Penthouse International Company, 1986), 347; *Forum*, September, 1986, 15(12): 5.
4. Media Coalition, Inc., *What Is the Media Coalition?* (New York: Media Coalition, Inc., 24 May 1986) *The Media Coalition 1985–1986: Highlights* (New York: Media Coalition, Inc., 13 June 1986).
5. ACLU, *The American Civil Liberties Union: Guardian of Freedom* (New York: American Civil Liberties Union, updated).
6. Jane M. Whicher, Testimony before the Attorney General's Commission on Pornography, Chicago, 24 July 1985, 1–13, 1, 6, 12.
7. Barry W. Lynn, "Polluting the Censorship Debate: A Summary and Critique of the Final Report of the Attorney General's Commission on Pornography" (Report prepared for the ACLU, New York, July 1986).
8. Ibid., 105.
9. Ibid., 27.
10. Ibid., 52.
11. Ibid., 60.
12. Ibid., 69.
13. Ibid., 107.
14. Attorney General's Commission on Pornography, *Final Report* (Washington, D.C.: United States Justice Department, 1986), 1381–82.
15. Letter from Bay Area FACT of San Francisco, California, to California assemblyman Art Arnos, 9 July 1985.
16. Nan D. Hunter, Testimony before the Attorney General's Commission on Pornography, Chicago, 25 July 1985, 1–9, 2–3.
17. Ibid., 3.
18. Ibid., 6, 7.
19. Ibid., 9.
20. Feminist Anti-Censorship Task Force, *Position Statement* (Feminist Anti-Censorship Task Force, *Position Statement* undated).
21. Joseph, "Presentation," 5–6.
22. Ibid., 9–10, 14.
23. Ibid., 16–17.
24. Hugh Hefner, "The Playboy Forum: The Playboy Philosophy," *Playboy*, December 1987, 41–44, 44.
25. "Problem Porn" (editorial response to letter to the editor), *Playboy*, March 1985, 54.
26. "What Sort of Man Reads Playboy? *Playboy*, June 1986, 69.
27. "The Playboy Forum: Commentary: Does Repression Cause Violence?" *Playboy*, May 1987, 53.
28. Hugh M. Hefner, "Sexual McCarthyism," *Playboy*, January 1986, 58–59.
29. "Southland a Victim, Too" (editorial response to letter to the editor), 11, "The Playboy Forum," 41–42; "Forum: On Censorship," 44; "Forum: Playboy Sues Meese," 46, *Playboy*, August, 1986.
30. "You call *that* being molested?" *Playboy*, October, 1971, cartoon.
31. Philip Nobile and Eric Nadler, *United States of America vs. Sex: How the Meese Commission Lied about Pornography* (New York: Minotaur Press, Ltd., 1986), 136, 143, 149.
32. Ibid., 43–44.
33. Ibid., 67, 69, 81, 82.
34. Ibid., 87, 89, 105, 108.
35. Ibid., 109–10.

36. "If You Think You Live In A Free Society . . . Think Again," *Penthouse Hot Talk*, Hot Talk No. 19, 1986, 43.

37. "The Experts Agree That Censorship Works," *Penthouse*, April 1985, 35.

38. Victor B. Cline, ed., *Where Do You Draw the Line?* (Provo, Utah: Brigham Young University Press, 1974), 3–7.

39. Eleanor Widmer, ed., *Freedom and Culture: Literary Censorship in the '70's* (Belmont, Calif.: Wadsworth Publishing, 1970), 2–4, 10–11.

40. Ibid., 15–16.

41. John Stuart Mill, quoted in Joseph, "Presentation," 18.

42. Harry M. Clor, *Censorship and Freedom of Expression* (Chicago: Rand McNally, 1971), 129–30.

43. Widmer, *Freedom and Culture*, 17.

44. Clor, *Censorship*, 96–97.

45. Widmer, *Freedom and Culture*, 16.

46. Ibid., 8.

47. Ibid., 19.

48. Clor, *Censorship*, 127.

49. Ibid., 105.

50. Alexander Meiklejohn, "The First Amendment Is Absolute," 1961 *Sup. Ct. Rev.* 257.

51. Clor, *Censorship*, 110.

52. Ibid., 110.

53. *Chaplinsky v. New Hampshire*, 315 U.S. 568, 572 (1942).

54. Widmer, *Freedom and Culture*, 23–26.

55. *Paris Adult Theatre I vs. Slaton*, 413 U.S. 49, 58 (1973).

56. *Miller v. California*, 413 U.S. 15, 34, rehearing denied 414 U.S. 881 (1973).

57. Christie Davies, "Preface," and "How our Rulers Argue about Censorship" in Rajeev Dhavan and Christie Davies, eds. *Censorship and Obscenity* (London: Martin Robertson & Co., Ltd., 1978), 1, 14–19.

58. Rajeev Dhavan, "Existing and Alternative Models of Obscenity Law Enforcement," in Rajeev Dhavan and Christie Davies, *Censorship and Obscenity*, 56–75.

59. D.N. MacCormick, "Privacy and Obscenity," in Rajeev Dhavan and Christie Davies *Censorship and Obscenity*, 76–87.

60. Ibid., 89–95.

61. John Trevelyan, "Film Censorship and the Law," in Rajeev Dhavan and Christie Davies, *Censorship and Obscenity*, 98–107.

62. T.M. Scanlon, "Freedom and Expression and Categories of Expression," in *Pornography and Censorship*, David Copp and Susan Wendell eds. (Buffalo, N.Y.: Prometheus Books, 1983), 139–65.

63. Ray C. Rist, *The Pornography Controversy* (New Brunswick, N.J.: Transaction Books, 1975), ix, 11, 12.

64. Alan Berger, "Pornography: Is Censorship the Answer?" *Boston Real Paper*, 14 September 1979.

65. Ibid.

66. Widmer, *Freedom and Culture*, 27, 35, 37.

67. Ibid., 37–41.

68. Ibid., 41–47.

69. Ibid., 55.

70. Judith Crist, [cited in H. Hart,] *Law, Liberty and Morality* New York: Vintage Books, 1966), 50, 58.

71. Carey McWilliams, [cited in Hart,] 63–91, 63, 73.

72. Charles Rembar, [cited in Hart,] 199–227, 227.

73. Clor, *Censorship*, 88.

74. Ibid., 182–89.

75. Meredith Gould, "Panel Discussion: Regulation of Pornography. "Colloquium: Violent Pornography: Degradation of Women versus Right of Free Speech," *New York University Review of Law and Social Change* 8 (1978–79): 281.

76. Ibid., 285–87.

77. Ibid., 288–90.

78. Herald Price Fahringer, "If the Trumpet Sounds an Uncertain Note . . ." "Colloquium: Violent Pornography . . ." 251–53.

79. Opening statement of Paul Chevigny, in "Panel Discussion: Effects of Violent Pornography," (Sylvia Law, moderator). "Colloquium: Violent Pornography . . ." 232–33, 235.

80. Varda Burstyn, ed., *Women Against Censorship* (Vancouver and Toronto: Douglas & McIntyre, Ltd., 1985), 1–3, 15–17, 160.

81. Ibid., 158–79.

82. Lisa Duggan, Nan Hunter and Carole S. Vance, "False Promises: Feminist Antipornography Legislation in the U.S.," in *Women Against Censorship*, Varda Burstyn, ed. (Vancouver and Toronto, Canada: Douglas & McIntyre, Ltd., 1985).

83. Ibid., 144–45.

84. Ibid., 144, 146–47.

85. Mariana Valverde and Larna Weir, "Thrills, Chills and the 'Lesbian Threat' or, The Media, the State and Women's Sexuality," in *Women Against Censorship*, Varda Burstyn, ed. (Vancouver and Toronto, Canada: Douglas & McIntyre, Ltd., 1985).

86. Lynn King, "Censorship and Law Reform: Will Changing the Laws Mean a Change for the Better?" In *Women Against Censorship*, Varda Burstyn, ed. (Vancouver and Toronto, Canada: Douglas & McIntyre, Ltd., 1985), 79–90.

87. Lisa Steele, "A Capital Idea: Gendering in the Mass Media," in *Women Against Censorship*, Varda Burstyn, ed. (Vancouver and Toronto, Canada: Douglas & McIntyre, Ltd., 1985), 58–75.

88. Sara Diamond, "Pornography: Image and Reality," in *Women Against Censorship*, Varda Burstyn, ed. (Vancouver and Toronto, Canada: Douglas & McIntyre, Ltd., 1985), 40–48, 52.

89. Ibid., 52–53.

90. Wendy Kaminer, "Pornography and the First Amendment: Prior Restraints and Private Action," in *Take Back the Night: Women on Pornography*, ed. Laura Lederer (New York: William Morrow & Co., 1980), 241–47.

91. FACT Book Committee, *Caught Looking*, 5, 20, 24.

92. Ibid., 35, 56, 58.

93. Meikert W. Titis, "The United States Supreme Court

and Obscenity: Reversed and Remanded," in *Pornography Solutions Through Law*, ed. Carol A. Clancy (Washington, D.C.: National Forum Foundation, 1985), 79.

94. "The Real Censor Is the Media Domination," *Media Report to Women*, September/October 1985, 8.

95. "Colloquium," 271–79. Judith Baat-Ada (Reisman)

96. Andrea Dworkin, "For Men, Freedom of Speech; for Women, Silence Please," in *Take Back the Night: Women on Pornography*, ed. Laura Lederer (New York: William Morrow & Co., 1980), 256–58.

97. Susan Brownmiller, "Opening Statement" in Dean Norman Redlich, moderator, "Panel Discussion: Regulation of Pornography," in "Colloquium: Violent Pornography . . .," 255–57.

98. Linda Rosenberg, *The Sapphire Matrix Voice* (Hawaii), Winter, 1983.

99. Women Against Sexist Violence in Pornography and Media, (position paper prepared by Women Against Sexist Violence in Pornography and Media, Pittsburgh, 20 October 1980).

100. Lorenne M.G. Clark, "Liberalism and Pornography,"
in *Pornography and Censorship*, eds. David Copp and Susan Wendell (Buffalo, N.Y.: Prometheus Books, 1983), 45–58.

101. Robert F. Fitch, "The Impact of Violence and Pornography on the Arts and Morality," in *Where Do You Draw the Line?* ed. Victor B. Cline (Provo, Utah: Brigham Young University Press, 1974), 15–24, 23.

102. Walter Berns, "Democracy, Censorship, and the Arts," in *Where Do You Draw the Line?* ed. Victor B. Cline (Provo, Utah: Brigham Young University Press, 1974), 25–44, 44.

103. Ibid., 53.

104. Irving Kristol, "The Case for Liberal Censorship," in *Where Do You Draw the Line?* ed. Victor B. Cline (Provo, Utah: Brigham Young University Press, 1974), 45–55, 46.

105. Reo M. Christenson, "Without Redeeming Social Value?" in *Where Do You Draw the Line?* ed. Victor B. Cline (Provo, Utah: Brigham Young University Press, 1974), 309–16.

106. Abraham Kaplan, "Obscenity and the Arts," *Law and Contemporary Problems* 20 (Autumn 1955): 559.

PART III

LEGAL ISSUES

9 OBSCENITY LAW: ITS PROSECUTION AND DEFENSE

Obscenity laws that exist federally and in most states are the primary mechanism for regulating pornographic material involving adults. Yet the Attorney General's Commission on Pornography and leading legal experts agree that, with a few exceptions, obscenity laws are not being enforced in the United States today. A new federal task force established by the attorney general is attempting to change that pattern. Experts acknowledge that the obscenity distribution network could be shut down by obscenity enforcement within a matter of a couple of years. (We agree and would encourage attempts to attain that goal.)

The Attorney General's Commission found that the lack of enforcement of obscenity laws is a major problem. From January 1, 1978, to February 27, 1986, only one hundred individuals were indicted for violating federal obscenity laws. Well over half of these were indicted in one major investigation called MIPORN.[1] In 1977, Harold Leventhal concluded, after lengthy study, that the *Miller* obscenity test established in 1973 had had little impact on the day-to-day regulation of obscene materials. In fact, he found that obscenity prosecutions had declined unexpectedly since *Miller* and that the easier-to-meet standards of *Miller* had failed to reduce the volume of sexually explicit materials available in the United States. In addition, pornography had grown more explicit since *Miller*. Leventhal said that limited prosecutorial resources, confusion over standards, the lack of meaningful standards, and increasing public tolerance of such materials may help explain why prosecutions did not increase. He also found that *Miller* did not cause the expected jump in the conviction rate.[2]

Bruce Taylor, an attorney for Citizens for Decency Through Law, Inc., (CDL) believes that, as a practical matter, obscenity law is practically uniformly applied in the United States despite differences in statutes, for only explicit sexual materials can be found obscene. The material must show at least simulated sexual conduct, explicit genital penetration, or ejaculation. Taylor believes that all the states should conform to the *Miller* standard to ensure uniform guidance about what is permitted. A good law would restrict obscenity while allowing honest uses of sexual matter, he states. Taylor, as detailed in chapter 1, has proposed a uniform law that would outlaw certain specific hardcore sexual depictions. Such a law, he says, may result in the court being "willing to admit the confusion and failure of its *Miller* 'test' to deter the traffic in obscenity."[3]

(We agree that obscenity laws should be enforced for the time being but suggest that a new law specifically detailing what should be prohibited as pornographic is desirable. In chapter 12, we propose such a law for consideration and debate.)

Major sources of material on obscenity law include George Weaver's *Handbook on the Prosecution of Obscenity Cases;* Frederick F. Schauer's *The Law of Obscenity;* Daniel S. Moretti's *Obscenity and Pornography: The Law under the First Amendment;* the National Obscenity Law Center's (NOLC's) *Obscenity Law Reporter;* the *Obscenity Law Bulletin* by the NOLC; and the *National Decency Reporter* by CDL.[4] Appendix A contains a model obscenity law and description of the law by CDL which should be consulted along with the various professional articles listed in the bibliography.

INTRODUCTION TO OBSCENITY LAW

It must be emphasized that obscenity laws are criminal, not civil, in nature. Although obscenity prosecutions are costly in terms of dollars and human resources, that cost can be recouped in fines and damages from convicted pornographers. As William A. Stanmeyer points out, the value of prosecuting such criminals includes "intangibles" such as preventing further attack on innocent persons, restoration of the moral order, safety of the community, and a sense of rightfulness.[5]

Where pornography is involved, the cost of *not* acting, as we have demonstrated in the behavioral sections of this book, can include making unwilling child and female victims act out pornographic scenarios and sexual assaults imitating pornography. While those costs are hard to measure in dollars, they can be presumed to be enormous in terms of harm to human lives (and resulting emotional, financial, career, and family problems).

Bruce Taylor notes that pornographers have caused great expense to states and cities by suing them under the Federal Civil Rights Act (Title 42 U.S.C. s. 1983) for hypothetical violations of their civil rights. Taylor calls this a misuse of the act. Such lawsuits allege that the procedure or law at issue is an unconstitutional violation of the defendant's rights and seek declaratory judgments and/or damages.[6]

In states which have racketeering and organized crime acts, it is advisable to include obscenity, sexual exploitation of children, and prostitution within the coverage of the Racketeer Influenced Corrupt Organizations Act (RICO) law, for these crimes are often committed by organized criminal enterprises. RICO prosecutions result in tougher penalties and more discovery rights than ordinary obscenity cases. Also, under RICO statutes, all profits of the crime can be reached by seizure of property, and civil remedies allow for treble damages. Lastly, under RICO laws, it is possible to order divestiture of the criminal pornography enterprise and to have it dissolved. The United States Supreme Court upheld the use of the Indiana RICO law in obscenity cases on February 21, 1989. (See *Fort Wayne Books, Inc.* v. *Indiana*, 57 *Law Week* 4180.)

(Consult chapter 1 for a short history of obscenity law in the United States. That chapter sets forth the key definitions of obscenity through the years as established in the important cases of *Hicklin*, *Roth*, *Memoirs*, and *Miller*. Those definitions are not repeated here.)

In *Roth* v. *United States/Alberts* v. *California*, the court held that "obscenity is not within the area of constitutionally protected speech or press."[7] The *Roth* court emphasized that the First Amendment was designed to ensure the free exchange of ideas to bring about social and political changes that the people desire. It said:

> All ideas having even the slightest redeeming social importance—unorthodox ideas, controversial ideas, even ideas hateful to the prevailing climate of opinion—have the full protection of the guaranties, unless excludable because they encroach upon the limited area of more important interests. But implicit in the history of the First Amendment is the rejection of obscenity as utterly without redeeming social importance.[8]

The court emphasized what it found to be a "universal judgment" that obscenity should be restrained, noting that more than fifty nations, forty-eight states, and Congress (passing twenty laws from 1842 to 1956) did so.

The *Roth* court also pointed out that certain types of speech have never been thought to be protected by the First Amendment. It quoted *Chaplinsky* v. *New Hampshire* (1942):

> There are certain well-defined and narrowly limited classes of speech, the prevention and punishment of which have never been thought to raise any constitutional problem. These include the lewd and obscene. . . . It has been well observed that such utterances are no essential part of any exposition of ideas, and are of such slight social value as a step to truth that any benefit that may be derived from them is clearly outweighed by the social interest in order and morality.[9]

The *Roth* court made it clear that because obscenity is not constitutionally protected speech, a "clear and present danger" need not be shown. At the same time, however, it cautioned that "sex and obscenity are not synonymous" and that "material which does not treat sex in a manner appealing to prurient interest" must be safeguarded.[10]

The standards of *Regina* v. *Hicklin*,[11] which were accepted as establishing the law of obscenity in our nation prior to *Roth*, were rejected by the *Roth* court primarily because *Hicklin* allowed material to be found obscene based upon its effect upon particularly susceptible persons and permitted isolated excerpts from material to be found obscene. *Roth* emphasized that the issue is not whether the material arouses impure sexual thoughts or sexual desires in one segment of a community while leaving others unmoved; rather, what is at issue is what impact the whole material has upon "all those whom it is likely to reach"—its "impact upon the average person in the community."[12] *Roth* established a new definition of obscenity (which is included in Chapter One).

Nine years later, in *Memoirs* v. *Massachusetts*, three justices of the U.S. Supreme Court issued an opinion that elaborated on and changed the *Roth* obscenity standards in a way that, in effect, gutted obscenity prosecutions in the United States.[13] Because legal principles said that cases did not have precedential value when a majority of justices could not agree on the principles involved, for many years confusion in the courts existed over whether *Roth* or *Memoirs* was the law of the land regarding obscenity standards.

Marks v. *U.S.* made it clear that when five justices do not agree on a single rationale explaining a case result, "[t]he holding of the Court may be viewed as that position taken by those Members who concurred in the judgments on the narrowest grounds' " (quoting *Gregg* v. *Georgia*). Thus, under *Marks,* the views of the *Memoirs* plurality were the holding of the court, and *Roth* was no longer the applicable standard.[14]

Memoirs said that under *Roth,* as elaborated in subsequent cases, three elements must coalesce:

[I]t must be established that (a) the dominant theme of the material taken as a whole appeals to a prurient interest in sex; (b) the material is patently offensive because it affronts contemporary community standards relating to the description or representation of sexual matters and (c) the material is utterly without redeeming social value.[15]

Two *Memoirs* justices rejected the new test, arguing that it conflicted with *Roth*'s basic holding that obscene material is "inherently without social value." It was the "utterly without redeeming social value" aspect of *Memoirs* that made prosecution of obscenity futile and, several years later, resulted in the court establishing a news test for obscenity in *Miller* v. *California:*

State statutes designed to regulate obscene materials must be carefully limited. . . . As a result, we now confine the permissible scope of such regulation to works which depict or describe sexual conduct. That conduct must be specifically defined by the applicable state law, as written or authoritatively construed. A state offense must also be limited to works which, taken as a whole, appeal to the prurient interest in sex, which portray sexual conduct in a patently offensive way, and which, taken as a whole, do not have serious literary, artistic, political, or scientific value.

The basic guidelines for the trier of fact must be: (a) whether "the average person, applying contemporary community standards" would find that the work, taken as a whole, appeals to the prurient interest. . . . (b) whether the work depicts or describes, in a patently offensive way, sexual conduct specifically defined by the applicable state law; and (c) whether the work, taken as a whole, lacks serious literary, artistic, political, or scientific value. We do not adopt as a constitutional standard the "*utterly* without redeeming social value" test of Memoirs v. Massachusetts.[16]

It is extremely important for the reader to understand that while the above test may appear vague and overbroad, in reality it is not, despite such arguments by pornographers and civil libertarians. Any vagueness or overbreadth problems are cured

by combining the *Miller* criteria with the specific definitions of sexual conduct set forth in the relevant state or federal law and by taking into consideration the myriad U.S. Supreme Court cases that have interpreted *Miller* and its obscenity test.

Miller gave examples of what a state could include within the sexual conduct/patent offensiveness standard.[17] The *Miller* court emphasized that in order to be obscene, materials must describe or depict "patently offensive 'hard core' sexual conduct."[18] The "contemporary community standards" of the *Miller* guidelines need not be national standards, the court concluded. The fact that the First Amendment limitations on state powers do not vary from state to state

does not mean that there are, or should or can be, fixed, uniform national standards of precisely what appeals to the "prurient interest" or is "patently offensive." These are essentially questions of fact, and our nation is simply too big and too diverse for this Court to reasonably expect that such standards could be articulated for all 50 States in a single formulation, even assuming the prerequisite consensus exists. . . . The adversary system, with lay jurors as the usual ultimate factfinders in criminal prosecutions, has historically permitted triers of fact to draw on the standards of their community, guided always by limiting instructions on the law. To require a State to structure obscenity proceedings around evidence of a *national* "community standard" would be an exercise in futility. . . .

It is neither realistic nor constitutionally sound to read the First Amendment as requiring that the people of Maine or Mississippi accept public depiction of conduct found tolerable in Las Vegas, or New York City.[19]

Nor were jurors required to consider statewide community standards, according to the *Miller* court.

As long as it is not aimed at a deviant group, material is to be judged "by its impact on an average person, rather than a particularly susceptible or sensitive person—or indeed a totally insensitive one," the *Miller* court said.[20] In regulating obscenity, the court emphasized the difference between the interchange of ideas to bring about social and political change desired by the public (which the First Amendment was intended to protect) and the "public portrayal of hard core sexual conduct for its own sake, and for the ensuing commercial gain."[21] The court did not find censorship of good or bad ideas or repression of political liberty "lurking" in regulations of commercial exploitation of sex.[22] *Miller* changed *Roth* in yet another way when it decided that appeal to pruriency must be judged based on the entire work, not just its dominant theme.

The Attorney General's Commission pointed out that because virtually every word of *Miller* has been litigated, there is a large body of legal opinion clarifying and explaining its concepts.[23] The impact of obscenity law, it said, is limited to hard-core material "devoid of anything except the most explicit and offensive representations."[24] The commission rejected proposals to make certain activities automatically obscene and definitions of obscenity broader than those of *Miller* because, it said, it had not been shown that existing laws are insufficient legal tools for those who care to enforce them.[25] (We feel that simplification and clarification of pornography definitions and laws could go a long way toward making enforcement of antipornography laws easier and more successful.)

It is important to emphasize that, since *Roth*, the U.S. Supreme Court has taken the position that obscenity is not speech. Thus, First Amendment theories need not be met, and harms or effects of obscenity need not be shown.[26]

A number of other Supreme Court cases have played major roles in defining the scope of obscenity law. The reader should keep in mind whether cases were decided under the *Roth*, *Memoirs*, or *Miller* obscenity standards and recognize that some aspects of these cases may no longer be valid. The most thorough source of information on obscenity cases is the *Obscenity Law Reporter*, which includes data on all state and federal court cases that were officially reported and is updated periodically.

Kingsley International Pictures Corp. v. *Regents* concerned a state motion picture licensing law. A license was denied for a film that presented adultery as proper behavior. The court found the license denial to be unconstitutional on the ground that the license was refused because the picture advocated an idea. Advocation of ideas is protected under the First Amendment. This case involved the motion picture *Lady Chatterley's Lover*.[27]

Manual Enterprises v. *Day* involved a two-justice opinion that obscenity under *Roth* "requires proof of two distinct elements: (1) patent offensiveness, and (2) 'prurient interest.'" This case established a definition of patent offensiveness that may still be the law—namely, "so offensive on their face as to affront current community standards of decency."[28] While this court found a "national standard of decency" to be the proper test under the federal law, it did not decide whether Congress could set other geographic boundaries.[29]

Manual Enterprises involved male homosexual magazines featuring nudity. The court found that the magazines at issue could not, taken as a whole, "be deemed to go beyond the pale of contemporary notions of rudimentary decency" and were not obscene. It declared that these magazines could not be seen as more objectionable than the "many portrayals of the female nude that society tolerates."[30]

In *Jacobellis* v. *Ohio*, the court stood by the *Roth* standard and found a film not obscene. However, two justices argued that under *Roth*, obscenity is unprotected only because it is "'utterly without redeeming social importance.'" Therefore, they said, material dealing with sex in a way that "advocates ideas" or has "literary or scientific or artistic value or any other form of social importance" is not obscene. And, they said, under *Roth*, material must go "'substantially beyond customary limits of candor in description or representation of such matters.'"[31] These two justices decided that, for purposes of obscenity law, the "community" is society at large and that a local definition of obscenity is improper. They argued that constitutional free expression cannot be allowed to vary with state and local lines. A national standard is required under *Roth*, they said. Two dissenting justices claimed that the proper standards are those of the local community.[32]

Ginzburg v. *United States* was a five-justice opinion. In that case, the court said that the question of whether material is obscene "may include consideration of the setting in which the publications were presented."[33] The background of this case involved "commercial exploitation of erotica solely for the sake of their prurient appeal," the justices said. This is the major case on pandering.[34] The publications involved in *Ginzburg* were pandered, which, according to the concurring opinion of Justice Earl Warren in *Roth*, is "'the business of purveying textual or graphic matter openly advertised to appeal to the erotic interest of their customers.'"[35]

In *Ginzburg* material was mailed from Middlesex, New York. Titles included *Eros* and *Liaison*. The "'leer of the sensualist'" also permeated the advertising for the publications, the court noted.[36] Solicitation for customers was "indiscriminate" rather than limited to those (such as physicians or psychiatrists) who might discern "therapeutic worth" in *The Housewife's Handbook on Selective Promiscuity*, the court said.[37] Here, the pandering issue was relevant to the obscenity issue, resolving "all ambiguity and doubt."[38] Representing the publications as "erotically arousing . . . stimulated the reader to accept them as prurient."[39] Readers looked for titillation, not saving intellectual content, the court concluded. Such appeal heightens the offensiveness of the material and also is relevant to deciding whether the social importance claimed by pornographers in the courtroom is "pretense or reality."[40] While such material might escape condemnation in other contexts, here the object of the material was commercial gain through appeal to "sexual curiosity and appetite."[41]

Schauer calls *Ginzburg* "perhaps the most controversial case in all of obscenity law." This decision was significant because some of the materials seemed to be serious literary efforts, he says. Materials not obscene by themselves became obscene because of the manner in which they were made publicly available.[42] He notes that mere open display and sale is not pandering, nor are lurid or enticing cover text or pictures. The most common kind of pandering evidence is "sensationalist advertising emphasizing the erotic or prurient aspects."[43]

Mishkin v. *New York* held that

[w]here the material is designed for and primarily disseminated to a clearly defined deviant sexual group, rather than the public at large, the prurient-appeal requirement of the Roth test is satisfied if the dominant theme of the material taken as a whole appeals to the prurient interest in sex of the members of that group.[44]

The appellant had argued that some of the books at issue (with "deviant" sexual practices such as lesbianism, fetishism, and flagellation) " 'disgust and sicken' " rather than appeal to "a prurient interest of the 'average person' in sex."[45] There was no substantial claim that the material did not have prurient appeal to sexually deviant groups, and the evidence showed that the books were, in fact, designed and marketed for such groups. The court said that it had adjusted the prurient appeal test to social reality—namely, assessing it in "terms of the sexual interests of its intended and probable recipient group."[46] According to Schauer, the deviant areas covered by the *Mishkin* decision include, but are not limited to, bestiality, bondage, sadomasochism, and homosexuality.[47]

In a confusing per curiam decision, the court, in *Redrup* v. *New York, Austin* v. *Kentucky, Gent et al.* v. *Arkansas*, refused to say what obscenity was but said whichever case law applied, the obscenity convictions involved in these cases could not stand. The justices did note that three court members held to the "utterly without redeeming social value" test.[48]

The issue in *Ginsberg* v. *New York* was whether a state statute could prohibit sale to minors of material defined as obscene based on appeal to minors regardless of whether it was obscene for adults. The "girlie" magazines involved in this case were not obscene for adults. In this variable obscenity case, the court held that the statute did not invade "the area of freedom of expression constitutionally secured to minors."[49] The state has the power to regulate the well-being of children, the court said. It was rational for the state to find that minors' exposure to such material might be harmful. The decision did not prevent parents from buying these materials for their children. The court said that it was adjusting the obscenity definition to social reality by allowing the appeal of the material to be looked at in terms of the sexual interests of minors.[50]

In *Stanley* v. *Georgia*, the defendant was charged with knowingly possessing obscene material. While searching for bookmaking evidence, authorities found three 8mm films in a desk drawer in Stanley's bedroom that, upon viewing, they said were obscene. Stanley argued that punishing mere possession of obscene material violated the First Amendment. Although the state argued that, under *Roth*, obscenity is without constitutional protection, the court held that "the mere private possession of obscene matter cannot constitutionally be made a crime."[51] *Roth* and other cases found an important interest in regulating the "commercial distribution" of obscenity, the court said.[52] Here, the constitutional right to "receive information and ideas" and to be free, except in limited circumstances, "from unwanted governmental intrusions into one's privacy" were controlling, the court said.[53] According to the court, "If the First Amendment means anything, it means that a State has no business telling a man, sitting alone in his own house, what books he may read or what films he may watch."[54]

The court said it was not certain that the state's claim of a right to protect "the individual's mind from the effects of obscenity . . . amounts to anything more than the assertion that the State has the right to control the moral content of a person's thoughts," which is inconsistent with the First Amendment.[55] It noted that a line cannot be drawn between the transmission of ideas and entertainment. States cannot "premise legislation of the desirability of controlling a person's private thoughts."[56] Here, there was no danger of the material intruding upon the general public's "sensibilities" or falling into children's hands.

In an interesting aside, the *Stanley* court commented that there seemed to be "little empirical basis" for the claim that exposure to obscene material may lead to sexually violent crimes or deviant sexual behavior.[57] It said:

But more important, if the State is only concerned about printed or filmed materials inducing anti-social conduct, we believe that in the context of private consumption of ideas and information we should adhere to the view that "[a]mong free men the deterrents ordinarily to be applied to prevent crime are education and punishment for violations of the law." (Brandeis, J. concurring in *Whitney* v. *California*.)[58]

The court did note that in *Roth,* the court rejected the necessity of proving that exposure to obscenity would induce recipients to antisocial conduct or create a clear and present danger of such conduct. However, that case dealt with the public distribution of obscenity, the court said.[59]

U.S. v. *Reidel* refused to extend the *Stanley* right to possess obscenity in the home to a right to sell (delivery through mail) to willing adult recipients.[60]

In *U.S.* v. *37 Photographs,* the defendant was arrested by customs officials when he returned to the United States from Europe with thirty-seven allegedly obscene photographs. The court refused to extend the *Stanley* possession of obscenity for private use in the home to a right to import obscenity from abroad.[61]

Rabe v. *Washington* involved a statute that allowed someone to be punished for showing an obscene film in a drive-in theater, but not in an indoor theater. (The statute had been so interpreted by the state supreme court.) The *Rabe* court said that the statute, as applied, was impermissibly vague for failing to give the defendant "fair notice that criminal liability is dependent upon the place where the film is shown." The statute itself said nothing about the location of an obscene exhibition being an element of the offense.[62]

Kois v. *Wisconsin* involved a published story about one of the newspaper *Kaleidoscope*'s photographers being arrested for possession of obscene material. The story was accompanied by two small photographs of a nude man and woman embracing in a sitting position. The pictures were said to be similar to those seized from the photographer.[63] The court thought that it would be unfair to say the article "was a mere vehicle for the publication of the pictures."[64] It said, "A quotation from Voltaire in the flyleaf of a book will not constitutionally redeem an otherwise obscene publication, but if these pictures were indeed similar to the one seized—they are relevant to the theme of the article."[65]

The court did not look at whether the pictures could be disseminated alone. The *Kois* court decided that here, in the context in which the pictures appeared in the newspaper, "they were rationally related to an article that itself was clearly entitled to the protection of the Fourteenth Amendment."[66]

The *Kois* court also dealt with a two-page spread of eleven poems in *Kaleidoscope,* one of which was titled "Sex Poem" and was about sexual intercourse. Here, the justices looked at the content and placement of the poem. They concluded that the poem bore "some of the earmarks of an attempt at serious art." It could not be said that the "dominant theme of this poem appeals to prurient interest."[67]

Pinkus v. *U.S.* held that in a prosecution under federal law for mailing obscene material, children were not to be included as part of the "community" under the *Miller* test. There was no evidence that children were the intended recipients of the material or that the petitioner had reason to know they were likely to receive the material. (The court emphasized that nothing suggested that insensitive or sensitive persons were to be excluded from the community as a whole but that such persons are not to be focused upon.) *Pinkus* also reaffirmed the right to give a jury instruction on appeal to "deviant" groups when the evidence supports such a charge. And it noted that methods of the materials' "creation, promotion, or dissemination are relevant" to the obscenity issue.[68]

SPECIFIC CONCERNS INVOLVING OBSCENITY LAW

Average Person

The interpretations of court decisions involving the "average person" concept of obscenity law are primarily based on information contained in the *Obscenity Law Reporter.* Consult pages 1011–12 of that book for conclusions about the average person standard reached by the attorneys at the National Obscenity Law Center (NOLC).

When defining the average person for obscenity law purposes, all persons in the community must be included. The *Pinkus* court said that average person "means what it usually means and is no less clear" than the term "reasonable person" used in other contexts.[69] Children might be included in the term average person where a defendant has reason to know that they are part of the audience, the NOLC believes.

The average person's role is primarily to judge the nature of the material. Secondarily, the average person embodies the reaction of the community. Jurors must evaluate the "average person" to determine the collective view of the community.[70]

According to *Mishkin,* when the evidence warrants it, special jury instructions can permit deviant material to be judged on its appeal to members of "deviant" groups rather than to the average person.

The old obscenity test established in *Hicklin* judged material by its impact on the most susceptible persons. *Roth* decided that such materials must be judged by their "impact on an average person, rather than a particularly susceptible or sensitive person—or indeed a totally insensitive one." Yet such people are not to be excluded from the community as a whole. The *Pinkus* court equated the average person with the "collective view of the community." Minors are not to be included in the average person equation unless they are intended or likely recipients of the material. George Weaver notes that it is best to think of the average person as one possessing "the mean values of all significant characteristics in the relevant community." The court has compared this person to the "reasonable person" concept used in other areas of the law."[71]

Schauer states that there is "a serious doubt as to whether the jury, especially in an obscenity case, despite instructions on the average man, can apply any evaluation of pruriency other than its own personal standard." It is hard, he feels, to decide what appeals to someone else's prurient interest, and most people think of themselves as having average sexual instincts.[72]

Contemporary Community Standards

As detailed earlier in this chapter, under *Miller*, juries and judges are not required to consider a national community or a statewide community. No precise geographical area is constitutionally required.[73] *Hamling* v. *United States* interpreted the *Miller* language as follows:

> A juror is entitled to draw on his own knowledge of the views of the average person in the community or vicinage from which he comes for making the required determination, just as he is entitled to draw on his knowledge of the propensities of a "reasonable" person in other areas of the law. . . . Our holding in Miller that California could constitutionally proscribe obscenity in terms of a "statewide" standard did not mean that any such precise geographic area is required as a matter of constitutional law.
> . . . The result of the Miller cases . . . is to permit a juror sitting in obscenity cases to draw on knowledge of the community or vicinage from which he comes in deciding what conclusion "the average person, applying contemporary community standards" would reach in a given case.[74]

In *Hamling*, a federal obscenity case was tried in a district court in California. The court said that jurors were presumably available from that district and it would be the standards of that " 'community' upon which the jurors would draw." Evidence of standards from outside that district could be admitted

if the judge felt it would assist the jurors in resolving the issues before them.[75]

Smith v. *United States* said that states could "impose a geographic limit on the determination of community standards by defining the area from which the jury could be selected in an obscenity case."[76]

There is disagreement about whether the fact that obscene material is tolerated or permitted by local law enforcement agencies creates a community standard. The *Obscenity Law Reporter* cites cases from across the United States that have found the relevant community to be the state, county, school district, area from which the jury is drawn, or municipality.[77]

Community standards may be looked at as "the standards of the average adult person." This ensures that fact finders cannot use their personal standards in determining what is obscene.[78]

Parrish believes that the word *community* adds confusion to the law and that the Constitution requires only that the contemporary standards of the average person be applied. He explains that *community* is a nongeographical concept, simply people in general or society at large, people in community with each other, with common interests or pursuits. He believes that it is unwise for states to draw geographic boundaries, for this can create troublesome proof problems for juries.[79]

Neil Gallagher suggests that civic action is the way to eliminate pornography and that community standards are substantially determined by the activity and concern of citizens.[80]

Taken as a Whole

While usually it is not difficult to determine what the "whole" is in relation to a work, problems arise when magazines and newspapers containing unconnected items are involved. This issue has not been settled by the U.S. Supreme Court. According to *Kois*, a pre-*Miller* case, deliberate attempts to add serious value to otherwise obscene works will not prevent findings of obscenity. *Kois* seems to indicate that a whole newspaper need not be considered as a whole when determining obscenity. If *Kois* can be read as applying to magazines also, then the rationally related test also applies to magazines and an entire magazine need not be considered as a whole. In *Kois*, when photographs in a newspaper that might be obscene were rationally related to an article clearly entitled to constitutional protection, the whole under consideration was the combination of the article and the photographs. There are many conflicting cases on this issue.[81]

In *Erznoznik* v. *City of Jacksonville*, the court

shed light on the meaning of "taken as a whole" when it said that "[s]cenes of nudity in a movie, like pictures of nude persons in a book, must be considered as a part of the whole book."[82] Weaver argues that the taken as a whole standard requires that materials be judged as "a single unit and not on the basis of isolated passages." He states that the standard applies to materials united by a common theme.[83]

Prurient Interest Appeal

Brockett v. *Spokane Arcades, Inc.* shed light on the *Miller* prurient interest test when it decided that a state statute that defined prurient as "that which incites lasciviousness or lust" must be interpreted to exclude from the meaning of *lust* a "normal interest in sex." The court found no fault with the lasciviousness aspect of the definition.[84]

The *Brockett* court relied on *Roth* for guidance in defining prurient interest. It said that *Roth* defined " 'material which deals with sex in a manner appealing to prurient interest,' " as,

> i.e., material having a tendency to excite lustful thoughts. Webster's New International Dictionary (Unabridged, 2d ed, 1949) defines *prurient*, in pertinent part, as follows:
> " . . . Itching; longing; uneasy with desire or longing; of persons, having itching, morbid, or lascivious longings; of desire, curiosity, or propensity, lewd. . . .
> *Pruriency* is defined, in pertinent part, as follows:
> " . . . Quality of being prurient; lascivious desire or thought."[85]

As *Brockett* noted, the *Roth* court also perceived no significant difference between its definition of obscenity and that of the American Law Institute Model Penal Code, which stated: " ' ". . . A thing is obscene if, considered as a whole, its predominant appeal is to prurient interest, i.e., a shameful or morbid interest in nudity, sex, or excretion, and if it goes substantially beyond customary limits of candor in description or representation of such matters." ' "[86]

The *Brockett* court commented:

> If, as we have held, prurience may be constitutionally defined for the purposes of identifying obscenity as that which appeals to a shameful or morbid interest in sex, . . . it is equally certain that if the statute at issue here is invalidated only insofar as the word "lust" is taken to include normal interest in sex, the statute would pass

constitutional muster and would validly reach the whole range of obscene publications.[87]

Unfortunately, the *Brockett* court did not define what is meant by a normal interest in sex. According to *Mishkin*, the prurient appeal requirement can also be targeted to "deviant" sexual groups when "the dominant theme of material taken as a whole appeals to the prurient interest in sex of the members of that group."[88] (This gets around the problem that many "deviant" sexual themes would disgust or sicken rather than appeal to the prurient interest of the average person.)

Attorney Bruce Taylor includes a definition of *prurient* in his proposed model law: "a lewd, lascivious, erotic, shameful, or morbid interest in sexual conduct or sexually explicit nudity, which would either have a tendency to excite lustful thoughts in or disgust and sicken the average person or members of its intended and probably recipient deviant group."[89]

Patent Offensiveness

Under current law (*Miller*), the appeal to prurient interest and the patent offensiveness prongs have contemporary community standards applied to them. However, the serious literary, artistic, or political value prong does not.[90] *Smith* v. *United States* said that "contemporary community standards must be applied by juries in accordance with their own understanding of the tolerance of the average person in their community." The entire community must be considered, "not simply their own subjective reactions or the reactions of a sensitive or of a callous minority."[91] Because of the use of the term *tolerance* in *Smith*, some courts have required community standards to be judged by community standards of tolerance rather than decency. The NOLC argues that the definition of patent offensiveness as " 'so offensive on their face as to affront current community standards of decency.' " (*Manual Enterprises* v. *Day*) is still the law because it has never been specifically overruled by the Supreme Court.[92] Weaver argues that the patent offensiveness test asks whether most people in the community would "immediately feel offended—or revolted, or disgusted—if they viewed the material."[93]

Hard-Core Sexual Conduct

Miller gave these examples of hard-core sexual conduct:

(a) Patently offensive representations or descriptions of ultimate sexual acts, normal or perverted, actual or simulated.

(b) Patently offensive representations or descriptions of masturbation, excretory functions, and lewd exhibition of the genitals.[94]

Miller emphasized that no one could be prosecuted for violating an obscenity law unless the material described or depicted "patently offensive 'hard core' sexual conduct specifically defined by the regulating state law, as written or construed." Simulated sexual activity can be hard-core pornography.[95]

Under *Miller*, *Jenkins* v. *Georgia* found that "nudity alone is not enough to make material legally obscene." In *Jenkins*, the film *Carnal Knowledge* was found not to depict sexual conduct in a patently offensive way. In that film, there were occasional nude scenes, but when sexual conduct was understood to be taking place, the camera did not focus on the actors' bodies and there was no exhibition of their genitals.[96]

Kaplan v. *California* held that words alone can be obscene. That case involved a book with no pictures made up "entirely of repetitive descriptions of physical, sexual conduct, 'clinically' explicit and offensive to the point of being nauseous."[97]

Ward v. *Illinois* also found books alone to be obscene. The *Ward* court rejected the argument that sadomasochistic materials including flagellation could not be prohibited because they were not expressly included in the examples of sexually explicit materials given in *Miller*. The court said that *Miller* gave examples not intended to be an exhaustive list.[98]

Mishkin v. *New York* found materials featuring "deviant" sexual practices such as fetishism, lesbianism, and flagellation to be obscene.[99]

According to the *Obscenity Law Reporter*, various cases have found materials featuring heterosexual intercourse, cunnilingus, fellatio, sodomy, bestiality, spread-eagled photographs of females, ejaculation, and use of sexual devices such as artificial vaginas and dildos to be obscene.[100]

Serious Value

One of the parts of the *Miller* obscenity test is "whether the work, taken as a whole, lacks serious literary, artistic, political, or scientific value." That case specifically rejected the *Memoirs* requirement that a work be "utterly without redeeming social value."[101] But states can adopt such stricter standards. The serious value test is an objective one, not couched in terms of contemporary community standards.[102] Under *Miller*, works with serious value, as defined,

receive First Amendment protection, regardless of whether most people or the government approves of the ideas presented in them.

Paris Adult Theatre I v. *Slaton* stated:

> If we accept . . . the well nigh universal belief that good books, plays, and art lift the spirit, improve the mind, enrich the human personality, and develop character, can we then say that a state legislature may not act on the corollary assumption that commerce in obscene books, or public exhibitions focused on obscene conduct, have a tendency to exert a corrupting and debasing impact leading to antisocial behavior?[103]

A political cartoon in a campus underground newspaper showing the Goddess of Justice and the Statue of Liberty being raped by policemen was not obscene according to *Papish* v. *Bd. of Curators of Missouri*. The court considered this to be the dissemination of ideas.[104]

The serious value test of *Miller* provides a major loophole for pornographers. For example, if pornographers insert enough articles of literary value in a magazine, despite the pornographic content of the rest of the magazine, it is likely that an obscenity requirement that the magazine *taken as a whole* must lack serious value could not be met. Yet, as feminists have suggested, if a human being is shown being sexually abused, it should not matter whether or not a work has such value.

Expert testimony is not required on the issue of serious value or for a court or jury to judge any aspect of obscenity.[105]

Schauer states that the value to be serious, "it must be a significant amount. It must also represent a major purpose of the material." There should be serious intent and serious effect.[106]

Weaver believes that "advocacy of ideas in a work counts toward serious value." Even a serious attempt may be enough. Pandering is a means of "probing the intent behind the material" in the serious value test.[107]

Schauer points out that the *Miller* court specified certain types of value as negating obscenity. It excluded entertainment value or educational value (as pornography could probably be said to "educate" about sexual techniques). The *Miller* exemptions of literary or artistic value seem to allow room for subjective judgment. As Schauer notes, advocacy of abolition of obscenity laws or of different standards of sexual conduct are examples of political views that would be protected if such ideas were a major theme of a work. He describes the serious value aspect of *Miller* this way:

Three elements of this change are significant. First, and probably most important, is the rejection of such language as "utterly" or "unqualifiedly" worthless, or "modicum of social value" found in *Memoirs*. The significance lies in the quantum of value required to redeem an otherwise obscene work. Under the *Memoirs* standard, some very slight degree of seemingly serious matter or intent would be significant. Under *Miller*, the value must be more predominant, more serious, and more pervasive throughout the entire work. . . . What the addition of the "serious" element does is to allow the jury and court to look beneath the argued or claimed value of the material to the relationship between the nonpornographic and the pornographic, and to the *intent* upon which the insertion of literary, artistic, political, or scientific value is based. If that intent is to convey a literary, artistic, political, or scientific idea or message, or to impart information, or advocate a position, then the purpose or intent is "serious" as the word appears to be used in *Miller*. If, on the other hand, it appears or is found that the purpose is to "dress up" or to try to "redeem" otherwise obscene matter, sold or distributed for its obscenity rather than for its ideas or message, then the value is not "serious." . . .

The second notable change embodied in the *Miller* test for value is the rejection of "the ambiguous concept of 'social importance.' " . . .

Finally, *Miller* specifically enumerated the kinds of value which would save an otherwise prurient and patently offensive work.[108]

Variable Obscenity

Variable obscenity means that material deemed suitable in one situation might be regulated in another. For example, material not considered obscene for the general adult population might be considered obscene if it was exhibited or distributed to minors. Such principles also might apply if material had no prurient appeal to normal adults but was directed at a "deviant" group. The intended audience and circumstances involved in the material's distribution become issues in variable obscenity cases. *Mishkin* established the principle that the obscenity definition may be varied or geared toward clearly defined "deviant groups," while *Ginsberg* followed the same rule for minors.

At the same time, however, legislators are not free to restrict the adult population to reading what is fit for children.[109] (*Butler* v. *Michigan*). Thus, some material might be protected activity if sold to adults but subject to restrictions if sold to children. Under the concept of variable obscenity, obscenity is not inherent in the material but rather is based on its

appeal to and effect on the audience at which it is primarily aimed.

Any law that regulates the flow of material harmful to minors must meet the rational basis test. The law in question must be rationally related to the purpose of safeguarding minors from harm due to obscenity.[110]

Erznoznik emphasized that laws aimed at keeping minors from viewing films must be directed against sexually explicit nudity and that "all nudity cannot be deemed obscene even as to minors." The court said that speech not deemed obscene for minors or legitimately proscribable for some other reason "cannot be suppressed solely to protect the young from ideas or images that a legislative body thinks unsuitable for them." Usually, the court said, the First Amendment is no less applicable to minors.[111]

Nudity

Nudity in itself is not obscene. In *Erznoznik*, a local ordinance prohibited drive-in theaters from showing films with nudity when their screens were visible from a public place or street. The movie at issue included images of female breasts and buttocks and could be viewed from public places. Although the locality conceded that the ordinance went beyond obscenity and applied to films protected by the First Amendment, it claimed that a movie involving nudity that is "visible from a public place may be suppressed as a nuisance." They claimed a need to protect citizens from unwilling exposure to offensive materials.[112]

The court that said states can "protect individual privacy by enacting reasonable time, place and manner regulations applicable to all speech irrespective of content" but cannot shield the public from speech on the ground of offensiveness unless it intrudes in the home or it is impractical to avoid exposure. Because people are captive audiences for many purposes in our society, the burden is usually on the viewer to avoid exposure by averting his or her eyes, the court said.[113]

In *Erznoznik*, the local law discriminated against movies solely on the basis of content. The privacy interests of persons on the public streets could not justify censoring otherwise protected speech on the basis of content, the court concluded. Even if the ordinance were aimed at keeping minors from viewing the films, it was too broad, for it was not directed at sexually explicit nudity. The court said authorities could not single out nude scenes as a traffic hazard justifying traffic regulation.[114]

California v. *La Rue* involved nude dancing in a bar. In that case, the court made it clear that not all conduct can be labeled speech. While not all performances covered by the law involved were without constitutional protection, the court found it important that the state had not prohibited such nude performances completely. The court said that it "was not irrational" to prohibit "certain sexual performances and the dispensation of liquor by the drink . . . at premises that have licenses."[115]

Doran v. *Salem Inn* concerned topless dancing in bars. A local ordinance prohibited bar owners from allowing entertainers, waitresses, and barmaids from appearing on their premises "with breasts uncovered or so thinly draped as to appear uncovered."[116] The ordinance was not limited to establishments that served liquor but forbade any female from appearing with her breasts uncovered. The court concluded that the lower court had not abused its discretion by granting a preliminary injunction against the law to the bar owners. However, it declined to issue an opinion as to the merits of the owners' arguments against the ordinance.[117]

In *Schad* v. *Borough of Mount Ephraim*, a local law prohibited all live entertainment, including nude dancing, in commercial zones. Some live entertainment escaped prohibition because it had existed prior to passage of the ordinance. The court said that this law prohibited a "wide range of expression that has long been held to be within the protection of the First and Fourteenth Amendments."[118] Again it emphasized that nudity alone does not make otherwise protected material unprotected. The court said, "[W]hen a zoning law infringes upon a protected liberty, it must be narrowly drawn and must further a sufficiently substantial governmental interest."[119] The court looked at whether the interest at stake could be served by less intrusive means. None of the justifications advanced by the locality were adequate:

1. The permitted uses went beyond the immediate needs of the residents.
2. There was no evidence that purposes of avoiding parking problems, trash, medical needs, or police protection were more significant with this type of use than with other uses.
3. It was not shown that a less intrusive regulation could not meet the needs.
4. It was not shown that live entertainment was incompatible with the allowed uses.
5. This was not a reasonable time, place, and manner restriction, and there was a lack of alternative communication channels.[120]

Nudity depictions, whether live or not, have been tested under the *Miller* obscenity standards. For example, nudity in sculpture, painting, or bona fide medical texts is not obscene if the material has serious literary, artistic, political, or scientific value. The NOLC argues that under *State* v. *Baysinger, Clark* v. *Indiana*, and *Dove* v. *Indiana* a state may prohibit nudity in a public place without having to meet the *Miller* test as long as exceptions are made for performances protected by the First and Fourteenth amendments. The differences appear to be based on a concept that mere nudity is conduct and not a communication, whereas nudity in connection with a performance might involve communication or speech.[121]

In *Southeastern Promotions Inc.* v. *Conrad*, a permit was denied for the showing of the rock musical *Hair* based on reports that it involved obscenity and nudity onstage. The court found this to be a prior restraint that was not allowable because minimal procedural safeguards were not included in the law. (Live theater productions are forms of expression protected by the First Amendment.)[122]

What Forms of Expression Can Be Obscene?

The following items involve expression protected by the First Amendment in some situations. However, such items, if they meet the *Miller* standards, could be found obscene.

Motion pictures
Books
Magazines
Newspapers
Poems and songs
Comic books, playing cards, and key chains
Pictures, photographs, and drawings
Language
Dildos and artificial vaginas
Advertisements
Telephone calls
Television, cable television, and radio programs

Language that is indecent but not obscene can sometimes be prohibited by law. (See chapter 11 for regulations of indecent language on television, cable television, and radio.) The *Obscenity Law Reporter* contains a detailed history of cases in which the types of expressions listed above have been found obscene.

Types of Allowable Regulation

Interstate transportation of obscene materials for sale or distribution can be and is prohibited by the federal government.[123] The federal government has, by civil forfeiture statute, prohibited the importation of obscenity since 1842.[124] Under *New York* v. *Ferber*, child pornography dissemination can be made illegal without having to meet the *Miller* obscenity test[125] (see chapter 14 on child pornography).

Prior Restraint and Search and Seizure Issues

A large number of the obscenity cases that have reached the U.S. Supreme Court have revolved around issues of prior restraint and/or search and seizure.

Ex Parte Jackson held that while packages are in the mail, they can be opened and examined only under warrant and Congress cannot give the U.S. Postal Service power to open mail. This was based on the Constitution's Fourth Amendment search and seizure clause.[126]

Kingsley International Pictures Corp. v. *Regents* was a motion picture licensing case. The picture at issue portrayed adultery in a positive way. The court said that the First Amendment guarantees the freedom to advocate ideas.[127]

Marcus v. *Search Warrants of Property* involved a state law that allowed a judge to issue a search and seizure warrant if the complaint of the police officer "states positively and not upon information and belief" facts from which the judge determines there is probable cause to believe obscene material is being held or kept in any place. The procedure did not provide for a hearing before issuance of the warrant. However, the judge had to set a date no later than twenty days after the seizure to determine whether the material was obscene. The owner could appear at the hearing, and there was no set time limit for the judge to give his or her decision. If the material was found obscene, it would be ordered destroyed. Otherwise, it would be returned to the owner.

In this case, the judge found 100 of the 280 items seized to be obscene. The court gave a history of search and seizure uses to suppress objectionable publications. Here the police officers just repeated the law's language in their request for a warrant and specified no named publications. The law gave broad discretion to the police in the warrants. No guide was given to exercise informed discretion. No step in the procedure focused searchingly on the question of obscenity. The court held that the statute lacked due process safeguards to ensure nonobscene material constitutional protection.[128]

Bantam Books, Inc. v. *Sullivan* involved a morals commission that tried to suppress books. It succeeded in stopping circulation by threatening to report persons it believed violated the law to authorities who could prosecute them. Lists of objectional publications were circulated to police departments, and book publishers and distributors were informed. Some of the books were not obscene. In reference to the discrimination of lists, the court said, "People do not lightly disregard public officers' thinly veiled threats to institute criminal proceedings against them."[129]

The court found this law unconstitutional, saying that it was a form of state regulation that made the state's criminal obscenity regulation "largely unnecessary." At the same time, the law eliminated criminal process safeguards. No safeguards against suppressing constitutionally protected, nonobscene material were provided. The court called it a system of "informal censorship." In overruling the law, it said:

> Any system of prior restraints of expression comes to this Court bearing a heavy presumption against its constitutional validity. . . . We have tolerated such a system only where it operated under judicial superintendence and assured an almost immediate judicial determination of the validity of the restraint.[130]

In this case, no judicial superintendence was provided for before notices were sent out by the commission, and there was no provision for judicial review.

A Quantity of Books v. *Kansas* involved the seizure of 1,715 copies of 31 novels. The state law authorized the seizure of books that were allegedly obscene prior to an adversary determination of obscenity. (An adversary hearing is one in which all parties have the right to be heard, including the defendant.) After a hearing, the books were ordered destroyed. The court said the law's procedures were "constitutionally insufficient because they did not adequately safeguard against the suppression of nonobscene books." Because an adversary hearing prior to the seizure of masses of books was not held, the seizure order was unconstitutional.[131]

The major case to set standards for making prior restraint on expression constitutional was *Freedman* v. *Maryland*. The case involved a motion picture censorship statute. The law at issue allowed the board to bar disapproved films "unless and until the exhibitor undertakes a time-consuming appeal to the Maryland courts and succeeds in having the Board's decision reversed."[132] No procedure was specified for court participation in the barring of films or for prompt judicial review. The *Freedman* court stated:

> Unlike a prosecution for obscenity, a censorship proceeding puts the initial burden on the exhibitor or distributor. Because the censor's business is to

censor, there inheres the danger that he may well be less responsive than a court—part of an independent branch of government—to the constitutionally protected interests in free expression. And if it is made unduly onerous, by reason of delay or otherwise, to seek judicial review, the censor's determination may in practice be final.

. . . [W]e hold that a noncriminal process which requires the prior submission of a film to a censor avoids constitutional infirmity only if it takes place under procedural safeguards designed to obviate the dangers of a censorship system. First, the burden of proving that the film is unprotected expression must rest on the censor. . . . Second, while the State may require advance submission of all films, in order to proceed effectively to bar all showings of unprotected films, the requirement cannot be administered in a manner which would lend an effect of finality to the censor's determination whether a film constitutes protected expression. The teaching of our cases is that, because only a judicial determination in an adversary proceeding ensures the necessary sensitivity to freedom of expression, only a procedure requiring a judicial determination suffices to impose a valid final restraint. . . . To this end, the exhibitor must be assured, by statute or authoritative judicial construction, that the censor will, within a specified brief period, either issue a license or go to court to restrain showing the film. Any restraint imposed in advance of a final judicial determination on the merits must similarly be limited to preservation of the status quo for the shortest fixed period compatible with sound judicial resolution. . . . [T]he procedure must also assure a prompt final judicial decision, to minimize the deterrent effect of an interim and possibly erroneous denial of a license.[133]

Because the state law at issue did not meet those criteria, the court reversed the appellant's conviction. The *Freedman* court suggested looking to *Kingsley Books, Inc.* v. *Brown* for a model. That case upheld a state injunctive procedure aimed at preventing the sale of obscene books. The procedure in *Kingsley* postponed restraints against sale after obscenity was judicially determined following "notice and an adversary hearing." That law allowed a hearing one day after joinder of issue and said the judge had to issue a decision within two days after the hearing terminated.[134]

Blount v. *Rizzi*, a case involving mailing obscenity, concluded that proper safeguards were lacking in the federal law's administrative censorship scheme. There was no "governmentally initiated judicial participation in the procedure" and no provision to ensure prompt judicial review. The court decision was based on *Freedman*.[135]

In *U.S.* v. *37 Photographs* the court found it possible to construe the law to meet constitutional requirements by reading the *Freedman* time limits into the it and finding them consistent with the legislative purpose. It therefore required that forfeiture proceedings begin within fourteen days and be completed within sixty days of commencement.[136]

In *Heller* v. *New York*, it was held that there is no right to an adversary hearing on the issue of probable obscenity before a warrant for seizure is issued. Importantly, *Heller* involved seizure of only one copy of one film. (A massive seizure of multiple copies may have resulted in a different outcome.) And, in this case, a fully adversary trial and a final judicial determination were complete within forty-eight days of the "temporary seizure." The court said that if it were shown that the exhibitor did not have other copies of the film available to exhibit, the court should allow the film to be copied so that it could continue to be shown pending "a judicial determination of the obscenity issue in an adversary proceeding."[137]

In *Roaden* v. *Kentucky*, a sheriff and prosecutor purchased tickets to and attended a film showing at a drive-in theater. At the conclusion of the film, the sheriff arrested the theater manager for exhibiting an obscene film to the public in violation of a state law. At the same time, the sheriff seized one copy of the film for evidence. While it was conceded that the film was obscene, the manager argued that the seizure of the film without a warrant violated the Fourth Amendment. The *Roaden* court said:

> Seizing a film then being exhibited to the general public presents essentially the same restraint on expression as the seizure of all the books in a bookstore. Such precipitate action by a police officer, without the authority of a constitutionally sufficient warrant, is plainly a form of prior restraint and is, in those circumstances, unreasonable under Fourth Amendment standards. . . . [P]rior restraint of the right of expression . . . calls for a higher hurdle in the evaluation of reasonableness.[138]

In *Roaden* there were no exigent circumstances (such as a need to preserve evidence of a crime), and the seizure could not be justified as a seizure of contraband. Nothing before the seizure had given a court or magistrate the chance to " 'focus searchingly on the question of obscenity' " (quoting *Heller*).[139]

Prior restraint was also an issue in *Southeastern Promotions Inc.* v. *Conrad*, the case involving the musical *Hair* described earlier in this chapter. In that case, use of a forum was denied prior to expression instead of allowing police to prosecute any illegalities after the fact. Again, minimal procedural safeguards were lacking. The *Freedman* procedures should have been followed, the court said.[140]

An open-ended search warrant that did not describe or list any specific items that were allegedly obscene was found to violate the Fourth Amendment in *Lo-Ji Sales Inc.* v. *New York.* This left it up to the local officials' discretion to determine which items were likely to be obscene during the search and seizure.[141]

Universal Amusement Co. v. *Vance* concerned a nuisance law that operated as a prior restraint. Orders temporarily prohibiting the exhibition of films were allowed to be entered ex parte (without the defendant being heard). Such injunctions could be extended upon a showing of probable success on the merits but without a final obscenity decision. The procedures were found deficient. *Freedman* should have been followed.[142]

In *Walter* v. *U.S.* and *U.S.* v. *Sanders,* sealed boxes with 871 boxes of 8mm film of homosexual activities were shipped by private carrier across state lines and delivered to the wrong place. The employees of the place where the boxes were delivered opened them and found suggestive drawings and explicit content descriptions on the sides of the boxes. They called the FBI. The FBI viewed the films without a warrant and without communication with the shipment cosignor or cosignee. Petitioners were indicted for interstate transportation of obscenity. The court held that "the unauthorized exhibition of the films constituted an unreasonable invasion of the owner's constitutionally protected interest in privacy. It was a search; there was no warrant; the owner had not consented; and there were no exigent circumstances."[143]

The *Walter* court said that the labels on the boxes gave probable cause that the films were obscene but were not enough to convict. Lawful possession of the boxes by the FBI did not give them authority to search the box contents. The fact that the packages and some boxes were opened by a private party before the FBI acquired them did not "excuse the failure to obtain a search warrant." There was nothing wrong with examining the contents to the extent already done by the private party; however, the government could not exceed the scope of the private search without a warrant. The additional search by the FBI—the screening of the films—was not justified and violated the Fourth Amendment. The fact that the cartons were opened by a third party did not "alter the cosignor's legitimate expectation of privacy."[144]

Maryland v. *Macon* made it clear that purchase of a magazine by a police officer was not a seizure, for there was no reasonable expectation of privacy and possessory interests were voluntarily transferred. The public was invited to enter the store and transact business therein.[145]

New York v. *P.J. Video, Inc.* established the probable cause standard applicable to seizure of materials presumtively protected by the First Amendment. A district attorney's investigator rented and viewed ten films, made affidavits summarizing film content, and attached these to police applications for a warrant to search the respondent's store. The warrant was issued, and police seized one or two copies of the movies described. Obscenity charges were brought concerning five of the ten movies. The respondent claimed that the movies should not be suppressed because the "warrant authorizing their seizure was not supported by probable cause because the issuing justice had not personally viewed the movies."[146] The court included the affidavit contents as an appendix. (This case also contains a good summary of other search and seizure cases.)

The court said that the First Amendment does not require a higher standard of probable cause. Thus, the regular standard should apply: Probable cause means " 'less than evidence which would justify condemnation. . . . It imports a seizure made under circumstances which warrant suspicion' " (citations omitted).[147] Only a " 'probability or substantial chance of criminal activity, not an actual showing of such activity' " is needed (citations omitted). The warrant was supported by probable cause.[148]

Search and seizure and prior restraint claims by pornographers are important, for failure to meet those constitutional requirements can result in dismissal of obscenity cases. Good sources of information on search and seizure law as it relates to obscenity include the books by Schauer and Weaver, the *Obscenity Law Reporter,* and Giampietro.[149]

Morality in Media, Inc., attorney Paul J. McGeady states that no adversary hearing prior to seizure of a copy of commercial motion pictures for use as evidence is necessary if these safeguards are met:

1. Prior Judicial Scrutiny.
2. By a Neutral Magistrate.
3. Which permits him to Focus Searchingly on the Question of Obscenity.
4. And who Determines that Probable Cause Exists.
5. And who Issues a Warrant For the Seizure of the Film.
6. And there is available following the Seizure a Prompt Judicial Determination of the Obscenity Issue in an Adversary Proceeding at the Request of Any Interested Party.[150]

(We recommend that attorneys and law enforcement personnel involved in searches and seizures obtain a copy of this article.)

The following sections on scienter, multiplicity and duplicity, vagueness, and overbreadth are based primarily on information obtained from the *Obscenity Law Reporter*.

Scienter

Scienter refers to the criminal intent element of criminal laws. It means "guilty knowledge." An example of a statutory term that denotes scienter is *knowingly*. Another such term is *willfully*. The term *intentionally* also can represent such knowledge. Under federal obscenity mailing statutes the only scienter required is that the material is sexually oriented.[151] To fulfill scienter requirements, courts look at the defendants' knowledge of the contents, nature, and character of the material.[152] It is not necessary for the defendants to have personal knowledge of the community standards in every place they distribute the material (films) in interstate commerce.[153]

In *Hays* v. *State*, the element of knowledge on the part of an adult bookstore manager was sufficiently shown by evidence that the storefront bore X-rated movie signs, only adults were admitted to the store, and a sign advertised sexually explicit movies.[154] The Indiana Supreme Court in *Sedelbauer* v. *State* ruled that the defendant would have been out of touch with reality if he did not know and understand the nature of the object he was selling. In *United States* v. *Sandy*, the court said that defendants need not have actually seen films to know the nature and character of them.[155] Other examples of proof of scienter in court cases include showing that the defendant was president of the corporation and helped build the peep show booths and evidence that a defendant had an ownership interest and worked in a peep show arcade on more than one occasion.[156]

According to *State* v. *I. and M. Amusements, Inc.*, in the ordinary operation of a motion picture theater, the knowledge of an agent acting within the scope of his employment will be attributed to a corporation.[157]

Smith v. *California* stated that obscenity ordinances require scienter. The reason for this is a concern that a law without a scienter clause will tend to impose restrictions on protected speech dissemination.[158] Because of this requirement, obscenity cannot be a strict liability crime. Scienter is usually proven by use of circumstantial evidence. It is not necessary to prove that the defendant actually saw or read the very materials in question.[159]

Various courts cited in the *Obscenity Law Reporter* found sufficient scienter on the part of obscenity

defendants to have been shown by proving the defendant was aware of the nature or contents of the magazine; showing the defendant was aware of the sexually explicit nature of the magazine; providing evidence that a clerk who covered explicit books with plastic had glanced at the covers; and showing that a clerk had checked the cover and price of a magazine. Many courts have found that observation of the cover of obscene magazines alone is sufficient to establish scienter.

Under scienter requirements, one need not show that a defendant had knowledge that material was obscene; rather one must show that he or she had notice of the material's contents. (*Rosen* v. *United States, Smith* v. *California, Ginsberg*, and *Hamling*). Under *Hamling*, the state must prove scienter beyond a reasonable doubt.[160]

Multiplicity and Duplicity

Multiplicity refers to the charging of a single criminal offense in multiple counts. Duplicity is the charging of two or more separate and distinct offenses in a single court.

A First Amendment rights issue arises when more than one magazine is sold by a single seller to a single police officer at the same time. If the magazines are separated into separate counts, the multiplicity problem can be raised. If the magazines are not separated, the appellate court and defendant cannot know which magazines were found obscene and which were not. *Street* v. *New York* appears to suggest that separate counts are in order where one or more of the acts charged may be protected speech.[161]

In *Adult Bookmart, Inc.*, v. *State*, the court found that it was *not* proper to separate a single sale of two magazines by one clerk to one police officer into two counts. However, the sale of the same magazine on the same day at two locations amounts to two separate offenses (*Stancil* v. *State*).[162]

Vagueness

Under the due process clause of the U.S. Constitution, a person may not be held criminally liable "for conduct which he could not reasonably understand to be proscribed."[163] Laws are held to be void for vagueness if their prohibitions are not clearly defined. The vagueness argument is commonly used to attack obscenity or antipornography laws, which suffer from inherent definitional problems. This concept centers on the belief that a person should not be held liable for obeying laws that do not give fair warning of what they prohibit.

A statute will be void for vagueness if its prohibitions are not clearly defined (*Grayned* v. *City of Rockford*).[164] Due process is violated if the law fails to give a person of ordinary intelligence fair notice that conduct is forbidden (*Papachristou* v. *City of Jacksonville*).[165] Another problem with vague laws is that they risk discriminatory and arbitrary enforcement (*Grayned*).

The court has said that a law is void for vagueness if persons of ordinary intelligence must "necessarily guess at its meaning and differ as to its application."[166] It is permissible, in drafting a law, to use words that are commonly used and understood (*Grayned*). Such words will be given their ordinary and popularly understood meaning.

A statute is not void for vagueness if its meaning is reasonably ascertainable by relying on previous judicial construction (*Ward* v. *Illinois*).

A statute that is so vague and indefinite as to permit punishment of conduct protected by the free speech and press guarantees is void on its face (*Winters* v. *New York*). *Winters* found that stricter standards of permissible vagueness may apply to laws having a potential of limiting speech.[167] Lack of precision alone is not enough to offend due process requirements (*Roth*). The obscenity laws of the *Roth* and *Miller* type have been found not to be vague. However, failure to define terms specifically in such laws may be grounds for voiding an obscenity law for vagueness.[168]

A statute that defines an obscene device as "any device designed or marketed as useful primarily for the stimulation of human genital organs is not vague."[169]

The *Obscenity Law Reporter* contains details of many cases in which antipornography laws were challenged on vagueness grounds. In criminal prosecutions, vagueness in a criminal complaint raises the issue of double jeopardy (a new prosecution for the same offense), another constitutional prohibition.[170]

Schauer suggests that *Miller* tackled the vagueness issue when it created the requirement that statutes specifically describe what sexual conduct may not be depicted. He believes that obscenity statues defined

in terms other than legal obscenity as established by the U.S. Supreme Court will be held to be unconstitutionally vague.[171]

Overbreadth

A law or statute is overbroad "when its prospective reach includes constitutionally protected activity." Often laws are overbroad because their vagueness makes it impossible to determine what conduct is prohibited. "Where conduct, and *not* merely speech is involved, the overbreadth of a statute must be not only real but substantial" in order for it to be voided. The overbreadth doctrine should be used only as a last resort.[172] A statute should not be declared facially overbroad and thus invalid unless it cannot be narrowly construed to prohibit only that conduct which may be regulated.[173] In other words, overbroad sections in obscenity laws may be excised without invalidating the entire law.

Although in general a person does not have standing to assert the rights of others, an exception has been made when First Amendment violations are alleged to be involved. In *Gooding* v. *Wilson*, facial overbreadth challenges were found to be most compelling where the statutes sought to regulate pure speech or to restrict the time, place, and manner of communication.[174] Yet under *Young* v. *American Mini Theatres, Inc.*, to be overbroad on its face, a law's deterrent effect on "legitimate" expression must be "real and substantial."[175]

Challenges to obscenity or related laws are often brought on overbreadth grounds. For example, in *Schad* v. *Borough of Mount Ephraim*, a ban on all live nude entertainment in a locality was held to be overbroad.[176]

The courts are concerned that an overbroad or vague law can have a chilling effect on free speech. For example, in *Winters* v. *New York*, obscenity in a statute included material "devoted to the publication, and principally made up of criminal news, police reports, or accounts of criminal deeds, or pictures, or stories of deeds of bloodshed, hurt, or crime." The court decided it was overbroad because it would include any material dealing with crime, whether obscene, violent, scholarly, or amusing.[177]

LEGAL STRATEGIES

Some of the common prosecutorial and defense strategies in obscenity cases are outlined in this section, to be considered in conjunction with the rest of this chapter when dealing with obscenity law.

Prosecution Tactics

Boston attorney Timothy O'Neill says that choosing the "field of combat" and letting the obscene materials' maximum impact reach the jury are the two decisions that should influence every decision in a prosecutor's case. Thus, he typically makes a motion for the jury to view the material before his opening statement.[178]

Hinson McAuliffe, the retired prosecutor responsible for the near elimination of pornographic outlets in Atlanta, made suggestions for prosecutors in 1985:

1. Have a prosecutor who specializes in obscenity and believes in the prosecution of such cases.
2. Show judges that the "small fry" on trial are under agreements with employers not to divulge the management's identity, to have the employee out on bond within a short time of arrest, to represent and pay for counsel for him or her, and to pay any fines assessed against him or her. As a result, judges are more willing to levy bigger fines.
3. If a prosecutor is unable to locate sufficient property upon which to levy judgments, file involuntary bankruptcy against the pornography corporations. This opens the possibility of discovering the true ownership of the corporations through interrogatories and depositions.

In Atlanta, after bankruptcy actions were filed, lawyers representing most of the pornographic stores and theaters came to the prosecutor's office and offered to close down all the remaining stores and theaters if he would dismiss all pending obscenity cases and forgo prosecution. The prosecutor agreed to remove them from the court calendar for one year. The porn businesses closed their doors.[179]

Larry E. Parrish warns prosecutors to make certain that the material to which the "taken as a whole" standard is applied is a single whole. There has to be a single, "contextually interdependent dominant theme connecting" the material. It does not matter if other works are bound in proximity to the pornographic material. If an illustration is rationally related to the written material to which it is in proximity, it cannot be evaluated apart from the written material.[180]

In dealing with the prurient interest prong, the defense may urge a definition of *appeals to* such as "arouse," Larry Parrish explained in 1981. This greatly increases the chances of success. Parrish said that *appeals to* merely means "urge toward" or "direct toward." A normal interest in sex is not prurient, he said. *Morbid* means "sick" or "pathological," a degrading or demented interest in sex such as a rapist or homosexual has. In his outline, he explained the concept as follows:

Prurient interest in sex is virtually a universal characteristic of all normal persons; however,

most normal persons have psychologically suppressed the prurient interest and when it is appealed to they react against the attempt to arouse it by emotions of repulsion, revulsion, fear, anger, shame, guilt, etc. Thus, the feelings most jurors have when exposed to obscene materials is the very best evidence there is of the objective fact of prurient appeal.[181]

In his statement to the Attorney General's Commission on Pornography then assistant U.S. attorney for the Eastern District of North Carolina Robert Showers (now head of the Attorney General's task force) stated that it is clear that the U.S. Supreme Court meant "directed towards" by the term *appeals to*, not to arouse or stimulate. He noted:

Many a case has turned on the fact that the jury could not find that sado-masochistic behavior, bestiality, and child pornography or picquesism could arouse or stimulate anyone. However, it is clear from case law that appeals to means directed towards a morbid interest in sex in context with the grosser graphic forms of pornography. Statutory definitions incorporating case law and common sense would end the confusion and useless lengthy arguments and allow the jury to understand and settle the issue at hand: whether the material violates what is acceptable by their local community standards.[182]

Bruce Taylor emphasized that the judge in an obscenity case must instruct the jury to determine whether the average person, applying contemporary community standards, would find that the appeal of the material at issue is "directed *to* the prurient interest." He said: "If a judge charges a jury that it must find the material obscene only if the material appeals to or excites a shameful or morbid interest *in* an average person or *in* the jury, confusion can result, and the purpose of obscenity law—to distinguish illegal from protected material—would be thwarted."[183]

According to Taylor, *Mishkin* sets out a duel test for "deviants" under the prurient appeal criteria. Only if material is designed for and primarily disseminated to a deviant class of persons must it be judged according to the prurient interest of that class. Otherwise, it must be judged according to the public at large. Thus, if it is sold in an adult bookstore, a defendant is not entitled to a special instruction to judge it according to the prurient interest of deviant groups, Taylor said. Prosecutors want the material to be judged under a "normal" person's view, he stated. He explained that prurient appeal material involves sex for its own sake and could either embrace or disgust a person, but does so for sexual reasons.

Taylor said that defense attorneys may put a bookstore clerk on the stand to try to buy sympathy for the "kid." It is wise for the prosecutor to show that the clerk voluntarily took the job, defends the material, feels it should not be against the law, and has close ties to the owner.[184]

Larry Parrish noted that the defense will constantly use the term *censorship*. He said that the prosecution should respond by pointing out that *censorship* means "prior restraint" and that does not occur in obscenity cases.[185]

Search warrants should be very specific in describing the content of the material to be seized so that the judge who issues the warrant can determine whether there is probable cause that the material is obscene. (For an example of such a warrant see Weaver.)[186]

Defense Strategies

The following are arguments we expect to be used by obscenity defendants:

The material is free expression protected by the First Amendment.

The material is not "obscene"—that is, it does not fall within the law's coverage.

The statute is unconstitutionally vague or overbroad in violation of the defendant's due process rights. Or the statute as applied to the specific material is overbroad or vague.

The defendant did not know the content of the material, so scienter (intent) cannot be shown.

The material has serious value.

The material is too repulsive to appeal to the prurient interest.

The "community" tolerates or accepts the pornography.

There was no commercial transaction (that is, possession, trade, or private use).

The defendant has a privacy right to consume the material.

The material incites only a normal, healthy interest in sex.

Obscene materials do not arouse the prurient interest of most females, which could be a loophole in the law.

The serious value test creates a major loophole for pornographers.

The ACLU details obscenity law from the defense perspective in a book titled *The Basic ACLU Guide to the Legal Rights of Authors and Artists*. The ACLU argues that there is no meaningful obscenity definition today and that obscenity laws clearly violate the First Amendment, which states that Congress may pass no law abridging freedom of the press or of speech. The ACLU seems to view obscene publications as advocating ideas. This book contains a good history of obscenity laws in the United States. It argues that terms such as "lewd exhibition of the genitals" are "ambiguous."

The serious value test of *Miller* is "the most effective protection for the author or artist who deals with sexual subjects," according to the ACLU book. The book asks, "Has the serious value standard lowered the obscenity threshold to the point where legitimate works by serious authors and artists will be threatened? The answer is probably no. Obscenity prosecutions against even arguably serious works are rare now, although they do occur." It states that child pornography laws also can affect works of serious value.[187]

According to Schauer, there are two main themes of obscenity defenses. First, there should be no obscenity laws for consenting adults. No one is hurt if some people have different tastes than most people. Second, pornographic material is no worse than a lot of other books, motion pictures, and magazines.

Schauer also suggests that it is to the defense's advantage to condition or desensitize the jury and prepare them for the shock of the pornography. To minimize the effect of the jury's seeing the pornography, Schauer suggests taking up days with unrelated information such as business practices or exposing the jury to a lot of comparable material and hoping for boredom.

He advises against trying to make a jury believe that sadomasochistic abuse or bestiality has any serious value, for the most likely result is that the jurors will not believe *any* of the defense contentions. Schauer also points out that if scienter is a contested issue, it could be harmful to put the defendant on the stand.[188]

Weaver details the following tactics used in obscenity defenses:

1. Argue that reasonable doubt exists as to one of the three *Miller* prongs or as to scienter.
2. Attempt to show that the material was possessed in a private home for the owner's private use (*Stanley* v. *Georgia*).
3. Suggest that pornography is not harmful and that everyone is using and distributing it. (The prosecution should object to such arguments because under *Roth*, one need not show that obscenity creates a clear and present danger of antisocial behavior or that it would likely induce its recipients to such behavior.)

4. Check the statutes to see if there are any applicable exemptions or defenses for the distribution of obscene materials.
5. Argue that the court should determine whether the material violates community standards by deciding whether it is tolerated by the community. (Note: This approach has been rejected by the courts.)
6. Claim that the material is distributed only to consenting adults to be used by them in the privacy of their own home and therefore the patent offensiveness standard is not met.[189]

According to Larry Parrish, defense tactics include causing as much confusion as possible and stating that the existence of pornography shows that the average person does not consider it to appeal to prurience.[190]

In states where community or local standards are allowed to be applied (instead of statewide standards) material could be found obscene in one community and nonobscene in another. The defense could argue that this violates the Fourteenth Amendment, which states that no state shall deny any person within its jurisdiction equal protection.[191]

It may be best for the defense to waive a jury if the material seems clearly constitutionally protected and the judge knows the obscenity law. However, if the material is clearly hard core, it may be best to have a jury. The likely makeup of the jury and the known attitudes of the judge should be considered.[192]

State courts may reject the U.S. Supreme Court obscenity findings by finding that their state constitutions permit less strict regulations of obscenity (under free speech type provisions).[193]

For examples of the types of surveys used by defense experts to attempt to show that pornography is acceptable to adults, see Michael Kent Curtis's article in the *Campbell Law Review*.[194]

Charging

Obscenity prosecution experts suggest that obscenity violations be prosecuted at the highest feasible level, but they note that even routine prosecutions of lower level employees can have an impact. Corporations should be prosecuted whenever possible, for they do not have a privilege against self-incrimination.

The hardest core pornography available should be targeted to maximize the prospect of conviction. It may be possible to prosecute sex devices and even advertisements if they are obscene or provide information on how to obtain obscene material.

When a particular item contains both obscene and nonobscene material, the charging document should name only the thematic unit that is believed to be obscene (for example, only a particular article in a magazine). It may be wise to state that the item is not related to any other articles contained in the magazine. Prosecutors can expect defense attorneys to take issue with this and argue that the entire magazine must be shown to be obscene.

Prosecutors also urge the use of multiple counts where possible to conserve resources and maximize the likelihood of conviction and punishment. Separate acts of distribution of the same material can be charged as separate offenses. It is wise to charge only one movie or magazine in each count. It must be alleged that the material is obscene, and scienter must be claimed.[195]

An indictment should not state that a specific issue of a magazine is obscene. Obviously, that usually cannot be true because many pornographic magazines also contain serious parts in an attempt to get around the obscenity law. In the charging document, only the obscene parts should be listed and the issue of the magazine should be referred to as the vehicle of distribution.

Schauer suggests that joinder of corporations be considered in charging in order to broaden subpoena and discovery rights. Also, he encourages prosecutors to make sure each separate offense is charged in a separate count and that violation of every applicable statute is charged for the same conduct.[196]

Plea Bargaining and Immunity

National Obscenity Law Center experts suggest that plea bargaining is a good approach in obscenity prosecutions because it allows speedy disposition. Caution is urged to ensure that the pornographers are not simply agreeing to a level of cost that is acceptable to them. Any probation offers should be made contingent upon a defendant's disassociation from "adult entertainment" businesses.

Offers of immunity to lower level employees may be used to obtain information about higher level organization members. Also, this will create a conflict of interest between the organization and employee and force separate legal representation of the employee, thus increasing cooperation with the prosecution.[197]

Pretrial Issues

Both sides need to know prior to a trial which community standards will be considered relevant. A motion should be made to clarify that issue.

Defense attorneys should consider a motion for

a bill of particulars aimed at advising the defendant of the substance of the charge and protecting against double jeopardy. The prosecution will likely oppose such a motion.

Schauer explains that defendants may make these motions to dismiss the indictment:

1. Attack the constitutionality of the statute on the ground of its being overbroad, vague, an incorrect obscenity test, and so on.
2. Allege that the material is obscene as a matter of law.
3. Address defects in the indictment.
4. Allege lack of a scienter allegation.
5. Allege lack of specificity.
6. If there are defects in the seizure of the pornography, make a motion to suppress (covering the trial material and any other material seized).

In discovery, the defendant has a right to obtain any defense statement and to demand documentary evidence, including scientific experiments or tests, expert evaluations of the material and any survey data, as well as any exculpatory evidence. Schauer suggests that the prosecution move for reciprocal discovery if a showing of need can be made.[198]

Prosecutors should make certain that the statute and jury instructions do not say that the material must appeal to the prurient interest of the average person (the defense can then argue that it is too disgusting to have prurient appeal to such persons). But they should keep in mind that one way of looking at the morbid interest description of prurient appeal is to view it as evoking feelings of disgust.

To defeat any suggestion of denial of a fair trial, an effort should be made to control prejudicial pretrial publicity.

Jury Selection

Although in criminal cases, juries are usually believed to be more favorable to defendants than are judges, a jury can be an advantage to the prosecution in obscenity cases where the judge is soft on pornography. Jury selection is critical in obscenity cases because people have deeply held views on pornography, sex, and sexual morality.

A major purpose of voir dire is to learn the views of the prospective jurors. Weaver lists characteristics of persons with more restrictive views toward pornography and types of persons to avoid having on juries. He argues that the court should refuse to disqualify those with antiobscenity views as long as

they can set aside their personal views and follow the law, but he admits that it is difficult to prevent the defense from excusing jurors favorable to the prosecution for cause. Ironically, Weaver urges the prosecution to challenge, for cause, persons with strong views against obscenity laws.

Sometimes defense attorneys try to get potential jurors to admit that they would have great difficulty viewing the material at issue. Weaver says that the defense attorney should not be allowed to describe the pornography.

Voir dire can be used to condition juries. Prosecutors should oppose sequestered voir dire because it is likely to result in disqualification of more jurors favorable to the prosecution, Weaver states. He gives an example of a conditioning question by the defense: "Do you believe that adults should have the right to read and see what they want?"

Weaver also suggests it is best for the prosecutor to avoid prying questions about views on sex and pornography and instead let the defense ask these questions and alienate jurors. He also says that technical legal questions should be avoided.[199]

Schauer's appendix A is a list of potential questions to ask prospective jurors on voir dire.[200] Kelly provides another good source of jury questions and the types of jurors to look for and avoid in obscenity trials.[201] O'Neill believes that limited voir dire is a tremendous advantage for prosecutors and that they should fight to limit questions so that the defense can not desensitize the jurors to the pornography.[202]

At a 1981 conference, obscenity prosecution experts Larry Parrish and Bill Kelly offered pointers for prosecutors. They said that jury selection is the point where the defense will try to win the case, for the defense usually needs only one favorable juror out of twelve. One defense tactic is to pick a housewife, explain in graphic detail what the pornography at issue shows (shocking her), then ask if she can discuss it with another juror (male) whom she has never met and be fair and impartial. If she hesitates or seems uncertain, the defense can get her excused for cause and not even have to use a preemptory challenge. This is where prosecutors can lose their cross-section of the community on the jury. The prosecutor could make a motion telling the judge that this tactic will undermine the entire process, ask the judge to describe the material, and tell the jurors they will not be excused for not wanting to see the material. The prosecutor might compare this to a murder case that involves unpleasant photographs. If the prosecutor makes this motion ahead of time, the defense will not try this tactic.[203]

Kelly also suggested that the jury questions for

voir dire, which are mailed to the panel in advance, and inquire whether potential jurors read or subscribe to pornography, have viewed sexually explicit videos or films, or have visited "adult" book stores.[204]

While judges may go overboard at first in excusing jurors (because of the First Amendment issue), they are less willing to excuse potential jurors later on. Kelly noted that sometimes 40 to 50 percent of the potential jurors are excused for cause.

Parrish and Kelly also suggested that prosecutors should look for more women on the jury because pornography is aimed against women. Older women with grandchildren are a good bet. Also, prosecutors should try to keep the religious moralists on the jury. They suggested persuading church leaders to tell congregations that it is not sinful to serve on a jury and see pornography. Also, an attempt should be made to find out whether a juror is active in religion.

Use of a simple jury questionnaire is a good technique: It is fast and revealing, and it speeds up the process. For instance, some jurors might be dismissed by the judge for being illiterate.

Prosecutors should seek to have average persons on the jury. As of 1981, such a person is 42 years old, has been married one time with two and a half children, holds a steady job, has 12.1 years of education, and is involved in nonsupervisory work as far as management is concerned. Some conduct of a religious nature is part of this person's weekly activity, and the person considers himself or herself to be religious. If the person has sown any wild oats, he or she is through doing so and the person's main concern is raising his or her children in a positive environment. The more average persons on the jury, the better for the prosecution.

Prosecutors also should be aware of persons who have the "consenting adults" view—that people should be free to read or see whatever they want. If a potential juror expresses such a view, he or she should be dismissed for cause, as this is contradictory to the law, and the person's ability to be fair and impartial is in doubt.[205]

Opening Statement

It is vital to make a good impression during the opening statement in obscenity cases. The prosecutor should explain and simplify the *Miller* test. Weaver states, "Basically, the issues are: would most people say that this magazine is *shameful,* would most people say it is *offensive,* and does it have any *serious value?*"

Prosecutors, Weaver says, should make it clear that the fact that other persons may be doing the same thing is not a defense. Also, they should diffuse the issue of whether there should be obscenity laws and emphasize the duty to uphold the law. He notes that the evidence should be outlined, an intent to use an expert in the case in chief should be mentioned, and a belief that the prosecution should prevail should be conveyed—without argument or personal opinion.

The prosecutor should say just enough about the obscene material to trigger a reaction against it but not describe it in detail. Weaver suggests terms such as *highly offensive* and *every imaginable perversion.* Finally, he notes, each side must watch to make certain that the law is not misstated and that extraneous issues are not interjected.[206]

Evidence

Chapter 9 of Weaver contains an excellent summary of prosecutorial evidentiary concerns in obscenity cases. Unlike many other types of criminal cases, obscenity need not be proved—the material itself is the best evidence of what it represents, Weaver states. However, the prosecution may want to offer expert testimony on prurient appeal if material is aimed at bizarre deviant groups or if the material is not offered as evidence.[207]

As of January 1, 1986, Illinois Revised Statutes provided that in obscenity prosecutions, evidence shall be admissible to show the following:

(1) The character of the audience for which the material was designed or to which it was directed;
(2) What the predominant appeal of the material would be for ordinary adults or a special audience, and what effect if any, it would probably have on the behavior of such people;
(3) The artistic, literary, scientific, educational or other merits of the material, or absence thereof;
(4) The degree, if any, of public acceptance of the material in this State;
(5) Appeal to prurient interest, or absence thereof, in advertising or other promotion of the material;
(6) Purpose of the author, creator, publisher or disseminator.[208]

Thus, Illinois, by statute, settles many of the questions that could be litigated regarding evidence and expert testimony admissibility.

One possible way to make proof of obscenity violations easier would be to state in the law that a person who possesses six or more obscene devices or articles is presumed to possess them with the intent to promote the same.

Serious Value and Pandering

It is common for the defense to argue that the material on trial has serious scientific value and to try to prove this with expert testimony. Weaver reminds prosecutors that serious value involves both intent and effect. An expert may testify that material does or does not advance a science, does or does not provide accurate information about reality, or provides harmful misinformation. He or she may distinguish material with real value from that at issue. Weaver suggests that prosecutors try to push defense experts into adopting "such broad definitions of serious value that everything passes."[209]

According to Weaver, the defense sometimes tries to get testimony that pornography is not harmful into evidence to back up its claim that the material at issue has serious value. A prosecutor who introduces testimony about the harms of pornography has raised that issue, and such testimony will probably be admitted. Weaver cautions prosecutors to make certain that defense experts cite no hearsay studies or opinions, such as the 1970 Pornography Commission report.[210]

While critical reviews might be cited as evidence of nonobscenity (or sometimes obscenity), this issue normally does not arise when hard-core pornography is involved, for such material is not reviewed in literary circles.

Weaver points out that, under the pandering doctrine, evidence of the "circumstances of presentation and dissemination of material" are admissible on the serious value question.[211]

Jury Instructions

In appendix D of his book, Weaver gives examples of jury instructions for prosecutors to use.[212] In chapter 12, he says that the following types of instructions should be sought:

Charges on the prosecutor's version of the patent offensiveness and prurient interest prongs
An instruction that "community standards are what is accepted, not tolerated, in the community"[213]
An instruction that all persons in the community, sensitive and insensitive, must be included
An instruction that the material need not sexually stimulate the average person; rather "the average person would find that the material appeals to a prurient interest"[214]

Obviously, defense attorneys may seek instructions contrary to those suggested by Weaver.

Schauer also includes an appendix of sample jury instructions.[215] He makes these additional suggestions:

The jury must understand that all the *Miller* standards must be satisfied. Each test should be fully explained.
The court should consider furnishing written instructions to the jury.

[T]he court should always instruct as to the type of sexual conduct the portrayal of which is included in the statute, the elements of the constitutional test for obscenity, the meaning of the most important concepts therein, such as 'appeal to the prurient interest,' 'as a whole,' 'patently offensive,' 'average person,' 'contemporary community standards,' and 'serious literary, artistic, political, or scientific value,' the other elements of the offense charged, and scienter.

The prosecution should make timely objections to instructions given by the court with which counsel disagrees or to the failure to give requested jury instructions.[216]

(We suggest that prosecutors and defense attorneys involved in obscenity cases consult Schauer and Weaver for jury instruction ideas and strategies.)

Expert Witnesses

Weaver notes that the court has shown general disapproval of the use of expert witnesses in obscenity cases because pornography speaks for itself, there probably is no such thing as an obscenity expert, and jurors are presumed to know community standards. Furthermore, experts usually testify based on their own feelings about the desirability of obscenity laws. Weaver suggests that the prosecution can benefit from saving evidence of obscenity, including expert testimony, for rebuttal. As a general rule, he believes, the prosecution should not call an expert unless the case is close, the opposition plans to use an expert, or the materials are directed at a bizarre deviant group.[217]

Weaver suggests that if an expert is used, his or her local experience or training should be emphasized (for example, knowledge of local attitudes on sexual issues). Only rehearsed questions should be used. Prosecution experts should be warned not to "wander into irrelevant matters, like the harmful effects of pornography" because this could bring a defense objection and open the door to defense evidence on the same issues.[218] Weaver suggests showing the other side's lack of familiarity with local attitudes and warns that prosecutors should be alert to attempts to admit hearsay evidence, such as results of studies done by other people and other people's opinions. Weaver appendix includes examples of the examination of a prosecution expert and the cross-examination of a defense expert.[219]

Weaver's warns that it may be dangerous for a prosecutor to fail to offer evidence of community standards, as one court concluded that the prosecution failed to meet its burden. The most natural way of showing community standards is to offer public opinion evidence such as surveys.[220]

Weaver notes that the defense sometimes argues that comparable materials are useful to prove community standards and tries to get such evidence admitted. The defense asserts that the material at issue does not violate community standards because similar explicit material is accepted in the community. Defense attorneys have successfully argued that widespread availability "supports an inference of acceptance." Most courts, however, have rejected jury tours of pornographic establishments because they say this shows only availability, not acceptance. Sales or circulation figures of the trial material are often offered by the defense and allowed as evidence. Weaver urges prosecutors to make sure that the figures used are for sales, not distribution. And, he argues, only local (community) circulation figures are relevant.[221]

Schauer deals with the use of expert testimony in obscenity cases. He notes that such testimony involving literary value or lack thereof was common in the pre-*Roth* period. Thereafter, such testimony increased in the area of explaining the standards. The court in *Paris Adult Theatre I* v. *Slaton* said that expert testimony that materials are obscene is not needed when the films are placed in evidence. However, the defense should be free to introduce "appropriate" expert testimony (*Kaplan* v. *California*). The major consideration is whether the expert will explain to jurors what they otherwise could not understand.[222]

According to Schauer,[223] experts can be used for the following purposes:

1. The witness can state that in his or her opinion, the material is or is not obscene. (Prosecutors should watch out for the rule against use of expert opinion as to the ultimate issue in the lawsuit and the principle of prohibiting testimony as to matters of law or mixed law/fact questions.) Schauer believes that such testimony provides no assistance but states that some courts have admitted it, while most have "properly" excluded it.

2. Expert testimony focused on helping the jury understand part of the obscenity test or some aspect of the material at issue is desirable.

3. The testimony must be legally relevant. For example, testimony about the presence or absence of harm or moral decay from pornography is immaterial and not relevant.

4. An expert can be used to identify the major purpose and theme of the material and what the whole (taken as a whole) is.

5. There is limited, and perhaps no, utility to use of an expert to explain the concept of the "average person."

6. Experts can explain the material's appeal to prurient interests. For example, literary specialists can explain the author's meaning or intent; psychological experts can explain the effect of the material on others and the difference between appeal to a "normal" as opposed to an "abnormal" or prurient interest. The expert must deal with the recipient group that is appropriate to the case (for instance, average person, deviant, or minor). Expert testimony may be required in deviant material cases because knowledge of what appeals to the deviant prurient interest would likely be beyond the ken of the average juror.

7. Experts can be helpful in determining contemporary community standards. Although local standards might be within the juror's knowledge, statewide standards (required by statute in some states) might not. There is a potential problem with the general rule that an expert be knowledgeable or experienced in the field about which he or she is testifying. As Schauer notes, "There is no field or acknowledged area of expertise for contemporary community standards."[224] Thus, most expert testimony in this arena involves statistical or sampling data about what the community believes. Some people may have knowledge of the community's views regarding depictions of sexual activity and would be good experts on this issue.

8. If the material is other than commercial hardcore pornography, experts can be useful in determining serious literary, artistic, political, or scientific value.

Schauer suggests what types of professionals should be selected as experts for various types of testimony. He points out that experts can be attacked for not having qualifications that relate to the specific matter at hand and for not having had the opportunity to observe the standards of the community at issue. He warns against using an expert as a general specialist on obscenity and cautions that experts should not be allowed to draw legal conclusions.[225]

On cross examination credentials, experience and bias can be attacked. Information about the expert should be obtained in advance.

McLaughlin deals with cross-examination issues by conducting a mock examination of himself as an expert witness.[226]

O'Neill told the Phoenix National Conference on Obscenity that prosecutors should have an attitude of cynicism toward experts on their own and the other side, never call them in the case in chief, and not call them in rebuttal unless the defense has done damage with experts. He suggested, however, that they have experts prepared and ready to testify.

O'Neill said that experts can be used to provide information about who the "average person" is and what he or she feels. He noted, however, that experts tend to cancel each other out.

While public opinion surveys are popular with obscenity defendants, O'Neill said, the prosecutor will need to impeach these. The defense will try to show that attitudes have become more liberal. The methods of the survey, the way it was handled, and the questions asked can often be attacked. It might be that many times the number of people surveyed were contacted but refused to participate. Was it a phone or direct contact survey? Were broad general questions asked? There is a big difference between broad questions and the specific material on trial. Prosecutors should try to show that the specific material was not described in the survey, and thus the survey does not reflect opinions about the specific material. Attempts can be made to keep such evidence out, but courts generally will allow expert evidence as long as it meets the general criterion that it must be helpful to the trier of fact.

O'Neill said that the prosecution should have psychiatrists willing to come in on rebuttal against defense experts. These experts could explain that prurience involves morbidity and that material that focuses on the genitals and has no plot falls into that category. Much testimony about literary or artistic value is made merely to protect the First Amendment absolutist ideology, O'Neill noted.[227]

Summation

Summation is important in obscenity cases because it allows direct argument. Weaver views this as an opportunity for the prosecutor to emphasize to the jurors their important "duty" and to remind them of the content of the material at issue. He suggests that prosecutors be brief, deal with the concept of reasonable doubt, outline the issues, make obscenity law understandable, and correct the other side's law distortions.

In summation, the prosecutor should directly confront the First Amendment issue and explain that obscenity is not protected speech, Weaver suggests. Also, he or she should emphasize that harmfulness of the material and other people's practices are not issues in the case. A prosecutor also may want to emphasize the jury's ability to determine community standards and urge that a defense expert be ignored. He or she also should point out the juror's duty to follow the law.

Attorneys must be careful not to give their own opinions. Rather, they should say, "It is clear from the evidence that . . ." If the prosecution does not have the last word, defense arguments should be anticipated and dealt with.[228]

Schauer also considers the closing statement to be important. He encourages prosecutors to emphasize the jurors' position in "embodying" the community's moral standards and their duty to that community. The prosecution should stress the facts that expert testimony is not a substitute for the jurors' common sense and that the validity of the law is not an issue. It should emphasize the hard-core nature of the material. The defense must stress that all of the elements of obscenity must be proven beyond a reasonable doubt, that "individual freedom is valuable," that jurors' personal views are not relevant, and that victims of obscenity do not exist.[229]

CONCLUSION

The fact that obscenity law is so complex may account for its lack of enforcement and effectiveness. However, there is no doubt that the law does work when used properly. At the same time, it is likely that a simpler, clearer law could be more effective, and we encourage governments to draft constitutionally valid laws against pornography that differ from the *Miller* standards and test them in the courts.

NOTES

1. Attorney General's Commission on Pornography, *Final Report* (Washington, D.C.: United States Department of Justice, 1986), 366–67, 502–3 (hereafter cited as AGCOP).

2. Harold Leventhal, "Project: An Empirical Inquiry into the Effects of Miller v. California on the Control of Obscenity," *New York University Law Review* 52 (1977): 810–939.

3. Bruce Taylor, "Pornography and the First Amendment," in *Criminal Justice Reform*, eds. Patrick B. McGuigan and Randall R. Rader (Washington, D.C.: Free Congress Research and Education Foundation, 1983), 155–70, 167.

4. George Weaver, *Handbook on the Prosecution of Obscenity Cases* (New York: National Obscenity Law Center, 1985); Frederick F. Schauer, *The Law of Obscenity* (Washington, D.C.: Bureau of National Affairs, 1976); Daniel S. Moretti, *Obscenity and Pornography: The Law under the First Amendment* (New York: Oceana Publications, 1984); *Obscenity Law Reporter* (New York: National Obscenity Center, 1986); *Obscenity Law Bulletin*; *National Decency Reporter*.

5. William A. Stanmeyer, "The Economics of Pornography Prosecutions," in *Pornography: Solutions through Law*, ed. Carol A. Clancy (Washington, D.C.: National Forum Foundation, 1985), 130–35.

6. Bruce Taylor, "State Prosecution of Pornography" in *Pornography: Solutions through Law*, ed. Carol A. Clancy (Washington, D.C.: National Forum Foundation, 1985), 117.

7. *Roth v. United States/Alberts v. California*, 354 U.S. 476, 481, 485, (1957).

8. Ibid., 484–85.

9. Ibid., 485.

10. Ibid., 486–88.

11. *Regina v. Hicklin*, 3 QB 360 (1868).

12. *Roth*, 489–90.

13. *Memoirs v. Massachusetts*, 383 U.S. 413 (1966).

14. *Marks v. U.S.*, 430 U.S. 188, 193 (1977).

15. *Memoirs*, 418.

16. *Miller v. California*, 413 U.S. 15, 24 (1973).

17. Ibid., 25.

18. Ibid., 27.

19. Ibid., 30–32.

20. Ibid., 33.

21. Ibid., 35.

22. Ibid., 36.

23. AGCOP, 1291.

24. Ibid., 259.

25. Ibid., 364–65.

26. Schauer, *The Law of Obscenity*, 34–39.

27. *Kingsley International Pictures Corp. v. Regents*, 360 U.S. 684 (1959).

28. *Manual Enterprises v. Day*, 370 U.S. 478, 486, 492 (1962).

29. Ibid., 488.

30. Ibid., 489–90.

31. *Jacobellis v. Ohio*, 378 U.S. 184, 191–92 (1964).

32. Ibid., 193–94.

33. *Ginzburg v. United States*, 383 U.S. 463, 464–65 (1966).

34. Ibid., 466–67.

35. Ibid.

36. Ibid., 468.

37. Ibid., 469.

38. Ibid., 470.

39. Ibid.

40. Ibid.

41. Ibid., 471, 475.

42. Schauer, *The Law of Obscenity*, 80–82.

43. Ibid., 84–85.

44. *Mishkin v. New York*, 383 U.S. 502, 508, *reh. den.* 384 U.S. 934 (1966).

45. Ibid., 508.

46. Ibid., 509.

47. Schauer, *The Law of Obscenity*, 79.

48. *Redrup v. New York, Austin v. Kentucky, Gent et al. v. Arkansas*, 386 U.S. 767, *reh. den.* 388 U.S. 924 (1967).

49. *Ginsberg v. New York*, 390 U.S. 629, 631, 634, 637 (1968).

50. Ibid., 638–41.

51. *Stanley v. Georgia*, 394 U.S. 557, 558–59 (1969).

52. Ibid., 563.

53. Ibid., 565.

54. Ibid.

55. Ibid.

56. Ibid., 566.

57. Ibid.

58. Ibid.

59. Ibid., 567.

60. *U.S. v. Reidel*, 402 U.S. 351 (1971).

61. *U.S. v. 37 Photographs*, 402 U.S. 363, 376 (1971).

62. *Rabe v. Washington*, 405 U.S. 313, 315–16 (1972).

63. *Kois v. Wisconsin*, 408 U.S. 229, 230 (1972).

64. Ibid., 231.

65. Ibid.

66. Ibid.

67. Ibid., 232.

68. *Pinkus v. U.S.*, 436 U.S. 293, 297–303 (1978), *on remand*, 579 F.2d 1174 (9th Cir. 1978), *cert. dismissed*, 439 U.S. 999 (1978).

69. Ibid., 300.

70. *Obscenity Law Reporter*, 2002.

71. *Weaver, Prosecution of Obscenity Cases*, 7–9.

72. Schauer, *The Law of Obscenity*, 73.

73. *Miller*, 30–32.

74. *Hamling v. United States*, 418 U.S. 37, 104, 105 (1974).

75. Ibid., 105–6.

76. *Smith v. United States*, 431 U.S. 291, 303 (1977).

77. *Obscenity Law Reporter*, 3020–21.

78. *Weaver, Prosecution of Obscenity Cases*, 9–10.

79. Larry E. Parrish, "The Non-Elusive Community Standard" (Paper September 1977).

80. Neil Gallagher, *The Porno Plague* (Minneapolis: Bethany House Publishers, 1981), 113.

81. *Kois, Obscenity Law Reporter,* 5009–10.

82. *Erznoznik v. City of Jacksonville,* 422 U.S. 205, 211, fn. 7 (1975).

83. Weaver, *Prosecution of Obscenity Cases,* 14–15.

84. *Brockett v. Spokane Arcades, Inc.,* 472 U.S. 491, 399, 406–7 (1985).

85. Ibid., 496–97.

86. Ibid., 497.

87. Ibid., 504.

88. *Mishkin,* 508.

89. Taylor, "Pornography and the First Amendment," 162.

90. *Smith,* 291, 300–301.

91. Ibid., 303–4.

92. *Obscenity Law Reporter,* 7009–10.

93. Weaver, *Prosecution of Obscenity Cases,* 25–29.

94. *Miller,* 94.

95. Ibid., 27.

96. *Jenkins v. Georgia,* 418 U.S. 153, 161 (1973).

97. *Kaplan v. California,* 413 U.S. 115, 116–17 (1973).

98. *Ward v. Illinois,* 431 U.S. 767, 773 (1977).

99. *Mishkin,* 502.

100. *Obscenity Law Reporter,* 8000–8023.

101. *Miller,* 24.

102. *Smith,* 300–301.

103. *Paris Adult Theatre I v. Slaton,* 413 U.S. 49, 63 (1973).

104. *Papish v. Bd. of Curators of Missouri,* 410 U.S. 667 (1973).

105. *Hamling,* 100.

106. Schauer, *The Law of Obscenity,* 147.

107. Weaver, *Prosecution of Obscenity Cases,* 30–33.

108. Schauer, *The Law of Obscenity,* 140–42.

109. *Butler v. Michigan,* 352 U.S. 380 (1957).

110. *Ginsberg,* 638.

111. *Erznoznik,* 213–14.

112. Ibid, 206–8.

113. Ibid., 209–11.

114. Ibid., 211–14.

115. *California v. La Rue,* 407 U.S. 109, 118 (1973).

116. *Doran v. Salem Inn,* 422 U.S. 922, 924 (1975).

117. Ibid., 933–34.

118. *Schad v. Borough of Mount Ephraim,* 452 U.S. 61, 65 (1981).

119. Ibid., 68.

120. Ibid., 70–74.

121. *Obscenity Law Reporter,* 11008–9, citing *State v. Baysinger,* 397 N.E. 2d 580 (Ind. Sup. Ct. 1979), *appeal dismissed sub. nom., Clark v. Indiana,* 446 U.S. 931 (1980), *appeal dismissed sub. nom., Dove v. Indiana,* 449 U.S. 806(1980).

122. *Southeastern Promotions Inc. v. Conrad,* 420 U.S. 546 (1975).

123. *United States v. Orito,* 413 U.S. 139 (1973); Title 18 U.S.C. s. 1462 and 1465.

124. Title 19 U.S.C. 1305 (a).

125. *New York v. Ferber,* 458 U.S. 747 (1982).

126. *Ex Parte Jackson,* 96 U.S. 727 (1878).

127. *Kingsley International Pictures Corp.,* 684.

128. *Marcus v. Search Warrants of Property,* 367 U.S. 717, 718–19 (1961).

129. *Bantam Books, Inc. v. Sullivan,* 378 U.S. 58, 68 (1963).

130. Ibid., 69–71.

131. *A Quantity of Books v. Kansas,* 378 U.S. 205, 208, 210 (1964).

132. *Freedman v. Maryland,* 380 U.S. 51, 54 (1965).

133. Ibid., 57–59.

134. Ibid., 60.

135. *Blount v. Rizzi,* 400 U.S. 410 (1971).

136. *U.S. v. 37 Photographs,* 363.

137. *Heller v. New York,* 413 U.S. 483, 490, 492–93 (1973).

138. *Roaden v. Kentucky,* 413 U.S. 496, 504 (1973).

139. Ibid.

140. *Southeastern Promotions Inc.,* 319.

141. *Lo-Ji Sales Inc. v. New York,* 442 U.S. 319 (1979).

142. *Universal Amusement Co. v. Vance,* 445 U.S. 308 (1980).

143. *Walter v. U.S. and U.S. v. Sanders,* 447 U.S. 649, 654 (1980).

144. Ibid., 655–59.

145. *Maryland v. Macon,* 472 U.S. 463 (1985).

146. *New York v. P.J. Video, Inc.,* 475 U.S. 868, 871, (1986).

147. Ibid., 874–75.

148. Ibid., 875–77.

149. *Nicholas L. Giampietro,* "First and Fourth Amendments—Obscenity and Police Purchases: A Purchase Is a Purchase Is a Seizure? Maryland v. Macon," *Journal of Criminal Law and Criminology* 76 (Winter 1985): 875–97.

150. Paul J. McGeady, "No Longer Necessary for Judge to Conduct a Prior Adversary Hearing or to See Film Prior to Its Seizure as Evidence," Paper presented at the National Conference on Obscenity, Scottsdale, Arizona, November 30 to December 2, 1981, 5–6.

151. *United States v. Hill,* 500 F.2d 733 (5th Cir. 1974), *cert. denied,* 420 U.S. 952 (1975).

152. *United States v. Sanders,* 592 F.2d 788 (5th Cir. 1979), *rev'd, sub nom. Walters v. United States,* 447 U.S. 649 (1980).

153. *United States v. Battista,* 646 F.2d 788 (5th Cir. 1979), *cert. denied,* 454 U.S. 1046 (1981).

154. *Hays v. State,* 243 S.E.2d 263 (Ga. Ct. App. 1978), *cert. denied,* 444 U.S. 984 (1978).

155. *Sedelbaver v. State,* 428 N.E. 2d 206, (Ind. Sup. Ct. 1981), *cert. denied,* 455 U.S. 1035, (1982) cited in *United States v. Sandy,* 605 F.2d 210 (6th Cir. 1979), *cert. denied,* 444 U.S. 984 (1979).

156. *Obscenity Law Reporter,* 38023.

157. *State v. I. and M. Amusements, Inc.* 226 N.E.2d 567 (Ohio Ct. App. 1966), *rev'd,* 389 U.S. 573 (1968).

158. *Obscenity Law Reporter,* 15003, 15020.

159. Schauer, *The Law of Obscenity,* 223–25.

160. *Obscenity Law Reporter,* 13026–29, 38000–38025.

161. *Street v. New York,* 394 U.S. 576, (1969) *on remand,* 250 N.E.2d 250 (N.Y. Ct. App. 1969).

162. *Obscenity Law Reporter,* 15014–15. citing *Adult Book-*

mart, Inc. v. State, 264 S.E. 2d 273 (Ga, Ct. App. 1979), *cert. denied,* 451 U.S. 975 (1981) and *Stancil v. State,* 272 S.E. 2d 511 (Ga. Ct. App. 1980), *cert. denied,* 451 U.S. 975 (1981).

163. Ibid., 31000.

164. *Grayned v. City of Rockford,* 408 U.S. 104 (1972).

165. *Papachristou v. City of Jacksonville,* 405 U.S. 156 (1972).

166. *Obscenity Law Reporter,* 31013.

167. *Winters v. New York,* 333 U.S. 507 (1948).

168. *Obscenity Law Reporter,* 31022–24.

169. Ibid., 31027.

170. Ibid., 31000–31034.

171. Schauer, *The Law of Obscenity,* 163–65.

172. *Obscenity Law Reporter,* 32012, 32013.

173. *Erznoznik,* 205.

174. *Obscenity Law Reporter,* 32018.

175. Ibid., 32019.

176. Ibid., 32000–32032.

177. Schauer, *The Law of Obscenity,* 155.

178. Timothy O'Neill, Speech to the Phoenix National Conference on Obscenity, 1 December 1981.

179. Hinson McAuliffe, Speech to the Denver National Conference on Pornography, 31 May 1985.

180. Larry E. Parrish, "The 'Taken as a Whole' Standard to Determine the Obscene," in "Colloquium: Violent Pornography: 268.

181. Larry E. Parrish, Speech to the Phoenix National Conference on Obscenity, 1 December 1981.

182. Robert Showers, "Statement of H. Robert Showers, Assistants United of North Carolina" (Testimony before the Attorney General's Commission on Pornography, date unknown), 1–24, 19.

183. Bruce A. Taylor, "Hard-Core Pornography: A Proposal for a Per Se Rule," *University of Michigan Journal of Law Reform,* Fall, 1987 and Winter, 1988. 21: 266–67.

184. Bruce Taylor, Speech to the Phoenix National Conference on Obscenity, 1 December 1981.

185. Parrish, Speech to the Phoenix National Conference on Obscenity.

186. Weaver, *Handbook on the Prosecution of Obscenity Cases,* 91–93.

187. Kenneth P. Norwick, *The Basic ACLU Guide to the Legal Rights of Authors and Artists* (New York: Bantam Books, 1984).

188. Schauer, *The Law of Obscenity,* 265–66, 273–74.

189. Weaver, *Prosecution of Obscenity Cases,* 12–13, 21–28, 78–79.

190. Parrish, "The Non-Elusive Community Standard."

191. Joseph Spoor Turner III, "Assessing the Constitu-

tionality of North Carolina's New Obscenity Law," *North Carolina Law Review* 65 (1987): 400–416.

192. Schauer, *The Law of Obscenity,* 267–68.

193. O'Neill, Speech to the Phoenix National Conference on Obscenity.

194. Michael Kent Curtis, "Obscenity: The Judges' Not So New Robes," *Campbell Law Review* 8 (1986): 387, 402, 417–19.

195. Weaver, *Prosecution of Obscenity Cases,* 44–46.

196. Schauer, *The Law of Obscenity,* 251–52.

197. Weaver, *Prosecution of Obscenity Cases,* 47–48.

198. Schauer, *The Law of Obscenity,* 248–49, 250–51.

199. Weaver, *Prosecution of Obscenity Cases,* 50, 49–54.

200. Schauer, *The Law of Obscenity,* 301–4.

201. Bill Kelly, Speech to the Phoenix National Conference on Obscenity, December 1981.

202. O'Neill, Speech to the Phoenix National Conference on Obscenity.

203. Parrish and Kelly, Speeches to the Phoenix National Conference on Obscenity.

204. Kelly, Ibid.

205. Parrish and Kelly, Speeches to the Phoenix National Conference on Obscenity.

206. Weaver, *Prosecution of Obscenity Cases,* 55–57.

207. Ibid., 58–78.

208. Ch. 38, s. 11-20 (c), *Illinois Revised Statutes* (1986).

209. Weaver, *Prosecution of Obscenity Cases,* 76.

210. Ibid.

211. Ibid., 75–77.

212. Ibid., 106–112.

213. Ibid., 85.

214. Ibid., 86.

215. Schauer, *The Law of Obscenity,* 305–9.

216. Ibid., 292–99.

217. Weaver, *Prosecution of Obscenity Cases,* 63–64.

218. Ibid., 67.

219. Ibid., 94–105.

220. Ibid., 69–72.

221. Ibid., 58–75.

222. Schauer, *The Law of Obscenity,* 276–91.

223. Ibid., 276–88.

224. Ibid., 286.

225. Ibid., 288–89.

226. Blaine D. McLaughlin, "The Psychiatrist as Expert Witness in Pornography Prosecutions," in *Where Do You Draw the Line?* ed. Victor B. Cline (Provo, Utah: Brigham Young University Press, 1974), 271–83.

227. O'Neill, Speech to the Phoenix National Conference on Obscenity.

228. Weaver, *Prosecution of Obscenity Cases,* 81–84.

229. Schauer, *The Law of Obscenity,* 274–75.

In the early 1980s, a coalition of feminists, pornography victims, and neighborhood organizations in Minneapolis started the movement to legally define pornography as a violation of civil rights and make it actionable in civil court. The civil rights antipornography ordinance, detailed in chapter 1 and included as appendix K, defines pornography as sex discrimination—"a systematic practice of exploitation and subordination based on sex that differentially harms women." The reader is asked to consider those parts of chapter 1 that relate to the civil rights law in conjunction with this chapter, for key terms such as *subordination, sex object,* and *submission* are defined in that chapter. In addition, chapter 7 details the feminist viewpoints that form the basis for the civil rights approach to pornography.

This chapter includes the history of the civil rights law, key arguments for and against the law, and legal strategies in support of and opposition to this approach.

A version of the civil rights ordinance was passed in Indianapolis in 1984. That ordinance was held to be unconstitutional by the district, circuit, and U.S. Supreme courts. Despite this, we believe that a human rights approach to fighting pornography in civil court will survive future court challenges.

The civil rights law proposed in Indianapolis gave victims of pornography the right to sue in civil court for damages and injunctions to get the specific pornography that harmed them off the market. It created four causes of action:

1. Coercion into pornography
2. Forcing pornography on a person
3. Assault or physical attack due to pornography
4. Trafficking in pornography

The civil rights approach has the potential to be highly effective in fighting pornography because it will be used by victims to seek redress, it will effectively cut into the profits of pornographers, it will compensate pornography victims for its harms, it will enable owners and investors in porno businesses to be publicly exposed, and it will get harmful pornography out of the stream of commerce.

HISTORY OF THE CIVIL RIGHTS ORDINANCE

An article by Paul Brest and Ann Vandenberg contains an excellent summary of the entire civil rights antipornography movement. The following information is based primarily on that article.

The civil rights approach to fighting pornography was born in Minneapolis out of the combined efforts of victims of pornography, feminists, and people from working-class neighborhoods who were trying to get rid of pornographic theaters and bookstores. This movement began with the recognition that existing obscenity law had not been an effective tool in fighting pornography.[1]

Feminists consider pornography a central part of a "political system in which men exercise power over women." They emphasize the Robin Morgan quote that "pornography is the theory, rape the practice."[2] However, the antipornography issue has caused controversy among feminists, Brest and Vandenberg point out. Some feel that the ordinance restates the premises of the old gender system by suggesting that women are less sexually safe than ever. The antipornography feminists point out that women in our society are not sexually safe and that, for many women, sex "is not a choice but something that must be done on demand" at risk of being beaten or abandoned or because they see it as their duty.[3]

Through the 1979 book *Sexual Harassment of Working Women,* Catharine MacKinnon and other attorneys established the legal point that under the Civil Rights Act of 1964, sexual harassment in the workplace is a form of sex discrimination. The antipornography civil rights ordinance began through a pornography course taught by MacKinnon and Andrea Dworkin at the University of Minnesota. During the same time period, residents of the central neighborhood of Minneapolis had established a

Neighborhood Pornography Task Force aimed at persuading the city to adopt a zoning ordinance to replace the law struck down by the courts. An associate professor at the university, Naomi Scheman, suggested that the task force invite MacKinnon and Dworkin to assist them in doing something about the pornography problem in the neighborhood.[4]

In testimony before a zoning and planning committee, Dworkin attacked the concept underlying the proposed zoning law because it permitted the dissemination of materials that upheld the inferior status of women. She said, " 'I think that you should say that you are going to permit the exploitation of live women, the sadomasochistic use of live women, the binding and torture of real women and then have the depictions of those women used in those ways sold in the City.' "[5] Pornography, according to Dworkin, is the actual practice of the idea that women are sexually subordinate people.[6]

MacKinnon also told the committee that she did not believe that pornography had to exist. She spoke against the zoning ordinance and urged the city to take a civil rights approach instead: " 'I suggest that you consider that pornography, as it subordinates women to men, is a form of discrimination on the basis of sex.' " She noted that Minneapolis had a law against sex discrimination and urged the city council to hold hearings aimed at extending that law to make pornography legally actionable.[7]

Dworkin and MacKinnon had first looked at treating pornography as a violation of women's civil rights several years before in response to the victimization of Linda Marchiano (known as Linda Lovelace in pornographic films). The complaint on behalf of Marchiano was never filed because the lawyers concluded that the suit was barred by the statute of limitations.

The zoning committee was receptive to the MacKinnon–Dworkin proposal. Charlee Hoyt, a liberal Republican on the city council, asked her aide to contact them and became the chief sponsor of the concept before the council. The zoning ordinance proposal was shelved. On Hoyt's motion, the council entered into a contract with Dworkin and MacKinnon to assist in developing a civil rights approach to fighting pornography. They were also contracted to develop testimony for hearings to show how pornography adversely affects women and is part of women's socially subordinate status. A great deal of public attention and publicity focused on this issue. The article by Brest and Vandenberg summarizes comments made at hearings and in the press and reviews the testimony of victims of pornography.

In November 1983, Hoyt and others introduced the civil rights ordinance. However, as Vandenberg and Brest note, aspects of the proposed law contrasted with most civil rights laws, which are phrased in neutral terms such as forbidding discrimination on the basis of sex rather than discrimination against women. This drew criticism that the ordinance was itself discriminatory and not a proper civil rights measure.[8]

As a result of the civil rights issue being raised, people who were victims of pornography came forward to tell their stories. (Many victim views appear in chapter 4.) The victim stories and those of therapists and others who work with porn victims built the case for passage of the ordinance.

A key point raised by MacKinnon is that pornography, "as an integral part of a system of sexual domination and subordination, makes women invisible and silences them." Thus, they are denied freedom of speech.[9] When women speak up to contradict the images of pornography, MacKinnon said, they are taken seriously, listened to, or believed, but " '[p]ornography makes women's speech impossible and where possible, worthless.' "[10]

Among the people and groups that opposed the ordinance were the editor of a gay publication, a person who emphasized the importance of adult bookstores as meeting places for gay men and places to be sexual together, the owner of a bookstore that sold romance novels who was concerned that the romances would be regulated by the ordinance, and a member of the civil rights commission who argued that merchants would resolve doubts about whether particular books were covered by not handling them.[11]

Representatives of the pornography industry, the civil liberties groups, and the radical right were, for the most part, absent from the Minneapolis hearings on the ordinance. The attorney for one of the pornographers who had successfully fought the city's zoning ordinance, said that they expected the ordinance to be adopted but would seek an injunction against it and would try to have it declared unconstitutional. The Minnesota Civil Liberties Union vigorously opposed the ordinance in the press, but its director, although invited to testify, did not appear.

MacKinnon attacked the local and national civil liberties unions as being the " 'pornographers' mouthpiece.' " She said that the ACLU and some of its local chapters had cozy ties with the pornographers. Sometimes, she said, they use pornography as fundraisers. Their projects are supported by the pornographers, MacKinnon noted: " '[M]any individuals who do national speaking on behalf of the ACLU are in fact privately paid attorneys of individual pornographers,' " she said. The public speaking of such people promotes their private interests, she concluded.[12]

The right-wing antipornography organizations were not among the supporters of the ordinance. The Morality in Media of Minnesota, Inc., president initially supported the law but later withdrew that support and said that existing obscenity laws should be enforced instead.

Council members were concerned about voting on the ordinance with little knowledge about whether it was constitutional. A serious oversight of the law's proponents was their failure to set up a meeting with the civil rights commission, the very agency that would hear complaints arising under the ordinance. That commission asked the city council to postpone voting on the ordinance for several months to allow it time for research.[13]

A variety of newspaper opinion columns responded to the hearings. One alleged that the law would establish special protection from "offensive" ideas or images for women as a class. Another did not find the "improbable" crime connection and pornography's repugnance sufficient enough to make an exception to the First Amendment. One person asked why the men who were defending the First Amendment were not protesting the fact that few people have any real First Amendment rights because they do not have the money and influence to get their opinions into the media.

Brest and Vandenberg note that feminists have defended the legitimacy of a wide variety of pornography and that a body of women's writing expresses women's sexuality in ways that might be covered by the ordinance. Some of these items include rape fantasies and mass-market romances that emphasize male dominance and female submission. MacKinnon, in fact, argued that women's enjoyment and fantasies of submission are rooted in the suppressive system of male-created sexuality that is basic to male dominance as a political system.[14]

Mayor Donald Fraser's wife, Arvonne, described the ordinance as a step backward because it treated women as a victimized class that had to be protected. She said that the law should not be based on the assumption that a class of people are helpless.[15]

In a January 5, 1984, letter to the city council, Mayor Fraser explained why he vetoed the antipornography civil rights ordinance. Fraser said that the ordinance as drafted was not appropriate or enforceable under the First Amendment. He concluded that the definition of pornography in the ordinance was so vague and broad as to make it impossible for booksellers and movie theater operators to change their conduct to keep from violating the law. The mayor also objected to letting an administrative body

(the civil rights commission), which some might call a "Board of Censors," decide whether violations took place. Fraser said the ordinance was redundant to the extent that it prohibited what was already prohibited by obscenity law. Sexually explicit material that is not obscene is protected by the First Amendment, Fraser said, even if it is degrading or it portrays women as sex objects. He called for more research into the issue of whether sexually explicit material that degrades women impairs women's full enjoyment of other rights and is thus not protected speech. Fraser's main concern was the "chilling effect" of an overly broad ordinance.[16]

Professor Laurence Tribe of the Harvard Law School responded to the mayor's veto, calling it "an abuse of the fundamental structure of our system of government." He said that the mayor had acted to deprive the courts of their unique constitutional function to pass on legislation that is not obviously unconstitutional. Here, the mayor usurped the judicial function, Tribe said.[17]

Tribe, a constitutional law expert, said:

> While many hard questions of conflicting rights will face any court that confronts challenges to the ordinance, as drafted it rests on a rationale that closely parallels many previously accepted exceptions to justly stringent First Amendment guarantees. While remaining uncertain myself as to the ultimate outcome of a judicial test, I urge you not to allow an executive to prevent the courts from adjudicating what may eventually be found to be the first sensible approach to an area which has vexed some of the best legal minds for decades.

In response, Dane County, Wisconsin, supervisor Kathleen Nichols said that "white male attorneys" had been the ordinance's "firmest naysayers" and that the Tribe letter "tends to take a lot of wind out of their sails."[18]

The veto was upheld by the council, which established a task force on pornography to continue to study the problem. During this same time period, the Pornography Resource Center (now called Organizing Against Pornography), a feminist-oriented antipornography organization, opened its office. Task force hearings focusing on social science research were conducted, and none of the witnesses recommended a policy aimed at suppressing pornography.

Randall Tigue, an attorney for the pornographers, criticized the ordinance on the ground that it defined pornography by the ideas advocated, prohibited protected expression, and embodied a concept that he called "pervert veto theory," which is a notion that the possibility of triggering violence in sex maniacs justifies denying access of the rest of the population to pornography.

MacKinnon in turn noted that the Supreme Court had never found the First Amendment to be absolute but had often balanced it against other important interests. Here the balance was between the rights of pornographers and those of women to equality and to freedom to speak out against the pornography (under the First Amendment).

David Gross of the city attorney's office argued that the ordinance could not be sustained on the basis of causing " 'a direct and immediate tangible harm.' " The experts, he said, agreed that there was no evidence that pornography caused sexual violence. The law attempted to regulate ideas, expressions, and thoughts, not conduct, and was unconstitutional.

While MacKinnon acknowledged that pornography was also expression, she argued that it was sexual subordination, not ideas, that the ordinance made actionable. Pornography was more actlike than thoughtlike in her view.

A therapist testified at the hearings that the real question was not whether pornography caused " 'violent acts to be perpetrated against women.' " Rather, the therapist said, " [p]orn is already a violent act against women.' "

The Task Force on Pornography issued its report on May 2, 1984, and proposed a narrower version of the civil rights ordinance. Among its recommendations were remedies for location-related harms such as zoning, opaque cover laws, and broadening the obscenity law to cover sexual violence. The proposal broadened the definition of pornography to refer to " 'sexually explicit subordination of persons' " and narrowed it to include only graphic depictions of violence. Significantly, it eliminated the trafficking provisions. Charlee Hoyt accused the task force of designing an ordinance that would sound good but not truly wanting to get rid of pornography.[19]

Michael A. Gershel says that the task force defined sexually explicit as follows:

> "(1) Actual or simulated sexual intercourse, including genital-genital, oral-genital, anal-genital or oral-anal, whether between persons of the same or opposite sex or between a person and animals; or
> (2) Uncovered exhibition of the breasts, genitals, pubic region, buttocks or anus of any person."

Importantly, as Gershel notes, this definition would not cover especially hard-core or deviant material such as bruises or lash marks on a victim, urination or defecation on a clothed victim, or bondage portrayals in which the victim's buttocks, breasts, and vagina are covered by the binding material.

The task force also defined *subordination* as ' "the treatment of another as inferior, submissive to, or controlled by another, made subject or subservient to another.' " Yet, as Gershel points out, this definition would greatly limit the scope of the ordinance, for it would exclude all portrayals in which a single person was depicted alone.[20] (We believe that this ignores the reality of pornography, which frequently portrays women being subordinated or as inferior without anyone else being included in the picture. One of the pornographic techniques is to make the male reader feel as though he is in control of the women pictured.)

Dworkin argued that the only real question before the city council was whether they were helping the pornographers or helping women. MacKinnon and Dworkin did go along with some revisions to the draft that retained the trafficking provision but eliminated language that allowed isolated passages to be actionable and emphasized the more violent material. The council rejected the task force proposal in favor of the Dworkin and MacKinnon's revised draft in June 1984. In July, the civil rights commission announced its opposition to the ordinance, stating that the commissioners would be required to act as censors and that it would divert the commission's energy " 'to the detriment of existing protected classes.' "[21]

On July 13, 1984, the council again passed the ordinance. A proposal to monitor the Indianapolis legislation also passed. The mayor again vetoed it.

Brest and Vandenberg state:

> The trauma experienced by the women who had testified before the City Council was compounded by unanticipated consequences of their testimony. Some found that they had become pariahs in their neighborhoods, stimatized and shamed by their revelations. Others, whose names had been printed in an article in *Forum* (a magazine published by *Penthouse*), received abusive and threatening letters and phone calls. By the end of the year many of the witnesses had been forced to change their phone numbers or move to different neighborhoods to avoid further harassment.[22]

In Minneapolis the Pornography Resource Center remains the only concrete legacy of the antipornography movement, Vandenberg and Brest say. However, they believe that it was no small achievement for MacKinnon, Dworkin, and their supporters to have affected the consciousness of so many people.[23]

Rebecca Benson offers another excellent summary of the civil rights perspective. She emphasizes that when the U.S. Supreme Court summarily affirmed the Seventh Circuit Court of Appeals decision in

American Booksellers v. *Hudnut,* (a court case that challenged the Indianapolis civil rights ordinance) the rationale on which the court relied remained unclear. Although the summary affirmance was a binding precedent, Benson says, the precedential value of such a decision is limited to "the precise issues presented and necessarily decided" in reaching the results under *Mandel v. Bradley.* Therefore, Benson concludes that the summary affirmance did not necessarily represent approval of the lower court's reasoning.

Benson argues that the more MacKinnon, Dworkin, and others oppose pornography on the basis that it perpetuates political and social hierarchy, the more pornography begins to resemble political speech of the very kind protected by the First Amendment rather than unprotected, low value speech. She emphasizes that the courts ignored the proposition that the state actually destroyed the speech rights of women by using the First Amendment to protect free speech (pornography). She notes that true " 'freedom of speech' is no more than an abstract and empty promise for women."

Benson says that the ordinance would not be in the best interests of women. She believes that it reinforced sexist stereotypes of women and might actually have discriminated on the basis of sex. She also argues that it could have been used against feminists.[24]

As mentioned previously, civil rights legislation was proposed in other cities besides Minneapolis. In Indianapolis, an hour after Mayor William H. Hudnut III signed the civil rights antipornography ordinance into law in 1984, the American Booksellers et al. filed a lawsuit in federal court. Judge Sarah Evans Barker promptly issued a preliminary injunction against enforcement of the law. The executive director of the Indiana Civil Liberties Union charged that the law would create "a cultural wasteland." And Michael A. Bamberger (a lawyer for the Media Coalition (a trade association of publication distributors) said that the definition of pornography would cover books such as *Gone with the Wind* and *The Taming of the Shrew,* as well as television programs such as "Dynasty" and "Dallas."[25]

Mayor Hudnut was quoted in the *Chicago Tribune* as stating that Indianapolis felt there was a "definite, traceable connection between pornography in our city and increasing crime rates and decreasing property values." He emphasized that First Amendment rights are not absolute. Opponents charged that James Bond movies and Sidney Sheldon novels would be prohibited by the ordinance, but supporters denied this. Beulah Coughenour, the council member who introduced the ordinance, explained that such items would not be covered because they are not graphic, sexually explicit subordination of women. Bamberger charged that it was a "thought-control law." Sheila Suess Kennedy, an attorney for the plaintiffs, said the ordinance read like a product of "fanaticism. Legally, this is a joke."[26]

A spokesman for the Indiana Civil Liberties Union said that the organization does not support pornography but it is committed to the protection of ideas that it both supports and loathes. A spokesman for an antipornography group said that the group had seen property values drop and neighborhoods deteriorate, as well as people grow afraid to go out at night, due to pornography. One of the reasons why Coughenour introduced the civil rights law was because jurors found it difficult to convict persons under the state obscenity law. Two law school professors charged that the ordinance might even make textbooks and news accounts actionable.[27]

In Cambridge, Massachusetts, the civil rights ordinance was forced onto the ballot as a binding municipal question. It received 9,419 votes but was defeated with 13,031 votes on the other side. The Cambridge Women's Alliance Against Pornography proposed the law. The group collected more than five thousand signatures of registered voters in order to put the question on the ballot. The city council voted 5 to 4 to keep the question off the ballot. The alliance sued to guarantee ballot access. Members of the group said they found a great deal of support for the ordinance from persons outside the feminist camp as well.[28]

Dane County, Wisconsin, supervisor Kathleen Nichols drafted an ordinance similar to the Minneapolis ordinance. At the same time (fall 1984), supervisor Stuart Levitan proposed a law under which a store would need a permit to sell what he called PM (perverse material). His proposal defined perverse material as "any magazine, poster, film, video, or other amusement which, taken as a whole, explicitly depicts or encourages sexual gratification derived from harming persons in ways prohibited by Chapter 940 of the Criminal Code" (dealing with crimes of bodily harm such as kidnapping, rape, false imprisonment, murder, and so on). It also said that no material would be considered perverse unless it does the following:

a. Fails to contain serious political, artistic, scientific or cultural value; and it

b. Depicts or encourages sexual gratification through sexual assault, or other acts of violence, or bestiality; and it

c. Appeals to the prurient interest through the graphic portrayal of buttocks, genitalia, or female breasts.[29]

Constitutional absolutest lawyer Gordon Baldwin of the University of Wisconsin–Madison Law School attacked Levitan's proposal, claiming that Levitan was saying "We know what's good for you." He expressed concern about where one would draw the line between what should be permitted and what excluded from First Amendment protection. He conceded that books can be very harmful or very good but said, "I'm not impressed by the knowledge that these things [pornography] are harmful."[30]

The Nichols proposal, unlike those in Minneapolis and Indianapolis, would not have had civil rights violations handled by an administrative commission. Instead, victims would have been able to go directly into court to seek redress.

Keenen Peck, associate editor of *The Progressive*, opposed the civil rights ordinance in Madison. He said that if pornography can be censored, "so can the publications of Democratic Socialists of America." He asked who can say what incites people to violence. "Does *Playboy*? Does the *Playboy* interview? Certainly the *Communist Manifesto* does." He termed the ordinance dangerous and repressive.[31]

When the civil rights approach was being considered on the county level in Madison, a chapter of the Feminist Anti-Censorship Task Force (FACT) formed. One spokeswoman said that FACT believed the ordinance would jeopardize the freedom of expression of feminists, gays, lesbians, and others who held unpopular beliefs and lifestyles. Representative David Clarenbach found the civil rights approach unacceptable because it would allow individuals to "use their personal preferences to decide for all others what should be said, seen or read."[32]

Attorney Robert O'Neil, University of Wisconsin president, called the civil rights approach to pornography "dangerously imprecise."[33] And Wisconsin Civil Liberties Union executive director Eunice Edgar expressed concern that any law to restrict pornography would have a chilling effect on free speech. She suggested that abhorrent ideas should be confronted by using free speech to condemn them rather than by restricting the freedom of expression.[34]

An author and First Amendment absolutist from Los Angeles spoke against the ordinance at a debate on the ground that people have the right to consider themselves sexual objects and to be filmed as sexual objects. She said that she opposed a ban on pornography because it is a "voluntary activity." She said, "If you can find one case where a photographer has held a camera in one hand and a Smith and Wesson in the other, I'll change my position."[35] (We point out that coercion, including use of weapons, is a reality in some pornography production. One

example is the treatment of Linda Marchiano-Lovelace.)

The University of Wisconsin–Madison student newspaper, *The Daily Cardinal*, ran a series of opinion items on the civil rights ordinance. Iris Christensen referred to pornography as "a body of hate literature used to terrorize women into silence and submission." Reverend Jeff Goldstein suggested that the civil rights law might be better understood if it were characterized as a product liability law under which pornographers would be held liable for damage caused by their product. Michelle Courier and Leslie J. Reagan argued that the law would be used by right-wing groups to attack lesbians, gays, and feminists and that it would empower courts, not women, to determine what is pornographic. They said that there are other ways to fight violence against women and sexism.[36]

In August 1984, conservative Suffolk County, New York, legislator Michael D'Andre introduced a version of the civil rights antipornography ordinance. Women Against Pornography and other feminists who supported the ordinance as drafted by MacKinnon and Dworkin actively opposed the D'Andre version because it failed to cover most pornography and was infused with "moralistic" language, raising a danger of its use against sexually explicit material that is not pornography.

Dworkin faulted the D'Andre proposal as being "absolutely inadequate" and having obscenity-based values that "do not establish a valid basis for sex discrimination claims." MacKinnon called for its defeat on the ground that it distorted the civil rights approach and "would do nothing for women." Feminist lobbying efforts against the D'Andre bill succeeded when it was defeated by the county by a vote of 9 to 8 on December 26, 1985.[37]

After lengthy investigation, including the taking of victim testimony, the Los Angeles Commission for Women proposed a version of the civil rights ordinance to the Los Angeles County Board of Supervisors. At one hearing, film director Peter Bogdanovich stated that many women in the entertainment industry support the ordinance but are afraid to state so publicly because of ties between pornographers and legitimate entertainment people. He stated, "In the name of freedom of speech, a lot of people are being silenced in Los Angeles."[38] The board adopted a measure to strengthen existing obscenity laws but did not pass the ordinance.

Groups such as FACT, Wages for Housework's prostitutes' collective, and the ACLU opposed the Los Angeles County ordinance. The concern that the right wing would take over the feminist law was raised. Some claimed that giving prostitutes a right to sue for coercion into pornography would make their lives more dangerous. In response to this claim, Catharine MacKinnon said that oppressed people often identify with their oppressors and succumb to the fear that any action to make their situation better will make their lives worse.[39]

A bill titled The Pornography Victims Protection Act was introduced in the U.S. Senate on October 3, 1985, by Senator Arlen Specter. The act would have enabled adults and children who were coerced, fraudulently induced, or intimidated into posing for pornography to civilly sue the distributors and producers of the material and to obtain injunctions to get the pornography off the streets. Three times the victims' actual damages and costs of the suit could be recovered under the proposal. This bill incorporated some of the features of the civil rights ordinance. The act was prompted by Senate hearings at which victims of pornography testified.[40] (The bill was not passed.)

PROPONENTS' VIEWS

In her testimony before the Attorney General's Commission, attorney Catharine MacKinnon said that pornography flourishes primarily because "its real harm was never identified: the violation of women and children that is essential to its making and inevitable through its use" and partly because the industry sets community standards. This harm is overlooked because the pornographers (whom she calls "pimps") "take the already powerless . . . and deepen their invisibility and their silence." Pornography plays a crucial role in institutionalizing a victimized, subhuman, second-class status for women, MacKinnon said. Pornography is an exception to the First Amendment precisely because it is harmful: It "undermines sex equality, a compelling state interest and legitimate concern of government, by harming people, differentially women." She stated that group libel, privacy, child pornography, and obscenity laws are partial precedents for the civil rights law. She said that pornography is at the center of a cycle of abuse.

A term that some allege is confusing—*subordination*—was defined by MacKinnon in her testimony: "A subordinate is the opposite of an equal. The term subordination refers to the active practice of making a person unequal."

MacKinnon stated:

> If speech interests become comparatively less valued for constitutional purposes when materials are false, obscene, indecent, lascivious, lewd, racist, provocative, dangerous, coercive, threatening, intrusive, inconvenient, or inaesthetic, we believe they should be able to be civilly actionable when they are, and can be proven to be, coerced, assaultive, and discriminatory.[41]

In "Pornography, Civil Rights, and Speech," MacKinnon details the need for a civil rights law, the reasons why pornography is discrimination, and how the ordinance would operate. She presents several case histories of pornography victims, case citations and background data, and sources on abuse of women in general. We include herein only a few of MacKinnon's main points, concentrating on those ideas not presented elsewhere in this book:

> What pornography does goes beyond its content: it eroticizes hierarchy, it sexualizes inequality. It makes dominance and submission sex. Inequality is its central dynamic; the illusion of freedom coming together with the reality of force is central to its working. Perhaps because this is a bourgeois culture, the victim must look free, appear to be freely acting. Choice is how she got there. Willing is what she is when she is being equal. It seems equally important that then and there she actually be forced and that forcing be communicated on some level, even if only through still photos of her in postures of receptivity and access, available for penetration. Pornography in this view is a form of forced sex, a practice of sexual politics, an institution of gender inequality.
>
> From this perspective, pornography is neither harmless fantasy nor a corrupt and confused misrepresentation of an otherwise natural and healthy sexual situation. It institutionalizes the sexuality of male supremacy, fusing the eroticization of dominance and submission with the social construction of male and female. To the extent that gender is sexual, pornography is part of constituting the meaning of that sexuality. Men treat women as who they see women as being. Pornography constructs who that is. Men's power over women means that the way men see women defines who women can be. Pornography is that way. Pornography is not imagery in some relation to a reality elsewhere constructed. It is not a distortion, reflection, projection, expression, fantasy, representation, or symbol either. It is a sexual reality.[42]

The point of the civil rights ordinance is to hold those who profit or benefit from the injury caused by pornography accountable, MacKinnon emphasizes. The injury should outweigh the pleasure and profits "or sex equality is meaningless." The ordinance defines pornography as a practice of sex discrimination and a violation of women's rights.[43]

MacKinnon argues that women who perform for or are otherwise harmed because of pornography need legal rights of redress for the same reasons that children do:

> [R]elative lack of power, inability to command respect for their consent and self-determination, in some cases less physical strength or lowered legitimacy in using it, specific credibility problems, and lack of access to resources for meaningful self-expression . . . also hold true for women's comparative social position to men.[44]

MacKinnon points out that the harm of child pornography cannot be effectively dealt with without addressing adult pornography, for such pornography is often used to induce children into sex and sometimes contains depictions in which adult women are made to appear childlike.[45]

It is necessary to reach trafficking in pornography in order to deal with the magnitude of the problem, MacKinnon states. She says that opposition to the ordinance centers on the trafficking provision:

> Pornography stimulates and reinforces, it does not cathect or mirror, the connection between one-sided freely available sexual access to women and masculine sexual excitement and sexual satisfaction. The catharsis hypothesis is fantasy. The fantasy theory is fantasy. Reality is: Pornography conditions male orgasm to female subordination. It tells men what sex means, what a real woman is, and codes them together in a way that is behaviorally reinforcing. . . . The behavioral data show that what pornography means *is* what it does.[46]

MacKinnon notes that under the First Amendment, restrictions with far less legislative basis have been allowed. For example, obscenity law is based on offensiveness, she says. Exceptions to the First Amendment exist because the harm done by certain speech outweighs its expressive value.

Comparing the ordinance to the "fighting words" exception created in *Chaplinsky*, MacKinnon states that perhaps the only reason why pornography has not been held to be fighting words—"words which by their very utterance tend to incite immediate

breach of peace—is that women have seldom fought back, yet."[47]

MacKinnon sheds light on the claim of supporters of the ordinance that pornography is a practice, not speech:

> The fact that pornography, in a feminist view, furthers the idea of the sexual inferiority of women, which is a political idea, doesn't make the pornography itself into a political idea. One can express the idea a practice embodies. That does not make that practice into an idea. Segregation expresses the idea of the inferiority of one group to another on the basis of race. That does not make segregation an idea. A sign that says "Whites Only" is only words. Is it therefore protected by the first amendment? Is it not an act, a practice, of segregation because of the inseparability of what it means from what it does?

Lastly, MacKinnon argues that it is erroneous to presuppose that population segments are not systematically silenced before government action. Thus, the equal power assumption built into the First Amendment freedom simply is not true, she believes.[48]

MacKinnon differentiates obscenity from pornography in "Pornography: Not a Moral Issue." She argues that obscenity law is concerned with morality from the perspective of male dominance. Pornography is a political practice, that of subordinating women to men. She sees obscenity law as covering nudity, sexual arousal, and other depictions of sex. At times birth control and abortion information were covered by such laws, she states. Pornography, MacKinnon says, "causes attitudes and behaviors of violence and discrimination which define the treatment and status of half of the population."[49]

According to MacKinnon, obscenity law tries to control what and how sex can be shown publicly. It exempts works of perceived male value. Thus, that which maintains male power is good, and that which undermines it is evil. Obscenity law, she says, protects what it sees as moral, which, from the feminist viewpoint, is often material that is damaging to women. Male morality considers that which feminists identify as central in women's subordination—the eroticization of dominance and submission—comparatively harmless, she says. She explains why feminists dislike obscenity law as defined in *Miller*. Feminists question whether a "gender neutral" average person exists and how community standards are defined. Feminists also ask why prurience is at issue but powerlessness is not under obscenity law. They also question basing the law on protection from offensiveness instead of protecting women from exploitation. They would define sexuality and its violation more broadly than obscenity law. Feminists, MacKinnon says, wonder "why a body of law which can't in practice tell rape from intercourse should be entrusted with telling pornography from anything less."[50]

In a letter to the editor of the *New York Times,* Catharine MacKinnon says that in opposing the civil rights ordinance, "you support the rights of pimps over the rights of women." She emphasizes that this law makes feeling offended "irrelevant" because harm to women is the real issue.[51]

After the Seventh Circuit Court of Appeals affirmed the district court's decision in *American Booksellers v. Hudnut,* Catharine MacKinnon stated that the ruling showed "women's rights are a joke." She said that "pornography is a violation of women. They're saying that violating women is protected by the Constitution." She also said that the court would not even listen to them and that they had been silenced in the name of free speech.[52]

Andrea Dworkin asked Minneapolis mayor Donald Fraser not to veto the civil rights ordinance. She told how she was sexually tortured by doctors in a prison and has spent the rest of her life "trying to understand precisely the relationship between power, sexuality, and torture." Members of her family survived concentration camp experiences in World War II. Everything that happened to them was sexual sadism, she said, "from rape to shaven heads to an infant son bayonetted in front of them." Likewise, pornography is an "entertainment" industry based on "torture," she said. She pointed out that when acts such as battery, rape, incest, and prostitution are perpetrated against men and boys, they are perceived as what they really are—torture. When these acts are perpetrated against women, however, they are made to seem natural.

Dworkin accused Fraser of showing concern for torture around the world through group activism but being indifferent "to the torture of women in and because of pornography." She suggested that it is harder to fight human rights violations when they happen around you and provide profit and pleasure for your peers. Dworkin said that Fraser had offered a baseball team $400,000 to stay in Minneapolis but that the city had no money to defend the civil rights bill against threatened litigation. "Can it be true that someone of conscience has money for baseball, but none to stop a trade in torture? I do not believe this of you," she wrote.[53]

In her testimony before the Attorney General's Commission on Pornography, Dworkin stated that the ACLU was colluding with the pornographers and taking money from them. She said that the group uses buildings that pornographers own without paying rent and uses pornography at benefits to raise money. In addition, she said, the ACLU is involved in defending pornographers in court and organizing events for them, as well as publishing in their magazines. According to Dworkin, the ACLU and a number of others are responsible for the fact that pornography has become a legitimate form of public entertainment. She also blames the lobby of lawyers who work for pornographers, the so-called legitimate media, politicians who collude with pornographers, the first national commission on pornography, and consumers for legitimizing pornography.

According to Dworkin, one of the reasons for the civil law is the fact that the process of civil discovery is an important one and could lead to criminal prosecutions against organized crime and pornographers. She opposes obscenity law because, she says, pornographers use it as part of their formula to make pornography—that is, community standards do not work for women because the community allows battering and pornography to occur. In addition, obscenity laws are based on a presumption that women's bodies are dirty and continue to allow pornography to be available to men in private.

Dworkin said that she would like to see a criminal conspiracy provision under the civil rights law making it a crime to conspire to deprive a person of civil rights by forcing him or her into pornography and conspiring to traffic in pornography. While Dworkin does not recommend enforcement of obscenity laws, she said that she supports use of laws against pandering and RICO laws. In her view, every woman who engages in hard-core pornography is a prostitute because the act of performing sex for money is prostitution.[54]

In 1986, the *Women Against Pornography Newsreport* reported that the ACLU wanted to suppress the Pornography Commission's list of pornographic books and magazines and descriptions of those items on the ground that the commission was being hypocritical in printing a list of dirty pictures. Feminist Dorchen Liedholdt responded by noting that *Playboy* had long funded the ACLU reproductive rights project and that the ACLU had shown pornographic films such as *Deep Throat* and *Sex World* to raise money for its projects.[55]

OPPONENTS' VIEWS

Barry Lynn, legislative counsel of the ACLU, says that the presumption that there is a difference between sexually oriented speech and all other types of speech is unwarranted. Sexually explicit material "fulfills the traditional functions of speech: transmitting ideas, promoting self-realization, and serving as a 'safety-valve' for both the speaker and the audience," he says. According to Lynn, pornography transmits ideas by being educational and promoting particular attitudes toward sexuality. He suggests that pornography also may have an effect or purpose of promoting political or ideological perspectives such as anger toward women. It is not low value speech.[56]

Lynn also considers pornography to be fostering self-expression or self-fulfillment. For example, material depicting or affirming lifestyles can be a means of self-affirmation for "sexual minorities." Lynn believes in the "safety-valve" or "cathartic" view of pornography. He states, "For many adolescent boys, pornography . . . is primarily an accompaniment to masturbation. As such, it serves as a substitute for sexual activity with young women which could lead to far more detrimental results of unwanted sexual relations and, possibly, undesired pregnancies."[57]

Lynn believes that there is no rational reason to assume that pornography plays a greater role than other negative images of women in our culture. If pornography truly plays a major role in the subordination of women, women should be much better off in places where pornography is not widely available, and they are not, he suggests.

Lynn argues that the civil rights ordinance would cover the same material that is currently covered by obscenity law and add more coverage.[58] He believes that Catharine MacKinnon does not understand how speech actually works:

> [T]he fact that it may stimulate a physical response does not distinguish pornography from other forms of speech; and, with respect to legitimating certain viewpoints and conditioning an audience toward a particular way of thinking, it should be clear that these are precisely the communicative intentions of political and commercial speech.[59]

The personal nature of individuals' responses to pornography makes it impossible to make distinctions between erotica and pornography, Lynn feels. While admitting that media violence is replicated during the commission of criminal acts at times, he denies that there is evidence that such portrayals cause the crimes. We should not, he states, return to the pre-*Roth* obscenity standard, which allowed regulation based on pornography's effect on the most suggestible person. He cites numerous cases in which liability was not found for imitative crimes.[60]

When pornography can be easily averted by turning away from it, there should be no cause of action, Lynn states. Women who are already sexually harassed by pornography have causes of action under current civil rights laws, so there is no need for the ordinance. However, because pornography is so prevalent, he believes that "the average American should not be legally offended by sexually explicit posters."[61]

Lynn accuses MacKinnon of blurring the distinction between acting and real life when she states that everything seen in pornography is happening to a real woman. Women who have been coerced into pornography have remedies under existing law, he claims.[62]

FACT attacked the civil rights ordinance in the June 1985 issue of *Off Our Backs*. FACT said:

1. The ordinance is sexist—it portrays women as helpless victims and people who cannot enjoy or seek sex and men as "aggressive beasts." Because it does not treat men and women equally, it violates the equal protection clause of the U.S. Constitution.
2. Terms in the ordinance are dangerously vague and could be used against feminists.
3. The ordinance is useless because it does not deal with the issues it purports to. FACT would prefer to punish acts of rape, coercion, and sexual abuse. It would rather change job segregation and provide day care. FACT does not believe that pornography is a central factor in sex discrimination. FACT would rather provide women with material resources to enable them to reject abusive marriages and jobs.
4. Sexually explicit speech needs more protection and sex is political.[63]

FACT details its opposition to the civil rights law in *Caught Looking: Feminism, Pornography and Censorship*. These arguments are covered in the legal briefs section of this chapter and in chapter 8.[64]

A series of articles that the Playboy Foundation helped fund appeared in the Fall 1983 issue of the *Journal of Popular Culture*. In that issue, Cynthia Toolin argues that pornography debases both women and men. She says that censorship will drive pornography underground: "It will not prevent violence against women; it will not eliminate objectification. Only a basic change in the tone and messages of our society's institutions can accomplish these things."[65]

In the same issue, William E. Brigman argues that pornography is a form of political speech. He says that court decisions stating that obscenity does not express ideas are inaccurate. Pornography, he believes, is not purely a sexual activity (as was argued by Professor Frederick Schauer and the U.S. Supreme Court) but also contains social, ideational, and political content. He believes that obscenity trials represent conflicts between groups or individuals with different values.[66]

Brigman cites Katz's view that the allegation that " 'pornography presents the debasement and dehumanization of man and that it involves no ideas is a contradiction.' "[67] Even Andrea Dworkin, co-author of the civil rights law, calls pornography "fascist propaganda," Brigman notes, stating that propaganda is protected by the First Amendment. He suggests that one cannot "seriously" deny that pornography consciously attempts to express a view of sexual and social life. And, he alleges, pornography "does not merely contain ideas: it is a statement of ideology." In fact, he suggests, pornography is found objectionable because it expresses an ideology that some want to suppress. Brigman states:

> In one sense, pornography is the archetypical political act or expression in that it seeks to challenge and undermine the foundations on which capitalistic economic and social systems are built. . . .

Pornography is political expression in that it attacks fundamental cultural values for displaying taboo sexual acts in a favorable light or by displaying acts that society prefers to treat as private in a public manner, thereby reversing the social designations of sacred and profane. . . . [A] swastika and a picture of a couple copulating . . . both constitute advocacy of cultural values that the producers and part of the audience wish to become dominant.[68]

In March 1985, *Newsweek* noted the contradiction between Americans bemoaning the recent wave of sexual abuse scandals on the one hand and supporting an industry that turns sexual abuse into entertainment on the other hand. It states that the ordinance has "troublesome" aspects in its definition and quotes Al Goldstein, publisher of *Screw* magazine, as summing up the conventional attack: " 'Frankly, I don't think it matters whether porn is degrading to women. It's a society of many voices and I don't want any of them silenced.' "[69]

In April 1985, *Ms.* magazine published an article by Mary Kay Blakely concerning the conflict within the feminist community about pornography. FACT, it said, questions whether a civil rights law is the best strategy to change woman-hating attitudes, whether images cause violence, and whether coalitions with the right wing will thwart feminist goals. Writer and poet Erica Jong is quoted as saying that she believes feminists would be the first to suffer under such a law. Support for the ordinance, however, came from feminists who believe that pornography shapes attitudes and that attitudes shape behavior.[70]

COURT OPINIONS

The Second Amended Complaint of the plaintiffs (American Booksellers Association, Inc., Association of American Publishers, Inc., Council for Periodical Distributors Associations, Freedom to Read Foundation, International Periodical Distributors Association, Inc., Koch News Co., National Association of College Stores Inc., Omega Satellite Products Co., Video Shack, Inc., and Kelly Bentley) in *American Booksellers Association, Inc. v. Hudnut* argued that the civil rights ordinance was unconstitutional for these reasons:

(a) It goes substantially beyond the standard for obscenity established by the United States Supreme Court;

(b) It imposes an unconstitutional prior restraint;

(c) It is unconstitutionally vague, incompre-

hensible and contains numerous substantive contradictions;

(d) It impermissibly empowers the Indianapolis "Office of Equal Opportunity" and "Equal Opportunity Advisory Board" . . . to act as censorship panels making determinations as to what materials can and cannot be read or viewed in Indianapolis, and to issue cease and desist orders and show cause orders in support thereof;

(e) It unconstitutionally interferes with interstate commerce by restricting the availability of First Amendment–protected materials only in the City of Indianapolis and Marion County. . . .

(f) It unconstitutionally restricts the access to First Amendment–protected material in Indianapolis by readers, viewers and other consumers thereof.[71]

Judge Sarah Evans Barker of the U.S. District Court, Southern District, Indiana, entered her judgment and reasons for the decision against the civil rights ordinance on November 19, 1984. The ruling was in support of the plaintiffs' motion for summary judgment. The ordinance was held to be unconstitutional.

Judge Barker made numerous conclusions of law, including the following:

1. The court need not abstain from jurisdiction because the ordinance is not susceptible to limiting constructions.
2. The plaintiffs had standing to challenge the amendment because their contentions were based on the First Amendment. The case was sufficiently ripe for adjudication.
3. Pornography, as defined in the ordinance, was speech, not conduct.
4. First Amendment protections extend to the regulation of pictures and words "to the extent that they express ideas and therefore, constitute 'speech' as that term is used in the First Amendment to the United States Constitution."[72]
5. Only speech that does not receive First Amendment protection may be regulated by government. The controls imposed by this ordinance do not fall within an established category of speech that can be regulated, such as obscenity, libel, or fighting words.
6. While the ordinance's pornography definition most clearly resembles obscenity, it fails to meet the legal definition of obscenity and therefore restricts speech that has been traditionally protected by the First Amendment. Because the ordinance goes beyond the definition of obscenity, the express purpose of regulation of pornography is the suppression of protected speech.
7. Only if the state's interest in prohibiting sex discrimination is so compelling as to outweigh the constitutional interest in free speech would pornography, as defined in the law, survive constitutional scrutiny. Here, the interest in prohibiting sex discrimination does not outweigh the interest in free speech.
8. Even assuming, for the purposes of argument, that the state's interest in prohibiting sex discrimination did outweigh the First Amendment interest, the ordinance is unconstitutional.
   a. It is unconstitutionally vague because it fails to give fair notice to persons of average intelligence about what material is intended to be prohibited.
   b. It is an unconstitutional prior restraint.[73]

The judge gave her reasons for her findings. On the standing issue, she found that because the claim related to the First Amendment, the plaintiffs could rely on the impact of the law on the speech activities of others as well as their own under *Schad* v. *Burrough of Mt. Ephraim*.[74] Such cases are allowable when claims of overbreadth and vagueness are made. Also, she found that the complaint alleged and it was true that the plaintiffs' interests were directly affected by the challenged ordinance. Therefore, they had standing both in their individual capacity and on behalf of others not before the court who might be similarly situated. Barker found that a case or controversy existed and the plaintiffs did not have to be the subjects of an administrative or judicial proceeding when they sued.

Judge Barker felt that it was key to the City of Indianapolis's defense of the ordinance that the court accept the plaintiffs' argument that it was not regulating speech but conduct. The judge found that the means the law used to combat sex discrimination was by regulating speech. The ordinance, she said, was clearly aimed at controlling the content of the speech and ideas that the city and county council found harmful and offensive.

The lower court emphasized that there are relatively few categories in which the government is allowed to regulate forms of individual expression. She gave child pornography, libel, and fighting words as examples. Pornography, she said, did not fall within the meaning of fighting words, which, by their very nature, carry the immediate potential for injury.

Judge Barker rejected the city's claim that this situation was similar to the *Ferber* (child pornography) case. *Ferber*, she said, applies solely to child pornography where the compelling state interest in preventing such pornography outweighs individual First Amendment rights. She rejected the argument that preventing sex discrimination was such a compelling interest. Adult women as a group do not need the same kind of protection that has been afforded children, she said.

> Adult women generally have the capacity to protect themselves from participating in and being personally victimized by pornography which makes the state interest in safeguarding the physical and psychological well-being of women by prohibiting the "sexually explicit subordination of women, graphically depicted, whether in pictures or in words" not so compelling as to sacrifice the guarantees of the First Amendment.[75]

The court rejected the city's claim that this was similar to the *Pacifica* case, which regulated the broadcasting of indecent words. Judge Barker specifically found that the civil rights ordinance did not attempt to regulate the airwaves. (We note that nothing in the ordinance states that the airwaves would not be regulated.) Therefore, she concluded, the law did not deal with a medium that invades the privacy of the home. The logical response is to avoid pornography, she suggested. The ordinance is not written to protect children from accessibility to pornography, she said, whereas the airwaves are accessible to children. (This does not recognize the reality that much pornography falls into the hands of children.)

The judge distinguished *Young* v. *American Mini Theatres, Inc.*, a zoning case, from the civil rights situation by stating that *Young* restricted only the time, place, and manner in which pornography could be distributed and the civil rights ordinance completely prohibited certain material.

If this law were allowed, legislative bodies could enact laws prohibiting other unfair expression, the court said, giving racist material and ethnic or religious slurs as examples. (We note that these other groups are not under a constant attack of hate literature as are women and that certain states do, in fact, prohibit hate literature directed at such groups.)

Importantly, Judge Barker found that the compelling state interest here is not so fundamental as to warrant a broad intrusion into free expression. Despite the claims that women were victimized and harmed by pornography, the district court specifically found that the First Amendment interest takes precedence over these other concerns. Such an exception to that amendment is not constitutionally warranted, she said.

> Free speech, rather than being the enemy, is a long tested and worthy ally. To deny free speech in order to engineer social change in the name of accomplishing a greater good for one sector of our society erodes the freedoms of all and, as such, threatens tyranny and injustice for those subjected to the rule of such laws. The First Amendment protections presuppose the evil of such tyranny and prevent a finding by this court upholding the Ordinance.[76]

The court said that, assuming for the sake of argument it had found that the state had a compelling interest in preventing sex discrimination which outweighed First Amendment rights, the ordinance would fail for other reasons. First, the court was struck by vagueness problems inherent in the definition of pornography and, specifically, of the term *subordination of women*. The judge felt that this decision was left up to censorship committees or individual plaintiffs to define. This, she said, was unfair under due process standards. She also stated

that the categories of pornography set out in the law were plagued by vagueness problems. Some of the terms had several different meanings, and a person of ordinary intelligence would not be on notice as to what was prohibited by the ordinance.

Second, the court refused to make a finding as to overbreadth on the ground that it had already found the ordinance in violation of the First Amendment on other grounds.

Third, the court concluded that the sections of the ordinance relating to trafficking in pornography and assault due to pornography were lawful regarding prior restraint requirements. However, those provisions relating to coercion into pornography and forcing pornography on a person did not meet the constitutional standards for prior restraint. The court said that obscenity and child pornography had been among the narrowly defined exceptions to the rule against prior restraint. *Freedman* v. *Maryland* had established the prior restraint requirements, she said.[77] Here, the *Freedman* standards were not met because the burden was placed on the defendants to initiate court proceedings and the law, in parts, lacked provisions for prompt judicial review. Judge Barker said that the entire ordinance failed as an unconstitutional prior restraint on free expression because the *Freedman* due process standard was not met in total.

The case was appealed to the U.S. Court of Appeals for the Seventh Circuit, which ruled on the case on August 27, 1985. This court emphasized that the definition of pornography in the ordinance was considerably different from obscenity. For example, there did not have to be an appeal to the prurient interest, the value of the work did not matter, and the work did not have to be judged as a whole. The court stated, "It is unclear how Indianapolis would treat works from James Joyce's *Ulysses* to Homer's *Iliad;* both depict women as submissive objects for conquest and domination."[78]

Importantly, the circuit court found that the ordinance discriminated based on the content of the speech and that the state may not ordain preferred viewpoints in this way. The Constitution, it said, forbids "a state to declare one perspective right and silence opponents."[79] The court also found that the interests of the plaintiffs and many of their members were directly affected by the ordinance, which gave them standing to attack it (*Buckley* v. *Valeo*).[80]

The court argued that pernicious beliefs such as those of the Nazis that led to the deaths of millions and those of the Ku Klux Klan that repressed millions may prevail and have a right to be heard. The court said that one of the things that separates American society from totalitarian governments is the "absolute right to propagate opinions that the government finds wrong or even hateful."[81] Thus, ideas of the Ku Klux Klan and the Nazi party can be propagated. People can seek to repeal laws that guarantee equal opportunity and employment or to revoke the constitutional amendments granting the vote to women and to blacks because the First Amendment means that the government has " 'no power to restrict expression because of its message (or) its ideas' " (Police Department v. Mosely).[82]

Under the ordinance, graphic, sexually explicit speech may or may not be pornography, depending on the perspective of the author, the court concluded.

> Speech that "subordinates" women and also, for example, presents women as enjoying pain, humiliation, or rape, or even simply presents women in "positions of servility or submission or display" is forbidden, no matter how great the literary or political value of the work taken as a whole. Speech that portrays women in positions of equality is lawful no matter how graphic the sexual content. This is thought control. It establishes an "approved" view of women, of how they may react to sexual encounters, of how the sexes may relate to each other. Those who espouse the approved view may use sexual images; those who do not, may not.[83]

The court said that Indianapolis justified the ordinance on the ground that pornography affects thoughts. In the view of the city, pornography is not an idea; it is the injury. The court admitted that there is much to this perspective—on the ground that beliefs are also facts and that people often act in accordance with the patterns and images they find around them. Importantly, and very cleverly, the court accepted the premises of the legislation—namely, that depictions of subordination tend to perpetrate subordination and that the subordinate status of women in turn leads to discrimination and lower pay at work, injury and insults at home, and rape and battery on the streets.

However, in a footnote, the court made it clear that they were not accepting the belief that pornography leads to "unhappy consequences" but rather saying that evidence to that effect is consistent with much human experience and that as judges they have to accept the legislative resolution of such disputed empirical questions. The court turned the argument around and said that this alleged effect simply demonstrates the power of pornography as speech. The court compared the effect to Hitler's speeches affecting how some Germans saw Jewish people. It emphasized that anti-Semitism, violence on television, and racial bigotry influence our culture, yet all of these are forms of protected speech, no matter how insidious. "Any other answer leaves the government in control of all of the institutions of culture, the great censor and director of which thoughts are good for us," the court concluded.[84]

Thus, while admitting that sexual responses are often unthinking and that associating sexual arousal with the subordination of women may have a substantial effect, the fact that speech plays a major role in the process of conditioning could end the freedom of speech if it were enough to permit regulation. The court noted that the image of pain is not necessarily pain and gave an example: a film in which a woman who is naked and presented as a sexually explicit display is murdered by an intruder with a drill running through her body. The court said that no one believes that the actress in the film died or suffered pain. (We note that, unfortunately, the reality of pornography suggests that, whether or not people believe the people presented were actually tortured or murdered, some people imitate such images.)

The court said the Constitution does not make dominance of truth a condition of freedom of speech. It noted that some cases have found that speech that is far removed from politics and other subjects of special concern to the Constitution's framers can be subject to special regulations. However, the court stated, these cases do not sustain statutes that select among viewpoints. Nonetheless, pornography is not low value speech within the meaning of these cases: "Indianapolis seeks to prohibit certain speech because it believes the speech influences social relations and politics on a grand scale, that it controls attitudes at home and in the legislature. This precludes a characterization of the speech as low value."[85]

The court suggested that group libel law may not be applicable to the civil rights ordinance case because it is not clear that depicting women as subordinate in sexually explicit ways would fit within the definition of group libel. Some material makes political statements and is not used to defame. A work must be a slur or insult for its own sake to be covered by group libel law they state.

The Seventh Circuit Court held that the definition of pornography in the Indianapolis ordinance was unconstitutional and that no construction or excision of particular terms could save it. The court expressed no view on the district court conclusion that the ordinance was vague and that it established a prior restraint.

Surprisingly, the circuit court suggested that, for example, the ordinance offense that made it unlawful to coerce someone to engage in pornography had elements that might be constitutional. Thus, a legislature could replace the term *pornography* with "any film containing explicit sex" and possibly create an actionable remedy on the ground that the state would have a strong interest in forbidding that conduct.

The section that provided remedies for injuries and assaults due to pornography also could have been salvaged, for the First Amendment does not prohibit redress of all injuries caused by speech. No damages could be awarded unless the harm flowed directly from the speech and there was an element of intent on the part of the speaker, the court said. The court admitted that the constitutional requirements for a valid recovery for assault might be too rigorous for a plaintiff to meet. It was not impossible that a state court could construe the limitation that the attack be directly caused by specific pornography in a constitutional way. But because the assault statute was tied to the definition of pornography, they could not find a way to repair the defects "without seizing power that belongs elsewhere."[86] (We note that the remedy suggested by the court may be to extend the scope of the ordinance to all speech.)

In February 1986, the U.S. Supreme Court affirmed the circuit court's decision without giving its reasoning.

THE LEGAL CASE FOR THE CIVIL RIGHTS ORDINANCE

In the district court, the City of Indianapolis filed a memorandum in opposition to the plaintiffs' motion for summary judgment. The city argued that the First Amendment could not be invoked to defend the dissemination of materials that are not the expression of ideas, that constitute harm, or that are an integral part of illegal activity. The city presented facts showing that pornography as defined in the amendment is harmful to women (similar to the facts outlined in chapters 4 and 5). The city stated that research substantiates what many women have known all along—namely, "that exposure to the types of pornography defined in the amendment effects a general pattern of discriminatory attitudes and behavior, both violent and non-violent that has the capacity to stimulate various negative reactions against women."[87]

The City of Indianapolis pointed out that these consequences are not abstract theories but real-life harms that women confront on a daily basis. The city noted that the use of pornography in the sexually violent abuse of women and children was documented to the city council before it passed the ordinance. Furthermore, the city stated, documentation of harm has never been required by courts for laws (such as those regulating obscenity) that deal with sexually explicit material (*Paris Adult Theatre I v. Slaton*).[88]

The city argued that pornography as defined by the amendment is a practice of sex discrimination and that sex equality is a legitimate governmental objective. The city called it a "practice of discrimination on the basis of sex" because it plays a central role in maintaining and creating sex as a basis for discrimination. It is sex discrimination because its victims, which can include men, are selected for victimization on the basis of their gender. Indianapolis argued that pornography, because it eroticizes the dominance of men and the submission of women and portrays women as objects to be sexually manipulated or exploited in a degrading fashion perpetuates the inferior status of women in society. Therefore, it "makes 'subordinate but equal' equality for women." As a result, women have difficulty getting hired for responsible positions in the work force and being taken seriously when they make sexual assault claims. The city said that pornography is central to maintaining the subordinate status of women.[89]

Pornography, it stated, is "not the free exchange of ideas." It does not play a role in human discourse because it does not communicate ideas. The law does not define pornography in terms of its idea content or its offensiveness but rather attacks what it actively does—subordinate women. It is not the *idea* of subordinating women that is prohibited but the actual subordination of women, the city said. "Pornography is no more the communication of ideas than segregation is," it concluded.[90]

The City of Indianapolis's memo quoted *Chaplinsky* v. *New Hampshire:* " 'Such utterances are no essential part of any exposition of ideas and are of such slight social value as a step to truth that any benefit that may be derived from them is clearly outweighed by the social interest in order and morality.' "[91] This same idea was quoted in *Ferber*, *Pacifica*, and *Roth*. According to the city, it applies to the antipornography ordinance as well. The city listed numerous examples of pornography to prove that "they contribute nothing to the free exchange of ideas." In a sense, the city said, pornography is no more dialogue than the racial epithet in *Beauharnais* v. *Illinois* or the fighting words in *Chaplinsky*. The First Amendment does not protect speech whose mere utterance inflicts injury (*Chaplinsky*). Pornography, Indianapolis stated, fits this category because "it inflicts injury on women which cannot be undone by a further exchange of ideas."[92]

Indianapolis compared the ordinance situation to that of the children in *Ferber* because of the coercive environment in which most pornography models work. This goes against any notion that they choose or consent to perform in the pornography, the city argued. The lack of choice is further shown by the pain and terror in the faces of the bound and gagged women, it noted. Other parts of this coercive environment include the use of alcohol, weapons, and drugs. The materials, like child pornography, become a permanent record of the forced participation, Indianapolis said. As a result of their continuing circulation, they cause continuing psychological harm to the participants.

In addition, other women suffer by, through, and in pornography, the city said. Basically, women get to be seen and treated the way pornography treats them: "objects and things to be bound, battered, tortured, humiliated and abused for the sexual arousal of men." These harms to women, the city noted, cannot be cured by further speech. Pornography "is the silence of women."[93]

Unlike the plaintiffs' claims, the obscenity standard is not the only constitutional way of separating protected from unprotected sexually explicit expression, the city said. It cited examples of the *Ferber* case involving child pornography, the *Pacifica* case involving indecent language, and *Young* v. *American Mini-Theatres* involving zoning. The city said that the *Ferber* reasoning applied to this case and quoted *Ferber* as follows:

> "Thus the question under the *Miller* test of whether a work, taken as a whole, appeals to the prurient interest of the average person bears no connection to the issue of whether a child has been physically or psychologically harmed in the production of the work. Similarly, a sexually explicit depiction need not be patently offensive in order to have required the sexual exploitation of a child for its production. In addition, a work which, taken on the whole, contains serious literary, artistic, political or scientific value may nevertheless embody the hardest core of child pornography. It is irrelevant to the child who has been abused whether or not the material has a literary, artistic, political or scientific value."[94]

Under the city's position, the same reasoning would apply to the use of women in pornography.

The city argued that the First Amendment does not protect speech that is an integral part of illegal activities. In this case, that would include sex discrimination and filming of actual sex acts that involve legally prohibited conduct such as battery, assault, rape, child abuse, prostitution, kidnapping, and murder. The law must reach the profit motive in pornography cases, Indianapolis said, because it is virtually impossible to enforce laws against the crimes being filmed given the way pornography is produced (in a clandestine industry) and the fact that the victimized women are typically relatively powerless.[95]

The city stated that the ordinance was not unconstitutionally vague under the vagueness standards developed by the Supreme Court. For example, *Conally* v. *General Construction Company* said that a law is impermissibly vague if " 'men of common intelligence must necessarily guess at its meaning and differ as to its application.' " But impossible standards were not required by the ordinance, the city pointed out (*U.S.* v. *Petrillo*). Under *Boyce Motor Lines* v. *United States,* " 'no more than a reasonable degree of certainty can be demanded.' " Quoting *Sproules* v. *Binford* the city noted that " 'the use of ordinary terms to express ideas which find adequate interpretation in common usage and understanding' " is allowed.[96]

The Supreme Court has upheld attacks on vagueness if the words used have a special or technical meaning that are well enough known for those reached by the law to correctly apply them, if they have a settled common meaning, or if there is a standard usage. The terms in the ordinance, according to the city, fit those criteria or are further defined within the amendment. *Pornography,* for example, is specifically defined in the amendment. This fact avoids vagueness and allows for objectivity. *The obscenity standard,* however, depends for its application on subjective, morally based elements.

In the ordinance, *sexually explicit* has a commonly understood meaning, the city argued. In *Webster's New Third International Dictionary of the English Language, sexually* is defined as " 'with regard to or by means of sex.' " *Explicit* is defined as that which is " 'characterized by full, clear expression, being without vagueness or ambiguity, leaves nothing implied.' " The city noted that the courts themselves have frequently used terms such as *sexually explicit* without further definition (*Island Trees Union Pre-School* v. *Pico*). Most adults know whether material is sexually explicit or not, the city said.

The same dictionary defines *subordination* as an " 'act of subordination (as by making secondary or subject)' " or " 'the quality of or state of being subordinate to another' " as in " 'inferiority or rank or dignity' " or as in " 'obedient submission' " or " 'an arrangement produced by an act of subordination' " as in " 'a position of inferior status.' " This is a commonly understood term, Indianapolis said, because most of society is divided into dominant–subordinate relationships such as parent–child and teacher–student.[97]

Importantly, the city said, the ordinance does not proscribe the idea or advocacy of the idea that women are sex objects who should be tied up; rather it outlaws the practice of placing women in an inferior status by subordinating them through words or pictures. For example, presenting them as sex objects tied up is what is proscribed, they explained. *Sex object* is another commonly understood term meaning reducing "a person to a thing used for sex." Likewise, the city said, *inferiority, conquest,* and *humiliation* are experiences common to people. The city listed other words alleged to be vague by the plaintiffs and detailed their commonly understood meanings.[98]

Indianapolis argued that the plaintiffs lacked standing under Article III of the U.S. Constitution and federal law. Based on previous cases, no definite or concrete conflict exists between the parties, the city said.[99]

The city gave examples of situations covered by the part of the law that allows men, children, or transsexuals to sue when they are used in the place of women. For example, cases in which pornographers use men, children, or transsexuals to portray women or feminize and subordinate them would be covered.

One of the reasons for not adopting the *Miller* standard of "taken as a whole" and instead stating that isolated words or passages will not be actionable is to show that pornographers have legitimized abuse of women by surrounding pornography with unquestionably legitimate speech, the city said. This "isolated words" part applies only to the trafficking cause of action under the ordinance. If pornography is forced on a woman or she is coerced into it or assaulted because of it, the city said, she does not suffer any less harm because part of a publication was used.[100]

The law could not be attacked for facial invalidation for vagueness, Indianapolis argued, because it would be subject to narrowing construction by state courts. Its deterrent effect on legitimate expression was not real and substantial, the city said, citing *Erzonznik* v. *City of Jacksonville* and *Young* v. *American Mini-Theatres, Inc.* In other words, statutes are to be construed in ways to avoid doubtful constitutional questions. This law reached only a hard core of conduct that is not subject to First Amendment protection, the city said.[101]

In its brief, Indianapolis gave examples of pornography that would violate the ordinance:

> The magazine entitled "Bondage Love" has a story subtitled "A Mild Case of Rape" with pictures and accompanying words which tell the story of a man raping a women because she is a "cock teaser." . . . She resists him when he violently abducts her, takes her home, ties her to a suspended bar and has intercourse with her. Eventually she submits totally to him and enjoys the rape. Sexual intercourse is graphically displayed throughout. This magazine is clearly an example of the sexually explicit subordination of women in which a woman is also presented as a sexual object who experiences pleasure in being raped.
>
> The magazine "Burning Asses" shows a series of photographs in which women are being hit on their buttocks by hands, hair brushes, whips, and paddles. The story lines indicate that the women are being spanked for not obeying their husbands or boyfriends. Their sexual body parts are exposed to view; they are often on their hands and knees or bending over the knee of another. Their faces show pain, but the story line indicates that they learn to enjoy these acts. . . . This magazine is an example of the sexually explicit subordination of women in which women are also shown as sexual objects who enjoy pain and humiliation.
>
> In the book "Betty's Animal Lover," a woman is penetrated numerous times by a dog. . . . In one instance the woman's brother prostitutes her by arranging for her and her dog to "perform" at a stag party for money. This is an example of the sexually explicit subordination of women in which the woman is presented being penetrated by an animal.
>
> In the magazine "Bondage Showcase" women are nude and painfully tied up. . . . The story line in one pictorial explains that the husband ties up and tapes shut his wife's mouth because she is a "frustrated housewife" and has "too much free time." This magazine shows women as tied up sexual objects.
>
> In the magazine "The Bitch Goddesses" women are shown in torture chambers with their nude body parts being tortured by their "master" for "even the slightest offense." . . . This magazine shows a woman in a scenario of torture.
>
> In the film 'Deep Throat' a woman is being shown as being ever eager for oral penetration by a series of men's penises, often on her hands and knees. There are repeated scenes in which her genitalia are graphically displayed and she is shown enjoying men ejaculating on her face. This film subordinates women and shows a woman as a sexual object for use by men and a sexual object in a position of servility.[102]

The vices of vagueness are not present in the law or its application, Indianapolis said. Those vices are failing to give people fair notice of what is prohibited so they can act accordingly, permitting arbitrary or discriminatory enforcement, and, when First Amendment freedoms are involved, having a chilling effect on the exercise of those freedoms. Vagueness, the city argued, is less of a concern in civil laws than in criminal laws because the penalties are less severe. Here, remedies would not issue until a court had independently determined that the material in question is pornography. It is worth noting that the law was not aimed at the individual person exercising constitutional rights but at a $8 billion per year pornography industry, the city said. The *Young* court said: " '[T]here is . . . a less vital interest in the uninhibited exhibition of material that is on the borderline between pornography and artistic expression than in the free dissemination of ideas of social and political significance.' "[103] This law, the city noted, did not threaten legitimate expressions of political or social ideas.

Finally, Indianapolis argued that the ordinance was not fatally overbroad. Laws are not voided on their face unless they reach a substantial amount of constitutionally protected conduct and are not readily subject to a saving construction. Here, the law could be construed constitutionally by state courts, the city said.

The examples cited by the plaintiffs do not come within the definition of pornography, Indianapolis said, for they are not, for the most part, sexually explicit, they do not subordinate women, or they do not contain one of the required scenarios in the definition of pornography.

Finally, the city refuted the claim that the amendment was an impermissible prior restraint. Prior restraints, the city said, occur prior to the communication and dissemination or take "place prior to 'an adequate determination that [the expression] is not protected by the First Amendment' " (*Pittsburgh Press Co.* v. *Pittsburgh Commission on Human Relations*). These types of restraints are not involved here, the city argued. Injunctive relief cannot be obtained prior to an independent de novo review by a court of law under the ordinance, the city pointed out.[104]

The City of Indianapolis also wrote a brief in the Seventh Circuit, again arguing that the plaintiffs lacked standing. It pointed out that the only injury alleged is the chilling effect the ordinance may have on their business. A chilling effect alone is inadequate for standing, Indianapolis said, because its existence has never been considered a sufficient basis by itself to prohibit state action (*Younger* v. *Harris*).[105]

Pornography, according to the city, is not protected expression because it is not the free exchange of ideas but is harm that cannot be undone by further speech. It is an integral part of illegal activity, some of which is criminal. Pornography, in fact, cuts off

debate by silencing women's speech. Here the record showed considerable testimony by women who said that pornography was used to break their self-esteem, to "train them to sexual submission, to season them to forced sex, to intimidate them out of job opportunities, to blackmail them into prostitution and keep them there, to terrorize and humiliate them into sexual compliance and to silence their dissent," Indianapolis said. As long as pornography exists, there will not be more speech by women because pornography cuts their value and ends their credibility. It is, in fact an illusion that a debate is possible because the $8 billion per year pornography industry is pitted against women who, in general, are economically poor and have no meaningful opportunity to participate in or contribute to the "free marketplace of ideas." This law actually furthered equal access to the means of speech, the city stated.[106]

The city quoted L. Tribe, *American Constitutional Law*, as saying " 'A government committed to the widest possible dissemination of information may find it essential to impose burdens on some in order that others might hear or be heard.' "[107]

At some point, the rights of the victims should outweigh and limit the pornographers' rights to enforce the subordination of women, the city argued. Pornography actually subordinates women, the city said, emphasizing that it is not the *idea* of subordination but the fact that it conditions the male sexual response to the subordination of women that is at issue.

Noting that the Supreme Court has said that prior restraints may be employed only in exceptional cases and has set forth procedural standards for use of such restraints, the city argued that the case of a woman being forced into a pornographic performance and the harm resulting from it constitute an exceptional case. Thus, the remedy of ending the dissemination of such material pending judicial review does not impose unreasonable strictures on individual liberties, the city said.

Finally, Indianapolis said that the ordinance was severable. Parts of it could be upheld even if the whole ordinance was not.

The city filed a reply brief in the Seventh Circuit, again emphasizing that the plaintiffs had not established a case or controversy. Indianapolis pointed out that the Supreme Court denied obscenity constitutional protection largely because it appeals to a prurient rather than an intellectual interest in sex (*Miller*).[108] Thus, its expressive value, which is minimal, can be outweighed by competing interests such as public safety or the quality of life (*Paris Adult Theatre* v. *Slaton*).[109] The city said, "In a similar vein, pornography triggers mere physical impulses instead of reasoned deliberation by conditioning male sexual response to the subordination of women. In no way does pornography inform its audience or promote consideration of new ideas and beliefs."[110] (We note that this statement contradicts the argument that pornography encourages certain attitudes toward women.) Indianapolis quoted from an article titled "Anti-pornography Laws and First Amendment Values":

> "To the extent that any form of expression influences its audience through means that bypass the process of conscious deliberation and choice, presupposed by the notion of marketplace of ideas, such expression cannot be said to further two important goals of the First Amendment: promoting self-government and fostering the search for truth."[111]

The city dealt with the plaintiffs' argument that the case of *Collin* v. *Smith* disposed of many of the issues in this case. It distinguished *Collin* by stating that there is a difference in the actual harm at issue. A small, sporadic circulation of Nazi literature was at issue in *Collin*, while pornography is an 8 billion dollar a year industry. The *Collin* case sought to fit the Nazi literature within the incitement exception to the First Amendment, the city noted. The anti-pornography ordinance did not do so. The ordinance was not predicated on an incitement rationale; rather it is based on "demonstrable concrete harm that women suffer by, through and in pornography." The city noted that the harm is not just psychological, as it was in *Collin*, but also physical, economic and a matter of dignity. Pornography involves sexually explicit speech, which, the city said, has always been given "less constitutional protection than the political speech in *Collin*."[112]

The city accused the opposition of picking the ordinance into parts instead of applying it as a whole. The ACLU amici brief had argued that the *Taming of the Shrew* uses the subordination of women and therefore would be banned by the ordinance. Indianapolis stated that the issue of whether it is also sexually explicit, whether it includes one of the sexually violent scenarios of the law, and whether it would form the basis of an assault would have to be considered as well.

Indianapolis petitioned for a rehearing in the Seventh Circuit. The panel, it argued, misapprehended clear First Amendment doctrine. The court failed to review the legal adequacy of the lower court ruling that the city had not established a compelling interest in reducing sex discrimination and did not look at the actual legislative record. A line of precedents under which First Amendment interests were outweighed by the governmental interest in eliminating sex inequality were not acknowledged by the court, which, the city said, should have balanced these interests (*Pittsburgh Press Co.* v. *Human Relations Comm'n*; *Roberts* v. *U.S. Jaycees*). While the court had found harm, it had precluded relief tailored to fit the harm, the city noted.[113]

The Seventh Circuit called the sex equality element of the ordinance "impermissible discrimination on the basis of viewpoint." This application is "radically at odds" with Seventh Circuit and Supreme Court precedents, according to Indianapolis. The viewpoint discrimination doctrine "is designed to prohibit government from discriminating between classes of ideas or classes of speakers on the basis of the content of their ideas."[114] If governmental regulations are covered by the First Amendment, the equal protection clause requires that they not discriminate on the basis of content but be narrowly tailored to meet legitimate objectives. When a compelling state interest exists, content-based distinctions *are* permitted, the city argued (*Police Department of Chicago* v. *Mosley*; *Carey* v. *Brown*; *Perry Education Association* v. *Perry Local Educators' Association*; *Wisconsin Action Coalition* v. *City of Kenosha*).[115]

In the civil rights ordinance case, the Seventh Circuit adopted a stance of absolute content neutrality that was never adopted by the Supreme Court, Indianapolis said (*Cornelius* v. *N.A.A.C.P. Legal Defense and Education Fund*). "Many prohibited materials express viewpoints," the city said. Examples cited included group libel, false advertising, and child pornography, which expresses the view that sex between children and adults is good. Importantly, the civil rights ordinance did not "restrict on the basis of content in the doctrinal sense," Indianapolis said. It explained that the second half of the definition alone would be a content regulation, but taken with the first part, it is not. For example, while *sexually explicit* might be a content term, *subordination* must be shown. Coercion, force, and trafficking are not ideas.

Discrimination is a practice, not merely a view, the city said. Citing *Planned Parenthood* v. *Kempiners*, the city argued that it is not viewpoint discrimination to " 'highlight government preference for one view while failing to recognize another' if a legitimate governmental interest is served." Sex equality, the city noted, is not "a mere viewpoint; it is a public policy."[116]

The city quoted *Roberts* v. *U.S. Jaycees*:

> [A]cts of invidious discrimination in the distribution of publicly available goods, services, and

other advantages cause unique evils that government has compelling interest to prevent—wholly apart from the point of view such conduct may transmit. Accordingly, like violence or other types of potentially expressive activities that produce special harms distinct from their communicative impact, such practices are entitled to no constitutional protection.[117]

The court ignored First Amendment methodology where a law is based on a showing of harm, the city said. It is not correct to say that laws that impinge on speech interests must fit within established exceptions, such as obscenity, or be content neutral. For example, the *Young* (zoning) and *Pacifica* (indecent words) cases are not content neutral, yet they are not restricted to the obscenity exception, Indianapolis pointed out. In deciding whether to create a new exception to the First Amendment, the court is to balance the interests at stake to determine whether " 'the evil to be restricted . . . overwhelmingly outweighs the expressive interests, if any, at stake' " (*New York* v. *Ferber*). According to the city, the Seventh Circuit wrongly held that no amount of harm through gender can outweigh the First Amendment interests in pornography. The court failed to apply the balancing test. While the court assumed that pornography is indistinguishable from all other "speech," the city argued differently.

The city said that the court allowed the case to proceed in the abstract, in violation of Article III of the U.S. Constitution. None of the plaintiffs had a personal stake in the outcome, the city said.[118]

The City of Indianapolis filed a jurisdictional statement in the Supreme Court aimed at convincing the court that the questions presented by the civil rights ordinance were substantial. Since *Roth* v. *United States* case, it said, the court has recognized that "pornographic materials exist which serve none of the purposes for which speech is constitutionally protected."[119] *Roth*, citing *Chaplinsky* v. *New Hampshire*, said, " 'The lewd and the obscene . . . are no essential part of any exposition of ideas.' "[120]

Differentiating civil rights law from obscenity law, the city noted that the civil approach allows "civil suits by victims of pornography's making and use rather than applying criminal bans on materials found to violate moral standards."[121]

The city argued that it is at the core of the Supreme Court's oversight function to pass on determinations of constitutionality of local legislation and that the erroneous opinions by the lower courts were widely perceived as authoritative in this case. Thus, if the Supreme Court failed to overturn those decisions, other jurisdictions not in the Seventh Circuit would be deterred from passing the civil rights ordinance. The Supreme Court, not a circuit court, should resolve this issue of national importance, the city argued.

The city alleged that the court of appeals had erred when it determined that the ordinance had to fall within a recognized exception to the First Amendment or be content neutral in order to be constitutional. The interests "to be furthered by this law—sex equality, including equal access to speech— are not only legitimate and substantial, they are compelling," Indianapolis stated.[122]

The court of appeals held that the ordinance impermissibly discriminated on the basis of viewpoint. However, the city noted, the ordinance did not restrict pornography on the basis of any point of view "articulated or affirmed by pornographers or the consumers" but instead restricted it on the basis of the harms of civil inequality engendered and exploited through its marketing, use, and making. Achieving sex equality, Indianapolis said, is not a viewpoint; rather it is a public policy. Force, assault, trafficking, and coercion are not viewpoints. Nor, in suing for those acts, is thought control being exercised, the city noted.

The city accused the Seventh Circuit of ignoring the line of cases holding that sex discrimination raises compelling state interests that can outweigh First Amendment rights (*Roberts*). The civil rights case showed much greater and pervasive harm than some of the cases that follow this line of legal reasoning. The city alleged that if the correct law had been followed, applying the balancing test, the court would have found a government purpose in eradicating sex discrimination, an interest that overwhelmingly " 'outweighs the expressive interest, if any, at stake' " (*Ferber*).[123]

The groups that sued in opposition to the ordinance are legitimate publishers, not pornographers, the city said. They were attempting to procure an advisory opinion in an abstract context that excluded real pornography, as well as victims and pornographers. Their complaint amounted only to an allegation of a chilling effect, which, the city said, "has never provided requisite injury in fact for constitutional adjudication" (*Younger* v. *Harris; Laird* v. *Tatum*). There was, the city argued, no Article III case or controversy between the parties. As a result, the opinion produced consisted of distorted statutory language, conjecture, abstract theorizing, and academic commentary.[124]

Pornography as defined in the ordinance is not protected speech, Indianapolis said. It noted that all the courts that had reviewed the law had affirmed the legislative findings and accepted the premises of the legislation. In other words, they did not disagree with the judgment that these harms are based on sex or question the concept that these acts are practices of sex discrimination. Thus, the issue became whether the harm of sex discrimination mattered under the Constitution. The city said:

> The legislative record shows that the pornography industry produces verbal and visual sexual entertainment made from coercion, rape, extortion, exploitation, intimidation, fraud and unequal opportunities. This material then engenders coercion, rape, extortion, exploitation, intimidation, fraud and unequal opportunities through its consumption. Pornography, as defined, and when coerced, forced on individuals, the cause of assault or actively trafficked, is inseparable from aggression and terror, crimes, torts and unspeakable indignities. Although men are also victimized and also covered, women and children are its primary targets and victims. Having accepted this reality, each court ruled that stopping this injustice is not as important to the Constitution as inflicting it. Legally, both courts assumed that the ordinance had to fit under an existing exception or counterbalance to the First Amendment, primarily obscenity.[125]

The overall effect, the city said, was "to legitimize sex inequality."[126]

According to the city, the court of appeals ignored accepted First Amendment methods in cases in which the exception was based on harm. It pointed out that such interests are not always absolute or paramount. When conflicting interests arise and speech is involved, the court should employ a balancing test. New exceptions that do not attempt to fit into preexisting ones could be fashioned. An example of this was the *Ferber* (child pornography) case. The city argued that because the court treated the First Amendment as if it were an absolute and did not balance the harms, it avoided the fact that most of the material covered by this ordinance had about as little First Amendment value as it was possible to have while still being words and pictures.

The city pointed out that the court in *Young* v. *American Mini-Theatres*, a zoning case, found that sexually explicit materials are not entitled to full First Amendment protection. And, it noted, obscenity has been found to be a crime without any showing of harm. Therefore, trafficking in pornography should be civilly actionable with a showing of harm.

The city asked, What is more important—the harm done to victims such as Linda Marchiano or the speech made from it? And what is more important—a film showing violent sexual acts or the interests of a young woman who gets abducted, cut, pierced, and so on, as a result of someone having read pornographic works? The city asked that the interests of someone trapped in prostitution by blackmail using pornography made of them be balanced against the speech interest in the existence of the marketplace that enforces enslavement. The city also asked that the pornographers' rights be balanced against the efforts to mitigate the sounds of women and their exclusion from access to speech, which reinforces their exclusion from full citizenship. The ordinance, the city stated, is "an effort to expand access to First Amendment rights by affecting the social determinants which currently preclude women from having effective access to speech." The interest in ending sex discrimination should have outweighed the expressive value (if any) of the pornography, the city said.[127]

Thus, Indianapolis said, if obscenity and mere indecent language can be regulated, a compelling state interest such as sex equality should stand on a comparable plane. Under *Kerry* v. *Brown*, even protected speech can be regulated when a compelling state interest exists.[128] Instead of balancing the interests, the court found that the ordinance was not content neutral and invalidated in per se. However, the city said, content neutrality is not legally required; if it was, cases such as *Miller, Young, Pacifica,* and *Ferber* would not have become law. In fact, the determination of whether something is or is not protected by the First Amendment often depends on the content of the speech.

The ordinance, the city said, was not a pure content restriction, although it did contain content terms in parts of the definition. Pornography is no more mental than obscenity, and obscenity is considered "not expression" at all, the city argued, citing *Roth*. Just as a book about slavery is not itself slavery, expressing the idea of subordination is not to subordinate, the city said. However, the city specifically amended the original definition, changing it from "sexually explicit subordination of women graphically depicted" to "graphic, sexually explicit subordination" in order to make that distinction. The city claimed that the ordinance did not make the mere depiction or description of a woman being subordinated actionable. The issue is whether materials that do subordinate women through their making or use are protected by the Constitution. (In our view, the ordinance attacked the subordination of women that results from pornography by regulating depictions or descriptions of women being sexually subordinated.)

The city said that the practice of segregating a community does not become protected speech because it expresses the idea that the races want separation any more than punching a person is protected speech because it delivers a point. Under the ordinance, nonspeech elements must be present in order for an action to be brought. People are prosecuted not for what they say or believe but for what they do, Indianapolis asserted, using the example of selling obscene books.

> Speakers can advocate sex inequality as the paradigm of sexual pleasure, promote subordination, urge rape, or incite sadism subject to pre-existing case law. What they may not do is practice coercion, force, assault or trafficking in localities that do not want women subjected by this means in their community.[129]

The core issue is whether a medium through which harm is done, when it is words or pictures, remains protected by virtue of that fact because "it delivers much of its harm at the same time it delivers its message."[130]

A similar case, in which a regulation against posting signs was upheld, is *Los Angeles* v. *Taxpayers for Vincent.* The court found that the adverse impact of the speech (visual blight) was not merely a possible by-product of the activity but was " 'created by the medium of expression itself.' " Pornography, the city argued, also is "inextricably interwoven" with crimes such as sexual abuse of children, pimping, battery, and rape. In other words, it is hard to separate the expression from the illegal action, the city said. The industry cannot exist without these acts.[131]

According to the city, the ordinance did not discriminate on the basis of viewpoint. The Seventh Circuit faulted the definition of *pornography* for restricting those sexually explicit materials that present a view of women and sex that favors inequality while permitting sex inequality to be favored through non–sexually explicit means and allowing sexually explicit materials that favor sex equality. This, the court said, is viewpoint discrimination. According to Indianapolis, this concept derives from the intersection of the equal protection clause and the First Amendment. Such cases typically look at statutes restricting which speakers can have access to a forum to see if the restriction is based on their political position or point of view.

This ordinance, the city stated, restricted nothing based on who the speaker is and instead defined pornography on the basis of what it does—namely, empowering those who are injured by giving them a means to sue. Furthermore, only if pornography is protected speech would the city have to justify its restriction against a charge of discrimination on the basis of viewpoint. Material that is unprotected because of the harm it causes does not become protected because it serves as a vehicle for a viewpoint. For example, the child pornography law is not invalidated because it takes the view that sex between adults and children is bad. Another example cited by the city was the *Pittsburgh Press* case in which the court did not find that the law was invalid because sex segregated ads express a view that the workplace should be segregated by sex.

Indianapolis said that the ordinance was not viewpoint discrimination because assault, trafficking, coercion, and force are a means of promoting a viewpoint, not viewpoints themselves. The city noted that there were no facts showing that it was impermissibly motivated by a desire to express a particular point of view. The ordinance was based on a harm theory, not a viewpoint theory; it only discriminated between materials that do damage and those that do not or do less. The ordinance did not make mere view actionable, the city insisted. The city compared this case to the *Dred Scott* v. *Sanford* decision, which considered it more important to the U.S. Constitution to require blacks to be slaves than it was to permit a legislature to recognize their full citizenship, including the right to sue. Similarly, Indianapolis said, this court had determined that women can be battered, tortured, raped, treated as merchandise, and trafficked whenever a profit can be made and that this is more important to the Constitution than women. The city wanted to recognize women as full citizens and to hold those who force them into inferiority accountable.

Finally, the city pointed out that no Article III case or controversy existed between the parties. The city called this suit a preenforcement challenge to a law and argued that Article III does not permit advisory opinions to be issued. Actual injury, the city said, should be shown. The plaintiffs should have alleged a personal stake in the outcome—that they suffered a threatened or actual injury. *Babbitt* v. *United Farmworkers National Union* listed the guidelines for allegations in a preenforcement challenge:

> [A] plaintiff who challenges a statute must demonstrate a realistic danger of sustaining a direct injury as a result of the statute's operation or enforcement. And plaintiff must allege an intention to engage in a course of conduct arguably affected with a constitutional interest but proscribed by a statute and there exists a credible threat of prosecution thereunder.[132]

Although, when First Amendment rights are involved, the doctrine of procedural overbreadth was fashioned to allow plaintiffs to raise interests of third parties not before the court whose speech will be chilled if the law is applied, this is not an issue in this case because the appellees did not raise the interest of others, only of themselves, the city noted. The Seventh Circuit did find that the special overbreadth standing rules do not apply to appellees. The appellees did not allege they had suffered any actual prosecution or threat of prosecution due to the ordinance. In other words, they had no intent to traffic in pornography; to produce, distribute, or sell it; to assault someone because of pornography; or to force it on persons. Despite the Seventh Circuit finding, the plaintiffs did not even allege that they read, made, or sold the material affected by the ordinance, Indianapolis said. Even the one consumer plaintiff did not allege an interest in reading pornographic material. What was sought was an advisory opinion based on a hypothetical set of facts. An alleged chilling effect on First Amendment rights alone is not sufficient to establish standing, the city argued (*Younger* v. *Harris*).[133] Therefore, the court of appeals should have granted abstention. It should not have adjudicated the merits of the ordinance before the Indiana courts had a chance to give it an authoritative construction.

An amici brief was filed by Women Against Pornography (WAP), the Pornography Resource Center, Men Against Pornography, and other groups against pornography, including battered women and sexual assault centers and professionals who work with sexual assault offenders. A major point of these amici was that they are "aware of the devastating physical, psychological, and societal injury caused by pornography and have engaged in various educational and political activities to eliminate such damage. The amici have found that existing laws fail to address adequately the harms of pornography and that its harms, as sex discrimination, are a compelling state interest."[134] Therefore, the amici supported the ordinance.

A key point of the amici brief was that pornography injures real women. The ordinance, the brief said, was an effective legal response to the "brutalization and forced inferiority amici have seen in their work." The amici said that pornography is a central practice of subordinating women and a major obstacle in achieving the goal of gender equality.[135]

At one point, these groups opposed legal solutions to the pornography problem. However, the drastic change of circumstances, including the staggering rate of multiplied injuries to women, caused them to endorse the civil rights approach, they said. The amici have acted to raise public awareness and to wage a public "intellectual battle" against pornography. These efforts, they said, have been difficult and unsuccessful because of the immense power of the pornography industry and the support it receives from the established media. The activities of the amici included demonstrations, sit-ins, boycotts, protests, and marches.

In the past, the amici were concerned about feminists using the legal system in the fight against pornography because powerful institutional agencies might misdirect efforts (for example, the concerns of obscenity law differ from feminist concerns). While feminists state that obscenity is a moral offensiveness concern, they view pornography as a "political practice involving the maltreatment of the powerless by the powerful." The amici's interest in fighting pornography is to curtail the systematic injury to women. Because their actions have not checked the pornography industry's abuse and violence, they said they now realize that education and political activism will not reduce pornography's harm to women or slow the growth of the industry.[136] They stated that an estimated half of the industry is controlled by organized crime and noted:

> It is not possible to challenge the pornography industry in the marketplace of ideas because much, if not most, of the business is controlled by individuals who operate instead in the arena of extortion, coercion, intimidation, violence and gross exploitation. Organized crime's control over pornography makes the industry especially dangerous to the women who work in it, and all but eliminates the possibility that women who have been coerced or abused in the production of pornography will ever come forward with a complaint under existing law.[137]

Pornography, the amici said, desensitizes its readers. They pointed out that rape and violent depictions have increased in pornography over the years. One of the amici went to two of New York's most popular pornography stores and found that between 25 and 30 percent of the material depicted bondage and domination. Much of that pornography showed models with welts, lash marks, burns, sores, cuts, and large bruises.

The amici detailed numerous cases where pornography was involved in the abuse of women. They said:

> The largest group of victims who have contacted amici consists of married women whose husbands forced pornography upon them and then coerced them into enacting scenes from the material. The next largest category of victims are working

women who were sexually harassed on the job through pornography, and little girls who have had pornography forced upon them during acts of incest and child molestation. Amici have also been sought out by women coerced to perform for pornography and by boys and young men who have been abused by men influenced by pornography. As the pornography has become more demeaning and brutal, so have the injuries reported by the victims.[138]

Importantly, several of the amici work with men who rape and batter women and sexually abuse children. These amici report that pornography instilled in many, "if not most," of their clients the belief that women are worthless and deserve abuse. Pornography, they said, conditioned the men to experience and associate sexual excitement and orgasm with the degradation and abuse of women. It was not uncommon for offenders to increase their use of pornography prior to a sexual assault and to use specific examples of pornography as scripts for attacks, they noted. These amici report that their efforts to help the clients change their abusive attitudes are continually undermined by pornography, which is widely available. A growing number of the offenders are pubescent and preteen boys.

Prosecution under the existing obscenity laws has not slowed the growth of the pornography industry, the amici stated. Zoning laws have been equally useless in restricting pornography, they said. Likewise, opaque cover laws have not diminished the sale of pornography or reduced the injury to children and women. They said that some of the laws have increased pornography sales by leading customers to think that they are participating in something illicit and, therefore, desirable. Even civil lawsuits by women who have been victims of nonconsensual sexual portrayals have not been successful in the past, the amici noted. Pornographers, they said, have successfully focused attention on First Amendment absolutism and diverted attention from their real practices. The abstractness of both obscenity and freedom of speech have fueled those efforts, they said. However, as Chief Justice Burger said in *Miller*,

"To equate the free and robust exchange of ideas and political debate with commercial exploitation of obscene material demeans the grand conception of the First Amendment and its high purpose in the historic struggle for freedom. It is misuse of the great guarantees of free speech and free press."[139]

These amici pointed out how pornographers try to thwart the obscenity law by attaching interviews with acceptable persons and institutions to their pornography in order to give the publications value when taken as a whole. Obscenity prosecutions, they said, will never solve the problems of pornography for the following reasons:

1. Such laws address public offensiveness, not private abuse.
2. The current constitutional law of obscenity protects men's right to possess pornography in the privacy of their homes, ignoring the fact that most sexual abuse of women occurs in the home.
3. The community standards provisions prevent such laws from protecting pornography victims because pornography creates and reflects those community standards that define the boundaries of the defense.
4. Obscenity laws are criminal and do not offer relief to pornography victims in the form of damages or injunctions to remove the injurious pornography from the market.
5. Often such laws are enforced only against local retailers, and the parties most responsible for the injury to victims—producers and assailants—continue to be free to go about their business.

A legal system that allows harm to continue without a remedy lacks justice, the amici said. Unlike current law, the ordinance would help the victims of pornography and should be available. Since the enactment of the ordinance in Indianapolis, victims have been coming forward in the belief that, for the first time, the legal system is recognizing the harm to them and offering them a remedy. According to the amici, the lower court did not perceive the existence and extent of the harm of pornography and in effect valued "pornographers' speech" interest over female victims' lives.

[T]he lower court employed certain cultural assumptions about the sexual abuse of women relative to the sexual abuse of children that do not accord with reality. First, it is evident that the character of sexual abuse—as commonly perceived in contemporary society—depends primarily upon the gender and age of the victims. The sexual assault of children, male and female, is deemed criminal: it represents in the view of society an unforgivable breach of the social order. The sexual abuse of women is viewed differently.

It is not intrinsically a crime, but rather, a regulated condition of normality. Forced intercourse in marriage is formally exempted from rape prohibitions in over 40 states; forced intercourse outside of marriage is informally exempted from rape sanctions unless the display of force has been brutal beyond imagining. Underlying this reality is the cultural belief that women are legitimate targets for sexual assault. . . . The lower court's application of this cultural belief below resulted in the complete denial of evidence of adult women's victimization through pornography, leading to the inaccurate conclusion "that adult women as a group do not, as a matter of public policy or applicable law, stand in need of the same type of protection which has long been afforded children. . . ."

Secondly, the lower court relied upon the unproven assertion that "adult women generally have the capacity to protect themselves from participating in and being personally victimized by pornography." This assertion is patently not true, and is legally incorrect. . . . If women had such capacity amici . . . would not have been contacted, as they have been, by scores of maltreated women. If women had such capacity pornography would not presently exist.[140]

The amici also argued that the court had before it concrete proof of pornography's harm, that it was not limited by the cultural misperceptions of the lower court, and that real injuries to real people should not be disregarded because of such misperceptions.

An amici brief was filed by Linda Marchiano and the Estate of Dorothy Stratten in the Seventh Circuit. Their attorney, Catharine A. MacKinnon (co-author of the ordinance) pointed out that both Marchiano (Linda Lovelace) and Stratten's estate were pornography victims, for both women had been coerced into pornography and wanted the photographs destroyed. If pornography did not exist, Dorothy Stratten "would have had a better life and would probably be alive today," the brief stated.[141] Key to the amici brief was the argument that pornography violates sex equality by harming women differentially and thus raises compelling state interests.

Pornography, the amici stated, is "inconsistent with the reasons speech is protected." They accused the groups that sued to prevent enforcement of the ordinance of trying to make it look as if there are no victims and of trying to litigate an imaginary conflict. The groups that sued (American Booksellers et al.) are not pornographers, pimps, or their customers, they noted. There was no case or controversy between the parties. The plaintiffs had no standing, even under the First Amendment facial overbreadth precedents. The amici said that the plaintiffs had not indicated that the ordinance would be applied to them; therefore, the facial overbreadth doctrine (which allows parties to assert the rights of others in limited situations) was the only possible right the Booksellers had to sue. This, they asserted, made it

extremely odd that the lower court made no finding as to overbreadth of the ordinance. The amici accused the plaintiffs of fronting for the pornographers. They argued that the ordinance could not be overbroad in all its applications because at least parts of it were constitutional as a matter of law under the obscenity and child pornography doctrines.

(In our view this is not an accurate interpretation of the ordinance, for it does not contain the *Miller* standards required by obscenity law and both the obscenity and child pornography laws are criminal in nature, while the ordinance was civil. Of course, much pornography covered by the ordinance would be obscene and/or child pornography.)

Pornography, the amici argued, is not protected speech. First, it is harmful. The women in pornography are harmed (for example, Linda Marchiano, known as Linda Lovelace in her pornographic films, was forced into pornographic performances).

> Many of these acts are illegal, either because they are not consensual, or because they cannot be legally consented to, or because they are sex acts for hire. But because consumers want to see these acts done by and to women, they are done, and nothing is done about it. It is argued and accepted below that the (so-called) speech that results, because it is pictures and words, must be constitutionally protected. But amici are here to say that so long as women's lives can be made pornographers' pictures and words, women's lives will be cheap compared with the value of the pornography.[142]

The civil rights of Linda Marchiano were violated when she was kept as a sexual slave for two and a half years, the amici stated. Dorothy Stratten was tortured and murdered on the basis of her sex and was thus deprived of her civil rights.

The amici argued that not only is pornography harmful to those who perform in it under coercion, but it is also harmful to the women and children it is forced on and to those who are assaulted and forced to do unwanted sex acts because of it.

Research further substantiates the fact of pornography's harm, they said. For example, they quoted Edward Donnerstein as saying that " '[t]he most important result of this research . . . is the finding that these changes in attitudes and arousal are directly related to aggression against women.' " Pornography, the amici said, leads to disbelief of women's claims of sexual abuse and thus silences them. The results in blaming the victim and normalizes sexual abuse.[143]

The amici said that pornography is sex discrimination. As such, it raises compelling state interests.

They also refuted the claim of the lower court that the City of Indianapolis said that pornography is conduct:

> Appellants do not have a conduct theory of speech interests raised here. They do argue that to define pornography as that sexually explicit material which subordinates women through pictures or words is to define it as an active practice, as something that does something. Accordingly, the definition does not cover the graphic "depiction of" anything.[144]

The word "depiction" was eliminated from the ordinance. Courts have recognized, the amici stated, that "some words, like libel or blackmail or obscenity or child pornography, amount to acts in the form of words, without ever suggesting that they are therefore doctrinally 'conduct' for purposes of First Amendment analysis." For example, coercion, force, trafficking, and assault are not speech. This active quality may explain why the courts have found that obscenity is not speech.[145] (It has been said that obscenity is not speech because it contributes nothing to the marketplace of ideas and causes a physical reaction—arousal—rather than mental contemplation.)

Pornography is sex discrimination because its victims (including men) are victimized on the basis of their sex, the amici said. It "is a practice of discrimination on the basis of sex in part because of its role in creating and maintaining sex as a basis for discrimination."[146]

This brief suggested that the absolutist approach to First Amendment issues is incorrect. The district court, it said, first determined whether the material at issue was speech, then looked to see if it fit an existing categorical exception (such as obscenity). This was not an accurate method of applying U.S. Supreme Court precedents, the brief said. The law requires a judicial balancing test in which the harms on both sides are balanced. In *Pittsburgh Press*, for example, the interest in stopping sex discrimination outweighed the First Amendment interests. The brief also noted that the following existing exceptions form a pattern of court recognition of harm: slander, misrepresentation, perjury, solicitation of crime, obscenity, false advertising, complicity by encouragement, bribery, conspiracy, blackmail, treason, fighting words, libel, clear and present danger, group libel, and indecency. In fact, the amici said, some of these exceptions are permitted with a great deal less harm than pornography causes.[147]

The amici denied that the ordinance was a group libel law. Speech, they said, can be restricted for " 'comfort and convenience' " (*Kovacs* v. *Cooper*,

which allowed a ban on sound trucks). Speech also can be restricted to avoid " 'the substantive evil—visual blight' ". Thus, *Los Angeles* v. *Taxpayers for Vincent* found that the adverse effect of signs on the landscape's appearance outweighed their speech value.[140] The amici said, "If speech interests can be outweighed to some degree because the materials are false, obscene, indecent, racist, coercive, threatening, intrusive, inconvenient, or inaesthetic, why can't they be actionable if they are coerced? What possible constitutional value can coerced 'speech' have?"[149]

According to the amici, the principles established in *Ferber* (the child pornography case) should be applied to women for the following reasons:

1. Child pornography, a form of child abuse, is not protected speech. Likewise, adult pornography, a form of abuse of women, is not protected speech.

2. Obscenity law was found not to be an appropriate definition/remedy for child pornography because work that contains value " 'may nevertheless embody the hardest core of child pornography.' "[150] Likewise, obscenity law is not an appropriate remedy for the harm to women resulting from adult pornography, for the value of the material, its prurient appeal (or lack thereof), and community standards have nothing to do with the fact that real women are injured in a real way by the pornography.

3. The *Ferber* court recognized that laws had to proceed against the traffickers in child pornography in order to do anything effective to stop the use and abuse of children in pornography. Likewise, the ordinance recognized that an action against trafficking in pornography must exist in order to effectively help those who are coerced into pornographic performances.

4. Children, as a class, are customarily "afforded greater legal protection than adults."[151] Women are not children. However, the amici noted that

> both groups share relative lack of power, inability to command respect for consent and self-determination, and comparative lack of access to resources for meaningful self-expression.
> . . . [The] assumptions that the law of the First Amendment makes about adults—that adults are *ipso facto* autonomous, self-defining, freely-acting, equal human beings—are exactly the qualities which pornography systematically denies and socially undermines for women.[152]

Importantly, the amici argued, pornography is not entitled to First Amendment protection because its nature is not that which the First Amendment intended to protect—speech of a political nature that contains ideas of advocacy. Pornography, because of its sexual nature, "works as a sexual behavior conditioner, reinforcer and stimulus, not as idea or advocacy." Pornography is not a constitutional right; it is a civil wrong. The amici compared the ordinance situation to that of segregation: "Is a sign that says 'Whites Only' protected speech because it is nothing but words?" They said it is not and cited *Brown* v. *Board of Education,* which held that separate but equal is inherently unequal.[153] Similarly, the injury of pornography is "differentially visited on one sex because of sex."[154]

In response to the claim that the best remedy for pornographic "speech" is speech in opposition to pornography, the amici said that such a remedy would not compensate or prevent their injury. No amount of speech remedies what is being done to Linda Marchiano, who, to this day, is being repeatedly raped for public entertainment each time the movies that are the product of her coercion into pornography are shown or sold. And, they noted, "[t]he pornographers and their pimps have silenced Dorothy Stratten forever."[155]

Andrea Dworkin, co-author of the civil rights law, wrote an amicus curiae brief in the Seventh Circuit. Dworkin was outraged that the appellees said pornography as defined under the ordinance was indistinguishable from her writings on pornography. The lower court, she said, protected abuses when it held that pornography is constitutionally protected speech. In her view, pornography, when it is photographic, is "indisputably action," not speech. Yet, according to the court, acts done by or to women are "speech." The founding fathers "could never have considered that there might be physical rights of people trampled on by rights of speech: that in protecting a photograph, for instance, one might be protecting an actual act of torture."[156]

Dworkin said that pornography "behaviorally conditions men to sex as dominance over and violence against women"—in other words, erection and orgasm are pleasurable responses to sexual abuse. Obscenity law recognizes that impact, she said, noting that the court ruled that obscenity is so different from any known form of speech that it is not speech even though it contains pictures or words. Yet, according to Dworkin obscenity laws are "woman-hating," set in a context of legal male ownership of women and male dominance and perpetuating a belief that sex by women is lewd and evil.[157] She noted, "Pornography creates the physiologically real conviction in men that women want abuse; that women are whores by nature; that women want to be raped and humiliated; that women get sexual pleasure from pain; even that women get sexual pleasure from being maimed or killed."[158]

Dworkin noted that most of the women who are exploited in pornography are incest and child sexual abuse victims who have been habituated to sexual abuse as children. Thus, no firm line between uses of children in pornography and uses of women in pornography exists. This, she said, is not a free and equal adult career choice. In addition, she noted, the production of pornography involves many abuses.

Pornography, in Dworkin's view, presents the rape and torture of women as entertainment. Judge Barker of the lower court was wrong to hold that pornography as defined under the ordinance expresses ideas and is protected speech, Dworkin argued, "unless one is prepared to say that murder or rape or torture with an ideology behind it also expresses ideas and might well be protected on that account."[159] Most acts and systems of exploitation and inequality express ideas, she said, giving segregation as an example. You cannot, however, protect exploitation because it expresses ideas that those being exploited are inferior.

Dworkin also took issue with Judge Barker's statement that adult women generally have the capacity to protect themselves from pornography victimization. This, she said, promotes a view that it is the victims' fault that they got hurt. Yet no one says it is a man's fault if he is murdered. It is not true that women can protect themselves from being victimized by pornography, Dworkin said. Its effect on women's civil status or its role in generating sexual abuse cannot be stopped because there is, under current law, no legal recourse available. For example, women in their homes do not have the economic power or social power to keep men from using it on them or making them participate in it. Women who are raped and photographed cannot win privacy actions to have the circulation of the material enjoined, for their compliance in its production is presumed. She noted, "[P]erhaps one effect of using $8 billion of pornography a year is that the basic premise of this law appears bizarre by contrast with the pornography—that women are human beings with rights of equality; and that being hurt by pornography violates those rights."[160]

Women, Dworkin stated (defining them as those who are sexually discriminated against), have been excluded from access to the means of speech because they cannot exercise their First Amendment rights. They are "too poor to buy speech, too silenced through sexual abuse to articulate in a credible way their own experiences, too despised because of their sex to be able to achieve the public significance required to exercise speech in a technologically advanced society."[161]

The First Amendment protects published speech

THE CIVIL RIGHTS ANTIPORNOGRAPHY LAW

but does not empower those who are excluded from speaking. The First Amendment, Dworkin said, existed in harmony with legal slavery and segregation. Despite such freedoms, blacks were denied the right to vote because of literacy tests, and teaching slaves to read and write was prohibited. Thus, rights of speech were denied to blacks. The laws passed after the Civil War acknowledged that "powerlessness is not cured simply by 'more speech.' " She suggested that, while the opposite should be true, perhaps the fact that women came into voting rights in 1920 and equality (Fourteenth Amendment) in 1971 helps account for the view that equality for women is "trivial" and the First Amendment is "fundamental." Thus, the lower court decided that equality does not matter, but expression does. The courts, Dworkin said, should give real weight to equality interests because of the systematic exclusion of those interests from the Bill of Rights. Otherwise, speech becomes a weapon used by haves against have-nots—"an intolerable instrument of dispossession, not a safeguard of human liberty." Judge Barker dignified pornographic abuse as an idea that warrants legal protection, Dworkin said. Under that decision, exploiters need only interject speech into practices of exploitation and hide behind it.[162]

Lastly, Dworkin argued that the mere presence of words in the process of discrimination does not turn it into protected activity. For example, a sexual proposition from an employer would not be protected speech.

Minneapolis City Council member Charlee Hoyt and numerous sexual assault and battered women's organizations from Minnesota submitted a brief in support of the civil rights law in the Seventh Circuit. Minneapolis, they said, was the birthplace of the law.

Hoyt argued that all former legal regulations of pornography have failed to remedy its harms. The new law will be the "only effective and adequate means of curbing the discrimination against women caused by pornography."[163] These amici detailed the inadequacies of current law:

1. Obscenity law is based on offensiveness and viewed as victimless. Its vagueness makes problems with prosecutions unpredictable. These are often expensive cases with small fines. In Minnesota, jury trials are mandated. As a result of this fact and the ruling that a defendant can refuse to produce a film for an adversarial hearing on the ground of self-incrimination, obscenity prosecutions were abandoned.

2. Zoning laws also have been ineffective. They have decreased property values and created crime areas due to clustered pornography shops. A Min-

neapolis zoning ordinance was held unconstitutional. Such laws have had no impact on the pornography industry or women's injuries.

3. Licensing and public nuisance statutes are equally inadequate. Licensing deals only with fire and health codes, not with injuries caused by the materials.

The amici emphasized the harms to actual victims of pornography: "For women in Minnesota, pornography has resulted in forced sex, forced prostitution, forced sexual submission, and enforced sexual inequality.[164]

The lower court, they noted, compared the effect of pornography to " 'other unfair expression' "—such as slurs—and other " 'literary depictions which are uncomplimentary, or oppressive.' "[165] In reality, pornography is responsible for specific injuries to actual women, the amici said, pointing to the Minneapolis hearings record, which contains cases of harm:

1. Coercion into pornographic performances. Pornography was used to blackmail women. It is critical to get it off the street to enable women to escape these conditions, the amici argued.

2. Forcing pornography on a person. Women, the amici stated, have been "sexually intimidated, humiliated, and shamed."[166] They gave examples of ex-husbands and coworkers forcing pornography on women.

3. Assault or physical attack due to pornography. Victims and professionals testified "to the pervasive use of pornography in demonstrating to men how, exactly, to rape, assault, and otherwise physically terrorize women."[167]

4. Trafficking in pornography. The lower court's view that when a government's interest in ending sex discrimination conflicts with the First Amendment protected values, the interest in discrimination must yield is wrong, amici said, citing *Roberts*. Despite its statements, the lower court implicitly rejected the finding of the City that trafficking in pornography is a "practice of sex discrimination," the amici said. This thinking, they said, is similar to that of the court in *Plessy* v. *Ferguson*, which said that it is a fallacy to think that the forced separation of the blacks and whites " 'stamps the colored race with a badge of inferiority' " and that if it was so, it was only because the blacks so construed it.[168]

The amici stated that pornography is "*central* in creating and maintaining the civil inequality of the sexes; that is, the subordinate legal, political, and social position of women to men." Acts of rape, assault, and so on, are made more likely by a high rate of pornography consumption, they argued. While victims and perpetrators cannot be predicted, the "perpetrator will be a man and the victim a woman." Pornography imposes daily constraints on women in employment, housing, and other areas. They fear for their lives daily. The amici pointed out that state and federal laws recognize that educational, employment, and contractual practices "which differentially harm women constitute actionable sex discrimination." The purpose of the ordinance was "social change," they said. Sex discrimination must be eradicated because only under conditions of equality "can speech be truly free."[169]

The Neighborhood Pornography Task Force of Minneapolis filed a brief in the Seventh Circuit. The task force is a voluntary organization working to halt the "deterioration of neighborhoods in South Minneapolis caused by the presence of increasing numbers of pornographic bookstores and theaters."[170]

Speech, the brief said, cannot fight the pornographers' power and money. In 1976, the group sought zoning laws to slow the growth of pornography in its neighborhood, but that law was held unconstitutional. The neighborhood conditions worsened:

1. Women who lived in the area were harassed, intimidated, and propositioned. They feared for the safety of themselves and their children.
2. Crime rates, especially for prostitution-related offenses, were higher in that area of the city.
3. Women from outside the area did not feel safe visiting it.
4. Children were forced to view pornography.
5. The once prosperous business community declined and deteriorated. The area lost shoppers because they did not feel safe.

A new effort to fight pornography through zoning proposed to allow pornography in poor and minority areas but not in affluent white areas. Thus, the task force pushed for the civil rights ordinance as an alternative. The group said it described the injuries of pornography that the residents had seen for years.

The court, the task force said, correctly perceived that the state has a legitimate interest in preserving neighborhoods. However, they said that zoning was not adequate to achieve that goal, for it only zones pornography from one place to another, putting it in areas of those without power, such as the poor and racially and ethnically disenfranchised. Rather than protecting neighborhoods, zoning supports pornography. Enforcement of zoning laws that force pornography on minority and poor neighborhoods denies those residents equal protection of the law, the task force argued. It also denies women who live there and want to visit there liberty in violation of the due process clause. And it denies them the right to exercise their First Amendment freedom of association. In effect, it makes these people second-class citizens and denies them a decent quality of life. The ordinance would give those who had pornography forced on them because of zoning laws a remedy, the task force stated.

The view that there are no rules to say that one publication is more dangerous or damaging than another is "incorrect," the task force said. The government *can* intrude to protect its citizens' lives, safety, and health and to ensure equality and justice. The task force wants government to ensure such equality and justice "because it believes that no one will be free until we all are free."[171]

The task force asked why material that subordinates women sexually is beyond legal remedy when housing, education, and the environment are not. The pornography industry cannot exist without coercion, it said. The task force said that by refusing to act against pornography, the state does the following:

1. Assents "to the brutal torture of women and children in pornography"
2. Assents "to the forced deterioration of neighborhoods"
3. Assents to the denial of a decent quality of life for the nonwhite and the poor (who live in these areas)
4. Encourages the proliferation of pornography
5. Protects pornographers' individual rights over rights to a decent life and women's rights to "dignity, equality and freedom"[172]

THE LEGAL CASE AGAINST THE CIVIL RIGHTS ORDINANCE

In their Seventh Circuit Court of Appeals Brief, the American Booksellers and others argued that the civil rights ordinance was attempting to do what criminal obscenity law could not—namely, collect major fines and damages. (We note that obscenity prosecutions under the RICO acts do, in fact, allow huge fines equal to or greater than the pornographers' profits to be collected.) Second, they argued that the ordinance restricted the availability of materials that depict the sexually explicit subordination of women by use of a censorship board. Third, they argued that the amendment created a new tort for women who have been assaulted "whether or not the assault was criminal in nature" at the expense of legitimate publishers, authors, and so on. (We note that based on commonly understood legal definitions, it is unlikely that an "assault" portrayed in pornography would not be a depiction of a criminal act such as rape, battery, or child molestation.)[173]

The appellees' three major arguments were as follows:

1. The ordinance was so vague and ambiguous that its chilling effects would reach far beyond what was intended and cause First Amendment protected works (by their definition, items that are not obscene) to be removed from stores and libraries.
2. The ordinance made no attempt to comply with the obscenity definition established by the court in *Miller*.
3. The ordinance constituted an impermissible prior restraint.

They said, "The amendment effectively bans all words and pictures which are said to engender a discriminatory attitude against women."[174] (We believe that this is an inaccurate description of the ordinance because it covered only material that is sexually explicit, subordinates women, *and* fits within one of the half dozen descriptions of forbidden acts.)

The appellees claimed to represent the parties against whom complaints may be brought under the ordinance. However, a specific examination of the parties and their clients makes it clear that such was not likely, for they did not represent pornographers but rather legitimate booksellers and retailers. They pointed to case law that argues that a constitutional Article III case or controversy can be established if a party reasonably fears that a law will be enforced against it for specific conduct on its part. (We note that Article III of the Constitution requires that a real case or controversy exist in order for federal lawsuits to be brought. In other words, the courts are not to issue advisory decisions.) The appellees, in their brief, attempted to make it appear that they met the case or controversy requirement, and the courts, in this case, accepted them as legitimate parties, despite the appellants' arguments to the contrary.

The appellees claimed that they had standing to challenge the ordinance despite the fact that they did not allege that they could be sued for forcing pornography on a person, coercing someone into performing for pornography, or assaulting someone because of pornography. The appellees cited *Secretary of State of Maryland* v. *Munson*, which, they said, ruled that a litigant can show that a statute substantially abridges the First Amendment rights of parties not before the court. They argued that because they demonstrated an injury in fact under the trafficking provision, they had standing to assert the rights of others under the forcing pornography on a person part of the law.[175]

Ironically, in the appellees' lower court brief on the motion for summary judgment, they listed specific "First Amendment protected works" sold by them that apparently fell within the scope of the law, yet argued that they could not tell what the law covered. (This listing certainly disputes their claim that the law was so vague that they could not tell what was covered.) They pointed to numerous parts of the law that they alleged were vague and ambiguous, such as the definition of pornography; the term *subordination;* the part that allowed men, children, and transsexuals to have claims if they were injured in the same way that a woman was injured; and the phrase "caused by specific pornography." As a result, they said, potential defendants cannot know what their rights are under this provision. Other vague terms (found to be so by the lower court) included degradation, abasement, inferiority, and "context that makes these conditions sexual." The appellees cited case law to the effect that, when First Amendment rights are involved, the government can regulate only "with narrow specificity" (*N.A.A.C.P.* v. *Button*).[176]

American Booksellers et al. also alleged that the authors and supporters of the civil rights antipornography ordinance could not, in their briefs, agree on the scope and meaning of the ordinance. Therefore, they said, how could the bookseller or distributor hope to comply with the law without "eliminating from the marketplace all words and pictures that arguably reveal women in an 'inferior' position?"[177] (We note that this again suggests a much broader scope to the ordinance than in reality exists.)

Only insulting or fighting words, child pornography, and the obscene, indecent, or libelous can be restricted as outside First Amendment coverage, the appellees said. (We point out that the appellant City of Indianapolis had made it clear that the ordinance attempted to create a new category of material outside of such coverage and pornography, as the ordinance defined it, was *not* speech. Child pornography, for example, was not found to be an exception to the First Amendment until 1982.) Relying on *Miller,* the appellees claimed that sexually explicit materials had to be obscene (that is, meet the court's current obscenity definition) in order to be regulated. For example, the works taken as a whole had to constitute hard-core pornography. The ordinance, they said, restricted far more than that. (We note that zoning, child pornography, and public display laws, to mention only a few, restrict sexually explicit material that is not obscene. Furthermore, many of those laws, including obscenity laws, are criminal in nature; in contrast, the ordinance was not.)

The appellees argued that popular fiction novels and standard motion pictures would be covered by the ordinance. (We believe that most would not fit the requirements of the ordinance—namely, that they are sexually explicit, subordinate women, and meet one of the six categories of covered acts.) Most women's romance and gothic novels would be covered by the ordinance, the appellees stated. (We note that coverage would depend on whether or not the specific book fit the definition of pornography under the ordinance.)

A key point of the appellees' position was that if damages were awarded for violating this civil law, it would have an impact on their exercise of First Amendment rights. Thus, it would restrict the pornographers (which, of course, is the intent of the law).

They attempted to distinguish *Roberts* v. *U.S. Jaycees* (which held that the interest of a state in ending discrimination based on sex is a superior interest to the First Amendment interest) from the ordinance case because *Roberts* "does not aim at the suppression of speech, does not distinguish between permitted and prohibited activity on the basis of viewpoint, and does not allow enforcement officials to administer it on the basis of constitutionally impermissible criteria." The ordinance, on the other hand, did so, the appellees said.[178]

They distinguished the ordinance from the zoning line of cases by pointing out that such cases permit only time, manner, or place restrictions (*Young*). Likewise, the decency case, *Pacifica*, was limited to such restrictions, they said. In contrast, the amendment bans "all expression that is said to engender a discriminatory attitude against women." (As we have noted, this is not the case.) They distinguished *Ferber* as being limited to actual pornographic depictions of children, which the court found to be a governmental objective of surpassing importance. They quoted the lower court opinion in *Hudnut* that adult women, as a group, do not need the same kind of protection as children.

The appellees compared the ordinance to *Near* v. *Minnesota*, which held that a statute banning an anti-Semitic newspaper was unconstitutional as an impermissible prior restraint. They said that the group libel case, *Beauharnais* v. *Illinois*, which upheld a statute making it a crime to disseminate material promoting racial or religious hatred toward groups, did not apply because the case did not remain good law. Calling the provisions that deal with trafficking a form of civil group libel law, they pointed out that a group loss without an injury that particularly affects an individual is not likely to be able to maintain an action under case precedents requiring that such injury be shown.[179]

The ordinance, according to the appellees, was not limited to depictions of torture, which would likely be obscene, but instead covered all depictions of women being subordinated. (We point out that many R-rated "slasher" films depict the torture of women and are not covered by obscenity law.) The fact that the ordinance was not restricted to violent pornography made it overbroad, the appellees stated. This suggests that the ordinance covered materials that are protected by the First Amendment. Coercion, assault, and other acts covered by the ordinance are already illegal, the appellees noted, and depictions of women in subordinate roles are protected speech unless they are obscene under *Miller*.

Unless there is actual incitement to unlawful action, producers of materials cannot be subjected to financial liabilities "for the aggressive acts of third parties, even if they are influenced by specific publications or films," the appellees stated. Again, the legal basis for this viewpoint is the First Amendment protection of speech. Quoting a Rhode Island state court opinion, they alleged that there is no power to restrict expression because of its ideas or message, subject matter, or content.[180] They cited these examples: parents sued a television station for broadcasting a movie stunt that was allegedly copied by their son and caused his death; a son read a sex-related article that allegedly led to his death; and a television movie allegedly caused a child to be sexually molested in a copycat crime. The reason given for not allowing such lawsuits to succeed is the alleged chilling effect on speech. The appellees suggested that if such lawsuits were successful, even news stories or documentaries that children imitated could be the basis for a victim suit. (We note that what the appellees failed to do was to distinguish between works that have value, such as news stories, documentaries, and films that realistically portray abuse without explicitly showing the abuse, and pornography, which lacks such value.) In another case cited by appellees, a man claimed he had been "subliminally intoxicated" by violence on television and therefore committed murder. The case had been dismissed by the court.

Lastly, the appellees argued that the ordinance

gave the civil rights commission of Indianapolis, a nonelected body, the power to act as an unrestricted censorship board. This, they said, is a prior restraint in violation of the First Amendment and has a chilling effect on speech. They listed certain procedural safeguards that must be provided before a system of censorship of unprotected material is constitutional. Those standards were set in *Southeastern Promotions Limited* v. *Conrad, Blount* v. *Rizzi,* and *Freedman* v. *Maryland.* They are as follows:

> (1) The burden of instituting judicial proceedings and of proving that the material is unprotected must rest on the censor. (2) Any restraint prior to judicial review can be . . . only for a specific brief period and only for the purpose of preserving the status quo. (3) A prompt final judicial determination must be assured.[181]

The civil rights ordinance did not meet those criteria, the appellees argued.

Other provisions in the law would allow censorship goals to be accomplished by cease and desist orders, they said. In addition, they stated that judicial review would not come for a long time in some situations.

A brief was filed in the Seventh Circuit by the Feminist Anti-Censorship Task Force (FACT) et al. The amici were feminists who opposed the ordinance. They stated: "We believe that the ordinance reinforces rather than undercuts central sexist stereotypes in our society and would result in state suppression of sexually explicit speech, including feminist images and literature which does not in any way encourage violence against women."[182]

While FACT condemned acts of violence against women, it said that the ordinance would not reduce such violence. Instead, the ordinance would "censor speech and imagery that properly belongs in the public realm."[183]

FACT organized as a feminist organization opposed to the civil rights law and is composed of community activists, writers, artists, and teachers. Other groups and persons were on the brief, including, among others, the Women's Legal Defense Fund, Inc. (with more than fifteen hundred members), which furthers women's rights and challenges sex-based inequities through the law, especially in domestic relations and employment discrimination; attorneys; lesbians; directors of rape crisis hot lines; the director of a street prostitutes ministry; well-known feminists such as Kate Millett, Betty Friedan, Del Martin, and Adrienne Rich; and people associated with the ACLU.

The amici argued that the ordinance suppressed constitutionally protected speech in a way that is particularly detrimental to women. Far from being limited to sexually violent or coercive images, it suppressed material that is sexually explicit but not violent. They said that an endless amount of material could be suppressed, for example, under the category "scenarios of degradation or abasement." At the same time, they said, the ordinance did not address, nor would the amici support suppression of, what they considered far more pervasive commercial images depicting women "as primarily concerned with the whiteness of their wash, the softness of their toilet tissue, and whether the lines of their panties show when wearing tight slacks."[184] These images (which impress young children, the amici stated) show women as people who are interested in matters that are not important and who are not capable of significant and serious roles in society's decision making.

"Historically," they said, "the law has incorporated a double standard denying women's interest in sexual expression."[185] These standards assumed that women were delicate and that voluntary sexual intercourse might harm them, the amici stated. Yet the same law set up a category of women who were not delicate and who were not worthy of protection—such as prostitutes. The other side of the standard was the suggestion that men were almost crazed by sex. The ordinance, the amici said, fit within the definition of the double standard: "It allows little room for women to openly express their sexual desires, and resurrects the notion that sexually explicit materials are subordinating and degrading to women."[186]

This law, by allowing one woman to sue under the trafficking provision, implied that individual women cannot choose for themselves what they consider to be enjoyable sexually arousing material without being humiliated or degraded, the amici said. The legal system enforces the sexual double standard to protect "good" women from sexual activity and explicit speech about sex. The law also has dealt harshly with "bad" women, they noted, such as prostitutes. The amici presented a unique definition of prostitution that does not coincide with most legal definitions and is taken from 63 AM. JUR. 2d Prostitution S.1. (1972): " 'the practice of a female offering her body to indiscriminate sexual intercourse with men' " or " 'submitting to such sexual intercourse which she invites or solicits.' "[187] Under this standard, a woman who is sexually active with many men becomes a prostitute and is considered criminal, while a sexually active man is considered normal. Laws such as those dealing with statutory rape, which punish men for consensual intercourse with females under a certain age, also reinforce the stereotype that, when sex is involved, the woman is the victim and the man the offender, the amici said. Under this idea, young men can have sex with older people, while young women cannot have sex with anyone.

In the past, the amici noted, among the sexually explicit material that was suppressed was birth control information. Such suppression was common until 1971, when the U.S. Supreme Court held that the right to privacy protects the person's right to access such information (*Eisenstadt* v. *Baird*).[188] The amici stated that contraceptive and abortion information was prosecuted under the federal Comstock Law passed in 1873, which prohibited mailing or transportation of obscene materials. Under this, women were jailed for distributing educational materials regarding birth control. These were deemed sexually explicit because they contained pictures of certain female organs. The Mann Act (an antiprostitution act) also was based on an idea that women require special protection from sexual activity, the amici noted. This act deals with coercing women into prostitution. It leaves no room for the possibility that prostitutes might willingly choose their activities. The upshot of all of this has been to restrict women's freedom to engage in sexual activity and to discuss it publicly, as well as to protect themselves from the risk of pregnancy. According to the amici, "The Indianapolis ordinance resonates with the traditional concept that sex itself degrades women and its enforcement would reinvigorate those discriminatory moral standards which have limited women's equality in the past."[189]

FACT et al. argued that the ordinance was unconstitutionally vague. They conceded that words and images do influence people's thinking and acts both negatively and positively and that pornography might have such influence. However, they said they were concerned about the fact that context often determines meaning—for example, the context would affect whether or not a particular image would be found to subordinate or degrade women. Yet the trafficking provision allowed suppression of images based on highly subjective criteria, the amici said. They asserted that the central parts of the ordinance had no fixed meaning and that the most common meanings of the terms were sexist and damaging to women because they reinforced a constrictive view of women's sexuality.

The amici said that feminist art that deals openly with sexual themes might be targeted for suppression under the ordinance. For example, the term *sexually explicit subordination* was not defined. They asked, What kinds of sexually explicit acts place a woman in an inferior status? Some people would say that

any graphic image of sexual acts is degrading to women and subordinates them. Some might say that an image of a woman lying on her back inviting intercourse fits the description, while others might view that image as "affirming women's sexual pleasure and initiative." Others might draw the line at acts outside of marriage or at acts of group sex. Still others might view the traditional heterosexual act as subordinate, with a man in a position of physical superiority and a woman in a position of physical inferiority.

The amici noted that the ordinance did not clearly state whether it was to be interpreted with an objective or a subjective standard. The objective standard would require a determination of whether the plaintiff's reaction to the material was in line with a general notion of images that do or do not degrade women. In other words, the judiciary would impose its views of correct sexuality on a diverse community. As a result, those images that are least conventional would be disapproved, and those closest to the majority belief would be approved. This type of inquiry profoundly threatens First Amendment freedoms and is inconsistent with feminist principles, the amici said. One cannot entrust image judgments of this type to legislative categories or judicial enforcement.

They noted that some women would say that any explicit lesbian scenes subordinated them and caused their dignity to suffer, while others would find such scenes affirming. They said that gays and lesbians encounter massive discrimination based on their sexual choices and that the trafficking provisions of the ordinance invited new manifestations of this prejudice. Other unclear terms they noted were *sex object, subordination,* and *degradation*. Historically, all sexually explicit images and words were thought to be abasing to women. There is no reason to believe that these terms would not be interpreted as they have in the past, from a subjective, moralistic viewpoint.

The amici stated that the First Amendment prohibits laws that regulate expression and would result in unpredictable and arbitrary interpretations. This is a concern with the chilling effect, they explained. They said that the ordinance perpetrated a belief that undermines "the principle that women are full, equal and active agents in every realm of life including the sexual."[190]

The amici argued that sexually explicit speech does not cause or incite violence in a way that is sufficiently direct to justify suppressing it under the First Amendment. This law, they said, called for invention of a new exception to the First Amendment. To justify such an exception, it must be shown that the speech to be suppressed will lead to immediate and concrete harm, they noted, citing *Brandenburg v. Ohio* and *Collin v. Smith*.[191]

According to the amici, the City of Indianapolis cited social science data in selective and distorted ways and failed to acknowledge that most of it is limited to a class of violent imagery. The ordinance, they said, left untouched most of the images that would cause negative effects and allowed suppression of many images that have not been shown to have any harmful effect. Also, debriefing of the experimental subjects suggests that many negative attitude changes can be corrected through further speech, they said. They quoted Edward Donnerstein as saying that a "good amount of research strongly supports the position that exposure to certain types of erotica can produce aggressive responses in people who are predisposed to aggression."[192] But they said that numerous methodological problems in the scientific studies make them too unreliable as predictors of real-world behavior to use them to sustain a limit on speech that is now permitted. None of the studies looked at the impact of words alone, they noted. Importantly, they said that violent and woman-hating images pervade our culture. Nothing in the research the city cited proves their theory that such messages are believed in a different way when communicated through the medium of sexually explicit material, so there is no reason to single out that form of expression.

"When more speech can effectively counter prejudicial and discriminatory messages, the First Amendment forbids the use of censorship to suppress even the most hateful content," the amici stated, citing *Collin v. Smith*.[193] Debriefing experimental subjects can deal with violent pornographic attitudes, they said. Sex education programs might provide another viable alternative to regulating pornography, they suggested. In the studies, debriefing sessions have shown that changes in attitude from pornography are not permanent or conditioned, they said. Furthermore, the studies undermine the city's claim that violent material causes the kind of concrete—immediate—harm that would justify a new exception to the First Amendment. In fact, behavior under laboratory conditions cannot predict behavior in real life with the degree of accuracy and specificity needed to justify "a new censorship law," the amici said. In most of the studies cited, they noted, the aggressive behavior happened only when the experimenter gave the subject cues indicating that such behavior was acceptable. In real life, a multitude of factors shape behavior. In Japan, pornography has more depictions of rape and bondage than in the United States, and pornography is more readily available in popular magazines and on television. Yet the Japanese have a substantially lower incidence of rape and violent crime in general, the amici said.

Images used in slasher films are not covered by the ordinance, amici claim. (In our view, this is not correct.)

The city's claim that a causal connection between the availability of pornography and rape exists, the amici said, "Such a claim is implausible on its face. Acts of rape and coercion long preceded the mass distribution of pornography, and, in many cultures pornography is unavailable, yet the incidence of rape, and of discrimination against women generally, is high."[194] Also, they state, there are places where pornography is widely available and the incidence of rape is low. Since it cannot be shown that pornography causes harm in the direct, immediate way that shouting "fire" in a crowded theater does, this new exception to the First Amendment should not be allowed, the amici argued. Constitutional protection for sexually explicit speech should be increased, not diminished.

Importantly, the amici argued that sexually explicit speech is political and one core insight of modern feminism is that personal matters are political: "The question of who does the dishes and rocks the cradle affects both the nature of the home and composition of the legislature," they said. Even clearly woman-hating pornography is political speech, they alleged. In fact, they noted, even antipornography advocates have often argued that pornography is political propaganda for male dominance. Here, the amici said, the city argued that sexually explicit speech is less important than other categories of speech. This reinforces structures that have identified women's concerns with relationships and intimacy as being less significant because they are regarded as not having a bearing on the structure of social and political life. The amici asserted, however, that depictions of life that are radically different from our own enlarge the range of human possibilities and make us open to the potentials of human behavior, good or bad. Rich fantasy images are part of this. And for sexual minorities, speech describing conduct can be a means of self-affirmation in a world that is generally hostile.

In one case, a woman was fired from her job because she told coworkers that she was bisexual, the amici noted. Sexually explicit expression, including some covered by the ordinance, can convey a message that sexuality need not be tied to reproduction, men, or domesticity and can have themes of sex for no other reason than pleasure, sexual adventure, and sex without commitment. All of these surely are ideas, they argued, citing *Kingsley Corp.*

v. *Regents*.[196] They quoted a passage suggesting that a woman could enjoy pornography even if it means enjoying a rape fantasy. One can, they stated, fantasize about a sexual encounter and refuse it at the same time. As more of women's writing and art on sexual themes "emerges unladylike, unfeminine, aggressive, power-charged, pushy, vulgar, urgent, confident and intense, the traditional foes of women's attempts to step out of their 'proper place' will find an effective tool of repression in the Indianapolis ordinance," they said.[197]

The amici also argued that the ordinance unconstitutionally discriminated on the basis of sex and reinforced sexist stereotypes. The ordinance claimed that there is a categorical difference between the makeup and needs of men and women. It presumed women as a class are subordinated by virtue of any sexually explicit image, while men are not. And it presumed that women cannot make a binding agreement to participate in the creation of sexually explicit material. Men as a class, however, are conditioned by sexually explicit depictions to commit acts of aggression and to believe woman-hating myths. The amici stated:

> Such assumptions reinforce and perpetuate sexist stereotypes; they weaken, rather than enhance, women's struggles to free themselves of archaic notions of gender roles. In so doing, this ordinance violates the equal protection clause of the Fourteenth Amendment. In treating women as a special class it repeats the errors of earlier protectionist legislation which gave women no significant benefits and denied their equality.[198]

Therefore, they said, the district court had erred when it accepted the assertion that pornography is a discriminatory practice based on sex.

The amici disagreed with the finding of the city and the county that pornography is central to " 'creating and maintaining sex as a basis for discrimination.' "[199] Instead, they said, the most significant factors in maintaining sex discrimination include sex segregated wage labor markets, devaluation of traditional women's work, sexist concepts of family and marriage, inadequate income maintenance programs for women who cannot find wage work, the lack of day-care services, the premise that child care is a woman's responsibility, barriers to reproductive freedom, and discrimination and segregation in athletics and education. Woman-hating images, whether sexually explicit or not, reflect and reinforce the inferior economic and social status of women, but none of the studies identified sexually explicit material as the central factor in oppression of women.

In history, they noted, pornography was not as prevalent as it is today, but women were treated as chattel property and husbands were allowed to rape or beat their wives. Thus, they disagreed with the claim that pornography as defined in the ordinance is a discriminatory practice denying women equal opportunity. Ideas can have an impact, but images of discrimination are not the discrimination. Antidiscrimination laws demand equality of treatment for men and women. The ordinance, on the other hand, purported to protect women. The amici said, "It assumes that women are subordinated by such images and that men act uncontrollably if exposed to them."[200] Thus, sexist stereotypes were built into the premises of the ordinance, and its effect would be to reinforce the stereotypes. Thus, the ordinance was fatally flawed not only for authorizing speech protected by the First Amendment, but also because it violated the constitutional guarantee of sex-based equality. According to the amici brief, this ordinance classified on the basis of sex and perpetuated sexist stereotypes. Its heart was the suppression of sexually explicit images of women based on a finding of subordination. It perpetuated images of women as helpless victims and people who could not seek sex. In addition, it reinforced sexist stereotypes of men and denied the possibility that sexually explicit images of men could ever degrade or subordinate them. The ordinance, the amici said, provided no remedies for images of men truncated or fragmented. (We note that this is not accurate, for men, if used in pornography the same way women are, would have a remedy.)

The ordinance, amici stated, allowed men a remedy only when used in place of women. Thus, the civil rights law assumed that "in sexuality, degradation is a condition that attaches to women."[201] It assumed that women as a class are hurt and subordinated by depictions of sex and men are not, thus reinforcing sexist stereotypes of men as aggressive beasts. Under the ordinance, men are conditioned into violent acts and negative beliefs by sexual images and women are not. The ordinance also reinforced sexist images of women as being incapable of consent, the amici said.

According to FACT et al., the law created a strong presumption that women who participate in pornography are coerced. Even the manifestations of consent such as binding contracts would not constitute a defense to women's subsequent claims of coercion under the ordinance. The women are deemed incompetent to consent and bad if they do so. The amici said that the city based its argument on the common points between women and children—namely, being incapable of consenting to engage in pornographic conduct and requiring special protection. Under this law, women would be incompetent to enter into legally binding contracts to produce sexually explicit material. The amici stated that the law would drive the production of such material even further into an underground economy in which the working conditions for women in the sex industry would be even worse.

Importantly, the amici argued that the ordinance was unconstitutional because it reinforced sexist stereotypes and classified on the basis of sex. Such classification can only stand up if it serves important governmental objectives and if the discriminatory means are substantially related to the achievement of those objectives, they said (*Mississippi University* v. *Hogan*).[202] This ordinance, they said, perpetuated traditional social views of sex-based differences, reinforcing the stereotype that good women do not seek and enjoy sex and that men are especially susceptible to violent imagery. They suggested that the law could be used to avoid directly blaming men who commit violent acts. It perpetuates a stereotype of women as helpless victims incapable of consent and needing protection. FACT et al. cited numerous laws, including labor laws, that were intended to protect women from exploitation, but that in reality hurt them. Gender-based classifications are premised on good-faith intent to help and protect women, they stated, but such classifications may actually hurt them.

The lower court found that adult women as a group do not need the type of protection afforded children when pornography is the issue. The particular stereotypes and sex-based classifications that the ordinance created "are not carefully tailored to serve important state purposes," the amici said. While preventing the sexual subordination of women is the sort of compelling public purpose that might justify such classifications, the benefits provided are minimal. They argued that this law was a misdirected response to real violence.[203]

The ordinance, amici claimed, would not have helped Linda Lovelace while she was a prisoner of the pornography industry. Individuals who commit acts of violence must be held legally and morally accountable, and this responsibility should not be displaced onto imagery. Laws should punish the abuser, not the image of abuse.

> To resist forced sex and violence, women need the material resources to enable them to reject jobs or marriages in which they are abused or assaulted, and the internal and collective strength to fight the conditions of abuse. The ordinance does nothing to enhance the concrete economic

and social power of women. Further, its stereotype of women as powerless victims undermines women's ability to act affirmatively to protect themselves.[204]

Suppression of sexually explicit material would not eliminate the sexist images in our mainstream culture or the discrimination against women, the amici stated. What is truly needed are social and economic equality; access to jobs, education, and day care; equal sharing of responsibility for children; recognition of the value of work women have traditionally done in the home; and access to birth control, sex education, and abortion. In conclusion, they stated that sexually explicit speech is not per se sexist or harmful to women.

The November 1984 *Newsletter on Intellectual Freedom* contained excerpts from the amicus curiae brief filed in the district court by the Freedom to Read Foundation on behalf of the Indiana Library Association and the Indiana Library Trustee Association. These amici called the scope of a library's collection "a measure of the community's access to ideas" necessary to the functioning of a democracy and the "predicate for the advancement of knowledge and the improvement of the human condition."[205] Many of the books on library shelves fall within the ordinance's "vague and boundless" pornography definition, they argued. (We note that if the law were truly vague, one could not tell what books were covered.) The law, these amici felt, "cuts to the heart of the library's mission to present the broadest range of ideas to the public."[206] Librarians would be threatened with lawsuits for doing their jobs—that is, responding to the public's need for access to information—they said. The interest of the librarians was immediate and direct, for their reason for professional existence—"intellectual freedom"—was threatened.

The amici argued that the ordinance was overbroad and based on an unconstitutional definition of pornography. The key point was that obscenity law controls the legal boundaries.

The ordinance, they said, was totally inconsistent with First Amendment philosophy, for "[g]overnment cannot constitutionally premise legislation on the desire to control the content of a person's private thoughts."[207] They also alleged that there was a complete lack of empirical evidence to support the claim that pornography promotes aggression and discrimination. They stated:

> [T]he Ordinance condemns shelf-upon-shelf of accepted literary works. Sex and sexuality have been subjects of absorbing interest to humanity since the beginning of time. . . . The *Bible* itself

contains passages which, to some, may present the "graphic sexually explicit subordination of women." The same can be said of a multitude of works from established classics. . . . Countless works could be accused of presenting women as "sex objects," "in scenarios of degradation," or as "inferior in a context that makes these conditions sexual."[208]

Even standard works of art history would be in violation of the ordinance, the amici claimed. They feared that "well-intentioned but zealous citizens" would use the law to purge the libraries of materials that were personally, socially, or morally reprehensible to them.

The amici also claimed that the ordinance was vague. For example, one person's concepts of subordination and domination are not the same as another's. Librarians are not trained to review books or to evaluate the merit of viewpoints and ideas contained in them, the amici stated. Such "content-based judgments" are "antithetical" to librarians and the First Amendment, they said, but the ordinance would force librarians to make such decisions. The response might be to avoid materials that might fall within the law's coverage rather than risk liability. They said that this chilling effect alone was sufficient to declare the civil rights law unconstitutional. The self-censorship decisions that would result would affect the "public's right to know and the public's right to read."[209] (We note that since libraries do not contain all of the published works available, librarians make decisions on a day-to-day basis to purchase some books and censor others. Logic dictates that some of those purchase decisions are based on judgments of the relative value of the works being considered.)

A version of the civil rights anti-pornography ordinance was placed on the ballot on November 8, 1988, in Bellingham, Washington, as a result of a citizens' initiative. The ordinance was approved by the voters 62 percent to 38 percent. The American Civil Liberties Union and others sued the City of Bellingham, challenging the constitutionality of the ordinance. The City (which had opposed placing the initiative on the ballot), agreed that the ordinance violates the First Amendment. Various groups and persons who favor the ordinance (including pornography victims) intervened in the lawsuit to defend the law. (The chief sponsor of the ordinance, Civil Rights Organizing for Women, sued the City to force the initiative onto the ballot).

Linda Marchiano (known as Linda Lovelace in pornographic movies) said she hoped to file a civil lawsuit under the Bellingham ordinance to obtain an injunction prohibiting the showing of the pornographic films she was coerced into performing for and seeking damages.

The complaint seeking to strike down the Bellingham civil rights ordinance was based on the same grounds as those presented in the Indianapolis (*Hudnut*) case, primarily involving alleged violations of the First Amendment. A theory that the initiative, in violation of the First Amendment, allows public figures to recover damages for defamation without having to show that a publication included a false factual statement made with knowledge of falsity or with reckless disregard as to whether it was true was created by the plaintiffs. The United States District Court for the Western District of Washington held the ordinance to be unconstitutional. (*Village Books, et al. v. The City of Bellingham*, No. C88-1470). The case is on appeal.[210]

CONCLUSION

We conclude that an approach similar to a civil rights ordinance is needed to effectively combat pornography. Such a law is proposed for purposes of debate in chapter 12.

NOTES

1. Paul Brest and Ann Vandenberg, "Essay: Politics, Feminism, and the Constitution: The Anti-Pornography Movement in Minneapolis," *Stanford Law Review* 39 (February 1987): 607–11.
2. Ibid., 611–12.
3. Ibid.
4. Ibid., 613–15.
5. Ibid., 615.
6. Ibid., 615–18.
7. Ibid., 615.
8. Ibid., 620.
9. Ibid., 621.
10. Ibid., 631.
11. Ibid., 629–30.

12. Ibid., 632–33.
13. Ibid., 633–35.
14. Ibid., 635–37.
15. Ibid., 639.
16. Gary E. McCuen, *Pornography and Sexual Violence* (Hudson, Wisc.: GEM Publications, 1985), 70–73.
17. Brest and Vandenberg, "Politics, Feminism, and the Constitution," 646–52.
18. *The Feminist Connection,* Annie Laurie Gaylor, "Pornography is a form of Discrimination." Madison, WI: June 1984.
19. Brest and Vandenberg, "Politics, Feminism, and the Constitution," 646–52.
20. Michael A. Gershel, "Evaluating a Proposed Civil Rights Approach to Pornography: Legal Analysis as if Women Mattered," *William Mitchell Law Review* 11 (1985): 48, fn. 28 and 29.
21. Brest and Vandenberg, "Politics, Feminism, and the Constitution," 652–53.
22. Ibid., 653.
23. Ibid., 661.
24. Rebecca Benson, "Pornography and the First Amendment: American Booksellers v. Hudnut," *Harvard Women's Law Journal* 9 (1986): 170, 154.
25. E.R. Shipp, "Civil Rights Law Against Pornography Is Challenged," *New York Times,* 15 May 1984.
26. Eileen Ogitz, "Porn Law Pits Women's Rights Against 1st Amendment," *Chicago Tribune,* 26 August 1984.
27. Dorothy Petrospy, "On the Card Anti-Porn Fight, Free Speech vs. Women's Rights," *Indianapolis Star,* 22 April 1984.
28. Susan Batpin, "42% of Cambridge Voters Support Anti-Porn Ordinance," *Women Against Pornography Newsreport* 7 (Spring/Summer 1986): 1 Jamie M. Moore, "Civil Rights Pornography Ordinances: A Status Report," *Response to the Victimization of Women and Children* 8 (Fall 1985): 17.
29. Doug Moe, "The New Censorship: Radical Feminists Join Religious Fundamentalists in a New Crusade," *Madison,* November 1984, 2, 7.
30. Ibid.
31. David Blaska, "Latest War Against Porn Dividing Liberal Politics," *Capital Times* (Madison, Wisc.), 16 August 1984.
32. Thomas M. Waller, "Group Disputes Civil-Suit Approach in Porno Fight," *Wisconsin State Journal,* 15 November 1984.
33. David Callender, "Caution Urged in Defining Smut," *Capital Times* (Madison, Wisc.), 25 September 1984.
34. Thomas M. Waller, "Group Seeking Alternative in Battle Against Pornography," *Wisconsin State Journal,* 13 November 1984.
35. Glen Mathison, "Feminists Disagree on Anti-Pornography Law," *Wisconsin State Journal,* 15 November 1984.
36. Iris Christensen, "Pornography Opinion: Civil Rights Ordinance Would Help Protect Women," 6–7; Jeff Goldstein, "Feminist Analysis Ignored in Pornography Debate," 7; Michele Courier and Leslie J. Reagan,

"Conservatives Can Use Pornography Ordinances . . . , *The Daily Cardinal,* 11 December 1984.
37. Dorchen Leidholdt, "Anti-Pornography Ordinance Update," *Women Against Pornography Newsreport* VII (No. 1) 1985: 4, 23.
38. Karen Davis, "Anti-Porn Initiative in L.A. Court," *Women Against Pornography Newsreport* VII (No. 1) 1985: 5, 17.
39. Ibid.; "L.A. Tightens Porn Law," *Off Our Backs* 15 (July 1985): 14.
40. Dorchen Leidholdt, "Senate Hearings Prompt Pornography Victims Act," *Women Against Pornography Newsreport* VII (No. 1) 1985: 1, 18.
41. Catharine A. MacKinnon, "The Civil Rights Approach to Pornography" (Testimony before the Attorney General's Commission on Pornography, Chicago, Illinois, 24–25 July 1985), 1, 2, 8, 11.
42. Catharine MacKinnon, "Pornography, Civil Rights, and Speech," *Harvard Civil Rights–Civil Liberties Law Review* 20 (1985): 18.
43. Ibid., 22.
44. Ibid., 36.
45. Ibid., 77, fn. 38.
46. Ibid., 58–59.
47. Ibid., 62.
48. Ibid., 65.
49. Catharine MacKinnon, "Pornography: Not a Moral Issue," *Yale Law and Policy Review* 9 (November 1984): 64–65.
50. Ibid., 69.
51. Catharine MacKinnon, Letter, *New York Times,* 31 May 1984.
52. Dorchen Liedholdt, "Indianapolis Ordinance Struck Down," *Women Against Pornography Newsreport* 7 (Spring/Summer 1986): 6.
53. Letter from Andrea Dworkin to Minneapolis mayor Donald Fraser, 5 July 1984.
54. Andrea Dworkin, "Pornography Is a Civil Rights Issue for Women" (Testimony before the Attorney General's Commission on Pornography, New York, 22 January 1986).
55. Dorchen Liedholdt, "ACLU Protests Commission Publication of Porn Information," *Women Against Pornography Newsreport* 7 (Spring/Summer 1986): 1, 18.
56. Barry Lynn, "Civil Rights' Ordinances and the New Developments in Pornography Regulations," *Harvard Civil Rights–Civil Liberties Law Review* 31 (Winter 1986): 48–49.
57. Ibid., 50–53, 58.
58. Ibid., 72, 78–79.
59. Ibid., 83.
60. Ibid., 85, 87.
61. Ibid., 98–99.
62. Ibid., 101–3.
63. "Struggle: Feminist Anti-Censorship Taskforce: The Case Against Indianapolis," *Off Our Backs* 15 (June 1985): 12–13.
64. FACT Book Committee, *Caught Looking: Feminism,*

Pornography and Censorship (New York: Caught Looking, Inc., 1986).

65. Cynthia Toolin, "Attitudes toward Pornography: What Have the Feminists Missed?" *Journal of Popular Culture* 17 (Fall 1983): 173.

66. William E. Brigman, "Pornography as Political Expression," *Journal of Popular Culture* 17 (Fall 1983): 129–34.

67. Ibid., 130.

68. Ibid., 132, 134.

69. Tessa Namuth, Gerald C. Lubenow, Michael Reese, David L. Friendly, and Ann McDaniel, "The War Against Pornography," *Newsweek*, 18 March 1985, 58, 66.

70. Mary Kay Blakeley, "Is One Woman's Sexuality Another Woman's Pornography?" *Ms.*, April 1985, 37, 38, 40, 44, 46, 47, 120, 123.

71. Second Amended Complaint, *American Booksellers Association, Inc. et al. v. Hudnut, et al.*, Case No. IP 84-791C (S.D. Indiana, Indianapolis Division), June 19, 1984, 2.

72. Sarah Evans Barker, *American Booksellers Association, Inc. et al. v. Hudnut et al.*, Case No. IP 84-791C, Judgement and Finding of Facts and Conclusions (S.D. Indiana, Indianapolis Division), November 19, 1984, 17–18.

73. Ibid., 18–19.

74. Ibid., 25, citing *Schad v. Burrough of Mt. Ephriam*, 452 U.S. 61 (1981).

75. Ibid., 38.

76. Ibid., 47.

77. Ibid., 54–58 citing *Freedom v. Maryland*, 380 U.S. 51 (1965).

78. *American Booksellers Association, Inc. v. Hudnut et al.*, Case No. 84-3147 (7th Cir. August 27, 1985), Judgement, 3.

79. Ibid.

80. Ibid., 7, citing *Buckley v. Valeo*, 424 U.S. 1 (1976).

81. Ibid., 9.

82. Ibid., 9, quoting *Police Department v. Mosely*, 408 U.S. 92 (1972).

83. Ibid., 9–10.

84. Ibid., 13.

85. Ibid., 16.

86. Ibid., 16–21.

87. Defendants' Memorandum in Opposition to Plaintiffs' Motion for Summary Judgment, *American Booksellers Association, Inc. v. Hudnut*, Cause No. IP 84-791C (S.D. Indiana, Indianapolis Division), July 3, 1984, 8.

88. Ibid., 13; *Paris Adult Theatre I v. Slaton*, 413 U.S. 49 (1965).

89. Ibid., 15–17.

90. Ibid., 17–19.

91. Ibid., 19, quoting *Chaplinsky v. New Hampshire*, 315 U.S. 568, 572 (1942).

92. Ibid., 19–22; *New York v. Ferber*, 458 U.S. 747 (1982); *FCC v. Pacifica Foundation*, 438 U.S. 726 (1978); *Roth v. United States*, 354 U.S. 476 (1957); *Beauharnais v. Illinois*, 343 U.S. 250 (1962); *Chaplinsky, ibid*, 571–72.

93. Ibid., 23–26.

94. Ibid., 27–30; *Ferber, Ibid;* 760-61; *Pacifica, Ibid; Young v. American Mini Theatres, Inc.* 425 U.S. 50 (1976).

95. Ibid., 31–34.

96. Ibid., 34–36; *Conally v. General Construction Co.* 269 U.S. 385 391 (1925); U.S. 1 (1946); *Boyce Motor Lines v. United States*, 342 U.S. *v. Petrillo*, 332 U.S. 1 (1946); 337, (1932); *Sproules v. Binford*, 286,340 U.S. 374, 392 (1932).

97. Ibid., 38. *Island Trees Union Pre-School v. Pico*, 457 U.S. 853 (1982).

98. Ibid., 43–47, 49–55.

99. Ibid., 49–50.

100. Ibid., 48, 56–57.

101. Ibid., 59–61. *Erzonznik v. City of Jacksonville*, 422 U.S. 205, 216 (1975); *Young v. American Mini Theatres, Inc.* 427 U.S. 50,60 (1976).

102. Ibid., 61–63.

103. Ibid., 69, quoting *Young, ibid.*, 61.

104. Ibid., 73–74; *Pittsburgh Press Co. v. Pittsburgh Commission on Human Relations*, 413 U.S. 376, 390 (1973).

105. Brief of Defendants–Appellants, *American Booksellers Association, Inc. et al. v. Hudnut et al.*, Case No. 84-3147 (7th Cir.), date unknown, 11. *Younger v. Harris*, 401 U.S. 37, 51 (1971).

106. Ibid., 19.

107. Ibid., 22.

108. Reply Brief of Defendants–Appellants, *American Booksellers Association, Inc. et al. v. Hudnut et al.*, Case No. 84-3147 (7th Cir.), April 1985, 6 citing *Miller v. California*, 413 U.S. 15, 24 (1973).

109. Ibid., 6, citing *Paris Adult Theatre I v. Slaton*, 413 U.S. 49, 57-8 (1973).

110. Ibid., 7.

111. Ibid.

112. Ibid., 7–8; *Collin v. Smith*, 578 F.2d 1197 (7th Cir. 1978);7.

113. Petition for Rehearing, Suggestion for Rehearing En Banc and Memorandum in Support Thereof, *American Booksellers Association, Inc. et al. v. Hudnut et al.*, Case No. 84-3147 (7th Cir.), September 10, 1985, 1–4; *Pittsburgh Press Co. v. Human Relations Comm'n*, 413 U.S. 376 (1973); *Roberts v. U.S. Jaycees*, 104 s. Ct. 3244 (1984).

114. Ibid., 4–5.

115. Ibid., 5; *Police Department Of Chicago v. Mosley*, 408 U.S. 92 (1972); *Carey v. Brown*, 447 U.S. 455 (1980); *Perry Education Association v. Perry Local Educators' Association*, 460 U.S. 37 (1983); *Wisconsin Action Coalition v. City Of Kenosha*, No. 84-2006, Slip op. 7th Cir., July 19, 1985.

116. Ibid., 5–8; *Cornelius v. N.A.A.C.P. Legal Defence and Education Fund*, 53 USLW 5116, 5121, June 25, 1985; *Planned Parenthood v. Kempiners*, 700 F.2d, 1115, 1129 (7th Cir. 1983).

117. Ibid., 9, quoting *Roberts v. U.S. Jaycees*, 104 S. Ct. 3244, 3255 (1983).

118. Ibid., 10–15; *New York v. Ferber*, 458 U.S. 742, 763-64 (1982).
119. Jurisdictional Statement of Hudnut et al., Appellants, in the Supreme Court of the United States, October Term, 1985, in *Hudnut et al. v. American Booksellers Association, Inc. et al.*, 6, citing *Roth v. United States*, 354 U.S. 476 (1957).
120. Ibid., 6, quoting *Roth, ibid.*, 485 citing *Chaplinsky v. New Hampshire*, 315 U.S. 568, 571-72 (1942).
121. Ibid., 7.
122. Ibid., 7–8.
123. Ibid., 8–9; *Ferber, supra*, at 763-64.
124. Ibid., 9; *Younger v. Harris*, 401 U.S. 37 (1971); *Laird v. Tatum*, 408 U.S. 1 (1972).
125. Ibid., 10–11.
126. Ibid., 11.
127. Ibid., 14.
128. Ibid., 15.
129. Ibid., 19.
130. Ibid.
131. Ibid., quoting *Los Angeles v. Taxpayers for Vincent*, 104 S. Ct. 2118, 2132 (1984).
132. Ibid., 25, quoting *Babbit v. United Farmworkers National Union*, 442 U.S. 289 (1979), 298.
133. Ibid., 28, citing *Younger v. Harris*, 401 U.S. 37, 41-42 (1972).
134. Brief Amici Curiae of Women Against Pornography; Pornography Resource Center; Men Against Pornography; Pornography Awareness; Alpha Human Resources; Citizens Against Pornography; Lincoln Women Against Pornography; Men's Task Force on Pornography; Minnesota Coalition for Battered Women: Northwest Women's Services; Pornography Education Center; Task Force on Prostitution and Pornography; Washington County Sexual Assault Center; and LaRaza Centro Legal, Inc., in *American Booksellers Association, Inc. et al. v. Hudnut et al.*, Seventh Circuit, Case 84-3147, date unknown, iv.
135. Ibid., viii.
136. Ibid., 2–4.
137. Ibid., 7–8.
138. Ibid., 13–14.
139. Ibid., 20.
140. Ibid., 26–27.
141. Brief of Linda Marchiano and the Estate of Dorothy Stratten Amici Curiae in Support of Appellant, *Hudnut et al. v. American Booksellers Association, Inc. et al.*, Seventh Circuit Court of Appeals, Case no. 84-3147, date unknown, 4–5.
142. Ibid., 16.
143. Ibid., 17.
144. Ibid., 21–22.
145. Ibid., 22–23.
146. Ibid., 24.
147. Ibid., 27, citing *Pittsburgh Press v. Pittsburgh Human Rights Commission*, 413 U.S. 376 (1973).
148. Ibid., 29; quoting *Kovacs v. Cooper*, 336 U.S. 77 (1949); citing *Los Angeles v. Taxpayers for Vincent*, 104 S. Ct. 2118 (1984).
149. Ibid.

150. Ibid., 30, quoting *New York v. Ferber*, 458 U.S. 747,761 (1982).
151. Ibid., 31.
152. Ibid., 31–32.
153. Ibid., 34; *Brown v. Board of Education*, 347 U.S. 483, 494 (1954).
154. Ibid., 33.
155. Ibid.
156. Brief Amicus Curiae of Andrea Dworkin, *American Booksellers Association, Inc. et al. v. Hudnut et al.*, Seventh Circuit Court of Appeals, Case No. 84-3147, 1–4.
157. Ibid., 4–5.
158. Ibid., 5–6.
159. Ibid., 9.
160. Ibid., 13.
161. Ibid., 13–14.
162. Ibid., 15, 17.
163. Brief of Minneapolis City Council Member Charlee Hoyt et al., Amicus Curiae in Support of Appellant, *American Booksellers Association, Inc. et al. v. Hudnut et al.*, Seventh Circuit Court of Appeals, Case No. 84-3147, 3.
164. Ibid., 13.
165. Ibid.
166. Ibid., 20.
167. Ibid., 24.
168. Ibid., 26, quoting *Plessy v. Ferguson*, 163 U.S. 537, 551, (1896).
169. Ibid., 27–31.
170. Amicus Curiae Brief of the Neighborhood Pornography Task of Minneapolis, *American Booksellers Association, Inc., et al. v. Hudnut, et al.*, Seventh Circuit Court Of Appeals, Case No. 84-3147, date unknown, 1.
171. Ibid., 17–18.
172. Ibid., 19.
173. Brief of Plaintiffs–Appellees, *American Booksellers Association Inc. et al. v. Hudnut et al.*, Seventh Circuit Court of Appeals, Case No. 84-3147, 3.
174. Ibid., 8.
175. Ibid., 11, citing *Secretary of State of Maryland v. Munson*, 81 L. Ed. 2d 786, 796 (1984).
176. Ibid., 17, 371 U.S. 415 (1963).
177. Ibid., 20.
178. Ibid., 25, citing *Roberts v. U.S. Jaycees*, 82 L. Ed. 2d 462,475 (1984).
179. Ibid., 26–27 citing *Young v. American Mini-Theatres Inc.*, 427 U.S. 50 (1976); *FCC v. Pacifica Foundation*, 438 U.S. 726 (1976); *Near Minnesota*, 283 U.S. 697, 718 (1931); *Beauharnais v. Illinois*, 343 U.S. 250 (1952).
180. Ibid., 34; *DeFilippo v. National Broadcasting Co., Inc.*, 446 A. 2d 1036 (R.I. 1982).
181. Ibid., 41, quoting *Southeastern Promotions Limited*, 560.
182. Brief Amici Curiae of Feminist Anti-Censorship Task Force et al., *American Booksellers Association, Inc. et al. v. Hudnut et al.*, Seventh Circuit Court of Appeals, Case No. 84-3147, April 8, 1985, xii.

183. Ibid.

184. Ibid., 3.

185. Ibid.

186. Ibid., 4.

187. Ibid., 5, quoting 63 AM JUR. 2d Prostitution s.1 (1971).

188. Ibid., 6.

189. Ibid., 8.

190. Ibid., 18.

191. Ibid.; *Brandenburg v. Ohio*, 395 U.S. 444 (1969); *Collin v. Smith*, 578 F. 2d 1197 (7th Cir.), *cert. denied*, 439 U.S. 916 (1978).

192. Ibid., 19, quoting Edward Donnerstein in a study placed before the court as Exhibit T.

193. Ibid., 22, citing *Collin;*

194. Ibid., 26.

195. Ibid., 28.

196. Ibid., 30, citing *Kingsley Corp. v. Regents*, 360 U.S. 684 (1959).

197. Ibid., 31–32.

198. Ibid., 33.

199. Ibid., 34.

200. Ibid., 37.

201. Ibid., 39.

202. Ibid., 41–42, citing *Mississippi University v. Hogan*, 458 U.S. 718, 724-25 (1982).

203. Ibid., 48.

204. Ibid., 50.

205. "Indianapolis Anti-Pornography Ordinance Challenged," *Newsletter on Intellectual Freedom*, November 1984, 176–78, 176.

206. Ibid., 176.

207. Ibid., 177.

208. Ibid.

209. Ibid., 178.

210. From correspondence, court documents and data from Organizing Against Pornography (Minneapolis, Minnesota) to the authors, May 18, 1989.

11 OTHER WAYS OF REGULATING PORNOGRAPHY THROUGH LAW

This chapter details ways of regulating pornography by use of civil or criminal laws. Obscenity, child pornography, and civil rights legislation are covered in other chapters. Pornography also can be regulated through zoning; nuisance laws; display to minors laws; indecency laws concerning television, radio, and cable television; and laws that govern telephone communication. Civil lawsuits are sometimes possible for libel, group libel, invasion of privacy, intentional infliction of emotional distress, and other torts. This chapter also discusses the First Amendment and how it relates to regulating pornography.

THE FIRST AMENDMENT—GENERALLY

As a general rule, "a direct and substantial limitation on protected activity cannot be sustained unless it serves a sufficiently strong, subordinating interest that the [government] is entitled to protect" (*Village of Schaumburg* v. *Citizens for a Better Environment*).[1] However, reasonable time, place, and manner restrictions are allowed if they are content neutral and necessary to advance a significant and legitimate state interest (*Members of City Council* v. *Taxpayers for Vincent*).[2] Such regulations should be narrowly tailored to serve the specific governmental interest and leave open "ample alternative channels for communication of the information" (*Clark* v. *Community for Creative Non-Violence*).[3] See also *Virginia State Board of Pharmacy* v. *Virginia Citizens Consumer Council, Inc.*[4] The court in *Vincent* upheld a law that prohibited the posting of signs (including political signs) on public property. While solicitation is protected by the First Amendment, reasonable time, place, and manner restrictions are permitted (*Heffron* v. *International Society for Krishna Consciousness, Inc.*).[5] Courts look at whether the type of expression is incompatible with the normal activity of a particular place and time (*Grayned* v. *City of Rockford*).[6]

The reader is cautioned that the law of the First Amendment is riddled with contradictions, confusion, frequent changes in whether or not certain speech is protected, and changes in which regulations of speech are allowable. In many cases, it is difficult to predict what the outcome will be when First Amendment questions are allegedly involved. The reader is cautioned to carefully research those First Amendment exceptions or issues that appear to relate to a particular situation.

This chapter contains only a short overview of First Amendment law and should not be used as a comprehensive source of information for such cases. Supreme Court interpretations of the First Amendment change frequently. Therefore, information and cases cited in this book should be updated by the reader before using them in legal arguments.

Political expression is at the core of First Amendment freedoms (*Williams* v. *Rhodes*).[7] Nonpolitical expression, such as commercial speech, sometimes receives less protection. Yet, in *Buckley* v. *Valeo*, limits on individual contributions to political campaigns, a limited restriction on freedom of association, were allowed based on the governmental interest in preventing corruption and the appearance of corruption. However, that same court found those justifications to be inadequate to support a ceiling on independent expenditures. It also overturned limits on expenditures by candidates and their families on the ground that it is important that candidates have an unobstructed chance to present their views. In the same case, the court held that limits on overall campaign expenditures were unconstitutional but stated that Congress could condition acceptance of public financing on expenditure limits.[8]

Buckley illustrates the unpredictability and lack of consistent principles in First Amendment cases. Nonetheless, because the First Amendment is the primary defense raised by pornographers against pornography regulation, it is important for antipornography advocates to understand this aspect of constitutional law.

OTHER CONSTITUTIONAL RIGHTS

On occasion, the Supreme Court has found that First Amendment protections must be sacrificed to guarantee the use of other constitutional rights. For example, in *Pittsburgh Press Co.* v. *Pittsburgh Commission on Human Relations,* the court held that a human rights commission order that prohibited "placement in sex-designated columns of advertisements for nonexempt job opportunities," did not infringe on the First Amendment rights of Pittsburgh Press. The newspaper had a practice of running help wanted ads under columns titled "Male Help Wanted" and "Female Help Wanted" before October 1969 and "Jobs—Male Interest" and "Jobs—Female Interest" after that time.

Pittsburgh Press argued that the order violated the First Amendment by restricting its editorial judgment. (The newspaper also claimed that the law violated due process because there was no rational connection between "sex-designated column headings and sex discrimination in employment." The court rejected that claim, ruling that common sense and evidence in the record showed that the two are connected.) There was no claim that the law was passed with a purpose of curbing the press, that it threatened the financial viability of the newspaper, or that it significantly impaired its ability to publish.

It was also important to the court that the advertisements at issue were "classic examples of commercial speech," which it said receives less First Amendment protection than other forms of speech. The court noted that even the exercise of editorial judgment does not "necessarily strip commercial advertising of its commercial character." The court also emphasized that the speech at issue was illegal commercial activity under the ordinance. The court compared it to the idea that a newspaper could be forbidden to publish an ad proposing a sale of narcotics or soliciting prostitutes. The court said:

> Any First Amendment interest which might be served by advertising an ordinary commercial proposal and which might arguably outweigh the governmental interest supporting the regulation is altogether absent when the commercial activity itself is illegal and the restriction on advertising is incidental to a valid limitation on economic activity.[9]

The order, the court said, did not endanger "arguably" protected speech. Nothing would prevent the newspaper from communicating advertisements that commented on the propriety of sex preferences in employment or on the law or commission practices.

Another case in which equal protection rights were found to outweigh First Amendment rights was *Bob Jones University* v. *United States.* That case involved the free exercise clause (religious freedom) of the First Amendment. The government interest at issue was the compelling, "fundamental, overriding" interest in ending racial discrimination in education. The court found that the governmental interest "substantially outweighs whatever burden denial of tax benefits places on petitioners' exercise of their religious beliefs."[10]

The court emphasized in *California Motor Transport Co.* v. *Trucking Unlimited* that First Amendment freedoms are not immune from regulation when they are used "as an integral part of conduct which violates a valid statute."[11] *Roth* v. *United States* stated: "All ideas having even the slightest redeeming social importance . . . have the full protection of the guarantees [of free speech and press] unless excludable because they encroach upon the limited area of more important interests."[12]

Under *Pittsburgh Press* and *Roberts* v. *United States Jaycees,* the compelling state interest in forbidding practices that foster sex discrimination was found to outweigh First Amendment rights. *Roberts* held that requiring that women be allowed to be members of the Jaycees did not interfere with freedom of association rights. In *Roberts,* it was important that the statute was not aimed at suppressing speech, did not prohibit or protect activity based on viewpoint, and could not achieve its purpose through significantly less restrictive means.[13]

Caryn Jacobs believes that there are options to control pornography without regulating speech. These include enforcing laws against slavery, rape, prostitution, and statutory rape. In addition, building code regulations, health laws, and fair labor laws should be enforced. These types of attacks on pornography will be less effective than a content-based attack because of the underground nature of pornography's production, Jacobs says.[14]

According to Jacobs, criminal sanctions only deter the small pornographer because the pornography is not taken off the streets and corporations that produce or distribute pornography do not get jail terms.[15]

Tort suits by models who were raped are another possible legal attack on pornography. Perhaps rapes of the throat caused by *Deep Throat* would reach the level of "incitement" needed to enable a victim to recover damages, Jacobs suggests. Another option would be a libel suit by an individual woman against an individual pornographer. A heavy tax could be levied on pornographic profits aimed at reducing profits, Jacobs says. However, she points out, this would give the government a vested financial interest in continued expansion of pornographic businesses and further their "public legitimization." A corrective fund could be created with money collected from pornographers' violations of laws to help pornography victims.[16]

Valerie Hamm raises the issue of whether violent pornography should be recognized as a new category of unprotected speech.[17] (Remember that the United States has a history of denying rights to groups of citizens. For example, at one time women were not allowed to vote or to practice law.)

SPEECH CONTENT REGULATION

As Geoffrey R. Stone notes, one of the major principles of the First Amendment is that "government may not excise specific viewpoints from public debate."[18] The U.S. Supreme Court said in *Police Department of Chicago* v. *Mosely* that the government cannot prohibit something on the basis of the content of the expression. *Mosely* involved an ordinance that allowed peaceful picketing relating to a school's labor–management dispute but prohibited all other picketing. (See also *Carey* v. *Brown* and *Schneider* v. *State*.) This concept is also known as viewpoint discrimination.[19]

The court has not followed the extreme principal of absolute content neutrality, however. In *Lehman* v. *City of Shaker Heights*, it failed to overturn a law prohibiting political advertising but not other advertising in a publicly owned bus.[20] In *Young* v. *American Mini Theatres, Inc.*, a zoning ordinance that prohibited the clustering of theaters showing pornographic movies but permitted the clustering of theaters showing movies with other content was upheld.[21] And in *FCC* v. *Pacifica Foundation*, regulations that prohibited the broadcast, during certain time periods, of sexually explicit speech but did not prohibit broadcast of other speech were upheld.[22]

These confusing and contrasting rulings by the Supreme Court make it impossible to predict when speech can be restricted on the basis of content and when it cannot. Numerous other court rulings in this area are listed in *First National Bank of Boston* v. *Bellotti*.[23]

(We point out that laws restricting certain types of speech, such as child pornography, obscenity, and commercial speech, could, under the principle of content discrimination, be considered to be restrictions based on content. We must, therefore, conclude that the court overturns laws based on speech content only when its members, based on personal biases, do not want a certain type of speech restricted and content discrimination becomes a convenient justification for voiding such laws. This, for example, is what we conclude happened in the civil rights ordinance case, *American Booksellers Association* v. *Hudnut*, in which the ordinance was invalidated because it discriminated on the basis of viewpoint.[24] Sunstein points out that the *Hudnut* court felt that the civil rights law singled out a particular viewpoint for suppression—a view of male–female relationships as expressed in pornography.[25] The claim that civil rights laws are aimed at harms from pornography rather than at a viewpoint was rejected by the court.

Our argument that court decisions concerning viewpoint discrimination are based on the biased views of individual justices or judges for or against restricting certain types of speech, rather than on a concrete and predictable constitutional principle is further supported by the fact that during the same week the Supreme Court summarily affirmed the *Hudnut* case, it issued a decision in *City of Renton* v. *Playtime Theatres, Inc.* in which it said that a statute prohibiting the showing of sexually explicit films within a specified distance of certain zones or dwellings was content neutral.[26] As Sunstein explains, the court said that the law was aimed at effects on neighborhoods and property values, not at the speech message. Why, then, did the court rule that the civil rights law was aimed at sex discrimination and physical abuse of women and children rather than at speech content?

As Sunstein notes, regulations prohibiting employers from speaking unfavorably about unionization effects before a union election if such speech is threatening, prohibitions of fighting words, and regulations of cigarette and casino advertisements are all viewpoint based, but these have been upheld by the U.S. Supreme Court. Why was pornography, as defined in the civil rights ordinance, singled out for differential treatment by the courts? According to Sunstein, "Whether a classification is viewpoint-based thus ultimately turns on the viewpoint of the decisionmaker." He suggests that obscenity law is considered "objective" because it prohibits a type of speech that most of society believes should be regulated. The pornography law, he says, prohibits a type of speech that is considered "subjective" because it deals with values that are less widely accepted and favors protecting the "relatively powerless."[27]

For the alternative view, that civil rights legislation is unconstitutional viewpoint discrimination, see Stone.[28]

EXCEPTIONS TO THE FIRST AMENDMENT

Obscenity

The obscenity exemption from the First Amendment is described at length in chapter 9. It addresses a different state interest than the civil rights approach and aims to prevent a different harm. While obscenity, defined in terms of offensiveness and prurience, seeks to preserve the social and moral order, civil rights antipornography law focuses on harms caused by the material.

Clear and Present Danger

The U.S. Supreme Court has denied constitutional protection under the First Amendment to speech that is a "clear and present danger of imminent lawless action."[29] Michael Gershel believes that pornography, because it contributes to violence against women, "raises a spectre of violence not associated with protected speech." He concludes that pornography does not meet the *imminent* requirement of the clear and present danger test; however, because it does create a serious and pervasive danger to women, a similar exception to the First Amendment should be made.[30]

Sunstein states that, after *Brandenburg,* speech cannot be "regulated because of the harm it produces unless it is shown that the speech is directed to produce harm that is both imminent and extremely likely to occur." Under *Hess,* one must connect particular harms to particular speech, for it is not enough to link a class of harm with a class of speech.[31]

Randall Tigue notes that *Terminello* v. *City of Chicago* held that speech " 'may indeed serve its high purpose when it induces a condition of unrest, creates dissatisfaction . . . or even stirs people to anger.' " He says that the civil rights ordinance could not meet the clear and present danger requirements.[32]

Hamm also doubts that pornography as defined in the ordinance would fall into the clear and present danger category of unprotected speech even if there is a causal connection between some pornography and violence against women. She states that while some pornography advocates the perpetration of crime, it lacks the immediacy element required by *Brandenburg,* even though pornography is arguably likely to incite the action advocated.[33]

James Branit argues that the depiction of sex crimes is not the same as advocating such crimes and that there is no evidence that pornography causes *imminent* lawless conduct; rather, it causes more subtle harm, such as attitude changes.[34]

In *Landmark Communications, Inc.* v. *Virginia,* the issue was whether a state could subject persons, including newspapers, to criminal sanctions for disclosing information about proceedings before a judicial review commission authorized to hear complaints about judicial misconduct when such proceedings are declared confidential by statute and the state constitution. The court said that the state could not make such conduct criminal.

The *Landmark* court questioned the relevancy of the clear and present danger test applied by the lower court. That test, it said, requires a court to "make its own inquiry into the imminence and magnitude of the danger said to flow from the particular utterance and then to balance the character of the evil, as well as its likelihood, against the need for free and unfettered expression."[35] The court should have gone behind the legislative decision and looked at the utterance at issue and the circumstances of its publication " 'to determine to what extent the substantive evil of unfair administration of justice was a likely consequence, and whether the degree of likelihood was sufficient to justify [subsequent] punishment' " (*Bridges* v. *California*).[36]

The court has rejected the claim that out-of-court comments about pending grand jury investigations or cases are a clear and present danger to the administration of justice (*Bridges* v. *California; Pennekamp* v. *Florida; Craig* v. *Harney; Wood* v. *Geor-*

gia).[37] These cases have a working principle " 'that the substantive evil must be extremely serious and the degree of imminence extremely high before utterances can be punished.' "[38] And they require that solid evidence be presented to meet the imminence: " 'The danger must not be remote or even probable; it must immediately imperil.' "[39]

In *Landmark,* although there was some risk of injury to the judge under scrutiny (of premature disclosure) and to the operation of the review commission, the risk fell "far short" of the clear and present danger requirements. Much of the risk could have been eliminated by careful internal procedures to protect confidentiality. In fact, the "danger" in this case was actually a type of activity the framers of the Constitution envisioned in proposing the First Amendment, the court said.

The graveness of the offense of incitement to riot is that incitement goes beyond argument or persuasion. In such cases, the speaker seeks to "arouse" one group against another and succeeds to the point where a "clear danger of disorder [is] . . . threatened." In *Feiner* v. *New York,* the defendant was found guilty of disorderly conduct after giving a speech on a street corner in which he "gave the impression that he was endeavoring to arouse the Negro people against the whites, urging that they rise up in arms and fight for equal rights." Because the court found that some of the audience seemed to be favoring Feiner's arguments, a clear danger of disorder was threatened.[40] (We pose this question: If the *Feiner* case was an incitement to riot, why is it not incitement to riot to constantly bombard American society with pornographic propaganda that endeavors to arouse males to commit acts of sexual violence and abuse against females?)

Fighting Words

The court held in *Chaplinsky* v. *New Hampshire* that states may prohibit the utterance of "fighting words." This concept permits regulation of communication that creates a threat of imminent violence. The *Chaplinsky* court said that "such utterances are no essential part of any exposition of ideas, and are of such slight social value as a step to truth that any benefit that may be derived from them is clearly outweighed by the social interest in order and morality."[41]

However, as Hamm notes, under *Chaplinsky,* in order to qualify for the fighting words exception to the First Amendment, words must be addressed to a person in a public place, not to a third person who

is not present. She concludes that while pornography might provoke a woman to violence, the woman so provoked could not regard pornography as a direct personal insult and thereby come within the fighting words criteria.[42]

Child Pornography

Under the 1982 case of *New York* v. *Ferber,* child pornography (visual depictions of children engaged in sexually explicit acts) can be made illegal without having to meet the *Miller* obscenity test. The court found a compelling state interest in "safeguarding the physical and psychological well-being of a minor" and balanced that against the minimal interest in permitting sexual performances by minors. The *Ferber* court found that those involved in the production of pornography may suffer harm, and that child pornography is related to the sexual abuse of children because (1) it is a permanent record of the child's participation in sex acts that could harm him or her in the future, and (2) the actual production of the pornography requires the sexual exploitation of children.[43]

Supporters of the civil rights approach to pornography have argued that the same reasoning used in *Ferber* applies to portrayals of adult women in pornography. Gershel states that adult women, like children, may be harmed by the knowledge that "people are buying, selling, and viewing displays of their bodies." And, he says, women who have been coerced or forced into pornography production have been exploited. He concludes that the pornographic traffic in women's bodies is sexual exploitation and is a form of harm.[44]

Jacobs believes that the harm and coercion in adult pornography should be presumed (as it has been in child pornography) because of the clandestine nature of the industry. She provides an excellent summary of the *Ferber* decision, breaking down the court's reasoning into five points:

1. The court acknowledged that preventing the sexual exploitation of children is a governmental interest of "surpassing importance." It also recognized that the state has a special interest in protecting the " 'physical and psychological well-being of a minor.' " It found the *Miller* obscenity standards to be unrelated to the issue of whether a child has been harmed in the production of pornography.

2. The court found the distribution of child pornography to be intrinsically related to the sexual abuse of children. The importance of controlling

child sexual abuse, combined with the clandestine nature of its production, justified regulating its distribution.

3. The court found the advertising and selling of child pornography to be an integral part of its production because it provides the incentive for the production. The First Amendment does not extend to such speech, which is part of the violation of valid criminal statutes.

4. The court found the value of commercial photographic depictions of children engaged in sex or live performances of such conduct to be " 'exceedingly modest, if not *de minimis.*' "

5. This situation was found to be consistent with prior First Amendment cases because content-based classifications of speech were sometimes regulated when the evils of the speech " 'overwhelmingly outweigh[ed]' " the expressive interests involved.[45]

Low Value Speech

According to Sunstein, if speech qualifies as low value, it may be regulated with a far less powerful demonstration of harm. Sunstein suggests that commercial speech, labor speech, and group libel may fit this category. The issue of low value depends on the speaker's purpose and how he or she communicates the message. Obscenity, for example, need not be subjected to the low value test because, according to the court, it is not speech. Sunstein lists four factors in deciding whether speech qualifies as low value:

> First, the speech must be far afield from the central concern of the first amendment, which, broadly speaking, is effective popular control of public affairs. . . . Second, a distinction is drawn between cognitive and noncognitive aspects of speech. Speech that has purely noncognitive appeal will be entitled to less constitutional protection. Third, the purpose of the speaker is relevant: if the speaker is seeking to communicate a message, he will be treated more favorably than if he is not. Fourth, the various classes of low-value speech reflect judgments that in certain areas, government is unlikely to be acting for constitutionally impermissible reasons or producing constitutionally troublesome harms.[46]

Sunstein explains the difference between cognitive and noncognitive speech. Whereas cognitive speech is intended to communicate a substantive message, noncognitive speech is not. Thus, pornography is noncognitive speech because it is intended primarily as a sex aid.[47]

Commercial Speech

The civil rights ordinance has nothing to do with proposing a commercial transaction, and thus it cannot come under the cases that reason that commercial speech has less First Amendment protection than other speech, Tigue argues. Unlike the discriminatory advertisement prohibited in *Pittsburgh Press*, pornography deals "solely with the advocacy of ideas," while the ad proposed an illegal commercial activity.[48] (Note that the court in *Pittsburgh Press* explained that not all advertisements are commercial speech. For example, it cited *New York Times Company* v. *Sullivan*, which found that an advertisement criticizing police action toward civil rights movement members was a political ad entitled to the same degree of protection as ordinary speech.[49]) The meaning of commercial speech established by the U.S. Supreme Court is that speech that does no more than propose a commercial transaction. An advertisement that offered the sale of admission to a submarine is an example of this (*Valentine v. Christensen*).[50]

At the heart of the court's distinction between commercial speech and other speech is a value judgment that commercial speech does not deal with social policies or issues of public interest and concern. Thus, it is of less value or importance and is not the type of speech the First Amendment was written to protect. In *Pittsburgh Press*, the court held that any First Amendment interest that might be met by an ordinary commercial ad that might outweigh the governmental interest in the regulation at issue is absent when "the commercial activity itself is illegal and the restriction on advertising is incidental to a valid limitation on economic activity."[51]

When commercial speech is untruthful, deceptive, or misleading, government can deal with the problem without violating First Amendment rights.[52] If commercial speech also addresses issues of public concern, it can enjoy complete protection.[53]

Commercial speech that is not misleading or fraudulent and concerns a lawful activity receives limited First Amendment protection. After determining that the First Amendment applies to the type of commercial speech at issue, a three-part test is applied. First, the speech may be restricted only if the governmental interest in doing so is substantial. Second, the restrictions used must directly advance the government's asserted interest. Third, the restrictions must be no more extensive than necessary to serve the interest.[54] For an example of how the test was applied to restrictions on advertising of gambling casinos in Puerto Rico, see *Posadas De Puerto Rico Association* v. *Tourism Co.*[55]

Regulating Speech to Enhance Others' Speech

In *Buckley* v. *Valeo,* the concept that government can restrict some people's speech in order to enhance the voice of others was rejected.[56] This conflicts with the finding in *Red Lion Broadcasting Co.* v. *FCC,* which upheld the FCC fairness doctrine. The fairness doctrine, which applies only to broadcast media, ensures fair coverage of public issues for all sides by requiring all viewpoints to be presented.[57]

Sunstein believes that the court's rejection of attempts to promote First Amendment values by regulating powerful private actors stems from three factors:

1. The belief that private power disparities do not significantly interfere with "a well-functioning system of free expression"

2. The belief that if we allow government to intervene on behalf of groups labeled powerless, it will be impossible to draw lines, and government would be allowed to act for impermissible reasons

3. The view that even if some people who have disproportionate power are not permitted to speak, "a genuine impairment of freedom results, even if that impairment is made in the interest of equality"

Sunstein calls it "fanciful" to claim that disparities in private power do not undermine free expression. He suggests that, in general, government should not be allowed to restrict one person's speech to ensure another's but says that there may be an exception to this principle in certain contexts, including that of pornography.[58]

ZONING

Some communities in the United States use zoning laws to concentrate adult entertainment businesses (pornography outlets) in specified areas. Others use zoning to prevent such outlets from locating next to each other by use of requirements of a minimum distance between pornographic businesses. Such outlets are often banned from residential neighborhoods.

The practice of zoning pornographic businesses derives from the belief that such outlets are detrimental to the neighborhoods in which they are located. The harms cited include creation of blight, deterioration of property values, harming existing traditional businesses by decreasing their patronage, attracting crime, and making people afraid to walk neighborhood streets. Several studies of the harms of pornography to neighborhoods are detailed in chapter 5.

While private property use and ownership in the United States is protected by the Fifth and Fourteenth amendments, government has the power to curtail certain uses that may be detrimental to the public in order to protect that same enjoyment of property rights. In *Village of Euclid* v. *Ambler Realty Co.,* the court held that zoning laws must be justified under some aspect of the police power " 'asserted for the public welfare.' " The reasonableness of zoning laws results from a comprehensive plan adopted by the local government. Failure to detail reasons for a particular restriction could result in zoning laws being declared unconstitutional as clearly arbitrary and unreasonable and having " 'no substantial relation to the public health, safety, morals, or general welfare.' " When such reasonable restrictions are adopted, claims that private property is being taken without compensation (by restricting its use) fail.[59]

Yet, although "municipalities are granted broad zoning power to enhance the quality of life in their communities," such laws must be carefully scrutinized if they infringe on constitutional rights.[60] For example, in *Schad* v. *Borough of Mount Ephraim,* the court said, "When a zoning law infringes upon a protected liberty, it must be narrowly drawn and must further a sufficiently substantial government interest."[61]

The frequently cited pornography zoning case, *Young* v. *American Mini Theatres,* involved a Detroit ordinance that prohibited an adult facility from locating less than one thousand feet from any two other adult facilities. The reason given by the city for passing the law was that concentration of such businesses downgraded neighborhoods. Two adult theaters challenged the law as an unconstitutional prior restraint of free speech and a violation of equal protection. The Supreme Court said that the law did not necessarily restrict access to adult centers and thus did not suppress protected speech. It left plenty of open lots in Detroit where such outlets could locate. The court agreed that concentration of pornographic centers " 'cause the area to deteriorate and become a focus of crime.' "

The *Young* court applied a two-part test: First,

there must be a reason for enacting the law. Second, it must be shown that the law is narrowly drawn to " 'infringe upon the least amount of protected speech.' " Justice Powell, in a concurring opinion, said that the law had to further an important or substantial governmental interest unrelated to the suppression of free expression and that the First Amendment restriction must be no greater than essential to further that interest.[62]

Moretti states that courts would not allow zoning laws that resulted in a blanket ban of pornographic entertainment centers. He uses the example of *Alexander* v. *City of Minneapolis*, which struck down a zoning law that did not provide for other economically viable sites where porno centers could locate. This is called the " 'commercial viability' " factor.[63]

It should be emphasized that zoning laws restrict the time, place, and manner of operation of pornography stores. They do not ban such outlets. Thus, some antipornography groups have claimed that zoning laws are not useful, noting that all they really do is determine which neighborhoods will be afflicted with the blight caused by such stores. This, some claim, results in such centers being located in neighborhoods in which poor and minority citizens live and kept out of wealthier white areas.

Importantly, zoning definitions of adult entertainment centers are not limited to *Miller* obscenity guidelines. In zoning, it is the "adult" nature of the business that defines it, not whether or not its merchandise is obscene. For example, "adult" establishments are those used to present material characterized by an emphasis on matter relating to "specified sexual activities" or "specified anatomical areas." In *Young*, *specified sexual activities* were defined as follows: " '(1) human genitals in a state of sexual stimulation or arousal; (2) acts of human masturbation, sexual intercourse, or sodomy; (3) fondling or other erotic touching of human genitals, pubic region, buttock, or female breast.' " *Specified anatomical areas* were defined this way: " '(1) less than completely and opaquely covered: (a) human genitals, pubic region, (b) buttock, and (c) female breast below a point immediately above the top of the areola; and (2) human male genitals in a discernibly turgid state, even if completely and opaquely covered.' "[64] These broader definitions are important because zoning authorities need not meet the difficult, time-consuming *Miller* test.

According to W.G. Roesler, the four-part test of *United States* v. *O'Brien* must be met by authorities who use zoning to combat pornography:

"(1) is the regulation within the constitutional power of government? (2) does it further an important or substantial government interest? (3) is this interest unrelated to suppression of free expression? and (4) is the restriction on First Amendment freedoms no greater than is essential to the furtherance of that interest?"[65]

In contrast, Ronald M. Stein says that the court in *City of Renton* v. *Playtime Theatres, Inc.* departed from its reliance on the *O'Brien* test and adopted a time, place, and manner analysis. Both *O'Brien* and *Schad* v. *Borough of Mount Ephraim* required adult business location ordinances to be analyzed under the "strict scrutiny" standard, which set forth a presumption of constitutional invalidity that the government had to overcome. Now, Stein says, such laws will be analyzed under the "rational basis" standard, which raises a presumption of validity.[66]

Renton approved a zoning ordinance that limited adult outlets to various locations in the community. While the community's interest in regulating adult businesses must be unrelated to suppressing free expression, it can be related to "the secondary effects of the adult businesses on surrounding neighborhoods," Stein says. Trying to " 'preserve the quality of urban life' serves this substantial governmental interest," the court found. Importantly, *Renton* held that a community may rely upon nearby community experiences and need not do its own studies in determining what the secondary effects are.[67]

Stein notes that during the period between *Young* and *Renton*, courts frequently invalidated antipornography zoning ordinances by applying the *O'Brien* rules. For example, in *Basiardanes* v. *City of Galveston*, the court held that the law was underinclusive because it did not cover other blighting influences such as pool halls and bars. In *Purple Onion* v. *Jackson*, the court found that the lack of alternative sites for pornographic outlets was a greater restriction on First Amendment rights than was needed to further the stated governmental interest.[68]

According to Stein, under the time, place, and manner analysis that is now the law under *Renton*, the court will look to the legislative record for two reasons: (1) to determine whether there are adequate findings to support the decision to regulate, and (2) to determine whether adequate evidence exists to support the findings. Yet, Stein cautions, *Renton* should not be viewed as giving communities carte blanche to eliminate pornographic businesses from their jurisdictions. Under the time, place, and manner analysis, a regulation is valid unless the plaintiff can show that the community passed the law for the express purpose of restraining speech based on its content. In *Renton*, the court said that the law was not aimed at the film content but at the secondary effects of the theaters on surrounding neighborhoods. The court emphasized that it would not strike down an otherwise valid law because of an alleged " 'illicit legislative motive.' "[69]

Under the *Renton* decision, municipalities need not wait until an adult entertainment center opens within their boundaries before deciding that such places can cause "secondary effects."

In *Renton*, only adult theatres were covered by the law. The Playtime Theatres argued that the law was underinclusive for failing to regulate other adult businesses that were likely to produce similar secondary effects. The court rejected that argument. The two dissenting justices agreed with Playtime.

Stein lists several guidelines for using zoning as a tool to regulate adult businesses after Renton:

1. Because pornography is protected by the First Amendment, any regulation of adult businesses must be backed up by an adequate record of the legislative meeting. (We dispute that pornography is protected by the First Amendment.)

2. Any law regulating adult businesses through zoning will be analyzed as a type of time, place, and manner regulation. Therefore, the record must contain evidence that:

    a. The ordinance's purpose was content neutral.

    b. The law was aimed at the secondary effects of the pornographic outlets on the community rather than at the content of adult films.

    c. The law "serves a substantial governmental interest and does not unreasonably limit alternative avenues of communication."

3. While there must be evidence in the record that adult businesses cause secondary effects such as loss of property value, the community need not show that those businesses present in it cause those effects. The experience and data of other communities can be used.

4. Citizens testifying at a hearing against adult businesses on the basis of content will not cause the law to be invalid, as long as the record shows that the predominant intent of the community was to eliminate secondary effects of such businesses. If such can be shown, the court will not overturn the law on the basis of an alleged illicit motive or intent.

5. Even if a city uses another city's study to prove harmful secondary effects, the city need not use the same remedy as the other city to deal with those effects.

6. The evidence must show that alternative "avenues of communication" are available to adult businesses.[70]

According to *Renton*, however, the First Amendment does not require that " 'speech-related businesses . . . be able to obtain sites at bargain prices.' " The author of an article on *Renton* argues that limiting adult theaters to 520 acres forced them to conduct business under severe restrictions. The article disagrees with the court's statement that the ordinance was consistent with its definitions of "content-neutral" regulations. It argues that the law was content based because it treated adult theaters differently than all others based on the content of the films exhibited. The author states that a majority of the Supreme Court now supports the idea that the government may rank speech "by the perceived importance of its content."[71]

Charles H. Clarke has noted that *Renton* "allows towns and small cities to virtually deny access altogether."[72]

Cities have the constitutional power to zone and license businesses and to prohibit their location in certain areas. Zoning power is part of the municipality's police power to protect the welfare, health, safety, and morals of the community. The *Young* case found that, based on the views of real estate experts and urban planners, the location of several pornographic businesses in the same neighborhood adversely affects property values, attracts undesirable transients, causes crime (especially prostitution) to increase, and encourages businesses and residents to move. The preservation of neighborhoods is a compelling state interest, the court said.[73]

Yet it is not enough for the government interest to be the dislike and opposition of area property owners and residents.[74] The government interest claimed must be specific. Thus, "a zoning ordinance completely prohibiting one form of protected speech must be 'narrowly drawn to further a sufficiently substantial governmental interest' and the zoning authority must be prepared to *articulate* and *support* a reasoned and *significant* basis for its decision."[75]

When a zoning ordinance involving First Amendment issues does not meet *Young's* requirements of supported and articulated significant government interest and regulates and attempts to ban adult uses, the law must be tested under the stricter *Schad* standard. That test makes the strictness of the standard of review proportional to the right allegedly violated or threatened. While in *Young* the law at issue merely dispersed the adult theaters and did not affect the number of theaters, the *Schad* law would have completely prohibited nude dancing. Under *Schad*, the law must advance a significant governmental interest and accomplish such purpose without undue restraint of speech. The interest involved must be important and substantial in *Schad*-type cases.[76]

The denial of a license to a business on the ground that it had live nude dancing was held to be unconstitutional when it was shown that the denial was unreasonable, arbitrary, and capricious in *Trombetta* v. *Mayor and Commissioners of Atlantic City*. In that case, city officials conceded that land value studies had not been done, that there had been no increase in criminal activity, and that they knew of no unsanitary conditions created by the pornographers involved. In addition, they could not explain why their law permitted live nude dancing in restaurants only.[77]

(Upon reviewing the case law, we believe that the wisest advice seems to be to encourage localities that want to enact antipornography zoning laws to back up their legislation with empirical studies and testimony about the negative effects of the pornographic businesses on the neighborhoods. We suggest that use of similar studies from other municipalities may also be useful tools to justify enactment of such laws. In fact, in *Genusa* v. *Peoria*, the court held that a legislative body may rely on the findings and experience of other legislative bodies as a basis for enacting such zoning laws. Thus, specific adverse effects from the presence of adult theaters did not have to be demonstrated. In *Renton*, the U.S. Supreme Court adopted the *Genusa* view.[78])

As long as a rational relationship exists between the objectives of the ordinance and the methods used, the court cannot substitute its judgment for that of the legislative body concerning the methods used to deal with preservation of neighborhoods. In *Young*, the court concluded that Detroit had demonstrated a legitimate and compelling interest in preserving social, economic, and aesthetic neighborhood values. Zoning can be based on spiritual values and aesthetic values, the court has held.[79] Zoning also can lay out areas where youth and family values and quiet seclusion make a sanctuary.[80]

A wrongful motive or purpose for enacting a zoning law does not justify a court's restraint on the exercise of lawful power.[81] Courts are bound by the legislative purposes stated in the laws.[82] In *Schad*, the stated reasons for a total ban on nude dancing could not withstand judicial scrutiny: "Immediate residents need . . . Parking . . . Police Protection . . . Medical facilities." Those reasons were given *after* the law's adoption.[83]

Importantly, in *Young* the court held that the state could legitimately use the content of the materials as a basis for placing them in a different classification from other motion pictures—despite the First Amendment. Prior to *Young*, cases held that standards based on the content of protected expression were impermissible. Thus, the zoning of sexually explicit materials became an exception. *Young* also emphasized that " '[t]here is a less vital interest in the uninhibited expression of material (that is on the borderline between pornography and artistic expression) than in the free dissemination of ideas of social and political importance.' "[84] Although some have argued that such classifications violate the equal protection clause of the U.S. Constitution, such claims fail once speech is classified and the "class" at issue is treated equally.[85]

Young found that reasonable regulations based on the time, place, and manner of protected speech are permitted by the First Amendment when necessary to further "significant" government interests. Note that these rules apply to sexually explicit material that is not obscene.[86]

Zoning ordinances can be used to disperse or concentrate pornographic outlets. In *Young*, for example, it was not impermissible to require pornographic outlets to be 1,000 feet apart.[87] While some courts have upheld bans on locating motion picture theaters in residential districts or near schools, a law that prohibited a pornographic store within 500 feet of a church, school, or liquor establishment or within 250 feet of a residential area was held invalid because it had the effect of an almost complete ban.[88] A community may not delegate legislative authority to a church to veto a liquor license within 500 feet of its premises.[89]

It is important to note that the antipornography zoning laws do not affect the operation of existing pornographic centers, only the location of new ones.[90] As with other laws that affect First Amendment rights, zoning laws must be careful not to be vague or overbroad.

Laws that restrict businesses to having one adult use under one roof (known as "sex supermarket laws") are valid under the *Young* criteria even though they are not based on zoning.[91]

NUISANCE ABATEMENT

The *Obscenity Law Reporter* points out that "as a general rule, activities which offend public morals and decency may be abated as public nuisances . . . provided they are fairly within the terms of an existing statute . . . or can be identified as common law nuisances." Nuisance laws are based on interference with the interest of the community. They include interference with public morals—for example, public profanity, houses of prostitution, and indecent exhibitions. The state police power can be used to abate a nuisance.[92]

A statute that puts a temporary restraint on the removal of contents and requires records of transactions to be kept prior to a judicial determination of obscenity is unconstitutional.[93] And padlocking (closing a store) is found to be unconstitutional in most courts. For example, in *Universal Amusement Co. Inc.* v. *Vance*, the court held that a one-year closing law in obscenity cases was an impermissible prior restraint because it would enjoin future operation of a business that "disseminates presumptively First Amendment protected material." Films not judicially found obscene also would be banned under the law at issue in *Vance*. The court said:

> "(a) that the regulation of a communicative activity such as the exhibition of motion pictures must adhere to more narrowly drawn procedures than is necessary for the abatement of an ordinary nuisance, and, (b) that the burden of supporting an injunction against a future exhibition is even heavier than the burden of justifying the imposition of a criminal sanction for a past communication."[94]

Yet the *Obscenity Law Reporter* states that padlocking of a pornographic bookstore that has been declared a nuisance remains an unsettled legal question. See the *Obscenity Law Reporter* for cases pro and con.[95]

Jeffrey Trachtman strongly disagrees with the *Obscenity Law Reporter*, stating that "the padlock order is a prior restraint on presumptively protected speech, unjustified by any extraordinary and compelling state interest."[96] Trachtman argues that padlock injunctions against pornographic bookstores (which close a store for a specified amount of time, such as one year) do not pass constitutional scrutiny:

> First, padlock orders are prior restraints on protected speech. Second, such orders do not meet procedural requirements for the suppression of obscenity. Third, even if the padlock sanction is not a prior restraint, and is not subject to the same procedural standards as a prior restraint, its incidental impact on protected speech is nevertheless too great to withstand scrutiny under standards originally developed to evaluate the impact on protected speech of municipal zoning ordinances.[97]

Trachtman says he would apply the *O'Brien* test discussed earlier in this chapter under Zoning to nuisance cases related to pornography. He traces the history of public nuisances, including display and sale of obscene material, which was a common law crime, and notes that it covers activities that endanger the safety, health, property, or comfort of a considerable number of people, as well as activities that violate public morals. Today, most nuisance actions against obscenity are grounded in state statutes.[98]

The unconstitutionality of padlock orders is, in Trachtman's view, also based on their failure to meet the strict requirements established by the courts to cover situations involving prior restraint of speech. (See the prior restraint section later in this chapter.) Specifically, he says, the *Freedman* v. *Maryland* standards must be met. Under the *O'Brien* test, Trachtman explains, padlock orders need not be characterized as prior restraint but would, instead, be scrutinized for their potential impact on protected speech. The means, ends, and impact of state regulation on protected speech would be assessed. Under *O'Brien*, laws that had an incidental impact on protected speech would have to be within the power of government, serve a substantial state interest, be unrelated to suppressing expression, and be narrowly drawn to avoid unnecessary curtailment of the speech at issue.[99]

Importantly, Trachtman's conclusion that the *O'Brien* criteria are not met by padlock orders is based on his position that the state interests underlying regulation of obscenity are weak. He attacks the state interests used by governments in support of pornography regulation. For example, he states that the state interests in protecting children and nonconsenting adults from exposure can be narrowly served by limiting obscenity to adults-only stores with appropriate notices posted to warn nonconsenting adults. Thus, padlock orders are greater than necessary restrictions. He also concludes that zoning laws are less restrictive and better ways to serve the interest in protecting the urban environment.

Trachtman determines, without examining cases or research, that there is no proof that obscenity causes crime, so that claim cannot be a substantial state interest. Even in the especially compelling area of adult stores selling child pornography (which, Trachtman agrees, is harmful to children), under *O'Brien* the prevention of the sexual abuse of children would have to be accomplished through less restrictive means than padlock orders, for such orders could curtail protected speech containing no child pornography.[100]

(We strongly disagree with Trachtman's conclusions regarding state interests. We believe that state interests in regulating pornography *are* compelling and grounded in the harm to victims, neighborhoods, and morality.)

A recent decision by the U.S. Supreme Court, *Arcara* v. *Cloud Books, Inc.*, sheds some light on the nuisance issue. In *Arcara*, the question before the court was whether the First Amendment bars enforcement of a statute authorizing closure of a premises used as a place of lewdness and prostitution because the premises also were used as a pornographic bookstore. In this case, the bookstore was closed as a public nuisance under state public health law. The court concluded that bookselling in a place used for prostitution does not confer First Amendment coverage to defeat a valid statute. The court of appeals had held that the *O'Brien* test for permissible government regulation applied to this case because the closure order would also impose an "incidental" burden on the defendant's bookselling activities. However, the Supreme Court found a critical distinction between the *O'Brien* circumstances and this case, stating that "unlike the symbolic draft card burning in *O'Brien*, the sexual activity carried on in this case manifests absolutely no element of protected expression." *O'Brien* was found to be irrelevant to a law directed at imposing sanctions on nonexpressive activity (prostitution).[101]

Some of the *Arcara* court's comments could be used by antipornography advocates. The court said that the severity of the burden on the "protected bookselling activities" was "dubious at best, and is mitigated by the fact that respondents remain free to sell the same materials at another location." This argument, it emphasized, is "too much," "since every civil and criminal remedy imposes some conceivable burden on First Amendment protected activities." The court gave examples: One liable for a civil damage award has less money to spend on political campaigns; a prisoner loses the right to speak in public places. The court said that the First Amendment was not implicated in the *Arcara* case.[102]

In *KMA, Inc.* v. *Newport News*, de facto closure of a pornography store resulted after the owner's conviction for knowingly permitting use of the building for presenting a pornographic performance. When the owner failed to pay the fine, the sheriff repossessed all personal property on the premises to satisfy the judgment.[103]

PRIOR RESTRAINT

In the antipornography arena, the two most common regulations influenced by the U.S. Supreme Court's First Amendment doctrine of prior restraint are the nuisance and film review board laws. The doctrine of prior restraint provides that no law may prevent publication or speech, but civil or criminal actions may result from that communication.[104] Although prior restraint is not absolutely prohibited, the most exigent circumstances must exist for its justification.[105] Frederick Schauer questions the prior restraint doctrine, noting that if the "evil" to be guarded against is suppression of constitutionally protected speech, prison terms or heavy fines may have a more chilling effect, "resulting in self-censorship," than procedures that determine legality without exposure to criminal sanctions.[106]

In *Freedman* v. *Maryland*, the court held that procedures of a state board of censors (which had the power to approve or disapprove of all motion pictures shown in Maryland) were unconstitutional for failing to provide for prompt judicial participation. The court established standards that have been frequently cited in subsequent cases involving prior restraint:

> Applying the settled rule of our cases, we hold that a noncriminal process which requires the prior submission of a film to a censor avoids constitutional infirmity only if it takes place under procedural safeguards designed to obviate the dangers of a censorship system. First, the burden of proving that the film is unprotected expression must rest on the censor. . . . Second, while the State may require advance submission of all films, in order to proceed effectively to bar all showings of unprotected films, the requirement cannot be administered in a manner which would lend an effect of finality to the censor's determination whether a film constitutes protected expression. The teaching of our cases is that, because only a judicial determination in an adversary proceeding ensures the necessary sensitivity to freedom of expression, only a procedure requiring a judicial determination suffices to impose a valid final restraint. . . . To this end, the exhibitor must be assured, by statute or authoritative judicial construction, that the censor will, within a specified brief period, either issue a license or go to court to restrain showing the film. Any restraint imposed in advance of a final judicial determination on the merits must similarly be limited to preservation of the status quo for the shortest period of time compatible with sound judicial resolution. Moreover, we are well aware that, even after expiration of a temporary restraint, an administrative refusal to license, signifying the

censor's view that the film is unprotected, may have a discouraging effect on the exhibitor. . . . Therefore, the procedure must also assure a prompt final judicial decision, to minimize the deterrent effect of an interim and possibly erroneous denial of a license.[107]

Schauer suggests that any system of censorship of written materials would probably be impermissible even if it complied with *Freedman*.[108]

The U.S. Supreme Court has decided numerous prior restraint cases, which should be consulted by anyone considering using nuisance or film review board laws to regulate pornography. *Teitel Films* v. *Cusack* found that a fifty- to fifty-seven-day period of an administrative process in a film licensing situation was impermissibly long and that the law had to contain a provision for a prompt judicial decision.

In *Blount* v. *Rizzi*, a U.S. Postal Service regulatory scheme of detaining obscene mail was declared unconstitutional and found not to comply with *Freedman* because it placed the burden of starting judicial review on the owner of the materials rather than on the censor. The *Blount* court expressed concern that a censor would be less responsive than a court to free expression interests.

United States v. *Thirty-Seven Photographs* concerned a federal law that allowed customs officials to seize obscene materials at the port of entry. While the general law conformed to the *Freedman* requirements, no time limits to ensure prompt commencement and completion of proceedings to minimize the prior restraint impact was included. However, the court, while stating clearly that time limits must be provided for, construed the law at issue to provide that judicial proceedings must be started within fourteen days of the initial seizure and completed (by a final court decision) within sixty days. The court emphasized that those particular time limits applied only to importation proceedings.[109] Schauer states that much shorter time periods are required when motion picture and other forms of licensing are involved.[110] The *Freedman* requirements were reaffirmed by the court in *Southeastern Promotions, Ltd.* v. *Conrad*.[111]

Times Film Corp. v. *Chicago* dealt with an ordinance that required all motion pictures to be submitted to a film board prior to their public exhibition. The petitioner did not attack the procedures set forth in the law but instead argued that the law was invalid as a prior restraint on freedom of speech. The court emphasized that First Amendment cases have made it clear that free speech is not an "absolute right."

The court held that prior restraints in the form of film review boards are not per se unconstitutional.[112]

In *Kunz* v. *New York*, the law at issue made it illegal to hold public worship meetings on the street without first obtaining a permit from the police. The petitioner's permit was revoked on the ground that he denounced and ridiculed other "religious beliefs in his meetings." In effect, the law allowed the police to control in advance a citizen's right to speak on religious grounds. The ordinance gave no reasons why a permit could be refused. The court held that the law was an invalid prior restraint. While a law can prevent serious "interference with normal usage of streets and parks," the court ruled that licensing systems cannot "vest in an administrative official discretion to grant or withhold a permit upon broad criteria unrelated to proper regulation of public places." Appropriate standards to guide discretion are required.[113]

In *Southeastern Promotions Ltd.* v. *Conrad*, the directors of a local theater denied use of the theater to show the rock musical *Hair* because they had heard it involved simulated sex, nudity, and obscenity. The lower court said that this was not speech or symbolic speech; rather it was pure conduct comparable to murder or rape and not entitled to First Amendment protection. The U.S. Supreme Court held that denial of the theater use was a prior restraint under a system that lacked constitutionally required minimal procedural safeguards. The danger of censorship is too great where officials have "unbridled discretion" over a forum's use, the court said. A system of prior restraint " 'comes to this Court bearing a heavy presumption against its constitutional validity,' " the court noted, quoting *Bantam Books, Inc.* v. *Sullivan*. The court pointed out that it is difficult to know in advance what a person will say. Here, the *Freedman* requirements were not met: A prompt judicial review was not provided for, and the petitioner bore the burden of seeking such a review.[114]

In *Bantam Books, Inc.* v. *Sullivan*, the Rhode Island Commission to Encourage Morality in Youth, created by statute, was granted the duty to educate the public about communications containing "obscene, indecent or impure language, or manifestly tending to the corruption of the youth" (as defined in state laws) and to investigate and recommend prosecution of all violations of said laws. Certain book companies were notified of objectionable publications such as *Playboy, Rogue, Frolic,* and *Peyton Place*. Copies of the list of objectionable publications were circulated to police departments. As a result, the book publishers and book sellers ceased selling and taking new orders for the books. The state conceded that some of the books were not obscene.

The court held that the law was unconstitutional as government censorship devoid of required safeguards. The state said that the commission did not suppress or regulate obscenity but merely "exhorts booksellers and advises them of their legal rights." They had no power to apply formal legal sanctions, the state said. The court found this "untenable." It said that the record showed that the commission had set out to suppress publications it deemed objectionable and had succeeded. According to the court, informal censorship "may sufficiently inhibit the circulation of publications to warrant injunctive relief." People do not "lightly disregard" threats by public officers to institute criminal proceedings, the court said. Here, letters were followed by police visits. Circulation of the publications stopped. The effect, the court said, was to make obscenity regulation largely unnecessary and to obviate the need to use criminal sanctions and thus eliminate the safeguards of the criminal process.

In addition, the law provided no safeguards against the suppression of nonobscene, constitutionally protected material. Here, the system of prior restraint had no saving features such as prompt judicial determination. The statute also was vague and deprived adults of publications (while the commission's jurisdiction applied only to youths). The U.S. Supreme Court held that the law violated the Fourteenth Amendment's procedural due process provisions.[115]

Trachtman argues that only "extraordinary and compelling state interests that cannot be served by less restrictive alternatives will constitutionally justify prior restraints, a standard of review that no prior restraint before the Court has survived."[116]

DISPLAY OF HARMFUL MATERIAL TO MINORS

Numerous states have laws that prohibit the display of harmful materials to minors. These are known as display statutes or harmful to minors laws.

The power of a state to regulate the distribution and access of "objectionable materials" to juveniles is grounded in its interest in youth.[117] This interest is sometimes expressed, such as in *Ferber* (the child pornography case), as a compelling interest in protecting children from physical and psychological harm.

The courts are divided over whether laws prohibiting the display of sexually explicit materials harmful to minors unless sealed or covered by an opaque wrapper are constitutional. The issue is whether adult rights to examine such material are violated by such laws. The interest of protecting minors must be balanced against the interest of adults in reading or viewing the material.[118]

The display laws can cover drive-in theaters [*Carey* v. *Starview Drive-In Theatre, Inc.*, 427 N.E.2d 201 (Ill. App. Ct. 1981), *appeal dismissed for want of a substantial federal question*, 457 U.S. 1113 (1982)]. This, according to the *Obscenity Law Reporter*, is a decision on the merits under *Hicks* v. *Miranda* and *Mandel*.[119]

In *Erznoznik* v. *City of Jacksonville*, the court struck down an ordinance related to drive-in theaters. The law at issue in that case made it illegal and a public nuisance to show any motion picture or other exhibit "in which the human male or female bare buttocks, human female bare breasts, or human bare pubic areas are shown, if such motion picture, slide, or other exhibit is visible from any public street or public place." The court said that the law prohibited drive-ins from showing any movies containing nudity—even if it was innocent or educational. The court also noted that a drive-in theater screen is not "so obtrusive as to make it impossible for an unwilling individual to avoid exposure to it." The court stated that the "limited" privacy interest of persons on the public streets could not justify censorship of otherwise protected speech on the basis of its content. But the justices left open the possibility of properly drawn zoning ordinances restricting the location of such theaters and nuisance laws creating a right to sue for invasion of privacy when the right to enjoy residences is diminished—regardless of the content.

The court found the Jacksonville law to be overly broad, for it did not limit coverage to "sexually explicit nudity." Even when minors are involved, all nudity cannot be held obscene, the court said. Interestingly, the court suggested that a narrowly drawn "nondiscriminatory traffic regulation" that required drive-in movie theaters to be screened from motorist view might be a valid and reasonable exercise of police power. A proper law, the court said, would limit the regulations to movies that are obscene as to minors.[120]

In a 1979 Citizens for Decency Through Law memorandum, Bruce Taylor suggested these approaches:

1. Prohibit the showing of drive-in films harmful or obscene to juveniles before 11 P.M.

2. Prosecute the operators of drive-in theaters for exhibiting obscene films or films that are harmful to juveniles.
3. Bring civil nuisance actions against the showing of such films.
4. Have those who live in the area of drive-in screens sue civilly for invasion of privacy. This pits one private interest against another and avoids pitting a state against a private interest that claims shelter under the First Amendment.[121]

Typical harmful to minors/outdoor theater laws prohibit the showing of sexually explicit movies or obscene acts in drive-in theaters unless the screen is out of public view. Punishments for violations include fines and revocation of licenses.

(We believe that the invasion of privacy caused by forcing adults or children to view pornographic motion pictures on drive-in theater screens from their backyards or streets is a far greater constitutional violation than any arguable minimal impact on freedom of speech created by requiring such movies to be shielded from unwanted view. Harmful to minors and outdoor theater laws should be carefully drafted to avoid successful constitutional challenges for being vague, overbroad, lacking safeguards or specific appeals procedures, and violating First Amendment rights.)

INDECENCY

Television and Radio

While the *Miller* obscenity definitions also apply to the broadcast media (radio and television), because of their pervasive impact on their audience, the broadcast media are much more strictly regulated. Such regulation extends beyond *Miller* to reach other speech termed "indecent." Broadcast is unique because the airwaves are limited. Therefore, Congress created the FCC to regulate broadcasting through the issuance and denial of licenses in the public interest.

Daniel S. Moretti has argued that federal statutes which regulate indecency conflict:

1. The Communications Act empowers the FCC to regulate broadcasters in the "public interest" and to suspend or revoke licenses.
2. A criminal statute prohibits the broadcast of indecent or obscene language.
3. The Communications Act prohibits the FCC from exercising censorship over broadcasters.

Moretti says, however, that these conflicts were partly resolved in *FCC* v. *Pacifica Foundation.*[122]

Pacifica involved a twelve-minute monologue by comedian George Carlin titled "Filthy Words." The following are excerpts:

[A]nd, uh, bastard you can say, and hell and damn so I have to figure out which ones you couldn't say ever and it came down to seven but the list is open to amendment. . . . The original seven words were, shit, piss, fuck, cocksucker, motherfucker, and tits. . . .

Now the word shit is okay for the man. At work you can say it like crazy. Mostly figuratively.

Get that shit out of here, will ya? I don't want to see that shit anymore. I can't cut that shit, buddy. I've had that shit up to here. I think you're full of shit myself. He don't know shit from Shinola. [You know that?] Always wondered how the Shinola people felt about that. . . . Oh, the shit is going to hit de fan. Built like a brick shit-house. [Up,] he's up shit's creek. . . . Hot shit, holy shit, tough shit, eat shit. . . . All the animals—Bull shit, horse shit, cow shit, rat shit, bat shit. . . . Shit or get off the pot. I got a shit-load full of them. . . . Shit-head, shit-heel, . . .

Fuck. Good word. . . . It means to make love. Right? . . . Oh, fuck you man. . . . Stupid fuck. . . . Stop me before I fuck again. . . .

I found three more words that had to be put on the list of words you could never say on television, and they were fart, turd and twat.[123]

A New York radio station owned by Pacifica Foundation broadcast Carlin's monologue. A listener, with his son, complained to the FCC. The FCC said the speech was not obscene but that it could be banned from the airwaves under Title 18 U.S.C. s. 1464, which required the FCC to prohibit the broadcast of indecent language. The Supreme Court upheld the FCC decision by a 5–4 vote, reasoning as follows. First, broadcasting has a pervasive presence in American society and therefore can be more stringently regulated than printed works. It reaches a large audience. Second, broadcasting media have unique access to children. Broadcasting interferes with the parental right to bring up children as they please. The court held that broadcast of indecent speech is unprotected by the First Amendment. While books must be deliberately purchased, broadcasting comes directly into the home—with or without invitation. The individual's right to be left alone outweighs the First Amendment rights of the intruder.

Pacifica Foundation argued that the listener could turn the channel or turn it off. This, the court said, is "like saying the remedy for an assault is to run away after the first blow." A prior warning would not necessarily prevent the listener from hearing such a program, it said.

The *Pacifica* court defined *indecency* as something that does not conform to "accepted standards of morality." Importantly, it was not necessary to show prurient appeal—that is, the speech need not arouse sexual thoughts. The court found Carlin's monologue "shocking," "vulgar," and "offensive." The dissenting justices in *Pacifica* argued that the listener has a right to hear such programs under the First Amendment. The listener can turn the channel. The dissenters feared that the decision could lead to unlimited censorship of protected speech. *Pacifica* required the FCC to look at the content and context (context might include time of day and the differences in content between radio, television, and cable or closed-circuit television). A nuisance law rationale was used.[124]

Pacifica, the major indecency case, is frequently cited by proponents and opponents of regulation of indecency on cable television and in rock music lyrics. Under it, definitions of *indecency* may cover "no more than that which portrays sexual or excretory organs or functions."[125]

Radio broadcasts also can be found obscene. In *Illinois Citizens Committee for Broadcasting* v. *FCC*, the FCC found a radio call-in show to be obscene under Title 18 U.S.C. s. 1464. The show, broadcast from 10 A.M. to 3 P.M., had explicit and repeated details of oral sex techniques. It was not presented for scientific or educational purposes; rather the sexual activity was portrayed in a context that could be described as pandering and titillating.[126]

In *Red Lion Broadcasting Co.* v. *FCC*, the court found that broadcasters have limited First Amendment protection due to the pervasive nature of the medium and its limited access. Thus, under the FCC's fairness doctrine, the broadcast media are required to offer airtime for opposing points of view. The print media, which enjoy greater First Amendment protection, need not offer such space (*Miami Herald Publishing Co., Inc.* v. *Tornillo*). In *FCC* v. *Midwest Video Corp.*, the court struck down FCC regulations requiring cable companies to grant access to basic cable channels to third parties in the franchised area and to furnish facilities and equipment for their use. The court said this " 'abrogated the cable operators' control over the composition of their programming.' "[127]

Cable Television

Cable television differs from broadcast television and radio because it is transmitted by wire rather than broadcast over airwaves. After studying the as yet unresolved issue of whether government should be able to regulate cable television for indecency, we conclude that such regulation should be permitted because of the substantial similarities between cable television and broadcast television and radio.

Sporn summarizes the arguments for and against regulation of the content of cable television. She notes the following arguments in favor of regulation:

1. Sexually explicit or indecent programming violates the right not to have offensive material intrude into the privacy of the home.
2. Children should be legally protected from such material.
3. The availability of indecent cable television to minors undermines parental authority in the home.
4. Such regulations are justified because indecent programs negatively affect private and public morality.

Arguments against regulation include the fact that the legal status of nonobscene sexually explicit material is "communication protected by the First Amendment guarantees of the right to speak, the right to receive information and ideas, the right to choose what to view in the privacy of one's home, and the Fourteenth Amendment rights of parents to exercise discretion in child-rearing." (See *Wisconsin* v. *Yoder* and *Prince* v. *Massachusetts*).[128]

While George and Moretti conclude that only *Miller* obscenity-type material can be regulated under the Cable Communications Act,[129] Wardle says that the act gives states and localities the authority to regulate cable indecency. These questions affect a large percentage of the American population. By January 1985, 43.7 percent of all U.S. homes with television sets subscribed to cable, which amounted to more than 37.2 million homes.

If regulation of indecency on cable is allowed, sanctions against cable operators who furnish such material could include revocation of the franchise, issuance of a cease and desist order, imposition of a monetary forfeiture, denying renewal of a franchise, or granting a short-term renewal. Wardle outlines approaches taken by various governments to regulate indecency on cable television:

1. Criminal sanctions for the knowing distribution of indecent material

2. Nuisance laws that impose time, place, and manner standards on cable programs
3. Laws that require cable operators to provide their customers with lockboxes
4. Laws that authorize revocation of operators' licenses
5. Statutes that make cable operators immune from liability for transmitting indecent programs they did not originate
6. Laws prohibiting local or state agencies from enacting regulations to control the content of cable programming.[130]

Defining Indecency on Cable. The *Pacifica* case, which some legal scholars believe should be extended to cover cable television, defined *indecency* broadly as "nonconformance with accepted standards of morality." However, it also approved the definition of *indecent* established by the FCC, which, in Rhoads's words, was "patently offensive, repetitive and deliberate use of words which refer to excretory or sexual activities used in an afternoon broadcast when children are likely to be in the audience." The court emphasized that "prurient appeal" was not a necessary element of indecent language. Rhoads says that indecent programming covers most nudity and soft-core sex.[131]

A model cable television law drafted by Morality in Media, Inc., defines indecent material as that which represents or verbally describes "1. a human sexual or excretory organ or function; or 2. nudity; or 3. ultimate sexual acts, normal or perverted, actual or simulated; or 4. masturbation; which under contemporary community standards for cable television is patently offensive."[132] The Utah statute, which was similar, also did not contain the *Miller* obscenity standard.[133]

(In our view, any regulation of indecency on television, radio, or cable should include depictions of sexual sadism and sexual masochism. A definition of *pornography* along the lines of that proposed in the civil rights antipornography law also might be considered.)

Rhoads discusses a proposed Pennsylvania cable indecency law that defined sexually explicit material as follows:

A depiction, representation or image or verbal description or narrative account of any of the following which the average person applying contemporary community standards for cable television would find, taken as a whole, is presented in a patently offensive way and which is harmful to minors:

(1) The showing of the human male or female genitals, pubic area or buttocks with less than a fully opaque covering, or the showing of the female breast with less than a fully opaque covering of any portion thereof below the top of the nipple, or the depiction of covered male genitals in a discernibly turgid state.

(2) Acts, actual or simulated, of masturbation, homosexuality, sexual intercourse, or physical contact with a person's clothed or unclothed genitals, pubic area, buttocks, or if such person be a female, breast.

(3) The condition of human male or female genitals when in a state of sexual stimulation or arousal.

(4) Flagellation, torture or other violence indicating a sadomasochistic sexual relationship.[134]

According to Rhoads, the Pennsylvania proposal stated that a depiction of sexual acts or nudity is harmful to minors when it "appeals to their prurient interests, offends prevailing standards of what is suitable for minors, and lacks redeeming social importance for minors." Under the bill, all material would be evaluated on a "variable" obscenity basis. (This is based on the *Ginsberg* v. *New York* decision that children and adults have different constitutional rights and that what is obscene for children might not be obscene for adults.) However, Rhoads notes the Pennsylvania bill was not closely tailored to its goal of protecting children because it called for a universal ban on material harmful only to children.[135] (*Butler* v. *Michigan* rejected a law that would restrict adults to reading only what is fit for children.[136])

It is important to remember that whatever definition is used, indecency laws allow much broader regulation of sexually explicit material than obscenity laws and that they need not meet the stringent three-part test of *Miller*.

Cable Television versus Broadcast Media. Much of the debate over whether cable television can be regulated for indecency centers on the issue of whether it is sufficiently similar to the broadcast media to permit similar regulation. In *Community Television of Utah, Inc.* v. *Roy City*, the court suggested perceived differences:

Cable	Broadcast
1. User needs to subscribe.	User need not subscribe
2. User holds power to cancel subscriptions.	User holds no power. May complain to F.C.C., station, network or sponsor.
3. Limited advertising.	Extensive advertising.
4. Transmittal through wires.	Transmittal through public airwaves.

5. User receives signal on private cable.	User appropriates signal from the public airwaves.
6. User pays a fee.	User does not pay a fee.
7. User receives a preview of coming attractions.	User receives daily and weekly listing in public press or commercial guides.
8. Distributor or distributee may add services and expanded spectrum of signals or channels and choices.	Neither distributor nor distributee may add services or signals or choices.
9. Wires are privately owned.	Airwaves are not privately owned but are publicly controlled.[137]

Other differences and similarities can be added:

1. Unlike broadcast television, cable television has an almost unlimited number of channels.
2. Both types of television pervade society.
3. Both come into the home.
4. Both are accessible to children.

As Wardle emphasizes, the list of differences by the *Roy City* court are irrelevant to the issue of whether regulation of indecency on cable television is constitutional. What matters is that when the *Pacifica* criteria for regulating indecency are applied to cable, no analytically significant differences between broadcast radio and television and cable television exist. The *Pacifica* court's three major reasons for allowing reasonable time, place, and manner restrictions on broadcast indecency were as follows:

1. Because of the pervasive presence of broadcasting in American society
2. Because citizens are confronted in the privacy of their homes by broadcast radio
3. Because broadcast programs are "uniquely accessible to children"[138]

The same reasoning applies to cable television. First, it has a pervasive presence in American society. Second, cable television confronts people in the privacy of their homes. Third, cable television programs are uniquely accessible to children.[139]

Wardle argues that the extent of allowable state regulation of indecent sexually explicit materials depends on factors that fall into two categories—intrusiveness of the speech and intrusiveness of the regulations:

Factors relating to the intrusiveness of the speech which are relevant to the analysis of cable television indecency regulations include: (1) the "pervasiveness" of the medium; (2) the monopolistic use of a public resource; (3) the privacy of the place into which the material intrudes; (4) the degree of audience captivity; (5) accessibility of inappropriate material to children; and (6) the offensiveness of the form of expression, especially if it is sexually explicit. Factors relevant to assessing the intrusiveness of the regulation include: (1) the characteristics of the medium of communication; (2) the necessity for other regulation in the public interest; (3) the type of regulation imposed; and (4) the context of enforcement. Finally, the balance of harm to the competing interests must be assessed.[140]

Wardle found that cable television was similar to broadcast television concerning the first five factors. (The sixth would depend on specific programs.) Cable television is pervasive because it is fast approaching the size of the broadcast television industry. Like broadcast television, it involves the monopolistic use of a public resource: broadcast uses limited air space; cable uses limited public ways, streets, alleys, easements, and condemnation authority, and those public resources can be used only by a very limited number of cable television operations at one time. Cable also comes into the home, and people, Wardle says, should be able to avoid intrusion of sexually explicit indecent material into their homes without having to give up cable television. Subscribers to cable television are just as "captive" an audience as broadcast users because they have no control over program content. The choice to tune in or tune out programs is the same, and such an affirmative act should not be required for avoidance of indecency. Both forms of communication are equally accessible to children.

Wardle points out that the nature of the First Amendment protection accorded communication depends on the character of the medium being regulated. Because cable is so similar to broadcast television, she concludes, it should be regulated in a similar fashion. There is a need to regulate cable in the public interest because the public has an interest in preventing the exploitation of public assets for private gain, she asserts. The greater the burden of the regulation, the greater the burden of justifying it. When only time, place, and manner regulations are imposed, strict scrutiny is no longer the standard of review; instead, the court looks at whether the regulation advances an important state interest.

Wardle states that a total ban on indecent cable communications would be subject to stricter scrutiny than laws that merely tried to channel indecent material "to times and channels where unsupervised children and unwilling adults would not be exposed to it." She feels that one of the reasons the laws passed in Roy City, Miami, and the State of Utah were invalidated was their failure to channel material. These laws totally banned indecent programming. Courts also look to the severity of the sanctions imposed in determining whether regulations on indecency are acceptable, Wardle states. For example, she says that courts probably will find civil sanctions more permissible than criminal sanctions. The context of the enforcement is a final factor of importance, she notes.

Next, according to Wardle, the regulator's rights must be balanced against the public's interest. This involves considering the comparative value and nature of the interests; the relative costs and burdens to people of vindicating those interests; the ability to receive redress for speech-created harm through other means; and the availability of less-restrictive, effective measures to protect legitimate public interests. There is an interest in protecting uncensored communications and in protecting sexually explicit indecent materials balanced against the interest in decency and in access to and use of cable systems. (Wardle states that the value of sexually explicit indecent material is "de minimis. At best it may have some entertainment value; at worst it may cause exploitive and demeaning anti-social behavior.") A total ban would be more onerous than channeling, which would merely place the burden of taking the initiative to obtain indecent programs on the customer. Private action against the kinds of injury inflicted by "offensive" indecent cable programs is unlikely because of the nature of the private interests affected and the unlikelihood that significant monetary damages could be recovered.[141]

Wardle suggests the following methods of channeling indecent cable programming:

(1) requiring cable system operators to disclose to potential customers at the time of the subscription the type of potentially offensive programming conveyed over specific channels; (2) restricting all offensive programming to certain channels or pay-for-viewing systems; (3) requiring that channels transmitting offensive programming be optional or extra-tier services; (4) requiring that transmission of offensive programming via cable be "scrambled" so that only viewers with decoding devices could receive it; (5) requiring that effective lockboxes that scramble unwanted signals be made available at no or low cost to subscribers; (6) restricting offensive programming to those times when children would be less likely to be in the viewing audience; or (7) requiring program guides that identify potentially offensive programming be provided at no or low cost to all subscribers.[142]

Sporn details the U.S. Supreme Court's views on privacy in the home and captive audiences. She notes that *Rowen* v. *U.S. Post Office Department* upheld a federal law under which unwilling recipients of sexually explicit mail can obtain a post office order requiring the mailer to stop future mailings. The court said that the person's right to privacy in the home outweighs the sender's right to communicate. The court also found that in one's home, one is always a captive audience. The theories of *Rowen* were found to apply to broadcasts in *Pacifica*. Television viewers were described as a captive audience in *Columbia Broadcasting System* v. *Democratic National Committee* and *Banzhaf* v. *FCC*. Unless the person is a captive audience, his or her privacy interest in avoiding offensive communications outside the home is insubstantial. The burden falls on the viewer to avert his or her eyes. (See *Erznoznik; Cohen* v. *California Kovacs . Cooper,* and *Lehman* v. *City of Shaker Heights*.)[143]

Robert Showers believes that when the U.S. Supreme Court reviews cable porn laws, it will look for the following things:

1. A precise and narrow definition based on *Pacifica* that the material is patently offensive "for the time, place, manner and context of its dissemination"
2. Enforcement procedures and rules that will protect the privacy of the home and children but be permissive enough to allow segregated, separately purchased channels for adults to view late at night
3. A clear intent by the legislature that the law was passed to protect legitimate local or state interests[144]

Rhoads, however, argues that indecency restraints undermine the principles of individualism that underlie the First Amendment. She also suggests there is no need to ask government to solve the indecent cable problem. If enough people believe such programming has "serious deleterious effects," they can solve the problem by applying market pressure on the cable industry—disconnecting or boycotting the service. "Questions of decency are better left to individual judgment," she says.[145]

Several courts have said indecency regulations of broadcasting are not applicable to cable, but the U.S. Supreme Court has not considered the issue. (See *Community Television of Utah, Inc.* v. *Roy City; Cruz* v. *Ferre;* and *Home Box Office* v. *Wilkinson*.) These cases (we believe erroneously) held that *Pacifica* has no application to cable, and in part suggested that sexually explicit material on cable can be regulated only if it is obscene.[146]

Federal Preemption. Some have argued that the supremacy clause of the Constitution preempts state and local cable porn laws. Showers points out that while the language of *Capital Cities Cable, Inc.* v. *Crisp* (which found that the FCC intended to preempt and, with congressional approval, did preempt state and local regulation of commercial advertising imported for retransmission on cable) was broad enough to sustain the FCC's preemption of all cable content regulation, the FCC clearly chose not to preempt regulation of obscenity and indecency on cable.[147] (In fact, Wardle notes, as of 1986, the FCC had never brought an enforcement action against a broadcast, cable television station, or programmer for violation of the obscenity or indecency standards.[148]

The Cable Communications Policy Act of 1984 (federal law) seems to have solved the preemption issue, Showers states. It expressly allows local laws on obscenity, and the legislative history shows an intent to include laws regulating indecency. [See Title 47 U.S.C. s. 544 (f) (1).[149]] However, Rhoads argues that, because Title 47 U.S.C. s. 556 (c) expressly preempted state and local laws inconsistent with the act, only material that meets the *Miller* obscenity test can be proscribed.[150] Yet, as Wardle notes, the act states that the law shall not be construed as prohibiting a franchising authority and a cable operator from providing in a franchise agreement or renewal that certain "cable services shall not be provided or shall be provided subject to conditions, if such cable services are obscene or are otherwise unprotected by the United States Constitution." Another section of the act grants state and local authorities the power to enforce obscenity and other similar laws (of which indecency would be one). The issue is whether Congress intended indecency to be included in the terms "otherwise unprotected" and "other similar laws." Wardle states that the legislative history clearly shows that Congress did not intend to preempt state and local regulation of indecent cable programming.[151]

Sporn states that the FCC has recognized the need for local licensing of cable because it uses public streets and local people can better follow up on service complaints with local authorities. Furthermore, she argues, licensing would place an unmanageable burden on the FCC.[152]

We conclude that cable indecency should be regulated in the same manner that broadcast (television and radio) is but that such regulation is best left to state and local governments.

Rock and Roll Lyrics

The National Parent Teacher Association and the Parents Music Resource Center have attacked heavy metal groups that promote rape, sadomasochism, incest, substance abuse, devil worship, and suicide. (See chapter 2 for a detailed description of rock porn images.) People in the recording industry oppose the efforts of these groups, maintaining that the lyrics imitate society's behavior more than they mold it. In November 1985, however, the industry voluntarily agreed to affix warnings to recordings containing "explicit" lyrics.[153] Importantly, First Amendment protections do not apply to censorship that is private, as opposed to governmental. According to Scheidemantel, the courts have found that rock music is protected expression under the First Amendment. For example, in *Cinevision Corporation* v. *City of Burbank*, the court said that an ordinance outlawing the playing of such music, based on its content, would violate the First Amendment.

Barriers exist to regulating obscene recordings, Scheidemantel believes. It would, for example, be difficult to apply the "taken as a whole" test of *Miller* to such recordings, he states. Would the "whole" be the entire record album or a single song? (We point out that there is some precedent for arguing that only those items that are united by a common theme make up the relevant "whole." Thus, one song on an album might be totally unrelated to another.

Scheidemantel believes that the music industry should not create a system of self-regulation similar to that of the motion picture industry because that system has been unsuccessful and abridges constitutional rights. (See the section on film review boards later in this chapter for his reasoning.)

Minors, although they may be shielded from material deemed obscene under *Miller*, have certain rights to receive the expression of others, Scheidemantel states. For example, in *Board of Education, Island Trees Union Free School District No. 26* v. *Pico*, the court said that a book review committee could not remove books from a school library if the committee's intent was to "deny [students] access to ideas with which [the board] disagreed." And, while *Ginsberg* approved a variable obscenity concept under which certain material could be deemed obscene as to minors but not adults, the court has never used that test to apply to four-letter expletives, violence, sacrilege, substance abuse, or brutality, Scheidemantel says.

He cites numerous cases in which the courts have upheld the rights of minors to receive nonobscene material. For speech to be considered obscene as to minors, it must in some way be "patently erotic," he argues. In addition, he says, the court has narrowly defined the type of speech that, in the interest of protecting minors, may be prevented from being aired under broadcast indecency criteria. The indecency definition does not include all references to lovemaking and sex or "violent, profane, occult or drug-related language," Scheidemantel notes.[154]

The reasoning of the *Pacifica* case (which dealt with broadcast television) does not apply to music lyrics, Scheidemantel argues. The arguments that broadcasting has a unique pervasiveness, especially intrusion into the home, and that it is highly accessible to young, unsupervised children whom government, in the interest of protecting youth, may shield from indecent broadcasts do not apply to music lyrics, he says. A captive audience is not involved. Thus, while indecent music lyrics could be kept off the airwaves, a "willing and interested listener" should have the option of purchasing recordings of such material, he believes.

If the Recording Industry Association of America "succumbs" to pressure from the public and regulates itself, it could, Scheidemantel fears,

[o]verstep otherwise constitutional bounds by: (1) regulating indecent content in a medium other than broadcasting; (2) constructing criteria for indecency in subjective, ill-defined terms; (3) applying those criteria to the entire nation; and (4) denying artists proper appellate procedures for unfavorable rating classifications applied to their works.[155]

(We argue in the section on film review boards that Scheidemantel's fears of constitutional infringement caused by voluntary film or record rating systems run by those industries are not credible.)

Scheidemantel does note a logistical problem: twenty-five thousand new songs annually would be time-consuming to rate. And, he asks, what happens with those songs already in the home? He says that requiring record sales personnel to be somewhat familiar with the music content would be a less restrictive means of providing parents with content information. He believes that it would be unfair to regulate only rock music when some other types of music also deal with sex and violence. Lastly, he believes that the subject matter that could be classified as indecent would be "potentially limitless." He concludes that if control of music lyrics is to occur, it should be done by legislation so that the courts will be able to ensure that controls are constitutional.

(We believe that any government regulation would be far more effective than industry self-regulation, but we do not oppose the use of "explicitness" warning labels, which would inform potential buyers of record content. We also believe that the teaching of sadistic sexuality, violence, and the like in some music lyrics has a harmful impact on some people's beliefs, which can lead to harmful or antisocial behavior.)

FILM REVIEW BOARDS

The preexhibition examination of motion pictures to permit denial of licenses to those that are obscene is allowed. (See *Star* v. *Preller* and Times Film Corp. v. *City of Chicago*.) However, the procedural safeguards to prevent censorship set forth in *Freedman* v. *Maryland* must be met.[156]

In 1915, films were considered to be merely a "business" and not a way of expressing protected ideas. Thus, in *Mutual Film Corporation* v. *Industrial Commission of Ohio*, the court permitted motion pictures to be censored by the state. However, forty years later, in *Joseph Burstyn, Inc.* v. *Wilson*, the court found that motion pictures were entitled to First Amendment protection because they are a "significant medium for the communication of ideas."

Today, films cannot be regulated by the government for indecent language, but they may be submitted to prior review by a licensing board in order to prevent the exhibition of obscene films.[157]

The movie industry has imposed a voluntary motion picture rating system on itself. According to Jack Valenti, 1982 President of the Motion Picture Association of America (MPAA), this was in response to the public interest of parents needing to know what kind of movie the local theater was exhibiting.

Valenti explains that under the rating system, a filmmaker can tell his story however he or she pleases. But the price of that freedom is the possible restriction on viewing by children. Importantly, no one is forced to submit a film to the rating board, but most "responsible" films are submitted. *Hard-core pornography is not* submitted, as most hard-core pornography producers instead apply an X rating, which is not registered by the board with the U.S. Patent and Trademark Office as a certification mark of the MPAA. Thus, the G, PG, and R ratings cannot be used by companies that have not submitted their films for rating, while the X rating can be used at will. (This strikes us as a major loophole that benefits pornographers.)

The board's criteria are language, theme, violence and nudity and sex. The rating placed on each film comes from an assessment of how each of these is treated in the film. All ratings are based on whether the films would be offensive to parents whose children (of various ages) viewed the film and would not be considered suitable for that age group. The four categories are as follows:

G All ages admitted
PG Parental guidance suggested (some material may not be suitable for children)
R Restricted (persons under 17 require an accompanying parent or guardian)
X No one under 17 admitted

An X rating does not necessarily mean the film is obscene or pornographic. Valenti says that it could, for example, involve accumulated sexually connected or brutal language or excessive and sadistic violence. It is important to emphasize that nothing gets banned under the movie-rating system.[158]

Scheidemantel criticizes the Motion Picture Rating System (MPRS). He cites opponents of the system as presenting the following arguments:

1. The board members and director can exercise an excessive amount of discretion due to the lack of well-defined rating criteria.

2. The lack of criteria results in a lack of reliable guidelines for the parents of moviegoing children.
3. Adults' rights are affected by the ratings because movies get reshaped and edited to conform to the "suitable for children" standards. This arguably violates the "right to receive the free expression of others."
4. Although the constitutional rights of minors are not equal to those of adults, minors do have significant First Amendment rights.
5. The constitutional right of parents to decide what is best for their children is disregarded by the MPRS. (Parents, he says, may want their children to accompany them to an X-rated film. This can, today, be accomplished through home video recorder use.)
6. The substantive rights of filmmakers are affected by the rating system. Because of the lack of well-defined standards, the classification criteria exceed permissible constitutional bounds (under due process and vagueness arguments). The vague standards fail to give producers fair warning as to what content will result in what rating. In addition, the rating system's appellate procedures do not meet the the due process requirements of *Freedman* v. *Maryland*.
7. In *Miller*, The court rejected a national definition of obscenity. The rating system violates that principle by creating a national standard.[159]

(We note that the rating system is in the private sector and need not be complied with by motion picture producers. Because governmental actions are not involved, the constitutional requirements of the First Amendment need not be complied with. Thus, arguments 3, 4, and 7 are invalid. It is also our belief that the requirements of *Freedman* v. *Maryland* would not have to be met by the MPRS because it, unlike the type of film review board at issue in *Freedman*, is not a governmentally controlled agency.)

TELEPHONE PORNOGRAPHY

As detailed in chapter 2, a massive business exists in the United States whereby customers receive obscene or otherwise sexually explicit communications by telephone. Many of these messages are heard by children. One type of dial-a-porn operation provides prerecorded sexually oriented messages. The other allows callers to speak to live persons who will provide sexually explicit fantasy stories.

A 1983 law (Amendment to Title 47 U.S.C. s. 223) declared any commercial telephone sex service with indecent or obscene language illegal if it is available to minors. It required the FCC to establish standards to determine when a telephone sex service had taken reasonable steps to block access by minors, thus making it immune from prosecution. In addition, Title 47 U.S.C. s. 223 (1976) prohibits obscene or harassing phone calls. Such laws, according to Daniel S. Moretti, are based on the belief that government has a "compelling interest in the protection of innocent individuals from fear, abuse or annoyance by persons who employed the telephone, not to *communicate,* but for other unjustifiable motives." Such use would be an unwarranted invasion of privacy.[160]

According to Elizabeth J. Mann, dial-a-porn services are of recent origin, beginning after the FCC ordered American Telephone & Telegraph (AT&T) to divest services such as dial-a-prayer and dial-a-joke and permitted other companies to competitively offer such services in 1982. While obscene dial-a-porn messages can be regulated without violating the First Amendment, messages that are merely indecent raise First Amendment issues under which the government must assert a compelling interest, and that interest must be balanced against free speech interests, Mann states. Here, the government asserted an interest in protecting minors from telephone indecency.[161]

At the time of this writing, FCC regulations issued on June 4, 1984, required dial-a-porn companies, if prosecuted, to prove that they required customers to pay by credit card before transmission of the message or that they operated only between 9 P.M. and 8 A.M. Eastern Standard Time. In *Carlin Communications, Inc.* v. *FCC,* the court held that the regulations were overly restrictive in violation of the First Amendment. The court said that the regulations had to be more closely scrutinized because they were content based (did not apply to all dial-a-porn services but only to obscene or indecent ones). Although the court agreed that the need to protect minors from " 'salacious matter' " was compelling, it concluded that the FCC regulations were not the least restrictive means of regulating constitutionally protected speech. As a result, the FCC adopted new regulations on October 10, 1985, which require adults wanting to call dial-a-porn companies to either pay by credit card before a message is transmitted or obtain a personal identification number.

According to Mann, the courts and the FCC do not believe that live pornographic conversations are a problem because children probably could not obtain the credit card numbers of their parents. Yet, she states, it is likely that children could access credit card numbers as easily as identification codes.[162]

While obscene speech is unprotected, indecent speech may be covered by the First Amendment, Mann states. The guidelines for regulating protected speech were set forth in *Central Hudson Gas & Electric* v. *Public Service.* That case required limits on

expression to be carefully designed to achieve the government's purpose. Any restrictions must "directly advance the state interest involved" and not provide only ineffective support for it. An excessive restriction is not allowable if a more limited restriction would serve that interest as well. Mann concludes that while the courts have "traditionally" upheld the government interest in protecting children from material related to sex, the least restrictive means must be used.[163]

According to Mann, the FCC has changed its original position that an identification code system would impose burdens on adults who do not have such codes and that children could access their parents' codes. In its new report, the FCC does not discuss those earlier views, she notes. Mann believes that customers find the system inconvenient and that vendors bear added burdens. Thus, ID code regulations violate the First Amendment "because they severely limit adult access to protected speech."

Mann would prefer to see blocking devices used to prevent access to dial-a-porn numbers—in much the same way they are used to prevent access to cable television channels. The FCC originally rejected such devices but later said there is " 'no patently insurmountable obstacle to development' " of such devices. Yet the FCC originally noted that children could use phones that are not blocked. Mann believes that the odds of children obtaining their parents' ID codes or fraudulently obtaining such codes are just as great. She says that the blocking device is a better solution because it would allow parents to decide whether their children may phone dial-a-porn services and "would not reduce adult access to protected speech." Mann believes that the telephone should be treated differently than the radio or broadcast television because it is not an "intrusive, uncontrollable communications media."[164]

Harvey C. Jassem notes that in 1983 Congress made it illegal to communicate obscenity or indecency by telephone to persons under eighteen or to anyone else without that person's consent. The Federal Communications Commission, in issuing regulations under the law, required dial-a-porn producers to scramble their messages (requiring use of a descrambler sold only to adults and required callers to use personal access identification/authorization codes to hear the messages. The U.S. Supreme Court refused to hear a dial-a-porn case which challenged FCC regulations.[165]

PORNOGRAPHY AS PROSTITUTION

One of the most effective ways to prosecute pornographers and to avoid having to deal with the complexity and uncertainty of the obscenity law is to charge them with prostitution-related crimes. Under most prostitution-related laws, pornographers are pimps, procurers, or panderers. Thus, pornographic producers can be jailed and/or fined for pimping and prostitution. As the Attorney General's Commission on Pornography stated,

> the production of obscene material almost always involves acts of prostitution. . . . By procuring an individual to do an act of prostitution the producer of obscene material is acting in the same capacity as a pimp. Like any other pimp he reaps his financial reward from these acts of prostitution.[166]

In most laws, a prostitute is someone who engages in sexual contact or conduct for a fee (or other form of remuneration). This makes pornographic "stars" prostitutes and pornography producers their pimps or procurers.

In Los Angeles, where many of the nation's best known pornographic motion pictures have been produced, the city launched an attack on the pornography industry in mid-1985 during which filmmakers were arrested for pandering (procuring prostitutes). California law mandates prison sentences for hiring people to perform sex acts. As a result, pornography production shifted out of the Los Angeles area. The pornographers raised a defense argument that convictions of this type violate porn producers' First Amendment rights.[167]

Lori Douglass Hutchins outlines the status of using prostitution statutes to prosecute pornography. She summarizes these cases:

Oregon v. *Kravitz*. The defendant offered theater audience customers money to engage in sex acts with a female dancer. A prostitution conviction was upheld.

People v. *Maita*. A theater owner who had female dancers perform nude and engage in sexual intercourse and oral sex with customers was convicted of pimping, pandering, and keeping a house of prostitution.

People v. *Fixler*. Two defendants paid a 14-year-old girl to engage in sexual acts while being photographed. The photos were to be published in a pornographic magazine. The defendants were convicted of pandering.

People v. *Kovner*. The defendant had a studio where he paid people to engage in sexual conduct, including intercourse, which was filmed and later sold on a wholesale basis. He was convicted of promoting prostitution.

People v. *Souter*. Several women were hired by the defendants to perform sexual acts with various men for pornography. The defendants were convicted of pandering (promoting prostitution).[168]

Hutchins says that two potential problems arise concerning the constitutionality of attacking pornography under the prostitution approach. First, because the due process clause requires that persons be convicted only of crimes when the prohibited conduct has been clearly defined, she asks whether the pornographers in these cases had adequate notice that their actions constituted promoting prostitution. She concludes that the pornographers had fair notice of what prostitution involves and therefore knew that aiding prostitution violated promotion of prostitution laws. Second, because the product of the prostitution—the pornography—may be protected speech, prosecution of pornographers under prostitution laws involves both a nonspeech and protected speech element. Therefore, it is arguable that the *O'Brien* test must be applied. The *Maita* court considered each step of that test. It found the following:

1. Pimping and pandering laws aim at discouraging prostitution by preventing third parties from expanding the supply of prostitutes or the size of their operations.
2. The government has a substantial interest in limiting prostitution and its related activities of pandering and pimping.
3. The governmental interest in preventing prostitution is unrelated to press or speech.
4. The restriction at issue is no greater than necessary to further the substantial governmental interest.

Hutchins points out that prosecuting pornographers under prostitution laws attacks the underlying criminal conduct and not the pornographic material.

(We support the use of pimping and pandering laws to attack pornographic producers. We caution that, due to the underground and clandestine nature of this crime-controlled industry, it might be difficult to obtain evidence to convict producers because those with information might not be willing to testify against them. While we believe that pornographic film and magazine actors and models who willingly engage in such prostitution also should be prosecuted under prostitution laws, we oppose prosecution of

actors and models who were not willing participants in the pornographic prostitution.)

PORNOGRAPHY AS SEX DISCRIMINATION UNDER CURRENT FEDERAL LAW

Women who have been sexually harassed by pornography have successfully sued under Title VII of the Civil Rights Act of 1964 as amended by the Equal Employment Opportunity Act of 1972 (Title 42 U.S.C. s. 2000e) to collect damages. (We suggest that persons who are sexually harassed by pornography on the job investigate the possibility of bringing such a lawsuit.)

Sex discrimination prevention was found to be a compelling state interest under *Roberts* v. *United States Jaycees*. In that case, the court said, "Like violence and other types of potentially expressive activities that produce special harms distinct from their communicative impact, such practices are entitled to no constitutional protection."[169]

Under *Henson* v. *City of Dundee*, a person must show the following to make a claim of sexual harassment in the workplace:

(1) The employee belongs to a protected group. (2) The employee was subject to unwelcome sexual harassment. (3) The harassment complained of was based on sex. (4) The employee's reaction to harassment complained of affected tangible aspects of the employee's compensation, terms, conditions or privileges of employment.[170]

One case, *Zabkowicz* v. *The West Bend Company*, relied on 29 C.F.R. s. 1604.11.. It described the fourth requirement slightly differently: "[T]he sexual conduct was sufficiently severe or pervasive that it unreasonably interfered with her work performance or created an intimidating, hostile or offensive working environment." That case, and the federal rules, added a fifth criteria—namely, that the employer knew or should have known of the sexual harassment and failed to take "immediate and appropriate corrective action."

Zabkowicz was repeatedly sexually harassed by a variety of coworkers. Some exposed their buttocks to her. At one time when she was pregnant and restricted to lifting twenty-five pounds, one male coworker allegedly grabbed his crotch and said he bet she would have trouble "handling this 25 pounder." Between 1979 and 1982, there were around seventy-five sexually oriented drawings posted in

conspicuous places in the warehouse. Many of the drawings showed a naked woman with exaggerated sexual characteristics and bore Zabkowicz's initials. The drawings were understood by fellow workers to refer to her. There were drawings showing her having oral sex, having sex with an animal, and birthing a black baby. Zabkowicz brought such drawings to her employer's representatives about fifty times, she testified. She suffered from vomiting, severe nausea, cramping, and diarrhea. A doctor diagnosed her illness as " 'psychophysiological gastro-intestinal disease due to harassment at work.' "

After Zabkowicz filed an Equal Employment Opportunity Commission complaint, an investigation occurred. One of the persons who tormented her was discharged, and three others were suspended. Because of the complaint, the close to four years of harassment ceased immediately. The five criteria were met, the court held. It called the harassment "more than merely unreasonable; it was malevolent and outrageous."[171]

In *Kyriazi* v. *Western Electric Co.*, a woman who was fired was found to have a claim for sexual harassment in employment. Three coworkers had tormented and teased Kyriazi by making loud remarks about her marital status, trumpeting their speculations, and making wagers about her virginity. They blocked her path when she tried to move in the aisle, treated her with contempt and ridicule, and tried to denigrate her position as a professional. Kyriazi weighs nearly two hundred pounds. She testified that the three men created an obscene cartoon (reprinted in the court opinion) and placed it on her desk. The cartoon depicted the back side of an obese woman squeezing a naked man between her buttocks. The court found that the cartoon was "created, disseminated and ultimately thrust upon this plaintiff to humiliate her as a woman." It also said her supervisors were aware of the harassment and disregarded her complaints.[172]

In *Arnold* v. *City of Seminole, Oklahoma*, Ramona Arnold established a Title VII claim for sex discrimination and harassment. Arnold, a female patrol officer, was sexually harassed by other police officers.

The harassment included vulgar and lewd sexual comments, as well as innuendoes "communicated" by sexually explicit and graphic photographs and pictures placed in rooms of the police department and comments that women are not fit to be police officers. Cartoons posted in the officers' quarters were pornographic and directed to Arnold. Pictures and cartoons were posted in the police station for public view with Arnold's name written on them. Some of these were explicit nude pictures depicting genitals in poses offensive to many persons and clearly offensive to Arnold.

> [O]ne picture showed a man and a woman naked engaging in a sex act with plaintiff's name written on it. Another showed a man having intercourse with a goat with plaintiff's name "Mona" written over the goat. Also posted was a picture of a naked woman lying down with legs apart and plaintiff's name written on private parts. . . . [O]n a posted schedule, written next to the plaintiff's name, was the word, "bitch."[173]

In *Rabidue* v. *Osceola Refining Co.*, however, the court failed to find that a fired female employee had established a sex discrimination and harassment claim. In this case, other employees called women "cunt," "pussy," and "tits" and once called the plaintiff a "fat ass." A number of male employees occasionally displayed pictures of partially clad or nude women in their work areas and offices. Rabidue saw these during many work days. The court found that she was a troublesome employee who was discharged for her inability to work "harmoniously" with coworkers and customers.

In *Rabidue*, the court said that a sexual harassment claim is rooted in s. 703 (a) (1) of Title VII, which makes it unlawful for an employer to "[F]ail or refuse to hire or to discharge any individual, or otherwise to discriminate against any individual with respect to his compensation, terms, conditions or privileges of employment, because of such individual's race, color, religion, sex or national origin."[174] The court explained that when a female employee is subjected to sexual harassment, the condition of her employment is "invidiously discriminatory" (because she is a woman), and Title VII is violated.

The *Rabidue* court found that the plaintiff had made a prima facie case because the language and posters at issue were "because of sex" and there was other physical or verbal conduct of a sexual nature. However, the court found that Rabidue's claim was insufficient because the harassment did not unreasonably interfere with her job performance, create an intimidating work environment, create a hostile work environment, or create an offensive work environment. Hostility could not be shown, the court said, because it did not affect the plaintiff's "psychological" well-being. An offensive work environment did not exist, for the posters had a "negligible effect." While the employer's language was "annoying," it was not so severe or shocking as "to actually affect the psyches of the females employees."

In order for an "offensive" work environment to be created, under an objective test, the conduct must be so significant a factor "that the average female employee finds that her overall work experience is substantially and adversely affected by the conduct. Under this standard the sex harassment need not be psychologically disabling. On the other hand, trivial and merely annoying vulgarity would not constitute sex harassment." The rules that the court applied are those in 29 CFR s. 1604.11 (a) (3).

Importantly, another comment by the *Rabidue* court shows that the court was totally insensitive to the harmful, humiliating, and debasing impact of sexually explicit depictions that objectify and humiliate women. The court said:

> For better or worse, modern America features open displays of written and pictorial erotica. Shopping centers, candy stores and prime time television regularly display pictures of naked bodies and erotic real or simulated sex acts. Living in this milieu, the average American should not be legally offended by sexually explicit posters.[175]

(We believe that the *Rabidue* court, in effect, bought the pornographers' propaganda: Pornography exists on a widespread scale in our nation; therefore, it is acceptable to the community and should not give rise to any legal action against it. That viewpoint is not the law in our nation, however. Obscenity is a crime. And, under Title VII, sexual harassment in the form of display of pornography, is illegal and the basis for recovery of civil damages and injunctions against it. We believe that pornography is a form of sex discrimination, for it is a propaganda tool used to maintain the inferior status of women in our society.)

LIBEL

An understanding of the principles of libel law is necessary to understand how victims of pornography may have libel or defamation claims against pornographers and why women as a class may have a claim for group libel against pornographers. The U.S. Supreme Court explained the purpose of libel laws this way:

> [T]he legitimate state interest underlying the law of libel is the compensation of individuals for the harm inflicted on them by defamatory falsehoods. . . . The individual's right to the protection of his good name 'reflects no more than our basic concept of the essential dignity and worth of every human being—a concept at the root of any decent system of ordered liberty.'[176]

In *New York Times* v. *Sullivan*, the court first recognized that libel law involves freedoms of the press and speech protected by the First Amendment.[177] (*The Basic ACLU Guide to the Legal Rights of Authors and Artists* summarizes the legal basis for libel and privacy claims. Much of the information about basic libel law that follows is based on that publication.) To be libelous, a statement must, according to the *Restatement* (Second) *of Torts,* tend to " 'harm the reputation of another as to lower him in the estimation of the community or to deter third persons from associating or dealing with him.' " Imputations of incompetence or dishonesty in one's profession, of crime, of a "loathsome" disease or of unchastity in a woman are examples of statements most frequently alleged to be libelous.[178]

True statements cannot be libelous. The person claiming libel must prove that the statement is false. Statements of opinion generally cannot be libelous, for "[u]nder the First Amendment there is no such thing as a false idea."[179] However, one is cautioned that merely using phrases such as "I believe" or "In my opinion" does not convert statements of fact into ones of opinion.

For a statement to be libelous, it must be published. It is published if it is shown to someone other than the subject of the libel. Defamatory statements, which are spoken rather than written, are termed slander.

Some statements that might otherwise be considered libelous are "privileged" and cannot be acted against. Comments made during official governmental activities and statements by legislators are often absolutely privileged. Statements made in good faith consistent with the purpose of the privilege are protected by a "qualified privilege." For example, statements to proper authorities accusing persons of crimes or improper conduct and statements by private detectives to clients may be privileged. There is also a qualified privilege that protects fair reports of government statements.

Prior to 1964, a libelous statement was presumed to be false, but since *Sullivan* it has been presumed true. In that case, the court recognized that the First Amendment principle of encouraging debate on public issues could result in sharp attacks on government officials.[180] In *Sullivan*, the court established a new libel standard:

> The constitutional guarantees require, we think, a federal rule that prohibits a public official from recovering damages for a defamatory falsehood relating to his official conduct unless he proves that the statement was made with "actual malice"—that is, with knowledge that it was false or with reckless disregard of whether it was false or not.[181]

In *Garrison* v. *Louisiana*, the court explained that actual malice required "a high degree of awareness of probable falsity." Negligence (acting in an unreasonable way, according to the ACLU definition) is not actual malice. Hatred or ill will does not, in itself, prove actual malice.[182] In most cases, public officials have failed to prove actual malice. An example of recklessness would be if a publisher had serious doubts about a statement but published it without further investigation or adequate verification. The publisher's subjective state of mind, not whether a reasonable person would have published the statement, is considered in determining recklessness. Examples of public officials include elected representatives and candidates for public office but not all public employees. "Public figures" (such as people who speak out on issues) must meet the actual malice standards.[183]

Under *Gertz*, "private figures" need not meet the actual malice criteria. The court reasoned that such persons are more vulnerable to injury than public officials and figures and are more deserving of recovery for injury. In order for a private individual to recover damages for libel or defamation, he or she must prove that the defendant made the statement negligently. The court allowed states to set more stringent criteria for recovery. A person can become a public figure by injecting himself or herself into a public controversy, but he or she becomes such for only a limited range of issues. Persons who believe they have been libeled in works of fiction or satire can sue for libel.[184]

Retraction of a libelous statement sometimes protects a person from a libel claim or shows an innocent or nonactionable intent. Sometimes it limits the recoverable damages. Importantly, only money damages can be recovered in libel and defamation actions. According to the ACLU, the government cannot grant injunctions against disseminating defamatory statements because of the line of prior restraint cases.[185]

(We argue that a successful libel plaintiff must be able to have the libelous material removed from the stream of commerce in order to prevent continuing injury. For example, a pornography victim whose photograph has been wrongly used in a defamatory manner should be able to stop future circulation of that photo and remove copies of it from the market.)

In *Pring* v. *Penthouse International, Ltd.*, a multimillion-dollar libel judgment was overturned on the ground that the plaintiff failed to prove that a satire about a Miss Wyoming in *Penthouse* contained statements of fact about her. (The plaintiff was a former Miss Wyoming.) Although there were similarities between the plaintiff and the person depicted, the court said that the story had to be "reasonably understood as describing actual facts about the plaintiff or her actual conduct." The court concluded that the allegedly defamatory events described were physically impossible and therefore could not reasonably be believed. Therefore, they were statements of opinion, not fact, and could not be libelous.[186]

(We find the outcome of *Pring* to be outrageous, for it gives pornographers a loophole: simply make up sexually explicit statements about people that are physically impossible and you cannot be sued for injuring their reputations. This is a ludicrous holding, especially considering that much pornography describes sexual activity that is physically impossible or harmful.)

GROUP LIBEL

Beauharnais v. *Illinois* upheld a state statute regulating group libel.[187] While the basic principle of this case—that false defamatory speech is not protected—remains true, some commentators have argued that subsequent court rulings have cast doubt on whether *Beauharnais* is still good law.

The harm of defamation, Gershel notes, is to reputation. Defamation law protects people against such harm by "regulating a class of communication that possesses minimal social value," he states. Citing *Gertz*, he points out that false statements fall outside the scope of First Amendment protection because they do not contribute to meaningful discussion and have no place in the free exchange of ideas. Thus, pornography, as a defamatory statement about women as a class, causes harm by tainting the image of women and adds little to the marketplace of ideas. Gershel found that the state interest in regulating pornography is greater than its interest in regulating defamation because "[p]ornography is symphonic defamation." He notes the weakness in attempting to pursue a group libel remedy against obscenity, as the courts have found that in order for a statement to be considered defamatory, it must "refer to a particular person."[188]

Jacobs states that a group libel plaintiff must show (1) that he or she is a member of the class defined, and (2) that the communication at issue has some "reasonable personal application of the words to himself."[189] (See also *Sullivan*.)

Group libel laws, which spring from an interest in protecting personal dignity and reputation, have fallen into disuse, some suggest.[190] However, some states have made group libel based on race, religion, or ethnic background a crime.

An article in the *Yale Law Journal* argues that the subcategory of group libel known as group vilification should be legally actionable. That article says that the common law (and often court-followed) rule that communication that would be libelous against an individual is not actionable when directed against a group of any "appreciable" size should not apply to group vilification because the reasons for not allowing such legal action do not apply to vilification. Such a prohibition is based on a belief that someone who hears a communication libeling a group will treat the statement rationally and not allow it to "affect his estimation of an individual member of the target group without reasonable grounds to believe that the general statement holds true for the particular individual." Thus, individual harm cannot result from the statement that libeled the group. When group "vilification"—that is, the targeting of a group because of a "racial, ethnic, or religious" distinction—is involved, that argument becomes "extremely doubtful," the article states. (We note that sex should be added as a category of vilification in order for pornography and women as a class to be covered by such laws.)

The article argues that those who hear defamatory statements about religious, ethnic, or racial (and we add sexual) groups are already prejudiced against the target group. The speaker thus reinforces and plays upon preexisting prejudices. The justification for limiting group vilification actions would have to depend on believing that racial, religious, sexual, and ethnic prejudices are rationally held. If they are not rationally held (and we believe they are not), the model that assumes a rational hearer is badly flawed.[191]

The article cites social science studies that concluded that the ability of prejudiced persons to evaluate new information rationally, "and to reason coherently in general, is substantially less than that of their more tolerant peers." Thus, group vilification is usually more persuasive than ordinary group libel, and the magnitude of its harm may be greater. That harm might include lowering the effectiveness of the group's participation in public affairs, as well as harm to the individual members by causing them to develop lower levels of self-esteem and "higher levels of repressed aggressiveness."[192] (We suggest that discriminatory harms such as decreased economic, professional, and educational opportunities, as well as and other unequal treatment, also result.)

For these reasons, the article says, group vilification is a kind of speech that is a "fit subject" for governmental concern. It encourages prejudicial behavior contrary to public policy. Interestingly, the article states that the offenses of incitement to riot, obscenity, and group vilification (all exceptions to First Amendment protections) are founded upon similar rationales: Each involves only speech that "threatens serious harm to some substantial public interest" and "includes only speech that bypasses the conscious faculties of its hearer in some way." The article uses the term *conscious faculties* to refer to the capacity in a hearer's mind that weighs contrary arguments and claims, evaluates information, and "decides how to respond to appeals to action, in a manner of which the hearer is aware." These can be distinguished from a hearer's ability to have unreflective, spontaneous, emotional reactions. Thus, the article states, each category causes harm in such a way "that it cannot be effectively counteracted by opposing speech."

According to the article, when speech fits those two rationales and when countervailing considerations are not present, it may be prohibited without violating the First Amendment. It suggests that under Alexander Meiklejohn's view of the First Amendment (which, the article asserts, has been adopted by the Supreme Court), the right to free speech derives from the principles of self-government, which include the right to receive all information that might affect the court's collective decisions. Thus, the only speech that must unquestionably receive protection is that which can be deliberated upon by the public. Speech of the emotion–reaction type should not be protected because it is not relevant to the process of "deliberative consent and self-government" from which the right to speak arises.

The article concludes that group vilification, which consists of true statements of fact or "simple statements of opinion," cannot be prohibited. (A statement of fact is defined as one that can have its truth or falsity objectively determined.) However, false statements of fact and "mixed statements of opinion that imply false assertions of fact" should not be protected. The article suggests that the lower standard of negligence (rather than actual malice) be applied to group vilification because it cannot be said that group defamation victims are public figures or officials.[193] It states:

> Currently, all group-libeling speech is widely viewed as protected by the First Amendment. But that view is simplistic and incorrect. It fails to take into account the psychological effects of prejudice; consequently, it applies the "marketplace of ideas" justification for freedom of speech to group vilification, which trades not in ideas but in pernicious and undeliberated passions.[194]

William Brigman notes that the original group libel laws made it a crime to portray certain groups in ways that would incite the general population to disparage, ridicule, or hate that group or create a danger of breach of the peace. He argues that the civil rights ordinance is a group libel law.[195] (We disagree but acknowledge that the civil rights law does acquire some of its principles from group libel concepts.)

Two major principles that have limited the success of group libel actions are the idea that defamation of a large group does not create a civil action right for the group and the idea that defamation of a large group does not create a civil action right by a group member unless the member can show that the defamatory material applies to himself or herself.

The most important group libel case is *Beauharnais* v. *Illinois*. The law at issue in that case made it a crime to publish a communication that "exposes the citizens of any race, color, creed or religion to contempt, derision, or obloquy or which is productive of breach of the peace or riots." (We note that England and Canada have long recognized the harmfulness of group vilification and have made such speech a crime.)

The leaflet at issue in *Beauharnais* called upon the white people of Chicago to unite against blacks to halt their further "encroachment, harassment and invasion of white people, their property, neighborhoods and persons." It also stated, "If persuasion and the need to prevent the white race from becoming mongrelized by the negro will not unite us, then the aggressions . . . rapes, robberies, knives, guns and marijuana of the negro, surely will."

The court noted that in most states, the constitutional guarantee of free speech is qualified by holding each person "responsible for the abuse of that right." It outlined how Illinois's experience with actual riots preceded by violently inflammatory speeches could cause the legislature to conclude that group libel played a large role in incitement. Thus, the state interest in keeping the peace and preventing violence seemed justified. Unless group libel laws were without purpose or unrelated to the state's well-being, the court said that it could not preclude a state from prohibiting such speech.

Brigman questions the continuing validity of *Beauharnais*, noting that more recent court decisions have required laws restricting free speech to show that they are necessary to achieve a compelling state interest, that the provisions of the First Amendment have been incorporated into those of the Fourteenth Amendment, and that the libel law from which the case law of group libel also developed was largely modified since *Beauharnais*.[196]

Brigman suggests that claims that pornography is a form of group libel are inaccurate because the differential treatment of women in it (claimed in the civil rights law) is nonexistent: Women, men, and children are all objectified and harmed in pornography. A group libel law, he states, must "protect something less than the entire population."[197] Brigman's views seem to be primarily based on his belief that "[t]here is a vast difference between Joseph Beauharnais' explicit attacks on blacks in his leaflets and the indirect commentary on women found in pornographic materials."[198]

(We find differences, but they are not those of Brigman. If anything, the woman hatred and promotion of and incitement to violence against women in pornography is much more extensive, much more graphic, and much more dangerous than the statements of Beauharnais. Both examples of group vilification deserve punishment under the laws of group libel.)

Various cases have considered group libel claims. In *Michigan United Conservation Clubs* v. *CBS News*, it was alleged that two CBS documentary films defamed the club and all Michigan hunters, more than a million people. The films criticized sports game hunting. The court emphasized that references to large groups do not constitute actionable defamation under *Schuster* v. *U.S. News and World Report, Inc.* Also, the individuals who sued did not show special personal application of the alleged defamation to them. The court rejected the claim that the clubs were defamed in the films because they were not even mentioned. In *Schuster*, the plaintiffs, who were among hundreds of people involved in selling, distributing, and advocating Laetrile, failed to make a claim for the same reasons cited in *Michigan United Conservation Clubs*.[199]

A suit by *Khalid Abdullah Tariq Al Mansour Faissal Fahd Al Talal* v. *Fanning* claimed that followers of the Islamic faith (more than 600 million people) were defamed by the film *Death of a Princess*, which depicted the death by public execution of a Saudi Arabian princess for adultery. The court concluded that to grant recovery ($20 billion in damages was sought) would render the First Amendment right to explore issues of public importance meaningless.[200]

In *National Nutritional Foods Association* v. *Whelan*, a group libel claim was dismissed because the allegedly defamatory communications—words such as "rip-off" and "quackery"—and excessive prices were not sufficiently condemnatory to amount to defamation. The plaintiffs failed to show that the alleged libels were addressed to them individually. The court cited other cases that found that a corporation may pursue a defamation action but an entire industry may not.[201]

In *Granger* v. *Time, Inc.*, a claim of group libel failed because the plaintiffs were unable to show that a general statement about arson applied to them specifically rather than to the large group of between two hundred and four hundred people in the community whose buildings were destroyed by fire.[202]

In *Kentucky Fried Chicken of Bowling Green, Inc.*, v. *Sanders*, general remarks made about chicken quality at Kentucky Fried Chicken restaurants were not defamatory because they did not pertain to any particular person or restaurant.[203]

In *Mikolinski* v. *Reynolds Production Co.*, persons of Polish descent (and an organization of such persons) did not have a group libel claim based on alleged defamation in a movie because the plaintiffs could not show any defamatory remarks directed at individuals.[204]

Articles about a lake's environmental conditions that allegedly defamed the community were the topic of litigation in *Ginert* v. *Howard Publications*. The claim failed because it involved a large group and there was no specific application to individual group members.[205]

In one of the most frequently cited group libel

cases, *Neiman-Marcus* v. *Lait*, an action for group libel was sustained for 9 models and 15 salesmen out of 25 salesmen who sued. But a group libel claim was dismissed for a group of 30 saleswomen out of 382 saleswomen employed by Neiman-Marcus. The court said, "Where the group or class libeled is large, none can sue even though the language used is inclusive [citations omitted]. Where the group or class libel is small, and each and every member of the group or class is referred to, then any individual member can sue."[206]

In *Collin* v. *Smith*, the Village of Stokie, Illinois (a primarily Jewish community) denied Nazis (National Socialist party of America) a permit to march in front of the village hall. A local law required a finding by officials that an assembly "will not portray criminality, depravity or lack of virtue in, or incite violence, hatred, abuse or hostility toward a person or group of persons by reason of reference to religious, racial, ethnic, national or regional affiliation." Another law prohibited the dissemination of material that "promotes and incites hatred against persons by reason of their race, national origin, or religion, and is intended to do so." This included clothing of symbolic significance and posters. Public demonstrations by party members wearing military-style uniforms also were prohibited. The court found that the activities in which the Nazis wanted to engage were of a type covered by the First Amendment (namely, wearing arm bands, carrying placards, marching, and so on). Although reasonable time, place, and manner regulations can cover speech assemblies, expression cannot be restricted because of its "message, its ideas, its subject matter, or its content."

Importantly, in *Collin*, the village did not rely on a fear of responsive violence to justify the law and did not suggest that such violence would occur if the march were held. This eliminated any claim based on the fighting words doctrine of *Chaplinsky*. However, it should be noted that the Illinois Supreme Court had previously ruled that the fighting words doctrine could not support prohibition of the demonstration.

The *Collin* court said that the Nazi ideology could not be treated as a "mere false 'fact' " and that there is no such thing as a false idea under the First Amendment. It said that *Beauharnais* did not apply because it relied on possible violence. The court also said that it doubted the validity of that case after the more recent libel cases. Finally, the court refused to criminalize protected First Amendment conduct in anticipation that the activity might be tortious conduct (intentional infliction of severe emotional distress on Holocaust survivors and other Jewish residents). It also refused to declare the village a "privacy" zone and suggested that, because the speech would not be offending people in their homes, it was not prohibitable on that theory.[207]

PRIVACY

Persons who have had sexually explicit depictions of them used without their consent can obtain legal relief by suing for invasion of privacy. The four legal causes of action based on privacy are as follows:

False Light: To make out a claim for false light, one must show that the person was publicly placed in a false light in a way that would be highly offensive to a person of ordinary sensibilities or to a reasonable person. Such statements must be public, about the plaintiff, unprivileged, and substantially and materially false.[208]

Under *Time, Inc.* v. *Hill*, when false reports of matters of public interest are involved, an action for invasion of privacy will fail unless it can be shown that the report was published with knowledge of its falsity or in reckless disregard of the truth (the *Sullivan* public official/figure principle applied to libel). See *Cantrell* v. *Forest City Publishing Co.* for a situation in which actual malice justified recovery for false light.[209]

Private Facts: To make out a claim for a "private facts" invasion of privacy, one must show that the person gave publicity to a matter concerning the private life of the plaintiff and that the matter is not of legitimate concern to the public and would be highly offensive to a reasonable person. Under this action, the statements made must be alleged to be true (unlike libel or false light claims).[210]

Appropriation Invasion of Privacy: This cause of action arises from the appropriation of a person's likeness or name for commercial benefit without renumeration or consent. This is sometimes called the right of publicity. In *Zacchini* v. *Scripps-Howard Broadcasting Co.*, the court found that misappropriation cases do not inherently violate First Amendment rights. However, such causes of action do not apply to communications about matters of legitimate public interest (such as newsworthy items).[211]

Intrusion: According to the *Restatement of Torts*, "One who intentionally intrudes, physically or otherwise, upon the solitude or seclusion of another or his private affairs or concerns, is subject to liability to the other for invasion of his privacy, if the intrusion would be highly offensive to a reasonable person."[212] The intrusion lawsuit attacks wrongful conduct (such as harassing pursuit by photographers) rather than a published work.

Ruth Colker argues persuasively that a new tort should be created to compensate persons for injury caused by unauthorized sexual portrayals. She proposes the following legislation:

Section 1. Publishers, filmmakers, producers, and all other persons who contribute to the production of pictorial or prose portrayals must obtain written consent from an individual before disseminating or modifying a pictorial or prose portrayal of that individual's sexual anatomical areas or sexual activities for commercial purposes in magazines, newspapers, movies or other forms of public portrayal. This written consent must specify the context of the dissemination or modification of each use of a portrayal. This obligation to obtain written consent applies to any pictorial or prose portrayal, as described above, in which a real person is portrayed in a recognizable manner, irrespective of whether the portrayal is considered fictional.

Section 2. An individual may bring an action against a publisher, filmmaker, producer, or any other individual who has intentionally or negligently failed to obtain his or her written consent, as required in section 1, to recover monetary damages for his or her injury, including but not limited to, damages to his or her reputation, career, personality, and emotional well-being. The fact that the individual portrayed has previously provided written consent to be portrayed sexually is not a defense to the requirement of written consent to the dissemination or modification of pictorial or verbal portrayals described in section 1.

Section 3. Definitions.

(a) "Sexual anatomical areas" are defined as:

1. less than completely and opaquely covered: (a) human genitals, pubic region. (b) buttocks, and (c) female breast below a point immediately above the top of the areola;

2. human male genitals in a discernibly turgid state, even if completely and opaquely covered.

(b) "Sexual activities" are defined as:

1. human genitals in a state of sexual stimulation or arousal;

2. acts of masturbation, sexual intercourse or sodomy;

3. fondling or other erotic touching of human genitals, pubic region, buttocks or female breast.

(c) Portrayals for "commercial purposes" are defined as: artwork, advertisements, nonfiction, fiction, movies, photographs, theatre productions, or other portrayals that are not used primarily for the purpose of disseminating news. Whether the primary purpose of a portrayal is to disseminate news shall be determined by analyzing the content, form and context of the portrayal as revealed by the publication in which the portrayal appears are not for the primary purpose of disseminating news then the portrayal will be considered commercial. If the primary purpose of the portrayal or the publication is to degrade, humiliate, or embarrass the individual portrayed on the basis of sex, then the portrayal is *per se* nonnewsworthy. Whether the individual portrayed is a public figure is not relevant to the determination of whether the primary purpose of the specific portrayal or publication is to disseminate news.

(d) "Dissemination" is defined as: publication, display, reproduction, or any other form of public portrayal.

(e) "Modification" is defined as: any dissemination of a portrayal that is not identical to the original portrayal.

(f) "Pictorial or prose portrayal" includes photographs, drawings, captions, descriptions, movies, or any other type of portrayal that does not include only verbal portrayals.

(g) "Written consent" is defined as: a signed statement by the individual portrayed that provides authorization for a portrayal to be used in a specified context. If the individual portrayed is a minor or not otherwise competent under local law, then written consent may be obtained from the individual's parent or guardian. However, once a minor reaches the age of majority, he or she acquires the right to consent to future publication of the portrayal.

Section 4. Severability.

If any of these sections, sub-sections, or phrases are found to be unlawful or unconstitutional, then these unlawful or unconstitutional sections, sub-sections, or phrases should be severed from the statute unless severing the invalid portion of the statute would clearly frustrate the intent of this statute.[213]

(We believe that Colker's proposed law is a good one. We would modify her proposal to include sadomasochistic sexual portrayals and modify the consent provisions to clarify that a lack of consent can exist when coercion, intimidation, fraud, or enticement occur—despite the fact that someone signed a consent form. In addition, injunctions to prevent further distribution of materials covered by the law should be permitted.)

Colker points out that actual malice should not be required in privacy actions involving consentless sexual portrayals. Rather, she suggests the use of a negligence standard. (We agree.) Unauthorized sexual portrayals, she notes, infringe upon the civil rights of the persons portrayed and rarely serve any newsworthy purpose. Colker suggests applying a balancing test, similar to that suggested by the *Ferber* (child pornography) court, to unauthorized sexual portrayals. Protecting the right of individuals to control dissemination of their sexual portrayals would be balanced against the publisher's free speech interests. She says that the "evil to be restricted" (in the words of *Ferber*) overwhelmingly outweighs the expressive interests (unless the primary purpose of the publication is to impart news). Importantly, Colker's proposed legislation would require that a person consent to each context in which his or her sexual portrayal was used. For example, a photograph intended for one magazine could not be published in another without new consent being given.[214]

The outcomes of cases for consentless sexual portrayals are detailed in Colker's "Published Consentless Sexual Portrayals: A Proposed Framework for Analysis." Footnote 7 of that work, which lists those cases and outcomes, is included as appendix J. Persons who have brought actions for consentless sexual portrayals under current laws are usually unsuccessful, Colker states. They usually fit into one of five categories:

1. Widely known persons who are not political figures (often actresses or models)
2. Private persons who have consentless information about their sexual victimization or behavior published
3. Persons who have fictionalized accounts of their sexual behavior portrayed
4. "[I]ndividuals who seek to enter the arena of political dialogue and face sexual invectives about their gender"
5. Private persons who appear in advertisements in a sexually suggestive context

Colker argues that the *Time, Inc.* v. *Hill* requirement of proving actual malice in false light privacy cases is not required in other types of privacy actions. The *Hill* case, she says, stated that its holding did not necessarily apply to other invasion of privacy actions, such as one for intentional infliction of emotional distress.[215] In *Douglass* v. *Hustler*, in which an actress sued for consentless sexual portrayal, the court suggested that a requirement that a plaintiff prove a defendant was negligent in mistaking the existence of a release form might be enough to protect First Amendment interests.[216]

An excellent description of the right of privacy and how it could be used to make a group defamation claim on behalf of all women for sexual display of their bodies as a class is found in Barbara S. Bryant's "Sexual Display of Women's Bodies—A Violation of Privacy." She points out that in *Griswold* v. *Connecticut,* the court held that use of contraceptives in a marital relationship cannot be prohibited because marital privacy is a fundamental right entitled to constitutional protection. *Roe* v. *Wade* upheld the right of women to decide whether or not to have an abortion (but only during the first trimester). That decision was based on the fact that it involved a right of personal privacy against governmental intrusion in matters of "intimate concern." *Eisenstadt* v. *Baird* found a privacy right of unmarried persons to receive birth control devices and information. *Eisenstadt* said, "If the right of privacy means anything, it is the right of the *individual,* married or single, to be free from unwarranted governmental intrusion into matters so fundamentally affecting a person as the decision whether to bear or beget a child." Bryant cites an argument that violations of personal privacy threaten individual liberty in much the same way as the torts of assault, battery, and false imprisonment.[217]

In *Ann-Margret* v. *High Society Magazine*, a pornographic magazine ran a photograph of actress Ann-Margret in which one of her breasts was visible. It was taken from a motion picture without consent for its use. The court ruled against Ann-Margret stating that the actual malice requirement could not be met and that the statute under which she had sued did not provide a right to consent to each context in which she was portrayed.[218]

In *Lerman* v. *Flynt Distributing*, author Jackie Collins Lerman was erroneously identified as an individual portrayed in nude photographs and labeled as a starlet who appeared in an orgy scene in a film based on a book she had written. She sued for violation of the New York privacy law, invasion of her common law right to publicity, and libel. Although the lower court awarded her injunctive relief and $10 million in damages, the appellate court reversed the decision based on her status as a public figure. The court decided that it could not be demonstrated that anyone in the defendant's company was subjectively aware of the probable falsity.[219] However, when *Playgirl* published a nude portrait of a black man who was unmistakably recognizable as Muhammad Ali, an injunction to stop distribution of the issue on right of privacy grounds was granted (*Ali* v. *Playgirl, Inc.*).[220]

In *Wood* v. *Hustler Magazine, Inc.*, nude photographs that a husband and wife took of each other in private were stolen. The photo of the wife was published in *Hustler* with a caption that her fantasy was being "tied down and screwed by two bikers."

The people who stole the photographs forged Wood's name to the consent form. Wood suffered mental anguish and humiliation and sought counseling because of publication of the photo. She sued under a privacy false light and disclosure of private facts claim. The court held that the *Gertz* standard of negligence (and not the actual malice standard) would be applied because Wood was a private figure. It ruled that *Hustler* had carelessly administered "a slipshod procedure that allowed LaJuan [Woods] to be placed in a false light in the pages of Hustler Magazine." The court suggested that because of the nature of the photographs and fantasies, great care should have been taken to verify consent. For example, a driver's license, Social Security number, or home phone verification could have been used. The court said that $150,000 in damages was not excessive.[221]

Kimerli Jayne Pring was awarded more than $14 million in damages by the jury in *Pring* v. *Penthouse International,* but the appellate court reversed the judgment. The object of the suit was a fictional story in which a Miss Wyoming in a Miss America contest performed acts of fellatio in front of a national television audience. There were similarities between the woman depicted and Pring, who had been Miss Wyoming in a Miss America contest. The appellate court said that Pring did not have a cause of action for defamation because the allegedly defamatory portions of the story "described something physically impossible in an impossible setting" and it was impossible to believe that a reader would not have understood that these portions were pure fantasy.[222]

Courts also have held that use of nude or sexually explicit photographs in films or magazines might not be in violation of laws prohibiting use of pictures for advertising or trade purposes. (See, for example, *McGray* v. *Watkins.*[223])

Occasionally, plaintiffs have won lawsuits for unauthorized publication of sexual portrayals. The elements of an action charging invasion of privacy are, in summary, as follows:

> (1) private affairs in which the public has no legitimate concern; (2) publication of such affairs, including identification of the facts disclosed with the complainant; (3) unwarranted publication, that is, absence of any waiver or privilege authorizing it; and (4) publication such as would cause mental suffering, shame, or humiliation to a person of ordinary sensibilities.[224]

PRIMA FACIE TORT

When a victim of pornography does not appear to have a cause of action in civil court under any of the established legal torts (such as libel, violation of right to privacy, false light, or assault), it might be possible for that person to file a prima facie tort claim. This is a remedy for harmful within the boundaries of any of the traditional tort actions.[225]

INTENTIONAL INFLICTION OF EMOTIONAL DISTRESS

In some cases, it could be argued that pornography has intentionally inflicted emotional distress—a common law tort. For example, in *Young* v. *Stensrude,* the plaintiff claimed that an employer "intentionally, recklessly, or negligently inflicted severe emotional distress upon plaintiff 'by showing Plaintiff an X-rated pornographic movie, to-wit, "Deep Throat," after representing to Plaintiff that the movie to be shown was an educational film.' " During the movie's showing, the employer uttered "sexual obscenities" to the plaintiff in the presence of four other men. The court held that the plaintiff had stated a cause of action and refused to dismiss the complaint.[226]

Richard Bernstein writes about First Amendment limits on tort liability for "words intended to inflict severe emotional distress." He notes that the conduct under this cause of action must be " 'extreme and outrageous.' " He notes that in *Falwell* v. *Flynt,* Reverend Jerry Falwell sued *Hustler* magazine for intentional infliction of emotional distress and was awarded $200,000 in compensatory and punitive damages by a jury. An "Ad Parody" in that magazine depicted Falwell as a " 'hypocritical, incestuous drunkard.' " A defamation claim was denied because the ad could not have been "reasonably understood to assert facts."[227]

It should be remembered, as Bernstein points out, that much speech, including that with First

Amendment protection, is intended to harm its target. One example of this is political debate speech. He expresses concern that the intentional infliction of emotional distress tort could create opportunities to suppress unpopular ideas because such ideas often include extreme, outrageous language.[228] (We believe that the courts can differentiate between political or other idea-oriented speech that would be protected under the First Amendment and speech, such as pornography, that should not receive such protection.)

IMITATIVE VIOLENCE

Another area in which pornography victims could sue under current law is that of imitative violence (for example, if a victim is raped by someone imitating pornography). However, current law is weak in this area and statutorily enacted laws are needed.

E. Barrett Prettyman, Jr., and Lisa A. Hook present three theories concerning media-related imitative violence:

1. According to the instructional, or modeling, theory, children "learn to behave aggressively from watching violent actors on television" just as they learn behavior from people. Imitation is more likely if an aggressor is rewarded for such behavior. Actors with valued characteristics are more likely to be imitated.
2. The attiduinal change theory says that a person becomes more "accepting of or desensitized to aggressive behavior" the more television he or she watches. This may lead to more aggression by the viewer.
3. The incitement or arousal theory asserts that the viewer is aroused by depictions of violence.[229]

Prettyman and Hook note that the FCC says it does not have the authority to develop regulations governing television violence under the Communications Act or the First Amendment.[230] They explain that imitative violence tort causes of action involve viewers who injure themselves or others while imitating an act portrayed in the media. Negligence is often the charge in such cases.[231]

The following four cases are in the forefront of this field; none allowed recovery:

Shannon v. *Walt Disney Productions, Inc.* An 11-year-old boy imitated an act on the *Mickey Mouse Club* and was partially blinded.
DeFilippo v. *National Broadcasting Co.* A boy imitated a hanging stunt done by Johnny Carson (despite a warning on the show that it could be dangerous) and died.
Olivia N. v. *National Broadcasting Co., Inc.* Minors who viewed the television movie *Born Innocent* imitated a scene by raping a 9-year-old girl with a bottle (a plunger was used in the movie).
Zamora v. *Columbia Broadcasting System.* A 15-year-old who shot and killed an elderly neighbor claimed he had been subliminally intoxicated since age 5 by violence on all three major networks.[232]

Prettyman and Hook state that, in order to show a cause of action for negligence, the plaintiff must prove the following:

(1) the existence of a duty requiring the defendant to conform to a certain standard of conduct for the protection of others against unreasonable risks; (2) a breach of the defendant's duty to conform to the required standard; (3) a casual relationship between the defendant's conduct and the plaintiff's injury, both actual and proximate; and (4) actual damages as a result of the plaintiff's injury.[233]

They address each of those aspects, applying them to case examples that relate to imitative violence, and stress the need to determine whether such a cause of action could be made out on a case-by-case basis. For example, imitative violence might be more foreseeable in some cases than in others. They stress that a plaintiff would usually have to show actual causation. This, they state, involves showing that the plaintiff would not "have been harmed 'but for' the defendant's conduct." (Such conduct is not a cause if the situation would have happened without the defendant's conduct). It should be a "material element and a substantial factor" in bringing about the event. Incitement or instruction/modeling effects can be argued.

Hook and Prettyman conclude that the causation issue involves showing that the harm done to the plaintiff is "sufficiently direct, natural and probable to justify imposing liability." Probability is hard to show because the inconclusive nature of scientific research and examples of violent programs being broadcast without adverse responses weigh against it. They note that proof of causation without modeling effect in addition to an incitement effect would be "virtually impossible."[234]

In the *Herceg* case, a mother sued *Hustler* magazine for the wrongful death of her son. He had read an article and seen pictures in *Hustler* that demonstrated the dangerous practice of autoerotic asphyxiation. He imitated the article and died of strangulation. He was found with the article nearby. Although the lower court and jury awarded damages to the mother (finding a sufficient factual connection between the pornography and the boy's death), the Fifth Circuit Court of Appeals overturned that decision on First Amendment grounds.[235] The case is on appeal to the U.S. Supreme Court. (We note that the cartoonist who draws the *Hustler* cartoon

"Chester The Molester" was arrested and charged with child molestation. The allegations against the man stemmed from an investigation of a teenage girl who was allegedly molested for years.[236])

(We suggest that any victim or attorney attempting to make out an imitative violence cause of action against pornographers read the Prettyman and Hook article. We believe that such causes of action should be upheld by the courts. However, due to the lack of success in this field in the past, we encourage enactment of specific state laws creating such a cause of action in order to make it clear to the courts that legislative bodies intend for such lawsuits to be permitted.)

LABOR AND HEALTH LAWS

Existing health laws could be used against pornography. For example, peep show booths in pornographic bookstores could be shut down or regulated based on the sex that takes place among booth patrons, for this is one way of spreading sexually transmitted diseases such as AIDS.

Labor and health laws could be used or enacted to prohibit use of persons in pornography. Again,

the theory is that performing for pornography is a health risk in the sense that there is a high risk of getting AIDS or another sexually transmitted disease. This type of work should be considered so dangerous to safety and health that it (or a pornographer's employing or using anyone for that purpose) is declared illegal.

PRODUCT LIABILITY

Pornography could be considered a product and its producers and distributors manufacturers. Linz et al. make a case for causes of action against pornographers based on product liability theories. It could be argued that the manufacturer's negligent or wrongful conduct harmed the plaintiff. A cause of action would involve similar types of proof as that described in the imitative violence section earlier in this chapter. They say that strict liability also could be applied. In that case, the plaintiff would have to show the following:

1. The manufacturer may be liable for product construction defects.

2. The manufacturer could be liable for "design defects in which the material does not perform in accordance with its own performance standards when put to ordinary use."
3. The manufacturer "may not have used adequate labels to warn the user of nonobvious dangers."

They suggest ways of using expert witnesses and scientific study data in civil lawsuits against pornographers to support claims of product liability or imitative violence.[237] (We encourage legislatures to enact laws creating causes of action for pornography victims that include product liability–type theories.)

CONCLUSION

We believe that it is essential for laws to be enacted creating a variety of civil causes of action for victims

of pornography. These laws would compensate victims for the harm done them, enable them to get the harmful pornography off the market, and, in the long run, make pornography production and distribution so unprofitable that it would not be produced or distributed. As a result, fewer people would be victimized by it.

NOTES

1. *Village of Schaumburg v. Citizens for a Better Environment*, 444 U.S. 620, 636 (1980).
2. *Members of City Council v. Taxpayers for Vincent*, 466 U.S. 789 (1984).
3. *Clark v. Community for Creative Non-Violence*, 104 S. Ct. 3065, 3069 (1984).
4. *Virginia State Board of Pharmacy v. Virginia Citizens Consumer Council, Inc.*, 425 U.S. 748 (1976).
5. *Heffron v. International Society for Krisha Consciousness, Inc.*, 452 U.S. 640 (1981).
6. *Grayned v. City of Rockford*, 408 U.S. 104 (1972).
7. *Williams v. Rhodes*, 393 U.S. 23 (1968).
8. *Buckley v. Valeo*, 424 U.S. 1 (1975).
9. *Pittsburgh Press Co. v. Pittsburgh Commission on Human Relations*, 413 U.S. 376 (1973).
10. *Bob Jones University v. United States*, 461 U.S. 574, 604 (1983).
11. *California Motor Transport Co. v. Trucking Unlimited*, 404 U.S. 508, 514 (1972).
12. *Roth v. United States*, 354 U.S. 476, 484 (1957).
13. *Roberts v. United States Jaycees*, 104 S. Ct. 3224 (1984).
14. Caryn Jacobs, "Patterns of Violence: A Feminist Perspective on the Regulation of Pornography," *Harvard Women's Law Journal* 7 (1984): 45–46.
15. Ibid., 47–48.
16. Ibid., 52–54.
17. Valerie J. Hamm, "The Civil Rights Pornography Ordinances—An Examination under the First Amendment," *Kentucky Law Journal* (1984–85): 1081–1108, 1101.
18. Geoffrey R. Stone, "Comment: Anti-Pornography Legislation as Viewpoint Discrimination," *Harvard Journal of Law and Public Policy* 9 (1981): 461–80, 461.
19. *Police Department of Chicago v. Mosely*, 408 U.S. 92 (1972); *Carey v. Brown*, 447 U.S. 455 (1980); *Schneider v. State*, 308 U.S. 151 (1939).
20. *Lehman v. City of Shaker Heights*, 418 U.S. 298 (1974).
21. *Young v. American Mini Theatres, Inc.*, 427 U.S. 50 (1976).
22. *FCC v. Pacifica Foundation*, 438 U.S. 726 (1978).
23. *First National Bank of Boston v. Bellotti*, 435 U.S. 765 (1978).
24. *American Booksellers Association v. Hudnut*, 771 F.2d 323 (7th Cir. 1985), *aff'd*, 106 S. Ct. 1172 (1986).
25. Cass R. Sunstein, "Pornography and the First Amendment," *Duke Law Journal* 4 (September 1986): 611–12.
26. *City of Renton v. Playtime Theaters, Inc.*, 106 S. Ct. 925 (1986).
27. Sunstein "Pornography and the First Amendment," 613–16.
28. Stone, "Anti-Pornography Legislation," 462–463.
29. Michael Gershel, "Evaluating a Proposed Civil Rights Approach to Pornography: Legal Analysis as if Women Mattered," *William Mitchell Law Review* 11 (1985): 68. See also *Mess v. Indiana*, 414 U.S. 105 (1973) (per curian); *Brandenburg v. Ohio*, 395 U.S. 444 (1969) (per curian); *Schenck v. United States*, 249 U.S. 47 (1919).
30. Gershel, "Evaluating a Proposed Civil Rights Approach," 69–70.
31. Sunstein, "Pornography and the First Amendment," 602–3.
32. Randall D.B. Tigue, "Civil Rights and Censorship—Incompatible Bedfellows," *William Mitchell Law Review* 11 (1985), 81, 111–12.
33. Hamm, "Civil Rights Ordinances," 1093.
34. James R. Branit, "Reconciling Free Speech and Equality—What Justifies Censorship?" Harvard Journal of Law and Public Policy 9 (1986): 429–60, 441–43.
35. *Landmark Communications, Inc. v. Virginia*, 435 U.S. 829, 843–44 (1978).
36. Ibid., quoting *Bridges v. California*, 314 U.S. 252 (1941); 830, 842–844.
37. *Pennekamp v. Florida*, 328 U.S. 331 (1946); *Craig v. Harney*, 331 U.S. 367 (1947); *Wood v. Georgia*, 370 U.S. 375 (1962).
38. *Bridges*, 263.
39. *Craig*, 376.
40. "Note: Group Vilification Reconsidered," *Yale Law Journal* 89 (1979): 308–332, 316. quoting *Feiner v. New York*, 340 U.S. 315, 320 (1951) 572.
41. *Chaplinsky v. New Hampshire*, 315 U.S. 568, 572 (1942).
42. Hamm, "Civil Rights Ordinances," 1093.
43. *New York v. Ferber*, 458 U.S. 747 (1982).
44. Gershel, "Evaluating a Proposed Civil Rights Approach," 71–72.
45. Jacobs, "Patterns of Violence," 37–40.
46. Sunstein, "Pornography and the First Amendment," 602–4.
47. Ibid., 606.
48. Tigue, "Civil Rights and Censorship," 113–14.
49. *Pittsburgh Press*, citing *New York Times Company v. Sullivan*, 376 U.S. 254 (1964). 376–391.
50. *Valentine v. Christensen*, 316 U.S. 52 (1942).
51. *Pittsburgh Press*, 376.
52. *Virginia State Board of Pharmacy*, 748.
53. *First National Bank*, 765.

54. *Central Hudson Gas and Electric Corp. v. Public Service Commission*, 447 U.S. 557 (1980).

55. *Posadas De Puerto Rico Association v. Tourism Co.*, 106 S. Ct. 2968 (1986).

56. *Buckley v. Valeo*, 424 U.S. 1 (1976).

57. *Red Lion Broadcasting Co.. v. FCC*, 396 U.S. 367 (1969).

58. Sunstein, "Pornography and the First Amendment," 618–24.

59. W.G. Roesler, "Regulating Adult Entertainment Establishments Under Conventional Zoning," *The Urban Lawyer* 1987 19(1): 125. quoting *Village of Euclid v. Ambler Realty Co.*, 272 U.S. 365.

60. Daniel S. Moretti, *Obscenity and Pornography: The Law under the First Amendment* (New York: Oceana Publications, 1984), 100.

61. *Schad v. Borough of Mount Ephraim*, 452 U.S. 61, 68 (1981).

62. Moretti, *Obscenity and Pornography*, 99–102. quoting *Young v. American Mini Theaters*, 427 U.S. 50 (1976).

63. Ibid., 103–4. citing *Alexander v. City of Minneapolis*, 698 F.2d 936 (1983).

64. Roesler, "Regulating Adult Entertainment," 137, fn. 31.

65. Ibid., 136. citing United States v. O'Brien, 391 U.S. 367 (1968).

66. Ronald M. Stein, "Regulation of Adult Business Through Zoning after Renton," *Pacific Law Journal* 18 (1987): 351.

67. Ibid., 352.

68. Ibid., 360–62.

69. Ibid., 362–68.

70. Ibid., 373–75.

71. David J. Macher, "City of Renton v. Playtime Theaters: Pornography Zoning Attains a Majority," *Western State University Law Review* 14 (1986): 287.

72. Charles H. Clarke, "Freedom of Speech and the Problem of the Lawful Harmful Public Reaction: Adult Use cases of *Renton* and *Mini Theaters*," *Akron Law Review* 20 (1986): 187, 188.

73. *Obscenity Law Reporter* (New York: National Obscenity Law Center, 1986), 42,017; *Young v. American Mini-Theaters*, 427 U.S. 50 (1976).

74. Ibid., 42,019; *Bayou Landin Ltd. v. Watts*, 563 F. 2d 1172 (5th Cir. 1977); *Cert. denied*, 439 U.S. 818 (1978).

75. Ibid., 42,020–21; citing *Schad v. Borough of Mount Ephraim*, 452 U.S. 61 (1981).

76. Ibid., 42,004–5, 42,048; *United States v. O'Brien*, 391 U.S. 367 (1968).

77. Ibid., 42,022; Trombetta v. *Mayor and Commissioners of Atlantic City*, 436 A. 2d 1349 (N.J. Super. Ct. 1981), *aff'd.* 454 A. 2d 900 (N.J. Super. Ct. App. Aiv. 1982).

78. *Genusa v. Peoria*, 619 F.2d 1203 (7th Cir. 1980); David J. Macher, *"City of Renton v. Playtime Theatres:* Pornography Zoning Attains a Majority," 14 Western S.U.L. Rev. 287 (1986).

79. *Obscenity Law Reporter*, 42,025. *Young; Berman v. Parker*, 348 U.S. 26 (1954).

80. Ibid., 42,025. *Village of Belle Terre v. Boraas*, 416 U.S. 1 (1974).

81. *United States v. O'Brien*, 391 U.S. 367 (1968); *McCray v. United States*, 195 U.S. 56 (1904).

82. *Obscenity Law Reporter*, 42,029. *Young.*

83. Ibid., 42,033.

84. Ibid., 42,034.

85. Ibid., 42,035.

86. Ibid., 42,036.

87. Ibid., 42,037. *Young; Northend Cinema, Inc. v. City of Seattle*, 585 P.2d 1153 (Wash. Sup. Ct. 1978). *Cert. denied* 441 U.S. 946 (1979).

88. Ibid., 42,038. *Keego Harbor Co. v. City of Keego Harbor*, 657 F. 2d 94 (6th Cir. 1981).

89. *Larkin v. Grendel's Den*, 459 U.S. 116 (1982).

90. *Obscenity Law Reporter*, 42,039.

91. Ibid., 42,053. *Hart Book Store, Inc. v. Edmisten*, 612 F.2d (4th Cir. 1979), *cert. denied*, 447 U.S. 929 (1980).

92. Ibid., 46,002, 46,009.

93. Ibid., 46,012.

94. Ibid., 46,013–15. OLR, 46,015 citing *Universal Amusement Co. Inc. v. Vance*, 445 U.S. 308 (1980).

95. Ibid., 46,502–5.

96. Jeffrey S. Trachtman, "Note: Pornography, Padlocks, and Prior Restraints—The Constitutional Limits of the Nuisance Power," *New York University Law Review* 58 (1983): 1478, 1529.

97. Ibid., 1480.

98. Ibid., 1484–86.

99. Ibid., 1515, 1517.

100. Ibid., 1520.

101. *Arcara v. Cloud Books, Inc.*, 478 U.S. 697, 705, 106 S. Ct. 3172, 92 L.Ed. 2d 568 (1986).

102. Ibid., 705.

103. *KMA, Inc. v. Newport News*, 228 Va. 365, 323 S.E.3d 78, *cert. denied*, 85 L.Ed. 2d 842, 105 S. Ct. 2324 (1984).

104. Frederick F. Schauer, *The Law of Obscenity* (Washington, DC: Bureau of National Affairs, 1976), 228.

105. *Near v. Minnesota*, 283 U.S. 697 (1931).

106. Schauer, *The Law of Obscenity*, 229.

107. *Freedman v. Maryland*, 380 U.S. 51, 58–59 (1965).

108. Schauer, *The Law of Obscenity*, 232.

109. *Teitel Films v. Cusack*, 390 U.S. 139 (1968); *Blount v. Rizzi*, 400 U.S. 410 (1971); *United States v. Thirty-Seven Photographs*, 402 U.S. 363 (1971).

110. Schauer, *The Law of Obscenity*, 233.

111. *Southeastern Promotions, Ltd. v. Conrad*, 420 U.S. 546 (1975).

112. *Times Film Corp. v. Chicago*, 365 U.S. 43 (1961).

113. *Kunz v. New York*, 340 U.S. 290, 294 (1951).

114. *Southeastern Promotions Ltd.*, 558.

115. *Bantam Books, Inc. v. Sullivan*, 372 U.S. 58, 59–60 (1963).

116. Trachtman, "Pornography, Padlocks, and Prior Restraints," 1501.

117. *Obscenity Law Reporter*, 43,009. *Ginsberg v. New York*, 390 U.S. 629 (1968).

118. Ibid., 43,010–11.

119. Ibid., 43,014.

120. *Erznoznik v. City of Jacksonville*, 422 U.S. 205, 207 (1975).

121. Bruce Taylor, Memorandum (Citizens for Decency Through Law, Phoenix, Arizona: 23 July 1979).

122. Moretti, *Obscenity and Pornography*, 65.

123. *Pacifica*, 751–55.

124. Moretti, *Obscenity and Pornography*, 66–74.

125. Paul E. Scheidemantel, "It's Only Rock and Roll but They Don't Like It: Censoring 'Indecent' Lyrics," *New England Law Review* 21 no. 2 (1985–1986): 467, 476.

126. *Illinois Citizens Committee for Broadcasting v. FCC*, 169 App. D.C. 166, 515 F.2d 397 (1974).

127. *Red Lion Broadcasting Co.*, 367; *Miami Herald Publishing Co., Inc. v. Tornillo*, 418 U.S. 241 (1974); *FCC v. Midwest Video Corp.*, 440 U.S. 689 (1979); [described in] Jessica Sporn, "Content Regulation of Cable Television: 'Indecency' Statutes and the First Amendment," *Rutgers Computer and Technology* 11 (1985)· 141–70, 154

128. Sporn, *Content Regulation of Cable*, 144–45; *Wisconsin v. Yoder*, 406 U.S. 205 (1972); *Prince v. Massachusetts*, 321 U.S. 158 (1944).

129. Moretti, *Obscenity and Pornography*, 85. Deborah A. George, "The Cable Communications Policy Act of 1984 and Content Regulation of Cable Television." *New England Law Review*, 1984–85. 20(4):779–804.

130. Lynn D. Wardle, "Cable Television Programming," *Denver University Review* 63 (1986): 621–95, 623, 627–28.

131. Ann E. Rhoads, "The Pig in the Parlor: Pennsylvania Senate Bill 645 and the Regulation of 'Cable Porn,' " *Dickinson Law Review* 90 (Winter 1985): 463–86, 468.

132. Moretti, *Obscenity and Pornography*, 137.

133. Ibid., 81–82.

134. Rhoads, "The Pig in the Parlor," 464.

135. Ibid., 477, 479.

136. *Butler v. Michigan*, 352 U.S. 380 (1957).

137. *Community Television of Utah, Inc. v. Roy City*, 555 F.Supp. 1164 (D. Utah 1982).

138. Wardle, "Cable Television Programming," 647–49.

139. Ibid.

140. Ibid., 649.

141. Ibid., 650–77, 670, 674.

142. Ibid., 678.

143. Sporn "Content Regulation of Cable," 148–49; *Rowen v. U.S. Post Office Department*, 397 U.S. 728 (1970); *Columbia Broadcasting System v. Democratic National Committee*, 412 U.S. 94 (1973); *Banzhaf v. FCC*, 405 F.2d 1082 (D.C. Cir. 1968), *cert. denied*, 396 U.S. 842 (1969); *Cohen v. California*, 403 U.S. 15 (1971); *Kovacs v. Cooper*, 336 U.S. 77 (1949); *Lehman v. City of Shaker Heights*, 418 U.S. 298 (1974).

144. Robert Showers, "Regulation of Pornography on Cable Television—Can It Be Done?" in ed. Carol A. Clancy, *Pornography: Solutions Through Law* (Washington, D.C.: National Forum Foundation, 1985), 22.

145. Rhoads, "The Pig in the Parlor," 482–84.

146. *Community Television of Utah, Inc. v. Roy City*, 555

F. Supp. 1164; (d. Utah, 1982; *Cruz v. Ferre*, 755 F.2d 1415 (11th Cir. 1985); *Home Box Office v. Wilkinson*, 531 F.Supp. 987, 611 F.Supp. 1104 (1982).

147. Showers, "Regulation of Pornography on Cable . . .," 20.

148. Wardle, 681.

149. Showers, "Regulation of Pornography on Cable" 21.

150. Rhoads, "The Pig in the Parlor," 471.

151. Wardle, "Cable Television Programming," 688.

152. Sporn, "Content Regulation of Cable," 155.

153. Scheidemantel, "It's Only Rock and Roll," 458–61.

154. Ibid., 489–94, 505–8. *Cinevision Corporation v. City of Burbank*, 745 F.2d 560 (1984); *Board of Education, Island Trees Union Free School District No. # 26 v. Pico*, 457 U.S. 853, (1982); 910.

155. Ibid., 514.

156. *Star v. Preller* 419 U.S. 43 (1961); *Times Film Corp.*, 43; *Freedman*, 51.

157. Scheidemantel, 477.

158. Jack Valenti, "The Movie Rating System" (Paper prepared for the Motion Picture Association of America, New York, 7 May 1982).

159. Scheidemantel, 484–88.

160. Moretti, *Obscenity and Pornography*, 107–10.

161. Elizabeth J. Mann, "Telephones, Sex and the First Amendment," *University of California Los Angeles Law Review* 33 (1986).

162. Ibid., 1224–36. *Carlin Communications, Inc. v. FCC*, 749 F.2d 113 (2d Cir. 1984).

163. Ibid., 1233.

164. Ibid., 1236–46.

165. Harvey C. Jassem, "Scrambling the Telephone: The FCC's Dial-a-Porn Regulations," *Communications and the Law*, December, 1988, 3–13.

166. Attorney General's Commission on Pornography, *Final Report* (Washington, DC: United States Department of Justice, 1986), 524.

167. "L.A. Finds a New Weapon in War on Pornography," *Milwaukee Journal*, 29 December 1985.

168. Lori Douglass Hutchins, "Pornography: The Prosecution of Pornographers under Prostitution Statutes—A New Approach," *Syracuse Law Review* 37(1986): 977–1002 summarizing: *Oregon v. Kravitz*, 14 Or. App. 243, 511 P.2d 844 (1973); *People v. Maita*, 157 Cal App. 3d 309, 203 Cal Rptr. 685 (1984); *People v. Fixler*, 56 Cal. App. 3d 321, 128 Cal. Rptr. 363 (1976); *People v. Kovner*, 96 Misc. 2d 414, 409 N.Y.S. 2d 349 (Sup. Ct. N.Y. Co. 1978); *People v. Souter*, 125 Cal. App. 3d 563, 178 Cal Rptr. 111 (1981).

169. *Roberts*, 104 S. Ct. 3244, 3255 (1984).

170. *Henson v. City of Dundee*, 682 F.2d 897, 898 (1982).

171. *Zabkowicz v. West Bend Co.*, 589 F.Supp. 780, 784 (E.D. Wisc. 1984); 601 F.Supp. 139 (1985); 789 F.2d 540 (7th Cir. 1986).

172. *Kyriazi v. Western Electric Co.*, 461 F.Supp. 894, 934 (1978).

173. *Arnold v. City of Seminole, Oklahoma*, 614 F.Supp. 853, 858 (D.C. E.D. Okl. 1985).

174. *Rabidue v. Osceola Refining Co.*, 584 F.Supp. 419, 429 (E.D. Mich. S.D. 1984).

175. Ibid., 433.
176. 383 U.S. 75, 92 (1966) *Gertz v. Robert Welch Inc.*, 418 U.S. 323, 341 (1974), quoting Justice Potter Stewart's concurring opinion in *Rosenblatt v. Baer.*
177. *New York Times v. Sullivan*, 376 U.S. 254 (1964).
178. Kenneth P. Norwick, *The Basic ACLU Guide to the Legal Rights of Authors and Artists* (New York: Bantam Books, 1984), 89.
179. *Gertz*, 339–40.
180. Norwick, *Legal Rights of Authors and Artists*, 96–97.
181. *Sullivan*, 279–80.
182. *Garrison v. Louisiana*, 379 U.S. 64 (1964).
183. Norwick, *Legal Rights of Authors and Artists*, 101.
184. Ibid., 105.
185. Ibid., 116.
186. *Pring v. Penthouse International Ltd..*, 8 Med. L. Rptr. 2409, *cert. denied*, 51 *U.S.L.W.* 3902 (1983), 695 F.2d 438 (1982).
187. *Beauharnais v. Illinois*, 343 U.S. 250 (1952).
188. Gershel, "Evaluating a Proposed Civil Rights Approach," 66–68.
189. Jacobs, "Patterns of Violence," 54.
190. Branit, "Reconciling Free Speech and Equality"; Tigue, "Civil Rights and Censorship"; "Anti-Pornography Law and First Amendment Values," *Harvard Law Review* 98 (1984): 460.
191. "Note: Group Vilification Reconsidered," 310–14.
192. Ibid., 312, fn. 19–20; 314, fn. 26.
193. Ibid., 325–28.
194. Ibid., 332.
195. William E. Brigman, "Pornography as Group Libel: the Indianapolis Sex Discrimination Ordinance," *Indiana Law Review*, 480, fn. 4.
196. Ibid., 487–88.
197. Ibid., 496.
198. Ibid., 505.
199. *Michigan United Conservation Clubs v. CBS News*, 665 F.2d 110 (6th Cir. 1981); *Schuster v. U.S. News and World Report, Inc.* 602 F.2d 850 (8th Cir. 1979).
200. *Khalid Abdullah Tariq Al Mansour Faissal Fahd Al Talal v. Fanning*, 506 F.Supp. 186 (N.D. Calif. 1980).
201. *National Nutritional Foods Association v. Whelan*, 492 F.Supp. 374 (1980).
202. *Granger v. Time, Inc.*, 568 P.2d 535 (1977).
203. *Kentucky Fried Chicken of Bowling Green, Inc. v. Sanders*, 563 S.W.2d 8 (S. Ct. Ky. 1978).
204. *Mikolinski v. Reynolds Production Co.*, 409 N.E.2d (App. Ct. Ma. 1980).
205. *Ginert v. Howard Publications*, 565 F.Supp. 829 (D.C. N.D. Indiana, 1983).
206. *Nieman-Marcus v. Lait*, 13 F.R.D. 311 (S.D. N.Y. 1952).
207. *Collin v. Smith*, 578 F.2d 1197 (7th Cir. 1978), *cert. denied*, 439 U.S. 916, 1199, 1202 (1978).
208. Norwick, *Legal Rights of Authors and Artists*, 119.
209. *Time, Inc. v. Hill*, 385 U.S. 374 (1967); *Cantrell v. Forest City Publishing Co.*, 419 U.S. 245 (1974).
210. *Restatement of the Law of Torts*, (St. Paul, MN: American Law Institute, 1934), s. 652 D.
211. Norwick, *Legal Rights of Authors and Artists*, 121–22. Citing *Zacchini v. Scripps-Howard Broadcasting Co.*, 433 U.S. 562 (1977).
212. *Restatement of the Law of Torts*, s. 652 B.
213. Ruth Colker, "Legislative Remedies for Unauthorized Sexual Portrayals: A Proposal," *New England Law Review* 20 (1984–85): 687, 703–5.
214. Ibid., 689, 696–97.
215. Ruth Colker, "Published Consentless Sexual Portrayals: A Proposed Framework for Analysis," *Buffalo Law Review* 35 (1986): 39, 42–43, 69–71.
216. *Douglass v. Hustler*, 769 F.2d 1128 (7th Cir. 1985).
217. Barbara S. Bryant, "Sexual Display of Women's Bodies—A Violation of Privacy," *Golden Gate University Law Review* 10 (1980): 1211; *Griswold v. Connecticut*, 381 U.S. 479 (1965); *Roe v. Wade*, 410 U.S. 113 (1973); *Eisenstadt v. Baird*, 405 U.S. 438, 453 (1972).
218. *Ann-Margret v. High Society Magazine*, 498 F.Supp. 401 (S. D.N.Y. 1980).
219. *Lerman v. Flynt Distributing*, 745 F.2d 123 (2nd Cir. 1984).
220. *Ali v. Playgirl, Inc.*, 447 F.Supp. 723 (1978).
221. *Wood v. Hustler Magazine, Inc.*, 736 F.2d 1084, *reh. denied*, 744 F.2d 94, *cert. denied*, 83 L.Ed. 2d 777, 105 S. Ct. 783, 1092 (1984).
222. *Pring*, 438.
223. *McGraw v. Watkins*, 373 N.Y.S.2d 663 (1975).
224. Jeffery F. Ghent, "Annotation: Invasion of Privacy by Radio or Television," 56 ALR3d 386–423, 395 (1974).
225. W.E. Shipley, "Prima Facie Tort" 16 ALR3d 1191 (1967).
226. *Young v. Stensrude*, 664 S.W.2d 263 (Mo. App. 1984).
227. Richard Bernstein, "Notes: First Amendment Limits on Tort Liability for Words Intended to Inflict Severe Emotional Distress," *Columbia Law Review* 85 (1985): 1749, 1752, fn. 19.
228. Ibid., 1755, 1759.
229. E. Barrett Prettyman, Jr., and Lisa A. Hook, "The Control of Media-Related Imitative Violence," *Federal Communications Law Journal* 38 (January 1987): 317–82, 326–30.
230. Ibid., 338.
231. Ibid., 344–45.
232. Ibid., 345–47; *Shannon v. Walt Disney Productions, Inc.*, 156 Ga. App. 545, 275 S.E.2d 121 (1980), *rev'd* 247 Ga. 402, 276 S.E.2d 580 (1980); *De Filippo v. National Broadcasting Co.*, 446 A.2d 1036 (R.I. 1980), 74 Cal. App. 3d 383, 141 Cal. Rptr. 511 (1977), *application for stay denied sub nom. Zamora v. Columbia Broadcasting* System, 480 F.Supp. 199 (S.D. Fla. 1979).
233. Prettyman and Hook, "The Control of Media-Related Imitative Violence." 347.
234. Ibid., 360–64.
235. *Herceg v. Hustler*, 814 F.2d 1017 (5th Cir. 1988).
236. "Cartoonist in Custody in Sex Case," *The Oregonian*, May 21, 1989.
237. Daniel Linz, Charles W. Turner, Bradford W. Hesse,

and Steven Penrod, "Bases of Liability for Injuries Produced by Media Portrayals of Violent Pornography," in *Pornography and Sexual Aggression,* eds. Neil Malamuth and Edward Donnerstein (New York: Academic Press, 1984), 277–304, 279, 286–301.

12 MODEL PORNOGRAPHY LAW

This model law drafted by the authors is meant to be considered by legislative bodies as a new legal way of dealing with pornography. Parts could be adopted in conjunction with current laws or could eventually (after found to be constitutional by the courts) replace current laws. The emphasis is on granting legal rights of redress to pornography victims and holding pornographers and offenders responsible for those injuries.

We have included some provisions (such as (2)(h)15, which includes in the definition of *pornography* sexually explicit portrayals of persons as sex objects and would likely cover most nudity and perhaps even ads emphasizing women's body parts) primarily for purposes of debate without expecting them to be adopted word for word or to withstand constitutional scrutiny. We decided to include such terminology in an effort to avoid unfairly eliminating it from debate. The emphasis of the law is on violent and degrading pornography, and it includes a strong child pornography section. The proposal draws on aspects of existing obscenity, civil rights, and child pornography laws for ideas and some language.

We drafted this law because current legal strategies to combat pornography and its harms are not working. We present a much more clear-cut and workable proposal and welcome comments and suggestions to improve it. Although the model law was drafted for states, it could be used by federal and local legislative bodies as well.

THE ANTI-SEXUAL-EXPLOITATION ACT

The people of the State of _____ do enact as follows:

SECTION 1. LEGISLATIVE INTENT. Consistent with section ____ of the (statutes, code), the provisions of this act are severable.

SECTION 2. 100.100 of the (statutes, code) is created to read: [Note: This number has been created merely for the sake of drafting convenience and readability.]

100.100 *PORNOGRAPHY: SEXUAL EXPLOITATION OF HUMANS*.

(1) DECLARATION OF POLICY.

The legislature finds that:

(a) Pornography, as defined and made actionable herein, is a form of sexual exploitation of humans. The prevention of sexual exploitation of humans constitutes a governmental objective of major importance. The State of _____ has a compelling interest in safeguarding the physical and psychological well-being of humans, and pornography, as a form of sexual exploitation, is a threat to that well-being. It is the policy of this state that it is necessary and essential in the public interest and for the public welfare to protect humans from sexual exploitation. Pornography, a form of sexual exploitation of humans, poses a substantial threat to the physical and psychological health, safety, peace, welfare, and equality of citizens of the State of _____, including through contributing to and creating an atmosphere of violence and sexual exploitation in which citizens are targeted for physical injury and in which women and children, in particular, are targeted for physical, sexual, and emotional abuse, hatred, and unequal treatment in their social, political, and economic lives.

(b) Pornography, a form of sexual exploitation, violates human rights and dignity and harms human beings by contributing to, encouraging, inciting, or advocating the commission of crimes, violation of human rights, and other wrongs against humans, including sexual abuse or exploitation; forced sex; forced prostitution; battery; physical injury; incest; child molestation; forced performances for pornography; torture; murder; sexual terrorism; and acts of violence or aggression. Pornography also inhibits passage and just enforcement of laws against these wrongful acts.

(c) Pornography, a form of sexual exploitation, differentially harms and discriminates against women and violates their right to equal protection under the law. It harms women by contributing to and helping create a culture of social and sexual terrorism and inferiority, sadism, woman hatred, and patriarchal supremacy. It harms women by contributing significantly to restricting them from full exercise of citizenship and participation in public life, including in neighborhoods; damaging relations between the sexes; and undermining women's exercise of rights to speech and action guaranteed to all citizens under the constitutions and laws of the United States and the State of _____. The bigotry and contempt pornography promotes toward women, with the acts of aggression it fosters, diminish opportunities for equality of rights for women in the economic, political, and social spheres. The legislature specifically finds that some types of pornography sexually exploit children, racial minorities, religious groups, handicapped or disabled persons, homosexuals, or lesbians in ways similar to the exploitation of women in most pornography.

(d) Pornography, a form of sexual exploitation, contributes to, advocates, encourages, or incites antisocial behavior. The legislature finds that a substantial body of evidence, in the form of scientific studies, statistics, data, and cases involving specific individuals, supports the belief that pornography contributes to anti-social, aggressive, and violent acts against human beings, most frequently women and children.

[Legislative Drafting Note: The legislative history of this measure documents the harms of pornography described in (1) above. Examples include studies that conclude that exposure to certain types of pornography desensitizes people to acts of sexual abuse, aggression, or violence, cases where humans were forced to perform for pornography, cases where children were enticed into sexual acts by use of pornography, cases where sex offenders acted out pornographic scenarios upon their victims, and countless other situations.]

(e) Pornography, whether pictures or words, communicates the sexual exploitation of human beings by depicting or describing such acts. The legislature recognizes that the women, children, and men who perform for pornography are sometimes physically, emotionally, or psychologically abused, harmed, or exploited.

(f) The legislature finds that the State's social interest in order and morality alone forms a sufficient basis for regulating pornography under this section and that it need not be proven that pornography will create a clear and present danger of antisocial conduct or will induce its recipients to such conduct.

(g) Pornography, a form of sexual exploitation, is unprotected speech under the United States and ___ constitutions, and therefore has no constitutional protection.

(2) Definitions.

In this section:

(a) *Child* means a person who has not attained the age of 18 years.

(b) *Coerce* means to force, intimidate, or fraudulently induce someone to do something. *Coerce* includes causing a person to do an act by:

1. Causing that person reasonably to believe that her or his act is the only means of preventing death, bodily injury, danger, or physical disfigurement to herself, himself, or another person, or threatening to inflict death, bodily injury, or physical disfigurement on someone; or

2. Using physical force, restraint, imprisonment, or violence to compel the person to engage in the act; or

3. Administering to the person without her or his consent or by threat or deception any alcoholic intoxicant, a drug as defined in (cite statute or code), or any poisonous, stupefying, overpowering, narcotic, or anesthetic substance; or

4. Threatening or causing that person reasonably to believe that her or his act is the only means of preventing the commission or accusation of a criminal offense or the communication to anyone of information, whether true or false, that would injure the reputation of the person or another; or

5. In the case of a person who has not yet attained the age of 18 years, or of a person who suffers from a mental disease or defect, by enticement; or

6. Causing the person to do the act without that person's consent; or

7. Instilling in the person a reasonable belief that, if the person refuses to do the act, someone will take or withhold action as an official or cause an official to take or withhold official action.

(bb) Proof of one or more of the following facts or conditions does not preclude a finding of coercion:

1. That the person is or has been a prostitute.

2. That the person has attained the age of 18 years.

3. That the person is connected by blood or marriage to anyone involved in or related to the making of pornographic or sexually explicit material.

4. That the person has previously had, or been thought to have had, sexual relations with anyone, including anyone involved in or related to the making of the pornographic or sexually explicit material at issue.

5. That the person has previously posed for pornographic or sexually explicit pictures with or for anyone, including anyone involved in or related

to the making of the pornographic or sexually explicit material at issue.

6. That anyone else, including a spouse or other relative, has given permission on the person's behalf.

7. That the person actually consented to the use of the performance that is changed into pornographic or sexually explicit material.

8. That the person knew that the purpose of the acts or events in question was to make pornographic or sexually explicit material.

9. That the person showed no resistance or appeared to cooperate actively in the photographic sessions or in the acts or events that produced the pornographic or sexually explicit material.

(c) *Commercial film and photographic print processor* means any person who, for compensation, develops exposed photographic film into negatives, slides, or prints into a movie film, videotape, or videodisc capable of producing or reproducing images on a screen, or who, for compensation, makes prints from negatives or slides. *Commercial film and photographic print processor* includes any employee of such a person but does not include a person who develops or makes prints for a public agency.

(d) *Force pornography on a person* means to communicate pornographic material to a person who does not want to view, read, or hear it, or to communicate it to a person who has not yet attained the age of 18 years.

(e) *Influenced in a material way by specific pornographic material* means:

1. That the perpetrator of the attack, assault, injury, battery, or molestation viewed, read, or heard, or the circumstances are such that the perpetrator can reasonably be believed to have viewed, read, or heard, the specific pornographic material at issue prior to or during the attack, assault, injury, battery, or molestation and, considering that fact and the entire circumstances of the incident, a reasonable person could conclude that the specific pornographic material contributed to or influenced the perpetrator in the commission of the act;

2. That the perpetrator of the attack, assault, injury, battery, or molestation acted out or imitated all or part of what was represented in the specific pornographic material upon the victim, or coerced, or if the victim is a person who has not yet attained the age of 18 years, coerced or enticed the victim to act out or imitate all or part of what was represented in the specific pornography; or

3. That the circumstances are such that it can reasonably be believed that the perpetrator viewed, heard, or read the specific pornography at issue and that the attack, assault, injury, battery, or molestation by the perpetrator upon the victim was so substantially similar to what was represented in the specific pornographic material at issue that a reasonable person could conclude that the specific pornography contributed to or influenced the perpetrator in the commission of the act.

(f) *Material* means anything tangible that is capable of being used or adapted to display, present, communicate, or portray pornography or any other word or picture whether through reading, observation, or sound or in any other manner, including, but not limited to, anything printed or written, any book, magazine, newspaper, pamphlet, picture, drawing, pictorial representation, motion picture, television broadcast, cable television broadcast, radio broadcast, photography, videotape, videodisc, film, transparency, animation, cartoon, or slide, or any other medium used to electronically produce or reproduce images on a screen, telephone communication, computer communication, satellite communication, or any mechanical, chemical, or electronic reproduction. *Material* includes undeveloped photographs, molds, printing plates, and other latent representational objects notwithstanding that processing or other acts may be required to make its content apparent. *Material* includes any play or live depiction or performance.

(g) *Perform for* or *engage in a performance* means to commit or engage in an act, including, but not limited to, modeling, posing, acting, or speaking, that is used or adapted or capable of being used or adapted into material that displays, presents, communicates, or portrays pornography or sexually explicit material.

(h) *Pornography* is material that communicates any of the following, whether actual or simulated or involving children or adults:

1. Sexual intercourse between children, a child(ren) and an adult(s), or a child(ren) and an animal(s) or object(s)

2. Bestiality

3. Necrophilia (sexual acts or expressions between live persons and dead persons or dead animals)

4. Fecal matter or urine or the exchange or inducement of fecal matter or urine in a sexual context

5. Enemas portrayed or described in a sexual context

6. Incest (as defined by the law of _____)

7. Sadism in a sexual context or in the context of a sexual encounter

8. Masochism in a sexual context or in the context of a sexual encounter

9. Ejaculation on another human being's body

10. Sexually explicit portrayals or descriptions of a female(s) as a nymphomaniac(s) or a male(s) as a satyr(s)

11. Sexually explicit vaginal, anal, or oral penetration by objects

12. Portrayals or descriptions of any of the following that (1) are sexually explicit, or (2) seek to, intend to, are for the apparent purpose of, or have the effect of sexually stimulating or gratifying normal or deviant viewers of, consumers of, producers of, or participants in the material:

   a. Murder

   b. Torture

   c. Mutilation of dismemberment

   d. Infliction of pain

   e. Physical or psychological coercion or abuse

   f. Physical bleeding, bruises, injury, or harm

   g. Bondage or other physical restraint

   h. Flagellation or beating

   i. Sexual assault or rape

   j. Discipline or punishment

   k. A sexually explicit power relationship that has the intention, apparent purpose, or effect of sexually stimulating or gratifying

   l. Sexual abuse or violence

   m. Sexual degradation or humiliation

   n. Subordination, submission, coercion, lack of consent, or debasement of any human body

   o. Self-infliction of physical harm

   p. A human being truncated, fragmented, or severed into body parts

13. Portrayals or descriptions of sexually explicit behavior that is degrading or abusive to one or more of the participants in such as way to endorse the degradation or abuse

14. Sexually explicit portrayals or descriptions of a human(s) enjoying or receiving sexual pleasure from any of the following:

   a. Violence

   b. Pain

   c. Sexual assault

   d. Humiliation

15. Sexually explicit portrayals or descriptions of a human(s) presented dehumanized as a sex object(s), thing(s), or commodity(ies)

16. Sexually explicit portrayals or descriptions of a person(s) as a sexual slave(s), prostitute(s), or pimp(s) in a manner that endorses, condones, or glamorizes prostitution, sexual slavery, or pimping

17. Sexually violent behavior

18. Sexually explicit sexual intercourse that depicts dominance and lacks affectionate or mutually pleasurable sexual interaction

19. Portrayals or descriptions of a child(ren) or of anyone represented to be a child(ren)

   a. Involved in masturbation; or

   b. With genitals, breast, pubic area, or buttocks lewdly exhibited; or

   c. Being touched, either directly or through clothing by the use of any body part or object, on the genitals, pubic area, buttocks, or breast if that touching can reasonably be said to be either for the purpose of satisfying the sexual or aggressive impulse of another person, or sexually arousing the child; or

   d. In the presence of anyone engaged in sexual activity

(i) *Sexual intercourse* includes actual or simulated genital-genital, oral-genital, anal-genital, or oral-anal intercourse, whether between persons of the same or opposite sex.

(j) *Sexually explicit* means any of the following:

   1. Nude

   2. Clad in undergarments or in a revealing costume

   3. A representation that emphasizes the vagina, breasts, buttocks, or genitals

   4. A sadistic, masochistic, or sadomasochistic representation in a sexual context or in the context of a sexual encounter

(k) *Traffic in* means to promote, produce, manufacture, issue, sell, give, trade, provide, lend, mail, deliver, transfer, transmute, publish, distribute, circulate, exchange, disseminate, present, exhibit, profit from, import, reproduce, or advertise, or offer or agree to do any of these activities, or to possess with intent to do any of these activities. When pornographic material depicting a child(ren) is involved, *traffic in* includes possession of the material.

(l) *Subordination* means the treatment of someone as inferior, submissive to, or controlled by another; made subject or subservient to another.

(m) *Degradation* means to depict someone as existing solely for the sexual satisfaction of another or others, to depict someone in a decidedly subordinate role in his or her sexual relations with another or others, or to depict someone engaged in sexual practices that would be considered humiliating.

(n) *Sexually stimulating* means causing or intended to cause sexual arousal.

There is a presumption that material seeks to, intends to, is for the apparent purpose of, or has the effect of sexually stimulating or gratifying someone when an act mentioned under (2)(h) of this law:

   1. Is shown associated with sexual acts, though not necessarily at the same time; or

   2. Is shown in conjunction with emphasis on the

vagina, penis, anus, buttocks, breasts, or mouth, whether nude or not; or

3. Emphasizes nude parts of the body;

4. Is consistently shown in the material as being perpetrated by the members of one sex on the other sex; or

5. Has an overall context that appears to have a primary purpose of sexually stimulating or intending to sexually stimulate the consumer.

When these factors are not present, material may still seek to, intend to, have the apparent purpose of, or have the effect of sexually stimulating or gratifying someone under this law, but the presumption does not apply.

(3) UNLAWFUL PRACTICES.

(a) *Child pornography.*

1. No person may employ, use, persuade, induce, entice, or coerce any child to engage in pornographic conduct for the purpose of photographing, filming, videotaping, recording the sounds of, reproducing, displaying, presenting, portraying, or communicating in any way the conduct or material containing that conduct or for the purpose of trafficking in material containing that conduct.

2. No person may knowingly photograph, film, videotape, record the sounds of, display, present, portray, reproduce, or communicate in any way a child or cartoon child engaged in pornographic conduct.

3. No person, having knowledge of or reason to know the character and content of the material, may traffic in material involving a child or cartoon child engaging in pornographic conduct.

4. No parent, legal guardian, or other person exercising temporary or permanent control of a child may knowingly permit, allow, or encourage the child to engage in pornographic conduct that is filmed, photographed, videotaped, recorded for sound, displayed, presented, or communicated in any way, or utilized in material that depicts pornographic conduct.

5. No parent, legal guardian, or other person exercising temporary or permanent control of a child may knowingly authorize, allow, or encourage material depicting the child engaging in pornographic conduct to be trafficked in.

6. No person may cause another, whether by employment, payment, inducement, enticement, coercion, use of force, threat, or fraud, or any other means, to engage in conduct that violates sub. (3)(a)1, 2, 3, 4, or 5.

7. Any commercial film and photographic print processor who has knowledge of or observes, within the scope of his or her professional capacity or employment, any material depicting a child or cartoon child engaged in pornographic conduct, including if the material came from out of state, shall report his or her observance or knowledge to a law enforcement agency having jurisdiction over the case immediately or as soon as practically possible by telephone and shall prepare and send a written report of it with a copy of the material attached within thirty-six hours of when he or she gains the knowledge or makes the observation. The processor shall not return the material to the customer and shall not make any prints or films of the material for the customer unless the law enforcement agency such material is reported to notifies the processor that the material does not depict a child or cartoon child engaged in pornographic conduct or a court having jurisdiction over the case finds that the material does not depict a child or cartoon child engaged in pornographic conduct. A person who is required to report under this paragraph is exempt from civil or criminal liability for reports made and actions taken in accordance with the paragraph. Failure to comply with this paragraph is against the law.

8.a. Consent of a child to engage in pornographic conduct is not a defense to alleged violations of sub. (3)(a).

b. It is an affirmative defense to prosecution under sub. (3)(a) that the defendant did not have a reasonable cause to believe or suspect that the child was under the age of 18 and did not rely solely on allegations or representations of the minor as to her or his age.

c. It is an affirmative defense to prosecution under sub. (3)(a) that the defendant did not have a reasonable cause to believe or suspect that the child was engaging in or had engaged in the pornographic conduct.

d. It is an affirmative defense to prosecution under (3)(a) that the defendant did not have a reasonable cause to believe or suspect that material depicting the child engaging in pornographic conduct was trafficked in.

9. Whoever violates sub. (3)(a) is guilty of a (misdemeanor or felony as described in the state law), except that a person who has not yet attained the age of 14 years shall be guilty of a (misdemeanor or felony, lesser charge).

[Legislative Drafting Note: We have not included specific penalties here because definitions of felonies and misdemeanors vary substantially among states. It is suggested that the penalties for sub. (3)(a)1, 2, 3, 4, 5, and 6 be higher than the penalty for violating sub. (3)(a)7. It is our strong feeling that violations of all unlawful practices in sub. (3)(a) except for 7 should be considered major crimes (usually called felonies) and should be subject to substantial potential prison terms.]

The court shall sentence the person convicted of violating sub. (3)(a)1, 2, 3, 4, 5, or 6 to at least one year in prison. The court shall not place the person on probation, nor shall said sentence be suspended. No person charged with a violation of sub. (3)(a)1, 2, 3, 4, 5, or 6 shall have said violation or violations read in at sentencing as part of a plea negotiation.

10. A person convicted of violating this section shall be prohibited from visitation with or having contact with the child or children involved in the violation, including during that time period after charges have been issued but not resolved. Whoever violates sub. (3)(a)10 is guilty of a (misdemeanor or felony as described in the state law).

(b) *Coercion into pornographic or sexually explicit performances.*

1. Whoever coerces a person into engaging in a pornographic or sexually explicit performance is guilty of a (misdemeanor or felony as described in the state law).

[Legislative Drafting Note: It is suggested that the penalty for this crime be high, at least a twenty-year maximum, because of the severity of injury to the person, including defamation and right to privacy concerns, as well as emotional and sometimes physical injury.]

A person convicted of violating this section shall receive a mandatory minimum sentence of two years in prison for each offense. The court shall not place a person convicted of said offense on probation, nor shall said sentence be suspended.

(c) *Trafficking in pornographic material.*

1. Whoever knowingly traffics in pornographic material is guilty of a (misdemeanor or felony as described in the state law).

[Legislative Drafting Note: This section is the new law's replacement for obscenity law. States would most likely consider a variety of penalties under this section, depending on the nature and extent of the trafficking.]

2. In this sub. (3)(c), persons who perform for pornography are not considered to be trafficking in pornography.

(d) *Racketeering.*

[Legislative Drafting Note: In this section, violations of 100.100 are made violations of the racketeering or organized crime sections of state law—if the additional criteria of those laws can be met.]

(e) *Production of physically harmful material.* Whoever knowingly produces or distributes pornographic material that was produced in such a way that actual physical harm was caused to a person or persons depicted is guilty of a (misdemeanor or felony as described in the state law.)

(f) *Pandering and pimping.* Anyone who does any of the following is guilty of a (misdemeanor or felony as described in the state law):

1. Solicits or arranges for someone to perform for pornography in exchange for money or other property

2. Arranges or offers to arrange or keeps or offers to keep a place for trafficking in pornography in exchange for money or other property.

(4) CIVIL REMEDIES.

(a) *Coercion into pornographic or sexually explicit performances.* It is unlawful to coerce a person into engaging in a pornographic or sexually explicit performance. The person who was coerced into performing for pornography may sue the person(s) who coerced her or him into the performance. The person who was coerced into performing for pornography may also sue the person(s) who traffic in any pornographic material that represents, displays, presents, communicates, or portrays the specific performance at issue, or any part thereof.

(b) *Production of injurious material.* Whoever produces or is involved in the production of pornographic or sexually explicit material that results in actual physical harm or injury to persons who perform for such material may be sued by the injured person(s). It does not matter whether the performer was coerced into performing for the pornography or consented to the performance. [Legislative Drafting Note: This strict liability provision is included in the realization that production of pornographic or sexually explicit material involves many health risks, including, but not limited to contraction of AIDS, sexually transmitted diseases, pregnancy, and potential injuries such as bleeding or bruising.]

(c) *Forcing pornography or sexually explicit material on a person.* It is unlawful to force pornography or sexually explicit material on a person in any place of employment or education, home, or public or private place. A person harmed under this paragraph may bring an action only against the perpetrator of the force and/or the responsible institution or person.

(d) *Assault, battery, or physical attack influenced by pornography*. It is unlawful to assault, physically attack, commit a battery against, molest, or injure any person in a way that is directly influenced in a material way by specific pornography.

1. The perpetrator(s) of the assault, attack, injury, battery, or molestation may be sued by the person who was injured or by her or his estate.

2. Any person who trafficked in the specific pornography may also be sued.

(e) *Trafficking in pornography*. Any person who traffics in pornography shall forfeit, for each such offense, the greater of $5,000 or an amount equal to three times the profits derived from the pornography trafficked in. Any person may commence a civil action for enforcement of sub. (e).

(f) *Coercing acceptance of pornographic materials*. No person shall, as a condition to any sale, allocation, consignment, or delivery for resale of any item require that the purchaser or consignee receive for resale any pornographic or sexually explicit material. No person shall deny or threaten to deny any franchise or impose or threaten to impose any penalty, financial or otherwise, by reason of the failure or refusal of any person to accept pornographic or sexually explicit materials or by reason of the return thereof.

(g) *Defamation through pornography*. It shall be defamation per se to make unauthorized use of the proper name, image, likeness, or recognizable personal evocation of any specific individual(s) in pornography or sexually explicit material. Authorization once given can be revoked in writing any time prior to any publication.

[Legislative Drafting Note: This provision recognizes that models may consent to use of sexually explicit or pornographic communications in one context but not in another and that they may, at some point, decide to invoke a right to privacy in their own bodies.]

(h) *Invasion of privacy*. It shall be an invasion of privacy to make unauthorized use of the proper name, image, likeness, or recognizable personal evocation of any specific individual(s) in any sexually explicit or pornographic communication. Authorization once given can be revoked in writing anytime prior to any publication.

(i) *Group libel/hate literature*. Any person who traffics in pornography that willfully promotes hatred against any identifiable group or that incites hatred against any identifiable group where such incitement is likely to lead to a breach of the peace, shall forfeit, for each such offense, the greater of $10,000 or an amount equal to six times the profits derived from the pornography trafficked in. Any person who is a member of the group at issue may commence a civil action for enforcement of sub. (i). An identifiable group is any section of the population distinguished by sex, sexual preference, color, race, religion, handicap, age, or ethnic origin.

(j) *Unfair labor and employment practice*. It shall be unlawful to employ any person to perform in pornography. The person(s) so employed and/or the state attorney general may sue, in civil court, any person who violates this section. Such violator shall forfeit the greater of $10,000 or an amount equal to six times the profits derived from any pornography trafficked in that features the person(s) employed. Any money recovered by the attorney general under sub. (j) shall be paid into the treasury of the state and used to fund programs to help victims of sexual assault and/or domestic abuse.

(5) ENFORCEMENT.

(a) Any person (if the injured person is dead or incapacitated, the person's representative may commence the action) aggrieved by a violation of sub. (4) may commence a civil action to recover any or all of the following:

1. Costs, including reasonable attorney fees and reasonable investigator fees.

2. Damages, as follows:

a. Compensatory damages based on the person's (plaintiff's) loss, including general damages for pain and suffering and loss of enjoyment and special damages.

b. Compensatory damages based on the defendant(s)' unjust enrichment when a violation of any part of sub. (4) except (e), (i), or (j) is involved.

c. Nominal damages.

d. Punitive or exemplary damages when a violation of sub. (4)(a), (b), (d), (f), (g), or (h) is involved.

(b) Except as quoted above, any person may commence a civil action for enforcement of sub. (4)(e) or (i). Any person suing under this provision shall recover, if said action is successful, all costs, including reasonable attorney fees and reasonable investigator fees. The forfeitures specified in sub. (4)(e) or (i) shall also be recovered by said person in the interest of the public and shall be paid into the treasury of the State and used to fund programs to help victims of sexual assault and/or domestic abuse.

(c) Any person aggrieved by a violation of sub. (4) or entitled to take action to enforce sub. (e)(i) or (j) may, in addition to those actions allowed under this section, bring a civil action to restrain or enjoin any violation of sub. (4), including to eliminate the specific pornographic or sexually explicit material or communication from public view, to remove it from the flow of commerce, and to stop it from being trafficked in.

(6) PROOF OF AGE.

When it becomes necessary for the purposes of this section to determine whether a person represented in pornographic or sexually explicit material or communications had attained the age of 18 years, the court or jury may make that determination by consideration of one or more of the following methods: personal inspection or testimony of the person; inspection of the material that displayed, presented, communicated, or portrayed the pornography or sexually explicit communication; oral testimony by a witness to the performance that resulted in the pornography or sexually explicit communication as to the age of the person based on the appearance of the person in the pornography or communication; testimony of a parent, police officer, guardian, teacher, or personal acquaintance of the person as to the age of the person; expert medical or scientific testimony based on the appearance of the person in the pornography or sexually explicit communication; and any other method authorized by law or by the rules of evidence.

(7) DEFENSES AND LIMITS ON LIABILITY.

(a) Any person who is coerced, or, in the case of a person who has not yet attained the age of 18 years, coerced or enticed, into violating any of the provisions of this section shall not be guilty of violating this section.

(b) Isolated passages or isolated parts of material shall not be actionable under (4)(e) or (i).

(c) It shall not be a defense to an action or complaint under (4) that the respondent did not know or intend that the material or communication at issue was pornography or sexually explicit. Except that no damages or compensation for losses shall be awarded under sub. (4)(e) or (i) for trafficking in pornography or against a defendant other than the perpetrator of the assault, attack, injury, battery, or molestation under sub. (4)(d) unless the defendant knew or had reason to know that the materials were pornography.

(d) *Scienter.* The crimes set forth in sub. (3)(c) and (e) require a showing of intent or knowledge on the part of the defendant, which the prosecution must prove. In this law, *intent, knowingly, intentionally,* and *with knowledge* mean that the person had knowledge of or reason to know the character and content of the material.

(e) This law shall not apply to the performance of bona fide official duties by law enforcement, prosecuting officers, court personnel, attorneys, or others involved in prosecuting, defending, or officially investigating cases under this law.

(f) This law shall not apply to the presentation of pornographic or sexually explicit material at bona fide educational programs conducted to demonstrate the illegality or harmfulness of the material.

(g) It shall be an affirmative defense to prosecute under sub. (3) or lawsuit for damages or compensation under sub. (4)(c), (e), or (i) to show that the material at issue, taken as a whole, (1) does not glamorize, exploit, sensationalize, legitimize or condone the activities portrayed or depicted, and (2) Has serious literary, artistic, political, or scientific value.

> [Legislative Drafting Note: The defenses and limits on liability in sub. (7)(e), (f), and (g) are intended to protect persons who have a legitimate reason for trafficking in pornography or sexually explicit material from prosecution or lawsuit. It is also intended to prevent prosecution and liability of persons, such as authors and speakers, who detail the contents of pornography in order to demonstrate its harmfulness or illegality.]

(8) STATUTE OF LIMITATIONS.

(a) Criminal prosecutions for violations of sub. (3) may be commenced at any time.

(b) Actions for injunctive relief or to recover damages or compensation or forfeitures for injuries set forth in sub. (4) may be commenced at any time.

(c) No criminal action may be commenced and no damages or compensation for losses or forfeitures shall be recoverable for trafficking in pornography prior to the effective date of this law.

(d) A cause of action accrues at the time of the wrongful act or injury. Each publication, communication, display, presentation, representation, or portrayal of pornography or sexually explicit material that is prohibited under this section shall constitute a separate act or injury and give rise to a new and separate cause of action.

> [Legislative Drafting Note: This law specifically provides that no statute of limitations will apply to most criminal prosecutions and civil causes of action under this section. This is necessary because of the nature of the pornography industry—for example, much pornography is clandestinely produced and produced through coercion. It can take victims a long time to identify and trace those responsible for their injury and to trace the pornography. Many victims are too fearful to report or take action against the injury until long

after standard (two- or three-year) statutes of limitations have run out. Many victims block out (do not remember) the pornography-related abuse until long afterward. (This is similar to the lack of memory experienced by incest victims.) Victims should not be penalized for these problems, which are inherent in the nature of the abuse. In addition, many of the harms of pornography are of a continuing nature—pornography continues to be trafficked in or, at a minimum, does not completely disappear.]

(9) REFUSAL TO PROSECUTE

If a prosecutor refuses to bring a prosecution under sub. (3) of this law, any citizen may go before a judge in the jurisdiction involved and seek an order requiring enforcement of this law.

(10) EXISTING LEGAL REMEDIES.

This law does not prohibit injured persons from using other existing legal remedies such as tort actions for assault, battery, and intentional infliction of severe emotional distress or product liability laws.

(11) PROCEDURE.

(a) Except as specified in this section, the procedures set forth in the Statutes apply to actions under this section.

(b) Filing and form of complaint. An action under sub. (3) shall be commenced by the filing of a complaint to which shall be attached as an exhibit a true copy of the pornographic or sexually explicit material that allegedly violates this section, if said material is available, or describing said material with specificity if not available.

(c) Any person interested in trafficking in the material involved or exhibited to the complaint may appear and may intervene as a respondent and file an answer.

(d) The public policy of this state requires that all proceedings in the section be heard and disposed of with the maximum promptness and dispatch commensurate with constitutional requirements, including due process, equal protection, right to privacy, right not to be defamed, freedom of the press, and freedom of speech.

(e) *Injunctions.*

1. In any action in which an injunction is sought under this section, any respondent named in the complaint, or any person who becomes a respondent by virtue of intervention under sub. (11)(c) shall be entitled to a trial of the issues within seven days after joinder of issue, and a decision shall be

rendered by the court within two days of the conclusion of the trial or by the jury upon conclusion of its deliberations.

2. No preliminary injunction shall be issued without at least two days' notice to the respondents.

3. If the court finds probable cause to believe specific material violates this section and so endorses the complaint, the court may, upon the motion of the plaintiff, issue a temporary restraining order against any respondent, prohibiting him or her from trafficking in the specific pornographic material at issue. No temporary restraining order may be granted without notice to the respondents unless it clearly appears from the specific facts shown by affidavit or by the verified complaint that immediate and irreparable injury to the plaintiff or the general welfare of persons in this state will result before notice can be served and a hearing had thereon. Every temporary restraining order granted hereunder shall state with specificity why the order was granted without notice and shall expire by its own terms within such time after entry, not to exceed three days, as the court fixes unless within the time so fixed the respondent against whom the order is directed consents that it may be extended for a longer period. If a restraining order is granted without notice, a motion for a preliminary injunction shall be set down for hearing within two days after the granting of the order and shall be given preference. When the motion comes on for hearing, the plaintiff shall proceed with the application for a preliminary injunction and, if he or she does not do so, the court shall dissolve the temporary restraining order.

(f) *Contempt.* Any respondent, or any officer, agent, servant, employee, or attorney of such respondent, or any person in active concert or participation by contract or arrangement with such respondent, who receives actual notice, by personal service or otherwise, of any injunction or restraining order entered under sub. (11)(e) and who disobeys any of the provisions thereof, shall be guilty of contempt of court and upon conviction is guilty of a felony.

(g) *Extradition.* If any person is convicted of sub. (11)(g) and cannot be found in this state, the governor or any person performing the functions of governor by authority of the law shall, unless such person shall have appealed from the judgment of contempt or conviction and such appeal has not been finally determined, demand his extradition from the executive authority of the state in which such person is found.

This chapter summarizes national studies of pornography from the United States, Canada, and Great Britain. We believe that these studies are important because of their extensiveness, thoroughness, and value as a resource for information about pornography. Both U.S. studies are included, while only the most recent studies from Canada and Britain are detailed.

The reader will find that the conclusions and approaches of the four national studies presented vary remarkably. We have concluded that the 1986 U.S. study and the 1985 Canadian study are the most accurate and helpful, while the British study lacks thoroughness and the 1970 U.S. study is unfairly biased in favor of pornographers, deals with a type of pornography much milder than that available today, and contains numerous inaccuracies.

THE ATTORNEY GENERAL'S COMMISSION ON PORNOGRAPHY

In July 1986, the U.S. Attorney General's Commission on Pornography (AGCOP) issued its *Final Report*. Its ninety-two important recommendations follow this summary. Among the major findings of the commission are the following:

1. The biggest problem is that obscenity laws are not being enforced; if they were, the pornography industry could be shut down within two years.
2. Some types of pornography do cause harm.
3. The pornography industry is controlled by organized crime.
4. The criminal method of dealing with pornography should continue to be through obscenity law as defined by *Miller*. (Proposals to create a more specific descriptive definition of pornography or to broaden the definition of covered material were rejected.)
5. Legislatures should consider enacting civil remedies for victims of pornography.
6. Victims of pornography do indeed exist.
7. The great majority of Americans oppose pornography, especially violent pornography.[1]

Importantly, when considering the harms of pornography and the different types of pornography, the commission created three separate categories for the material:

1. *"Sexually Violent Material."* This category was defined as "material featuring actual or unmistakeably simulated or unmistakeably threatened violence presented in sexually explicit fashion with a predominant focus on the sexually explicit violence."[2] The most prevalent forms of pornography are increasingly fitting this category, the commission said. It includes depictions such as sadomasochism (torture, bondage, beatings, and so on); sexual assaults (including rapes in which the woman rebuffs the assailant(s), is forced into sex, then becomes sexually aroused and begs for more); and sexual activity or "sexually suggestive nudity" combined with extreme violence such as murder or disfigurement (as in slasher films).[3]

The commission concluded that clinical and experimental research that has focused on sexually violent material has unanimously found that exposure to such materials "has indicated an increase in the likelihood of aggression."[4] The research specifically found that there is a "causal relationship between exposure to material of this type and aggressive behavior towards women."[5] Clinical evidence and other evidence supports the view that for an aggressive population, increased aggressive behavior toward women is causally related to increased sexual violence, the commission said.[6]

> [W]e have reached the conclusion, unanimously and confidently, that the available evidence strongly supports the hypothesis that substantial exposure to sexually violent materials as described here bears a causal relationship to antisocial acts of sexual violence and, for some subgroups, possibly to unlawful acts of sexual violence.[7]

As the commission pointed out, this conclusion is logical, for it simply states that "the images that people are exposed to bears a causal relationship to their behavior."[8]

In addition, the commission found that, when dealing with sexually violent material, "significant attitudinal changes" occur in those who are substantially exposed to such pornography. Specifically, sexual violence victims "are likely to be perceived by people so exposed as more responsible for the assault, as having suffered less injury, and as having been less degraded as a result of the experience."[9] In addition, they are likely to view the sexual offender as deserving of less punishment and as less responsible for the act. Such exposure leads to greater acceptance of the rape myth—that is, that a woman who says no means yes; that women enjoy being coerced into sex; that they enjoy being physically hurt in a sexual context; and that a man who sexually forces himself on a woman "is in fact merely acceding to the 'real' wishes of the woman, regardless of the extent to which she seems to be resisting."[10]

The commission found that this attitude is "both pervasive and profoundly harmful" and that anything that increases or reinforces this myth is harmful.[11] The harms are more pronounced when the material shows the woman enjoying or becoming aroused by sexual assault, the commission said. Importantly, the harms *do not vary with the extent of sexual explicitness, so long as the violence is presented in an undeniably sexual context.*[12] Thus, slasher films are likely to produce the harms discussed to a greater extent than most material available in pornographic outlets, the commission concluded. The class of sexually violent materials is harmful to society on the whole, it said.[13]

2. *"Nonviolent Materials Depicting Degradation, Domination, Subordination, or Humiliation."* The commission used the term *degrading* to include all four characteristics, then defined it as follows:

> The degradation we refer to is degradation of people, most often women, and here we are referring to material that, although not violent, depicts people, usually women, as existing solely for the sexual satisfaction of others, usually men, or that depicts people, usually women, in decidedly subordinate roles in their sexual relations with others, or that depicts people engaged in sexual practices that would to most people be considered humiliating.[14]

The commission found that forms of degradation predominate in commercially produced pornography.[15] According to the summary of the commission report prepared by Richard E. McLawhorn, executive vice president and general counsel of the National Coalition Against Pornography (NCAP), the following are examples of pornography covered by this category:

a. Two women engaged in sex while a man watches
b. A spread-eagled woman holding her labia open with her fingers
c. Men urinating on a woman who is kneeling
d. A woman lying on a bed begging for sex from a large number of different men
e. A woman being "non-physically coerced" into sex with a male authority figure such as a priest, boss, or teacher[16]

While the commission's conclusions about the harmful effects of degrading material were "substantially similar" to those concerning violent material, it expressed less confidence in those findings.[17] Specifically, the commission found that exposure to degrading material is likely to increase the extent to which sexual assault victims and offenders will be viewed as described under the section on sexually violent material.[18] These beliefs will result in more acts of sexual violence and coercion than would occur in a population holding these beliefs "to a lesser extent."[19] The commission concluded that substantial exposure to degrading pornography "bears some causal relationship to the level of sexual violence, sexual coercion, or unwanted sexual aggression in the population so exposed."[20] It said:

> Substantial exposure to materials of this type bears some causal relationship to the incidence of various non-violent forms of discrimination against or subordination of women in our society. To the extent that these materials create or reinforce the view that women's function is disproportionately to satisfy the sexual needs of men, then the materials will have pervasive effects on the treatment of women in society far beyond the incidence of identifiable acts of rape or other sexual violence.[21]

The commission emphasized that it was not claiming that every person who is exposed to sexually degrading material has his or her attitude toward sexual violence changed, only that substantial exposure "increases the likelihood for an individual and the incidence over a large population that these attitudinal changes will occur."[22] The commission emphasized that everyone with such attitudes will not necessarily commit an act of sexual coercion or violence, but such attitudes will increase the likelihood for individuals, and the incidence for a population, of such acts.[23]

3. *"Non-Violent and Non-Degrading Materials."* Stating that this category is quite small in proportion to all currently available pornography, the commission defined this as "materials in which the participants

THE NATIONAL STUDIES 433

appear to be fully willing participants occupying substantially equal roles in a setting devoid of actual or apparent violence or pain."[24] The commission was persuaded, based on the small amount of evidence available, that this material "does not bear a causal relationship to rape and other acts of sexual violence."[25] However, the commission members expressed divergent views concerning whether or not this material is harmful for the following reasons:

a. Some depicts sexual practices frequently condemned in American and other societies, and it could legitimize or bear a causal relationship to such sexual acts.[26]
b. It promotes promiscuity (sexual activity outside of marriage, love, commitment, and affection). Some commissioners saw this as a matter of individual choice.[27]
c. "The very publicness of what is commonly taken to be private [sexual activity] is cause for concern." At the same time, some commissioners were concerned that sexual issues were too private in the past.[28]
d. Some of this material has been used to coerce or encourage women to engage in sexual practices in which they do not choose to engage. Alternatively, some people have used it in mutually pleasurable ways.[29]
e. It harms sexual morality in society.[30]

The commissioners agreed that exposure of children to these materials is harmful because it teaches that sex is public and commercial and that it can be divorced from love, affection, commitment, and marriage.[31]

4. "*Nudity.*" None of the commissioners thought that the portrayal of the human body was harmful. There were concerns about nudity portrayed in a sexual context where issues similar to those discussed under categories 1–3 might exist. The commission said, however, that nudity that did not fit in the previous categories was not much cause for concern.[32]

The commission emphasized the need for more research into the effects of pornography.[33]

The *Final Report* contains extensive summaries of the testimony of victims of pornography and social science research. These results are dealt with in chapters 4 and 5 of this book and are not repeated here. Excerpts from the AGCOP findings concerning details of the organized crime control of the pornography industry appear in chapter 3. The questionnaire for victims of pornography contained in chapter 4

was based primarily on the questionnaire contained in the commission report.[34]

The commission report, apparently in recognition of the fact that many Americans still visualize pornography as mere pinup-style depictions of nude, glamorous women, includes hundreds of pages of descriptions of actual pornography. Not surprisingly, pornographers and their civil libertarian defenders launched a major campaign to discredit the report, including hiring a public relations firm to orchestrate that campaign with the media.

We conclude that the most important results of the report are the recognition that pornography causes harm, useful recommendations for legal change, creation of more public awareness, and creation of a major task force to prosecute pornographers and shut down the industry.

In its *Final Report,* AGCOP made the following recommendations:

I. Recommendations For The Justice System And Law Enforcement Agencies.
A. *Recommendations For Changes In Federal Law*
1. Congress should enact a forfeiture statute to reach the proceeds and instruments of any offense committed in violation of the federal obscenity laws.
2. Congress should amend the federal obscenity laws to eliminate the necessity of proving transportation in interstate commerce. A statute should be enacted to only require proof that the distribution of the obscene material "affects" interstate commerce.
3. Congress should enact legislation making it an unfair business practice and an unfair labor practice for any employer to hire individuals to participate in commercial sexual performances.
4. Congress should amend the Mann Act to make its provisions gender neutral.
5. Congress should amend Title 18 of the United States Code to specifically proscribe obscene cable television programming.
6. Congress should enact legislation to prohibit the transmission of obscene material through the telephone or similar common carrier.
B. *Recommendations For Changes In State Law*
7. State legislatures should amend, if necessary, obscenity statutes containing the definitional requirement that material be "utterly without redeeming social value" in order to be obscene to conform with the current standard enunciated by the United States Supreme Court in *Miller v. California.*
8. State legislatures should amend, if necessary, obscenity statutes to eliminate misdemeanor status for second offenses and make any second offense punishable as a felony.

9. State legislatures should enact, if necessary, forfeiture provisions as part of the state obscenity laws.

10. State legislatures should enact a racketeer influenced corrupt organizations (RICO) statute which has obscenity as a predicate act.

C. *Recommendations For the United States Department of Justice*

11. The Attorney General should direct the United States attorneys to examine the obscenity problem in their respective districts, identify offenders, initiate investigations, and commence prosecution without further delay.

12. The Attorney General should appoint a high ranking official from the Department of Justice to oversee the creation and operation of an obscenity task force. The task force should consist of special assistant United States attorneys and federal agents who will assist United States attorneys in the prosecution and investigation of obscenity cases.

13. The Department of Justice should initiate the creation of an obscenity law enforcement data base which would serve as a resource network for federal, state, and local law enforcement agencies.

14. The United States attorneys should use law enforcement coordinating committees to coordinate enforcement of the obscenity laws and to maintain surveillance of the nature and extent of the obscenity problem within each district.

15. The Department of Justice and United States attorneys should use the Racketeer Influenced Corrupt Organization Act (RICO) as a means of prosecuting major producers and distributors of obscene material.

16. The Department of Justice should continue to provide the United States attorneys with training programs on legal and procedural matters related to obscenity cases and also should make such training available to state and local prosecutors.

17. The United States attorneys should use all available federal statutes to prosecute obscenity law violations involving cable and satellite television.

D. *Recommendations For State And Local Prosecutors*

18. State and local prosecutors should prosecute producers of obscene material under existing laws including those prohibiting pandering and other underlying sexual offenses.

19. State and local prosecutors should examine the obscenity problem in their jurisdiction, identify offenders, initiate investigations, and commence prosecution without further delay.

20. State and local prosecutors should allocate sufficient resources to prosecute obscenity cases.

21. State and local prosecutors should use the bankruptcy laws to collect unpaid fines.

22. State and local prosecutors should use all available statutes to prosecute obscenity violations involving cable and satellite television.

23. State and local prosecutors should enforce existing corporate laws to prevent the formation, use and abuse of shell corporations which serve as a shelter for producers and distributors of obscene material.

24. State and local prosecutors should enforce the alcoholic beverage control laws that prohibit obscenity on licensed premises.

25. Government attorneys, including state and local prosecutors, should enforce all legal remedies authorized by statute.

E. *Recommendations For Federal Law Enforcement Agencies*

26. Federal law enforcement agencies should conduct active and thorough investigations of all significant violations of obscenity laws with interstate dimensions.

27. The Internal Revenue Service should aggressively investigate violations of the tax laws committed by producers and distributors of obscene material.

F. *Recommendations For State And Local Law Enforcement Agencies*

28. State and local law enforcement agencies should provide the most thorough and up-to-date training for investigators involved in enforcing the obscenity laws.

29. State and local law enforcement agencies should allocate sufficient personnel to conduct intensive and thorough investigations of any violations of the obscenity laws.

30. State and local law enforcement officers should take an active role in the law enforcement coordinating committees.

31. State and local revenue authorities must insure taxes are collected from businesses dealing in obscene materials.

32. State and local public health authorities should investigate conditions within "adults only" pornographic outlets and arcades and enforce the laws against any health violations found on those premises.

G. *Recommendations For The Judiciary*

33. Judges should impose substantial periods of incarceration for persons who are repeatedly convicted of obscenity law violations and when appropriate should order payment of restitution to identified victims as part of the sentence.

H. *Recommendations For The Federal Communications Commission*

34. The Federal Communications Commission should use its full regulatory powers and impose appropriate sanctions against providers of obscene dial-a-porn telephone services.

35. The Federal Communications Commission should use its full regulatory powers and impose appropriate sanctions against cable and satellite television programmers who transmit obscene programs.

I. *Recommendation For Other Federal Organizations*

36. The President's Commission On Uniform Sentencing should consider a provision for a minimum of one year imprisonment for any second or subsequent violation of federal law involving obscene material that depicts adults.

II. Recommendations For The Regulation Of Child Pornography

37. Congress should enact legislation requiring producers, retailers, or distributors of sexually explicit visual depictions to maintain records containing consent forms and proof of performers' ages.

38. Congress should enact legislation prohibiting producers of certain sexually explicit visual depictions from using performers under the age of twenty-one.

39. Congress should enact legislation to prohibit the exchange of information concerning child pornography or children to be used in child pornography through computer networks.

40. Congress should amend the Child Protection Act forfeiture section to include a provision which authorizes the postal inspection service to conduct forfeiture actions.

41. Congress should amend 18 U.S.C. S2255 to define the term "visual depiction" and include undeveloped film in that definition.

42. Congress should enact legislation providing financial incentives for the states to initiate task forces on child pornography and related cases.

43. Congress should enact legislation to make the acts of child selling or child purchasing, for the production of sexually explicit visual depictions, a felony.

B. *Recommendations For State Legislation*

44. State legislatures should amend, if necessary, child pornography statutes to include forfeiture provisions.

45. State legislatures should amend laws, where necessary, to make the knowing possession of child pornography a felony.

46. State legislatures should amend, if necessary, laws making the sexual abuse of children through the production of sexually explicit visual depictions, a felony.

47. State legislatures should enact legislation, if necessary, to make the conspiracy to produce, distribute, give away or exhibit any sexually explicit visual depictions of children or exchange or deliver children for such purpose a felony.

48. State legislatures should amend, if necessary, child pornography laws to create an offense for advertising, selling, purchasing, bartering, exchanging, giving or receiving information as to where sexually explicit materials depicting children can be found.

49. State legislatures should enact or amend legislation, where necessary, to make child selling or child purchasing for the production of sexually explicit visual depictions, a felony.

50. State legislatures should amend laws, where necessary, to make child pornography in the possession of an alleged child sexual abuser which depicts that person engaged in sexual acts with a minor sufficient evidence of child molestation for use in prosecuting that individual whether or not the child involved is found or is able to testify.

51. State legislatures should amend laws, if necessary, to eliminate the requirement that the prosecution identify or produce testimony from the child who is depicted if proof of age can otherwise be established.

52. State legislatures should enact or amend legislation, if necessary, which requires photo finishing laboratories to report suspected child pornography.

53. State legislatures should amend or enact legislation, if necessary, to permit judges to impose a sentence of lifetime probation for convicted child pornographers and related offenders.

C. *Recommendations For Federal Law Enforcement Agencies*

54. The State Department, The United States Department of Justice, The United States Custom Service, The United States Postal Inspection Service, The Federal Bureau Of Investigation and other federal agencies should continue to work with other nations to detect and intercept child pornography.

55. The United States Department of Justice should direct the law enforcement coordinating committees to form forces of dedicated and experienced investigators and prosecutors in major regions to combat child pornography.

56. The Department of Justice or other appropriate federal agency should initiate the creation of a data base which would serve as a resource network for federal, state and local law enforcement agencies to send and obtain information regarding child pornography trafficking.

57. Federal law enforcement agencies should develop and maintain continuous training programs for agents in techniques of child pornography investigations.

58. Federal law enforcement agencies should have personnel trained in child pornography investigation and when possible they should form specialized units for child sexual abuse and child pornography investigation.

59. Federal law enforcement agencies should use search warrants in child pornography and related cases expeditiously as a means of gathering evidence and furthering overall investigation efforts in the child pornography area.

60. Federal law enforcement agents should ask the child victim in reported child sexual abuse cases if photographs or films were made of him or her during the course of sexual abuse.

61. The Department of Justice should appoint a national task force to conduct a study of cases throughout the United States reflecting apparent patterns of multi-victim, multi-perpetrator child sexual exploitation.

D. *Recommendations For State And Local Law Enforcement Agencies*

62. Local law enforcement agencies should participate in the law enforcement coordinating committees to form regional task forces of dedicated and experienced investigators and prosecutors to combat child pornography.

63. State and local law enforcement agencies should develop and maintain continuous training programs for officers in identification, apprehension, and undercover techniques of child pornography investigation.

64. State and local law enforcement agencies should participate in a national data base established to serve as a center for state and local law enforcement agencies to submit and receive information regarding child pornography trafficking.

65. State and local law enforcement agencies should have personnel trained in child pornography investigation and when possible they should form specialized units for child sexual abuse and child pornography investigations.

66. State and local law enforcement agencies should use search warrants in child sexual exploitation cases expeditiously as a means of gathering evidence and furthering overall investigation effort in the child pornography area.

67. State and local law enforcement officers should ask the child victim in reported child sexual abuse cases if photographs or films were made of him or her during the course of sexual abuse.

E. *Recommendations For Prosecutors*

68. The United States Department Of Justice should direct United States attorneys to participate in law enforcement coordinating committee task forces to combat child pornography.

69. Federal, state, and local prosecutors should participate in a task force of multi-disciplinary practitioners and develop a protocol for courtroom procedures for child witnesses that would meet constitutional standards.

70. Prosecutors should assist state, local, and federal law enforcement agencies to use search warrants in potential child pornography and related child sexual abuse cases.

71. State, local, and federal prosecutors should ask the child victim in reported child sexual abuse cases if photographs or films were made of him or her during the course of sexual abuse.

72. State and local prosecutors should use the vertical prosecution model in child pornography and related cases.

F. *Recommendations For The Judiciary And Correctional Facilities*

73. Judges and probation officers should receive specific education so they may investigate, evaluate, sentence and supervise persons convicted of child pornography and related cases appropriately.

74. Judges should impose appropriate periods of incarceration for convicted child pornographers and related offenders.

75. Judges should use, when appropriate, a sentence of lifetime probation for convicted child pornographers.

76. Pre-sentence reports concerning individuals found guilty of violations of child pornography or related laws should be based on sources of information in addition to the offender himself or herself.

77. State and federal correctional facilities should recognize the unique problems of child pornographers and related offenders and designate appropriate programs regarding their incarceration.

78. Federal, state, and local judges should participate in a task force of multi-disciplinary practitioners and develop a protocol for courtroom procedures for child witnesses that would meet constitutional standards.

G. *Recommendations For Public And Private Social Service Agencies*

79. Public and private social service agencies should participate in a task force of multi-disciplinary practitioners and develop a protocol for courtroom procedures for child witnesses that would meet constitutional standards.

80. Social, mental health and medical services should be provided for child pornography victims.

81. Local agencies should allocate victims of crimes funds to provide monies for psychiatric evaluation and treatment and medical treatment of child pornography victims and their families.

82. Clinical evaluators should be trained to assist

children victimized through the production and use of child pornography more effectively and to better understand adult psychosexual disorders.

83. Behavioral scientists should conduct research to determine the effects of the production of child pornography and the related victimization of children.

84. States should support age appropriate education and prevention programs for parents, teachers and children within public and private school systems to protect children from victimization by child pornographers and child sexual abusers.

85. A multi-media educational campaign should be developed which increases family and community awareness regarding child sexual exploitation through the production and use of child pornography.

III. Victimization

86. State, county and municipal governments should facilitate the development of public and private resources for persons who are currently involved in the production or consumption of pornography and wish to discontinue this involvement and for those who suffer mental, physical, educational, or employment disabilities as a result of exposure or participation in the production of pornography.

IV. Civil Rights

87. Legislatures should conduct hearings and consider legislation recognizing a civil remedy for harms attributable to pornography.

V. "Adults Only" Pornographic Outlets

88. "Adults Only" pornographic outlet peep show facilities which provide individual booths for viewing should not be equipped with doors. The occupant of the booth should be clearly visible to eliminate a haven for sexual activity.

89. Holes enabling interbooth sexual contact between patrons should be prohibited in the peep show booths.

90. Because of the apparent health hazards posed by the outlet environment generally, and the peep show booth in particular, such facilities should be subject to periodic inspection and licensing by appropriate governmental agents.

91. Any form of indecent act by or among "adults only" pornographic outlet patrons should be unlawful.

92. Access to "adults only" pornographic outlets should be limited to persons over the age of eighteen.[35]

Readers should remember that the reasons for each of the ninety-two recommendations are detailed in the report. We concur with many of the recommendations but again emphasize that we would like to see a new definition of pornography adopted by the legislatures and courts.

THE COMMISSION ON OBSCENITY AND PORNOGRAPHY

On September 30, 1970, the Commission on Obscenity and Pornography issued its report.[36] The commission found that general release films were becoming more sexually explicit, with increasing scenes of simulated intercourse. Even in the so-called skin flicks and exploitation films, however, acts of sexual intercourse and oral-genital contact were not shown, only strongly implied. Full male nudity was virtually unknown except in the tiny male homosexual market. Sexual foreplay was graphically depicted. In the late 1960s, "[h]ybrid" films, however, some of which graphically depicted actual sexual intercourse, began to appear and were exhibited in some one thousand to two thousand theaters.[37] The commission specifically found that the "vast majority" of exploitation films were directed at the male heterosexual market, as were the adult paperbacks.[38]

In 1970, X-rated films accounted for only a small percentage of gross receipts in the film industry.[39] Adult paperback receipts totaled $550 million in 1968 (or 21 percent of the entire book industry).[40] Forty-one million "men's sophisticates" magazines, which devoted a substantial portion of content to photo-

graphs of partially nude females, sold in 1969 (sixty-two different magazines).[41] In that year, just under sixty-four million *Playboy* magazines were sold, with retail dollar sales of approximately $64 million.[42] Adults-only magazines contained implied sexual activity, but actual sexual activity and physical arousal of males was not depicted.[43] The commission estimated that the total of all adults-only magazines and books in the United States amounted to only between $70 million and $90 million in retail sales in 1969.[44] Fetish and sadomasochistic materials made up less than 5 percent of the total.[45]

In the late 1960s, more than twenty-one billion pieces of mail soliciting purchases or advertising products annually inundated American consumers. Less than 0.25 percent attempted to sell sexually oriented materials.[46] In 1968, a new federal law allowed recipients of unsolicited sexually provocative advertisements to request the U.S. Postal Service to issue orders to the mailer prohibiting further mailings to the address. During the first two years of enforcement of this law, the Postal Service issued more than 370,000 orders and received more than

450,000 requests for such orders.[47] The estimated volume of sexually oriented mail (advertisements) was forty-five to forty-eight million letters in 1969.[48]

While the commission found much disagreement among law enforcement officials regarding whether "organized crime" was involved in the pornography business, it concluded that "at present, there is insufficient data to warrant any conclusion in this regard."[49]

Although 85 percent of men and 70 percent of women in the United States had been exposed at some time to depictions (visual or text) of explicit sexual material, the commission noted that between 20 and 25 percent of the male population had "somewhat regular experience with sexual materials as explicit as depictions of heterosexual intercourse."[50] For most, their first experience with such materials occurred during adolescence.[51] The commission characterized the patrons of adult theaters and bookstores as mainly white, middle-class, middle-age married males.[52]

The commission conducted elaborate studies of the effects of explicit sexual materials, the results of which can be found in its technical reports and some of which are discussed in chapter 5 in this book. The commission concluded that sexual behavior was, in general, "not altered substantially by exposure to erotica."[53] It also found that substantial numbers of males and females are sexually aroused by exposure to "erotic stimuli."[54] The commission said that "exposure to erotic stimuli appears to have little or no effect on already established attitudinal commitments regarding either sexuality or sexual morality."[55]

The commission said that the relationship between the changes in sex crime rates and the availability of erotica "neither proves nor disproves the possibility that availability of erotica leads to crime, but the massive overall increases in sex crimes that have been alleged do not seem to have occurred."[56] It found that sex offenders, while having less experience with "erotica" as adolescents than other persons, had the same experiences during adulthood as nonoffenders.[57] The commission concluded:

> In sum empirical research designed to clarify the question has found no evidence to date that exposure to explicit sexual materials plays a significant role in the causation of delinquent or criminal behavior among youths or adults. The Commission cannot conclude that exposure to erotic materials is a factor in the causation of sex crime or sex delinquency.[58]

The commission advocated sex education in the schools and adequate sexual information as alterna-

tives to pornography and ways of counteracting some of the incorrect sexual information communicated in pornography.[59]

In the legal arena, the *Roth* standard was the law at the time of the commission report. The commission stated that "a great deal of subjective judgment" is required to apply the *Roth* standard to specific material "because the criteria refer to emotional, aesthetic and intellectual responses to the material rather than to descriptions of its content."[60] In addition, the meaning of the *Roth* criteria was unclear, the commission said.[61] This subjectivity and vagueness produced uncertainty about what is obscene and made it impossible for publishers and distributors to know in advance whether they would be charged with a criminal offense for a particular work.

The commission also suggested that U.S. Supreme Court opinions had greatly narrowed the coverage of obscenity laws to only the most graphic pictorial depictions of actual sex, making the law for adults "largely ineffective."[62] A definition of *obscenity*, it concluded, should describe the covered material specifically and objectively. However, because the commission decided that insufficient "social justification" existed to retain or enact "broad legislation prohibiting the consensual distribution of sexual materials to adults,"[63] it refused to comply with its congressional mandate to provide a definition of *obscenity* for adults.

Interestingly, about two-thirds of those surveyed on a national level who opposed legal restrictions on pornography said that their views would change "if it were clearly demonstrated that certain materials have harmful effects."[64]

The commission said that much of the "problem" regarding sexually explicit materials stemmed from "the inability or reluctance of people in our society to be open and direct in dealing with sexual matters."[65] It believed that interest in sex is good, normal, and healthy. Clandestine sources of sexual information (such as pornography) might be distorted and inaccurate.[66] Thus, the commission presented what it called "positive" approaches to dealing with pornography:

1. Launch a massive sex education program.
2. Continue to discuss openly the issues surrounding pornography and obscenity.
3. Develop additional factual information.
4. Motivate citizens groups to aid in implementing these recommendations by providing a forum for all views to be heard.[67]

The commission also made legislative recommendations. It said that, in general, legislation should "not seek to interfere with the right of adults who wish to do so to read, obtain, or view explicit sexual materials."[68] Thus, it recommended the repeal of all existing laws prohibiting the sale, distribution, or exhibition of sexual materials to consenting adults. (This proposal was opposed by five of seventeen commissioners.)[69] That recommendation was based primarily on the conclusion that pornography did not have a significant role in causing social or individual harms.[70] Also, the commission noted that a substantial number of adults seek sexual materials (which the commissioners saw as positive).[71] Other reasons for the recommendation included the lack of past success in enforcing obscenity laws; the lack of consensus about whether pornography should be available to adults; the value of individuals' exercising free speech rights; the belief that the objective of protecting young people does not outweigh the denial of materials to adults; the belief that making pornography available will not adversely affect the business of other book, film, and magazine producers; and the belief that pornography does not adversely affect morality.[72] The commission said that the pornography business is not "an especially profitable one"[73] and that it is "unwise" to try to legislate individual moral values and standards of independent behavior.[74]

The commission decided it should be against the law to commercially communicate pornography to children unless parents consent to such communication. Only pictorial pornographic material would be prohibited for sale or commercial display to children.[75] The commission was influenced considerably by its finding that most Americans "believe that children should not be exposed to certain sexual materials."[76] Also, it found that while its finding that pornography did not cause harm applied to children, it could not reach that conclusion as confidently as it did its conclusion about adult exposure because few data were available on exposing children to "erotic" materials. The commission said that sometimes exposing children to sexual materials might facilitate communication about sex between a child and his or her parents.[77] The model statute proposed by the commission would not have prohibited sale to juveniles through the mails (because it said that "juveniles rarely purchase sexually explicit materials through the mail"), did not include verbal materials, and did not cover television or radio.[78]

Interestingly, the commission supported laws prohibiting the "public display" of pornography on the ground that such material should not be thrust upon people without their consent. It also supported prohibiting unsolicited sexually explicit advertisements through the mails.[79] If antipornography laws existed, it proposed requiring prosecutors to obtain civil declaratory judgments against pornography in lieu of prosecution in all cases except where the materials at issue were unquestionably covered by the statute.[80]

In its proposed law for minors, the commission defined explicit sexual material as

> any pictorial or three dimensional material including, but not limited to, books, magazines, films, photographs and statuary, which is made up in whole or in dominant part of depictions of human sexual intercourse, masturbation, sodomy (i.e. bestiality or oral or anal intercourse), direct physical stimulation of unclothed genitals, or flagellation or torture in the context of a sexual relationship, or which emphasizes the depiction of uncovered adult human genitals; provided however, that works of art or of anthropological significance shall not be deemed to be within the foregoing definition.[81]

Interestingly, the commission's emphasis was on getting rid of what it considered to be vague and subjective standards under *Roth* and substituting specific descriptions of what would be prohibited. That same concept is often advanced today. The commission's proposed public display law also would have prohibited any depiction emphasizing adult human genitals, whether or not they were unclothed.[82]

Not surprisingly, the commission's report was overwhelmingly rejected by the president and Congress. Several commissioners filed minority reports.

The minority report filed by Commissioners Hill and Link and concurred in by Commissioner Keating called the majority report "a Magna Carta for the pornographer."[83] The report said that the conclusions and recommendations were "fraudulent."[84] The inference that pornography is "harmless" is "not only insupportable on the slanted evidence presented; it is preposterous," the commissioners said.[85] The minority report said:

> We believe that pornography has an eroding effect on society, on public morality, on respect for human worth, on attitudes toward family love, on culture.
>
> We believe it is impossible, and totally unnecessary, to attempt to prove or disprove a cause-effect relationship between pornography and criminal behavior.
>
> Sex education, recommended so strongly by the majority, is the panacea for those who advocate license in media. . . .
>
> Children cannot grow in love if they are trained with pornography. Pornography is loveless; it degrades the human being, reduces him to the level of animal. . . .

[W]e find . . . that the majority of the American people favor tighter controls.[86]

The minority had Victor B. Cline, a psychologist and social science research methodology and statistics expert, review the commission's Effects Panel Report. Cline concluded that it was "seriously flawed, and omitting some critical data on negative effects."[87] Importantly, he concluded that the evidence the commission presented did not clearly indicate "no harm" and that the presentation contained "frequent errors and inaccuracies in their reporting of research results as well as in the basic studies themselves."[88] The minority report stated:

> Frequently, conclusions which are not warranted are drawn inappropriately from data. There is a frequent failure to distinguish or discriminate between studies which are badly flawed and weak and those of exceptional merit. But, most serious of all, data from a number of studies which show statistical linkages between high exposure to pornography and promiscuity, deviancy, affiliation with high criminality groups, etc. have gone unreported. This suggests a major bias in the reporting of results which raises a major issue of credibility of the entire report.[89]

(Having reviewed both viewpoints, we have concluded that the minority report more correctly presented the truth about pornography and more accurately interpreted the research results.) Importantly, the minority report accused the majority of misinterpreting the law of obscenity by presenting as legal precedents U.S. Supreme Court rulings made by only a minority of the justices. At the time of the commission report, such nonmajority rulings were not of precedential value, and the minority report correctly emphasized that fact in great detail. Under present law, such nonmajority holdings *are* the law of the land. The minority report recognized the need for a new test for obscenity (and the U.S. Supreme Court developed one in *Miller* a few years later).

Commissioner Keating also issued a minority report. Like the Hill–Link minority report, the Keating report alleged that the commission and its staff and resources were all biased in favor of pornographers.[90]

In our opinion, it is unfortunate that the *Report of the Commission on Obscenity and Pornography* served, for years, as the basis for pornographers to claim that their products were harmless and influenced public attitudes in a way that resulted in much more pornography being circulated in the United States.

CANADA'S SPECIAL COMMITTEE ON PORNOGRAPHY AND PROSTITUTION

In 1985, the Special Committee on Pornography and Prostitution (known as the Fraser Committee) issued its report, *Pornography and Prostitution in Canada*.[91] The Canadian committee disagreed with the idea that criminal law should be confined to conduct that causes "tangible harm" to an individual.[92] While great care must be taken to establish society's values, the need to protect those values is legitimate, the committee said. Laws dealing with pornography and prostitution must "be founded upon the rights of women and men to legal, social and economic equality."[93] According to the committee, pornography and prostitution reflect (if not cause) "perceptions that women are inferior, and that men can expect women to be available to service their sexual needs."[94] Pornography inhibits improvement of the status of women, the committee said. It called upon Canada to reject the view of women espoused in much contemporary pornography.[95]

As a general rule, the committee noted, adults must be responsible for their actions. The committee did not accept the idea that criminal law should be

based on the belief that women are victims of pornography. In contrast, children were seen as vulnerable victims.[96] The committee explained: "We see the zone of no regulation as that where the adult's conduct does not coerce others, and where it does not impinge unacceptably on the values which are basic to our society."[97]

In the pornography area, the right of some persons to equality will run counter to the right of others to create or enjoy pornography, the committee recognized. Two values that they said deserve protection are "human dignity and voluntary sexual expression." Basic physical integrity is an important part of human dignity, and the committee found no room in a civilized society for "activities which threaten the physical well-being of others." Humans, it said, benefit from "open and caring sexual relationships, characterized by mutuality and respect."[98]

Importantly, the committee urged a shift from focusing on sexual immorality as the reason for criminal prohibitions against pornography to a view of pornography as an assault on human rights—that is, offenses to "equality, dignity and physical integrity." The committee strove to create a clear and specific description of prohibited conduct.[99]

In 1982, Canada passed the Charter of Rights and Freedoms, a law similar to the U.S. Constitution, which granted rights to Canadian citizens and divided governmental powers between the federal government and the provincial legislatures. While the charter includes rights of free speech and equal rights under the law (while allowing affirmative action for disadvantaged persons and groups), interpretations of it are slowly making their way through the courts. The charter aimed partly at correcting inequalities and injustices. There is also a notion that rights are not absolute but must sometimes be balanced against "the greater claims of the community." Rights can be overridden by the Parliament and provincial legislatures.[100]

The Canadian law at the time of the report stated that any publication "a dominant characteristic of which is the undue exploitation of sex, or of sex and any one or more of the following subjects, namely crime, horror, cruelty and violence," is obscene. In addition, the publication had to exceed the "contemporary Canadian community standards of tolerance."[101] Other parts of the Canadian law attacked disgusting objects or indecent shows, as well as representations of "an immoral or indecent character."[102] The lack of uniform terminology created problems with enforcement of these laws. There was, according to the committee, dissatisfaction with the law, lack of use of the law, and inconsistent results.[103] A 1983 proposal would have detached the term *sex* from *violence and cruelty* to permit things to be obscene without being pornographic.[104]

Finding that opinions of what is offensive varied widely among Canadians, the committee concluded that subjectivity does not belong in the criminal law. Thus, it decided to recommend elimination of the community standards of tolerance requirement.[105]

The committee found two main types of pornography—that which is merely sexually explicit and that which is, in addition, degrading or abusive, combines sex and violence, or promotes woman hating.[106] The description of pornography that the committee created—we would say that a work is pornographic if it combines the two features of explicit sexual representations (context) and an apparent or purported intention to arouse its audience sexually—was not totally satisfying to the members.[107]

The civil rights definitions proposed by Dworkin and MacKinnon were too imprecise and broad to be used in the criminal law, the committee said.[108] It also felt strongly that the criminal law should not stifle "erotic art."[109] The committee recommended that the term *obscene* be retired from use because it does not cover the new pornography, which combines sex and violence.

The range of viewpoints at the public hearings included those that supported regulation of any depiction of sexual activity to those that found all pornography except that depicting children acceptable. The large majority agreed that something should be done about violent pornography.[110] Most participants were concerned

> that pornography degrades women, robs them of their dignity as individual human beings and equal partners within a relationship and treats them as objects or possessions to be used by men; that male violence against women is treated as socially acceptable and viewers are desensitized to the suffering of others and thirdly, that these two influences will have a strong negative influence on children and on the family.[111]

The committee detailed some of the reasons why people are opposed to pornography, including arguments about harms and effects. Among those were the following:

- The Concerned Morality League of Winnipeg stated that (in the report's words) "[t]he values which support family love, mutual respect, and generosity are undermined, and lust, exploitation, selfishness are promoted."[112]
- According to the Ontario Advisory Council on the Status of Women, "Pornography is unacceptable not because it portrays explicit sex but because it promotes hatred, violence, degradation and dehumanization." Pornography also promotes hostility toward women. "Women are . . . terrorized by the message that male violence and power is so prevalent and menacing. Pornography alienates women and men. In no way does it foster healthy sexual or human relations any more than other forms of hate literature would foster healthy relations between races or religions."[113]
- The Provincial Advisory Council on the Status of Women in St. John's said that pornography promotes an idea that "a woman's value lies in her physical appearance and her ability to sexually satisfy a man." And it leads to an increase in aggressive antisocial behavior and violent sex crimes.[114]
- Carl Beigie, an economist from Toronto, suggested that only an "intrinsically sexist society" could wholeheartedly support the massive amounts of pornography available.[115]

- The United Church of Canada in Toronto made this comment: "It cannot be a coincidence that pornography exists in a society where women are raped, beaten by husbands, pushed into low income work and generally not taken seriously. . . . [T]he Church has transmitted and shaped male domination in western culture."[116]
- Media Watch of Calgary found that "male dominance and female submissiveness are at the very heart of the stereotype of men and women. Pornography is the extreme portrayal of dominance-submissiveness, the objectification and the abuse of women."[117]

The committee noted that most Canadians believe that exposure to pornography should be limited to adults and many believe that the proliferation of pornography is related to the fact that Canadian society is controlled by men.[118] Opposition to controls on pornography came from civil liberties groups, those who profit from pornography, and gay rights organizations, but even some of these groups agreed to censor *actual* abuse of real people.

The committee analyzed porn effects research and concluded that the available research is of very limited use in addressing the issue of pornography's harm to society and individuals. The committee said:

> [W]e have had to conclude, very reluctantly, that the available research is of very limited use in addressing these questions. We want to articulate our position very clearly: the Committee is not prepared to state, *solely on the basis of the evidence and research it has seen,* that pornography is a significant causal factor in the commission of some forms of violent crime, in the sexual abuse of children, or the disintegration of communities and society. Pornography may, indeed, be a prime factor in each of the undesirable consequences mentioned but, *based solely on the evidence we have considered,* we cannot at this time conclude that such is the case.
>
> . . . [T]he research is so inadequate and chaotic that no consistent body of information has been established. We know very well that individual studies demonstrate harmful or positive results from the use of pornography. However, overall, the results of the research are contradictory or inconclusive.[119]

The Canadian committee recognized pornography as a human rights/discrimination against women issue involving hatred toward and group defamation of women. It decided that the term *obscenity* had outlived its usefulness. It noted that elimination of false depictions of women cannot be achieved through the criminal code; rather, a reorientation of the priorities and values of the media is needed. The committee concluded however, that some sexual material is so "damaging to individuals and society" that it must be criminally punished.[120]

The committee established the three-tier system for regulating pornography criminally that is quoted in chapter 1. These categories are critical, for they create harsh penalties for the more extreme forms of pornography such as child pornography and for pornography that causes actual harm to participants. Fairly strict penalties are suggested for sexually violent pornography and depictions of bestiality, incest, or necrophilia. The system would, however, allow the private exhibition and sale of other forms of pornography and decriminalize most live sex shows. The committee said that treating live shows differently from magazines, films, and other pornography could not be justified. Thus, much pornography would be decriminalized as long as it was available in public only with a warning as to its nature and a prohibition on access to persons under 18.

It is unclear from the study whether or not degrading pornography would be permitted, but the proposed legal terminology suggests that it would be allowed. The committee defined "sexually violent behaviour" as "(i) sexual assault, (ii) physical harm, including murder, assault or bondage of another person or persons, or self-infliction of physical harm, depicted for the apparent purpose of causing sexual gratification to or stimulation of the viewer."[121]

In recommending elimination of the community standards test, the committee suggested that it is impossible to tell what the national standard is and that material gets measured against the most extreme pornography. It said that criminal charges should be based on clearly stated principles and not on "majoritarian impulses." The committee recommended standardizing pornographic definitions regarding all media and forms of distribution such as films, books, live performances, importation, and domestic mail. It noted that the context of a presentation would play an important role in deciding whether the portrayal of physical harm was wrongful and gave as an example the difference between incest portrayals in pornography and such portrayals in a medical or educational setting.[122]

> In essence we see two forms of harm flowing from pornography. The first is the offense which it does to members of the public who are involuntarily subjected to it. The second is the broader social harm which it causes by undermining the right to equality which is set out in section 15 of the *Charter of Rights and Freedoms.*[123]

The first harm, it said, should be handled by penalties for failing to protect the public from involuntary encounters with pornography. The second requires proscription of certain forms of pornography.[124]

The committee noted that some human rights authorities in Canada are already dealing with pornography in ways similar to the Minneapolis/ Indianapolis civil rights approach by redressing complaints of unwilling exposure to pornography in employment, education, and public places. Such material is seen as violating equal rights for women and men, which are guaranteed by the charter. (This differs from U.S. court holdings that pornography is not a form of sex discrimination.)

Importantly, the Canadian committee recommended that [jurisdictions enact] civil causes of action "focusing on the violation of civil rights inherent in pornography."[125] It also recommended the enactment in each province and territory of civil causes of action regarding the promotion of hatred through pornography. The criminal law that makes it unlawful to willfully promote hatred against any identifiable group would, under the committee's proposals, be amended to include women as an identifiable group. And it would no longer be necessary to show that a defendant specifically intended to promote hatred.[126]

The committee view is perhaps best summarized in this way: "Our recommendations thus include a complete reworking of the *Criminal Code* prohibitions in this area, to create offenses based not on concepts of sexual immorality but rather on the offenses to equality, dignity, and physical integrity that we believe are involved in pornography."[127]

GREAT BRITAIN'S COMMITTEE ON OBSCENITY AND FILM CENSORSHIP

The Committee on Obscenity and Film Censorship in Great Britain issued its report in October 1979. The committee was chaired by Bernard Williams, who published an abridged version of the report with the Cambridge University Press in 1981.[128] The Williams committee did not do original research or conduct public opinion surveys.[129]

Great Britain's antipornography laws at the time of the report lacked uniformity. Different definitions of pornography applied to different categories such as imports, mailing, and public display. Some obscenity tests were easier to apply than others. Contradictions abounded. For example, it was a defense for a publication to be "for the public good on account of its literary, artistic or scientific value." The committee asked how something found to "deprave and corrupt" could be in the public good.[130] Private clubs managed to escape the film certification system, which applied only to public exhibitions of pornography.[131] The committee estimated the market of pornographic magazines in Great Britain to be 3 million per month with a gross readership of 8 million.[132]

The Williams committee accepted the philosophy that no conduct should be suppressed "by law unless it can be shown to harm someone."[133] In other words, it is not enough for something to be morally wrong. There is, the committee said, a presumption in favor of individual freedom that can be overcome by a showing of harm beyond a reasonable doubt.[134] And, if a class of publications (such as pornography) is to be banned, the harms must be ascribable to that *class* of publications, not just one book that caused harm.[135]

The committee studied two types of evidence of harm from pornography:

1. *Anecdotal and clinical evidence.* Although the murderers in a well-known murder case (the Moors Murders) actually created pornography, the committee concluded that nothing suggested that they would not have committed the crimes if they had not been exposed to pornography. None of the psychiatrists and psychologists the committee consulted produced a case with evidence of a causal link between pornography and a violent sexual crime. The committee said that "it is striking that one can study case after case of sex crimes and murder without finding any hint at all that pornography was present in the background."[136] (We note that this differs remarkably from U.S. findings.) The committee then concluded that all kinds of literature can have a destructive effect on those "susceptible."[137]

2. *Research.* Research into the effects of pornography leaves no clear impression and much disagreement about what conclusions can be drawn, the committee said.[138] While pointing out that criminal and antisocial behavior cannot ethically be experimentally produced, the committee noted that "[c]orrelation experiments in artificial conditions are regarded by many competent critics as an unilluminating and unreliable way of investigating complex behaviour."[139]

The committee concluded that there did not appear to be any "strong evidence" that exposure to sexually explicit material triggers antisocial behavior.[140] Likewise, studies of television violence produced no firm evidence that television has a socially harmful effect or that it does not.[141] The committee argued that even if there is a correlation between pornography and sex crime, there is no proof that one influences the other because the causes of crime are complex and cannot be isolated. The committee spent much space attacking experts who have argued that there is a link between pornography and crime. While the committee did not deny the possibility of a link between pornography and sexual offenses, it rejected the suggestion that "available statistical information for England and Wales lends any support at all to the argument that pornography acts as a stimulus to the commission of sexual violence."[142]

(As an example of the absurdity of the committee's findings, we point out that they went into elaborate detail concerning a Danish study that found that the dramatic reduction in sex offenses against children between 1967 and 1969 was "difficult to explain other than in relation to the availability of pornography."[143] Pornography, the study suggested, could be a substitute for child molestation.[144] Not only does this fly in the face of common sense, but it contrasts markedly with current U.S. reports that show that most child molesters are pornography users and that many use it to entice children into sexual acts, while some also photograph the children they abuse in sexual acts. The committee declined to draw any firm conclusions about the Danish study.)

The committee said that research results indicate that "sexual patterns of behaviour are fixed before reading pornography can exercise any influence."[145] It concluded that there is no evidence that exposure to deviant pornography creates a taste for it, but rather that such pornography appeals to those with a preexisting interest established by life experience.[146] (Again, we suggest that this finding lacks common sense because most people would learn of sexual practices such as bondage and sadomasochism only through pornography.)

The committee listened to claims that pornography could damage marital relationships by giving husbands the desire to experiment with sexual practices that wives abhor and creating dissatisfaction with existing partners and a desire to look elsewhere. Having received little concrete evidence of this, the committee concluded that the evidence was too insubstantial to "suggest overall that pornography was a significant cause of harm to marriages or other personal relationships."[147] And, while accepting the viewpoint that pornography is one *symptom* (rather than a cause) of women's subservient role in society, the committee argued that there was no reason to single out pornography for attack in the goal of altering society's attitudes.[148]

Even though the committee concluded that participation in child pornography involves the commission of a sex offense, it said that the participation of adults in pornography is not a cause of harm because most models see it as a way to make money and physical injury is already prohibited by the law.[149] The committee said that the role of pornography in influencing society is minor compared to many other problems.[150]

Despite its conclusions that pornography is harmless, the Williams committee did propose certain restrictions on it. Such restrictions were justifiable as long as they were not directed against the advocacy of an opinion and they did not apply to those who wanted to obtain it.[151]

The committee recommended that publications consisting solely of the written word not be suppressed or restricted.[152] Interestingly, the committee declared that it "emphatically" rejected the viewpoint that books have no bad or good effects at all.[153] It also said that although most pornography is totally worthless as an art form, it would be possible for pornography to have some artistic merit.[154]

Pornography, the committee said, is always a representation combining two features: "[I]t has a certain function or intention, to arouse its audience sexually, and also a certain content, explicit representations of sexual material (organs, postures, activity, etc.)"[155]

The committee concluded that a "public good" defense relating to literary or artistic merit is "misconceived" because it would tend to favor successful writers and artists over unknowns even if the content was similar.[156]

In general, the committee aimed at containing, rather than suppressing, pornography: "[T]he law should primarily aim to restrict pornography so that it will not be offensive to the public, and to satisfy the widespread feeling that young people should not be exposed to material of this kind."[157] In reaching that goal, the committee proposed making it unlawful to sell or display pornography except in separate premises or in a part of the premises having a street access to which no one under age 18 would be admitted. Warnings that what is inside could be offensive and that minors will not be admitted would have to be posted, and the public display of such material would not be allowed. In other words, only those adults who wished to consume the pornography could obtain it, and others would not have to be exposed to it.[158]

The committee concluded that the words *obscene, indecent,* and *tendency to deprave and corrupt* in the law were useless and should be replaced by the offensiveness concept. It rejected proposals to be extremely specific in defining what pornography is because it felt such a definition would provide loopholes for pornographers.[159] The committee's primary proposal was to restrict that "[w]hich, not consisting of the written word, is such that its unrestricted availability is offensive to reasonable people by reason of the manner in which it portrays, deals with or relates to violence, cruelty or horror, or sexual, faecal or urinary functions, or genital organs."[160] The effect of the restrictions would be to force any material to which the definition applied to be available only in shops specializing in pornography and to which children had no access.[161]

The committee found no need to allow exemptions for any material because literary (written) works were not covered and artistic works and medical texts would not be found offensive.[162] The penalties the committee proposed for violations were low in comparison to those for many criminal offenses. In addition, the committee proposed taking away the right of private individuals to prosecute violators out of fear that some would find offensive what most people do not and suc.[163]

Only the following materials would be prohibited under the committee's recommendations:

> Material whose production appears to the court to have involved the exploitation for sexual purposes of any person where either:
> (a) that person appears from the evidence as a whole to have been at the relevant time under the age of sixteen years; or
> (b) the material gives reason to believe that actual physical harm was inflicted on that person.
> Consent would not be a defense to such charges.[164]

The committee refused to prohibit bestiality on the ground that it could find no reason to prohibit such depictions.[165]

The Williams committee decided to apply the same rules to live entertainment as to pictorial publications—that is, to allow a consensual audience to view such entertainment as long as it was found not to be offensive to reasonable adults. If the live performance involved actual sexual activity of an offensive kind, it would be prohibited. Live performances involving the sexual exploitation of anyone

under age 16 also would be prohibited. Interestingly, it also would be a crime to take part in such performances.[166] (We note that the Williams committee apparently did not recognize the fact that some so-called actresses are not willing participants in sexual activity.)

The committee rejected the idea that all media should be treated uniformly.[167] For example, it concluded that film is a "uniquely powerful instrument" with an impact unlike that of other media. Here, the committee sidestepped its earlier conclusions about the lack of harm from pornography and stated:

> It may be that this very graphically presented sadistic material serves only as a vivid object of fantasy, and does no harm at all. There is certainly no conclusive evidence to the contrary. *But there is no conclusive evidence in favour of that belief, either, and in this connection it seems entirely sensible to be cautious.*[168]

Thus, it seems that the committee did not subscribe to the catharsis theory. In fact, it expressed concern that the "vividness" of film might make it harder for some people to tell the difference between reality and fantasy.[169]

Therefore, in the arena of film, the committee proposed that the power to censor films no longer rest with local authorities and called for the creation of a new statutory body at the national level. The same principles would apply as those proposed for publications. Restricted showings of certain films that the censors did not approve would be allowed in adults-only theaters designated for the showing of such films. It would be up to the local authorities to decide whether they wanted to have such a cinema in their area and to control the number of such theaters. A film certificate from the national board would guarantee immunity from prosecution.[170] (We point out that the impact of the committee's proposals regarding film censorship would have been to ensure censorship of less material.) The committee declined to make it an offense for teenagers to sneak into age-restricted films, claiming that seeing an X-rated film before age 18 is "so hallowed a teenage tradition."[171]

According to a book by A.W.B. Simpson, who served on the Williams committee, the government shelved the report with no real legislative debate on its provisions. Readers interested in learning more about the background of antipornography laws in Great Britain, the Williams committee, and changes in laws since the report was issued should consult Simpson's book.[172]

(We suggest that, as far as British pornography studies are concerned, the one chaired by Lord Longford, which resulted in *Pornography: The Longford Report*, took a much more realistic approach.[173])

NOTES

1. Attorney General's Commission on Pornography, *Final Report* (Washington, DC: United States Department Of Justice, 1986) (hereafter cited as AGCOP).
2. Ibid., 323.
3. Ibid., 323–24.
4. Ibid., 324.
5. Ibid.
6. Ibid., 325.
7. Ibid., 326.
8. Ibid.
9. Ibid., 326–27.
10. Ibid., 327.
11. Ibid.
12. Ibid., 328.
13. Ibid., 328–29.
14. Ibid., 329, 331.
15. Ibid., 331–32.
16. Richard E. McLawhorn, *Summary of the Final Report of the Attorney General's Commission on Pornography* (Cincinnati: National Coalition Against Pornography, Inc., 1986), 8.
17. AGCOP, 332.
18. Ibid., 333.
19. Ibid., 333.
20. Ibid., 333–34.
21. Ibid., 334.
22. Ibid., 333.
23. Ibid.
24. Ibid., 335.
25. Ibid., 337.
26. Ibid., 338.
27. Ibid., 339–40.
28. Ibid., 340–42, 340.
29. Ibid., 342–43.
30. Ibid., 345–47.
31. Ibid., 343–45.
32. Ibid., 347–49.
33. Ibid., 349–51.
34. Ibid., 739–45.
35. Ibid., 433–58.
36. *The Report of the Commission on Obscenity and Pornography* (New York: Bantam Books, 1970).
37. Ibid., 9–11.
38. Ibid., 10–11, 18.
39. Ibid., 90.
40. Ibid., 106.
41. Ibid., 110.
42. Ibid.
43. Ibid.
44. Ibid., 20.
45. Ibid., 18.
46. Ibid., 20.
47. Ibid., 21.
48. Ibid.
49. Ibid., 22–23.
50. Ibid., 23–24.
51. Ibid., 24–25.
52. Ibid., 25.
53. Ibid., 29.
54. Ibid., 28.
55. Ibid., 29.
56. Ibid., 31.
57. Ibid.
58. Ibid., 32.
59. Ibid., 33–37.
60. Ibid., 45.
61. Ibid.
62. Ibid., 45–46.
63. Ibid., 47–48.
64. Ibid., 49–50.
65. Ibid., 53.
66. Ibid., 53–54.
67. Ibid., 54–56.
68. Ibid., 57.
69. Ibid.
70. Ibid., 58.
71. Ibid., 59.
72. Ibid., 59–61.
73. Ibid., 61.
74. Ibid.
75. Ibid., 63–64.
76. Ibid., 63.
77. Ibid.
78. Ibid., 64–67.
79. Ibid., 67–68.
80. Ibid., 70–71.
81. Ibid., 77.
82. Ibid., 78–79.
83. Ibid., 456.
84. Ibid.
85. Ibid., 457.
86. Ibid., 458–59.
87. Ibid., 463.
88. Ibid., 489.
89. Ibid.
90. Ibid., 578–700.
91. *Pornography and Prostitution in Canada: Report of the Special Committee on Pornography and Prostitution* (Ottawa: Minister of Supply and Services, 1985).
92. Ibid., 22.

93. Ibid., 23–24.
94. Ibid., 24.
95. Ibid.
96. Ibid., 25.
97. Ibid., 26.
98. Ibid.
99. Ibid., 27.
100. Ibid., 31–39.
101. Ibid., 45–46.
102. Ibid., 46–47.
103. Ibid., 47–48.
104. Ibid., 48.
105. Ibid., 50.
106. Ibid., 52–54.
107. Ibid., 53.
108. Ibid., 56.
109. Ibid., 58.
110. Ibid., 63.
111. Ibid., 67.
112. Ibid.
113. Ibid., 68.
114. Ibid.
115. Ibid., 69.
116. Ibid., 71.
117. Ibid.
118. Ibid., 73–74.
119. Ibid., 99.
120. Ibid.
121. Ibid., 279.
122. Ibid., 259, 272–74.
123. Ibid., 259.
124. Ibid., 260.
125. Ibid., 310, 313, 315.
126. Ibid., 314, 317–24.
127. Ibid., 27.
128. Bernard Williams, ed., *Obscenity and Film Censorship: An Abridgement of the Williams Report* (Cambridge, England: Cambridge University Press, 1981).
129. Ibid., 4.
130. Ibid., 9–15, 15.
131. Ibid., 25, 26.
132. Ibid., 44.
133. Ibid., 50.
134. Ibid., 51, 57, 59.
135. Ibid., 60.
136. Ibid., 62–63.
137. Ibid., 64.
138. Ibid., 65.
139. Ibid.
140. Ibid., 66.
141. Ibid., 67.
142. Ibid., 80.
143. Ibid., 84.
144. Ibid.
145. Ibid., 86.
146. Ibid., 86–87.
147. Ibid., 87–88.
148. Ibid., 88.
149. Ibid., 90–92.
150. Ibid., 95.
151. Ibid., 100–101.
152. Ibid., 102.
153. Ibid., 109.
154. Ibid., 103.
155. Ibid., 103.
156. Ibid., 109–10.
157. Ibid., 114.
158. Ibid., 116–17.
159. Ibid., 119 123.
160. Ibid., 124.
161. Ibid., 125.
162. Ibid.
163. Ibid., 129.
164. Ibid., 131.
165. Ibid., 132–133.
166. Ibid., 137–41.
167. Ibid., 144.
168. Ibid., 145, emphasis added.
169. Ibid., 145.
170. Ibid., 148–57.
171. Ibid., 158.
172. A.W.B. Simpson, *Pornography and Politics: A Look Back to the Williams Committee* (London: Waterloo Publishers, Ltd., 1983).
173. *Pornography: The Longford Report* (London: Coronet Books, 1972).

14   CHILD PORNOGRAPHY

We believe that vendors of child pornography can damage children physically, emotionally, and spiritually. While co-author Osanka played a key role in the national anti–child pornography movement in the 1970s, co-author Johann was involved in legislative drafting aimed at strengthening the Wisconsin child pornography legislation in 1985. Osanka also helped draft the 1977–78 federal child pornography law.

The effects of pornography on children and child victimization in pornography are covered extensively in chapters 4 and 5, and the reader is encouraged to consult those chapters for case histories and relevant scientific research.

Our suggestions for new, strengthened legislation regulating child pornography appear in chapter 12. The proposed law presented in that chapter contains civil remedies for victims of pornography in addition to criminal penalties for some activities. Appendix H also contains a list of state statutory citations indicating where the state child pornography laws can be found.

In *New York* v. *Ferber,* the U.S. Supreme Court accepted the argument first made by Osanka that pornography is, in fact, evidence of the crime of child abuse—namely, pictorial proof of the crime of child sexual abuse. Thus, Osanka argued, child pornography should be legally treated as a form of child sexual abuse, and the First Amendment and obscenity law should be irrelevant to that issue. The court also accepted Osanka's argument that stopping distribution of child pornography is the only effective way to end the abuse. The court quoted his statement to the U.S. House: " '[W]e have to be very careful . . . that we don't take comfort in the existence of statutes that are on the books in connection with the use of children in pornography. . . . There are usually no witnesses to these acts of producing pornography.' "[1]

Osanka, whose mother died when he was born and whose father died three years later, lived in two juvenile institutions, twenty-three foster homes, and three orphanages during his first fifteen years of life. He suffered much abuse. In his introduction to Clifford Linedecker's book *Children in Chains,* Osanka urges the public to "send a strong message" to child pornographers "that we will not tolerate their behavior." He also urges compassion, not scorn, for the children involved in child pornography and prostitution.[2]

Osanka was the lead-off expert witness in the 1977 U.S. House and Senate hearings leading to the passage of the federal child pornography law. He also appeared as an expert witness at Illinois House of Representatives hearings that resulted in passage of the state child pornography law in 1978 and at Chicago City Council hearings that resulted in passage of a local ordinance. Osanka also testified at the 1980 Illinois House of Representatives Legislative Investigations Commission hearings on the sexual exploitation of children. He has been an expert witness in numerous child pornography and obscenity cases.

Osanka played a key role in persuading Congress to enact anti–child pornography legislation. Excerpts from his May 23, 1977, testimony before a congressional committee investigating the issue follow:

> I think it is important to point out in the context of these hearings that my mother died the day I was born, my father a few years later, so I was raised in the foster care and institutional care systems, and, as such, I became street-sophisticated far earlier than I became intellectually sophisticated. I think it is important to establish that base line because we are dealing with, in many cases, vulnerable children who are dependent on the child care systems of the United States.
>
> The act and the depiction of the act of children in explicit sexual interaction is a clear case of child abuse and/or child neglect. Existing child abuse and neglect statutes should be strengthened to provide strong criminal penalties for all adult participants, from the camera person to the "adult" bookstore clerk. The law should be so specific that even the act of selling such pornography be interpreted as a party to child abuse and neglect. I realize that these are extreme measures, but the socially corrupting nature of child pornography and the current inability of the criminal justice system to stop it, demand strong protective legislation. In my view, a person who purchases child pornography is a party to child abuse since his purchase will insure a profit for the pornographer and thereby guarantee abuse of additional children through the production of new items. The purchase is also a reward to the pornographer for the child abuse he has already commissioned.

The incidence of child abuse and/or child sexual abuse is on the rise in the United States, and this form of social deviance will be made worse by the introduction and widespread distribution of various forms of pornography utilizing children as the principal sex object. Such materials, in my mind, represent a socially disintegrating assault upon basic moral principles of American society. More immediate, child pornography is a clear case of child abuse and neglect with the potential for immediate and long-term damage to the children, and perhaps the adult readers, involved.

As a concerned citizen, a responsible scholar, and a startled father of four, I urge the Congress of the United States to take immediate remedial action to provide adequate legal provisions guaranteed to secure maximum protection for American children from this insidious commercial exploitation of children's vulnerabilities which, at the same time, clearly is child abuse and/or neglect. I urge the designer of such legislation to go to great length to insure that the sexual use of children in pornography be viewed as child abuse and/or neglect. H.R. 3913, Child Abuse Prevention Act, which is now under consideration by the United States Congress, seems so directed.

Legislation must take care to word protective laws regarding the sexual abuse of children in pornography with such precision that time-consuming, and often futile, debates on the prevailing definitions of obscenity and pornography be avoided. Such debates do not provide protection for the victimized and often traumatized child. The sexual abuse of children in pornography is demonstrably child abuse and/or neglect, and is a clear danger to the dependent children involved and to the basic moral fiber of the American society. Children in American society are conditioned to obey adults and very young children operationally do not have the right of refusal. Persons who coerce children into pornographic activities are violating the civil rights of these children. The sexual abuse of children for commercial pornographic purposes is not guaranteed by the first amendment. Some may debate the degree of obscenity that is involved in the sexual exploitation of children, but none can deny that such insidious manipulations are clearly child abuse and/or neglect.

Offenders under this definition must be vigorously pursued and severely punished. While I personally favor punishment coupled with clinical treatment of individual child sexual molesters, I urge the provision of strong penalties for American pornographers convicted of using children in pornography. Further, serious penalties should be provided for the importation and exploitation of child pornography. In brief, protective legislation in this area must take the

profit out of child pornography. It is not social or cultural need, but individual greed that has given birth to the wholesale introduction of child pornography. In my view, Ellen Goodman's words reflect the majority opinion of Americans when she says, "This is not a first amendment issue. It is not a matter of legislating the sexual fantasies of adults. It's a matter of protecting the lives of the young models."—Chicago Sun-Times of March 15, 1977, p. 32.

I suspect that child pornographers hope that the judicial system gets bogged down in lengthy debate over the first amendment and obscenity definitions, thereby postponing, perhaps for years, meaningful action against child pornography. The result, of course, will be an avalanche of depictions of the sexual abuse of children.

With all due respect to men and women legislators, I would urge you to avoid the very understandable inclination to decline from a personal examination of representative samples of child pornography. It is a painful, sickening, and often very sad experience, but you are obligated to view these items in private to be satisfied in your own mind that none of this material realistically contains any cultural or scientific value. Through such an examination you will fully appreciate the challenging psychological and social implication of most examples of child pornography.

On February 4, 1977, Dr. Judianne Densen-Gerber and I held a closed press conference in the Executive House Hotel in Chicago. The assembled newspersons, many of them hardened veterans of the "crime beat," reacted emotionally by expressing shock and verbalizing anger. Indeed, a tape recording of the press conference indicates that one Chicago Sun-Times columnist and popular "talk show" hostess said:

I'd like to just say that it is the worst thing I have ever seen in my entire life and I wish they (child pornographers) were all dead.

After the press conference, many of the assembled newspersons expressed their concerns in their respective media, and some became active crusaders for public awareness and public demand for protective legislation against the sexual molestation of children. . . .

Responsible citizens have learned of child pornography and have demonstrated their disapproval through press conferences, TV, and radio, and by physically demonstrating outside of "adult bookstores" that sell child pornography. The press has investigated and responsibly reported this new form of social degenerateness. The elected legislation must act now. In my view, local, State and Federal legislators must now take the ball and run toward the goal of adequate protection for children from sexual exploitation and provide strong criminal penalties for all guilty of this new form of child abuse.

I began researching sexual abuse of children last year in seeking data for my special 3-credit-hour course at Lewis University, Glen Ellyn, Ill., entitled "Child Abuse and Neglect Prevention and Treatment." Scholarly research into the sexual abuse of children usually takes into consideration intra-family sexual abuse (incest), molestation by strangers, and child prostitution. However, in the last 2 years there has been a massive introduction of pornographic materials depicting children in explicit sexual acts with each other and with adults. Such materials constitute a fourth, and heretofore unsuspected, type of sexual abuse of children. Many of my social justice students are active law enforcement officials, and they began to bring confiscated examples of child pornography to class. My research and their samples so startled me that I initiated my own public awareness campaign through radio and television "talk shows" and through cooperation with the newspapers and law enforcement agencies. More shocking than even the crass nature of the child pornography, itself, was the discovery that there is a total lack of protective laws or that the existing laws are so vague that meaningful prosecution is not possible.

My aim was and is to heighten public awareness, mobilize public disapproval against the child pornographer, and to urge voters to demand the enactment of protective legislation.

Let's be clear what we are talking about. I am referring to books, pamphlets, playing cards, and 8mm films which vividly depict children in sexual poses and/or in explicit sexual acts with each other or with adults. Much of the materials have clear themes of sadomasochism. The pamphlet, "Child Discipline," is a prime example of this theme. "Child Discipline" advocated adult sexual satisfaction through the spanking of children. It provides both written and pictorial depictions of adults spanking children.

The theme of sadomasochism prevails in much of the material. The children are represented as powerless and the adults all-powerful. The dominant theme is that sexual abuse of children is enjoyable and socially sanctioned by the sexually liberated members of society.

It is interesting to point out that the same themes prevail in a monthly cartoon in Hustler Magazine. I would like to draw attention to this cartoon. Hustler Magazine has a monthly installment of "Chester, the Molester." It is a full-page color depiction of the intent of sexual molestation of children. If I may briefly describe the Easter installment, in that installment is a picture of a public park scene where children are on an Easter egg hunt. The depiction shows a little girl following a trail of Easter eggs. When she turns the corner, the trail leads to the bushes where Chester the Molester is sitting in a rabbit outfit with a baseball bat and his testicles laying on the grass colored with different colored spots, and it is clear that the last "eggs" will be Chester's testicles.

The issue of March 1977 shows a typical playground scene. The scene involves a child, young girl, going down the slide, her dress flying in the air, her panties showing, and Chester the Molester has his chin at the bottom of the slide with his body hidden under the slide and his tongue is wiggling at the bottom of the slide. I would like to point out to the committee that the publisher of Hustler has been appearing on national TV and making statements that he does not approve the use of children in pornography. I suggest that the implications of these so-called cartoons, while not physical depictions of children being sexually abused, are in some ways sanctioning of the sexual abuse of children. They also are making fun of a great many of the legitimate fears of parents that their children can be molested by strangers where, in fact, according to the record, children are molested by strangers, and that is in public places, in particular playgrounds. Each issue has the "Chester the Molester" series. They also have an ad for "Chester the Molester" T-shirts. I won't read the description of the ad, but it is in the public record. . . .

. . . If your Federal law included provisions for punishment for the producers and the sellers, I think that would stop the child abuse through sexual molestation and pornography primarily because it would stop the marketability of the materials. If it included even the bookstore manager, that person who sits up in the high booth in the adult bookstores, and requires the 50 cents of everybody who comes in, a couple might test it, but if it is successfully prosecuted, there will be no volunteers for that kind of work, and it will stop the flow of dollars to pornographers, and in my view take them out of the child pornography business. My goal would be to insure, and I think that would, that they not further molest children. There is no justice for children at the present time in this category, and there is very little justice in the categories of other sexual molestation.[3]

In 1977, Osanka's college course on child abuse and neglect prevention and treatment was the only one of its kind in the United States. When Osanka taught child abuse and neglect at a university, a police officer student showed an example of child pornography and asked how it related to child abuse. Osanka learned that it was not considered child abuse legally. He countered the First Amendment issue by asking " '[W]here were the free speech rights of the children?' " He said that survival techniques used by children involved in pornography " 'can lead them into lives of drug dependency and crime.' "[4] Osanka also said that child pornography is " 'morally repugnant. It's slavery and rape of a child.' "[5] He noted that greed, not social or cultural need, gave birth to the " 'wholesale introduction of child pornography.' "[6]

Osanka has stated that those who are making money from child pornography are criminals. He has emphasized the need to protect children and to keep the issue of child pornography out of the First Amendment debate and away from the obscenity law requirements of *Miller* v *California.* [7] Osanka believes that America's founding fathers did not intend to protect child pornography with the First Amendment. He has expressed concern that the existence of such material legitimizes the material in the view of some users. This presents the danger of sexual abuse of children becoming " 'a social norm by default.' "[8] Osanka has argued that legislation can stop child pornography, as it has in Illinois. Public pressure also influenced the federal government to enforce customs laws against pornography.[9]

Osanka emphasizes that children run away from the " 'best families' " and that anyone's child can be involved in child pornography. He says he hopes that the child pornography issue will make people realize that " 'children are used as sexual objects' " and open up discussion of the " 'whole issue of sexual abuse of children and the lack of protection afforded them.' "[10]

Osanka has called managers of bookstores that sell child pornography accessories to child abuse. He believes that by removing the profit, you can kill the abuse. Osanka has said that pedophiles patronize pornographic bookstores and buy child pornography to excite themselves. When there is media attention, he has said, public attention and outrage follow, and then legislation is enacted.[11] Child pornography became scarce in the cities where the leaders of the anti–child pornography movement spoke, but went back on the shelves after they left, according to Dr. Osanka.

Osanka emphasizes the need to alleviate "alienation" in the home in an effort to reduce the number of runaways and thus the pool of "talent" for the child pornographers. Parents need to reestablish communication with children and always leave the door open for children to retreat from their stands without losing face. Osanka points out that many runaways are running away from abuse in the home and that some parents even put their children into pornography. He believes that if child pornography had been as active when he grew up as an orphan, he might have become one of its victims.[12]

An excellent summary of child pornography and prostitution issues, including details about federal and state laws, is the 1987 *Child Pornography and Prostitution: Background and Legal Analysis* by Howard A. Davidson and Gregory A. Loken.[13] Richard Van Why provides excellent abstracts of numerous publications concerning child pornography.[14]

In the introduction to her book *Child Pornography,* Shirley O'Brien notes that child pornography can be "defined as children seeking attention and affection, adults seeking sexually explicit material with children as subject, and profiteers realizing substantial profit margins."[15]

For an excellent review of the definitions, history and content of child pornography, see Lore Stone's doctoral dissertation. Stone studied child pornography, with an emphasis on paperback books. Stone would define child pornography to include pictorial, written, and audiovisual materials depicting children in explicit sexual acts or poses. Such activities would be covered whether homosexual or heterosexual and whether the children were by themselves or with adults, animals, or other children. To be considered pornography the material would have to be produced to perpetuate victimization, sexually stimulate the user, seduce victims, or achieve commercial gain.[16]

O'Brien notes that according to a 1977 estimate, child pornography (involving minors under 18) was 5 to 10 percent of the total pornography trade.[17] In May 1987, Carolyn Huebner, president of Texas Child Search, Inc., said that more than $500 million nationwide is generated annually by the trade in child pornography.[18]

The best known child sex organization, Paedophile Information Exchange (PIE), was founded in England in 1974. The North American Man-Boy Love Association was founded in Boston in 1978 to "promote pedophilia as a lifestyle, to defend men accused of sex crimes involving boys, and to lobby against age of consent laws for sexual activity."[19]

In 1978, Beverly Heinrich reported that Houston, Texas, had earned the title of "Kid-Porn Capital of the World" because of the local case of Roy Clifton Ames in which 6 1/4 tons of pornography and equipment were seized, including homosexual material involving local boys that had a nationwide distribution. Heinrich said that organized crime controlled pornography distribution in Texas. She reported that a grand jury had found that minors were not excluded from adult theaters and teen prostitutes plied their trade at one theater. In addition, magazines in pornography stores advertised young boys for sexual use and homosexual pornography camps.[20]

An article in the July 21, 1986, *Atlanta Journal* stated that a nationwide industry of child pornography was flourishing through molesters in groups that advocate sexual acts with minors through "widely circulated newsletters." The groups produce vast collections of child pornography and trade collections.[21]

Robert Pierce says that child pornography is a form of child abuse that flourishes relatively unnoticed and suggests that this might be partly due to the societal disbelief that adults would sexually exploit children for profit. The purpose of such pornography is to sexually arouse, he says, and little in it contributes to education or science. Even today, he says, despite child pornography laws, little is done to prevent such victimization and to intervene. He believes that there is a lack of planned control of the problem.[22]

Kenneth Herrmann and John Jupp report on the international child pornography problem. They detail the 1959 United Nations Declaration of the Rights of the Child, which includes protecting children from exploitation, cruelty, and neglect and provides that they shall not be the subjects of trafficking. Under this declaration, children are not to be employed before an "appropriate minimum age" or permitted or caused to "engage in any occupation or employment which prejudice(s) his health or education, or interfere(s) with his physical, mental, or moral development."[23] (Obviously, these would include pornography and prostitution.)

Herrmann and Jupp also discuss Defense for Children International (DCI), which was founded in 1979 to carry out the UN mandate. It is concerned with child pornography, prostitution, trafficking, and pedophilia. A 1982 DCI study found that "child sex package tours" were offered in the United States, Japan, West Germany, and the Netherlands, taking people to Thailand, Sri Lanka, and the Philippines. They report that the United States is the biggest producer and importer of child pornography and the biggest purchaser of sex tourism. Early findings of a DCI study to be released in 1985 showed that lack of public pressure to combat child pornography resulted in the industry's prospering.[24]

Herrmann and Jupp note that $5 billion would be a conservative estimate of the international trafficking in children. There are sophisticated international networks and hundreds of millions of children involved, they claim. They state that the more sophisticated networks involve organized crime. They call for more funding, enforcement of laws, and intervention. A clearinghouse to identify child pornography producers and distributors and those engaged in international trafficking in children should be created, they say. Such a clearinghouse also would identify the children involved and return them to their families.

According to Herrmann and Jupp, pedophiles need child pornography for "psychopathological needs" and the "seduction process." Such molesters appear to have ready access to children who are vulnerable and "large, well-organized, and indexed supplies of obscene material."[25]

Sale of child pornography has created an incentive for American child pornographers, Dr. Frank Osanka believes. What had been mainly an underground network of child molesters who exchanged personal photographs has become an open market. He believes that the child pornography industry also was fueled by the desire for more variety in pornography, the lack of concern in the United States about children, and the growing awareness that there were weaknesses in legal protection of children, such as children's testimony being disqualified and parents refusing to allow their children to testify. Osanka has said that evidence based on the purchasing of child pornography suggests that pedophiles are not " 'a small portion of our population.' "[25]

EXAMPLES OF CHILD PORNOGRAPHY

Child pornography contains the same types of sexual activities as those shown in adult pornography (see chapter 2) but involves children, children and adults, or children and animals or objects. We have found that a great deal of the material in the adult pornography market sexualizes children. For example, incestuous acts are common. Another common theme is adult women made to like children in childlike clothing or settings. For example, adult women are shown behaving like children in sexually explicit fairy tales. Diaper sex video porn and magazines are available, showing adults dressed up like babies and performing sex acts. Paperback books openly discuss sex between children or teenagers and adults.

We recommend that these forms of substitute child pornography be regulated under child pornography laws. We believe there is a danger that some persons who are exposed to such materials will be influenced by them to carry out sexually abusive acts against children.

In the late 1970s, child pornography film loops "cost only pennies to produce" but sold for as much as hundreds of dollars. Magazines were produced for 25 cents or less and sold for up to $10. Titles of child pornography magazines included *Moppets, Lillitots, Chicken Brats, (chicken* is the term for child prostitutes; adults who use such children are called hawks), and *Incest, the Game the Whole Family Can Play.* [27]

David Sonenschein argues that 9- to 17-year-old girls are portrayed as sex symbols in our culture through advertising and entertainment. Examples of such portrayals include advertisements for jeans, other clothing, and cosmetics. Sonenschein provides other examples of how young girls are portrayed as sex symbols and offers an extensive bibliography. [28]

Various sources list other examples of child pornography magazines. One magazine titled *Baby Sex* showed a 6-month-old baby engaged in sexual acts with an adult. [29] Another, *Child Discipline,* taught readers how to be sexually satisfied by beating children. *Lust for Children* instructed readers how to avoid successful prosecution for molestation. It said that the screams of a little girl when she is "being sexually attacked are actually cries of pleasure." [30]

Baker reports that according to the 1977 *Report to the Attorney General on Child Pornography in California,* a 1972 Hollywood pamphlet called *Where the Young Ones Are* listed 378 places in 34 states where readers would find young children to sexually exploit. The pamphlet allegedly sold seventy thousand copies at $5 each. The same report showed that Los Angeles police interviewed more than a hundred victims and suspects in more than forty child molesting cases over five months. Pornography, often involving children, was present in every one of those cases. [31]

Dr. Frank Osanka testified in *U.S.* v. *Nunes, et al.* (a child pornography case) in 1982. He commented on two eight-minute child pornography films. One showed a man sexually penetrating an 8-year-old girl's unruptured hymen and her bleeding profusely. In the other, the same girl was molested by a man and a woman who looks like her mother. Osanka told the court that these films " 'are potentially dangerous to other children because of their instructional nature' to would-be molesters." Such films, he said, "appeal to deviant behavior because they 'activate the arousal to sexually abuse a child.' "

The court agreed with Osanka that it is much more serious to widely distribute "something that is morally reprehensible" than for it to happen once. The court said that the "wide distribution of child pornography would seem . . . to encourage more of it to be produced, encourage more abuse of children." [32]

HARMS SUFFERED BY CHILDREN INVOLVED IN CHILD PORNOGRAPHY

In the 1977 Senate report titled *Protection of Children against Sexual Exploitation,* the Los Angeles Police Department presented a profile of the typical boy participant in pornography:

1. Between the ages of 8 and 17;
2. An underachiever in school or at home;
3. Usually without previous homosexual experience;
4. From a home where the parents were absent either physically or psychologically;
5. Without any strong moral or religious affiliations;
6. Suffering from poor sociological development. [33]

Burgess and Clark provide profiles of child pornography victims and pedophile pornographers, as well as numerous case histories of victims and abusers. [34]

Burgess, Groth, and McCausland provide a detailed study of thirty-six children involved as victim witnesses in child sex ring cases. They describe how initiation occurs, how rings are organized, and methods used in accessing children. They also detail offender relationships to victims and describe the use of peer pressure. They explain that sex rings depend on secrecy and outline the physical, social, psychological, and behavioral symptoms of victims. [35]

Gulo, Burgess, and Kelly studied the structure of child sex rings. They found that the explicitness of the photographs available ranges from children in brief attire to children performing explicit sexual acts. Much child pornography is "laundered" through the mails so that the persons buying it do not know the source and the police have a hard time tracing it. Suppliers of child pornography include professional procurers, pedophiles, and parental figures. Clandestine film processors and photo labs also play a role. Blackmail files are kept on each child to ensure secrecy. Subscribers may be screened, and a system of trading photos is used. The researchers found that production costs are low and profits high. They report that syndicated child pornography includes six factors: "time, storage space, fictitious names, preference for children, camaraderie, and photo collections."[36]

Burgess et al. point out that adult pornography is used in sex rings "for instruction." Introducing child pornography to the ring provides a further link, letting the children think they used the adult for money. In addition, pornography is used as blackmail—for example, telling the child that betraying the group could result in exposure of the picture to his or her parents. The promise of money plays "a key role in enticing the child." In eight of the eleven sex rings studied by these researchers, the children were used in producing pornography. The adults involved used it to stimulate themselves and traded it among their associates. In four of the rings, children received money for their sexual activities and child pornography was commercially sold.[37]

These researchers found four response patterns to stress at follow-up interviews with the children involved in the rings: "integration of the event, avoidance of the event, repetition of symptoms, and identification with the exploiter." After the sex rings were exposed, many children experienced post-traumatic stress response. The majority reexperienced the sex ring event through flashbacks and intrusive thoughts. There were fears that the offender would return or carry out threats. Forty-one of the sixty-six children studied had diminished responsiveness to the environment and to other people. Many developed symptoms that they did not have before involvement in the rings, such as crying spells, sleep disturbances, and hyperalertness. A few children continued to be abused and victimized, some by becoming prostitutes. Five children performed acts with young children similar to those they had experienced ("such as inserting an object vaginally, sodomizing a younger brother, or urinating on a classmate"). Three worked as pimps.

The researchers found that those children who were used longer for child pornography and in sex rings were more likely to become involved in an exploitive cycle. A strong association was found between the development of "deviant and symptomatic behaviors" and children being used in pornography and involved in a sex ring for more than a year. If children or adolescents show antisocial behaviors such as alcohol or drug abuse, gender confusion, acting out, sexual anxiety, or avoidance, these researchers suggest that professionals consider the possibility that they were (or are) involved in pornography or sex rings.[38]

Some of the children who are in child pornography " 'never get back into the mainstream,' " Dr. Frank Osanka has said. Accepting the brainwashing from pornographers that they are no good, such children become involved in a deviant lifestyle. The children blame themselves, thinking something is wrong with them. Involvement in child pornography can lead to believing that sex is bad or, conversely, to promiscuity. Osanka believes that people sometimes view children in pornography as criminals instead of victims. Partly because of this, children who have been in pornography worry about when the pictures will show up. According to Osanka, " 'One photograph . . . can haunt a child for a lifetime.' "[39]

Osanka also has noted that many of the producers of child pornography are businesspeople making money, not perverts. He has said that photographs of children in pornography show the pain they undergo when they are prematurely introduced to sex. According to Osanka, Charles Manson is an example of what happens to children who are sexually abused. Osanka has reported that Manson was sodomized at age 10 and suffered other physical abuses and that today he " 'can't separate sex and violence.' "[40]

According to a 1982 U.S. General Accounting Office (GAO) study, some children participate in pornography to survive after running away from home. Others have said they were enticed into it by other children, neighbors, or relatives. Often these young people are from unstable homes, are underachievers at home and in school, lack love and attention at home, are abused or neglected, lack parental supervision, are runaways, and spend much time in public places such as arcades, theaters, and parks.

The GAO study says that pornography victims experience psychological scarring, see themselves as objects to be sold rather than people who are important, and are fearful, cynical, and exploitive. Some feel dirty and unwanted and become bitter toward adults. Some "have difficulty experiencing normal sexual fulfillment as adults." Some wind up as prostitutes, drug addicts, criminals, and adolescent parents.

While finding that only 8.8 percent of the children whom police departments surveyed by the GAO estimated were involved in child pornography were referred to social service providers, the report concluded that needed services are generally available for those wishing to leave pornography.[41]

According to Robert Pierce, many child pornography stars start as teenage runaways who sell themselves to survive. These children mistake seduction for affection. Some are introduced into the child pornography trade by mothers who are in the pornography business.[42]

According to Pierce, the current views on the effects of pornography on children come from a small sample of clinical reports and "untested assumptions." Concrete empirical evidence is lacking. Thus, he feels, it is impossible to show a direct cause–effect relationship between child pornography, prostitution, and molestation. Experts believe that sexually exploited children suffer psychological damage, he points out. Such children are unable to "integrate the physical, emotional and psychological dimensions of this experience." They undergo feelings of guilt, betrayal, rage, and worthlessness. Pierce argues that there is a cycle in which sexually exploited children become child sexual exploiters as adults. (We strongly disagree, pointing out that many abused children do not become abusers when they grow up. Dr. Osanka is an example of such a person.) The issue of the link between child pornography and molestation is unresolved, Pierce believes.[43] (We point out that the many case histories linking pornography and abuse of persons set forth in chapter 4 dispute this claim.)

Shirley O'Brien outlines how child pornography is damaging:

1. It is psychologically damaging to the child.
2. It ruins a child's self-image.
3. It is exploitive. It depicts children as wanting to be molested, raped, and exploited and implies that children are not harmed because they want this experience.
4. It makes children vulnerable to adults in unnatural ways.
5. It spreads incorrect information about sex, which hinders a child's normal sexual functioning later in life.
6. It forever invades a child's privacy.
7. It complicates a child's moral development.

O'Brien believes that abuse and neglect of children at home serves as the "springboard" to prostitution, sexual molestation, and pornography. She emphasizes that many children will do whatever is asked of them by an adult because they crave adult love, affection, and attention. While children working the street often do not want to be photographed at first, later their values are confused, their self-esteem declines, and their inhibitions are lowered. At that point, they will do almost anything for money, gifts, and rewards. O'Brien also notes that rectal hemorrhage is a major cause of death among runaway boys engaged in prostitution.[44]

Chief Investigator Thomas R. Hampson told the State of Illinois Legislative Investigating Commission in 1980 that the commission's investigation found "that child molesters are generally also interested in child pornography." In addition, he said, they often produce child pornography, often for private use.[45]

According to Peter Bridges, an undercover New York Police Department operation that involved running a pornography shop showed that child pornography customers were "usually white middle-class men" who would be considered seemingly well-adjusted people.[46]

Tyler and Stone report that child molesters realize that their victim(s) will age beyond the stages of development or age they prefer and that there may be times when they do not have children to molest. Therefore, they develop "a compelling need to record the acts of sexual molestation with their victims," using tools such as written diaries, computerized diaries, photos, videotapes, and motion pictures. The researchers say that molesters supply such materials to commercial child pornographers.[47]

Gwen Ingram quotes Judianne Densen-Gerber as stating that men whose fantasies are stimulated by adult pornography can " 'find a consenting female, either for money or for companionship,' " but men whose fantasies are stimulated by child pornography involving a 5-year-old cannot find healthy, legitimate sources of stimulation.[48] (We note that this type of comment fails to recognize the harms done to women due to adult pornography.)

R. S. Anson conducted an interview with Serena, a child pornography victim, who wondered " 'what it would have been like to have been a real kid, you know, with proms and bubble baths and all that.' " Of her 1-year-old daughter, Serena said, ' 'I was fucking at 12, so she'll probably be fucking at 10.' " She noted that a friend's daughter was already doing pornography at age 5.[49]

Schoettle presents a case report of a 12-year-old girl involved in a pornography ring. The girl experienced more than three years of being photographed in genital, anal, and oral sex acts with other children and adults. Her younger siblings also were involved. The girl had the following reactions to her experiences:

1. She felt guilty for involving her siblings.
2. She threatened suicide when her family's involvement was exposed and her family was harassed by neighborhood children.
3. She feared perpetrator "recrimination."
4. She had projective testing themes, including "helplessness, depression, victimization, and a denial of, or pulling away from, sexual concerns."[50]

In treatment, the family's children provided investigators with detailed accounts of their experiences. The result was a flood of emotion from the 12-year-old victim, ambivalent relief about the broken secret, and guilt feelings because she was placed in the juvenile system and the adults involved were jailed.

The victim also experienced anger at her parents for failing to protect the children from adult perpetrators, ambivalence toward the molesters—including viewing them as "father-like," "warm," and "giving"—and attempts to split the good and bad parts of herself and the adults involved.[51]

Schoettle states that in contrast to most adolescents, pornography victims often freely discuss sexual matters at first, then deny doing so later as transference with the therapist develops. Other adolescents become less inhibited as a "therapeutic alliance develops."

The pornography victim seems able to reintegrate into an age-appropriate lifestyle, Schoettle believes. In the integration phase of treatment, the normal development process gradually resumes and the person can appreciate the good and bad parts of himself or herself and others. Schoettle warns that countertransference can be a problem for the therapist and can hamper treatment. The sex descriptions in a case can be enticing, stimulating, and threatening to the therapist, he says.[52]

THE 1977 ANTI–CHILD PORNOGRAPHY CAMPAIGN

Payton credits the "barnstorming" efforts of the following four people as the key to legislative action taken against child pornography:

Judianne Densen-Gerber, psychiatrist, lawyer, and founder of an agency working with drug addicts

Robin Lloyd, author of *For Money or Love: Boy Prostitution in America*

Lloyd H. Martin, head of the Los Angeles Police Department's Sexually Exploited Child Unit, the only one of its kind in 1977

Frank Osanka (co-author of this book), then an associate professor of social justice and sociology who "learned of child pornography while teaching a class on child abuse, but cites his own experience as an orphan as a major impetus to his involvement."[53]

McCaghy and Beranbaum provide an excellent history of the early anti–child pornography movement.[54] We found much of this information verified in other sources. While disagreeing with some of their conclusions (namely, that the 1977 anti–child pornography movement was a "moral crusade" or part of a national crusade to prosecute major pornographers, clean up sex-related businesses in several major cities, and a "backlash against the gay rights movement"), we found their paper to be helpful. The following text is a summary based on that paper.

The anti–child pornography movement began in New York City in March 1975, when the Beame administration received a Law Enforcement Administration grant to campaign against the sex businesses, especially in Times Square. (New York City was to be the site of the 1976 Democratic National Convention.) Over the next few months, four pornography shops were targeted and raided because they featured child pornography.

Robin Lloyd's book about boy prostitution and pornography was published in 1976. On January 6, 1977, six men from a Times Square pornography shop were arrested for selling pornography. One week later, state representative Edward I. Koch announced he had set up a meeting with a federal attorney to see what could be done to prosecute child pornographers. Dr. Judianne Densen-Gerber, a lawyer and psychiatrist who owned and directed Odyssey Institute, a private drug rehabilitation program in New York City, said she had contacted the Manhattan district attorney. The next day the district attorney and deputy police commissioner said that existing laws severely hampered prosecution and discovery of child pornography cases. Material usually had to be found obscene or laws on endangering the morals and health of children had to be used. Four days later, Father Bruce Ritter announced that Covenant House, a shelter for teen-age runaways, would be established in New York City. Ritter said that many of the children used in pornography came from the streets where the pornography shops were located.

On January 30, 1977, the *Washington Post* did the first lengthy media piece on child pornography. It mentioned that one week earlier, the Los Angeles Police Department had set up a sexually exploited child unit in its juvenile division, the first of its kind in the nation. It also cited William Simon, a sociologist who claimed that police were exaggerating when they said that child molesters always possess child pornography when arrested. According to McCaghy and

Beranbaum, national media attention reached its peak in four months.

The crusade for national legislation against child pornography was officially launched at a news conference by Dr. Frank Osanka and Judianne Densen-Gerber in Chicago on February 4, 1977. During the following weeks Osanka and Densen-Gerber separately held news conferences around the United States, and media coverage grew.

On March 8, 1977, the first child pornography bill was introduced in Congress. It defined such pornography as abuse, not obscenity, which was considered difficult to define.

In March 1977, nationally syndicated columnist Ellen Goodman described child pornography as a symptom of power relationships—in this case, the adult–child power relationship. The movement received national publicity in *Time* on April 4, 1977. On April 11, 1977, the *Washington Star* detailed the movement's themes and printed statements by Robin Lloyd that there were 264 child pornography magazines and by Fred Cohen, executive director of Odyssey Institute, that 90 percent of all child pornography originates in the United States. Lloyd Martin of the Los Angeles Police Department was quoted as saying that every child molestation case involves child pornography. On May 15, 1977, a twenty-three-minute segment of CBS's "60 Minutes" dealt with "kiddie porn." Beginning on May 15, the *Chicago Tribune* did a four-day feature on child pornography and prostitution. (It was Dr. Frank Osanka who convinced a *Tribune* reporter to do this series.[55]

From May through September, three congressional committees held hearings on the subject. In October 1977, the Protection of Children Against Sexual Exploitation Act of 1977 passed both houses of Congress. It was signed into law by President Jimmy Carter on February 6, 1978.

McCaghy and Beranbaum believe that the legislative approach toward child pornography (outlawing its production and distribution) will be no more effective than that same approach toward illegal drugs. They say that there is no reason to expect a supply decrease unless the demand for child pornography decreases. They would prefer attacking the problem of preventing the abuse by dealing with homeless children who need protection.

We disagree and note that child pornography laws appear to have been fairly effective in getting commercial child pornography off of the open market. Many states currently struggle to find ways to deal with such molester-type (homemade) pornography. Many laws do not outlaw the possession or trading of child pornography, so molesters with such collections often cannot be prosecuted. And it is usually impossible to locate the child victims to prove actual molestation. With child pornography less available, the demand for it will fall because fewer people will have been exposed to it. Realistically, the best way to reduce the amount of abuse in child pornography is by strictly penalizing distributors and traders in it, thus reducing profits and making its marketing very risky. This, in turn, would cut the production of it, so fewer children would be abused in the making of it. The U.S. Supreme Court accepted this argument, made by Dr. Osanka, in *New York* v. *Ferber*.

PRE-FERBER LEGAL ISSUES

Payton describes the 1978 federal child pornography legislation. Title 18 U.S.C. s. 2251 prohibits the use of minors in sexually explicit conduct for the purpose of producing any " 'visual or print medium' " depicting such conduct. This includes abuse by parents or guardians.[56]

Title 18 U.S.C. s. 2252 deals with receiving child pornography for the purpose of sale or distribution, as well as the sale and distribution of it. It prohibits knowing transport or shipment by mail or by interstate or foreign commerce " 'for the purpose of sale or distribution for sale' " any " 'obscene visual or print medium' " in which the production of the material involved the use of a minor engaged in sexually explicit conduct.[57]

The law calls for a maximum fine of $10,000 and a maximum prison sentence of ten years for the first conviction; the penalty for subsequent convictions is a maximum fine of $15,000 and a maximum prison sentence of fifteen years with a two-year minimum sentence.

Title 18 U.S.C. s. 2253 defines *sexually explicit conduct* as " 'actual or simulated' "

(A) sexual intercourse, including genital-genital, oral-genital, anal-genital, or oral-anal, whether between persons of the same or opposite sex;
(B) bestiality;
(C) masturbation;
(D) sado-masochistic abuse (for the purpose of sexual stimulation); or
(E) lewd exhibition of the genitals or pubic area of any person.[58]

Minor means anyone under 16.

Payton contains an excellent history of the many child pornography bills introduced in and considered by Congress and the pros and cons of each. One bill, for example, argued that those who distribute or sell child pornography 'are accessories after the fact to the crime of child abuse.' Major debate arose over the issue of whether the parts of the legislation dealing with distribution of child pornography had to contain an obscenity requirement in order to be constitutional. While the U.S. Senate adopted a law without the obscenity provision, the obscenity provision became part of the final legislation at the suggestion of a conference committee comprising members of both houses. The vague term *any other sexual activity* was taken out, and mere nudity was not prohibited.[59]

For a federal child pornography prosecution to occur, an interstate commerce or mailing connection must be shown. Thus, the states also needed to pass child pornography legislation. Prior to 1977, only Tennessee had a law prohibiting the use of children in pornography. Other states had general child sexual abuse laws and obscentiy laws. As a result of the national campaign to regulate child pornography, some states passed laws incorporating obscenity standards into child pornography, while others did not include the *Miller* test. Some prohibited showing a minor observing sexual conduct, and some incorporated a concept of "merit" as an affirmative defense. Payton provides an excellent review of state child pornography laws. Proponents of child pornography laws came to the following conclusions:

1. Child pornography should not have First Amendment protection because it is a product of child abuse.
2. "[E]rotic materials that involve child actors or models are child pornography."
3. Such materials "may be excluded from first amendment protection, even if no child abuse activity occurs."[60]

Two early court cases dealt with child pornography laws. *St. Martin's Press* v. *Carey* challenged a New York law concerning "promoting a sexual performance by a child." The suit was brought by the retail sellers and publishers of *Show Me! A Picture Book of Sex for Children and Parents.* (Some have argued that this is a sex education book, while others have argued that it is obscenity or child pornography.) The plaintiffs argued that the statute was unconstitutional because it did not limit its coverage to obscene works. The book in question, they said, was photographed in Germany, so it was not relevant to the exploitation of children in New York. They claimed it also infringed on parents' constitutional privacy right "to teach their children about sex." The court said *Show Me* was not obscene because it did not lack serious value. (Three other state courts held it not obscene.) The court issued a preliminary injunction but did not declare the law unconstitutional. It said that suppressing nonobscene speech is not a legal way to "indirectly" reach "illegal conduct."[61]

In *Graham* v. *Hill,* the court ruled against a child pornography statute that did not require prohibited material to be obscene. The court suggested, however, that a statute grounded in preventing abuse could permit a more lenient standard. The court also found the statute to be overbroad because it was not confined to sexual exploitation.[62]

Payton outlines future issues relating to child pornography legislation, including the following:

1. Should child pornography be viewed as pure speech or child abuse?
2. Do government interests in regulating non-speech elements of laws that cover both conduct and speech justify " 'incidental limitations on First Amendment freedoms' " under *U.S.* v. *O'Brien?*
3. Is child pornography incitement to " 'imminent lawless action' " as envisioned in *Brandenburg* v. *Ohio?*
4. How should legislatures deal with the concept that offensive speech cannot be proscribed (*Cohen* v. *California*)?
5. St. Martin's Press argued on appeal that the publisher and the seller cannot be said to be "an accomplice of the child abuser." Others have disagreed. Which is the best course of action?
6. Could child pornography be prohibited on the idea that the child lacks ability to consent? (Payton notes that if the pornography is photographed outside the United States, this would not apply.)
7. Is enforcement of obscenity laws the basic requirement, since most child pornography is obscene?
8. Group homes, camps, and other places that care for children should be licensed, inspected, and supervised to make certain they are safe.
9. A better job of coping with the runaway problem, such as by providing jobs for youths and shelters, is needed.
10. Should constitutional principle changes be used only as the last resort?[63]

Donnelly has suggested looking at the child pornography business as two tiered. The first tier consists of the producers, who obtain children, abuse them, and photograph them. The second tier is the distributors—the sellers and theater and bookstore operators who provide producers with the incentives for production.

Donnelly points out that even if visual pornography shows only simulated acts, the producers have often sexually abused the child before and after the photo session. In addition, he says, child pornography "appears to play a special role in the sexual molestation of children"—namely, stimulating both adult and child and being used to overcome the child's inhibitions. It could, he argues, affect moral principles and lead to family value decay.[64]

Donnelly believes that prior legislation was inadequate. Sex offense laws covering crimes such as rape, incest, and immoral conduct with children would reach pornographers only in cases where the adult sexually molested the child (not in cases where the child posed alone or where there was sex between children). It is hard to obtain evidence of molestation, as young children may not be considered competent witnesses and the victim may be too frightened or confused to testify properly. In addition, many abuse laws apply only to guardians or parents, contain weak penalties, or outlaw only physical abuse (Donnelly argues that many child pornography victims are harmed psychologically.) Donnelly notes that obscenity laws do not cover children whose pictures are in nonobscene works. In addition, obscenity cases are difficult to prosecute, are given a low priority by officials, and often result in light sentences.

Donnelly details what each of the thirty-nine state child pornography laws in 1978 provided. (Thirty-four of these laws were enacted in 1977 or 1978.) State laws are needed because the federal law covers only interstate transportation of pornography. All of the laws made production of visual material of children in sexually explicit conduct criminal. Some made it illegal for a parent or guardian to allow a child's involvement. Half of the states required the material to be legally obscene. Several required it to be distributed for commercial gain. Knowledge of the defendant had to be shown.

Regulation of *producers'* acts is a "reasonable exercise of a state's police power to protect its children," Donnelly says. While these acts of abuse also involve speech, not all acts that "incidentally involve speech" have a protected speech element. Under the balancing of interests test, the state interest of protecting children outweighs the free speech right of the producer because of the harm involved. The same reasoning applies to the *coercers* —those who coerce children into pornography. Coercers have no First Amendment interest, Donnelly states. While *parents* and *guardians* are a subset of coercers, they

have certain rights concerning marital privacy and raising of children. The courts have, however, upheld child abuse laws and laws regulating child labor and requiring school attendance, all of which enter into the area of parental rights.[65]

Distributors are one step removed from the abuse. Distribution of visual material has traditionally been given a high degree of First Amendment protection. However, the court has allowed the distribution of *obscene* materials to be regulated, Donnelly notes, and it has permitted prohibition of dissemination of material not considered obscene under adult standards to minors. A balancing test between the free speech interests and other state interests, such as harm to children, must be applied. The least restrictive alternative must be used—preferably one that does not infringe on individual rights. Donnelly says that legislation could be unconstitutionally overbroad. While there is a state interest in protecting children, the distributor is not directly engaged in abuse, even though the distributor arguably aids and abets the producer's abuse by being a vital link between the producer and the market. The distributor provides economic incentives to produce child pornography, and without this, production and abuse "would be severely curtailed."

As Donnelly notes, those who support distributor legislation argue that targeting the economic center of the industry is the only effective way to end the abuse. If production alone is targeted, it will simply move farther underground, making prosecution even more difficult. Donnelly says that there is a state interest in protecting the child from the psychological harm of "knowing the material has been publicly circulated." He compares the distributor proposals to federal labor laws that prohibit both the use of children and shipment interstate of goods manufactured by children (Title 29 U.S.C. s. 212, 1976).[66]

Laws regulating all sexual abuse in pornography could be overbroad when applied to distributors, Donnelly suggests, as harm varies. For example, he says, while sadomasochism would always be harmful, there would be less harm from depicting an older child's genitals and sometimes no harm from certain depictions. (We disagree with this position, for the constant fear of public exposure and ridicule would follow the child throughout life.)

A law might be overbroad if it covers someone who appears to be under 16. Also, it is necessary to define what sexual conduct is covered and to determine what sexual conduct could justifiably be covered. Donnelly suggests (we believe erroneously) that it might be too broad to cover masturbation, fondling, or exhibition of genitals in cases where the child would not be psychologically harmed in production or by the knowledge that the material has been distributed. One could define *prohibited genital exhibition* as that which "according to accepted psychiatric evidence, tends to harm the child psychologically or emotionally." An expert would be free to consider the context of the depiction and the child's age. For example, an ad of a naked boy in a diaper would not be harmful, Donnelly suggests.[67]

Donnelly deals with the knowledge requirement, which, under U.S. Supreme Court precedents, must be a part of criminal laws of this nature. When producers are at issue, one need show only production, for knowledge of the materials' nature is inherent. When distributors are involved, one would show that they knew or had reason to know the character and content of the material. The law could make possession of several copies of the same work prima facie proof of intent to disseminate.

Knowledge of the child's age should not be an element of a child pornography offense, Donnelly argues. However, the law could allow an affirmative defense showing a bona fide or reasonable attempt to ascertain a child's age. The California law requiring that distributors keep records of the source of child pornography is an effective deterrent to distribution, but it could be unconstitutional unless immunity is granted to the record keeper, as it is arguable that this compels self-incrimination, which is protected against by the Fifth Amendment. Donnelly says that when seizures or injunctions are involved, prior restraint guidelines must be followed. In addition, he believes that child pornography laws should cover live performances and that visual materials should include undeveloped or unprocessed materials.[68]

According to Gwen Ingram, the goals of the federal child pornography law were to prohibit the use of children, to reduce the profit motive with stiff penalties, and to curtail out-of-state imports. As a result, child pornography went underground. She argues that legislation would have little impact because tracing the children used in child pornography would be "almost impossible" and authorities would not be aware of when pornography is produced.[69]

Haven Gow quotes child psychologist Dr. Sam Janus as stating that child pornographers pervert the First Amendment's intent and ignore " 'one of the most basic humanistic rights of man: the right not to be exploited.' "[70]

Herald Price Fahringer, an attorney who specializes in obscenity cases, testified before the House Committee on the Judiciary on September 20, 1977. He did not oppose the portions of the proposed federal child pornography law that attacked the producers of such pornography, and he said that he endorsed efforts to "protect children from any form of mistreatment." But, he argued, it is unconstitutional to restrict printing of "pictures dealing with child abuse." He noted that it is legal to propagate photographs and films of murder, assault, and rape.[71]

Fahringer said that the proposed law would cover not only child pornography, but also articles about child pornography by legitimate sources such as newspapers. People should be free to read about different attitudes toward sex, he said. He expressed confidence that the public could read or see anything "without being corrupted" and cited the 1970 Commission on Obscenity's finding that pornography does not contribute to sexual offenses or alter sexual desires.

According to Fahringer terms such as "any other sexual activities" and "nudity—for the purpose of sexual stimulation or gratification" in the proposed law were too vague and violated the due process requirements of the U.S. Constitution by not giving fair warning about what is against the law. He said that obscenity prosecutions are "ill-conceived" and that people should put up with thoughts they hate. He echoed the concern of civil libertarians that if one is not able to see or read everything, the right to see or read may include nothing. Persons who are appalled by frank sexual descriptions (including of those of child abuse or child pornography) do not have to read them, Fahringer said.[72]

Even Charles Rembar, an attorney who specializes in obscenity law, told a U.S. Senate subcommittee that child pornography would be an exception (along with libel and privacy) to the First Amendment, which, he said, is not absolute. The purpose would be protecting children. Rembar said that the only way to deal with the child pornography problem is to attack the sale of the publications.[73]

Burton Joseph, an executive committee member of the ACLU, spoke to the Illinois house subcommittee investigating child pornography. While claiming that he found the use of children in pornography " 'disgusting and reprehensible,' " he disputed the call for new laws. The problem could be covered by criminal child abuse laws and should not be dealt with by free press and speech restraints, Joseph argued. He said that child pornography could not be legislated against by creating a new obscenity law without violating First Amendment rights.[74]

Baker argues that the child abusing producer of child pornography should be regulated separately from the distributor or retailer. He suggests that producers should be categorized broadly as abusers and not protected by the First Amendment, while retailers and distributors should be prosecuted under obscenity laws.[75]

Pope notes that "the primary purpose of the

dissemination offense might be to prohibit speech not because it is inherently evil, but because it directly encourages the sexual abuse that is the subject of depiction." However, even he says that the New York law regulating child pornography dissemination without requiring it to be obscene was unconstitutional on the ground that it did not fit into any "recognized category of exceptions to first amendment protection."[76]

In Pierce's view, obscenity law disregards any consideration of children's dehumanizing experiences and of safeguarding them. The abuse arises from the *entire* operation, including subject recruitment, material production, and trade. He encourages use of child pornography laws, child protection laws, criminal laws, sexual conduct laws, and laws about contributing to the delinquency of a minor to tackle the child pornography problem.[77]

Thomas R. Hampson, the chief investigator for the Illinois Legislative Investigating Commission, said at public hearings on October 9 and 10, 1980, that the commission's three-year investigation into child pornography and prostitution had found that most persons who were arrested and charged with child pornography violations (felonies) did not receive any jail sentence. The majority had plea bargaining agreements under which they pled guilty to misdemeanors. Many received only probationary sentences.[78]

In his statement to a congressional committee in May 1977, San Francisco district attorney Joseph Freitas, Jr., explained that

> in order to avoid prosecution, child pornographers will recruit their victims in one city, send them to another city to do the filming, send the film yet to another city for processing, send the film for wholesale marketing to Denmark (in order to suggest it was made out of the United States),

and then have it sent back to the city in which the film was made for ultimate sale.[79]

A 1977 California law required those involved in the sale or distribution of material depicting children engaged in sexual contact to keep, for three years, confidential records of names and addresses from which the material was obtained and to make these available to law enforcement officials upon request. The law made failure to keep these records a misdemeanor with a civil penalty of not more than $5,000.[80]

In 1982, the U.S. GAO said the 1977 hearings in the Senate and the House showed that no one knew how many children were involved in child pornography and prostitution. Estimates of the number of teen prostitutes ranged from 90,000 to 2.4 million, and state governments that had responded to a GAO survey believed that the number of such prostitutes had not declined, but there was also a feeling that commercially produced child pornography had declined since 1977 for the following reasons:

1. The 1977 federal law
2. Tougher state child pornography laws
3. "Stricter enforcement of obscenity laws involving child pornography"
4. The likelihood that juries would convict child pornographers as opposed to adult pornographers
5. The 1979 banning of child pornography in Sweden and Denmark (among the major overseas suppliers)
6. Media attention

The GAO report concluded that much of the 1982 child pornography was part of an underground pedophile network involving homemade pornography that is traded, not sold.[81]

THE FERBER CASE

In 1981, the New York Court of Appeals struck down part of the 1977 New York law that prohibited nonobscene depictions of children in sex acts. It said that the law violated the First Amendment. In encouraging passage of child pornography laws that did not require obscenity standards to be met, Dr. Frank Osanka had argued that obscenity was "academic and debatable and could not be defined." After learning of the New York court ruling, he expressed concern that the decision could mean a return to the open sale of child pornography that had existed in the late 1970s. He noted that the court

seemed to say it was okay to sexually exploit children in certain circumstances.[82] On August 24, 1982, Bruce A. Taylor, an attorney with Citizens for Decency Through Law, congratulated Osanka by letter because the U.S. Supreme Court quoted his views in the *Ferber* child pornography case.[83]

The U.S. Supreme Court decided the major child pornography case, *New York* v. *Ferber,* on July 2, 1982. Ferber, a distributor of two child pornography films involving male masturbation, had challenged the constitutionality of a New York statute that made it a crime to knowingly promote sexual performances by children under age 16 by distributing material depicting such performances. The primary issue was whether it was constitutional to prohibit distribution of material "depicting children engaged in sexual conduct" without requiring the material to be legally obscene. Twenty states, including New York, had child pornography statutes that did not require the material to be obscene.[84]

Importantly, in the *Ferber* case a jury had found Ferber guilty of violating the law that did not require proof of obscenity but had acquitted him on charges of promoting an obscene sexual performance. (We note that obscenity prosecutions of child pornography present a difficult problem because juries may not find that such pornography appeals to the prurient interest.) The New York Court of Appeals had found that the New York statute violated the First Amendment because it "discriminated against visual portrayals of children engaged in sexual activity by not also prohibiting the distribution of films of other dangerous activity." The court also found the statute to be overbroad in prohibiting materials such as educational works and medical books dealing with adolescent sex in a nonobscene, realistic way and in prohibiting materials produced outside the state.[85]

The U.S. Supreme Court said that the *Miller* obscenity standard, and those obscenity standards that had preceded it, balanced the state interests in protecting unwilling recipients from exposure to pornography and "the dangers of censorship inherent in unabashedly content-based laws."[86] It concluded that states are entitled to "greater leeway" in regulating pornographic depictions of children for these reasons:

1.–The states have a compelling interest in " 'safeguarding the physical and psychological well being of a minor' " (*Globe Newspapers* v. *Superior Court*).[87] This applies even in areas of constitutionally protected rights. The court said:

> The prevention of sexual exploitation and abuse of children constitutes a government objective of surpassing importance.
> . . . The legislative judgment, as well as the judgment found in the relevant literature, is that the use of children as subjects of pornographic materials is harmful to the physiological, emotional, and mental health of the child. That judgment, we think, easily passes muster under the First Amendment.[88]

2.–The distribution of child pornography relates to the sexual abuse of children in two ways. First, the pornography is a permanent record of the child's involvement, and circulation of the materials exac- erbates the harm to the child (that is, pornography can haunt the person throughout his or her life). Second, if the production of materials requiring "the sexual exploitation of children is to be effectively controlled," its distribution network must be closed.[89] (In pushing for legislation regulating child pornography, Dr. Frank Osanka had repeatedly made that argument. His testimony before the U.S. House was cited by the *Ferber* court.) The court found legislatures to be justified in concluding that pursuit of child pornography producers alone would not halt the exploitation of children. Production, it emphasized, is clandestine, while marketing the pornography requires visible distribution. Testimony and literature supports the conclusions of the U.S. Congress and thirty-five states that the problem can be combated effectively only through restraining the distribution of the pornography, the court noted.

The court said that the *Miller* obscenity standard did not solve the state's compelling interest in prosecuting those who promote child sexual exploitation. It noted that the *Miller* issue "of whether a work, taken as a whole, appeals to the prurient interest of the average person bears no connection to the issue of whether a child has been physically or psychologically harmed in the production of the work." In addition, it said, "a sexually explicit depiction need not be 'patently offensive' in order to have required the sexual exploitation of a child for its production." Lastly, a work that, as a whole, contains serious literary, artistic, political, or scientific value "may nevertheless embody the hardest core of child pornography." That issue is irrelevant to the child who was abused. *Miller*, the court concluded, is not a satisfactory resolution to the child pornography dilemma. (In a footnote, the court commented that applying contemporary community standards, or a community's tolerance for pornography, would be unrealistic in dealing with child pornography.)[90]

3.–Because it provides an economic incentive for production of child pornography, the advertising and selling of it becomes an "integral part" of its production, the court said. Production is illegal. The First Amendment does not extend immunity to writing or speech that is part of conduct violating a valid criminal law.

4.–The court said:

> The value of permitting live performances and photographic reproductions of children engaged in lewd sexual conduct is exceedingly modest, is not *de minimis*. We consider it unlikely that visual depictions of children performing sexual acts or lewdly exhibiting their genitals would often constitute an important and necessary part of a

literary performance or scientific or educational work.[91]

The court suggested that if such a portrayal is necessary for literature or art, someone over the statutory age who looked younger could be used.

5.—Making child pornography a category of unprotected speech is compatible with earlier court decisions, for the question of whether speech is protected often depends on its content. Here, the balance of competing interests comes down on the side of considering the material without First Amendment protection.

The court limited the scope of permissible child pornography legislation by requiring that the conduct prohibited be "adequately defined by the applicable state law"; that the law be limited to works "that *visually* depict sexual conduct by children below a specified age"; and that the term "sexual conduct" be described and suitably limited. Lastly, some element of scienter (or knowledge) on the defendant's part would be required. The law at issue in *Ferber* met those requirements.[92]

The court also found that there was nothing unconstitutionally "underinclusive" about a law singling out child pornography for proscription and that the First Amendment did not bar states from prohibiting distribution of such materials produced outside the state. (We note that it is usually impossible to prove where child pornography was produced.) The court found child pornography to be "unprotected speech subject to content-based regulation."[93]

The court traced the history of its overbreadth doctrine. It concluded that the statute at issue was not substantially overbroad and any existing overbreadth could be cured by case by case fact analysis.

Herald Price Fahringer, Paul J. Cambria, Jr., and Barbara Davies Ebert, attorneys for Paul Ira Ferber, wrote a brief in opposition to the state's petition to be heard before the U.S. Supreme Court. These attorneys argued that the New York Court of Appeals decision had been correct. They said that by striking down the provisions of the law prohibiting distribution of child pornography that is not obscene, the state lost "none of the protections of innocent children from the supposed harm attendant their participation in the making of sexual films and photographs." The persons "responsible for the possible danger to" children are the producers, not the distributors, they argued. Viewing pictures of sexual acts of children harms no one, they said, and the states that included the obscenity requirement in their child pornography laws were "enlightened."[94]

According to Ferber's attorneys, films such as

Luna (with Jill Clayburgh masturbating her son), *Pretty Baby* (with Brooke Shields engaging in simulated sex), and *The Exorcist* (with Linda Blair masturbating), as well as *Lolita* and *Taxi Driver*, "could have been condemned under this bad law." Even works depicting "coming of age" rituals would have been covered, they said. The greatest harm from such a law would be preventing the writing of works that could be useful to society.[95]

Ferber's attorneys argued that in order to be constitutional, child pornography laws must contain the *Miller* obscenity standards. They said, "No matter how offensive the material in question may be, whether it be bestiality, necrophilia, or pedophilia, a free society should be permitted to decide for itself what is enjoyable or worthwhile so long as the material chosen is not legally obscene."[97] Throughout the *Ferber* litigation, the ACLU defended child pornography as speech.[97]

At issue in the *Ferber* case was a film showing a naked boy lying face down on a bed rubbing against it. Later, he turns onto his back and masturbates to ejaculation twice. The boy then lies on his side and places a dildo between his buttocks as if "to insert it into his anus." Also at issue was a second film showing a young naked boy who masturbates to ejaculation and inserts a dildo into his anus. Other naked boys, some only 8 or 9 years old, were shown moving about and reclining on a mattress and engaged in conduct suggesting oral-genital contact and mutual and solo masturbation. Ferber sold the films to an undercover police officer.[98]

The state, in its brief in *Ferber*, presented the theories and arguments that the U.S. Supreme Court echoed in its ruling. The arguments centered on the harm to children involved and the lack of less restrictive effective alternatives for dealing with the problem. The state also emphasized that

such materials may be dangerous to children other than the child depicted. Law enforcement officers observed that child molesters use pornography, including child pornography, to seduce their young victims. And the danger exists that child pornography, like pornography of any kind, will stimulate its adult users to act out in real life the fantasies it engenders. A direct causal link between child pornography and child molestation has not so far been scientifically established. Nevertheless, child abusers are avid consumers of child pornography, and it is impossible to rule out the danger that pornography is one factor among the complex causes which precipitate the abuse, particularly where the pornography is of a violent, sadistic nature and the user is sexually disturbed.

. . . What is primary and beyond dispute

is that the production of child pornography necessarily entails the criminal sexual abuse of the boys and girls who are made to perform. The psychological and physical damage to these children demonstrates conclusively that child pornography is not a victimless crime, but a substantial social evil.[99]

In its brief in the *Ferber* case, Covenant House argued that the First Amendment guarantee of free expression does not allow children's privacy to be invaded nonconsensually through "public display of their most intimate conduct." An appendix explained why children could not, in a meaningful way, consent to sexual performances. This brief also detailed the harms to children from pornography involvement, one of which is the endless fear of exposure. The presumed lack of the child's voluntary participation "removes a critical aspect of protected 'speech'—that it somehow expresses one's own, as opposed to one's master's thoughts."[100]

The ACLU filed a brief in support of child pornography distributor Ferber in the Supreme Court case.[101]

CURRENT CHILD PORNOGRAPHY ISSUES

In drafting proposed changes for Wisconsin's child pornography law, co-author and attorney Sara Lee Johann found that changes such as the following were needed:

1. Prohibit possession of child pornography (with exceptions for legitimate possession, such as by law enforcement officers and expert witnesses in court cases). This would address the problem of pedophiles collecting it.
2. Include cartoon children in the definitions.
3. Cover all forms of communication. For example, by covering writings (not just pictures) of child pornography, the problem of children being abused by persons aroused by such writings would be dealt with.
4. Expand the type of sexual conduct covered.
5. Require a minimum prison term for persons convicted of this offense.
6. Create a duty for commercial film and photographic print processors to report child pornography and make it a crime not to report.
7. Allow experts to testify about the age of the child portrayed in the pornography. (The child will usually be unknown and unavailable.)
8. Remove statutes of limitations in child pornography cases so that victims who come forward long into adulthood will still have legal remedies against their abusers.

Concerning the first point in the list, the U.S. Supreme Court has not yet decided whether states may regulate possession of child pornography. The Ohio Supreme Court held that prohibiting possession of child pornography does not violate First Amendment rights,[102] and as of 1987, thirteen states had made possession of child pornography a criminal offense. Such laws should be upheld as constitutional because of the states' compelling interests in safeguarding minors' psychological and physical well-being.

The following states prohibit possession of child pornography: Alabama s. 13A-12-192 (1984), and see *Felton* v. *State*, 8 Div. 547 (1986), Aff'd by the Ala. Sup. Ct. on 4-8-88, reh. den. 5-20-88, which upheld this law; Arizona s. 13-3553 (1983); Colorado s. 18-6-403 (1988); Florida s. 827.071 (1985); Idaho s. 18-1507(3)(b) and 18-1507A (1987); Georgia s. 16-12-100 (1987); Illinois s. 11-20.1 (1985), upheld on March 23, 1988, by the Illinois Supreme Court in *People* v. *Geever;* Kansas s. 21-3516 (1986); Minnesota s. 617.247 (1983); Missouri s. 573.037 (1987); Nebraska—check 1988 laws; Nevada s. 200.730 (1983); Ohio s. 2907.321, 2907.322, 2907.323 (1984), upheld in *State* v. *Meadows*, 28 Ohio St.3d 43, 503 N.E.2d 697 (1986), *cert. denied* 94 L.Ed. 2d 771, 107 S. Ct. 1581 (1987); Oklahoma s. 1021.2 (1984); Texas s. 43.26 (1985); and Washington s. 9.68A.070 (1984).

(We encourage states to develop standardized statewide sex-related crime reports to be filled in by local police whenever sex crimes occur. These should include portions aimed at identifying the relationship of pornography to such offenses.)

Legal problems that occur in child pornography situations include (1)statutes of limitations running out before victims come forward or remember being abused, and (2)child victims being found incompetent to testify.

The 1982 U.S. General Accounting Office (GAO) report proposed solutions to minimize the sexual exploitation of children:

• Parental love, attention, and awareness and instilling appropriate sexual ethics and values

- School sex education, including telling children about pimps
- Public pressure and services
- Use of the news media to educate
- Increased legislative sanctions
- Better law enforcement
- Commercial licensing of all uses of children in modeling or performing
- Requiring film processors and labs to turn over child pornography to authorities
- Training of professionals.[103]

In October 1983, the *Juvenile Justice Digest* reported on federal legislation intended to strengthen the child pornography (sexual exploitation of children) law. New provisions were proposed because existing laws were inadequate. There had been only fifty prosecutions under the federal act in the six years (since 1978) it had been on the books. The proposed law eliminated the requirement that the pornography be sold (or commercial), thus reaching the underground network of pedophiles who trade such material. It also did away with the requirement that, when distribution is involved, obscenity must be proven. The age of minors was proposed to be raised from 16 to 18. And fines were to be raised from $10,000 to $100,000 maximum for a first offense and from $15,000 to a $200,000 maximum for additional offenses. (The Child Protection Act, passed in 1984, removed obscenity requirements and made receipt of, mailing of, or trafficking in child pornography illegal.)[104]

In 1983, the American Bar Association, Young Lawyers Division, produced a monograph titled *Child Sexual Exploitation*. The monogram concludes that sexual offense statutes, child labor laws, obscenity laws, child abuse statutes, and contributing to the delinquency of a minor laws are inadequate to deal with the child pornography problem. The following problems with some child pornography laws are listed:

1. Typical traffickers in or collectors of child pornography could not be prosecuted under laws that covered only distribution for commercial purposes.
2. Use of expert testimony to establish a child's age should be allowed. Otherwise, it is often impossible for the prosecutor to prove that the child was a minor at the time of the offense, for the child's identity and location are rarely known.
3. Statutes could provide that possession of three or more child pornography items is prima facie evidence of the distribution or intent to sell crimes.

4. Obscenity requirements should be removed from child pornography laws.

The report concludes that production and distribution of child pornography should be banned by all states and that laws should not require that such material be disseminated or produced for commercial profit. The report also suggests that child pornography victims be taken into custody of social services agencies for proceedings, as in other abuse and neglect cases.[105]

Lorri Staal reported on proposals pending in the 1985 U.S. Congress to amend the child pornography laws. Various bills would have amended the organized crime laws to permit civil lawsuits on behalf of victims of child prostitution and child pornography; allowed child pornography prosecution without proof of age; amended the interstate trafficking in prostitutes (Mann Act) to be gender neutral; prohibited distribution of advertisements depicting minors involved in sexual conduct; enacted new penalties for child kidnapping; and provided victims of pornographic performances and those who are coerced into performing for pornography a civil right to sue. Staal focuses on the feminist reactions to child pornography legislation, noting that feminists have been mostly silent on such proposals, while conservatives have been active. However, feminists, she says, lack the resources to be active lobbyists on Capitol Hill. Feminists also feel that the focus on child pornography avoids tackling the problem of violence against women due to pornography.[106]

Beverly Heinrich suggests requiring background checks on all employees working with children. She found that police and social workers did not ask children whether their abusers took pictures of them or showed them child pornography because the role of pornography in sexual abuse of children was not given serious consideration. She also mentions the lack of money and manpower devoted to investigating interstate trafficking in children. Heinrich calls for vigorous enforcement of federal obscenity laws and the Mann Act (concerning prostitution), as well as interagency, multidisciplinary cooperation and specialized training.[107]

The need for programs for child pornography victims is emphasized by Robert Pierce. He suggests using street workers rather than detached social workers in these cases. The proactive street workers can search for victims in need of help instead of waiting for victims to approach social services. They also can work with the victims during the hours when they are active and operate within the community environment rather than in the bureaucracy. Pierce cautions against too much flexibility, however.[108]

Even in the Netherlands, where child pornography was openly produced, distributed, and marketed, authorities have cracked down on the use of children in production of pornography.[109]

1986 AMENDMENTS TO THE FEDERAL LAW

Davidson and Loken report on changes in the federal law regulating child pornography passed in 1986. The Child Sexual Abuse and Pornography Act of 1986 did two things. First, it created a separate offense for transporting a child in foreign or interstate commerce when an intent to have the child engage in sexual acts "for the purpose of producing child pornography" could be shown.[110] Second, it created new offenses for "knowingly advertising or causing a notice to be made that a person was either seeking or offering to: a) receive, exchange, buy, produce, display, distribute, or reproduce child pornography; or b) secure the participation of a child for sexual conduct in order to produce child pornography.[111]

Davidson and Loken also explain the Child Abuse Victims' Rights Act of 1986, which allows any minor who is a victim of a violation of the federal child pornography law and who is personally injured as a result of such violation to sue to recover actual damages plus the cost of the lawsuit, including a reasonable attorney's fee. A minor who is so victimized is deemed under the law to have suffered damages of no less than $50,000. Such civil lawsuits must be initiated within six years after the cause of action accrues or, if the child was a minor at the time, no later than his or her twenty-first birthday. This law increased penalties for repeat offenders under the criminal child pornography law from a two-year to a five-year minimum prison sentence.

Federal laws concerning child pornography can be found at 18 U.S.C. ss. 2251–2256 and 2421–2423. Davidson and Loken provide an excellent summary of those laws. They also include a short summary of each of the fifty states' child pornography and child prostitution laws.

Davidson and Loken note that child pornography victims are eligible for victim services under 42 U.S.C. s. 10601, et. seq.; the federal Victims of Crime Act of 1984; and state crime victim compensation funds.

CONCLUSION

We believe that child pornography remains a major problem in the United States, although it is less open today than in the late 1970 and more centered on molester rather than commercial types of situations. We urge passage of some of the suggested legal reforms and, most importantly, devotion of more resources and time to investigating, solving these crimes, helping victims, and enforcing the child pornography laws.

Notes

1. Dr. Frank Osanka, Testimony of Frank Osanka, Hearings on Sexual Exploitation of Children before the Subcommittee on Crime of the Committee on the Judiciary, House of Representatives, 95th congress, May 23 1977, 4–33. 11 quoted in *New York v. Ferber*, SLIP Opinion (1982), 13, fn, 11.
2. Frank Osanka, "Introduction," in *Children in Chains*, Clifford L. Linedecker (New York: Everest House, 1981),?.
3. Frank Osanka, Testimony at the Hearings on Sexual Exploitation of Children, House Subcommittee on Crime, 95th Cong., 23 May 1977, 4–9.
4. [Carol Datt Mattar,] "No Age Limit: Child Pornography Is Abuse, Too, Wright State Workshop Told," (Dayton, Ohio) *Journal Herald*, 19 June 1978.
5. Jeff Trewhitt, "Child Pornography Trade Slammed by Professor," *The State Journal-Register* (Springfield, Ill.) 27 February 1977.
6. Arthur Siddon, "Take Profit out of the Child Porn: Expert," *Chicago Tribune*, 24 May 1977.
7. Elsie Mueller, "Calls for Strong Laws on Child Porno," *Du Page County Star* (DuPage County, Ill.), 9 June 1977.
8. Molly Stocking, "Children in Pornography: Sociologist

Condemns Increase of New 'Child Abuse' Form," (Bloomington, Ind.) *Sunday Herald*, 6 March 1977.

9. Frank Osanka, "Can Legislation Stop Child Pornography?" *Youth Forum*, January 1978.

10. "Pornography in America: Now They're Using Children," *PTA Today*, October 1977.

11. Elizabeth Ciancone, "Gibault Alumnus Given School's High Honor," *Terre Haute Star*, 16 July 1977.

12. Peter Bridges, "What Parents Should Know and Do about 'Kiddie Porn,' " *Parents Magazine*, January 1978, 42 ff.

13. Howard A. Davidson and Gregory A. Loken, *Child Pornography and Prostitution: Background and Legal Analysis* Child Pornography section copyrighted by American Bar Association (Washington, D.C., Child Prostitution section copyrighted by Covenant House, New York, 1987, available from the National Center for Missing and Exploited Children, 1835 K Street NW, Suite 700, Washington, DC 20006).

14. Richard P. Van Why, *Sex, Children and the Law: Explorations in the Problems of Child Pornography and Prostitution* (New York: R.P. Van Why Books, 1981).

15. Shirley O'Brien, *Child Pornography* (Dubuque, Iowa: Kendall/Hunt Publishing Co., 1983), viii.

16. Lore E. Stone, "Child Pornography Literature: A Content Analysis" (Doctoral dissertation, International College, Los Angeles, 1985), 15.

17. O'Brien, *Child Pornography*, 19.

18. Thomas Edwards, "Official: Pedophiles Are Now Using Computers," *Citizens Against Pornography Newsletter* (Austin, Tex.) 4 (May 1987), 1.

19. Clifford L. Linedecker, *Children in Chains* (New York: Everest House, 1981), 110–12.

20. Beverly Heinrich, "Texas House Select Committee on Child Pornography: Related Causes and Control: Extent Report," 66th sess., 14 September 1978, 1–45, 6.

21. *Atlanta Journal*, 21 July 1986.

22. Robert Lee Pierce, "Child Pornography: A Hidden Dimension of Child Abuse and Neglect," *Child Abuse and Neglect* vol. 8 (1984): 483–93.

23. Kenneth J. Herrmann, Jr., and Michael John Jupp, "Commercial Child Pornography and Pedophile Organizations: An International Report," *Response* 8 (Spring 1985): 7–10, 7.

24. Ibid., 8–10.

25. Ibid., 9–10.

26. "Sex and Children: It's Not a Pretty Picture," *Checkpoints for Children* 3 (January 1978):?.

27. Bridges, "What Parents Should Know."

28. David Sonenschein, "Children, Sex, and the Media: An Introductory Documentation," *Journal of Popular Culture* (1983):?.

29. Haven Bradford Gow, "Child Pornography Linked to Sexual Abuse," *Human Events*, 7 January 1984, 13.

30. Bridges, "What Parents Should Know."

31. D. Baker, "Preying on Playgrounds: The Sexploitation of Children in Pornography and Prostitution," in *The Victimology of Youth*, ed. L.G. Schultz (Springfield, Ill.: Charles C. Thomas, 1980), 813.

32. Mike Keller, "An Appeal to Deviant Behavior: Kiddie

Porn in Living, Queasy Color, "*Honolulu Advertiser*, 25 March 1987.

33. *Protection of Children Against Sexual Exploitation*, Report of the Senate Subcommittee to Investigate Juvenile Delinquency, 95th Cong., 1st sess., 27 May 1977, 16 June 1977 (Washington, DC: GPO, 1977), 8, 9.

34. Ann Wolbert Burgess with Marieanne Lindquist Clark, *Child Pornography and Sex Rings* (Lexington, Mass.: Lexington Books, 1984).

35. Ann Wolbert Burgess, A.N. Groth, and M. Mc-Causland, "Child Sex Initiation Ring," *American Journal of Orthopsychiatry* 51 (January 1981): 110–19.

36. Michael V. Gulo, Ann W. Burgess, and Ronald Kelly, "Child Victimization: Pornography and Prostitution," *Journal of Crime and Justice* 3 (1980): 65–81, 67–70.

37. A.W. Burgess, C.R. Hartman, M.P. McCausland, and P. Powers, "Response Patterns in Children and Adolescents Exploited through Sex Rings and Pornography," *American Journal of Psychiatry* 141 (May 1984): 656–62, 657–58.

38. Ibid., 658–62.

39. Rita Rooney, "Innocence for Sale," *Ladies' Home Journal*, April 1983,??.

40. Jeff Trewhitt, "Specialist Wants Child Abuse Laws Strengthened," *State Journal–Register* (Springfield, ILL.) 22 May 1977.

41. U.S. General Accounting Office (GAO), "Sexual Exploitation of Children—A Problem of Unknown Magnitude," Report to the Chairman, Subcommittee on Select Education, House Committee on Education and Labor, *GAO*, 20 April 1982, 16.

42. Pierce, "Child Pornography," 485.

43. Ibid., 486–87.

44. O'Brien, *Child Pornography*, 5, 19, 20, 22.

45. Thomas R. Hampson, Statement before the Illinois Legislative Investigating Commission on the Sexual Exploitation and Molestation of Children, 9, 10 October 1980, 1–15, 1.

46. Bridges, "What Parents Should Know," 69.

47. "Toby" R.P. Tyler and Lore E. Stone, "Child Pornography: Perpetuating the Sexual Victimization of Children," *Child Abuse and Neglect* 9 (1985): 313–18, 315.

48. Gwen Ingram, "A Commentary: The Law and Child Pornography," *Youth Forum*, January 1978, 5.

49. R.S. Anson, "The Last Porno Show," in *The Victimology of Youth*, ed. L. G. Schultz (Springfield Ill.: Charles C. Thomas, 1980), 275–91, 287–88.

50. Ulrich C. Schoettle, "Treatment of the Child Pornography Patient," *American Journal of Psychiatry* 139 (September 1980): 1109.

51. Ibid., 1110.

52. Ibid., 1110.

53. J.M. Payton, "Child Pornography Legislation—Notes," *Journal of Family Law* 17 (1979):505–43.

54. Charles H. McCaghy and Tina M. Beranbaum, "Child Pornography: The Rise of a Social Problem" (Paper presented at the annual meeting of the American Society of Criminology, Denver, 9–13 November 1983).

55. "Nobody Thought It Would Be Done," *PTA Today*, October 1977, 2.
56. Payton, "Child Pornography Legislation," 512.
57. Ibid.
58. Ibid., 513.
59. Ibid., 518.
60. Ibid., 529–30, 519–28, 528.
61. Ibid., 531–36.
62. Ibid. *Graham v. Hill*, 444 F.Supp. 584 (W.D. Tex. 1978).
63. Ibid., 537–43; *U.S. v. O'Brien*, 391 U.S. 367 (1968); *Brandenburg v. Ohio*, 395 U.S. 444, 447 (1967); Cohen v. California, 403 U.S. 15 (1971).
64. Christopher T. Donnelly, "Protection of Children from Use in Pornography: Toward Constitutional and Enforceable Legislation," *University of Michigan Journal of Law Reform* 12 (Winter 1979): 295–37, 298, 300–301.
65. Ibid., 302–3, 305–12.
66. Ibid., 312–16.
67. Ibid., 316–17, 322–23.
68. Ibid., 324–26, 327–35.
69. Ingram, "The Law and Child Pornography," 5.
70. Gow, "Child Pornography Linked to Sexual Abuse," 13.
71. Herald Price Fahringer, Statement before the House Committee on the Judiciary, H.R. 3913, 20 September 1977, 1–8, 1–2.
72. Ibid., 4, 4–5.
73. Siddon, "Take Profit out of Child Porn."
74. Michael Sneed and Rudolph Unger, "Carey: Child Porn Encourages Abuse," *Chicago Tribune*, 4 February 1977.
75. Baker, "Preying on Playgrounds," 832.
76. R.S. Pope, "Child Pornography—A New Role for the Obscenity Doctrine," *University of Illinois Law Forum* (1978): 711–57, 725, 742–44.
77. Pierce, "Child Pornography," 489.
78. Hampson, Statement before the Illinois Commission on the Sexual Exploitation and Molestation of Children, 5.
79. Joseph Freitas, Jr., Statement before the Select Education Subcommittee of the Education and Law Committee, U.S. Congress, 27 May 1977, 1–16, 11.
80. U.S. GAO, "Sexual Exploitation of Children," 31.
81. Ibid., 4–7.
82. Cliff Linedecker, "New York Ruling Might Bring 'Kiddie Porn' out of the Closet, " *Chicago Tribune*, 13 September 1981.
83. Letter from Bruce A. Taylor to Dr. Frank Osanka, 24 August 1982.
84. *Ferber*, 2.
85. Ibid., 5.
86. Ibid., 9.
87. Ibid.
88. Ibid., 10.
89. Ibid., 12.
90. Ibid., 13.
91. Ibid., 15.
92. Ibid., 17.
93. Ibid., 18.
94. Herald Price Fahringer, Paul J. Cambria, Jr., and Barbara Davies Ebert, "Brief for the Respondent in Opposition to Petition for Writ of Certiorari," *New York v. Ferber*, U.S. Supreme Court Case No. 81–55, August 1981, 1–18, 5, 8–9.
95. Ibid., 12–13.
96. Ibid., 17.
97. "First and Fourteenth Amendments," *Women Against Pornography Newsreport* 6 (Spring/Summer 1984): 21.
98. Robert P. Morgenthau, Robert M. Pitler, Mark Dwyer, and Donald J. Siewert, "Brief and Appendices for Petitioner," *New York v. Ferber*, U.S. Supreme Court Case No. 81–55, January 15, 1982, 1–33, 3.
99. Ibid., 13a–15a.
100. Edmund J. Burns, Gregory A. Loken, David P. Shouvlin, and William A. Cahill, Jr., "Motive for Leave to File a Brief *Amicus Curiae* and *Amicus Curiae* Brief," *New York v. Ferber*, U.S. Supreme Court Case No. 81–55, September 9, 1981, 1–20, 2, 18.
101. Gregory A. Loken, "Child Pornography: A Turning Point," *The Prosecutor* 16 (Summer 1982): 15–17, 16.
102. Davidson and Loken, *Child Pornography and Prostitution*, 10–11.
103. U.S. GAO, "Sexual Exploitation of Children,"??. 53–56.
104. "Washington Report—Child Pornography Legislation Is Sent to Full House," *Juvenile Justice Digest*, 17 October 1983, 7–8.
105. American Bar Association, Young Lawyers Division, *Child Sexual Exploitation: Background and Legal Analysis* (Washington, DC: National Legal Resource Center for Child Advocacy and Protection, 1981), 9, 15, 21, 34.
106. Lorri Staal, "Child Pornography: Federal and Feminist Responses," *Response* 8 (Summer 1985): 17–19.
107. Beverly Heinrich, "Texas House Select Committee on Child Pornography: Related Causes and Control: Extent Report. 66th sess." 14 September 1978, 1–45, 6.
108. Robert Lee Pierce, "Child Pornography," 190.
109. Jaap E. Doek, "Child Pornography and Legislation in the Netherlands," *Child Abuse and Neglect* (1985) 9: 411–12.
110. Davidson and Loken, *Child Pornography and Prostitution*, 7–8.
111. Ibid., 7.

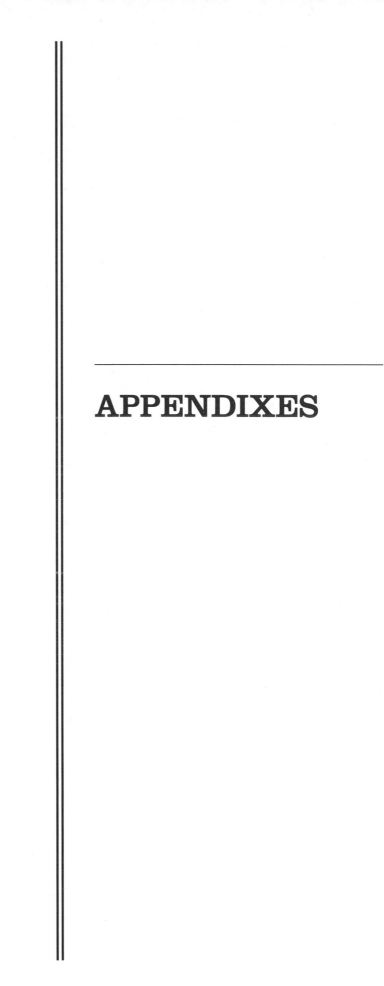

APPENDIXES

A MODEL STATE OBSCENITY STATUTE AND MEMO ON HARD-CORE PORNOGRAPHY

The following obscenity statute is intended as a model. Before it is adopted, it will, in all likelihood, need to be modified to avoid potential conflict with particular state constitutional or statutory constraints. As a matter of U.S. constitutional law, however, it is correct in its present form.

MODEL OBSCENITY CHAPTER

An Act to create and enact chapter _____ of the _____ Code, relating to definitions, pandering of obscenity, wholesale pandering of obscenity, promoting or wholesale promoting of a sexual device, making obscene drawings, disseminating matter harmful to minors, unlawful exhibition or display of harmful materials to minors, unlawful exhibition of harmful performances at outdoor theaters, deception to obtain matter harmful to minors, compelling acceptance of objectionable materials, commercial nudity, sexual exploitation of children, presumption and evidence of knowledge, injunctive actions, jury instructions concerning evidence of pandering, and legislative purpose and severability.

BE IT ENACTED BY THE CITY OR STATE OF

Chapter _____ of the _____ Code is hereby created and enacted to read as follows:

SECTION 1. *Definitions*. As used in this chapter, unless the context clearly indicates otherwise:

(a) "Community" when used in connection with "contemporary community standards," means the geographical area within the jurisdiction of the court or vicinage of the jury hearing the case, whichever is larger.

(b) "Harmful to minors" includes any material or performance, whether through pictures, photographs, drawings, writings, cartoons, recordings, telephonic transmissions, films, videotapes, or other such media, which shall be "harmful to minors" if the following apply:

(1) The average person, applying contemporary community standards, would find that the material or performance, taken as a whole, appeals to the prurient interest; and

(2) The material or performance depicts or describes sexually explicit nudity, sexual conduct, or sadomasochistic sexual abuse in a way which is patently offensive to prevailing standards in the adult community with respect to what is suitable for minors; and

(3) The material or performance, taken as a whole, lacks serious literary, artistic, political, or scientific value for minors.

(c) "Knowledge of character" means having general knowledge or reason to know, or a belief or ground for belief which warrants further inspection or inquiry, of the nature and character of the material or performance involved. A person has such knowledge when he or she knows or is aware that the material or performance contains, depicts, or describes sexually explicit nudity, sexual conduct, sadomasochistic sexual abuse, or lewd exhibition of the genitals, whichever is applicable, whether or not such person has precise knowledge of the specific contents thereof. Such knowledge may be proven by direct or circumstantial evidence, or both.

(d) "Material" means any book, magazine, newspaper, advertisement, pamphlet, poster, print, picture, figure, image, drawing, description, motion picture film, phonographic record or recording tape, videotape, or other tangible thing capable of producing or reproducing an image, picture, sound, or sensation through sight, sound, or touch.

(e) "Minor" means any person under the age of eighteen years.

(f) "Obscene" means any material or performance,

whether through pictures, photographs, drawings, writing, cartoons, recordings, films, videotapes, telephonic transmissions, or other media, is "obscene" if the following apply:

(1) The average person, applying contemporary adult community standards, would find that the material or performance, taken as a whole, appeals to the prurient interest; and

(2) The average person, applying contemporary adult community standards, would find that the material or performance depicts or describes sexual conduct or sadomasochistic sexual abuse in a patently offensive way; and

(3) The material or performance, taken as a whole, lacks serious literary, artistic, political, or scientific value.

(g) "Performance" means any motion picture, film, videotape, played record, phonograph or tape, broadcast, preview, trailer, play, show, skit, dance, or other exhibition performed or presented to or before an audience of one or more, or transmission by means of electrical, radio, television, telephone, or other communicative device or facility to a known closed or open circuit audience of one or more or to the general public.

(h) "Person" means any individual, corporation, cooperative, company, partnership, firm, association, joint venture, business, establishment, organization, or other legal entity of any kind.

(i) "Promote" means to manufacture, issue, sell, give, provide, advertise, produce, reproduce, lend, mail, deliver, transfer, transmit, publish, distribute, circulate, disseminate, present, display, exhibit, or advertise or to offer or agree, or possess with intent, to do any of the foregoing.

(j) "Prurient" means an unhealthy lustful or erotic interest, a lascivious or degrading interest, or a shameful or morbid interest, in sexual conduct, sexually explicit nudity, sadomasochistic sexual abuse, or lewd exhibition of the genitals. Materials or performances may be deemed to appeal to the prurient interest when they have a tendency to excite such thoughts or desires or when they are designed, marketed, promoted, or disseminated to cater or appeal to such an interest. Where the material or performance is designed for and primarily disseminated or promoted to a clearly defined deviant sexual group, rather than the public at large, the prurient appeal requirement is satisfied if the dominant theme of the material or performance, taken as a whole, appeals to the prurient interest in sex of the members of that intended and probable recipient group.

(k) "Sadomasochistic sexual abuse" means actual or simulated flagellation, rape, torture, or other physical or sexual abuse, by or upon a person who is nude or partially denuded, or the condition of being fettered, bound, or otherwise physically restrained, for the actual or simulated purpose of sexual gratification or abuse or represented in the context of a sexual relationship.

(1) "Sexual conduct" means ultimate sexual acts, normal or perverted, actual or simulated, involving a person or persons, or a person or persons and an animal, including acts of masturbation, vaginal or anal intercourse, fellatio, cunnilingus, analingus; physical contact with a person's nude or partially denuded genitals, pubic area, perineum, anal region, or female breast; excretory functions; or lewd exhibition of the genitals.

(m) "Sexual device" means any artificial human penis, vagina, or anus, or other device primarily designed, promoted, or marketed to physically stimulate or manipulate the human genitals, pubic area, perineum, or anal area, including dildos, penisators, vibrators, vibrillators, penis rings, and erection enlargement or prolonging creams, jellies, or other such chemicals or preparations.

(n) "Sexually explicit nudity" means the sexually oriented and explicit showing, by any means, including but not limited to, close-up views, poses, or depictions in such position or manner as to present or expose such areas to prominent, focal, or obvious viewing attention, of any of the following: postpubertal, fully or partially developed, human female breast with less than a fully opaque covering of any portion thereof below the top of the areola; the depiction of covered human male genitals in a discernible turgid state; or lewd exhibition of the human genitals, pubic area, perineum, buttocks, or anal region with less than a fully opaque covering.

(o) "Visibly displayed" means that the material or performance is visible on a billboard, viewing screen, marquee, newsstand, display rack, window, showcase, display case, or other similar display area that is visible from any part of the premises where a minor is or may be allowed, permitted, or invited as part of the general public or otherwise, or that is visible from a public street, sidewalk, park, alley, residence, playground, school, or other place to which a minor, as part of the general public or otherwise, has unrestrained and reasonably anticipated access and presence.

(p) "Wholesale promote" means to promote for purpose of resale.

SECTION 2. *Pandering obscenity.*

(a) No person, with knowledge of the character of the material or performance involved, shall do any of the following:

(1) Create, photograph, produce, reproduce, or

publish any obscene material, when the offender knows that such material is to be commercially or publicly promoted or when reckless in that regard.

(2) Exhibit or advertise for promotion or promote any obscene material.

(3) Create, photograph, tape, direct, produce, or reproduce an obscene performance, when the offender knows that it is to be commercially or publicly promoted or when reckless in that regard.

(4) Advertise an obscene performance for presentation, or promote or participate in promoting an obscene performance, when such performance is presented publicly, or when admission is charged, or when presented or to be presented before an audience of one or more.

(5) Possess or control any obscene material with the purpose to violate this section.

(6) Participate in the acting or posing for any obscene material or performance, or portion thereof which is obscene, when the offender knows that it is to be commercially or publicly promoted or when reckless in that regard.

(b) It is an affirmative defense to a charge under this section that the material or performance involved was disseminated or promoted for a bona fide medical, psychological, legislative, judicial, or law enforcement purpose, by or to a physician, psychologist, legislator, judge, prosecutor, law enforcement officer, or other person having such a bona fide interest in such material or performance.

(c) A person who violates this section is guilty of pandering obscenity, a class __ misdemeanor. If the offender has previously been convicted of a violation of this section or of Section 6 relating to disseminating matters harmful to minors, then pandering obscenity is a class __ felony.

SECTION 3. *Wholesale pandering obscenity.*

(a) No person, with knowledge of the character of the material involved, shall wholesale promote any obscene material or offer or agree, or possess with intent, to wholesale promote any obscene material.

(b) It is an affirmative defense to a charge under this section that the material or performance involved was wholesale promoted for a bona fide medical, psychological, legislative, judicial, or law enforcement purpose, by or to a physician, psychologist, legislator, judge, prosecutor, or law enforcement officer.

(c) A person who violates this section is guilty of wholesale pandering obscenity, a class __ felony. If the offender has previously been convicted of a violation of this section, then wholesale pandering obscenity is a class __ felony.

SECTION 4. *Promoting or wholesale promoting a sexual device.*

(a) No person, with knowledge that the device involved is a "sexual device," shall do either of the following:

(1) Promote, or offer or agree, or possess with intent, to promote, any sexual device.

(2) Wholesale promote, or offer or agree, or possess with intent, to wholesale promote, any sexual device.

(b) It is an affirmative defense to a charge under this section that the sexual device was promoted or wholesale promoted for a bona fide medical, psychological, legislative, judicial, or law enforcement purpose by or to a physician, psychologist, legislator, judge, prosecutor, or law enforcement officer.

(c) A person who violates this section is guilty of promoting or wholesale promoting a sexual device. A person violating subdivision (1) of subsection (a) of this section is guilty of a class __ misdemeanor. If the offender has previously been convicted of a violation of subdivision (1) of subsection (a) of this section, promoting a sexual device is a class __ felony. Violation of subdivision (2) of subsection (a) is a class __ felony. If the offender has previously been convicted of a violation of subdivision (2) of section (a) of this section, wholesale promoting a sexual device is a class __ felony.

SECTION 5. *Making obscene drawings.*

(a) No person shall make, draw, color, paint, scratch, cut, or otherwise produce any obscene drawing, writing, graffiti, picture, or other material in public or on a public place, including a public or private building, billboard, utility pole, wall, sidewalk, roadway, or poster.

(b) A person who violates this section is guilty of making an obscene drawing, a class __ misdemeanor.

SECTION 6. *Disseminating matter harmful to minors.*

(a) No person, with knowledge of its character, shall promote or otherwise furnish or present to a minor any material or performance which is obscene or harmful to minors, or possess or control any such materials with the purpose or intent to violate this section.

(b) The following are affirmative defenses to a charge under this section, involving material or a performance which is harmful to minors but not obscene:

(1) The minor exhibited to the defendant or his agent or employee a draft card, driver's license, birth certificate, marriage license, or other governmental or educational document purporting to show that such minor was eighteen years of age or

over and the person to whom such document was exhibited did not otherwise have reasonable cause to believe that such minor was under the age of eighteen and did not rely solely upon the oral allegations or representations of the minor as to his or her age.

(2) At the time the material or performance was promoted or otherwise furnished or presented to the minor involved, a parent or lawful guardian of such minor, with knowledge of its character, accompanied the minor or consented to the material or performance being promoted or otherwise furnished or presented to the minor.

(c) The following are affirmative defenses to a charge under this section, involving material or a performance which is obscene or harmful to minors:

(1) The defendant is the parent, lawful guardian, or spouse of the minor involved.

(2) The material or performance was promoted or otherwise furnished or presented to the minor for a bona fide medical, psychological, judicial, or law enforcement purpose by a physician, psychologist, judge, prosecutor, or law enforcement officer.

(d) A person who violates this section is guilty of disseminating harmful to minors. If the material or performance involved is harmful to minors but not obscene, violation of this section is a class ___ misdemeanor. If the material or performance involved is obscene, violation of this section is a class ___ felony.

SECTION 7. *Unlawful exhibition or display of harmful materials to minors.*

(a) No person, having custody, control, or supervision of any business or commercial establishment or premises, with knowledge of the character of the material involved, shall do any of the following:

(1) Visibly display, exhibit, or otherwise expose to view in that part of the premises where a minor is or may be allowed, permitted, or invited as part of the general public or otherwise, all or any part of any book, magazine, newspaper, or other form of material which is harmful to minors.

(2) Visibly display, exhibit, or otherwise expose to view all or any part of such material which is harmful to minors in any business or commercial establishment where minors, as part of the general public or otherwise, are, or will probably be, exposed to view all or any part of such material from any public or private place.

(3) Hire, employ, or otherwise place, supervise, control, or allow in any business or commercial establishment or other place, any minor under circumstances which would cause, lead, or allow such minor to engage in the business or activity of

promoting or otherwise handling such material which is harmful to minors, either to or for adults or minors.

(b) The following are affirmative defenses to a charge under this section:

(1) The minor exhibited to the defendant or his agent or employee a draft card, driver's license, birth certificate, marriage license, or other governmental or educational document purporting to show that such minor was eighteen years of age or over, and the person to whom such document was exhibited did not otherwise have reasonable cause to believe that such minor was under the age of eighteen and did not rely solely upon the oral allegations or representations of the minor as to his or her age or as to the knowing consent of the minor's parent or lawful guardian.

(2) At the time the material was visibly displayed or otherwise furnished or presented to the minor involved, a parent or lawful guardian of such minor, with knowledge of its character, accompanied the minor or consented to the material being visibly displayed or otherwise furnished or presented to the minor.

(3) The defendant is the parent, lawful guardian, or spouse of the minor involved.

(c) A person who violates subdivisions (1) or (2) of this subsection (a) is guilty of displaying harmful materials to minors, a class ___ misdemeanor. If the offender has previously been convicted of a violation of either of these subdivisions, then such offense is a class ___ misdemeanor. Whoever violates subdivision (3) of subsection (a) is guilty of unlawfully employing a minor, a class ___ misdemeanor.

SECTION 8. *Unlawful exhibition of harmful performances at outdoor theaters.*

(a) No person, having custody, control, or supervision of any outdoor or drive-in motion picture theater or arena, with knowledge of the character of the performance involved, shall knowingly present or participate in presenting the exhibition of a performance which is harmful to minors upon any outdoor or drive-in motion picture theater or arena screen, when such screen is visible from public highway or street, sidewalk, park, alley, residence, playground, school, or other such place to which minors, as part of the general public or otherwise, have unrestrained and reasonably anticipated access and presence.

(b) A person who violates this section is guilty of exhibiting a harmful performance at an outdoor theater, a class ___ misdemeanor. If the offender has previously been convicted of a violation of this section, then such offense is a class ___ misdemeanor.

SECTION 9. *Deception to obtain matter harmful to minors.*

(a) No person, for the purpose enabling a minor to obtain any material or gain admission to any performance which is obscene or harmful to minors, shall do either of the following:

(1) Falsely represent that he or she is the parent, guardian, or spouse of such minor.

(2) Furnish such minor with any identification or document purporting to show that such minor is eighteen years of age or over.

(b) No minor, for the purpose of obtaining any material or gaining admission to any performance which is harmful to minors, shall do either of the following:

(1) Falsely represent that he or she is eighteen years of age or over.

(2) Exhibit any identification or document purporting to show that he or she is eighteen years of age or over.

(c) A person who violates this section is guilty of deception to obtain matter harmful to minors, a class ___ misdemeanor.

SECTION 10. *Compelling acceptance of objectionable materials.*

(a) No person, as a condition to the sale or delivery of any material or goods of any kind, shall, over the objection of the purchaser or consignee, require the purchaser or consignee to accept any other material reasonably believed to be obscene or which if furnished or presented to a minor would be harmful to minors.

(b) A person who violates this section is guilty of compelling acceptance of objectionable materials, a class ___ misdemeanor.

SECTION 11. *Commercial nudity.*

(a) In any establishment or premises where alcoholic beverages are dispensed, no person shall knowingly provide service without a fully opaque cloth covering of the human male or female genitals, pubic hair, buttocks, anal region, or postpubertal female breast below the top of the areola, where such person is exposed to the view of the public, patrons, guests, invitees, or customers.

(b) No person, being the owner, lessor, lessee, or having control, custody, or supervision of any commercial business, establishment, tavern, store, shop, massage parlor, or other place of public accommodation, commerce, or amusement, shall recklessly use or promote the use of, or permit or tolerate others to use or promote the use of, such premises in violation of subsection (a) of this section, or, if given or having actual notice of such violation, shall negligently fail or refuse to cease or stop such violation, or to cause an agent, employee, or other subordinate to cease or stop such violation, or to notify a law enforcement agency of such violation.

(c) "Provide service" means the provision or allowance of services, advertisement, or entertainment to the public, patrons, guests, invitees, or customers, including hostessing, bartending, food or beverage serving or preparing, table setting or clearing, waitering or waitressing, singing, dancing, massaging, counseling, and also including beauty or figure contests, modeling, or exhibitions.

(d) It is an affirmative defense to a charge under this section if any full or partial nudity has serious literary, artistic, political, or scientific value.

(e) A person who violates subsection (a) of this section is guilty of commercial nudity, a class ___ misdemeanor. Whoever violates subsection (b) of this section is guilty of promoting commercial nudity, a class ___ felony. If the offender has previously been convicted of a violation of this section, the degree of offense shall be one degree higher than that above provided for the particular subsection involved.

SECTION 12. *Sexual exploitation of children.*

(a) No person, with knowledge of the character of the material or performance involved, shall employ, consent to, authorize, direct, or otherwise induce or allow a minor to engage or participate in the production, filming, photographing, acting, posing, or other manner of making any material or performance, when the minor will or does engage or participate in sexually explicit nudity, sexual conduct, or sadomasochistic sexual abuse.

(b) No person, with knowledge of the character of the material or performance involved, shall promote or wholesale promote any material or performance which includes, depicts, represents, or contains a minor engaged or participating in the acting, posing or otherwise the subject of sexually explicit nudity, sexual conduct, or sadomasochistic sexual abuse.

(c) No person, with knowledge of the character of the material or performance involved, shall promote or wholesale promote any obscene material or performance which includes, depicts, represents, or contains a minor engaged or participating in the acting, posing, or otherwise being the subject of sexually explicit nudity, sexual conduct, or sadomasochistic sexual abuse.

(d) It is an affirmative defense to a charge under subsection (a) that the minor exhibited to the defendant, prior to engaging or participating in the material or performance, a draft card, driver's license, birth certificate, or other governmental or educational document purporting to show that such minor was eighteen years of age or over and the defendant did not otherwise have reasonable cause to believe or suspect that such minor was under the age of eighteen and did not rely solely upon the oral allegations or representations of the minor as to his or her age.

(e) It is an affirmative defense to a charge under subsections (b) and (c) of this section that the defendant, in good faith, had a reasonable factual basis to conclude that the subject of the sexually explicit nudity, sexual conduct, or sadomasochistic sexual abuse was not a minor but was in fact over the age of eighteen years.

(f) In any prosecution or action under this section, the court or jury, as trier of fact, shall make the determination of whether the subject of the sexually explicit nudity, sexual conduct, or sadomasochistic sexual abuse is, beyond a reasonable doubt, a minor, and the following methods of proof shall be competent for the admission of direct or circumstantial evidence on this issue:

(1) Personal inspection or testimony of the minor or alleged minor.

(2) Testimony of the parent, lawful guardian, teacher, or other personal acquaintance of the minor or alleged minor.

(3) Inspection of the material or performance involved.

(4) Testimony of a witness to the production, filming, photographing, acting, posing, or other manner of making the material or performance involved or testimony of a physician, scientist, or other expert witness as to the age or appearance of the minor or alleged minor.

(5) Any other method authorized by law or by the rules of evidence.

(g) The subject of the sexual exploitation is presumed to be a minor if he or she is portrayed, advertised, marketed, cast, represented, or otherwise promoted or appears as being a minor.

(h) A person who violates subsection (a) of this section is guilty of sexual exploitation of a minor, a class ___ felony. A person who violates subsection (b) of this section is guilty of pandering the sexual exploitation of a minor, a class ___ misdemeanor. A person who violates subsection (c) of this section is guilty of pandering obscenity involving the sexual exploitation of a minor, a class ___ felony. If the offender has previously been convicted of a violation of this section, then the degree of the offense shall be one higher than that above provided for the particular subsection involved.

SECTION 13. *Presumption and evidence of knowledge.*

(a) An owner or manager, or his agent or employee, of a bookstore, newsstand, theater, distributing firm, warehouse, or other commercial establishment engaged in promoting materials or performances or distributing or handling materials for promotion or wholesale promotion, may be presumed to have knowledge of the character of the material or performance involved if he or she has actual or constructive notice of the nature of such material or performance, whether or not he or she has precise knowledge of its contents.

(b) In any prosecution or action in which knowledge of the character of material or a performance or knowledge that a device is a "sexual device" is at issue, it is evidence of such knowledge that actual notice of the nature of the material was previously provided. Without limitation on the manner in which such notice may be given, actual notice of the character of material or a performance may be given in writing by the state's attorney, city attorney, or similar prosecuting authority of the jurisdiction in which the person to whom the notice is directed does business. Such notice, regardless of the manner in which it is given, shall identify the sender, identify the material or performance, state whether it is obscene or harmful to minors, and bear the date of such notice. Such notice shall also give a brief description of the contents of the material or performance and indicate whether the material or performance contains sexually explicit nudity, sexual conduct, sadomasochistic sexual abuse, or lewd exhibition of the genitals or is a "sexual device."

(c) In any prosecution or action in which knowledge of the character of material or a performance or knowledge that a device in a "sexual device" is at issue, evidence of any of the following is relevant proof of such knowledge:

(1) The sexually explicit nature and character of the material or performance involved is advertised, marketed or otherwise publicly exploited for the purpose of attracting patrons or purchasers.

(2) The bookstore, newsstand, theater, distributor, firm, warehouse or establishment is advertised, held out, or otherwise represented as possessing sexually explicit materials for promotion or wholesale promotion or as promoting or wholesale promoting a sexually explicit performance.

(3) The bookstore, newsstand, theater, distributor, firm, warehouse, or establishment is primarily engaged in promoting or wholesale promoting sexually explicit materials or sexually explicit performances.

(d) In any prosecution or action under this chapter, knowledge of the character of the material or performance involved may be proven by direct or circumstantial evidence, or both.

SECTION 14. *Injunctive actions.*

(a) When there is reason to believe that any person is violating, is about to violate, or is possessing any material with intent to violate any of the provisions of this chapter, the attorney general, state's attorney, city attorney, or prosecutor for a city may institute and maintain an action for preliminary and permanent injunctive relief, to enjoin the violation in an appropriate court having equitable jurisdiction. No bond shall be required of the official bringing the action, and the official and the political subdivision shall not be liable for costs or damages, other than court costs, by reasons of the injunctive orders not being granted or where judgment is entered in favor of the defendant by the trial or an appellate court. A citizen of the county may also bring such an action, but shall post a bond in an amount not less than five hundred dollars. Such actions shall be brought in the name of the state.

(b) The court shall hold the hearing on the preliminary injunction within two days, not counting Saturdays, Sundays, or legal holidays, after service of the complaint and motion for preliminary injunction upon the defendants. The court shall then issue an order granting or denying the preliminary injunction within twenty-four hours after the conclusion of the hearing, regarding the material or performance adjudged obscene or harmful to minors. No right of jury trial shall attach to the hearing on a preliminary injunction but the duty rests on the plaintiff to prove by clear and convincing evidence that the offense is being or is about to be committed. If the defendants who have been served fail to appear at said hearing, then a preliminary injunction shall be issued on the date of the hearing. The finding of the court regarding the obscenity or that the subject matter is harmful to minors at the preliminary injunction stage shall not be binding upon the final order on the merits at trial on the permanent injunction. The court shall reserve the right to reconsider its preliminary finding based upon any further evidence or testimony which may be introduced at such trial. If the court enters final order denying a permanent injunction on the basis that the material or performance is not obscene or harmful to minors as a whole, then no contempt shall be found for violation of the preliminary injunction relating thereto.

(c) The court shall set the matter for a hearing on the permanent injunction according to the provisions of the rules or other order of court. The defendant shall have the right to demand a hearing on the permanent injunction within ten days of the issue or denial of the preliminary injunction. Either party shall have the right of trial by jury on the issue of the obscenity or harmful to minors nature of the material or performance involved at the hearing for the permanent injunction, and such jury shall render a special and separate verdict as to the nature of the subject matter. The duty rests on the plaintiff to prove by clear and convincing evidence that the offense is being or is about to be committed by the defendants. It shall be the duty of the trier of fact to determine all issues of fact concerning the obscene or harmful to minors nature of the subject matter, including the elements of appeal to prurient interest, community standards, patent offensiveness, and serious value, without the need for expert testimony or other evidence other than the material or performance itself. Expert testimony or other evidence on these issues may be entered by either party and will be entitled to such weight as the trier of fact deems appropriate under the circumstances. The court shall then issue an order granting or denying the permanent injunction within five days after the conclusion of the trial, regarding the material or performance adjudged obscene or harmful to minors.

(d) In the event that the court issues a permanent injunction, it shall also issue an order directing a law enforcement officer to seize and hold all copies of the subject matter which are in the possession of the defendants. Such material shall be held until the exhaustion of all appellate remedies and may then be disposed of by order of the court.

(e) Violation of a preliminary or permanent injunction shall be punishable as contempt of court.

SECTION 15. *Jury instructions—evidence of pandering.*

The following instruction may be read to the jury in a criminal prosecution or civil action under this chapter:

"In determining the question of whether the allegedly obscene material or performance involved, when taken as a whole, lacks serious literary, artistic, political, or scientific value, the jury may consider the circumstances of promotion, advertisement, or editorial intent and particularly whether such circumstances indicate that the material or performance was being commercially exploited for the sake of its prurient appeal and whether any serious value claimed was, under the circumstances, a pretense or reality.

"Such evidence is probative with respect to the nature of the material or performance, and if the jury concludes that the sole emphasis was on the sexually provocative aspect, this can justify the conclusion that the material or performance is lacking in serious literary, artistic, political, or scientific value.

"The weight, if any, which such evidence is entitled is a matter for the jury to determine."

SECTION 16. *Legislative purpose and severability.*

(a) Nothing in this chapter shall be presumed to invalidate, supersede, repeal, prevent, or preempt any ordinance or resolution or any county or city covering the subject matter of this chapter. Cities or counties may adopt ordinances and resolutions which are consistent with this chapter and must employ the language of this chapter, as written or judicially construed, for all offenses which are covered by this chapter. Cities and counties further retain the right to regulate and define offenses, locations, or requirements regarding any activities, displays, exhibitions, or materials, whether by zoning, licensing, or criminal laws, not specifically regulated by this chapter.

(b) If any provision of this chapter, including any part, phrase, or word of any section, or the application thereof, to any person or circumstance is held invalid, such invalidity shall not affect other provisions or applications of this chapter which can be given effect without the invalid provision or application, and to this end, the provisions of this chapter are declared to be severable. It is the purpose of this chapter to comply with constitutional and police power limitations, and this chapter shall be interpreted and construed to adopt or change in compliance with controlling court decisions.

OUTLINE OF MEMORANDUM IN SUPPORT OF MODEL OBSCENITY CHAPTER

SECTION 1. *Definitions.*

(a) "Community" allows the determination of community standards by the jury or judge in relation to the area where the materials are being promoted, rather than a difficult to apply concept such as a statewide standard would engender. This method of judging standards was approved by the U.S. Supreme Court in *Miller v. California*, 413 U.S. 15, at 31–33 (1973); *Jenkins v. Georgia*, 418 U.S. 153, at 157 (1974); and *Hamling v. United States*, 418 U.S. 87, at 103–8 (1974).

(b) "Harmful to minors" is adapted from the New York statute which was approved by the U.S. Supreme Court in *Ginsberg v. New York*, 390 U.S. 629 (1968), with revisions to comply with the modernized version of certain phrases as changed in the *Miller v. California* case. This allows the issue of what is suitable for juveniles to be determined on a "variable obscenity" basis, which is less than the standards for obscenity for adults.

(c) "Knowledge of character" defines the requirement of *scienter* as required by *Smith v. California*, 361 U.S. 147, at 154 (1959). The use of the word "character" to describe this knowledge was intended to deal with the erroneous contention that a person must be proven to know the specific and exact contents of the material. Since it is not innocent but calculated purveyance of pornography which is being regulated, it would be unfair to hold a person liable for dealing in a work which was thought to be something entirely harmless and nonsexual. If a person knows that a work is sexually oriented and contains the types of sexual representations which are defined in this code, then that person also knows that such work may be judged as to its obscene or

harmful nature and must then take precautions not to violate the law. The use of this standard of *scienter* has been approved in *Mishkin v. New York*, 383 U.S. 502, at 510–12 (1966); *Hamling v. United States*, 418 U.S. 87, at 119–20 (1974); and also by the Supreme Court of Ohio in *State v. Burgun*, 384 N.E.2d 255 (1978).

(d) "Material" defines the types of physical objects which are covered under this code in order to give specificity and clarity to courts and persons.

(e) "Minor" specifies all persons under the age of eighteen.

(f) "Obscene" is taken from and adopts the guidelines for determining obscenity announced by the U.S. Supreme Court in the cases of *Miller v. California*, 413 U.S. 15, at 24–25 (1973) and *Brockett v. Spokane Arcades, Inc.*, __ U.S. __ (June 29, 1985), taking into consideration that the Court also said that it is an adult standard which must be applied, as stated in *Pinkus v. United States*, 436 U.S. 293 (1978).

(g) "Performance" defines the types of exhibitions subject to the code.

(h) "Person" specifies types of natural and legal entities which are responsible for the provisions of the code.

(i) "Promote" is defined in a way which can be consistently applied throughout the code. It is taken from the codes of New York, Texas, and several other states and is meant to encompass the various methods of commercial traffic in materials and performances.

(j) "Prurient" is defined in such a manner to allow a proper consideration of the nature of the material's appeal. The definition is from *Brockett v. Spokane Arcades, Inc.*, __ U.S. __ (June 19, 1985); *Miller v.*

California, supra at 24, 30–31; *Mishkin v. New York, supra* at 508–9 (1966); and *Hamling v. United States, supra* at 104–6. The exception is where the material is aimed and promoted primarily to a known deviant group, and then the appeal can be judged according to whether it would appeal to the prurient interest of the group, as approved in *Mishkin v. New York, supra* at 508–9.

(k) "Sadomasochistic sexual abuse" is defined in language similar to that of other statutes, such as those of New York, Texas, and other states, and delineates a type of material which has been upheld as a subject of regulation by the cases of *Mishkin v. New York, supra; Ginsberg v. New York, supra;* and *Ward v. Illinois,* 431 U.S. 767 (1977).

(l) "Sexual conduct" adopts the examples suggested by the Court in *Miller v. California,* 413 U.S., at 25, and specifies in further detail the exact types of conduct which must be present in order for any material or performance to be judged as to its obscene or harmful nature.

(m) "Sexual device" is defined in a manner similar to that of the Georgia statute, Section 26-2101(c), but with added specificity and detail. The regulation of such devices is provided for in Section 4, and an explanation of its legality is included in the discussion of that section, *infra.*

(n) "Sexually explicit nudity" defines the term, as used in the harmful to minors and display sections of the proposed code, to limit such nudity to a form of sexually oriented exhibition so as to comply with the cases of *Ginsberg v. New York, supra,* and *Erznoznik v. Jacksonville,* 422 U.S. 205, at 213, and at 216, footnote 15 (1975).

(o) "Visibly displayed" is adapted from the provision of statutes and ordinances in several states, including New York, Virginia, Tennessee, Utah, and Rhode Island, with added specification to ease application.

(p) "Wholesale promote" is also taken from New York and Texas codes and provides that only sales, distributions, etc., for resale purposes will be subject to the stricter penalties provided.

SECTION 2. *Pandering obscenity.*

(a) This section provides the elements of the offense. The structure is adopted from Ohio Revised Code Section 2907.32, with added specificity and detail to encompass all foreseeable methods of violation of the law.

(b) The only defense which can be justified for dealing in matter which is outside the protection of the Constitution is for proper persons who are seriously engaged in medical or psychological treatment, law enforcement authorities engaged in enforcement of the law or educating the public to the law and its abuses, and also provides for a defense for any "other person having such a bona fide interest" in a medical, psychological, legislative, judicial, or law enforcement purpose. This would protect all serious uses of sexually expressive materials which if pandered to the public could be obscene, but allows use, research, and study of such material for these valid purposes.

SECTION 3. *Wholesale pandering obscenity.*

(a) This section provides the elements of the offense, dealing with obscenity for purpose of resale. This crime is more serious because it reaches those who distribute obscenity on a scale which seriously affects the entire State and allows a greater penalty and justifies greater efforts by law enforcement in identifying and apprehending those most responsible for the influx of obscenity in and across the State.

(b) The defenses are the same, in order to protect legitimate interests.

SECTION 4. *Promoting or wholesale promoting a sexual device.*

(a) The elements of this offense require that the offender know that the illegal device is a "sexual device" [see "Definitions," (m)] which clearly establish it as an object of sexual perversion or abuse. Such an item is "obscene as a matter of law," with no requirement that it meet the tests for obscenity in formal fashion. This crime is adopted from Georgia law, which has been upheld by appellate courts and the Supreme Court of Georgia, and which has been approved by the U.S. Supreme Court by its refusal to reverse those decisions and dismiss appeals on this law "for want of a substantial federal question" [*Sewell v. State,* 233 S.E.2d 187 (Sup. Ct. Ga. 1977) and *Teal v. State* (Ct. App. Ga. 1977)]. (Both *Sewell* and *Teal* were dismissed "for want of a substantial federal question" by the U.S. Supreme Court on April 24, 1978, 435 U.S. 982, 435 U.S. 989.)

(b) The defenses to this section provide for legitimate use of such devices for medical, psychological, and governmental–judicial purposes.

SECTION 5. *Making obscene drawings.*

(a) This offense is one to prevent defacing walls, streets, public places, etc., with exhibitions, paint, scratchings, etc., which meet all the tests for obscenity. Nonobscene expression is not covered under this section, for that is encompassed under the general criminal laws against malicious destruction of property.

SECTION 6. *Disseminating matter harmful to minors.*

(a) This subsection provides the elements of the offense. Matter is harmful to minors if it satisfies the definition of Section 1(b) whether or not it is fully obscene, but matter is also harmful if it meets the test of obscenity. The difference in criminality is one of degree, and the offense is a misdemeanor if harmful but not obscene, but is a felony if obscene material is furnished to a juvenile.

(b) The affirmative defenses are meant to protect innocent persons from liability if the juvenile presents false identification or when the parents accompany or consent to the juvenile's exposure to the material, but only when the matter is not obscene but still harmful as defined.

(c) This defense applies to harmful and obscene materials as related to receipt by juveniles, but is limited to defending parents, guardians, and spouses of juveniles and proper persons engaged in scientific or governmental functions where the material is seriously required.

SECTION 7. *Unlawful exhibition or display of harmful materials to minors.*

(a) This offense requires *scienter* of the displayed material of business personnel. Subsection (a)(1) prohibits the allowance of unsupervised minors in any establishment where harmful matter is displayed. This provision does not require the business to restrict the displays of its materials unless minors are allowed into the establishment without parental supervision. Any store which values the trade of juveniles would have to conduct its premises accordingly, but the interests in protecting children from seeing explicit covers or harmful works must be protected and this regulation does so in a manner giving stores a choice between nonoffensive displays and restricting access to adults. Subsection (a)(2) prohibits the actual display of such materials which are harmful to minors but only when such displays can be seen from places where minors cannot be protected from their exposure except by the minors themselves. Subsection (a)(3) forbids the employment or use of minors when such materials would be handled or displayed to them.

(b) Affirmative defenses protect innocent business personnel who take precautions as to proper identification and parental consent and prevent the law from interfering with the parental right to direct children.

SECTION 8. *Unlawful exhibition of harmful performances at outdoor theaters.*

(a) This section prohibits the showing of movies which are "harmful to minors" on any outdoor screen which is both visible from a place where minors are likely to be, such as public streets and residences, and where the screen can be seen from these places.

The provisions for protecting minors from harmful displays has been the subject of state regulation in New York, Rhode Island, Arizona, Ohio, Utah, and local regulation in several other states. As to drive-in movies, the U.S. Supreme Court held in *Erznoznik v. Jacksonville, supra,* that such a law could not merely prohibit movies containing *any* nudity, but must restrict such regulations to nudity which is "harmful to minors" under *Ginsberg v. New York.* Likewise, see *Cinecom Theatres v. City of Fort Wayne,* 473 F.2d 1297 (9th Cir. 1973). Display statutes using Ginsberg's Test have also been upheld in *M.S. News v. Casado,* 712 F.2d 1281 (10th Cir. 1983); *Upper Midwest Booksellers v. Minneapolis,* 602 F.Supp 136 (D. Minn. 1985); *American Booksellers v. Rendell,* 481 A.2d 919 (Pa. Super. 1984).

(b) There are no affirmative defenses to this section since drive-in operators cannot protect juveniles, nor can the law, except by foregoing the display of such harmful movies on screens which are visible from streets, playgrounds, residences, and other such places where minors are expected to be.

SECTION 9. *Deception to obtain matter harmful to minors.*

(a) This section prohibits any person's attempt to aid a minor to obtain or see any harmful or obscene materials by false pretense.

(b) This section prohibits any minor from using false identification or other means to obtain or see any harmful or obscene materials.

SECTION 10. *Compelling acceptance of objectionable materials.*

(a) This offense is common to many states and provides protection for a business that wishes to refrain from dealing in materials which the business "reasonably" believes to be either obscene or harmful to minors. This section prohibits any distributor or other person from linking the sale and right to receive any nonsexual materials, such as general papers and sports and topic magazines, with pornography and so-called "adult" or "men's" magazines which the business retailer could reasonably feel are not desired in the store in order to be able to allow family shopping without restriction.

SECTION 11. *Commercial nudity.*

(a) This section bans nudity in establishments dispensing liquor and was upheld in *New York State Liquor Authority v. Bellanca,* 452 U.S. 714 (1981) and *California v. LaRue,* 409 U.S. 109 (1972).

(b) Those who operate nudity exploitation establishments are given greater responsibility under the law, as opposed to the dancers, hostesses, models, etc.

(c) The section only prohibits conduct if it involves certain types of "service," which is defined to limit the scope of the law.

(d) It is a defense to this section that the nudity was for certain serious value rather than exploitation. This would protect such legitimate acts as African ballet or dance groups, serious plays, etc.

SECTION 12. *Sexual exploitation of children.*

This section generally is a combination child abuse and child pornography statute. The offenses are serious and are felonies. The approach taken to the use of minors in sexually explicit films and materials has been of two types. The federal government, as well as many states such as Ohio, have forbidden the use of minors to engage in sex for purposes of producing materials, and then provide for a crime of dealing in "obscene" materials which feature child performances. Other states, such as New York, Texas, and Kentucky, provide for a crime of using minors in sexual materials and prohibit the dealing in materials which feature minors as actors, without proof that the child pornography is also obscene. This latter approach is adopted for the State in order to provide maximum protection for minors and allow efficient prosecution in order to take the profit motive out of child exploitation without the defenses inherent in obscenity cases. This law was upheld in *New York v. Ferber*, 458 U.S. 747 (1982).

(a) This section provides the elements of exploiting minors, whether married or not, for use in sexual materials.

(b) This section prohibits the promotion of any material which contains a sexual performance by a minor.

(c) This section prohibits the promotion of any "obscene" material which contains a sexual performance by a minor and provides for a greater penalty.

(d) Under (a), there is a defense that the minor presented false identification but this prohibits the reliance upon the oral allegations of the minor as to his or her age to act as a defense, in order to eliminate fraud.

(e) Under (b) and (c), the merchant in sexual materials which are obscene and feature a child, or merely are sexual and feature a child, has the defense of proving "a reasonable factual basis to conclude that the subject . . . was not a juvenile but was in fact over the age of eighteen." If the work is obscene, the lesser offense of Pandering Obscenity could apply.

(f) This section provides guidance for the courts in arriving at a finding that the actor is a minor. Among other methods, the jury or judge may rely on the material or performance itself to determine the age or apparent age of the actor, and provides for expert testimony on this point. Since the actor will almost never be found, the court must be able to rely on the appearance of the actor and the manner of presentation to determine if the book or film holds itself out as containing a minor to prevent abuse.

(g) The actor must be eighteen years old, whether or not married. This is to prevent the actors from wearing wedding bands or getting married solely to frustrate the protections sought to be enforced by the law.

SECTION 13. *Presumption and evidence of knowledge.*

(a) This provision makes a presumption that a dealer in materials or performances knows the character of that which is dealt in if the proof is that the offender has "actual or constructive notice of the nature of such material or performance whether or not he or she has precise knowledge of its contents." This allows proof that the establishment is obviously dealing in sexually explicit works and must therefore be aware that they contain the types of conduct and exhibitions which form the basis for obscenity law. This is meant to prosecute only the calculated purveyance of such materials.

(b) This section provides a method for law enforcement to provide conclusive and actual notice of the type of material or performance upon the dealer by notifying him or her in writing of the content of the work. This provision is similar to Ohio law on this point and allows fair and effective notice to a suspect business, allowing it to adjust if desired. Ohio has such a statutory provision, and it has been employed fairly and effectively to provide advance notice to certain businesses and to aid in the prosecution of certain offenses, usually movies and certain magazines.

(c) This section allows for the introduction of various facts which bear on the circumstances of distribution which give rise to the conclusion that the dealer must be aware of that which he sells or exhibits. Such proof can consist of the manner in which the material is held out to the public, or the manner and reputation of the course of business of the dealer.

(d) This provision specifies that proof of guilty knowledge can be established by direct or circumstantial evidence, or both. Such proof has been used historically in obscenity prosecutions and upheld by the courts. See, for example, *Splawn v. California*, 431 U.S. 595 (1977), and *State of Ohio v. Burgun*, *supra*, 384 N.E.2d 255 (1978).

SECTION 14. *Injunctive actions.*

This section provides for the granting of preliminary and permanent injunctions against the present or imminent promotion of obscene or harmful materials and performances. *Ex parte* temporary restraining orders are not provided for, but under common law and established equity case law, the courts may still use such orders to preserve only the *status quo* and not restrict the promotion of the material or performance itself without hearing.

The general format of these provisions is adapted from the New York provisions approved by the U.S. Supreme Court in *Kingsley Books v. Brown,* 354 U.S. 436 (1957). The Supreme Court has held that the duty is on the government to initiate judicial proceedings to interfere with the promotion of any materials or performances, and requires specific guidelines for the court to follow to ensure a speedy and effective resolution of the issues. See: *Southeastern Promotions v. Conrad,* 420 U.S. 546, at 560 (1975), and *Vance v. Universal Amusements Co., Inc.,* 445 U.S. 308 (1980).

SECTION 15. *Jury instructions—evidence of pandering.*

This provides jury instructions, which also serve as a statement of law which can also be applied by a judge sitting without a jury, allowing any material or performance to be judged in part by the manner in which it was held out or promoted to the public or its intended audience. If a sexually explicit work is promoted and marketed solely for its prurient appeal, rather than for a serious purpose or interest, then these circumstances bear on whether the material is obscene or harmful to juveniles as the case may be. The U.S. Supreme Court approved the use of evidence of "pandering" to help determine obscenity in *Ginzburg v. United States,* 383 U.S. 463 (1966), and specifically approved of the wording of this proposed jury instruction in *Splawn v. California, supra,* 431 U.S., at 597–98, 600.

SECTION 16. *Legislative purpose and severability.*

(a) Due to the changing nature of obscenity law, and the strict viewpoints taken by many courts regarding regulatory statutes affecting the First Amendment, this provision requires that the court save all parts of these statutory provisions which cannot be said to be clearly invalid, even when certain parts are struck down. The duty is upon the court to first attempt to save the statute by authoritative construction to include the proper statements of law and legislative intent, in order to preserve the working of the statutes and eliminate the necessity for the legislature to constantly revise these provisions unnecessarily.

(b) This is a statement of legislative intent to adopt and comply with all applicable constitutional, statutory, and judicial safeguards and rules of law, both in the past and in the future.

MEMO ON HARD-CORE PORNOGRAPHY

"Hard-core pornography" refers to visual materials that depict explicit sexual acts, where penetration of the genitals or ejaculation is clearly visible. The U.S. Supreme Court has historically dealt with the developing "test" for obscenity in relation to the justices' common agreement in the illegality of "hard-core pornography." The "Miller Test," like the "Roth Test," allows material to be found obscene even if it is *not* "hard-core pornography" as commonly understood. In *Roth v. U.S.,* 354 U.S. 476 (1957), the court upheld the convictions of Roth under federal law and Alberts under state law. As Justice Harlan said in his separate opinion, at 500–8, the materials were not "hard-core pornography" (they were not explicit) and the state conviction should be upheld, because the states should have more freedom to regulate pornographic materials, but the federal case should be dismissed, because he felt the U.S. government should be allowed to criminalize only "hard-core" matter. In 1962, Justice Harlan again expressed his view that only "hard-core" pornography should be regulated by the federal government and that pictures of male nudes with covered genitals could not be banned from the mails [*Manual Enterprises v. Day,* 370 U.S. 478 (1962)]. In 1966, a majority of the court recognized that "hard-core" meets the illegality test and that the test for obscenity as expressed in *Roth* reaches materials that are not as explicit as "hard-core pornography." In *Mishkin v. New York,* 383 U.S. 502, at 506 and 508, the court noted:

> Indeed, the definition of "obscene" adopted by the New York courts in interpreting §1141 delimits a narrower class of conduct than delimited under the Roth definition.

> The New York courts have interpreted obscenity in §1141 to cover only so-called "hard-core pornography," . . . Since that definition of obscenity is more stringent than the Roth definition, the judgment that the constitutional criteria

are satisfied is implicit in the application of §1141 below.

The court upheld Mishkin's conviction for books that depicted "deviant sexual practices, such as flagellation, fetishism, and lesbianism" as well as "those dominated by descriptions of relatively normal heterosexual relationships" (see p. 508 and fn. 6).

In *Miller v. California*, 413 U.S. 15, at 24–25 (1973), the court announced the modern "test" for "obscenity." The court explicitly reaffirmed *Roth* as its basis and made it clear that it was reaching more than "hard-core pornography" (in the sense of the "street term" of "PCV"—penetration clearly visible) when it gave its examples of what a state statute could define for regulation under part (b) of the standard ("sexual conduct specifically defined by the applicable state law") on page 25:

(a) Patently offensive representations or descriptions of ultimate sexual acts, normal or perverted, actual or simulated.
(b) Patently offensive representations or descriptions of masturbation, excretory functions, and lewd exhibition of the genitals.

The court referred to these examples as types of sex that comprise "hard-core sexual conduct" (p. 27). The court said such a test—which includes "ultimate sexual acts, normal or perverted, actual or simulated . . . and lewd exhibition of the genitals"— was necessary to prevent "hard-core pornography" from being "exposed without limit to the juvenile, the passerby, and the consenting adult alike" (p. 28).

Had the court followed the Harlan view, it would have limited the "Miller Test" to actual depictions of ultimate sex acts and not included simulated depictions and lewd exhibitions of the genitals. To so limit the federal government, or the states, would have provided little protection against the growing explicitness and deviance of the porno industry—in effect allowing only the worst forms of pornography to be targeted and thereby guaranteeing that much "hard-core" and offensive "medium-core" materials would be openly distributed. Such a "hard-core" limitation would have required the court to abandon the "pandering" concept, established in *Ginzburg v. U.S.*, 383 U.S. 463 (1966), where materials which were not "hard-core," and the court notes may not even be "obscene" standing alone, to be subject to conviction if the pornographer panders them as if they were obscene and highly prurient. The court said if someone exploits the prurient—erotic— qualities of a work, then this is evidence that the treatment of sex is for solely commercial purposes rather than for legitimate social value. In other words,

if you act as a pornographer and hold out your items as pornography, then the courts can take you at your word and convict you. Only by restraining sexual materials, both the explicit and the pandered, can a "decent society" be protected from "the crass commercial exploitation of sex," as the court discusses in *Paris Adult Theatre v. Slaton*, 413 U.S. 49, 63–70 (1973).

There is a difference between hard-core sexual conduct and "hard-core pornography." Hard core conduct refers to *types* of sex—ultimate sexual acts and lewd exhibitions of the genitals. "Hard-core pornography" refers to a *way* of depicting ultimate sexual acts—explicitly depicting genital penetration or ejaculation. Hard-core conduct—the "Miller Examples"—can be depicted in a "hard-core" way (PCV), a "medium-core" way (simulated), or even a "soft-core" way (posing of nudes with focus on genitals). These three kinds of pornography can all be found "obscene" under *Miller* (such as *Deep Throat*, *Vixen*, and *Penthouse*), but only if presented in a patently offensive way under community standards of decency and in a way which appeals to the prurient interest and then only when the work has no serious value. As stated in *Miller*, at 26: "At a minimum, prurient, patently offensive depiction or description of sexual conduct must have serious literary, artistic, political, or scientific value to meet First Amendment protection."

There is always more agreement by researchers, and even the public, that child porn, violent porn (soft and hard), and other more degrading or bizarre porn is harmful and causes or contributes to antisocial and criminal behavior, as noted by the Attorney General's Commission. However, the Supreme Court has never required obscenity laws to be based on or limited by current research or the opinions of college professors and doctors who wish to change the present law. The court has been steadfast in allowing the Congress and state legislatures to define the crime of obscenity to the limits that the "Miller Test" makes constitutionally permissible. The court set out three prongs of the test in *Miller*, and characteristics of materials are relevant to these three prongs. Prosecutors and police have no right, though they have the actual power, to add prongs to the test or diminish the law's constitutional reach. Material is not illegal only if it is obscene under *Miller* and also violent or degrading or deviant. There is no fourth prong, and to allow or condone the limitation of the "Miller Test" to only violent hard-core pornography, or violent "soft-core" pornography, or degrading hard-core or degrading soft-core material makes the enforcement of the law all the more difficult even against the targets that a particular person wants to have enforcement on. Prosecutors can set community standards by their cases and if they only prosecute "A, B, C, D, E," then other obscene and "hardcore" material will be in effect legalized—a clear and improper departure from *Miller* and a usurpation of legislative and judicial prerogatives.

Obviously, simulated and normal sexual acts and lewd exhibitions of the genitals (even without conduct) are not "hard-core pornography" in the strict sense, even though they are types of hard-core sexual activities—as opposed to mere nudity and fondling—and yet these can be found "obscene" and illegal under the federal and state "Miller Test." It is "implicit," as stated in *Mishkin*, that if such hardcore types of sex are depicted in a "hard-core" fashion (meaning explicitly—"PCV"), then the material is clearly and obviously illegal and can be subject to criminal and civil penalties as obscene under federal and state statutes. Under the "Miller Test," issues of *Penthouse* and *Oui* magazines, but not *Playboy*, were found obscene by one of the biggest federal courts in the country in *Penthouse v. McAuliffe*, 610 F.2d 1353 (5th Cir. 1980). In Ohio, the movie "Vixen" was enjoined as obscene under the pre-Miller "Roth Test" and then re-affirmed as obscene by the Ohio Supreme Court after *Miller* and by applying the "Miller Test" in *State of Ohio, ex rel. Keating v. A Film Entitled "Vixen"*, 35 Ohio St.2d. 215, 301 N.E.2d 880 (1973), where the Supreme Court of Ohio stated, at page 218:

> Doubt can no longer remain that the depiction of purported acts of sexual intercourse on the movie screen and the public exhibition thereof "for commercial exploitation rather than for a genuine, scientific, educational, sociological, moral, or artistic purpose" is forbidden by Ohio law. Here, there is no dispute as to the fact that "Vixen does depict numerous acts of purported sexual intercourse, and obviously it does so for a commercial purpose. . . .
>
> Therefore, where scenes in a motion picture film depict purported acts of sexual intercourse and are exhibited for commercial exploitation, those scenes are violative of R. C. 2905.34 and 2905.35, constitute a "nuisance" within the meaning of R. C. 3767.01 and their exhibition may be enjoined as provided in R. C. 3767.02 et seq.
>
> This court is of the opinion that the statutes applied in this case initially by the court comport with the standards enunciated in Miller. Therefore, we adhere to our holding that the motion picture film Vixen "does depict numerous acts of purported sexual intercourse . . . for a commercial purpose," in violation of R. C. 2905.34 and 2905.35, and that its "exhibition may be enjoined as provided in R. C. 3767.02, et seq.

Former assistant U.S. attorney Larry Parish obtained federal convictions for conspiracy to distribute the hard-core film *School Girl* in *U.S. v. Sandy*, 605 F.2d 210, 213 (6th Cir. 1979). *Deep Throat* was also subject to conviction, and after two trials with guilty verdicts, the obscenity of the film and convictions were upheld in *U.S. v. Battista*, 646 F.2d 237, 243 (6th Cir. 1981), cert. denied 454 U.S. 1046 (1981). *Deep Throat* has been found obscene by more state and federal appeal courts than any other movie. A list of some of these cases is set out in the civil complaint filed by the county attorney in Phoenix against the showing of the film by Arizona State University college students. A permanent injunction was issued as a result.

It is not open to debate that all explicit sexual materials can be found obscene and that nonexplicit, simulated material can also violate the *Miller* standards. That much the Supreme Court has made clear. Whether the theme or context of the sex is violent, consensual, degrading, or bizarre is an element only of how "patently offensive" a *way* the sex is depicted. The court in *Miller* did not require patently offensive sexual acts—but rather sexual acts in a patently offensive way. *Miller* requires an average person, applying contemporary community standards, to find that the work depicts or describes ultimate sexual acts, normal or perverted, actual or simulated, masturbation, excretory functions, or lewd exhibition of the genitals in a *patently offensive way*. As made clear in *Mishkin*, and by Justice Harlan, and in the cases sustained on appeal since *Miller*, these materials can include the violent ("Devil in Miss Jones") as well as non-violent ("Deep Throat"), the simulated ("Vixen"), and the so-called "soft-core" or "medium-core" ("Penthouse"). Just as clearly, all "hard-core pornography" must remain subject to federal and state regulation in order to curtail the ravages of a pornography syndicate, dominated by organized crime, which creates and controls an industry of prostitution to provide the current explosion of "hard-core," explicit, XXX, "adult" films, magazines, and videotapes.

Although prosecutors do not ordinarily prosecute magazines such as "Hustler" and "Penthouse," the courts agree that all "PCV," "hard-core pornography," is fair game for obscenity statutes. It has been argued by the defense attorneys for the porn industry and the AFAA (Adult Film Association of America) that the only items which should be considered "hard-core" or obscene are "A, B, C, D, E" items (Animals, Bondage, Children, Deviants, and Excretion); and they don't think even these should be prosecuted if it is just "acting" rather than actual—which, of course, they don't do! The porn magazine lobby—Grey & Co.—has also advertised the concept that only "blood and goats" and child porn with little kids are illegal and proper targets for "censorship." The Supreme Court states that all obscenity is illegal and that all "hard-core pornography" is obscene. CDL [Citizens for Decency Through Law, Inc.] is dedicated to this position and has even expressed the opinion that federal and state statutes which would make all "hard-core pornography" per se unlawful to sell or distribute would be constitutional and upheld by the Supreme Court. (See *Criminal Justice Reform*, chapter 11, "Pornography and the First Amendment," by Bruce Taylor, pp. 165–68.)

If law enforcement agents, prosecutors, and especially citizen and religious leaders drop "community standards" to the level of the AFAA, then prosecutions would only be *considered* against the most secretive and out of the ordinary materials. This would tend to legitimize, if not legalize, the bulk of the industry's hard-core trade—which is the main problem facing America's communities in the form of "adult" bookstores and theaters ("hard-core shops"), video stores renting and selling hard-core tapes, and the massive interstate mailing and shipment of the syndicate's lifeblood.

The U.S. Supreme Court and the highest courts of our states have given communities the right to fight to remove all obscene materials. CDL will take this fight to the death. To this we dedicate our talents and energy. The fight may go 15 rounds, but the result must be a knock-out, even if a TKO, in order to sustain the burden we have been blessed with.

—Bruce A. Taylor
  General Counsel
  Citizens for Decency Through Law, Inc.

B HOW PASSAGE OF PORNOGRAPHY LAWS IS PREVENTED

In 1983, Kathleen Nichols, a county supervisor in Dane County, Wisconsin, proposed a civil rights ordinance. She received dozens of abusive phone calls and false invitations to meetings around the nation. Someone broke into her apartment, left her pornography files strewn across a desk, and stole her mail. Nichols believes that "someone was trying to scare her away from backing the anti-porn bill." It worked. She dropped the proposal.

Also in Madison, Wisconsin, on April 11, 1985, Wisconsin state representative James A. Rutkowski asked the Legislative Reference Bureau (LRB) to draft a state law modeled after the Minneapolis and Indianapolis ordinances and to improve the state's weak child pornography statute. Attorney Sara Lee Johann, co-author of this book, was Representative Rutkowski's legislative aide. In the months that followed, she did extensive research on the effects of pornography and legal approaches to its regulation. She played a major role in drafting the proposed civil rights and child pornography bills in Wisconsin.

The Wisconsin civil rights bill and the child pornography bill were scheduled to be formally introduced in the legislature in September 1985. In late August, Rutkowski's state capitol office was burglarized. Intruders used a wire device to gain entrance through an office window. They stole a tape player (conspicuously leaving the tape that had been in it behind) and some one-of-a-kind pens with Rutkowski's name on them (which suggests the burglary was aimed specifically at him and his office). The cover was pulled off the air conditioner. Rutkowski's desk drawer was sprayed full of shaving cream, and the empty can was left open on top of the desk. An open, used bottle of typewriter eraser fluid was left on an aide's desk. A pencil sharpener was moved from Rutkowski's desk to that of aide Sara Lee Johann. A radio antenna was bent, and a

wastebasket was moved from out in the hall into Rutkowski's office.

On the evening of Friday, August 23, 1985, an attorney from the LRB had slipped handwritten notes for changes in Johann's draft of the civil rights bill under the door of Rutkowski's office. He was planning to go away on vacation the next week, and Johann was expected to work on the draft during that time.

When Johann discovered the break-in on the afternoon of Sunday, August 25, 1985, the LRB attorney's notes were found conspicuously leaning on the other aide's chair arm *and* desk. The word *Sorry* was written in typewriter eraser fluid on the desk directly in front of the law draft. Johann believes that the break-in was timed to stop introduction of the legislation by threatening, frightening, or blackmailing Rutkowski.

It worked. The next week, Rutkowski told Johann that he was dropping the civil rights bill.

Rutkowski never introduced that bill or the child pornography bill and did what he could to see that other legislators did not take up those proposals. A bill to create a new constitutional obscenity bill in Wisconsin (to replace the one ruled unconstitutional by the state's supreme court) had been pending in the Assembly Judiciary Committee (chaired by Rutkowski) since January 1985. Rutkowski made it clear to Johann that he never supported *that* bill. Part of his motivation for proposing the civil rights and child pornography bills had been to find alternatives to the obscenity bill. Rutkowski's lack of support for the obscenity bill is proven by the fact that he refused to hold a public hearing on the bill until December 1985, despite repeated demands from constituents, legislators, and others. He also had arranged for a fiscal note to be attached to the bill—which had the effect of requiring the bill to be passed by the Joint Finance Committee in addition to the Judiciary Committee. Lastly, he had allowed the bill out of his committee (in weakened form) only in the concluding weeks of the legislative session, with the

---

This appendix is based on the personal knowledge of Sara Lee Johann and "Hell Is for Children," which appears as appendix I.

result that it never got to the assembly floor for a vote.

Despite these facts, Rutkowski, who disputes that his office was burglarized because of the pornography proposals, told a reporter in May 1986 that "he gave up on the legislation because he became more concerned with the obscenity bill which was before his Judiciary Committee." Most frightening about all of this is that by threatening, blackmailing, or frightening Rutkowski, the propornography forces managed to prevent any consideration of antipornography legislation in the assembly during the 1985–86 session—and possibly in the future—if Rutkowski remains as chairman of the Judiciary Committee.

At the December 3, 1985, public hearing on the obscenity bill, Johann went public with the story about the break-in to Rutkowski's office. Rutkowski fired her a couple of weeks later, giving no reason for the firing. Johann believes that she was fired for exercising her First Amendment right to take a stand against pornography. In mid-1988, an obscenity law finally passed the Wisconsin legislature—but only after the governor had made it part of a special legislative session.

C CLICHÉ ARGUMENTS

PORNOGRAPHY, OBSCENITY LAW

1. Are you advocating censorship?

Answer: Absolutely not. We are advocating enforcement of obscenity laws. Censorship is prior restraint by government. No American would stand still for this. However, there are laws prohibiting the dissemination of obscenity. Anyone can produce anything he pleases, but he is responsible after the fact if he is violating the law.

2. Freedom of expression is protected by the First Amendment.

Answer: It most certainly is. But the Supreme Court has said, and has always held, that obscenity is not protected by the First Amendment. It is not protected expression, any more than libel or slander is. Obscenity is *not* a First Amendment issue. It is a *crime*, and 90% of the traffic in hardcore pornography in the country is controlled by *organized* crime.

3. The porno industry is flourishing and growing, so the American people must want it or must accept it.

Answer: a. Certainly there are some who want it. That's what makes it so profitable. But all surveys show that the majority of Americans are vehemently opposed to the traffic in pornography and want it stopped. The majority *do* care; but they are confused and discouraged in the face of a highly organized industry and the loud prophets of false freedom. This is the reason the organization Morality in Media exists: to expose the false prophets, to vindicate the true freedoms of responsibility under law, and to raise in an organized way, the voice of the majority who care very much about standards of public morality.

One of the major factors in the growth of the pornography traffic is the lack of vigorous enforcement of obscenity laws, particularly at the federal level.

b. Because pornography is so available does not mean it is acceptable to the people. The U.S. Supreme Court said in 1974, "Mere availability of similar materials by itself means nothing more than that other persons are engaged in similar activities."

4. Obscenity is a "victimless crime."

Answer: a. There is no such thing as a "victimless" crime. In every crime there is a seller or seducer and the person who purchases, or the seduced. That person is the immediate victim, and society is the ultimate victim, for with each seduction the moral fabric of society is diminished. The "victimless crime" theory is an active and insidious attack on almost all laws dealing with public morality, maintaining there is "no victim" when "consenting adults" indulge in drugs, prostitution, obscenity, incest, etc.

b. A glaring instance of victimization in obscenity is the use of children in child pornography.

c. For centuries, civil communities have maintained laws against such behavior as detrimental to the public health, morals, and welfare.

d. The Boston Combat Zone has vividly proved that an increase in commercial pornography causes concentration of violent prostitution and organized crime.

e. In a 1970 study 55% of rapists interviewed reported they had been triggered into action by pornography.

5. How do *you* define obscenity?

Answer: How I define obscenity is not the issue. The Supreme Court has defined obscenity, to the satisfaction of most, as materials which "taken as a whole appeal to the prurient interest in sex, which portray sexual conduct in a patently offensive way, and which, taken as a whole, do not have serious literary, artistic, political or scientific value."

6. Well, the Supreme Court has said a lot of things, but it still can't define obscenity clearly.

Answer: This statement is incorrect. The Supreme Court defined obscenity in June of 1973, and the definition is adequate.

These arguments and answers were originally published in pamphlet form by Morality in Media, Inc., New York. They are reprinted here with permission.

7. But the Supreme Court left it to communities to decide what is obscene.

Answer: This is an oversimplification and a misleading one. Community standards is not *the* test for obscenity, but a *part* of the test for obscenity, and has been part of the test for obscenity since 1957. In 1973 the court said: "The basic guidelines for the trier of the fact must be: a. whether 'the average person, applying contemporary community standards' would find that the work, taken as a whole appeals to the prurient interest . . . . b. whether the work depicts or describes, in a patently offensive way, sexual conduct specifically defined by the applicable state law, and c. whether the work, taken as a whole, lacks serious . . . value." It is the "trier of the fact," a jury or a judge, who decides what is obscene under the guidelines, putting themselves in the place of the average person to determine or apply community standards.

8. When "consenting adults" watch porno videocassettes at home, no one is being harmed. I have a right to watch what I choose to watch in my own home.

Answer: Regarding so-called "consenting adults," the United States Supreme Court said in *Paris Theatre* in June of 1973: "We categorically disapprove the theory that obscene films acquire constitutional immunity from state regulation simply because they are exhibited for consenting adults only. Rights and interests other than those of the advocates are involved. These include the interest of the public in the quality of life, the total community environment, the tone of commerce and, possibly, the public safety itself."

Videoporn is no different than other pornography. There is no such thing as a constitutional "right" to watch pornography. And it is against the law for any merchant to sell or rent obscene material to you. The law is not aimed at you, but at the distributor and seller of obscene videocassettes. Obscenity laws apply to videocassettes as they do to any type of obscenity, in whatever medium it is produced.

9. If you don't like porn films and books, you don't have to see them or buy them, but don't interfere with my right to see or buy them.

Answer: a. I don't see or buy pornography, but it is there polluting the environment in which I am trying to raise my children. Society says it does not want it there and has enacted laws against it.

b. The United States Supreme Court has said that what you do in the privacy of your home is your own business, but your privacy right does not extend to the marketplace. It is against the law for anyone to sell or exhibit obscenity to you.

10. You can't legislate morality.

Answer: a. On its face this cliché is absurd, because every law legislates morality. Every law sets some standard for its citizens, and every citizen must ultimately make the moral decision to obey or disobey.

b. Private morals are private; public morals are the business of the entire community and of the officers empowered by the community to defend its welfare against the willful minority. Commercial obscenity is public business. It is public morality that obscenity laws are designed to safeguard, not private morality.

11. Obscenity is in the eye of the beholder. What is obscene to you may not be obscene to me.

Answer: This implies that obscenity is subjective. It is not. It is the description or depiction of specific sexual activity—the description or depiction of which is prohibited by law, to protect the common good. It is as objective as stealing or murder.

12. Who are you to tell me what I can see or read? You are imposing your morality on me.

Answer: a. Nobody can tell you what to see or to read, but the community can tell you what commercial materials cannot be sold or distributed to you—if you choose to live in that community. The community sets up standards for itself and has a right to legislate to protect those standards.

b. Nobody is imposing his morality on anybody. It is only the consensus of the community that determines the standards of public decency. When that consensus is properly manifested in public law, that is community or public morality, not "ours."

c. Judge Robert Bork, former solicitor general of the United States, has said, "One of the freedoms, the major freedom of the society, is the freedom to choose to have a public morality."

13. Pornography is harmless. The 1970 Presidential Commission report said so.

Answer: a. The 1970 Majority Report of the Presidential Commission on Obscenity and Pornography was called a "scientific scandal" by many in the scientific community. It was rejected by the U.S. Senate by a vote of 60 to 5. The Hill–Link Minority Report of that Commission was read into the record in both Houses of Congress as a "responsible position on the issues." The Hill–Link report cited numerous instances where evidence was suppressed when it went counter to the predetermined "findings" of the majority report. The Hill–Link report and the chapters by Dr. Victor B. Cline in "Where Do You Draw the Line?" expose the majority report for what it is. In addition, studies in the Hill–Link report show linkages between exposure to obscene material and sexual deviancy, promiscuity, affiliation with criminal groups, and more. However, pornographers and their defenders who want obscenity laws repealed will continue to resurrect this discredited report.

b. The Supreme Court in *Paris Theatre v. Slaton* (June 1973) said: "The sum of experience, including that of the past two decades, affords an ample basis for legislatures to conclude that a sensitive, key relationship of human existence, central to family life, community welfare and the development of human personality, can be debased and distorted by crass commercial exploitation of sex."

14. Why bother enforcing the law? The "adult" bookstores and porno movie houses keep operating while their owners are in the courts.

Answer: Continuous, vigorous enforcement of the law is the answer. When arrests and prosecutions begin, the sex industry is put on warning. Prison sentences, fines, legal fees will put the pornographers out of business. Atlanta, Jacksonville, and Cincinnati are clean cities because of vigorous, continuous enforcement of the law. And experts say that with aggressive enforcement of federal law, the back of the porno industry would be broken in 18 months. Also, the inclusion of obscenity in the federal RICO (Racketeer Influenced and Corrupt Organizations) law provides for confiscation of all of the pornographers' porno-related assets. Some states have also enacted RICO laws and included obscenity.

15. How is a producer or publisher to know his material is obscene when the court can't even decide what is obscene?

Answer: The court has decided what is obscene, and it is up to a person who traffics in pornography to be alert to Supreme Court decisions. The court said in its landmark *Miller* decision when it defined obscenity, "We are satisfied that these prerequisites (the three-part test) will provide fair notice to a dealer in such materials that his public and commercial activities may bring prosecution."

16. Why be concerned about obscenity when there is so much violent crime?

Answer: They're related. Pornography outlets breed and attract violent crime.

17. If you'd let pornography flow freely, people would get bored and the problem would take care of itself.

Answer: a. This boredom or satiation theory is invalid. Heavy users of pornography do not get bored. They go deeper and deeper into more and more bizarre forms of it.

b. Professor Irving Kristol has said: "I would like to go along with this theory (boredom), but I cannot. I think it is false. The sexual pleasure one gets from pornography is autoerotic and infantile; put bluntly, it is a masturbatory exercise of the imagination when it is not masturbation pure and simple. Now, people who masturbate do not get tired of masturbation, just as sadists don't get bored with sadism and voyeurs don't get bored with voyeurism. In other words, infantile sexuality is not only a permanent temptation—it can easily become a self-reinforcing neurosis."

c. Remember, every day a new generation of children is being exposed to pornography for the first time. Pornography strikes at children in the mails, on newsstands, etc., and creates new markets for the vulnerable.

18. I'd rather see people make love than make violence.

Answer: There is no love in pornography. It is totally loveless, debasing women, children, and all humanity. In addition, violence is inherent in all pornography, even in that described as "nonviolent."

19. War, poverty, hunger, and violence are the real obscenities. Sex is not obscene.

Answer: a. The extension of the word *obscenity* to cover all kinds of social evils is a recent development in our language. It is a well-known technique to confuse and blunt the force of obscenity law.

b. Of course sex is not obscene. It is the design and creation of God. It is the debasing abuse of sex that is obscene. And, as in the past, so now all over the country, legislatures and the judiciary definitely specify certain depicted abuses of sex as obscene.

CABLEPORN

1. If you don't want to see pornography on cable TV, turn the dial.
Answer: I have no obligation to do this. The obligation is on the cable operator not to transmit pornography. The U.S. Supreme Court said, in the case of broadcasting, in 1978 that the "turn the dial" argument does not hold water. I have already been assaulted. The court said it's like running away after I have been attacked by a mugger.

2. A law prohibiting indecency on cable would interfere with the First Amendment rights of the cable operator, with the free flow of information.
Answer: There is already a federal law prohibiting the *broadcasting* of the obscene, indecent, and profane, and it has never interfered with the free flow of information in broadcasting. Cablecasting, the U.S. Department of Justice has decided, does not come under the purview of the broadcasting law because it is transmitted through wires. Only obscene cable TV is presently prohibited by law. But there should be the same regulation of cable as there is of broadcasting. Different technology or not, it comes through the same instrument, the TV set, into the home.

3. In trying to get a law passed that prohibits cableporn, you're trying to tell me what I can see.
Answer: Nobody can tell you what you can see. But the community can tell you what cannot be transmitted through the cable wires. The community sets up standards for itself, and has a right to legislate to protect those standards.

4. But I want to see porno programming in my home, and I pay to see it.
Answer: You might pay for it, but once the cable operator transmits pornography through that wire, it is released on the community; it then becomes the community's business; and the community can legislate against it. And the law is aimed, not at you, but at the cable operator who transmits the cableporn to you. You might also want to pay $5 to see a porno movie in a movie house, but it is against the law for the owner to exhibit it to you. You might want to watch a porno videocassette in your home, but it is against the law for a dealer to sell or rent it to you. You might want heroin in your home, and pay for it, but it is against the law for the seller to sell it to you.

5. The cable operator says only those who pay for cableporn will get it, so if you don't want it, you don't have to subscribe to it.
Answer: Again, once the cableporn is released on the community, it is the community's business. In addition, there have been complaints from many areas of the country that the signals of cableporn channels are "bleeding" over onto the sets of people who don't subscribe to them. Audio signals are clear and unscrambled; video signals fade in and out clearly.

There is also cableporn on public access channels, which come into homes for the basic cable fee; and any child can tune in these channels at any time.

6. If you don't want your children to see cableporn, the cable operator can offer lockout boxes.
Answer: There is no lockout box that is a match for a child's curiosity. Children have found ways to bring a cableporn channel into nonsubscribing homes simply by jiggling the key on the cable channel selector. Today's children are high-tech experts and just as curious as ever.

7. If you don't want cableporn bleeding over onto your set, don't subscribe at all.
Answer: Nobody should have to deprive himself of cable TV because a few porno peddlers are giving the industry a bad name. Cable TV is a medium of great potential, of infinite variety. It should be regulated in the same manner as broadcasting.

8. What about "consenting adults" who want to see porn movies in their home?
Answer: The U.S. Supreme Court said in *Paris Theatre* v. *Slaton*, "we categorically disapprove the theory . . . ." See question 8 in the previous section.

D MORALITY GROUPS

American Family Association
Rev. Donald E. Wildmon, Executive Director
107 Parkgate
P.O. Drawer 2440
Tupelo, MS 38803
(601) 844-5036

Citizens for Decency Through Law, Inc.
Charles H. Keating, Jr., Founder
2845 East Camelback Road
Suite 740
Phoenix, AZ 85016
(602) 381-1322

Morality in Media, Inc.
and National Obscenity Law Center
Paul J. Murphy, S.J., President
475 Riverside Drive
New York, NY 10015
(212) 870-3222
(212) 870-3232

National Christian Association
Brad Curl, President
P.O. Box 40945
Washington, DC 20016
(202) 296-7155

National Coalition Against Pornography, Inc.
Jerry R. Kirk, President
Richard E. McLawhorn, Esq., Executive Director
800 Compton Road
Suite 9248
Cincinnati, OH 45231
(513) 521-6227

Religious Alliance Against Pornography
c/o National Coalition Against Pornography, Inc.
800 Compton Road
Suite 9248
Cincinnati, OH 45231
(513) 521-6227

E FEMINIST GROUPS

Citizens for Media Responsibility Without Law
(Outlaws for Social Responsibility)
P.O. Box 671
Oshkosh, WI 54902

Feminist Anti-Censorship Task Force (FACT)
Box 135
660 Amsterdam Avenue
New York, NY 10025
(201) 756-2665

National Organization for Women
1401 New York Avenue NW
Suite 800
Washington, DC 20005
(202) 347-2279

Organizing Against Pornography:
A Resource Center for Education and Action
310 East 38th Street
Minneapolis, MN 55409
(612) 822-1476

Task Force on Prostitution and Pornography
P.O. Box 1602
Madison, WI 53701

Women Against Pornography
358 West 47th Street
New York, NY 10036
(212) 307-5055

WOMEN AGAINST PORNOGRAPHY: FEMINIST ANTIPORNOGRAPHY CRUSADES IN AMERICAN SOCIETY*

R. George Kirkpatrick
Department of Sociology
San Diego State University
San Diego, California

Louis A. Zurcher, Jr.
School of Social Work and
Department of Sociology
The University of Texas, Austin

PORNOGRAPHY AND ITS DISCONTENTS

In *Citizens for Decency*, (1) we explained the opposition to pornography of Christian groups in the midwestern and southwestern parts of the United States as attempts on the part of a declining old middle class to protect the endangered prestige of its style of life. Pornography is understood as a collective representation of "social fact" in the tradition of the sociology of Emile Durkheim (2). Pornography is part of the ideological superstructure of modern industrial society (3), according to the Marxian model of society (4). Pornography will be seen by future generations of sociologists in future civilizations as a concrete artifact of the patriarchal civilization of the West.

In the last ten years, feminists in and out of the universities have been developing a powerful critique of pornography (5) as "the ideology of rape" and the "ideological justification for male dominance." The present article is a sociological analysis of the feminist social movement which has grown up around the issues of male violence and male culture. We present original data from survey research including 35 questionnaires completed by feminist antipornogra-phy crusaders in 12 cities around the United States. Data on the ideology, beliefs, attitudes, goals, social and demographic and demographic composition and strategy and tactics used by feminist antipornography organizations and their active members are presented and analysed in the light of Feminist, Marxist and traditional "Labelling School" explanations of the characterological and motivational substructure of such mass movements of moral indignation against male dominated culture.

We believe that it is easy to justify the sociological and social importance of such research, given the amount of money involved in the pornography industry and the large numbers of women participating in these moral crusades, especially in California, New York and Massachusetts. With memberships over 1,000 and marches of over 1,000 participants and rallies estimated at 1,000 participants or more, the strength of the feminist moral crusade seems greater than that of the opposition of the Christian old middle class. Feminists estimate the pornography industry as an industry in the billions of dollars a year, with a potential increase in the near future in the field of home video; it seems clear that the political and economic aspects of the pornography industry make it a serious topic for sociological study.

The word "pornography" usually implies that sexually explicit materials are in some way bad, evil or harmful. Sometimes, the word can have a positive connotation, but in either case there is the implicit

*Paper read at meetings of the Popular Culture Association, Wichita, Kansas, April 23–26, 1983. Reprinted with permission.

Authors wish to gratefully acknowledge the assistance of Rolf Shultz, George N. Katsiaficas, Joseph R. Gusfield, Armund L. Mauss, Jim Wood, Ralph Turner, Mary Lou Emery, Anne Rossi, Jack Delaura, Frank Balzer, Marilee Coombs, and the members of the San Francisco Women Against Pornography and Violence in Media.

notion that such materials lead to sexual arousal, at least among men, and in some cases to actual sexual behaviour.

Studies of sexual behaviour which have attempted to take a neutral scientific point of view included the famous Kinsey researches, which treated sexual behaviour of the 10,000 men and 12,000 women that were interviewed as they would the sexual behaviour of any other mammal, without concerning themselves with the content of the mores or social norms involved (6).

Social anthropologists and comparative sociologists have a better chance to hold such value judgments constant, because they are involved in comparing institutions and practices concerned with sexually explicit cultural artifacts of one culture with the next. But whatever the value judgment attached to sexually explicit or sexually arousing material in a particular culture, pornography is undoubtedly a "social fact."

American sociologists have been more concerned with reactions to and creation of social facts by the audience or public that responds to it than with the social facts themselves as things. In other words, Americans have been more interested in the origins of social facts in the responses of individuals, organisations, courts, legislative bodies to certain social phenomena, and how such reactions create social facts of various kinds (7).

We see the laws and social movements that oppose pornography as similar to the laws passed against and the social movements which have opposed alcohol (8) and marijuana. Alcohol prohibition, marijuana prohibition and the prohibition of sexually explicit materials have in common the characteristic of being moral crusades.

To understand the proclivity of American culture for moral crusades, one need only to go back to the Puritan beginnings of our society (9). The New England states were settled primarily and first by upright, abstinent, sexually repressive Protestants, and we have never fully been able to escape this heritage in the two hundred years of immigration of peoples from cultures not similarly Puritan. The lifestyle of the Christian old rural middle class had a need to be sober, sexually proper, industrious, hardworking and morally pure.

We have argued that the primary impetus of right wing antipornography crusades came from the descendents of rural, old middle class Christians, who see defense of sexual abstinent life-styles as part of a defense of their overall status as the representatives of "real America." These are the same elements that supported the Prohibition movement.

The word pornography originally comes from the Greek word *porne* which referred to one of the five classes of prostitutes in the ancient Greek city state (10). The *porne* were the common or street prostitutes as opposed to the courtesans, the dancers, the concubines (who occupied a position within the Greek family or household) and the temple prostitutes. Pornography then implies the art, writings, pictures, statues, etc., produced by the prostitutes with the sole or primary purpose of sexual arousal of their male clients. It is fair to say then, that historically and philologically speaking, pornography is writings or pictures designed to arouse men sexually and ultimately, perhaps, to increase the trade of these common prostitutes.

Today, and since the publication of the Report of the Presidential Commission on Obscenity and Pornography, there are no laws restricting the sale of pornographic materials, except to minors, or unsolicited through the mail, or materials which depict criminal activity such as sexually explicit materials involving juveniles. The conclusions of the Presidential Commission, of which our study *Citizens for Decency* was a part, included the following:

> Extensive empirical investigation . . . provides no evidence that exposure to or use of explicit sexual materials play a significant role in the causation of social or individual harms such as crime, delinquency, sexual or nonsexual deviancy or severe emotional disturbances.

Today, however, in addition to opponents of pornography on the Christian right that can be viewed in the context of right wing extremism, (11) are the new feminist opponents of pornography that can be found on the left. It is a somewhat ironic situation that right wing persons are in essential agreement on the issue of pornography with such notable radical feminists as Susan Brownmiller and Andrea Dworkin. Brownmiller, author of the feminist attack on rape, *Against Our Will*, (12) argues that there is a direct *causal* link between pornography and rape including child molestation and incest. She describes pornography as "anti-woman propaganda" and she believes it should be suppressed in a fashion similar to the suppression of racist, anti-Black and anti-Semitic propaganda. Andrea Dworkin, in her book *Women Hating*, (13) suggests that pornography is part of heterosexual culture in general which she calls "misogynist" because it portrays women in degrading and subordinate relationships to men.

On the right, we find Rev. Morton Hill, a Roman Catholic priest and the president of Morality in Media, a national antipornography organisation, and Charles Keating, a Nixon appointee to the Commission on Obscenity and Pornography and the founder of Citizens for Decent Literature, Inc. According to Rev. Hill:

> We believe that pornography has an eroding effect on society, on public morality, on respect for human worth, on attitudes toward family love, on culture. . . . We believe it is impossible and totally unnecessary to attempt to prove or disapprove a cause–effect relationship between pornography and criminal behaviour. . . . Pornography is loveless: it degrades the human being, reduces him to the level of animal. . . . We believe government must legislate to regulate pornography, in order to protect the social interest in order and morality (pp. 458–459).

It is interesting to note in this context that one of the persons interviewed in our previous study *Citizens for Decency* who was a public health official in an industrial city in the Midwest felt that pornography was the cause of illegitimacy, sexual promiscuity and V.D. He also believed that V.D. had reached epidemic proportions because of the flood of pornography available.

It is not our task to explain pornography. Pornography is a social fact of our society whatever value judgment one might place upon it, from the right or the left. Our task, somewhat more modest, is to explain the social movements which oppose pornography, the structure of and participation in such movements, and the creation of laws or other strategies which such movements undertake to achieve their goals of changing, modifying or protecting moral norms regarding sexually explicit materials (14).

The basic theory of status politics is based on the sociology of Max Weber (15). According to Weber, there are three autonomous spheres of social differentiation which can become arenas of social conflict and political struggle. These are class, status and party. Class conflict and class politics, often discussed by Marx, (16) should be familiar to all of us. Power politics, or politics as such, separate from class is as old as Aristotle and Machiavelli, Hobbes and Rousseau. Status politics, or the politics of prestige and life-style, however, have not been examined as much by political scientists, economists and sociologists. And it is this third dimension that, according to Gusfield, holds the key to an understanding of moral crusades.

There seems little doubt that antipornography crusades are moral crusades. They are collective attempts to change, modify or preserve moral norms relevant to sexually explicit materials. The rural, old middle class Christians, whose life-style does tend to dominate the right wing antipornography crusades, are trying to protect and conserve a life-style based on sobriety and sexual repression—or at least sexuality which is narrowly contained within marriage in the Christian Ideal—from a hedonistic life-style based on pleasure, sexual promiscuity or moral lapses with drugs, alcohol and sexual activity. The left wing antipornography crusader, the feminist, is engaged in a similar status struggle. She desires to raise the status of women and perceives the submission of women to nude photography as a ceremonial degradation of the status of woman, to which, had she enough power or a high enough status, she would not have to submit. The feminists demand that women do not have to submit to the pornographer's camera is like the civil rights leader's demand that blacks sit in the front of the bus or at the white lunch counter. The ceremonies of degradation that southern blacks were forced to submit to prior to the civil rights movement of the 1960s are similar to the ceremonies of degradation that female Go Go dancers and nude models are required to submit to in America today.

In either case we are dealing with status politics. In the case of the right, women and Christian puritans generally strive to preserve the status of a sexless life except within marriage. In the case of the feminist left, we are dealing with an attempt by women to raise the status of women as a group by demanding that they no longer be required to submit to rituals of degradation portrayed in or involved in the production of pornographic materials. The rituals of female degradation involve the use of fetish clothings symbolic of subordinate status (and the use of particular positions or poses including masturbation or lesbianism which imply the lower status of the female sex object).

We have argued that the right wing antipornography crusade was a Norm Oriented Social Movement. In Southtown, one of the communities we studied, the entire focus of the right-wing Christian social movement was on passing a state law which would prohibit the sale of pornography. In Midville, the midwestern community we studied, it was not as clear-cut. There was a combination of persuasion, direct action against adult bookstores and theatres, and attempts at legislative change. We elaborated several hypotheses about the conditions under which a Norm Oriented Movement or attempts at legislative change were more likely, and conditions under which direct action against pornographers was more likely, or the gentler tactic of persuasion was adopted. In Midville, citizens would enter the adult bookstore, buy books and magazines and then make citizens' complaints with the police department. It is interesting to note that the feminist strategy is a combination of persuasion (or the use of propaganda such as slide shows) and the encouraging of participants to write to advertisers and record company owners who use "violent and pornographic images" to sell products, and boycott such products until these images are removed. Also, the feminists (at least in New York, London, and San Francisco) plan direct action including sit-down demonstrations in pornography shops. In London, where the history of the feminist movement is very militant, there have already been cases of women "trashing" adult bookstores in Picadilly in 1978, and more recently in 1980 of women throwing eggs at movie screens of theatres showing pornographic films. In San Francisco, the feminists give guided tours of the "tenderloin" district where most of the adult theatres and bookstores are located.

Although their strategy and tactics are similar, it may be suggested that in addition to the fact that the feminist antipornography crusades more often develop into hostile outbursts than do the right wing movements, the feminist movement itself may be a Value Oriented Movement rather than a Norm Oriented Movement like the right wing groups. The right wing antipornography crusaders basically want to maintain and preserve the life-style of the Protestant Old Rural Middle Class. The feminists want to transform the entire society according to the utopian and moralistic values of the Women's Liberation Movement, which require the transformation of sex roles, socialisation practices and the distribution of economic and political power of women, as well as a change in the status of women as a group.

THE EMPIRICAL RESEARCH

In 1980, a list of all known Feminist Antipornography organisations was obtained from the San Francisco-based Women Against Violence in Pornography and Media. Ten questionnaires were sent to all organisations except those in San Francisco and San Diego, which received 25 questionnaires each. Responding to our questionnaire were Feminist Crusaders from Los Angeles; San Francisco; San Diego; Springfield, Massachusetts; Chicago; Cleveland; Pittsburgh; New York; New Haven, Connecticut; Long Beach; Denver; and Boston. The only organisations or areas which are overrepresented are San Francisco, San Diego, and Springfield, Massachusetts. The other organisations responded with one or two questionnaires from their leaders or most active members. This gave us a total of 35 completed, usable questionnaires. The questionnaire contained basic demographic characteristics such as age, sex, religion, income, two feminist scales, and standard attitude scales measuring alienation, authoritarianism, a scale measuring social movement involvement and aware-

ness, attitude toward sex and censorship scales, self-esteem, and an attitude toward sex in the home scale. We also had open-ended questions concerning exposure to pornography as a child, and questions concerning organizational structure, activity, goals, etc. Finally, the questionnaire included questions asking the feminists to judge what books, magazines, movies and TV shows they deem pornographic. Additional questions probed the feminists' attitudes toward different types of pornography and their perceptions of the people who produce/consume pornography. Also, other questions probing the relationship between pornography and violence were asked, including the respondent's own history regarding being a victim of sexual assault or rape. The questionnaire was identical to the one used 10 years ago on Christian Right Wing antipornography crusaders, except for the questions concerning violence, feminism and the self-esteem scale, which were added for the present study, making the data roughly comparable.

RESULTS

A preliminary analysis of our data yields the following results. The strongest concentration of feminist crusaders who responded to our questionnaire are in the Northeast—principally Springfield, Massachusetts, and in the West, around the San Francisco Bay area. Both areas are well known for both radical political activity and feminism. In all, 17 respondents

are from the West, including Colorado and California, while 15 are from the East and only one response came from the Midwest, from Chicago. This finding contrasts sharply with the midwestern origins of the right wing Christian opponents to pornography (see Table F–1A).

The feminist crusaders are a highly educated

Table F–1A
City of Activism for Feminist Antipornography
Crusaders

	Number	Percent
Los Angeles, California	1	3
San Francisco Bay Area, California	9	26
San Diego, California	5	15
Springfield, Massachusetts	8	24
Chicago, Illinois	1	3
Cleveland, Ohio	2	6
Pittsburgh, Pennsylvania	2	6
New York, New York	1	3
New Haven, Connecticut	2	6
Denver, Colorado	1	3
Long Beach, California	1	3
Boston, Massachusetts	1	3
Total number	34	

Table F–1B
Educational Background of Feminist
Antipornography Crusaders

	Number	Percent
High school	1	2
Some college	10	29
Completed bachelor's degree	8	23
Some graduate work	3	9
Completed MA degree	7	20
PhD	2	6
Professional degree (MSW, LLD)	4	11
Total number	35	

Table F–2
Occupations of Feminist Antipornography
Crusaders

	Number	Percent
Feminist community organiser	5	15
College teacher/researcher	4	12
Graduate student	3	9
Student	1	3
Unemployed	2	6
Manager/proprietor	2	6
Professional, technical	8	24
Waitress, cook	3	9
Secretary	1	3
Housewife	1	3
Bus Driver	1	3
Teacher	2	6
Total number	33	

Table F–3
Social Class of Feminist Antipornography
Crusaders

	Number	Percent
Old middle class	2	6
New middle class	17	52
Professional feminist activist	5	15
Working class	5	3
Student	1	3
Unemployed	2	6
Housewife	1	3
Total number	33	

Table F–4
Religious Preferences of Feminist
Antipornography Activists

	Number	Percent
Pagan feminist religions	5	15
Jewish	6	12
Unitarian	2	6
Quaker	1	2
Baptist	1	2
Catholic	1	2
None	19	55
Total number	35	

group, with all but one of the respondents reporting some college, with 13 possessing graduate degrees and half (17) with some experience with graduate education (see Table F–1B). The high educational attainment is one of the reasons the feminist crusaders seem to fit the characterisation of "New Middle Class" (18). We are arguing that the feminists are New Middle Class status discontents, responding to the declining status of the New Middle Class. We are also arguing that as women, these feminists oppose sexist and degrading portrayals of women in general—*status protest* as the motivational substratum of the Moral Crusade. Occupationally the data support the same sort of interpretation. One half of the respondents reported occupations that were clearly part of the New Middle Class.

An interesting and somewhat unexpected finding was that several (5) of the feminists thought of themselves as Pagan Witches or Wiccas. Six were Jewish but the vast majority, 19, were secular and reported no religion (see Table F–4). These secular feminists were largely young women, produced by

the Women's Liberation Movement of the 1970s, with 18 in their 20s and 10 in their 30s, while only six were 40 years or older. No apparent trend in the rural or urban origins of feminist crusaders was indicated by the data, as seen in Table F–6. Nor were there definite income differences among the feminists, but given the high education and high occupational status of over half of the feminist

Table F–5
Age Distribution for Feminist
Antipornography Activists

	Number	Percent
20s	18	53
30s	10	30
40s	4	12
50s	2	6
Total number	34	

Table F–6
Rural or Urban Origins of Feminist
Antipornography Crusaders

Population	Number	Percent
Below 2,500	1	3
2,500–24,999	7	23
25,000–49,999	5	16
50,000–99,999	3	10
100,000–499,999	2	6
Above 500,000	13	42
Total number	31	

Table F–7
Income Characteristics of Feminist
Antipornography Crusaders

Monthly Income ($)	Number	Percent
Below 400	9	28
400–599	3	9
600–799	2	6
800–999	2	6
1,000–1,199	3	9
1,200–1,399	3	9
1,400–1,599	2	6
1,600–1,999	3	9
2,000–2,999	5	16
Total number	32	

Table F–8
Political Party Preferences of Feminist
Antipornography Crusaders

	Number	Percent
Republican	1	3
Democrat	13	42
Socialist	5	16
Citizens' party	2	6
Independent	3	10
Socialist feminist	1	3
Feminist	1	3
None	5	16
Total number	31	

Table F–9
Political Orientation of Feminist
Antipornography Crusaders

	Number	Percent
Conservative	2	6
Liberal	6	18
Radical	23	71
Feminist	1	3
Total number	32	

Table F–10
Feminist Antipornography Crusaders' Attitude
toward Social Movement Commitment
in Terms of Self-Concept Indentification
(Feminist Subscale No. 1)

	Number	Percent
As a radical feminist	22	62
As a feminist	12	34
As a supporter of women's rights, but not a feminist	2	5
As a lesbian feminist*	1	2
Total number	35	

*Lesbians were also counted as radicals.

Table F–11
Feminist Antipornography Crusaders' Ties to
Feminist Organisations

	Number	Percent
Leader or officer	17	49
Official member	11	31
Supporter but not an official member	7	20
Total number	35	

crusaders the income data seem to indicate that the income distribution is what one would expect, with roughly half of the crusaders making over 1,000 dollars a month (see Table F–7).

As one would expect, only one of the feminist crusaders was a Republican. It is outstanding that five of the crusaders mentioned Socialist as their political party preference, with 13 Democrats. See Tables F–8 and F–9. It was very significant that 23 of 32 respondents who responded to the item considered themselves radicals. With regard to feminism as such, as exhibited in Table F–10, the self-concept of feminist crusaders was largely "Radical

Table F–12
Antipornography Organisations with Which
Feminist Crusaders Are Associated*

	Number	Percent
Women Against Violence in Pornography and Media	17	50
Women Against Violence Against Women	8	23
Feminist Committee for Media Reform	1	3
Women's Institute for Freedom of the Press	1	3
Women's Forum Against Media Violence	4	11
Women Against Pornography	5	14
Feminists Against Pornography	2	6
Women Against Sexist Violence in Media	3	9
Wipe Out Media Abuse Now (W.O.M.A.N.)	1	3
Coalition for Women to Take Back the Night	2	6
Preying Mantis Women's Brigade	1	3
Total number	45	

*Double membership counted twice.

Feminist." Twenty-two feminist crusaders thought of themselves as Radical Feminists and 12 as feminists.

Altogether, the feminist crusaders mentioned 11 antipornography organisations, and unquestionably the most important group is the Women Against Violence in Pornography and Media. This group, which has branches around the U.S., has its strongest branch in San Francisco. As part of our documentary research, we have obtained copies of all of WAVPM (wave pam)'s monthly newsletter for the whole period of the existence of the organisation. The first issue of this newsletter is dated August 1977. At that time, the headquarters of WAVPM was in the Berkeley Women's Centre. On November 17–19 in 1978, WAVPM sponsored a conference at San Francisco State University called "Feminist Perspectives on Pornography." This conference was comparable to the "Upsurge for Decency" conference held in Southtown and reported in our previous research in *Citizens for Decency*. This feminist antipornography conference included speeches by prominent feminists including Andrea Dworkin (author of *Women Hating*), Susan Brownmiller (author of *Against Our Will*), Susan Griffin, Juidith Reisman, Cathy Barry, and Adrienne Rich. This conference concluded with a march and rally on Saturday night, November 18, which according to the WAVPM newsletter drew 1,000 strong women. There was a similar march on the same night in New York City which marched down Broadway, and we have examined pictures of

this match which indicate massive participation. The march organisers estimated 3,000 women in attendance.

In April of 1979, WAVPM started a membership drive in which they tried to obtain 1,000 additional dues-paying members (dues at that time were 10 dollars a year; they have subsequently been raised to 15 a year). With these kind of numbers and dues, the feminist antipornography movement has been able to generate several "paid positions" for full-time or part-time professional feminist activists. Five of the respondents in our sample listed "Feminist Community Organiser" as their occupation. On October 10, 1979, a massive march against pornography was held at Times Square in New York. The New York Organisation, Women Against Pornography is described by San Francisco based WAVPM as a "sister organisation." On July 28, 1970, 1,500 women marched in New Haven, Connecticut in a Take Back the Night March.

One of the ideologists of the feminist antipornography movement, feminist sociologist Kathleen Barry, in her book *Female Sexual Slavery* (20) suggests that pornography is the ideology of cultural sadism. This analysis was strongly supported by San Francisco WAVPM. The other feminist antipornography organisations mentioned, about whom we have less historical and documentary data, include the Women Against Violence Against Women, which was mentioned by eight women in our sample, and which according to our data is the second most influential feminist antipornography organisation. Women Against Pornography based in New York was mentioned by five respondents, ranking third, Women's Forum Against Media Violence was mentioned by four respondents, ranking fourth, and the fifth ranking feminist antipornography organisation was Women Against Sexist Violence in Media. The other organisations were mentioned only once each, and we can conclude that they are either local in scope or groups which might have only one or two active leaders.

The feminist antipornography group operating out of Chicago is unique, in that it is called People Against Pornography, and is consciously designed to be feminist but is not composed entirely of women. The leader of that group, now defunct, a woman graduate student in sociology at Northwestern University, was cooperative in our study, completed our questionnaire, and mailed us considerable literature about her organisation.

The only explicit reference in the literature written by the feminist crusaders to the right wing opponents of pornography was in the newsletter of WAVPM for January of 1980. In that issue they made the following statement:

. . . we have observed that the antipornography forces have almost always been conservative, homophobic, antisex and protraditional patriarchal family. They have equated nudity and explicit sex with pornography. They are often against abortion, the ERA, and the women's liberation movement. We have been so put off by the politics of these people that our knee-jerk response is that we must be *for* whatever they are *against*.

So the feminist crusaders seem to be aware of the "strange bedfellows" aspect of their antipornography movement. It may be the case, that pornography is more of a pragmatic rather than ideological issue. That is, the issue is used to organise women, and to cut across differences that might divide women, such as age, income, race, politics. It is generally felt that all women "instinctively" oppose pornography because it is "degrading" so the issue serves as a strategic one for broad based, grass roots organising of women around other feminist issues. On the other hand, it may be that the majority of these women actually believe that pornography causes rape, assault and incest, and is indeed a threat to women's lives and well-being. To try to determine the answer to this and similar questions concerning feminist organising and the content of pornography as a male ideology which might promote violence against women, let us look at the responses made by women who completed our questionnaire to questions concerning the goals of their organisations.

The goal most often mentioned by feminist antipornography crusaders as being important was to ". . . educate people about pornography and violence against women in media and in reality. . . ." These feminists primarily see their work as educational, and it was mentioned a number of times by different respondents that "censorship is not our goal" and "we are opposed to censorship in any form." Even so, second to education in importance as an organisational goal was to ". . . eliminate violent, sexist, degrading and physically and sexually abusive images of women in media. . . ." The tactics mentioned, however, do not include censorship, although they do include marches, demonstrations, direct action, boycott, protests, etc. In fact, one of the most interesting and colorful tactics of WAVPM in San Francisco is their "Feminist Tours of the Pornography District" which they reported on in their newsletter of October 1980. These feminist tours serve to publicise and politicise the issue of pornography in a manner similar to the newspaper campaign against the Adult Bookstore in Midville, described in our earlier work *Citizens for Decency*. In fact the imagery is remarkably similar. According to the WAVPM newsletter:

Tours start with a shortened version of the WAVPM slide show, "Abusive Images of Women in Pornography and Mass Media." Then the 10–20 participants are taken into several pornography stores with names like "Fantasy 'N Flesh," where typical porn offerings can be observed. Most stores have a large selection of family incest books featuring titles such as Do It With Daddy, Daddy's Little Girl and Sex Before Six, and an entire wall of magazines displaying women bound in various contorted positions, tortured and humiliated for male sexual stimulation, and a section of books bearing swastikas portraying Nazi look-alikes beating women. These books have titles like Sex Under the Swastika and Dachau Mistress. Film loops, available for viewing at the back of the stores for a series of 25 cent deposits, shows scenes ranging from a man undressing to a bound woman being molested by a pig.

The feminist moral indignation exhibited in this quote recalls similar moral indignation that the Christian Right Wing crusaders felt about "Plain & Flat Filth" and "Moral Degeneracy worse than the fall of Rome" and horror at such book titles as *Bitches in Heat* and *Humping Homos*.

Returning to the goals mentioned by our feminist crusader respondents, we find the third most mentioned goal (see Table F–13) to be to "stop violence against women" and to "remove pornography from legal and public sale, distribution and promotion by direct action and confrontation with dealers." Other stated organisational goals included "to end male dominance and establish equality for women," "to build a strong women's movement" and, significantly, "to increase the desire for more erotica." Other goals mentioned were to "confront consumers of pornography," "to use boycotts to stop sexist and abusive images of women on record album covers, in films and in advertising," and "to prevent the production of pornography." Comparing the goals mentioned by feminist crusaders to the official goals of the WAVPM organisation, we find that WAVPM's stated goals given in the July 1980 edition of their newsletter are:

1. To educate women and men about the hatred of women expressed in pornography and other media violence to women, and to increase understanding of the destructive consequences of these images.
2. To confront those responsible for perpetuating media violence: producers, distributors, store owners, porn consumers.
3. To put an end to all portrayals of women being degraded, raped, tortured, or murdered for entertainment or profit.

Table F–13
Goals of Feminist Antipornography Organisations*

	Number	Percent
Educate people about pornography and violence against women in media and reality	14	40
Eliminate sexist violent degrading and physically and sexually abusive images of women	6	17
Stop violence against women	4	11
Remove pornography from legal and public sale, distribution and promotion by direct action and confrontation with dealers	4	11
To end male dominance and establish equality for women	3	9
To build a strong women's movement (feminist)	2	6
To eliminate violent and abusive images of women on record album covers	2	6
To increase the desire for more erotica	2	6
To confront consumers of pornography	1	3
Use boycott to stop sexist and abusive images of women on album covers, films and advertising	1	3
To prevent the production of pornography	1	3
Total number	40	

*Organisations had multiple and overlapping goals.

Table F–14
Movies Judged Pornographic by Feminist Crusaders*

	Number	Percent
Deep Throat	11	31
Dressed to Kill	10	29
Story of O	8	23
"Snuff" films	7	20
X-rated films	6	17
Tatoo	4	11
The Devil in Miss Jones	3	9
Recent horror movies	3	9
Behind the Green Door	2	6
Pretty Baby	2	6
Flesh Gordon	2	6
James Bond movies	2	
Windows	2	
He Knows You're Alone	2	
Dachau Mistress Ilsa: She Wolf of the SS	2	6
Total number	64	

*Multiple answers coded per respondent.

Table F–15
Books Judged Pornographic by Feminist Crusaders

	Number	Percent
The Story of O	6	17
Henry Miller, *Tropic of Cancer*	5	14
Norman Mailer, *An American Dream*	4	11
Books by deSade	3	9
Gone with the Wind	1	3
Hawaii	1	3
100 Ways to Cut up a Woman	1	3
Cristie	1	3
The Bible	1	3
Books in porn shops (adult bookstores)	1	3
Lolita	1	3
Gothic quasi-porn "women's bodice rippers"	1	3
Hitler's Girls	1	3
Raped by Daddy	1	3
Virgin Whore	1	3
Total number	29	

So far, much has been said about pornography, but again as we found in our earlier study of *Citizens for Decency*, there seems to exist little agreement even among feminist activists as to what exactly pornography is and what examples of it consist of. Or more clearly just where does one "draw the line"? We asked our feminist crusader respondents to judge what movies they felt were "pornographic." Thirty percent of our respondents felt that the classic porno film *Deep Throat* was pornographic. Surprisingly, however, 29 percent felt that the violent exploitation and horror film *Dressed to Kill* was pornographic. Twenty-three percent of our respondents felt that *Story of O* was pornographic. Twenty percent of them felt that "Snuff" films were pornographic. Seventeen percent felt that traditional X-rated films shown in adult theatres were pornographic. There were some respondents that felt that James Bond movies were pornographic (see Table F–14).

We also asked feminist crusaders to judge what books they felt to be pornographic. In Table F–15 these data are presented. Seventeen percent of our respondents felt that *The Story of O* was pornographic, while fourteen percent mentioned Henry Miller and eleven percent said Norman Mailer, and nine percent said the words of deSade. Other than these four, which are traditionally considered to be pornographic by Citizens for Decency and by legal history regarding obscenity decisions in American courts, the respondents variously felt that books such as *Gone With the Wind*, *The Bible*, and *Hawaii* were pornographic.

Table F–16
Magazines Judged Pornographic by Feminist Crusaders*

	Number	Percent
Hustler	22	63
Playboy	20	57
Penthouse	17	49
Oui	7	20
Chic	3	9
Playgirl	3	9
Easy Rider Motorcycle Magazine	3	9
National Lampoon	2	6
Detective Magazine	2	6
Screw	2	6
Breast Bondage	1	3
Fetish Times	1	3
Velvet	1	3
All magazines in adult bookstores	1	3
Cosmopolitan	1	3
Gun magazines	1	3
Cop magazines	1	3
Ms.	1	3
Cherry	1	3
Vogue	1	3
Hustle	1	3
Total number	94	

*Multiple responses coded.

Table F–17
Feminist Crusaders' Attitudes toward People Who Make Pornography

	Number	Percent
Profiteers out to make easy money	17	49
Women haters	5	14
Normal Madison Avenue big business men	4	11
Exploiters of women's bodies	4	11
Dangerous, sexist, oppressive, violent men	3	9
White men	2	6
Greedy male capitalists	2	6
Women who need to make money	2	6
Male mafia	1	3
Irresponsible men with no self-respect	1	3
Amoral men	1	3
Moral majority	1	3
Rich racist, classist males	1	3
Women who are forced	1	3
Impotent men	1	3
Total number	36	

*Multiple responses coded.

Table F–18
Feminist Antipornography Crusaders' Attitudes toward Consumers of Pornography

	Number	Percent
Women haters	7	20
Depressed, needy, lonely, sexually insecure men and teenaged boys with no sexual outlet	5	14
All kinds of men	7	20
Men who objectify women for arousal	2	6
Most all types of people	2	6
Middle and upper class rich men in suburbia	2	6
Men who define sex as power	2	6
Men and women who want to improve their relationships	1	3
Men for masturbation	1	3
Deviants for justification	1	3
Sexually repressed	1	3
Men who cannot deal with women as equals	1	3
Men who see sex as dirty	1	3
The moral majority	1	3
Poor males	1	3
Creeps who aspire to be tyrannical perverts	1	3
Women who are extremely male identified	1	3
Men uneducated about the sexist roots of porn	1	3
The sexually dysfunctional	1	3
Rapists	1	3
Wife beaters	1	3
Sadomasochists	1	3
Total number	43	

Table F–19
Feminist Crusaders' Attitudes toward Violence and Pornography: Does Pornography Cause Violence?

	Number	Percent
Yes	23	66
No	6	17
No response	6	17
Total number	35	

Although such responses may have been given as humour, the tone of most questionnaires carried the seriousness usually associated with moral crusades.

Looking now to magazines, we find that in response to questions concerning what magazines were felt to be pornographic, 63 percent of our feminist crusader respondents felt *Hustler* to be pornographic, and one feminist even said it was the cover of a *Hustler* magazine, which depicted a woman being put into a meat grinder, that precipitated her involvement in the antipornography movement. Fifty-seven percent of our respondents felt *Playboy* to be pornographic, and one of the major projects of one of the feminist antipornography organisations was to stop a Playboy Club from locating in their community. Forty-nine percent of the feminist crusaders felt that *Penthouse* was pornographic. There can be no doubt, then, that when these crusaders say pornography, they do not generally mean underground publications in adult bookstores, but they mean mainstream publications like *Hustler, Penthouse,* and *Playboy.* Other interesting magazines mentioned include *Easy Rider Motorcycle Magazine, National Lampoon,* detective magazines, *Cosmopolitan,* gun magazines, cop magazines, *Ms.* and *Vogue.*

Let us proceed to examine the stereotypes feminist crusaders hold about producers and consumers of pornography. Forty-nine percent of the respondents felt that the producers of pornography were "profiteers out to make easy money." Fourteen percent felt that they were "women haters" and eleven percent felt that they were "normal Madison Avenue big business men." Other responses included "exploiters of women's bodies," "dangerous, sexist, oppressive violent men," "white men," "greedy capitalists," "women who need to make money," "male mafia," "irresponsible men with self-respect," "moral men," "the moral majority," "rich racist, classist men," "women who are forced," "impotent men."

The most significant responses to the question concerning the consumers of pornography, with whom the feminists presumably have more experience, included twenty percent who said "women haters" while another twenty percent said "all kinds of men." Fourteen percent said "depressed, needy, lonely, sexually insecure men and teenage boys with no sexual outlets." Other interesting responses included "sadomasochists," "wife beaters," "rapists," "men for masturbation," "deviants for justification," "women who are extremely male identified," "sexually repressed," "men who cannot deal with women as equals," and "creeps who aspire to be tyrannical perverts."

Sixty-eight percent of our feminist crusader respondents felt that pornography causes violence, and evidence cited (see Table F–20) as follows:

Y. Jaffe, N. Malamuth, J. Feingold, and S. Feshbach, "Sexual Arousal and Behavioral Aggression," *Journal of Personality and Social Psychology,* vol. 32, 1975; N. Malamuth, S. Feshbach and Y. Jaffe, "Sexual Arousal and Aggression: Recent Experiments and Theoretical Issues," *Journal of Social Issues,* vol. 33, 1977; and E. Donnerstein and G. Barrett, "The Effects of Erotic Stimuli on Male

Table F–20

Specific Responses Regarding Research on Cases of Violence Causing Pornography

Edward Donnerstein, "The Porno Commission Revisited" Feshbach, et al., recent research.

"Testing Hypotheses Regarding Rape: Exposure to Sexual Violence, Sex Differences, and the 'Normality' of Rapists," *Journal of Research in Personality* (in press), p. 8 of unpublished manuscript.

Seymour Feshbach and Neal Malamuth, "Sex and Aggression: Proving the Link," *Psychology Today,* November 1978, pp. 116–117.

"Testing Hypotheses Regarding Rape," *op. cit.,* pp. 5–6.

D. Zillmann, "Exciting Transfer in Communication-Mediated Aggressive Behavior," *Journal of Experimental Social Psychology,* Vol. 7, 1971; Y. Jaffe, N. Malamuth, J. Feingold, and S. Feshbach, "Sexual Arousal and Behavior Aggression," *Journal of Personality and Social Psychology,* Vol. 30, 1974; E. Donnerstein, M. Donnerstein, and R. Evans, "Erotic Stimuli and Aggression: Facilitation or Inhibition," *Journal of Personality and Social Psychology,* Vol. 32, 1975; R.A. Baron and P.A. Bell, "Sexual Arousal and Aggression by Males: Effects of Type of Erotic Stimuli and Prior Provocation," *Journal of Personality and Social Psychology,* Vol. 35, 1977; and E. Donnerstein and G. Barrett, "The Effects of Erotic Stimuli on Male Aggression towards Females," *Journal of Personality and Social Psychology,* Vol. 36, 1978.

R.A. Baron. "The Aggression-Inhibiting Influence of Heightened Sexual Arousal," *Journal of Personality and Social Psychology,* Vol. 30, 1974; A. Frodi, "Sexual Arousal, Situational Restrictiveness, and Aggressive Behaviour," *Journal of Research in Personality,* Vol. 11, 1977; and N. Malamuth, S. Feshbach, and Y. Jaffe, "Sexual Arousal and Aggression: Recent Experiments and Theoretical Issues," *Journal of Social Issues,* Vol. 33, 1977.

"Pornography Commission Revisited: Aggressive Erotica and Violence Against Women," Unpublished paper presented to the New York Academy of Science, October 1979, p. 4.

E. Donnerstein, "Pornography and Violence Against Women: Experimental Studies" (unpublished, undated paper), p. 13.

"Sexual Aggression in American Pornography: The Stereotype of Rape," Unpublished paper presented at the American Sociological Association Meetings, New York, August 1976, p. 5.

"A Longitudal Content Analysis of the Best-Selling Erotica Magazines," Unpublished manuscript, p. 8.

Time, August 27, 1979, p. 64.

The New York Times, October 21, 1979, p. 41.

Aggression Towards Females," *Journal of Personality and Social Psychology,* vol. 30, 1974 (21) and the case of the "Born Innocent" TV suit. A quote from the October 1978 newsletter of the WAVPM group explains the "Born Innocent" case:

On August 8, 1978 Judge Robert Dossee dismissed the $11 million "Born Innocent" damage suit

Table F–21
Feminist Crusaders' Experience as Victims of Sexual Assault and Rape

	Number	Percent
Experienced sexual assault	22	63
Not experienced sexual assault	8	23
No response	5	14
Total number	35	

Table F–22
Feminist Antipornography Crusaders' Theory of the Cause of Child Pornography

	Number	Percent
Men need to dominate something powerless	7	20
Men are terrified and threatened by older women	5	14
Child porn is motivated by profit, money and economic gain	4	11
As women become less available as sex objects, children are feminised and used instead	3	9
Impotent old men	2	6
Children are the most easily exploited group in society	2	6
Children are innocent (virgin), lovely, loving and men get enjoyment from despoiling and debasing innocence	2	6
Desire for the new and the taboo	1	3
The media pushes it (e.g., Lolita and Brooke Shields)	1	3
Patriarchy	1	3
Fantasy fulfillment	1	3
Sexual violation and access to women is no longer taboo, so new taboos and violations are needed to sell the product	1	3
Men's sick minds	1	3
Resentment by adults who want to remain children against young people	1	3
Total number	32	

against NBC on the grounds that the 1974 televised drama falls under the protection of the First Amendment. Marven E. Lewis, the attorney suing the network and its local affiliate, KRON-TV, based his lawsuit on the theory that NBC and KRON-TV were either negligent or reckless in broadcasting "Born Innocent" at a time when children would watch it. The lawsuit said that the 9-year-old girl was raped with a beer bottle four days after a similar sexual attack was shown in "Born Innocent," and presented evidence to indicate that the attack was inspired by the TV drama.

As shown in Table F–22, twenty percent of our feminist activists felt that the cause of child pornography was that "men need to dominate something powerless." Fourteen percent of our feminist activists feel that child pornography is caused by the fact that "men are terrified and threatened by older women." Eleven percent felt that child pornography was motivated by the desire for profit, money and economic gain. Other interesting responses include the notion that "as women become less available as sex objects, children are feminised and used instead." Other feminist activists suggested that "children are innocent (virgin), lovely, loving, and men get enjoyment from despoiling or debasing innocence." Another suggestion that, "Sexual violation and access to women is no longer taboo, so new taboos and violations are needed to sell the product."

Thirty-seven percent of our respondents felt that there was a difference between pornography and erotica. The felt difference is neatly summarised in the responses given in specific to this question. Forty-three percent of the feminist activists said that *erotica* "involves mutual pleasure, is passive, voluntary, sensual, involves shared experience, is loving, giving, celebratory, consensual, equal and non-violent." They conversely felt *pornography* "involves violence, conquest, control, subjugation, objectification, rape, degradation, dominance, submission and exploitation."

If the feminist analysis of pornography seems persuasive in the areas of abnormal and social psychology, perhaps it should also be taken seriously on issues of political economy. In the June 1978 issue of their newsletter, the feminist activists suggest that pornography is a very big business. They estimate sales of pornographic films in Los Angeles alone at 8.5 million dollars. *Hustler* Magazine has a readership of seven million and *Playboy* of six million. The San Francisco Chronicle and the San Francisco Examiner earn about one million dollars a year on advertisements for pornography theatres. They estimate that twenty million dollars a year are generated by selling pornography in San Francisco.

And now for the future. If pornography is indeed an issue which cuts across differences among feminists and unites women, it serves as an excellent organising tool for the feminist activist and as a social barometer of the strength of the feminist movement and its prospects for the 1980s. The feminist activists see their antipornography movement as a real response of female victims of male violence to real or potential attacks, assaults and rapes. They therefore make predictions about the strength of their movement based on the incidence and prevalence of male

Table F–23
Feminist Crusaders' Views on the Difference between Pornography and Erotica

	Number	Percent
Yes	13	37
Erotica involves mutual pleasure, is passive, voluntary, sensual, shared experience, loving, giving, celebratory, and equal and nonviolent	8	23
Pornography involves violence, conquest, control, subjugation, objectification, rape, degradation, dominance and submission and exploitation	7	20
Pornography portrays pain and humiliation as pleasure	1	3
Etymologically pornography is the depiction of whores	1	3
Etymologically erotica is the depiction of love (Eros)	1	3
Pornography and Erotica differ in the way the subject is exposed or posing	1	3
Erotica exists in many cultures and societies, but pornography is recent and involves profit	1	3
Not sure	3	9
No response	3	9
No	1	3
Total number	40	

*Multiple responses coded per respondent.

Table F–24
Exposure to Pornography as a Child

	Number	Percent
Exposure as a child to Playboy or other "porn" magazine	19	54
No exposure as child to porn	10	28
No response	6	17
Total number	35	

violence against women, which they see as being on the rise. In an essay entitled "Will WAVPM Survive the Eighties?" by Bridget Wynne, several interesting notions are suggested. WAVPM has been in existence for five years, from 1977 to 1982. Their strategy for survival is discussed below. According to Bridget Wynne, the feminist antipornography activists have "made media violence against women an important issue for thousands of concerned people, and are now the leaders of a national growing movement." WAVPM's strategy is to maintain funding self-sufficiency through the use of 1) canvassing for donations and memberships (which currently nets between 800 and 3,300 dollars a month); 2) showing their slide show on abusive images of women in media (which currently nets 200 to 600 dollars a month); and 3) benefits (which currently net between 150 and 1,700 dollars each quarter). If the social movement against sexist and violent pornography and media is indeed fueled by the rage of victims of sexual assault, and this is perhaps borne out by the fact that 63 percent of these feminist activists who responded to our questionnaires indicated that they had been victims of sexual assault or rape, then this movement is likely to continue as long as real violence against women and rape continue. If this movement, on the other hand, has its motivational roots in the status protest of women, or in the status protest of dissatisfied members of the New Middle Class, then it is likely to continue only so long as other avenues of status protest are blocked, or other means are not available for resolving status difficulties, such as additional jobs or avenues of upward mobility or increased on-the-job power and meaning for under-employed women professionals.

NOTES

1. Louis A. Zurcher, Jr. and R. George Kirkpatrick, *Citizens for Decency: Antipornography Crusades as Status Defense*, University of Texas Press, 1976 and Louis A. Zurcher, Jr., R. George Kirkpatrick, Robert G. Cushing and Charles K. Bowman, "Ad Hoe Antipornography Organisations," *Journal of Social Issues*, 29 (3) 1973, pp. 69–93.

2. It will become clear below that we view pornography as a collective representation or "social fact" in the tradition of Emile Durkheim's discussion on *The Rules of the Sociological Method*, Free Press, 1938.

3. For a good sociological description of the current situation with regard to the production and consumption of pornography, and a discussion of the social issues involved, *not* from a feminist point of view, see John H. Gagnon, *Human Sexualities*, Scott Foresman, 1977, Ch. 17, "The Erotic Environment," pp. 341–361, or Ned Polsky's classic discussion of pornography in *Hustlers, Beats and Others*, Aldine, 1967.

4. Using the basic Marxist model of society, we see pornography as part of the cultural superstructure of society, which perhaps in this case has its own unique

Table F–25
Comparison of Conporns, Proporns, Controls and Feminists on Social Psychological Scales*

Characteristic	Conporns (N = 36)	Midville Proporns (N = 25)	Controls (N = 12)	Conporns (N = 49)	Southtown Proporns (N = 26)	Controls (N = 38)	Feminists (N = 35)
Powerlessness	1.82	2.61	2.61	2.25	2.09	2.41	2.08
Normlessness	0.75	1.84	1.20	0.63	1.48	0.97	1.24
Alienation	1.38	2.32	2.05	1.60	1.85	1.84	1.67
Authoritarianism	2.06	1.32	2.40	2.62	0.80	2.49	0.56
Religiosity	3.95	2.44	4.00	4.45	2.02	4.04	1.70
Traditional family ideology	2.56	1.54	3.25	3.27	1.23	2.97	0.45
Political intolerance	2.47	0.34	2.45	3.11	0.38	2.85	0.15
Traditional attitude toward sex	2.41	1.69	2.60	2.80	1.49	2.72	0.85
Approval of censorship	3.15	1.45	2.89	3.25	1.47	3.17	1.38

*From Louis A. Zurcher, Jr. and R. George Kirkpatrick, *Citizens for Decency*, University of Texas Press, 1976, p. 245.

Table F–26
Comparison of Conporns, Proporns, Controls and Feminists on Social Psychological Scales*

Characteristic	Conporns (N = 85)	Proporns (N = 51)	Controls (N = 50)	Feminists (N = 35)
Powerlessness	2.04	2.35	2.51	2.08
Normlessness	0.69	1.66	1.09	1.24
Alienation	1.49	2.09	1.95	1.67
Authoritarianism	2.34	1.06	2.45	0.56
Traditional family ideology	2.92	1.39	3.11	0.45
Political intolerance	2.79	0.36	2.65	0.15
Traditional view of sex	2.65	1.59	2.66	0.85

*From Zurcher, *et al.*, "Ad Hoc Antipornography Organisations and Their Active Members: A Research Summary," *Journal of Social Issues*, 29 no. 3, 1973, p. 82.

economic base in the money made from the pornography industry, estimated at in excess of one billion dollars a year. For a good discussion of this basic Marxist model of society, see Howard Sherman and James L. Wood, *Sociology: Traditional and Radical Approaches*, Harper and Row, Irving M. Zeitlin, *Marxism: A Re-Examination*, Van Nostram Reinhold, 1967, 1962, & Patrick Goode, [Readings in *Marxists*, Dell and Tom B. Bottomore. Marxist Sociology, Oxford, 1983]

5. The most interesting recent feminist critique of pornography as an ideology of patriarchical civilisation is Laura Lederer, (Ed.) *Take Back the Night: Women on Pornography*, Morrow Quill Paperbacks, 1980. See also Andrea Dworkin, *Pornography: Men Possessing Women*, Perigee Books by G.P. Putnam's Sons, 1981, Angela Carter, *The Sadeian Women and the Ideology of Pornography*, Harper Colophon, 1978, and Susan Griffin, *Pornography and Silence: Culture's Revenge Against Nature*, Harper, 1981.

6. Alfred Kinsey, Wardell Pomeroy and C. Martin, *The Sexual Behavior of the Human Male*, Saunders, 1948. This is still, because of its scientific rigor, its use of depth interviews the majority of which were conducted by Kinsey himself, and the use of 10,000 respondents and multivariate analysis, the best study to date on sexual behaviour.

7. Many of the studies of deviance commonly referred to as the Labeling School fall into this category. The classic study in this tradition is by Howard S. Becker, *Outsiders: Studies in the Sociology of Deviance*, 1963, The Free Press. Becker starts out studying deviants—Marijuana users—and ends up studying the Marijuana Tax Act and the social movements and moral crusaders responsible for its passage.

8. See Joseph R. Gusfield, *Symbolic Crusade: Status Politics and the American Temperance Movement*, 1963, University of Illinois Press, for the classical study of a moral crusade against alcohol.

9. See Edmund S. Morgan, *The Puritan Family: Religion and Domestic Relations in Seventeenth-Century New England* Harper Torchbooks, 1944, 1966.

10. See Hans Licht, *Sexual Life in Ancient Greece*, New York: E.P. Dutton, 1934.

11. Richard F. Hofstadter, *The Paranoid Style in American Politics*, Vintage, 1967.

12. Susan Brownmiller, *Against Our Will*, Simon, 1975.

13. Andrea Dworkin, *Women Hating*, New York: E.P. Dutton, 1974.

14. See Louis A. Zurcher, R. George Kirkpatrick, Charles K. Bowman and Robert G. Cushing, "The Anti-Pornography Campaign: A Symbolic Crusade," *Social Problems*, 19, 1971, pp. 217–238.

15. Hans Gerth and C. Wright Mills (ed.), *From Max Weber: Essays in Sociology*, 1946, Oxford, and Max Weber, *The Protestant Ethic and the Spirit of Capitalism, and Social and Economic Organisation*, Charles Scribner's Sons, 1958, New York Free Press, 1968.

16. Marx's best analysis and description of class politics and the relationship between class struggle and social change can be found in *The Civil War in France*, Peking: Foreign Languages Press, 1966.

17. Neil J. Smelser, *A Theory of Collective Behavior*, The Free Press, 1963.

18. See C. Wright Mills, *White Collar*, Oxford, 1955, or more recent use of the theory of the New Middle Class in James L. Wood, *The Sources of American Student Activism*, Heath, 1974.

19. Nicos Poulantzas, *Classes in Contemporary Capitalism*, New Left Books, 1975. See especially Part Three: "The Petty Bourgeoisie, Traditional and New."

20. Kathleen Barry, *Female Sexual Slavery*, Prentice-Hall, 1979.

21. Y. Jaffe, N. Malamuth, J. Feingold, and S. Feshbach, "Sexual Arousal and Aggression," *Journal of Personality and Social Psychology*, 32, 1975; N. Malamuth, S. Feshbach, and Y. Jaffe, "Sexual Arousal and Aggression: Recent Experiments and Theoretical Issues," *Journal of Social Issues*, 33, 1977; and E. Donnerstein and G. Barrett, "The Effects of Erotic Stimuli on Male Aggression Towards Females," *Journal of Personality and Social Psychology*, 30, 1974. See Table 20.

G PRIVATE ENTERPRISE AND CIVIL LIBERTARIAN GROUPS

American Civil Liberties Union
132 West 43rd Street
New York, NY 10036
(212) 944-9800

Family Affairs
Distributed by Kable News Co.
777 Third Avenue
New York, NY 10017
Published by
Letters Magazine, Inc.
P.O. Box 1314
Teaneck, N.J. 07666

Feminist Anti-Censorship Task Force
P.O. Box 135
660 Amsterdam Avenue
New York, NY 10025

Media Coalition, Inc.
425 Park Avenue
New York, NY 10022
(212) 687-2288

Penthouse
1965 Broadway
New York, NY 10023-5965

Playboy
919 N. Michigan Avenue
Chicago, Illinois 60611

CITATIONS TO SPECIALIZED CHILD PORNOGRAPHY STATUTES

Ala. §§13A-12-190 to 198
Alaska §§11.41.455, 11.61.125
Ariz. §§13-3552 to 3553
Ark. §§41-4203, 4206 to 4210
Calif. Penal Code, 311.2 to 4, 311.10 to 312.3
   Labor Code, §1309.5
Colo. §18-6-403 to 404
Conn. §53a-196a, 196b
Del. tit. 11, §§1108
D.C. §§22-2011 to 2014
Fla. §827.071
Ga. §26-9943a
Hawaii §§707-750, 751
Idaho Labor Code, §18-1507
Ill. ch 38, §11-20.1; §3-6(c)
Ind. §35-42-4-4
Iowa §728.12
Kans. §21-3516
Ky. §531.300 -.360
La. §14:81.1
Maine tit. 17, §§2921-2923
Md. art. 27, §419A
Mass. ch 272, §§29A to 29B
Mich. §750.145c
Minn. §§617.246;617.247

Miss. §§97-5-31 to 37
Mo. §568.06, 808 to 100; §573.010 to 050
Mont. §45-5-625
Nebr. §§28-1463, 1464
N.H. §649-A
N.J. §2C:24-4
N. Mex. §0-6A-1 to 3
N.Y. Penal Law, §§263.00 to 25
N.C. §14.190.13 to .17
N. Dak. §§12.1-27.2-01,-06
Ohio §2907.321 to 323
Okla. tit. 21, §§1021.2, to 3
Oreg. §163.483, to 485
Pa. tit. 18, §6312
R.I. §11-9-1
S.C. §§22-22-22 to 25
Tenn. §§39-6-1137, 1138
Tex. Penal Code §43.25, .26
Utah §76-5a-1 to 4
Vt. tit. 13, §2821 to 2826
Va. §18.2 -374.1
Wash. §§9.68A.040-.130
W.Va. §§61-8C-1, to 5
Wis. §940.203
Wyo. §6-4-403

AGE AT WHICH PORTRAYED OR INVOLVED PERSON NO LONGER CONSIDERED A CHILD

18 (30 states); 17 (5 states); 16 (16 states)

The information in this appendix is from Howard Davidson, Esq., Director, National Legal Resource Center for Child Advocacy and Protection, American Bar Association, 1800 M Street NW, Washington, DC 20036, (202) 331-2250. It was correct as of August 1987.

OFFENSES COVERED

Production of materials (all states)

Coercion of child (41 states; all but Ala., Conn., Hawaii, Ill., Ind., Minn., N.H., Ohio, R.I., Utah)

Distribution of material (46 states; all but Del., Ga., Iowa, R.I., Wyo.)

Parents named as possible facilitators of child's involvement (or law penalizes consenting to or permitting use of child) (48 states; all but Hawaii, N.H., Va.)

REPORTING OF EXPLOITED CHILD TO CHILD PROTECTION AGENCY REQUIRED

41 states; all but D.C., Hawaii, Kans., Mass., Miss., Mo., N.J., N.Dak., Tex., Wyo.

LAWS FACILITATING PROOF OF CRIME

Possession of three or more of same photo, film, etc., infers intention to distribute [8 states: Ala., Colo., Fla., Idaho, La., Ky. (1 or more), Conn. (2 or more), Maine (10 or more)]

Permits portrayed child's age to be inferred (or established by expert testimony) rather than conclusively proven (19 states: Ala., Ariz., Ark., Mass., Mich., Nev., N.J., N.Y., Pa., R.I., Tex., Vt., Hawaii, Ky., Md., Mo., N.Dak., S.C.)

Defendant is legally presumed to know that involved child was a minor (or a mistake of age is not a defense) (6 states: Hawaii, La., Minn., Wash., Va., N.C.)

LAWS THAT SPECIFICALLY PROHIBIT NONCOMMERCIAL DISTRIBUTION (SHOWING OF PECUNIARY GAIN NOT NECESSARY)

39 states; all but Ala., Idaho, Iowa, Mich., Miss., Oreg., Pa., R.I., S.Dak., Wash., Wyo.

LAWS THAT PROHIBIT THE MERE POSSESSION OF CHILD PORNOGRAPHY

15 states: Ariz., Fla., Ga., Ill., Kans., La., Minn., Mo., Nev., S.Dak., Ohio, Okla., Tex., Utah, Wash.

OTHER INNOVATIVE PROVISIONS

Use of videotaped testimony of child victim (Ariz.)

Use of videotaped deposition of child victim (Ark.)

Mandatory reporting of case by police to state department of justice/state provides local police with training and procedural guidelines for handling cases/local police sex crime investigation units encouraged/retailers must keep records on sellers of child pornography (Calif.)

Aggressive law enforcement action is encouraged (N.H.)

Child welfare agency must immediately assume custody of child pornography victims (Conn.)

Use of child pornography (or distribution of same) is labeled "promoting child abuse" or criminal "abuse of a child" (Hawaii, Mo.)

Law has excellent preamble that states the purpose of its enactment (Idaho, Minn., N.H., Utah)

Unusually creative sentencing provisions (Maine: Judge shall consider mental and physical well-being of a child and suspend a sentence only when the case has "exceptional features"; Mass.: Additional penalty for distribution is a fine of up to three times the monetary value of the economic gain derived from the dissemination; Nev.: Provides for forfeiture of assets of convicted defendant with the value going toward a fund for child victim counseling and treatment; N.C.: Convicted defendant can be sent to a psychiatric facility for treatment and counseling for up to ninety days)

Mandatory reporting by commercial film processors to local police (6 states: Alaska, Ariz., Calif., Ill., S.C., Wash.)

Advertising is prohibited. (Twenty states: Ark., Calif., Colo., Conn., D.C., Fla., Ga., La., Mont., Miss., Nebr., Nev., N.J., N.Y., N.Dak., Ohio, S.C., Tenn., Tex., Vt., Wis.)

Forfeiture of assets provisions (7 states: Ala., Calif., Ill., Nev., Okla., Va., Wash.)

I   HELL IS FOR CHILDREN

Margaret Camlin

Louise starred in films as a child, but never saw herself. Nor would she want to. For years Louise, her sister and other children were drugged, tied up, sexually molested and filmed by Louise's parents and their friends in Madison.

"We were put on a stage and told it was a game," recalls Louise, now 40, who asked to remain anonymous. "We were hypnotized and drugged. They would give us an enema with our legs tied up in the air. Things were poked into us, then they had sex with us."

The Madison police refuse to pursue the matter, she says, because of a lack of evidence and the statute of limitations, under which an arrest must be made within six years of the crime.

"We went to four different law-enforcement people, then gave up," Louise says. "They said there was nothing they could do unless the film was sold or unless a murder took place. They said I should go home and find proof."

Louise has no proof to show the police. "I remember nude photos being taken of me from the time I was two or three," she says. Sometimes the photo sessions took place in a downtown room with cameras and bright lights. But usually the porn was produced in her own basement. She has no idea where the pictures and films are today.

Twenty-five years passed before Louise even remembered. "You block it, you suppress it any way you can," she says. "I thought I was crazy when these memories started coming." Now she spills out those memories to a therapist. Her horror has not gone away.

"Animals were used on us," Louise recalls, her voice quaking. "We saw dogs being tortured and killed in front of us. They all threatened that we'd be killed if we said anything."

Louise's parents and others who molested her still live in Madison. Some, she says, would be considered "pillars of the community." And she knows they often babysit for her relatives' small children.

"But nobody will listen or help," she says, even though she has given the police names of those who preyed upon her and details of what took place. "They think it's wacko—they act like we're nuts."

LARGER PROBLEM

Louise's case points to what some say is a fundamental failure of present legal and criminal-justice systems to effectively combat the problem of child pornography.

Victims of child abuse and exploitation often repress the experience for many years, waiting until adulthood before telling anyone. Evidence of the crime—the porn itself—travels from the pornographer to distributors to pedophiles in the United States and abroad.

Complicating matters further is the fact that children's faces are often hidden beneath hoods, or the photos focus only on private parts, making identification an impossible task. And victims of child pornography usually make poor witnesses in court, especially when they are too young to talk.

New video technology lends itself well to porn production. Today's inexpensive video cameras eliminate the need for a studio and fancy equipment and reduce the risk of getting caught by having the film developed by a commercial processor.

"Of course there's more of a problem," says Jody Urso, a detective with the Dane County Sheriff's Department. "The ease is there. It can be produced in the child's home—anywhere and everywhere."

According to Urso, investigators have just scraped the surface of a vast underworld of child pornogra-

This article was originally published in *Isthmus: The Weekly Newspaper of Madison* (Wisc.), May 30–June 5, 1986. Reprinted with permission.

phers. "We catch one or two and it makes the papers," she says, sighing. "We don't usually find out about them."

Most child porn circulates through the mail, leaving postal inspectors with the trying task of detecting it and contacting law enforcement officials. Personal computers linked by telephone lines have become stations in national and international networks of people involved in child pornography. Pedophiles routinely help each other locate child victims and exchange fantasies and accounts of sexual encounters with children.

"Kiddie porn exists because someone has a passion for kids," says Urso, who's in charge of investigating child abuse and child exploitation cases in Dane County. "Someone's in it for the money. It's a matter of supply and demand." Some law enforcement officials suspect organized crime is making a bundle from child porn.

Pedophiles—people, usually males, who have a sexual craving for children—often use "kiddie porn"

to lower the inhibitions of children before molesting them. They sometimes film or photograph these incidents for later viewing when no prey can be found. Or they sell it to other pedophiles for a hefty price.

Recently a Dane County man was about to sell seven sexually explicit shots of his stepson for $600 to a buyer in California when he was arrested, and eventually convicted, on charges of sexually enticing the child. The man produced pornography in his basement using all four of his children and peddled it around the country, according to the children's social worker. Masses of child porn were found in the man's home, including photos of boys being sexually tortured.

"I was shocked at what this fellow was involved in," the social worker says. "If he died, I'd shed no tears except for tears of joy." All four children have been placed in foster homes and are, as the social worker puts it, "far from over it."

THE PORN AT HOME

Law enforcement officials and mental health professionals concede that children are being used for pornography in Madison, but no one knows the extent of the problem.

Recently, Dane County detectives have begun asking child victims of sexual assault if they were photographed or filmed during the incident. Detective Urso reports that many children answer yes. "But we can't find the pictures," she says.

Counselors at Madison's Oasis Parental Stress Center have seen a "handful" of sexually abused teenagers this year who say they've been used for pornography. "My guess is that there's a lot more going on," remarks one counselor. She notes that "a lot of child porn takes place in the home" and that at least 50% of the abusers are fathers or stepfathers.

A Madison police lieutenant says most "homemade" child porn in Madison is being sold out of town or out of state. But he believes commercial child pornography can be purchased within the city limits, despite severe penalties for selling it—$10,000, 10 years in prison or both. He says he thinks it can be purchased at a particular adult bookstore in Madison.

"We've never done a raid on the place," he says. "We could send someone in there, but you have to

prove all kinds of statutes. There isn't much incentive to go in and find child pornography." The lieutenant adds that it is often difficult to prove the age of the person filmed or photographed. The legal age limit for pornographic depiction is 18 years. But sometimes a 22-year-old can be made to look 14, and vice versa.

Some pedophile literature is sold at ordinary bookstores, since it does not always legally qualify as child pornography. One area bookstore, for instance, carries a book called *Chicken* that contains nude photographs of young males and explicit poetry describing sex between men and boys.

Madison law enforcement agents say they respond to child pornography no differently than they respond to other crimes. Most investigations begin only after the crime has been committed. "We don't have a proactive approach," the police lieutenant confesses. "Unless someone brings it to our attention," department investigators do not pursue child porn.

Another source, who asked not to be identified, charges that legitimate businesses in Madison operate as fronts for pornographers and distributors of porn. "It's an underground, quiet thing," she says. "They've got their system. Everything's running smoothly and has been for years."

LACK OF RESOURCES

According to Madison officials, the root problem is a shortage of trained personnel to track down the producers of child porn. "Certainly more investigators are needed," says Dane County District Attorney Hal Harlowe. "That would allow us to focus in on the people who are involved in it as a commercial enterprise."

But pursuing child pornographers is a harrowing, time-consuming task. Often years pass before a search warrant can even be obtained, as was the case with Harry Wald, the child pornographer in the Dane County town of Oregon who was convicted last year of nine counts of sexual assault and exploitation of children.

The charges were based on hundreds of sexually explicit photographs of little girls, some of them infants. Wald had sent several batches of these pictures to postal inspector Paul Groza, who was using a phony name and address and playing the role of a purchaser of child pornography. Many photos showed no faces, only children's bottoms. Some showed hard objects like combs and brushes inserted into little girls' vaginas.

Groza says he obtained Wald's name as a source of kiddie porn from a Milwaukee man and began corresponding with Wald in 1981. Investigators had to trace the photographs to identify the children, contact parents, find out how Wald had access to the girls and determine when and where the incidents occurred. According to Detective Urso, who investigated the case, Wald is a "dyed in the wool" pedophile who befriended families with young daughters and volunteered to babysit or take children on excursions.

Investigators determined early on that Wald was not only selling kiddie porn, but was also producing it. Given a choice between trying to nab a dirty old man who peddles child pornography and nailing down a clear-cut case of sexual abuse, police chose the latter. Wald was prosecuted for crimes committed while producing the porn, and not for possession or sale.

Some officials say that the state should strengthen its child porn laws. In Wisconsin it's a felony to produce, sell or distribute sexually explicit visual material of children. It's also a felony to coerce or entice a child for pornographic purposes or for parents and guardians to allow a child to be so used.

It is not against the law, however, to purchase or possess child porn. Nor are film and photo processors legally required to report sexually explicit material depicting children. Harlowe said a requirement such as this would be "worth pursuing" because it would greatly help investigators track down the actual producers.

A CHANGE IN THE LAW?

"Any change would be better than what we have now," remarks Rep. John Medinger (D-La Crosse), who says he might sponsor a bill to revise the child porn laws during the next legislative session. "What we have is really nothing."

Other states have criminalized mere possession of child pornography, with mixed results. Illinois made possession a felony last November, and the first person arrested under the new law also published a homemade magazine, ironically called Pure, that extolled child serial murder and torture.

But such legislation almost invariably faces legal challenges. Last December in Ohio a Court of Appeals ruled that a law prohibiting private possession of child pornography was unconstitutional. Various city ordinances prohibiting possession of kiddie porn have been struck down on grounds that they were overly broad and violate the First Amendment.

Nevertheless, Rep. Medinger and a number of sheriffs and district attorneys across the state want to criminalize possession of child porn. Currently, police must establish a suspect's intent to distribute before they can obtain a search warrant or make an arrest.

Milwaukee's assistant district attorney, John DiMotto, says it is "ludicrous" to outlaw the distribution of child porn without also outlawing its possession. "To allow the private possession gives an incentive to distributors to take a chance and attempt to produce and distribute since there is a market for such materials," DiMotto stated last year in a letter to a legislative aide.

The Milwaukee chief of police and a Waukesha police captain both claim that outlawing possession would make it easier to obtain search warrants, investigate suspects and prosecute more effectively.

But Madison law enforcement officials are less enthusiastic about such a change in the law. Outlawing possession won't help the victims of child pornography, Urso maintains. "These little laws come in real handy," she says, "but if they get out of jail in a couple of months, so what."

Rep. Medinger says that although "strong support exists in the legislature" to toughen child pornography laws, it is not an easy task. "The tricky thing is to draft legislation that doesn't interfere with First Amendment rights," he says.

Harlowe also sees problems with restricting private possession of child porn, however revolting. "You're not going to get at the producer by creating penalties for possession," he says. "The hazard is it's very easy to end up overregulating."

The district attorney adds: "We're going to end up in a constitutional mire, and I think properly so, if we focus in on the question of possession of any kind of literature for personal use."

VULNERABILITY

Laws regulating pornography face other challenges as well. Last year a legislative aide to Rep. Jim Rutkowski (D-Hales Corners) drafted a bill to revise the state's child porn laws, including a section outlawing possession. The new law would require commercial film and photo processors to report child pornography and expand the definition of pornography as it pertains to children. It also would allow expert witnesses to testify about the age of individuals used in porn.

Rutkowski and his legislative assistant also drafted a civil rights antipornography bill, modeled after ordinances passed by city councils in Minnesota and Indiana. Both the child pornography and civil antiporn bill were to be introduced in the legislature last September. Rep. Medinger had agreed to co-sponsor the proposal.

Then Rutkowski's office was burglarized. Intruders crawled in through an office window, stole a tape player and some pens, sprayed Rutkowski's desk drawers full of shaving cream and left the word "Sorry" in white-out on another desk, according to Capitol Police reports.

"The break-in was specifically timed to stop introduction of the legislation," says attorney Sara Johann, formerly Rutkowski's legislative aide. "All they had to do was convince Jim [Rutkowski] they were after him. They just wanted the legislation stopped. And they were successful at that."

Johann says the break-in fit a pattern of harassment against those who seek to impose legislative controls on pornography. She referred to threats received by proponents of Minneapolis' civil antiporn legislation and by Ald. Kathleen Nichols of Madison, who had proposed a civil rights antipornography ordinance for Dane County in 1983.

During the time she pushed for the ordinance, Nichols received dozens of abusive phone calls, as well as several false invitations to meetings around the country. Someone also stole Nichols' mail and broke into her apartment, leaving her files on pornography strewn across a desk. Eventually the FBI was called in to investigate.

Nichols believes someone was trying to scare her away from backing the antiporn bill. She warned Rutkowski's staff that they, too, might be singled out for harassment. "I felt concerned that they were about to take up the flag on a state level," says Nichols, who thought the state workers were "even more vulnerable" than she had been regarding legislation on a local level.

Rutkowski, who disputes that his office was burglarized because of the child pornography proposal, says he gave up on the legislation because he became more concerned with the obscenity bill, which was before his Judiciary Committee.

Still, Rutkowski does feel there are "some gaps or improvements we could make in terms of other state laws" regarding child pornography. He adds, however, that such legislation is no longer among his priorities. "I'm not really interested in working on the issue any further," he says.

J CONSENTLESS SEXUAL PORTRAYAL CASES

See, e.g., Keeton v. Hustler Mag., 465 U.S. 770 (1984) (female plaintiff having personal jurisdiction to bring libel suit against defendant); Lerman v. Flynt Distrib. Co., 745 F.2d 123 (2d Cir. 1984) (reversing jury award of ten million dollars for female plaintiff who was allegedly misidentified as the subject of nude magazine photographs), *cert. denied*, 105 S.Ct. 2114 (1985); Faloona v. Hustler Mag. 799 F.2d 1000 (5th Cir. 1986) (affirming dismissal of invasion of privacy case stemming from publication of plaintiff's nude photographs in the *Sex Atlas*); Wood v. Hustler Mag., 736 F.2d 1084 (5th Cir. 1984) (affirming damages for female plaintiff who was allegedly depicted nude in Hustler's "Beaver hunt" section without her consent), *cert. denied*, 105 S. Ct. 783 (1985); Boddie v. ABC, 731 F.2d 333 (6th Cir. 1984) (reversing lower court's dismissal of action brought under federal wiretap statute regarding information obtained about female plaintiff's sexual activity); Braun v. Flynt, 726 F.2d 245 (5th Cir.) (affirming female plaintiff's damage award in privacy action concerning allegedly unauthorized publication of a female plaintiff's photograph), *cert. denied sub nom.*, Chic Mag. v. Braun, 105 S.Ct. 252 (1984); Pring v. Penthouse Int'l, 695 F.2d 438 (10th Cir. 1982) (reversing jury award on behalf of plaintiff and dismissing action where magazine allegedly portrayed plaintiff as performing aberrant sexual acts with her baton), *cert. denied*, 462 U.S. 1132 (1983); Clark v. ABC, 684 F.2d 1208 (6th Cir. 1982) (reversing and remanding summary motion for defendant in defamation action involving defendant's alleged portrayal of plaintiff as a street prostitute), *cert. denied*, 460 U.S. 1040 (1983); Street v. NBC, 645 F.2d 1227 (6th Cir. 1981) (affirming summary judgment for defendant in libel action arising out of defendant's allegedly inaccurate portrayal of plaintiff as a whore), *cert. granted*, 454 U.S. 815, *cert. dismissed*, 454 U.S. 1095 (1981); Geisler v. Petrocelli, 616 F.2d 636 (2d Cir. 1980) (reversing dismissal of female plaintiff's action relating to publication of story which allegedly

depicted plaintiff as engaging in "untoward sexual conduct"); Douglass v. Hustler Mag., 607 F. Supp. 816 (N.D. Ill. 1984) (granting defendant magazine's motion for new trial unless plaintiff agreed to remittitur of jury award in action stemming from defendant's alleged publication of female plaintiff's photograph without her consent), *rev'd in part*, 769 F.2d 1128 (7th Cir. 1985); Jackson v. Playboy Enters., 574 F. Supp. 10 (S.D. Ohio 1983) (granting defendant's motion to dismiss an action brought by three minor plaintiffs allegedly photographed while being assisted by a female policewoman in fixing a bicycle. This photo was included in the publication of a spread of nude photographs of the policewoman without the plaintiffs' consent); Parnell v. Booth Newspapers, 572 F. Supp. 909 (W.D. Mich. 1983) (denying defendant's motions for dismissal and summary judgment where defendant allegedly published plaintiff's photograph in "false light" in connection with newspaper articles on prostitution); Barger v. Playboy Enters., 564 F. Supp. 1151 (N.D. Cal. 1983) (granting defendant's summary judgment motion in defamation action relating to publisher's allegedly inaccurate description of female plaintiff as engaging in aberrant sexual behavior), *aff'd*, 732 F.2d 163 (9th Cir. 1984), *cert. denied*, 105 S. Ct. 175 (1984); Hamilton v. United Press Int'l, 9 Media L. Rep. (BNA) 2453 (S.D. Iowa 1983) (granting defendant's motion for summary judgment in action brought by male plaintiff for story that allegedly incorrectly stated that he was married to a woman who had been arrested for indecent exposure; denying motion for summary judgment in action brought by wife of male plaintiff); Wynberg v. Nat'l Enquirer, 564 F. Supp. 924 (C.D. Cal. 1982) (granting defendant's motion for summary judgment in libel action brought by male plaintiff arising from publication of information about a close personal relationship); McCable v. Village Voice, 550 F. Supp. 525 (E.D. Pa. 1982) (granting defendant's motion for summary judgment on libel and false light claims while denying motion as to the publication of private facts claim in action brought by female plaintiff who was allegedly depicted nude without her authorization); Lerman v. Chuckleberry Publishing, 544 F.

This appendix is taken from Ruth Colker, "Published Consentless Sexual Portrayals: A Proposed Framework For Analysis," *Buffalo Law Review* 35 (?? 1986): 41–43, fn. 7. Reprinted with permission.

Supp. 966 (S.D.N.Y. 1982) (reversing verdict that had been granted to plaintiff in suit alleging invasion of privacy based on publication of nude photographs), *rev'd sub nom.* Lerman v. Flynt Distrib. 745 F.2d 123 (1984); Clark v. Celeb. Publishing, 530 F. Supp. 979 (S.D.N.Y. 1981) (awarding female plaintiff damages in action relating to allegedly unauthorized publication of photographs of her on the cover of and in advertisements for defendant's magazine); Miss America Pageant v. Penthouse, 524 F. Supp. 1280 (S.D.N.Y. 1981) (granting defendant's motion for summary judgment in libel action brought by plaintiff pageant after magazine story depicting sexual behavior by contestants); Ann-Margaret v. High Soc'y Mag., 498 F. Supp. 401 (S.D.N.Y. 1980) (dismissing action brought by female plaintiff for publication of her partially nude photograph allegedly without her authorization); Neiman-Marcus v. Lait, 13 F.R.D. 311 (S.D.N.Y. 1952) (granting motion to dismiss the claim of saleswomen who were allegedly depicted as prostitutes and denying motion to dismiss claim of salesmen who were allegedly described as "faggots" and "fairies"); Martin v. Penthouse, 12 Media L. Rep. (BNA) 2058 (Cal. Ct. App. 1986) (affirming summary judgment for defendant's invasion of privacy action challenging publication of photographs of plaintiffs at "exotic erotic ball"); Diaz v. Oakland Tribune, 139 Cal. App.3d 118, 188 Cal. Rptr. 762 (1983) (reversing jury award for plaintiff who had undergone gender "corrective" surgery); Herrell v. Twin Coast, 7 Media L. Rep. (BNA) 1216 (Cal. Ct. App. 1981) (affirming dismissal of plaintiff's complaint in action arising from a story stating that male plaintiffs had been suspended from the police force for an alleged sexual assault); Spradley v. Sutton, 9 Media L. Rep. (BNA) 1481 (Fla. Cir. Ct. 1982) (granting defendant's motion for summary judgment in invasion of privacy action against television station for defendant's allegedly unauthorized broadcast of male plaintiff partially nude); Brooks v. Stone, 253 Ga. 565, 322 S.E.2d 728 (1984) (granting defendant's motion for summary judgment in defamation action relating to allegedly sexually critical statements about plaintiff); Shields v. Gross, 58 N.Y.2d 338, 448 N.E.2d 108, 461 N.Y.S.2d 254 (1983) (dismissing female plaintiff's action relating to allegedly nonconsensual publication of her photographs); Cohen v. Herbal Concepts, 100 A.D.2d 175, 473 N.Y.S.2d 426 (reversing dismissal of plaintiff's complaint where mother and child were photographed partially nude for an advertisement), *aff'd*, 63 N.Y.2d 379, 472 N.E.2d 307, 482 N.Y.S.2d 497 (1984); Springer v. Viking Press, 90 A.D.2d 315, 457 N.Y.S.2d 246 (1982) (dismissing plaintiff's action arising from unauthorized publication of a fictional novel in which plaintiff was allegedly portrayed as a whore), *aff'd*, 60 N.Y.2d 916, 458 N.E.2d 1256, 470 N.Y.S.2d 579 (1983); Berkley v. Casablance, 80 A.D.2d 428, 458 N.Y.S.2d 1004 (1981) (granting partial summary judgment on behalf of plaintiff where defendant allegedly published female plaintiff's photographs without authorization); Giaimo v. Literary Guild, 79 A.D.2d 917, 434 N.Y.S.2d 419 (1981) (affirming defendant's motion for dismissal where male and female plaintiffs' photograph was published without authorization in an advertisement); Creel v. Crown Publishers, 115 A.D.2d 414, 496 N.Y.S.2d 219 (1985) (dismissing plaintiff's invasion of privacy action stemming from publication of plaintiff's nude photograph in a guide to nude beaches); Moore v. Stonehill Communications, 7 Media L. Rep. (BNA) 1438 (N.Y. Sup. Ct. 1981) (granting plaintiff's motion for summary judgment where defendant published an allegedly unauthorized sexual photograph of plaintiff in advertisement for a book); Guccione v. Hustler, 7 Media L. Rep. (BNA) 2077 (Ohio Ct. App. 1981) (affirming on the issue of liability but reversing and remanding on the issue of damages in action by male plaintiff arising from publication of a magazine photograph depicting him engaged in sexually aberrant activity); Miller v. Charleston Gazette, 9 Media L. Rep. (BNA) 2540 (W. Va. Cir. Ct. 1983) (granting defendant's motion for summary judgment in action arising from allegedly depicting male plaintiff in a cartoon as a person who engaged in deviant sexual activities); Doe v. Sarasota-Bradenton Television, 436 So.2d 328 (Fla Dist. Ct. App 1983) (dismissing plaintiff's complaint in action relating to unauthorized publication of plaintiff's identity as a rape victim); Cape Publications v. Bridges, 423 So.2d 426 (Fla. Dist. Ct. App. 1982) (reversing award for female plaintiff where her partially nude photograph was allegedly published without authorization), *cert. denied*, 464 U.S. 893 (1983). *Cf.* Schrottman v. Boston Globe, 7 Media L. Rep. (BNA) 1487 (Mass. Super. Ct. 1981) (granting defendant's motion for summary judgment in libel action arising from defendant's alleged false attribution of the use of an offensive, racial epithet to plaintiff); Arrington v. New York Times, 55 N.Y.2d 433, 434 N.E.2d 1319, 449 N.Y.S.2d 941 (1982) (granting defendant's motion to dismiss an action arising from newspaper's unauthorized publication of plaintiff's photograph in article on upward mobility of the black middle class), *cert. denied* 459 U.S. 1146 (1983). For further discussion of issues arising from racial epithets, see Delgado, *Words That Wound: A Tort Action for Racial Insults, Epithets, and Name-Calling,* 17 Harv. C.R.-C.L. L. Rev. 133 (1982).

K MODEL ANTIPORNOGRAPHY LAW

An Ordinance of the City of Minneapolis

(As passed by the City Council and Vetoed by the Mayor)

Amending Title 7, Chapter 139 of the Minneapolis Code of Ordinances Relating to Civil Rights: In General.

The City Council of the City of Minneapolis do ordain as follows:

Section 1. That Section 139.10 of the above-entitled ordinance be amended to read as follows:

139.10 *Finding, declaration of policy and purpose.*

(a) *Findings.* The council finds that discrimination in employment, labor union membership, housing accommodations, property rights, education, public accommodations and public services based on race, color, creed, religion, ancestry, national origin, sex, including sexual harassment AND PORNOGRAPHY, affectional preference, disability, age, marital status, or status with regard to public assistance or in housing accommodations based on familial status adversely affects the health, welfare, peace and safety of the community. Such discriminatory practices degrade individuals, foster intolerance and hate, and create and intensify unemployment, sub-standard housing, under-education, ill health, lawlessness and poverty, thereby injuring the public welfare.

> (1) *SPECIAL FINDINGS ON PORNOGRAPHY:* THE COUNCIL FINDS THAT PORNOGRAPHY IS CENTRAL IN CREATING AND MAINTAINING THE CIVIL INEQUALITY OF THE SEXES, PORNOGRAPHY IS A SYSTEMATIC PRACTICE OF EXPLOITATION AND SUBORDINATION BASED ON SEX WHICH DIFFERENTIALLY HARMS WOMEN. THE BIGOTRY AND CONTEMPT IT PROMOTES, WITH THE ACTS OF AGGRESSION IT FOSTERS, HARM WOMEN'S OPPORTUNITIES FOR EQUALITY OF RIGHTS IN EMPLOYMENT, EDUCATION, PROPERTY RIGHTS, PUBLIC ACCOMMODATIONS AND PUBLIC SERVICES; CREATE PUBLIC HARASSMENT AND PRIVATE DENIGRATION; PROMOTE INJURY AND DEGRADATION SUCH AS RAPE, BATTERY AND PROSTITUTION AND INHIBIT JUST ENFORCEMENT OF LAWS AGAINST THESE ACTS; CONTRIBUTE SIGNIFICANTLY TO RESTRICTING WOMEN FROM FULL EXERCISE OF CITIZENSHIP AND PARTICIPATION IN PUBLIC LIFE, INCLUDING IN NEIGHBORHOODS; DAMAGE RELATIONS BETWEEN THE SEXES; AND UNDERMINE THE WOMEN'S EQUAL EXERCISE OF RIGHTS TO SPEECH AND ACTION GUARANTEED TO ALL CITIZENS UNDER THE CONSTITUTIONS AND LAWS OF THE UNITED STATES AND THE STATE OF MINNESOTA.

(b) *Declaration of policy and purpose.* It is the public policy of the City of Minneapolis and the purpose of this title:

(1) To recognize and declare that the opportunity to obtain employment, labor union membership, housing accommodations, property rights, education, public accommodations and public services without discrimination based on race, color, creed, religion, ancestry, national origin, sex, including sexual harassment AND PORNOGRAPHY, affectional preference, disability, age, marital status, or status with regard to public assistance or to obtain housing accommodations without discrimination based on familial status is a civil right;

(2) To prevent and prohibit all discriminatory practices based on race, color, creed, religion, ancestry, national origin, sex, including sexual harassment AND PORNOGRAPHY, affectional preference, disability, age, marital status, or status with regard to public assistance with respect to employment, labor union membership, housing accommodations, property rights, education, public accommodations, or public services;

(3) To prevent and prohibit all discriminatory practices based on familial status with respect to housing accommodations;

(4) TO PREVENT AND PROHIBIT ALL DISCRIMINATORY PRACTICES OF SEXUAL SUBORDINATION OR INEQUALITY THROUGH PORNOGRAPHY;

(5) To protect all persons from unfounded charges of discriminatory practices;

(6) To eliminate existing and the development of any ghettos in the community; and

(7) To effectuate the foregoing policy by means of public information and education, mediation and conciliation, and enforcement.

Section 3. That Section 139.20 of the above-entitled ordinance be amended by adding thereto a new subsection (gg) to read as follows:

(gg) *Pornography.* Pornography is a form of discrimination on the basis of sex.

(1) Pornography is the sexually explicit subordination of women, graphically depicted, whether in pictures or in words, that also includes one or more of the following:

   (i) women are presented dehumanized as sexual objects, things or commodities; or

   (ii) women are presented as sexual objects who enjoy pain or humiliation; or

   (iii) women are presented as sexual objects who experience sexual pleasure in being raped; or

   (iv) women are presented as sexual objects tied up or cut up or mutilated or bruised or physically hurt; or

   (v) women are presented in postures of sexual submission; or

   (vi) women's body parts—including but not limited to vaginas, breasts, and buttocks—are exhibited, such that women are reduced to those parts; or

   (vii) women are presented as whores by nature; or

   (viii) women are presented being penetrated by objects or animals; or

   (ix) women are presented in scenarios of degradation, injury, abasement, torture, shown as filthy or inferior, bleeding, bruised, or hurt in a context that makes these conditions sexual

(2) The use of men, children, or transsexuals in the place of women in (1) (i - ix) above is pornography for purposes of subsections (1) - (p) of this statute.

Section 4. That Section 139.40 of the above-entitled ordinance be amended by adding thereto

new subsections (*l*), (m), (n), (o), (p), (q), (r) and (s) to read as follows:

(*l*) *Discrimination by trafficking in pornography.* The production, sale, exhibition, or distribution of pornography is discrimination against women by means of trafficking in pornography:

(1) City, state, and federally funded public libraries or private and public university and college libraries in which pornography is available for study, including on open shelves, shall not be construed to be trafficking in pornography but special display presentations of pornography in said places is sex discrimination.

(2) The formation of private clubs or associations for purposes of trafficking in pornography is illegal and shall be considered a conspiracy to violate the civil rights of women.

(3) Any woman has cause of action hereunder as a woman acting against the subordination of women. Any man or transsexual who alleges injury by pornography in the way women are injured by it shall also have a cause of action.

(m) *Coercion into pornographic performances.* Any person, including transsexual, who is coerced, intimidated, or fraudulently induced (hereafter, "coerced") into performing for pornography shall have a cause of action against the maker(s), seller(s), exhibitor(s) or distributor(s) of said pornography for damages and for the elimination of the products of the performance(s) from the public view.

(1) *Limitation of action.* This claim shall not expire before five years have elapsed from the date of the coerced performance(s) or from the last appearance or sale of any product of the performance(s), whichever date is later;

(2) Proof of one or more of the following facts or conditions shall not, without more, negate a findings of coercion;

   (i) that the person is a woman; or

   (ii) that the person is or has been a prostitute; or

   (iii) that the person has attained the age of majority; or

   (iv) that the person is connected by blood or marriage to anyone involved in or related to the making of the pornography; or

   (v) that the person has previously had, or been thought to have had, sexual relations with anyone, including anyone involved in or related to the making of the pornography; or

   (vi) that the person has previously posed for sexually explicit pictures for or with anyone, including anyone involved in or related to the making of the pornography at issue; or

(vii) that anyone else, including a spouse or other relative, has given permission on the person's behalf; or

(viii) that the person actually consented to a use of the performance that is changed into pornography; or

(ix) that the person knew that the purpose of the acts or events in question was to make pornography; or

(x) that the person showed no resistance or appeared to cooperate actively in the photographic sessions or in the sexual events that produced the pornography; or

(xi) that the person signed a contract, or made statements affirming a willingness to cooperate in the production of pornography; or

(xii) that no physical force, threats, or weapons were used in the making of the pornography; or

(xiii) that the person was paid or otherwise compensated.

(n) *Forcing pornography on a person.* Any woman, man, child, or transsexual who has pornography forced on him/her in any place of employment, in education, in a home, or in any public place has a cause of action against the perpetrator and/or institution.

(o) *Assault or physical attack due to pornography.* Any woman, man, child, or transsexual who is assaulted, physically attacked or injured in a way that is directly caused by specific pornography has a claim for damages against the perpetrator, the maker(s), distributor(s), seller(s), and/or exhibitor(s), and for an injunction against the specific pornography's further exhibition, distribution, or sale. No damages shall be assessed (A) against maker(s) for pornography made, (B) against distributor(s) for pornography distributed, (C) against seller(s) for pornography sold, or (D) against exhibitors for pornography exhibited prior to the ENFORCEMENT date of this act.

(p) *Defenses.* Where the materials which are the subject matter of a cause of action under subsections (l), (m), (n), or (o) of this section are pornography, it shall not be a defense that the defendant did not know or intend that the materials were pornography or sex discrimination.

(q) *Severability.* Should any part(s) of this ordinance be found legally, invalid, the remaining part(s) remain valid.

(r) Subsections (l), (m), (n), and (o) of this section are exceptions to the second clause of section 141.90 of this title.

(s) *Effective date.* Enforcement of this ordinance of December 30, 1983, shall be suspended until July 1, 1984 ("enforcement date") to facilitate training, education, voluntary compliance, and implementation taking into consideration the opinions of the City Attorney and the Civil Rights Commission. No liability shall attach under (1) or as specifically provided in the second sentence of (o) until the enforcement date. Liability under all other sections of this act shall attach as of December 30, 1983.

City-County General Ordinance No. 35, 1984, § 2, amending the Code of Indianapolis and Marion County, Indiana, Ch. 16, Human Relations; Equal Opportunity, § 16-3, Definitions, subd. (q):

(q) Pornography shall mean the graphic sexually explicit subordination of women, whether in pictures or in words, that also includes one or more of the following:

(1) Women are presented as sexual objects who enjoy pain or humiliation; or

(2) Women are presented as sexual objects who experience sexual pleasure in being raped; or

(3) Women are presented as sexual objects tied up or mutilated or bruised or physically hurt, or as dismembered or truncated or fragmented or severed into body parts; or

(4) Women are presented being penetrated by objects or animals; or

(5) Women are presented in scenarios of degradation, injury, abasement, torture, shown as filthy or inferior, bleeding, bruised, or hurt in a context that makes these conditions sexual;

(6) Women are presented as sexual objects for domination, conquest, violation, exploitation, possession, or use, or through postures or positions of servility or submission or display.

The use of men, children, or transsexuals in the place of women in paragraphs (1) through (6) above shall also constitute pornography under this section.

BIBLIOGRAPHY

CHAPTER 1

Attorney General's Commission on Pornography. *Final Report*. Washington, D.C.: U.S. Department of Justice, 1986.

Barry, Kathleen. *Female Sexual Slavery*. Englewood Cliffs, N.J.: Prentice – Hall, 1979.

"Constitutional Law—Obscenity—the Definitional Dilemma." *Georgia State Bar Journal* 10 (November 1973): 327–35.

Dershowitz, Alan M. "What Is Porn? Should the First Amendment Protect Pornography?" *American Bar Association Journal* 72 (November 1986): 36.

"From Roth to Miller: The Continuing Redefinition of Obscenity." *Idaho Law Review* 10 (Spring 1974): 193–211.

Gardiner, Harold C. "Moral Principles towards a Definition of the Obscene." *Law and Contemporary Problems* 20 (Autumn 1955): 560–71.

Gilboa, Netta. "Defining Pornography: Why the Experts Disagree." Paper presented to the Popular Culture Association, Cincinnati, 28 March 1981.

Houston, J., et al. "On Determining Pornographic Material." *Journal of Psychology* 88 (November 1974): 277–87.

Hughes, Ann. "What Is Pornography: Discussion Paper." *Bulletin of the Hong Kong Psychological Society* 16–17 (January–July 1986): 33–40.

Kirk, Dr. Jerry R. *The Mind Polluters*. Nashville, Tenn.: Thomas Nelson, 1985.

MacDonald, Michael. "Obscenity, Censorship, and Freedom of Expression: Does the Charter Protect Pornography?" *University of Toronto Faculty of Law Review* 43 (Fall 1985): 130–52.

McTeer, Maureen. "How Should Our Laws Define Pornography?" *Chatelaine* 58 (March 1985): 46.

Mewett, Alan W. "Pornography and Erotica." *Criminal Law Quarterly* (Canada) 29 (September 1987): 401–2.

"Miller, Jenkins, and the Definition of Obscenity." *Montana Law Review* 36 (Summer 1975): 285–99.

Moretti, Daniel S. *Obscenity and Pornography: The Law Under The First Amendment*. New York: Oceana Publications, 1984.

Price, D.G. "Role of Choice in a Definition of Obscenity." *Canadian Bar Review* 57 (June 1979): 301–24.

Report of the Special Committee on Pornography and Prostitution. Ottawa: Minister of Supply and Services, 1985.

Schauer, Frederick. *The Law of Obscenity*.: BNA Books, 1976.

Steinem, Gloria. "Erotica and Pornography: A Clear and Present Difference." *Ms.*, November 1978, 53.

Taylor, Bruce A. "Hard–Core Pornography: A Proposal for a Per Se Rule." *University of Michigan Journal of Law Reform* 21 (Fall 1987, Winter 1988): 255–82.

Weaver, George A. *Handbook on the Prosecution of Obscenity Cases*. New York: National Obscenity Law Center, Division of Morality in Media, Inc., 1985.

CHAPTER 2

Abramson, P., and B. Mechanic. "Sex and the Media: Three Decades of Best-Selling Books and Major Motion Pictures." *Archives of Sexual Behavior* 12, no. 3 (1983): 185–205.

Adult Movies. New York: Pocket Books, 1982.

American Psychiatric Association. *Diagnostic and Statistical Manual of Mental Disorders III, Revised*. Washington, D.C.: American Psychiatric Association, 1980.

Anchell, Melvin. *Sex and Sanity*. New York: Macmillan, 1971.

Ashley, Barbara Renchkowvsy, and David Ashley. "Sex as Violence: The Body Against Intimacy." *International Journal of Women's Studies* 7, no. 4 (1984): 352–71.

Attorney General's Commission on Pornography. *Final Report*. Washington, D.C.: U.S. Department of Justice, 1986.

Baker, Ann. "Hard-Sell or Hard-Core? Critics Say Ads Use Pornographic Themes." *St. Paul Pioneer Press*, 16 October 1983.

Barbach, Lonnie, ed. *Pleasures: Women Write Erotica*. Garden City, N.Y.: Doubleday, 1984.

Baxter, R.L., C. DeRiemer, L.L. Landini, and M.W. Singletary. "A Content Analysis of Music Videos." *Journal of Broadcasting and Electronic Media* 29, no. 3 (1985): 333–40.

Brown, Jane D., and Kenneth Campbell. "Race and Gender in Music Videos: The Same Beat but a Different Drummer." *Journal of Communication* 36 (Winter 1986): 94–105.

Burn, G., and R. Thompson. "Music and Television: Some Historical and Esthetic Considerations." Paper presented to the Popular Culture Association, Toronto, April 1984.

Byrne, D. "The Imagery of Sex." In *Handbook of Sexology,* edited by J. Money and H. Musaph, 327–50. Amsterdam: Excerpta Media, 1977.

Caplan, R. "The Image of Women in Music Videos." Paper presented to the Popular Culture Association, Toronto, April 1984.

Center for Media Awareness and National Institute for Media Education and Research. "Content Analysis of Five Leading Pornographic Magazines (Playboy, Hustler, Penthouse, Oui and Playgirl)." Report submitted to the Texas House of Representatives Select Committee on Child Abuse/Neglect and Pornography, Houston, 31 January 1984.

Check, J.V.P. "A Survey of Canadians' Attitudes Regarding Sexual Content in Media." Report to the Lamarch Research Programme on Violence and Conflict Resolution and the Canadian Broadcasting Corporation, Toronto, 1985.

Clarens, C. *An Illustrated History of the Horror Film.* New York: Capricorn, 1967.

Cornillon, Susan Koppelman, ed. *Images of Women in Fiction.* Bowling Green, Ohio: Bowling Green University Popular Press, 1972.

Courtney, A., and T. Whipple. *Sex Role Stereotyping in Advertising.* Lexington, Mass.: Lexington Books, 1983.

Dietz, P.E. and B. Evans. "Pornographic Imagery and Prevalence of Paraphilia." *American Journal of Psychiatry* 139 (1982): 1493–94.

Dietz, P.E., B. Harry, and R.R. Hazelwood. "Detective Magazines: Pornography for the Sexual Sadist?" *Journal of Forensic Sciences* 31 (January 1986): 197–211.

Dietz, P.E., and A.E. Sears. "Pornography and Obscenity Sold in 'Adult Bookstores': A Survey of 5132 Books, Magazines, and Films in Four American Cities." *University of Michigan Journal of Law Reform* 21 (Fall 1987, Winter 1988): 7–46.

Di Lauro, Al. *Dirty Movies: An Illustrated History of the Stag Film, 1915–1970.* New York: Chelsea House, 1976.

Dixon, K. (director). *Filmgore.* Filmgore Productions. Film.

Douglas, D. *Horror.* New York: Macmillan, 1966.

Drakeford, John W., and Jack Hamm. *Pornography: The Sexual Mirage.* Nashville, Tenn.: Thomas Nelson, 1973.

Duncan, Carol. "The Esthetics of Power in Modern Erotic Art." *Heresies.* January 1977.

Eisenberg, Daniel. "Toward a Bibliography of Erotic Pulps." *Journal of Popular Culture* 15 (Spring 1982): 175–84.

Ellis, John. "Photography/Pornography/Art/Pornography." *Screen.* Spring 1980, 81–108.

Fedler, F., J. Hall, and L. Tanzi. "Popular Songs Emphasize Sex, Deemphasize Romance." *Mass Communication Review* 9 (Spring–Fall 1982): 10–15.

Fishburn, K. *Women in Popular Culture: A Reference Guide.* Westport, Conn.: Greenwood Press, 1982.

Foxon, David. *Libertine Literature in England, 1660–1745.* Hyde Park, N.Y.: University Books, 1965.

Friedman, Herbert. "Sex Wars: Lesbianism, Rape, Bestiality and Adultery—Porn Propaganda, the Military's Secret Weapon." *Oui.* September 1983.

Gerhard, Paul. *Pornography in Fine Art from Ancient Times up to the Present.* Los Angeles: Elysium, 1969.

Goffman, Erving. *Gender Advertisements.* New York: Harper & Row, 1976.

Gordon, M., and R.R. Bell. "Medium and Hardcore Pornography: A Comparative Analysis." *Journal of Sex Research* 5 (1969): 260–68.

Gould, L. *Pornography for Women.* New York: New York Times Co., 1975.

Gould, L. "Pornography for Women." In *Human Sexuality in Today's World,* edited by J. Gagnon. Boston: Little, Brown, 1977.

Griffin, Susan. *Pornography and Silence: Culture's Revenge Against Nature.* New York: Harper & Row, 1981.

Haskell, Molly. "Rape in the Movies: Update on an Ancient War." *Village Voice,* 8 October 1979.

Hazen, Helen. *Endless Rapture: Rape, Romance and the Female Imagination.* New York: Charles Schribner's Sons, 1983.

Herrman, Margaret S., and Diane C. Bordner. "Attitudes toward Pornography in a Southern Community." *Criminology* 21 (August 1983): 349–74.

Holmes, Ronald M., *The Sex Offender and the Criminal Justice System.* Springfield, Ill.: Charles C. Thomas, 1983.

Hommel, Teresa. "Images of Women in Pornography and Media: Colloquium: Violent Pornography: Degradation of Women Versus Right of Free Speech." *New York University Review of Law and Social Change* 8, no. 2 (1978–79): 207–15.

Houston, J.A. "Capturing Policies of Pornographic Pictorial Representations by Normative Judgment Analysis." *Dissertation Abstracts International* 34 (1974): 5713–14.

Hurwood, Bernhardt J. *The Golden Age of Erotica.* Los Angeles: Sherbourne Press, 1965.

Kaite, B. "A Survey of Canadian Distributors of Pornographic Material." Working paper 17. Prepared by the Canadian Department of Justice for the Special Committee on Pornography and Prostitution, 1984.

Kearney, Patrick J. *The Private Case: An Annotated Bibliography of the Private Case Erotica Collection in the British (Museum) Library.* London: J. Landesman, 1981.

Kendrick, William. *The Secret Museum: The History of Pornography in Literature.* New York: Viking Press, 1987.

Kerin, K., W. Lundstrum, and D. Sciglimpaglia. "Women in Advertisements: Retrospect and Prospect." *Journal of Advertising* (November 1979): 37–41.

Key, Wilson Bryan. *Media Sexploitation.* Englewood Cliffs, N.J.: Prentice-Hall, 1977.

Kiedrowski, John S., and J.M. Van Dijk. "Pornography and Prostitution in Denmark, France, West Germany, The Netherlands and Sweden." Working paper 1.

Prepared by the Canadian Department of Justice for the Special Committee on Pornography and Prostitution, 1984.

Klenow, D.J., and L. Jeffrey. "Selected Characteristics of the X-rated Movie Audience: Toward a National Profile of the Recidivist." *Sociological Symposium* 20 (1977): 73–83.

Knipe, E. "The Semantics of Sex: An Analysis of 8-mm 'Porn' Movies." Paper presented to the Southern Sociological Society, 1978.

Kramer, Robert, ed. *Obscenity and the Arts*. Durham, N.C.: Duke University School of Law, 1955.

Kronhausen, E., and P. Kronhausen. *Pornography and the Law*. New York: Ballantine Books, 1959.

Kronhausen, E., and P. Kronhausen. "The Psychology of Pornography." In *The Encyclopedia of Sexual Behavior*. rev. ed., edited by A. Ellis and A. Abarbanel. New York: Hawthorn Books, 1967.

Kronhausen, P. *The Complete Book of Erotic Art: Erotic Art, Volumes 1 and 2: A Survey of Erotic Fact and Fancy in the Fine Arts*. New York: Bell Publishing Co., 1978.

Kurland, Morton L. "Pedophilia Erotica." *Journal of Nervous and Mental Disease* 131 (1960): 394–403.

Kurti, Laszlo. "Dirty Movies—Dirty Minds: The Social Construction of X-Rated Films." *Journal of Popular Culture* 17 (Fall 1983): 187–92.

Lebegue, Breck J. "Paraphilias in Pornography: A Study of Perversions Inherent in Title." *Australian Journal of Sex, Marriage and Family* 6, no. 1: 33–36.

Leidholdt, Dorchen. "WAP and NOW Protest *Pieces*." *Womanews* 4 (November 1983): 10.

Leventhal, H. "An Empirical Inquiry into the Effect of Miller v. California on the Control of Obscenity." *New York Review* 52 (1977): 810–935.

Linz, Daniel, and Edward Donnerstein. "Methodological Issues in the Content Analysis of Pornography." *University of Michigan Journal of Law Reform* 21 (Fall 1987, Winter 1988): 47–54.

Loth, David Goldsmith. *The Erotic in Literature: A Historical Survey of Pornography as Delightful as It Is Indiscreet*. New York: J. Messner, 1961.

Lowary, D.T., G. Love, and M. Kirby. "Sex on the Soap Operas: Patterns of Intimacy." *Journal of Communication* 31 (1981): 90–96.

Marcus, Steven. *The Other Victorians: A Study of Sexuality and Pornography in Mid-Nineteenth Century England*. New York: Basic Books, 1974.

Matacin, Mala L., and Jerry M. Berger. "A Content Analysis of Sexual Themes in *Playboy* Cartoons." *Sex Roles* 17 (August 1987): 179–86.

McDonald, W.K., K.B. Perkings, R.R. Sheehan, and J.H. Curtis. "The Pornography Controversy: A Study of Attitudes in a Southern Georgian Community." *Journal of Humanics* 5 (1977): 64–78.

McKenna, K. "Videos—Low in Art, High in Sex and Sell." *Los Angeles Times Calendar*, 21 August 1983.

McKinstry, William C. "The Pulp Voyeur: A Peek at Pornography in Public Places." In *Deviance: Field Studies and Self-Disclosures*, edited by Jerry Jacobs, 30–40. Palo Alto, Calif.: National Press Books, 1974.

Michelson, Peter. *The Aesthetics of Pornography*. New York: Herder and Herder, 1971.

Miller, Paul. "The Miller Report: A Survey of Swingers in America Today." *Gallery*, November 1984, 59–77.

National Coalition on Television Violence. "TV/Film Violence Bibliography, 1933–1983." *NCTV News* (Canada), Special Issue, May 1983, 1–12.

Nawy, Harold. "In the Pursuit of Happiness?: Consumers of Erotica in San Francisco." *Journal of Social Issues* 29, no. 3 (1973): 147–60.

'OJJDP Concedes Flaws in Study of Cartoons in Adult Magazines." *Criminal Justice Newsletter*, 1 December 1986.

"OJJOP Study Finds 6000 Images of Children in Soft Porn." *Criminal Justice Newsletter*. 16 September 1986.

Otto, H.A. "Sex and Violence on the American Newsstand." *Journalism Quarterly* 40 (1963): 19–26.

Palmer, C. "Pornographic Comics: A Content Analysis." *Journal of Sex Research* 15 (1979): 285–97.

Palys, T.S. "A Content Analysis of Sexually Explicit Videos in British Columbia." *Working Papers on Pornography and Prostitution, Report No. 15*. Ottawa: Prepared by the Canadian Department of Justice for the Special Committee on Pornography and Prostitution, 1984.

Palys, T.S. "Testing the Common Wisdom: The Social Content of Video Pornography." *Canadian Psychology* 27 (January 1986): 22–35.

Paul, J., C. Miller, and J. Hanson. "Music Television: Technological Advancement or Passing Fancy." Paper presented to the Popular Culture Association, Toronto, April 1984.

Peat Marwick and Partners. "National Population Study on Pornography and Prostitution." Working paper 6. Prepared by the Canadian Department of Justice for the Special Committee on Pornography and Prostitution, 1984.

Peckham, Morse. *Art and Pornography: An Experiment in Explanation*. New York: Basic Books, 1969.

Peters, Dan, and Steve Peters. *Rock's Hidden Persuader: The Truth about Backmasking*. Minneapolis: Bethany House Publishers, 1985.

Pfaus, James G., Lonn D.S. Myronuk, and W.J. Jacobs. "Soundtrack Contents and Depicted Sexual Violence." *Archives of Sexual Behavior* 15 (June 1986): 231–37.

Pornography: The Longford Report. London: Coronet Books, Hodder Paperbacks, Ltd., 1972.

"Pornography: Love or Death?" *Film Comment* 20 (December 1984): 29.

Prehn, John W. "Invasion of the Male Strippers: Role Assignment in a Small-Town Strip Club." *Journal of Popular Culture* 17 (Fall 1983): 182–86.

Reage, P. "Consensus in Pornography Definitions: A Content Analysis." *International Behavioral Scientist* 5 (1973): 1–12.

Reisman, J.A. "About My Study of 'Dirty Pictures'." *Washington Post*, 18 June 1985.

Reisman, J.A., D.F. Reisman, and B.S. Elman. "Sexual Exploitation by Health Professionals in Cartoons of a Popular Magazine." In *Sexual Exploitation of Patients by Health Professionals,* edited by Ann W. Burgess and Carol R. Hartman, 107–19. New York: Praeger, 1986.

Reynolds, J. "Special Issues: Dial-a-Porn." Paper presented at the obscenity prosecution seminar conducted by the Department of Legal Education, U.S. Department of Justice, Washington, D.C., 17 May 1984.

Richards, Abe. *An Illustrated History of Pornography.* Los Angeles: Athena Books, 1968.

Rochelle, Larry. "Now You See 'Em—Now You Don't: Those Sexy Sublims." *Journal of Popular Culture* 17 (Fall 1983): 161–66.

Rosegrant, John. "Contributions to Psychohistory: X Fetish Symbols in *Playboy* Centerfolds." *Psychological Reports* 59 (October 1986): 623–31.

Sansfacon, D. "Agreements and Conventions of the United Nations with Respect to Pornography and Prostitution." Working paper 3. Prepared by the Canadian Department of Justice for the Special Committee on Pornography and Prostitution, 1984.

Schell, Bernadette, Helen Sherritt, Jennifer Arthur, Lisa Beatty, et al. "Development of a Pornography Community Standard: Questionnaire Results of Two Canadian Cities." *Canadian Journal of Criminology* 29 (April 1987): 133–52.

Scott, D.A. ed. *Symposium on Media Violence and Pornography: Proceedings, Resource Book and Research Guide.* Toronto: Media Action Group, 1984.

Scott, D.A. *Pornography: Its Effects on the Family, Community and Culture.* Washington, D.C.: The Free Congress Foundation, 1985.

Scott, J.E. "An Updated Longitudinal Content Analysis of Sex References in Mass Circulation Magazines." *Journal of Sex Research* 22 (1986): 385.

Scott, J.E., and S.J. Cuvelier. "Violence in Playboy Magazine: A Longitudinal Analysis." *Archives of Sexual Behavior* 16 (August 1987): 279–88.

Sherman, Barry L., and Joseph R. Dominick. "Guns, Sex and Rock and Roll: A Content Analysis of Music Television." Paper presented to the Speech Communication Association. Chicago, November 1984.

Sherman, Barry L., and Joseph R. Dominick. "Violence and Sex in Music Videos: TV and Rock 'n' Roll." *Journal of Communication* 36 (Winter 1986): 79–93.

Shulman, S.G. "Pornography: A Poll." *Time,* 21 July 1986, 22.

Simpson, Maria. "Jeans Ads." *Journal of Popular Culture* 17 (Fall 1983): 146–53.

Slade, Joseph. "Pornographic Theaters Off Times Square." in *The Pornography Controversy,* edited by Ray C. Rist, 119–39. New Brunswick, N.J.: Transaction Books, 1975.

Slade, Joseph. "Violence in the Hard-Core Pornographic Film: A Historical Survey." *Journal of Communication* 34 (Summer 1984): 148–63.

Smith, D. "The Social Content of Pornography." *Journal of Communication* 36 (1976): 16–24.

Smith, M.A., J.V.P. Check, and M.J. Henery. *Sexual Violence in the Mass Media: A Content Analysis of Feature-Length Films.* Paper presented to the Canadian Psychological Association, Ottawa, May–June 1984.

Snitow, Ann, Christine Stansell, and Sharon Thompson, eds. *Powers of Desire: The Politics of Sexuality.* New York: Monthly Review Press, 1983.

"Spiers Confirmation on Hold; Reisman Porn Study at Issue. (Vern L. Spiers as Head of Federal Juvenile Justice Office)." *Criminal Justice Newsletter.* 15 July 1987.

Sprankin, J.N., L.T. Silverman, and E.A. Rubinstein. "Update: Physically Intimate or Sexual Behavior on Prime Time Television: 1978–1979." *Journal of Communication* 31, no. 1 (1981): 34–40.

Sprankin, J.N., L.T. Silverman, and E.A. Rubinstein. "Reactions to Sex on Television: An Exploratory Study." *Public Opinion Quarterly* 44 (1980): 303–15.

Stoller, R.J. *Perversion: The Erotic Form of Hatred.* New York: Pantheon Books, 1975.

Stoller, R.J. *Sexual Excitement: Dynamics of Erotic Life.* New York: Pantheon Books, 1979.

Sun, Se-Wen, and James Lull. "The Adolescent Audience for Music Videos and Why They Watch." *Journal of Communication* 36 (Winter 1986): 115–25.

Task Force on Sex-Role Stereotyping in the Broadcast Media. "Images of Women." Report to the Minister of Supply and Services, Hull, Quebec, 1982.

Thatcher, J.C. *Report of the Royal Commission on Violence in the Communications Industry.* Volume 4: *Violence in Print and Music.* (Toronto: 1977).

Thompson, Roger. *Unfit for Modest Ears: A Study of Pornographic, Obscene and Bawdy Works Written or Published in England in the Second Half of the Seventeenth Century.* London: Macmillan, 1979.

Tieger, T., and J. Aronstam. "Brutality Chic: Images and Endorsement of Rape Myths." Paper presented to the American Psychological Association, Los Angeles, August 1981.

Tinkler, Arlene. "Reactions: Not a Love Story." *Obiter Dicta* (Canada), 8 February 1982, 54.

Turan, Kenneth. *Sinema: American Pornographic Films and the People Who Make Them.* New York: Praeger, 1974.

Wallace, D.H. "Obscenity and Contemporary Community Standards: A Survey." *Journal of Social Issues* 29, no. 3, (1973): 53–67.

Wallace, D.H., and G. Wehmer. "Evaluations of Visual Erotica by Sexual Liberals and Conservatives." *Journal of Sex Research* 8 (1972): 147–53.

Waller, Gregory. "Auto-Erotica: Some Notes on Comic Softcore Films for the Drive-In Circuit." *Journal of Popular Culture* 17 (Fall 1983): 135–41.

Wein, Betty. "The Chilling Effects of Pornography: A Jewish Perspective." Paper prepared for the Seventh World Media Conference, Tokyo, November 1984.

Weyr, Thomas. *Reaching for Paradise: The Playboy Vision of America.* New York: Times Books, 1978.

"What Do *You* Think Is Erotic? 10 Women Explain What Turns Them On . . ." *Ms.,* November 1978, 56.

Winick, C. "A Content Analysis of Sexually Explicit Magazines Sold in Adult Bookstores." *Journal of Sex Research* 21 (1985): 206–10.

"Womanpoll: Your Views about Pornography." *Chatelaine* 59 (February 1986): 44.

Yang, N., and D. Linz. "Sexual, Violent, Sexually Violent, and Prosocial Behavior in R- and X-rated Videotapes." Unpublished manuscript, University of California, Los Angeles, 1988.

Your Movie Guide to Adult Video Tapes and Discs. New York: New American Library, 1985.

Zellinger, D.A., H.L. Fromkin, D.E. Spesler, and D.A. Kohn. "A Commodity Theory Analysis of the Effects of Age Restrictions on Pornography Materials." *Journal of Applied Psychology* 60 (February 1975): 94–99.

Ziplow, Steven. *The Film Maker's Guide to Pornography.* New York: Drake Publishers, 1977.

CHAPTER 3

Abadsky, J. *Organized Crime.* New York: Allyn & Bacon, 1981.

Albini, J. *The American Mafia: Genesis of a Legend.* New York: Appleton, 1971.

Andrews, P., C. Longfellow, and F. Martens. "Zero-Sum Enforcement: Some Reflections on Drug Control." *Federal Probation,* March 1982, 14–20.

Attorney General's Commission on Pornography. Final Report. Washington, D.C.: U.S. Department of Justice, 1986.

Barzini, L. *The Italians.* New York: Atheneum, 1965.

Benes, Cindy. "The Current Status of Pornography and Its Effects on Society." Report to the Los Angeles Police Department Administrative Vice Division, Los Angeles, November 1984.

Bergsman, S. "Local Porno Businesses Tied to Organized Crime: Phoenix's Largest Porno Operation Part of Rubin Sturman's Cleveland Syndicate." *Phoenix Weekly Gazette,* 22 July 1980.

"The Big Business of Selling Smut." *Parade Magazine,* 19 August 1979.

Bliss, George, and Robert Davis. "Tie N.Y. Mob to Porn Here: Chicago Syndicate Gets Half of Profits." *Chicago Tribune,* 7 July 1977.

Brockett, D., A. Frank, and M. Diernan. "Mystery Man Quietly Gives up Holdings in the World of Smut" and "Pornography Cash Is an Invitation to Corruption." *Washington Star,* 13 February 1978.

California Assembly Committee on Criminal Justice. Hearing on Obscenity and the Use of Minors in Pornographic Material. San Diego, 31 October 1977.

"Crime Tie Found in Porno Films." *New York Times,* 21 April 1972.

Daniels, A. "The Supreme Court and Obscenity: An Exercise in Empirical Constitutional Policy-Making." *San Diego Law Review* 17 (1980): 757, 795, 107–108.

Denison, George. "Sultan of Smut: The Life and Times of Mike Thevis, Operator of America's Largest Network." *Reader's Digest,* November 1975, 107–8.

"Diary of Slain Smut Peddlar." *Charlotte News,* 12 June 1978.

Dorschmer, J. "The Case of the Naive Porn Lawyer: Inside Miami's FBI Scam." *Miami Herald/Tropic Magazine,* 8 June 1980.

Dworin, W. "State and Local Enforcement Efforts Related to Obscenity." Paper presented at the obscenity prosecution seminar conducted by the Department of Legal Education, U.S. Department of Justice, Washington, D.C., 16 May 1984.

Edelhertz, H., R. Cole, and B. Berk. *The Containment of Organized Crime.* Lexington, Mass.: Lexington Books, 1983.

Ehrlich, I. "Participation in Illegitimate Activities: A Theoretical and Empirical Investigation." In *The Economics of Crime and Law Enforcement,* edited by L. McPheters and W. Stronge, Springfield, Ill.: Charles C. Thomas, 1976.

Farley, E., and W. Knoedelseder. "Family Business, Episode 1, 'The Pornbrokers.' " *Los Angeles Times/Calendar,* 13 June 1982;" Family Business, Episode 2, 'The Hollywood Years,' " 20 June 1982; "Family Business, Episode 3, 'The Fall,' " 27 June 1982.

"FBI Raids Operation Run by Porn King Here." *Cleveland Press,* 14 February 1980.

Federal Bureau of Investigation Report Regarding the Extent of Organized Crime Development in Pornography. Federal Bureau of Investigation: Washington, D.C.: 1978.

"55 Persons Indicted in Piracy of Films and in Pornography." *New York Times,* 15 February 1980.

"51 Arrested in Miami-Area Porno Raids." *St. Petersburg Times,* 2 December 1982.

Gallagher, Neil. *The Porno Plague.* Minneapolis: Bethany House Publishers, 1981.

Gardiner, J. *The Politics of Corruption: Organized Crime in an American City.* New York: Russell Sage, 1970.

Gillaspy, James A. " 'Deep Throat' Changed Image: Porn Films Have New, Slicker Look." *Indianapolis Star,* 25 November 1981; "Vague, Confusing: Obscenity Law Hinders Closing of Porn Shops" and "Do Kings of Porn Run Legit Businesses or Obscenity Stores?" 22 November 1981; "Little Is Taboo: Adult Bookstores Flourish in Cities throughout State" and "Big Business Alters 'Tame' Porn Trade of '60s, Early '70s," 23 November 1981; "Porn Video Tape Cassette Business Booms," 26 November 1981; "Cable TV Systems Jockey for Pieces of Sexy Film Action," 27 November 1981; "Muncie Sheds Old 'Middletown' Image," 30 November 1981.

Hanlon, M. "The Caper That Caught a Porn King." *Toronto Star/Saturday Magazine,* 2 March 1985; "Can Rayne Beat the Test?" 9 March 1985.

Helms, Jesse. *Congressional Record,* 30 January 1984.

Hess, H. *Mafia and Mafiosi: The Structure of Power.* Translated by E. Osers. Lexington, Mass.: Lexington Books, 1983.

Ianni, F., and E. Reuss-Ianni. *A Family Business: Kinship and Social Control in Organized Crime.* New York: Russell Sage, 1972.

"An Investigation of Racketeer Infiltration into the Sex-oriented Materials Industry in New York City." Report of the New York Select Committee on Crime to the State of New York Commission of Investigation, 26 July 1982.

"An Investigation into the Sex-Oriented Materials Industry in New York City." In *Thirteenth Annual Report of the Temporary Commission of Investigation of the State of New York to the Governor and the Legislature of the State of New York.* New York: Commission of Investigation, 1971.

"Investigative Report on Organized Crime and Pornography." Report to the Attorney General of California, Sacramento, 1984.

"Kogan, Rick, and Toni Ginnetti. "Sex for Sale: Boom of the 80's." Twelve-part series. *Chicago Sun Times,* August 1982.

Kranes, Marsha. "Outrage over Taxpayer Handout to Porn Palace." *New York Post,* 9 June 1982.

"La Cosa Nostra." In *1984 Report: Pennsylvania Law Enforcement,* 38–43. St. Davids, Pa.: Pennsylvania Crime Commission, 1984.

Langelan, M. "The Political Economy of Pornography." *Oasis,* 1980.

Lawrence, Ronald J. "Mafia Linked to St. Louis Pornography Operations." *St. Louis Post-Dispatch,* 3 July 1977.

Lewis, N. *The Honored Society.* New York: G.P. Putnam's Sons, 1964.

Lovelace, Linda. *Ordeal.* Secaucus, N.J.: Citadel Press, 1980.

"Mafia Controls Distribution of Smut Books." *Cleveland Plain Dealer,* 13 October 1975.

May, D., and M. Hosenball, "Worldwide Tentacles of Mr. Porn," *London Times,* 6 September 1981.

McGuigan, P., and R. Rader, eds. *Criminal Justice Reform: A Blueprint.* Washington, D.C.: Free Congress Foundation, 1983.

Messick, H. *Lansky.* New York: G.P. Putnam's Sons, 1971.

Miller, Carl, and Jay Whearly. "Ties to Organized Crime: Denver Pornography $3 Million Scene." *Denver Post,* 21 August 1977.

"Mob Here Reaps Child Porn Cash." *Chicago Daily News,* 17 May 1977.

"Mob's Role Is Target in Fight Against Porno." *Miami Herald,* 25 March 1974.

Mori, C. *The Last Struggle with the Mafia.* Translated by O. Williams. New York: G.P. Putnam, 1933.

Nelli, H. *The Business of Crime: Italians and Syndicate Crime in the United States.* New York: Oxford University Press, 1976.

O'Brien, John. "Porn Theater Owner Reported Missing." *Chicago Tribune,* 26 July 1985.

"Obscenity Now Covered by 'RICO' Statute (18 U.S.C. 1961) as a Result of Congressional Passage on October 11, 1984 of the 'Helms Amendment' to the 'Compre-hensive Crime Control Act of 1984.' " News release. Morality in Media, Inc., New York.

"Once Closed by Police: Porno Club Got Uncensored Government Loan." *Chicago Tribune,* 11 June 1982.

"Organized Crime Involvement in Pornography." Report of the U.S. Department of Justice, Washington, D.C., 8 June 1977.

Organized Crime Task Force Report. Presidential Commission on Law Enforcement and Administration of Justice, Washington, D.C., 1967.

"Organized Crime's Involvement in the Pornography Industry." Report of the Investigative Services Division, Metropolitan Police Department, Washington, D.C., November 1978.

Pace, D., and J. Styles. *Organized Crime: Concepts and Control.* Englewood Cliffs, N.J.: Prentice-Hall, 1975.

Pantaleone, M. *The Mafia and Politics.* New York: Coward-McCann, 1966.

Payne, D. "Shy Pornographers." *MacLean's,* 3 May 1975, 34–41.

Peterson, V. *The Mob: 200 Years of Organized Crime in New York.* Ottawa, Ill.: Green Hill Publishers, 1983.

Pianin, Erick, and Patrick Marx. "Officials Fear Porn Near Monopoly." *Minneapolis Star,* 17 November 1975.

"Plea Bargain Offer Made in Pornography Distribution Case." *St. Petersburg Times,* 24 October 1982.

"Police Link 'Porn' to Crime Syndicate." *Christian Science Monitor,* 8 July 1977.

"Porno Trade in Capital Tied to Mob." *Staten Island Advance,* 22 May 1978.

"Pornography Said Linked to Underworld." *Indianapolis Star,* 10 October 1981.

"Pornography: The Real Story—A Portrait of the Mob's Man." *Washington Star,* 15 February 1978.

Raab, Selwyn, and Nathaniel Sheppard, Jr. "Mobsters Skim New York City Sex Industry Profits." *New York Times,* 27 July 1977.

Report of the Commission on Obscenity and Pornography. Washington, D.C.: GPO, 1970.

"Report to the Governor of Ohio: Organized Crime." Ohio Law Enforcement Consulting Committee, Columbus, 1982.

Report on the Multi-Billion Dollar Traffic in Pornography. New York: Morality in Media, Inc., 1985.

Satchell, M. "The Big Business of Selling Smut; Five Little Known Men Dominate Sleazy Network of Pornography That May Gross $4 Billion a Year." *Parade Magazine,* 19 August 1979.

Schiavo, G. *The Truth about the Mafia and Organized Crime in America.* New York: Vigo Press, 1962.

Scott, David Alexander. *Pornography—Its Effects on the Family, Community and Culture.* Washington, D.C.: Free Congress Foundation, 1985.

Secter, Bob, and Phillip J. O'Connor. "Porno Landlord Blames Plight on the Crosstown." *Chicago Daily News,* 7 July 1977.

Selle. "Pornography Warehouse Target of Irate Protesters." *New York Tribune,* 29 October 1984.

Serrano, Richard A., and Richard D. Balles. "Porn a

Risky Business." *Kansas City (Missouri) Times*, 9 September 1978.

Servaido, G. *Mafioso: A History of the Mafia from Its Origins to the Present Day*. New York: Stein & Day, 1976.

Smith, W. "Enforcement of Anti-Pornography Laws." Memo. U.S. Department of Justice, 1982.

Sobel, Lester A., ed. *Pornography, Obscenity and the Law*. New York: Facts on File, 1979.

Stanmeyer, William A. *The Seduction of Society: Pornography and Its Impact on American Life*. (Ann Arbor, Mich.: Servant Books, 1984.

Suk, Tom. "Smut Empire Linked to Iowa Outlets." *Des Moines Register*, 26 August 1985.

"Summary Report: Federal Bureau of Investigation." White House Working Group on Pornography, Washington, D.C., 6 December 1983. See also J. Baker.

"An Approach to Pornography as a Copyright Problem." Memo to the working group, 27 July 1984.

U. S. Congress. Senate. Kefauver Committee to Investigate Organized Crime. *Investigation of Organized Crime in Interstate Commerce: Hearing on S. 202*. 81st Cong. 2d sess., and 82d Cong., 1st sess.

Thomas, William. "Organized Crime: The American Shakedown." *Editorial Research Reports* 1. no. 23 (1981): 451–68.

Washington, Betty, and Art Petacque. "Three Area Men Arrested in FBI's Pornography 'Sting.' " *Chicago Sun Times*, 15 February 1980.

Whalen, E. "Prince of Porn." *Cleveland Magazine*, August 1985.

"Who's Who in Smut Shows Mob Influence." *Indianapolis Star*, 30 December 1977.

CHAPTER 4

Attorney General's Commission on Pornography. Final Report. Washington, D.C.: U.S. Department of Justice, 1986.

Barry, Kathleen. *Female Sexual Slavery*. Englewood Cliffs, N.J.: Prentice-Hall, 1979.

Benes, C. "The Current Status of Pornography and Its Effects on Society," Report to the Los Angeles Police Department Administrative Vice Division, Los Angeles, November 1984.

Bogdanovich, Peter. *The Killing of the Unicorn: Dorothy Stratten, 1960–1980*. 1984.

Brownmiller, Susan. *Against Our Will: Men, Women and Rape*. New York: Simon & Schuster, 1975.

Burgess, Ann Wolbert, with Marieanne Lindequist Clark. *Child Pornography and Sex Rings*. Lexington, Mass.: Lexington Books, 1984.

Champion, Cheryl A. "Clinical Perspectives on the Relationship Between Pornography and Sexual Violence." *Law and Inequality: A Journal of Theory and Practice* 4 (May 1986): 22–27.

Clor, Harry M. *Obscenity and Public Morality: Censorship in a Liberal Society*. Chicago: University of Chicago Press, 1969.

DiGioia, Donna Waldron. "Pornography and Its Relation to Violence." In *The Violent Family: Victimization of Women, Children and Elders*, edited by Nancy Hutchins, 131–49. New York: Human Sciences Press, 1988.

Dworkin, A. "Effects of Pornography on Women and Children." Testimony before the Committee on the Judiciary, Subcommittee on Juvenile Justice. 98th Cong., 2d sess.

Gallagher, Neil. *The Porno Plague*. Minneapolis: Bethany House Publishers, 1981.

Hazelwood, Robert R., Park Elliott, Dietz, and Ann Wolbert Burgess. *Autoerotic Fatalities*. Lexington, Mass.: Lexington Books, 1983.

Hite, Shere. *The Hite Report on Male Sexuality: How Men Feel about Love, Sex, and Relationships*. New York: Ballantine Books, 1985.

Holland, Elizabeth. "I Don't Have the Right." *Bible Advocate*, December 1985.

Hoover, J. Edgar. "Combating Merchants of Filth: The Role of the FBI." *University of Pittsburgh Law Review* 25 (March 1964): 469–78.

Johnson, Hilary. "Violence Against Women—Is Porn to Blame?" *Vogue*, September 1985.

Keating, Charles Jr. "Minority Report." In *Report of the Commission on Obscenity and Pornography*. Washington, D.C.: GPO, 1970.

Kirk, Jerry R. *The Mind Polluters*. Nashville, Tenn.: Thomas Nelson, 1985.

Lederer, Laura, ed. *Take Back the Night: Women on Pornography*. New York: Bantam Books, 1980.

Linedecker, Clifford L. *The Man Who Killed Boys*. New York: St. Martin Press, 1980.

Linedecker, Clifford L. *Children in Chains*. New York: Everest House, 1981.

Lloyd, Robin. *For Money or Love: Boy Prostitution in America*. New York: Vanguard Press, 1976.

Lovelace, Linda. *Ordeal*. Secaucus, N.J.: Citadel Press, 1980.

Lovelace, Linda. *Out of Bondage*. Secaucus, N.J.: L. Stuart, 1986.

Matusinka, Alexandra. *Bibliography: Pornography, Rape and Child Molestation*. New York: Women Against Pornography, 1983.

McCuen, Gary E. *Pornography and Sexual Violence*. Hudson, Wisc.: Gary McCuen Publications, 1985.

Miller, Russell. *Bunny: The Real Story of Playboy*. London: Corgi Books, 1985.

Minnery, Tom, ed. *Pornography: A Human Tragedy*. Wheaton, Ill.: Tyndale House Publishers, 1986.

Morgan, Robin. "Pornography and Rape." In Robin Morgan, *Going Too Far: The Personal Chronicle of a Radical Feminist*, 163–69. New York: Vintage Books, 1977.

Not a Love Story. Film. National Film Board of Canada,

Pope, Darrel. "Does Pornographic Literature Incite Sexual Assaults?" Report to the Western Michigan Committee for Decency in Media, 1 May 1979.

"Public Hearings on Ordinances to Add Pornography as Discrimination Against Women." Committee on Government Operations, City Council, Minneapolis, 12–13 December 1983.

Report of the Commission on the Status of Women. State of Illinois, February 1985.

Report of the Committee on Sexual Offenses Against Children and Youths. Ottawa: Communications and Public Affairs, Department of Justice, 1985.

Report of the Municipality of Metropolitan Toronto Task Force on Public Violence Against Women and Children, 1984.

Report of the Special Committee on Pornography and Prostitution. Ottawa: Minister of Supply and Services, 1985.

Rhodes, Dusty, and Sandra McNeill, eds. *Women Against Violence Against Women.* London: Onlywoman Press, 1985.

Rosenblum, S., and M. Faber. "The Adolescent Sexual Asphyxia Syndrome." *Journal of Child Psychiatry* 18, no. 3 (1979): 546–58.

Russell, D.E.H. "Testimony Against Pornography: Witness from Denmark." In *Take Back the Night: Women on Pornography,* edited by Laura Lederer, 82–85. New York: William Morrow, 1980.

Russell, D.E.H. "Research on How Women Experience the Impact of Pornography." In *Pornography and Censorship,* edited by David Copp and Susan Wendell, 213–18. New York: Prometheus Books, 1983.

Russell, D.E.H., and N. Van de Ven, eds. *Crimes Against Women: Proceedings of the International Tribunal.* Millbrae, Calif.: Les Femmes, 1976.

Schlafly, Phyllis, ed. *Pornography's Victims.* Westchester, Ill.: Crossway Books, 1987.

Schultz, Gladys Denny. "What Sex Offenders Say about Pornography." *Reader's Digest,* July 1971.

Scott, David Alexander. *Pornography: Its Effects on the Family, Community and Culture.* Washington, D.C.: Free Congress Foundation, 1985.

Silbert, Mimi H., and Ayala M. Pines. "Pornography and Sexual Abuse of Women." *Sex Roles* 10, nos. 11 and 12 (1984): 857–67.

Stanmeyer, William A. *The Seduction of Society: Pornography and Its Impact on American Life.* Ann Arbor, Mich.: Servant Books, 1984.

Steinem, Gloria. "Linda Lovelace's Ordeal." *Ms.,* May 1980, 72–77.

Sundah, Deborah. "My Work in the Sex Industry." *The Advocate,* 13 October 1983.

Task Force on Public Violence Against Women and Children. *Final Report.* Toronto: 1984.

Todasco, Ruth. "Women in the Sex Industry." *Gay Community News,* 24 November 1984.

U.S. Congress. Senate. Committee on the Judiciary. Subcommittee on Juvenile Justice. *Effect of Pornography on Women and Children.* 98th Cong., 2d sess.

Van der Maag, Ernest. "Is Pornography a Cause of Crime?" In *The Case Against Pornography,* edited by David Holbrook, 161–68. London: Tom Stacey, 1972.

Violent Pornography: What It Is and Who It Hurts. Milwaukee: Freedom from Sexual Violence, 1985.

Wathen, P.W. "Schiro's Sexual Behavior Linked to Pornography." *Evansville (Indiana) Courier,* 12 September 1981.

Wertham, Frederic. *Seduction of the Innocent.* New York: Holt, Rinehart & Winston, 1953.

Wheeler, Hollis. "Pornography and Rape: A Feminist Perspective." In *Rape and Sexual Assault,* edited by Ann Wolbert Burgess, 374–91. New York: Garland Publishing, 1985.

Wildmon, Donald E. *The Case Against Pornography.* Wheaton, Ill.: Victor Books, 1986.

Wilson, Carolyn F. *Violence Against Women: An Annotated Bibliography.* Boston: G.K. Hall, 1981.

Womongold, Marsha. *Pornography: A License to Kill.* Private publication, 1978. (Send $2 to M. Womongold, 16B Cedar St., Somerville, MA 02143.)

CHAPTER 5

Abel, G.G. "Evaluating and Treating Rapists and Child Molesters: Current Status." Report to U.S. Congress, House Committee on Science and Technology, Washington, D.C., 1978.

Abel, G.G., et al. "Identifying Specific Erotic Cues in Sexual Deviations by Audiotaped Descriptions." *Journal of Applied Behavioral Analysis* 8 (Fall 1975): 247–60.

Abel, G.G., D.H. Barlow, E.B. Blanchard, and M. Mavissakalian. "Measurement of Sexual Arousal in Male Homosexuals: Effects of Instructions and Stimulus Modality." *Archives of Sexual Behavior* 4, no. 6 (1975): 623–29.

Abel, G.G., D.H. Barlow, and D. Guild. "The Components of Rapists' Sexual Arousal." *Archives of General Psychiatry* 34 (1977): 895–903.

Abel, G.G., J.V. Becker, W. Murphy, and B. Flanagan. "Identifying Dangerous Child Molesters." In *Violent Behavior: Social Learning Approaches to Predicting Management and Treatment,* edited by R.B. Stuart, New York: Brunner-Mazel, 1981.

Abel, G.G., J.V. Becker, and L.T. Skinner. "Aggressive Behavior and Sex." *Psychiatric Clinics of North America* 3, no. 1 (1980): 131–51.

Abel, G.G., and E.B. Blanchard. "The Measurement and Generation of Sexual Arousal in Male Deviation." In *Progress in Behavior Modification.* Vol. 2, edited by M. Mersen, R.M. Eisler, and P.M. Miller, Academic Press, 1976.

Abel, G.G., and E.B. Blanchard. "The Role of Fantasy in the Treatment of Sexual Deviation." *Archives of General Psychiatry* 30 (1977): 467–75.

Abel, G.G., E.B. Blanchard, and D.H. Barlow. "Measurement of Sexual Arousal in Several Paraphilias: The

Effects of Stimulus Modality, Instructional Set and Stimulus Context on the Objective." *Behavior Research and Therapy* 19, no. 1 (1981): 25–33.

Abel, G.G., E.B. Blanchard, D.H. Barlow, et al. "Identifying Specific Erotic Cues in Sexual Deviations by Audiotaped Descriptions." *Archives of General Psychiatry* 30 (1977): 467–75.

Abel, G.G., E.B. Blanchard, D.H. Barlow, and M. Mavissakalian. "Identifying Specific Erotic Cues in Sexual Deviations by Audiotape Descriptions." *Journal of Applied Behavior Analysis* 8 (1975): 247–60.

Abel, G.G., E.B. Blanchard, and J.V. Becker. "Psychological Treatment of Rapists." In *Sexual Assault: The Victim and the Rapist*, edited by Marcia J. Walker and Stanley L. Brodsky, 99–116. Lexington, Mass.: Lexington Books, 1976.

Abel, G.G., E.B. Blanchard, and J.V. Becker. "An Integrated Treatment Program for Rapists." In *Clinical Aspects of the Rapist*, edited by R. Rada, . New York: Grune and Stratton, 1978.

Abel, G.G., E.B. Blanchard, J. Becker, and A. Djenderedjian. "Differentiating Sexual Aggressives with Penile Measures." *Criminal Justice and Behavior* 5 (1978): 315–32.

Abel, G.G., D.J. Lewis, and J. Clancy. "Effects of Aversive Therapy on Sexual Deviants: A Preliminary Report." Paper presented to the American Psychiatric Association, May 1969.

Abel, G.G., D.J. Lewis, and J. Clancy. "Aversion Therapy Applied to Taped Sequences of Deviant Behavior in Exhibitionism and Other Sexual Deviations: A Preliminary Report." *Journal of Behavior Therapy and Experimental Psychiatry* 1, no. 1 (1970): 59–66.

Abel, G.G., Mittelman, and J.V. Becker. "The Effects of Erotica on Paraphiliacs' Behavior." Unpublished paper, Emory University, 1985.

Abel, G.G., J. Rouleau, and R. Cunningham. "Sexually Aggressive Behavior." In *Modern Legal Psychiatry and Psychology*, edited by W. Curran, A. McGarry, and S. Shah, Philadelphia: F.A. Davis Co.

Abelson, H., R. Cohen, E. Heaton, and C. Suder. "National Survey of Public Attitudes toward and Experience with Erotic Materials." In *Technical Reports of the Commission on Obscenity and Pornography*. Vol. 6, . Washington, D.C.: GPO, 1971.

Abramson, P.R. "Ethical Requirements for Research on Human Behavior: From the Perspective of Participating Subjects." *Journal of Social Issues* 33 (1977): 184–92.

Abramson, P.R., P.A. Goldberg, D.L. Mosher, L.M. Abramson, and M. Gottesdiener. "Experimenter Effects on Responses to Erotic Stimuli." *Journal of Research in Personality* 9 (1975): 136–46.

Abramson, P.R., and M. Hayashi. "Pornography in Japan: Cross-Cultural and Theoretical Considerations." In *Pornography and Sexual Aggression*, edited by N. Malamuth and E. Donnerstein, 173–88. New York: Academic Press, 1984.

Abramson, P.R., and D.L. Mosher. "An Empirical Investigation of Experimentally Induced Masturbatory

Fantasies." *Archives of Sexual Behavior* 8 (1979): 27–29.

Abramson, P.R., C.A. Repczynski, and L.R. Merrill. "The Menstrual Cycle and Response to Erotic Literature." *Journal of Consulting and Clinical Psychology* 44 (1976): 1018–19.

Achampong, Francis. "Death from Autoerotic Asphyxiation and the Double Indemnity Clause in Life Insurance Policies: the Latest Round in Accidental Death Litigation." *Akron Law Review* 21 (Fall 1987): 191–200.

Adamson, J.D., K.R. Romano, J.A. Burdick, C.L. Corman, and F.S. Chebib. "Physiological Responses to Sexual and Unpleasant Film Stimuli." *Journal of Psychosomatic Research* 16 (1972): 153–62.

"Adult Business Study" Report of the City of Phoenix Planning Department, 25 May 1979.

Ageton, S.S. *Sexual Assault among Adolescents*. Lexington, Mass.: Lexington Books, 1983.

Agrawal, K.G. "Obscene in Erotica: A Study in Affective Meanings." *Manus* 24 (1977): 51–63.

Alder, C. "An Explanation of Self-Reported Sexually Aggressive Behavior." *Crime and Delinquency* 31 ( ): 306–11.

Alder, C. "The Convicted Rapist: A Sexual or a Violent Offender?" *Criminal Justice and Behavior* 11 (1984): 157–77.

Alger, I. "Therapeutic Use of Videotape Playback." *Journal of Nervous Mental Disorders* 150 (1969): 148–205.

Amoroso, Donald M., and Marvin Brown. "Problems in Studying the Effects of Erotic Material." *Journal of Sex Research* 9 (1973): 18–95.

Amoroso, Donald M., Marvin Brown, Manfred Pruesse, Edward E. Ware, and Dennis W. Pilkey. "An Investigation of Behavioral Psychological and Physiological Reactions to Pornographic Stimuli." In *Technical Reports of the Commission on Obscenity and Pornography*. Vol. , 1 40. Washington, D.C.: GPO, 1971.

Anderson, F.S. "TV Violence and Viewer Aggression: A Culmination of Study Results." *Public Opinion Quarterly* 41 (1956): 314–31.

Anderson, J. "The Theorical Lineage of Critical Viewing Curricula." *Journal of Communication* 30 (1980): 64–70.

Antell, M.J., and L. Goldberger. "The Effects of Subliminally Presented Sexual and Aggressive Stimuli on Literary Creativity." *Psychological Research Bulletin* (1978): 18.

Anthanasiou, R. "Pornography: A Review of Research." In *Handbook on Human Sexuality*, edited by John Money, 252–65. Englewood Cliffs, N.J.: Prentice-Hall, 1980.

Anthanasiou, R., and P. Shawuer. "Correlates of Heterosexuals' Reactions to Pornography." *Journal of Sex Research* 7 (1971): 298–311.

Armentrout, J.A., and A.I. Hauer. "MMPI's of Rapists and Adults, Rapists of Children, and Non-Rapist Sexual Offenders." *Journal of Clinical Psychology* 34 (1978): 330–32.

Ashley, Barbara Renchkovsky, and David Ashley. "Sex as

Violence: The Body Against Intimacy." *International Journal of Women's Studies* 7 ( ): 3521–371.

Attorney General's Commission on Pornography. *Final Report*. Washington, D.C.: U.S. Department of Justice, 1986.

Bachy, Victor. "Danish 'Permissiveness' Revisited." *Journal of Communication* 26 (Winter 1976): 40–43.

Bain, James Lewton. *The Last Taboo: Sex and the Fear of Death*. Garden City, N.Y.: Doubleday. 1978.

Bancroft, J.A. "Aversion Therapy on Homosexuality." *British Journal of Psychiatry* 115 (1969): 1417–31.

Bancroft, J.A. "A Comparative Study of Aversion and Desensitization in the Treatment of Homosexuality." In *Behaviour Therapy in the 1970's*, edited by L.E. Burns and J.L. Worsley, Bristol, England: Wright, 1970.

Bancroft, J.A. *Deviant Sexual Behavior: Modification and Assessment*. Oxford, England: Clarendon Press, 1974.

Bancroft, J.H.J. "Treatment of Deviant Sexual Behavior." In *Current Themes in Psychiatry*. Vol. 2, edited by R. Gaind and B.D. Mudson, London: Macmillan, 1979.

Bancroft, J.H.J., H.J. Jones, and B.R. Pullan. "A Simple Transducer for Measuring Penile Erection with Comments on Its Use in the Treatment of Sexual Disorders." *Behavior Research and Therapy* 4 (1966): 239–41.

Bancroft, J., and I. Marks. "Electrical Aversion Therapy in Sexual Deviations." *Proceedings of the Royal Society of Medicine* 61 (1968): 796–99.

Bandura, A. "What TV Violence Can Do to Your Child." *Look*, 22 October 1963, 46–52.

Bandura, A. *Principles of Behavior Modification*. New York: Holt, Rinehart & Winston, 1969.

Bandura, A. *Aggression: A Social Learning Process*. Englewood Cliffs, N.J.: Prentice-Hall, 1973.

Bandura, A. *Social Learning Theory* Englewood Cliffs, N.J.: Prentice-Hall, 1977.

Bandura, A. "Psychological Mechanisms of Aggression." In *Aggression: Theoretical and Empirical Reviews*. Vol. 1, edited by Russell G. Green and Edward I. Donnerstein, 1–40. New York: Academic Press, 1983.

Bandura, A., E.B. Blanchard, and B. Ritter. "The Relative Efficacy of Desensitization and Modeling Approaches for Inducing Behavioral, Affective, and Attitudinal Changes." *Journal of Personality and Social Psychology* 13 (1968): 173–99.

Bandura, A., and F.L. Menlove. "Factors Determining Vicarious Extinction of Avoidance Behavior through Symbolic Modeling." *Journal of Personality and Social Psychology* 8 (1968): 99–108.

Bandura, A., D. Ross, and S. Ross. "Imitation of Film-Mediated Aggressive Models." *Journal of Abnormal and Social Psychology* 66 (1986): 3–11.

Baran, S.J. "How TV and Film Portrayals Affect Sexual Satisfaction in College Students." *Journalism Quarterly* 53, no. 3 (1976): 468–73.

Barbach, L. "Group Treatment of Anorgasmic Women." In *Principles and Practice of Sex Therapy*, edited by S.R. Leiblum and L.A. Perwin. London: Tavistock, 1980.

Barbaree, H.F., W.L. Marshall, and R.D. Lanthier. "Deviant Sexual Arousal in Rapists." *Behaviour Research and Therapy* 17 (1979): 215–22.

Barclay, A.M. "The Effect of Hostility on Physiological and Fantasy Responses." *Journal of Personality* 37 (1969): 651–67.

Barclay, A.M. "The Relation of Aggressive to Sexual Motivation." *Journal of Personality* 37 (1969): 651–67.

Barclay, A.M. "The Effect of Female Aggressiveness on Aggressive and Sexual Fantasies." *Journal of Projective Techniques and Personality Assessment* 34 (1970): 19–26.

Barclay, A.M. "Linking Sexual and Aggressive Motives: Contribution of 'Irrelevant' Arousals." *Journal of Personality* 39 (1971): 481–92.

Barclay, A.M. "Sexual Fantasies in Men and Women." *Medical Aspects of Human Sexuality* 7 (1973): 205–16.

Barclay, A.M., and R.N. Haber. "The Relation of Aggressive to Sexual Motivation." *Journal of Personality* 33 (1965): 462–75.

Barclay, A.M., and D.M. Little. "Urinary Acid Phophatase Secretion Resulting from Different Arousals." *Psychophysiology* 9 (1972): 69–77.

Bardwick, J.M., and S.J. Behrman. "Investigation into the Effects of Anxiety, Sexual Arousal, and Menstrual Cycle Phase on Uterine Contractions." *Psychosomatic Medicine* 29 (1967): 468–82.

Barker, J.C. "Behaviour Therapy for Transvestism: A Comparison of Pharmacological and Electrical Aversion Techniques." *British Journal of Psychiatry* 111 (1965): 268–76.

Barker, J.C., J.G. Thorpe, C.B. Blakemore, N.I. Lavin, and C.G. Conway. "Behaviour Therapy in a Case of Transvestism." *Lancelot* 1 (1961): 510.

Barker, W.J., and D. Perlman. "Volunteer Bias and Personality Traits in Sexual Standards Research." *Archives of Sexual Behavior* 4 (1975): 161–71.

Barlow, D.H. "The Treatment of Sexual Deviation: Towards a Comprehensive Behavioral Approach." In *Innovative Treatment Methods in Psychopathology*, edited by Karen S. Calhoun, Henry E. Adams, and Kevin M. Mitchell, 121–48. New York: John Wiley, 1974.

Barnes, G.E., N.M. Malamuth, and J.V.P. Check. "Psycholicism and Sexual Arousal to Rape Depictions." *Personality and Individual Differences* 5, no. 3 (1984): 273–79.

Baron, L. "Immoral, Inviolate or Inconclusive?" *Society* 24 (July/August 1987): 6–12.

Baron, L., and M.A. Straus. "Conceptual and Ethical Problems in Research on Pornography." Paper presented to the Society for the Study of Social Problems, Detroit, 5 August 1983.

Baron, L., and M.A. Straus. "Sexual Satisfaction, Pornography and Rape in American States." Unpublished manuscript, 18 November 1983.

Baron, L., and M.A. Straus. "Legitimate Violence, Pornography, and Sexual Inequality as Explanations for State and Regional Differences in Rape." Unpublished manuscript, Yale University 1985.

Baron, L., and M. Straus. "Rape and Its Relation to Social Disorganization, Pornography, and Sexual Inequality." Paper presented at the International Congress on Rape, Israel, April 1986.

Baron, L., and M.A. Straus. "Four Theories of Rape: A Macrosociological Analysis." *Social Problems* 34 (December 1987): 467–89.

Baron, R.A. "The Aggression-Inhibiting Influence of Heightened Sexual Arousal." *Journal of Personality and Social Psychology* 30 (1974): 318–32.

Baron, R.A. "Sexual Arousal and Physical Aggression: The Inhibiting Influence of 'Cheesecake' and Nudes." *Bulletin of the Psychonomic Society* 3 (1974): 337–39.

Baron, R.A. *Human Aggression.* New York: Plenum Press, 1977.

Baron, R.A. "Aggression Inhibiting Influence of Sexual Humor." *Journal of Personality and Social Psychology* 36 (1978): 189–98.

Baron, R.A. "Heightened Sexual Arousal and Physical Aggression: An Extension to Females." *Journal of Research in Personality* 13 (1979): 91–102.

Baron, R.A. "The Control of Human Aggression: An Optimistic Perspective." *Journal of Social and Clinical Psychology* 1 (1983): 97–119.

Baron, R.A. "The Control of Human Aggression: A Strategy Based on Incompatible Responses." In *Aggression: Theoretical and Empirical Reviews.* Vol. 2, edited by Russell G. Geen and Edward I. Donnerstein, 173–90. New York: Academic Press, 1983.

Baron, R.A., and P.A. Bell. "Sexual Arousal and Aggression by Males: Effects of Type of Erotic Stimuli and Prior Provocation." *Journal of Personality and Social Psychology* 35, no. 2 (1977): 79–87.

Baron, R.A., and R.J. Eggleston. "Performance on the Aggression Machine: Motivation to Help or Harm?" *Psychonomic Science* 26 (1972): 321–22.

Barr, R., and A. Blaszcynski. "Autonomic Responses of Transsexual and Homosexual Males to Erotic Film Sequences." *Archives of Sexual Behavior* 5 (1976): 211–22.

Barr, R.F., and N. McConaghy. "Penile Volume Responses to Appetitive and Aversive Stimuli in Relation to Sexual Orientation and Conditioning Performance." *British Journal of Psychiatry* 119 (1971): 377–83.

Barry, Kathleen. *Female Sexual Slavery.* Englewood Cliffs, N.J.: Prentice-Hall, 1979.

Bart, P.B., L. Freeman, and P. Kimball. "The Different Worlds of Women and Men: Attitudes toward Pornography and Responses to *Not a Love Story,* a Film about Pornography." *Women's Studies International Forum* 9, no. 4 (1985): 307–22.

Bart, P.B., and M. Jozsa. "Dirty Books, Dirty Films and Dirty Data." In *Take Back the Night: Women on Pornography,* edited by Laura Lederer, 204–17. New York: William Morrow, 1980.

Bauman, K.E. "Volunteer Bias in a Study of Sexual Knowledge, Attitudes, and Behavior." *Journal of Marriage and Family* 35 (1973): 27–31.

Becker, Michael A., and Donn. Byrne. "Self-Regulated Exposure to Erotica, Recall Errors, and Subjective Reactions as a Function of Erotophobia and Type A Coronary-Prone Behavior." *Journal of Personality and Social Psychology* 48 (March 1985): 760–67.

Beech, H.R., H. Watts, and A.D. Pook. "Classical Conditioning of a Sexual Deviation: A Preliminary Note." *Behavior Therapy* 3 (1971): 400–402.

Beis, R.H. "Pornography: The Harm It Does." *International Journal of Moral and Social Studies* 2 (Spring 1987): 81–92.

"Behavior Modification For Child Molesters." *Corrections Magazine* 1 (January/February 1975): 77–80.

Bell, R. "Pornography." In *Social Deviance,* edited by , 120–51, Homewood, Ill.: Dorsey Press, 1976.

Belson, W.A. *Television Violence and the Adolescent Boy.* London: Saxon House, 1981.

Bender, W.R.G. "The Effect of Pain, Emotional Stimuli and Alcohol Upon Pupillary Reflex Activity." *Psychological Monographs* 44 (1933): 1–32.

Benjamin, J. "The Bonds of Love: Rational Violence and Erotic Domination." *Feminist Studies* 6 (1980): 144–74.

Benke, T. *Men on Rape.* New York: St. Martin's Press, 1982.

Ben-Veniste, Richard. "Pornography and Sex Crime: The Danish Experience." In *Technical Reports of Commission on Violence and Pornography.* Vol. 7, 245–62. Washington, D.C.: GPO, 1971.

Berest, J.J. "Report on a Case of Sadism." *Journal of Sex Research* 6 (1970): 210–19.

Berger, S. "Conditioning through Vicarious Instigation." *Psychological Review* 69 (1962): 405–56.

Berger, A.S., W. Simon, and J.H. Gagnon. "Youth and Pornography in a Social Context." *Archives of Sexual Behavior.* 2, no. 4 (1973): 279–308.

Bergman, J. "The Influence of Pornography on Sexual Development: Three Case Histories." *Family Therapy* 9, no. 3 (1982): 263–69.

Berkowitz, L. "Sex and Violence: We Can't Have It Both Ways." *Psychology Today* 5, no. 7 (1971): 14–23.

Berkowitz, L. "Some Determinants of Impulsive Aggression: Role of Mediated Associations with Reinforcements for Aggression." *Psychological Review* 81 (1974): 165–79.

Berkowitz, L. "Some Effects of Thoughts on Anti- and Pro-Social Influences of Media Events: A Cognitive-Neoassociation Analysis." *Psychological Bulletin* 95 (1984): 410–27.

Berkowitz, L. "Situational Influences on Reactions to Observed Violence." *Journal of Social Issues* 42, no. 3 (1986): 93–105.

Berkowitz, L., and J. Alioto. "The Meanings of an Observed Event as a Determinant of Its Aggressive Consequences." *Journal of Personality and Social Psychology* 28 (1973): 206–17.

Berkowitz, L., and E. Donnerstein. "External Validity Is More Than Skin Deep." *American Psychologist* 37 (1982): 245–57.

Berkowitz, L., and A.W. Edfeldt. "Report from a Media

Violence Symposium in Stockholm, April 25, 1974." University of Stockholm, 1974.

Berkowitz, L., and R.G. Geen. "Film Violence and the Cue Properties of Available Targets." *Journal of Personality and Social Psychology* 3 (1966): 525–30.

Berkowitz, L. and R.G. Geen. "Stimulus Qualities of the Target of Aggression: A Further Study." *Journal of Personality and Social Psychology* 5, 1967: 364–68.

Berkowitz, L., and E. Rawlings. "Effects of Film Violence on Inhibitions Against Subsequent Aggression." *Journal of Abnormal and Social Psychology* 66 (1963): 405–12.

Berkowitz, L., and K.H. Rodgers. "A Priming Effect Analysis of Media Influences." In *Perspective on Media Effects Research*. Vol. 4, edited by J. Bryan and D. Zillman, 57–75. Hillsdale, N.J.: Lawrence Erlbaum Associate Publishers, 1986.

Berns, Walter. "Pornography vs. Democracy—A Case for Censorship." *The Public Interest* 22 (1971): 3–24.

Bicher, M., and E. Tyndale. "Symposium on Media Violence and Pornography." *Perception* 7 (March/April 1984): 10–11.

Bjorksten, Oliver J.W. "Sexually Graphic Material in the Treatment of Sexual Disorders." In *Clinical Management of Sexual Disorders*, edited by Jon K. Meyer, 161–94. Baltimore: Williams & Williams, 1976.

Blackburn, R. "Psychopathy, Arousal and the Need for Stimulation." In *Psychopathic Behavior: Approaches to Research*, edited by R.D. Hare and D. Schalling, 165–86. London: Wiley, 1978.

Blader, Joseph C., and William L. Marshall. "The Relationship between Cognitive and Erectile Measures of Sexual Arousal in Non-Rapist Males as a Function of Depicted Aggression." *Behavior Research and Therapy* 22, no. 6 (1984): 623–30.

Blakemore, C.B., J.G. Thorpe, J.C. Barker, G.C. Conway, and N.I. Lavin. "The Application of Faradic Aversion Conditioning to a Case of Transvestism." *Behavior Research and Therapy* 1 (1963): 29–34.

Blanchard, D. Caroline, Barry Graczyk, and Robert J. Blanchard. "Differential Reactions of Men and Women to Realism, Physical Damage and Emotionality in Violent Films." *Aggressive Behavior* 12 (1986): 45–55.

Blount, Winton M. "Pornography and Its Effect on Society." *Florida Bar Journal* 44 (November 1970): 518–21.

Blumer, H., and P.M. Hauser. *Movies, Delinquency, and Crime*. New York: Macmillan, 1933.

Bogart, Leo. "After the Surgeon General's Report: Another Look Backwards." In *Television and Social Behavior: Beyond Violence and Children*, edited by S.B. Withey and R.P. Abeles, 103–34. Hillsdale, N.J.: Lawrence Erlbaum Associates, 1980.

Botto, R.W., G.G. Galbraith, and R.M. Stern. "Effects of False Heart Rate Feedback and Sex-Guilt upon Attitudes toward Sexual Stimuli." *Psychological Reports* 35 (1974): 267–74.

Boulding, E. "Women and Social Violence." *International and Social Science Journal* 30 (1978): 801–15.

Bowen, Nancy H. "Pornography: Research Review and

Implications for Counseling." *Journal of Counseling and Development* 65 (March 1987): 345–50.

Brady, J.P., and E.E. Levitt. "The Relation of Sexual Preferences to Sexual Experience." *Psychological Record* 15 (1965): 377–84.

Brannigan, Augustine. "Is Obscenity Criminogenic?" *Society* 24 (July/August 1987): 12–19.

Brannigan, Augustine. "Pornography and Behavior: Alternative Explanations." *Journal of Communication* 37, no. 3 (Summer 1987): 185–89.

Brannigan, Augustine, and Andros Kapardis. "The Controversy over Pornography and Sex Crimes: The Criminological Evidence and Beyond." *Australian and New Zealand Journal of Criminology* 19 (December 1988): 259–84.

Brickman, J.R. "Erotica, Sex Differences in Stimulus Preferences and Fantasy Context." *Dissertation Abstracts International* 39, no. 7B (1979): 3500–3501E.

Briddell, D.W., D.C. Rinn, G.R. Caddy, G. Kravitz, D. Sholis, and R.J. Wunderlun. "Effects of Alcohol and Cognitive Set on Sexual Arousal to Deviant Stimuli." *Journal of Abnormal Psychology* 87 (1978): 418–30.

"Brief of the Neighborhood Pornography Task Force, Amicus Curiae, in Support of Appellant in *Mudrut v. American Booksellers Association, Inc*." 7th Circuit Court of Appeals, 25 February 1985.

Briere, J., S. Carre, and M. Runtz. "The Rape Arousal Inventory: Predicting Actual and Potential Sexual Aggression in a University Population." Paper presented to the American Psychological Association, Toronto, 1984.

Briere, J., and N. Malamuth. "Self-Reported Likelihood of Sexually Aggressive Behavior: Attitudinal Versus Sexual Explanations." *Journal of Research in Personality* 17 (1983): 315–23.

Briere, J., N. Malamuth, and J.V.P. Check. "Sexuality and Rape-Supportive Beliefs." In *Sex Roles*. Vol. 2: *Feminist Psychology in Transition*, edited by P. Caplan, Toronto: Eden, 1981.

Briggs, M.M. "The Use of Audio-Visual Materials in Sexuality Programs." In *Sex Education for the Health Professional: A Curriculum Guide*, edited by N. Rosenzweig and F.P. Pearsall, . New York: Grune and Stratton, 1978.

Brissett, Dennis, and Robert P. Snow. "Vicarious Behavior: Leisure and the Transformation of *Playboy* Magazine." *Journal of Popular Culture* 3 (Winter 1969): 428–40.

Brittain, R.P. "The Sadistic Murderer." *Medicine, Science and the Law* 10 (1970): 198–207.

Brodsky, S.L. "Sexual Assault: Perspectives on Prevention and Assailants." In *Sexual Assault*, edited by M.J. Walker and S.L. Brodsky, . Lexington, Mass.: D.C. Health, 1976.

Brody, S. "Screen Violence and Film Censorship: A Review of Research." Home Office Research Study No. 40. Her Majesty's Stationery Office, London, 1977.

Bross, M. "Mitigating the Effects of Mass Media Sexual Violence." Master's thesis, University of Wisconsin, Madison, 1985.

Brown, C., J. Anderson, L. Burggraf, and N. Thompson.

"Community Standards, Conservatism, and Judgments of Pornography." *Journal of Sex Research* 14 (1978): 81–95.

Brown, M. "Viewing Time of Pornography." *Journal of Psychology* 102 (May 1979): 83–95.

Brown, M., D.M. Amoroso, and E.F. Ware. "Behavioral Effects of Viewing Pornography." *Journal of Social Psychology* 98 (1976): 235–45.

Brown, M., D.M. Amoroso, E.E. Ware, M. Pruesse, and D.W. Pilkey. "Factors Affecting Viewing Time of Pornography." *Journal of Social Psychology* 90 (1973): 125–35.

Brown, P.T. "On the Differentiation of Homo- or Hetero-Erotic Interest in the Male: An Operant Technique Illustrated in a Case of Motor-Cycle Fetishist." *Behaviour Research and Therapy* 2 (1964): 31–37.

Brownell, K.D., S.C. Hayes, and D.H. Barlow. "Patterns of Appropriate and Deviant Sexual Arousal: The Behavioral Treatment of Multiple Sexual Deviations." *Journal of Consulting and Clinical Psychology* 45 (1977): 1144–55.

Bryant, Jennings, and Dolf Zillman. *Perspectives on Media Effects.* Hillsdale, N.J.: L. Erlbaum Associates, 1986.

Buhrich, N. "The Association of Erotic Piercing with Homosexuality, S-M, Bondage, Fetishism, and Tattoos." *Archives of Sexual Behavior* 12 (1983): 167–71.

Bullock, Donald H. "Note on 'Looking at Pictures' Behavior." *Perceptual and Motor Skills* 9 (1959): 333.

Bullough, V., and B. Bullough. *Sin, Sickness, and Sanity: A History of Sexual Attitudes.* New York: New American Library, 1977.

Burdick, J.A. "The Relationship between Cardiac Variability and the Evaluation of Pictorial Sexual Stimuli." *Dissertation Abstracts International* 38, no. 12B (1978): 6188–89.

Burditt, T.C., Jr. "Social Abuse of Children and Adolescents." Texas Legislature House Select Committee on Child Pornography, Austin, 1978.

Burgess, A. "The Effects of Pornography on Women and Children Including an Analysis of Sexual Homicide Crime Scene Data." Testimony before the Senate Committee on the Judiciary, Subcommittee on Juvenile Justice, Washington, D.C., 12 September 1984.

Burstyn, Varda, ed. *Women Against Censorship.* Toronto: Douglas & McIntrye, 1985.

Burt, M.E.H. "Use of Pornography of Women: A Critical Review of the Literature." *Case Western Reserve Journal of Sociology* 8 (1976): 1–16.

Burt, M.R. "Cultural Myths and Supports for Rape." *Journal of Personality and Social Psychology* 38 (1980): 217–30.

Burt, M.R. "Justifying Personal Violence: A Comparison of Rapists and the General Public." *Victimology: An International Journal* 8 (1983): 131–50.

Burt, M.R., and R.S. Allun. "Rape Myths, Rape Definitions and Probability of Conviction." *Journal of Applied Social Psychology* 11 (1981): 212–30.

Byeff, P. "Helping Behavior in Audio and Audio-Visual Conditions." Senior honors thesis, University of Pennsylvania, 1970.

Byrne, D. "Social Psychology and the Study of Sexual Behavior." *Personality and Social Psychology Bulletin* 3 (1977) 3–30.

Byrne, D. "The Imagery of Sex." In *Handbook of Sexology*, edited by J. Money and H. Musaph, Amsterdam: Elseveier/North-Holland Biomedical Press, 1977.

Byrne, D., F. Cherry, J. Lamberth, and H.E. Mitchell. "Husband-Wife Similarity in Response to Erotic Stimuli." *Journal of Personality* 41 (1973): 385–94.

Byrne, D., J.D. Fisher, J. Lamberth, and H.E. Mitchell. "Evaluations of Erotica: Facts or Feelings?" *Journal of Personality and Social Psychology* 29 (January 1974): 111–16.

Byrne, D., and K. Kelley. "Internal and External Imagery as Determinants of Individual Differences in Sexual Expression." Unpublished manuscript, State University of New York at Albany, 1983.

Byrne, D., and K. Kelley. "Introduction: Pornography and Sex Research." In *Pornography and Sexual Aggression*, edited by N. Malamuth and E. Donnerstein, 1–16. New York: Academic Press, 1984.

Byrne, D., and K. Kelley, eds. *Approaches to the Study of Sexual Behavior.* Hillsdale, N.J.: Lawrence Erlbaum Associates, 1985.

Byrne, D., and J. Lamberth. "The Effect of Erotic Stimuli on Sex Arousal, Evaluative Responses, and Subsequent Behavior." In *Technical Reports of the Commission on Obscenity and Pornography.* Vol. 8, . Washington, D.C.: GPO, 1971.

Byrne, D., and J. Sheffield. "Response to Sexually Arousing Stimuli as a Function of Repressing and Sensitizing Defenses." *Journal of Abnormal Psychology* 70 (1965): 114–18.

Caird, W.K., and J.P. Wincze. *Sex Therapy: A Behavioral Approach.* Hagerstown, Md.: Harper & Row, 1977.

Cairns, R.B., J.C.N. Paul, and J. Wishner. "Sex Censorship: The Assumptions of Anti-Obscenity Laws and the Empirical Evidence." *Minnesota Law Review* 46 (1962): 1009–41.

Cairns, R.B., J.C.N. Paul, and J. Wishner. "Psychological Assumptions in Sex Censorship." In *Technical Reports of the Commission on Obscenity and Pornography.* Vol. 8, . Washington, D.C.: GPO, 1971.

Calderone, M.S. "Eroticism as a Norm." *Family Coordinator* 23 (1974): 337–41.

Cantor, J.R., D. Zillmann, and J. Bryant. "Enhancement of Experienced Sexual Arousal in Response to Erotic Stimuli through Misattribution of Unrelated Residual Excitation." *Journal of Personality and Social Psychology* 32 (1975): 69–75.

Cantor, J.R., D. Zillman, and E.F. Einsiedel. "Female Responses to Provocation after Exposure to Aggressive and Erotic Films." *Communication Research* 5 (1978): 395–411.

Carlson, J.M. "Crime Show Viewing by Preadults: The Impact on Attitudes toward Civil Liberties." *Communication Research* 10 (1983): 527–52.

Carroll, J.S. "The Effects of Imagining an Event on Expectations for the Event: An Interpretation in Terms of the Availability Heuristic." *Journal of Experimental Social Psychology* 14 (1978): 88–96.

Carruthers, M., and P. Taggart. "Vagotonicity of Violence: Biochemical and Cardiac Responses to Violent Films and Television Programmes." *British Medical Journal* 3 (1973): 384–89.

Carter, Daniel L., Robert A. Prentky, Raymond A. Knight, Penny L. Vanderveer, et al. "Use of Pornography in the Criminal and Developmental Histories of Sexual Offenders." *Journal of Interpersonal Violence* 2 (June 1987): 196–211.

Casey, C.E., and L. Martin. "Pornography and Obscenity." In *Police Yearbook 1978*. Gaithersburg, Md.: International Association of Chiefs of Police, 1979.

Cash, T.F., D.N. Cash, and J.W. Butters. "Mirror, Mirror, On the Wall? Contrast Effects and Self Evaluations of Physical Attractiveness." *Personality and Social Psychology Bulletin* 9 (1983): 351–58.

Cattell, R.B., G.F. Kawash, and G.E. DeYoung. "Validation of Objective Measures of Ergic Tension: Response of the Sex Erg to Visual Stimulation." *Journal of Experimental Research in Personality* 6 (1972): 76–83.

Cerny, J.A. "Biofeedback and the Voluntary Control of Sexual Arousal in Women." *Behavior Therapy* 9 (1978): 847–55.

Chaffee, S. "Television and Adolescent Aggressiveness." In *Television and Social Behavior*. Vol. 3: *Television and Adolescent Aggressiveness*, edited by G. Comstock and E.A. Rubenstein, . Washington, D.C.: GPO, 1972.

Chamberlin, F.M. "The Faces of Pornography." In *Pornography and Human Sexuality*, edited by J.N. Santamaria, . Victoria, Australia: Human Life Research Foundation, 1974.

Chapin, M. *Debriefings of Females Exposed to Film Depictions of Violence Against Women*. Master's thesis, University of Wisconsin, Madison, 1985.

Chapman, L.J., Jean P. Chapman, and T. Brelje. "Influence of the Experimenter on Pupillary Dilation to Sexually Provocative Pictures." *Journal of Abnormal Psychology* 74 (1969): 396–400.

Check, J.V.P. "The Effects of Violent and Nonviolent Pornography." Report to the Department of Justice, Ottawa, 1985.

Check, J.V.P. *The Hostility towards Women Scale*. Doctoral dissertation, University of Manitoba, 1985.

Check, J.V.P., B. Elias, and S.H. Barton. "Hostility towards Men in Female Victims of Male Sexual Aggression." In *Violence in Intimate Relationships*, edited by G.W. Russell, . Jamaica, N.Y.: Spectrum, 1985.

Check, J.V.P., and N.H. Heapy. "Report for the LaMarsh Research Programme. A Survey of Canadians' Attitudes Regarding Sexual Context in the Media." York University, Toronto, July 1985.

Check, J.V.P., and N. Malamuth. "Can Exposure to Pornography Have Positive Effects?" Paper presented to the American Psychological Association, Los Angeles, August 1981.

Check, J.V.P., and N. Malamuth. "Pornography Effects and Self-Reported Likelihood of Committing Acquaintance versus Stranger Rape." Paper presented to the Midwestern Psychological Association, Minneapolis, May 1982.

Check, J.V.P., and N. Malamuth. "The Hostility towards Women Scale." Paper presented at the Western Meetings of the International Society for the Research on Aggression, Victoria, Canada, June 1983.

Check, J.V.P., and N. Malamuth. "Violent Pornography, Feminism, and Social Learning Theory." *Aggressive Behavior* 9 (1983): 106–7.

Check, J.V.P., and N.M. Malamuth. "Can There Be Positive Effects of Participation in Pornography Experiments?" *Journal of Sex Research* 20 (February 1984): 1–31.

Check, J.V.P., and N.M. Malamuth. "Pornography and Sexual Aggression: A Social Learning Theory Analysis." In *Communication Yearbook*. Vol. 9, edited by M.L. McLaughlin, . Beverly Hills, Calif.: Sage Publications, 1985.

Check, J.V.P., and N. Malamuth. *Ethical Considerations in Sex and Aggression Research*. Unpublished manuscript, York University, 1986.

Check, J.V.P., N.M. Malamuth, B. Elias, and S. Barton. "On Hostile Ground." *Psychology Today* 19 (1985): 56–61.

Christie, W., and M. Christie. "Pedophilia and Aggression." *Criminal Justice and Behavior* 8 (1981): 145–50.

Clark, D.F. "Fetishism Treated by Negative Conditioning." *British Journal of Psychiatry* 109 (1963): 404–8.

Clark, L. "Pornography's Challenge to Liberal Ideology." *Canadian Forum* 3 (1980): 9–12.

Clark, L., and D.J. Lewis. *Rape: The Price of Coercive Sexuality*. Toronto: Canadian Women's Educational Press, 1977.

Clark, R.A. "The Projective Measurement of Experimentally Induced Levels of Sexual Motivation." *Journal of Experimental Psychology* 44 (1952): 391–99.

Clark, R.A. "The Effects of Sexual Motivation on Fantasy." *Journal of Experimental Psychology* 44 (1953): 3–11.

Clark, R.A. "The Effects of Sexual Maturation on Fantasy." In *Studies in Motivation*, edited by D.C. McClelland, 44–57. New York: Appleton-Century-Crofts, 1955.

Clayson, D.E., and W. Eshler. "Evaluation of Self, Ideal Self and Pornography in Relation to Handedness and Sex." *Journal of Psychology* 111 (1982): 87–90.

Cline, V.B. "Critique of Commission on Behavioral Research." In *The Report of Commission on Obscenity and Pornography*, 463–90. New York: Bantam Books, 1970.

Cline, V.B., ed. *Where Do You Draw the Line? An Exploration into Media Violence, Pornography, and Censorship*. Provo, Utah: Brigham Young University Press, 1974.

Cline, V.B. "The Scientists vs. Pornography: An Untold Story." *Intellect*, February 1976, 574–76.

Cline, V.B. "The Effects of Pornography on Human Behavior: Data and Observations." Testimony before the Attorney General's Commission on Obscenity and Pornography, 11 September 1985.

Cline, V.B., R.G. Croft, and S. Courrier. "Desensitization of Children to Television Violence." *Journal of Personality and Social Psychology* 27 (1973): 360–65.

Cobb, C., and B. Avery. *Rape of a Normal Mind.* Markham, Ontario: Paperjacks, 1977.

Cochrane, P. "Sex Crimes and Pornography Revisited." *International Journal of Criminology and Penology* 6 (1978): 307–17.

Cohen, M.L., R. Garofalo, R. Boucher, and T. Seghorn. "The Psychology of Rapists." *Seminars in Psychiatry* (1971): 307–27.

Coles, Claire, D., and Johanna Shamp. "Some Sexual, Personality, and Demographic Characteristics of Women Readers of Erotic Romances." *Archives of Sexual Behaviour* 13 (June 1984): 187–209.

Collins, B.G. A Discriminant Analysis of the Attitudes, Psychological Characteristics, and Behavior of Male Readers and Non-Readers of Soft-Core Pornography. Doctoral dissertation, Rutgers University, 1988.

Collins, W.A., B.L. Sobol, and S. Westby. "Effects of Adult Commentary on Children's Comprehension and Inferences about a Televised Aggressive Portrayal." *Child Development* 52 (1981): 158–63.

Colson, Charles E. "The Evaluation of Pornography: Effects of Attitude and Perceived Physiological Reactions." *Archives of Sexual Behavior* 3 (1974): 307–23.

Committee on Obscenity and Film Censorship. *The Report of the Committee on Obscenity and Film Censorship.* London: Her Majesty's Stationery Office, 1979.

Comstock, G. "The Impact of Television on American Institutions." *Journal of Communications* 28 (1978): 12–28.

Comstock, G. "New Emphasis in Research on the Effects of Television and Film Violence." In *Children and the Faces of Television: Teaching, Violence, and Selling,* edited by Edward L. Palmer and Aimée Dorr, 129–48. New York: Academic Press, 1980.

Comstock, G., S. Chaffee, N. Katzman, M. McCombs, and D. Roberts. *Television and Human Behavior.* New York: Columbia University Press, 1978.

Conrad, S.R., and J.P. Winze. "Orgasmic Reconditioning: A Controlled Study of Its Effects upon the Sexual Arousal and Behavior of Adult Male Homosexuals." *Behavior Therapy* 7 (1976): 155–66.

Cook, R.F., and R.H. Fosen. "Pornography and the Sex Offenders: Patterns of Exposure and Immediate Arousal Effects of Pornographic Stimuli." In *Technical Reports of the Commission on Obscenity and Pornography.* Vol. 7, 149–62. Washington, D.C.: GPO, 1971.

Cook, R.F., R.H. Fosen, and A. Pacht. "Pornography and the Sex Offender: Patterns of Previous Exposure and Arousal Effects of Pornographic Stimuli." *Journal of Applied Psychology* 55 (1971): 503–11.

Cook, T.D., and B.R. Flay. "The Persistence of Experimentally Induced Attitude Change." In *Advances in Experimental Social Psychology.* Vol. 11, edited by L. Berkowitz, . New York: Academic Press, 1978.

Cook, T.D., D.A. Kenedzierski, and S.V. Thomas. "The Implicit Assumptions of Television Research: An Analysis of the 1982 N.I.M.H. Report on Television and Behavior." *Public Opinion Quarterly* 47 (1983): 161–201.

Cooper, A.J. "A Case of Fetishism and Impotence by Behavior Therapy." *British Journal of Psychiatry* 109 (1963): 649–52.

Corder-Bolz, Charles R. "Television Literacy and Critical Television Viewing Skills." In *Television and Behavior: Ten Years of Scientific Progress and Implications for the Eighties.* Vol. 2: *Technical Reviews,* edited by David Pearl, Lorraine Bouhilet, and Joyce Lanzer, 91–102. Rockville, Md.: U.S. Department of Health and Human Services, 1982.

Corman, C. "Physiological Response to a Sexual Stimulus." Undergraduate thesis, University of Manitoba, 1968.

Corry, J. "The Networks Shrug off Violence." *New York Times,* 31 July 1983.

Costin, F. "Beliefs about Rape and Women's Social Roles." *Archives of Sexual Behavior* 14 (1985): 319–25.

Court, J.H. *Changing Community Standards.* Adelaide, Australia: Lutheran Publishing House, 1972.

Court, J.H. "The Place of Censored Material in the Treatment of Behavior Disturbances." *Australian Psychologist* 8 (July 1973): .

Court, J.H. "Pornography—Personal and Societal Effects." In *Liberation Movements and Psychiatry. Geigy Psychiatric Symposium.* Vol. 2, edited by N. McConaghy, . 1974.

Court, J.H. *Law, Light and Liberty.* Adelaide, Australia: Lutheran Publishing House, 1975.

Court, J.H. "Pornography and Sex-Crimes: A Re-evaluation in the Light of Recent Trends around the World." *International Journal of Criminology and Penology* 5 (1977): 129–57.

Court, J.H. "Rape and Pornography in White South Africa." *De Sure* ( ) 12, no. 2 (1979): 236–41.

Court, J.H. *Pornography and the Harm Condition.* : Finders University of South Australia, 1980.

Court, J.H. "Aspects of Sexual Medicine: Pornography Update." *British Journal of Sexual Medicine* (May 1981): .

Court, J.H. "Pornography and Harm." *Swansea* (July 1982): .

Court, J.H. "Rape Trends in New South Wales: A Discussion of Conflicting Evidence." *Australian Journal of Social Issues* 17, no. 3: 202–6.

Court, J.H. "The Relief of Sexual Problems through Pornography." *Australian Journal of Sex, Marriage and Family* 5 (May 1984): 97–106.

Court, J.H. "Sex and Violence: A Ripple Effect." In *Pornography and Sexual Aggression,* edited by N. Malamuth and E. Donnerstein, 143–72. New York: Academic Press, 1984.

Court, J.H. "Contemporary Pornography as a Contributor to Sexual Offenses Against Women." In *Women's Worlds,* edited by M. Safir, M. Mednick, D. Israeli, and J. Bernard . New York: Praeger, 1985.

Court, J.H. Testimony before the Attorney General's Commission on Pornography, 12 September 1985.

Cowan, G. *See No Evil: The Backstage Battle over Sex and Violence on Television.* New York: Simon & Schuster, 1978.

Cox, M. "Dynamic Psychotherapy with Sex-offenders." In *Sexual Deviation,* edited by I. Rosen, Oxford, England: Oxford University Press, 1979.

Crawford, D.A. "Modification of Deviant Sexual Behavior: The Need for a Comprehensive Approach." *British Journal of Medical Psychology* 52 (1979): 151–56.

Crepault, C. "Sexual Fantasies and Visualization of 'Pornographic Scenes.'" *Journal of Sex Research* 8 (1972): 154–55.

Crepault, C. "Men's Erotic Fantasies." *Archives of Sexual Behavior* 9, no. 6 (1980): 565–81.

Crepault, C., G. Abraham, R. Porto, and M. Couture. "Erotic Imagery in Women." In *Progress in Sexology,* edited by R. Gemme and C.C. Wheeler, . New York: Plenum Press, 1977.

Crepault, C., R. Abraham, R. Porto, and M. Couture. *Erotic Sexology.* New York: Plenum Press, 1977.

Crepault, C. and M. Couture. "Mens Erotic Fantasies." *Archives of Sexual Behavior* 9 (1980) 565–81.

Csillag, E.R. "Modification of Penile Erectile Response." *Behavior Research and Experimental Psychiatry* 7 (1976): 27–29.

Davidson, G.C., and G.T. Wilson. "Processes of Fear Reduction in Systematic Desensitization: Cognitive and Social Reinforcement Factors in Humans." *Behavior Therapy* 4 (1973): 1–21.

David, J., and T. Smith. "National Opinion Research Center, General Social Survey, 1972–1982." *Cumulative Codebook.* Chicago: University of Chicago Press, 1982.

Davis, K.E., and G.N. Braucht. "Exposure to Pornography, Character and Sexual Deviance: A Retrospective Survey." In *Technical Reports of the Commission on Obscenity and Pornography.* Vol. 7, 173–244. Washington, D.C.: GPO, 1971.

Davis, K.E., and G.N. Braucht. "Reactions to Viewing Films of Erotically Realistic Heterosexual Behavior." In *Technical Reports of the Commission on Obscenity and Pornography.* Vol. 8, 68–96. Washington, D.C.: GPO, 1971.

Davis, K.E., and G.N. Braucht. "Exposure to Pornography, Character and Sexual Deviance: A Retrospective Survey." *Journal of Social Issues* 29 (1973): 183–96.

Davis, R.C., and A.M. Buchwald. "An Exploration of Somatic Response Patterns: Stimulus and Sex Differences." *Journal of Comparative and Physiological Psychology* 50 (1957): 44–52.

Davison, G. "Elimination of a Sadistic Fantasy by Client-Controlled Counterconditioning Technique." *Journal of Abnormal Psychology* 73 (1968): 84–90.

Dean, S.J., R.B. Martin, and D.L. Steiner. "The Use of Sexually Arousing Slides as Unconditioned Stimuli for the GSR in a Discrimination Paradigm." *Psychonomic Science* 13 (1968): 99.

Deitz, S.R., K.T. Blackwell, and P.C. Daley. "Measurement of Empathy toward Rape Victims and Rapists." *Journal of Personality and Social Psychology* 43 (1982): 372–84.

Deitz, S.R., and L.E. Byrnes. "Attribution of Responsibility for Sexual Assault: The Influence of Observer Empathy and Defendant Occupation and Attractiveness." *Journal of Psychology* 108 (1981): 17–29.

Demare, D. "The Effects of Erotic and Sexually Violent Mass Media on the Attitudes toward Women and Rape." Unpublished manuscript, University of Winnipeg, 1985.

Dengerink, H.A. "Personality Variables as Mediators of Attack-Instigated Aggression." In *Perspectives on Aggression,* edited by Russell G. Geen and Edgar C. O'Neal, 61–98. New York: Academic Press, 1976.

Dehnoltz, M. "An Extension of Covert Procedures in the Treatment of Male Homosexuals." *Journal of Behavior Therapy and Experimental Psychiatry* 4 (1973): 305.

Dermer, M., and T.A. Pyszcynski. "Effects of Erotica upon Men's Loving and Linking Responses for Women They Love." *Journal of Personality and Social Psychology* 36 (1978): 1302–10.

Diener, E., and R. Crandell. *Ethics in Social and Behavioral Research.* Chicago: University of Chicago Press, 1978.

Diener, E., K.L. Westford, S.C. Fraser, and A.L. Beaman. "Selected Demographic Variables in Altruism." *Psychology Reports* 33 (1973): 226.

Dienstbier, R.A. "Sex and Violence: Can Research Have It Both Ways?" *Journal of Communication* 27 (1977): 176–88.

Dominick, J., and B.S. Greenberg. "Attitudes towards Violence: Interaction of Television, Social Class, and Family Attitudes." In *Television and Social Behavior.* Vol. 3: *Television and Adolescent Aggressiveness,* edited by G. Comstock and E.A. Rubinstein, . Washington, D.C.: GPO,

Donnerstein, E. "Pornography and Sexual Violence." *Medical Aspects of Human Sexuality* 13 (1979): 103.

Donnerstein, E. "Aggressive Erotica and Violence Against Women." *Journal of Personality and Social Psychology* 39 (1980): 269–77.

Donnerstein E. "Pornography and Violence Against Women." *Annals of the New York Academy of Sciences* 347 (1980): 277–88.

Donnerstein, E. "Pornography and Violence Against Women: Experimental Studies." In *Forensic Psychology and Psychiatry,* edited by Fred Wright, Charles Bahn, and Robert W. Rieber, 277–88. New York: New York Academy of Sciences, 1980.

Donnerstein, E. "Aggressive Pornography: Can It Influence Aggression Against Women?" In *Promoting Sexual Responsibility and Preventing Sexual Problems,* edited by G. Albee, S. Gordon, and H. Leitenberg, Hanover, N.H.: University of New England Press, 1983.

Donnerstein, E. "Erotica and Human Aggression." In *Aggression: Theoretical and Empirical Reviews.* Vol. 2, edited by Russell G. Geen and Edward I. Donnerstein, 127–54. New York: Academic Press, 1983.

Donnerstein, E. "Pornography and Violence Against Women." In *Pornography and Censorship,* edited by

David Copp and Susan Wendell, 219–32. New York: Prometheus Books, 1983.

Donnerstein, E. "Pornography: Its Effect on Violence Against Women." In *Pornography and Sexual Aggression,* edited by N. Malamuth and E. Donnerstein, . New York: Academic Press, 1984.

Donnerstein, E., and G. Barrett. "The Effects of Erotic Stimuli on Male Aggression toward Females." *Journal of Personality and Social Psychology* 36 (February 1978): 180–88.

Donnerstein, E. and L. Berkowitz. "Victim Reactions in Aggressive Erotic Films as a Factor in Violence Against Women." *Journal of Personality and Social Psychology* 41 (1981): 710–24.

Donnerstein, E., and L. Berkowitz. "Effects of Film Contents and Victim Association on Aggressive Behavior and Attitudes." Unpublished manuscript, University of Wisconsin, Madison, 1983.

Donnerstein, E., and L. Berkowitz. "Victim Reactions in Aggressive Erotic Films as a Factor in Violence Against Women." In *Pornography and Censorship,* edited by David Copp and Susan Wendell, 233–56. New York: Prometheus Books, 1983.

Donnerstein, E., L. Berkowitz, and D. Linz. "Role of Aggressive and Sexual Images in Violent Pornography." Unpublished manuscript, University of Wisconsin, Madison, 1986.

Donnerstein, E., C.A. Champion, Cass R. Sunstein, and Catharine A. MacKinnon. "Pornography: Social Science, Legal and Clinical Perspectives." *Law and Inequality* 4 (May 1986): 17–49.

Donnerstein, E., M. Donnerstein, and G. Barrett. "Where Is the Facilitation of Media Violence? The Effects of Nonexposure and Placement of Anger Arousal." *Journal of Research in Personality* 10 (1976): 386–98.

Donnerstein, E., M. Donnerstein, and R. Evans. "Erotic Stimuli and Aggression: Facilitation or Inhibition?" *Journal of Personality and Social Psychology* 32 ( ): 237–44.

Donnerstein, E., and J. Hallam. "The Facilitation Effects of Erotica on Aggression toward Females." *Journal of Personality and Social Psychology* 36 (1978): 1270–77.

Donnerstein, E., and D. Linz. "Sexual Violence in the Media: A Warning." *Psychology Today,* January 1984, 14–15.

Donnerstein, E., and D. Linz. "Mass Media Sexual Violence and Male Viewers: Current Theory and Research." *American Behavioral Science* 29 (May/June 1986): 601–18.

Donnerstein, E., D. Linz, and S. Penrod. *The Question of Pornography: Research Findings and Policy Implications.* New York: Free Press, 1987.

Donnerstein, E., and N. Malamuth. "Mitigating the Effects of Exposure to Sexually Violent Mass Media Stimuli." In *Advances in the Study of Aggression.* Vol. 2, edited by R. Blanchard and C. Blanchard, . New York: Academic Press, .

Donnerstein, E., and N. Malamuth. "Pornography: Its Consequences on the Observer." In *Sexual Dynamics of Antisocial Behavior,* edited by Louis B. Schlesinger

and Eugene Revitch, 31–47. Springfield, Ill.: Charles C. Thomas, 1982.

Donnerstein, E., C. Mueller, and J. Hallam. "Erotica and Aggression towards Women: The Role of Aggressive Models." Unpublished manuscript, University of Wisconsin, Madison, 1983.

Donnerstein, E., and D.W. Wilson. "Effects of Noise and Perceived Control on Ongoing and Subsequent Aggressive Behavior." *Journal of Personality and Social Psychology* 34 (November 1976): 774–81.

Doolittle, J. "Immunizing Children Against the Possible Anti-Social Effects of Viewing Television Violence: A Curricular Intervention." Doctoral dissertation, University of Wisconsin, Madison, 1976.

Dorr, A. "Television Viewing and Fear of Functioning: Maybe This Decade." *Journal of Broadcasting* 25 (1981): 334–45.

Dorr, A., S. Graves, and E. Phelps. "Television Literacy for Young Children." *Journal of Communication* 30 (Summer 1980): 71 83.

Dorr, A., P. Kovaric. "Some of the People Some of the Time—But Which People? Televised Violence and Its Effects." In *Children and the Faces of Television,* edited by Edward L. Palmer and Aimée Dorr, 183–200. New York: Academic Press, 1980.

Drabman, R., and M. Thomas. "Does Media Violence Increase Children's Toleration of Real-Life Aggression?" *Development Psychology* 10 (1974): 418–21.

Dunn, Angela Fox. "The Dark Side of Erotic Fantasy." *Human Behavior* 7 (November 1978): 18–23.

Dunwoody, V., and K. Pezdek. "Factors Affecting the Sexual Arousal Value of Pictures." *Journal of Sex Research* 15 (1979): 276–84.

Dutcher, L.W. "Scarcity and Erotica: An Examination of Commodity Theory Dynamics." *Dissertation Abstracts International* 37, no. 6B (1975): 3069.

Dysinger, W.S., and C.A. Rickmick. *The Emotional Responses of Children to the Motion-Picture Situation.* New York: Macmillan, 1983.

"The Effects of Explicit Sexual Materials: The Report of the Commission on Obscenity and Pornography." In *The Pornography Controversy,* edited by Ray C. Rist, 217–24. New Brunswick, N.J.: Transaction Books, 1975.

Einsiedee, E. "Social Behavior Science Research Analysis." In Attorney General's Commission on Pornography, *Final Report,* . Washington, D.C.: U.S. Department of Justice, 1986.

Eisenman, R. "Sexual Behavior as Related to Sex Fantasies and Experimental Manipulation of Authoritarianism and Creativity." *Journal of Personality and Social Psychology* 43, no. 4 (1982): 853–60.

Eliasberg, W.G. "Psychiatric Viewpoints on Indecency, Obscenity and Pornography in Literature and the Arts." *American Journal of Psychotherapy* 16 (1962): 477–83.

Eliasberg, W.G., and I.R. Stuart. "Authoritarian Personality and the Obscenity Threshold." *Journal of Social Psychology* 55 (1961): 143–51.

"The Psychology of Pornography." In *the Encyclopedia of Sexual Behavior*. Vol. 2, edited by Albert Ellis and Albert Aibarbanel, 848–59. New York: Hawthorn Books, 1961.

Ellis, L., and C. Beattie. "The Feminist Explanation for Rape: An Experimental Test." *Journal of Sex Research* 19 (February 1983): 74–93.

Englar, Z.C., and C.E. Walker. "Male and Female Reactions to Erotic Literature." *Psychology Reports* 32 (1973): 481–82.

English, Dierdre. "The Politics of Pornography: Can Feminists Walk the Line?" *Mother Jones*, April 1980, 20.

Eron, L.D. "Prescription for a Reduction of Aggression." *American Psychologist* 35 (1980): 244–52.

Eron, L.D. "Interventions to Mitigate the Psychological Effects of Media Violence on Aggressive Behavior." *Journal of Social Issues* 42, no. 3 (1986): .

Eron, L.D., and L.R. Huesmann. "Adolescent Aggression and Television. *Annals of the New York Academy of Sciences* 347 (1980): 319–31.

Esses, Victoria. "Field Data on Availability of Pornography and Incidence of Sex Crime in Denmark: Fuel for a Heated Debate." *Canadian Criminology Forum* 7, no. 2 (1985): 83–91.

Evans, D.R. "Masturbatory Fantasy and Sexual Deviation." *Behavioral Research and Therapy* 6 (1958): 17.

Evers, , and Stanmeyer. "Insight Pornography—Extent of Pornography in Modern Society and Its Harm." *Journal of Current Adolescent Medicine* 3 (1981): 13.

Eysenck, H.J. "The Uses and Abuses of Pornography." In *Psychology Is about People*, edited by H.J. Eysenck, 236–86. London: Allen Lane, The Penguin Press, 1972.

Eysenck, H.J. "Psychology and Obscenity: A Factual Look at Some of the Problems." In *Censorship and Obscenity*, edited by R. Dhavan and Christie Davies, 148–81. London: Martin Robertson & Co., 1978.

Eysenck, H.J., and S.B.G. Eysenck. *Psychoticism as a Dimension of Personality*. London: University of London Press, 1976.

Eysenck, H.J. and D.K.B. Nias. *Sex, Violence and the Media*. London: Maurice Temple Smith, 1978.

Farkas, G.M. "Trait and State Determinants of Male Sexual Arousal to Description of Coercive Sexuality." Doctoral dissertation, University of Hawaii, 1979.

Farkas, G.M., L.F. Sine, and I.M. Evans. "Personality, Sexuality, and Demographic Differences between Volunteers and Nonvolunteers for a Laboratory Study of Male Sexual Behavior." *Archives of Sexual Behavior* 87 (1978): 513.

Farkas, G.M., L.F. Sine, and I.M. Evans. "Personality, Sexuality, and Demographic Differences between Volunteers and Nonvolunteers for a Laboratory Study of Male Sexual Behavior." *Behavior Research and Therapy* 17 (1979): 25–32.

Faust, B. "Why Don't Humanists Do Their Homework?" *Australian Humanist* 28 (1973): 4–7.

Faust, B. *Women, Sex and Pornography: A Controversial Study*. New York: Macmillan, 1980.

Fehr, F.S., and M. Schulman. "Female Self-Report and Autonomic Responses to Sexually Pleasurable and Sexually Aversive Readings." *Archives of Sexual Behavior* 7 (1978): 443–53.

Field, H.S. "Attitudes towards Rape: A Comparative Analysis of Police, Rapists, Crisis Counsellors and Citizens." *Journal of Personality and Social Psychology* 36 (1978): 156–79.

Feldman, M.P. "Aversion Therapy for Sexual Deviations: A Critical Review." *Psychological Bulletin* 65 (1966): 65–79.

Feldman, M.P., and M.J. MacCulloch. "The Application of Anticipatory Avoidance Learning to the Treatment of Homosexuality, I Theory, Technique and Preliminary Results." *Behavior Research and Therapy* 2 (1965): 165–84.

Feldman, M.P., and M.J. MacCulloch. "Aversion Therapy in the Management of Homosexuals." *British Medical Journal* 1 (1967): 594.

Feldman, M.P., and M.J. MacCulloch. *Homosexual Behavior: Therapy and Assessment*. Oxford, England: Pergamon Press, 1971.

Feshbach, S. "Reality and Fantasy in Film Violence." In *Television and Social Behavior*. Vol. 2, edited by J. Murray, E. Rubinstein, G. Rubinstein, and G. Comstock, . Washington, D.C.: U.S. Department of Health, Education and Welfare, .

Feshbach, S., and N. Malamuth. "Sex and Aggression: Providing the Link." *Psychology Today* 12 (1978): 111–22.

Finklehor, D., and S. Arajl. "Explanation of Pedophilia: A Four Factor Model." unpublished paper, University of New Hampshire, 1983.

Finklehor, D. *Child Sexual Abuse: New Theory and Research*. New York: Free Press, 1984.

Fisher, S., and H. Osofsky. "Sexual Responsiveness in Women, Physiological Correlates." *Psychological Reports* 22 (1968): 215–26.

Fisher, W.A. "Individual Differences in Behavioral Responsiveness to Erotica: Cognitive Labeling, Transfer of Arousal, and Disinhibition Considerations." Master's thesis, Purdue University, 1976.

Fisher, W.A., and D. Byrne. "Individual Differences in Socialization to Sex as a Mediator of Responses to an Erotic Film: Teach Your Children Well." Paper presented to the Midwestern Psychological Association, Chicago, May 1976.

Fisher, W.A., and D. Byrne. "Individual Differences in Affective, Evaluative, and Behavioral Responses to an Erotic Film." *Journal of Applied Social Psychology* 8 (1978): 355–65.

Fisher, W.A., C.T. Miller, D. Byrne, and L.A. White. "Talking Dirty: Responses to Communicating a Sexual Message as a Function of Situational and Personality Factors." *Basic and Applied Social Psychology* 1 (1980): 115–26.

Flay, B.R. "Psychosocial Approaches to Smoking Prevention: A Review of Findings." *Health Psychology* 4 (1985): 449–88.

Flay, B.R., and J.L. Sobel. "The Role of Mass Media in

Preventing Adolescent Substance Abuse." In *Preventing Adolescent Drug Abuse: Intervention Strategies*, edited by T. Glynn, C. Leufeld, and J. Ludlord, . Research Monograph 47, National Institute on Drug Abuse, Washington, D.C., 1983.

Foddy, W.H. "Obscenity Reactions: Toward a Symbolic Interactionist Explanation." *Journal for the Theory of Social Behavior* 11 (1981): 125–46.

Follingstad, Diane R., and C. Dawne Kimbrell. "Sex Fantasies Revisited: An Expansion and Further Clarification of Variables Affecting Sex Fantasy Production." *Archives of Sexual Behavior* 15 (December 1986): 475–86.

Francoeur, R.T. "Sex Films." *Society* 14 (1977): 33–37.

Frank, A.D. "The Problem of Pornography in Cities Large and Small." *Family Weekly,* 28 January 1979, 5.

Freedman, J.L. "Longterm Behavioral Effects of Cognitive Dissonance." *Journal of Experimental Social Psychology* 1 (1965): 145–55.

Freidman, H., and R.L. Johnson. "Mass Media and Aggression: A Pilot Study." In *Television and Social Behavior*. Vol. 3: *Television and Adolescent Aggressiveness*, edited by G.A. Comstock and E.A. Rubinstein, . Washington, D.C.: GPO, 1972.

Freund, K. "Laboratory Differential Diagnosis of Homo- and Hetero-sexuality—An Experiment with Faking." *Rev. Czech. Med.* 7 (1961): 20–31.

Freund, K. "A Laboratory Method for Diagnosing Predominance of Homo- and Hetero-Erotic Interest in the Male." *Behavior Research and Therapy* 1 (1963): 85–93.

Freund, K. "Diagnosing Heterosexual Pedophilia by Means of a Test for Sexual Interest." *Behavior Research and Therapy* 3 (1965): 229–34.

Freund, K. "Diagnosing Homo- and Heterosexuality and Erotic Age Preference by Means of a Test for Sexual Interest." *Behaviour Research and Therapy* 5 (1967): 209–28.

Freund, K., J. Diamant, and V. Pinkava. "On the Validity and Reliability of the Phalloplethysmographic Diagnosis of Some Sexual Deviations." *Rev. Czech. Med.* 4 (1958): 145–51.

Freund, K., F. Sedlacek, and K.A. Knob. "Simple Transducer for Mechanical Plethysmography of the Male Genital." *Journal of Experimental Analysis of Behavior* 8 (1965): 169–70.

Frodi, A. "Sexual Arousal, Situational Restrictiveness and Aggressive Behavior." *Journal of Research in Personality* 11 (1977): 48–58.

Frodi, A., J. Macauley, and P.R. Thome. "Are Women Always Less Aggressive Than Men? A Review of the Experimental Literature." *Psychological Bulletin* 84 (1977): 634–60.

Fromkin, H.L., and T.C. Brock. "Erotic Materials: A Commodity Theory Analysis of the Enhanced Desirability That May Accompany Their Unavailability." *Journal of Applied Social Psychology* 3 (1973): 219–31.

Fu, Lee L. "The Constitution of Arousing Images in Pornography." *Bulletin of the Hong Kong Psychological Society* 16–17 (January–July 1986): 25–28.

Furnham, A., and B. Gunter. "Sex Presentation Mode and Memory for Violent and Non-Violent News." *Journal of Educational Television* 11 (1985): 99–105.

Gaertner, S.L., and J.F. Dovidio. "The Subtlety of White Racism, Arousal, and Helping Behavior." *Journal of Personality and Social Psychology* 35 (1977): 691–707.

Gager, H., and C. Schurr. *Sexual Assault: Confronting Rape in America.* New York: Grosset & Dunlap, 1976.

Gagnon, J.H. "The Erotic Environment." In *Human Sexualities*, edited by John H. Gagnon, 341–61. Glenview, Ill.: Scott Foresman, 1977.

Gagnon, J.H., and W. Simon. *Sexual Deviance.* New York: Harper & Row, 1967.

Gaier, E.L., and L. Hurowitz. "Adolescent Erotica and Female Self-Concept Development." *Adolescence* 11 (1976): 497–508.

Galbraith, G.G. "Effects of Sexual Arousal and Guilt upon Free Associative Sexual Responses." *Journal of Consulting and Clinical Psychology* 32 (1968): 707–11.

Galbraith, G.G., and D.L. Mosher. "Associative Sexual Responses in Relation to Sexual Stimulation, Guilt, and External Approval Contingencies." *Journal of Personality and Social Psychology* 10 (1968): 142–47.

Garanson, R.E. "Media Violence and Aggressive Behavior: A Review of Experimental Research." In *Advances in Experimental Social Psychology*. Vol. 5, edited by L. Berkowitz, . New York: Academic Press, 1970.

Garcia, Luis T. "Exposure to Pornography and Attitudes about Women and Rape: A Correlational Study." *Journal of Sex Research* 22 (August 1986): 378–85.

Garcia, Luis T., et al. "Sex Differences in Sexual Arousal to Different Erotic Stories." *Journal of Sex Research* 20 (November 1984): 391–402.

Garry, A. "Pornography and Respect for Women." *Social Theory and Practice* 4 (1979): 395–421.

Gaughan, E., and W. Michael. "College Students Rating of Arousal Value of Pornographic Photographs." *Proceedings of the 81st Annual Convention of the American Psychological Association* 8 (1973): 409–10.

Gebhard, P.H. "Sex Differences in Sexual Responses." *Archives of Sexual Behavior* 2 (1973): 201–3.

Gebhard, P.H., J.H. Gagnon, W.B. Pomeroy, and C.V. Christenson. *Sex Offenders: An Analysis of Types.* New York: Harper Row, 1965.

Geen, R.G. "The Meaning of Observed Violence: Real vs. Fictional Violence and Consequent Effects on Aggression and Emotional Arousal." *Journal of Research in Personality* 9 (1975): 270–81.

Geen, R.G. "Observing Violence in the Mass Media: Implications of Basic Research." In *Perspectives on Aggression*, edited by Russell G. Geen and Edgar C. O'Neal, 193–34. New York: Academic Press, 1976.

Geen, R.G. "Some Effects of Observing Violence upon the Behavior of the Observer." In *Progress in Experimental Personality Research*. Vol. 8, edited by Brendan A. Maher, 49–93. New York: Academic Press, 1978.

Geen, R.G. "Behavioral and Physiological Reactions to Observed Violence: Effects of Prior Exposure to Aggressive Stimuli." *Journal of Personality and Social Psychology* 40 (1981): 868–75.

Geen, R.G., and L. Berkowitz. "Film Violence and the Cue Properties of Available Targets." *Journal of Personality and Social Psychology* 3 (1966): 525–30.

Geen, R.G., and L. Berkowitz. "Name-Mediated Aggressive Cue Properties." *Journal of Personality* 34 (1966): 456–65.

Geen, R.G., and L. Berkowitz. "Some Conditions Facilitating the Occurrence of Aggression after the Observation of Violence." *Journal of Personality* 35 (1967): 666–76.

Geen, R.G., and L. Berkowitz. "Stimulus Qualities of the Target of Aggression: A Future Study." *Journal of Personality and Social Psychology* 5 (1967): 364–68.

Geen, R.G., and E. O'Neal, eds. *Perspectives on Aggression.* New York: Academic Press, 1976.

Geen, R.G., and M. Quanty. "The Catharsis of Aggression: An Evaluation of a Hypothesis." *Advances in Experimental Sociology* 10 (1975): 1–37.

Geen, R.G., and M.B. Quanty. "The Catharsis of Aggression: An Elevation of a Hypothesis." In *Advances in Experimental Social Psychology.* Vol. 10, edited by L. Berkowitz, . New York: Academic Press, 1970.

Geen, R.G., and J.J. Rakosky. "Interpretations of Observed Violence and Their Effects on GSR." *Journal of Experimental Research in Personality* 6 (1973): 289–92.

Geen, R.G., D. Stonner, and G.L. Shope. "The Facilitation of Aggression by Aggression: Evidence Against the Catharsis Hypothesis." *Journal of Personality and Social Psychology* 31 (1975): 721–26.

Geer, J.H., and R. Fuhr. "Cognitive Factors in Sexual Arousal: The Role of Distraction." *Journal of Consulting and Clinical Psychology* 44 (1976): 238–43.

Geer, J.H., P. Morokoff, and P. Greenwood. "Sexual Arousal in Women: The Development of a Measurement Device for Vaginal Blood Volume." *Archives of Sexual Behavior* 3 (1974): 559–64.

Geis, G. "Forcible Rape: An Introduction." In *Forcible Rape: The Crime, the Victim and the Offender,* edited by D. Chappel, R. Geis, and G. Geis, 1–47. New York: Columbia University Press, 1977.

Geis, G., and R. Geis. "Rape in Stockholm: Is Permissiveness Relevant?" *Criminology* 17 (1979): 311.

Geiser, R.L. *Hidden Victims—The Sexual Abuse of Children.* Boston: Beacon Press, 1979.

Gerbner, G. "Violence in Television Drama: Trends and Symbolic Functions." In *Television and Social Behavior.* Vol. 1: *Media Context and Control,* edited by G.A. Comstock and E.S. Rubinstein, . Washington, D.C.: GPO, 1972.

Gerbner, G. "Science or Ritual Dance? A Revisionist View of Television Violence Effects Research." *Journal of Communication* 34 (Summer 1984): 164–73.

Gerety, T. "Pornography and Violence." *University of Pittsburgh Law Review* 40 (1979): 627–51.

Giarrusso, R., P. Johnson, B.D. Goodshield, and G. Zeilman. "Adolescents' Cues and Signals: Sex and Assaults." Paper presented to the Western Psychological Association, San Diego, April 1979.

Gibbons, F.X. "Sexual Standards and Reactions to Pornography: Enhancing Behavioral Consistency through Self-Focused Attention." *Journal of Personality and Social Psychology* 36 (1978): 976–87.

Giglio, Ernest D. "Pornography in Denmark: A Public Policy Model for the United States?" *Comparative Social Research* 8 (1985): 281–300.

Gillan, P. "Objective Measures of Female Sexual Arousal." *Proceedings of the Physiological Society* 66 (May 1976): 678.

Gillan, P. "Therapeutic Uses of Obscenity." In *Censorship and Obscenity,* edited by R. Dhavan and E. Davies, 127–47. London: Martin Robertson, 1978.

Gillan, P., and C. Frith. "Male-Female Differences in Responses to Erotica." In *Love and Attraction: An International Conference,* edited by M. Cook and G.D. Wilson, . Oxford, England: Pergamon, 1979.

Gillette, P.P. "A Study of Rapists." Undergraduate honors thesis, University of California at Los Angeles, 1971.

Glassman, M.B. "Uses and Gratifications Approach to the Study of Sexual Materials." *Dissertation Abstracts International* 40 (1979): 467.

Glide Foundation. "Effects of Erotic Stimuli Used—National Sex Forum Training Courses in Human Sexuality." In *Technical Reports of the Commission on Obscenity and Pornography.* Vol. 5, 354. Washington, D.C.: GPO, 1970.

Gold, S., and I.L. Neufeld. "A Learning Approach to the Treatment of Homosexuality." *Behaviour Research and Therapy* 2 (1965): 201–4.

Goldstein, M.J. "Exposure to Erotic Stimuli and Sexual Deviance." *Journal of Social Issues* 29, no. 3 (1973): 197–219.

Goldstein, M.J. "A Behavioral Scientist Looks at Obscenity." In *The Criminal Justice System,* edited by B.D. Saks, . New York: Plenum, 1977.

Goldstein, M.J., H.S. Kant, and J.J. Hartmann. *Pornography and Sexual Deviance.* Berkeley: University of California Press, 1973.

Goldstein, M.J., H. Kant, L. Judd, C. Rice, and R. Green. "Experiences with Pornography: Rapists, Pedophiles, Homosexuals, Transsexuals, and Controls." *Archives of Sexual Behavior* 1 (1971): 1–15.

Goldstein, M.J., H.S. Kant, L.J. Judd, C.J. Rice, and R. Green. "Exposure to Pornography and Sexual Behavior in Deviant and Normal Groups." In *Technical Reports of the Commission on Obscenity and Pornography.* Vol. 7, 1–90. Washington, D.C.: GPO, 1971.

Gordon, G. *Erotic Communications: Studies in Sex, Sin, and Censorship.* New York: Hastings House, 1980.

Gosselin, C. "Personality Attributes to the Averse Rubber Fetishist." In *Love and Attraction: An International Conference,* edited by M. Cook and G.D. Wilson, . Oxford, England: Pergamon, 1978.

Graber, B., K. Hartmann, J.A. Coffman, C.D. Huey, and C.J. Golden. "Brain Damage among Mentally Disordered Sex Offenders." *Journal of Forensic Sciences* 27 (January 1982): 125–34.

Gray, C. "Pornography and Violent Entertainment: Exposing the Symptoms." *Canadian Medical Journal* 130 (1984): 769–72.

Gray, Susan H. "Exposure to Pornography and Aggression toward Women: The Case of the Angry Male." *Social Problems* 29, no. 4 (1982): 387–98.

Green, R. "Exposure to Explicit Sexual Materials and Sexual Assault: A Review of Behavioral and Social Science Research." Paper presented to the Attorney General's Commission on Pornography, Houston 1985.

Green, S.E., and D.L. Mosher. "A Casual Model of Sexual Arousal to Erotic Fantasies." *Journal of Sex Research* 21 (1985): 1–23.

Griffitt, W. "Response to Erotica and the Projection of Response to Erotica in the Opposite Sex." *Journal of Experimental Research in Personality* 6 (1973): 330–38.

Griffitt, W. "Sexual Experience and Sexual Responsiveness: Sex Differences." *Archives of Sexual Behavior* 4 (1975): 529–40.

Griffitt, W., et al. "Sexual Stimulation and Interpersonal Behavior: Heterosexual Evaluative Responses, Visual Behavior, and Physical Proximity." *Journal of Personality and Social Psychology* 30 (September 1974): 367–77.

Griffitt, W., and D.L. Kaiser. "Affect, Sex Guilt, Gender, and the Rewarding-Punishing Effects of Erotic Stimuli." *Journal of Personality and Social Psychology* 36 (1978): 850–58.

Griffitt, W., J. May, and R. Veitch. "Sexual Stimulation and Interpersonal Behavior: Heterosexual Evaluative Responses, Visual Behavior, and Physical Proximity." *Journal of Personality and Social Psychology* 30 (1974): 367–77.

Gross, L. "Pornography and Social Science Research: Serious Questions." *Journal of Communication* 33 (Autumn 1983): 111–14.

Gross, L.S. *Telecommunications: An Introduction to Radio, Television and the Developing Media.* Dubuque, Iowa: W.C. Brown, 1983.

Grossberg, J.M. "Behaviour Therapy: A Review." *Psychological Bulletin* 62 (1964): 73–88.

Groth, N.A., and H.J. Birnbaum. *Men Who Rape: The Psychology of the Offender.* New York: Plenum, 1979.

Groth, N., and A.W. Burgess. "Rape: A Sexual Deviation." *American Journal of Orthopsychiatry* 47 (1977): 400–406.

Groth, N., A.W. Burgess, and L.L. Holmstrom. "Rape: Power, Anger, and Sexuality." *American Journal of Psychiatry* 134 (1977): 1239–43.

Groth, N.A., and W.F. Hobson. "The Dynamics of Sexual Assault." In *Sexual Dynamics of Anti-Social Behavior,* edited by L.B. Schlesinger and E. Revitch, 159–72. Springfield, Ill.: Charles C. Thomas, 1983.

Grusec, J. "Effects of Co-Observer Evaluation on Imitation: A Developmental Study." *Developmental Psychology* 8 (1973): 141.

Gunter, B. "Personality and Perceptions of Harmful and Harmless T.V. Violence." *Personality and Individual Differences* 4 (1983): 665–70.

Gunter, B., and A. Furnham. "Personality and the Perception of T.V. Violence." *Personality and Individual Differences* 4 (1983): 315–21.

Gustafson, J.E., G. Winokey, and S. Reichlin. "The Effect of Psychic and Sexual Stimulation on Urinary and Serum Acid Phosphatase and Plasma Nonesterified Fatty Acids." *Psychosomatic Medicine* 25 (1963): 101–5.

Gutierres, S., D.T. Kenrick, and L. Golbert. "Adverse Influence on Exposure to Popular Erotica: Effects on Judgments of Others and Judgments of One's Spouse." Paper presented to the Midwestern Psychological Association, Chicago, 1985.

Hain, J.D., and P.H. Linton. "Physiological Response to Visual Sexual Stimuli." Paper presented at the National Association for Mental Health Scientific Conference on Research in the South, New Orleans, November 1966.

Hain, J.D., and P.H. Linton. "Physiological Responses to Visual Sexual Stimuli." *Journal of Sex Research* 5 (1971): 292–302.

Haines, W.H. "Juvenile Delinquency and T.V." *Journal of Social Therapy* 1 (1955): 192.

Hall, E.R., and P.I. Flannery. "Prevalence and Correlates of Sexual Assault Experiences in Adolescents." *Victimology: An International Journal* 9 (1984): 398–406.

Halpern, James W. "Projection: A Test of the Psychoanalytic Hypothesis." *Journal of Abnormal Psychology* 86 (1977): 536–42.

Hammer, E.F. "A Comparison of H-T-Ps of Rapists and Pedophiles." *Journal of Projective Techniques* 18 (1954): 346–54.

Hamrick, N.D. "Physiological and Verbal Responses to Erotic Visual Stimuli on a Female Population." *Behavioral Engineering* 2 (1974): 9–16.

Haney, R., M.H. Harris, and L. Tipton. "Impact of Reading on Human Behavior." *Advances in Librarianship* 6 (1976): 104–26.

Hans, V.P. "Pornography and Feminism: Empirical Evidence and Directors For Research." Paper presented to the American Psychological Association, Montreal, September 1980.

Hansknecht, M. "The Problem of Pornography." *Dissent* 25 (1978): 193–98.

Hariton, B., and J. Singer. "Women's Fantasies during Sexual Intercourse." *Journal of Consulting and Clinical Psychology* 42, no. 3 (1974): 313–22.

Harris, M.B., and L.C. Huang. "Arousal and Attribution." *Psychological Reports* 34 (June 1974): 747–53.

Harris, R., S. Ullis, and D. Lacoste. "Relationships among Sexual Arousability, Imagery, Ability and Introversion-Extraversion." *Journal of Sex Research* 16 (1980): 72–86.

Hatfield, E., S. Sprecher, and J. Traupmann. "Men's and Women's Reactions to Sexually Explicit Films: A Serendipitous Finding." *Archives of Sexual Behavior* 7 (1978): 583–92.

Haward, L.R.C. "Admissibility of Psychological Evidence in Obscenity Cases." *Bulletin of the British Psychological Society* 28 (1975): 466–69.

Hawkins, R.P., and S. Pingree. "Television's Influence on Constructions of Social Reality." In *Television and Behavior: Ten Years of Scientific Progress and Implications for the Eighties.* Vol. 2: *Technical Reports,* edited by David Pearl, Lorraine Bouthilet, and Joyce Lazar,   . Rockville, Md.: U.S. Department of Health and Human Services, 1982.

Hayes, S.C., K.D. Brownwell, and D.H. Barlow. "The Use of Self-Administered Covert Sensitization in the Treatment of Exhibitionism and Sadism." *Behavior Therapy* 9 (1978): 283–89.

Hazelwood, R.R., P.E. Dietz, and A.W. Burgess. "Sexual Fatalities: Behavioral Reconstruction in Equivocal Cases." *Journal of Forensic Sciences* 27 (October 1982): 762–73.

Hearold, S.L. *Meta-Analysis of the Effect of Television on Social Behavior.* Doctoral dissertation, University of Colorado, 1979.

Heffner, R. "Presentation to the Film Regulators Second International Conference." *Film Classification*, September 1984.

Hefley, James C. *Are Textbooks Harming Your Children?* Milford, Mich.: Mott Media, 1981.

Heiby, E., and J.D. Becker. "Effect of Filmed Modeling on the Self-Reported Frequency of Masturbation." *Archives of Sexual Behavior* 9 (1980): 115–21.

Heiman, J.R. "Women's Sexual Arousal: The Physiology of Erotica." *Psychology Today* 8 (April 1975): 90–94.

Heiman, J.R., and J.P. Hatch. "Affective and Physiological Dimensions of Mate Sexual Response to Erotica and Fantasy." *Basic and Applied Social Psychology* 1 (1980): 314–27.

Henley, N.M. *Body Politics: Power, Sex and Nonverbal Communication.* Englewood Cliffs, N.J.: Prentice-Hall, 1977.

Henn, F.A. "The Aggressive Sexual Offender." In *Victimology: A New Focus*, edited by L. Kutash, S.B. Kutash, and L.B. Schlesinger,   . Lexington, Mass.: Lexington Books, 1978.

Henson, D.E., et al. "Analysis of the Consistency of Objective Measures of Sexual Arousal in Women." *Journal of Applied Behavior Analysis* 12 (Winter 1979): 701–11.

Henson, D.E. and H. Rubin. "Voluntary Control of Eroticism." *Journal of Applied Behavior Analysis* 4 (1971): 37–44.

Henson, D.E., H.B. Rubin, and C. Henson. "Labial and Vaginal Blood Volume Responses to Visual and Tactile Stimuli." *Archives of Sexual Behavior* 11 (1982): 23–31.

Herman, S.H., D.H. Barlow, and W.S. Agras. "An Experimental Analysis of Exposure to 'Explicit' Heterosexual Stimuli as an Effective Variable in Changing Arousal Patterns in Homosexuals." *Behaviour Research and Therapy* 12 (1974): 335–45.

Herrell, J.M. "Sex Differences in Emotional Responses to 'Erotic Literature.' " *Journal of Consulting and Clinical Psychology* 43 (1975): 921.

Hess, E.H., and J.M. Polt. "Pupil Size as Related to the Interest Value of Visual Stimuli." *Science* 132 (1960): 349–50.

Hess, E.H., A. Seltzer, and J. Shlien. "Pupil Response of Hetero- and Homosexual Males to Pictures of Men

and Women." *Journal of Abnormal Psychology* 70 (1965): 165–68.

Hicks, D. "Effects of a Co-Observer's Sanctions and Adult Presence on Imitative Aggression." *Child Development* 38 (1968): 303–8.

Hicks, R.A., T. Reany, and L. Hill. "Effects of Pupil Size and Facial Angle on Preference for Photographs of a Young Woman." *Perceptual and Motor Skills* 24 (1967): 388–90.

High, R.W., H.B. Rubin, and D. Henson. "Color as a Variable in Making an Erotic Film More Arousing." *Archives of Sexual Behavior* 8 (1979): 263–67.

Hill, J.H., R.M. Liebert, and D.E.W. Mott. "Vicarious Extinction of Avoidance Behavior through Films: An Initial Test." *Psychology Reports* 22 (1968): 192.

Hindelang, M. "Variations in Sex-Race-Age Specific Incidence of Offending." *American Sociological Review* 46 (1981): 461–74.

Holmes, Ronald M. *The Sex Offender and the Criminal Justice System.* Springfield, Ill.: Charles C. Thomas, 1983.

Holmstrom, L.L., and A.W. Burgess. "Rape and Everyday Life." *Society* 6 (1983): 33–40.

Hoover, J.E. "The Fight Against Filth." *The American Legion Magazine* 70, no. 16: 48–49.

Hoover, J.E. "Combating the Merchants of Filth: The Role of the FBI." *University of Pittsburgh Law Review* 25 (1964): 469–75.

Horowitz, M.I. "Psychic Trauma: Return of Images after a Stress Film." *Archives of General Psychiatry* 20 (1969): 552–59.

Horowitz, M.J., and S.S. Becker. "Cognitive Response to Erotic and Stressful Films." *Archives of General Psychiatry* 29 (1973): 81–84.

Houston, J.A. "Capturing Policies of Pornographic Pictorial Representations by Normative Judgment Analysis." *Dissertation Abstracts International* 34, no. 9B (1974): 5713–14.

Houston, J.A., and S. Houston. "Identifying Pornographic Materials with Judgment Analysis." *Journal of Experimental Education* 42 (1974): 18–26.

Houston, J.A., S. Houston, and E. Ohlson. "The Atypicality of Pornography and Public Policy: A Pilot Investigation." *Psychology* 11, no. 4 (1974): 3–7.

Houston, J.A., S. Houston, and E. Ohlson. "On Determining Pornographic Material." *Journal of Psychology* 88 (1974): 277–87.

Howitt, D. *Mass Media and Social Problems.* New York: Pergamon, 1982.

Howard, J.L., M.B. Liptzin, and C.B. Reifler. "Is Pornography a Problem?" *Journal of Social Issues* 29 (1973): 133–45.

Howard, J.L., C.B. Reifler, and M. Liptzin. "Effects of Exposure to Pornography." In *Technical Reports of the Commission on Obscenity and Pornography.* Vol. 8, 97–132. Washington, D.C.: GPO, 1971.

Huesmann, L.R. "Television Violence and Aggression Behavior." In *Television and Behavior: Ten Years of Scientific Progress and Implications for the Eighties*, edited by David Pearl, Lorraine Bouthilet, and Joyce

Lazar, . Rockville, Md.: U.S. Department of Health and Human Services, 1982.

Huesmann, L.R., L. Eron, R. Klein, P. Brice, and P. Fischer. "Mitigating the Imitation of Aggression Behaviors." Technical report, Department of Psychology, University of Illinois at Chicago Circle, 1981.

Huesmann, L.R., L. Eron, R. Klein, P. Brice, and P. Fischer. "Mitigating the Imitation of Aggressive Behavior to Changing Children's Attitudes about Media Violence." *Journal of Personality and Social Psychology* 44 (1985): 899–910.

Huesmann, L.R., K. Lagerspetz, and L.D. Eron. "Intervening Variables in the TV Violence Aggression Relation: Evidence from Two Countries." *Developmental Psychology* 20 (1984): 746–55.

Hui, C. Harry. "Fifteen Years of Pornography Research: Does Exposure to Pornography Have Any Effects?" *Bulletin of the Hong Kong Psychological Society* 16–17 (January–July 1986): 41–62.

Hunt, M. *Sexual Behavior in the 1970's.* New York: Dell, 1974.

Huvos, K. "The Eroticization of the American Woman in French Literature." *The French Review* 49 (1976): 1062–71.

Inciardi, James A. "Little Girls and Sex: A Glimpse at the World of the 'Baby Pro.' " *Deviant Behavior* 5 (1984): 71–78.

Ireland, J. "Reform Rape Legislation: A New Standard for Sexual Responsibility." *University of Colorado Law Review* 49 (1978): 185–204.

"Is Pornography a Threat to Society or Just a Nuisance?" *Medical Aspects of Human Sexuality* 2 (1968): 4–11.

Iwawaki, S., and G. Wilson. "Sex Fantasies in Japan." *Personality and Individual Differences* 4 (1983): 543–45.

Izard, Carroll E., and Sanford Caplan. "Sex Differences in Emotional Responses to Erotic Literature." *Journal of Consulting and Clinical Psychology* 42 (June 1974): 468.

Jackson, B.T. "A Case of Voyeurism Treated by Counterconditioning." *Behaviour Research and Therapy* 7 (1969): 133–34.

Jaffee, David, and Murray A. Straus. "Sexual Climate and Reported Rape: A State-Level Analysis." *Archives of Sexual Behavior* 16 (April 1987): 107–23.

Jaffe, Y. "Sex and Aggression: An Intimate Relationship." Doctoral dissertation, University of California, Los Angeles, 1975.

Jaffe, Y. "Sexual Stimulation: Effects on Prosocial Behavior." *Psychological Reports* 48 (1981): 75–81.

Jaffe, Y., and A. Berger. "A Cultural Generality of the Relationship between Sex and Aggression." *Psychological Reports* 41 (1977): 335–36.

Jaffe, Y., N. Malamuth, J. Feingold, and S. Feshbach. "Sexual Arousal and Behavioral Aggression." *Journal of Personality and Social Psychology* 30 (1974): 759–64.

Jakobovitz, L.A. "Evaluational Reactions to Erotic Literature." *Psychological Reports* 16 (1965): 985–94.

James, B. "Case of Homosexuality Treated by Aversion Therapy." *British Medical Journal* 1 (1962): 768–70.

Jankovich, R., and P. Miller. "Response of Women with Primary Organic Dysfunction to Audiovisual Education." *Journal of Sex and Marital Therapy* 4 (1978): 16–19.

Johnson, Pamela Hansford. *On Iniquity.* New York: Charles Scribner's Sons, 1967.

Johnson, Paula, and Jacqueline D. Goodchilds. "Pornography, Sexuality, and Social Psychology." *Journal of Social Issues* 29, no. 3 (1973): 231–38.

Johnson, Weldon T., Lenore R. Kupperstein, and Joseph J. Peters. "Sex Offenders Experience with Erotica." In *Technical Reports of the Commission on Obscenity and Pornography.* Vol. 7, 163–72. Washington, D.C.: GPO, 1971.

Jones, R.J., K.J. Gruber, and M.H. Freeman. "Reactions of Adolescents of Being Interviewed About Their Sexual Assault Experiences." *Journal of Sex Research* 19 (1983): 160–72.

Jones, R.N., and V.C. Joe. "Pornographic Materials and Commodity Theory." *Journal of Applied Social Psychology* 10 (1980): 311–22.

Julien, E., and R. Over. "Male Sexual Arousal with Repeated Exposure to Erotic Stimuli." *Archives of Sexual Behavior* 13 (1984): 311–22.

Kaats, G.R., and Davis. "Effects of Volunteer Biases in Studies of Sexual Behavior and Attitudes." *Journal of Sex Research* 7 ( ): 26–34.

Kahnemann, D., and A. Tversky. "The Framing of Decisions and the Psychology of Choice." *Science* 211 (1981): 453–58.

Kanin, E.J. "Male Aggression in Dating—Courtship Relations." *American Journal of Sociology.* 63 (1957): 197–204.

Kanin, E.J. "Male Sex Aggression and Three Psychiatric Hypotheses." *Journal of Sex Research* 1 (1965): 221–31.

Kanin, E.J. "Rape as a Function of Relative Sexual Frustration." *Psychological Reports* 52 (1983): 133–34.

Kanin, E.J. "Date Rape: Unofficial Criminals and Victims." *Victimology: An International Journal* 9 (1984): 95–108.

Kanin, E.J. "Date Rapists: Differential Sexual Socialization and Relative Deprivation." *Archives of Sexual Behavior* 14 (1985): 209–31.

Kanin, E.J., and S.R. Parcell. "Sexual Aggression: A Second Look at the Offended Female." *Archives of Sexual Behavior* 6, no. 1 (1977): 67–76.

Kant, H.S. "Exposure to Pornography and Sexual Behavior in Deviant and Normal Groups." *Corrective Psychiatry and Journal of Social Therapy* 17 (1971): 15–17.

Kant, H.S., and M.J. Goldstein. "Pornography and Its Effects." In *Crime in Society,* edited by D. Savity and J. Johnson, . New York: John Wiley 1978.

Kant, H.S., J. Goldstein, and D.J. Lepper. "A Pilot Comparison to Two Research Instruments Measuring Exposure to Pornography." In *Technical Reports of the Commission on Obscenity and Pornography.* Vol. 7, 325–40. Washington, D.C.: GPO, 1971.

Kaplan, R. "The Measurement of Human Aggression." In *Aggression in Children and Youth,* edited by R. Kaplan,

V. Koenic, and R. Novaco, . Ryin, Netherlands: Sijthoff & Noordhuff International, 1983.

Karacon, I., R.L. Williams, M. Guerraro, P.J. Salis, J.I. Thornby, and C.J. Hursch. "Nocturnal Penile Tumescence and Sleep of Convicted Rapists and Other Prisoners." *Archives of Sexual Behavior* 3 (1974): 19–26.

Karpman, J.J. *The Sexual Offender and His Sex Offenses.* New York: Julian Press, 1954.

Kassner, J.S. "Obscenity Leads to Perversion." *New York Law Forum* 20 (Winter 1975): 551–68.

Kazdin, A.E., and L.A. Wilcoxin. "Systematic Desensitization and Nonspecific Treatment Effects: A Methodological Evaluation." *Psychological Bulletin* 83 (1976): 729–58.

KeBler, B.H., and J. Schuickerath. "Reactions to Erotic Stimuli and Their Relationship to Biological and Psychological Sex." *Psychologische Beirtrage* 23 (1981) 421–33.

Kefauver, E. "Obscene and Pornographic Literature and Juvenile Delinquency." *Federal Probation* 24 (December 1960): 3.

Kelley, H.H. *Attribution in Social Interaction.* Morristown, N.J.: General Learning Corporation, 1971.

Kelley, K. "Heterosexuals' Homophobic Attitudes and Responses to Mildly Stimulating Erotica." Paper presented to the Midwestern Psychological Association, Detroit, May 1981.

Kelley, K. "Predicting Attraction to the Novel Stimulus Person: Affect and Concern." *Journal of Résearch in Personality* 16 (1981): 32–40.

Kelley, K. "Sexual Fantasy and Attitudes as Functions of Sex and Subject and Content of Erotica." *Imagination, Cognition and Personality* 4, no. 4 (1984–85): .

Kelley, K. "The Effects of Sexual and/or Aggressive Film Exposure on Helping, Hostility, and Attitudes about the Sexes." *Journal of Research in Personality* 19 (1985): 472–83.

Kelley, K. "Sex, Sex Guilt, and Authoritarianism: Differences in Responses to Explicit Heterosexual and Masturbatory Slides." *Journal of Sex Research* 21 (February 1985): 68–85.

Kelley, K. "Sexual Attitudes as Determinants of the Motivational Properties of Exposure to Erotica." *Personality and Individual Differences* 6 (1985): 391–93.

Kelley, K., and D. Byrne. "The Function of Imaginative Fantasy in Sexual Behavior." *Journal of Mental Imagery* 2 (1978): 139–46.

Kelley, K., and D. Byrne. "Assessment of Sexual Responding: Arousal, Affect, and Behavior." In *Social Psychophysiology,* edited by J. Capioppo and R. Petty, 467–90. New York: Guilford, 1983.

Kelley, K., C. Miller, D. Byrne, and P. Bell. "Facilitating Sexual Arousal via Anger, Aggression, or Dominance." *Motivation and Emotion* 7, no. 2 (1983): 191–202.

Kelley, K., and D. Musialowski. "Repeated Exposure to Sexually Explicit Stimuli: Novelty, Sex, and Sexual Attitudes." *Archives of Sexual Behavior* 15, no. 6 (1986): 487–98.

Kenrick, D.T., and S.E. Gutierres. "Contrast Effects and Judgments of Physical Attractiveness: When Beauty Becomes a Social Problem." *Journal of Personality and Social Psychology* 38 (1980): 131–40.

Kenrick, D.T., S.E. Gutierres, and L. Goldbert. "Adverse Influence of Popular Erotica on Attraction." Paper presented to the American Psychological Association, Washington, D.C., 1982.

Kenrick, D.T., D.O. Stringfield, W.L. Wagenhals, R.H. Dahl, and H.J. Ransdell. "Sex Differences, Androgyny, and Approach Responses to Erotica: A New Variation on the Old Volunteer Program." *Journal of Personality and Social Psychology* 38 (1980): 517–24.

Kenyon, F.E. "Pornography, the Law, and Mental Health." *British Journal of Psychiatry* 126 (March 1975): 225–33.

Kercher, G.A., and C.E. Walker. "Reactions of Convicted Rapists to Sexually Explicit Stimuli." *Journal of Abnormal Psychology* 81 (1973): 46–50.

Kilman, P.R., R.F. Sabalis, M.L. Gearing, L.H. Bukstell, and A.W. Scovern. "The Treatment of Sexual Paraphilia; A Review of Outcome Research." *Journal of Sex Research* 18, no. 3 ( ): 193–252.

Kinsey, A.C., W.B. Pomeroy, and C.E. Martin. *Sexual Behavior in the Human Male.* Philadelphia: Saunders, 1948.

Kinsey, A.C., W.B. Pomeroy, C.E. Martin, and P.H. Gebhard. *Sexual Behavior in the Human Female.* Philadelphia: Saunders, 1953.

Kirchener, Neil M. "Effects of Need for Approval and Situational Variables on the Viewing of Erotic Material." *Journal of Consulting and Clinical Psychology* 44 (October 1976): 869.

Kirkpatrick, C., and E. Kanin. "Male Sex Aggression on a University Campus." *American Sociological Review* 22 (1957): 52–58.

Kirkpatrick, R.G. "Collective Consciousness and Mass Hysteria: Collective Behavior and Antipornography Crusades in Durkheimian Perspective." *Human Relations* 28 (1975): 63–84.

Klein, D. "Violence Against Women: Some Considerations Regarding Its Causes and Its Elimination." *Crime and Delinquency* 27 (1981): 64–80.

Knaffo, D. "Sexual Fantasizing in Males and Females." *Journal of Research in Personality* 18 (1984): 461–62.

Koegler, R.R., and L.Y. Kline. "Psychotherapy Research: An Approach Utilizing Autonomic Response Measurement." *American Journal of Psychotherapy* 19 (1965): 268–79.

Koenig, K.P. "The Differentiation of Hetero- and Homo-Erotic Interests in the Male." *Behaviour Research and Therapy* 2 (1965): 305–7.

Kolarsky, A., and J. Madlafousek. "Female Behavior and Sexual Arousal in Intersexual Male Deviant Offenders." *Journal of Nervous and Mental Disease* 155 (1972): 110–18.

Kolarsky, A., and J. Madlafousek. "The Inverse Role of Preparatory Erotic Stimulation in Exhibitionists: Phallometric Studies." *Archives of Sexual Behavior* 12, no. 2 ( ): 123–48.

Kolarsky, A., and J. Madlafousek. "Variability of Stimulus Effect in the Course of Phallometric Testing." *Archives of Sexual Behavior* 6 (1977): 135–41.

Kolarsky, A., J. Madlafousek, and V. Novotra. "Stimuli Eliciting Sexual Arousal in Males Who Offend Adult Women: An Experimental Study." *Archives of Sexual Behavior* 7 (1978): 79–87.

Konecni, V.G. "Annoyance, Type and Duration of Post-Annoyance Activity, and Aggression: The Cathartic Effect." *Journal of Experimental Psychology* 104 (1975): 76–102.

Koop, E. "Presentation to the National Coalition on Television Violence." Department of Health and Human Services, Washington, D.C. October 1983.

Koss, M.F., and K.E. Leonard. "Sexually Aggressive Men: Empirical Findings and Theoretical Implications." In *Pornography and Sexual Aggression*, edited by N.M. Malamuth and E. Donnerstein, . New York: Academic Press, 1984.

Koss, M.P., and C.J. Oros. "Sexual Experiences Survey: A Research Instrument Investigating Sexual Aggression and Victimization." *Journal of Consulting and Clinical Psychology* 50, no. 3: 455–57.

Krafka, C.L. "Sexually Explicit, Sexually Violent, and Violent Media: Effects of Multiple Naturalistic Exposures and Debriefing on Female Viewers." Doctoral dissertation, University of Wisconsin, Madison, 1985.

Kraft, T. "A Case of Homosexuality Treated by Systematic Desensitization." *American Journal of Psychotherapy* 21 (1967): 815–21.

Krattenmaker, T.G., and L.A. Powe, Jr. "Televised Violence: First Amendment Principles and Social Science." *Virginia Law Review* 64 (1978): 1123–1297.

Kraus, J. "Trends in Violent Crime and Public Concern." *Australian Journal of Social Issues* 14, no. 3 (1979): 175–91.

Krogh, I. "British Report Proven Wrong on Impact of Pornography in Denmark." *Newsweekly* (Melbourne), November 1980, 8–9.

Kronhausen, E., and P. Kronhausen. *Pornography and the Law*. New York: Ballantine Books, 1964.

Kruglanski, A. "The Human Subjects in the Psychology Experiments: Facts and Artifacts." In *Advances in Experimental Social Psychology*. Vol. 8, edited by L. Berkowitz, . New York: Academic Press, 1975.

Kruttschnitt, Candice, Linda Heath, and David A. Ward. "Family Violence, Television Viewing Habits, and Other Adolescent Experiences Related to Violent Criminal Behavior." *Criminology* 24 (May 1986): 235–67.

Kupperstein, Lenore, R., and W. Cody Wilson. "Erotica and Antisocial Behavior: An Analysis of Selected Social Indicator Statistics. In *Technical Reports of the Commission on Obscenity and Pornography*. Vol. 7, 311–24. Washington, D.C.: GPO, 1971.

Kushner, M. "The Reduction of a Long-Standing Fetish by Means of Aversion Conditioning." In *Case Studies in Behavior Modification*, edited by Leonard Ullmann and Leonard Krasner, 239–42. New York: Holt, Rinehart and Winston, 1985.

Kushner, M., and J. Sandler. "Aversion Therapy and the Concept of Punishment." *Behaviour Research and Therapy* 4 (1966): 179–86.

Kutchinsky, Berl. "Pornography in Denmark: Pieces of a Jigsaw Puzzle Collected around New Year 1970." In *Technical Reports of the Commission on Obscenity and Pornography*. Vol. 4, . Washington, D.C.: GPO, 1970.

Kutchinsky, Berl. "The Effect of Pornography. A Pilot Experiment on Perception, Behavior, and Attitudes." In *Technical Reports of the Commission on Obscenity and Pornography*. Vol. 8, 133–69. Washington, D.C.: GPO, 1971.

Kutchinsky, Berl. "Towards an Explanation of the Decrease in Registered Sex Crimes in Copenhagen." In *Technical Reports of the Commission on Obscenity and Pornography*. Vol. 7, 263–310. Washington, D.C.: GPO, 1971.

Kutchinsky, Berl. "The Effect of Easy Availability of Pornography on the Incidence of Sex Crimes: The Danish Experience." *Journal of Social Issues* 29, no. 3 (1973): 163–81.

Kutchinsky, Berl. "Eroticism without Censorship: Sociological Investigations on the Production and Consumption of Pornographic Literature in Denmark." *International Journal of Criminology and Penology* 1, no. 3 (1973): 217–25.

Kutchinsky, Berl. "Deviance and Criminality: The Case of Voyeur in a Peeper's Paradise." *Diseases of the Nervous System* 37 (1976): 145–51.

Kutchinsky, Berl. "The Effects of Not Prosecuting Pornography." *British Journal of Sexual Medicine* 3 (1976): .

Kutchinsky, Berl. "Pornography in Denmark–A General Summary." In *Censorship and Obscenity,* edited by R. Dhavan and C. Davies, . London: Martin Robertson, 1978.

Kutchinsky, Berl. "The Effect of Easy Availability of Pornography on the Incidence of Sex Crimes: The Danish Experience." In *Pornography and Censorship*, edited by David Copp and Susan Wendell, 295–312. New York: Prometheus, 1983.

Kutchinsky, Berl. "Obscenity and Pornography: Behavioral Aspects." In *Encyclopedia of Crime and Justice*. Vol. 3, edited by Sanford Kadish, 1079–85. New York: Free Press, 1983.

Kutchinsky, Berl. "Pornography and Its Effects in Denmark and the United States: A Rejoinder and Beyond." *Comparative Social Research* 8 (1985): 301–30.

Lader, M.H., and A.M. Matthews. "A Physiological Model of Phobic Anxiety and Desensitization." *Behaviour Research and Therapy* 6 (1968): 411–21.

Lang, A.R. "Sexual Guilt, Expectancies and Alcohol as Determinants of Interest in and Reaction to Sexual Stimuli." *Dissertation Abstracts International* 39 (1979): 5075–76.

Lang, A.R., J. Scarles, R. Layerman, and V. Adesso. "Expectancy, Alcohol and Sex Guilt as Determinants of Interest in and Reaction to Sexual Stimuli." *Journal of Abnormal Psychology* 89 (1980): 644–53.

Lang, P.J. "Imagery in Therapy: An Information Processing Analysis of Fear." *Behavior Therapy* 8 (1977): 862–86.

Lang, P.J. "Cognition in Emotion: Concept and Action." In *Emotions, Cognition, and Behavior,* edited by Carroll E. Izard, Jerome Kagan, and Robert B. Zajonc, 192–228. Cambridge, Mass.: Cambridge University Press, 1984.

Langevin, R., and M. Martin. "Can Erotic Responses Be Classically Conditioned? *Behavior Therapy* 6 (1975): 3509–55.

Langevin, R., D. Paitich, and A.E. Russon. "Are Rapists Sexually Anomalous, Aggressive or Both?" In *Erotic Preference, Gender Identity, and Aggression in Men: New Research Studies,* edited by Ron Langevin, 17–38. Hillsdale, N.J.: Lawrence Erlbaum Associates, 1985.

Largen, Mary Ann. "History of the Women's Movement in Changing Attitudes, Laws, and Treatment toward Rape Victims." In *Sexual Assault,* edited by Marcia J. Walker and Stanley L. Brodsky, 69–74. Lexington, Mass.: D.C. Health, 1976.

LaTorre, R.A. "Sexual Stimulation and Displaced Aggression." *Psychology Reports* 33 (1973): 123–25.

Lavin, N.I., J.C. Thorpe, J.C. Barker, C.B. Blakemore, and C.G. Conway. "Behavior Therapy in a Case of Transvestism." *Journal of Nervous and Mental Disease* 133 (1961): 346–53.

Lawless, J.C. "Sex Differences in Pupillary Response to Visual Stimuli." Paper presented to the Society for Psychophysiological Research, Washington, D.C., October 1968.

Laws, D.R. "A Comparison of the Measurement Characteristics of Two Circumferential Penile Transducers." *Archives of Sexual Behavior* 6 (1977): 45–51.

Laws, D.R. "Treatment of Bisexual Pedophiles by a Biofeedback Assisted Self-Control Procedure." *Behaviour Research and Therapy* 18 (1980): 207–11.

Laws, D.R., and M.L. Holmes. "Sexual Response Faking by Pedophiles." *Criminal Justice and Behavior* 5 (1978): 343–56.

Laws, D.R., J. Meyer, and M.L. Holmes. "Reduction of Sadistic Sexual Arousal by Olfactory Aversion: A Case Study." *Behaviour Research and Therapy* 16 (1978): 281–85.

Laws, D.R., and J.A. O'Neil. "Variations on Masturbatory Conditioning." *Behavioral Psychotherapy* 9 (1981): 111–36.

Laws, D.R., and H.B. Rubin. "Instructional Control of an Autonomic Sexual Response." *Journal of Applied Behavioral Analysis* 2 (1969): 93–99.

Lazarus, A. "A Case of Pseudonecrophilia Treated by Behavior Therapy." *Journal of Clinical Psychology* 24 (1968): 113–115.

Lazarus, R.S., and E. Alfert. "Short-Circuiting of Threat by Experimentally Altering Cognitive Appraisal." *Journal of Abnormal and Social Psychology* 69 (1964): 195–205.

Lazarus, R.S., J.C. Speisman, A.M. Mordkoff, and L.A. Davidson. "A Laboratory Study of Psychological Stress Produced by Motion Picture Film." *Psychological Monographs* 76, no. 533 (1962).

LeBeque, Breck J. "Paraphilias in Pornography: A Study of Perversions Inherent in Title." *Australian Journal of Sex, Marriage and Family* 6 (February 1985): 33–36.

Lederer, Laura, ed. *Take Back the Night: Women on Pornography*. New York: Morrow, 1980.

LeFave, M.K., and R.W. Neufeld. "Effect of Stimulus Context and Repeated Aversive Visual Stimulation on the Cardiac Correlate of Attention." *Perceptual and Motor Skills* 44 (1977): 215–21.

Lefkowitz, M.M., L.D. Eron, L.O. Walder, and L.R. Huesmann. "Television Violence and Child Aggression: A Follow-up Study." In *Television and Social Behavior*. Vol. 3: *Television and Adolescent Aggressiveness,* edited by G.A. Comstock and E.A. Rubinstein,. Washington, D.C.: GPO, 1972.

Lefkowitz, M.M., L.D. Eron, L.O. Walder, and L.R. Huesmann. *Growing Up to Be Violent: A Longitudinal Study of the Development of Aggression*. New York: Pergamon, 1977.

Lehman, R.E. "The Disinhibiting Effects of Visual Material in Treating Orgasmically Dysfunctional Women." *Behavior Engineering* 1 (1974): 1–3.

Leifer, A.D., and D.F. Roberts. *"Children's Responses to Television and Social Behavior*. Vol. 2: *Television and Social Learning*. Washington, D.C.: GPO, 1972.

Leiman, A.H., and S. Epstein. "Thermatic Sexual Responses as Related to Sexual Drive and Guilt." *Journal of Abnormal and Social Psychology* 63 (1961): 169–75.

Lenes, M.S., and E.J. Hart. "The Influence of Pornography and Violence on Attitudes and Guilt." *Journal of School Health* 45 (1975): 447–51.

Leonard, K., and S. Taylor. "Exposure to Pornography, Permissive and Nonpermissive Cues, and Male Aggression toward Females." *Motivation and Emotion* 7 (1983): 291–99.

Leone, Bruno. *Is Pornography Harmful?* St. Paul, Minn.: Greenhaven Press, 1983.

Leone, Bruno, and M. Teresa O'Neill. *Sexual Values*. St. Paul, Minn.: Greenhaven Press, 1983.

Lepper, M.R. "Dissonance, Self-Perception and Honesty in Children." *Journal of Personality and Social Psychology* 25 (1973): 65–74.

Lerner, M.J. "The Effect of Responsibility and Choice on a Partner's Attractiveness Following Failure." *Journal of Personality* 33 (1965): 178–87.

Lerner, M.J. "Observer's Evaluation of a Victim: Justice, Guilt, and Veridical Perception." *Journal of Personality and Social Psychology* 20 (1971): 127–35.

Lester, D. "Rape and Social Structure." *Psychological Reports* 35 (1974): 146.

Lester, D. "Pornographic Films and Unconscious Homosexual Desires: An Hypothesis." *Psychological Reports* 54 (April 1984): 606.

Lester, D. "Topic: Males Who Habitually Attend Pornography Films May Be Gratifying Unconscious Homosexual Desires." *Psychology Reports* 54 (1984): 606.

Levi, L. "Sympatho-Adrenomedullary Responses to Emotional Stimuli: Methodologic, Physiologic and Pathologic Consideration." In *An Introduction to Clinical*

Neuroendocrinology, edited by Eors Bajusz, 78–105. Baltimore: Williams & Wilkins, 1967.

Levi, L. Sympatho-Adrenomedullary Activity, Diuresis and Emotional Reactions during Visual Sexual Stimulation in Human Females and Males." *Psychosomatic Medicine* 31 (1969): 251–68.

Levitt, E.E. "Pornography: Some New Perspectives on an Old Problem." *Journal of Sex Research* 5 (1969): 247–59.

Levitt, E.E., and R.K. Hensely. "Some Factors in the Valences of Erotic Visual Stimuli." *Journal of Sex Research* 3 (1967): 63–68.

Levy, N., L. Lipsitt, and J. Rosenblith. "Psychology Committee Reports on Censorship Statements." *Brown Daily Herald,* special edition, 6 November 1958.

Lewittes, D.J., and W.L. Simmons. "Impression Management of Sexually Motivated Behavior." *Journal of Social Psychology* 96 (1975): 39–44.

Leyens, J.P., L. Camino, R.D. Parke, and L. Berkowitz. "Effects of Movie Violence on Aggression in a Field Setting as a Function of Group Dominance and Cohesion." *Journal of Personality and Social Psychology* 32 (1975): 346–60.

Libby, R.W., and M.A. Strauss. "Make Love Not War? Sex, Sexual Meanings, and Violence in a Sample of University Students." *Archives of Sexual Behavior* 9 (1980): 133–48.

Liebert, R.M., and N.S. Schwartzberg. "Effects of Mass Media." *Annual Review of Psychology* 28 (1977): 141–73.

Liebert, R.N., J.M. Sprafkin, and E.S. Davidson. *The Early Window: Effects of Television on Children and Youth.* 2d ed. New York: Pergamon, 1982.

Lifshitz, K. "The Average Evoked Cortical Response to Complex Visual Stimuli." *Psychophysiology* 3 (1966): 55–68.

Lindquist, J.H., and M.L. Cave. "Myths and Realities of Dirty Book Buyers." *Free Inquiry in Creative Sociology* 7 (1979): 48–51.

Lindsey, Gardner, and Elliott Aronson. *Handbook of Social Psychology.* Vol. 2. New York: Random House, 1985.

Linz, D. "Sexual Violence in the Media: Effects on Male Viewers and Implications for Society." Doctoral dissertation, University of Wisconsin, Madison, 1985.

Linz, D., E. Donnerstein, and M. Chapin. "Mitigating the Influence of Violence on Television and Sexual Violence in the Media." In *Advances in the Study of Aggression.* Vol. 2, edited by R. Blanchard, . New York: Academic Press, 1986.

Linz, D., E. Donnerstein, and S. Penrod. "The Effects of Multiple Exposures to Filmed Violence Against Women." *Journal of Communication* 34 (Summer 1984): 130–47.

Linz, D., E. Donnerstein and S. Penrod. "The Findings and Recommendations of the Attorney General's Commission on Pornography: Do the Psychological 'Facts' Fit the Political Fury?" *American Psychologist* 42 (1987): 10.

Linz, D., C. Krafka, E. Donnerstein, and S. Penrod. *Combining the Results of Several Studies on the Effects of Nonviolent Pornography on Male and Female Views.* Unpublished manuscript, University of Wisconsin, Madison, 1986.

Linz, D., S. Penrod, and E. Donnerstein. "Media Violence and Antisocial Behavior: Alternative Legal Policies." *Journal of Social Issues* 42, no. 3 (1986): 1–6.

Lipton, M. "The Problem of Pornography." In *Phenomenology and Treatment of Psychosexual Disorders,* edited by W.E. Fann, I. Karacan, A.D. Pokorny, and R.L. Williams, 132. Jamaica, N.Y.: Spectrum Publications, 1983.

Loisell, R.H., and S. Mollenauer. "Galvanic Skin Responses to Sexual Stimuli in a Female Population." *Journal of General Psychology* 68 (1964): 307–12.

London, J. "Images of Violence Against Women." *Victimology: An International Journal* 2 (1977–78): 510–24.

Longford, Lord ed. *Pornography: The Longford Report.* London: Coronet, 1972.

LoPiccolo, J. "Case Study: Systematic Desensitization of Homosexuality." *Behavior Therapy* 2 (1971): 394–99.

Lovas, O.I. "Effect of Exposure to Symbolic Aggression on Aggressive Behavior." *Child Development* 32 (1971): 37–44.

Love, R.E., L.R. Sloan, and M.J. Schmidt. "Viewing Pornography and Sex Guilt: The Priggish, the Prudent and the Profligate." *Journal of Consulting and Clinical Psychology* 44 (1976): 624–29.

Luria, Z., and U. Tufts. "Sexual Fantasy and Pornography. Two Cases of Girls Brought Up with Pornography." *Archives of Sexual Behavior* 11 (1982): 395–404.

MacCulloch, M.J., C.J. Birtles, and M.P. Feldman. "Anticipatory Avoidance Learning for the Treatment of Homosexuality: Recent Developments and an Automatic Aversion Therapy System." *Behavior Therapy* 2 (1971): 151–69.

MacCulloch, M.J., and M.P. Feldman. "Aversion Therapy in the Management of 43 Homosexuals." *British Medical Journal* 2 (1967): 594–97.

MacCulloch, M.J., P.R. Snowden, P.J.W. Wood, and E.H. Mills. "Sadistic Fantasy, Sadistic Behavior, and Offending." *British Journal of Psychiatry* 143 (1983): 20–29.

MacDonald, A.P., Jr. "A Little Bit of Lavender Goes a Long Way: A Critique of Research on Sexual Orientation." *Journal of Sex Research* 19 (February: 1983) 94–100.

MacDonough, T.S. "A Critique of the First Feldman and MacCulloch Avoidance Conditioning Treatment for Homosexuals." *Behavior Therapy* 3 (1972): 104–11.

MacNamara, Donald E.J., and Edward Sagavin. "Pornography and Its Relationship to Crime." In *Sex, Crime, and the Law,* 199–213. New York: Free Press, 1977.

Maddison, D. "Mental Health in a Permissive Society." *Medical Journal of Australia* 58 no. 1 (1970): 17.

Malamuth, N.M. *Erotica, Aggression and Perceived Appropriateness.*" Paper presented to the American Psychological Association, Toronto, September 1978.

Malamuth, N.M. "Rape Fantasies as a Function of Exposure to Violent Sexual Stimuli." *Archives of Sexual Behavior* 10 (1981): 33–47.

Malamuth, N.M. "Rape Proclivity among Males." *Journal of Social Issues* 37 (1981): 138–57.

Malamuth, N.M. *Predictors of Aggression Against Female as Compared to Male Targets of Aggression.* Paper presented to the American Psychological Association, Washington, D.C., 1982.

Malamuth, N.M. "Factors Associated with Rape as Predictors of Laboratory Aggression Against Women." *Journal of Personality and Social Psychology* 45, no. 2 (1983): 432–42.

Malamuth, N.M. "Aggression Against Women: Cultural and Individual Causes:" In *Pornography and Sexual Aggression,* edited by N.M. Malamuth and E. Donnerstein, . New York: Academic Press, 1984.

Malamuth, N.M. "The Mass Media and Aggression Against Women." *American Academy of Psychiatry and the Law Newsletter* 10 (1985): 22–24.

Malamuth, N.M. "The Mass Media and Aggression Against Women: Research Findings and Prevention." In *Rape and Sexual Assault,* edited by Ann Wolbert Burgess, 392–412. New York: Garland Publishing, 1985.

Malamuth, N.M. "Predictors of Naturalistic Sexual Aggression." *Journal of Personality and Social Psychology* 50 (1986): .

Malamuth, N.M., and V. Billings. "Why Pornography? Models of Functions and Effects." *Journal of Communication* 34 (Summer 1984): 117–29.

Malamuth, N.M. and V. Billings. "The Functions and Effects of Pornography: Sexual Communication versus the Feminist Models in Light of Research Findings." In *Perspectives on Media Effects.* Vol. 5, edited by J. Bryant and D. Zillman, 83–104. Hillsdale, N.J.: Lawrence Arlbaum Associates, 1986.

Malamuth, N.M., and J. Briere. "Sexually Violent Media: Indirect Effects on Aggression Against Women." *Journal of Social Issues* 42, no. 3 (1986): 75–89.

Malamuth, N.M. and J. Ceniti. "Repeated Exposure to Violent and Nonviolent Pornography: Likelihood of Raping Ratings and Laboratory Aggression Against Women." *Aggressive Behavior* 12 (1986): 129–37.

Malamuth, N.M. and J.V.P. Check. "Penile Tumescence and Perceptual Responses to Rape as a Function of Victims' Perceived Reactions." *Journal of Applied Social Psychology* 10 (1980): 528–47.

Malamuth, N.M., and J.V.P. Check. "Sexual Arousal to Rape and Consenting Depictions: The Importance of the Woman's Arousal." *Journal of Abnormal Psychology* 89 (1980): 763–66.

Malamuth, N.M., J.V.P. Check, and J. Briere. "Sexual Arousal in Response to Aggression: Ideological, Aggressive and Sexual Correlates." *Journal of Personality and Social Psychology* 50 (1986): 330–40.

Malamuth, N.M., and J.V.P. Check. "The Effects of Mass Media Exposure on Acceptance of Violence Against Women: A Field Experiment." *Journal of Research in Personality* 15 (September 1981): 436–46.

Malamuth, N.M., and J.V.P. Check. "Penile Tumescence and Perceptual Responses to Rape as a Function of Victims' Perceived Reactions." In *Pornography and Censorship,* edited by David Copp and Susan Wendell, 257–74. New York: Prometheus, 1983.

Malamuth, N.M., and J.V.P. Check. "Sexual Arousal to Rape Depictions: Individual Differences." *Journal of Abnormal Psychology* 2, no. 92 (1983): 55–67.

Malamuth, N.M., and J.V.P. Check. "Debriefing Effectiveness Following Exposure to Pornographic Rape Depictions." *Journal of Sex Research* 20 (February 1984): 1–13.

Malamuth, N.M., and J.V.P. Check. "The Effects of Aggressive Pornography on Beliefs in Rape Myths: Individual Differences." *Journal of Research in Personality* 19 (September 1985): 299–320.

Malamuth, N.M., and E. Donnerstein. "The Effects of Aggressive-Erotic Stimuli." In *Advances in Experimental Social Psychology,* edited by L. Berkowitz, . New York: Academic Press, 1982.

Malamuth, N.M., and E. Donnerstein. *Pornography and Sexual Aggression.* New York: Academic Press, 1984.

Malamuth, N.M., S. Feshbach, T. Fera, and J. Kunath. "Aggressivity in Erotica." Paper presented to the Western Psychological Association, Los Angeles, April 1976.

Malamuth, N.M., S. Feshbach, and Y. Jaffe. "Sexual Arousal and Aggression: Recent Experiments and Theoretical Issues." *Journal of Social Issues* 33 (1977): 110–33.

Malamuth, N.M., S. Haber, and S. Feshbach. "Testing Hypotheses Regarding Rape: Exposure to Sexual Violence, Sex Differences and the 'Normality' of Rapists." *Journal of Research in Personality* 14 (1980): 121–37.

Malamuth, N.M., M. Heim, and S. Feshbach. "Sexual Responsiveness of College Students to Rape Depictions: Inhibitory and Disinhibitory Effects." *Journal of Personality and Social Psychology* 38, no. 3 (1980): 399–408.

Malamuth, N.M., I. Reisin, and B. Spinner. "Exposure to Pornography and Reactions to Rape." Paper presented at the 86th Annual Convention of the American Psychological Association, New York, 1979.

Malamuth, N.M., and B. Spinner. "A Longitudinal Content Analysis of Sexual Violence in the Best-Selling Erotic Magazines." *Journal of Sex Research* 16 (1980): 226–37.

Malcolm, P.B., P.R. Davidson, and W.L. Marshall. "Control of Penile Tumescence: The Effects of Arousal Level and Stimulus Content." *Behaviour Research and Therapy* 23, no. 3 (1985): 273–80.

Mallory, C.H. "An Investigation of Motor Response Measure of the Approach-Avoidance Aspects of Subjective Reactions to Filmed Erotic Stimuli." *Dissertation Abstracts International* 34, no. 9B (1974): 4635.

Mann, J., L. Berkowitz, J. Sidman, S. Starr, and S. West. "Satiation of the Transient Stimulating Effect of Erotic Films." *Journal of Personality and Social Psychology* 30 (1974): 729–35.

Mann, J., J. Sidman, and S. Starr. "Effect of Erotic Films on the Sexual Behavior of Married Couples." In *Technical Reports of the Commission on Obscenity and*

Pornography. Vol. 8, 170–254. Washington, D.C.: GPO, 1971.

Mann, J., J. Sidman, and S. Starr. "Evaluating Social Consequences of Erotic and Sexual Deviance: A Retrospective Survey." *Journal of Social Issues* 29 (1973): 133–39.

Mann, J., J. Sidman, and S. Starr. "Evaluating Social Consequences of Erotic Films: An Experimental Approach." *Journal of Social Issues* 29, no. 3 (1973): 113–31.

Mann, L., and I.L. Janis. "A Follow-up Study on the Long Term Effects of Emotional Role Playing." *Journal of Personality and Social Psychology* 8 (1981): 339—42.

Marks, I.M., and M.G. Gelder. "Transvestism and Fetishism: Clinical and Psychological Changes during Faradic Aversion." *British Journal of Psychiatry* 113 (1967): 711–29.

Marks, I.M., S. Rachman, and M.G. Gelder. "Methods for Assessment of Aversion Treatment in Fetishism with Masochism." *Behaviour Research and Therapy* 3 (1965): 253–58.

Marquis, J.N. "Orgasmic Reconditioning: Changing Sexual Object Choice by Controlling Masturbatory Fantasies." *Journal of Behavior Therapy and Experimental Psychology* 30 (1970): 729–35.

Marshall, W.L. "The Use of Pornography by Sex Offenders." Paper, Queen's University, Department of Psychology, Kingston, Ontario, no date.

Marshall, W.L. "Satiation Therapy: A Procedure for Reducing Deviant Sexual Arousal." *Journal of Applied Behavior Analysis* 12 (1979): 377–89.

Marshall, W.L. "Report on the Use of Pornography by Sexual Offenders." Report to the Federal Department of Justice, Ottawa, 1983.

Marshall, W.L. "The Use of Pornography by Sex Offenders." Paper presented to the Attorney General's Commission on Pornography, Houston, September 1985.

Marshall, W.L. "The Use of Sexually Explicit Stimuli by Rapists, Child Molesters, and Nonoffenders." *Journal of Sex Research* 25 (May 1988): 267–88.

Marshall, W.L., and H.E. Barbaree. "The Reduction of Deviant Arousal: Satiation Treatment for Sexual Aggressors." *Criminal Justice Behavior* 5 (1978): 294–303.

Marshall, W.L., and H.E. Barbaree. "A Behavioral View of Rape." *International Journal of Law and Psychiatry* 7 (1984): 51–77.

Marshall, W.L., and Christie. "Pedophilia and Aggression." *Criminal Justice and Behavior* 8 (1981): 145–58.

Marshall, W.L., C.M. Earls, Z. Segal, and J. Darke. "A Behavioral Program for the Assessment and Treatment of Sexual Aggressors." In *Advances in Clinical Behavior Therapy,* edited by Kenneth D. Craig and Robert J. McMahon, 148–74. New York: Brunner-Mazel, 1983.

Martin, B. "Expression and Inhibition of Sex Motive Arousal in College Males." *Journal of Abnormal and Social Psychology* 68 (1964): 307–12.

Masters, W.H., and V.E. Johnson. *Human Sexual Response.* Boston: Little, Brown, 1966.

Masters, W.H., V.E. Johnson, and R.C. Kolodny, eds. *Ethical Issues in Sex Therapy and Research.* Vol. 1. Boston: Little, Brown, 1977.

Masters, W.H., V.E. Johnson, R.C. Kolodny, and S.M. Weems, eds. *Ethical Issues in Sex Therapy and Research.* Vol. 2. Boston: Little, Brown, 1980.

Masterson, John. "The Effects of Erotica and Pornography on Attitudes and Behavior: A Review." *Bulletin of the British Psychological Society* 37 (August 1984): 249–52.

Mavissakalian, M., E. Blanchard, G. Abel, and D. Barlow. "Responses to Complex Erotic Stimuli in Homosexual and Heterosexual Males." *British Journal of Psychiatry* 126 (1975): 252–57.

Mayerson, Suzin E., and Dalmas A. Taylor. "The Effects of Rape Myth Pornography on Women's Attitudes and the Mediating Role of Sex Role Stereotyping." *Sex Roles* 17 (September 1987): 321–38.

McCauley, C., and C.P. Swann. "Male-Female Differences in Sexual Fantasy." *Journal of Research in Personality* 12 (1978): 76–86.

McConaghy, N. "Penile Volume Change to Moving Pictures of Male and Female Nudes in Heterosexual and Homosexual Males." *Behaviour Research and Therapy* 5 (1967): 43–48.

McConaghy, N. "Subjective and Penile Plethysmograph Responses Following Aversion Relief and Apomorphine Aversion Therapy for Homosexual Impulses." *British Journal of Psychiatry* 115 (1969): 723–30.

McConaghy, N. "Penile Response Conditioning and Its Relationship to Aversion Therapy in Homosexuals." *Behavior Therapy* 1 (1970): 213–21.

McConaghy, N. "Penile Volume Responses to Moving and Still Pictures of Male and Female Nudes." *Archives of Sexual Behavior* 3 (1974): 565–70.

McConaghy, N., and J. Check. "Explorations in Sex and Violence." Unpublished manuscript, Yale University, 1973.

McConahay, S.A., and J.B. McConahay. "Sexual Permissiveness, Sex Role Rigidity, and Violence across Cultures." *Journal of Social Issues* 33 (1977): 134–43.

McCormack, T. "Machismo in Media Research: A Critical Review of Research on Violence and Pornography." *Social Problems* 25, no. 5 (1978): 544–55.

McCormack, T. "Passionate Protests: Feminists and Censorship." *Canadian Forum* (March 1980): 697.

McCormack, T. "Making Sense of Research on Pornography." In *Women Against Censorship,* edited by Varda Burstyn, 181–205. Toronto: Douglas and McIntyre, 1985.

McGaugh, James L. "Preserving the Presence of the Past: Hormonal Influence on Memory Storage." *American Psychologist* 38 (February 1983): 161–74.

McGuire, R.J., J.M. Carlisle, and B.G. Young. "Sexual Deviations as Conditioned Behavior: A Hypothesis." *Behaviour Research and Therapy* 2 (1965): 185.

McGuire, R.J., and M. Vallance. "Aversion Therapy by Electric Shock: A Simple Technique." *British Medical Journal* 1 (1964): 151–53.

McGuire, W.J. "The Myth of Massive Media Impact: Savagings and Salvagings." In *Publication Communication and Behavior*, Vol. 1, edited by G. Comstock, . New York: Academic Press, 1985.

McIntire, J., and J. Teevan. "Television Violence and Deviant Behavior." In *Television and Social Behavior*. Vol. 3: *Television and Adolescent Aggressiveness*, edited by G.A. Comstock and E.A. Rubinstein, . Washington, D.C.: GPO, 1972.

McKay, H.B., and D.J. Dolff. "The Impact of Pornography: An Analysis of Research and Summary of Findings." Working paper 13 prepared by the Canadian Department of Justice for the Special Committee on Pornography and Prostitution, 1984.

McMullen, S. "The Use of Film or Manual for Anorgasmic Women." In *Love and Attraction*, edited by M. Cook and G.D. Wilson, . Oxford, England: Pergamon Press, 1978.

McNamara, P.H., and A. St. George. " 'Porno' Litigation, Community Standards, and the Phony Expert: A Case Study of Fraudulent Research in the Courtroom." *Sociological Practice* 3 (1979): 45–60.

Medoff, Norman J., Dolf Zillmann, Jennings Bryant, and Paul W. Cominsky. "Excitation and Hedonic Valence in the Effect of Erotica on Motivated Intermale Aggression." In *Pornography and Censorship*, edited by David Copp and Susan Wendell, 275–94. New York: Prometheus, 1983.

Mees, H. "Sadistic Fantasies Modified by Aversive Conditioning and Substitution: A Case Study." *Behaviour Research and Therapy* 4 (1966): 317–20.

Merritt, C.G., J.E. Gerstl, and L.A. LoSciuto. "Age and Perceived Effects of Erotica-Pornography: A National Sample Study." *Archives of Sexual Behavior* 4 (1975): 605–21.

Meyer, T.P. "The Effects of Sexually Arousing and Violent Films on Aggressive Behavior." *Journal of Sex Research* 8 (1972): 324–33.

Meyer, T.P. "The Effects of Viewing Justified and Unjustified Real Film Violence on Aggressive Behavior." *Journal of Personality and Social Psychology* 23 (1972): 21–29.

Milavsky, J. Ronald, Ronald Kessler, Horst Stipp, and William S. Rubens. "Television and Aggression: The Results of a Panel Study." In *Television and Behavior: Ten Years of Scientific Progress and Implications for the Eighties*. Vol. 2: *Technical Reviews*, edited by David Pearl, Lorraine Bouthilet, and Joyce Lazar, 138–57. Rockville, Md.: U.S. Department of Health and Human Services, 1982.

Miller, C.T. *Generalizability of the Facilitating Effects of Anger on Sexual Arousal*. Master's thesis, Purdue University, 1977.

Miller, C.T., D. Byrne, and J.D. Fisher. "Order Effects and Responses to Sexual Stimuli by Males and Females." *Journal of Sex Research* 16 (1980): 131–47.

Miller, R., P. Brickmann, and D. Bolan. "Attribution versus Persuasion as for Modifying Behavior." *Journal of Personality and Social Psychology* 31 (1975): 430–41.

Miller, W.R.C., and H.E. Leif. "The Sexual Knowledge and Attitude Test (SKAT)." *Journal of Sex and Marital Therapy* 5 (1979): 282–87.

Minnery, Tom, ed. *Pornography: A Human Tragedy*. Wheaton, Ill.: Tyndale House Publishers, 1986.

Mitchell, F.B. "A Preliminary Investigation of Reported Sex Attitudes in a Sexually Deviant Group as a Function of a Stimulus Presentation and Group Interaction." *Dissertation Abstracts International* 38, no. 7B (1978): 3407.

Moan, C.E., and R.G. Heath. "Septal Stimulation for the Initiation of Heterosexual Behavior in a Homosexual Male." *Journal of Behavior Therapy and Experimental Psychiatry* 3 (1972): 23–30.

Money, J. "Pornography in the Home: A Topic in the Medical Education." In *Contemporary Sexual Behavior: Critical Issues in the 1970's*, edited by, J. Zubin and J. Money, . Baltimore: Johns Hopkins University Press, 1972.

Money J. "Gender: History, Theory and Usage of the Term in Sexology and Its Relationship to Nature/Nurture." *Journal of Sex and Marital Therapy* 11 (1985): 71–79.

Money, J., and R. Athanasiou. "Pornography in the Home: A Topic in Medical Education." In *Critical Issues in Contemporary Sex Research*, edited by J. Zubin and J. Money, . Baltimore: Johns Hopkins University Press, 1973.

Money, J., and G.K. Lehne. "Biomedical and Criminal Justice Concepts of Paraphilia: Developing Convergence." *Medicine and Law* 2 (1983): 257–61.

Moreault, D.M. "Women's Sexual Fantasies: As a Function of Sex Guilt and Experimental Sexual Stimulation." *Dissertation Abstracts International* 38, no. 9B (1978): 4989.

Moreault, D.M., and D.R. Follingstad. "Sexual Fantasies of Females as a Function of Sex Guilt and Experimental Response Cues." *Journal of Clinical Psychology* 46 (1978): 1385–93.

Moreland, R.L., and R.B. Zajonc. "A Strong Test of Exposure Effects." *Journal of Experimental Social Psychology* 12 (1976): 170–79.

Morokoff, P.J., and J.R. Heiman. "Effects of Erotic Stimuli on Sexually Functional and Dysfunctional Women: Multiple Measures before and after Sex Therapy." *Behaviour Research and Therapy* 18 (1980): 127–37.

Mosher, D.L. "Psychological Reactions to Pornographic Films" and "Sex Callousness toward Women." In *Technical Reports of the Commission on Obscenity and Pornography*. Vol. 8, 225–325. Washington, D.C.: GPO, 1971.

Mosher, D.L. "Sex Differences, Sex Experience, Sex Guilt, and Explicitly Sexual Films." *Journal of Social Issues* 29 (1973): 95–112.

Mosher, D.L. "Sex Guilt and Sex Myths in College Men and Women." *Journal of Sex Research* 15 (1979): 224–34.

Mosher, D.L., and P.R. Abramson. "Subjective Sexual Arousal to Films of Masturbation." *Journal of Consulting and Clinical Psychology* 45 (1977): 796–807.

Mosher, D.L., and R.D. Anderson. "Macho Personality, Sexual Aggression, and Reactions to Guided Imagery of Realistic Rape." *Journal of Research in Personality* 20 (1986): 77–94.

Mosher, D.L., and I. Greenberg. "Females' Affective Responses to Reading Erotic Literature." *Journal of Consulting and Clinical Psychology* 33 (1969): 472–77.

Mosher, D.L., and H. Katz. "Pornography Films, Male Verbal Aggression Against Women, and Guilt." In *Technical Reports of the Commission on Obscenity and Pornography*, 357–59. Washington, D.C.: GPO, 1971.

Mosher, D.L., and K.E. O'Grady. "Homosexual Threat, Negative Attitudes toward Masturbation, Sex Guilt, and Males' Sexual and Affective Reactions to Explicit Sexual Films." *Journal of Consulting and Clinical Psychology* 47 (October 1979): 860–73.

Mosher, D.L., and K.E. O'Grady. "Sex Guilt, Trait Anxiety, and Females' Subjective Sexual Arousal to Erotica." *Motivation and Emotion* 3 (1979): 235–50.

Mosher, D.L., and B.B. White. "Effects of Committed or Casual Erotic Guided Imagery on Females' Subjective Sexual Arousal and Emotional Response." *Journal of Sex Research* 16 (1980): 273–99.

Mueller, C.W., and E. Donnerstein. "The Effects of Humor-Induced Arousal upon Aggressive Behavior." *Journal of Research in Personality* 11 (1977): 73–82.

Mueller, C.W., and E. Donnerstein. "Film-Facilitated Arousal and Prosocial Behavior." *Journal of Experimental Social Psychology* 17 (1981): 31–41.

Mueller, C.W., R. Nelson, and E. Donnerstein. "Facilitative Effects of Media Violence on Helping." *Psychological Reports* 40 (1977): 775–78.

Mulvey, E.P., and J.L. Haugaard, eds. "Report of the Surgeon General's Workshop on Pornography and Public Health." U.S. Public Health Service and U.S. Department of Health and Human Services, Washington, D.C., 4 August 1986.

Mussen, P.H., and A. Scodel. "The Effects of Sexual Stimulation under Varying Conditions on TAT Sexual Responsiveness." *Journal of Consulting Psychology* 19 (1955): 90.

National Association of Broadcasters Code Authority. "Television Code (19th edition)." In *Documents of American Broadcasting*. 2d ed., edited by F.J. Kahn, . New York: Appleton-Crofts, .

National Commission on the Causes and Prevention of Violence. *Report*. Washington, D.C.: GPO, 1969.

Neird, J.S. "Exposure to Homoerotic Stimuli: Effects on Attitudes and Affects of Heterosexual Viewers." *Journal of Social Psychology* 119 (1983): 249–55.

Nelson, E.C. "Pornography and Sexual Aggression." In *The Influence of Pornography on Behavior*, edited by M. Yaffe and E.C. Nelson, 171–248. New York: Academic Press, 1982.

Nelson, G.K. "The Findings of the National Viewers' Survey." In *Video Violence and Children*, edited by G. Barlow, and A. Hill, . New York: St. Martin's Press, 1985.

Ng, M.L., and Peter W. Lee. "Psychological Characteristics and Attitudes Toward Pornography: A Preliminary Report." *Bulletin of the Hong Kong Psychological Society* 16–17 (January–July 1976): 63–72.

O'Grady, K.E. "Affect, Sex Guilt, Gender, and the Rewarding-Punishing Effects of Erotic Stimuli: A Reanalysis and Reinterpretation." *Journal of Personality and Social Psychology* 43 (1982): 618–22.

Orne, Martin T. "Demand Characteristics and Quasi-Controls." In *Artifacts in Behavior Research*, edited by Robert Rosenthal and Ralph L. Rosnow, 147–81. New York: Academic Press, 1969.

Osborn, C.A., and R.H. Pollack. "The Effects of Two Types of Erotic Literature on Physiological and Verbal Measures of Female Sexual Arousal." *Journal of Sex Research* 13 (1977): 250–56.

Packer, Herbert L. "The Pornography Caper." *Commentary*, February 1971, 72–77.

Palmer, C. "Pornographic Comics: A Content Analysis." *Journal of Sex Research* 15 (1979): 285–97.

Palys, T.S., and J. Lowman. "A Study of the Definition and Contents of Pornographic Media." Application for a research grant from the Social Science and Humanities Research Council of Canada, 1984.

Paris, J., and L.D. Goodstein. "Responses to Death and Sex Stimulus Materials as a Function of Repression-Sensitization." *Psychological Reports* 19 (1966): 1283–91.

Parke, R.D., L. Berkowitz, J.P. Levine, S.G. West, and R.J. Sebastian. "Some Effects of Violent and Non-Violent Movies on the Behavior of Juvenile Delinquents." In *Advances in Experimental Social Psychology*. Vol. 10, edited by L. Berkowitz, . New York: Academic Press, 1977.

Paul, G.L., and D.A. Bernstein. *Anxiety and Clinical Problems: Systematic Desensitization and Related Techniques*. Morristown, N.Y.: General Learning Press, 1973.

Pawlowski, W. "Response to Sexual Films as a Function of Anxiety Level." *Psychological Reports* 44 (1979): 1067–73.

Penrod, S., and D. Linz. "Using Psychological Research on Violent Pornography to Inform Legal Change." In *Pornography and Sexual Aggression*, edited by N.M. Malamuth and E. Donnerstein, . New York: Academic Press, 1984.

Perdue, W.C., and D. Lester. "Personality Characteristics of Rapists." *Perceptual and Motor Skills* 35 (1972): 514.

Perkins, K.B., and J.K. Skipper, Jr. "Pornographic and Sex Paraphernalia Shops: An Ethnography of Expressive Work Settings." *Deviant Behavior* 2 (1981): 187–99.

Perlman, B.J., and S.J. Weber. "The Effects of Pre-Information on Reactions to a Violent Passage and an Erotic Passage." *Journal of Social Psychology* 109 (1979): 127–38.

Philipson, Irene. "The Repression of History and Gender: A Critical Perspective on the Feminist Sexuality Debate." *Signs* 10 (Fall 1984): 113–18.

Phillips, David. "Natural Experiments on the Effects of Mass Media Violence on Fatal Aggression: Strengths and Weaknesses of a New Approach." *Studies in Experimental Social Psychology* 19 (1986): 207.

Phillips, David, and John Hensley. "When Violence Is Rewarded or Punished: The Impact of Mass Media Stories on Homicide." *Journal of Communication* 34 (Summer 1984): 101–16.

Piliavin, J.A., I.M. Piliavan, and B. Trudell. "Incidental Arousal, Helping, and Diffusion of Responsibility." Unpublished data, University of Wisconsin, Madison, 1974.

Pirke, K., G. Kockott, and F. Dittmar. "Psychosexual Stimulation and Plasma Testosterone in Man." *Archives of Sexual Behavior* 3 (1974): 577–84.

Polsky, Ned. "Pornography." In *Problems of Sex Behavior*, edited by Edward Sagarin and Donel E. McNamera, 268–84. New York: Crowell, 1968.

Pomeroy, W.B. "Transsexualism and Sexuality: Sexual Behavior of Pre- and Post-Operative Male Transsexuals." In *Transsexualism and Sex Reassignment*, edited by R. Green and J. Money, 183–88. Baltimore: Johns Hopkins University Press, 1969.

Powell, C.C., P. Blakney, H. Croft, and G. Pullian. "Rapid Treatment Approach to Human Sexual Inadequacy." *American Journal of Obstetrics and Gynecology* 119, no. 1 (1974): 89.

Prescott, J.W. "Body Pleasure and the Origins of Violence." *Futurist*, March–April 1975, 64–80.

Przybla, D.P.J., and D. Byrne. "The Mediating Role of Cognitive Processes in Self-Reported Sexual Arousal." *Journal of Research in Personality* 18 (1984): 54–63.

Przybla, D.P.J., D. Byrne, and K. Kelley. "The Role of Imagery in Sexual Behavior." In *Imagery: Current Theory, Research, and Application*, edited by A.A. Sheikh, 436–67. New York: John Wiley, 1983.

Quanty, Michael B. "Aggression Catharsis: Experimental Investigations and Implications." In *Perspectives on Aggression*, edited by Russell G. Geen and Edgar C. O'Neal, 99–132. New York: Academic Press, 1976.

Quinsey, V.L. "Prediction of Recidivism and Evaluation of Treatment Programs for Sex Offenders." In *Sexual Aggression and the Law*, edited by S.N. Verdun-Jones and A.A. Keltner, . Burnaby, B.C.: Criminology Research Center, Simon Fraser University, 1983.

Quinsey, V.L., and W.F. Carrigan. "Penile Responses to Visual Stimuli." *Criminal Justice and Behavior* 5 (1978): 333–41.

Quinsey, V.L., and T.C. Chaplin. "Penile Responses to Nonsexual Violence among Rapists." *Criminal Justice and Behavior* 9 (September 1982): 372–81.

Quinsey, V.L., T. Chaplin, and W. Carrigan. "Biofeedback and Signalled Punishment in the Modification of Inappropriate Sexual Age Preferences." *Behavior Therapy* 11 (1980): 567–76.

Quinsey, V.L., T.C. Chaplin, and D. Upfold. "Sexual Arousal to Nonsexual Violence and Sadomasochistic Themes among Rapists and Nonsexual Offenders." *Journal of Consulting and Clinical Psychology* 52 (1984): 651–57.

Quinsey, V.L., T.C. Chaplin, and G. Varney. "A Comparison of Rapists' and Nonsex Offenders' Sexual Preferences for Mutually Consenting Sex, Rape and Physical Abuse of Women." *Behavioral Assessment* 3 (1981): 127–35.

Quinsey, V.L., and W.L. Marshall. "Procedures for Reducing Inappropriate Sexual Arousal: An Evaluation Review." In *The Sexual Aggressor: Current Perspectives on Treatment*, edited by Joanne G. Greer and Irving R. Stuart, 267–92. New York: Von Nostrand Reinhold, 1983.

Quinsey, V.L., C.M. Steinman, S.G. Bergersen, and T. Holmes. "Penile Circumference, Skin Conductance, and Ranking Responses of Child Molesters and 'Normals' to Sexual and Nonsexual Visual Stimuli." *Behavior Therapy* 6 (1975): 213–19.

Rachman, S. "Aversion Therapy: Chemical or Electrical?" *Behaviour Research and Therapy* 2 (1965): 289–99.

Rachman, S. "Sexual Disorders and Behavior Therapy." *American Journal of Psychiatry* 118 (1961): 235–40.

Rachman, S. "Sexual Fetishism: An Experimental Analogue." *Psychological Record* 16 (1966): 293–96.

Rachman, S., and R.J. Hodgson. "Experimentally Induced 'Sexual Fetishism,' Replication and Development." *Psychological Record* 18 (1968): 25–27.

Rada, R.T. Clinical Aspects of the Rapist. New York: Grune & Stratton, 1978.

Rada, R.T., D. Laws, and R. Kellner. "Plasma Testosterone Levels in the Rapist." *Psychosomatic Medicine* 38 (1976): 257–68.

Ragault, M. "Pornography and Violent Sexual Offenders: A Preliminary Research Report." Department of Justice, Ottawa, 1983.

Ramirez, John, Jennings Bryant, and Dolf Zillman. "Effects of Erotica on Retaliatory Behavior as a Function of Level of Prior Provocation." *Journal of Personality and Social Psychology* 43, no. 5 (1982): 971–78.

Rapaport, K. "Sexually Aggressive Males: Characterological Features and Sexual Responsiveness to Rape Depictions." Doctoral dissertation, Auburn University, 1984.

Rapaport, K., and B.R. Burkhart. "Personality and Attitudinal Characteristics of Sexually Coercive College Males." *Journal of Abnormal Psychology* 93 (1984): 216–21.

Ray, R.E., and W.D. Thompson. "Autonomic Correlates of Female Guilt Responses to Erotic Visual Stimuli." *Psychological Reports* 34 (June 1974): 1299–1306.

Ray, R.E., and C.E. Walker. "Biographical and Self-Report Correlates of Female Guilt Responses to Visual Erotic Stimuli." *Journal of Consulting and Clinical Psychology* 41 (1973): 93–96.

Raymond, J.J. "Case of Fetishism Treated by Aversion Therapy." *British Medical Journal* 2 (1956): 854–56.

Reed, J.P., and R.S. Reed. "P.R.U.D.E.S. (Pornography Research Using Direct Erotic Stimuli)." *Journal of Sex Research* 8 (1972): 237–46.

Reid, L.D. "Processes of Fear Reduction in Systematic Desensitization: An Addendum to Wilson and Davidson. *Psychological Bulletin* 79 (1973): 107–9.

Reifler, C.B., J. Howard, A. Lipton, M.B. Liptzin, and D.E. Widmann. "Pornography: An Experimental

Study of Effects." *American Journal of Psychiatry* 128 (1971): 575–81.

Reisinger, J.J. "Masturbatory Training in the Treatment of Primary Orgasmic Dysfunction." *Journal of Behavior Therapy and Experimental Psychiatry* 5 (1974): 179–83.

Reisinger, J.J. "Effects of Erotic Stimulation and Masturbatory Training upon Situational Orgasmic Dysfunction." *Journal of Sex and Marital Therapy* 4 (1978): 177–85.

Reisinger, J.J. "Effects of Erotic Stimulation and Masturbatory Training with Erotic Stimuli." *Journal of Behavior Therapy and Experimental Psychiatry* 10 (1979): 247–50.

Reisman, Judith A. "A Content Analysis of *Playboy, Penthouse,* and *Hustler* Magazines with Special Attention to the Portrayal of Children, Crime and Violence." Report to the Attorney General's Commission on Pornography, , January 1986.

Revitch, E., and R.G. Wiess. "The Pedophilic Offender." *Diseases of the Nervous System* 23 (1962): 73–78.

Rhodes, P. "The Use of Aids in the Management of Disorders of Sexual Function." *Clinics in Obstetrics and Gynecology* 7 (1980): 421–32.

Richard, S.F. "The Business of Pornography: Methodological and Ethical Considerations in the Study of an Adult Bookstore Chain." *Society for the Study of Social Problems* (1983): 2155.

Rieber, R.W., C. Wiedmann, and J. Damato. "Obscenity: Its Frequency and Context of Usage as Compared in Males, Nonfeminist Females and Feminist Females." *Journal of Psycholinguistic Research* 8 (1979): 201–23.

Riger, , and M.T. Gordon. "The Fear of Rape: A Study in Social Control." *Journal of Social Issues* 37 (1981): 71–92.

Rist, R. "Policy, Politics, and Social Research: A Study in the Relationship of Federal Commissions and Social Science." *Social Problems* 21 (Summer 1973): .

Rist, R. "Policy, Politics and Social Research: A Study in the Relationship of Federal Commissions and Social Science." In *The Pornography Controversy,* edited by Ray C. Rist, 244–68. New Brunswick, N.J.: Transaction Books, 1975.

Roberts, Donald F., and Christine M. Bachen. "Mass Communication Effects." *Annual Review of Psychology* 32 (1981): 307.

Roberts, Elizabeth J. "Television and Sexual Learning in Childhood." In *Television and Behavior: Ten Years of Scientific Progress and Implications for the Eighties.* Vol. 2: *Technical Reviews,* edited by David Pearl, Lorraine Bouthilet, and Joyce Lanzer, 209–24. Rockville, Md.: U.S. Department of Health and Human Services, 1982.

Robinson, C.H. "The Effects of Observational Learning on Sexual Behavior and Attitudes in Orgasmic Dysfunctional Women." Doctoral dissertation, University of Hawaii, 1974.

Romano, K. "Psychophysiological Responses to a Sexual and an Unpleasant Motion Picture." Undergraduate thesis, University of Manitoba, 1969.

Roper Organization, Inc. "Sex, Profanity, and Violence: An Opinion Survey about Seventeen Television Programs." A survey conducted for the National Broadcasting Company and presented to the New York Advertising Company, July 1981.

Rose, V.M. "Rape as a Social Problem: A By-Product of the Feminist Movement." *Social Problems* 25 (1977): 75–89.

Rosen, Lawrence, and Stanley H. Turner. "Exposure to Pornography: An Exploratory Study." *Journal of Sex Research* 5 (November 1969): 235–46.

Rosen, R.C., and F.J. Keefe. "The Measure of Human Penile Tumescence." *Psychophysiology* 15 (1978): 366–76.

Rosenblum, S., and M. Faber. "The Adolescent Sexual Asphyxia Syndrome." *Journal of the American Academy of Child Psychiatry* 18 (1979): 546.

Rosene, J.M. "The Effects of Violent and Sexually Arousing Film Content: An Experimental Study." Doctoral dissertation, Ohio State University, 1971.

Rosenthal, R. "The 'File Drawer Problem' and Tolerance for Nill Results." *Psychological Bulletin* 86 (1976): 638–41.

Rosenthal, R., and R.L. Rosnow. *The Volunteer Subject.* New York: John Wiley, 1975.

Roth, M. "Sexual Pornography in Society: A Psychiatric Perspective." Fifth Goodman Lecture, Society of Opticians, London, 1977.

Rowland, Willard D., Jr. *The Politics of TV Violence: Policy Uses of Communication Research.* Beverly Hills, Calif.: Sage Publishing Co., 1983.

Rubin, H.B., and D.E. Henson, R.E. Falvo, and R.W. High. "The Relationship between Men's Endogenous Levels of Testosterone and Their Penile Responses to Erotic Stimuli." *Behaviour Research and Therapy* 17 (1979): 305–12.

Rubin, Z. "Measurement of Romantic Love." *Journal of Personality and Social Psychology* 14 (1970): 265–73.

Rule, B.J., and T.J. Ferguson. "The Immediate Effects of Media Violence on Attitudes, Emotions and Cognitions." *Journal of Social Issues* 42, no. 3 (1986): 7–23.

Russell, D.E.H. *The Politics of Rape.* New York: Stein & Day, 1975.

Russell, D.E.H. "Pornography and Violence: What Does the New Research Say?" In *Take Back the Night: Women on Pornography,* edited by Laura Lederer, 218–37. New York: Morrow 1980.

Russell, D.E.H. *Rape and Marriage.* Beverly Hills, Calif.: Sage Publishing Co., 1982.

Russell, D.E.H. "The Prevalence and Incidence of Forcible Rape and Attempted Rape of Females." *Victimology: An International Journal* 7 (1983): 1–4.

Russell, D.E.H. *Sexual Exploitation: Rape, Child Sexual Abuse and Workplace Harassment.* Beverly Hills, Calif.: Sage Publishing Co., 1984.

Sandford, D.A. "Patterns of Sexual Arousal in the Heterosexual Male." *Journal of Sex Research* 10 (1974): 150–55.

Sapolsky, B.S. "The Effect of Erotica on Annoyance and

Hostile Behavior in Unprovoked Males." *Dissertation Abstracts International* 38, no. 8A (1977): 4433.

Sapolsky, B.S. "Arousal, Affect, and the Aggression-Moderating Effect of Erotica." In *Pornography and Sexual Aggression*, edited by N.M. Malamuth and E. Donnerstein, . New York: Academic Press, 1984.

Sapolsky, B.S., and D. Zillman. "The Effect of Soft-Core and Hard-Core Erotica on Provoked and Unprovoked Hostile Behavior." *Journal of Sex Research* 17, no. 4 (1981): 319–43.

Schaefer, H.H., and A.H. Colgan. "The Effect of Pornography on Penile Tumescence as a Function of Reinforcement and Novelty." *Behavior Therapy* 8 (1977): 938–46.

Schell, Bernadette, Helen Sherritt, Jennifer Arthur, Lisa Beatty, Lorraine Berry, Lisa Edmonds, Joanne Kaashoek, and Deborah Kempny. "Development of a Pornography Community Standard: Questionnaire Results for Two Canadian Cities." *Canadian Journal of Criminology* 29 (April 1987): 133–52.

Schill, T., and J. Chapin. "Sex Guilt and Males' Preference for Reading Erotic Magazines." *Journal of Consulting and Clinical Psychology* 39 (1972): 516.

Schill, T., M. Van Tuinen, and D. Doty. "Repeated Exposure to Pornography and Arousal Levels of Subjects Varying in Guilt." *Psychological Reports* 46 (April 1980): 467–71.

Schindler, Gordon Wenezel. *A Report on Denmark's Legalized Pornography*. Torrance, Calif.: Banner Books, 1969.

Schmidt, G. "Male-Female Differences in Sexual Arousal and Behavior during and after Exposure to Sexually Explicit Stimuli." *Archives of Sexual Behavior* 4 (1975): 353–65.

Schmidt, G., and V. Sigusch. "Sex Differences in Responses to Psychosexual Stimulation by Films and Slides." *Journal of Sex Research* 6 (1970): 268–83.

Schmidt, G., V. Sigusch, and U. Meyberg. "Psychosexual Stimulation in Men: Emotional Reactions, Changes of Sex Behavior, and Measures of Conservative Attitudes." *Journal of Sex Research* 5 (1969): 199–217.

Schmidt, G., V. Sigusch, and S. Schafer. "Responses to Reading Erotic Stories: Male-Female Differences." *Archives of Sexual Behavior* 2 (1973): 181–99.

Schwarz, N., and J.F. Brand. "Effects of Salience of Rape on Sex Role Attitudes, Trust, and Self-Esteem in Non-Rape Women." *European Journal of Social Psychology* 13 (1983): 71–76.

Schwendinger, J., and H. Schwendinger. *Rape and Inequality*. Beverly Hills, Calif.: Sage Publishing Co., 1983.

Scott, D., ed. *Symposium on Media Violence and Pornography: Proceedings, Resource Book and Research Guide*. Toronto: Media Action Group, 1984.

Scott, D. *Pornography—Its Effects on the Family, Community and Culture*. Washington, D.C.: Free Congress Foundation, 1985.

Scott, D. "The Blurred Distinction between the Effects of Violent and Nonviolent Pornography." Paper submitted to the Attorney General's Commission on Pornography, 1 May 1986.

Scott, J.E. "Rape Rates and the Circulation Rates of Adult Magazines." Paper presented to the American Association for the Advancement of Science, Los Angeles, May 1985.

Scott, J.E. "Violence and Erotic Material: The Relationship between Adult Entertainment and Rape." Paper presented to the American Association for the Advancement of Science, Los Angeles, May 1985.

Scott, T.R., W.H. Wells, D.D. Wood, and D.I. Morgan. "Pupillary Response and Sexual Interest Reexamined." *Journal of Clinical Psychology* 23 (1967): 433–38.

Sears, D.O. "College Sophomores in the Laboratory: Influence of Narrow Data on Social Psychology's View of Human Nature." *Journal of Personality and Social Psychology* 51 (1986): 515–30.

Segal, Z.V., and W.L. Marshall. "Heterosexual Social Skills in a Population of Rapists and Child Molesters." *Journal of Consulting and Criminal Psychology* 53 (February 1985): 55–63.

Segal, Z.V., and L. Stermac. "A Measure of Rapists' Attitudes towards Women." *International Journal of Law and Psychology* 7 (1984): 437–40.

Senn, C.H. "A Comparison of Women's Reactions to Nonviolent Pornography, Violent Pornography and Erotica." Master's thesis, University of Calgary, 1985.

Serber, M. "Shame Aversion Therapy: A New Aversive Technique with Sexual Deviants." In *Advances in Behavior Therapy*, edited by R.D. Rubin, . London: Academic Press, 1970.

Sharp, Imogen. "Pornography and Sex-Related Crime: A Sociological Perspective." *Bulletin of the Hong Kong Psychological Society* 16–17 (January–July 1986): 73–81.

Shaughnessy, E.J., and D. Trebbi. *Standard for Miller: A Community Response to Pornography*. Washington, D.C.: University of America Press, 1980.

Shenken, L.E. "Some Clinical and Psychological Aspects of Bestiality." *Journal of Nervous and Mental Disease* 139 (1964): 137–42.

Sherif, Carolyn Wood. "Comment on Ethical Issues in Malamuth, Heim and Feshbach's 'Sexual Responsiveness of College Students to Rape Depictions: Inhibitory and Disinhibitory Effects.'" *Journal of Personality and Social Psychology* 38, no. 3 (1980): 409–12.

Shohom, S.G. "The Interdisciplinary Study of Sexual Violence." *Deviant Behavior:* 3 (1982): 245–74.

Siegman, , and Dintur. "The Catharsis of Aggression and Hostility." *Psychological Reports* 41 (1977): 399.

Sigusch, V., G. Schmidt, A. Reinfeld, and I. Wiedemann-Sutor. "Psychosexual Stimulation: Sex Differences." *Journal of Sex Research* 6 (1970): 10–24.

Silbert, M.H. "Sexual Assault of Prostitutes." Report prepared by the National Center for the Prevention and Control of Rape, November 1980.

Silbert, M.H., and A.M. Pines. "Pornography and Sexual Abuse of Women." *Journal of Sex Research* 6 (1970): 10–24.

Simons, G.L. *Pornography without Prejudice*. London: Abelard Schuman, 1972.

Sims, T.M. "Pupillary Response of Male and Female Subjects to Pupillary Difference in Male and Female Picture Stimuli." *Perception and Psychophysics* 2 (1967): 553–55.

Sirkin, Mark I., and Donald L. Mosher. "Guided Imagery of Female Sexual Assertiveness: Turn On or Turn Off?" *Journal of Sex and Marital Therapy* 11 (Spring 1985): 41–50.

Smeaton, George, and Donn Byrne. "The Effects of R-Rated Violence and Erotica, Individual Differences and Victim Characteristics on Acquaintance Rape Proclivity." Paper, State University of New York at Albany, 1987.

Smith, D.D. "The Social Content of Pornography." *Journal of Communication* 26 (1976): 16–23.

Smith, D.G. "Sexual Aggression in American Pornography: The Stereotype of Rape." Paper presented to the American Sociological Association, New York, 1976.

Smith, M. Dwayne, and Carl Hand. "The Pornography/Aggression Linkage: Results from a Field Study." *Deviant Behavior* 8, no. 4 (1987): 389–99.

Soble, A. "Pornography: Defamation and the Endorsement of Degradation." *Social Theory Practice* 11 (Spring 1985): 61–87.

Soble, A. *Pornography: Marxism, Feminism, and the Future of Sexuality*. New Haven, Conn.: Yale University Press, 1986.

Sobrero, A.J., H.E. Stearns, and J.H. Blair. "Technique for the Induction of Ejaculation in Humans." *Fertility and Sterility* 16 (1965): 765–67.

Solyom, L., and S. Miller. "A Differential Conditioning Procedure as the Initial Phase of the Behaviour Therapy of Homosexuality." *Behaviour Research and Therapy* 3 (1965): 147–60.

Sonenschein, D. "Dynamics in the Uses of Erotica." *Adolescent* 7 (1972): 233–44.

Sorenson, R. *Adolescent Sexuality in Contemporary America*. New York: World, 1972.

Sparks, Glenn G. "Developing a Scale to Assess Cognitive Responses to Frightening Films." *Journal of Broadcasting and Electronic Media* 30 (Winter 1986): 65–73.

Speisman, J.C., R.S. Lazarus, L. Davison, and A.M. Mordkoff. "Experimental Analysis of a Film Used as a Threatening Stimulus." *Journal of Consulting Psychology* 28 (1964): 23–33.

Spence, J.T., and R.L. Helmreich. *Masculinity and Femininity*. Austin: University of Texas Press, 1978.

Spengler, . "Manifest Sadomasochism of Males: Results of an Empirical Study." *Archives of Sexual Behavior* 6 (1977): 441.

Stanley, E. "Perspectives on the Need for Continuity of Physical Stimulation in Female Sexual Arousal." *Medical Aspects of Human Sexuality* 8 (1974): 98.

Stauffer, J., and R. Frost. "Explicit Sex: Liberation or Exploitation? Male and Female Interest in Sexually Oriented Magazines." *Journal of Communication* 26 (Winter 1976): 25–30.

Steele, D. Female Responsiveness to Erotic Films and Its Relation to Attitudes, Sexual Knowledge, and Selected Demographic Variables." Doctoral dissertation, Baylor University, 1973.

Steele, D., and E. Walker. "Male and Female Differences in Reaction to Erotic Stimuli as Related to Sexual Adjustment." *Archives of Sexual Behavior* 3 (1974): 459–70.

Steele, D., and E. Walker. "Female Responsiveness to Erotic Films and the 'Ideal' Erotic Film from a Feminine Perspective." *Journal of Nervous and Mental Disease* 162 (1976): 266–73.

Steffy, R.A. "Progress Report on the Treatment of the Pedophile Sex Offender." Paper presented to the Alex G. Brown Memorial Clinic Fourth Annual Conference on Addictions and on Sexual Deviation, Mimico, Ontario, April 1967.

Steinman, D.L., J.P. Wincze, B.A. Sakheim, D.H. Barlow, and M. Mavissakalian. "A Comparison of Male and Female Patterns of Sexual Arousal." *Archives of Sexual Behavior* 10 (1981): 529–47.

Sterling, B. "The Effects of Anger, Ambiguity, and Arousal on Helping Behavior." *Dissertation Abstracts International* 38 (1977): 1962.

Stern, M.L. "The Effects of Erotic Film-Induced or Exercise-Induced Physiological Arousal on an Instrumental Measure of Altruistic Behavior." *Dissertation Abstracts International* 39, no. 3B (1978): 1463.

Sternberg, Barbara A., and Aaron Weissman. "Comment: Television Violence: Censorship and the First Amendment." *University of Western Los Angeles Law Review* 12 (1980): 81–96.

Stock, W.E. "The Effects of Violent Pornography on Women." Paper presented to the Society for the Scientific Study of Sex, San Francisco, November 1982.

Stock, W.E. "The Effects of Violent Pornography on the Sexual Responsiveness and Attitudes of Women." Doctoral dissertation, State University of New York at Stony Brook, 1983.

Stock, W.E. "The Effects of Violent Pornography on Women." Paper presented to the American Psychological Association, Anaheim, Calif., 1983.

Stock, W.E. *Women's Affective Response and Subjective Reactions to Exposure to Violent Pornography*. Unpublished manuscript, Texas A&M University, 1984.

Stock, W.E. "Male Power, Hostility, and Sexual Coercion." In *Sexual Coercion*, edited by E. Allgeier, R. Allgeier, T. Perper, and W. Stock, . New York: SUNY Press, 1985.

Stock, W.E., and J. Geer. "A Study of Fantasy-Based Sexual Arousal in Women." *Archives of Sexual Behavior* 11 (1982): 33–47.

Stoller, R.J. "Pornography and Perversion." *Archives of General Psychiatry* 22 (1970): 490–99.

Stoller, R.J. *Perversion: The Erotic Form of Hatred*. Hassocks: Harvester Press, 1976.

Stoller, R.J. "Centerfold." *Archives of General Psychiatry* 36 (1979): 1019–24.

Stone, L.E. "Child Pornography Literature: A Content

Analysis." Doctoral dissertation, International College, San Diego, 1985.

Storms, M.D. "Theories of Sexual Orientation." *Journal of Personality and Social Psychology* 38 (May 1980): 783–92.

Straus, M. "A General Systems Theory Approach to a Theory of Violence Between Family Members." *Social Science Information* 12 (1973): 105–25.

Stuart, I.R., and J.G. Greer. *Victims of Sexual Aggression. Treatment of Children, Women, and Men.* New York: Van Nostrand Reinhold, 1984.

Study of the Effects of the Concentration of Adult Entertainment Establishments in the City of Los Angeles. Department of City Planning, June 1977.

Sue, D. "Erotic Fantasies of College Students during Coitus." *Journal of Sex Research* 15 (1979): 299–305.

Surgeon General's Scientific Advisory Committee. *Television and Growing Up: The Impact of Televised Violence.* Rockville, Md.: National Institute of Mental Health, 1972.

Tamborini, Ron, James Stiff, and Dolf Zillman. "Preference for Graphic Horror Featuring Male versus Female Victimization: Personality and Past Film Viewing Experiences." *Human Communication Research* 13 (Summer 1987): 529–52.

Tannenbaum, P.H. "Emotional Arousal as a Mediator of Erotic Communication Effects." In *Technical Reports of the Commission on Obscenity and Pornography*, Vol. 8, Washington, D.C.: GPO, 1970.

Tannenbaum, P.H. "Emotional Arousal as a Mediator of Erotic Communication Effects." In *Technical Reports of the Commission on Obscenity and Pornography.* Vol. 8, 326–56. Washington, D.C.: GPO, 1971.

Tannenbaum, P.H., and D. Zillmann. "Emotional Arousal in the Facilitation of Aggression through Communication." In *Advances in Experimental Social Psychology.* Vol. 8, edited by L. Berkowitz, . New York: Academic Press, 1975.

Taylor, S.P. "Aggressive Behavior and Physiological Arousal as a Function of Provocation and the Tendency to Inhibit Aggression." *Journal of Personality* 35 (1967): 297–310.

Taylor, S.P., and S. Epstein. "Aggression as a Function of the Interaction of the Sex of the Victim." *Journal of Personality* 35 (1967): 474–86.

Thomas, M.H. "Physiological Arousal, Exposure to a Relatively Lengthy Aggressive Film, and Aggressive Behavior." *Journal of Research in Personality* 16 (1982): 72–81.

Thomas, M.H., and R.S. Drabman. "Toleration of Real Life Aggression as a Function of Exposure to Televised Violence and Age of Subject." *Merrill-Palmer Quarterly* 21 (1975): 227–32.

Thomas, M.H., R.W. Horton, E.C. Lippencott, and R.S. Drabman. "Desensitization to Portrayals of Real-Life Aggression as a Function of Exposure to Television Violence." *Journal of Personality and Social Psychology* 35 (1977): 450–58.

Thomas, M.H., and P.M. Tell. "Effects of Viewing Real Versus Fantasy Violence upon Interpersonal Aggres-

sion." *Journal of Research in Personality* 8 (1974): 153–60.

Thompson, J.J., and P.W. Dixon. "A Power Function Between Ratings of Pornographic Stimuli and Psychophysical Responses in Young Normal Adult Women." *Perceptual and Motor Skills* 38 (1974): 1236–38.

Thorne, F.C., T.D. Haupt, and R.M. Allen. "Objective Studies of Adult Male Sexuality Using the Sex Inventory." *Journal of Clinical Psychology* 21 (1966): 1–43.

Thorpe, J.G., E. Schmidt, and D. Castell. "A Comparison of Positive and Negative (Aversive) Conditioning in the Treatment of Homosexuality." *Behaviour Research and Therapy* 1 (1963): 357–62.

Tieger, T. "Self-Rated Likelihood of Raping and the Social Perception of Rape." *Journal of Research in Personality* 15 (1981): 147–58.

Tillich, Hannah. *From Time to Time.* Briarclif Manor, N.Y.: Stein & Day, 1974.

Tjaden, P.G. "Pornography and Sex Education." Paper presented to the American Society of Criminology, San Diego, November 1985.

"Toward a Consent Standard in the Law of Rape." *University of Chicago Review* 43 (1976): 613–645.

Travis, C., and C. Offir. *The Longest War: Sex Differences in Perspectives.* New York: Harcourt Brace Jovanovich, 1977.

Tsang, Adolph. "Pornography as Cause or Pornographic Experience as Constituted?" *Bulletin of the Hong Kong Psychological Society* 16–17 (January –July 1986): 29–32.

Valentich, M., and I. Berry. "Social Work and Pornography." *The Social Worker/Le Travailleur Social* 55, no. 1 (1987): 19–22.

Van Deventer, A.D., and D.R. Laws. "Orgasmic Reconditioning to Redirect Sexual Arousal in Pedophiles." *Behavior Therapy* 9 (1978): 748–65.

Van Dyke, Michael S., Augustine Brannigan, and Andros Kapardis. "The Controversy over Pornography and Sex Crimes: The Criminological Evidence and Beyond." *Australian and New Zealand Journal of Criminology* 19 (December 1986): 259–84.

Vandervoort, H.E., and T. McIlvenna. "Sexually Explicit Media in Medical School Curricula." In *Human Sexuality: A Health Practitioner's Test*, edited by R. Green, . Baltimore: Williams and Wilkins, 1975.

Walker, C. Eugene. "Erotic Stimuli and the Aggressive Sexual Offender." In *Technical Reports of the Commission on Obscenity and Pornography.* Vol. 8, 91–148. Washington, D.C.: GPO, 1971.

Wallace, D.H., and G. Wehmer. "Pornography and Attitude Change." *Journal of Sex Research* 7, no. 2 (1971): 116–25.

Wallace, D.H., and G. Wehmer. "Evaluation of Visual Erotica by Sexual Liberals and Conservatives." *Journal of Sex Research* 8 (1972): 147–53.

Ware, E., M. Brown, D. Amoroso, W. Pilkey, and M. Pruesse. "The Semantic Meaning of Pornographic Stimuli for College Males." *Canadian Journal of Behavioral Science* 4 (1972): 204–9.

Waring, E.M., and J.J. Jefferies. "The Conscience of a Pornographer." *Journal of Sex Research* 10 (1974): 40–46.

"Washington's Attempt to View Sexual Assault as More Than a Violation of the Moral Woman: The Revision of the Rape Laws." *Gonzaga Law Review* 11 (1975): 145–77.

Weaver, J.B. "Effects of Portrayals of Female Sexuality and Violence Against Women on Perceptions of Women." Doctoral dissertation, Indiana University, 1987.

Weaver, J.B., J. Masland, and D. Zillmann. "Effects of Erotica on Young Men's Aesthetic Perception of Their Female Sexual Partners." *Personality and Motor Skills* 50 (1984): 929–30.

Weber, S.J., and D.T. Cook. "Subject Effects in Laboratory Research: An Examination of Subject Roles, Demand Characteristics, and Valid Inference." *Psychological Bulletin* 77 (1972): 273–95.

Weidner, G., and W. Griffitt. "Rape: A Sexual Stigma?" *Journal of Personality* 51 (1983): 152–66.

Weidner, J.B., G. Istuan, and W. Griffitt. "Beauty in the Eyes of the Horny Beholders." Paper presented to the Midwestern Psychological Association, Chicago, 1979.

Weis, K., and S.S. Borges. "Victimology and Rape: The Case of the Legitimate Victim." *Issues in Criminology* 8 (1973): 71–115.

Wertham, F. "The Comics . . . Very Funny!" *Saturday Review of Literature*, 24 May 1948, 19.

Wesselius, C.L., and R. Bally. "A Male with Autoerotic Asphyxia Syndrome." *American Journal of Forensic Medicine and Pathology* 4 (1983): 341–45.

West, D.J. "Victims of Sexual Crime." *British Journal of Sexual Medicine* 8 (1982): 30–35.

"What Should Parents Do When They Find Their Children in Possession of Pornographic Material?" *Medical Aspects of Human Sexuality* 3 (1969): 6–12.

White, L.A. "Affective Response to Erotic Stimulation and Human Aggression." *Dissertation Abstracts International* 39, no. 2B (1978): 965.

White, L.A. "Erotica and Aggression: The Influence of Sexual Arousal, Positive Affect, and Negative Affect on Aggressive Behavior." *Journal of Personality and Social Psychology* 37 (April 1979): 591–601.

White, L.A., W. Fisher, D. Byrne, and R. Kingmen. "Development and Validation of an Affective Orientation to Erotic Stimuli." Paper presented to the Midwestern Psychological Association, Chicago, May 1977.

Wilcox, B.L. "Pornography, Social Science, and Politics: When Research and Ideology Collide." *American Psychologist* 42 (October 1987): 941–43.

Wilkins, W. "Desensitization: Social and Cognitive Factors Underlying the Effectiveness of Wolpe's Procedure." *Psychological Bulletin* 76 (1971): 311–17.

Williams, Bernard. *Report of the Commission on Obscenity and Film Censorship*. London: Her Majesty's Stationery Office, 1979.

Williams, J., and R.A. Holmes. *The Second Assault: Rape and Public Attitudes*. Westport, Conn.: Greenwood Press, 1981.

Williams, Tannis MacBeth, ed. *The Impact of Television: A Natural Experiment in Three Communities*. Orlando, Fla.: Academic Press, 1986.

Wills, Garry. "Measuring the Impact of Erotica." *Psychology Today*. August 1977, 31.

Wilson, G.T., D.M. Lawson, and D.B. Brams. "Effects of Alcohol on Sexual Arousal in Male Alcoholics." *Journal of Abnormal Psychology* 87 (1978): 609–16.

Wilson, James Q. "Violence, Pornography and Social Science." In *The Pornography Controversy*, edited by Ray C. Rist, 225–43. New Brunswick, N.J.: Transaction Books, 1975.

Wilson, K.L., and L.A. Zurcher. "Status Inconsistency and Participation in Social Movements: An Application of Goodman's Hierarchical Modeling." *Sociological Quarterly* 17 (Autumn 1976): 520–33.

Wilson, W. "Sex Differences in Response to Obscenities: Bawdy Humor." *Psychological Reports* 37 (1975): 1074.

Wilson, W., and V. Liedtke. "Movie-Inspired Sexual Practices." *Psychological Reports* 54 (1984): 328.

Wilson, W.C. "Facts vs. Fears: Why Should We Worry about Pornography?" *Annals of the American Academy of Political and Social Science* 397 (1971): 105–17.

Wilson, W.C. *The Use of Explicit Sexual Materials in the Training of Professional Sex Educators and Counselors*. Washington, D.C.: AASEC, 1972.

Wilson, W.C. "The Distribution of Selected Sexual Attitudes and Behaviors Among the Adult Population of the United States." *Journal of Sex Research* 11 (1975): 46–64.

Wilson, W.C. "Can Pornography Contribute to the Prevention of Sexual Problems?" In *The Prevention of Sexual Disorders: Issues and Approaches*, edited by C. Brandon Qualls, John P. Wincze, and David H. Barlow, 159–82. New York: Plenum Press, 1978.

Wilson, W.C., and H.I. Abelson. "Experience with and Attitudes toward Explicit Sexual Materials." *Journal of Social Issues* 39, no. 3 (1973): 19.

Wilson, W., and V. Liedtke. "Movie-Inspired Sexual Practices." *Psychological Reports* 54 (1984): 328.

Wincze, J.P., E.F. Hoon, and P.W. Hoon. "Physiological Responsivity of Normal Sexually Dysfunctional Women during Erotic Stimulus Exposure." *Journal of Psychosomatic Research* 20 (1976): 445–51.

Wincze, J.P., P.W. Hoon, and E.F. Hoon. "Sexual Arousal in Women: A Comparison of Cognitive and Physiological Responses by Continuous Measurement." *Archives of Sexual Behavior* 6 (1977): 121–33.

Wincze, J.P., E. Venditti, D. Barlow, and M. Mavissakalian. "The Effects of a Subjective Monitoring Task in the Physiological Measure of Genital Response to Erotic Stimulation." *Archives of Sexual Behavior* 9 (1980): 533–45.

Winick, C. "A Content Analysis of Sexually Explicit Magazines Sold in an Adult Bookstore." *Journal of Sex Research* 21 (1985): 206–10.

Wishnoff, R. "Modeling Effects of Explicit and Nonexplicit Sexual Stimuli on the Sexual Anxiety and Behavior of

Women." *Archives of Sexual Behavior* 7 (1978): 455–61.

Wolchik, S.A., et al. "Effect of Emotional Arousal On Subsequent Sexual Arousal in Men." *Journal of Abnormal Psychology* 89 (August 1980): 595–98.

Wolchik, S.A., S.L. Braver, and K. Jensen. "Volunteer Bias in Erotica Research: Effects of Intrusiveness of Measure and Sexual Background." *Archives of Sexual Behavior* 14 (1985): 93–107.

Wolchik, S.A., L. Spencer, and I.S. Lisi. "Volunteer Bias in Research Employing Vaginal Measures of Sexual Arousal." *Archives of Sexual Behavior* 12 (1983): 399–408.

Wolfe, J., and V. Baker. "Characteristics of Imprisoned Rapists and Circumstances of the Rape." In *Rape and Sexual Assault*, edited by Carmen Germaine Warner, . Germantown, Md.: Aspen Systems Corp., 1980.

Wood, Michael, and Michael Hughes. "The Moral Basis of Moral Reform: Status Discontent vs. Culture and Socialization as Explanations of Anti-Pornography Social Movement Adherence." *American Sociological Review* 49 (February 1984): 86–99.

Woodmansee, J.J. "Methodological Problems in Pupillographic Experiments." *Proceedings of 74th Annual Convention of the American Psychological Association* (1966): 133–34.

Wyer, R., G.V. Bodenhausen, and T.F. Gorman. "Cognitive Mediators of Reaction to Rape." *Journal of Personality and Social Psychology* 48 (1985): 324–38.

Yaffe, M. "Research Survey." In *Pornography: The Longford Report*. London: Coronet Books, 1972.

Yaffe, M. "Pornography and Violence." *Bethlem and Maudsley Hospital Gazette*, Winter 1976, 11–14.

Yaffe, M. "Pornography: An Updated Review (1972–77)." In *The Williams Report*. 1979.

Yaffe, M. "Pornography and Violence." *British Journal of Sexual Medicine* 5 (1979): 32–36.

Yaffe, M. "The Law Relating to Pornography: A Psychological Overview." *Medicine, Science and the Law* 20 (1980): 20–27.

Yaffe, M. "Therapeutic Uses of Sexually Explicit Material." In *The Influence of Pornography on Behavior*, edited by M. Yaffe and E. Nelson, 120–50. London: Academic Press, 1982.

Yaffe, M., and E. Nelson, eds. *The Influence of Pornography on Behavior*. New York and London: Academic Press, 1982.

Yaffe, M., and T.G. Tennent. "Pornography: A Psychological Appraisal." *British Journal of Hospital Medicine* 9 (1973): 379–83.

Yllö, Kersti. "Using a Feminist Approach in Quantitative Research: A Case Study." In *The Dark Side of Families*, edited by David Finkelhor, Richard J. Gelles, Gerald T. Hotaling, and Murray A. Straus, 277–88. Beverly Hills, Calif.: Sage Publishing Co., 1983.

Young, M. "Sexual Attitudes and Behavior of Female Readers and Non-Readers of Erotic Literature." *Psychological Reports* 45 (December 1979): 932–34.

Yuen, Kenneth, and William Ickes. "'Prudes' and 'Pornographiles': Effects of Subject and Audience Attitudes on the Viewing and Rating of Pornographic Materials." *Journal of Social and Clinical Psychology* 2 (February 1984): 215–29.

Zajonc, R.B. "The Attitudinal Effect of Mere Exposure." *Journal of Personal Psychology* (Monograph Supplement) 9 (1968): 1–27.

Zamansky, H.S. "A Technique for Assessing Homosexual Tendencies." *Journal of Personality* 24 (1956): 436–48.

Zellinger, D.A., H.L. Fromkin, D.E. Speller, and C.A. Kohn. "A Commodity Theory Analysis of the Effects of Age Restrictions upon Pornographic Materials." *Journal of Applied Psychology* 60 (1975): 94–99.

Zellman, G.L., J.D. Goodchilds, P.B. Johnson, and R. Giarrusso. "Teenagers' Application of the Label 'Rape' to Nonconsensual Sex between Acquaintances." Symposium presented at the American Psychological Association, Los Angeles, August 1981.

Zetterberg, Hans Lennart. *The Consumers of Pornography Where It is Easily Available: The Swedish Experience.* Stockholm: SIFO, 1971.

Zillman, D. "Excitation Transfer in Communication-Mediated Aggressive Behavior." *Journal of Experimental Social Psychology* 7 (1971): 419–34.

Zillman, D. *Hostility and Aggression*. Hillsdale, N.J.: Lawrence Erlbaum Associates, 1979.

Zillman, D. "Anatomy of Suspense." In *The Entertainment Function of Television*, edited by P.H. Tannenbaum, . Hillsdale, N.J.: Lawrence Erlbaum Associates, 1980.

Zillman, D. *The Connection between Sex and Aggression*. Hillsdale, N.J.: Lawrence Erlbaum Associates, 1984.

Zillman, D., and J. Bryant. "Pornography, Sexual Callousness and the Trivialization of Rape." *Journal of Communication* 32 (Autumn 1982): 10–21.

Zillman, D., and J. Bryant. "Pornography and Social Science Research: Higher Moralities." *Journal of Communication* 33 (Autumn 1983): 107–11.

Zillman, D., and J. Bryant. "Effects of Massive Exposure to Pornography." In *Pornography and Sexual Aggression*, edited by N.M. Malamuth and E. Donnerstein, 115–38. New York: Academic Press, 1984.

Zillman, D., and J. Bryant. *Pornography's Impact on Sexual Satisfaction*. Unpublished manuscript, Indiana University, 1986.

Zillman, D., and J. Bryant. "Shifting Preferences in Pornography Consumption." *Communication Research* 12 (October 1986): 560–78.

Zillman, D., and J. Bryant. " 'Pornography and Behavior: Alternative Explanations': Reply." *Journal of Communication* 37 (Summer 1987): 189–92.

Zillman, D., J. Bryant, and R.A. Carveth. "The Effect of Erotica Featuring Sadomasochism and Bestiality on Motivated Intermale Aggression." *Personality and Social Psychology Bulletin* (1981): .

Zillman, D., J. Bryant, P.W. Comisky, and N.J. Medoff. "Excitation and Hedonic Valance in the Effect of Erotica and Motivated Intermale Aggression." *European Journal of Social Psychology* 2 (1981): 233–52.

Zillman, D., J.L. Hoyt, and K.D. Day. "Strength and Duration of the Effects of Aggressive, Violent and

Erotic Communications on Subsequent Aggressive Behavior." *Communication Research* 1 (1974): 286–306.

Zillmann, D., and R.C. Johnson. "Motivated Aggressiveness Perpetuated by Exposure to Aggressive Films and Reduced by Exposure to Nonaggressive Films." *Journal of Research in Personality* 7 (1973): 261–76.

Zillmann, D., A.H. Katcher, and B. Milavsky. "Excitation Transfer from Physical Exercise to Subsequent Aggressive Behavior." *Journal of Experimental Social Psychology* 8 (1972): 247–59.

Zillmann, D., and N. Mundorf. *Effects of Sexual and Violent Images in Rock-Music Videos on Music Appreciation.* Paper presented at the 31st Annual Convention of the Broadcasting Education Association, Dallas, April 1986.

Zillmann, D., and B. Sapolsky. "What Mediates the Effect of Mild Erotica on Annoyance and Hostile Behavior in Males?" *Journal of Personality and Social Psychology* 35 (1977): 587–96.

Zillmann, D., and J. Wakshag. "Fear of Victimization and the Appeal of Crime Drama." In *Selective Exposure to Communication,* edited by D. Zillman and J. Bryant, . Hillsdale, N.J.: Lawrence Erlbaum Associates 1985.

Zillman, D., J. Weaver, N. Mundorf, and C. Aust. "Effects of an Opposite-Gender Companion's Affect to Horror on Distress, Delight, and Attraction." *Journal of Personality and Social Psychology* 51 (1986): 586–94.

Zuckerman, M. "Psychological Measures of Sexual Arousal in the Human." *Psychological Bulletin* 75 (1971: 297–329.

Zuckerman, M. "Research on Pornography." In *Sex and the Life Cycle,* edited by W.W. Oaks, G.A. Melchiode, and I. Ficher, . New York: Grune & Stratton, 1976.

Zuckerman, M. *Sensation Seeking: Beyond the Optimal Level of Arousal.* Hillsdale, N.J.: Lawrence Erlbaum Associates, 1979.

CHAPTER 6

Allen, Ray. "The War on Children." *Bible Advocate,* December 1985.

Anchell, Melvin. *Sex and Sanity.* New York: Macmillan, 1971.

Anchell, Melvin. "A Psychiatrist Looks at Pornography." *Liberty Magazine,* July/August 1977.

Attorney General's Commission on Pornography. *Final Report.* Washington, D.C.: U.S. Department of Justice, 1986.

Barnett, W. "Corruption of Morals—The Underlying Issue of the Pornography Commission Report." *Law and Social Order* 189 (1971): 201–5.

Beck, M., and V.E. Smith. "How to Make It Hot for Porn." *Newsweek,* 25 May 1981.

Brown, , Anderson, Burggraf, and Thompson. "Community Standards, Conservatism, and Judgments of Pornography." *Journal of Sex Research* 14 (1978): 81.

Brown, Beverley, and John Court. "Pornography—Erotica or Violence?" *Counterpoint Forum.* Murdoch University Australia, 11 October 1984.

Caron, Yves. "The Legal Enforcement of Morality and the So-Called Hart-Devlin Controversy." *McGill Law Journal* 15 (1969): 9–47.

Cavnar, Nick. "The Victims of a 'Victimless' Crime." *Bible Advocate,* December 1985.

Chemerinsky, E. and McGeady, P.J. "Outlawing Pornography: What We Gain, What We Lose." *Human Rights* 12 (Spring 1985): 24–6.

Christenson, Reo. "The Truth about Pornography." *Bible Advocate,* January 1985.

Citizens for Decency Through Law. *Legal Aspects.* Phoenix, Ariz.: Citizens for Decency Through Law.

Cline, Victor. *Where Do You Draw the Line?* Provo, Utah: Brigham Young University Press, 1974.

Cline, Victor. "The Effects of Pornography on Behavior." *Bible Advocate,* January 1985.

Court, John H. "Censorship—A Conservative Viewpoint." In *Conservatism as Heresy,* edited by J.J. Ray, 314–35. Sydney, Australia: A.N.Z. Books, 1974.

Court, John H. *Pornography: A Christian Critique.* Australia: Inter-Varsity Press, 1980.

Court, John H. *Pornography and the Harm Condition.* Australia: Finders University, 1981.

Court, John H. "What Then Shall We Say or Do?" *Bible Advocate,* December 1985, 22–26.

Curl, Brad. *A Strategy for Decency.* 2d ed. Washington, D.C.: National Christian Association, 1986.

Devlin, Patrick. *The Enforcement of Morals.* London: Oxford University Press, 1965.

"Did You Know? Some Facts about Pornography and the Victories Being Won Against It." *Bible Advocate,* January 1985, 8.

Dobson, James. "Combatting the Darkness." *Focus on the Family,* August 1986.

Dworkin, Ronald. "Lord Devlin and the Enforcement of Morals." *Yale Law Journal,* (1966): 75.

Emrich, Richard S. "A New and Dangerous Evil." *Bible Advocate,* January 1985, 10–12.

Feinberg, Joel. " 'Harmless Immoralities' and Offensive Nuisances." In *Issues in Law and Morality,* edited by Norman S. Care and Thomas K. Trelogan, . Cleveland: Case Western Reserve University, 1973.

Feinberg, Joel. *Offense to Others: The Moral Limits of the Criminal Law.* New York: Oxford University Press, 1985.

Fortune, Marie Marshall. *Sexual Violence . . . the Unmentionable Sin: An Ethical and Pastoral Perspective.* New York: Pilgrim, 1983.

Frankel, Charles. "The Moral Environment of the Law." *Minnesota Law Review* 61 (1977): 921.

Gallagher, Neil. *The Porno Plague.* Minneapolis: Bethany House Publishers, 1981.

Gardiner, Harold J. "Moral Principles towards a Definition of the Obscene." In *The Pornography Controversy*, edited by Ray C. Rist 159–74. New Brunswick, N.J.: Transaction Books, 1975.

Glock, Charles, and R. Stuart. *Religion and Society in Tension*. Chicago: Rand McNally, 1965.

Hart, H.L.A. *Law, Liberty and Morality*. London: Oxford University Press, 1963.

Holbrook, D. "Mary Whitehouse." *Political Quarterly* 51 (April 1980): 154–63.

Holland, Elizabeth. "I Don't Have the Right." *Bible Advocate*, January 1985.

Jelen, Ted G. "Fundamentalism, Feminism and Attitudes Toward Pornography." *Review of Religious Research* 28 (December 1986): 97–103.

Jones, A. "Fit to Be Tied." *The Nation*, 28 May 1983, 21.

Kirk, Jerry R. *The Mind Polluters*. Nashville, Tenn.: Thomas Nelson, 1985.

Kirkpatrick, R.G. "Moral Indignation and Repressed Sexuality: The Sociosexual Dialectics of Antipornography Crusades." *Psychoanalytic Review* 61 (1974): 141–49.

Kirkpatrick, R.G. "Collective Consciousness and Mass Hysteria: Collective Behavior and Anti-Pornography Crusades in Durkheimian Perspective." *Human Relations* 28 (February 1975): 63–84.

Kohl, H. "Pornography." *Canadian Living*, April 1984.

Kopecky, Frank J. "Morality on Trial: Should Prostitution and Pornography Be Against the Law?" *Update on Law-Related Education* 4 (Winter 1980): 6.

Lanning, Kenneth V. "The Pedophile and Pornography." *Bible Advocate*, December 1985.

McCuen, Gary E. "Pornography and Sexual Violence." *Ideas in Conflict Series*. Hudson, Wisc.: GEM Publications, 1985.

"Men Confronting Pornography." *Changing Men* (Madison, Wisc.) (Fall 1985): .

National Decency Reporter. (Phoenix, AZ: Citizens for Decency Through Law).

National Federation for Decency Journal. (Tupelo, Mississippi: National Federation for Decency).

National Coalition Against Pornography. *Mission and Objectives of the N-CAP, Inc*. Cincinnati: National Coalition Against Pornography, 1985.

Polsky, Ned. "On the Sociology of Pornography." In *Hustlers, Beats, and Others*, edited by , . New York: Doubleday, Anchor Books, 1969.

"The Porn Peddlers." *San Diego Reader*, 13 March 1986.

Pretty Poison: The Selling of Sexual Warfare. *Village Voice*, 9 May 1977, 18–23.

Religious Alliance Against Pornography. "Policy Statement." Cincinnati, 1986.

Report of the Commission on Obscenity and Pornography. New York: Bantam Books, 1970.

Richards, D.A. "Free Speech and Obscenity Law: Toward a Moral Theory of the First Amendment." *University of Pennsylvania Law Review* 123 (1974–75): 45–91.

Richards, D.A. *The Moral Criticism of Law*. Encino and Belmont, Calif.: Dickinson Publishing Co., 1977.

Rist, Ray C. "Pornography as a Social Problem: Reflections on the Relation of Morality and the Law." In *The Pornography Controversy*, edited by Ray C. Rist, 1–15. New Brunswick, N.J.: Transaction Books, 1975.

Schell, B., H. Sherritt, J. Arthur, L. Beatty, L. Berry, L. Edmonds, J. Kaashoek, and D. Kempny. "Development of a Pornography Community Standard: Questionnaire Results for Two Canadian Cities." *Canadian Journal of Criminology* 29 (April 1987): 133–52.

Showers, H. Robert. "Myths and Misconceptions of Pornography: What You Don't Know Can Hurt You." *Christian Lawyer in American Culture* 5 (Fall 1988): 8–10.

Skolnick, Jerome H. "Coercion to Virtue: The Enforcement of Morals." *Southern California Law Review* 41, no. 3 (1968): 581–641.

Stanmeyer, William A. *The Seduction of Society: Pornography and Its Impact on American Life*. Ann Arbor, Mich.: Servant Books, 1984.

Tanner, Paul. *A Call to Righteousness: A Plan of Action Against Pornography and Obscenity*. Denver: Bible Advocate Press, 1985.

Tanner, Paul. "10 Steps to Action." *Bible Advocate*, January 1985.

Thompson, Edward. "Morality, Pornography and the Law." *Communication and the Law* 4 (Spring 1982): 43–68.

Trumbull, Charles Gallaudet. *Anthony Comstock, Fighter*. New York: Fleming H. Revell Co., 1913.

"The War Against Pornography." *Newsweek*, 18 March 1985, 58–67.

Wasserstrom, Richard, ed. *Morality and the Law*. Belmont, Calif.: Wadsworth Publishing Co., 1971.

Wasserstrom, Richard, ed. *Today's Moral Problems*. New York: Macmillan, 1979.

Watchtower Bible and Tract Society. *Awake*. New York: Watchtower Bible and Tract Society, 1982.

Wein, Betty. "The Chilling Effects of Pornography: A Jewish Perspective." Paper prepared for the Seventh World Media Conference, Tokyo, November 1984.

Wildmon, Donald E. *The Home Invaders*. Wheaton, Ill.: Victor Books, 1985.

Wood, Michael, and Michael Hughes. "The Moral Basis of Moral Reform: Status Discontent vs. Culture and Socialization as Explanations and Anti-Pornography Social Movement Adherence." *American Sociological Review* 49 (February 1984): 86–99.

Yen, M. "A Morality Who's Who." *Publisher's Weekly*, 11 July 1986, 42–43.

Zurcher, Louis A., Jr., and R. George Kirkpatrick. *Citizens for Decency: Antipornography Crusades as Status Defense*. Austin: University of Texas Press, 1976.

Zurcher, Louis A., Jr., R. George Kirkpatrick, and Robert G. Cushing. "The Anti-Pornography Campaign: A Symbolic Crusade." *Social Problems* 19 (1971): 217–38.

Zurcher, Louis A., Jr., R. George Kirkpatrick, Robert G. Cushing, and Charles K. Bowman. "Ad Hoc Antipornography Organizations." *Journal of Social Issues* 29, no. 3 (1973): 69–93.

CHAPTER 7

Bart, Pauline B. "Pornography: Institutionalizing Women-Hating and Eroticizing Dominance and Submission for Fun and Profit." *Justice Quarterly* 2 (1985): 283–92.

Bart, Pauline B. "Pornography: Hating Women and Institutionalizing Dominance and Submission for Fun and Profit: Response to Alexis M. Durham III." *Justice Quarterly* 3 (1986): 103–6.

Benjamin, Loretta. "The Porno Business." New York: Women for Racial and Economic Equality, .

Blakely, Mary Kay. "Is One Woman's Sexuality Another Woman's Pornography?" *Ms.*, April 1985, 37–47.

Brants, Chrisje, and Erna Kok. "Penal Sanctions a Feminist Strategy: A Contradiction in Terms? Pornography and Criminal Law in the Netherlands." *International Journal of the Sociology of the Law* 14 (August–November 1986): 269–86.

Braudy, Susan. "The Article I Wrote on Women That *Playboy* Wouldn't Publish." *Glamour*, May 1971, 202.

Bryden, David. "Between Two Constitutions: Feminism and Pornography." *Constitutional Commentary* 2 (Winter 1985): 147–89.

Carter, Angela. *The Sadian Woman and the Ideology of Pornography*. New York: Pantheon Books, 1979.

Coderre, Cecile. "Les Luttes de Femmes Contre la Pornographie: Bref Historique Quebecois" (Women's Struggle Against Pornography: A Brief Review of Quebec). *Resources for Feminist Research* 15 (December/January 1986–87): 4.

Cottingham, L. "Pornography: Expression or Oppression." *WIN Magazine*, 15 July 1982, 10–14.

Delcoste, F., and F. Newman. "Stack O' Wheats: An Exercise in Issues." *Fight Back!* 1981, 255.

Diamond, Irene. "Pornography and Repression: A Reconsideration." *Signs:* (1980): 686–781.

di Lenardo, M. "Why We Can't Wait: Pornography as a Socialist-Feminist Issue." *Solidarity Discussion Bulletin*, Winter 1981–82, 51–54.

Duggan, L., "Censorship in the Name of Feminism." *Village Voice*, 16 October 1984.

Durham, Alexis M., III. "Pornography, Social Harm, and Legal Control: Observations on Bart." *Justice Quarterly* 3 (1986): 95–102.

Dworkin, A. *Woman Hating*. New York: E.P. Dutton, 1974.

Dworkin, A. "Pornography: The New Terrorism." *The Body Politic*, August 1978, 11–12.

Dworkin, A. "Pornography: The New Terrorism." *New York University Review of Law and Social Change* 8 (1979): 215–18.

Dworkin, A. *Pornography: Men Possessing Women*. New York: G.P. Putnam's Sons, 1981.

Dworkin, A. "Against the Male Flood: Censorship, Pornography and Equality." *Harvard Women's Law Journal* 8 (1985): 1–29.

Dworkin, A. "Pornography Is a Civil Rights Issue for Women." *University of Michigan Journal of Law Reform* 21, nos. 1, 2 (Fall 1987, and Winter 1988): 55–68.

Eckersley, Robyn. "Whither the Feminist Campaign?: An Evaluation of Feminist Critiques of Pornography." *International Journal of the Sociology of the Law* 15 (May 1987): 149–78.

Ellis, Kate. "42nd Street Porn Shop Tour Belies Simplistic Views." *In These Times* 12–25 March 1980, 16.

Ellis, Kate. "Pornography Won't Go Away." *In These Times*, 15–21 September 1982, 13.

Ellis, Kate. "Pornography and the Feminist Imagination." *Socialist Review*, Summer 1984, 103ff.

Ellis, M., and U. Barnsley. "Pornography's Real Intent: Control of Women." *Kinesis*, March 1983, .

Elshtain, J.B. "The Victim Syndrome: A Troubling Turn in Feminism." *Progressive* 42 (June 1982): 42–47.

English, D. "The Politics of Porn: Can Feminists Walk the Line?" *Mother Jones* 5 (April 1980).

Faust, Beatrice. *Women, Sex and Pornography*. Harmondsworth: Penguin Books, 1980.

"Film of Violence Snuffed Out by Angered Pickets' Protests." *San Diego Union*, 29 September 1977.

Fraser, D.M. "Minneapolis Veto: 'Cherished, Protected Speech.'" *Human Rights* 12 (Spring 1985): 27.

Friday, N. *Men in Love*. New York: Delacorte, 1980.

Friedan, Betty. *The Feminine Mystique*. New York: Dell, 1963.

Friedman, Deb, and Lois Yankowski. "Snuffing Sexual Violence." *Quest*, Fall 1976.

Frye, Marilyn. "Rape and Respect." In *Feminism and Philosophy*, edited by Vetterling-Braggin, Elliston, and English, . Totowa, N.J.: Littlefield, Adams and Co., 1977.

Garry, Ann. "Pornography and Respect for Women." *Social Theory and Practice* 4 (Spring 1978): 395–421.

Garry, Ann. "Pornography and Respect for Women." In *Pornography and Censorship*, edited by David Copp and Susan Wendell, 61–82. New York: Prometheus, 1983.

Gilboa, Netta. "Violent Art and Interest Groups: The Feminist Response to Pornography." Paper presented to the Popular Culture Association, Toronto, April 1984.

Good Girls/Bad Girls—Feminists and Sex Trade Workers in Dialogue. Seattle: Seal Press, 1987.

Griffin, Moira K. "Women, Pornography, and the First Amendment." *Student Lawyer* 9 (December 1980): 24.

Griffin, Susan. "On Pornography." *Chrysalis* 1, no. 4 (1978): .

Griffin, Susan. *Pornography and Silence: Culture's Revenge Against Nature.* New York: Harper & Row, 1981.

Gubar, Susan. "Representing Pornography: Feminism, Criticism, and Depictions of Female Violation." *Critical Inquiry* 13 (1987): 712.

Guettel, Charnie. *Marxism and Feminism.* Toronto: Women's Press, 1974.

Henry, Alice. "Porn Is Subordination?" *Off Our Backs,* November 1984, .

Hoffman, Eric. "Feminism, Pornography and Law." *University of Pennsylvania Law Review* 133 (January 1985): 497–534.

Kaminer, Wendy. "A Woman's Guide to Pornography and the Law." *Nation* 230 (21 June 1980): 754.

Kirkpatrick, R. George, Louis A. Zurcher, Jr., and David Snow. "Feminist Anti-Pornography Crusades in American Society." *International Journal of Sociology and Social Policy* (19): 1–30.

Kostash, M. "Pornography: A Feminist View." *This Magazine,* 1978, 46–50.

Kostash, M. "Power and Control: A Feminist View of Pornography." *This Magazine,* July/August 1978, 4–7.

Langelan, Martha. "The Political Economy of Pornography." *Aegis: Magazine on Ending Violence Against Women* 5 (Autumn 1981): .

Lederer, Laura, ed. *Take Back the Night: Women on Pornography.* New York: Morrow, 1980.

Leidholdt, Dorchen. "Where Pornography Meets Fascism." *WIN,* 15 March 1983, 18–22.

Linden, Robin, et al., eds. *Against Sadomasochism: A Radical Feminist Analysis.* East Palo Alto, Calif.: Frog in the Well Press, 1982.

Liston, Angela A. "Pornography and the First Amendment: The Feminist Balance." *Arizona Law Review* 27, no. 2 (1985): 415–35.

Longino, H.E. "Pornography, Oppression and Freedom: A Closer Look." In *Take Back the Night: Women on Pornography,* edited by Laura Lederer, 40–54. New York: Morrow, 1980.

Lootens, Tricia, and Alice Henry. "Interview: Nikki Craft, Activist and Outlaw." *Off Our Backs,* July 1985, .

MacDonald, S. "Confessions of a Feminist Porn Watcher." *Film Quarterly* 36 (Spring 1983): 10–17.

MacKinnon, C. "Feminism, Marxism, Method and the State: An Agenda for Theory." *Signs* 7 (Spring 1982): 515–44.

MacKinnon, C. "Feminism, Marxism, Method and the State: Toward Feminist Jurisprudence." *Signs* 8 (Summer 1983): 635–58.

MacKinnon, C. "Not a Moral Issue." *Yale Law and Policy Review* 2 (1984): 321–45.

MacKinnon, C. "Feminist Discourse, Moral Values, and the Law: A Conversation." *Buffalo Law Review* 34 (1985): 11.

MacKinnon, C. "Pornography, Civil Rights, and Speech: Commentary." *Harvard Civil Rights–Civil Liberties Law Review* (1985): 20 1–70.

Mahoney, K. "Obscenity, Morals and the Law: A Feminist Critique. *Ottawa Law Review* 17 (1984): 33–71.

Manion, Eileen. "We Objects Object: Pornography and the Women's Movement." *Canadian Journal of Political and Social Theory* 9 (1985): 65–80.

McCarthy, Sarah J. "Pornography, Rape, and the Cult of Macho." *The Humanist* 40 (September/October 1980): 11–16.

McCormack, T., ed. "Feminism, Censorship and Sadomasochistic Pornography." *Studies in Communication* 1 (1980): 37–61.

McCormack, T. "Passionate Protests: Feminists and Censorship: *Canadian Forum* 59 (March 1980): 6–8.

Media Report to Women. (This publication, by the Women's Institute for Freedom of the Press, Washington, D.C., frequently contains information on sexism in the media.)

Millet, Kate. *Sexual Politics.* New York: Doubleday, Equinox Edition, Avon Books, 1969.

Millet, K. *The Prostitution Papers.* New York: Basic Books, 1971.

Milne, Kirsty. "Porn: What Do Women Want?" *Society,* 23 October 1987, 82:18–20.

Morgan, Robin. *Going Too Far.* New York: Vintage Books, 1978.

Morgan, Robin. "How to Run the Pornographers out of Town (and Preserve the First Amendment)." *Ms.,* November 1978, 55.

Morgan, Robin. "Theory and Practice: Pornography and Rape." In *Take Back the Night: Women on Pornography,* edited by Laura Lederer, 134–40. New York: Morrow, 1980.

O'Dair, Barbara. "Sex, Love and Desire: Feminist Debate over the Portrayal of Sexuality." *Alternative Media,* Spring 1983, 12ff.

"Passionate Protests: Feminists and Censorship." *Canadian Forum* 59 (March 1980): 697.

Philipson, Ilene. "The Repression of History and Gender: A Critical Perspective on the Feminist Sexuality Debate." *Signs* 10 (Fall 1984): 113–18.

Ratterman, Debbie. "Pornography: The Spectrum of Harm." *Aegis,* Autumn 1982, .

Rich, Adrienne. "We Don't Have to Come Apart over Pornography." *Off Our Backs,* July 1985, 30.

Ridington, Jill. "Freedom from Harm or Freedom of Speech?" Discussion paper prepared for the National Association of Women and the Law, Ottawa, 1983.

Rosenberg, Linda. "Pornography Is Hazardous to Our Health." *Sapphire Matrix Voice* (Panhoa, Hawaii), Winter 1983, .

Rubin, Gayle. "Anti-Porn Laws and Women's Liberation." *Gay Community News,* 22 December 1984.

Russell, D.E.H. "Pornography: A Feminist Perspective." Presentation at the Women Against Violence and Pornography in the Media symposium, San Francisco, 1977.

Russell, D.E.H. "Pornography: A Feminist Perspective." In *Women Against Violence in Pornography and Media,* edited by , 7–13. Berkeley, Calif.: Berkeley Women's Center, 1977.

Russell, D.E.H. "On Pornography." *Chrysalis* 4 ( ): 11–15.

Russell, D.E.H. "Pornography and the Women's Liberation Movement." In *Take Back the Night: Women on Pornography*, edited by Laura Lederer, 301–6. New York: Morrow, 1980.

Russell, D.E.H. "Censorship Issue Is Muting the Feminists' Attacks on Pornography." *Center Magazine* 14 (May/June 1981): 42–43.

Russo, Ann. "Conflicts and Contradictions among Feminists over Issues of Pornography and Sexual Freedom." *Women's Studies International Forum* 10, no. 2 (1987): 103–12.

Schmidt, G., and V. Sigusch. "Women's Sexual Arousal." In *Contemporary Sexual Behavior*, edited by J. Zubin and J. Money, . Baltimore: Johns Hopkins University Press, 1973.

Shear, Marie. "Free Meat Talks Back." *Journal of Communication* (Winter 1976): 26.

Shepher, Joseph, and Judith Reisman. "Pornography: A Sociobiological Attempt at Understanding." *Ethology and Sociobiology* 6 no. 2 (1985): 103–4.

Smith, . "Violent Pornography and the Women's Movement." *Civil Liberties Review* 4 (January/February 1978): 50.

Smith, Margaret, and Barbara Waisberg. *The Pornography Workshop for Women: A Leader's Handbook*. Toronto: Birch, 1984.

Smith, Marjorie M. " 'Violent Pornography' and the Women's Movement." *Civil Liberties Review* (January/February 1978): .

Soble, Alan. *Pornography: Marxism, Feminism, and the Future of Sexuality*. New Haven, Conn.: Yale University Press, 1986.

Sontag, Susan. "The Pornographic Imagination." In *Perspectives on Pornography*, edited by Douglas A. Hughes, New York: St. Martin's Press, 1970.

Sontag, Susan. *Styles of Radical Will*. New York: Delta, 1978.

Steinem, Gloria. "Pornography: Not Sex but the Obscene Use of Power." *Ms.*, August 1977, 43–44.

Steinem, Gloria. "Erotica and Pornography: A Clear and Present Difference." In *Take Back the Night: Women on Pornography*, edited by Laura Lederer, 35–39. New York: Morrow, 1980.

Steinem, Gloria. *Outrageous Acts and Everyday Rebellions*. New York: Holt, Rinehart & Winston, 1983.

Stever, Ellyn J. "Violent Pornography: Degradation of Women versus Right of Free Speech—A Colloquium." *New York University Review of Law and Social Change* 8–9 (1978–80): 181–204.

Thornton, Neil. "The Politics of Pornography: A Critique of Liberalism and Radical Feminism." *Australian and New Zealand Journal of Sociology* 22 (March 1988): 25–45.

Tong, R. "Feminism, Pornography and Censorship." *Social Theory and Practice* 8 (Spring 1982): 1–17.

Toolin, Cynthia. "Attitudes toward Pornography: What Have the Feminists Missed?" *Journal of Popular Culture* 17 (Fall 1983): 167–74.

Tribe, Laurence. "Between Two Constitutions: Feminism and Pornography." *Constitutional Commentary* 2 (1985): 147–80.

Vance, Carole S., ed. *Pleasure and Danger: Exploring Female Sexuality*. Boston, Routledge and Kegan Paul, 1984.

Vance, Carole S., and Ann Barr Snitow. "Toward a Conversation about Sex in Feminism: A Modest Proposal." *Signs* 10 (Autumn 1984): 128–29.

Vivar, N.A. "The New Anti-Female Violent Pornography: Is Moral Condemnation the Only Justifiable Response?" *Law and Psychology Review* 7 (1982): 53–70.

Wachtel, Eleanor. "Our Newest Battleground: Pornography." *Branching Out* (1979): 6.

Waring, Nancy W. "Coming to Terms with Pornography: Toward a Feminist Perspective on Sex, Censorship, and Hysteria." *Research in Law, Deviance and Social Control* 8 (1986): 86–112.

Willis, Ellen. "Feminism, Moralism, and Pornography." In *Beginning to See the Light: Pieces of a Decade*, edited by , . New York: Knopf, 1981.

Willis, Ellen. "Nature's Revenge: Review of *Pornography and Silence and Pornography*." *New York Times* 12 July 1981.

Willis, Ellen. "Who Is a Feminist?" *Village Voice Literary Supplement*, December 1982, 16–17.

Wolfgang, . "Women's War on Porn." *Time*, 27 August 1979, 64.

Zima, Elizabeth. "There She Is . . . 'Myth America' . . ." *Cedar Rapids Gazette*, 29 September 1984.

CHAPTER 8

Adams, Michael. *Censorship: The Irish Experience*.: University of Alabama Press, 1968.

Allain, A.P. "First and Fourteenth Amendments as They Support Libraries, Librarians, Library Systems, and Library Development." *Women's Law Journal* 60 (Spring 1974): 55–72.

Allan, T.R.S. "A Right to Pornography?" *Oxford Journal of Legal Studies* 3 (Winter 1983): 376–81.

Alput, Leo M. "Judicial Censorship of Obscene Literature." *Harvard Law Review* 52 (November 1938): 40–76.

Appleson, Gail. "Out of Reach: Drive to Ban Library Books Opens New Chapter on Censorship." *American Bar Association Journal* 67 (July 1981): 825–27.

Bachman, Albert *Censorship in France from 1715 to 1750: Voltaire's Opposition*. New York: B. Franklin, 1971.

Baier, K. "Response: The Liberal Approach to Pornography." *University of Pittsburgh Law Review* 40 (Summer 1979): 567–651.

Bailey–Jones, Bonnie B. "Education Law: Local School Board Authority v. Students' First Amendment Rights." *Journal of Juvenile Law* 7 (1983): 40–53.

Baker, Edwin C. "Scope of the First Amendment. Freedom of Speech." *University of California Los Angeles Law Review* 15 (1978): 964–1040.

Balmuth, Daniel. *Censorship in Russia: 1865–1905.* Washington D.C.: University Press of America, 1979.

Baratz, Ellen M. "Constitutional Law—First Amendment: Freedom of Speech." *New York Law School Law Review* 29 (Spring/Summer   ): 469–89.

Barber, John. "Sex and Censorship." *MacLean's* 99 (September 1986): 36–40.

Baren, Charles H. "Protecting News Sources: Playboy Extends Publisher's Rights." *Loyola Entertainment Law Journal* 6 (1986): 221–29.

Barker, Martin, ed. *The Video Nasties: Freedom and Censorship in the Media.* Sydney, Australia: Pluto Press, 1984.

Bartlett, Jonathan, ed. *The First Amendment in a Free Society.* New York: H.W. Wilson Co., 1979.

Beman, Lamar Taney. *Selected Articles on Censorship of the Theater and Moving Pictures.* New York: H.W. Wilson Co., 1931.

Bennett, Mike. "School Library Book Removals." *Arkansas Law Review* 36 (Fall 1983): 551–69.

Berger, Alan. "Pornography: Is Censorship the Answer?" *Boston Real Paper,* 14 September 1979.

Berger, F. "Pornography, Sex, and Censorship." *Social Theory and Practice* 4 (Spring 1977): 183–209.

Berger, F. "Pornography, Sex and Censorship." In *Pornography and Censorship,* edited by David Copp and Susan Wendell, 83–104. New York: Prometheus, 1983.

Berns, Walter. "Pornography vs. Democracy." *The Public Interest* 22 (Winter 1971): 3–24.

Berns, Walter. "Beyond the (Garbage) Pale, or Democracy, Censorship and the Arts." In *The Pornography Controversy,* edited by Ray C. Rist, 40–63. New Brunswick, N.J.: Transaction Books, 1975.

Bernstein, Sidney. "School Censorship." *Trial* 24 (May 1988): 93–94.

Black, Martha L. "School Library Censorship: First Amendment Guarantees and the Student's Right to Know." *University of Detroit Journal of Urban Law* 57 (Spring 1980): 523–45.

Blanchard, Paul. *The Right to Read: The Battle Against Censorship.* Boston: Beacon Press, 1955.

Bodensteiner, Ivan E., and Rosalie Berger Levison. "Civil Liberties: Adherence to Established Principles." *Chicago–Kent Law Review* 58 (Spring 1982): 269–347.

Bogutz, Allan D. "Protection of the Adult's Right to Pornography." *Arizona Law Review* 11 (Winter 1969): 792–806.

Bosmajian, Haig A., ed. *Obscenity and Freedom of Expression.* New York: B. Franklin, 1976.

Bosmajian, Haig A. *Censorship, Libraries and the Law.* New York: Neal–Schuman, 1983.

Bowerman, George Franklin. *Censorship and the Public Library: With Other Papers.* Freeport, N.Y.: Books for Libraries Press, 1967.

Bowers, Kelly. "Banning Books in Public Schools" *Pepperdine Law Review* 10 (March 1983): 545–78.

Boyd, Julian, ed. *The Papers of Thomas Jefferson.* 7 Vol. 6. Princeton, N.J.: Princeton University Press, 1952, 304, 316.

Boyd, N. "Censorship and Obscenity: Jurisdiction and the Boundaries of Free Expression." *Osgoode Hall Law Journal* (Canada) 23 (Spring 1985): 37–66.

Boyer, Paul S. *Purity in Print: The Vice-Society Movement and Book Censorship in America.* New York: Charles Scribner's Sons, 1968.

Braun, Stefan. "Freedom of Expression v. Obscenity Censorship: The Developing Canadian Jurisprudence." *Saskatchewan Law Review* 50, no. 1 (1985–86): 39–73.

Brigman, William E. "Pornography as Political Expression." *Journal of Popular Culture* 17 (Fall 1983): 129–34.

Brookhiser, Richard. "Why Enshrine the First Amendment?" *American Bar Association Journal* 72 (November 1986): 37.

Brooks, Betty. "Censorship Not the Answer to Violence." *Los Angeles Frontiers,* 20–27 March 1985.

Bryson, Joseph E., and Elizabeth W. Detty. *Censorship of Public School Library and Instructional Material.* Charlottesville, Va.: Michie Co., 1982.

Buckley, T.D., Jr., "Student Publications, the First Amendment, and State Speech." *Cleveland State Law Review* 34 (Spring 1985): 267–309.

Burstyn, V. "Censoring Who? Why State Censorship Backfires." *Our Times,* November 1984, 27–44.

Burstyn, V., ed. *Women Against Censorship.* Toronto: Douglas & McIntyre, 1985.

Burstyn, V. "Porn Again: Feeling the Heat of Censorship." *FUSE,* 10 (Spring 1987): 10–18.

Cabe, Robert D. "School Board Censorship: Undemocratic and Unconstitutional." *Arkansas Lawyer* 19 (July 1985): 118–20.

Canadian Civil Liberties Association. *Pornography and the Law.:* Canadian Civil Liberties Association, 1984.

"Censorship." *Encyclopedia Britannica.* Vol 5, 1970:161.

"Censorship and the English Teacher." *Arizona English Bulletin* 11, no. 2 (1969).

Censorship and Freedom of Expression: Essays on Obscenity and the Law. Chicago: Rand McNally, 1971.

"Censorship of Obscene Literature by Informal Government Action." *University of Chicago Law Review* 22 (1954–55): 216–33.

Censorship Litigation and the Schools. Chicago: American Library Association, 1983.

"Censorship and Obscenity: A Panel Discussion (Specter, Ball, Roche, Goldberg)." *Dickinson Law Review* 66 (Summer 1962): 421–41.

Chandos, John, ed. *To Deprave and Corrupt: Original Studies in the Nature and Definition of Obscenity.* New York: Association Press, 1962.

Chemerinsky, Erwin. "Outlawing Pornography: What We

Gain, What We Lose; 'Offensiveness Is Not Enough to Justify Suppressing Free Speech.' " *Human Rights* 12 (Spring 1985): 24.

"The Chilling Effect in Constitutional Law." *Columbia Law Review* 69 (May 1969): 808–42.

Clark, L. "Pornography's Challenge to Liberal Ideology." *Canadian Forum* 59 (March 1980): 9–12.

Clark, L. "Liberalism and Pornography." In *Pornography and Censorship,* edited by David Copp and Susan Wendell, 45–60. New York: Prometheus, 1983.

Clor, Harry. *Obscenity and Public Morality: Censorship in a Liberal Society.* Chicago: University of Chicago Press, 1969.

Clor, Harry. *Censorship and Freedom of Expression.* Chicago: Rand McNally, 1971.

Coggins, Timothy L. "A School Board's Authority v. a Student's Right to Receive Information." *North Carolina Central Law Journal* 14 (Winter 1983): 255–77.

Coggins, Timothy L. "Book Removals from School Libraries and Students' First Amendment Rights." *School Law Bulletin* 17 (Summer 1986): 17–21.

Coleman, Peter. *Obscenity, Blasphemy, Sedition: 100 Years of Censorship in Australia.* Rev. ed. Sydney: Angus & Robertson, 1974.

"Colloquium: Violent Pornography: Degradation of Women versus Right of Free Speech." *New York University Review of Law and Social Change* 8, no. 2 (1978–79): 181.

Comstock, Anthony *Traps for the Young.* Cambridge, Mass.: Belknap Press, 1967.

Conrad, M. "Censorship in America." *Human Rights* 10 (Winter 1982): 28–31.

Cook, Earleen H. *Obscenity: The First Amendment and the Courts.* Monticello, Ill.: Vance Bibliographies, 1979.

Copp, David, and Susan Wendell, eds. *Pornography and Censorship.* New York: Prometheus, 1983.

Cox, Charles Benjamin. *The Censorship Game and How to Play It.* Arlington, Va.: National Council for the Social Studies, 1977.

Craig, Alec. *Suppressed Books: A History of the Conception of Literary Obscenity.* Cleveland: World Publishing Co., 1963.

Daily, Jay Elwood. *The Anatomy of Censorship.* New York: M. Dekker, 1973.

Daniels, Walter M., ed. *Censorship of Books.* New York: H.W. Wilson Co., 1954.

Davenport–Binetsch, Joan. "The First Amendment and Public School Library Censorship." *St. Louis University Law Journal* 27 (April 1983): 461–81.

Davies, Patrick S., Charles R. Shreffler, Jr., and Nancy H. Wilder. "Relevance of Improper Motive to First Amendment Incidental Infringement Claims." *Notre Dame Law Review* 61 (Spring 1986): 272–88.

Davis, Murray S. *Smut, Erotic Reality/Obscene Ideology.* Chicago: University of Chicago Press, 1983.

DeGrazia, E. *Censorship Landmarks.* New York: Bowker, 1969.

DeGrazia, E., and R.K. Newman. *Banned Films: Movies, Censors, and the First Amendment.* New York: Bowker, 1982.

de Sola Pool, Ithiel. *Technologies of Freedom.* Cambridge, Mass.: Belknap Press, 1983.

Dhavon, Rajeev, and Christie Davies, eds. *Censorship and Obscenity.* London: Martin Robertson & Company, 1978.

"Dirty Words and Dirty Politics: Cognitive Dissonance in the First Amendment." *University of Chicago Law Review* 34 (Winter 1967): 367–86.

Donohue, William. *The Politics of the American Civil Liberties Union.* New Brunswick, N.J.: Transaction Books, 1985.

Douglas, William. *Right of the People.* New York: Doubleday, 1958.

Douglas, William. *Is Pornography Protected by the First Amendment? Justice William O. Douglas vs. Ernest van den Haag.* Minneapolis: Greenhaven Press, 1977.

Duggan, Lisa. "Censorship in the Name of Feminism." *Village Voice,* 16 October 1984.

Dunn, Donald J. "Pico and Beyond: School Library Censorship Controversies." *Law Library Journal* 77 (Summer 1985): 435–64.

Dutton, Geoffrey, and Max Harris, eds. *Australia's Censorship Crisis.* Melbourne: Sun Books, 1970.

Dybikowski, J.C. "Law, Liberty, and Obscenity." *University of British Columbia Law Review* 7 (Summer 1972): 33–54.

Ellis, Tottie, and Peter McGrath. "Pornography Must Be Censored." In *Censorship—Opposing Viewpoints,* edited by Terry O'Neill, . St. Paul: Greenhaven Press, 1985.

Elshtain, J. "The New Porn Wars: The Indecent Choice between Censorship and Civil Libertarianism." *New Republic,* 25 June 1984, 15–20.

Emerson, Thomas. *The System of Freedom of Expression.* New York: Vintage Books, 1970.

Ernst, Morris L. *The First Freedom.* New York: Macmillan, 1946.

Ernst, Morris L. *The Censor Marches On: Recent Milestones in the Administration of the Obscenity Law in the United States.* New York: DaCapo Press, 1971.

Ernst, Morris L., and Alan U. Schwartz. *Censorship: The Search for the Obscene.* New York, Macmillan, 1974.

Ernst, Morris L., and William Seagle. *To the Pure: A Study of Obscenity and the Censor.* New York: Viking Press, 1978.

Esposito, Joseph P. "First Amendment Rights—Freedom of Speech." *Annual Survey of American Law* (1978): 135–59.

"Extralegal Censorship of Literature." *New York University Law Review* 33 (1958): 989–1026.

Fact Book Committee. *Caught Looking: Feminism, Pornography and Censorship.* New York: Caught Looking, Inc., 1986.

Fahringer, H.P., and P.C. Cambria, Jr. "The New Weapons Being Used in Waging War Against Pornography." *Capital University Law Review* 7 (1978): 553–78.

Feinberg, Joel. "Limits to the Free Expression of Opinion."

In *Philosophy of Law*. edited by Joel Feinberg and Hyman Gross, Encino and Belmont, Calif.: Dickinson Publishing Co., 1975.

Feinberg, Joel. "Obscenity, Pornography and the Arts: Sorting Things Out." In *Contemporary Value Conflicts*, edited by Burton M. Leiser,   . New York: Macmillan, 1975.

Feinberg, Joel. "Pornography and the Criminal Law." In *Pornography and Censorship,* edited by David Copp and Susan Wendell, 105–38. New York: Prometheus, 1983).

Fellman, David *The Censorship of Books.* Madison: University of Wisconsin Press, 1957.

"Film Censorship: An Administrative Analysis." *Columbia Law Review* 39 (December 1939): 1383–65.

Finch, J.D. "Conspiracy, Society and the Press: The Recent Experience in English Law." *Canadian Bar Review* 50 (September 1972): 522–31.

Finkel, D.B. "Protection or Censorship?" *L. A. B. Journal* 51 (May 1976): 534–38.

Fleishman, S. "Mr. Justice Douglas on Sex Censorship." *L.A.B. Journal* 51 (May 1976): 560–62.

"Flight of the Phoenix: The Censor Returns." *South Dakota Law Review* 19 (Winter 1974): 121–42.

Ford, Paul Leicester, ed. *The Writings of Thomas Jefferson.* Vol. 10. New York: G.P. Putnam's Sons, 1905, 89–90.

Ford, Robert A. "Constitutional Law: Right of School Board to Remove Books from Secondary School Libraries." *Wake Forest Law Review* 19 (February 1983): 119–39.

Frank, John Paul. *Obscenity, the Law, and the English Teacher.* Champaign, Ill.: National Council of Teachers of English, 1966.

"Freedom of Speech and Association: Removing Books from School Libraries." *Harvard Law Review* 96 (November 1982): 151–60.

Friendly, Fred W. *The Good Guys, the Bad Guys, and the First Amendment.* New York: Random House, 1977.

Friendly, Fred W., and Martha J.H. Elliott. *The Constitution—That Delicate Balance.* New York: Random House, 1984.

Gamsky, Elizabeth M. "Judicial Clairvoyance and the First Amendment: The Role of Motivation in Judicial Review of Book Banning in the Public Schools." *University of Illinois Law Review* (Summer 1983): 731–55.

Gardner, Gerald C. *The Censorship Papers: Movie Censorship Letters from the Hays Officer, 1934–1968.* New York: Dodd, Mead, 1987.

Gardiner, Harold. *Catholic Viewpoint on Censorship.* Garden City, N.Y.: Doubleday, Image Books, 1961.

Gellhorn, Walter. "John A. Sibley Lecture: Dirty Books, Disgusting Pictures and Dreadful Laws." *Georgia Law Review* 8 (Winter 1974): 291–312.

Gerhard, Paul. *Pornography in Fine Art from Ancient Times up to the Present.* Los Angeles: Elysium, 1969.

Glass, Marvin. "Left, Pornography and Censorship." *Canadian Dimension* 21 (March 1987): 13–15.

Goodman, Paul. "Pornography, Art and Censorship." In *Perspectives on Pornography,* edited by Douglas A. Hughes,   . New York: St. Martin's Press, 1970.

Grant, Sidney S., and S.E. Angoff. "Massachusetts and Censorship." *Boston University Law Review* 10 (1930): 36–60.

Greeley, John T. *Obscenity: Liberty or License?* Cincinnati: Pamphlet Publications, 1977.

Groarke, L. "Pornography: From Liberalism to Censorship." *Queens Quarterly.* 90 (Winter 1983): 1108–20.

Haiman, Franklin S. *Speech and Law in a Free Society.* Chicago: University of Chicago Press, 1981.

Halfhill, Robert. "Pornography, Free Speech and Gay Separatism." *Gay Community News* (Boston), 8 December 1984.

Haney, Robert W. *Comstockery in America: Patterns of Censorship and Control.* Boston: Beacon Press, 1960.

Haney, Robert W. *Comstockery in America: Patterns of Censorship and Control.* New York: DaCapo Press, 1974.

Harris, Albert W., Jr. "Comment, Movie Censorship and the Supreme Court–What Next?" *California Law Review* 42 (1954): 122–38.

Hart, H.L.A. *Law, Liberty and Morality.* New York: Vintage Books, 1966.

Hart, Harold H., ed. *Censorship, For and Against.* New York: Hart Publishing Co., 1971.

Hawkins, Gordon. *Pornography in a Free Society.* Cambridge, Mass.: Cambridge University Press, 1988.

Hawkins, Kenneth B., and Williard L. King. "Lady Chatterley." *American Bar Association Journal* 48 (January 1962): 43–49.

Hefner, Hugh. "The Playboy Philosophy." *Playboy.* December 1962, and February 1963,   .

Hentoff, N. "Covering a Hustler: Media Watch." *Civil Liberties Review* 4 (August 1977): 50–54.

Hentoff, N. *The First Freedom: The Tumultuous History of Free Speech in America.* New York: Dell, 1980.)

Hinderks, Mark U. "Constitutional Law—Schools: School Board Removal of Books from Libraries and Curricula." *University of Kansas Law Review* 30 (Fall 1981): 146–58.

Hobbes, Thomas. *Leviathan.* London: Routledge and Sons, 1887.

Hoyt, Olga, and Edwin P. Hoyt. *Censorship in America.* New York: Seabury Press, 1970.

Hughes, Patricia. "Pornography: Alternatives to Censorship." *Canadian Journal of Political and Social Theory* 9 (1985): 96–126.

Hunnings, Neville March. *Film Censors and the Law.* London: Allen & Unwin, 1967.

Hunt, Gaillard, ed. *The Writings of James Madison.* Vol. 6. New York: G.P. Putnam's Sons, 1906, 389–92.

Hunter, Nan D. "Power and Pornography." *Village Voice,* 27 November 1984.

Hurley, Dan, ed. "Is It Human or Is It Art? Right to Life Painting Stirs Censorship Controversy." *Student Lawyer* 12 (May 1984): 6.

Hutchins, Peter E. "The First Amendment in the Classroom: Library Book Removals and the Right of

Access to Information." *Boston College Law Review* 23 (September 1982): 1471–1527.

Hyman, Stanley Edgar. "In Defense of Pornography." In *Perspectives on Pornography,* edited by Douglas A. Hughes,   . New York: St. Martin's Press, 1970.

Irvine, Janice. "Carol Vance Discusses FACT." *Sojourner,* December 1985.

Jansen, Sue Curry. *Censorship: The Knot That Binds Power and Knowledge.* New York: Oxford University Press, 1988.

Jenkins, Bruce S. Review of *Pornography and Censorship,* edited by David Copp and Susan Wendell. *Journal of Contemporary Law* 10 (1984): 281–86.

Jenkins, Iredell. "The Legal Basis of Literary Censorship." *Virginia Law Review* 31 (December 1944): 83–118.

Jenkinson, Edward B. *Censors in the Classroom: The Mind Benders.* Carbondale, Ill.: Southern Illinois University Press, 1979.

Jones, Larry, with C.A. Roberts. *Hustler for the Lord.* Plainfield, N.J.: Logos International, 1978.

Jowett, B., trans. *The Dialogues of Plato.* New York: Oxford University Press, 1842.

Kamiat, Walter A. "State Indoctrination and the Protection of Non-State Voices in the Schools: Justifying a Prohibition of School Library Censorship." *Standford Law Review* 35 (February 1983): 497–535.

Kaplan, Abraham. "Obscenity and the Arts." *Law and Contemporary Problems* 20 (Autumn 1955):   .

Kaplan, Abraham. "Obscenity as an Esthetic Category." In *The Pornography Controversy,* edited by Ray C. Rist, 16–39. New Brunswick, N.J.: Transaction Books, 1975.

Karst, Kenneth L. "Equality as a Central Principle in the First Amendment." *University of Chicago Law Review* 43 (1975): 20–68.

Kecskes, Stephen J. "Removal of Library Books vs. Students' Right to Receive Information and Ideas." *University of Toledo Law Review* 14 (Summer 1983): 1329–70.

Kennedy, Jeff. "Constitutional Law: First Amendment Limitations on the Authority of School Boards to Remove Library Books." *Washburn Law Journal* 22 (Spring 1983): 553–63.

Kramer Faaborg, Karen. "High School Play Censorship: Are Students' First Amendment Rights Violated When Officials Cancel Theatrical Productions?" *Journal of Law and Education* 14 (October 1985): 575–94.

Kristol, Irving. "Pornography, Obscenity and the Case for Censorship." *New York Times Magazine,* 28 March 1971.

Kuh, Richard. *Foolish Figleaves?* New York: Macmillan, 1967.

Langvardt, Arlen W. "Not on Our Shelves: A First Amendment Analysis of Library Censorship in the Public Schools." *Nebraska Law Review* 61 (Winter 1982): 98–137.

Larrabee, Eric. "The Cultural Context of Sex Censorship." *Law and Contemporary Problems* 20 (Autumn 1955): 673–88.

Lawrence, David Herbert. *Pornography and Obscenity.* London: Faber & Faber, 1929.

Lawrence, D. H. *Sex, Literature and Censorship.* (New York: The Viking Press, 1953).

Lawrence, D.H. (Harry T. Moore, Editor). *Sex, Literature and Censorship.* (New York: Twayne Publishers, 1953).

Lawrence, David Herbert *Pornography and Obscenity: Handbook for Censors* (Michigan City, Indiana: Fridtjof-Karla, 1958).

Lempinen, Edward W. "The Censor's Voice of America." *Student Lawyer* 17 (October 1988): 4.

"Less Drastic Means and the First Amendment." *Yale Law Journal* 78 (1969): 464–74.

Levy, Leonard W. *Emergence of a Free Press.* New York: Oxford University Press, 1985.

Linde, Hans A. "Courts and Censorship." Part 1. *Minnesota Law Review* 66 (November 1981): 171–208.

Liston, Robert A. *The Right to Know: Censorship in America.* New York: Franklin Watts, 1973.

Lockhart, W.B. "Escape from the Chill of Uncertainty: Explicit Sex and the First Amendment." *Georgia Law Review* 9 (Spring 1975): 533–87.

Lockhart, W.B., and R.C. McClure. "Obscenity Censorship: The Core Constitutional Issue—What Is Obscene?" *Utah Law Review* 7 (Spring 1961): 289–303.

Lorde, Audre. *Uses of the Erotic: The Erotic as Power.* New York: Out and Out Books, 1978.

Lynn, Barry W. "Civil Rights Ordinances and the Attorney General's Commission: New Developments in Pornography Regulation." *Harvard Civil Rights–Civil Liberties Law Review* 21 (Winter 1986): 27–125.

Lynn, Barry W., and Al Goldstein. "Pornography Should Not Be Censored." In *Censorship—Opposing Viewpoints,* edited by Terry O'Neill,   . St. Paul: Greenhaven Press, 1985.

MacMillan, Peter R. *Censorship and Public Morality.* Aldershot, England: Gower, 1983.

Marcuse, F.L. "Some Reflections on Pornography and Censorship." *Canadian Forum* 54 (March 1975): 13–16.

Marcuse, Herbert. "Repressive Tolerance." in *A Critique of Pure Tolerance.* edited by Robert Wolff, Barrington Moore, Jr., and Herbert Marcuse, 81–123. Boston: Beacon Press, 1965.

Marlin, Randall. "Censoring Pornography: With French Summary." *Policy Options Politiques* 7 (November 1986): 9–13, 46.

McClosky, Herbert, and Alida Brill. *Dimensions of Tolerance: What Americans Believe about Civil Liberties.* New York: Basic Books, 1984.

McCormack, Thelma. "Censorship and 'Community Standards' in Canada." In *Communications in Canadian Society.* Vol. 4, edited by Benjamin D. Singer, 320–41. Toronto: Copp Clark Publishing, 1972.

McCormack, Thelma. "Deregulating the Economy and Regulating Morality: The Political Economy of Censorship." *Studies in Political Economy* 18 (1985): 173–85.

McDonald, Fran, and Matthew Stark. *Censorship in Public Elementary and High School Libraries and Public Li-*

braries in Minnesota. Minneapolis: Minnesota Civil Liberties Union, 1983.

Meek, Oscar. *Pornography, Obscenity and Censorship: A Selected Bibliography.* Santa Fe: New Mexico Research Library of the Southwest, 1969.

Meiklejohn, A. *Political Freedom: The Constitutional Powers of the People.* New York: Oxford University Press, 1965.

Meiklejohn, D. "Reconciliation of First Amendment Freedoms with Local Control over the Moral Development of Minors." *Suffolk University Law Review* 12 (Fall 1978): 1205–24.

Menzel, Kelsey. "School Library Book Removal and the First Amendment." *St. Mary's Law Journal* 14 (Fall 1983): 1063–81.

Messall, Rebecca S. "The Public School Library: Who Will Control?" *University of Missouri Kansas City Law Review* 50 (Summer 1982): 567–602.

Michelson, Peter. "The Pleasures of Commodity, or How to Make the World Safe for Pornography." In *The Pornography Controversy*, edited by Ray C. Rist, 140–58. New Brunswick, N.J.: Transaction Books, 1975.

Mill, John Stuart. *On Liberty.* Indianapolis: Bobbs–Merrill, 1956.

Miller, Henry. *Obscenity and the Law of Reflection.* New York: Chapbooks, 1945.

Miller, Janella. "The First Amendment Does Not Protect Pornography." In *Censorship—Opposing Viewpoints*, edited by Terry O'Neill,　. St. Paul: Greenhaven Press, 1985.

Miller, R. *Bunny.* New York: Holt, Rinehart & Winston, 1980.

Mishan, Edward J. *Pornography, Psychedelics and Technology: Essays on the Limits to Freedom.* Boston: Allen & Unwin, 1980.

Mitchell, Richard H. *Censorship in Imperial Japan.* Princeton, N.J.: Princeton University Press, 1983.

Munic, Martin U. "Education or Indoctrination: Removal of Books from Public School Libraries." *Minnesota Law Review* 68 (October 1983): 213–53.

Murphy, Earl F. "Value of Pornography." *Wayne Law Review* 10 (Summer 1964): 655–80.

Murphy, Terrence J. *Censorship: Government and Obscenity.* Baltimore: Garamond Press, 1963.

National College Competition Winning Essays on the Subject Obscenity: Censorship or Free Choice? San Diego: Greenleaf Classics, 1971.

Nelson, Jack, and Gene Roberts, Jr. *The Censors and the Schools.* Boston: Little, Brown, 1963.

Nestle, Joan. "My History with Censorship." *Bad Attitude*, Spring 1985, 2ff.

New York Public Library. *Censorship: 500 Years of Conflict.* Oxford, England: Oxford University Press, 1984.

Nielsen Forbes, Christopher. "Constitutional Law—First Amendment: School Officials Entitled to Regulate Contents of School Sponsored Newspaper in Reasonable Manner." *St. Mary's Law Review* 19 (Spring 1988): 1133–39.

Nordquist, Joan. *Pornography and Censorship.* Santa Cruz, Calif.: Reference and Research Services, 1987.

Noyce, John L. *Censorship in Public Libraries.* Brighton: Noyce, 1977.

Oboler, Eli M. *The Fear of the Word: Censorship and Sex.* Metuchen, N.J.: Scarecrow Press, 1974.

Oboler, Eli M., ed. *Censorship and Education.* New York: H.W. Wilson Co., 1981.

Office for Intellectual Freedom of the American Library Association. *Intellectual Freedom Manual.* Chicago: American Library Association, 1983.

O'Higgins, Paul. *Censorship in Britain.* London: Nelson, 1972.

O'Neill, Terry, ed. *Censorship—Opposing Viewpoints.* St. Paul: Greenhaven Press, 1985.

Pally, Marcia. "Ban Sexism, Not Pornography." *Nation*, 29 June 1985, 794ff.

Parker, Barbara, and Stefanie Weiss. *Protecting the Freedom to Learn.* Washington, D.C.: People for the American Way, 1983.

Pascal, C.B. "A Question of Censorship: Science of Moral Persuasion." *Contemporary Psychology* 22 (1977): 579–80.

Patterson, Annabel M. *Censorship and Interpretation: The Conditions of Writing and Reading in Early Modern England.* Madison: University of Wisconsin Press, 1984.

Paul, James C.N. *Federal Censorship: Obscenity in the Mail.* Westport, Conn.: Greenwood Press, 1961.

Paul, James C.N., and Murray L. Schwartz. *Federal Censorship: Obscenity in the Mail.* New York: Free Press, 1961.

Paulus Sorenson, Gail. "Removal of Books from School Libraries 1972–1982: Board of Education v. Pico and Its Antecedents." *Journal of Law and Education* 12 (July 1983): 417–41.

Peary, Gerald. "Woman in Porn." *Take One*, September 1978, 28–32.

Peckham, Morse. *Art and Pornography.* New York: Basic Books, 1969.

Perry, Stuart. *Indecent Publications: Control in New Zealand.* Wellington: P.D. Hasselberg, Government Printer, 1980.

Peterson, Christine R. "Protecting the Pornographer's Constitutional Right to Free Speech." *Ohio Northern University Law Review* 13 (Summer 1986): 553–60.

Pherigo, Cherlyn. "Book Removal in Secondary Schools: A Violation of the First Amendment?" *Akron Law Review* 17 (Winter 1984): 483–93.

Pilpel, H.F. "Dirty Business in Court." *Civil Liberties Review* 1 (Fall 1974): 30–41.

"Playboy, Penthouse Sue Porn Commission Over 'Threat' Against Magazine Retailers." *News Media and the Law* 10 (Summer 1986): 22.

Poole, Howard. "Obscenity and Censorship." *Ethics* 93 (October 1982): 39–44.

"Pornography: Love or Death?" *Film Comment*, December 1984,　.

Pornography and Obscenity Handbook for Censors: Two Essays By D.H. Lawrence and Henry Miller. Michigan City, Ind.: Fridtjof–Karla Publications, 1958.

Pray, Lee. "What Are the Limits to a School Board's Authority to Remove Books from School Library

Shelves?" *Wisconsin Law Review* (Summer 1982): 417–71.

Pressy, James Boyce, Jr. "Constitutional Law—Freedom of Expression and the Censor." *South Carolina Law Review* 22 (1970): 115–25.

Preuhs, Sandra. "Constitutional Law—First Amendment—Book Removals—School Boards: The United States Supreme Court Has Held That Removals of Books from High School Libraries May Not Be Motivated by the Political, Moral or Social Tastes of School Board Members, or a Desire of the Board to Suppress Access to Ideas with Which They Disagree." *Duquesne Law Review* 21 (Summer 1983): 1055–82.

Purdon, R.L. "Pornography in the Dormitories: A Commander's Dilemma." *A.F. J.A.G. Law Review* 14 (May 1973): 146.

Quenemoen, Helen M. "The Supreme Court's Answer to School Library Censorship." *Ohio State Law Journal* 44 (Winter 1983): 1103–24.

Quick, Albert T. "What Johnny Can't Read: The Supreme Court Book Removal." *Journal of Law and Education* 12 (January 1983): 116–26.

Randall, Richard S. *Censorship of the Movies.* Madison: University of Wisconsin Press, 1968.

Rapping, Elayne. "Banning Pornography Solves No Problems and Worsens Some." *Guardian,* 19 December 1984.

Redish, Martin H. "The Value of Free Speech." *University of Pennsylvania Law Review* 130 (January 1982): 591–645.

Reed, Michael. "What Johnny Can't Read: School Boards and the First Amendment." *University of Pittsburgh Law Review* 42 (Spring 1981): 653–67.

Regan Henry, Susan. "The Perimeters of School Boards' Censorship." *Brooklyn Law Review* 48 (Summer 1982): 869–96.

Rembar, Charles. *The End of Obscenity: The Trials of Lady Chatterley, Tropic of Cancer and Fanny Hill.* New York: Random House, 1968.

Rembar, Charles. "Obscenity—Forget It." *Atlantic,* May 1977, 37–41.

Ricci, Richard. "Public School Library Book Removals: Community Values v. First Amendment Freedoms." *Notre Dame Lawyer* 57 (October 1981): 166–88.

Rist, Ray C., ed. *The Pornography Controversy.* New Brunswick, N.J.: Transaction Books, 1975.

Rohrer, Daniel M. *Mass Media, Freedom of Speech, and Advertising: A Study in Communication Law.* Dubuque, Iowa: Kendall/Hunt Publishing Co., 1979.

Rolph, Cecil Hewitt. *Books in the Dock.* London: Deutsch, 1969.

Scanlon, T.M. "Freedom of Expression and Categories of Expression." *University of Pittsburgh Law Review* 40 (1979): 519–50.

Scanlon, T.M. "Freedom of Expression and Categories of Expression." In *Pornography and Censorship,* edited by David Copp and Susan Wendell, 139–67. New York: Prometheus, 1983.

Schenkkan, P.M. "Comment: Power in the Marketplace of Ideas: The Fairness Doctrine and the First Amendment." *Texas Law Review* 52 (April 1974): 727–72.

Schexhaydre, Linda, Nancy Burns, and Emporia State University School of Library and Information Management. *Censorship: A Guide for Successful Workshop Planning.* Phoenix: Oryx Press, 1984.

Schmitz, Anthony. "The Purity Patrol (Censorship Pressures)." *Student Lawyer* 10 (October 1981):

Schopflin, George, ed. *Censorship and Political Communication in Eastern Europe.* London: Frances Pinter, 1983.

Schroder, Theodore Albert. *'Obscene' Literature and Constitutional Law: A Forensic Defense of Freedom of the Press.* New York: DaCapo Press, 1972.

Sheinfeld, Lois. "Banning Porn: The New Censorship." *Nation,* 8 September 1984,

Sheinfeld, Lois. "The First Amendment Forbids Censorship." In *Censorship—Opposing Viewpoints,* edited by Terry O'Neill. St. Paul: Greenhaven Press, 1985.

Smith, Marjorie M. "'Violent Pornography' and the Women's Movement." *Civil Liberties Review* (January/February 1978): 50–53.

Stomer, Curtis V. "Curbing Media Sex and Violence by Means Other Than Censorship." *Christian Science Monitor,* 25 May 1985.

Sutherland, John Andrew. *Offensive Literature: Decensorship in Britain 1960–1982.* Totowa, N.J.: Barnes and Noble Books, 1983.

Tadman, Martin. "Obscenity, Civil Liberty and the Law." *Chitty's Law Journal* 21 (1973): 226–33.

Thomas, Donald. *A Long Time Burning: The History of Literary Censorship in England.* New York: Praeger, 1969.

Toward a General Theory of the First Amendment. New York: Random House, 1966.

Tribe, David H. *Questions of Censorship.* London: Allen & Unwin, 1973.

Tudzarov, Louise E. "Censorship in the Public School Library: State, Parent and Child in the Constitutional Arena." *Wayne Law Review* 27 (Fall 1980): 167–91.

van Dyke, Michael S. "Regulation of Pornography: Is Erotica Self-Expression Deserving of Protection?" *Loyola Law Review* 33 (Summer 1987): 445–68.

Vance, C.S. "What Does the Research Prove?" *Ms.,* April 1985.

Veal Singleton, Sherrill. "Constitutional Law—Book Removals from Public School Libraries—First Amendment Rights of Secondary School Students and School Board Authority—Establishing a Constitutional Standard for Review." *Land and Water Law Review* 18 (Fall 1983): 837–55.

Waggoner, Tracy A. "The First Amendment and Censorship of Books in Schools." *Washington University Journal of Urban and Contemporary Law* 25 (1983): 385–409.

Warren, Earl Jr. "Obscenity Laws—A Shift to Reality." In *The Pornography Controversy,* edited by Ray C. Rist, 96–118. New Brunswick, N.J.: Transaction Books, 1975.

Watson, William G. "Pornography and Liberalism." *Political Options* 6 (June 1985): 18–21.

Wenglin, Barbara Nedell. *The Effects of the 1973 Supreme Court Obscenity Ruling on the Public Library: A Survey.* Washington, D.C.: Educational Resources Information Center, 1974.

Wellington, H. "On Freedom of Expression." *Yale Law Journal* 88 (1979): 1105–42.

Wexton, Jane L. "A School Board's Decision to Remove Books." *Hofstra Law Review* 12 (Winter 1984): 581–92.

Widmer, Eleanor, ed. *Freedom and Culture: Literary Censorship in the 70's.* Belmont, Calif.: Wadsworth Publishing Co., 1970.

Williams, Bernard. "Offensiveness, Pornography, and Art." In *Pornography and Censorship,* edited by David Copp and Susan Wendell, 185–206. New York: Prometheus, 1983.

Woods, L.B. *A Decade of Censorship in America: The Threat to Classrooms and Libraries.* Metuchen, N.J.: Scarecrow Press, 1979.

CHAPTER 9

Abel, Robert M. "Constitutional Law—First Amendment: Obscenity Not Constitutionally Protected." *American University Law Review* 7 (January 1958): 39–41.

Abelson, David, and Robert Crow. "Note: The Scienter Element in California's Obscenity Laws: Is There a Way to Know?" *Hastings Law Journal* 24 (May 1973): 1303–25.

Ablard, C.D. "Obscenity, Advertising, and Publishing: The Impact of Ginzburg (Ginzburg v. U.S., 86 S. Ct. 942) and Mishkin (Mishkin v. New York, 86 S. Ct. 958)." *George Washington Law Review* 35 (October 1966): 85–92.

Abse, D.W. "Psychodynamic Aspects of the Problem of Definition of Obscenity." *Law and Contemporary Problems* 20 (Autumn 1955): 572–88.

"Administrative Law: Scope of Judicial Review: Constitutional Questions in a Determination of Obscenity." *University of California Los Angeles Law Review* 8 (May 1961): 634–38.

Alexander, Judy. "Obscenity as Protected Speech: A Proposal for a New Analytic Approach to a Persistent Judicial Problem." *Beverly Hills Bar Association Journal* 17 (Fall 1983): 229.

"Alleged Obscenity as a Cause for Suppression." *Virginia Law Review* 9 (1923): 216.

Alpert, L.M. "Judicial Censorship of Obscene Literature." *Harvard Law Review* 52 (November 1938): 40–76.

Alschuler, M. "Origins of the Law and Obscenity." In *Presidential Commission on Obscenity and Pornography.* Vol. 2, Washington, D.C.: GPO, 1970.

Amen, M. "Church Legislation on Obscenity." *Catholic Lawyer* 10 (Spring 1964): 109–28.

Amen, M. "Church versus Obscene Literature." *Catholic Lawyer* 11 (Winbter 1965): 21–32.

Anastapio, G. "Obscenity and Common Sense: Toward a Definition of 'Community' and 'Individuality.' " *St. Louis University Law Journal* 16 (Summer 1972): 527.

Anderson, Robert L. "Free Speech and Obscenity: A Search for Constitutional Procedures and Standards." *University of California Los Angeles Law Review* 12 (January 1965): 532–60.

Andre, Judith. "Poole on Obscenity and Censorship. (Howard Poole's Obscenity and Censorship, from the

93 Ethics 1982, 39044)." *Ethics* 94 (April 1984): 496–500.

Andrews, John. "Freedom of Expression and the Export of Pornography." *European Law Review* 9 (June 1984): 203.

Antrim, Stanley E. "Obscene Publications and the Constitution—Censorship v. Freedom of the Press." *Washburn Law Journal* 4 (Winter 1964): 114–27.

"Application of a Local or National Standard of Decency in the Use of the Roth-Memoirs Obscenity Test." *Washington University Law Quarterly* (Fall 1971): 691–95.

Arnebergh, Roger. "Pornography and 'Community Standards.' " *Dicta* 37 (July/August 1960): 231–36.

Aronson, Stephen D. "Constitutional Law—Criminal Law—Obscenity: Constitutionality of Massachusetts Obscenity Statute." *Suffolk University Law Review* 9 (Fall 1974): 255–67.

Arthur, Stephen E., and Christopher D. Seigel. "Constitutional Law (Survey of Indiana Law)." *Indiana Law Review* 14 (January 1981): 185–222.

Asencio, José Benito Diaz. "Freedom of Speech and Obscenity Standards in the United States: Their Applicability to Puerto Rico." *Revista of Juridica University of Puerto Rico* 35, no.3 (1966): 423–50.

"Attack on Confessional as Obscenity." *Law Notes* (N.Y.) 11 (1907): 85.

"Attorney-General ex rel McWhirter v. Independent Broadcasting Authority (1973)." *Law Quarterly Review* 89 (July 1973): 329–31.

Balter, Harry Graham. "Obscenity: Some Observations Concerning the Federal Statutes." *Southern California Law Review* 8 (1935): 267.

Banner, Tim K. "Constitutional Law—Criminal Law—Obscenity." *Texas Law Review* 44 (July 1966): 1382–89.

Barber, John Linder. "Note: The Geography of Obscenity's Contemporary Community Standard." *Wake Forest Law Review* 8 December (1971): 81–92.

Barish, Lawrence. *Determining the Limits of Free Expression: A New Look at the Obscenity Issue.* Madison, Wisc.: Legislative Reference Bureau, 1971.

Barnett, C.S. "Obscenity and s.150(8) of the Criminal

Code." *Criminal Law Quarterly* 12 (December 1969): 10–29.

Barth, Roger V. "Pennsylvania—A Cinematic Gomorrah." *Buffalo Law Review* 11 (Winter 1962): 389.

Bates, Frank. "Pornography and the Expert Witness." *Criminal Law Quarterly* 20 (March 1978): 250–64.

Baughman, Thomas H. "Obscenity—Obscene Publications—Pandering." *Case Western Reserve Law Review* 19 (April 1968): 748–56.

Baum, T.L. "California's New Law on Obscene Matter." *California State Bar Journal* 36 (September/October 1961): 625–35.

Beckett, J.S. "Obscenity: Ward v. Illinois—The Miller Promise Abandoned." *Chicago Bar Record* 60 (January/February 1979): 183–84.

Beckett, Steven J., and Roderick A. Bell. "Community Standards: Admitting a Public Opinion Poll into Evidence in an Obscenity Case." *Case and Comment* 84 (1979): 18–24.

Beckwith, Harry G., Jr. "Comments: Oregon's Obscenity Bill: New Fig Leaves, Old Faux Pas." *Oregon Law Review* 53 (Spring 1973–74): 375–92.

Bell, Roderick A., "Determining Community Standards." *American Bar Association Journal* 63 (September 1977): 1202–7.

Benjoya, M., R.L. Zisson, and D.J. LaCroix. "Obscenity: The New Law and Its Enforcement—Two Views." *Suffolk University Law Review* 8 (Fall 1973): 1–37.

Bentil, J. Kodwo. "Obscenity Law and Foreigners." *Solicitor's Journal* 126 (16 July 1982): 473–76.

Berbysse, E.J. "Conflict in the Courts: Obscenity Control and First Amendment Freedoms." *Catholic Lawyer* 20 (Winter 1974): 1–29.

Berk, Steven N. "Expert Testimony in Obscenity Litigation." *Annual Survey of Massachusetts Law* 30 (1983): 354–60.

Berman, J.B. "Use of Advisory Juries in Obscenity Cases." *Missouri Bar Journal* 33 (July/August 1977): 282–89.

Berndt, Frank. "Constitutional Law—Anti-Obscenity Legislation." *Western Reserve Law Review* 12 (March 1961): 425–30.

Bertelsman, William O. "Injunctions Against Speech and Writing: A Re-Evaluation." *Kentucky Law Journal* 59 (1970): 319–50.

Betts, Brenda Bowe. "Pennsylvania Obscenity Law: A Pornographer's Delight." *University of Pittsburgh Law Review* 41 (Winter 1980): 251–73.

"Bills v. Brown (1974)." *University of Tasmania Law Review* 5 (1976): 194–97.

Black, Robert C. "Obscenity and Freedom of Expression in Michigan." *University of Detroit Journal of Urban Law* 56 (Fall 1978): 27–97.

Blakey, James. "Postal Obscenity Prosecutions after Miller v. California: Mandatory Venue in the Federal District of Intended Receipt." *Boston University Law Review* 58 (January 1978): 79–94.

"Blasphemy and Obscenity." *C.L. Ten. Brit. J. L. Soc.* 5 (Summer 1978): 89–96.

Blodgett, Nancy. "RICO v. First Amendment: Statute Used to Seize Assets in Fight Against Pornography." *American Bar Association Journal* 73 (November 1987): 17.

Bloomberg, Mitchell R. "Pornography: An Obscene Clarification." *University of Miami Law Review* 28 (Fall 1973): 238–46.

"Book Banning: The Complete Findings and Rulings in the Case of Commonwealth v. 'Forever Amber.' " *Massachusetts Law Quarterly* 32 (May 1947): 79–84.

"Bookcase, Inc. v. Broderick (NY) 218 N.E. 2d 668." *Kansas Law Review* 15 (December 1966): 198–201.

Borman, Susan, and William Rush. "Obscenity: A Matter of Individual Conscience?" *Journal of Urban Law* 47 ( ): 490–521.

Boyd, Neil. "Censorship and Obscenity: Jurisdiction and the Boundaries of Free Expression." *Osgoode Hall Law Journal* (Canada) 23 (Spring 1985): 37–66.

Boyer, Ronald L. "Bee See Books, Inc. v. Leary, 291 F. Supp. 622." *Arkansas Law Review* 23 (Fall 1969): 487–92.

Bradley, Lawrence James, and Joseph A. Marino. "Constitutional Law—Freedom of Speech—Obscenity 1958–1960." *Notre Dame Law Review* 35 (August 1960): 537–46.

Bradley, Michael R. "Constitutional Law—Obscenity—The Evolving Definition of Obscenity." *Villanova Law Review* 7 (Winter 1961–62): 287–91.

Brannigan, Augustine. "Crimes from Comics: Social and Political Determinants of Reform of the Victoria Obscenity Law 1938–1954." *Australian and New Zealand Journal of Criminology* 19, no. 1 (1986): 23–42.

Bray, J.J. "The Juristic Basis of the Law Relating to Offenses Against Public Morality and Decency." *Australian Law Journal* 46 (March 1972): 100–108.

Breuer, Peter, and J.C. Smith. "Indecent or Obscene Articles: Whether Goods Which Can Be Lawfully Made and Sold within the United Kingdom Can Be Held to Be Prohibited from Importation by Section 42 of the Customs Consolidation Act 1876—Section 2 European Communities Act 1972—Articles 30 and 36 of the Treaty of the European Communities—Obscene Publications Act 1959." *Criminal Law Review* (Great Britain) (August 1986): 562–64.

Brigman, William E. "The Controversial Role of the Expert in Obscenity Litigation." *Capital University Law Review* 7 (1978): 519–51.

Bromberg, Benjamin. "Five Tests for Obscenity." *Chicago Bar Record* 41 (May 1960): 416–22.

Bronson, Peter C. "New Prosecutorial Techniques and Continued Judicial Vagueness: An Argument for Abandoning Obscenity as a Legal Concept." *University of California Los Angeles Law Review* 21 (October 1973): 181–241.

Brown, Gene D. "Florida's Obscenity Statutes—Some Recommendations." *University of Florida Law Review* 18 (Summer 1965): 135–41.

Brown, Ray W. "Constitutional Law: Freedom of the Press: Injunctions: Obscene Literature." *Cornell Law Quarterly* 42 (Winter 1957): 256–61.

Buchanan, G.S. "Obscenity and Brandenburg: The Missing

Link?" *Houston Law Review* 11 (March 1974): 537–82.

Bucknell, Patrick, and J.C. Smith. "Trial of Retailer of Obscene Videos Where a Supplier Had Been Acquitted at an Earlier Trial: Obscene Publications Act, 1959." *Criminal Law Review* (Great Britain) (January 1986): 46–47.

Buckner, David E. "Constitutional Law—Regulation of Obscene Matter." *North Carolina Law Review* 36 (Fall 1958): 189–98.

"Burger Court's Crunch on 'Hard Core.'" *Ohio Northern Law Review* 1 (1973): 97–110.

Burgess, Wells D. "Obscenity Prosecution: Artistic Value and the Concept of Immunity." *New York University Law Review* 39 (December 1964): 1063–86.

Burkoff, J.M., and V.T. Adamo. "Obscenity under the Michigan Constitution: Protected Expression?" *Michigan State Bar Journal* 54 (December 1975): 964–75.

Burnett, A.L. "Obscenity: Search and Seizure and the First Amendment." *Denver Law Journal* 51 (1974): 41–74.

Burt, Kristin M. "Nude Entertainment as Protected Expression: A Federal/State Law Conflict after Crownover v. Musick." *Santa Clara Law Review* 22 (Winter 1982): 211–34.

Bustamante, Luis C. "Comment: Pornography, The Local Option." *Baylor Law Review* 26 (Winter 1974): 97–107.

Buttarazzi, Ronald J. "Enjoining Distribution of Obscene Literature Not an Unconstitutional 'Prior Restraint.'" *Syracuse Law Review* 8 (Fall 1956): 106–9.

Byrne, Edward T. "Government Seizures of Imported Obscene Matter: Section 305 of the Tariff Act of 1930 and Recent Supreme Court Obscenity Decisions." *Columbia Journal of Transnational Law* 13, no. 1 (1974): 114–42.

Caesar, Cary Douglas. "First Amendment—Freedom of Speech—Obscenity. *Pinkus v. United States*, 98 Supreme Court 1808 (1978)." *Akron Law Review* 12 (Fall 1978): 309–16.

Cairns, R.B., J.C.N. Paul, and J. Wishner. "Sex Censorship: The Assumptions of Anti-Obscenity Laws and the Empirical Evidence." *Minnesota Law Review* 46 (May 1962): 1009–41.

Caldwell, John L. "Judicial Review—Locus Standi." *New Zealand Law Journal* (July 1987): 203–5.

Canada. Law Reform Commission. *Limits of Criminal Law: Obscenity, A Test Case.* Ottawa: Information Canada, 1975.

"Candor or Shame? Defining Obscenity by Statute." *Oklahoma Bar Association Journal* 38 (24 June 1967): 1333–45.

Cappi, P. "Handyside Case." *New Law Journal* 127 (3 November 1977): 1064–66.

Cardin, Tom. "Constitutional Law—Obscenity and Minors." *Arkansas Law Review* 22 (Winter 1969): 768–72.

Carpenter, Edwin P. "Walton's Castle: The Spectrum of 'I Am Curious Yellow.'" *Washburn Law Journal* 10 (Fall 1970): 163–76.

Cartolano, F.J., and A.B. Dennison. "Hustler Trial: Two Opinions on the Use of Comparative Evidence in Determining Community Standards in Obscenity Litigation." *Northern Kentucky Law Review* 4 (1977): 195–224.

"Censorship of Motion Pictures." *Yale Law Journal* 49 (1939): 87–113.

"Changing Standards for Obscenity." *Santa Clara Law Review* 6 (Spring 1966): 206.

Charles, John. "Criminal Law: Seizure of Allegedly Obscene Material—Requirement of a Prior Adversary Hearing." *Ohio State Law Journal* 32 (Summer 1971): 668–73.

Charles, W.H. "Obscene Literature and the Legal Process in Canada." *Canadian Bar Review* 44 (1966): 243–92.

Chew, Deborah. "Informal Prosecutorial Communications and Prior Restraint in Obscenity Cases: Resolving the Conflict of Interests." *Columbia-VLA Journal of Law and the Arts* 12 (Winter 1988): 249–76.

Cihlar, Frank P., Michael K. Cook, Joseph P. Martor, Jr., and Paul J. Meyer. "Obscenity." *Notre Dame Law Review* 41 (June 1966): 753–85.

Clancy, Carol A. *Pornography: Solutions through Law.* Washington, D.C.: National Forum Foundation, 1985.

Clardy, Bert L. "Recent Decisions: Constitutional Law—Obscenity—Film Censorship." *Baylor Law Review* 17 (Winter 1965): 119–21.

Clark, C.D.L. "Obscenity, the Law and Lady Chatterley." *Criminal Law Records* (March/April 1961): 156–224.

Clor, H. "Obscenity and the First Amendment: Round Three." *Loyola University of Los Angeles Law Review* 7 (June 1974): 207–26.

Clor, H. "Obscenity and the Law. Public Morality and Free Expression: the Judicial Search for Principles of Reconciliation." *Hastings Law Journal* 28 (July 1977): 1275–1358.

Cockburn, Ruth Barkley. "Criminal Law—Constitutional Law—Obscenity—'Immoral Publications.'" *South Texas Law Journal* 6 (Fall 1961): 57–59.

Coen, Ronald S. "Note: Cohen v. California: A New Approach to an Old Problem." *California Western Law Review* 9 (1972): 171–83.

Cohen, F. "Obscenity Cases: Anatomy of a Winning Defense." *Criminal Law Bulletin* 14 (May/June 1978): 225–31.

Cohen, Steven I. "Constitutional Law—Obscene Literature: Wisconsin Statute Provides Civil Action Against a Book." *Wisconsin Law Review* (March 1960): 309–24.

Cohen, W. "A Look Back at Cohen v. California." *University of California Los Angeles Law Review* 34 (June/August 1987): 1595–614.

Collins, Isobel. "Information Alleging Possession of Five Obscene Articles for Publication for Gain: Whether Information Charging Only One Criminal Activity. *Criminal Law Review* (Great Britain)." (April 1985): 219–20.

Collins, John J. "New York—Laws of the 178th Session—Publication and Distribution of Comic Books—Sale to Minors." *Villanova Law Review* 1 (May 1956): 323–31.

Commons, Glenn D. "Washington's 'Anti-Pornography' Initiative Declared Unconstitutional." *Gonzaga Law Review* 14, no. 1 (1978): 237–50.

"Community Standards, Class Actions, and Obscenity Under Miller v. California." *Harvard Law Review* 88 (June 1975):1838–74.

Conner, J.S. "Obscenity: Its Moral Meaning and Scope." *Catholic Law* 27 (Winter 1981): 70–78.

Connors, Francis P. "Constitutional Law—Freedom of Speech—Obscenity Statutes." *Villanova Law Review* 3 (November 1957): 71–79.

"Constitutional Law—Censorship—Obscenity: Nonmailability." *Tennessee Law Review* 30 (Winter 1963): 291–96.

"Constitutional Law—Censorship: Standard for Suppression of 'Filthy' Material Distinct from That for Obscenity." *Iowa Law Review* 49 (1964): 552–60.

"Constitutional Law—Due Process—Mens Rea. Invalidity of Ordinance Imposing Absolute Criminal Liability on Bookseller Processing Obscene Material." *New York University Law Review* 35 (May 1960): 1086–96.

"Constitutional Law—Federal Censorship: Revised Standard for Obscenity." *Fordham Law Review* 31 (Fall 1963): 570–77.

"Constitutional Law—Federal and State Obscenity Statutes: No Violation of First Amendment Rights When Interpreted by Community Standard." *Howard Law Journal* 4 (January 1958): 105–9.

"Constitutional Law—First Amendment Freedoms: Statute Prohibiting Obscene Materials in the Mails." *Brooklyn Law Review* 29 (April 1963): 325–28.

"Constitutional Law—First Amendment—Obscenity: Within a Period of Less Than Four Months, the Supreme Court of Georgia Issued Two Opinions Upholding the Application of Georgia's Obscenity Statutes to Cases Begun Prior to the Formulation of the New Constitutional Guidelines but Reached Apparently Opposite Results on the Issue of Which 'Community Standard' to Be Applied in Obscenity Cases." *Georgia Law Review* 8 (Fall 1973): 225–53.

"Constitutional Law—First Amendment: Statute Prohibiting the Importation of Obscene Material into the United States Does Not Violate Constitutional Rights of Persons Importing Such Material for Private Use." *Alabama Law Review* 24 (Fall 1971): 120–30.

"Constitutional Law—First Amendment: Statute Prohibiting the Importation of Obscene Matter into the United States Infringes the Right of Adults to Possess Such Matter." *Alabama Law Review* 23 (Fall 1970): 135–42.

"Constitutional Law—Free Press—Prior Restraints of Obscenity." *Minnesota Law Review* 41 (January 1957): 222–28.

"Constitutional Law: Freedom of Expression of Minors Not Infringed by a Variable Obscenity Standard Stating Sufficiently Definite Classifications." *Brooklyn Law Review* 35 (Fall 1968): 109–17.

"Constitutional Law—Freedom of Press—Obscenity Standards: Memoirs v. Massachusetts, Ginzberg v. United States, Mishkin v. New York (United States Supreme Court, 1966)." *Albany Law Review* 31 (January 1967): 143–52.

"Constitutional Law—Freedom of Speech: Lack of Scienter Element in City Ordinance Against Obscenity Violates First Amendment." *William and Mary Law Review* 2 (1960): 491–96.

"Constitutional Law–Freedom of Speech and Press: Determination of Obscenity." *West Virginia Law Review* 62 (February 1960): 179–81.

"Constitutional Law—Freedom of Speech: Statute Proscribing Conscious Possession of Obscene Materials Is Upheld Only for Failure to Obtain Exceptional Majority Required by Ohio Constitution for Invalidation." *Harvard Law Review* 74 (February 1961): 779–81.

"Constitutional Law: Legal History of the Problems Posed by the Publication of 'Obscene' Literature Traced—Protection of First and Fourteenth Amendments and Standard of Obscenity Discussed." *New York Law Forum* 6 (April 1960): 313–20.

"Constitutional Law—Obscenity." *West Virginia Law Review* 60 (December 1957): 89–91.

"Constitutional Law–Obscenity—Evidence: Failure of the Prosecution to Introduce Evidence of National Contemporary Community Standards for Determining Patent Offensiveness Requires Dismissal." *Georgetown Law Journal* 55 (December 1966): 555–60.

"Constitutional Law—Obscenity: The First Amendment Does Not Preclude State Regulation of Material Which, According to Contemporary Community Standards, as a Whole Appeals to Prurient Interest in Sex, Depicts or Describes in a Patently Offensive Way Sexual Conduct Specifically Defined by Applicable State Law, and Lacks Serious Literary, Artistic, Political or Scientific Value." *Brooklyn Law Review* 40 (Fall 1973): 442–60.

"Constitutional Law—Obscenity: Materials May Be Obscene for Minors without Being Obscene for Adults." *Vanderbilt Law Review* 21 (October 1968): 844–50.

"Constitutional Law: Obscenity Not Protected by First or Fourteenth Amendments; 'Prurient Interest' Is Declared Current Constitutional Test for Obscenity." *New York Law Forum* 5 (January 1959): 93–96.

"Constitutional Law—Obscenity—'Pandering' Activities.'" *Tennessee Law Review* 33 (Summer 1966): 516–22.

"Constitutional Law—Obscenity—Protection of Minors: No Necessity of Scienter as to Age of Purchaser." *Brooklyn Law Review* 33 (Winter 1967): 329–34.

"Constitutional Law—Obscenity Redefined." *University of Richmond Law Review* 8 (Winter 1974): 325–33.

"Constitutional Law—Obscenity: The Right to an Adversary Hearing on the Issue of Obscenity Prior to the Seizure of Furtively Distributed Films." *Michigan Law Review* 69 (April 1971): 913–57.

"Constitutional Law—Obscenity: State Statute Allowing Injunction Against Dissemination of Allegedly Obscene Material Prior to Adversary Hearing Not Violative of

First Amendment." *Vanderbilt Law Review* 23 (November 1970): 1352–59.

"Constitutional Law—Obscenity: Supreme Court Looks to Local Standards in Determining Obscenity." *Valparaiso Law Review* 8 (Fall 1973): 166–79.

"Constitutional Law—Obscenity: United States Supreme Court Adopts a New Test." *St. Louis University Law Journal* 18 (Winter 1973): 297–325.

"Constitutional Law: Ohio Supreme Court Upholds Conviction Under Statute Prohibiting 'Knowing Possession' of Obscene Literature." *DePaul Law Review* 10 (Autumn/Winter 1960): 156–61.

"Constitutional Law: Power of the State and Federal Government to Suppress the Obscene through Post-Publication Criminal Conviction and through Injunctive Procedures." *Illinois Bar Journal* 46 (December 1947): 323.

"Constitutional Law: Refusal of Police Commissioner to Permit Showing of Film on Ground of Obscenity Upheld." *University of Pennsylvania Law Review* 106 (November 1957): 132–35.

"Constitutional Law (Survey of Ohio Law: Ohio Supreme Court Decisions 1982–1983)." *Ohio Northern University Law Review* 10 (Fall 1983): 731–34.

"Constitutional Law: The Standards of Obscenity in Missouri." *University of Missouri Kansas City Law Review* 37 (Winter 1969): 109–27.

"Constitutional Law: Test for Obscenity—Requirement of Patent Offensiveness and Necessity of Judicial Determination Prior to Postal Censorship." *Rutgers Law Review* 17 (Fall 1962): 213–18.

"Constitutional Law: Utterly without Redeeming Social Value Test Is Rejected as a Constitutional Standard for Determining Obscenity in Favor of a Jury Measurement of Issues of Prurient Appeal and Patent Offensiveness by the Standards That Prevail in the Forum Community." *Houston Law Review* 11 (October 1973): 224–26.

"Constitutional Law: Variable Definitions of Obscenity Based on Its Appeal to Minors Is Constitutional." *Albany Law Review* 33 (Fall 1968): 173–191.

"Construction and Constitutionality of Statutes Regulating Obscene Literature." *New York University Law Review* 28 (April 1953): 877–90.

"Controlling Obscenity: A Non-Legal Approach." *Osgoode Hall Law Journal* (Canada) 1 (1958–59): 72.

Cook, Earleen H. *Obscenity, the First Amendment and the Courts.* Monticello, Ill.: Vance Bibliographies, 1979.

Cook, G. Bradford. "Recent Problems in Obscene Publication Regulation and Motion Picture Censorship." *Nebraska Law Review* 40 (April 1961): 481.

Cooksey, James Peter. "Constitutional Law (Eleventh Annual Tenth Circuit Survey, June 1, 1983–May 31, 1984)." *Denver University Law Review* 62 (Winter 1985): 91–107.

Coons, W.H., and P.A. McFarland. "Obscenity and Community Tolerance." *Canadian Psychology* 26, no. 1 (1985): 30–38.

Corn-Revere, Robert. 'They'll Know It When They Seize It: The Government Is Using RICO to Round Up Pornography—But It Isn't Just Pornography They're Hauling In." *Student Lawyer* 16 (May 1988): 14–18.

Coupe, Bradford. "Roth Test and Its Corollaries." *William and Mary Law Review* 8 (Fall 1966): 121–32.

Coutts, J.A. 'Five Obscene Articles, One Crime." *Journal of Criminal Law* (Great Britain) 50 (February 1986): 9–11.

Crabtree, James, and Daniel Kearney. "Constitutional Law: A Revised Standard of Obscenity?" *University of Florida Law Review* 19 (Summer 1966): 185–93.

Craig, Alec. *The Banned Books of England and other Countries: A Study of the Conception of Literary Obscenity.* London: Allen & Unwin, 1962.

"Criminal Law: Obscene Literature Statutes." *Wisconsin Law Review* (May 1955): 492.

"Criminal Law—Obscenity—Criteria: Publication Not Obscene Unless Tests of Patent Offensiveness and Prurient Interest Appeal Are Met." *Albany Law Review* 27 (January 1963): 127–31.

"Criminal Law—Obscenity: First Amendment Permits Showing Obscene Film in Public Theater to Paying Adult Audience That Was Forewarned of Film's Nature." *Albany Law Review* 34 (Spring 1970): 708–15.

"Criminal Law—Obscenity: Information Charging Defendant with Selling and Distributing Obscene Magazine Dismissed." *Albany Law Review* 26 (January 1962): 102–5.

"Criminal Law: Survey Evidence of Community Standards in Obscenity Prosecutions." *Canadian Bar Review* 50 (1972): 315–30.

"Criminal Law: Test of Obscenity Held to Be What Reasonable Men Think Would Corrupt Public Morals or Order." *Virginia Law Review* 32 (February 1946): 408–12.

"Criminal Obscenity Statute Held Unconstitutional for Lack of Scienter." *Ohio State Law Journal* 23 (1962): 355–60.

"Criminal Procedure: Transfer of Venue and the Contemporary Community Standards Test in Federal Obscenity Prosecutions." *New York University Law Review* 52 (June 1977): 629–50.

Crocker, Leslie. "Constitutional Law: Deprivation of Personal Rights—Possessing and Exhibiting Film—Evolution of an Obscenity Standard." *Western Reserve Law Review* 16 (May 1965): 780–88.

Crocker, Leslie. "Ginzburg et al.: An Attack on Freedom of Expression." *Western Law Review* 17 (June 1966): 1325–41.

Cross, Fred M., Jr. "Constitutional Law—Due Process: Delineation of Procedures Used in Seizing Obscene Films." *Journal of Urban Law* 47 (1969–70): 746–52.

Cross, Scott. "Obscenity: Determined by Whose Standards?" *University of Florida Law Review* 26 (Winter 1974): 324–29.

Currin, Samuel T., and H. Robert Showers. "The State of Pornography." *Campbell Law Observer* (22 February 1985): 21.

Currin, Samuel T., and H. Robert Showers. "Regulation

of Pornography—The North Carolina Approach." *Wake Forest Law Review* 21 (Summer 1988): 263–361.

Curtis, Anne M.K. "Criminal Law—Obscenity—Test of Obscenity: Whether Hicklin Test Superseded: Whether Criminal Code Test Exhaustive: Whether Devices and Articles Constitute Publications: Whether Criminal Code Definition Applicable to Such Devices and Articles." *Ottawa Law Review* 11 (1979): 501–8.

Curtis, M.K. 'Obscenity: The Justices' (Not So) New Robes." *Campbell Law Review* 8 (1986) 387–419.

DaMeron, Charles E., III. "Constitutional Law: Obscenity Statute—Proof of Scienter." *North Carolina Law Review* 38 (June 1960): 634–38.

Daniels, Stephen. "The Supreme Court and Obscenity: An Exercise in Empirical Constitutional Policy-Making." *San Diego Law Review* 17 (July 1980): 757–99.

David, Anshal. "Obscenity: In the Matter or in the Mind?" *Brooklyn Law Review* 46 (Summer 1980): 695–715.

Davidow, Robert P., and Michael O'Boyle. "Obscenity Laws in England and the United States: A Comparative Analysis." *Nebraska Law Review* 56 (1977): 249–87.

Day, J. Edward. "Mailing Lists and Pornography." *American Bar Association Journal* 52 (December 1966): 1103–9.

"Declaratory Judgments—Massachusetts Provides for Declaratory Action Against Obscene Book with Jury Trial on the Issue of Obscenity." *Harvard Law Review* 59 (May 1946): 813–16.

DeGrazia, Edward. "Obscenity and the Mail: A Study of Administrative Restraint." *Law and Contemporary Problems* 20 (Autumn 1955): 608–20.

Denniston, Lyle. "A Shifting Argument and a Stand-up Routine." *American Lawyer* 7 (May 1985): 108–9.

DeSimone, Judith A. "Criminal Law." *University of Arkansas at Little Rock Law Journal* 3 (Spring 1980): 191–97.

Diamond, Judith E. "First Amendment Onstage." *Boston Law Review* 53 (November 1973): 1121–41.

Dibble, J. Rex. "Obscenity: A State Quarantine to Protect Children." *Southern California Law Review* 39 (1966): 345–77.

Dickey, Anthony. "Legal Concept of Obscenity in Western Australia." *University of Western Australia Law Review* 10 (June 1972): 223–42.

"Distinction between Obscene and Potentially Obscene Article." *Law Quarterly Review* 78 (October 1962): 477–78.

"Double Standard of Obscenity: The Ginsberg Decision." *Valperasio University Law Review* 3 (Fall 1968): 57–68.

Doyle, M.W. "Obscenity Revisited: From Morality to Manners." *New Zealand University Law Review* 6 (April 1974): 68–73.

Dunaj, Sherryll M. "Constitutional Law: Private Possession of Obscene Films Where There Is No Intent to Sell, Circulate or Distribute." *University of Miami Law Review* 24 (Fall 1969): 179–83.

Dyson, Richard B. "Looking-Glass Law: An Analysis of the Ginzburg Case." *University of Pittsburgh Law Review* 28 (October 1966): 1–18.

Eads, Arthur C. "Stanley v. Georgia (89 S. Ct. 1243)—A Private Look at Obscenity." *Baylor Law Review* 21 (Fall 1969): 503–11.

Eddy, J.P. "Obscene Publications: Society of Authors' Draft Bill." *Criminal Law Review* (Great Britain) (April 1955): 218–26.

Edelstein, Stephen J. and Kenneth Mott. "Collateral Problems in Obscenity Regulation: A Uniform Approach to Prior Restraints, Community Standards, and Judgment Preclusion." *Seton Hall Law Review* 7 (Spring 1976): 543–87.

Edhlund, Sandra. "Candor or Shame? Defining Obscenity by Statute." *Catholic Lawyer* 13 (Spring 1967): 3–144, 170.

Edmiston, James P. "Proof of Scienter in Criminal Obscenity Prosecutions." *Akron Law Review* 9 (Summer 1975): 131–57.

Edmondson, N.H., and J.A. Wright. "Canadian Obscenity Law—Archaic Trends." *Faculty Law Review* (Canada) 16 (April 1958): 93–98.

Eich, William. "From Ulysses to Portnoy: A Pornography Primer." *Marquette Law Review* 53 (Summer 1970): 156–71.

Eissinger, James. "Notes: 'Prurient Interests' as a Guide to the State Courts." *North Dakota Law Review* 39 (July 1963): 308–22.

Elias, E.A. "Obscenity: The Law, A Dissenting Voice." *Baylor Law Review* 15 (Winter 1963): 1–38.

Elias, E.A. 'Sex Publications and Moral Corruption: The Supreme Court Dilemma." *William and Mary Law Review* 9 (Winter 1967): 302–26.

Elison, Larry M., and Gary L. Graham. "Obscenity: A Compromise Proposal." *Montana Law Review* 30 (Spring 1969): 123–39.

Elkin, Susan. "Taking Serious Values Seriously: Obscenity, Pope v. Illinois, and an Objective Standard." *University of Miami Law Review* 41 (March 1987): 855–77.

Ellis, Steven D. "Constitutionality of Obscenity Statutes: People v. New Horizons." *University of Colorado Law Review* 52 (Summer 1981): 575–85.

Emerson, Thomas. "First Amendment Doctrine and the Burger Court." *California Law Review* 68 (1980): 422–81.

"Encore for Roth: United States v. Reidel, United States v. Thirty-Seven Photographs." *University of Pittsburgh Law Review* 33 (Winter 1971): 367.

Engdahl, David E. "Requiem for Roth: Obscenity Doctrine Is Changing." *Michigan Law Review* 68 (December 1969): 185–235.

Erbe, Norman A., and A.F. Craig, Jr. "Freedom from Obscenity." *Cleveland-Marshall Law Review* 10 (January 1961): 123–35.

"Evidence: Admission of Contemporary Critical Evaluation of Libeled Book." *Minnesota Law Review* 35 (February 1951): 326–30.

"Expert Witnesses: An Interview with Lord Longford." *New Law Journal* (Great Britain) (20 December 1973): 1171–74.

"Extralegal Censorship Held Valid." *Utah Law Review* 8 (Summer 1962): 70–84.

"Extralegal Censorship of Literature." *New York University Law Review* 33 (November 1958): 989–1026.

Fagan, Edward T. "Symposium—Obscenity and the Law." *Catholic Lawyer* 10 (Fall 1964): 270–84.

Fahringer, H.P. "Obscenity: The Defense of an Obscenity Prosecution." *Trial* 14 (May 1978): 31–37.

Fahringer, H.P., and M.J. Brown. "Rise and Fall of Roth: A Critique of the Recent Supreme Court Obscenity Decisions." *Kentucky Law Journal* 62 (1973–74): 731–68.

Fahringer, H.P., and M.J. Brown. "Rise and Fall of Roth: A Critique of the Recent Supreme Court Obscenity Decisions." *Criminal Law Bulletin* 10 (November 1974): 785–826.

Fahringer, H.P., and P.J. Cambria, Jr. "Obscenity and the First Amendment: The New Weapons Being Used in Waging War Against Pornography." *Capital University Law Review* 7 (1978): 227.

Falk, G. "Roth Decision in the Light of Sociological Knowledge." *American Bar Association Journal* 54 (March 1968): 288–92.

Farber, Daniel A. "Civilizing Public Discourse: An Essay on Professor Bikel, Justice Marlan and the Enduring Significance of Cohen v. California." *Duke Law Journal* (1980): 283–303.

"Federal Mail Obscenity Statute Held Inapplicable to Voluntary Private Correspondence by Adults." *Utah Law Review* (December 1966): 717–35.

Feinberg, Joel. "Pornography and the Criminal Law." *University of Pittsburgh Law Review* 40 (Summer 1979): 567–604.

Fiander, Jeanne. "A Stealthy Encroachment: Obscenity and the Fourth Amendment." *American University Law Review* 36 (Spring 1987): 773–99.

Finnegan, Jeremiah D. "Constitutional Law—Search and Seizure: Procedures for Seizure of Obscene Publications." *Missouri Law Review* 26 (November 1961): 501–5.

Finnis, John M. ' "Reason and Passion': The Constitutional Dialectic of Free Speech and Obscenity." *University of Pennsylvania Law Review* 116 (December 1967): 222–43.

Firmage, E.B. "Utah Supreme Court and the Rule of Law: Phillips and the Bill of Rights in Utah." *Utah Law Review* (Fall 1975): 593–627.

"First Amendment I: Freedom of Religion in the Employment and Education Arenas; Religious Expression in the Public Forum; and Obscenity." *1982 Annual Survey of American Law* (April 1983): 579–602.

Fitzgerald, Edward. "Obscene Publications Act 1959, s. 1(2)—Pornographic Video Cassette: Whether Video Cassette an Article for Purposes of Act." *Criminal Law Review* (Great Britain) (November 1980): 723–24.

Fleishman, S. "Obscenity and Post Office Censorship. *Law in Transition Quarterly* 22 (Winter 1963): 222–30.

Fleishman, S. "Obscenity: The Exquisitely Vague Crime." *Law in Transition Quarterly* 24 (Spring 1965): 97–110.

Fleishman, S. "Seamy Side of Life." *Journal of Beverly Hills Bar Association* 2 (December 1968): 10.

Fleishman, S. *The Supreme Court Obscenity Decisions.* San Diego: Greenleaf Classics, 1973.

Flournoy, Peter H., and J. Brian O'Donnell. "Private Correspondence and Federal Obscenity Prosecutions." *San Diego Law Review* 4 (January 1967): 76–117.

Forbes, M.Z. "Obscene Publications." *Australian Law Journal* 20 (July 1946): 92–99.

Ford, John. *Criminal Obscenity: A Plea for Its Suppression.* New York: F.H. Revell, 1926.

"Forfeiture of Obscene Articles Intended for Export." *Journal of Criminal Law.* (Great Britain) (November 1981): 214–16.

Forkosch, M.D. "Obscenity, Copyright, and the Arts." *New England Law Review* 10 (Fall 1974): 1–24.

Forkosch, M.D. "Obscenity and the First Amendment: Porno-Obscenity, Morals, and Judicial Discrimination." *Capital University Law Review* 7 (1978):.

Foster, Henry H., Jr. " 'Comstock Load'—Obscenity and the Law." *Journal of Criminal Law* 48 (September/October 1957): 245–58.

Foth, J.R. "Judges Read Dirty Books." *Journal of Kansas Bar Association* 47 (Fall 1978): 191–203.

Fox, Donald R. "Obscenity: A Step Forward by a Step Back?" *Albany Law Review* 38 (1974): 764–97.

Fox, R.G. "Crown v. Graham (1968) 41 ALJR 402." *Adelaide Law Review* Australia 3 (May 1969): 392–402.

Fox, R.G. "Criminal Law: Survey Evidence of Community Standards in Obscenity Prosecutions." *Canadian Bar Review* 50 (May 1972): 315.

Fox, R.G. "Obscenity." *Alberta Law Review* (Canada) 12 (1974): 172–235.

Frank, John P. "Obscenity: Some Problems of Values and the Use of Experts." *Washington Law Review* 41 (August 1966): 631.

Franke, Lewis. "Constitutional Law—Censorship of Obscenity in Literature—Prior Restraint." *American University Law Review* 12 (June 1963): 211–16.

"Free Speech: Obscenity Regulation (6th Annual Survey of Alabama Law: 1978–79)." *Alabama Law Review* 31 (Summer 1980): 677–79.

Freund, P.A., and R.H. Kuh. "Political Libel and Obscenity." *Federal Rules Decisions* 42 (November 1967): 491–518.

Friedman, Jon Lewis. "New Approach to Obscenity." *University of Pittsburgh Law Review* 19 (Fall 1957): 166–73.

Friedman, Leon, ed. *Obscenity: The Complete Oral Arguments before the Supreme Court in the Major Obscenity Cases.* New York: Chelsea House, 1970. Rev. ed. New York: Chelsea House, 1983.

Froessel, C.W. "Law and Obscenity." *Albany Law Review* 27 (January 1963): 1–10.

Frost, Peter. "People Ex. Rel. Gow v. Mitchell Brothers: California Gropes for a Civil Obscenity Standard." *COMM-ENT* 5 (Fall 1982): 109–26.

Fullmer, Mark A. "Obscenity Regulation." *Louisiana Law Review* 35 (Spring 1975): 601–8.

Gamma, Richard Luke. "Massachusetts' Three-Prong

Obscenity Test." *Annual Survey of Massachusetts Law* 33 (1986): 78–85.

Gastil, Raymond D. "The Moral Right of the Majority to Restrict Obscenity and Pornography through Law." *Ethics* (1976): 3.

Gaylin, Willard M. "The Prickly Problems of Pornography." *Yale Law Journal* 77 (1967–68): 579–603.

Gaylord, C.L. "The Writing on the Wall." *Case & Comment* 89 (July/August 1984): 48.

Gegan, B.E. "Twilight of Nonspeech." *Catholic Lawyer* 15 (Summer 1969): 210–20.

"Geography of Obscenity's 'Contemporary Community Standards.' " *Wake Forest Law Review* 8 (December 1971): 81.

George, B.J. "Obscenity Litigation: An Overview of Current Legal Controversies." *National Journal of Criminal Defense* 3 (Fall 1977): 189–217.

George, B.J. "United States Supreme Court 1980–1981 Term: Criminal Law Decisions." *New York Law School Law Review* 27 (Winter 1981): 1–101.

Gerber, Albert B. "A Suggested Solution to the Riddle of Obscenity." *University of Pennsylvania Law Review* 112 (1964): 834–56.

Gertz, Elmer. "The Illinois Battle over 'Tropic of Cancer.' " *Chicago Bar Record* 46 (January 1965): 161–72.

Getz, Leon. "The Problem of Obscenity." *University of British Columbia Law Review* 2 (March 1965): 216–32.

Giampietro, Nicholas L. "First and Fourth Amendments—Obscenity and Police Purchases: A Purchase Is a Purchase Is a Seizure?" *Journal of Criminal Law and Criminology* 76 (Winter 1985): 875–96.

Gibbens, Daniel G. "Constitutional Law—Due Process: Freedom of the Press in Obscenity Cases." *Oklahoma Law Review* 11 (May 1958): 197–98.

Gillespie, Hal Keith. "Constitutional Law—Obscenity: Federal Statute Allowing Prosecution for Mailing 'Non-Mailable' Obscene Material to Requesting Adults Is An Unconstitutional Infringement of First Amendment Free Speech." *Texas Law Review* 49 (March 1971): 575–81.

Gillis, Kenneth L. "Obscenity: The Man, Not the Book." *Illinois Bar Journal* 55 (February 1967): 462–72.

Gilloti, Chris F. "Book Censorship in Massachusetts: The Search for a Test for Obscenity." *Boston University Law Review* 42 (Fall 1962): 476.

Glassman, M.B. "Community Standards of Patent Offensiveness: Public Opinion Data and Obscenity Law." *Public Opinion Research* (1978): 161–70.

Gliedman, Wendy L. "Obscenity Law: Definitions and Contemporary Standards." *1985 Annual Survey of American Law* (October 1986): 915–27.

Gold, Alan D. "Charter of Rights—Search and Seizure—Obscenity." *Criminal Law Quarterly* (Canada) 27 (December 1984): 24–25.

Gold, Alan D. "Search and Seizure—Obscene Books." *Criminal Law Quarterly* (Canada) 28 (March 1986): 156–59.

Gordon Klein, Margaret. "Criminal Law and Procedure—Search and Seizure: Viewing a Movie Constitutes a 'Search.' " *Tennessee Law Review* 48 (Spring 1981): 765–84.

Grant, Sidney S., and S.E. Anzoff. "The Constitutionality of the Obscenity and Birth Control Statutes." *Boston University Law Review* 10 (1930): 176.

Grant, Sidney S., and S.E. Anzoff. "Massachusetts and Censorship." *Boston University Law Review* 10 (1930): 36.

Grant, Sidney S. and S.E. Anzoff. "Recent Developments in Censorship." *Boston University Law Review* 10 (1930): 488.

Graphin, Anthony J. "Criminal Law—The Louisiana Obscenity Statute and Freedom of Speech and Press." *Louisiana Law Review.* 23 (April 1963): 604–9.

Gray, Ronald D. "Balancing Community Standards Against Constitutional Freedoms of Speech and Press." *Southwestern Law Journal* 41 (November 1987): 1023–39.

Green, B. "Obscenity, Censorship, and Juvenile Delinquency." *University of Toronto Law Journal* 14 (1962): 229.

Green, Ronald L. "The Obscenity Defense to Copyright Revisited." *Kentucky Law Journal* 69 (Winter 1980–81): 161–84.

Greenstone, Richard J. "Protection of Obscene Parody as Fair Use." *Entertainment and Sports Lawyer* 4 (Winter/Spring 1988): 3–6.

Gregory, David D. "Substantive Issues of the Supreme Court's Method of Dealing with Obscenity Regulation." *Maine Law Review* 18 (1966): 284–96.

Grunes, Rodney A. "Obscenity Law and the Justices: Reversing Policy of the Supreme Court." *Seton Hall Law Review* 9, no. 3 (1978): 403–73.

Gruntz, Louis G., Jr. "Obscenity 1973: Remodeling the House That Roth Built." *Loyola Law Review* 20 (1973–74): 159–75.

Gumer, Robert. "Communications Law—The Family Viewing Hour—Obscenity—Indecency." *Annual Survey of American Law* (1978): 783–98.

Hafen, B.C. "Restraint and the Regulation of Obscenity." *Oklahoma City University Law Review* 12 (Fall 1987): 787–93.

Haimbaugh, George D., Jr. "Obscenity: An End to Weighing?" *South Carolina Law Review* 21 (1969): 357–73.

Haldane, Robert Mayer. "Constitutional Law–Private Possession of Obscene Materials: *Stanley v. Georgia,* 89 S. Ct. 1243 (1969)." *William and Mary Law Review* 11 (Fall 1969): 261–63.

Haller, Scot. "Simon Pure: Prosecutor of Pornography." *American Lawyer* 2 (February 1980): 23–25.

Hardy, John, Jr. "Miller v. California and Adult Theatre I v. Slaton: The Obscenity Doctrine Reformulated." *Columbia Rights Law Review* 6 (Spring 1974): 219–37.

Harlech, R.T. "Film Censorship in Britain: Past, Present and Future." Presentation at the International Conference of Film Regulators, London, March 1982.

Harrington, John. "The Evolution of Obscenity Control Statutes." *William and Mary Law Review* 3, no. 2 (1962): 302–10.

Harris, Richard H. "Obscenity Law in Ohio." *Akron Law Review* 13 (Winter 1980): 520–39.

Hart, Thomas D. "Constitutional Law—Obscenity: Weighing Social Import Against Prurient Appeal Unconstitutional Test." *American University Law Review* 14 (June 1965): 226–30.

Haward, L. "Admissibility of Psychological Evidence in Obscenity Cases." *Bulletin of the British Psychological Society* (1975): 28.

Haward, L. "Obscenity and the Forensic Psychologist." *New Behavior* 3 (July 1975):.

Hawkins, Laura A. "Criminal Procedure—Search and Seizure: Observance of Two Men Entering Adjoining Glory Hole Booths in an Adult Theater." *Thurgood Marshall Law Review* 9 (Fall 1983): 208–17.

Hayes, Arthur S. "A Jury Wrestles with Pornography." *American Lawyer* 10 (March 1988): 96.

Hayes, J.C. "Obscenity: The Intractable Legal Problem." *Catholic Lawyer* 15 (Winter 1969): 5–15.

' "He That Hath Eyes to See, Let Him See'; He That is Offended, Let Him Look the Other Way: Obscenity Law and Artistic Expression." *Utah Law Review* (Winter 1972): 503.

Heath, E.D. "Police Problems in Enforcement of Laws Pertaining to Obscenity and Sex-Related Criminal Offenses." *Police Chief* 45 (1978): 52–54.

Heck, E.V. "Justice Brennan and the Development of Obscenity Policy by the Supreme Court." *California Western Law Review* (Spring 1982): 18.

Heilman, John. "Pornography Prosecutions: New Skirmishes in an Age-Old War." *Los Angeles Lawyer* 10 (May 1987): 25.

"Helpful Decision." *Justice Policies* 123 (31 January 1959): 70.

Henkin, Louis. "Morals and the Constitution: The Sin of Obscenity." *Columbia Law Review* 63 (March 1963): 391–414.

Hennessey, Paul F. "Attorney General v. a Book Named John Cleland's Memoirs of a Woman of Pleasure (Mass) 106 N.E. 2d 403." *Portia Law Journal* 1 (Spring 1966): 250.

Hibbard, Paul R. "Constitutional Law–Obscenity Laws: Community Standards Test." *South Carolina Law Review* 16 (1964): 639–45.

Hicks, Randolph S. "Federal Obscenity Prosecutions: Dirty Dealing with the First Amendment?" *Santa Clara Law Review* 18 (Summer 1978): 720–56.

Hidayatullah, M. "Thoughts on Obscenity." *Southern Illinois University Law Journal* (1976–77): 283–98.

Hoellrich, Gene R. "Stanley v. Georgia (89 S. Ct. 1243): A First Amendment Approach to Obscenity Control." *Ohio State Law Journal* 31 (Spring 1970): 364–70.

Hofstadter, S.H., and S.R. Levittan. "No Glory, No Beauty, No Stars—Just Mud." *New York State Bar Journal* 37 (February–April 1965): 38–116.

Holcomb, Franklin. "Texas' New Obscenity Law: Redefining Taste." *Houston Law Review* 17 (May 1980): 835–72.

Holley, Ira H. "Obscenity Law—The Bane of the Courts." *Criminal Law Bulletin* 1 (July/August 1965): 3–26.

Homer, Kenneth D. "Constitutional Law—Obscenity: The Ohio Statute Prohibiting the Pandering of Obscenity Is Neither Unconstitutionally Overbroad nor Void for Vagueness When Authoritatively Construed in Pari Materia with the Constitutional Standard for the Determination of Obscenity Set Forth by the United States Supreme Court in Miller v. California, Turoso v. Cleveland Municipal Court." *University of Cincinnati Law Review* 51, no. 3 (1982): 669–81.

Hotchkiss, Glenn Buchanan. "Is Expert Testimony Necessary to Obscenity Litigation? The Arizona Supreme Court Answers—NO!" *Arizona State Law Journal* 19 (Winter 1988): 821–47.

Hunsaker, D.M. "1973 Obscenity-Pornography Decisions: Analysis, Impact, and Legislative Alternatives." *San Diego Law Review* 11 (June 1974): 906–56.

Hunt, Chris. "Community Standards in Obscenity Adjudication." *California Law Review* 66 (1978): 1277–91.

Hunter, I.A. "Strange Passion in the County Court." *Criminal Law Quarterly* 13 (March 1971): 184.

Hunter, A. "Obscenity, Pornography and Law Reform." *Dalhousie Law Journal* 2 (1975–76): 482–504.

Huston, Alice. "Miller v. California: A Search for a New Community." *University of Western Los Angeles* 5 (Fall 1974): 63–67.

Hutchins, Shelby V. "Obscenity Law Imposing Strict Liability Declared Unconstitutional." *Ohio State Law Journal* 21 (Spring 1960): 242–44.

"I Know It When I Seize It: Selected Problems in Obscenity." *Loyola University Law Review* 4 (February 1971): 9.

Iliffe, J.A. "Australian 'Obscene Publications' Legislation of 1953–55." *Sydney Law Review* 2 (January 1956): 134–39.

Iliffe, J.A. "Objectionable Literature." *Sydney Law Review* (Australia) 2 (January 1957): 374.

"In Quest of a 'Decent Society': Obscenity and the Burger Court." *Washington Law Review* 49 (November 1973): 89–135.

Jacobs, D.H. "Control of Obscenity in Connecticut." *Connecticut Bar Journal* 41 (June 1967): 172.

Jaffary, K.D. "An Approach to the Criminal Provisions Regarding Obscenity." *Faculty Law Review* 21 (April 1962): 5–19.

"The Japanese Law of Obscenity." *Law Quarterly Review* 75 (April 1959): 183–87.

Jeffries, James H., IV. "Seizing Obscenity: The Waning of Presumptive Protection." *North Carolina Law Review* 65 (April 1987): 799–815.

"Jenkins v. Georgia and Hamling v. United States: Testing the Miller Obscenity Test." *Columbia Human Rights Law Review* 7 (Spring/Summer 1975): 349–63.

"John Calder (Publications) Ltd. v. Powell. (1965) 1 Q.B. 509." *Law Quarterly Review* 82 (January 1966): 23–24.

Jones, Teddy M., Jr. "Obscenity Standards in Current Perspective." *Southwestern Law Journal* 21 (Spring 1967): 285–305.

Jorgensen, Herbert W. "Constitutional Law—Injunctions—Obscene Matter—Freedom of the Press."

American University Law Review 7 (January 1958): 41–44.

Josephson, Ralph S. "Obscenity and Pornography: Forging Decency through the Law." *Colorado Lawyer* 17 (January 1988): 45.

"Judicial Process in the Law of Obscenity." *Manchester Law Journal* 4 (1971): 380.

"Judicial Regulation of Birth Control under Obscenity Laws." *Yale Law Journal* 50 (February 1941): 682–89.

"Jury's Role in Criminal Obscenity Cases: A Closer Look." *Kansas Law Review* 28 (Fall 1979): 111–39.

Kalash, Dwight F. "Obscenity—Protection of Speech: Necessity of Hearing to Determine Obscenity Prior to Seizure of Property." *North Dakota Law Review* 46 (Winter 1970): 257–63.

Kalven, Harry, Jr. "Metaphysics of the Law of Obscenity." *Supreme Court Review* (1960): 1–45.

Kamp, John. "Obscenity and the Supreme Court: A Communication Approach to a Persistent Judicial Problem." *Communication and the Law* 2 (Summer 1980): 1–42.

Kanowitz, L. "Love and Lust in New Mexico and the Emerging Law of Obscenity." *Natural Resources Journal* 10 (April 1970): 339.

Kaplan, Abraham. "Obscenity as an Esthetic Category." *Law and Contemporary Problems* 20 (Autumn 1955): 544–59.

"Karalexis v. Byrne and the Regulation of Obscenity: 'I am Curious (Stanley).'" *Virginia Law Review* 56 (October 1970): 1205–22.

Karp, I. "From Roth to Rohauer: Twenty Years of Amicus Briefs." *Bull Creek Society* 25 (October 1977): 1–18.

Karre, Richard A. "Stanley v. Georgia: New Directions in Obscenity Regulations?" *Texas Law Review* 48 (Fall 1970): 646–60.

Katz, A. "Free Discussion v. Final Decision: Moral and Artistic Controversy and the *Tropic of Cancer* Trials." *Yale Law Journal* 79 (December 1969): 209.

Katz, A. "Privacy and Pornography: Stanley v. Georgia." *Supreme Court Review* (1969): 203–17.

Katz, Ellen Edge. "Regulating Obscenity." *Whittier Law Review* 5 (Winter 1983): 1–35.

Kay, Maurice R. "Notes of Case: Depravity and Corruption for the Public Good." *Modern Law Review* 32 (March 1969): 198–202.

Kelley, Oliver. "Constitutional Law—Freedom of Speech—Tests of Obscenity." *Southwestern Law Journal* 15 (1961): 336–40.

Kemp, Karl H. "Comment: Recent Obscenity Cases." *Arkansas Law Review* 28 (Fall 1974): 357–72.

Keup, Erwin J. "Constitutional Law: Obscenity Not within the Area of Constitutionality Protected Speech or Press." *Marquette Law Review* 41 (Winter 1957–58): 320–428.

Kiefer, George Gerard. "Constitutional Law: Minors and Variable Obscenity." *Loyola Law Review* 15 (1968–69): 97–107.

Killough, James G. "Criminal Procedure—Search Warrants in Obscenity Cases: Sufficient Information upon Which to Base Probable Cause." *Journal of Public Law* 18 (1969): 205–13.

Kintner, Earl W. "Survey of a Decade of Decisions on the Law of Obscenity." *Catholic Lawyer* 8 (Spring 1962): 93–96.

Kopesky, John P. "Constitutional Law—Obscenity: 1977 Amendments to the Pennsylvania Obscenity Statute." *Villanova Law Review* 23 (September 1978): 1137–58.

Krislov, S. "From Ginzburg to Ginsberg: The Unhurried Children's Hour in Obscenity Litigation." *Supreme Court Review* (1968): 153.

Kronhausen, Eberhard, and Phyllis Kronhausen. *Pornography and the Law*. New York: Ballentine Books, 1964.

Krotter, Mark M. "Censorship of Obscenity in British Columbia: Opinion and Practice." *University of British Columbia Law Review* 5 (June 1970): 123–63.

Kuh, R. *Foolish Figleaves*. New York: Macmillan, 1967).

Kuh, R. "Rational Approach to Pornography Legislation." *Brooklyn Law Review* 37 (Winter 1971): 354–64.

Kupferman, Theodore R. and Philip J. O'Brien. "Motion Picture Censorship—The Memphis Blues." *Cornell Law Quarterly* 36 (Winter 1951): 273–300.

Kutz, Ellen. "Regulating Obscenity." *Whittier Law Review* 5, no. 3 (1983): 1–35.

LaBarre, Weston. "Obscenity: An Anthropological Appraisal." *Law and Contemporary Problems* 20 (Autumn 1955): 532–43.

Lachman, Andrea S., Thomas B. Stoddard, and Max Von Hollweg. "First Amendment Rights—Obscenity." *Annual Survey of American Law* (1976): 521–41.

" 'Lady Chatterley's Lover': An Historico-Literary Retrospect." *Justice Policies* 125 (7 January 1961): 5.

Lamont, John M.H. "Public Opinion Polls and Survey Evidence in Obscenity Cases." *Criminal Law Quarterly* 15 (February 1973): 135–59.

Langston, Robert. "*Southeastern Promotions Ltd. v. Conrad*: Construing the Constitutional Obscenity Ordinance." *Baylor Law Review* 28 (1976): 737–44.

LaPenta, Philip. "Motion Picture Seizures and the Adversary Hearing: Settled Law of Fertile Ground for Change." *American University Law Review* 21 (April 1972): 444–55.

"Larkin v. G.P. Putnam's Sons (NY) 200 N.E. 2d 760." *New York Law Forum* 10 (December 1964): 593.

Laughlin, S.K., Jr. "Requiem for Requiems: The Supreme Court at the Bar of Reality." *Michigan Law Review* (June 1970): 1389.

Laurencelle, U.G. "Censorship and Obscenity." *Canadian Bar Journal* 4 (June 1961): 223–32.

"The Law of Obscenity: New Significance of the Receiving Group." *Indiana Law Journal* 34 Spring (1959): 426–520.

Law Reform Commission of Canada. "Limits of the Criminal Law: Obscenity, A Test Case." Working paper 10, Minister of Supply and Services, Ottawa, 1977.

Lawrence, D.H. *Pornography and Obscenity*. New York: Knopf, 1930.

Lebowitz, Edward S. "Conviction for Mailing a Private

'Filthy' Letter Upheld." *Stanford Law Review* 16 (March 1964): 463–69.

Lederman, S.N. "Obscenity: Interpretation and Application of Section 150(8) of Criminal Code." *Faculty Law Review* 24 (April 1966): 106–14.

"Legal Responsibility for Extra-Legal Censure." *Columbia Law Review* 62 (March 1962): 475-500.

Leigh, L.H. "Aspects of the Control of Obscene Literature in Canada." *Modern Law Review* (Canada) 27 (November 1964): 669–81.

Leith, Patricia. "Regulation and Trial of Obscenity in Utah: Questions Raised by Salt Lake City v. Peipenburg." *Utah Law Review* (1978): 375–88.

Lelli, Alexander J., Jr. "Constitutional Law—Obscenity: First Amendment Rights Are Not Violated by a Jury Instruction Permitting a Jury to Consider Evidence of Pandering in Circumstances of Production, Distribution and Sale in a Determination of Obscenity." *University of Detroit Journal of Urban Law* 55 (Winter 1978): 458–74.

Lentz, Marguerite Munson. "Comparison Evidence in Obscenity Trials." *University of Michigan Journal of Legal Reform* 15 (Fall 1981): 45–76.

Leonard, Thomas A. "Constitutional Law: First Amendment Rights of Freedom of Speech and Press Violated by State Statute Prohibiting Possession of Obscene Matter." *Temple Law Quarterly* 43 (Fall 1969): 89–91.

Leventhal, H. "1973 Round of Obscenity-Pornography Decisions." *American Bar Association Journal* 59 (November 1973): 1261–66.

Leventhal, H. "Project: An Empirical Inquiry into the Effects of Miller v. California on the Control of Obscenity." *New York University Law Review* 52 (October 1977): 810–939.

Leverson, Bruce. "Copyright and Obscenity: Towards a National Standard?" *Performing Arts Review* 7 (1977): 495–525.

Levine, G.D. "Sexual Sensationalism and the First Amendment: The Supreme Court's Questionable Regime of Obscenity Adjudication." *New York State Bar Journal* 42 (April–June 1970): 193.

Levine, James P. "Empirical Approach to Civil Liberties: The Bookseller and Obscenity Law." *Wisconsin Law Review* (1969): 153–69.

Levine, S. "Pornography and Law: Latest U.S. Developments." *New Zealand Law Journal* (20 November 1973): 497–502.

Levy, Bernard S. "Obscenity: A Perusal and a Proposal." *Temple Law Quarterly* 32 (Spring 1959): 322–31.

Lewis, Felice F. *Literature, Obscenity, and the Law.* Carbondale: Southern Illinois University Press, 1976.

Lezin, Valerie. "First Amendment: Illinois Statute Defining Obscenity Is Neither Void for Vagueness nor Overbroad." *Illinois Bar Journal* 66 (April 1978): 481–84.

Licker, Jessica A. "Constitutionality of Federal Obscenity Legislation: Roth and Stanley on a Seesaw." *Boston University Law Review* 52 (Spring 1972): 443–63.

Lieberman, Marvin S. "Constitutional Law: Obscenity Is not within the Area of Constitutionality Protected Speech and Press." *University of Illinois Law Forum* (Fall 1957): 499–505.

Linz, D. "Assessing Courtroom Performance from the Perspective of the Social Science Observer, the Trial Practice Attorney, and the 'Jury Box.' " Paper presented to the Law and Society Association, Toronto, June 1982.

Linz, D., S. Penrod, D. Coates, M. Atkinson, L. Heuer, and S. Hertzberg. "The Use of Expert Witness Credibility." Paper presented to the Academy of Criminal Justice Sciences, March 1982.

"Literary Obscenity in New York." *Columbia Law Review* 42 (May 1947): 686–89.

"Literature and the Law." *L.J.* 105 (22 April 1955): 244–47.

"Local Regulation of Pornography." *University of Colorado–Denver Law Review* 10 (1977): 309–30.

Lockhart, William B. "Obscenity and the Law. Schauer: The Law of Obscenity." *Hastings Law Journal* 28 (July 1977): 1275–1358.

Lockhart, William B., and Robert McClure. "Literature, the Law of Obscenity and the Constitution." *Minnesota Law Review* 38 (1954): 295–395.

Lockhart, William B., and Robert McClure. "Obscenity in the Courts." *Law and Contemporary Problems* 29 (Autumn 1955): 589–607.

Lockhart, William B., and Robert McClure. "Censorship of Obscenity: the Developing Constitutional Standards." *Minnesota Law Review* 45, no. 5 (1960): 70–78.

Loewy, A.H. "Abortive Reasons and Obscene Standards: A Comment on the Abortion and Obscenity Cases." *North Carolina Law Review* 52 (December 1973): 223–43.

Loewy, A.H. "A Better Test for Obscenity: Better for the States—Better for Libertarians." *Hastings Law Journal* 28 (July 1977): 1315–23.

Loewy, A.H. "Free Speech: The 'Missing Link' in the Law of Obscenity." *Journal of Public Law* 16 (1967): 81.

Loewy, A.H. "A New Test for Obscenity." *Trial* 14 (May 1978): 31–37.

Loewy, A.H. "Why the 1985 North Carolina Obscenity Law Is Fundamentally Wrong." *North Carolina Law Review* 65 (1987): 793.

"Look at Thought Control: Obscenity in the Eyes of the Supreme Court." *Suffolk University Law Review* 7 (Spring 1973): 649.

Lord, Richard A. "Film Is a Four Letter Word." *Memphis State University Law Review* 5 (Fall 1974): 41–58.

Lovett, Anthony. "Constitutional Law—First Amendment: States May Not Prohibit Mere Private Possession of Obscene Material." *San Diego Law Review* 7 (January 1970): 111–19.

Lowman, Walker B. "Federal Pandering Advertisements Statute: The Right of Privacy versus the First Amendment." *Ohio State Law Journal* 32 (Winter 1971): 149–63.

Luce, Robert L. "Obscenity: Nature and Elements of

Offenses in General—Statutory Provisions." *Kansas Law Review* 10 (March 1962): 453–60.

Luchsinger, John A. "Blueprint for Censorship of Obscene Material: Standards for Procedural Due Process." *Villanova Law Review* 11 (Fall 1965): 125–38.

Ludwig, F.M. "Private Correspondence under the Mail Obscenity Law." *Denver Law Center Journal* 41 (May/June 1964): 152–64.

MacDougall, Cynthia A. "The Community Standards Test of Obscenity." *University of Toronto Faculty Law Review* 42 (1984): 79–92.

Mackay, R.S. "Criminal Law—Judicial Censorship: Recent Developments in the Law on Obscenity." *Canadian Bar Review* 32 (November 1954): 1010–18.

MacKinnon, Catherine A. "Pornography, Civil Rights, and Speech." *Harvard Civil Rights–Civil Liberties Law Review* 20 (Winter 1985): 1–70.

MacMillan, P.R. *Censorship and Public Morality.* Aldershot, England: Gower, 1983.

Magrath, C. Peter. "Obscenity Cases: Grapes of Roth." *Supreme Court Review* (1966): 7–77.

Maher, W.F. "Constitutional Law: Possession of Obscene Material in the Home Is Constitutionally Protected." *University of Florida Law Review* 22 (Summer 1969): 138–44.

Mahoney, Kathleen E. "Obscenity and Public Policy: Conflicting Values—Conflicting Statutes." *Saskatchewan Law Review* 50, no. 1 (1985–86): 75–109.

Main, E.J. "The Neglected Prong of the Miller (Miller v. California, 93 S. Ct. 2607) Test for Obscenity: Serious Literary, Artistic, Political, or Scientific Value." *Southern Illinois University Law Journal* 11 (Summer 1987): 1159–77.

Makowski, Kenneth W. "Constitutional Law: Obscenity Statute Declared Unconstitutional Due to Vagueness." *Temple Law Quarterly* 33 (Spring 1960): 359–65.

Manchester, Colin. "Customs Control of Obscene Materials." *Criminal Law Review* (Great Britain) (August 1981): 531–42.

Mann, J. "Fahringer Plays to a Hostile Court." *American Lawyer* 4 (1982): 39.

"Man's Prerogative." *Justice Policies* 122 (18 October–22 November 1958): 680.

Marcin, R.B. "Obscenity and the First Amendment: Ideological Pluralism and Government Regulation of Private Morality." *Capital University Law Review* 7 (1978): 227.

Marks, S. "What Is Obscene Literature Today?" *U.S.L. Review* 73 (April 1939): 217–23.

Marvin, James S. "Legal Censorship of Obscene Literature." *Syracuse Law Review* 12 (Fall 1960): 58–66.

Mayberry, Richard S. "Obscenity in New York: Law, Fact—or Both?" *Buffalo Law Review* 12 (April 1963): 369–84.

Mayer, M.F. "Obscenity Revolution of June 21, 1973." *Performing Arts Review* 4 (Fall/Winter 1973): 122–37.

Mayer, Shelly B., and Michael F. Mayer. "New Approach to Obscenity—The Conspiracy Doctrine." *St. Louis University Law Journal* 21 (1977): 366–84.

Mays, Richard L. "Gent v. State (Ark) 393 S.W. 2d 219." *Arkansas Law Review* 20 (Summer 1966): 178–80.

Maxwell, Robert. "Constitutional Law: Obscenity Regulation in Kansas—A New Standard." *Washburn Law Journal* 6 (Fall 1976): 204–11.

Mazurczak, Michael J. "An Assessment of the Value Inquiry of the Obscenity Test." *Illinois Bar Journal* 76 (May 1988): 512–15.

McCarty, Bryan K. "Obscenity from *Stanley Karalexis*: A Back Door Approach to First Amendment Protection." *Vanderbilt Law Review* 23 (March 1970): 369–87.

McColloch, Mike, and David W. Coody. "Criminal Law. (Annual Survey of Texas Law—1983)." *Southwestern Law Journal* 37 (April 1983): 379–401.

McCommon, P., B. Bull, and B. Taylor. *Preparation and Trial of Obscenity Cases: A Guide for Prosecuting Attorneys.* Phoenix: Citizens for Decency through Law, 1985.

McConnell, John Lithgow Chandos. *To Deprave and Corrupt: Original Studies in the Nature and Definition of "Obscenity".* London: Souvenir Press, 1962.

McDonald, L.D. "Youth, Obscenity, and the Law." *Washburn Law Journal* 1 (Spring 1961): 220–31.

McGaffney, Ruth. "A Realistic Look at Expert Witnesses in Obscenity Cases." *Northwestern Univesity Law Review* 69 (May/June 1974): 218–32.

McKay, R.S. "Hicklin Rule and Judicial Censorship." *Canadian Bar Review* 36 (March 1958): 1.

McKenna, Edward. "Constitutional Law—Due Process: Variable Standard for Determining Obscenity—Ginsberg v. New York. 390 U.S. 629." *American University Law Review* 18 (December 1968): 195–201.

McLaughlin, Blane D. "The Psychiatrist as Expert Witness in Pornography Prosecutions." In *Where Do You Draw the Line?* edited by Victor B. Cline, 271–83. Salt Lake City: Brigham Young University Press, 1974.

McPheeters, Hugh, Jr. "Obscenity—Variable Concept—Ginzburg v. U.S." *Missouri Law Review* 32 (Winter 1967): 127–30.

McTeague, Marie. "Neither Rain, nor Sleet . . . nor the United States Congress . . . Will Prevent the U.S. Postal Service from Delivering Hustler Magazine." *Loyola Entertainment Law Journal* 8 (Winter 1988): 159–67.

Melott, Robert A. "Constitutional Law—Obscenity." *North Carolina Law Review.* 43 (December 1964): 172–87.

"The Metaphysics of the Law of Obscenity." In *The 1959 Supreme Court Review,* edited by Philip P. Kurland, Chicago: University of Chicago Press, 1960.

Meyer, P.R., D.J. Seifer. "Censorship in Oregon: New Developments in an Old Enterprise." *Oregon Law Review* 51 (Spring 1972): 537.

Miller, Beverly G. "Miller v. California: A Cold Shower for the First Amendment." *St. John's Law Review* 48 (March 1974): 568–610.

Miller, C.J. "Recent Developments in the Law of Obscenity." *Criminal Law Review* (Great Britain) (August 1973): 467–83.

Miller, Henry. "Obscenity and the Law of Reflection." In

Remember to Remember. New York: New Directions, 1947.

Miller, Henry. "Offense of Obscenity: A Symposium of Views." *Kentucky Law Journal* 51 (Summer 1963): 577–90.

Miller, J.G. "Some Obscene Thoughts." *Faculty Law Review* 25 (May 1967): 128–41.

Miller, Robert H., II. "Control of Obscenity through Enforcement of a Nuisance Statute." *Campbell Law Review* 4 (1981): 139–67.

"Miller v. California: A Mandate for New Obscenity Legislation." *Mississippi Law Journal* 45 (1975): 435.

Milligan, William W. "Obscenity: Malum in Se or Only in Context? The Supreme Court's Long Ordeal." *Capital University Law Review* 7 (1978): 631–45.

Minnesota Library Association. *Intellectual Freedom in Minnesota: The Continuing Problem of Obscenity*. Minneapolis: Minnesota Library Association, 1979.

Mohan, John J., Jr. "Constitutional Law: First Amendment Protection of Public Commercial Dissemination of Obscene Material." *St. Louis University Law Journal* 14 (Summer 1970): 732–40.

Monaghan, Henry P. "Obscenity, 1966: The Marriage of Obscenity Per Se and Obscenity Per Quod." *Yale Law Journal* 76 (November 1966): 127–57.

Monoghan, Henry P. "First Amendment 'Due Process.' " *Harvard Law Review*. 83 (1969–70): 518–51.

Montgomery, Donald E. "Obscenity: 30 Years of Confusion and Still Counting." *Creighton Law Review* 21 (Fall 1987): 379–407.

"Montreal Newsdealer Supply Co. v. Board of Cinema Censors of the Province of Quebec (1969) C.S. 83." *McGill Law Journal* 15 (June 1969): 350–52.

"More Ado about Dirty Books." *Yale Law Journal* 75 (July 1965): 1364–1405.

Moretti, Daniel S. *Obscenity and Pornography: The Law under the First Amendment*. New York: Oceana Publications, 1984.

Morreale, Justin P. "Obscenity: An Analysis and Statutory Proposal." *Wisconsin Law Review* (1969) 421–68.

Morrison, Ted. V. "Note: Constitutionality of Enjoining Publication of Obscene Literature." *Journal of Public Law* 6 (1957): 548–55.

Morton, J.F. "Our Foolish Obscenity Laws." *Case and Comment* 23 (1916): 23.

Moskin, M. "Criminal Law—Legislation: Inadequacy of Present Tests as to What Constitutes Obscene Literature." *Cornell Law Quarterly* 34 (Spring 1949): 442–47.

"Motion Picture Censorship: License Denial on Grounds of Indecency Held Invalid." *St. John's Law Review* 32 (December 1957): 126–31.

Mott, K., and C. Kellett. "Obscenity, Community Standards, and the Burger Court: From Deference to Disarray." *Suffolk University Law Review* 13 (Winter 1973): 14–26.

Muchmore, Clyde. "Holding v. Nesbitt, 259 Supp. 694." *Oklahoma Law Review* 20 (May 1967): 184–89.

Mulroy, T.R. "Obscenity, Pornography, and Censorship."

American Bar Association Journal 49 (September 1963): 869–75.

"Multi-Venue and the Obscenity Statutes." *University of Pennsylvania Law Review* 115 (January 1967): 399–438.

Myers, Michael. 'Venue: Its Impact on Obscenity." *South Dakota Law Review* 11 (Spring 1966): 363–73.

Myers, Thomas E. "Contemporary Community Standards in Obscenity Prosecutions—*Smith v. United States*." *Baylor Law Review* 30 (Spring 1978): 317–31.

Nagel, S. "Judicial Behavior in Pornography Cases." *Journal of Urban Law* 52 (August 1974): 1–23.

Nash, Brian J. "Constitutional Law—First Amendment—Obscenity: On Appellate Review Obscenity Is a Question of Fact Not a Mixed Question of Law and Fact." *Catholic University Law Review* 22 (Winter 1973): 479–86.

Newman, Bruce L. "Constitutional Law: The Problems with Obscenity." *Western Reserve Law Review* 11 (September 1960): 669–79.

Nichols, John E. "Vulgarity and Obscenity in the Student Press." *Journal of Law and Education* 10 (April 1981): 207–18.

Nightingale, G.M. "Vulgar Postcards." *Just P.* 118 (2 January 1954): 5–6.

"Non-Criminal Obscenity Regulation and Freedom of Expression." *Washington University Law Quarterly*. (December 1962): 474–14.

Northrop, David E. "Constitutional Law—Obscenity: Injunctive Proceedings Against the Display or Sale of Obscene Materials." *Ohio State Law Journal* 33 (Winter 1972): 236–46.

Nutting, C.B. "Definitive Standards in Federal Obscenity Legislation." *Iowa Law Review* 23 (November 1937): 24–40.

Obley, Loren L. "Commonwealth v. Jacobs (Mass) 191 N.E. 2d 873." *Kansas Law Review* 12 (May 1964): 547–49.

"Obscene Libel." *Criminal Law Review* (Great Britain) (August 1954): 593–97.

"Obscene Literature." *Legal Times* 115 (1903): 75.

"Obscene Literature." *Marquette Law Review* 34 (Spring 1951): 301–9.

"Obscene Literature." *Vanderbilt Law Review* 18 (October 1965): 2084–90.

"Obscene Publications." *Legal Times* 223 (12 April 1957): 189.

"Obscene Publications Bill." *Justice Policies* 121 (20 April 1957): 243.

"Obscene Publications—Cinema Club Showing Obscene Films—Offender with Recent Conviction for Similar Offence: Whether Sentence of Immediate Imprisonment Appropriate—Length of Sentence: Whether Appropriate to Impose Fine in Addition to Sentence of Imprisonment." *Criminal Law Review* (Great Britain) (June 1985): 396–97.

"Obscene Publications, Pictures, and Articles." *Chicago-Kent Law Review* 38 (March 1950): 163–70.

"Obscenity: Admissibility of Evidence of Contemporary

Community Standards." *DePaul Law Review* 12 (Spring/Summer 1963): 337–42.

"Obscenity and the Arts—A Symposium." *Law and Contemporary Problems* 20 (Autumn 1955):531.

"Obscenity: A Change in Approach." *Loyola Law Review* 18 (1971–72): 319.

"Obscenity: Comparison Evidence Is Inadmissible for Purpose of Establishing Community Standards under 'Hard-Core Pornography' Test." *Harvard Law Review* 76 (May 1963): 1498–1501.

"Obscenity—Constitutional Obscenity: The Supreme Court's Interpretation." *DePaul Law Review* 12 (Autumn/ Winter 1962): 103–15.

"Obscenity and Copyright: An Illustrious Past and Future?" *Southern Texas Law Journal* 22 (1982): 87–101.

"Obscenity: Court Holds 1978 Act Unconstitutional." *Suffolk University Law Review* 14 (Summer 1980): 755–63.

"Obscenity Defense to Copyright Revisited." *Kentucky Law Journal* 69 (1980 81): 161 81.

"Obscenity Defense Denied: The Rise of a Rational View of Copyright." *Washington State University Law Review* 9 (Fall 1981): 85–95.

"Obscenity: Dissection of Theatrical Plays into Speech and Conduct Components: An Exception to the Roth Rule?" *Seton Hall Law Review* 4 (Fall/Winter 1972): 379.

"Obscenity: Federal Statutes Prohibiting Importation and Mail Distribution of Obscene Materials Do Not Violate First Amendment." *Vanderbilt Law Review* 25 (January 1972): 196.

"Obscenity and the First Amendment: The Search for an Adequate Test." *Duke Law Journal* 7 (Spring 1958): 116.

"Obscenity: Jury Determination of Contemporary Community Standards Constitutionally Requested in Missouri." *Missouri Law Review* 43 (Winter 1978): 141–48.

"Obscenity Law: Après Stanley, Le Deluge? Le Deluge Postponed." Parts 1 and 2 *Catholic Lawyer* 17 (Winter/ Summer 1971): 45, 255.

"Obscenity Law in Ohio." *Akron Law Review* 13 (Winter 1980): 520–39.

"Obscenity: Mailability of Magazines Which Appeal to Homosexuals." *Vanderbilt Law Review* 16 (December 1962): 251–57.

"Obscenity in the Mails: Post Office Department Procedures and the First Amendment." *Northwestern University Law Review* 58 (November/December 1963): 664–84.

"Obscenity and Minors: Another Attempt—Penal Law Sections 484-h and 484-i." *Albany Law Review* 30 (January 1966): 133.

"Obscenity in the Movies." *Loyola Law Review* 19 (1971–72): 354.

"Obscenity—Motion Pictures." *American Jurisprudence Proof of Facts* 18 (1971): 465.

"Obscenity: A New Direction in Regulation." *John Marshall Journal* 4 (Spring 1971): 268.

"Obscenity, 1969: Another Attempt to Define Scienter." *Pacific Law Journal* 1 (January 1970): 364.

"Obscenity Not a Defense in Copyright Infringement Action." *Art and Law* 5 (Spring 1980): 68–69.

"Obscenity: The Pig in the Parlor." *Santa Clara Law Review* 10 (Spring 1970): 288.

"Obscenity and the Post Office: Removal from the Mail under Section 1461." *University of Chicago Law Review* 27 (Winter 1960): 354–68.

"Obscenity in Private Communications." *Ohio State Law Journal.* 23 (Summer 1962): 553–56.

"Obscenity, Profanity and the High School Press." *Williamette Law Review* 15 (Summer 1979): 507–29.

"Obscenity: A Quick Look at Stanley v. Georgia." *Tulsa Law Journal* 6 (August 1970): 277.

"Obscenity Regulation and Enforcement in St. Louis and St. Louis County." *Washington University Law Quarterly* (February 1964): 98–127.

"Obscenity Regulation: The Rhode Island Experience." *Suffolk University Law Review.* 13 (1979): 524 52.

"Obscenity and the Right to Be Left Alone: The Balancing of Constitutional Rights." *Indiana Law Review* 6 (March 1973): 490.

"Obscenity '73: Something Old, a Little Bit New, Quite a Bit Borrowed, but Nothing Blue." *Maryland Law Review* 33 (1973): 421–60.

"Obscenity: The Wavering Line of Pornography—How Hard the Core?" *USFV Law Review* 1 (January 1968): 210.

O'Connor, Craig Ryan. "Obscenity vel None!" *Law and Social Order* 2 (1972): 300–12.

O'Donnell, Michael F. "Obscenity—Evidence—Contemporary Community Standards—Prurient Interest— Literary Merit." *Catholic University Law Review* 12 (January 1963): 53–57.

O'Mara, John T. "Obscenity: Roth Goes to the Movies." *Buffalo Law Review* 14 (Spring 1965): 512.

O'Meara, Joseph, and Thomas L. Shaffer. "Obscenity in the Supreme Court: A Note on Jacobellis v. Ohio." *Notre Dame Law Review* 40 (1964): 1–12.

"One Result." *Stetson Law Review* 15 (Summer 1986): 1018 20.

O'Neil, R.M. "Federalism and Obscenity." *University of Toleda Law Review* 9 (Summer 1978): 731–53.

Oswald, Edwin G. "Court of Appeals Adopts Elevated Standard in Determining Probable Cause for Alleged Obscenity Violations." *St. John's Law Review* 61 (Fall 1986): 196–203.

Owens, Jesse Samuel, Jr. "Note: Miller v. California: A Mandate for New Obscenity Legislation." *Mississippi Law Journal* 45 (1974): 435–53.

Paine, Donald F. "Obscenity Legislation in Tennessee." *Tennessee Law Review* 29 (Summer 1962): 562–72.

Palumbo, Norman A., Jr. "Obscenity and Copyright: An Illustrious Past and Future?" *South Texas Law Journal* 22 (Winter 1982) 87–101.

Parker, Graham. "Developments in Criminal Law: The 1984–85 Term." *Supreme Court Law Review* 8 (1986): 165–93.

Parker, Paul Abbott. "Constitutional Law (Survey of

Developments in North Carolina Law, 1982)." *North Carolina Law Review* 61 (August 1983): 1052–59.

Paul, J.C.N. "Post Office and Non-Mailability of Obscenity: An Historical Note." *University of California Los Angeles Law Review* 8 (January 1961): 44–68.

Paul, J.C.N., and M.L. Schwartz. "Obscenity in the Mails: A Comment on Some Problems of Federal Censorship." *University of Pennsylvania Law Review* 106 (December 1957): 214.

Paul, J.C.N., and M.L. Schwartz. *Federal Censorship? Obscenity in the Mail.* New York: Free Press, 1961.

Peavy, D. Kirk. "Constitutional Law—Obscenity—Private Possession." *Mercer Law Review* 21 (Winter 1970): 337–40.

Penrod, S., D. Linz, D. Coates, L. Heur, M. Atkinson, and S. Herzberg. "First Impressions in the Courtroom: Juror Impressions of Prosecution and Defense Attorneys in Voir Dire and Opening Statements." Paper presented to the Academy of Criminal Justice Sciences, March 1982.

"People v. Fritch (NY) 192 N.E. 2d 713." *New York Law Forum* 9 (August 1963): 371–84.

"People v. Rothenberg (NY) 228 N.E. 2d 379." *New York Law Forum* 13 (Summer 1967): 389–435.

Peterson, James M. "Constitutional Law—Freedom of Speech: Pandering Held Relevant to the Application of the Roth Obscenity Test." *Tulane Law Review* 41 (December 1966): 126–31.

Phillips, Jeremy. "Copyright in Obscene Works: Some British and American Problems." *Anglo-American Law Review* 6 (July–September 1977): 138–71.

Pines, Burt. "The Obscenity Quagmire." *California State Bar Journal* 49 (November/December 1974): 509–14, 561–65.

Pinkepank, Jane. "Notes on Use: Obscenity: Jury Determination of Contemporary Community Standards Constitutionally Requested in Missouri." *Missouri Law Review* 43 (1978): 141.

Playton, Vernon P. "Obscenity Control: A Search for Validity." *Land and Water Law Review* 4, no. 2 (1969): 575–85.

Poole, Howard. "Obscenity and Censorship." *Ethics* 93 (October 1982): 39–44.

Port, Manuel L. "Standards of Judging Obscenity—Who? What? Where?" *Chicago Bar Record* 46 (June 1965): 405–11.

Posey, Allen M. Jr. "Criminal Law." *Louisiana Law Review* 40 (Winter 1980): 437–56.

Pratt, Ralph E. "Obscene Publications, Pictures, and Articles—Prohibition of Importation." *Kansas Law Review* 7 (December 1958): 216–19.

Prevezer, S. "Obscene Publications." *Modern Law Review* 17 (November 1954): 571–74.

Pritchard, John F. "Interstate Circuit, Inc. v. Dallas, 366 F. 2d 590." *California Law Review* 55 (August 1967): 926–37.

"The Prior Adversary Hearing: Solution to Procedural Due Process Problems in Obscenity Seizures?" *New York University Law Review* 46 (1971): 80–119.

"Prior Adversary Hearings on the Question of Obscenity." *Columbia Law Review* 70 (December 1970): 1403–25.

"Private Ratings of Motion Pictures as a Basis for State Regulation." *Georgetown Law Journal* 59 (1971): 1205–36.

"Procedural Problems in the Seizure of Obscenity." *Albany Law Review* 37, no. 1 (1972): 203–27.

"Prohibition on Importation of Pornography Upheld." *New Law Journal* (Great Britain) 130 (17 April 1980): 389–91.

"Proposed Amendment to the Obscene and Indecent Publications Act 1901–1946." *Australian Law Journal* 27 (November 1953): 457–58.

Provizer, Norman W. "Of Lines and Men: The Supreme Court, Obscenity, and the Issue of the Avertable Eye." *Tulsa Law Journal* 13 (1977): 52–81.

Ramey, Carl. "Constitutional Law—Obscenity Laws: Knowledge of Obscenity May Be Imputed to a Book Dealer to Satisfy Scienter Requirement." *George Washington Law Review* 34 (March 1966): 552–57.

Ratner, Leonard G. "Social Importance of Prurient Interest—Obscenity Regulation v. Thought-Privacy." *Southern California Law Review* 42 (1969): 587–99.

Rault, Gerard A. "Constitutional Law: The 1966 Obscenity Cases." *Louisiana Law Review* 27 (December 1966): 100–109.

Reagan, Robert D. "Constitutional Law: Recent Obscenity Decisions—A Pliant Approach." *Washburn Law Journal* 17 (Winter 1978): 400–406.

Reeves, George E. "Obscenity: What Is the Test?" *Arizona Law Review* 5 (Spring 1964): 265–73.

Regan, J.J. "An Unhurried Look at Obscenity." *Catholic Lawyer* 13 (Fall 1967): 297–324.

"Regina v. Calder and Boyars Ltd. (1968) 3 W.L.R. 974." *Law Quarterly Review* 85 (January 1969): 6–15.

Reidel, Stanley. "Still More Ado about Dirty Books (and Pictures): Stanley, Reidel, and Thirty-Seven Photographs." *Yale Law Journal* 81 (December 1971–72): 309–33.

"Reidel, 37 Photographers and Luros: The Disinterring of Roth." *San Francisco Law Review.* 6 (April 1972): 399.

Reifin, Melvin H. "The Constitutionality of Obscenity Laws: U.S. and Ohio." *University of Cincinnati Law Review* 31 (Summer 1962): 285–96.

Reisman, Joseph M. "The Legal Obsession with Obscenity: Why Are the Courts Still Being Challenged?" *Journal of Arts Management and Law* 13 (Fall 1983): 54–79.

Reiss, Bernard F. "Supreme Court and Obscenity: Mishkin (Mishkin v. New York, 86 S. Ct. 958), and Ginzburg (Ginzburg v. U.S. 86 S. Ct. 942)—Expansion of Freedom of Expression and Improved Regulation through Flexible Standards of Obscenity." *Rutgers Law Review* 21 (Fall 1966): 43–55.

Rembar, Charles. *The End of Obscenity: The Trials of Lady Chatterley, Tropic of Cancer, and Fanny Hill.* New York: Random House, 1968.

"Removal of Supreme Court Appellate Jurisdiction a Weapon Against Obscenity?" *Duke Law Journal* (April 1969): 291–325.

Reno, D.M. Jr. "Obscenity Revisited—1972." *American Bar Association Journal* 58 (July 1972): 736.

Reno, D.M., Jr. "People v. Ridens: The Witchcraft of the Illinois Obscenity Law Survives." *Illinois Bar Journal* 63 (July 1975): 640–45.

"Report of the Saskatchewan Subcommittee on Civil Liberties on Censorship and Obscenity." *Saskatchewan Bar Review* 25 (September 1960): 80–87.

"Requirement and Techniques for Holding an Adversary Hearing Prior to Seizure of Obscene Material." *North Carolina Law Review* 48 (June 1970):830.

"Requirement of Scienter in Obscenity Statutes." *DePaul Law Review* 9 (Spring/Summer 1960): 250–54.

"Restricting the Pandering of Obscenity: A Case of Legislative Overkill." *Pacific Law Journal* 1 (January 1970): 373.

Reynolds, Richard R., "Our Misplaced Reliance on Early Obscenity Cases." *American Bar Association Journal* 61 (February 1975): 220–22.

Rice, Hamilton H. "Youth—Obscenity Problem—A Proposal." *Kentucky Law Journal* 52 (1964): 429–47.

Richards, D.A. "Free Speech and Obscenity Law: Toward a Moral Theory of the First Amendment." *University of Pennsylvania Law Review* 123 (November 1974): 45–91.

Richards, I. "Obscenity and Film: An Empirical Dilemma." *Loyola Entertainment Law Journal* 6 (1986): 7–30.

Richardson, N.A. "Obscenity Law in Colorado: The Struggle to Pass a Constitutional Statute." *Denver Law Journal* 60 (1982): 49–76.

Riggs, R.E. "Miller v. California Revised: An Empirical Note." Brigham Young University Law Review 2 (1981): 247–73.

Ringel, William E. *Obscenity Law Today.* Jamaica, N.Y.: Gould Publications, 1970.

Rittenhouse, David C. "Obscenity and Social Statics." *William and Mary Law Review* 1, no. 2 (1958): 303–24.

Roberts, H. Buswell, Jr. "Supreme Court Takes Another Look at Obscenity." *University of Toledo Law Review* 5 (Fall 1973): 113–32.

Robertson, Geoff. *Obscenity: An Account of Censorship Laws and Their Enforcement in England and Wales.* London: Weidenfeld & Nicolson, 1979.

Roet, M.J. "Interpretation of Objectionable Literature Act 1954 (Queensland)—'Objectionable'—Undue Emphasis on Sex—Admissibility of Evidence Concerning Effect of Publications on Abnormal Persons." *Melbourne University Law Review* 1 (November 1958): 552–55.

Rogers, Charles H. "Police Control of Obscene Literature." *Journal of Criminal Law* 57 (December 1966): 430–82.

Rogers, L. "The Freedom of the Press." *Yale Law Journal* 23 (1914): 559.

Rogge, O.J. "State Power over Sedition, Obscenity and Picketing." *New York University Law Review* 34 (May 1959): 817–60.

Rogge, O.J. "Obscenity Litigation." *American Jurisprudence Trials.* Vol. 10, edited by Rochester, N.Y.: Lawyers

Co-Operative Publishing Company; San Francisco: Bancroft-Whitney Company, 1965, 1–254.

Rogge, O.J. "High Court of Obscenity." *University of Colorado Law Review* 41 (February–May 1969): 201.

Rogge, O.J. "Obscenity Terms of the Court." *Villanova Law Review* 17 (Fall 1972): 393.

Rolph, C.H. "Obscene Publications Bill." *Solicitors' Journal* 103 (24 April 1959): 317–18.

Rolph, C.H. "Obscene Publications: The New Act." *Solicitors' Journal* 103 (20 November 1959): 904–5.

Rooney, Daniel G. "Constitutional Law—First Amendment—Obscenity: A Work May Be Subject to State Regulation Where That Work, Taken as a Whole, Appeals to the Prurient Interest in Sex, Portrays, in a Patently Offensive Way, Sexual Conduct Specifically Defined by the Applicable State Law, and Taken as a Whole, Does Not Have Serious Literary, Artistic, Political, or Scientific Value." *Journal of Urban Law* 51 (November 1973): 314–21.

Rosenblum, R. "Judicial Politics of Obscenity." *Pepperdine Law Review* 3 (Winter 1975): 1–25.

Ross, Terry D. "Expert Testimony in Obscenity Cases." *Hastings Law Journal* 18 (November 1966): 161–79.

Rowell, G.B. "Argument in 'Forever Amber' Case." *Case and Comment* 54 (March/April 1949): 43–49.

Rubenstein, B.J. "Obscenity." *Brooklyn Law Review* 24 (December 1957): 49.

Rudolph, Glenn. "RICO: The Predicate Offense of Obscenity, the Seizure of Adult Bookstore Assets, and the First Amendment." *Northern Kentucky Law Review* 15 (1988): 585–609.

Russell, Thomas B. "Criminal Law—Obscenity: The Need for Legislative Reform." *Kentucky Law Journal* 57 (1968 69): 582 91.

Ryan, James J. "Seizure of Allegedly Obscene Films." *South Dakota Law Review* 15 (Spring 1970): 399–411.

St. John-Stevas, N. "Obscenity, Literature and the Law." *Catholic Lawyer* 3 (Autumn 1957): 301.

St. John-Stevas, N. *Obscenity and the Law.* New York: DaCapo Press, 1974.

Ste-Marie, J-P. "L'obscenite." *Revue Juridique Themis* 1 (1969): 125.

Samuels, A. "Obscenity and the Law: The Balance between Freedom to Publish and Public Decency." *Law Society's Gazette* 61 (November 1964): 729.

Samuels, A. "Obscenity and the Law." *Nothern Ireland Legal Quarterly* 20 (September 1969): 231–54.

Sanders, William C. "Constitutional Law—Obscenity: Constitutionality of Georgia Statute Proscribing Obscene Language in the Presence of Women or Children Upheld." *Mercer Law Review* 25 (Winter 1974): 371–79.

Sands, Alexander P., III. "Requirement and Techniques for Holding an Adversary Hearing Prior to Seizure of Obscene Material." *North Carolina Law Review* 48 (1970): 830–47.

Sauvey, Marian Weilert. "Constitutional Law: McNary v. Carlton—The Binding Advisory Jury in Missouri Obscenity Cases." *University of Missouri Kansas City Law Review* 45 (Fall 1976): 159–67.

Schaberg, John I. "Constitutional Law—Obscenity: The State May Not Prohibit Future Exhibitions of Motion Pictures through a Nuisance Abatement Statute Which Allows a State Trial Judge, on the Basis of a Finding That a Theater Has Shown Specific Obscene Films in the Past, to Issue Such Injunction Against Future Activity, Unless Procedural Safeguards Govern the Entry of Orders Restraining the Exhibition of Named or Unnamed Films with Regard to the Context in Which They Are Displayed." *American Journal of Criminal Law* 8 (July 1980): 199–208.

Schauer, F. "Obscenity and the Conflict of Laws." *West Virginia Law Review* 77 (April 1975): 377–400.

Schauer, F. *The Law of Obscenity*. Washington, D.C.: Bureau of National Affairs, 1976.

Schauer, F. "Obscenity and the Law: The Return of Variable Obscenity?" *Hastings Law Journal* 28 (July 1977): 1275–1358.

Schauer, F. "Reflections on 'Contemporary Community Standards': The Perpetuation of an Irrelevant Concept in the Law of Obscenity." *North Carolina Law Review* 56 (January 1978): 1–28.

Schauer, F. "Speech and 'Speech'—Obscenity and 'Obscenity': An Exercise in the Interpretation of Constitutional Language." *Georgia Law Journal* 67 (April 1979): 899–933.

Schauer, F. "Response: Pornography and the First Amendment." *University of Pittsburgh Law Review* 40 (Summer 1979): 567–651.

Schauer, F. "Categories and the First Amendment: A Play in Three Acts." *Vanderbilt Law Review* 34 (March 1981): 265–307.

Schauer, F. "Slippery Slopes." *Harvard Law Review* 99 (1985): 361.

Schell, B. "Development of a Pornography Community Standard—Questionnaire Results for Two Canadian Cities." *Canadian Journal of Criminology* 29 (April 1987): 133–52.

Schleef, Joan. "Constitutional Law—Appellate Procedure—Obscenity: In Determining Whether Materials Are Obscene, the Trier of Fact May Rely upon the Widespread Availability of Comparable Materials to Indicate That the Materials Are Accepted by the Community and Hence Not Obscene under the Miller Test." *University of Cincinnati Law Review* 52, no. 4 (1983): 1131–41.

Schmalz, Kurt L. "Problems in Giving Obscenity Copyright Protection: Did Jartech and Mitchell Brothers Go Too Far?" *Vanderbilt Law Review* 38 (March 1983): 403–30.

Schmarak, Barry. "Haralampopoulos v. Capital News Agency, Inc. (Ill) 217 N.E. 2d 366." *DePaul Law Review* 16 (Autumn/Winter 1966): 249–54.

Schmidt, G.P. "Justification of Statutes Barring Pornography from the Mail." *Fordham Law Review* 26 (Spring 1957): 70.

Schnall, Marc. "United States Supreme Court: Definitions of Obscenity." *Crime and Delinquency* 18 (January 1972): 59–67.

Schneider, D.W. "Authority of the Register of Copyrights to Deny Registration of a Claim to Copyright on the Ground of Obscenity." *Chicago-Kent Law Review* 51 (1975): 691–724.

Schoen, R.B. "Billy Jenkins and Eternal Verities: The 1973 Obscenity Cases." *North Dakota Law Review* 50 (Summer 1974): 567–91.

Schopler, E.H. "Comment Note: Validity of Procedures Designed to Protect the Public Against Obscenity." In *American Law Reports*. 3d ed. Vol. 5, edited by Rochester, N.Y.: Lawyers Co-Operative Publishing Company; San Francisco: Bancroft-Whitney Company, 1966. 1214–35.

Schroeder, Theodore. "What Is Criminally Obscene?" *Albany Law Journal* 68 (1906): 211.

Schroeder, T. "Legal Obscenity and Sexual Psychology." *Medical Legal Journal* 25 (1907): 195.

Schroeder, Theodore. "Obscene Literature at Common Law." *Albany Law Journal* 69 (1907): 146.

Schroeder, Theodore. "Varieties of Official Modesty." *Albany Law Journal* 70 (1908): 226.

Schwab, H.J. "Obscene but Not Heard." *Los Angeles Bar Bulletin* 46 (October 1971): 483.

Schwartz, L.B. "Criminal Obscenity Law: Portents from Recent Supreme Court Decisions and Proposals of the American Law Institute in the Model Penal Code." *Pennsylvania Bar Association Quarterly* 29 (October 1957): 8.

Schwartz, L.B. "Morals Offenses and the Model Penal Code." *Columbia Law Review* 63 (March 1963): 669–86.

"Scienter Requirement in Criminal Obscenity Prosecutions." *New York Univeristy Law Review* 41 (October 1966): 791–820.

Scileppi, John F. "Obscenity and the Law." *New York Law Forum* 10 (September 1964): 297–306.

"Scope of Statutes Censoring Obscene Literature." *Illinois Law Review* 40 (January/February 1946): 417–21.

"Scope of Supreme Court Review in Obscenity Cases." *Duke Law Journal* (Summer 1965): 596–607.

Scoville, Stanley E. "Private Morality and the Right to Be Free: The Thrust of Stanley v. Georgia." *Arizona Law Review* 11 (Winter 1969): 731–48.

"Search, Seizure and Obscenity—Confusion in the Test for Probable Cause." *Ohio State Law Journal* 24 (Summer 1963): 562–66.

Seaton, Richard H. "Obscenity: The Search for a Standard." *Kansas Law Review* 13 (October 1964): 117–24.

Sebastian, Raymond F. "Note: Obscenity in the Supreme Court: Nine Years of Confusion." *Stanford Law Review* 19 (November 1966): 167–89.

"Seizing Obscenity: New York v. P.J. Video, Inc. (106 S. Ct. 1610) and the Waning of Presumptive Protection." *North Carolina Law Review* 65 (April 1987): 799–815.

Semonche, John E. "Definitional and Contextual Obscenity: The Supreme Court's New and Disturbing Accommodation." *University of California Los Angeles Law Review* 13 (August 1966): 1173–1213.

Serritos, Manuel S. "Illinois' Obscenity Statute Revisited: The Legacy of Ward v. Illinois, the Unresolved

Vagueness Problem." *Illinois Bar Journal* 75 (September 1986): 20.

Shapiro, M. "Obscenity Law: A Public Policy Analysis." *Journal of Public Law* 20 (1971): 503.

Sharma, K.M. "Obscenity and the Law: The Indian Experience through the American Looking-Glass." *Houston Law Review* 6 (January 1969): 425–53.

Sharp, Donald S. *Commentaries on Obscenity.* Metuchen, N.J.: Scarecrow Press, 1970.

Sharp, Frederick, L. "Obscenity: Prurient Interests and the Law." *University of Toronto Faculty Law Review* 34 (Spring 1976): 244–54.

Shaughnessy, Edward J. *A Standard for Miller: A Community Response to Pornography.* Lanham, Md.: University Press of America, 1980.

Shearer, William B., Jr. "Corinth Publications, Inc. v. Westberry (Ga) 146 S.E. 2d 764." *Mercer Law Review* 17 (Spring 1966): 478–79.

Shepherd, Robert E., Jr. "The Law of Obscenity in Virginia." *Washington and Lee Law Review* 17 (Fall 1960): 322–28.

Shubow, Michael Z. "Constitutional Law–Obscenity: Supreme Court Decisions as to 'Obscenity' of a Particular Work May Not Be Binding on State Courts." *Wayne Law Review* 13 (Winter 1967): 410–17.

Shugrue, Richard E., and Patricia Zieg. "An Atlas for Obscenity: Exploring Community Standards." *Creighton Law Review* 7 (1974): 157–81.

Silber, Alan. "Supreme Court and Obscenity: The Ginzburg (Ginzburg v. U.S., 86 S. Ct. 942) Test—Restriction of First Amendment Freedoms through Loss of Predictability." *Rutgers Law Review* 21 (Fall 1966): 56–72.

Simmons, E.B. "Obscene Publication." *Solicitors' Journal* 107 (March 1963): 165–67.

Simner, J.S. "Obscene Literature—Its Suppression." *Case and Comment* 23 (1916): 16.

Sinclair, Kent. "Note: Constitutional Law—First Amendment: The New Metaphysics of the Law of Obscenity." *California Law Review* 57 (1969): 1257–80.

Skrabut, Paul A. "Constitutional Law—Obscenity—Evidence—Ginzberg v. United States." *Cornell Law Quarterly* 51 (Summer 1966): 785–94.

Skrinseth, Karen. "Constitutional Law—First Amendment: Evidence of Pandering in the Advertising and Sale of Material May Be Probative with Respect to the Obscene Nature of the Material." *American University Law Review* 16 (December 1966): 122–36.

Slivka, William J. "Obscenity through the Mails." *Case Western Reserve Law Review* 11 (June 1960): 480–92.

Slough, M.C. "Obscenity, Freedom, and Responsibility." *Creighton Law Review* 3 (1969–70): 218.

Slough, M.C. "Miller v. California: An Attempt to Control Obscenity." *Journal of the Bar Association of Kansas* 42 (Winter 1973): 317–23.

Slough, M.C., and P.D. McAnany. "Obscenity and Constitutional Freedom." *St. Louis University Law Journal* 8 (Spring 1964): 279–357.

Slough, M.C., and P.D. McAnany. "Obscenity and Constitutional Freedom." *St. Louis University Law Journal* 8 (Summer 1964): 449–532.

Smith, Leo H. "Constitutional Law—Obscenity: The Principle of Pandering Promotion." *University of Colorado Law Review* 39 (Fall 1966): 152–55.

Snowden, John R. "Case Note: Constitutional Law—Obscenity: A Return to the First Amendment?" *Nebraska Law Review* 49 (March 1970): 660–69.

Sobel, Lester A., ed. *Pornography, Obscenity and the Law.* Facts on File, 1979.

Sorenson, Karen L. "Community Standards and the Regulation of Obscenity." *DePaul Law Review* 24 (Fall 1974): 185–94.

Spacone, Andrew C. "Topless Dancing and the Constitution: A New York Town's Experience." *Buffalo Law Review* 25 (Spring 1976): 753–72.

Spencer, J.R. "Blasphemy: the Law Commission's Working Paper." *Criminal Law Review* (Great Britain) (December 1981): 810–20.

Staal, Lorri. "First Amendment: The Objective Standard for Social Value in Obscenity Cases: Pope v. Illinois (107 S. Ct. 1918)." *Journal of Criminal Law and Criminology* 73 (Winter 1988): 735–62.

"Stanley v. Georgia: New Directions in Obscenity Regulations." *Texas Law Review* 48 (1970): 646.

Stanmeyer, W.A. "Obscene Evils v. Obscure Truths: Some Notes on First Amendment Principles." *Capital University Law Review* 7 (1978): 647–82.

Stanmeyer, W.A. "Keeping the Constitutional Republic Civic Virtue vs. Pornographic Attack." *Hastings Constitutional Law Quarterly* 14 (Spring 1987): 561–93.

"Statutory Innovation in the Obscenity Field." *Buffalo Law Review* 6 (Spring 1957): 305.

Steinkamp, Robert T. "Constitutional Law: The Scale of Obscene Material to Minors." *University of Missouri Kansas City Law Review* 34 (Winter 1969): 127–42.

Stephenson, D. Grier, Jr. "State Appellate Courts and Written Obscenity: The Georgia Experience." *Mercer Law Review* 19 (Summer 1968): 287–311.

Stephenson, D. Grier., Jr. "State Appellate Courts and the Judicial Process: Written Obscenity." *William and Mary Law Review* 11 (Fall 1969): 106–37.

Stern, C.M. "Toward a Rationale for the Use of Expert Testimony in Obscenity Litigation." *Case Western Reserve Law Review* 20 (April 1969): 527–69.

Stern, Jill Abeshouse, Edwin G. Krasnow, and R. Michael Senkowski. "The New Video Marketplace and the Search for a Coherent Regulatory Philosophy." *Catholic University Law Review* 32 (Spring 1983): 529–602.

Stevens, Pamela J. "Community Standards and Federal Obscenity Prosecutions." *Southern California Law Review* 55 (March 1982): 693–726.

Stewart, S. Jean. "Constitutional Law–Pornography: Colorado Municipal Government Authority to Regulate Obscene Materials." *Denver Law Journal* 51 (1974): 75–94.

Stone, R.T.H. "Obscene Publications—The Problems Persist." *Criminal Law Review* (Great Britain) (March 1986): 139–45.

Stone, R.T.H. "Obscenity Law Reform: Some Practical Problems." *New Law Journal* (Great Britain) 130 (25 September 1980): 872–740.

Stout, Ed., and Richard Schneider. "Private Search and Prior Restraint of Obscene Materials: The Interaction of Two Doctrines." *Mercer Law Review* 31 (Summer 1980): 1029–45.

Strahan, J.A. "Obscene Literature and Constitutional Law." *Chicago Legal Notes* 44 (1911): 70.

"Substantive Law of Obscenity: An Adventure in Quicksand." *New York Law Forum* 13 (Spring 1967): 81.

Summers, Robert C. "Constitutional Protection of Obscene Material Against Censorship as Correlated with Copyright Protection of Obscene Material Against Infringement." *Southern California Law Review* 31 (April 1958): 301–12.

Sunderland, Lane V. *Obscenity: The Court, the Congress and the President's Commission.* Washington, D.C.: American Enterprise Institute for Public Policy Research, 1974.

"The Supreme Court, 1968 Term: Private Possession of Obscene Material." *Harvard Law Review* 83 (1969–70): 147–54.

"Supreme Court Rules Undercover Purchase of Obscene Material Not a Search or Seizure." *Search and Seizure Law Reporter* 12 (October 1985): 164.

Swanson, Edward T. "New Obscenity Standard." *Connecticut Law Review* 6 (Fall 1973): 165–95.

Swingen, Amy L. "Federal Court Interpretation of the Washington Obscenity Statute." *Washington Law Review* 61 (July 1986): 1237–52.

"Tariff Act, Ban Against Importation of Obscene Books, Standard for Test of Obscenity. (Parmelee v. United States, 113 F. 2d 729)." B. Globman, *Buffalo University L. Review*, Rev. 20: 740-3, November, 1940; A.C. Seward, Jr., *Georgetown Law Journal*, 29: 664-6, February, 1941; R.C. Souder, Jr., *Georgian Bar Journal* 3: 67-8, November, 1940.

Tarlow, Barry. "RICO: The New Darling of the Prosecutor's Nursery." *Fordham Law Review* 49 (1980): 165–206.

Taylor, Bruce. "Pornography and the First Amendment." In Patrick B. McGuigan and Randall R. Rader, *Criminal Justice Reform*, edited by Washington, D.C.: Free Congress Foundation, 1983: 155–70.

Taylor, Charles E. "New Standard of Obscenity." *Ohio State Law Journal* 19 (Winter 1958): 137.

Taylor, Glen E. "Constitutional Law—Freedom of Speech: Obscenity Not Entitled to Constitutional Protection as Free Speech under First or Fourteenth Amendments." *Texas Law Review* 36 (December 1957): 226–29.

Taylor, Michael B. "Constitutional Law—Freedom of Speech and Press—Censorship of Obscenity." *Mississippi Law Journal* 37 (March 1966): 310–13.

Taylor, Wallace L. "Status of Iowa's Obscenity Laws." *Drake Law Review* 21 (January 1972): 314–30.

Teachout, P.R. "Obscenity and the First Amendment: Chains of Tradition, Instruments of Freedom: Contours of the Emerging Right to Community in Obscenity Law." *Capital University Law Review* 7 (1978): 227.

Teeter, D.L., Jr., and D.R. Pember. "Retreat from Obscenity: Redrup v. New York." *Hastings Law Journal* 21 (November 1969): 175–89.

Teeter, D.L. Jr., and D.R. Pember. "Obscenity, 1971: The Rejuvenation of State Power and the Return to Roth." *Villanova Law Review* 17 (December 1971): 211.

Telling, David. "Defense of 'Public Good.' " *New Law Journal* (1979): 299–301.

Terry, B.G. "Effect of Recent Obscenity Cases." *Washburn Law Journal* 13 (Winter 1974): 26–32.

Tessaro, Nancy. "Is the Pig in the Parlor? (First Amendment Symposium)." *Northern Kentucky Law Review* 15 (Spring 1988): 205–25.

"Test of Obscene Literature: Work of Possible Scientific Interest Obscene When Circularized as Pornography." *Harvard Law Review* 53 (June 1940): 1403–4.

"Texas' New Obscenity Laws: Redefining Taste." *Houston Law Review* 17 (May 1980): 835–72.

Thomas, Elizabeth T. "Obscenity Statute Deemed Unconstitutionally Overbroad. (Annual Survey of South Carolina Law: January 1, 1986–December 31, 1986.)" *South Carolina Law Review* 39 (Autumn 1987): 53–57.

Thomson, John M. "Case Comment: Constitutional Law—Obscenity Statutes—Freedom of Speech." *Miami Law Quarterly* 11 (1957): 523–26.

Tierney, Kevin. "Criminal Law—Obscenity: An Anglo-American Dilemma." *New Law Journal* 116 (3 November 1966): 1483–84.

Tobolowsky, E. "Obscenity: A Continuing Dilemma." *Southwestern Law Journal* 24 (December 1971): 827.

Tongg, Trudie L. "Criminal Law—State v. Kam: Do Community Standards on Pornography Exist?" *University of Hawaii Law Review* 9 (Fall 1987): 727–41.

"Trans-Lux Distribution Corporation v. Board of Regents, 14 N.Y. 2d 88, 198 N.E. 2d 242." *Ohio State Law Journal* 25 (Summer 1964): 417–34.

Trillope, A. "Proceeding Against Defendant in Respect of Allegedly Obscene Film Where Trial of Same Issue Against Different Defendant Had Resulted in Aquittal—All Proceedings Capable of Being Brought Together before Same Court: Whether Abuse of Process." *Criminal Law Review* (Great Britain) (June 1984): 350–52.

Trimmier, C. Stephen, Jr. "Criminal Law—Obscenity: A New Dimension in Which to Judge Previous Criteria." *Alabama Law Review* 19 (Fall 1966): 187–93.

Tucker, E.W. "Law of Obscenity: Where Has It Gone?" *University of Florida Law Review* 22 (Spring/Summer 1970): 547.

Turner, Joseph Spoor, III. "Assessing the Constitutionality of North Carolina's New Obscenity Law." *North Carolina Law Review* 65 (January 1987): 400–16.

Turney, H.L. "Road to Respectability: A Woman of Pleasure and Competing Conceptions of the First Amendment." *University of Dayton Law Review* 5 (Summer 1980): 271–99.

Tushnet, M. "Obscenity and the First Amendment: Technical and Economic Aspects of the Production of Sexually Explicit Materials." *Capital University Law Review* 7 (1978): 227.

Twomey, John E. "The Citizens' Committee and Comic-Book Control: A Study of Extragovernmental Restraint." *Law and Contemporary Problems* 20 (Autumn 1955): 621–29.

Upchurch, Virgil. "Constitutional Law—Due Process—Obscenity." *Oklahoma Law Review* 11 (November 1958): 435–37.

U.S. Congress. House. Committee on Post Office and Civil Service. Subcommittee on Postal Operations. "Obscene Matter Sent Through the Mail" 87th Cong. 1st sess., 1962.

"U.S. v. West Coast News Co., 228 F. Supp. 171." *University of Pennsylvania Law Review* 113 (January 1965): 464–72.

"U.S. v. Zuideveld, 316 F. 2d 873." *University of Pennsylvania Law Review* 112 (Fall 1961): 601 5.

Vamplew, J.L.K. "Obscene Literature and Section 150A." *Criminal Law Quarterly* 7 (August 1964): 187–92.

Van Smith, Larry. "United States v. Reidel: Resolving an Ambiguity in Obscenity Control." *Southwestern Law Journal* 25 (December 1971): 819–23.

Vollersen, Melva M. "Constitutional Law—Obscenity: California Penal Code Section 311 Defining Obscene Matter Is Not Unconstitutionally Vague." *Santa Clara Law Review* 17 (Winter 1977): 236–45.

Wade, E.C.S. "Obscene Publications Act, 1959." *Cambridge Law Journal* (Great Britain) (November 1959): 179–82.

Wald, Emil W. "Constitutional Law—First Amendment: Obscene Literature Standards Re Examined." *South Carolina Law Review* 18 (1966): 497–503.

Wallahan, Franklin J. "Immorality, Obscenity and the Law of Copyright." *South Dakota Law Review* 6 (Spring 1961): 109–29.

Waples, Gregory L., and Mary Jo White. "Choice of Community Standards in Federal Obscenity Proceedings: The Role of the Constitution and the Common Law." *Virginia Law Review* 64 (April 1978): 399–446.

Warren, E., Jr. "Obscenity Laws: A Shift to Reality?" *Santa Clara Law Review* 11, (Fall 1970): 1.

Weaver, George M. *Handbook on the Prosecution of Obscenity Cases.* New York: National Obscenity Law Center, 1985.

Weaver, Timothy A. "Constitutional Law: States May Regulate Material Depicting Obscene Sexual Conduct Specifically Defined by Applicable State Law." *Illinois Bar Journal* 62 (December 1973): 218–21.

Weber, J.W. "First Amendment—Obscenity and Indecency." *Journal of Criminal Law and Criminology* 69 (Winter 1978): 474–83.

Weinberg, Richard A. "The Right to a Jury Trial in Obscenity Prosecutions: A Sixth Amendment Analysis for a First Amendment Problem." *Fordham Law Review* 50 (May 1982): 1311–27.

Weisberger, Joseph R. "The Bill of Rights and Benevolent Despotism: A Look at the Supreme Court's Role in

Education, Regulation of Attorney Advertising and Obscenity." *Suffolk University Law Review* 17 (Spring 1983): 23–52.

Weitzel, Stephen E. "Constitutional Law—Obscenity: Constituent Elements of Tripartite Definition of Obscenity to Be Determined by Applying Contemporary Community Standards, Not National Standards." *Emory Law Journal* 23 (Spring 1974): 551–65.

Werne, Naomi. "Obscenity Prosecutions: Maryland v. Macon and Other Recent Developments." *Search and Seizure Law Report* 13 (February 1988): 9–15.

Wessling, John J. "Comment: Constitutional Law: A New Test for Determining Obscenity." *Glendale Law Review* 3 no. 1 (1978–79): 39–54.

Whitmore, Harry. "Obscenity in Literature: Crime of Free Speech." *Sydney Law Review* (Australia) 4 (March 1963): 179–204.

Whitmore, Harry. "Australian Censorship 1964." *Sydney Law Review* 4 (August 1964): 396–403.

Whyte, George K., Jr. "Notes: The Use of Expert Testimony in Obscenity Litigation." *Wisconsin Law Review* (Winter 1965): 113–32.

Wien, Daniel P. "Constitutional Law: Taking a Soft Look at Probable Cause: An Obscene Result for First Amendment Protections." *Loyola Entertainment Law Journal* 7 (1987): 111–22.

Wiesman, M.W. "Obscenity: The Court Tries Again." *Missouri Business Journal* 30 (March 1974): 81–92.

Wilcox, Jamison. "The Craft of Drafting Plain-Language Jury Instructions: A Study of Sample Pattern Instruction on Obscenity." *Temple Law Quarterly* 59 (Winter 1986): 1159–87.

Wilkins, Stan N. "Obscenity Law's Application in Kansas: Issues and Procedures." *Washburn Law Journal* 12 (Winter 1973): 185–202.

Williams, D.G.T. "Sex and Morals in the Criminal Law." *Criminal Law Recorder* (April 1964): 253.

Williams, D.G.T. "Control of Obscenity." *Criminal Law Recorder* (August/September 1965): 471–522.

Williams, J.E. Hall. "Obscenity in Modern English Law." *Law and Contemporary Problems* 20 (Autumn 1955):630–47.

Williams, J.E. Hall. "Statutes: The Obscene Publications Act, 1959." *Modern Law Review* 23 (May 1960): 285–90.

Wilson, Hnter. "California's New Obscenity Statute: The Meaning of 'Obscene' and the Problem of Scienter." *Southern California Law Review* 36, no. 4 (1963): 513–45.

Wilson, John D. "Criminal Law—Obscenity: Interpretation of Criminal Statutes." *Canadian Bar Review* 64 (December 1986): 740–54.

Wilson, Thomas Buck. "Constitutional Law—Obscenity—Formulation of Standards—Commercial Exploitation." *Connecticut Bar Journal* 40 (December 1966): 670–79.

Wisener, Randolph N. "Criminal Law—Obscenity: State Police Powers Justify the Legislative Proscription and Criminalization of the Sale or Promotion of Devices Which Are Designed or Manufactured for the Purpose of Stimulating Human Genital Organs." *St. Mary's Law Journal* 17 (Summer 1986): 1125–51.

Wolf, Steven M. "Obscenity: The Lingering Uncertainty." *New York University Review of Law and Social Change* 2 (Spring 1972): 1–19.

Wolfe, Stacy E. "Constitutional Law—Obscenity—New First Amendment Standards." *Akron Law Review* 7 (Fall 1973): 179–87.

The Working Party. *The Obscenity Laws.* London: Deutsch, 1969.

Wright, R.G. "Defining Obscenity: The Criterion of Value." *New England Law Review* 22 (December 1987): 315–39.

Wszolek, Dennis F. "Application of Miller v. California in Ohio." *Capital University Law Review* 4 (1975): 315–24.

"X-Rated Motion Pictures: From Restricted Theatres and Drive-Ins to the Television Screen?" *Virginia University Law Review* 8 (Fall 1973): 107–24.

Yoakum, Robert. "An Obscene, Lewd, Lascivious, Indecent, Filthy and Vile Tabloid Entitled Screw." *Columbia Journalism Review* 15 (March/April 1977): 38–49.

Young, James B. "McCauley v. Tropic of Cancer (Wis) 121 N.W. 2d 545." *Marquette Law Review* 47 (Fall 1963): 275–314.

Young, R., "Right to Counsel . . . Conflict of Interests." *American Bar Association Journal* 67 (May 1981): 636–37.

Zellick, Graham. "Obscene or Pornographic? Obscenity and the Public Good." *Cambridge Law Journal* (Great Britain) 27 (November 1969): 177–81.

Zellick, Graham. "A New Approach to the Control of Obscenity." *Modern Law Review* 33 (May 1970): 289–98.

Zellick, Graham. "Films and the Law of Obscenity." *Criminal Law Review* (Great Britain) (March 1971): 126.

Zellick, Graham. "Two Comments on Search and Seizure under the Obscene Publications Act." *Criminal Law Review* (Great Britain) (September 1971): 504–14.

Zellick, Graham. "Offensive Advertisements in the Mail." *Criminal Law Review* Great Britain (December 1972): 724.

Zuckman, Harvey Lyle. "Obscenity in the Mails." *Southern California Law Review* 33 (Winter 1960): 171–88.

CHAPTER 10

"Anti-Pornography Law Voided." *News Media and the Law.* 9 (Fall/Winter 1985): 32–33.

Ashman, Allan "Indianapolis Porno Law Violates First Amendment. (American Booksellers Association Inc. v. Hudnut)." *American Bar Association Journal* 71 March 1985: 118.

Ayim, M. "Pornography and Sexism: A Thread in the Web." *University of Western Ontario Law Review* 23 (December 1985): 189–96.

Baldwin, Margaret. "The Sexuality of Inequality: The Minneapolis Pornography Ordinance." *Law and Inequality: A Journal of Theory and Practice* 2 (August 1984): 629–53.

Beck, Melinda, et al. "A Court Test for Porn." *Time.* 13 August 1984.

Benson, Rebecca. "Pornography and the First Amendment: American Booksellers v. Hudnut." *Harvard Women's Law Journal* 9 (Spring 1986): 153–72.

Brèst, Paul, and Ann Vandenberg. "Politics, Feminism, and the Constitution: The Anti-Pornography Movement in Minneapolis." *Stanford Law Review* 39 (February 1987): 607–61.

Carr, Edward A. "Feminism, Pornography, and the First Amendment: An Obscenity-Based Analysis of Proposed Antipornography Laws." *University of California Los Angeles Law Review.* 34 (April 1987): 1265–1304.

Duggan, Lisa, Nan Hunter, and Carol S. Vance. "False Promise: New Antipornography Legislation in the U.S." *SIECUS Report* (May 1985).

Duggan, Lisa, and Ann Snitow. "Porn Law is About Images, Not Power." *Newsday,* 26 September 1984.

Dworkin, Andrea. "Against the Male Flood: Censorship, Pornography, and Equality." *Harvard Women's Law Journal* 8 (Spring 1985): 1–30.

Dworkin, Andrea, and Catharine MacKinnon. "Pornography Violates Women's Civil Rights." In *Censorship—Opposing Viewpoints,* edited by Terry O'Neill. St. Paul: Greenhaven Press, 1985.

Elshtain, Jean Bethke. "The New Porn Wars." *New Republic.* 25 June 1984,.

Emerson, Thomas I. "Pornography and the First Amendment: A Reply to Professor MacKinnon." *Yale Law and Policy Review* 3 (1984–85): 130–43.

Emerson, Thomas I. "Censoring Pornography Would Violate Civil Rights." In *Censorship—Opposing Viewpoints,* edited by Terry O'Neill, St. Paul: Greenhaven Press, 1985.

Epstein, R.A. "Products Liability: The Search for the Middle Ground." *North Carolina Law Review* 56 (1978): 643–62.

Gamso, Jeffrey M. "Sex Discrimination and the First Amendment: Pornography and the Free Speech." *Texas Technological Law Review* 17 (June 1986): 1577–1602.

Gaze, Beth. "Pornography and Freedom of Speech: An American Feminist Approach." *Legal Service Bulletin* 11 (June 1986): 123–27.

Gerety, T. "Pornography and Violence." *University of Pittsburgh Law Review* 40 (1979:).

Gershel, Michael A. "Evaluating a Proposed Civil Rights Approach to Pornography: Legal Analysis As If Women Mattered." *William Mitchell Law Review* 11, no. 1 (1985): 41–80.

Goldstein, Leslie F. "The New Pornography Laws." *Delaware Lawyer* 4 (Fall 1985): 32–39.

Hamm, Valerie. "The Civil Rights Pornography Ordinances—An Examination under the First Amendment." *Kentucky Law Journal* 73 (1984–85): 1081–1108.

Hoffman, Eric. "Feminism, Pornography, and Law." *University of Pennsylvania Law Review* 133 (January 1985): 497–534.

Hoyt, Charlee. "Pornography and Women's Civil Rights." *Response To The Victimization of Women and Children* (Fall 1984): 507.

Hunter, Nan D., and Sylvia A. Law. "Brief Amici Curiae of Feminist Anti-Censorship Taskforce, et al., in *American Booksellers Association v. Hudnut.*" *University of Michigan Journal of Law Reform* 20 (Fall 1987 and Winter 1988): 69–136.

Hutchins, Lori Douglass. "Pornography: The Prosecution of Pornography Under Prostitution Statutes—A New Approach." *Syracuse Law Review* 37 (1986): 977–1002.

Jacobs, Caryn. "Patterns of Violence: A Feminist Perspective on the Regulation of Pornography." *Harvard Women's Law Journal* 7 (1984): 5–55.

Klausner, Marian Leslie. "Redefining Pornography as Sex Discrimination: An Innovative Civil Rights Approach." *New England Law Review* 20 (1984–85): 721–58.

Krauthammer, Charles. "Pornography is a Moral, Not a Civil Rights, Issue." In *Censorship—Opposing Viewpoints*, edited by Terry O'Neill, St. Paul: Greenhaven Press, 1985.

Layman, William K. "Violent Pornography and the Obscenity Doctrine: The Road Not Taken." *Georgetown Law Journal* 75 (April 1987): 1475–1508.

Liston, Angela A. "Pornography and the First Amendment: The Feminist Balance." *Arizona Law Review* 27 (Spring 1985): 416–39.

Lubert, Jane. "Constitutional Law: Death of an Ordinance: Pornography Unconstitutionally Defined as Sex Discrimination." *Loyola Entertainment Law Journal* 7 (Winter 1987): 89–109.

Maag, Marilyn J. "The Indianapolis Pornography Ordinance: Does the Right to Free Speech Outweigh Pornography's Harm to Women?" *University of Cincinnati Law Review* 54, no. 1 (1985): 249–69.

MacKinnon, Catharine. "Commentaries: Not a Moral Issue." *Yale Review of Law and Policy* 2 November 1983: 321–45.

MacKinnon, Catharine. "Pornography, Civil Rights, and Speech." *Harvard Civil Rights–Civil Liberties Law Review* 20 (Winter 1985): 1–70.

Martin, Del. "An Open Letter to Feminists about Antipornography Laws." *Gay Community News* (Boston), 4 May 1985.

McWalters, Thomas. "An Attempt to Regulate Pornography through Civil Rights Legislation: Is It Constitutional?" *University of Toledo Law Review* 16 (Fall 1984): 231–313.

"The Minneapolis Civil Rights Ordinance, with Proposed Feminist Pornography Amendments." *Constitutional Commentary* 2 (Winter 1985): 181–89.

Moore, Jamie M. "A New Legal Approach to Pornography." *Response to the Victimization of Women and Children* 9, no. 1 (1986): 13–15.

"Pornography as Civil Rights Violation: Right Enemy, Wrong Attack." *American Bar Association Journal* 71 (March 1985): 46.

"Press at Home and Abroad: Local Governments Attempt to Ban Pornography as a Form of Sex Discrimination." *News Media and Law* 9 (Spring 1985): 45–47.

Quade, Vicki. "Smut Furor: Women's Rights v. Free Speech." *American Bar Association Journal* 70 (March 1984): 42.

Sandler, Winifred Ann. "The Minneapolis Anti-Pornography Ordinance: A Valid Assertion of Civil Rights." *Fordham Urban Law Journal* 13 (1984–85): 909–46.

Seator, Penelope. "Judicial Indifference to Pornography's Harm: *American Booksellers v. Hudnut.*" *Golden Gate University Law Review* 17 (Fall 1987): 297–358.

Tigue, Randall D.B. "Civil Rights and Censorship—Incompatible Bedfellows." *William Mitchell Law Review* 11 (1985): 81–125.

Vadas, Melinda. "A First Look at the Pornography/Civil Rights Ordinance: Could Pornography be the Subordination of Women?" *Journal of Philosophy* 84 (September 1987): 487–511.

Van Dyke, Michael S. "Regulation of Pornography: Is Erotica Self-Expression Deserving of Protection?" *Loyola Law Review* 33 (Summer 1987): 445–68.

Waring, Nancy W. "Coming to Terms with Pornography: Toward a Feminist Perspective on Sex, Censorship, and Hysteria." *Research in Law, Deviance and Social Control* 8 (1986): 85–112.

Warshay, D.W., and L.H. Warshay. "The Use of Obscenity in the Subordination of Women." *Midwest Sociological Society* (1978).

CHAPTER 11

Abrams, F. "Negligent Programming? Some First Amendment Ramifications." *Communications Lawyer* 1 (Winter 1983): 1, 8-9.

Abrams, F. "Content Neutrality: Some Thoughts on Words and Music." *Harvard Journal of Law and Public Policy* 10 Winter 1986: 61-65.

Addison, Roger G. "Constitutional Law: Can Offensive Language Be Punished in Oklahoma?" *Oklahoma Law Review* 29 (Spring 1976): 395-409.

"Adult Theatre Zoning Overturned for Failure to Justify Restrictions." *Zoning and Planning Law Report* 8 (May 1985): 127.

"Agency Won't Define Indecency: Broadcasters Can Assume Children Aren't Listening between Midnight and 6:00 a.m.; At Other Times Stations Must Guess Whether FCC Will Say Programs Violate Policy." *News Media and the Law* 12 (Winter 1988): 47-48.

"Airways Theater v. Canale, 366 F Supp 343." *Memphis State University Law Review* 4 (Spring 1974): 619-22.

Albaugh, B. Kay. "Regulation of Obscenity through Nuisance Restraint—Statutes and Injunctive Remedies," *Wake Forest Law Review* 19 (1983): 7-31.

Albert, James A. "The Federal and Local Regulation of Cable Television." *University of Colorado Law Review* 48 (Summer 1977): 501-23.

Allen, Peter. "Public Nuisances, Private Lawyers." *California Lawyer* 5 (July 1985): 10-11.

Allen, Samuel N. "Constitutional Law: First Amendment Protection of Adult Establishments." *Washington and Lee Law Review* 38 (Spring 1981): 495-505.

Alpert, James A. "Constitutional Regulation of Televised Violence." *Virginia Law Review* 64 (December 1978): 1299-1345.

Anderson, Robert M., and Thomas W. Mayo. "Zoning and the First Amendment." *Syracuse Law Review* 35 (Winter 1984): 492-97.

"Anti-Pornography Law and First Amendment Values." *Harvard Law Review* 98 (December 1984): 460-81.

Arenson, Kenneth J. "Prior Restraint: A Rational Doctrine or an Elusive Compendium of Hackneyed Cliches?" *Drake Law Review* 38 (Spring 1987): 265-96.

Arkes, Hadley. "Civility and the Restriction of Speech: Rediscovering the Defamation of Groups." *Supreme Court Review* (1974): 281-325.

Arthurs, H.W. "Hate Propaganda—An Argument Against Attempts to Stop It by Legislation." *Chitty's Law Journal* 18 (January 1970): 1-5.

Atleson, James B. "Obscenities in the Workplace: A Comment on Fair and Foul Expression and Status Relationships." *Buffalo Law Review* 34 (Fall 1985): 693-723.

Aver, Raymond H. "The Zoning of Adult Entertainment: How Far Can Planning Commission Go?" *COMMENT* 5 (Winter 1983): 293-315.

Ayer, Douglas, Roy E. Bates, and Peter J. Herman. "Self-Censorship in the Movie Industry: An Historical Perspective on Law and Social Change." *Wisconsin Law Review* 3 (1970): 791-838.

Ayim, Maryann. "Pornography and Sexism: A Thread in the Web." *University of Western Ontario Law Review* 23 (December 1985): 189-96.

Baker, Edwin C. "Constitutional Speech: A Problem in the Theory of Freedom." *Iowa Law Review* 62 (1976): 1-56.

Bakewell, Caroline D. "Constitutional Law: The Constitutionality of North Carolina's Nuisance Abatement Statute: A Prior Restraint on Non-Obscene Speech." *North Carolina Law Review* 61 (April 1983): 685-713.

Ballou, Gail. "Note: Recourse for Rape Victims: Third Party Liability." *Harvard Women's Law Journal* 4 (1981): 105-60.

Bals, Beth. "Comment: The Growing Pains of Cable Television." *Campbell Law Review* 7 (1984): 175-98.

Barlow, N.L.A. "Indecent and Obscene Language in New Zealand," *New Zealand Law Journal* (30 July 1974): 319-26.

Barnes, R.L. "Commercial Speech Concerning Unlawful Conduct—A Clear and Present Danger." *Brigham Young University Law Review* (1984): 457-508.

Barnes, R.L. "Regulation of Speech Intended to Affect Behavior." *Denver University Law Review* 63 (1985): 37-83.

Barnett, Stephen R. "State, Federal and Local Regulation of Cable Television." *Notre Dame Law Review* 47 (1972): 685-814.

Barrow, Roscoe L. "The Fairness Doctrine: A Double Standard for Electronic and Print Media." *Hastings Law Journal* 26 (January 1975): 659-708.

Bates, Roy Eugene. "Note: Private Censorship of Movies." *Stanford Law Review* 22 (February 1970): 618-56.

Batterman, Scott I. "Constitutional Law—First Amendment: FCC Regulation of Indecent Speech." *New York Law School Law Review* 25 (1979): 347-76.

Baxter, Richard L., Cynthia De Riemer, Ann Landini, Larry Leslie, and Michael W. Singletary. "A Content Analysis of Music Videos." *Journal of Broadcasting and Electronic Media* 29 (Summer 1985): 333-40.

Bazelon, David L. "The First Amendment and the News Media—New Directions in Regulating Telecommunications." *Federal Communications Law Journal* 31 (1979): 201-13.

Beany, William M. "The Right to Privacy and American Law." *Law and Contemporary Problems* 31 Spring 1966: 253-71.

Been, Jeffrey A. "Erhardt v. State: Nude Dancing Stripped of First Amendment Protection. (Survey of Recent Developments in Indiana Law June 1, 1984–May 31, 1985)." *Indiana Law Review* 19 (Winter 1986): 1-16.

Bender, Susan A. "Regulating Pornography through Zoning: Can We 'Clean Up' Honolulu?" *University of Hawaii Law Review* 8 (Spring 1986): 75-131.

Benevenia, Marianne. "Constitutional Law—First Amendment: First Amendment Does Not Preclude Closure of Adult Bookstore Where Illegal Activity Occurs on Premises." *Seton Hall Law Review* 17 (Spring 1987): 382–401.

Bernstein, Richard, "Constitutional Law—Obscenity—Liquor Regulations. *California v. La Rue*, 93 Supreme Court 390 (1972)." *Akron Law Review* 6 (Spring 1973): 247–54.

Bernstein, Richard. "Notes: First Amendment Limits on Tort Liability for Words Intended to Inflict Severe Emotional Distress." *Columbia Law Review* 85, no. 8 (1985): 1749–85.

Berry, Cecelie, and David Wolin. "Regulating Rock Lyrics: A New Wave of Censorship?" *Harvard Journal on Legislation* 23 (Summer 1986): 595–619.

Beschle, Donald L. "An Absolutism That Works: Reviving the Original 'Clear and Present Danger' Test." *Southern Illinois University Law Journal* (Spring 1983): 127–59.

Beth, Loren P. "Group Libel and Free Speech." *Minnesota Law Review* 39 (1955): 167–84.

Biasi, Vincent. "Toward a Theory of Prior Restraint: The Central Linkage." *Minnesota Law Review* 66 (November 1981): 11–93.

Bijleveld, W.H. "Group Defamation in the Netherlands." *Cleveland Marshall Law Review* 13 (January 1964): 73–94.

Billingsley, Robert T. "'Indecent' Language: A New Class of Prohibitable Speech?" *University of Richmond Law Review* 13 (Winter 1979): 297–311.

Blalock, Hubert. *Casual Inferences in Nonexperimental Research.* Chapel Hill: University of North Carolina Press, 1964.

Blalock, Hubert. "Multiple Causation, Indirect Measurement and Generalizability in the Social Sciences." *Synthese* 68 (July 1986): 13–36.

Bloodworth, Jon M., III. "Compelling Extension of First Amendment Infringement." *Golden Gate University Law Review* 13 (Spring 1983): 475–94.

Bloomfield, Louis J. "Defamation of Corporations." *Cleveland Marshall Law Review* 13 (January 1964): 95–101.

Bloustein, Edward J. "Privacy as an Aspect of Human Dignity: An Answer to Dean Prosser." *New York University Law Review* 39 (1964): 962–1007.

Bloustein, Edward J. "The First Amendment and Privacy: The Supreme Court Justice and the Philosopher." *Rutgers Law Review* 28 (Fall 1974): 41–95.

Bobo, Jim. "Constitutional Law—First Amendment: Cities May Restrict Location of Adult Theaters through Narrowly Tailored Content-Neutral, Time, Place and Manner Restrictions." *Mississippi Law Journal* 56 (August 1986): 401–16.

Bonicksen, A.L. "Obscenity Reconsidered: Bringing Broadcasting into the Mainstream Commentary." *Valparaiso University Law Review* 14 (Winter 1980): 261–93.

Boyce, William J. "Restraining Prior Restraint, or Call for Balancing in Evaluating Obscenity Abatement Statutes: City of Paducah v. Investment Entertainment, Inc."

Northwestern University Law Review 82 (Fall 1987): 181–211.

Boyle, L.M., and Sheila Noonan. "Prostitution and Pornography: Beyond Formal Equality." *Dalhousie Law Journal* Canada 10 (October 1986): 225–65.

Bragg, Dabney Elizabeth. "Note: Regulation of Programming Content to Protect Children after Pacifica." *Vanderbilt Law Review* 32 (November 1979): 1377–1417.

Branit, James R. "Reconciling Free Speech and Equality: What Justifies Censorship?" *Harvard Journal of Law and Public Policy* 9 (Spring 1986): 429–60.

Brenner, D. "Censoring the Airwaves: The Supreme Court's Pacifica Decision." In *Free but Regulated: Conflicting Traditions in Media Law*, edited by D. Brenner and W. Rivers, 1982.

Brigman, William E. "Pornography as Group Libel: The Indianapolis Sex Discrimination Ordinance." *Indiana Law Review* 18 (1985): 479–505.

"Broadcast Negligence and the First Amendment: Even Mickey Mouse Has Rights." *Mercer Law Review* 33 (1981): 423.

Brookfield, F.M. "Indency and Rules of Precedent." *New Zealand University Law Review* 9 (December 1981): 376–90.

Brown, James Jay, and Carl L. Stern. "Group Defamation in the U.S.A." *Cleveland Marshall Law Review* 13 (January 1964): 7–32.

Bryant, Barbara S. "Sexual Display of Women's Bodies—A Violation of Privacy." *Golden Gate University Law Review* 10 (Spring 1980): 1211–35.

Burkhart, Lori A. "976 Audiotax Service: Lost Innocence." *Public Utilities Fortnightly* 121 (3 March 1988): 48.

Burns, Kathleen. "Constitutional Law—First Amendment: Zoning Prohibition Which Impinges upon First Amendment Activity Must Be Adequately Justified by Municipality." *Seton Hall Law Review* 12 (Spring 1982): 311–26.

Busselmaier, Leona R. "Television Violence: What Is the Networks' Civil Liability?" *Glendale Law Review* 3 no. 4 (1978–79): 95–103.

"Cable Porn Law Unconstitutional." *News Media and the Law* 10 (Fall 1986): 43–45.

Calabresi, Guido. "Concerning Cause and the Law of Torts: An Essay for Harry Kalven Jr." *University of Chicago Law Review* 43 (1975): 69–108.

Caldwell, J.L. "The Determination of Indecency under the Indecent Publications Act: A Need for a New Criterion." *New Zealand Law Journal* (October 1986): 340.

Caldwell, J.L. "The Text for Indecency—Is Evidence Required?" *New Zealand Law Journal* (December 1987): 375–377, 380.

Caldwell, J.L. "The Video Recordings Act 1987." *New Zealand Universities Law Review* 12 (December 1987): 438–45.

Calvin Jeffries, John. "Rethinking Prior Restraint." *Yale Law Journal* 67 (January 1982): 245–82.

Campbell, I.D. "Indecent Publications Amendment Act,

1954: A Commentary." *New Zealand Law Journal* 30 (28 September 1954): 293–94.

Campisano, Mark S. "Notes: Group Vilification Reconsidered." *Yale Law Journal* 89 (December 1979): 308–32.

Capin, Beth Jaye. "The Regulation of Potentially Protected Expression through the Control of Liquor Dispensation." *Arizona Law Review* 23 (Winter 1981): 395–410.

Cardin, Tom. "Constitutional Law—Obscenity and Minors." *Arkansas Law Review* 22 (Winter 1969): 768–72.

Cartwright, Nancy. "Causal Laws and Effective Strategies." *Nous* 13 (November 1979): 419–38.

Catlett, Steven I. "Enjoining Obscenity as a Public Nuisance and the Prior Restraint Doctrine." *Columbia Law Review* 84 (October 1984): 1616–29.

"Censorship of Motion Pictures." *Yale Law Journal* 49 (1939): 87–113.

Chappelle, Pamela. "Note: Can an Adult Theater or Bookstore Be Abated as a Public Nuisance in California?" *University of San Francisco Law Review* 10 (1975): 115–32.

Cherry, Jonathan B. "Note: Obscenity and Ohio Nuisance Statutes." *University of Toledo Law Review* 5 (1973): 171–80.

"Children—Defense of 'Pied Piper' Injury Cases." *Defense Law Journal* 30 (1981): 473–76.

Christiansen, David J. "Zoning and the First Amendment Rights of Adult Entertainment." *Valparaiso University Law Review* 22 (Spring 1988): 695–724.

Clancy, Carol A., ed. *Pornography: Solutions through Law.* Washington, D.C.: National Forum Foundation, 1985.

Clark, Tom C. "The Problem of Group Defamation." *Cleveland Marshall Law Review* 13 (January 1964): 1–3.

Clarke, Charles H. "Freedom of Speech and the Problem of the Lawful Harmful Public Reaction: Adult Use Cases of Renton 106 S. Ct. 925 and Mini Theatres 96 S. Ct. 2440." *Akron Law Review* 20 (Fall 1986): 187–208.

"The Clear and Present Danger Test as Applied to Sexually Oriented Films: Some Pitfalls." *Washington University Law Quarterly* (Fall 1967): 585–90.

Cleary, John C. "Telephone Pornography: First Amendment Constraint on Shielding Children from Dial-a-Porn." *Harvard Journal on Legislation* 22 (Summer 1985): 503–50.

Cohen, Maxwell, chairman. *Report of the Special Committee on Hate Propaganda in Canada.* Ottawa: Queen's Printer, 1966.

Cohen, Robert S. "Constitutional Law—First Amendment—Prior Restraint—Class Actions: Silence Is Golden, but a Rule 23(3) Judicial Order Is an Unconstitutional Prior Restraint on Speech." *Florida State University Law Review* 8 (Fall 1980): 771–88.

Cole, David. "Getting There: Reflections from Trashing from Feminist Jurisprudence and Critical Theory." *Harvard Women's Law Journal* 8 (Spring 1985): 59–92.

Coletti, Michael A. "First Amendment Implication of Rock Lyric Censorship." *Pepperdine Law Review* 14 (January 1987): 421–51.

Colker, R. "Published Consentless Sexual Portrayals: A Proposed Framework for Analysis." *Buffalo Law Review* 35 (Winter 1976): 39–83.

Colker, R. "Pornography and Privacy: Towards the Development of a Group Based Theory for Sex Based Intrusions of Privacy." *Law and Inequality: A Journal of Theory and Practice* 1 (November 1983): 191–238.

"Communications Law—Obscene and Indecent Language: Under the Communications and Censorship Provision, the FCC May Not Prohibit the Broadcasting of Nonobscene Speech with Consideration of Context." *George Washington Law Review* 46 (January 1987): 324–37.

"Communications Law: Political Advertising: Cable Television and Indecent Programming; and Broadcasters' Responsibilities to Children" *Annual Survey of American Law* (June 1985): 401–34.

"Constitutional Law: Freedom to Communicate versus Right to Privacy: Regulation of Offensive Speech Limited by Captive Audience Doctrine." *Washington Law Review* 48 (May 1973): 667–85.

"Constitutional Law: Freedom of Expression of Minors Not Infringed by a Variable Obscenity Standard Stating Sufficiently Definable Classifications." *Brooklyn Law Review* 35 (Fall 1968): 109–17.

"Constitutional Law—Obscenity—Prior Restraint: A Nuisance-Abatement Statute that, When Applied to Obscenity, Authorizes a Prior Restraint on the Future Exhibition of Unnamed Films, Violates the United States Constitution." *Georgia Law Review* 13 (Spring 1979): 1076–85.

"Constitutional Law: Tennessee Nuisance Statute Declared Unconstitutional." *Memphis State University Law Review* 4 (1974): 619–22.

"Constitutional Law: Variable Definition of Obscenity Based on Its Appeal to Minors Is Constitutional." *Albany Law Review* 33 (Fall 1968): 173–82.

"Content Regulation and the Dimensions of Free Expression." *Harvard Law Review* 96 (June 1983): 1854–73.

Cooper, J.H. "Right of Individual Member of Class or Group Referred to in a Defamatory Publication to Maintain Action for Libel or Slander." In *American Law Reports. 2d ed. Vol. 70,* Rochester, N.Y., 1382–92. Lawyers Co-Operative Publishing Company; San Francisco: Bancroft-Whitney Company, 1960.

Cooper, R.J. "Sex Establishments—Licensing." *Journal of Criminal Law* (Great Britain) 51 (February 1987): 49–51.

Coulter, Ann H. "Note: Restricting Adult Access to Material Obscene as to Juveniles." *Michigan Law Review* 85, no. 2 (1987): 1681.

Court, J.H., and W.A. Gardiner. "Classification of Publications in South Australia: A Board Simulations Experiment." *Politics* (15 May 1980): 61–68.

"Court Says Chic Photo Use Puts Woman in False Light; Idea Given That Diving Pig Aide Posed for Pornographer. (Texas)." *News Media and Law* 9 (Summer 1985): 10–11.

"Crime Comics and the Constitution." *Stanford Law Review* 7 (1955): 237.

Cronin, Philip M. "Constitutional Law—Prior Restraint: Collateral Attack on Court Orders in Contempt Proceedings." *Massachusetts Law Review* 72 (June 1987): 91.

Cox, Lawrence A. "Brubaker v. Board of Education: Teacher Dismissals for Use of Objectionable Material in the Classroom." *Connecticut Law Review* 7 (Spring 1975): 580–608.

Coyne, David M. "Note: The Future of Content Regulation in Broadcasting." *California Law Review* 69 (1981): 555–98.

Dalby, J. Thomas. "Is Telephone Scatologia a Variant of Exhibitionism?" *International Journal of Offender Therapy and Comparative Criminology* 32 (April 1988): 45–49.

Davis, Stephanie Marie. "Employment Contracts: New York Law Is No Shield for Brooke." *Loyola Entertainment Law Journal* 6 (1986): 177–82.

Davis, Thomas L. "Defects in Indiana's Pornographic Nuisance Act." *Indiana Law Journal* 49 (1973–74): 320–33.

Dean, Steven D. "First Amendment Restrictions on Local Zoning Powers." *Ohio Northern University Law Review* 9 (January 1982): 121–30.

Dee, Juliet Lushbough. "Media Accountability for Real-Life Violence: A Case of Negligence or Free Speech?" *Journal of Communication* 37 (Spring 1987): 106–39.

Delgado, Richard. "Words That Wound: A Tort Action for Racial Insults, Epithets and Name-Calling." *Harvard Civil Rights–Civil Liberties Law Review* 17 (Spring 1982): 133–81.

Diamond, John L., and James L. Primm. "Rediscovering Traditional Tort Typologies to Determine Media Liability for Physical Injuries: From the *Mickey Mouse Club* to *Hustler Magazine*." *Hastings Law Journal* 10 (1988): 969–97.

Dickey, Jay W., Jr. "Broadcast-Transmission of Pornography: A Serious Matter." *Arkansas Lawyer* 20 (January 1986): 21–22.

Dihan, John N. "Constitutional Law—Nuisance Abatement: Alabama's 'Red Light' Abatement Act Held Applicable to Obscene Movies as Permanently Enjoinable Nuisances." *Cumberland Law Review* 10 (Fall 1979): 593–603.

Dobbins, H.W. "Regulation of Adult Theaters by Zoning." *Pub. Mgt.* 59 (February 1977): 14–16.

Dobbins, Richard E. "Ohio Liquor Control Commission's Right to Regulate." *Akron Law Review* 9 (Spring 1976): 695–711.

Donaldson, W.D. "Minnesota's Approach to the Regulation of Cable Television." William Mitchell Law Review 10 no. 3 (1984): 413–32.

Donnelly, P. "Running the Gauntlet: The Moral Order of Pornographic Movie Theaters." *Urban Life* 10 (October 1981): 239–64.

Downs, Donald A. *Nazis in Skokie*. Notre Dame, Ind.: Notre Dame Press, 1985.

Downs, Donald A. "Skokie Revisited: Hate Group Speech and the First Amendment." *Notre Dame Law Review* 60, no. 2 (1985): 629–85.

Doyle, M.W. "Indecent Publications." *New Zealand Law Review* 6 (October 1975): 374–77.

Drechsel, Robert E. "Media Tort Liability for Physical Harm." *Journalism Quarterly* (Spring 1987): 99–105.

Drysdale, William. "Indecency and the First Amendment: Special Problems of the Broadcast Industry." *Lincoln Law Review* 13 (1982): 101–11.

Duffala, Donald Paul. "Validity and Application of Statute Authorizing Forfeiture of Use on Closure of Real Property from Which Obscene Materials Have Been Disseminated or Exhibited." In *American Law Reports*. 4th ed. Vol. 25, Rochester, N.Y.: 395–412. Lawyers Co-Operative Publishing Company; San Francisco: Bancroft-Whitney Company, 1983.

Dugan, Thomas E. "FCC—Constitutional Right to Free Speech: Limp Libidinal Language." *Marquette Law Review* 61 (Spring 1978): 534–43.

Dunlap, Mary C. "Sexual Speech and the State: Putting Pornography in Its Place." *Golden Gate University Law Review* 17 (Fall 1987): 359–78.

Dwight, George, II, Peter A. Levitan, and Laura A. DeFelice. "One Small Step for Smut." *Art and Law* 8 (Winter 1984): 431–32.

Dyson, Richard B. "Looking-Glass Law: An Analysis of the Ginzburg Case," *University of Pittsburgh Law Review* 28 (October 1966): 1–18.

Eades, R.W. "Control of Seditious Libel as a Basis for the Development of the Law of Obscenity." *Akron Law Review* 11 (Summer 1977): 29–58.

Eberle, Edward J. "Prior Restraint of Expression through the Private Search Doctrine." *University of San Francisco Law Review* 17 Winter 1983: 171–201.

"Education Law—Censorship of Motion Pictures—N.Y. Licensing Statute—Indecency." *Albany Law Review* 22 (January 1958): 186–97.

Edwards, Joseph E. "Validity, Construction, and Application of Federal Criminal Statute (18 U.S.C.S.S. 1464) Punishing Utterance of Obscene, Indecent, or Profane Language by Means of Radio Communication." In *American Law Reports, Federal*. Vol. 17. 900–17 Rochester, N.Y.: Lawyers Co-Operative Publishing Company; San Francisco: Bancroft-Whitney Company, 1973.

Eels, Ellery. "Probabilistic Causal Interaction." *Philosophy of Science* 53 (March 1986): 52–64.

Emerson, Thomas I. "The Doctrine of Prior Restraint." *Law and Contemporary Problems* 20 (Autumn 1955): 648–71.

"Enjoining Obscenity as a Public Nuisance and the Prior Restraint Doctrine." *Columbia Law Review* 84 (1984): 1616.

Faber, Daniel A. "Content Regulation and the First Amendment: A Revisionist View." *Georgetown Law Journal* 68 (February 1980): 727–63.

Faber, Daniel A., and John E. Nowak. "The Misleading

Nature of Public Forum Analysis: Content and Context in First Amendment Adjudication." *Virginia Law Review* 70 (September 1984): 1219–66.

"FCC Fines Station; Voids 4 Complaints." *News Media and the Law* 12 (Summer 1988): 53–54.

"FCC Launches Pornography Inquiries: Complaints Rise." *News Media and the Law* 11 (Winter 1987): 31–32.

Federal Communications Commission. *Report on the Broadcast of Violent, Indecent, and Obscene Material.* Washington, D.C.: Federal Communications Commission, 1975.

Fee, Charles T., Jr. "Note: Using Constitutional Zoning to Neutralize Adult Entertainment—Detroit to New York." *Fordham Urban Law Journal* 5 (1977): 455–74.

Fendleman, Doug. "Civilizing Pornography: The Case for an Exclusive Obscenity Nuisance Statute." *University of Chicago Law Review* 44 (Spring 1977): 509–61.

"Filthy Words, the FCC and the First Amendment: Regulating Broadcast Obscenity." *Virginia Law Review* 61 (April 1975): 579–642.

Finer, J.J. "Regulation and Prohibition of Sensual Performances under Nonobscenity Statutes." *Criminal Law Bulletin* 10 (October 1974): 717–36.

"First Amendment Overrides Municipal Attempt to Zone Adult Bookstores and Theaters." *William Mitchell Law Review* 10, no. 2 (1984): 331–39.

Fleishman, Stanley. "Times Film Corporation v. City of Chicago: Obscenity and Prior Restraint." *Law in Transition Quarterly* 21 (Winter 1962): 235–43.

Fleming, Horace W. "Georgia Literature Commission." *Mercer Law Review* 18 (Summer 1967): 325–36.

Fleming, H.W., Jr. "Oklahoma Literature Commission: A Case Study in Administrative Regulation of Obscenity." *Oklahoma Law Review* 29 (Fall 1976): 882–910.

" 'For Adults Only': The Constitutionality of Governmental Film Censorship by Age Classification." *Yale Law Journal* 69 (1959): 141–52.

Forshay, Andrew E. "The First Amendment Becomes a Nuisance: Arcara v. Cloud Books, Inc." *Catholic University Law Review* 37 (Fall 1987): 191–217.

Fredricks, Laura. "Note: Tort Law—Televiolence: Should Broadcasters Be Liable?" *Western New England Law Review* 6 (1984): 897–915.

"Freedom of Expression in a Commercial Context." *Harvard Law Review* 78 (April 1965): 1191–1211.

Friedlander, Samuel D. "Constitutional Law—First Amendment: When Concepts Collide: Display Provisions and the First Amendment." *Western New England Law Review* 10 (Winter 1988): 133–73.

Friedman, Jane M. "The Motion Picture Rating System of 1968: A Constitutional Analysis of Self-Regulation by the Film Industry." *Columbia Law Review* 73 (February 1973): 185–240.

Friedman, Jane M. "Obscenity and the Law. Zoning 'Adult' Movies: The Potential Impact of Young v. American Mini Theaters." *Hastings Law Journal* 28 (July 1977): 1275–1358.

Fritz, Leah. "Pornography as Gynocidal Propaganda."

New York University Review of Law and Social Change 8–9 (1979–80): 219–23.

Fryer, David R. "Group Defamation in England." *Cleveland Marshall Law Review* 13 (January 1964): 33–51.

Fulton, E.D., Maureen Porrester, Reva Landau, Tina Head, John G. Inge, Jan Bauer, E. Ratushny, John McLaren, and Alan Walker. "Comment on Crime Comics and Pornography." *Ottawa Law Review* (Canada), 20 (Winter 1988): 25–31.

Gard, Stephen W. "Fighting Words as Free Speech." *Washington University Law Quarterly* 58, no. 3 (1980): 531–81.

Geller, Henry, and Donna Lampert. "Cable, Content Regulation and the First Amendment." *Catholic University Law Review* 32 (1983): 603–31.

George, Deborah A. "The Cable Communications Policy Act of 1984 and Content Regulation of Cable Television." *New England Law Review* 20 (1984–85): 779–804.

Gerard, Jules B. "Supreme Court Restricts Adult Entertainment: A Critique of City of Newport v. Iacobucci." *Zoning and Planning Law Report* 10 (March 1987): 105–10.

Gerety, T. "Pornography and Violence." *University of Pittsburgh Law Review* 40 (Summer 1979): 567–651.

Gey, Steven G. "The Apologetics of Suppression: The Regulation of Pornography as Act and Idea." *Michigan Law Review* 86 (June 1988): 1584–1634.

Ghent, Jeffrey F. "Invasion of Privacy by Radio or Television." *American Law Reports.*3d ed. vol. 56, edited by Rochester, N.Y., 386–423: Lawyers Co-Operative Publishing Company; San Francisco: Bancroft-Whitney Company, 1974.

Giglio, Ernest. "Prior Restraint of Motion Pictures." *Dickinson Law Review* 69 (1965): 379–90.

Gillmor, D.M., and J.A. Barron. *Mass Communication Law: Cases and Comment.* St. Paul: West Publishing, 1984.

Giokaris, Virginia M. "Zoning and the First Amendment: A Municipality's Power to Control Adult Use Establishments." *University of Missouri Kansas City Law Review* 55 (Winter 1987): 263–83.

Givelber, Daniel. "The Right to Minimum Social Decency and the Limits of Evenhandedness: International Infliction of Emotional Distress by Outrageous Conduct. *Columbia Law Review* 82 (January 1982): 42–76.

Glasser, Theodore L. and Harvey Jassem. "Indecent Broadcasts and the Listener's Right of Privacy." *Journal of Broadcasting* 24 (Summer 1980): 285–99.

Glover Moore, Barbara E. "Prohibition of 'Indecent' Material on Cable Television Struck Down." *Stetson Law Review* 15 (Summer 1986): 975–76,

Glover Moore, Barbara E. "Zoning Ordinance Restricting Adult Theaters to Concentrated Area 1000 Feet from Residential Areas, Parks and Churches Is Constitutionally Valid." *Stetson Law Review* 15 (Summer 1986): 1091–2.

Goldman, Roger L. "The Doctrine of Worthier Speech:

Young v. American Mini Theatres, Inc." *St. Louis University Law Journal* 21 (1977): 281–307.

Goldstein, Leslie F. "The New Pornography Laws." *Delaware Lawyer* 4 (Fall 1985): 32–39.

Good, I.J. "A Causal Calculus I-II." *British Journal for the Philosophy of Science* 11 (1961): 305.

Goodchild, Seth. "Twisted Sister, Washington Wives and the First Amendment: The Movement to Clamp Down on Rock Music." *Entertainment and Sports Law Journal* 3 (Fall 1986): 131–97.

Goodman, Jonathan. "The Death of a Princess Case: Television Programming by State-Owned Public Broadcasters and Viewers' First Amendment Rights." *University of Miami Law Review* 26 (July 1982): 779–805.

Gorman, Rosalee C. "The Demise of Civil Nuisance Actions in Obscenity Control." *Loyola University of Chicago Law Journal* 14 (1982–83): 31–56.

Graglia, Lino A. "Permissible and Impermissible Content-Based Restrictions on Freedom of Speech." *Harvard Journal of Law and Public Policy* 10 (Winter 1987): 67–73.

Graham, Arthur F. "Film Censorship Upheld." *Ohio State Law Journal* 20 (Winter 1959): 161–64.

Graham, Marcia A. "Obscenity and Profanity at Work." *Employee Relations Law Journal* 11 (Spring 1986): 662–77.

Graham McFadden, Cynthia. "Inviting the Pig to the Parlor: The Case Against the Regulation of Indecency and Obscenity on Cable Television." *Art and the Law* 8 (Winter 1984): 317–68.

Greenstone, Richard J. "Protection of Obscene Parody as Fair Use." *Entertainment and Sports Lawyer* 4 (Winter-Spring 1986): 3–6.

Grobaty, Michael J. "Miami Ordinance Regulating Cable Television Transmission of 'Indecent' Material: The First Amendment to the Rescue." *Loyola Entertainment Law Journal* 5–6 (1985): 198–204.

Groskaufmanis, Karl A. "What Films We May Watch: Videotape Distribution and the First Amendment." *University of Pennsylvania Law Review* 136 (April 1988): 1263–1300.

"Group Libel Laws: Abortive Efforts to Combat Hate Propaganda." *Yale Law Journal* 61 (1952): 252–64.

Gurney, D. Scott. "Celebrities and the First Amendment: Broader Protection Against the Unauthorized Publication of Photographs." *Indiana Law Journal* 61 (Fall 1986): 697–719.

Haiman, Franklyn S. "Speech v. Privacy: Is There a Right Not to Be Spoken To?" *Northwestern University Law Review* 67 (1972): 153–99.

Halliwell, Thomas L. "Defamation and Invasion of Privacy: Piggie Porn in the Fifth Circuit." *Loyola Entertainment Law Journal* 6 (1986): 167–76.

Hamm, Valerie J. "The Civil Rights Pornography Ordinances: An Examination under the First Amendment." *Kentucky Law Journal.* 73 (1984–85): 1081–1108.

Hanks, William, and Steve Coran. "Federal Preemption of State Obscenity Law Applied to Broadcasting." *COMM-ENT* 5 (Fall 1982): 21–41.

Harrison, Regina. "Access and Pay Cable Rates: Off Limits to Regulators after Midwest Video II?" *Columbia Journal of Law and Social Problems* 16, no. 4 (1981): 591–669.

Hart, H.L.A., and Tony Honore. *Causation in the Law.* 2d ed. Oxford, England: Clarendon Press, 1985.

Hassman, Phillip E. "Taking Unauthorized Photographs as Invasion of Privacy." *American Law Reports.* 3d ed. vol. 86, 374–84, edited by Rochester, N.Y.: Lawyers Co-Operative Publishing Company; San Francisco: Bancroft-Whitney Company, 1978.

Heins, Marjorie. "Banning Words: A Comment on 'Words that Wound'." *Harvard Civil Rights–Civil Liberties Law Review* 18 (Summer 1983): 585–92.

Henry, James F., and Thomas R. Schutt. "Adult Use Zoning: How Far Can a Municipality Go?" *Illinois Bar Journal* 71 (November 1982): 158.

Herbst, Adrian E., Gary R. Matz, and John F. Gibbs. "A Review of Federal, State and Local Regulations of Cable Television in the United States." *William Mitchell Law Review* 10, no. 3 (1984): 377–411.

Hilker, Anne K. "Tort Liability of the Media for Audience Acts of Violence: A Constitutional Analysis." *Southern California Law Review* 52 (1979): 529–71.

Hill, Alfred. "Defamation and Privacy under the First Amendment." *Columbia Law Review* 76 (December 1976): 1203–1313.

Hill, Lawrence, H. "State v. Rabe: No Preseizure Adversary Hearing Required under Nuisance Theory of Obscenity." *Utah Law Review* (Winter 1971): 582–93.

Hoak, Jon. "Obscenity: Court Upholds the Activities of the Federal Communications Commission in Curtailing Sex-Oriented Talk Show on Radio." *Drake Law Review* 25 (Fall 1975): 257–65.

Hoets, Pieter J. "Symposium Conclusion" (Group Defamation Symposium). *Cleveland Marshall Law Review* 13 (January 1964): 111–17.

Hofbauer, Diane L. " 'Cableporn' and the First Amendment: Perspectives on Content Regulation of Cable Television." *Federal Communications Commission Law Journal* 35 (1983): 139–208.

Hoffman, J.M. "From Random House to Mickey Mouse: Liability for Negligent Publishing and Broadcasting." *Tort and Insurance Law Journal* 21 (Fall 1985): 65–89.

Hogue L.L. "Regulating Obscenity through the Power to Define and Abate Nuisances." *Wake Forest Law Review* 14 (February 1978): 1–49.

Hsiung, James C. "Indecent Broadcast: An Assessment of Pacifica's Impact." *Communications and the Law* 9 (February 1987): 41–56.

Humphreys, Paul. "Causation in the Social Sciences: An Overview." *Synthese* 68 (July 1986): 1–12.

Hunter, Howard O. "Toward a Better Understanding of the Prior Restraint Doctrine: A Reply to Professor Mayton." *Cornell Law Review* 67 (January 1982): 283–96.

"Hustler Magazine v. Jerry Falwell" *Arkansas Law Review* 41 (Fall 1988): 926–27.

"Hustler Not Liable for Youth's Hanging: Article on Dangerous Sexual Practice Privileged; Didn't Cause

Youth to Hang Self." *News Media and the Law* 11 (Summer 1987): 27–28.

"Indecency on Cable Television." *Entertainment and Sports Law Journal* 1 (1984): 79.

" 'Indecency' Policy Clear as Mud: FCC Tells Broadcasters, Beware; Agency Sets Vague Standard to Decide Case-by-Case, after Broadcast, Whether Show is Indecent; Denies WBAI Request for Ruling." *News Media and the Law* 11 (Summer 1987): 3–4.

"Indecent Programming on Cable Television and the First Amendment." *George Washington Law Review* 51 (January 1983): 254–68.

"Industry-Wide Liability and Market Share Allocation of Damages." *Georgia Law Review* 15 (Winter 1981): 423–50.

"Injunctive Relief Against Nuisance in Alabama." *Alabama Law Review* 28 (Summer 1977): 677–716.

"Invasion of Privacy: Publication of Minors' Nude Photographs in Hardcore Magazine Is Not Invasion of Privacy When Parent Signs Release; Court Approval of Parental Consent Is Not Required for Publication of Nude Photographs of Minors." *Journal of Family Law* 24 (January 1986): 357–62.

Jacobs, Caryn. "Patterns of Violence: A Feminist Perspective on the Regulation of Pornography." *Harvard Women's Law Journal* 7 (Spring 1984): 5–55.

Jacobson, Nancy G. "Restricting the Public Display of Offensive Materials: The Use and Effectiveness of Public and Private Nuisance Actions." *University of San Francisco Law Review* 10 (Fall 1975): 232–51.

Jassem, Harvey C. "Scrambling the Telephone: The FCC's Dial-a-Porn Regulations." *Communications and the Law* (December 1988): 3–13.

Jaynes, Peter M. "Sticks and Stones May Break My Bones. . . F.C.C. v. Pacifica Foundation (The Seven Dirty Words Case)." *Glendale Law Review* 3 (Winter 1978): 192–206.

Kalvan, Harry, Jr. "Privacy in Tort Law—Were Warren and Brandeis Wrong?" *Law and Contemporary Problems* 31 (Spring 1966): 326–41.

Kassner, Minna F. "Radio Censorship." *Air Law Review* 8 (January 1937): 99–111.

Katz, Al. "Privacy and Pornography: Stanley v. Georgia (89 S. Ct. 1243)." *Supreme Court Review* (1969): 203–17.

Kaufman, Wendy B. "Song Lyric Advisories: The Sound of Censorship." *Cardozo Arts and Entertainment Law Journal* 5 (January 1986): 225–63.

Kellam, R.B., and T.S. Lovelace. "To Bare or Not to Bare: The Constitutionality of Local Ordinances Banning Nude Sunbathing." *University of Richmond Law Review* 20 (Spring 1986): 589–628.

Kelly, John. "Criminal Libel and Free Speech." *University of Kansas Law Review* 6 (1958): 295–333.

Khosla, Gopal Das. *Pornography and Censorship in India.* New Delhi: Indian Book Co., 1976.

Keifer, George Gerard. "Constitutional Law—Minors and Variable Obscenity." *Loyola Law Review* 15 (1968–69): 97–107.

Kimbell, Linda. "First Amendment: Zoning of Adult Business No Cure-All." *Loyola Entertainment Law Journal* 6 (1986): 183–90.

Kinczewski, Greg. "Keeping the Airwaves Safe for 'Indecency.' " *DePaul Law Review* 27 (Fall 1977): 155–73.

Kirchick, C.R. "Young v. American Mini Theatres, Inc.: The War on Neighborhood Deterioration Leaves First Amendment Casualty." *Environmental Affects* 6, no. 1 (1977): 101–25.

Kleiman, Howard M. "Indecent Programming on Cable Television: Legal and Social Dimensions." *Journal of Broadcasting and Electronic Media* (Summer 1986):.

Kobylka, Joseph F. "A Court-Created Context for Group Litigation: Libertarian Groups and Obscenity." *Journal of Politics* 49 (November 1987): 1061–77.

"Kodak Can Refuse to Develop Explicit Film." *New Jersey Law Journal* 107 (22 January 1981): 3.

Krattenmaker, Thomas G., and Marjorie L. Esterlow. "Censoring Indecent Cable Programs: The New Morality Meets the New Media." *Fordham Law Review* 51 (1983): 606–36.

Krattenmaker, Thomas G., and L.A. Powe. "Televised Violence: First Amendment Principles and Social Science Theory." *Virginia Law Review* 64 (December 1978): 1123–1297.

Kreiss, Robert A. "Deregulation of Cable Television and the Problem of Access under the First Amendment." *Southern California Law Review* 54 (July 1981): 1001–52.

Krislov, Samuel. "From Ginzburg to Ginsberg: The Unhurried Children's Hour in Obscenity Litigation." *Supreme Court Review* (1968): 153–97.

Kronlund, Michael C. "Crimes—Distribution of Obscene Matter: Telephone Information-Access Service Providers. (Review of Selected 1987 California Legislation.)" *Pacific Law Journal* 19 (January 1988): 550–51.

Kuchel, Thomas H. "The Fright Peddlers." *Cleveland Marshall Law Review* 13 (January 1964): 4–6.

Lahey, Kathleen A. "The Canadian Charter of Rights and Pornography: Toward a Theory of Actual Gender Equality." *New England Law Review* 20 (1984–85): 649–85.

Laidlaw, R. Bruce. "Ann Arbor's Adult Entertainment Ordinance." *Municipal Attorney* 27 (September–October 1986): 7–10.

Lambert, J.L. "Reproduction Victoriana: The Indecent Displays (Control) Act of 1981." *Public Law* (Great Britain) (Summer 1982): 226–29.

Landes, William, and Richard Posner. "Causation in Tort Law: An Economic Approach." *Journal of Legal Studies* 12 (1983): 109–34.

Lane, James M. "Constitutional Law: Pacifica Foundation v. FCC: First Amendment Limitations on FCC Regulation of Offensive Broadcasts." *North Carolina Law Review* 56 (April 1978): 584–601.

Lasson, Kenneth. "Racial Defamation as Free Speech: Abusing the First Amendment." *Columbia Human Rights Law Review* 17 (1985–86): 11.

Lawlor, P. "Group Defamation." A report prepared for the Attorney General of Ontario, 1984.

Lazarus, Alan Jay. "Rock Is a Four-Letter Word: The Potential for FCC Regulation of (Un)Popular Music." *COMM/ENT Law Journal* 9 (1987): 423–522.

Lee, Leon Harvey, Jr. "Constitutional Law: Policing the Parlor and the First Amendment: City of Renton v. Playtime Theatres, Inc. (106 S. Ct. 925)." *Wake Forest Law Review* 22 (1987): 673–96.

Leigh, L.H. "Vagrancy, Morality and Decency: Indency and Obscenity—Indecent Exposure." *Criminal Law Review* (Great Britain) (July–August 1975): 381–90, 413–20.

Levine, Ken. "Constitutional Law: Utah's Cable Decency Act: An Indecent Act?" *Loyola Entertainment Law Journal* 7 (Spring 1987): 401–15.

Lewis J. "The Individual Member's Right to Recover for a Defamation Leveled at the Group." *Miami Law Review* 17 (1963): 519.

"The Libel-Proof Plaintiff Doctrine." *Harvard Law Review* 98 (June 1985): 1909–26.

Linde, Hans. "Clear and Present Danger Re-Examined: Dissonance in the Brandenburg Concerto." *Stanford Law Review* 22 (June 1970): 1163–86.

Linz, D., et al. "Issues Bearing on the Legal Regulation of Violent and Sexually Violent Media." *Journal of Social Issues* 42 (Fall 1986): 171–93.

Linz, D., E. Donnerstein, M. Bross, and M. Chapin. "Mitigating the Influence of Violence on Television and Sexual Violence in the Media." In *Advances in the Study of Aggression* vol. 2, edited by Robert J. Blanchard, New York Academic Press, 1986.

Linz, D., C.W. Turner, B.W. Hesse, and S.D. Penrod. "Bases of Liability for Injuries Produced by Portrayals of Violent Pornography." In *Pornography and Sexual Aggression,* edited by N. Malamuth and E. Donnerstein, 277–304. New York: Academic Press, 1984.

Louis, Stephen E. "Broadcasting Offensive Programming under a New Communications Act." *Columbia Journal of Law and Social Problems* 15, no. 4 (1980): 427–53.

Lupo, Cynthia M. "Constitutional Law—First Amendment—Freedom of Expression: Prior Restraint of Obscenity as a Public Nuisance." *New York Law School Law Review* 26 (Fall 1981): 1122–34.

Lupo, Frank. "Adult Entertainment Zoning Ordinances." *Loyola Entertainment Law Journal* 4 (1984): 108–12.

Lynd, Staughton. "Brandenburg v. Ohio: A Speech Test for All Seasons?" *University of Chicago Law Review* 43 (Fall 1975): 151–91.

Lyons, Richard J. "Constitutional Law: Board of Regents May Direct Removal of Obscene Scenes from Motion Picture." *Syracuse Law Review* 16 (1964–65): 131–32.

Macher, David J. "City of Renton v. Playtime Theatres: Pornography Zoning Attains a Majority." *Washington State University Law Review* 14 (Fall 1986): 287–308.

Malamuth, N., and E. Donnerstein eds. *Pornography and Sexual Aggression.* New York: Academic Press, 1984.

Maltz, Earl M., and L. Lynn Hogue. "On Keeping Pigs out of the Parlor: Speech as Public Nuisance after FCC v. Pacifica Foundation." *South Carolina Law Review* 31 (1980): 377–93.

Mandelker, Daniel. "The Free Speech Revolution in Land Use Control." *Chicago-Kent Law Review* 60 (Winter 1984): 51–62.

Mann, Elizabeth J. "Telephones, Sex and the First Amendment." *University of California Los Angeles Law Review* 33 (April 1986): 1221–46.

Marcus, N. "Zoning Obscenity: Or, the Moral Politics of Porn." *Buffalo Law Review* 27 (Winter 1977): 1–46.

Martin, Jack Anton. "When Speech Is Not Speech: A Perspective on Categorization in First Amendment Adjudication." *Wake Forest Law Review* 19 (February 1981): 33–57.

Mayo, Thomas William. "Land Use Control." *Syracuse Law Review* 33 (1982): 401–22.

Mayton, William T. "Toward a Theory of First Amendment Process: Injunctions of Speech, Subsequent Punishment, and the Costs of the Prior Restraint Doctrine." *Cornell Law Review* 67 (January 1982): 245–82.

McAllister, Marlis. "Zoning and the Suppression of Free Speech: Playtime Theaters v. City of Renton 748 F.2d 527 (9th Cir. 1984)." *Golden Gate University Law Review* 15 (Spring 1985): 216–20.

McCommon, Paul C. "Cable Pornography: Problems and Solutions." January 1985. (Phoenix, Arizona: Citizens for Decency Through Law.)

McDaniel, Bruce I. "Prohibition of Obscene or Harassing Telephone Calls in Interstate or Foreign Communications under 47 USCS S. 223." In *American Law Reports, Federal.* vol. 50, edited by, 541–46. Rochester, N.Y.: Lawyers Co-Operative Publishing Company; San Francisco: Bancroft-Whitney Company, 1980.

McFadden, Cynthia Graham. "Inviting the Pig to the Parlor: The Case Against the Regulation of Indecency and Obscenity on Cable Television." *Art and Law* 8 (Winter 1984): 317–68.

McHugh, John J. "Constitutional Law: Validity of State Statute Requiring Denial of a License to Motion Picture Films Presenting Acts of Sexual Immorality as Desirable, Acceptable or Proper Patterns of Behavior." *Illinois Bar Journal* 48 (November 1959): 213–16.

McKenna, Edward. "Constitutional Law—Due Process: Variable Obscenity Standard for Determining Obscenity—Ginsburg v. New York, 390 U.S. 629 (1968)." *American University Law Review* 18 (December 1968): 195–201.

McMillin, Nancy. "State Ex. Rel. Kidwell v. U.S. Marketing, Inc.: Prior Restraint and Obscenity under the Idaho Moral Nuisance Abatement Act." *Idaho Law Review* 18 (Winter 1983): 135–55.

Meisler, Linda. "A New Approach to the Regulation of Broadcast Programming: The Public Nuisance Doctrine." *American University Law Review* 28 (Winter 1979): 239–77.

Melnick, Alison. "Note: Access to Cable Television: A Critique of the Affirmative Duty Theory of the First Amendment." *California Law Review* 70 (1982): 1393–1420.

Meyers, Mark B. "Fourth Amendment Remedies in Civil Proceedings." *Louisiana Law Review* 38 (Summer 1978): 1086–96.

Meyerson, Michael I. "The Cable Communications Policy Act of 1984: A Balancing Act on the Coaxial Wires." *Georgetown Law Review* 19 (1985): 543.

Meyerson, Michael I. "The Right to Speak, the Right to Hear, and the Right Not to Hear: The Technological Resolution to the Cable/Pornography Debate." *University of Michigan Journal of Law Reform* 21 (Fall 1987 and Winter 1988): 137–200.

Michaud, Leonard J. "Decent Exposure: An Inquiry into the Constitutionality of State Statutes Proscribing Expressive Public Nudity." *Loyola Law Review* 22 (Fall 1975–76): 1018–35.

Miller, Diana K. "Constitutional Law—First Amendment: Suppression of Demonstration Permits Represents Invalid Prior Restraint on Free Speech, for Which Temporary Injunctive Relief Appropriate." *St. Mary's Law Journal* 3 (Winter 1981): 372–80.

Miller, Nancy L. "Media Liability for Injuries That Result from Television Broadcasts to Immature Audiences." *San Diego Law Review* 22 (1985): 377–400.

Miller, Neal. "Facts, Expert Facts, and Statistics: Descriptive and Experimental Research Methods in Litigation." Part 2. *Rutgers Law Review* 40 (Winter 1988): 467–520.

Miller, Nicholas P., and Alan Beals. "Regulating Cable Television." *Washington Law Review* 57 (1981): 85–118.

Miller, Robert H., II. "Constitutional Law: Control of Obscenity through Enforcement of a Nuisance Statute." *Campbell Law Review* 4 (Fall 1981): 139–67.

Minnesota Crime Prevention Center. *Neighborhood Deterioration and the Location of Adult Entertainment Establishments in St. Paul.* Minneapolis: Minnesota Crime Prevention Center, 1978.

Mitchell, Robert G. "Aid or Obstruction? Government Regulation of Cable Television Meets the First Amendment." *Washington Law Review* 61 (April 1986): 665–701.

"A Model Movie Censorship Ordinance." *Harvard Journal on Legislation* 5 (March 1968): 395–412.

Moliterno, James E., "First Amendment—Freedom of Speech—Broadcasting—Obscenity." *Akron Law Review* 12 (Fall 1978): 284–90.

Monaghan, H.P. "First Amendment 'Due Process.' " *Harvard Law Review* 83 (January 1970): 518.

Moody, George Randall. "Broadcast Negligence and the First Amendment." *Mercer Law Review* 33 (1981): 423–32.

Moore, Barbara E. Glover. "City Zoning Ordinance Restricting Nude Dancing Held Unconstitutional as Applied." *Stetson Law Review* 15 Summer 1986: 1088–90.

Moore, Barbara E. Glover. "Prohibition of Indecent Material on Cable Television Struck Down." *Stetson Law Review* 15 (Summer 1986): 975–76.

Moore, Barbara E. Glover. "Zoning Ordinance Restricting Adult Theaters to Concentrated Area 1000 Feet from Residential Areas, Parks and Churches Is Constitutionally Valid." *Stetson Law Review* 15 (Summer 1986): 1091–92.

"Morality and the Broadcast Media: A Constitutional Analysis of FCC Regulatory Standards." *Harvard Law Review* 84 (January 1971): 664–99.

Moretti, Daniel S. *Obscenity and Pornography: The Law under the First Amendment.* New York: Oceana Publications, 1984.

"Motion Pictures and the First Amendment." *Yale Law Journal* 60 (1951): 696–719.

Munro, Colin. "Indecent Displays (Control) Act 1981." *New Law Journal* 132 (Great Britain) (1 July 1982): 629–30.

Murphy, William P. "The Prior Restraint Doctrine in the Supreme Court: A Reevaluation." *Notre Dame Law Review* 51 (1976): 898–918.

Mustin, Scott H. "FCC Content Regulation of Cable Pay Television: The Threat of Pacifica." *Cumberland Law Review* 9 (Winter 1979): 811–29.

Nagel, Ellen L. "First Amendment Constraints on the Regulation of Telephone Pornography." *University of Cincinnati Law Review* 55 (1986): 237–56.

Neier, Aryeh. *Defending My Enemy: American Nazis, the Skokie Case and the Risks of Freedom.* New York: E.P. Dutton, 1979.

Nelson, Eric M. "Communications Law: Political Advertising; Cable Television and Indecent Programming; and Broadcasters' Responsibilities to Children." *Annual Survey of American Law* (1984): 401–34.

Nelson, Kristen Carol. "Notes: 'Offensive Speech' and the First Amendment." *Boston University Law Review* 53 (1973): 834–57.

Němečková, Zdena."A New Strategy for Censorship: Prosecuting Pornographers as Panderers." *Cardozo Arts and Entertainment Law Journal* 6 (1988): 539–63.

Nemeroff, Milton A. "Criminal Law—Obscene Language: Conviction Absent Statute and Judicial Precedent." *Temple Law Quarterly* 29 (Fall 1955): 106–9

"New York Law Controlling The Dissemination of Obscene Materials to Minors." *Fordham Law Review* 34 (May 1966): 692–774.

Nickerson, Steven C. "Injunctions Pursuant to Public Nuisance Obscenity Statutes and the Doctrine of Prior Restraints." *Washington University Law Quarterly* 61 (Fall 1983): 775–98.

Nimmer, Melville B. "The Constitutionality of Official Censorship of Motion Pictures." *University of Chicago Law Review* 25 (Summer 1958): 625–57.

Nolte, M. Chester. "New Pig in the Parlor: Official Constraints on Indecent Words." *NOLPE Sch. L. J.* 9 (Spring 1980): 1–22.

Noto, Thomas A. "FCC Regulation of Cable Television Content." *Rutgers Law Review* 31 (July 1978): 238–68.

O'Brien, Bridget. "Magazine Cleared in Death: Auto-Erotic Asphyxiation" *National Law Journal* 9 (11 May 1987): 8.

O'Brien, David M. "Reassessing the First Amendment and the Public's Right to Know in Constitutional Adjudication." *Villanova Law Review* 26 (November 1980): 1–62.

O'Connor, P.J. "Nuisance Abatement Law as a Solution

to New York City's Problem of Illegal Sex Related Businesses in the Mid-Town Area." *Fordham Law Review* 46 (October 1977): 57–90.

"Offensive Speech and the FCC." *Yale Law Journal* 79 (June 1970): 1343–68.

Oglesby, Roger. "Porno non est pro bono Publico: Obscenity as a Public Nuisance in California." *Hastings Constitutional Law Quarterly* 4 (Spring 1977): 385–419.

Olson, Paul E. "Texas Harassment Statute: Is It Constitutional?" *Southern Texas Law Journal* 17 (1976): 283–300.

Paines, George P. "Obscenity, Cable Television and the First Amendment: Will FCC Regulation Impair the Marketplace of Ideas?" *Duquesne Law Review* 21 (Summer 1983): 965.

Palumbo, Norman A., Jr. "Obscenity and Copyright: An Illustrious Past and Future?" *Southern Texas Law Journal* 22 (Winter 1982): 87–101.

Papineau, David. "Probabilities and Causes." *Journal of Philosophy* 82 (February 1985): 57–74.

Papineau, David. "Causal Asymmetry." *British Journal for the Philosophy of Science* 36 (September 1985): 273–89.

Parish, William P. "Communications Law—Broadcasting Indecent but Not Obscene Language: When the FCC Finds That a Pig Has Entered the Parlor during Times of the Day When Children Are in the Audience, the Exercise of Its Regulatory Power Does Not Depend on Proof That the Pig is Obscene." *University of Detroit Journal of Urban Law* 57 (Fall 1979): 95–121.

Park, Aloma H. "Regulation of Music Videos: Should the FCC 'Beat It'?" *Computer-Law Journal* 8 Summer 1988: 287–310.

Pearlman, T.J., and M.J. Marko. "Broadcast Negligence: Television's Responsibility for Programming." *Trial* 16 (August 1980): 40–43, 71.

Pearson, R.L. "Commentary: State Regulation of Obscene Motion Pictures: The Red Light Nuisance Statute." *Alabama Law Review* 31 (1980): 274–305.

Pemberton, John De J., Jr. "Can the Law Provide a Remedy for Race Defamation in the United States?" *New York Law Forum* 14 (Spring 1968): 33–48.

Perry, Michael J. "Modern Equal Protection: A Conceptualization and Appraisal." *Columbia Law Review* 79 (October 1979): 1023–84.

Peytel, Jean. "Group Defamation in France." *Cleveland Marshall Law Review* 13 (January 1964): 64–72.

Picard, R.G. "Media Self-Censorship: 'The Public Will Never Know.'" In *Readings in Mass Communication: Concepts and Issues in the Mass Media*, 521–25, edited by M. Emoery and T.C. Smythe; Dubuque, Iowa: William C. Brown, 1983.

Pignanelli, Frank R. "Comment: Regulation of Indecent Television Programming: HBO v. Wilkinson." *Journal of Contemporary Law* 9 (1983): 207–16.

Pless Davidson, Laurance. "Constitutional Law: Short Shrift for the Prior Restraint Doctrine." *North Carolina Law Review* 59 (January 1981): 417–27.

Plummer, Margery. "Verbal Rape: The Obscene Phone Call," *Victimology: An International Journal* 9 (Winter 1984): 15–16.

Pohorelsky, Viktor V. "Constitutional Law—First Amendment: FCC May Regulate Broadcast of Nonobscene Speech." *Tulane Law Review* 53 (1978): 273–83.

Polifka, John C. "A Legitimate Time, Place, and Manner Restriction on Speech in the Public Schools." *South Dakota Law Review* 32 (Spring 1987): 156–66.

Postawko, Edmund J. "The Conflict between the First Amendment and Ordinances Regulating Adult Establishments." *Washington University Journal of Urban and Contemporary Law* 30 (Spring 1986): 315–31.

Powe, L.A., Jr. "Cable and Obscenity." *Catholic University Law Review* 24 (Summer 1975): 719–54.

Powe, L.A., Jr. "American Voodoo: If Television Doesn't Show It Maybe It Won't Exist." *Texas Law Review* 59 (May 1981): 879–918.

Powe, L.A., Jr. "Consistency over Time: The FCC's Indecency Rerun." *COMM-ENT* 10 (Winter 1988): 571–77.

Power, David F. "Communications Law: FCC Empowered to Regulate Radio Broadcasts That Are Indecent but Not Obscene." *Temple Law Quarterly* 52 (1979): 170–97.

Prettyman, E.B., Jr., and L.A. Hook. "The Control of Media-Related Imitative Violence." *Federal Communications Law Journal* 38 (January 1987): 317–82.

"Prior Restraints." *News Media and the Law* 7 (September/October 1983): 33–41.

"Prior Restraints." *News Media and the Law* 6 (June/July 1982): 49.

"Prior Restraints." *News Media and the Law* 8 (January/February 1984): 4–11.

"Prior Restraints." *News Media and the Law* 8 (November/December 1984): 4–8.

Prosser, W. "Privacy." *California Law Review* 48 (1960): 383–423.

Prosser, W., and J.W. Wade. *Casas and Material on Torts.* 5th ed. Mineola, N.Y.: Foundation Press, 1971.

Quadres, Harold. "The Applicability of Content-Based Time, Place, and Manner Regulations to Offensive Language: The Burger Court." *Santa Clara Law Review* 21 (Fall 1981): 995–1045.

Quigg, Richard J. "Defenses to Group Defamation Actions." *Cleveland Marshall Law Review* 13 (January 1964): 102–10.

Rabin, R.J. "Some Comments on Obscenities, Health and Safety, and Workplace Values." *Buffalo Law Review* 34 (Fall 1985): 725–34.

"Race Defamation and the First Amendment." *Fordham Law Review* 34 (1966): 653–91.

Reaves, Lynne. "Smut by Phone: FCC Looks into Porn Service." *American Bar Association Journal* 89 (December 1983): 1815–16.

"Recent Decisions Approve Decency Statutes." *University of Cincinnati Law Review* 27 (Winter 1958): 61.

Redish. "The Content Distinction in First Amendment Analysis." *Stanford Law Review* 34 (1981): .

Regina, Maria T. "Broadcasting Obscene Language: The Federal Communications Commission and Section

1464 Violations." *Arizona State Law Journal* (1974): 457–84.

"Regulating Rock Lyrics: A New Wave of Censorship?" *Harvard Journal on Legislation* 23 (1986): 595.

"Regulation of Live Entertainment: Schad v. Borough of Mount Ephraim." *Harvard Law Review* 95 (1981): 231.

"Regulation of Program Content by the FCC." *Harvard Law Review* 77 (February 1964): 701–16.

Reidinger, Paul. "Thrills That Kill: Hustler Not Liable." *American Bar Association* 73 (July 1987): 80.

Rendleman, D. "Civilizing Pornography: The Case for an Exclusive Obscenity Nuisance Statute." *Chicago Law Review* 44 (Spring 1977): 509–60.

Rhoads, Ann E. "The Pig in the Parlor: Pennsylvania Senate Bill 645 and the Regulation of 'Cableporn.' " *Dickinson Law Review* 90 (Winter 1985): 463–86.

Riesman, David. "Democracy and Defamation: Control of Group Libel." *Columbia Law Review* 42 (May 1942): 727–80.

Riggs, Robert E. "Indecency on the Cable: Can It Be Regulated?" *Arizona Law Review* 26 (Spring 1984): 269–328.

Riggs, Robert E. "Regulation of Indecency on Cable Television." *Florida Bar Journal* 59 (March 1985): 9–12.

Rist, R.C. *The Pornography Controversy: Changing Moral Standards in American Life.* New Brunswick, N.J.: Transaction Books, 1975.

Robbins, Vicky Hallick. "Indecency on Cable Television: A Barren Battleground for Regulation of Programming Content." *St. Mary's Law Journal* 18 (Spring 1984): 417–41.

Robilliard, St. John A. "The Indecent Displays (Control) Act 1981." *Law and Justice* (Spring 1982): 24–30.

Roeseler, W.G. "Regulating Adult Entertainment Establishments under Conventional Zoning." *Urban Law* 19 (Winter 1987): 125–40.

Roldan, Jonathan Michael. "Radio-Active Fallout and Uneasy Truce: The Aftermath of the Porn Rock Wars." *Loyola Entertainment Law Journal* 7 (Spring 1987): 217–61.

"The Role of 'Secondary Effects' in First Amendment Analysis: Renton v. Playtime Theatres, Inc." *University of San Francisco Law Review* 22 (Fall 1987): 161–87.

Rosen, Deborah. "In Defense of a Probabilistic Theory of Causality." *Philosophy of Science* 45 (December 1978):604–13.

Rosen, Deborah. "A Critique of Deterministic Causality." *Philosophical Forum* 14 (Winter 1982–83): 101–30.

Rouder, Wendy P. "If You Can't Say It, Why Can You Show It? An Open Letter to the FCC." *Golden Gate University Law Review* 9, no. 2 (1978–79): 617–30.

Russ, Lee R. "Validity of Statutes or Ordinances Requiring Sex-Oriented Businesses to Obtain Operating Licenses." In *American Law Reports*, 130–440. 4th ed. vol. 8, edited by Rochester, N.Y.: Lawyers Co-Operative Publishing Company; San Francisco: Bancroft-Whitney Company, 1981.

Rutzick, Mark C. "Offensive Language and the Evolution

of First Amendment Protection." *Harvard Civil Rights–Civil Liberties Law Review* 9 (January 1974): 1–28.

Salmon, Wesley C. "Probabilistic Causality." *Pacific Philosophical Quarterly* 61 (January–April 1980): 50–74.

Sandler, Winifred Ann. "The Minneapolis Anti-Pornography Ordinance: A Valid Assertion of Civil Rights?" *Fordham Urban Law Journal* 13 (Fall 1985): 909–46.

"Sarong Gals: Green Light for the Red Light Abatement Law." *Pepperdine Law Review* 1 (1973): 126–28.

Savell, L. "Right of Privacy: Appropriation of a Person's Name, Portrait or Picture for Advertising or Trade Purposes without Written Consent: History and Scope in New York." *Albany Law Review* 48 (1983): 1–47.

Savitz, Leonard. "Obscene Phone Calls." In *Critique and Explanation: Essays in Honor of Gwynne Nettler*, edited by Timothy F. Hartnagel and Robert A. Silverman, 149–58; New Brunswick, N.J.: Transaction Books, 1986.

Schabert, John I. "Constitutional Law—Obscenity: The State May Not Prohibit Future Exhibitions of Motion Pictures through a Nuisance Abatement Statute Which allows a State Trial Judge, on the Basis of a Finding That a Theater Has Shown Specific Obscene Films in the Past, to Issue Such Injunction Against Future Activity, Unless Procedural Safeguards Govern the Entry of Orders Restraining Exhibition of Named or Unnamed Films with Regard to the Context in Which They Are Displayed." *American Journal of Criminal Law* 8 (July 1980): 199–208.

"Schad v. Borough of Mount Ephraim: A Pyrrhic Victory for Freedom of Expression?" *Loyola of Los Angeles Law Review* 15 (1982): 321.

Schaper, Joseph R. "Constitutional Law—First Amendment—Municipal Zoning—Pornography: The Supreme Court Has Held That a Municipal Zoning Ordinance Prohibiting Adult Motion Picture Theaters from Locating within 1,000 feet of Any Residential Zone Single- or Multiple-Family Dwelling, Church, Park, or School, Does Not Violate the First Amendment." *Duquesne Law Review* 26 (Fall 1987): 163–80.

Schauer, Frederick. *The Law of Obscenity.* Washington, D.C.: Bureau of National Affairs, 1976.

Schauer, Frederick. "Causation Theory and the Causes of Sexual Violence." *American Bar Foundation Research Journal* (1987): 737–70.

Scheidemantel, Paul E. "It's Only Rock-and-Roll but They Don't Like It: Censoring 'Indecent' Lyrics." *New England Law Review* 21 (1985–86): 467–508.

Schiffres, Irvin J. "Invasion of Privacy by Use of Plaintiff's Name or Likeness for Non-Advertising Purposes." In *American Law Reports*. 3d ed. Vol. 30, edited by Rochester, N.Y.: Lawyers Co-Operative Publishing Company; San Francisco: Bancroft-Whitney Company, 1970: 203–83.

Schmalz, Kurt L. "Problems in Giving Obscenity Copyright Protection: Did Jartech and Mitchell Brothers Go Too Far?" *Vanderbilt Law Review* 36 (March 1983): 403–30.

Schmidt, G. Booker. "Subsequent Use of Civil Adjudications of Obscenity." *Tulsa Law Journal* 13 (1977): 146–77.

Schneider, Dan W. "Authority of the Register of Copyrights to Deny Registration of Claim to Copyright on the Ground of Obscenity." *Chicago-Kent Law Review* 51, no. 3 (1975): 691–723.

Schooner, Steven L. "Obscene Parody: The Judicial Exception to Fair Use Analysis." *Journal of Arts Management and Law* 14 (Fall 1984): 69–94.

Schopler, Ernest H. "Supreme Court's View as to Overbreadth of Legislation in Connection with First Amendment Rights."

Schwartz, Allan L. "Right of Telephone or Telegraph Company to Refuse, or Discontinue, Service Because of Use of Improper Language." In *American Law Reports* 3d ed. Vol 32, 1041–46, edited by Rochester, N.Y.: Lawyers Co-Operative Publishing Company; San Francisco: Bancroft-Whitney Company, 1970.

Scott, George Ryley. *"Into Whose Hands": An Examination of Obscene Libel in its Legal, Sociological and Literary Aspects.* New York: Waron Press, 1961.

"Second Class Speech: The Court's Refinement of Content Regulation: Schad v. Borough of Mount Ephraim." *Nebraska Law Review* 61 (1982): 361.

Shapiro, G., P. Kurland, and F. Mercurio. " 'Cable Speech': The Case for First Amendment Protection." 1983. 42-48. Available from Pennsylvania Cable Television Association, 325 N. Front Street, Harrisburg, PA 17101.

Shapiro, Jacqueline. " 'Filthy Words': One Man's Lyric or Broadcasting's Indecency?" *University of Miami Law Review* 34 (November 1979): 147–59.

Shavell, Steven. "An Analysis of Causation and the Scope of Liability in the Law of Torts." *Journal of Legal Studies* 9 (1980): 463–516.

Shaw, Jack W., Jr. "Exhibition of Obscene Motion Pictures as Nuisance." In *American Law Reports.* 3d ed. Vol. 50, 969–91, edited by Rochester, N.Y.: Lawyers Co-Operative Publishing Company; San Francisco: Bancroft-Whitney Company, 1970.

Shinners, Gary W. "Offensive Personal Product Advertising on the Broadcast Media: Can it be Constitutionally Censored?" *Federal Communications Law Journal* 34 (1982): 49–91.

Shipley, W.E. "Comment Note: Prima Facie Tort." In *American Law Reports* 3d ed. Vol 16, 1191–1231, edited by Rochester, N.Y.: Lawyers Co-Operative Publishing Company; San Francisco: Bancroft-Whitney Company, 1967.

Slater, Robert Bruce. "Parents Purport to Purify Porn Rock." *Business and Society Review* (Winter 1988): 60–62.

Sloan, Martin C. "Note: Regulating Indecent Speech: A New Attack on the First Amendment." *University of Pittsburgh Law Review* 41 (1979): 321–41.

Smith, Jeffrey A. "Prior Restraint: Original Intentions and Modern Interpretations." *William and Mary Law Review* 28 (Spring 1987): 439–72.

Smith, Rosemary C. "Indecent Programming on Cable

Television and the First Amendment." *George Washington Law Review* 51 (January 1983): 254–68.

Spahn, Elizabeth. "On Sex and Violence." *New England Law Review* 20 (1984–85): 629–47.

Spak, Michael I. "Predictable Harm: Should the Media Be Liable? *Ohio State Law Journal* 42 (1981): 671–87.

Spindel, Frederic T. "Constitutional Law: A City Ordinance That Prohibits the Exhibition with View of a Public Highway of Films Deemed Objectionable to Children Does Not Violate the First Amendment." *Texas Law Review* 45 (December 1966): 345–56.

Sporn, Jessica. "Content Regulation of Cable Television: 'Indecency' Statutes and the First Amendment." *Rutgers Computer and Technology Law Journal* 11 (1985): 141–70.

"Statutory Prohibition of Group Defamation." *Columbia Law Review* 47 (May 1947): 595–612.

Stein, Ronald M. "Regulation of Adult Businesses through Zoning after Renton." *Pacific Law Journal* 18 (January 1987): 351 75.

Steiner, George. "Night Words: High Pornography and Human Privacy." In *Perspectives on Pornography*, edited by Douglas A. Hughes, New York: St. Martin's Press, 1970.

Steinkamp, Robert T. "Constitutional Law: The Sale of Obscene Material to Minors." *University of Missouri Kansas City Law Review* 37 (Winter 1969): 127–42.

Stephenson, Saskia A. "Constitutional Law—Freedom of Speech—Radio and Television—Obscenity—Right of Privacy: The FCC May Constitutionally Sanction a Radio Station for Broadcasting Language Which Is Indecent but Not Obscene." *University of Cincinnati Law Review* 47 (Summer/Fall 1978): 678–85.

Sternberg, Barbara A., and Aaron J. Weissman. "Television Violence: Censorship and the First Amendment." *University of West Los Angeles Law Review* 12 (Spring 1980): 81–96.

Stevenin, Cynthia D. "Note: Young v. American Mini Theatres, Inc.: Creating Levels of Protected Speech." *Hastings Constitutional Law Quarterly* 4 (Spring 1977): 321–59.

Stewart, C. Jean. "Note: Constitutional Law—Pornography: Colorado Municipal Government Authority to Regulate Obscene Materials." *Denver Law Journal* 51 (1974): 75–94.

Stokes, Gerald Cat. "Distribution of Obscene Material Subject to Civil Prosecution as Unfair Competition." *U.W.I.A. Law Review* 13 (Spring 1981): 183–202.

Stone, Geoffrey R. "Restrictions of Speech Because of Its Content: The Peculiar Case of Subject Matter Restrictions." *University of Chicago Law Review* 46 (Fall 1978): 81–115.

Stone, Geoffrey R. "Comment: Anti-Pornography Legislation as Viewpoint Discrimination." *Harvard Journal of Law and Public Policy* 9 (Spring 1986): 461–80.

Strong, Frank R. "Fifty Years of 'Clear and Present Danger': From Schenck to Brandenburg—and Beyond." *Supreme Court Review* (1969): 41–80.

Stuart, Shelley R. "Young v. American Mini Theatres,

Inc.: A Limit on First Amendment Protection." *New England Law Review* 12 (Fall 1976): 391–418.

Sunkel, William M. "Court-Approved Censorship through Zoning." *Pace Law Review* 7 (Fall 1986): 251–90.

Sunstein, C.R. "Pornography and the First Amendment." *Duke Law Journal* (September 1986): 589–627.

Suppes, Patrick. *A Probabilistic Theory of Causality.* Amsterdam: North Holland Publishing Company, 1970.

Suppes, Patrick. "Scientific Causal Talk: A Reply to Martin." *Theory and Decision* 13 (December 1981): 363–79.

Suppes, Patrick. *Probabilistic Metaphysics.* Oxford, England: Basil Blackwell, 1984.

"Supreme Court and Obscenity." *Vanderbilt Law Review* 11 (March 1958): 585.

Tanenhaus, Joseph. "Group Libel." *Cornell Law Quarterly* 35 (Winter 1950): 261–302.

Tanner, Eric. "First Amendment Due Process and the University." *University of Missouri Kansas City Law Review* 42 (Spring 1974): 390–95.

Taylor, Paul Renwick. "Constitutional Law—Obscenity: Washington's Pornography and Moral Nuisance Act of 1982 Withstands First Amendment Challenge." *Gonzaga Law Review* 18, no. 1 (1982–83): 143–52.

Tell. "Cable TV's Sex Problem." *National Law Journal* 4 15 (February 1982): 1.

Tessaro, Nancy. "Is the Pig in the Parlor? (First Amendment Symposium)." *Northern Kentucky Law Review* 15 (Spring 1988): 205–25.

Torke, James W. "Some Notes on the Proper Use of the Clear and Present Danger Test." *Brigham Young University Law Review* 1 (1978): 1–37.

"Torts—Liability on TV." *American Bar Association Journal* 67 (July 1981): 921–22.

Tovey, Morgan W. "Dial-a-Porn and the First Amendment: The State Action Loophole." *Federal Communications Law Journal* 40 (April 1988): 267–93.

Tozier, Deborah A. ". . . But the Eleventh Circuit Court of Appeals Teaches the Other." (Restriction of Topless Dancing in Bars). *Stetson Law Review* 15 (Summer 1986): 1020–21.

Trachtman, Jeffrey S. "Pornography, Padlocks, and Prior Restraints: The Constitutional Limits of the Nuisance Power." *New York University Law Review* 58, no. 2 (1983): 1478–1529.

Trenkner, Thomas R. "Validity of 'War Zone' Ordinances Restricting Location of Sex-Oriented Businesses." In *American Law Reports.* 4th ed. Vol. 1, 1297–1304, edited by Rochester, N.Y.: Lawyers Co-Operative Publishing Company; San Francisco: Bancroft-Whitney Company, 1980.

Truchi, Kenneth L. "Municipal Zoning Restrictions on Adult Entertainment: Young, Its Progeny, and Indianapolis' Special Exceptions Ordinance." *Indiana Law Journal* 58 (Summer 1982–83): 505–29.

Turney, Harriet L. "The Road to Respectability: A Woman of Pleasure and Competing Conceptions of the First Amendment." *University of Dayton Law Review* 5 (Summer 1980): 271–99.

Urwin,. "Tort Liability of Broadcasters for Audience Acts of Imitative Violence." *Public Entertainment Advertisement and Allied Fields Law Quarterly* 19 (1981): 315.

U.S. Congress Senate. *Record Labeling: Hearing before the Senate Committee on Commerce, Science and Transportation.* 99th Cong. 1st Sess., 1985.

"Using Constitutional Zoning to Neutralize Adult Entertainment—Detroit to New York." *Fordham Urban Law Journal* 5 (1977): 455.

Van Lente, Scott. "Obscenity, Indecency and the Excitable Boy: Is Pay Cable Different?" *Cooley Law Review* 1 (May 1983): 391–420.

Verani, John R. "Motion Picture Censorship and the Doctrine of Prior Restraint." *Houston Law Review* 3 (Spring/Summer 1965): 11–57.

Vicinaiz, Victor V. "The Content Distinction and Freedom of Expression: Arcara v. Cloud Books, Inc. (106 S. Ct. 172)." *Creighton Law Review* 20 (1986–87): 893–915.

"Video Censorship." *Legal Service Bulletin* 10 (Australia) (February 1985): 38–40.

Vinar, Benjamin. "Right of Privacy: A Model's Naked Past: Recent New York Ruling Highlights Issue." *New York Law Journal* 183 (19 February 1980): 1.

"Violence and Obscenity—Chaplinsky Revisited." *Fordham Law Review* 42 (1973): 141–60.

"Violent Pornography: Degradation of Women versus Right of Free Speech." *New York University Review of Law and Social Change* 8, no. 2 (1978–79): 181–300.

"The Void-for-Vagueness Doctrine in the Supreme Court." *University of Pennsylvania Law Review* 109 (November 1960): 67–116.

Wade, J.W. "On the Nature of Strict Tort Liability for Products." *Mississippi Law Journal* 44 (1973): 825–51.

Wakshlag, J., V. Vial, and R. Tambori. "Selecting Crime Drama and Apprehension about Crime." *Human Communication* 10 (1983): 227–42.

Waldbillig, Deborah A. "Padlock Orders and Nuisance Laws: The First Amendment in Arcara v. Cloud Books." *Albany Law Review* 51 (Spring/Summer 1987): 1007–46.

Wallace, Jeffrey E. "Contextual Regulation of Indecency: A Happy Medium for Television." *Valparaiso University Law Review* 21 (Fall 1986): 193–220.

Wardle, Lynn D. "Cable Comes of Age: A Constitutional Analysis of the Regulation of 'Indecent' Cable Television Programming." *Denver University Law Review* 63 (1986): 621–95.

Warren, Samuel D., and Louis D. Brandeis. "The Right to Privacy." *Harvard Law Review* 4 (December 1890): 193–220.

Washburn, A. "Regulating the Airwaves Is Not the Same as Censoring Them." *Barrister* 6 (Summer 1979): 52–55 +.

Waters, K. "Pacifica and the Broadcast of Indecency." *Houston Law Review* 16 (1979): 551–601.

Watkins, Sharon Anne. "Note: The Devil and the D.A.: The Civil Abatement of Obscenity." *Hastings Law Journal* 28 (July 1977): 1329–58.

Weingarten, Steven J. "Tort Liability for Nonlibelous

Negligent Statements: First Amendment Considerations." *Yale Law Journal* 93 (1984): 744–62.

Weinstein, Alan C. "The Renton Decision: A New Standard for Adult Business Regulation." *Washington University Journal of Urban and Contemporary Law* 32 (Summer 1987): 91–122.

Weller, Christopher W. "See No Evil: The Divisive Issue of Minors' Access Laws." *Cumberland Law Review* 18 (Winter 1988): 141–79.

Westen, Peter, "The Empty Idea of Equality." *Harvard Law Review* 95 (January 1982): 537–96.

Wheeler, Tom. "Comment: Drug Lyrics, the FCC and the First Amendment." *Loyola of Los Angeles Law Review* 5 (1972): 329–67.

Whitley, Jack. "Note: Cable Television: The Practical Implications of Local Regulation and Control." *Drake Law Review* 27 (1978): 391–420.

Wilkinson, Bonnie. "Copyright: The Obscenity Defense in Actions to Protect Copyright." *Fordham Law Review* 46 (April 1978): 1037–47.

Winer, Laurence H. "The Signal Cable Sends." Part 2: "Interference from the Indecency Cases?" *Fordham Law Review* 55 (March 1987): 459–527.

Wing, Susan. "Note: Morality and Broadcasting: FCC Control on 'Indecent' Material Following Pacifica." *Federal Communications Law Journal* 31 1978: 145–73.

Winter, Bill. "Channel X: Cable TV Smut Battles Growing." *American Bar Association Journal* 69 (July 1983): 886–87.

Witt, John W. "The First Amendment and Cable Television." *Municipal Attorney* 25 (March/April 1984): 1–4.

Witt, John W. "Cable Television Regulation after Crisp: Is There Anything Left." *Urban Law Review* 17 (1985): 277–97.

Woito, L.N., and P. McNulty. "Privacy Disclosure Tort and the First Amendment: Should the Community Decide Newsworthiness?" *Iowa Law Review* 64 (January 1979): 185–232.

Wolff, Robert. "Pacifica's Seven Dirty Words: A Sliding Scale of the First Amendment." *University of Illinois Law Forum* 4 (1979): 969–1107.

Wolin, David, and Cecelic Berry. "Regulating Rock Lyrics:

A New Wave of Censorship?" *Harvard Journal on Legislation* 73 (Summer 1986): 595–619.

Yahig, Laurance. "Note: Tort Law: First Amendment Bars Suit for Alleged Negligence in Programming." *Suffolk University Law Review* 17 (1983): 456–61.

Yen, Alfred C. "Judicial Review of the Zoning of Adult Entertainment: A Search for the Purposeful Suppression of Protected Speech." *Pepperdine Law Review* 12, no. 2 (1985): 651–78.

York, Gary A. "Recent Developments: Summary Termination of Telephone Service for Suspected Illegal Use." *Stanford Law Review* 20 (1967): 136–45.

Zabin, S. "Obscenity Indictment or Information—Whether Use of Obscene Language over a Telephone Amounts to a Criminal Offense." *Chicago-Kent Law Review* 33 (September 1955): 370–73.

Zellick, G. "Violence as Pornography." *Criminal Law Records* (April 1970): 188.

Ziegler, Edward H., Jr. "City of Renton v. Playtime Theatres, Inc.: Supreme Court Reopens the Door for Zoning of Sexually Oriented Businesses." *Zoning and Planning Law Report* 9 (May 1986): 33–39.

Ziegler, Edward H., Jr. "Sexually Oriented Business, the First Amendment, and the Supreme Court's 1985–1986 Term: The New Prerogatives of Local Community Control." *Washington University Journal of Urban and Contemporary Law* 32 (Summer 1987): 123–46.

Zillman, D. "Victimization of Women through Pornography." Proposal to the National Science Foundation, Indiana University, 1984.

"The Zoning of Adult Entertainment: How Far Can Planning Commissions Go?" *COMM/ENT Law Journal* 5 (1983): 293.

Zuckerman, H.L. "There Is Tort Liability for Negligent Programming." *Communications Lawyer* 1 (Winter 1983): 1, 8–9.

Zuleeg, Manfred. "Group Defamation in West Germany." *Cleveland Marshall Law Review* 13 (January 1964): 52–63.

Zupanec, Donald M. "Validity, Construction, and Effect of Statutes or Ordinances Prohibiting the Sale of Obscene Materials to Minors." In *American Law Reports.* 3d ed. Vol. 93, 297–320, edited by Rochester, N.Y.: Lawyers Co-Operative Publishing Company; San Francisco: Bancroft-Whitney Company, 1979.

CHAPTER 13

Attorney General's Commission on Pornography. *Final Report.* Washington, D.C.: U.S. Department of Justice, 1986.

Barnett, Walter, "Corruption of Morals: The Underlying Issue of the Pornography Commission Report." *Law and Social Order* (1971): 189–243.

Blodgett, Nancy. "Porno Blacklist? Magazines Fight Meese Panel." *American Bar Association Journal* 72 (July 1986): 28.

Bruce, E. Edward. "Prostitution and Obscenity: A Com-

ment upon the Attorney General's Report on Pornography." *Duke Law Journal* (February 1987): 123–39.

Canada. Special Committee on Pornography and Prostitution. *Pornography and Prostitution in Canada.* Ottawa: Canadian Government Publishing Centre, 1985.

Cline, Victor B. "The Scientists vs. Pornography: An Untold Story." *Intellect* 104 (May/June 1976): 574–76.

Clor, Harry M. "Science, Eros and the Law: A Critique

of the Obscenity Commission Report." *Duquesne Law Review* 10 (Fall 1971): 63–76.

Coldham, Simon. "Reports of the Committee on Obscenity and Film Censorship." *Modern Law Review* 43 (Great Britain) (May 1980): 306–18.

Cunningham, S. "Motives, Mission Unclear in Pornography Probe." *American Psychological Association Monitor* 16 (August 1985): 26–27.

Donnerstein, Edward. "The Pornography Commission Report: Do Findings Fit Conclusions?" In *Sexual Coercion and Assault: Issues and Perspectives*, 185–88, edited by Bellingham, Wash.: 1986.

Feldman-Summers, Shirley. "A Comment on the Meese Commission Report and the Dangers of Censorship." In *Sexual Coercion and Assault: Issues and Perspectives*, 179–84, edited by Bellingham, Wash.: 1986.

Hughes, P. "Tensions in Canadian Society: The Fraser Committee Report." *Windsor Yearbook of Access to Justice* 6 (1986): 282–323.

Ince, John. "Sex and the Justice Department: A Fear of Erotica." *Canadian Lawyer* 12 (March 1988): 22–25.

Johansen, Bruce E. "The Meese Police on Porn Patrol." *Progressive* 52 (June 1988): 20.

Johnson, Weldon T. "Pornography Report: Epistemology, Methodology and Ideology." *Duquesne Law Review* 10 (Winter 1971): 190–219.

Kanter, Michael. "Prohibit or Regulate? The Fraser Report and New Approaches to Pornography and Prostitution." *Osgoode Hall Law Journal* 23 (Canada) (Spring 1985): 171–94.

"Legislative Recommendations: Report of the Committee on Obscenity and Pornography." In *The Pornography Controversy*, edited by Ray C. Rist, 64–84, New Brunswick, N.J.: Transaction Books, 1975.

Lipton, M.A. "Fact and Myth: The Work of the Commission on Obscenity and Pornography." In *Contemporary Sexual Behavior: Critical Issues in the 1970's*, edited by J. Zubin and J. Money, Baltimore: Johns Hopkins University Press, 1973.

Lockhart, W.B. "Findings and Recommendations of the Commission on Obscenity and Pornography: A Case Study of the Role of Social Science in Formulating Public Policy." *Oklahoma Law Review* 24 (May 1971): 126.

Longford, Lord. "*Pornography: The Longford Report.*" London: Coronet Books, 1972.

Manchester, Colin. "The Scope of Obscenity Control in England and Wales: A Critique of the Williams Committee's Approach." *Northern Ireland Legal Quarterly* 31 (Summer 1980): 103–13.

Marcotte, Paul. "See No Evil: Sex Magazines Go Undercover." *American Bar Association Journal* 72 (February 1986): 33.

"Meese Commission Releases Porn Report, Can't Agree on Harm on 'Indecent' Matter." *News Media and the Law* 10 (Fall 1986): 40–42.

"Meese Creates Task Force to Enforce Anti-Pornography Laws." *Criminal Justice Newsletter* 17 (1 December 1986): 3.

"Meese Panel Begins Search for Crime-Pornography Connection." *Criminal Justice Newsletter* 16 (1 August 1983): 4–5.

National Coalition Against Censorship. *Meese Commission Exposed: Proceedings of an NCAC Public Information Briefing on the Attorney General's Commission on Pornography*. New York: National Coalition Against Censorship, 1986.

Nobile, P., and E. Nadler. *United States of America vs. Sex: How the Meese Commission Lied about Pornography*. New York: Minotaur, 1986.

O'Dair, Barbara. "Meese Commission: 'A License to Clamp Down' on Sexuality." *Guardian*, 19 February 1986, 7.

"Playboy, Penthouse Sue Porn Commission over 'Threat' Against Magazine Retailers." *New Media and the Law* 10 (Summer 1986): 22.

"Porn Panel May Advocate Ban." *News Media and the Law* 10 (Summer 1986): 20–21.

"Pornography in Canada: Report of the Special Committee." *Response to the Victimization of Women and Children* 9 (1986): 3.

Quade, Vicki. "The Lawyer Behind the Government's Pornography Report." *Barrister* 13 (Fall 1986): 13.

Richards, David A.J. "Pornography Commissions and the First Amendment: On Constitutional Values and Constitutional Facts." *Maine Law Review* 39 (July 1987): 275–320.

Simpson, A.W.B. *Pornography and Politics*. London: Waterlow, 1983.

Stanmeyer, William A. "The Pornography Commission Report: A Plea for Decency." *Benchmark* 2 (September–December 1986): 227.

Stengel, Richard. "Sex Busters." *Time*, 21 July 1986, 21.

Stoltz, Craig. "Porn in the U.S.A.: The Attorney General's Commission on Pornography Goes Public—And on the Road—To Find out the Difference between Bad Taste and Bad Influence." *Student Lawyer* 14 (September 1985): 40–41.

Sunderland, Lane V. *Obscenity: The Court, the Congress and the Presidential Commission*. Washington, D.C.: American Enterprise Institute for Public Policy Research, 1975.

Tarbet, Don. "How to Lie with Pornography: Lies, Damn Lies, Statistics—and the Meese Commission." *Student Lawyer* 15 (December 1985): 32.

Vance, Carole S. "The Meese Commission on the Road." *Nation*, 2–9 August 1986, 80.

CHAPTER 14

Able-Peterson, Trudee. *Children of the Evening*. New York: G.P. Putnam's Sons, 1981.

American Bar Association, Young Lawyers Division. *Child Sexual Exploitation: Background and Legal Analysis*. Washington, D.C.: National Legal Resource Center for Child Advocacy and Protection, 1981.

Anson, R.S. "The Last Porno Show." In *The Sexual Victimization of Youth*, 275–91, edited by L.G. Schultz, Springfield, Ill: Charles C. Thomas, 1980.

Arnett, Peter. "Use of Children Opens New Front in Porn War." *Blade* (Toledo, Ohio), 17 April 1977, 25.

Attorney General's Commission on Pornography. *Final Report*. Washington, D.C.: U.S. Department of Justice, 1986.

Baker, C. David. "Comment: Preying on Playgrounds: The Sexploitation of Children in Pornography and Prostitution." *Pepperdine Law Review* 5 (1978): 809–46.

Baker, D. "Preying on Playgrounds: The Sexploitation of Children in Pornography and Prostitution." *The Sexual Victimization of Youth*, edited by L.G. Schultz, Springfield, Ill.: Charles C. Thomas, 1980.

Baratz, Ellen M. "Constitutional Law—First Amendment—Freedom of Speech: New York v. Ferber 458 U.S. 747 (1982)." *New York Law School Law Review* 29 (Spring/Summer 1984): 469–89.

Barry, Kathleen. *Female Sexual Slavery*. Englewood Cliffs, N.J.: Prentice-Hall, 1979.

Berger, A.S., W. Simon, and J.H. Gagnon. "Youth and Pornography in Social Context." *Archives of Sexual Behavior* 2, no. 4 (1973): 279–308.

Blodgett, Nancy. "Child Porn Curb: Bill Limits Computer Sex Data." *American Bar Association Journal* 72 (February 1986): 32–33.

Bloodworth, Jon M., III. "New York v. Ferber: Compelling Extension of First Amendment Infringement." *Golden Gate University Law Review* 13 (Spring 1983): 475–94.

Bosarge, Betty. "Who Will Help the Kids? JJS Personnel Call for Action on Child Porno Murders: 'Who Then Will Become Outraged?' " *Juvenile Justice Digest*. 11 December 1981, 9:23.

Bosarge, Betty. "National Symposium: Police 'Handcuffed' Trying to Stop Nationwide Sex Abuse, Porno Rings Involving Children. 'Turn in America's Sacred Cows.' " *Juvenile Justice Digest*, 23 December 1981, 7.

Bridge, Peter. "What Parents Should Know and Do About 'Kiddie Porn.' " *Parents Magazine*, January 1978, 42ff.

Brown, Sandra Zunker. "First Amendment: Nonobscene Child Pornography and Its Categorical Exclusion from Constitutional Protection." *Journal of Criminal Law and Criminology* 73 (Winter 1982): 1337–64.

Burgess, Ann Wolbert et al. "Executive Summary: Research on the Use of Children in Pornography." Report to the National Center on Child Abuse and Neglect, 8 December 1982.

Burgess, Ann Wolbert, with Marieanne Lindequist Clark. *Child Pornography and Sex Rings*. Lexington, Mass: Lexington Books, 1984.

Burgess, Ann Wolbert, A.N. Groth, and M. McCausland. "Child Sex Initiation Ring." *American Journal of Orthopsychiatry* 51 (January 1981): 110–19.

Burgess, Ann Wolbert and Carol R. Hartman. "Child Abuse Aspects of Child Pornography." *Psychiatric Annals* 17 (April 1987): 248–53.

Burgess, Ann Wolbert, Carol R. Hartman, Maureen P. McCausland, and Patricia Powers. "Response Patterns in Children and Adolescents Exploited through Sex Rings and Pornography." *American Journal of Psychiatry* 141 (May 1984): 656–62.

California. Assembly. Committee on Criminal Justice. "Obscenity and the Use of Minors in Pornographic Material." 31 October 1977, 22 November 1977.

California. Attorney General's Advisory Committee on Obscenity and Pornography. "Report to the Attorney General on Child Pornography in California," 24 June 1977.

Campagna, Daniel S., and Donald L. Poffenberger. *The Sexual Trafficking in Children: An Investigation of the Child Sex Trade*. Dover, Mass: Auburn House, 1988.

Canada. Committee on Sexual Offenses Against Children and Youths. *Sexual Offenses Against Children*, 1984.

Casey, C.E., and L. Martin. "Pornography and Obscenity." *Police Yearbook* 1978:.

Caso, Anthony T. "Free Speech and Self-Incrimination: The Constitutionality of California's New Child Pornography Laws." *Pacific Law Journal* 10 (January 1979): 119–40.

Caughlan, Susan G. "Private Possession of Child Pornography: The Tensions between Stanley v. Georgia and New York v. Ferber." *William and Mary Law Review* 29 (Fall 1987): 187–214.

"Child Porn: Is the Issue 1st Amendment Freedom?" *Washington Star*, 11 April 1977.

"Child Pornography: Outrage Starts to Stir Some Action." *U.S. News and World Report*, 13 June 1977, 66.

"Child Pornography: Sickness for Sale." *Chicago Tribune*, 15 May 1977.

"Child's Garden of Perversity." *Time*, 4 April 1977, 56.

Chock, Patricia N. "The Use of Computers in the Sexual Exploitation of Children and Child Pornography." *Computer Law Journal* 7 (Summer 1987): 383–407.

Clark, Jayne. "Child Pornographers: A Secretive Danger." *Phoenix Gazette*, 27 June 1983.

Clinton, Robert J. "Notes: Child Protection Act of 1984—Enforceable Legislation to Prevent Sexual Abuse of Children." *Oklahoma City University Law Review* 10 (Spring 1985): 121–51.

Colen, Joan S. "Child Pornography: Ban the Speech and Spare the Child? New York v. Ferber." *DePaul Law Review* 32 (1983): 685–711.

Connor, Patricia S. "Children" (Survey of Virginia Law,

1978–79). *Virginia Law Review* 66 (March 1980): 253–57.

"Constitutional Problems in Obscenity Legislation Protecting Children." *Georgetown Law Journal* 54 (Summer 1966): 1379–1414.

"Contents of Pornography." In *Sexual Offenses Against Children*. Vol. 2, 1213–41, edited by Ottawa: Canadian Government Publishing Center, 1984.

"Crimes: Child Pornography" (1984 California legislation). *Pacific Law Journal* 16 (January 1985): 595–614.

Cropper, Gregory. "Child Pornography Law." *Utah Law Review* (Winter 1986): 171–78.

Dauber, Eric L. "Constitutional Law—Child Pornography: A New Exception to the First Amendment." *Florida State University Law Review* 10 (Winter 1982): 684–701.

Davidson, Howard. "Sexual Exploitation of Children: An Overview of Its Scope, Impact and Legal Ramifications." *Prosecutor* 16 (1982): 7.

Davis, E. "Kid Porn: Is It 'The Nadir of Man's Depravity'?" *Los Angeles Times*, 18 September 1977.

Densen-Gerber, J. "What Pornographers Are Doing to Children: A Shocking Report." *Redbook*, August 1977, 86–89.

Densen-Gerber, J. "Child Prostitution and Child Pornography: Medical, Legal and Societal Aspects of the Sexual Exploitation of Children." In *Sexual Abuse of Children: Selected Readings*, edited by U.S. Department of Health and Human Services, 77–82. Washington, D.C., 1980.

Densen-Gerber, J., and S.F. Hutchinson. "Medical-Legal and Societal Problems." In *Whoring Children: Child Prostitution, Child Pornography and Drug Related Abuse—Recommended Legislation*, edited by Baltimore: University Park Press, 1978.

Densen-Gerber, J., and S.F. Hutchinson. *Medical-Legal and Societal Problems Involving Children: Child Prostitution, Child Pornography and Drug-Related Abuse—Recommended Legislation*. Baltimore: University Park Press, 1978.

Densen-Gerber, J.D., and S.F. Hutchinson. "Sexual and Commercial Exploitation of Children: Legislative Responses and Treatment Challenges." In *Child Abuse and Neglect*, edited by New York: Pergamon Press, 1979, 61–66.

Dibble, J. Rex. "Obscenity: A State Quarantine to Protect Children." *Southern California Law Review* 39, no. 3 (1966): 345–77.

DiSantis, L. "Vetoed Bill: Distribution and Display of Sexually Explicit Materials to Minors." *Georgia State University Law Review* 3 (Spring/Summer 1987): 406–10.

Ditkoff,. "Child Pornography." *American Humane*, April 1978, 29–32.

Doek, Jaap E. "Child Pornography and Legislation in the Netherlands." *Child Abuse and Neglect* 9 (1985): 411–12.

Dong, S. "N.Y. Court Lifts Ruling Protecting 'Show Me'—St. Martin's Press Case." *Publisher's Weekly* 215 (22 January 1979): 283–84.

Donnelly, T. Christopher. "Note: Protection of Children from Use in Pornography." *University of Michigan Journal of Law Reform* 12 (Winter 1979): 295–337.

Dudar, Helen. "America Discovers Child Pornography." *Ms.*, August 1977, 45ff.

Durdines, David. "New York, Petitioner, v. Paul Ira Ferber, Respondent—U.S.—102 S. Ct. 3348 (1982)." *Journal of Juvenile Law* 7 (1983): 180–81.

Ferguson, Robert Warner. "Constitutional Law: A New Standard for the State's Battle Against Child Pornography." *Wake Forest Law Review* 19 (February 1983): 95–117.

Finkelhor, David. *Child Sexual Abuse*. New York: Free Press, 1984.

Finkelhor, David. *Sexually Victimized Children*. New York: Free Press, 1981.

Finkelhor, David. *Child Sexual Abuse: New Theory and Research*. New York: Free Press, 1981.

"First Amendment—Freedom of Speech: Child Pornography, Obscene or Not, Possesses No First Amendment Protection." *Santa Clara Law Review* (Spring 1983): 23: 675–84.

Flanagan, Thomas J. "Constitutional Law: Supreme Court Upholds Prohibition of Nonobscene Depictions of Sexual Conduct by Children." *Suffolk University Law Review* 17 (Spring 1983): 86–107.

Fox, R.G. "Censorship Policy and Child Pornography." *Australian Law Review* 52 (July 1978): 361–71.

Frank, G. "Child Pornography Industry Finds a Home in Los Angeles." *Los Angeles Daily Journal*, 28 November 1977.

Fraser, Morris. "Child Pornography." *New Statesman* 95 (17 February 1978): 213.

"Freedom of Speech and Association: Child Pornography and Unprotected Speech." *Harvard Law Review* 96 (November 1982): 141–50.

Geiser, R.L. *Hidden Victims—The Sexual Abuse of Children*. Boston: Beacon Press, 1979.

General Accounting Office. "Sexual Exploitation of Children—A Problem of Unknown Magnitude." Report to the House Committee on Education and Labor, Subcommittee on Select Education," Gaithersburg, MD. 20 April 1982.

Ginn, Robert W. "Constitutional Law: Child Pornography and the First Amendment: Abrogation of the Obscenity Doctrine in *New York v. Ferber*." *Creighton Law Review* 16 (1983): 509–31.

Goetz, John D. "Children's Rights under the Burger Court: Concern for the Child but Deference to Authority." *Notre Dame Law Review* 60 (Fall 1985): 1214–32.

Gow, Haven Bradford. "What Pornography Does." *Christian News*, 30 March 1981.

Gow, Haven Bradford. "Child Pornography Linked to Sexual Abuse." *Human Events*, 7 January 1984, 13.

Green, William. "Children and Pornography: An Interest Analysis in System Perspective." *Valparaiso University Law Review* 19 (Winter 1985): 441–70.

Grossberg, Scott J. "Child Pornography." *Journal of Juvenile Law* 9 (Summer 1985): 344–48.

Gulo, Michael V., Ann W. Burgess, and Ronald Kelly.

"Child Victimization: Pornography and Prostitution." *Journal of Crime and Justice* (1980): 65–81.

Hazelwood, Robert, Park Elliott Dietz, and Ann Wolbert Burgess. *Autoerotic Fatalities*. Lexington, Mass: Lexington Books, 1983.

Herrmann, K.J., Jr. "Children Sexually Exploited for Profit: A Plea for a New Social Work Priority." *Social Work* 32 (November/December 1987): 523–25.

Herrmann, K.J., Jr., and M.J. Jupp. "Commercial Child Pornography and Pedophile Organizations: An International Report." *Response to the Victimization of Women and Children* 8 (Spring 1985): 2, 7, 10.

Hershberg, Jim, and Dennis Bell. "Cops Raid Home in Child Sex Ring." *Newsday*, 14 July 1981.

Humphreys, Laud. Review of *For Money or Love*, by Robin Lloyd. *Contemporary Sociology* 7 (1978): 37–39.

Hurst, J. "Children—A Big Profit Item for the Smut Producer." *Los Angeles Times*, 26 May 1977.

Illinois. Legislative Investigating Commission. "Sexual Exploitation of Children." Chicago, August 1980.

Inciardi, James A. "Little Girls and Sex: A Glimpse at the World of the 'Baby Pro.'" *Deviant Behaviour* 5 (1984): 71–78.

Israel, Jerold H., and Rita Ann Burns. "Juvenile Obscenity Statutes: A Proposal and Analysis." *University of Michigan Journal of Law Reform* 9 (Spring 1976): 413–527.

Jaworski, Cynthia A. "Constitutional Law—First Amendment: New York Statute Proscribing Distribution of Nonobscene Materials Depicting Minors Engaged in Sexual Conduct Does Not Violate the First Amendment Because the Materials Are Outside First Amendment Protection and the Statute Is Not Substantially Overbroad." *Villanova Law Review* 28 (January 1983): 416–33.

Kaltenheuser, Skip. "They Don't Understand My Art: Accused of Kiddy Porn, Artist Had to Fight to Keep Children." *Legal Times* 11 (26 September 1988): 1.

Keitel, David. "Child Pornography Not Protected Speech in New York." *Loyola Entertainment Law Journal* 4 (1984): 192–96.

Keller, Mike. "An 'Appeal to Deviant Behavior': Kiddie Porn—In Living, Queasy Color." *Honolulu Advertiser*, 25 March 1987.

Kellogg, E.H., and J. Stepan. "Legal Aspects of Sex Education." *American Journal of Computer Law* 26 (Fall 1978): 573–608.

"'Kid Sex': Pornography's All-Time Low." *Reader's Digest*, July 1977, 45–50.

Kraft, M. "Computer Game Helps Pedophiles Woo Children for Sex." *Los Angeles Times*, 16 September 1985.

Lab, Steven P. "Pornography and Aggression: A Response to the U.S. Attorney General's Commission." *Criminal Justice Abstracts* 19 (June 1987): 301–21.

Linedecker, Clifford L. *Children in Chains*. New York: Everest House, 1981.

Lloyd, Robin. *For Money or Love: Boy Prostitution in America*. New York: Ballantine Books, 1977.

Loken, Gregory. "Child Pornography—A Turning Point." *Prosecutor* 16 (Summer 1982): 15–17.

Loken, Gregory. "The Federal Battle Against Child Sexual Exploitation: Proposals for Reform." *Harvard Women's Law Journal* 9 (Spring 1986): 105–34.

"Lolita. In re (1961) NZLR 542." *New Zealand University Law Review* 1 (September 1965): 535.

MaCarthy, M.A., and R.A. Moodie. "Parliament and Pornography: The 1978 Child Protection Act." *Parliamentary Affairs* 34 Winter 1981: 47–62.

MacPherson, Myra. "Children: The Limits of Porn." *Washington Post*, 30 January 1977.

Martin, L., and J. Haddad. *We Have a Secret*. Newport Beach, Calif.: Summit Books, 1982.

Massey, Donald C. "No First Amendment Protection for the Sexploitation of Children. *Loyola Law Review* 29 (Winter 1983): 227–35.

Mattar, Carol Datt. "No Age Limit: Child Pornography Is Abuse, Too, Wright State Workshop Told." *Journal Herald* (Dayton, Ohio), 19 June 1978.

McCaghy, Charles H. "The Moral Crusade Against Child Pornography: Some Reflections." Paper presented to the American Society of Criminology, Philadelphia, 7–10 November 1979.

McCaghy, Charles H., and Tina M. Beranbaum. "Child Pornography: The Rise of a Social Problem." Paper presented to the American Society of Criminology, Denver, 9–13 November 1983.

McKinnon, Isaiah. "Child Pornography." *FBI Law Enforcement Journal* (February 1979): 18–20.

Mitchell, Greg. "Innocence for Sale." *Police Magazine* 6 (1983): 52–60.

Moore, James W. "Child Pornography, the First Amendment, and the Media: The Constitutionality of Super-Obscenity Laws." *Comment* 4 (Fall 1981): 115–39.

"The Mother of Kiddie Porn." *Newsweek*, 23 January 1984.

Nash, D. *Child Sexual Exploitation: Background and Legal Analysis*. Washington, D.C.: American Bar Association, Young Lawyers Division, 1981.

Nash, D. "Legal Issues Related to Child Pornography: Legal Response." *Child Advocacy and Protection* 2 (1981): 8–9.

O'Brien, Shirley. *Child Pornography*. Dubuque, Iowa: Kendall/Hunt Publishing Co., 1983.

Page, Roger A. "Constitutional Law: Child Pornography Is Outside the Scope of First Amendment Protection." *Memphis State University Law Review* 12 (Summer 1982): 613–23.

Payton, Jennifer M. "Note: Child Pornography Legislation." *Journal of Family Law* 17 (1982): 505–43.

Pierce, Robert Lee. "Child Pornography: A Hidden Dimension of Child Abuse." *Child Abuse and Neglect* 8 (1984): 483–93.

Polnik, A. "'Show Me!' Publisher Shows 'em." *American Libraries* 7 (November 1976): 642.

Pope R.S. "Child Pornography—A New Role for the Obscenity Doctrine." *University of Illinois Law Forum* 3 (1978): 771–57.

"Pornography in America: Now They're Using Children." *PTA Today*, October 1977.

"Pornography and Children." *America*, 30 May 1981, 435.

Postic, Lionel J. "Constitutional Law—Obscenity: Child Pornography Laws Need Not Comply with the Legal Definition of Obscenity." *University of Detroit Journal of Urban Law* 61 (Fall 1983): 154–64.

Potuto, Josephine R. "Stanley and Ferber: The Constitutional Crime of At-Home Child Pornography Possession." *Kentucky Law Journal* 76 (October 1987): 15–80.

Radatz, Clark. *Child Pornography: Selective Legislative Solutions to the Sexual Exploitation of Minors.* Madison, Wisc.: Legislative Reference Bureau, 1977.

Rader, D. "Child on the Run: A Deepening American Tragedy." *Parade*, 5 September 1982, 4–7.

Reuter, Madalynne. "Child Sexual Portrayals Ruled Legal Unless Obscene." *Publishers Weekly* 219 (29 May 1981): 10.

Rooney, Rita. "Innocence for Sale." *Ladies' Home Journal*, April 1983, 128ff.

Rossman, P. *Sexual Experience between Men and Boys.* New York: Association Press, 1976.

Roth, R.A. "Child Sexual Abuse—Incest, Assault, and Sexual Exploitation: A Special Report from the National Center on Child Abuse and Neglect." Center on Child Abuse and Neglect, Washington, D.C., 1978.

Rush, F. *The Best Kept Secret: Sexual Abuse of Children.* New York: McGraw-Hill, 1980.

Rush, F. "Child Pornography." In *Take Back the Night: Women on Pornography*, edited by Laura Lederer, 71–81, New York: Morrow, 1980.

Russell, Vicki. "A Kiddie Porn Assault." *Macleans*, 7 June 1982, 50.

Schauer, Frederick. "Codifying the First Amendment: New York v. Ferber." *Supreme Court Review* (1982): 285–317.

Schoettle, U.C. "A Study of Pornography." *Journal of the American Academy of Child Psychiatry* 19 (1980): 289–99.

Schoettle, U.C. "Treatment of the Child Pornography Patient." *American Journal of Psychiatry* 137 (September 1980): 1109–10.

Schultz, L.G. "The Child Sex Industry." In *The Sexual Victimology of Youth*, edited by L.G. Schultz, Springfield, Ill.: Charles C. Thomas, 1980.

"See No Evil, Speak No Evil, Read No Evil: The Child vs. the First Amendment." *Children's Legal Rights Journal* 4 (August 1982): 20–27.

"Separate Obscenity Standard for Youth: Potential Court Escape Route from Its 'Supercensor' Role." *Georgia Law Review* 1 (Summer 1967): 707.

"A Special Report on Child Pornography." *Ladies' Home Journal*, April 1984.

Shelanski, Vivian B. "First Amendment I ...Child Pornography: New York. Ferber." *Annual Survey of American Law* (1983): 531–44.

Shewaga, Duane. "First Amendment—Freedom of Speech: Child Pornography, Obscene or Not, Possesses No First Amendment Protection." *Santa Clara Law Review* 23 (Spring 1983): 675–84.

Shouvlin, David P. "Preventing the Sexual Exploitation of Children: A Model Act." *Wake Forest Law Review* 17 (August 1981): 535–60.

Siddon, Arthur. "Take Profit out of Child Porn: Expert." *Chicago Tribune*, 24 May 1977.

Smith, S.M., ed. *Maltreatment of Children.* Baltimore: University Park Press, 1978.

Staal, Lorri. "Child Pornography: Federal and Feminist Responses." *Response* 8 (Summer 1985): 17–19.

Stack, Elaine Jackson. "Preventing the Sexual Exploitation of Children: The New York Experience." *New York State Bar Journal* 56 (February 1984): 11–18.

"Status Offenders in Los Angeles County: Focus on Runaway and Homeless Youth." Report of the UCLA Bush Foundation, 1985.

Stone, L.E. "Child Pornography Literature: A Content Analysis." Doctoral Dissertation, International College, San Diego, 1985.

Stone, L.E. "Child Pornography: Perpetuating the Sexual Victimization of Children." *Child Abuse and Neglect* 9 (1985): 313–18.

Temples, D. "Sexual Exploitation of Children: Provide for Criminal and Civil Penalties." *Georgia State University Law Review* 6 (Spring/Summer 1987): 403–5.

Texas. House. Select Committee on Child Pornography. *Related Causes and Control: Interim Report.* 66th legislative sess., 1978.

Thompson, Mark. "Congress Considers Means to Fight Sex Abuse of Children." *Criminal Justice Newsletter* 16 16 (November 1984): 4–6.

"Tightening the Reins on the Child Pornographer." *Children's Legal Rights Journal* 5 (Summer 1984): 2–9.

Trewhitt, Jeff. "Specialist Wants Child Abuse Laws Strengthened." *State Journal-Register* (Springfield, Ill.), 22 May 1977.

Tyler, R.P. "Toby." *Child Abuse and Neglect* 9 (1985):.

U.S. Congress. House. Committee on Education and Labor. Subcommittee on Select Education. *Teenage Prostitution and Child Pornography.* 97th Cong., 2d sess., Pittsburgh, 23 April 1982; Washington, D.C., 24 June 1982.

U.S. Congress. Senate. Committee on Governmental Affairs. Subcommittee on Investigations. *Child Pornography and Pedophilia.* 99th Cong., 1st sess., 1985.

U.S. Congress. Senate. Committee on the Judiciary. Subcommittee on Juvenile Justice. *Exploitation of Children.* 97th Cong., 1st sess., 1981.

U.S. Congress. Senate. Committee on the Judiciary. Subcommittee on Juvenile Justice. 97th Cong., 2d sess., 1982.

U.S. Congress. Senate. Committee on the Judiciary. Subcommittee on Juvenile Justice. *Computer Pornography and Child Exploitation Prevention Act, S. 1305.* 99th Cong., 1st sess., 1985.

U.S. Congress. Senate. Committee on the Judiciary. Subcommittee on Juvenile Justice. *Child Abuse Victims Rights Act of 1985.* 98th Cong., 2d sess., 1985.

U.S. Congress. Senate. Committee on the Judiciary. Subcommittee on Juvenile Justice. *Child Sexual Abuse and Pornography Act of 1986.* 99th Cong., 2d sess., 1986.

U.S. Congress. Senate. Committee on the Judiciary. Subcommittee on Security and Terrorism. *The Use of Computers to Transmit Material Inciting Crime.* 99th Cong., 1st sess., 1985.

U.S. Congress. Subcommittee on Crime. *Sexual Exploitation of Children.* 95th Cong., 1st sess., 1977.

U.S. Congress. Senate. Subcommittee to Investigate Juvenile Delinquency. *Protection of Children Against Sexual Exploitation.* 95th Cong., 1st sess., Chicago, 27 May 1977, 16 June 1977.

Van Why, Richard P. *Sex, Children and the Law: Explorations in the Problems of Child Pornography and Prostitution: A Sourcebook.* New York: R.P. Van Why Books, 1981.

Voyle, Glover. "Child Pornography Outrage." *American Bar Association Journal* 63 (May 1977): 600.

Wagner, S. "Court Removes Children from Obscenity Definition." *Publishers Weekly* 213 (5 June, 1979): 17.

Wall, Patrick M. "Obscenity and Youth: The Problem and a Possible Solution." *Criminal Law Bulletin* 1 (October 1965): 28–39.

"Washington Report...Child Pornography Legislation Is Sent to Full House." *Juvenile Justice Digest,* 17 October 1983.

Weiss, Todd J. "The Child Protection Act of 1984: Child Pornography and the First Amendment." *Seton Hall Legislation Journal* 9 (1985): 327–53.

Whitcomb, Debra, Elizabeth R. Shapiro, and Lindsey D. Stellwagen. "When the Victim Is a Child: Issues for Judges and Prosecutors." Report to the U.S. National Institute of Justice, Washington, D.C., 1985.

Woolsey, Robin Edward. "Child Pornography: Greater State Power to Protect the Interest of the Child." *Journal of Juvenile Law* 7 (Spring 1983): 227–31.

Woolsey, Robin Edward. "Child Pornography and the Initial Impact of New York v. Ferber." *Journal of Juvenile Law* 8 (1984): 237–39.

Yaffe, M. "The Assessment and Treatment of Paedophilia." In *Perspective on Paedophilia,* edited by B. Taylor, London: Bratsford, 1981.

Yates, Alayne. *Sex without Shame: Encouraging the Child's Healthy Sexual Development.* New York: Morrow, 1978.

Young, Rowland L. "Freedom of Speech...Child Pornography." *American Bar Association* 68 (September 1982): 1153.

"The Youth-Obscenity Problem—A Proposal." *Kentucky Law Journal* 52 (1964): 429.

"Youth for Sale on the Street." *Time,* (28 November 1977):23.

ADDITIONAL SOURCES

Allan, T.R.S. "A Right to Pornography?" *Oxford Journal of Legal Studies* (Great Britain) 3 (Winter 1983): 376–81.

Allen, "What Those Women Want in Pornography." *Humanist,* November/December 1978.

Anchell, Melvin. "Pornography Is Not the Harmless Recreation It Is Said to Be." *Liberty Magazine,* July/August 1977, 11–12.

Ayim, Maryann. "Pornography and Sexism: A Thread in the Web." *University of Western Ontario Law Review* 14 (August–November 1986): 269–86.

Baken, Joel. "Pornography, Law and Moral Theory." *Ottawa Law Review* 17, (Winter 1985): 1–32.

"Ban on Importation of Pornographic Articles Not Contrary to E.E.C. Treaty." *Journal of Criminal Law* 44 (August 1980): 165–67.

Barber, Dulan Friar. *Pornography and Society.* London: Skilton, 1972.

Beauvoir, Simone de. "Must We Burn Sade?" In *The Marquis de Sade,* edited by Simone de Beauvoir. London: New English Library, 1972.

Beckton, C.F. "Obscenity and Censorship Re-Examined under the Charter of Rights." *Manchester Law Journal* 13 (1983): 351–69.

Benjamin, Loretta. *The Porno Business.* New York: Women for Racial and Economic Equality.

Bessmer, S. "Anti-Obscenity: A Comparison of the Legal and the Feminist Perspectives." *W. Pol. Q.* 34 (March 1981): 143–55.

Bies, W.J. "La Danseuse nue et les Articles 163 et 170 du Code Criminel." *C de D.* 14 (1973): 535–40.

Bishop, Katherine. "Porn in the USA." *California Lawyer* 6 (December 1986): 60.

Blachford, Gregg. "Looking at Pornography: Erotica and the Socialist Morality." *Radical America,* January/February 1979, 7–18.

Blowers, Geoffrey. "Pornography: Some Points for Consideration in the Continuing Debate." *Bulletin of the Hong Kong Psychological Society* 16–17 (January–July 1986): 7–24.

Boyd, N. "Sexuality and Violence, Imagery and Reality: Censorship and the Criminal Control of Obscenity." Working paper 16 prepared by the Canadian Department of Justice for the Special Committee on Pornography and Prostitution, 1985.

Brannigan, Augustine. "Crimes from Comics: Social and Political Determinants of Reform of the Victoria Obscenity Law 1938–54." *Australian and New Zealand Journal of Criminology* 19 (March 1986): 23–42.

Brants, Chrisje, and Erna Kok. "Penal Sanctions as a Feminist Strategy: A Contradiction in Terms? Pornography and Criminal Law in the Netherlands." *International Journal of the Sociology of the Law* 14 (August–November 1986): 269–86.

Bronski, Michael. "What Does Soft Core Porn Really Mean to the Gay Male?" *Gay Community News.* 28 January 1978, 6–7.

Buruma, I. "Aesthetics East and West: The Bare Facts of

Life." (Hong Kong's adult magazines). *Far East Economic Review* 126 (4 October 1984): 51–53.

Bushdoony, Rousas J. *The Politics of Pornography*. New Rochelle, N.Y.: Arlington House Publishers, 1974.

Byerly, G., and R. Rubin. *Pornography: The Conflict over Sexually Explicit Material in the United States—An Annotated Bibliography*. New York: Garland, 1980.

Cahan, Catherine G. "One Man's Trash Is Another Man's Free Speech." *Student Law* 13 (February 1985): 8.

Caldwell, J.L. "The Video Recordings Act 1987." *New Zealand University Law Review* 12 (December 1987): 438–45.

Canada. House of Commons. *Report of the Standing Committee on Justice and Legal Affairs*. 3d Session of the 30th Parliament, 1977–78.

Cancel Hegron, R. "En Torno a la Obscenidad: un Concepto Juridico Impreciso." *Rev. C. Abo. P.R.* 29 (Fall 1969): 169.

Chervenak, Mary Francesca. "Selected Bibliography on Pornography and Violence." *University of Pittsburgh Law Review* 40 (Summer 1979): 652–60.

Chevrette, F., and H. Marx. "Le Droit Canadien en Mattere d'obscenite: Aspects Constitutionnels." *Canadian Bar Review* 54 (September 1976): 499–562.

Cihlar, Frank P., Michael K. Cook, Joseph P. Martori, Jr., and Paul J. Meyer. "Note: Church-State: Religious Institutions and Values." *Notre Dame Law Review* 41 (1966): 681–785.

Clandon, John. *To Deprave and Corrupt*. New York: Association Press, 1962.

Clark, Marc. "New Pornography Wars." *Maclean's*, 18 May 1987.

Cook, James. "The X-Rated Economy." *Forbes*, 18 September 1978, 81–92.

Cooper, R.J. "Sex Establishments—Licensing." *Journal of Criminal Law* (Great Britain) 51 (February 1987): 49–51.

Court, John Hugh. *Changing Community Standards*. Adelaide, Australia: Lutheran Publishing House, 1972.

Court, John Hugh. *Pornography: A Christian Critique*. Downers Grove, Ill.: Intervarsity Press, 1980.

Coutts, J.A. "Limitations Imposed by Treaty of Rome." *Journal of Criminal Law* (Great Britain) 51 (August 1987): 259–60.

Curtis, L.A. "Sexual Combat." *Society* 13 (1976): 69–72.

Dearn, Edmund Lawrence. *Pornography Degrades*. Sydney, Australia: Renda Publications, 1974.

"Debate on Pornography." *Film Comment*. December 1984,.

Dennett, Mary. *Who's Obscene?* New York: Vanguard, 1930.

Devlin, Patrick. *The Enforcement of Morals*. London: Oxford University Press, 1965.

"Doctrine of Margin of Appreciation and the European Convention on Human Rights." *Notre Dame Lawyer* 53 (October 1977): 90–106.

Donnelly, Harrison. "Pornography: Setting the Limits." *Editorial Research Reports* 1 (16 May 1986): 351–68.

Drouin, J. *Rapport Preliminaire du Comite Interminsteriel de Moralite Publique. Vol. 2: Jurisprudence et Difficultes d'application de la Legislation Federale en Materiere d'obscenite*. Quebec: Ministere de la Justice, 1969.

D'Souza, D. "National Endowment for Pornography." *Pol. R.* 20 (Spring 1982): 146–55; 21 (Summer 1982): 153–62.

El Komos, M. "Canadian Newspapers' Coverage of Pornography and Prostitution." Working paper 5 prepared by the Canadian Department of Justice for the Special Committee on Pornography and Prostitution, 1978–83.

Ellis, William H. "Obscenity and the Law: The Christian Lawyer in American Culture: Taking a Stand on Issues of the Day." *Quarterly (CLS)*. 9 (Fall 1988): 10–11.

Epstein, "The Problem of Pornography." *Dissent*. (Spring 1978):.

"Expert Evidence." *Solicitors' Journal* (Great Britain) 129 (19 April 1985): 305.

Falwell, J. *Listen America*. Garden City, N.Y.: Doubleday, 1980.

Faust, Beatrice. *Women, Sex and Pornography*. Harmondsworth: Penguin, 1980.

Feinberg, J. *The Moral Limits of Law*. New York: Oxford University Press, 1983.

Forkosch, M.D. "Pornobscenity, Morals, and Judicial Discrimination." *Capital University Law Review* 7 (1978): 579–619; 8: (1979): 1–30.

"Forum: The Place of Pornography." *Harper's*, November 1984.

Fox, R.G. "Depravity, Corruption and Community Standards." *Adelaide Law Review* (Australia) 7 (January 1980): 66–78.

Frankel, C. "Moral Environment of the Law." *Minnesota Law Review* 61 (June 1977): 921–60.

Gagnon, John H., and William Simon. "Pornography—Raging Menace or Paper Tiger?" In *The Pornography Controversy*, edited by Ray C. Rist, 85–95. New Brunswick, N.J.: Transaction Books, 1975.

Gellhorn, W. "Dirty Books, Disgusting Pictures, and Dreadful Laws." *Georgia Law Review* 8 (Winter 1974): 291–312.

Gerber, Albert Benjamin. *Sex, Pornography, and Justice*. New York: L. Stuart, 1965.

Goldman, Harry. "In-Depth: Pornography." *Journal of Popular Culture* 17 (Fall 1983): 123–28.

Goldstein, Leslie F. "The New Pornography Laws." *Delaware Lawyer* 4 (Fall 1985): 32–39.

Goodman, W. "Battle on Pornography Spurred by New Tactics." *New York Times*, 3 July 1984.

Gordon, George N. *Erotic Communications: Studies in Sex, Sin and Censorship*. New York: Hastings House, 1980.

Gordon, Gerald H. "Shameless Indecency and Obscenity: An Analysis." *Journal of the Legal Society of Scotland* 25 (July 1980): 262.

Gorman, Carol. *Pornography*. New York: Franklin Watts, 1988.

Grant, J.H. "Pornography." *Medicine Science and Law* 13 (October 1973): 232–38.

Greek, Cecil, and Mary Wright. "Law Enforcement and

Antipornography Laws." *American Journal of Police* 7, no. 1 (1988): 29–51.

Greene, Gerald, and Caroline Greene. *S-M: The Last Taboo.* New York: Grove Press, 1974.

Grey, Thomas. "Eros, Civilization and the Burger Court." *Law and Contemporary Problems* 43, no. 3 (1980): 83–100.

Griffiths, Richard. *Art, Pornography and Human Value: A Christian Approach to Violence and Eroticism in the Media.* Bramcote, England: Grove Books, 1975.

Hague, Amy. *Regulation of Pornography: Striking a Balance among Competing Interests.* Madison, Wisc.: Legislative Reference Bureau, 1986.

Harper, Phillip Brian. "Gay Men and Pornography." *Gay Community News,* 2 October 1982, 8ff.

Hausknecht,. "The Problem of Pornography." *Dissent* (Spring 1978):.

Hawkins, Gordon J. "Problem of Pornography." *Sydney Law Review* (Australia) 5 (September 1966): 221–38.

Heron, R.A. "Indecent Publications Tribunal: A Legal Practitioner's Viewpoint." *Otago Law Review* 3 (August 1974): 205–44.

Hertzberg, Hendrik. "Big Boobs," *New Republic,* 14 and 21 July 1986, 21.

Hewitt, Cecil Rolph. *Books in the Dock.* London: Deutsch, 1969.

Holbrook, D. *The Case Against Pornography.* La Salle, Ill.: Library Press, 1972.

Holbrook, D. "Mass Law-Breaking in the Mass Media." *New Law Journal* 123 (26 July 1973): 701–3.

Holbrook, D. "Politics of Pornography." *Pol. Q.* 48 (January 1977): 44–53.

Huer, Jon. *Art, Beauty, and Pornography: A Journey through American Culture.* Buffalo, N.Y.: Prometheus Books, 1987.

Hughes, Douglas A. *Perspectives on Pornography.* New York: St. Martin's Press, 1970.

Hughes, Patricia. "Tensions in Canadian Society: The Fraser Committee Report." *Windsor Yearbook of Access to Justice* 6 (1986): 282–323.

Hunter, I.A. "Obscenity, Pornography and Law Reform." *Dalhousie Law Journal* (Canada) 2 (September 1975): 482–504.

Hunter, I.A., P.J.T. O'Hearn, and R. Murrant. "Limits of Criminal Law." *Ottawa Law Review* 8 (Summer 1976): 299–321.

Hutchinson, Allan C. "Pornography." *New Law Journal* (Canada) 136 (10 January 1986): 31–32.

Hyde, H. Montgomery. *A History of Pornography.* New York: Farrar, Strauss & Girous, 1965.

Irvine, Janice, and Sue Hyde. "Porn, Politics and Pleasure." *Gay Community News.* 23 February 1985, .

Jayewardene, C.H.S., T.J. Juliani, and C.K. Talbot. "Prostitution and Pornography." Working paper 4 prepared by the Canadian Department of Justice for the Special Committee on Pornography and Prostitution.

Jones, Larry W. "Limiting the Burdeau Shield: Walter v. United States 100 S. Ct. 2395 (1980)." *Criminal Justice Journal* 4 (Fall 1980): 299–311.

Jonigan, Mary. "Confronting Pornography." *Maclean's,* 29 October 1984.

Kilpatrick, James Jackson. *The Smut Peddlers.* Garden City, N.Y.: Doubleday, 1960.

Kim, C. "Constitution and Obscenity: Japan and the U.S.A." *American Journal of Computer Law* 23 (Spring 1975): 255–83.

Kirkendall, Lester. "My Stance on Pornography." *Humanist,* November/December 1978.

Knight, Graham, and Berkeley Kaite. "Patriarchy and Pleasure: The Pornographic Eye/I; With Reply "Fetishism and Pornography." *Canadian Journal of Political and Social Theory.* 9, nos. 1–2 (1985): 81–95; 9no. 3 (1985): 64–71.

Kos, J. Stephen. "Obscene Language—Objective Community Standard—Time, Place, and Circumstances—Policy Factors—Police Offences Act 1927 (N.Z.) s. 48 (1), Summary Offences Act 1981 (N.Z.), s. 4(2). *Criminal Law Journal* (Great Britain) 5 (April 1982): 105–7.

Krueger, Robert. "What's All This . . . about Pornography?" *Los Angeles Bar Bulletin* 40 (August 1965): 505–20.

Kuh, Richard H. *Foolish Figleaves? Pornography in and out of Court.* New York: Macmillan, 1967.

Kyle-Keith, Richard. *The High Price of Pornography.* Washington, D.C.: Public Affairs Press, 1961.

Lambert, J.L. "Reproduction Victoriana: The Indecent Displays (Control) Act 1981." *Public Lawyer* (Great Britain) (Summer 1982): 226–29.

Leader, Sheldon. "Blasphemy and Human Rights." *Modern Law Review* (Great Britain) 48 (May 1983): 338–45.

Lee, Bartholomew, " 'Brass Checks' Return: An Excursus in Erotic Numismatics, or *The Spintriae Roll Again.*" *Journal of Popular Culture* 17 (Fall 1983): 142–45.

"Legislating Obscenity. Controlling Obscenity by Administrative Tribunal. A Study of the Ontario Board of Cinema Censors. Controlling Obscenity by Criminal Sanction." *Osgoode Hall Law Journal* (Canada) 9 (November 1971): 385–413.

Levine, S. "Indecent Publications Tribunal: Some Political Observations." *Otago Law Review* 3 (August 1974): 205–44.

Lewis, Felice Flanery. *Literature, Obscenity and Law.* Carbondale: Southern Illinois University Press, 1976.

Lutes, R.E. "Obscenity Law in Canada." *University of New Brunswick Law Journal* 23 (May 1974): 30–52.

MacDonald, Michael. "Obscenity, Censorship, and Freedom of Expression: Does the *Charter* Protect Pornography?" *University of Toronto Faculty of Law Review* 43 (1985): 130–52.

MacGregor, John. "The Modern Machiavellians: The Pornography of Sexual Game-Playing." In *The Pornography Controversy,* edited by Ray C. Rist, 175–202. New Brunswick, N.J.: Transaction Books, 1975.

Macklin, Tony. "Censorship in Queensland." *Queensland Law Society Journal* (Australia) 13 (June 1983): 129–37.

Manchester, C. "Note on England's Proposals for Restricting and Prohibiting Pornography." *U.W.A. Law Review* 14 (December 1979): 172–83.

Manchester, C. "Defining Indecency: A Recent New Zealand Decision." *International and Comparative Law Quarterly* 30 (April 1981): 455–61.

Manchester, C. "Customs Control of Obscene Materials." *Criminal Law Review* (Great Britain) (August 1981), 531–42.

Manchester, C. "Much Ado about the Location of Sex Shops." *Journal of Planning and Environment Law* (Great Britain) (February 1982): 89–95.

Mann, J. "Uncommon Conscience." *Stanford Law Review* 26 (June 1974): 1343–52.

McCarthy, S.J. "Pornography, Rape, and the Cult of Macho." *Humanist*, September/October 1980, 11–20.

McKay, R.B. "One Nation, Divisible—With Pornography for Some." *Bull Creek Society* 21 (December 1973): 73–88.

Meek, Oscar. *Pornography, Obscenity and Censorship: A Selected Bibliography*. Santa Fe, N.Mex.: New Mexico Research Library of the Southwest, 1969.

Metsker, Vidy. "The Curse of Pornography." *Psychology for Living* (March 1985):.

Michael, Richard. *The ABZ of Pornography*. London: Panther, 1972.

Mishan, E.J. "Making the World Safe for Pornography." In *Making the World Safe for Pornography and Other Intellectual Fashions*, edited by London: Alcove Press, 1973.

Mishkin, Barry D. *Pornography: Who, Where and Why?* Cincinnati: Pamphlets Publications, 1981.

Money, J., and R. Athanasiou. "Pornography: Review and Bibliographic Annotations." *American Journal of Obstetrics and Gynecology* 115 (1973): 130–46.

Nelson, Eric M. "Communications Law." *Annual Survey of American Law* (June 1985): 401–34.

New Zealand Psychological Society. "Submission to the Select Committee on the Cinematographic Films Bill and Cinematographic Films Amendment Bill." *New Zealand Psychologist* 5 (1976): 98–105.

Norwick, Kenneth P. *Pornography: The Issues and the Law*. New York: Public Affairs Committee, 1972.

Oberst, Paul, and Jeffrey B. Hunt. "Administrative and Constitutional Law." *Kentucky Law Journal* 71 (Spring 1983): 417–43.

Palys, T.S. "Testing the Common Wisdom: The Social Content of Video Pornography." *Canadian Psychology* 27 (January 1986): 22–35.

Peek, C.W., D.D. Witt, and D.A. Gay. "Pornography: Important Political Symbol or Limited Political Issue?" *Sociological Focus* 15 (1982): 41–51.

Perry, S. "Indecent Publications Tribunal: A View from the Inside." *Otago Law Review* 3 (August 1974): 205–44.

Perry, S. *Indecent Publications Control in New Zealand*. Wellington, New Zealand: McCrae, 1975.

Persky, Stan. "Canada's Curious Customs: Gay Lit, Censorship and the Law." *This* 21 (March/April 1987): 33–36.

Pilpel, Harriet F. *Obscenity and the Constitution*. New York: Bowker, 1973.

"Porn Prone." *Humanist*, July/August 1985: 28.

"The Porno Plague." *Time* 5 (April 1978): 58–63.

"Pornographic Articles in the Crown Court." *Journal of Criminal Law* (Great Britain) 49 (November 1985): 304–6.

"The Pornography Explosion." *Ladies' Home Journal*, October 1985, 104.

"Pornography and Its Discontents." *Society*, July/August 1987, 26.

"Pornography: Social Science, Legal, and Clinical Perspectives." *Law and Inequality* 4 (May 1986): 17–49.

Post, Robert C. "Cultural Heterogeneity and Law: Pornography, Blasphemy, and the First Amendment." *California Law Review* 76 (March 1988): 297–335.

Potter, Gary W. *The Porn Merchants*. Dubuque, Iowa: Kendall/Hunt Publishing Co., 1986.

Power, Richard W. "Candy Case: A Defense of the Intellect." *St. Louis University Law Journal* 13 (Summer 1969): 544–63.

Press, Aric, et al. "The War Against Pornography." *Newsweek*. 18 March 1985, .

"Prohibition on Importation of Pornography Upheld." *New Law Journal* (Great Britain) 130 (17 April 1980): 389–91.

Rangel Medina, D. "Mexican Law on Obscenity." *Law Am.* 7 (June 1975): 337–48.

"Regina v. Commissioner of Metropolitan Police, ex parte Blackburn (1973)." *Law Quarterly Review* 89 (July 1973): 329–31.

Reichenbach, Hans. *The Direction of Time*. Berkeley: University of California Press, 1956.

Reimann, Mathias. "Prurient Interest and Human Dignity: Pornography Regulation in West Germany and the United States." *University of Michigan Journal of Law Reform*. 21 (Fall 1987, Winter 1988): 201–54.

Robilliard, J.A. "Law or Licence? Local Government (Miscellaneous Provisions) Act 1982, Schedule Three and Cinematograph (Amendment) Act 1982." *Modern Law Review* 45 (November 1982): 676–82.

Robison, James. *Pornography: The Polluting of America*. Wheaton, Ill.: Tyndale House Publishers, 1982.

Rolph, C.H. *Does Pornography Matter?* London: Routledge & Kegan Paul, 1961.

Sachs, W. "Sex Magazines: No Business Like Show Business." *Business and Society Review* 20 (Winter 1976–77): 21–25.

Salfrank, Linda J. "The Fraser Balancing Test: Leaving Cohen's Jacket at the Schoolhouse Gate." *Missouri Law Review* 52 (Fall 1987): 913–24.

Samek, R.A. "Pornography as a Species of Second-Order Sexual Behaviour: A Submission for Law Reform." *Dalhousie Law Journal* (Canada) 1 (December 1973): 265–93.

Sansfacon, D. "Pornography and Prostitution in the United States." Working paper 2 prepared by the Canadian Department of Justice for the Special Committee on Pornography and Prostitution.

Scott, G.H. "Sex and the Law." *New Law Journal* 123 (22 February 1973): 168–72.

See, Carolyn. *Blue Money: Pornography and the Pornographers—An Intimate Look at the Two-Billion Dollar Fantasy Industry.* New York: McKay, 1974.

"Selected Materials on Censorship and Obscenity." *Record* 3 (December 1948): 410–13.

Sharma, V.D., and F. Wooldridge. "Law Relating to Obscene Publications in India." *International & Comparative Law Quarterly* 22 (October 1973): 632–47.

Showers, H. Robert. "Myths and Misconceptions of Pornography: What You Don't Know Can Hurt You." *Quarterly (CLS)* 9 (Fall 1988): 8–10.

Shuker, Roy, " 'Video Nasties': Censorship and the Politics of Popular Culture." *New Zealand Sociology* 1 (1 May 1986): 64–73.

Simons, G.L. *Pornography without Prejudice: A Reply to Objectors.* London: Abeland-Schuman, 1972.

Sklar, Ronald. "Pornography. (Bill C-19: Reforming the Criminal Law)." *Ottawa Law Review* 16 (Spring 1984): 387–99.

Slough, M.C. "Pornography and Sane Legal Control." *Journal of the Bar Association of Kansas* 40 (Spring 1971): 25.

Smith, George P., II. "Nudity, Obscenity and Pornography: The Streetcars Named Lust and Desire." *Journal of Contemporary Health Law and Policy* 4 (Spring 1988): 155–201.

Spitz, . "The Problem of Pornography." *Dissent* Spring 1978, .

Stanmeyer, William A. "Keeping the Constitutional Republic: Civic Virtue vs. Pornographic Attack." *Hastings Constitutional Law Quarterly* 145 (Spring 1987): 561–93.

Steiner, George. "Night Words: High Pornography and Human Privacy." In *The Pornography Controversy,* edited by Ray C. Rist, 203–16, New Brunswick, N.J.: Transaction Books, 1975.

Stoddart, Charles N. "Shameless Indecency—Again." *Journal of Criminal Law* (Scotland) 46 (May 1982): 91–92.

Stone, R.T.H. "Indecent Performances: The Law Commission's Proposals." *New Law Journal* 127 (12 May 1977): 452–54.

Stone, R.T.H. "Out of Sight, Out of Mind." *Modern Law Review* (Great Britain) 45 (January 1982): 62–68.

Tacker, Susan, and David Wellman. "Bibliography of Useful Articles on First Amendment Issues, Arranged by Area of Interest." *Media Law Notes* 14 (Winter 1987): 4.

Talbot, P.K., comp. *Pornography: A Brief Annotated Bibliography.* Ottawa: House of Commons, 1983.

Taylor, Ian. "The Development of Law and Public Debate in the United Kingdom in Respect of Pornography and Obscenity." Working paper 14 prepared by the Canadian Department of Justice for the Special Committee on Pornography and Prostitution.

Teachout, Terry. "The Pornography Report That Never Was." *Commentary* 84 (August 1987): 51.

Telling, D. "Defence of 'Public Good.' " *New Law Journal* 129 (22 March 1979): 299–301.

Toner, William J. *Regulating Sex Businesses.* Chicago: American Society of Planning Officials, 1977.

Ursel, Susan. "Pornography and Violence." *Obiter Dicta* (Canada) 54 (25 January 1982): 6–7.

Ursel, Susan, and Robert Spenceley. "Violence Against Women Deserves Recognition." *Obiter Dicta* (Canada) 54 (15 February 1982): 1.

van den Haag, Ernest. "Outlaw Porn." *American Spectator,* July 1987: 30–32.

"Video Cassette an Obscene Article?" *Journal of Criminal Law* (Great Britain) 45 (May 1981): 79–81.

Wallace, Rebecca M. "Public Morality: The Terms of Article 36 of the EEC Treaty." *Journal of the Legal Society of Scotland* 25 (June 1980): 234.

"War Declared on Obscene Materials." *Beijing Review* (China) 28 (5 August 1985): 8–9.

Waugh, Tom. "A Heritage of Pornography." *Body Politic,* January/February 1983, 29.

Weatherford, J. McIver. *Porn Row.* New York: Arbor House, 1986.

Weiler, J.H.H. "Europornography—First Reference of the House of Lords to the European Court of Justice." *Modern Law Review* (Great Britain) 44, 91–96.

West, Woody. "Pornography's Cultural Pollution." *Insight,* 4 August 1986, 72.

Wilkinson, H.W. "Control of Sex Establishments." *New Law Journal* (Great Britain) 60 (30 September 1983): 51–62.

Williamsen, M.A. "Justice Tobriner and the Tolerance of Evolving Lifestyles: Adapting the Law to Social Change." *Hastings Law Journal* 29 (September 1977): 73–97.

Wollheim, Richard. "A Charismatic View of Pornography." *London Review of Books,* 7 (February 1980):.

Yoakum, Robert. "The Great *Hustler* Debate." *Columbia Journalism Review* 16 (May/June 1977): 53–58.

Zellick, Graham. "Sex under License." *Public Law* (Great Britain) (Summer 1982): 167–71.

Zillman, Dolf. "Effects of Prolonged Consumption of Pornography." In *Report of the Surgeon General's Workshop on Pornography and Public Health,* edited by E.P. Mulvey and J.L. Haugaard, Washington, D.C.: U.S. Public Health Service and U.S. Department of Health and Human Services, 1986.

Zurcher, Louis A. *Citizens for Decency: Antipornography Crusades as Status Defense.* Austin: University of Texas Press, 1976.

INDEX

ABOUT THE AUTHORS

Franklin Mark Osanka, Ph.D., is a behavioral consultant who practices as president of Behavioral Consultants, Naperville, Illinois. Dr. Osanka travels the nation presenting pornography-influence workshops and family violence prevention/intervention workshops and conducts seminars on university campuses and to community professional groups. He also presents seminars and lectures on child sexual-abuse prevention, child abuse, and other abuse topics. Dr. Osanka has been an expert witness/consultant in a number of murder, child sexual abuse, pornography influence, and domestic violence cases. He also has practical experience evaluating battered women who kill their abusers and has testified at such trials as an expert witness. Dr. Osanka has run for the state senate in Illinois, is listed in **American Men of Science,** and is the recipient of many awards including a distinguished service award presented by the World Congress of Victimology in 1980. His academic specialties in the American Sociological Association are social psychology; crime, law, and deviance; the family; and Asia and Asian Americans. Dr. Osanka earned an M.A. and a Ph.D. in sociology from Northwestern University. He earned his B.A. and another M.A. from Northern Illinois University. In 1979, Dr. Osanka was the recipient of the NIU Distinguished Alumnus Award for his outstanding service to child-abuse and domestic-violence education and prevention.

Sara Lee Johann, J.D., is an attorney who practices nationally out of Cedarburg, Wisconsin. While with the Wisconsin state assembly, she drafted legislation on child pornography, civil rights for victims of pornography, and other issues of concern to victims of crime. Attorney Johann travels the nation presenting workshops on the legal and social aspects of pornography, domestic violence, and sexual abuse. She has served as an expert witness/consultant in major cases involving pornography, murder, and battered women who kill. She also does consulting in cases involving pornography victimization and law, battered women who kill, domestic abuse, therapist-client sexual abuse, and related issues. She has been an executive director of a center for battered women. Attorney Johann earned a J.D. from the University of Wisconsin/Madison Law School. Her B.A., with honors, is from the University of Wisconsin/Milwaukee where she majored in political science and studied journalism and economics extensively. She ran for the state senate in Wisconsin, has seventeen years of experience in civic, political, and artistic organizations, and has been a newspaper reporter.

Franklin Mark Osanka and Sara Lee Johann have co-authored a book on battered women who kill and are co-authoring books on therapist-client sexual abuse, and children and pornography. They have presented their research before many learned organizations including the American Society of Criminology, the American Sociological Association, the Midwestern Criminal Justice Association, the Wisconsin Bench and Bar Conference, and the Illinois Sociological Association; and they have been expert guests of numerous television programs including "Sally Jesse Raphael," "Pittsburgh 2Day," and "Thirty on 2."